The
Essential
Desk Reference

OXFORD

The
Essential
Desk Reference

OXFORD
UNIVERSITY PRESS

OXFORD
UNIVERSITY PRESS

Oxford New York

Auckland Bangkok Buenos Aires Cape Town Chennai
Dar es Salaam Delhi Hong Kong Istanbul Karachi Kolkata
Kuala Lumpur Madrid Melbourne Mexico City Mumbai Nairobi
São Paulo Shanghai Singapore Taipei Tokyo Toronto

with an associated company in Berlin

Published by Oxford University Press, Inc.
198 Madison Avenue, New York, NY 10016
www.oup.com

Oxford is a registered trademark of Oxford University Press

Library of Congress Cataloging-in-Publication data is available.

ISBN 0-19-512873-7

Project manager: Mary Kay Linge
Design: Mary Neal Meador
Illustrations: Gary Tong

1 3 5 7 9 8 6 4 2

Printed in the United States of America on acid-free paper

Contents

Contents *(cont.)*

UNITED STATES

Contents *(cont.)*

THE SCIENCES

Contents *(cont.)*

ARTS AND LEISURE

Contents *(cont.)*

PRIZES AND AWARDS

WORK AND HOME

Contents (cont.)

How to Use This Book

Do you need to know the location of the 512 telephone area code? What is the difference between vitamin A and vitamin B12? How do hurricanes get their names? *The Essential Desk Reference* can help you find the answers to these questions—and thousands of others—in seconds.

The *Essential Desk Reference* is intended to be the quickest way to find facts on a wide variety of subjects. The book is arranged thematically in broad sections such as The World, The United States, and The Sciences, which proceed generally from global to personal; the section on The Sciences is followed by Arts and Leisure, Prizes and Awards, and Work and Home.

There are many ways to use the *Desk Reference*. Perhaps the most enjoyable is simply to browse its pages in any category that interests you. "Inventors and Discoverers," in The Sciences, is a fascinating list of scientific geniuses, explorers, and creative minds who have changed the way we live; or count the number of Booker Prize–winning authors you have read, in the Prizes and Awards section.

Fast facts: the index. The easiest way to find a specific fact quickly is to look up the subject in the index. While some organizations' or individuals' names can be found in the index, you will sometimes be more successful looking up a slightly broader category. For instance, you are unlikely to find the Boston Bruins in the index, but you can find out what years they won the Stanley Cup if you look under "Stanley Cup" or "ice hockey." Likewise, if you want to know the dates of carnival week in Brazil, look under "holidays (U.S. and global)," not under "carnival."

The big picture: the table of contents. While the index is a tool for looking up specific facts, the table of contents will tell you the range of information available in the *Desk Reference* on any subject of interest. If you simply wanted to know the population of China, you would look up "China, population" in the index. But if you are interested in China in general, scan the World section of the table of contents. You will see that this section offers a list of "UN Members." Is China a member? There is an atlas. What countries border China? In China's listing under "Nations" you can find not only the population, but a breakdown of religions, ethnicities, and languages in China, the highest and lowest points in its geography, and the Chinese currency. Finally, "World History" offers "Dynasties of China." The table of contents is a tool for the curious mind.

Websites and other sources for further information. After each section or list in the book, the ☉ symbol indicates the sources of the information in that section as well as related references of special interest, whether books, government documents, or websites. Websites are correct at the time of publication but if you encounter a problem with one of them, search for the name of the website's host institution (as listed in the *Desk Reference*) using a standard search engine. With more than 300 source lists throughout the book, the *Desk Reference* is an excellent starting point for further research.

WORLD: *International Organizations and Alliances*

United Nations Members

Member	Date of Admission	Member	Date of Admission
Afghanistan	Nov. 19, 1946	Democratic People's Republic	
Albania	Dec. 14, 1955	of Korea	Sep. 17, 1991
Algeria	Oct. 8, 1962	Democratic Republic	
Andorra	July 28, 1993	of the Congo	Sep. 20, 1960
Angola	Dec. 1, 1976	Denmark	Oct. 24, 1945
Antigua and Barbuda	Nov. 11, 1981	Djibouti	Sep. 20, 1977
Argentina	Oct. 24, 1945	Dominica	Dec. 18, 1978
Armenia	Mar. 2, 1992	Dominican Republic	Oct. 24, 1945
Australia	Nov. 1, 1945	Ecuador	Dec. 21, 1945
Austria	Dec. 14, 1955	Egypt	Oct. 24, 1945
Azerbaijan	Mar. 9, 1992	El Salvador	Oct. 24, 1945
Bahamas	Sep. 18, 1973	Equatorial Guinea	Nov. 12, 1968
Bahrain	Sep. 21, 1971	Eritrea	May 28, 1993
Bangladesh	Sep. 17, 1974	Estonia	Sep. 17, 1991
Barbados	Dec. 9, 1966	Ethiopia	Nov. 13, 1945
Belarus	Oct. 24, 1945	Fiji	Oct. 13, 1970
Belgium	Dec. 27, 1945	Finland	Dec. 14, 1955
Belize	Sep. 25,1981	France	Oct. 24, 1945
Benin	Sep. 20, 1960	Gabon	Sep. 20, 1960
Bhutan	Sep. 21, 1971	Gambia	Sep. 21, 1965
Bolivia	Nov. 14, 1945	Georgia	July 31, 1992
Bosnia and Herzegovina	May 22, 1992	Germany	Sep. 18, 1973
Botswana	Oct. 17, 1966	Ghana	Mar. 8, 1957
Brazil	Oct. 24, 1945	Greece	Oct. 25, 1945
Brunei Darussalam	Sep. 21, 1984	Grenada	Sep. 17, 1974
Bulgaria	Dec. 14, 1955	Guatemala	Nov. 21, 1945
Burkina Faso	Sep. 20, 1960	Guinea	Dec. 12, 1958
Burundi	Sep. 18, 1962	Guinea-Bissau	Sep. 17, 1974
Cambodia	Dec. 14, 1955	Guyana	Sep. 20, 1966
Cameroon	Sep. 20, 1960	Haiti	Oct. 24, 1945
Canada	Nov. 9, 1945	Honduras	Dec. 17, 1945
Cape Verde	Sep. 16, 1975	Hungary	Dec. 14, 1955
Central African Republic	Sep. 20, 1960	Iceland	Nov. 19, 1946
Chad	Sep. 20, 1960	India	Oct. 30, 1945
Chile	Oct. 24, 1945	Indonesia	Sep. 28, 1950
China	Oct. 24, 1945	Iran, Islamic Republic of	Oct. 24, 1945
Colombia	Nov. 5, 1945	Iraq	Dec. 21,1945
Comoros	Nov. 12, 1975	Ireland	Dec. 14, 1955
Congo	Sep. 20, 1960	Israel	May 11, 1949
Costa Rica	Nov. 2, 1945	Italy	Dec. 14, 1955
Côte d'Ivoire	Sep. 20, 1960	Jamaica	Sep. 18, 1962
Croatia	May 22, 1992	Japan	Dec. 18, 1956
Cuba	Oct. 24, 1945	Jordan	Dec. 14, 1955
Cyprus	Sep. 20, 1960	Kazakhstan	Mar. 2, 1992
Czech Republic	Jan. 19, 1993	Kenya	Dec. 16, 1963

Member	Date of Admission	Member	Date of Admission
Kiribati	Sep. 14, 1999	Portugal	Dec. 14, 1955
Kuwait	May 14, 1963	Qatar	Sep. 21, 1971
Kyrgyzstan	Mar. 2, 1992	Republic of Korea	Sep. 17, 1991
Lao People's Democratic		Republic of Moldova	Mar. 2, 1992
Republic	Dec. 14, 1955	Romania	Dec. 14, 1955
Latvia	Sep. 17, 1991	Russian Federation	Oct. 24, 1945
Lebanon	Oct. 24, 1945	Rwanda	Sep. 18, 1962
Lesotho	Oct. 17, 1966	Saint Kitts and Nevis	Sep. 23, 1983
Liberia	Nov. 2, 1945	Saint Lucia	Sep. 18, 1979
Libyan Arab Jamahiriya	Dec. 14, 1955	Saint Vincent and the	
Liechtenstein	Sep. 18, 1990	Grenadines	Sep. 16, 1980
Lithuania	Sep. 17, 1991	Samoa	Dec. 15, 1976
Luxembourg	Oct. 24, 1945	San Marino	Mar. 2, 1992
Madagascar	Sep. 20, 1960	São Tomé and Príncipe	Sep. 16, 1975
Malawi	Dec. 1, 1964	Saudi Arabia	Oct. 24, 1945
Malaysia	Sep. 17, 1957	Senegal	Sep. 28, 1960
Maldives	Sep. 21, 1965	Seychelles	Sep. 21, 1976
Mali	Sep. 28, 1960	Sierra Leone	Sep. 27, 1961
Malta	Dec. 1, 1964	Singapore	Sep. 21, 1965
Marshall Islands	Sep. 17, 1991	Slovakia	Jan. 19, 1993
Mauritania	Oct. 7, 1961	Slovenia	May 22, 1992
Mauritius	Apr. 24, 1968	Solomon Islands	Sep. 19, 1978
Mexico	Nov. 7, 1945	Somalia	Sep. 20, 1960
Micronesia, Federated States of	Sep. 17, 1991	South Africa	Nov. 7, 1945
Monaco	May 28, 1993	Spain	Dec. 14, 1955
Mongolia	Oct. 27, 1961	Sri Lanka	Dec. 14, 1955
Morocco	Nov. 12, 1956	Sudan	Nov. 12, 1956
Mozambique	Sep. 16, 1975	Suriname	Dec. 4, 1975
Myanmar	Apr. 19, 1948	Swaziland	Sep. 24, 1968
Namibia	Apr. 23, 1990	Sweden	Nov. 19, 1946
Nauru	Sep. 14, 1999	Syrian Arab Republic	Oct. 24, 1945
Nepal	Dec. 14, 1955	Tajikistan	Mar. 2, 1992
Netherlands	Dec. 10, 1945	Thailand	Dec. 16, 1946
New Zealand	Oct. 24, 1945	The former Yugoslav Republic	
Nicaragua	Oct. 24, 1945	of Macedonia	Apr. 8, 1993
Niger	Sep. 20, 1960	Tonga	Sep. 14, 1999
Nigeria	Oct. 7, 1960	Togo	Sep. 20, 1960
Norway	Nov. 27, 1945	Trinidad and Tobago	Sep. 18, 1962
Oman	Oct. 7, 1971	Tunisia	Nov. 12, 1956
Pakistan	Sep. 30, 1947	Turkey	Oct. 24, 1945
Palau	Dec. 15, 1994	Turkmenistan	Mar. 2, 1992
Panama	Nov. 13, 1945	Uganda	Oct. 25, 1962
Papua New Guinea	Oct. 10, 1975	Ukraine	Oct. 24, 1945
Paraguay	Oct. 24, 1945	United Arab Emirates	Dec. 9, 1971
Peru	Oct. 31, 1945	United Kingdom of Great	
Philippines	Oct. 24, 1945	Britain and Northern Ireland	Oct. 24, 1945
Poland	Oct. 24, 1945	United Republic of Tanzania	Dec. 14, 1961

Member	Date of Admission	Member	Date of Admission
United States of America	Oct. 24, 1945	Vietnam	Sep. 20, 1977
Uruguay	Dec. 18, 1945	Yemen	Sep. 30, 1947
Uzbekistan	Mar. 2, 1992	Yugoslavia	Oct. 24, 1945
Vanuatu	Sep. 15, 1981	Zambia	Dec. 1, 1964
Venezuela	Nov. 15, 1945	Zimbabwe	Aug. 25, 1980

⊙ United Nations. "United Nations Member States," www.un.org/Overview/unmember.html

United Nations Permanent Observer Missions

States

Holy See   Switzerland

Non-Governmental Organizations

Asian-African Legal Consultative Committee
Caribbean Community
Commonwealth Secretariat
European Community
International Committee of the Red Cross
International Federation of Red Cross and Red
   Crescent
International Organization of La Francophonie
International Organization for Migration

International Seabed Authority
International Tribunal for the Law of the Sea
International Union for the Conservation of
   Nature and Natural Resources
League of Arab States
Organization of African Unity
Organization of the Islamic Conference
Palestine
Sovereign Military Order of Malta

⊙ United Nations. "Permanent Missions to the United Nations," www.un.org/Overview/
   missions.htm#nperm

Principal Organs of the United Nations

Organ: General Assembly
Members: all members of the United Nations
Function: serves as a forum for members to launch initiatives on international questions of peace,
economic progress, and human rights; initiates studies; makes recommendations; develops and
codifies international law; promotes human rights and other economic, social, cultural, and educational programs

Organ: Economic and Social Council
Members: 54 members, elected for 3-year terms
Function: promotes higher standards of living, full employment, and conditions of economic and social
progress and development; solutions to international economic, social, health, and related problems;
international cultural and educational cooperation; universal respect for, and observance of, human
rights and fundamental freedoms for all

Organ: International Court of Justice
Members: 15 judges, elected for 9-year terms; may not include more than one judge of any nationality
Function: settles in accordance with international law legal disputes submitted to it by member coun-
tries and gives advice on legal questions

Organ: Security Council
Members: 5 permanent members (China, France, Russian Federation, United Kingdom, United States)
and 10 elected for 2-year terms; presidency rotates monthly

Principal Organs of the United Nations *(cont.)*

Function: maintains international peace and security; investigates disputes and recommends solutions; calls on members to take non-aggressive action in cases of threats to peace; takes military action when necessary; recommends admission of new members; exercises UN trusteeship functions; recommends appointment of the secretary-general and elects judges of the International Court

Organ: Trusteeship Council

Members: 5 permanent members; suspended 11/1/94 after Palau, last UN trust territory, gained independence

Functions: examines and discusses reports from administering authority on political, economic, social and educational advancement of peoples of trust territories and examines petitions from and undertakes special missions to trust territories

Organ: Secretariat

Members: more than 8,600 employees, headed by the Secretary-General

Functions: carries out the day-to-day work of the United Nations, servicing the other principal organs and administering their programs and policies worldwide

⊙ United Nations. "About the United Nations," www.un.org/aboutun/

United Nations Secretaries-General

Name	*Country*	*Term of Office*
Trygve Lie	Norway	1946–1952
Dag Hammarskjöld	Sweden	1953–1961
U Thant	Myanmar	1961–1971
Kurt Waldheim	Austria	1972–1981
Javier Perez de Cuellar	Peru	1982–1991
Boutros Boutros-Ghali	Egypt	1992–1996
Kofi Annan	Ghana	1997–

⊙ United Nations. "UN Secretaries-General," www.un.org/Overview/SG/index.html

International Organizations and Groups

African Development Bank (AfDB)

Established: 4 August 1963

Aim: to promote economic and social development

Regional members (53): Algeria, Angola, Benin, Botswana, Burkina Faso, Burundi, Cameroon, Cape Verde, Central African Republic, Chad, Comoros, Democratic Republic of the Congo, Republic of the Congo, Côte d'Ivoire, Djibouti, Egypt, Equatorial Guinea, Eritrea, Ethiopia, Gabon, Gambia, Ghana, Guinea, Guinea-Bissau, Kenya, Lesotho, Liberia, Libya, Madagascar, Malawi, Mali, Mauritania, Mauritius, Morocco, Mozambique, Namibia, Niger, Nigeria, Rwanda, São Tomé and Príncipe, Senegal, Seychelles, Sierra Leone, Somalia, South Africa, Sudan, Swaziland, Tanzania, Togo, Tunisia, Uganda, Zambia, Zimbabwe

Nonregional members (25): Argentina, Austria, Belgium, Brazil, Canada, China, Denmark, Finland, France, Germany, India, Italy, Japan, South Korea, Kuwait, Netherlands, Norway, Portugal, Saudi Arabia, Spain, Sweden, Switzerland, U.A.E., U.K., U.S.

Andean Community of Nations (CAN)

Established: 26 May 1969

Aim: to promote harmonious development through economic integration

Members (5): Bolivia, Colombia, Ecuador, Peru, Venezuela

Arab Bank for Economic Development in Africa (ABEDA)

Established: 18 February 1974 (effective 16 September 1974)
Aim: to promote economic development
Members (18): Algeria, Bahrain, Egypt, Iraq, Jordan, Kuwait, Lebanon, Libya, Mauritania, Morocco, Oman, Qatar, Saudi Arabia, Sudan, Syria, Tunisia, U.A.E., Palestine Liberation Organization

Arab League (AL)

Established: 22 March 1945
Aim: to promote economic, social, political, and military cooperation
Members (22): Algeria, Bahrain, Comoros, Djibouti, Egypt, Iraq, Jordan, Kuwait, Lebanon, Libya, Mauritania, Morocco, Oman, Qatar, Saudi Arabia, Somalia, Sudan, Syria, Tunisia, U.A.E., Yemen, Palestine Liberation Organization

Asia Pacific Economic Cooperation (APEC)

Established: 7 November 1989
Aim: to promote trade and investment in the Pacific basin
Members (19): Australia, Brunei, Canada, Chile, China, Hong Kong, Indonesia, Japan, South Korea, Malaysia, Mexico, N.Z., Papua New Guinea, Philippines, Singapore, Taiwan, Thailand, U.S., Vietnam

Association of Southeast Asian Nations (ASEAN)

Established: 9 August 1967
Aim: to encourage regional economic, social, and cultural cooperation among the non-Communist countries of Southeast Asia
Members (9): Brunei, Burma, Indonesia, Laos, Malaysia, Philippines, Singapore, Thailand, Vietnam

Australia Group

Established: 1984
Aim: to consult on and coordinate export controls related to chemical and biological weapons
Members (30): Australia, Argentina, Austria, Belgium, Canada, Czech Republic, Denmark, Finland, France, Germany, Greece, Hungary, Iceland, Ireland, Italy, Japan, Luxembourg, Netherlands, New Zealand, Norway, Poland, Portugal, Romania, Slovak Republic, South Korea, Spain, Sweden, Switzerland, U.K., U.S.
Observer: European Union

Big Seven

Established: 1975
Aim: to discuss and coordinate major economic policies
Members (7): Canada, France, Germany, Italy, Japan, U.K., U.S.

Commonwealth (Commonwealth of Nations)

Established: 31 December 1931
Aim: to foster multinational cooperation and assistance, as a voluntary association that evolved from the British Empire
Members (52): Antigua and Barbuda, Australia, The Bahamas, Bangladesh, Barbados, Belize, Botswana, Brunei, Cameroon, Canada, Cyprus, Dominica, Fiji, Gambia, Ghana, Grenada, Guyana, India, Jamaica, Kenya, Kiribati, Lesotho, Malawi, Malaysia, Maldives, Malta, Mauritius, Mozambique, Namibia, N.Z., Nigeria (suspended), Pakistan, Papua New Guinea, Saint Kitts and Nevis, Saint Lucia, Saint Vincent and the Grenadines, Samoa, Seychelles, Sierra Leone, Singapore, Solomon Islands, South Africa, Sri Lanka, Swaziland, Tanzania, Tonga, Trinidad and Tobago, Uganda, U.K., Vanuatu, Zambia, Zimbabwe
Special members (2): Nauru, Tuvalu

Commonwealth of Independent States (CIS)

Established: 8 December 1991 (effective 21 December 1991)
Aim: to coordinate intercommonwealth relations and to provide a mechanism for the orderly dissolution of the USSR
Members (12): Armenia, Azerbaijan, Belarus, Georgia, Kazakhstan, Kyrgyzstan, Moldova, Russia, Tajikistan, Turkmenistan, Ukraine, Uzbekistan

European Monetary Union (EMU)

Proposed: 7 February 1992 (full implementation 1 July 2002)
Aim: to promote a single market by creating a single currency, the euro
Members (11): Austria, Belgium, Finland, France, Germany, Ireland, Italy, Luxembourg, Netherlands, Portugal, Spain

European Union (EU)

Established: 7 February 1992 (effective 1 November 1993)
Aim: to coordinate policy among members in economics, building on the European Economic Community's efforts to establish a common market; defense, within the concept of a Common Foreign and Security Policy (CFSP); and justice and home affairs, including immigration, drugs, terrorism, and labor
Members (15): Austria, Belgium, Denmark, Finland, France, Germany, Greece, Ireland, Italy, Luxembourg, Netherlands, Portugal, Spain, Sweden, U.K.
Membership applicants (12): Albania, Bulgaria, Cyprus, Czech Republic, Estonia, Hungary, Latvia, Lithuania, Malta, Poland, Romania, Slovakia

International Atomic Energy Agency (IAEA)

Established: 26 October 1956 (effective 29 July 1957)
Aim: to promote peaceful uses of atomic energy
Members: 127 nations

International Bank for Reconstruction and Development (IBRD or World Bank)

Established: 22 July 1944 (effective 27 December 1945)
Aim: to provide economic development loans as a UN specialized agency
Members: 181 nations

International Committee of the Red Cross (ICRC)

Established: 1863
Aim: to provide humanitarian aid in wartime
Members: 25 individual Swiss nationals

International Court of Justice (ICJ)

Established: 26 June 1945 (effective 24 October 1945)
Aim: primary judicial organ of the United Nations
Members: 15 judges elected by the UN General Assembly and Security Council to represent all principal legal systems

International Labor Organization (ILO)

Established: 11 April 1919 (affiliated with the UN 14 December 1946)
Aim: to deal with world labor issues as a UN specialized agency
Members: 174 nations

International Monetary Fund (IMF)

Established: 22 July 1944 (effective 27 December 1945)
Aim: to promote world monetary stability and economic development as a UN specialized agency
Members: 182 nations

International Organization for Standardization (ISO)

Established: February 1947
Aim: to promote the development of international standards with a view to facilitating international exchange of goods and services and to developing cooperation in the sphere of intellectual, scientific, technological, and economic activity
Members: 85 national standards organizations

North Atlantic Treaty Organization (NATO)

Established: 17 September 1949
Aim: to promote mutual defense and cooperation
Members (19): Belgium, Canada, Czech Republic, Denmark, France, Germany, Greece, Hungary, Iceland, Italy, Luxembourg, Netherlands, Norway, Poland, Portugal, Spain, Turkey, U.K., U.S.

Organization for Economic Cooperation and Development (OECD)

Established: 14 December 1960 (effective 30 September 1961)
Aim: to promote economic cooperation and development
Members (29): Australia, Austria, Belgium, Canada, Czech Republic, Denmark, Finland, France, Germany, Greece, Hungary, Iceland, Ireland, Italy, Japan, Luxembourg, Mexico, Netherlands, N.Z., Norway, Poland, Portugal, South Korea, Spain, Sweden, Switzerland, Turkey, U.K., U.S.

Organization of African Unity (OAU)

Established: 25 May 1963
Aim: to promote unity and cooperation among African states
Members (53): Algeria, Angola, Benin, Botswana, Burkina Faso, Burundi, Cameroon, Cape Verde, Central African Republic, Chad, Comoros, Democratic Republic of the Congo, Republic of the Congo, Côte d'Ivoire, Djibouti, Egypt, Equatorial Guinea, Eritrea, Ethiopia, Gabon, Gambia, Ghana, Guinea, Guinea-Bissau, Kenya, Lesotho, Liberia, Libya, Madagascar, Malawi, Mali, Mauritania, Mauritius, Mozambique, Namibia, Niger, Nigeria, Rwanda, Sahrawi Arab Democratic Republic, São Tomé and Príncipe, Senegal, Seychelles, Sierra Leone, Somalia, South Africa, Sudan, Swaziland, Tanzania, Togo, Tunisia, Uganda, Zambia, Zimbabwe

Organization of American States (OAS)

Established: 30 April 1948 (effective 13 December 1951)
Aim: to promote regional peace and security as well as economic and social development
Members (35): Antigua and Barbuda, Argentina, The Bahamas, Barbados, Belize, Bolivia, Brazil, Canada, Chile, Colombia, Costa Rica, Cuba (excluded from formal participation since 1962), Dominica, Dominican Republic, Ecuador, El Salvador, Grenada, Guatemala, Guyana, Haiti, Honduras, Jamaica, Mexico, Nicaragua, Panama, Paraguay, Peru, Saint Kitts and Nevis, Saint Lucia, Saint Vincent and the Grenadines, Suriname, Trinidad and Tobago, U.S., Uruguay, Venezuela
Observers (40): Algeria, Angola, Austria, Belgium, Bosnia and Herzegovina, Croatia, Cyprus, Czech Republic, Egypt, Equatorial Guinea, EU, Finland, France, Germany, Greece, Holy See, Hungary, India, Israel, Italy, Japan, Kazakhstan, Latvia, Lebanon, Morocco, Netherlands, Pakistan, Poland, Portugal, Romania, Russia, Saudi Arabia, South Korea, Spain, Sri Lanka, Sweden, Switzerland, Tunisia, Ukraine, U.K.

Organization of Petroleum Exporting Countries (OPEC)

Established: 14 September 1960
Aim: to coordinate petroleum policies
Members (11): Algeria, Indonesia, Iran, Iraq, Kuwait, Libya, Nigeria, Qatar, Saudi Arabia, U.A.E., Venezuela

World Health Organization (WHO)

Established: 22 July 1946 (effective 7 April 1948)
Aim: to deal with health matters worldwide as a UN specialized agency
Members: 191 nations

World Trade Organization (WTO)

Established: 15 April 1994 (effective 1 January 1995)
Aim: to provide a means to resolve trade conflicts between members and to carry on negotiations with the goal of further lowering and/or eliminating tariffs and other trade barriers
Members: 134 nations

⊙ www.cia.gov/cia/publications/factbook/appc.html
 Central Intelligence Agency (CIA). *The World Factbook 1999.* Washington, D.C.: Central Intelligence Agency, 1999.
 McFarlane, Theresa. *Encyclopedia of Associations: International Organizations.* 33rd ed. 2 vols. Detroit: Gale Research, 1998.

WORLD: *Geography*

Global Statistics

Circumference:

Equatorial: 24,902 mi. (40,067 km.)
Polar: 24,860 mi. (40,000 km.)

Diameter:

Equatorial: 7926 mi. (12,753 km.)
Polar: 7899 mi. (12,709 km.)

Surface area:

Total surface area: 196,939,000 sq. mi.
 (510,072,520 sq. km.)
Land area: 57,506,000 sq. mi.
 (148,940,689 sq. km.)
Water surface: 139,433,000 sq. mi.
 (361,131,831 sq. km.)
Note: 70.8% of the world's surface is water,
 29.2% is land
Coastline: 221,208 mi. (356,000 km.)
Greatest ocean depth: Mariana Trench, 35,839 ft.
 (10,924 m.) in the Pacific Ocean
Elevation extremes: lowest point: Dead Sea
 −1339 ft. (−408 m.); *highest point:* Mount
 Everest 29,028 ft. (8,848 m.)

Land use:

Arable land: 10%
Permanent crops: 1%
Meadows and pastures: 26%
Forests and woodland: 32%
Other: 31%
Irrigated land: 958,016 sq. mi.
 (2,481,250 sq. km.)

Population:

6,080,671,215 (July 2000)
Population growth rate: 1.3% (2000 est.)
Birth rate: 22 births/1,000 population (2000
 est.)
Sex ratio: (2000 est.)
 at birth: 1.05 male(s)/female
 under 15 years: 1.05 male(s)/female

15–64 years: 1.02 male(s)/female
65 years and over: 0.78 male(s)/female
Infant mortality rate: 54 deaths/1,000 live births
 (2000 est.)
Life expectancy at birth: (2000 est.)
 total population: 64 years
 male: 62 years
 female: 65 years
Total fertility rate: 2.8 children born/woman
 (2000 est.)
Literacy rate (% of those age 15 and over who can
 read and write, 1999 est.):
 Combined: 79.4%
 Male: 85.2%
 Female: 73.6%

Economy:

GDP (GWP: gross world product): purchasing
 power parity—USD$40.7 trillion (1999 est.)
GDP (real growth rate): 3% (1999 est.)
GDP (per capita): purchasing power parity—
 USD$6800 (1999 est.)
Inflation rate (consumer price index): all
 countries 25%; developed countries 1% to 3%
 typically; developing countries range from 5%
 to 60% (1999 est.)

Labor force:

Total: 2.24 billion (1992 est.)
Unemployment rate: 30% combined unemployment and underemployment in many non-
 industrialized countries; developed countries
 typically 4–12% unemployment (1999 est.)

Railways:

Total: 746, 476 mi. (1,201,337 km.) (1997 est.)

Merchant marine:

Total: 27,825 ships (Jan. 1999)

Military expenditures:

(Percent of GDP): roughly 2% of gross world
 product (1998 est.)

⊙ www.cia.gov/cia/publications/factbook/geos/xx.html
 Central Intelligence Agency, *The World Factbook,* 1998. Washington, D.C.: CIA Printing and
 Photography Group, 1999.
 Brunner, Borgna, ed. *Time Almanac 2000.* Boston: Information Please, 1999.

Continents

Continent	Africa	Antarctica	Asia	Europe	North America	Oceania	South America
Population*	805,243,217	0	3,688,072,099	728,981,999	480,545,248	30,794,760	346,504,360
Percent of world population**	13%	0	61%	12%	8%	1%	6%
Pop. density	27	0	118.9	31.9	22.5	3.7	19.8
Pop. growth rate	2.27	0	1.33	0.00	1.14	1.35	1.25
Life expectancy at birth	50.8	0	66	74.1	73.7	73.2	67.7
Area, sq. mi. (sq. km.)	11,507,729 (29,805,048)	3,355,209 (8,690,000)	11,979,613 (31,027,230)	8,813,096 (22,825,942)	8,260,131 (21,393,762)	3,254,321 (8,428,702)	6,765,387 (17,522,371)

*all figures as of July 2000

**percentages may not add to 100 due to rounding

Oceania includes American Samoa, Australia, Cook Islands, Fiji, French Polynesia, Guam, Kiribati, Marshall Islands, Federated States of Micronesia, Nauru, New Caledonia, New Zealand, Northern Mariana Islands, Palau, Papua New Guinea, Samoa, Solomon Islands, Tonga, Tuvalu, Vanuatu, and Wallis and Futuna.

⊙ U.S. Census Bureau. "International Data Base (IDB)," www.census.gov/ipc/ www/idbnew.html

World Population: Future Estimates

Year	Estimated World Population	Estimated Average Annual Growth Rate (%)	Average Annual Population Increase
2000	6,080,141,683	1.26	77,258,877
2005	6,460,553,564	1.14	73,759,794
2010	6,823,634,553	1.03	70,770,206
2015	7,175,675,066	.97	69,613,925
2020	7,518,010,600	.88	66,371,114
2025	7,840,660,355	.78	61,682,010
2030	8,140,344,240	.70	57,189,977
2035	8,416,742,278	.62	52,278,271
2040	8,668,391,454	.55	47,462,555
2045	8,897,075,495	.48	43,234,092

⊙ U.S. Census Bureau. "Total Midyear Population for the World: 1950–2050,"
   www.census.gov/ipc/www/worldpop.html

World Population: Historical Estimates

Year	Population Estimates in millions (lower to upper)*	Year	Population Estimates in millions (lower to upper)*
−10000	1 to 10	1300	360 to 432
−5000	5 to 20	1400	350 to 374
−4000	7	1500	425 to 540
−3000	14	1600	545 to 579
−2000	27	1650	470 to 545
−1000	50	1700	600 to 679
−500	100	1750	629 to 961
−400	162	1800	813 to 1,125
−200	150 to 231	1850	1,128 to 1,402
1	170 to 400	1900	1,550 to 1,762
200	190 to 256	1910	1,750
400	190 to 206	1920	1,860
500	190 to 206	1930	2,070
600	200 to 206	1940	2,300
700	207 to 210	1950	2,556
800	220 to 224	1960	3,039
900	226 to 240	1970	3,706
1000	254 to 345	1980	4,453
1100	301 to 320	1990	5,283
1200	360 to 450	2000	6,080
1250	400 to 416		

*Single figures indicate no variation in estimates.

⊙ U.S. Census Bureau. "Historical Estimates of World Population," www.census.gov/
   ipc.www.worldhis.html

Largest Islands

Island	National Sovereignty	Area sq. mi. (sq. km.)
Greenland	Denmark	839,900 (1,175,600)
New Guinea	Papua New Guinea, Indonesia	309,000 (800,000)
Borneo	Indonesia, Malaysia, Brunei	283,400 (734,000)
Madagascar	Madagascar	226,658 (587,040)
Baffin	Canada	195,928 (507,451)
Sumatra	Indonesia	167,600 (434,000)
Honshu	Japan	87,805 (227,414)
Great Britain	Great Britain	88,795 (229,978)
Victoria	Canada	81,930 (212,199)
Ellesmere	Canada	75,767 (192,236)
Celebes (Sulawesi)	Indonesia	73,057 (189,216)
South Island	New Zealand	58,676 (151,971)
Java	Indonesia	48,900 (126,602)
North Island	New Zealand	44,204 (114,489)
Cuba	Cuba	42,800 (110,851)
Newfoundland	Canada	42,031 (108.860)
Luzon	Philippines	40,420 (104,688)
Iceland	Iceland	39,699 (103,000)
Mindanao	Philippines	36,537 (94,630)
Ireland	Ireland, U.K.	32,589 (84,406)
Hokkaido	Japan	30,144 (78,073)
Sakhalin	Russia	29,500 (76,400)
Hispaniola	Haiti, Dominican Republic	29,418 (76,192)
Banks	Canada	27,038 (70,028)
Tasmania	Australia	26,383 (68,332)

⊙ Wright, John W., ed. *The New York Times Almanac, Millennium Edition*. New York: Penguin, 1999.

Largest Deserts

Desert	Location	Area sq. mi. (sq. km.)
Sahara	North Africa	3,320,000 (8,600,000)
Gobi (Shamo)	Mongolia, China	500,000 (1,294,994)
Libyan	Libya, Egypt, Sudan	450,000 (1,165,495)
Rub' al-Khali	Saudi Arabia	200,000 (517,998)
Great Basin	United States	189,000 (489,500)
Chihuahuan	Mexico	175,000 (450,000)
Great Sandy	Australia	150,000 (388,498)
Great Victoria	Australia	150,000 (388,498)
Atacama	Chile	140,000 (362,598)
Takla Makan	China	140,000 (362,598)
Kalahari	South Africa	120,000 (310,798)
Sonoran	Arizona, California, Mexico	120,000 (310,800)
Kara Kum	Turkmenistan	115,000 (297,849)
Kavir	Iran	100,000 (258,999)
Kyzyl Kum	Uzbekistan and Kazakhstan	100,000 (258,999)
Nubian	North Africa	100,000 (258,999)
Syrian (Al-Hamad)	Iraq, Jordan, Saudi Arabia, Syria	100,000 (258,999)
Thar (Indian)	Pakistan-India	100,000 (258,999)
Namib	Namibia	52,000 (134,679)
Mojave	California	25,000 (64,750)

⊙ Allan, Tony, and Andrew Warren, eds. *Deserts: The Encroaching Wilderness*. New York: Oxford University Press, 1993.

Highest Mountains

Mountain Peak	Range	Country	Elevation ft. (m.)
Everest	Himalayas	Nepal, Tibet	29,028 (8,848)
K2 (Godwin Austen)	Karakoram	Pakistan, China	28,250 (8,611)
Kanchenjunga	Himalayas	India, Nepal	28,169 (8,586)
Lhotse I	Himalayas	Nepal, Tibet	27,940 (8,516)
Makalu I	Himalayas	Nepal, Tibet	27,766 (8,463)
Cho Oyu	Himalayas	Nepal, Tibet	26,906 (8,201)
Dhaulagiri	Himalayas	Nepal	26,795 (8,167)
Manaslu I	Himalayas	Nepal	26,781 (8,163)
Nanga Parbat	Himalayas	Pakistan	26,660 (8,125)
Annapurna	Himalayas	Nepal	26,545 (8,091)
Gasherbrum I	Karakoram	Pakistan, China	26,470 (8,068)
Broad Peak	Karakoram	Pakistan, China	26,400 (8,047)
Gosainthan (Shishma Pangma)	Himalayas	Tibet	26,397 (8,046)
Gasherbrum II	Karakoram	Pakistan, China	26,360 (8,035)
Annapurna II	Himalayas	Nepal	26,041 (7,937)
Gyachung Kang	Himalayas	Nepal	25,910 (7,897)
Disteghil Sar	Karakoram	Pakistan	25,858 (7,882)
Himalchuli	Himalayas	Nepal	25,801 (7,864)
Nuptse	Himalayas	Nepal	25,726 (7,841)
Nanda Devi	Himalayas	India	25,663 (7,824)
Masherbrum	Karakoram	Kashmir	25,660 (7,821)
Rakaposhi	Karakoram	Pakistan	25,551 (7,788)
Kanjut Sar	Karakoram	Pakistan	25,461 (7,761)
Kamet	Himalayas	India, Tibet	25,446 (7,756)
Namcha Barwa	Himalayas	Tibet	25,445 (7,756)
Gurla Mandhata	Himalayas	Tibet	25,355 (7,728)
Ulugh Muztagh	Kunlun	Tibet	25,340 (7,723)
Kungur	Muztagh Ata	China	25,325 (7,719)
Tirich Mir	Hindu Kush	Pakistan	25,230 (7,690)
Saser Kangri	Karakoram	India	25,172 (7,672)
Makalu II	Himalayas	Nepal	25,120 (7,657)
Minya Konka (Gongga Shan)	Daxue Shan	China	24,900 (7,590)
Kula Kangri	Himalayas	Bhutan	24,783 (7,554)
Chang-tzu	Himalayas	Tibet	24,780 (7,553)
Muztagh Ata	Muztagh Ata	China	24,757 (7,546)
Skyang Kangri	Himalayas	Kashmir	24,750 (7,544)
Ismail Samani Peak (formerly Communism Peak)	Pamirs	Tajikistan	24,590 (7,495)
Jongsong Peak	Himalayas	Nepal	24,472 (7,459)
Pobeda Peak	Tien Shan	Kyrgyzstan	24,406 (7,439)
Sia Kangri	Himalayas	Kashmir	24,350 (7,422)
Haramosh Peak	Karakoram	Pakistan	24,270 (7,397)
Istoro Nal	Hindu Kush	Pakistan	24,240 (7,388)

Tent Peak	Himalayas	Nepal	24,165 (7,365)
Chomo Lhari	Himalayas	Tibet, Bhutan	24,040 (7,327)
Chamlang	Himalayas	Nepal	24,012 (7,319)
Kabru	Himalayas	Nepal	24,002 (7,316)
Alung Gangri	Himalayas	Tibet	24,000 (7,315)
Baltoro Kangri	Himalayas	Kashmir	23,990 (7,312)
Muztagh Ata (K-5)	Kunlun	China	23,890 (7,282)
Mana	Himalayas	India	23,860 (7,237)
Baruntse	Himalayas	Nepal	23,688 (7,220)
Nepal Peak	Himalayas	Nepal	23,500 (7,163)
Amne Machin	Kunlun	China	23,490 (7,160)
Gauri Sankar	Himalayas	Nepal, Tibet	23,440 (7,145)
Badrinath	Himalayas	India	23,420 (7,138)
Nunkun	Himalayas	Kashmir	23,410 (7,135)
Lenin Peak	Pamirs	Tajikistan, Kyrgyzstan	23,405 (7,134)
Pyramid	Himalayas	Nepal	23,400 (7,132)
Api	Himalayas	Nepal	23,399 (7,132)
Pauhunri	Himalayas	India, China	23,385 (7,128)
Trisul	Himalayas	India	23,360 (7,120)
Korzhenevski Peak	Pamirs	Tajikistan	23,310 (7,105)
Kangto	Himalayas	Tibet	23,260 (7,090)
Nyainqentanglha	Nyainqentanglha Shan	China	23,255 (7,088)
Trisuli	Himalayas	India	23,210 (7,074)
Dunagiri	Himalayas	India	23,184 (7,066)
Revolution Peak	Pamirs	Tajikistan	22,880 (6,974)
Aconcagua	Andes	Argentina	22,834 (6,960)
Ojos del Salado	Andes	Argentina, Chile	22,664 (6,908)
Bonete	Andes	Argentina, Chile	22,546 (6,872)
Tupungato	Andes	Argentina, Chile	22,310 (6,800)
Moscow Peak	Pamirs	Tajikistan	22,260 (6,785)
Pissis	Andes	Argentina	22,241 (6,779)
Mercedario	Andes	Argentina, Chile	22,211 (6,770)
Huascarán	Andes	Peru	22,205 (6,768)
Llullaillaco	Andes	Argentina, Chile	22,057 (6,723)
El Libertador	Andes	Argentina	22,047 (6,720)
Cachi	Andes	Argentina	22,047 (6,720)
Kailas	Himalayas	Tibet	22,027 (6,714)
Incahuasi	Andes	Argentina, Chile	21,720 (6,620)
Yerupaja	Andes	Peru	21,709 (6,617)
Kurumda	Pamirs	Tajikistan	21,686 (6,610)
Galan	Andes	Argentina	21,654 (6,600)
El Muerto	Andes	Argentina, Chile	21,463 (6,542)
Sajama	Andes	Bolivia	21,391 (6,520)
Nacimiento	Andes	Argentina	21,302 (6,493)
Illampu	Andes	Bolivia	21,276 (6,485)
Illimani	Andes	Bolivia	21,201 (6,462)
Coropuna	Andes	Peru	21,083 (6,426)

Mountain Peak	Range	Country	Elevation ft. (m.)
Laudo	Andes	Argentina	20,997 (6,400)
Ancohuma	Andes	Bolivia	20,958 (6,388)
Cuzco (Ausangate)	Andes	Peru	20,945 (6,384)
Toro	Andes	Argentina, Chile	20,932 (6,380)
Tres Cruces	Andes	Argentina, Chile	20,853 (6,356)
Huandoy	Andes	Peru	20,852 (6,356)
Parinacota	Andes	Bolivia, Chile	20,768 (6,330)
Tortolas	Andes	Argentina, Chile	20,745 (6,323)
Chimborazo	Andes	Ecuador	20,702 (6,310)
Ampato	Andes	Peru	20,702 (6,310)
El Condor	Andes	Argentina	20,669 (6,300)
Salcantay	Andes	Peru	20,574 (6,271)
Huancarhuas	Andes	Peru	20,531 (6,258)
Famatina	Andes	Argentina	20,505 (6,250)
Pumasillo	Andes	Peru	20,492 (6,246)
Solo	Andes	Argentina	20,492 (6,246)
Polleras	Andes	Argentina	20,456 (6,235)
Pular	Andes	Chile	20,423 (6,225)
Chañi	Andes	Argentina	20,341 (6,200)
McKinley (Denali)	Alaska	Alaska	20,320 (6,194)
Aucanquilcha	Andes	Chile	20,295 (6,186)
Juncal	Andes	Argentina, Chile	20,276 (6,180)
Negro	Andes	Argentina	20,184 (6,152)
Quela	Andes	Argentina	20,128 (6,135)
Condoriri	Andes	Bolivia	20,095 (6,125)
Palermo	Andes	Argentina	20,079 (6,120)
Solimana	Andes	Peru	20,068 (6,117)
San Juan	Andes	Argentina, Chile	20,049 (6,111)
Sierra Nevada	Andes	Argentina	20,023 (6,103)
Antofalla	Andes	Argentina	20,013 (6,100)
Marmolejo	Andes	Argentina, Chile	20,013 (6,100)

⊙ Wright, John W., ed. *The New York Times Almanac, Millennium Edition.* New York: Penguin, 1999.

Largest Lakes

Name	Location	Area sq. mi. (sq. km.)	Maximum Depth ft. (m.)
Caspian Sea	Azerbaijan, Russia, Kazakhstan, Turkmenistan, Iran	143,550 (371,800)	3,363 (1,025)
Superior	U.S., Canada	31,800 (82,362)	1,333 (406)
Victoria	Tanzania, Uganda	26,820 (68,000)	279 (85)
Aral Sea	Kazakhstan, Uzbekistan	24,904 (64,500)	220 (67)
Huron	U.S., Canada	23,000 (59,570)	750 (227)
Michigan	U.S.	22,400 (58,000)	923 (281)

Tanganyika	Tanzania, Congo	12,350 (31,986)	4,800 (1,463)
Baikal	Russia	12,160 (31,494)	5,315 (1,620)
Great Bear	Canada	12,028 (31,152)	1,356 (413)
Nyasa	Malawi, Mozambique, Tanzania	11,150 (28,878)	2,280 (695)
Great Slave	Canada	11,030 (28,568)	2,015 (614)
Erie	U.S., Canada	9,910 (25,666)	210 (64)
Winnipeg	Canada	9,417 (24,390)	92 (28)
Ontario	U.S., Canada	7,600 (19,684)	802 (244)
Balkhash	Kazakhstan	7,115 (18,428)	87 (27)
Ladoga	Russia	6,835 (17,703)	755 (230)
Chad	Chad, Niger, Nigeria	6,300 (16,317)	36 (11)
Maracaibo	Venezuela	5,200 (13,468)	115 (35)
Eyre	Australia	3,920 (10,153)	4 (1.5)*
Onega	Russia	3,720 (9,635)	394 (120)
Titicaca	Bolivia, Peru	3,200 (8,288)	990 (301)
Nicaragua	Nicaragua	3,150 (8,158)	230 (70)
Athabaska	Canada	3,064 (7,936)	407 (124)
Reindeer	Canada	2,568 (6,651)	720 (219)
Rudolf	Kenya	2,473 (6,405)	240 (73)
Issyk Kul	Kyrgyzstan	2,355 (6,099)	2,303 (702)
Torrens	South Australia	2,230 (5,776)	.5 (.15)*
Vänern	Sweden	2,156 (5,584)	325 (99)
Nettilling	Baffin Island, Canada	2,140 (5,543)	38 (11)
Winnipegosis	Canada	2,075 (5,374)	38 (11)
Lake Albert	Uganda, Democratic Republic of the Congo	2,075 (5,374)	168 (51)
Kariba	Uganda	2,050 (5,309)	390 (119)
Nipigon	Canada	1,872 (4,848)	540 (165)
Urmia	Iran	1,815 (4,701)	49 (15)
Manitoba	Canada	1,800 (4,662)	92 (28)

*Depth varies dramatically with rainfall in wet season

⊙ United States Department of Commerce, National Oceanic and Atmospheric Administration, *Principal Rivers and Lakes of the World*, 1982.
Wright, John W., ed. *The New York Times Almanac 2000*. New York: Penguin Reference, 1999.

Longest Rivers

River	Continent	Length mi. (km.)
Nile	Africa	4,145 (6,669)
Amazon	South America	3,860 (7,148)
Mississippi-Missouri	North America	3,740 (6,018)
Yangtze (Chang Jiang)	Asia	3,720 (5,985)
Yenisei-Angara	Asia	3,650 (5,873)
Amur	Asia	3,590 (5,776)
Ob	Asia	3,360 (5,406)
Río de la Plata-Paraná	South America	3,030 (4,875)
Yellow (Huang He)	Asia	2,903 (4,671)
Congo (Zaire)	Africa	2,900 (4,666)
Lena	Asia	2,730 (4,393)

River	Continent	Length mi. (km.)
Mackenzie	North America	2,635 (4,240)
Niger	Africa	2,600 (4,183)
Mekong	Asia	2,600 (4,183)
Murray-Darling	Australia	2,330 (3,749)
Volga	Europe	2,290 (3,685)
Madeira	South America	2,013 (3,239)
São Francisco	South America	1,988 (3,199)
Yukon	North America	1,979 (3,665)
Rio Grande	North America	1,885 (3,491)
Purus	South America	1,860 (2,993)
Indus	Asia	1,800 (2,896)
Danube	Europe	1,776 (2,858)
Brahmaputra (Tsangpo)	Asia	1,770 (2,848)
Salween (Saluen, Chiama Ngu Chu)	Asia	1,750 (2,816)
Tocantins-Para	South America	1,710 (2,751)
Zambezi	Africa	1,700 (2,735)
Paraguay	South America	1,610 (2,590)
Saskatchewan	North America	1,600 (2,574)
Amu Darya	Asia	1,578 (2,539)
Ural	Europe	1,575 (2,534)
Ganges	Asia	1,560 (2,510)
Euphrates	Asia	1,510 (2,430)
Colorado	North America	1,450 (2,333)
Arkansas	North America	1,450 (2,333)
Dnieper	Europe	1,420 (2,285)
Kasai	Africa	1,338 (2,153)
Orange	Africa	1,300 (2,092)
Irrawaddy	Asia	1,300 (2,092)
Kolyma	Asia	1,300 (2,092)
Orinoco	South America	1,280 (2,060)
Columbia	North America	1,243 (2,000)
Don	Europe	1,224 (1,969)
Dniester	Europe	875 (1,408)
Rhine	Europe	820 (1,319)
Brazos	North America	800 (1,287)
Saint Lawrence	North America	800 (1,287) *
Vistula	Europe	663 (1,067)
Loire	Europe	625 (1,006)
Tagus	Europe	625 (1,006)

*not including waterway provided by the Great Lakes

⊙ *The World Almanac and Book of Facts, 2000: Millennium Collector's Edition.* Mahwah, N.J.: World Almanac Books, 1999.

Ocean	Area (in millions) sq. mi. (sq. km.)	Coastline mi. (km.)	Maximum Depth ft. (m.)	Location of Maximum Depth	Marginal Seas
Pacific	69.35 (179.68)	84,246 (135,663)	35,839 (10,924)	Mariana Trench	Bali, Bellingshausen, Bering, Coral, Flores, Java, Philippine, Ross, Savu, Sea of Japan, Sea of Okhotsk, South China, Tasman, Timor
Atlantic	35.65 (92.37)	69,468 (111,866)	28,231 (8,605)	Puerto Rico Trench	Baltic, Black, Caribbean, Mediterranean, North, Norwegian, Scotia, Weddell
Indian	28.53 (73.91)	41,312 (66,526)	23,812 (7,258)	Java Trench	Arabian, Bass Strait, Bay of Bengal
Arctic	5.44 (14.09)	28,186 (45,389)	17,881 (5,450)	Eurasia Basin	Barents, Beaufort, Chukchi, East Siberian, Greenland, Hudson Bay, Kara, Laptev

⊙ Central Intelligence Agency. *The World Factbook*, 1998. Washington, D.C.: CIA Printing and Photography Group. 1999.

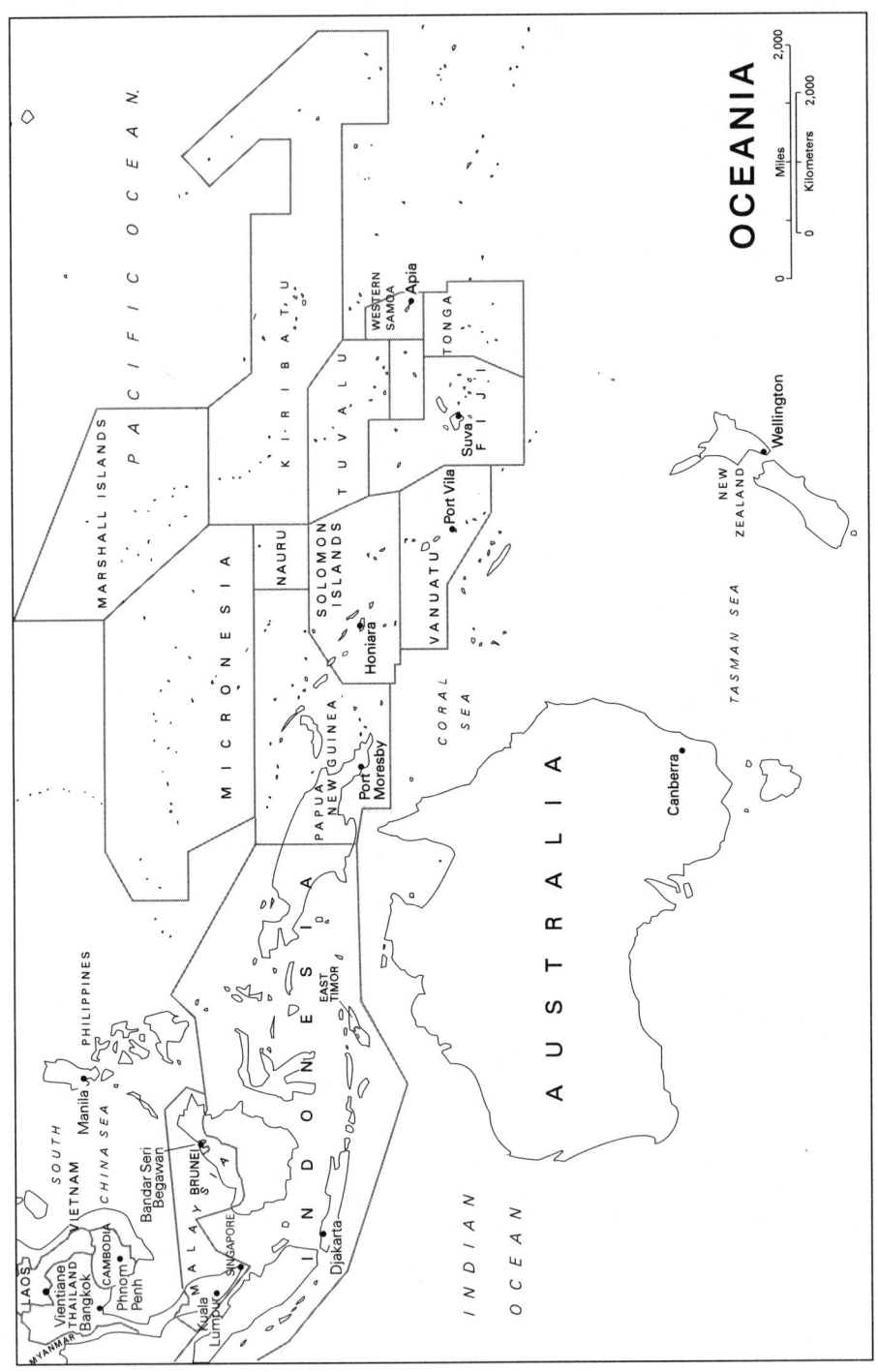

OCEANIA

CARIBBEAN SEA

SAINT VINCENT AND THE GRENADINES — SAINT LUCIA

GRENADA

BARBADOS

Port of Spain

TRINIDAD AND TOBAGO

Panama

Caracas

VENEZUELA

ATLANTIC OCEAN

PANAMA

Bogotá

Georgetown

Paramaribo

GUYANA

SURINAME

French Guiana

COLOMBIA

Quito

ECUADOR

P E R U

Lima

B R A Z I L

Brasília

La Paz

B O L I V I A

C H I L E

PACIFIC OCEAN

PARAGUAY

Asunción

A R G E N T I N A

Santiago

URUGUAY

Buenos Aires

Montevideo

SOUTH AMERICA

0   Miles   1,000

0   Kilometers   1,000

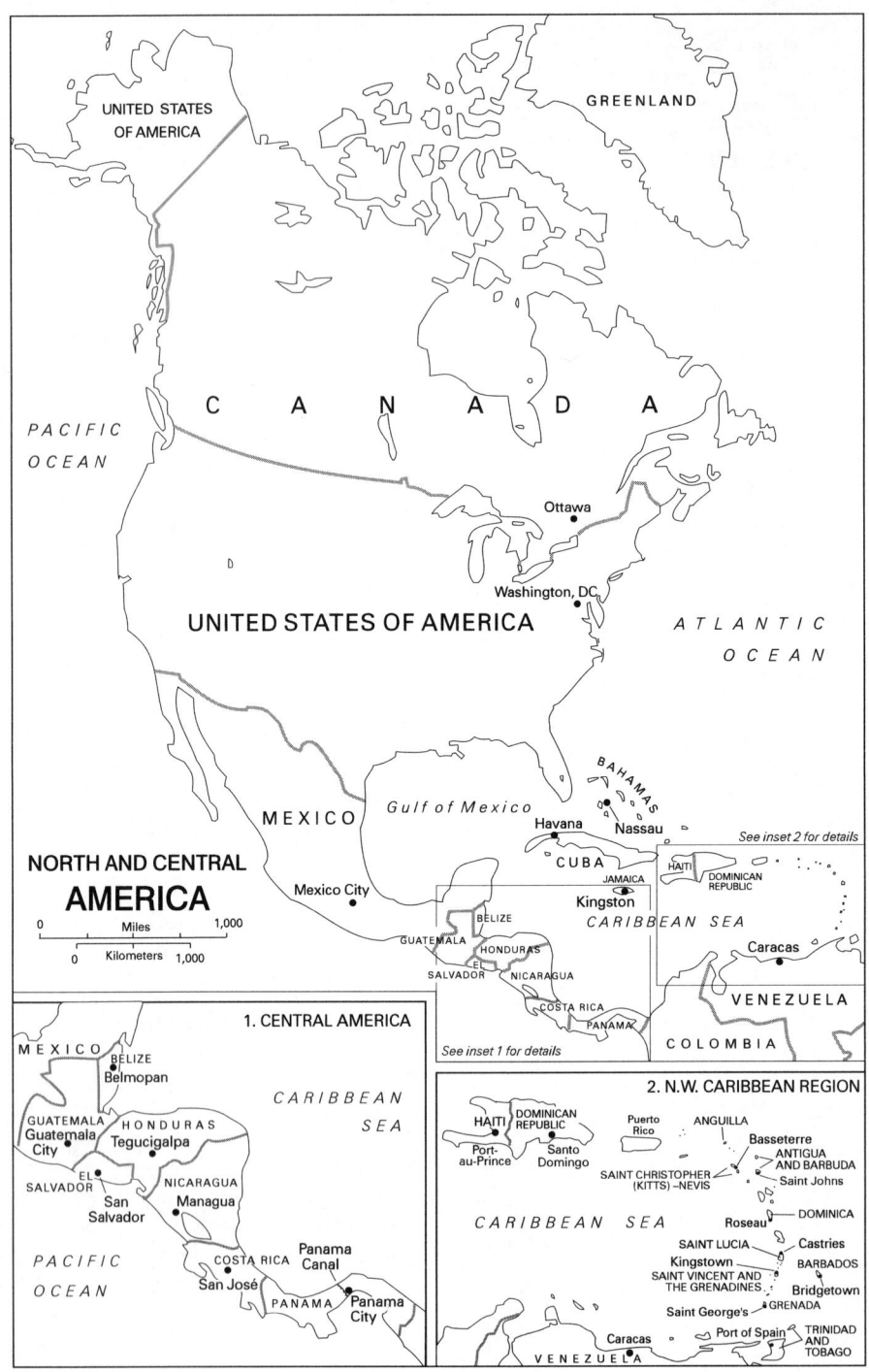

UNITED STATES
OF AMERICA

GREENLAND

C A N A D A

PACIFIC
OCEAN

Ottawa

Washington, DC

UNITED STATES OF AMERICA

ATLANTIC
OCEAN

MEXICO *Gulf of Mexico*

BAHAMAS

Havana   Nassau

NORTH AND CENTRAL

AMERICA

0	Miles	1,000
0	Kilometers	1,000

Mexico City

CUBA

HAITI DOMINICAN
REPUBLIC

See inset 2 for details

JAMAICA
Kingston

BELIZE

GUATEMALA

HONDURAS

EL
SALVADOR   NICARAGUA

COSTA RICA

PANAMA

CARIBBEAN SEA

Caracas

VENEZUELA

COLOMBIA

See inset 1 for details

1. CENTRAL AMERICA

MEXICO   BELIZE
Belmopan

CARIBBEAN
SEA

GUATEMALA
Guatemala
City   HONDURAS
Tegucigalpa

EL
SALVADOR   NICARAGUA
San   Managua
Salvador

Panama
Canal

PACIFIC
OCEAN

COSTA RICA   PANAMA   Panama
San José   City

2. N.W. CARIBBEAN REGION

HAITI   DOMINICAN
REPUBLIC   Puerto
Rico   ANGUILLA

Port-
au-Prince   Santo
Domingo   Basseterre   ANTIGUA
AND BARBUDA

SAINT CHRISTOPHER   Saint Johns
(KITTS) –NEVIS

CARIBBEAN   SEA   Roseau   DOMINICA

SAINT LUCIA   Castries
Kingstown   BARBADOS
SAINT VINCENT AND
THE GRENADINES   Bridgetown
Saint George's   GRENADA

Port of Spain   TRINIDAD
AND
Caracas   TOBAGO

VENEZUELA

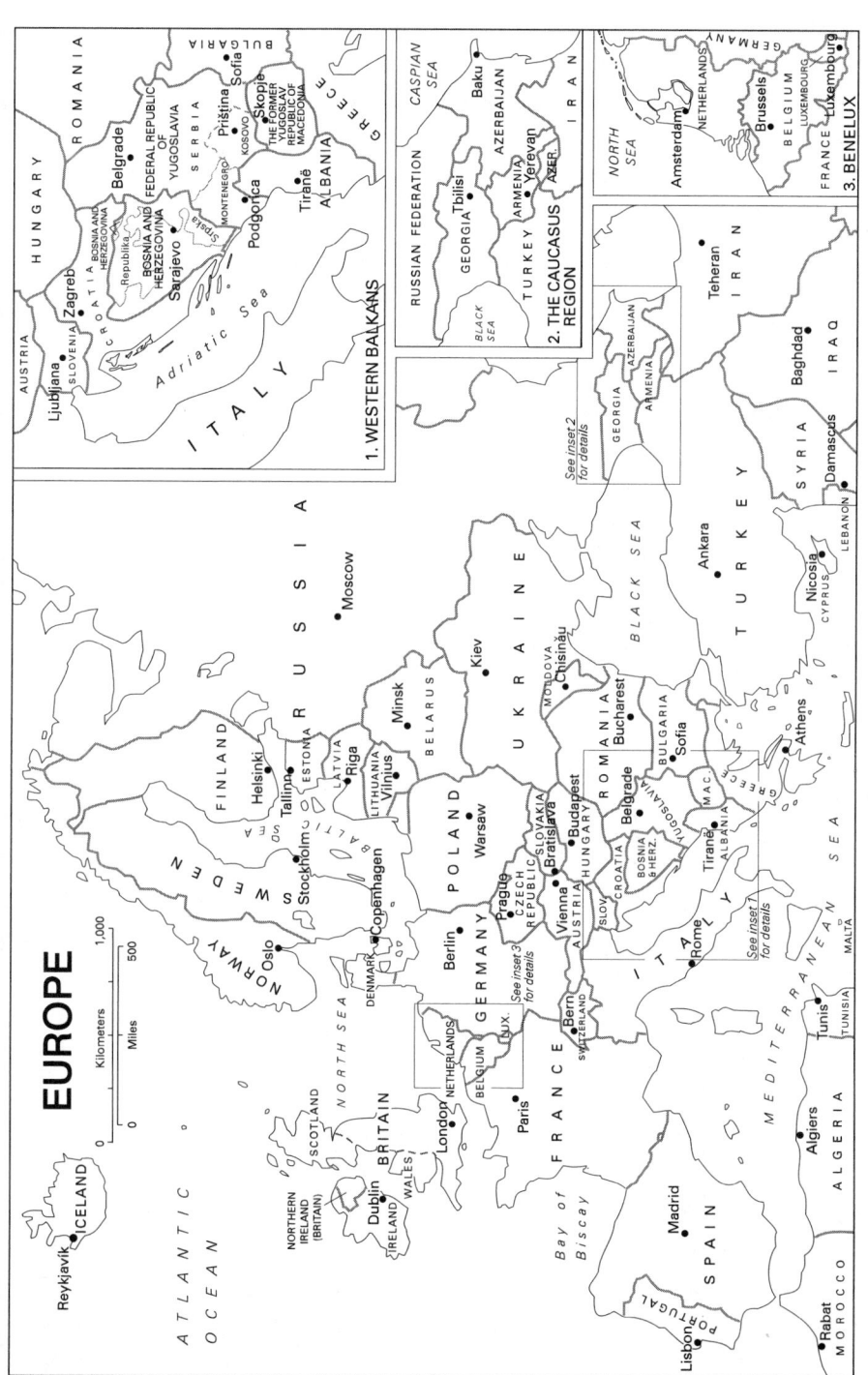

EUROPE

1. WESTERN BALKANS

2. THE CAUCASUS REGION

3. BENELUX

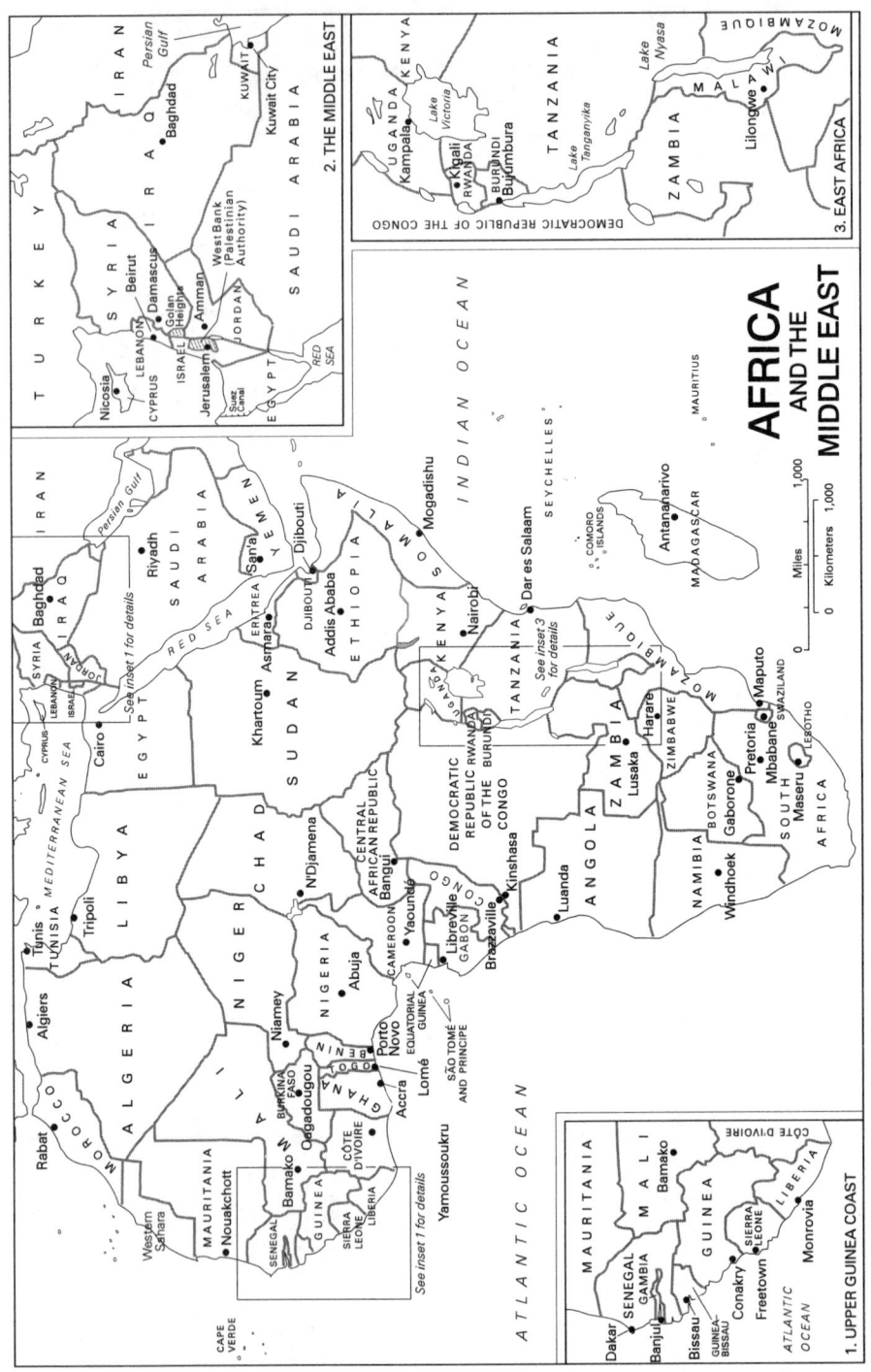

AFRICA AND THE MIDDLE EAST

2. THE MIDDLE EAST

TURKEY

SYRIA

IRAQ
Baghdad

IRAN

Persian Gulf

KUWAIT
Kuwait City

SAUDI ARABIA

Nicosia
CYPRUS

LEBANON
Beirut
Damascus
Golan Heights
ISRAEL
Jerusalem
Suez Canal

West Bank (Palestinian Authority)
Amman
JORDAN

RED SEA

EGYPT

3. EAST AFRICA

DEMOCRATIC REPUBLIC OF THE CONGO

UGANDA
Kampala
Lake Victoria

RWANDA
Kigali
BURUNDI
Bujumbura
Lake Tanganyika

KENYA

TANZANIA

ZAMBIA

Lake Nyasa

MALAWI
Lilongwe

MOZAMBIQUE

1. UPPER GUINEA COAST

MAURITANIA

MALI
Bamako

SENEGAL
Dakar
GAMBIA
Banjul
GUINEA-BISSAU
Bissau

GUINEA
Conakry

SIERRA LEONE
Freetown

LIBERIA
Monrovia

CÔTE DIVOIRE

ATLANTIC OCEAN

TURKEY
SYRIA
CYPRUS
LEBANON
ISRAEL
IRAQ
Baghdad
IRAN

Persian Gulf

JORDAN

EGYPT
Cairo

MEDITERRANEAN SEA

MOROCCO
Rabat

ALGERIA
Algiers

TUNISIA
Tunis
Tripoli

LIBYA

Western Sahara

MAURITANIA
Nouakchott

CAPE VERDE

SENEGAL

GUINEA

SIERRA LEONE
LIBERIA
CÔTE DIVOIRE

Bamako
MALI
Ouagadougou
BURKINA FASO

NIGER
Niamey

NIGERIA
Abuja

BENIN
TOGO
GHANA
Accra
Lomé
Porto Novo

Yamoussoukro

CHAD
N'Djamena

CENTRAL AFRICAN REPUBLIC
Bangui

CAMEROON
Yaoundé

EQUATORIAL GUINEA
Libreville
GABON
CONGO
Brazzaville

SÃO TOMÉ AND PRINCIPE

SUDAN
Khartoum

EGYPT

SAUDI ARABIA
Riyadh

YEMEN
Sana'a

ERITREA
Asmara

DJIBOUTI
Djibouti

ETHIOPIA
Addis Ababa

SOMALIA
Mogadishu

RED SEA

Persian Gulf

IRAQ
Baghdad

IRAN

DEMOCRATIC REPUBLIC OF THE CONGO
Kinshasa

RWANDA
BURUNDI

KENYA
Nairobi

TANZANIA
Dar es Salaam

ANGOLA
Luanda

ZAMBIA
Lusaka

ZIMBABWE
Harare

NAMIBIA
Windhoek

BOTSWANA
Gaborone

SOUTH AFRICA
Pretoria
Maputo
Mbabane
SWAZILAND
Maseru
LESOTHO

MOZAMBIQUE

MALAWI

INDIAN OCEAN

SEYCHELLES

COMORO ISLANDS

MADAGASCAR
Antananarivo

MAURITIUS

ATLANTIC OCEAN

See inset 1 for details

See inset 3 for details

0 1,000 Miles
0 1,000 Kilometers

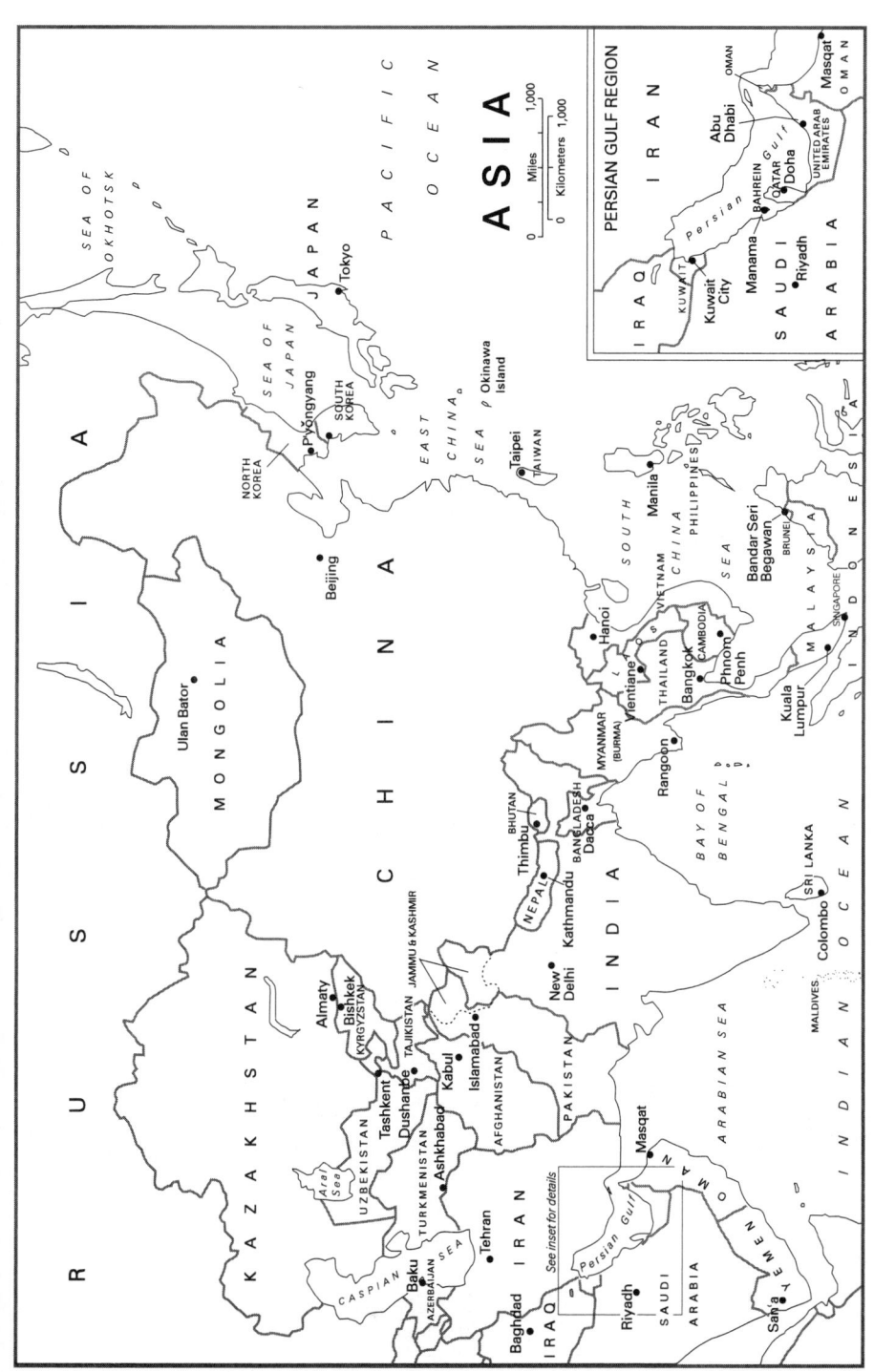

WORLD: *Nations and Territories*

Nations

Afghanistan

Geography

Location: Southern Asia

Area: 250,000 sq. mi.; 647,500 sq. km. (slightly smaller than Texas)

Climate: arid to semiarid; cold winters and hot summers

Terrain: mostly rugged mountains; plains in north and southwest

Elevation: lowest point: Amu Darya 846 ft. (258 m.); highest point: Nowshak 24,557 ft. (7,485 m.)

Natural resources: natural gas, petroleum, coal, copper, talc, barites, sulfur, lead, zinc, iron ore, salt, precious and semiprecious stones

People

Population: 25,824,882

Population growth rate: 4.21%

Infant mortality rate: 143.63 deaths/1,000 live births

Life expectancy at birth: total population: 46.83 years; male: 47.35 years; female: 46.29 years

Major ethnic groups: Pashtun 38%, Tajik 25%, Uzbek 6%, Hazara 19%

Major religions: Sunni Muslim 84%, Shi'a Muslim 15%

Major languages: Pashtu 35%, Afghan Persian (Dari) 50%, Turkic languages (primarily Uzbek and Turkmen) 11%

Government

Official name: Islamic Emirate of Afghanistan

Government type: transitional government

National capital: Kabul

Independence: August 19, 1919

Legal system: Shari'a (Islamic law)

Economy

Industries: small-scale production of textiles, soap, furniture, shoes, fertilizer, and cement; handwoven carpets; natural gas, oil, coal, copper

Agricultural products: wheat, fruits, nuts, karakul pelts; wool, mutton

Currency: 1 afghani (AF) = 100 puls

Albania

Geography

Location: Southeastern Europe, bordering the Adriatic Sea and Ionian Sea, between Greece and Serbia and Montenegro

Area: 11,100 sq. mi. (28,750 sq. km.); slightly larger than Maryland

Climate: mild temperate; cool, cloudy, wet winters; hot, clear, dry summers; interior is cooler and wetter

Terrain: mostly mountains and hills; small plains along coast

Elevation: lowest point: Adriatic Sea 0 ft. (0 m.); highest point: Maja e Korabit 1,063 ft. (2,753 m.)

Natural resources: petroleum, natural gas, coal, chromium, copper, timber, nickel

People

Population: 3,364,571 (July 1999 est.)

Population growth rate: 1.05% (July 1999 est.)

Infant mortality rate: 42.9 deaths/1,000 live births

Life expectancy at birth: total population: 67 years; male: 65.92 years; female: 72.33 years

Major ethnic groups: Albanian 95%, Greeks 3%, other 2% (Vlachs, Gypsies, Serbs, and Bulgarians). NOTE: in 1989, other estimates of the Greek population ranged from 1% (official Albanian statistics) to 12% (from a Greek organization)

Major religions: Muslim 70%, Albanian Orthodox 20%, Roman Catholic 10%

Major languages: Albanian (Tosk is the official dialect), Greek

Government

Official name: Republic of Albania

Government type: emerging democracy

National capital: Tirana
Independence: November 28, 1912 (from Ottoman Empire)
Legal system: has not accepted compulsory ICJ jurisdiction

Economy

Industries: food processing, textiles and clothing; lumber, oil, cement, chemicals, mining, basic metals, hydropower
Agricultural products: wide range of temperate-zone crops and livestock
Currency: 1 lek (L) = 100 qintars

Algeria

Geography

Location: Northern Africa, bordering the Mediterranean Sea, between Morocco and Tunisia
Area: 919,590 sq. mi. (2,381,740 sq. km.); slightly less than 3.5 times the size of Texas
Climate: arid to semiarid; mild, wet winters with hot, dry summers along coast; drier with cold winters and hot summers on high plateau; sirocco is a hot, dust/sand-laden wind especially common in summer
Terrain: mostly high plateau and desert; some mountains; narrow, discontinuous coastal plain
Elevation: lowest point: Chott Melrhir –131 ft. (–40 m.); highest point: Tahat 9,852 ft. (3,003 m.)
Natural resources: petroleum, natural gas, iron ore, phosphates, uranium, lead, zinc

People

Population: 31,133,486 (July 1999 est.)
Population growth rate: 2.1%
Infant mortality rate: 43.82 deaths/1,000 live births
Life expectancy at birth: total population: 69.24 years; male: 68.07 years; female: 70.46 years
Major ethnic groups: Arab-Berber 99%, European less than 1%
Major religions: Sunni Muslim (state religion) 99%, Christian and Jewish 1%

Major languages: Arabic (official), French, Berber dialects

Government

Official name: Democratic and Popular Republic of Algeria
Government type: republic
National capital: Algiers
Independence: July 5, 1962 (from France)
Legal system: socialist, based on French and Islamic law; judicial review of legislative acts in ad hoc Constitutional Council composed of various public officials, including several Supreme Court justices; has not accepted compulsory ICJ jurisdiction

Economy

Industries: petroleum, light industries, natural gas, mining, electrical, petrochemical, food processing
Agricultural products: wheat, barley, oats, grapes, olives, citrus, fruits; sheep, cattle
Currency: 1 Algerian dinar (DA) = 100 centimes

American Samoa

Geography

Location: Oceania, group of islands in the South Pacific Ocean, about one-half of the way from Hawaii to New Zealand
Area: 77 sq. mi. (199 sq. km.); slightly larger than Washington, D.C.
Climate: tropical marine, moderated by southeast trade winds; annual rainfall averages 124 inches; rainy season from November to April, dry season from May to October; little seasonal temperature variation
Terrain: five volcanic islands with rugged peaks and limited coastal plains, two coral atolls (Rose Island, Swains Island)
Elevation: lowest point: Pacific Ocean 0 ft. (0 m.); highest point: highest point: Lata 373 ft. (966 m.)
Natural resources: pumice, pumicite

People

Population: 63,786 (July 1999 est.)
Population growth rate: 2.64 %

Infant mortality rate: 10.19 deaths/1,000 live births

Life expectancy at birth: total population: 75.46 years; male: 71.23 years; female: 79.95 years

Major ethnic groups: Samoan (Polynesian) 89%, Caucasian 2%, Tongan 4%, other 5%

Major religions: Christian Congregationalist 50%, Roman Catholic 20%, Protestant denominations and other 30%

Major languages: Samoan (closely related to Hawaiian and other Polynesian languages), English; most people are bilingual

Government

Official name: Territory of American Samoa

Government type: unincorporated and unorganized territory of the U.S.; administered by the U.S. Department of Interior, Office of Territorial and International Affairs

National capital: Pago Pago

Independence: none (territory of the U.S.)

Legal system: N/A

Economy

Industries: tuna canneries (largely dependent on foreign fishing vessels), meat canning, handicrafts

Agricultural products: bananas, coconuts, vegetables, taro, breadfruit, yams, copra, pineapples, papayas, dairy

Currency: 1 U.S. dollar (US$) = 100 cents

Andorra

Geography

Location: Southwestern Europe, between France and Spain

Area: 174 sq. mi. (450 sq. km.); comparative area: 2.5 times the size of Washington, D.C.

Climate: temperate; snowy, cold winters and warm, dry summers

Terrain: rugged mountains dissected by narrow valleys

Elevation: lowest point: Riu Valira 2,756 ft. (840 m.); highest point: Coma Pedrosa 9,665 ft. (2,946 m.)

Natural resources: hydropower, mineral water, timber, iron ore, lead

People

Population: 65,939 (July 1999 est.)

Population growth rate: 2.24%

Infant mortality rate: 4.0 deaths/1,000 live births

Life expectancy at birth: total population: 83.46 years; male: 80.55 years; female: 86.55 years

Major ethnic groups: Spanish 61%, Andorran 30%, French 6%

Major religions: Roman Catholic (predominant)

Major languages: Catalan (official), French, Castilian

Government

Official name: Principality of Andorra

Government type: parliamentary democracy that retains as its heads of state a coprincipality; the two princes are the president of France and Spanish bishop of Seo de Urgel, who are represented locally by officials called veguers

National capital: Andorra la Vella

Independence: 1278

Legal system: based on French and Spanish civil codes; no judicial review of legislative acts; has not accepted compulsory ICJ jurisdiction

Economy

Industries: tourism (particularly skiing), sheep, timber, tobacco, banking

Agricultural products: small quantities of tobacco, rye, wheat, barley, oats, vegetables; sheep raising

Currency: 1 French franc (F) = 100 centimes; 1 peseta (Pta) = 100 centimos; the French and Spanish currencies are used

Angola

Geography

Location: Southern Africa, bordering the South Atlantic Ocean, between Namibia and Zaire

Area: 481,351 sq. mi. (1,246,700 sq. km.); comparative area: slightly less than twice the size of Texas

Climate: semiarid in south and along coast to Luanda; north has cool, dry season (May to October) and hot, rainy season (November to April)

Terrain: narrow coastal plain rises abruptly to vast interior plateau

Elevation: lowest point: Atlantic Ocean 0 ft. (0 m.); highest point: Moro de Moco 8,596 ft. (2,620 m.)

Natural resources: petroleum, diamonds, iron ore, phosphates, copper, feldspar, gold, bauxite, uranium

People

Population: 11,177,537 (July 1999 est.)

Population growth rate: 2.84%

Infant mortality rate: 129.19 deaths/1,000 live births

Life expectancy at birth: total population: 48.93 years; male: 46.08 years; female: 50.82 years

Major ethnic groups: Ovimbundu 37%, Kimbundu 25%, Bakongo 13%, mestico (mixed European and Native African) 2%, European 1%, other 22%

Major religions: indigenous beliefs 47%, Roman Catholic 38%, Protestant 15%

Major languages: Portuguese (official), Bantu and other African languages

Government

Official name: Republic of Angola

Government type: transitional government nominally a multiparty democracy with a strong presidential system

National capital: Luanda

Independence: November 11, 1975 (from Portugal)

Legal system: based on Portuguese civil law system and customary law; recently modified to accommodate political pluralism and increased use of free markets

Economy

Industries: petroleum; diamonds, iron ore, phosphates, feldspar, bauxite, uranium, and gold; fish processing; food processing; brewing; tobacco; sugar; textiles; cement; basic metal products

Agricultural products: bananas, sugarcane, coffee, sisal, corn, cotton, manioc (tapioca), tobacco, vegetables, plantains; livestock; forest products; fish

Currency: 1 new kwanza (NKz) = 100 lwei

Anguilla

Geography

Location: Caribbean, island in the Caribbean Sea, east of Puerto Rico

Area: 35 sq. mi. (91 sq. km.); about half the size of Washington, D.C.

Climate: tropical; moderated by northeast trade winds

Terrain: flat and low-lying island of coral and limestone

Elevation: lowest point: Caribbean Sea 0 ft. (0 m.); highest point: Crocus Hill 213 ft. (65 m.)

Natural resources: salt, fish, lobster

People

Population: 11,510 (July 1999 est.)

Population growth rate: 3.16%

Infant mortality rate: 18.72 deaths/1,000 live births

Life expectancy at birth: total population: 77.71 years; male: 74.72 years; female: 80.78 years

Major ethnic group: black African

Major religions: Anglican 40%, Methodist 33%, Seventh-Day Adventist 7%, Baptist 5%, Roman Catholic 3%, other 12%

Major language: English (official)

Government

Official name: Anguilla

Government type: dependent territory of the U.K.

National capital: The Valley

Independence: none (dependent territory of the U.K.)

Legal system: based on English common law

Economy

Industries: tourism, boat building, offshore financial services

Agricultural products: pigeon peas, corn, sweet potatoes; sheep, goats, pigs, cattle, poultry; fishing (including lobster)

Currency: 1 East Caribbean dollar (EC$) = 100 cents

Antigua and Barbuda

Geography

Location: Caribbean, islands between the Caribbean Sea and the North Atlantic Ocean, east-southeast of Puerto Rico

Area: 170 sq. mi. (440 sq. km.) comparative area: 2.5 times the size of Washington, D.C.

Climate: tropical marine; little seasonal temperature variation

Terrain: mostly low-lying limestone and coral islands with some higher volcanic areas

Elevation: lowest point: Caribbean Sea 0 ft. (0 m.); highest point: Boggy Peak 1,319 ft. (402 m.)

Natural resources: negligible; pleasant climate fosters tourism

People

Population: 64,246 (July 1999 est.)

Population growth rate: 0.36%

Infant mortality rate: 20.69 deaths/1,000 live births

Life expectancy at birth: total population: 71.46 years; male: 69.06 years; female: 73.98 years

Major ethnic groups: black, British, Portuguese, Lebanese, Syrian

Major religions: Anglican (predominant), other Protestant sects, some Roman Catholic

Major languages: English (official), local dialects

Government

Official name: Antigua and Barbuda

Government type: parliamentary democracy

National capital: Saint John's

Independence: November 1, 1981 (from U.K.)

Legal system: based on English common law

Economy

Industries: tourism, construction, light manufacturing (clothing, alcohol, household appliances)

Agricultural products: cotton, fruits, vegetables, bananas, coconuts, cucumbers, mangoes, sugarcane; livestock

Currency: 1 East Caribbean dollar (EC$) = 100 cents

Argentina

Geography

Location: Southern South America, bordering the South Atlantic Ocean, between Chile and Uruguay

Area: 1,068,296 sq. mi. (2,766,890 sq. km.); slightly less than three-tenths the size of the U.S.

Climate: mostly temperate; arid in southeast; subantarctic in southwest

Terrain: rich plains of the Pampas in northern half, flat to rolling plateau of Patagonia in south, rugged Andes along western border

Elevation: lowest point: Salinas Chicas –131 ft. (–40 m.); highest point: Cerro Aconcagua 22,841 ft. (6,962 m.)

Natural resources: fertile plains of the pampas, lead, zinc, tin, copper, iron ore, manganese, petroleum, uranium

People

Population: 36,737,664 (July 1999 est.)

Population growth rate: 1.29%

Infant mortality rate: 18.41 deaths/1,000 live births

Life expectancy at birth: total population: 74.76 years; male: 71.13 years; female: 78.56 years

Major ethnic groups: white 85%, mestizo, Indian, or other nonwhite groups 15%

Major religions: nominally Roman Catholic 90% (less than 20% practicing), Protestant 2%, Jewish 2%, other 6%

Major languages: Spanish (official), English, Italian, German, French

Government

Official name: Argentine Republic

Government type: republic

National capital: Buenos Aires

Independence: July 9, 1816 (from Spain)
Legal system: mixture of US and West European legal systems, has not accepted compulsory IJC jurisdiction

Economy

Industries: food processing, motor vehicles, consumer durables, textiles, chemicals and petrochemicals, printing, metallurgy, steel
Agricultural products: wheat, corn, sorghum, soybeans, sugar beets; livestock
Currency: 1 nuevo peso argentino = 100 centavos

Armenia

Geography

Location: Southwestern Asia, east of Turkey
Area: 11,506 sq. mi. (29,800 sq. km.); slightly larger than Maryland
Climate: highland continental, hot summers, cold winters
Terrain: high Armenian Plateau with mountains; little forest land; fast flowing rivers; good soil in Aras River valley
Elevation: lowest point: Debed River 1,312 ft. (400 m.); highest point: Aragats Lerr 13,435 ft. (4,095 m.)
Natural resources: small deposits of gold, copper, molybdenum, zinc, alumina

People

Population: 3,409,234 (July 1999 est.)
Population growth rate: -0.38%
Infant mortality rate: 41.12 deaths/1,000 live births
Life expectancy at birth: total population: 66.56 years; male: 62.21 years; female: 71.13 years
Major ethnic groups: Armenian 93%, Azeri 3%, Russian 2%
Major religions: Armenian Orthodox 94%
Major languages: Armenian 96%, Russian 2%,

Government

Official name: Republic of Armenia
Government type: republic
National capital: Yerevan

Independence: May 28, 1918 (First Armenian Republic); September 23, 1991 (from Soviet Union)
Legal system: based on civil law system

Economy

Industries: much of industry is shut down; metal-cutting machine tools, forging-pressing machines, electric motors, tires, knitted wear, hosiery, shoes, silk fabric, washing machines, chemicals, trucks, watches, instruments, microelectronics
Agricultural products: fruit (especially grapes), vegetables; vineyards near Yerevan are famous for brandy and other liqueurs; minor livestock sector
Currency: 1 dram = 100 luma (introduced new currency in November 1993)

Aruba

Geography

Location: Caribbean, island in the Caribbean Sea, north of Venezuela
Area: 75 sq. mi. (193 sq. km.); slightly larger than Washington, D.C.
Climate: tropical marine; little seasonal temperature variation
Terrain: flat with a few hills; scant vegetation
Elevation: lowest point: Caribbean Sea 0 ft. (0 m.); highest point: Mount Jamanota 617 ft. (188 m.)
Natural resources: negligible

People

Population: 68,675 (July 1999 est.)
Population growth rate: 0.55%
Infant mortality rate: 7.84 deaths/1,000 live births
Life expectancy at birth: total population: 77.04 years; male: 73.33 years; female: 80.94 years
Major ethnic groups: mixed European/Caribbean Indian 80%
Major religions: Roman Catholic 82%, Protestant 8%, Hindu, Muslim, Confucian, Jewish
Major languages: Dutch (official), Papiamento (a Spanish, Portuguese, Dutch, English dialect), English (widely spoken), Spanish

Government

Official name: Aruba

Government type: part of the Dutch realm; full autonomy in internal affairs obtained in 1986 upon separation from the Netherlands Antilles

National capital: Oranjestad

Independence: none (part of the Dutch realm; in 1990, Aruba requested and received from the Netherlands cancellation of the agreement to automatically give independence to the island in 1996)

Legal system: based on Dutch civil law system, with some English common law influence

Economy

Industries: tourism, transshipment facilities, oil refining

Agricultural products: aloes; livestock; fishing

Currency: 1 Aruban florin (Af.) = 100 cents

Australia

Geography

Location: Oceania, continent between the Indian Ocean and the South Pacific Ocean

Area: 2,967,893 sq. mi. (7,686,850 sq. km.) slightly smaller than the U.S.

Climate: generally arid to semiarid; temperate in south and east; tropical in north

Terrain: mostly low plateau with deserts; fertile plain in southeast

Elevation: lowest point: Lake Eyre −49 ft. (−15 m.); highest point: Mount Kosciusko 7,313 ft. (2,229 m.)

Natural resources: bauxite, coal, iron ore, copper, tin, silver, uranium, nickel, tungsten, mineral sands, lead, zinc, diamonds, natural gas, petroleum

People

Population: 18,783,551 (July 1999 est.)

Population growth rate: 0.99%

Infant mortality rate: 5.11 deaths/1,000 live births

Life expectancy at birth: total population: 80.14 years; male: 77.22 years; female: 83.23 years

Major ethnic groups: Caucasian 92%, Asian 4%, aboriginal and other 1%

Major religions: Anglican 26.1%, Roman Catholic 26%, other Christian 24.3%

Major languages: English, native languages

Government

Official name: Commonwealth of Australia

Government type: federal parliamentary state

National capital: Canberra

Independence: January 1, 1901 (federation of U.K. colonies)

Legal system: based on English common law

Economy

Industries: mining, industrial and transportation equipment, food processing, chemicals, steel

Agricultural products: wheat, barley, sugarcane, fruits; cattle, sheep, poultry

Currency: 1 Australian dollar ($A) = 100 cents

Austria

Geography

Location: Central Europe, north of Italy

Area: 32,374 sq. mi. (83,850 sq. km.); slightly smaller than Maine

Climate: temperate; continental, cloudy; cold winters with frequent rain in lowlands and snow in mountains; cool summers with occasional showers

Terrain: in the west and south mostly mountains (Alps); along the eastern and northern margins mostly flat or gently sloping

Elevation: lowest point: Neusiedler See 377 ft. (115 m.); highest point: Grossglockner 12,457 ft. (3,797 m.)

Natural resources: iron ore, oil, timber, magnesite, lead, coal, lignite, copper, hydropower

People

Population: 8,139,299 (July 1999 est.)

Population growth rate: 0.09%

Infant mortality rate: 5.1 deaths/1,000 live births

Life expectancy at birth: total population: 77.48 years; male: 74.31 years; female: 80.82 years

Major ethnic groups: German 99.4%, Croatian 0.3%, Slovene 0.2%, other 0.1%

Major religions: Roman Catholic 85%, Protestant 6%, other 9%

Major languages: German

Government

Official name: Republic of Austria

Government type: federal republic

National capital: Vienna

Independence: November 12, 1918 (from Austro-Hungarian Empire)

Legal system: civil law system with Roman law origin; judicial review of legislative acts by the Constitutional Court; separate administrative and civil/penal supreme courts

Economy

Industries: food, iron and steel, machines, textiles, chemicals, electrical, paper and pulp, tourism, mining, motor vehicles

Agricultural products: grains, fruit, potatoes, sugar beets; cattle, pigs, poultry; sawn wood

Currency: 1 Austrian schilling (S) = 100 groschen

Azerbaijan

Geography

Location: Southwestern Asia, bordering the Caspian Sea, between Iran and Russia

Area: 33,436 sq. mi. (86,600 sq. km.); slightly larger than Maine

Climate: dry, semiarid steppe

Terrain: large, flat Kur-Araz Lowland (much of it below sea level) with Great Caucasus Mountains to the north, Qarabag (Karabakh) Upland in west; Baku lies on Abseron (Apsheron) Peninsula that juts into the Caspian Sea

Elevation: lowest point: Caspian Sea −92 ft. (−28 m.); highest point: Bazarduzu Dagi 14,714 ft. (4,485 m.)

Natural resources: petroleum, natural gas, iron ore, nonferrous metals, alumina

People

Population: 7,908,224 (July 1999 est.)

Population growth rate: 0.63%

Infant mortality rate: 82.52 deaths/1,000 live births

Life expectancy at birth: total population: 63.08 years; male: 58.76 years; female: 67.63 years

Major ethnic groups: Azeri 90%, Dagestani Peoples 3.2%, Russian 2.5%, Armenian 2.3%

Major religions: Muslim 93.4%, Russian Orthodox 2.5%, Armenian Orthodox 2.3%, other 1.8%

Major languages: Azeri 89%, Russian 3%, Armenian 2%, other 6%

Government

Official name: Azerbaijani Republic

Government type: republic

National capital: Baku (Baki)

Independence: August 30, 1991 (from Soviet Union)

Legal system: based on civil law system

Economy

Industries: petroleum and natural gas, petroleum products, oilfield equipment; steel, iron ore, cement; chemicals and petrochemicals; textiles

Agricultural products: cotton, grain, rice, grapes, fruit, vegetables, tea, tobacco; cattle, pigs, sheep, goats

Currency: 1 manat = 100 gopik

Bahamas, The

Geography

Location: 24 15 N, 76 00 W; Caribbean, chain of islands in the North Atlantic Ocean, southeast of Florida

Area: 5,382 sq. mi. (13,940 sq. km.) slightly larger than Connecticut

Climate: tropical marine; moderated by warm waters of Gulf Stream

Terrain: long, flat coral formations with some low rounded hills

Nations (cont.)

Elevation: lowest point: Atlantic Ocean 0 ft.
(0 m.); highest point: Mount Alvernia 207 ft.
(63 m.)
Natural resources: salt, aragonite, timber

People

Population: 283,705 (July 1999 est.)
Population growth rate: 1.36%
Infant mortality rate: 18.38 deaths/1,000 live
births
Life expectancy at birth: total population:
74.25 years; male: 70.94 years; female:
77.64 years
Major ethnic groups: black 85%, white 15%
Major religions: Baptist 32%, Anglican 20%,
Roman Catholic 19%, Methodist 6%, Church
of God 6%, other Protestant 12%
Major languages: English, Creole (among
Haitian immigrants)

Government

Official name: Commonwealth of The
Bahamas
Government type: commonwealth
National capital: Nassau
Independence: July 10, 1973 (from U.K.)
Legal system: based on English common law

Economy

Industries: tourism, banking, cement, oil refining and transshipment, salt production, rum,
aragonite, pharmaceuticals, spiral-welded steel
pipe
Agricultural products: citrus, vegetables;
poultry
Currency: 1 Bahamian dollar (B$) = 100 cents

Bahrain

Geography

Location: Middle East, archipelago in the Persian
Gulf, east of Saudi Arabia
Area: 239 sq. mi. (620 sq. km.); 3.5 times the
size of Washington, D.C.
Climate: arid; mild, pleasant winters; very hot,
humid summers

Terrain: mostly low desert plain rising gently to
low central escarpment
Elevaton: lowest point: Persian Gulf 0 ft. (0 m.);
highest point: Jabal ad Dukhan 400 ft.
(122 m.)
Natural resources: oil, associated and nonassoci-
ated natural gas, fish

People

Population: 629,090 (July 1999 est.)
Population growth rate: 2.27%
Infant mortality rate: 14.81 deaths/1,000 live
births
Life expectancy at birth: total population:
75.32 years; male: 72.25 years; female:
77.96 years
Major ethnic groups: Bahraini 63%, Asian 13%,
other Arab 10%, Iranian 8%
Major religions: Shi'a Muslim 75%, Sunni
Muslim 25%
Major languages: Arabic, English, Farsi,
Urdu

Government

Official name: State of Bahrain
Government type: traditional monarchy
National capital: Manama
Independence: August 15, 1971 (from U.K.)
Legal system: based on Islamic law and English
common law

Economy

Industries: petroleum processing and refining,
aluminum smelting, offshore banking, ship
repairing
Agricultural products: fruit, vegetables; poultry,
dairy products; shrimp, fish
Currency: 1 Bahraini dinar (BD) = 1,000 fils

Bangladesh

Geography

Location: Southern Asia, bordering the Bay of
Bengal, between Burma and India
Area: 55,598 sq. mi. (144,000 sq. km.); slightly
smaller than Wisconsin

Climate: tropical; cool, dry winter (October to March); hot, humid summer (March to June); cool, rainy monsoon (June to October)

Terrain: mostly flat alluvial plain; hilly in southeast

Elevation: lowest point: Indian Ocean 0 ft. (0 m.); highest point: Keodradong 4,035 ft. (1,230m.)

Natural resources: natural gas, arable land, timber

People

Population: 127,117,967 (July 1999 est.)

Population growth rate: 1.59%

Infant mortality rate: 69.68 deaths/1,000 live births

Life expectancy at birth: total population: 60.6 years; male: 60.73 years; female: 60.46 years

Major ethnic groups: Bengali 98%, Biharis 250,000, tribals less than 1 million

Major religions: Muslim 83%, Hindu 16%, other 1.2%

Major languages: Bangla (official), English

Government

Official name: People's Republic of Bangladesh

Government type: republic

National capital: Dhaka

Independence: December 16, 1971 (from Pakistan)

Legal system: based on English common law

Economy

Industries: jute manufacturing, cotton textiles, food processing, steel, fertilizer

Agricultural products: jute, rice, wheat, tea, sugarcane, potatoes; beef, milk, poultry

Currency: 1 taka (Tk) = 100 poiska

Barbados

Geography

Location: Caribbean, island between the Caribbean Sea and the North Atlantic Ocean, northeast of Venezuela

Area: 166 sq. mi. (430 sq. km.); 2.5 times the size of Washington, D.C.

Climate: tropical; rainy season (June to October)

Terrain: relatively flat; rises gently to central highland region

Elevation: lowest point: Atlantic Ocean 0 ft. (0 m.); highest point: Mount Hillaby 1,102 ft. (336 m.)

Natural resources: petroleum, fish, natural gas

People

Population: 259,191 (July 1999 est.)

Population growth rate: 0.04%

Infant mortality rate: 16.74 deaths/1,000 live births

Life expectancy at birth: total population: 74.98 years; male: 72.22 years; female: 77.81 years

Major ethnic groups: African 80%, European 4%, other 16%

Major religions: Protestant 67% (Anglican 40%, Pentecostal 8%, Methodist 7%, other 12%), Roman Catholic 4%, none 17%,

Major languages: English

Government

Official name: Barbados

Government type: parliamentary democracy

National capital: Bridgetown

Independence: November 30, 1966 (from U.K.)

Legal system: English common law; no judicial review of legislative acts

Economy

Industries: tourism, sugar, light manufacturing, component assembly for export

Agricultural products: sugarcane, vegetables, cotton

Currency: 1 Barbadian dollar (Bds$) = 100 cents

Belarus

Geography

Location: Eastern Europe, east of Poland

Area: 80,154 sq. mi. (207,600 sq. km.); slightly smaller than Kansas

Climate: cold winters, cool and moist summers; transitional between continental and maritime

Terrain: generally flat and contains much marshland

Elevation: lowest point: Nyoman River 295 ft. (90 m.); highest point: Dzyarzhynskaya Hara 1,135 ft. (346 m.)

Natural resources: forests, peat deposits, small quantities of oil and natural gas

People

Population: 10,401,784 (July 1999 est.)

Population growth rate: -0.09%

Infant mortality rate: 14.39 deaths/1,000 live births

Life expectancy at birth: total population: 68.13 years; male: 62.04 years; female: 74.52 years

Major ethnic groups: Byelorussian 77.9%, Russian 13.2%, Polish 4.1%, Ukrainian 2.9%, other 1.9%

Major religions: Eastern Orthodox 60%, other (including Roman Catholic and Muslim) 40%

Major languages: Byelorussian, Russian

Government

Official name: Republic of Belarus

Government type: republic

National capital: Minsk

Independence: August 25, 1991 (from Soviet Union)

Legal system: based on civil law system

Economy

Industries: tractors, metal-cutting machine tools, off-highway dump trucks up to 110-metric-ton load capacity, wheel-type earth movers for construction and mining, eight-wheel-drive, high-flotation trucks, equipment for animal husbandry and livestock feeding, motorcycles, television sets, chemical fibers, fertilizer, linen fabric, wool fabric, radios, refrigerators, other consumer goods

Agricultural products: grain, potatoes, vegetables; meat, milk

Currency: Belarusian rubel (BR)

Belgium

Geography

Location: Western Europe, bordering the North Sea, between France and the Netherlands

Area: 11,780 sq. mi. (30,510 sq. km.); slightly larger than Maryland

Land boundaries: total: 1,385 km.

Climate: temperate; mild winters, cool summers; rainy, humid, cloudy

Terrain: flat coastal plains in northwest, central rolling hills, rugged mountains of Ardennes Forest in southeast

Elevation: lowest point: North Sea 0 ft. (0 m.); highest point: Signal de Botrange 2,277 ft. (694 m.)

Natural resources: coal, natural gas

People

Population: 10,182,034 (July 1999 est.)

Population growth rate: 0.06%

Infant mortality rate: 6.17 deaths/1,000 live births

Life expectancy at birth: total population: 77.53 years; male: 74.31 years; female: 80.9 years

Major ethnic groups: Fleming 55%, Walloon 33%

Major religions: Roman Catholic 75%, Protestant or other 25%

Major languages: Dutch 56%, French 32%, German 1%, legally bilingual 11%

Government

Official name: Kingdom of Belgium

Government type: constitutional monarchy

National capital: Brussels

Independence: October 4, 1830 (from the Netherlands)

Legal system: civil law system influenced by English constitutional theory; judicial review of legislative acts

Economy

Industries: engineering and metal products, motor vehicle assembly, processed food and beverages, chemicals, basic metals, textiles, glass, petroleum, coal

Agricultural products: sugar beets, fresh vegetables, fruits, grain, tobacco; beef, veal, pork, milk

Currency: 1 Belgian franc (BF) = 100 centimes

Belize

Geography

Location: Central America, bordering the Caribbean Sea, between Guatemala and Mexico

Area: 8,865 sq. mi. (22,960 sq. km.) slightly larger than Massachusetts

Climate: tropical; very hot and humid; rainy season (May to February)

Terrain: flat, swampy coastal plain; low mountains in south

Elevation: lowest point: Caribbean Sea 0 ft. (0 m.); highest point: Victoria Peak 3,806 ft. (1,160 m.)

Natural resources: arable land potential, timber, fish

People

Population: 235,789 (July 1999 est.)

Population growth rate: 2.42%

Infant mortality rate: 31.57 deaths/1,000 live births

Life expectancy at birth: total population: 69.2 years; male: 67.23 years; female: 71.26 years

Major ethnic groups: mestizo 44%, Creole 30%, Maya 11%, Garifuna 7%

Major religions: Roman Catholic 62%, Protestant 30%

Major languages: English (official), Spanish, Mayan, Garifuna (Carib)

Government

Official name: Belize

Government type: parliamentary democracy

National capital: Belmopan

Independence: September 21, 1981 (from U.K.)

Legal system: English law

Economy

Industries: garment production, food processing, tourism, construction

Agricultural products: bananas, coca, citrus, sugarcane; lumber; fish, cultured shrimp

Currency: 1 Belizean dollar (Bz$) = 100 cents

Benin

Geography

Location: Western Africa, bordering the North Atlantic Ocean, between Nigeria and Togo

Area: 43,483 sq. mi. (112,620 sq. km.); slightly smaller than Pennsylvania

Climate: tropical; hot, humid in south; semiarid in north

Terrain: mostly flat to undulating plain; some hills and low mountains

Elevation: lowest point: Atlantic Ocean 0 ft. (0 m.); highest point: Mount Tanekas 2,103 ft. (641 m.)

Natural resources: small offshore oil deposits, limestone, marble, timber

People

Population: 6,305,567 (July 1999 est.)

Population growth rate: 3.32%

Infant mortality rate: 97.76 deaths/1,000 live births

Life expectancy at birth: total population: 54.08 years; male: 51.98 years; female: 56.24 years

Major ethnic groups: African 99% (42 ethnic groups, most important being Fon, Adja, Yoruba, Bariba)

Major religions: indigenous beliefs 70%, Muslim 15%, Christian 15%

Major languages: French (official), Fon and Yoruba (most common vernaculars in south), tribal languages (at least six major ones in north)

Government

Official name: Republic of Benin

Government type: republic under multiparty democratic rule dropped Marxism-Leninism December 1989; democratic reforms adopted February 1990; transition to multiparty system completed April 4, 1991

National capital: Porto-Novo

Independence: August 1, 1960 (from France)

Legal system: based on French civil law and customary law, has not accepted compulsory IJC jurisdiction

Economy

Industries: textiles, cigarettes; beverages, food; construction materials, petroleum

Agricultural products: corn, sorghum, cassava (tapioca), yams, beans, rice, cotton, palm oil, peanuts; poultry, livestock

Currency: 1 Communauté Financière Africaine franc (CFAF) = 100 centimes

Bermuda

Geography

Location: North America, group of islands in the North Atlantic Ocean, east of North Carolina (U.S.)

Area: 19 sq. mi. (50 sq. km.); about 0.3 times the size of Washington, D.C.

Climate: subtropical; mild, humid; gales, strong winds common in winter

Terrain: low hills separated by fertile depressions

Elevation: lowest point: Atlantic Ocean (0 m.); highest point: Town Hill 249 ft. (76 m.)

Natural resources: limestone, pleasant climate fostering tourism

People

Population: 62,472 (July 1999 est.)

Population growth rate: 0.72%

Infant mortality rate: 13.16 deaths/1,000 live births

Life expectancy at birth: total population: 76.97 years; male: 75.19 years; female: 78.83 years

Major ethnic groups: black 61%, white and other 39%

Major religions: Anglican 37%, Roman Catholic 14%, African Methodist Episcopal (Zion) 10%, Methodist 6%, Seventh-Day Adventist 5%, other 28%

Major language: English

Government

Official name: Bermuda

Government type: dependent territory of the U.K.

National capital: Hamilton

Independence: none (dependent territory of the U.K.)

Legal system: English law

Economy

Industries: tourism, finance, structural concrete products, paints, pharmaceuticals, ship repairing

Agricultural products: bananas, vegetables, citrus, flowers; dairy products

Currency: 1 Bermudian dollar (Bd$) = 100 cents

Bhutan

Geography

Location: Southern Asia, between China and India

Area: 18,147 sq. mi. (47,000 sq. km.); slightly more than half the size of Indiana

Climate: varies; tropical in southern plains; cool winters and hot summers in central valleys; severe winters and cool summers in Himalayas

Terrain: mostly mountainous with some fertile valleys and savanna

Elevation: lowest point: Dangme Chu 318 ft. (97 m.); highest point: Khula Kangri I 24,780 ft. (7,553 m.)

Natural resources: timber, hydropower, gypsum, calcium carbide

People

Population: 1,951,965 (July 1999 estimate, other estimates range as low as 600,000)

Population growth rate: 2.25%

Infant mortality rate: 109.33 deaths/1,000 live births

Life expectancy at birth: total population: 52.75 years; male: 53.19 years; female: 52.29 years

Major ethnic groups: Bhote 50%, ethnic Nepalese 35%, indigenous or migrant tribes 15%

Major religions: Lamaistic Buddhism 75%, Indian- and Nepalese-influenced Hinduism 25%

Major languages: Dzongkha (official), Bhotes speak various Tibetan dialects, Nepalese speak various Nepalese dialects

Government

Official name: Kingdom of Bhutan

Government type: monarchy; special treaty relationship with India

National capital: Thimphu

Independence: August 8, 1949 (from India)

Legal system: based on Indian law and English common law

Economy

Industries: cement, wood products, processed fruits, alcoholic beverages, calcium carbide

Agricultural products: rice, corn, root crops, citrus, foodgrains; dairy products, eggs

Currency: 1 ngultrum (Nu) = 100 chetrum; note—Indian currency is also legal tender

Bolivia

Geography

Location: Central South America, southwest of Brazil

Area: 424,162 sq. mi. (1,098,580 sq. km.) slightly less than three times the size of Montana

Climate: varies with altitude; humid and tropical to cold and semiarid

Terrain: rugged Andes Mountains with a highland plateau (Altiplano), hills, lowland plains of the Amazon Basin

Elevation: lowest point: Rio Paraguay 295 ft. (90 m.); highest point: Nevado Sajama 6,542 m.

Natural resources: tin, natural gas, petroleum, zinc, tungsten, antimony, silver, iron, lead, gold, timber

People

Population: 7,982,850 (July 1999 est.)

Population growth rate: 1.96%

Infant mortality rate: 62.02 deaths/1,000 live births

Life expectancy at birth: total population: 61.43 years; male: 58.51 years; female: 64.51 years

Major ethnic groups: Quechua 30%, Aymara 25%, mestizo (mixed European and Indian ancestry) 25%–30%, European 5%–15%

Major religions: Roman Catholic 95%, Protestant (Evangelical Methodist)

Major languages: Spanish (official), Quechua (official), Aymara (official)

Government

Official name: Republic of Bolivia

Government type: republic

National capital: La Paz (seat of government); Sucre (legal capital and seat of judiciary)

Independence: August 6, 1825 (from Spain)

Legal system: based on Spanish law and Napoleonic Code

Economy

Industries: mining, smelting, petroleum, food and beverages, tobacco, handicrafts, clothing

Agricultural products: coffee, coca, cotton, corn, sugarcane, rice, potatoes; timber

Currency: 1 boliviano ($B) = 100 centavos

Bosnia and Herzegovina

Geography

Location: Southeastern Europe, bordering the Adriatic Sea and Croatia

Area: 19,781 sq. mi. (51,233 sq. km.); comparative area: slightly smaller than West Virginia

Climate: hot summers and cold winters; areas of high elevation have short, cool summers and long, severe winters; mild, rainy winters along coast

Terrain: mountains and valleys

Elevation: lowest point: Adriatic Sea 0 ft. (0 m.); highest point: Maglic 7,828 ft. (2,386 m.)

Natural resources: coal, iron, bauxite, manganese, forests, copper, chromium, lead, zinc

People

Population: 3,482,495 (July 1999 est.) Note—all data dealing with population is subject to considerable error because of the dislocations caused by military action and ethnic cleansing

Population growth rate: 3.2%
Infant mortality rate: 43.2 deaths/1,000 live
  births
Life expectancy at birth: total population:
  66.98 years; male: 62.55 years; female:
  71.71 years
Major ethnic groups: Serb 40%, Muslim 38%,
  Croat 22% (est.-Croats claim they now make
  up only 17% of the total population)
Major religions: Muslim 40%, Orthodox 31%,
  Catholic 15%, Protestant 4%, other 10%
Major languages: Serbo-Croatian 99%

Government
Official name: Bosnia and Herzegovina
Government type: emerging democracy
National capital: Sarajevo
Independence: April 1992 (from Yugoslavia)
Legal system: based on civil law system

Economy
Industries: steel, coal, iron ore, lead, zinc, manganese, bauxite, vehicle assembly, textiles,
  tobacco products, wooden furniture, tank and
  aircraft assembly, domestic appliances, oil
  refining
Agricultural products: wheat, corn, fruits, vegetables; livestock
Currency: 1 convertible marka (KM) = 100 convertible pfenniga

Botswana

Geography
Location: Southern Africa, north of South
  Africa
Area: 231,803 sq. mi. (600,370 sq. km.); slightly
  smaller than Texas
Climate: semiarid; warm winters and hot sum-
  mers
Terrain: predominately flat to gently rolling
  tableland; Kalahari Desert in southwest
Elevation: lowest point: junction of the
  Limpopo and Shashe Rivers 1,683 ft. (513 m.);
  highest point: Tsodilo Hill 4,885 ft.
  (1,489 m.)

Natural resources: diamonds, copper, nickel, salt,
  soda ash, potash, coal, iron ore, silver

People
Population: 1,464,167 (July 1999 est.)
Population growth rate: 1.05%
Infant mortality rate: 59.08 deaths/1,000 live
  births
Life expectancy at birth: total population:
  39.89 years; male: 39.42 years; female:
  40.37 years
Major ethnic groups: Batswana 95%, Kalanga,
  Basarwa, and Kgalagadi 4%, white 1%
Major religions: indigenous beliefs 50%,
  Christian 50%
Major languages: English (official), Setswana

Government
Official name: Republic of Botswana
Government type: parliamentary republic
National capital: Gaborone
Independence: September 30, 1966 (from
  U.K.)
Legal system: based on Roman-Dutch law and
  local customary law; judicial review limited to
  matters of interpretation

Economy
Industries: diamonds, copper, nickel, coal, salt,
  soda ash, potash; livestock processing
Agricultural products: sorghum, maize, millet,
  pulses, groundnuts (peanuts), beans, cowpeas,
  sunflower seed; livestock
Currency: 1 pula (P) = 100 thebe

Brazil

Geography
Location: Eastern South America, bordering the
  Atlantic Ocean
Area: 3,286,470 sq. mi. (8,511,965 sq. km.);
  slightly smaller than the U.S.
Climate: mostly tropical, but temperate in
  south
Terrain: mostly flat to rolling lowlands in north;
  some plains, hills, mountains, and narrow
  coastal belt

Elevation: lowest point: Atlantic Ocean 0 ft. (0 m.); highest point: Pico da Neblina 9,888 ft. (3,014 m.)
Natural resources: bauxite, gold, iron ore, manganese, nickel, phosphates, platinum, tin, uranium, petroleum, hydropower, timber

People

Population: 171,853,126 (July 1999 est.)
Population growth rate: 1.16%
Infant mortality rate: 35.37 deaths/1,000 live births
Life expectancy at birth: total population: 64.06 years; male: 59.35 years; female: 69.01 years
Major ethnic groups: white (includes Portuguese, German, Italian, Spanish, Polish) 55%, mixed white and African 38%, African 6%
Major religions: Roman Catholic (nominal) 70%
Major languages: Portuguese (official), Spanish, English, French

Government

Official name: Federative Republic of Brazil
Government type: federal republic
National capital: Brasilia
Independence: September 7, 1822 (from Portugal)
Legal system: based on Roman codes

Economy

Industries: textiles, shoes, chemicals, cement, lumber, iron ore, tin, steel, aircraft, motor vehicles and parts, other machinery and equipment
Agricultural products: coffee, soybeans, wheat, rice, corn, sugarcane, cocoa, citrus; beef
Currency: 1 real (R$) = 100 centavos

Brunei

Geography

Location: Southeastern Asia, bordering the South China Sea and Malaysia
Area: 2,228 sq. mi. (5,770 sq. km.); slightly larger than Delaware
Climate: tropical; hot, humid, rainy

Terrain: flat coastal plain rises to mountains in east; hilly lowland in west
Elevation: lowest point: South China Sea 0 ft. (0 m.); highest point: Bukit Pagon 6,069 ft. (1,850 m.)
Natural resources: petroleum, natural gas, timber

People

Population: 322,982 (July 1999 est.)
Population growth rate: 2.38%
Infant mortality rate: 22.83 deaths/1,000 live births
Life expectancy at birth: total population: 71.84 years; male: 70.35 years; female: 73.42 years
Major ethnic groups: Malay 64%, Chinese 20%, other 16%
Major religions: Muslim (official) 63%, Buddhism 14%, Christian 8%, indigenous beliefs and other 15%
Major languages: Malay (official), English, Chinese

Government

Official name: Negara Brunei Darussalam
Government type: constitutional sultanate
National capital: Bandar Seri Begawan
Independence: January 1, 1984 (from U.K.)
Legal system: based on Islamic law

Economy

Industries: petroleum, petroleum refining, liquefied natural gas, construction
Agricultural products: rice, cassava (tapioca), bananas; water buffalo, pigs
Currency: 1 Bruneian dollar (B$) = 100 cents

Bulgaria

Geography

Location: Southeastern Europe, bordering the Black Sea, between Romania and Turkey
Area: 42,822 sq. mi. (110,910 sq. km.); slightly larger than Tennessee
Climate: temperate; cold, damp winters; hot, dry summers
Terrain: mostly mountains with lowlands in north and southeast

Elevation: lowest point: Black Sea 0 ft.
(0 m.); highest point: Musala 9,596 ft.
(2,925 m.)
Natural resources: bauxite, copper, lead, zinc,
coal, timber, arable land

People
Population: 8,194,772 (July 1999 est.)
Population growth rate: −0.52%
Infant mortality rate: 12.37 deaths/1,000 live
births
Life expectancy at birth: total population:
72.27 years; male: 68.72 years; female:
76.03 years
Major ethnic groups: Bulgarian 85.3%, Turk
8.5%, Gypsy 2.6%, Macedonian 2.5%
Major religions: Bulgarian Orthodox 85%,
Muslim 13%
Major languages: Bulgarian, secondary
languages closely correspond to ethnic break-
down

Government
Official name: Republic of Bulgaria
Government type: emerging democracy
National capital: Sofia
Independence: September 22, 1908 (from
Ottoman Empire)
Legal system: based on civil law system with
Soviet law influence; accepts compulsory IJC
jurisdiction

Economy
Industries: machine building and metal working, food processing, chemicals, textiles, construction materials, ferrous and nonferrous
metals
Agricultural products: grain, oilseed, vegetables,
fruits, tobacco; livestock
Currency: 1 lev (Lv) = 100 stotinki

Burkina Faso

Geography
Location: Western Africa, north of Ghana
Area: 105,869 sq. mi. (274,200 sq. km.); slightly
larger than Colorado

Climate: tropical; warm, dry winters; hot, wet
summers
Terrain: mostly flat to dissected, undulating
plains; hills in west and southeast
Elevation: lowest point: Black Volta River 656 ft.
(200 m.); highest point: Tena Kourou 2,457 ft.
(749 m.)
Natural resources: manganese, limestone,
marble; small deposits of gold, antimony,
copper, nickel, bauxite, lead, phosphates, zinc,
silver

People
Population: 11,575,898 (July 1999 est.)
Population growth rate: 2.7%
Infant mortality rate: 107.19 deaths/1,000 live
births
Life expectancy at birth: total population:
45.89 years; male: 44.97 years; female:
46.84 years
Major ethnic groups: Mossi about 24%,
Gurunsi, Senufo, Lobi, Bobo, Mande,
Fulani
Major religions: indigenous beliefs 40%,
Muslim 50%, Christian 10%
Major languages: French (official), tribal lan-
guages belonging to Sudanic family, spoken
by 90% of the population

Government
Official name: Burkina Faso
Government type: parliamentary
National capital: Ouagadougou
Independence: August 5, 1960 (from France)
Legal system: based on French civil law system
and customary law

Economy
Industries: cotton lint, beverages, agricultural
processing, soap, cigarettes, textiles, gold
Agricultural products: peanuts, shea nuts,
sesame, cotton, sorghum, millet, corn, rice;
livestock
Currency: 1 Communauté Financière Africaine
franc (CFAF) = 100 centimes

Burma

Geography

Location: Southeastern Asia, bordering the Andaman Sea and the Bay of Bengal, between Bangladesh and Thailand

Area: 261,969 sq. mi. (678,500 sq. km.); slightly smaller than Texas

Climate: tropical monsoon; cloudy, rainy, hot, humid summers (southwest monsoon, June to September); less cloudy, scant rainfall, mild temperatures, lower humidity during winter (northeast monsoon, December to April)

Terrain: central lowlands ringed by steep, rugged highlands

Elevation: lowest point: Andaman Sea 0 ft. (0 m.); highest point: Hkakabo Razi 19,294 ft. (5,881 m.)

Natural resources: petroleum, timber, tin, antimony, zinc, copper, tungsten, lead, coal, some marble, limestone, precious stones, natural gas

People

Population: 48,081,302 (July 1999 est.)

Population growth rate: 1.61%

Infant mortality rate: 76.25 deaths/1,000 live births

Life expectancy at birth: total population: 54.74 years; male: 53.24 years; female: 56.32 years

Major ethnic groups: Burman 68%, Shan 9%, Karen 7%, Rakhine 4%, Chinese 3%, Mon 2%

Major religions: Buddhist 89%, Christian 4%

Major languages: Burmese, minority ethnic groups have their own languages

Government

Official name: Union of Burma (regime refers to Burma as Myanmar)

Government type: military regime

National capital: Rangoon (regime refers to the capital as Yangon)

Independence: January 4, 1948 (from U.K.)

Legal system: NA, does not accept compulsory IJC jurisdiction

Economy

Industries: agricultural processing; textiles and footwear; wood and wood products; petroleum refining; copper, tin, tungsten, iron; construction materials; pharmaceuticals; fertilizer

Agricultural products: paddy rice, corn, oilseed, sugarcane, pulses; hardwood

Currency: 1 kyat (K) = 100 pyas

Burundi

Geography

Location: Central Africa, east of Zaire

Area: 10,745 sq. mi. (27,830 sq. km.); slightly larger than Maryland

Climate: temperate; warm; occasional frost in uplands; dry season from June to September

Terrain: hilly and mountainous, dropping to a plateau in east, some plains

Elevation: lowest point: Lake Tanganyika 2,533 ft. (772 m.) highest point: Mount Heha 9,055 ft. (2,760 m.)

Natural resources: nickel, uranium, rare earth oxides, peat, cobalt, copper, platinum (not yet exploited), vanadium

People

Population: 5,735,937 (July 1999 est.)

Population growth rate: 3.54%

Infant mortality rate: 99.36 deaths/1,000 live births

Life expectancy at birth: total population: 45.44 years; male: 43.54 years; female: 47.41 years

Major ethnic groups: Africans: Hutu (Bantu) 85%, Tutsi (Hamitic) 14%, Twa (Pygmy)

Major religions: Christian 67% (Roman Catholic 62%, Protestant 5%), indigenous beliefs 32%

Major languages: Kirundi (official), French (official), Swahili (along Lake Tanganyika and in the Bujumbura area)

Government

Official name: Republic of Burundi

Government type: republic

National capital: Bujumbura

Independence: July 1, 1962 (from UN trusteeship under Belgian administration)

Legal system: based on German and Belgian civil codes and customary law

Economy

Industries: light consumer goods such as blankets, shoes, soap; assembly of imported components; public works construction; food processing

Agricultural products: coffee, cotton, tea, corn, sorghum, sweet potatoes, bananas, manioc; meat, milk, hides

Currency: 1 Burundi franc (FBu) = 100 centimes

Cambodia

Geography

Location: Southeastern Asia, bordering the Gulf of Thailand, between Thailand and Vietnam

Area: 69,900 sq. mi. (181,040 sq. km.); slightly smaller than Oklahoma

Climate: tropical; rainy, monsoon season (May to November); dry season (December to April); little seasonal temperature variation

Terrain: mostly low, flat plains; mountains in southwest and north

Elevation: lowest point: Gulf of Thailand 0 ft. (0 m.); highest point: Phnum Aoral 5938 ft. (1,810 m.)

Natural resources: timber, gemstones, some iron ore, manganese, phosphates, hydropower potential

People

Population: 11,626,520 (July 1999 est.)

Population growth rate: 2.49%

Infant mortality rate: 105.06 deaths/1,000 live births

Life expectancy at birth: total population: 48.24 years; male: 46.81 years; female: 49.75 years

Major ethnic groups: Khmer 90%, Vietnamese 5%

Major religions: Theravada Buddhism 95%

Major languages: Khmer (official), French

Government

Official name: Kingdom of Cambodia

Government type: multiparty liberal democracy under a constitutional monarchy established in September 1993

National capital: Phnom Penh

Independence: November 9, 1949 (from France)

Legal system: currently being defined

Economy

Industries: rice milling, fishing, wood and wood products, rubber, cement, gem mining

Agricultural products: rice, rubber, corn, vegetables

Currency: 1 new riel (CR) = 100 sen

Cameroon

Geography

Location: Western Africa, bordering the North Atlantic Ocean, between Equatorial Guinea and Nigeria

Area: 183,567 sq. mi. (475,440 sq. km.); slightly larger than California

Climate: varies with terrain, from tropical along coast to semiarid and hot in north

Terrain: diverse, with coastal plain in southwest, dissected plateau in center, mountains in west, plains in north

Elevation: lowest point: Atlantic Ocean 0 ft. (0 m.); highest point: Fako 13,434 ft. (4,095 m.)

Natural resources: petroleum, bauxite, iron ore, timber, hydropower potential

People

Population: 15,456,092 (July 1992 est.)

Population growth rate: 2.79%

Infant mortality rate: 75.69 deaths/1,000 live births

Life expectancy at birth: total population: 51.32 years; male: 49.75 years; female: 52.94 years

Major ethnic groups: Cameroon Highlanders
31%, Equatorial Bantu 19%, Kirdi 11%, Fulani
10%, Northwestern Bantu 8%, Eastern Nigritic
7%, other African 13%
Major religions: indigenous beliefs 51%,
Christian 33%, Muslim 16%
Major languages: 24 major African language
groups, English (official), French (official)

Government

Official name: Republic of Cameroon
Government type: unitary republic; multiparty
presidential regime (opposition parties legalized 1990)
National capital: Yaounde
Independence: January 1, 1960 (from UN trusteeship under French administration)
Legal system: based on French civil law system,
with common law influence

Economy

Industries: petroleum production and refining,
food processing, light consumer goods, textiles, lumber
Agricultural products: coffee, cocoa, cotton, rubber, bananas, oilseed, grains, root starches;
livestock; timber
Currency: 1 Communauté Financière Africaine
franc (CFAF) = 100 centimes

Canada

Geography

Location: Northern North America, bordering
the North Atlantic Ocean and North Pacific
Ocean, north of the conterminous U.S.
Area: 3,851,788 sq. mi. (9,976,140 sq. km.);
slightly larger than U.S.
Climate: varies from temperate in south to sub-
arctic and arctic in north
Terrain: mostly plains with mountains in west
and lowlands in southeast
Elevation: lowest point: Atlantic Ocean 0 ft.
(0 m.); highest point: Mount Logan 19,520 ft.
(5,950 m.)
Natural resources: nickel, zinc, copper, gold,
lead, molybdenum, potash, silver, fish, timber,
wildlife, coal, petroleum, natural gas

People

Population: 31,006,347 (July 1999 est.)
Population growth rate: 1.06%
Infant mortality rate: 5.47 deaths/1,000 live
births (1996 est.)
Life expectancy at birth: total population:
79.37 years; male: 76.12 years; female:
82.79 years
Major ethnic groups: British Isles origin 40%,
French origin 27%, other European 20%,
indigenous Indian and Eskimo 1.5%, other
(mostly Asian) 11.5%
Major religions: Roman Catholic 45%, United
Church 12%, Anglican 8%, other 35%
Major languages: English (official), French
(official)

Government

Official name: Canada
Government type: confederation with parliamen-
tary democracy
National capital: Ottawa
Independence: July 1, 1867 (from U.K.)
Legal system: based on English common law,
except in Quebec, where civil law system
based on French law prevails

Economy

Industries: processed and unprocessed minerals,
food products, wood and paper products,
transportation equipment, chemicals, fish
products, petroleum and natural gas
Agricultural products: wheat, barley, oilseed,
tobacco, fruits, vegetables; dairy products; forest products; commercial fisheries provide
annual catch of 1.5 million metric tons, of
which 75% is exported
Currency: 1 Canadian dollar (Can$) = 100 cents

Cape Verde

Geography

Location: Western Africa, group of Islands in the
North Atlantic Ocean, west of Senegal
Area: 1,556 sq. mi. (4,030 sq. km.); slightly larger
than Rhode Island
Climate: temperate; warm, dry summer; precipi-
tation meager and very erratic

Terrain: steep, rugged, rocky, volcanic
Elevation: lowest point: Atlantic Ocean 0 ft.
(0 m.); highest point: Mt. Fogo 9,281 ft.
(2,829 m.)
Natural resources: salt, basalt rock, pozzolana,
limestone, kaolin, fish

People
Population: 405,748 (July 1999 est.)
Population growth rate: 1.44%
Infant mortality rate: 45.5 deaths/1,000 live
births
Life expectancy at birth: total population:
70.96 years; male: 67.66 years; female:
74.36 years
Major ethnic groups: Creole (mulatto) 71%,
African 28%, European 1%
Major religions: Roman Catholicism fused with
indigenous beliefs
Major languages: Portuguese, Crioulo, a blend of
Portuguese and West African words

Government
Official name: Republic of Cape Verde
Government type: republic
National capital: Praia
Independence: July 5, 1975 (from Portugal)
Legal system: derived from the legal system of
Portugal

Economy
Industries: fish processing, salt mining, garments, ship repair, food and beverages
Agricultural products: bananas, corn, beans,
sweet potatoes, sugarcane, coffee, peanuts; fish
Currency: 1 Cape Verdean escudo (CVEsc) = 100
centavos

Cayman Islands

Geography
Location: Caribbean, island group in Caribbean
Sea, nearly one-half of the way from Cuba to
Honduras
Area: 100 sq. mi. (260 sq. km.) 1.5 times the size
of Washington, D.C.

Climate: tropical marine; warm, rainy summers
(May to October) and cool, relatively dry winters (November to April)
Terrain: low-lying limestone base surrounded by
coral reefs
Elevation: lowest point: Caribbean Sea 0 ft.
(0 m.); highest point: The Bluff 141 ft. (43 m.)
Natural resources: fish, climate and beaches that
foster tourism

People
Population: 39,335 (July 1999 est.)
Population growth rate: 4.19%
Infant mortality rate: 8.4 deaths/1,000 live births
Life expectancy at birth: total population: 77.1
years; male: 75.37 years; female: 78.81 years
Major ethnic groups: mixed 40%, white 20%,
black 20%, expatriates of various ethnic
groups 20%
Major religions: United Church, Anglican,
Baptist, Roman Catholic, Church of God, other
Protestant denominations
Major languages: English

Government
Official name: Cayman Islands
Government type: dependent territory of the U.K.
National capital: George Town
Independence: none (dependent territory of the
U.K.)
Legal system: British common law and local
statutes

Economy
Industries: tourism, banking, insurance and
finance, construction, construction materials,
furniture
Agricultural products: vegetables, fruit; livestock;
turtle farming
Currency: 1 Caymanian dollar (CI$) = 100 cents

Central African Republic

Geography
Location: Central Africa, north of Zaire
Area: 240,533 sq. mi. (622,980 sq. km.); slightly
smaller than Texas

Climate: tropical; hot, dry winters; mild to hot, wet summers

Terrain: vast, flat to rolling, monotonous plateau; scattered hills in northeast and southwest

Elevation: lowest point: Oubangui River 1099 ft. (335 m.); highest point: Mount Gaou 4659 ft. (1,420 m.)

Natural resources: diamonds, uranium, timber, gold, oil

People

Population: 3,444,951 (July 1999 est.)

Population growth rate: 2.04%

Infant mortality rate: 103.42 deaths/1,000 live births

Life expectancy at birth: total population: 47.19 years; male: 45.35 years; female: 49.09 years

Major ethnic groups: Baya 34%, Banda 27%, Sara 10%, Mandjia 21%, Mboum 4%, M'Baka 4%

Major religions: indigenous beliefs 24%, Protestant 25%, Roman Catholic 25%, Muslim 15%

Major languages: French (official), Sangho (lingua franca and national language), Arabic, Hunsa, Swahili

Government

Official name: Central African Republic

Government type: republic

National capital: Bangui

Independence: August 13, 1960 (from France)

Legal system: based on French law

Economy

Industries: diamond mining, sawmills, breweries, textiles, footwear, assembly of bicycles and motorcycles

Agricultural products: cotton, coffee, tobacco, manioc (tapioca), yams, millet, corn, bananas; timber

Currency: 1 Communauté Financière Africaine franc (CFAF) = 100 centimes

Chad

Geography

Location: Central Africa, south of Libya

Area: 495,752 sq. mi. (1,284,000 sq. km.); slightly more than three times the size of California

Climate: tropical in south, desert in north

Terrain: broad, arid plains in center, desert in north, mountains in northwest, lowlands in south

Elevation: lowest point: Djourab Depression 574 ft. (175 m.); highest point: Emi Koussi 11,204 ft. (3,415 m.)

Natural resources: petroleum (unexploited but exploration under way), uranium, natron, kaolin, fish (Lake Chad)

People

Population: 7,557,436 (July 1999 est.)

Population growth rate: 2.65%

Infant mortality rate: 115.27 deaths/1,000 live births

Life expectancy at birth: total population: 48.56 years; male: 46.13 years; female: 51.09 years

Major ethnic groups: Muslims (Arabs, Toubou, Hadjerai, Fulbe, Kotoko, Kanembou, Baguirmi, Boulala, Zaghawa, and Maba); South: non-Muslims (Sara, Ngambaye, Mbaye, Goulaye, Moundang, Moussei, Massa)

Major religions: Muslim 50%, Christian 25%, indigenous beliefs (mostly animism) 25%

Major languages: French (official), Arabic (official), Sara and Sango (in south), more than 100 different languages and dialects

Government

Official name: Republic of Chad

Government type: republic

National capital: N'Djamena

Independence: August 11, 1960 (from France)

Legal system: based on French civil law system and Chadian customary law, does not accept compulsory IJC jurisdiction

Economy

Industries: cotton textiles, meat packing, beer brewing, natron (sodium carbonate), soap, cigarettes, construction materials

Agricultural products: cotton, sorghum, millet, peanuts, rice, potatoes, manioc (tapioca); cattle, sheep, goats, camels

Currency: 1 Communauté Financière Africaine franc (CFAF) = 100 centimes

Chile

Geography

Location: Southern South America, bordering the South Atlantic Ocean and South Pacific Ocean, between Argentina and Peru

Area: 292,258 sq. mi. (756,950 sq. km.) slightly smaller than twice the size of Montana

Climate: temperate; desert in north; cool and damp in south

Terrain: low coastal mountains; fertile central valley; rugged Andes in east

Elevation: lowest point: Pacific Ocean 0 ft. (0 m.); highest point: Cerro Aconcagua 22,841 ft. (6,962 m.)

Natural resources: copper, timber, iron ore, nitrates, precious metals, molybdenum

People

Population: 14,973,843 (July 1999 est.)

Population growth rate: 1.23%

Infant mortality rate: 10.02 deaths/1,000 live births

Life expectancy at birth: total population: 75.46 years; male: 72.33 years; female: 78.75 years

Major ethnic groups: European and European-Indian 95%, Indian 3%

Major religions: Roman Catholic 89%, Protestant 11%

Major languages: Spanish

Government

Official name: Republic of Chile

Government type: republic

National capital: Santiago

Independence: September 18, 1810 (from Spain)

Legal system: based on Code of 1857 derived from Spanish law and subsequent codes influenced by French and Austrian law; judicial review of legislative acts in the Supreme Court

Economy

Industries: copper, other minerals, foodstuffs, fish processing, iron and steel, wood and wood products, transport equipment, cement, textiles

Agricultural products: wheat, corn, grapes, beans, sugar beets, potatoes, fruit; beef, poultry, wool; timber; fish

Currency: 1 Chilean peso (Ch$) = 100 centavos

China

Geography

Location: Eastern Asia, bordering the East China Sea, Korea Bay, Yellow Sea, and South China Sea, between North Korea and Vietnam

Area: 3,705,386 sq. mi. (9,596,960 sq. km.); slightly larger than the U.S.

Climate: extremely diverse; tropical in south to subarctic in north

Terrain: mostly mountains, high plateaus, deserts in west; plains, deltas, and hills in east

Elevation: lowest point: Turpan Pendi −505 ft. (−154 m.); highest point: Mount Everest 29,028 ft. (8,848 m.)

Natural resources: coal, iron ore, petroleum, mercury, tin, tungsten, antimony, manganese, molybdenum, vanadium, magnetite, aluminum, lead, zinc, uranium, hydropower potential

People

Population: 1,246,871,951 (July 1999 est.)

Population growth rate: 0.77%

Infant mortality rate: 43.31 deaths/1,000 live births

Life expectancy at birth: total population: 69.92 years; male: 68.57 years; female: 71.48 years

Major ethnic groups: Han Chinese 91.9%, Zhuang, Uygur, Hui, Yi, Tibetan, Miao, Manchu, Mongol, Buyi, Korean, and other nationalities 8.1%

Major religions: Daoism (Taoism), Buddhism, Muslim 2%–3%

Major languages: Standard Chinese or Mandarin (Putonghua, based on the Beijing dialect), Yue (Cantonese), Wu (Shanghaiese), Minbei (Fuzhou), Minnan (Hokkien-Taiwanese), Xiang, Gan, Hakka dialects

Government

Official name: People's Republic of China
Government type: Communist state
National capital: Beijing
Independence: 221 BC (unification under the Qin or Ch'in Dynasty 221 BC; Qing or Ch'ing Dynasty replaced by the Republic on February 12, 1912; People's Republic established October 1, 1949)
Legal system: a complex amalgam of custom and statute, largely criminal law; rudimentary civil code in effect since 1 January 1987; continuing efforts are being made to improve civil, administrative, criminal, and commercial law

Economy

Industries: iron and steel, coal, machine building, armaments, textiles and apparel, petroleum, cement, chemical fertilizers, consumer durables, food processing, autos, consumer electronics, telecommunications
Agricultural products: rice, potatoes, sorghum, peanuts, tea, millet, barley, cotton, other fibers, oilseed; pork and other livestock products; fish
Currency: 1 yuan (•) = 10 jiao

Christmas Island

Geography

Location: Southeastern Asia, island in the Indian Ocean, south of Indonesia
Area: 52 sq. mi. (135 sq. km.); about 0.7 times the size of Washington, D.C.
Climate: tropical; heat and humidity moderated by trade winds
Terrain: steep cliffs along coast rise abruptly to central plateau
Elevation: extremes: lowest point: Indian Ocean 0 ft. (0 m.); highest point: Murray Hill 1,184 ft. (361 m.)
Natural resources: phosphate

People

Population: 2,373 (July 1999 est.)
Population growth rate: 7.77%
Major ethnic groups: Chinese 61%, Malay 25%, European 11%

Major religions: Buddhist 55%, Christian 15%, Muslim 10%, other 20%
Major languages: English

Government

Official name: Territory of Christmas Island
National capital: The Settlement
Independence: none (territory of Australia)
Legal system: under the authority of the governor general of Australia and Australian law

Economy

Industries: tourism, phosphate extraction (near depletion)
Currency: 1 Australian dollar ($A) = 100 cents

Colombia

Geography

Location: Northern South America, bordering the Caribbean Sea, between Panama and Venezuela, and bordering the North Pacific Ocean, between Ecuador and Panama
Area: 439,733 sq. mi. (1,138,910 sq. km.); slightly less than three times the size of Montana
Climate: tropical along coast and eastern plains; cooler in highlands
Terrain: flat coastal lowlands, central highlands, high Andes Mountains, eastern lowland plains
Elevation: lowest point: Pacific Ocean 0 ft. (0 m.); highest point: Nevado del Huila 18,865 ft. (5,750 m.)
Natural resources: petroleum, natural gas, coal, iron ore, nickel, gold, copper, emeralds

People

Population: 39,309,422 (July 1999 est.)
Population growth rate: 1.85%
Infant mortality rate: 24.3 deaths/1,000 live births
Life expectancy at birth: total population: 70.48 years; male: 66.54 years; female: 74.54 years
Major ethnic groups: mestizo 58%, white 20%, mulatto 14%, black 4%, mixed black-Indian 3%, Indian 1%
Major religions: Roman Catholic 95%
Major languages: Spanish

Government

Official name: Republic of Colombia

Government type: republic; executive branch dominates government structure

National capital: Bogota

Independence: July 20, 1810 (from Spain)

Legal system: based on Spanish law; a new criminal code modeled after U.S. procedures was enacted in 1992–93; judicial review of executive and legislative acts

Economy

Industries: textiles, food processing, oil, clothing and footwear, beverages, chemicals, cement; gold, coal, emeralds

Agricultural products: coffee, cut flowers, bananas, rice, tobacco, corn, sugarcane, cocoa beans, oilseed, vegetables; forest products; shrimp farming

Currency: 1 Colombian peso (Col$) = 100 centavos

Comoros

Geography

Location: Southern Africa, group of islands in the Mozambique Channel, about two-thirds of the way between northern Madagascar and northern Mozambique

Area: 838 sq. mi. (2,170 sq. km.); slightly more than 12 times the size of Washington, D.C.

Climate: tropical marine; rainy season (November to May)

Terrain: volcanic islands, interiors vary from steep mountains to low hills

Elevation: lowest point: Indian Ocean 0 ft. (0 m.); highest point: Mount Kartala 7,743 ft. (2,360 m.)

Natural resources: negligible

People

Population: 562,723 (July 1999 est.)

Population growth rate: 3.11%

Infant mortality rate: 81.63 deaths/1,000 live births

Life expectancy at birth: total population: 60.85 years; male: 58.39 years; female: 63.38 years

Major ethnic groups: Antalote, Cafre, Makoa, Oimatsaha, Sakalava

Major religions: Sunni Muslim 86%, Roman Catholic 14%

Major languages: Arabic (official), French (official), Comoran (a blend of Swahili and Arabic)

Government

Official name: Federal Islamic Republic of the Comoros

Government type: independent republic

National capital: Moroni

Independence: July 6, 1975 (from France)

Legal system: French and Muslim law in a new consolidated code

Economy

Industries: tourism, perfume distillation, textiles, furniture, jewelry, construction materials, soft drinks

Agricultural products: vanilla, cloves, perfume essences, copra, coconuts, bananas, cassava (tapioca)

Currency: 1 Comoran franc (CF) = 100 centimes

Congo, Democratic Republic of the

Geography

Location: Central Africa, northeast of Angola

Area: 905,568 sq. mi. (2,345,410 sq. km.); slightly less than one-fourth the size of U.S.

Climate: tropical; hot and humid in equatorial river basin; cooler and drier in southern highlands; cooler and wetter in eastern highlands; north of Equator—wet season April to October, dry season December to February; south of Equator—wet season November to March, dry season April to October

Terrain: vast central basin is a low-lying plateau; mountains in east

Elevation: extremes: lowest point: Atlantic Ocean 0 m. (0 ft.); highest point: Margherita Peak (Mount Stanley) 5,110 m. (16,765 ft.)

Natural resources: cobalt, copper, cadmium, petroleum, industrial and gem diamonds, gold, silver, zinc, manganese, tin, germanium, uranium, radium, bauxite, iron ore, coal, hydropower potential, timber

People

Population: 50,481,305 (July 1999 est.)

Population growth rate: 2.96%

Infant mortality rate: 99.45 deaths/1,000 live births

Life expectancy at birth: total population: 49.44 years; male: 47.28 years; female: 51.67 years

Major ethnic groups: over 200 African ethnic groups of which the majority are Bantu; the four largest tribes—Mongo, Luba, Kongo (all Bantu), and the Mangbetu-Azande (Hamitic) make up about 45% of the population

Major religions: Roman Catholic 50%, Protestant 20%, Kimbanguist 10%, Muslim 10%, other syncretic sects and traditional beliefs 10%

Major languages: French (official), Lingala (a lingua franca trade language), Kingwana (a dialect of Kiswahili or Swahili), Kikongo, Tshiluba

Government

Official name: Democratic Republic of the Congo (formerly Zaire)

Government type: dictatorship; presumably undergoing a transition to representative government

Independence: June 30, 1960 (from Belgium)

Legal system: based on Belgian civil law system and tribal law, has not accepted compulsory IJC jurisdiction

Economy

Industries: mining, mineral processing, consumer products (including textiles, footwear, cigarettes, processed foods and beverages), cement, diamonds

Agricultural products: coffee, sugar, palm oil, rubber, tea, quinine, cassava (tapioca), palm oil, bananas, root crops, corn, fruits; wood products

Currency: 1 zaire (Z) = 100 makuta

Congo, Republic of the

Geography

Location: Western Africa, bordering the South Atlantic Ocean, between Angola and Gabon

Area: 132,046 sq. mi. (342,000 sq. km.); slightly smaller than Montana

Climate: tropical; rainy season (March to June); dry season (June to October); constantly high temperatures and humidity

Terrain: coastal plain, southern basin, central plateau, northern basin

Elevation: lowest point: Atlantic Ocean 0 ft. (0 m.); highest point: Mount Berongou 2,963 ft. (903 m.)

Natural resources: petroleum, timber, potash, lead, zinc, uranium, copper, phosphates, natural gas

People

Population: 2,716,814 (July 1999 est.)

Population growth rate: 2.16%

Infant mortality rate: 100.58 deaths/1,000 live births

Life expectancy at birth: total population: 47.14 years; male: 45.42 years; female: 48.92 years

Major ethnic groups: Kongo 48%, Sangha 20%, M'Bochi 12%, Teke 17%, Europeans

Major religions: Christian 50%, Animist 48%, Muslim 2%

Major languages: French (official), Lingala and Monokutuba (lingua franca trade languages)

Government

Country name: Republic of the Congo

Government type: republic

National capital: Brazzaville

Independence: August 15, 1960 (from France)

Legal system: based on French civil law system and customary law

Economy

Industries: petroleum extraction, cement kilning, lumbering, brewing, sugar milling, palm oil, soap, cigarette making

Agricultural products: cassava (tapioca) accounts for 90% of food output, sugar, rice, corn, peanuts, vegetables, coffee, cocoa; forest products

Currency: 1 Communauté Financière Africaine franc (CFAF) = 100 centimes

Cook Islands

Geography

Location: Oceania, group of islands in the South Pacific Ocean, about one-half of the way from Hawaii to New Zealand

Area: 93 sq. mi. (240 sq. km.); slightly more than one times the size of Washington, D.C.

Climate: tropical; moderated by trade winds

Terrain: low coral atolls in north; volcanic, hilly islands in south

Elevation: lowest point: Pacific Ocean 0 ft. (0 m.); highest point: Te Manga 2,139 ft. (652 m.)

Natural resources: negligible

People

Population: 20,200 (July 1999 est.)

Population growth rate: 1.04%

Infant mortality rate: 24.7 deaths/1,000 live births

Life expectancy at birth: total population: 71.14 years; male: 69.2 years; female: 73.1 years

Major ethnic groups: Polynesian (full blood) 81.3%, Polynesian and European 7.7%, Polynesian and non-European 7.7%, European 2.4%

Major religions: Christianity

Major languages: English (official), Maori

Government

Official name: Cook Islands

Government type: self-governing parliamentary government in free association with New Zealand; Cook Islands is fully responsible for internal affairs; New Zealand retains responsibility for external affairs, in consultation with the Cook Islands

National capital: Avarua

Independence: none (became self-governing in free association with New Zealand on August 4, 1965 and has the right at any time to move to full independence by unilateral action)

Economy

Industries: fruit processing, tourism

Agricultural products: copra, citrus, pineapples, tomatoes, bananas, yams, taro

Currency: 1 New Zealand dollar (NZ$) = 100 cents

Costa Rica

Geography

Location: Central America, bordering both the Caribbean Sea and the North Pacific Ocean, between Nicaragua and Panama

Area: 19,730 sq. mi. (51,100 sq. km.); slightly smaller than West Virginia

Climate: tropical; dry season (December to April); rainy season (May to November)

Terrain: coastal plains separated by rugged mountains

Elevation: lowest point: Pacific Ocean 0 ft. (0 m.); highest point: Cerro Chirripo 12,500 ft. (3,810 m.)

Natural resources: hydropower potential

People

Population: 3,674,490 (July 1999 est.)

Population growth rate: 1.89%

Infant mortality rate: 12.89 deaths/1,000 live births

Life expectancy at birth: total population: 76.04 years; male: 73.6 years; female: 78.61 years

Major ethnic groups: white (including mestizo) 96%, black 2%

Major religions: Roman Catholic 95%

Major languages: Spanish (official), English spoken around Puerto Limon

Government

Official name: Republic of Costa Rica

Government type: democratic republic

National capital: San Jose
Independence: September 15, 1821 (from Spain)
Legal system: based on Spanish civil law system; judicial review of legislative acts in the Supreme Court

Economy

Industries: food processing, textiles and clothing, construction materials, fertilizer, plastic products
Agricultural products: coffee, bananas, sugar, corn, rice, beans, potatoes; beef; timber (depletion of forest resources has resulted in declining timber output)
Currency: 1 Costa Rican colon (C) = 100 centimos

Côte d'Ivoire

Geography

Location: Western Africa, bordering the North Atlantic Ocean, between Ghana and Liberia
Area: 124,502 sq. mi. (322,460 sq. km.); slightly larger than New Mexico
Climate: tropical along coast, semiarid in far north; three seasons—warm and dry (November to March), hot and dry (March to May), hot and wet (June to October)
Terrain: mostly flat to undulating plains; mountains in northwest
Elevation: lowest point: Atlantic Ocean 0 ft. (0 m.); highest point: Mont Nimba 5,748 ft. (1,752 m.)
Natural resources: petroleum, diamonds, manganese, iron ore, cobalt, bauxite, copper

People

Population: 15,818,068 (July 1999 est.)
Population growth rate: 2.35%
Infant mortality rate: 94.17 deaths/1,000 live births
Life expectancy at birth: total population: 46.05 years; male: 44.48 years; female: 47.67 years
Major ethnic groups: Baoule 23%, Bete 18%, Senoufou 15%, Malinke 11%, Agni,
Major religions: indigenous 25%, Muslim 60%, Christian 12%

Major languages: French (official), 60 native dialects with Dioula the most widely spoken

Government

Official name: Republic of Côte d'Ivoire
Government type: republic; multiparty presidential regime established 1960
National capital: Yamoussoukro
Independence: August 7, 1960 (from France)
Legal system: based on French civil law system and customary law; judicial review in the Constitutional Chamber of the Supreme Court; has not accepted compulsory IJC jurisdiction

Economy

Industries: foodstuffs, beverages; wood products, oil refining, automobile assembly, textiles, fertilizer, construction materials, electricity
Agricultural products: coffee, cocoa beans, bananas, palm kernels, corn, rice, manioc, sweet potatoes, sugar; cotton, rubber; timber
Currency: 1 Communauté Financière Africaine franc (CFAF) = 100 centimes

Croatia

Geography

Location: Southeastern Europe, bordering the Adriatic Sea, between Bosnia and Herzegovina and Slovenia
Area: 21,829 sq. mi. (56,538 sq. km.); slightly smaller than West Virginia
Climate: Mediterranean and continental; continental climate predominant with hot summers and cold winters; mild winters, dry summers along coast
Terrain: geographically diverse; flat plains along Hungarian border, low mountains and highlands near Adriatic coast, coastline, and islands
Elevation: lowest point: Adriatic Sea 0 ft. (0 m.); highest point: Dinara 6,004 ft. (1,830 m.)
Natural resources: oil, some coal, bauxite, low-grade iron ore, calcium, natural asphalt, silica, mica, clays, salt

People

Population: 4,676,865 (July 1999 est.)

Population growth rate: 0.1%

Infant mortality rate: 7.84 deaths/1,000 live births

Life expectancy at birth: total population: 74 years; male: 70.69 years; female: 77.52 years

Major ethnic groups: Croat 78%, Serb 12%

Major religions: Catholic 76.5%, Orthodox 11.1%

Major languages: Serbo-Croatian 96%

Government

Official name: Republic of Croatia

Government type: parliamentary democracy

National capital: Zagreb

Independence: June 25, 1991 (from Yugoslavia)

Legal system: based on civil law system

Economy

Industries: chemicals and plastics, machine tools, fabricated metal, electronics, pig iron and rolled steel products, aluminum, paper, wood products, construction materials, textiles, shipbuilding, petroleum and petroleum refining, food and beverages

Agricultural products: wheat, corn, sugar beets, sunflower seed, alfalfa, clover, olives, citrus, grapes, vegetables; livestock breeding, dairy farming

Currency: 1 Croatian kuna (HRK) = 100 paras

Cuba

Geography

Location: Caribbean, island between the Caribbean Sea and the North Atlantic Ocean, south of Florida

Area: 42,803 sq. mi. (110,860 sq. km.); slightly smaller than Pennsylvania

Climate: tropical; moderated by trade winds; dry season (November to April); rainy season (May to October)

Terrain: mostly flat to rolling plains with rugged hills and mountains in the southeast

Elevation: lowest point: Caribbean Sea 0 ft. (0 m.); highest point: Pico Turquino 6,578 ft. (2,005 m.)

Natural resources: cobalt, nickel, iron ore, copper, manganese, salt, timber, silica, petroleum

People

Population: 11,096,395 (July 1999 est.)

Population growth rate: 0.44%

Infant mortality rate: 7.81 deaths/1,000 live births

Life expectancy at birth: total population: 75.78 years; male: 73.41 years; female: 78.3 years

Major ethnic groups: mulatto 51%, white 37%, black 11%

Major religions: nominally Roman Catholic 85% prior to Castro assuming power

Major languages: Spanish

Government

Official name: Republic of Cuba

Government type: Communist state

National capital: Havana

Independence: May 20, 1902 (from Spain, December 10, 1898; administered by the U.S. from 1898 to 1902)

Legal system: based on Spanish and American law, with large elements of Communist legal theory; does not accept compulsory ICJ jurisdiction

Economy

Industries: sugar, petroleum, food, tobacco, textiles, chemicals, paper and wood products, metals (particularly nickel), cement, fertilizers, consumer goods, agricultural machinery

Agricultural products: sugarcane, tobacco, citrus, coffee, rice, potatoes and other tubers, beans; livestock

Currency: 1 Cuban peso (Cu$) = 100 centavos

Cyprus

Geography

Location: Middle East, island in the Mediterranean Sea, south of Turkey

Area: 3,571 sq. mi. (9,250 sq. km.); about 0.7 times the size of Connecticut

Climate: temperate; Mediterranean with hot, dry summers and cool, wet winters

Terrain: central plain with mountains to north and south; scattered but significant plains along southern coast

Elevation: lowest point: Mediterranean Sea 0 ft. (0 m.); highest point: Olympus 6,404 ft. (1,952 m.)

Natural resources: copper, pyrites, asbestos, gypsum, timber, salt, marble, clay earth pigment

People

Population: 754,064 (July 1999 est.)

Population growth rate: 0.67%

Infant mortality rate: 7.68 deaths/1,000 live births

Life expectancy at birth: total population: 77.1 years; male: 74.91 years; female: 79.39 years

Major ethnic groups: total: Greek 78% (99.5% of the Greeks live in the Greek area), Turkish 18% (98.7% of the Turks live in the Turkish area)

Major religions: Greek Orthodox 78%, Muslim 18%

Major languages: Greek, Turkish, English

Government

Official name: Republic of Cyprus

Government type: republic

National capital: Nicosia; note: the Turkish area's capital is Lefkosa (Nicosia)

Independence: August 16, 1960 (from U.K.)

Legal system: based on common law, with civil law modifications

Economy

Industries: food, beverages, textiles, chemicals, metal products, tourism, wood products

Agricultural products: potatoes, vegetables, barley, grapes, olives, citrus, vegetables

Currency: 1 Cypriot pound (£C) = 100 cents; 1 Turkish lira (TL) = 100 kurus

Czech Republic

Geography

Location: Central Europe, southeast of Germany

Area: 30,387 sq. mi. (78,703 sq. km.); slightly smaller than South Carolina

Climate: temperate; cool summers; cold, cloudy, humid winters

Terrain: Bohemia in the west consists of rolling plains, hills, and plateaus surrounded by low mountains; Moravia in the east consists of very hilly country

Elevation: lowest point: Elbe River 377 ft. (115 m.); highest point: Snezka 5,256 ft. (1,602 m.)

Natural resources: hard coal, soft coal, kaolin, clay, graphite

People

Population: 10,280,513 (July 1999 est.)

Population growth rate: -0.01%

Infant mortality rate: 6.67 deaths/1,000 live births

Life expectancy at birth: total population: 74.35 years; male: 71.01 years; female: 77.88 years

Major ethnic groups: Czech 94.4%, Slovak 3%

Major religions: atheist 39.8%, Roman Catholic 39.2%, Protestant 4.6%, Orthodox 3%

Major languages: Czech, Slovak

Government

Official name: Czech Republic

Government type: parliamentary democracy

National capital: Prague

Independence: January 1, 1993 (from Czechoslovakia)

Legal system: civil law system based on Austro-Hungarian codes

Economy

Industries: fuels, ferrous metallurgy, machinery and equipment, coal, motor vehicles, glass, armaments

Agricultural products: grains, potatoes, sugar beets, hops, fruit; pigs, cattle, poultry; forest products

Currency: 1 koruna (Kc) = 100 haleru

Denmark

Geography
Location: Northern Europe, bordering the Baltic Sea and the North Sea, on a peninsula north of Germany

Area: 16,629 sq. mi. (43,070 sq. km.); slightly more than twice the size of Massachusetts

Climate: temperate; humid and overcast; mild, windy winters and cool summers

Terrain: low and flat to gently rolling plains

Elevation: lowest point: Lammefjord −23 ft. (−7 m.); highest point: Ejer Bavnehoj 568 ft. (173 m.)

Natural resources: petroleum, natural gas, fish, salt, limestone

People
Population: 5,356,845 (July 1999 est.)

Population growth rate: 0.38%

Infant mortality rate: 5.11 deaths/1,000 live births

Life expectancy at birth: total population: 76.51 years; male: 73.83 years; female: 79.33 years

Major ethnic groups: Scandinavian, Eskimo, Faroese, German

Major religions: Evangelical Lutheran 91%

Major languages: Danish, Faroese, Greenlandic (an Eskimo dialect)

Government
Official name: Kingdom of Denmark

Government type: constitutional monarchy

National capital: Copenhagen

Independence: 10th century first organized as a unified state; in 1849 became a constitutional monarchy

Legal system: civil law system; judicial review of legislative acts

Economy
Industries: food processing, machinery and equipment, textiles and clothing, chemical products, electronics, construction, furniture, and other wood products, shipbuilding

Agricultural products: grain, potatoes, rape, sugar beets; meat, dairy products; fish

Currency: 1 Danish krone (DKr) = 100 oere

Djibouti

Geography
Location: Eastern Africa, bordering the Gulf of Aden and the Red Sea, between Eritrea and Somalia

Area: 8,494 sq. mi. (22,000 sq. km.); slightly larger than Massachusetts

Climate: desert; torrid, dry

Terrain: coastal plain and plateau separated by central mountains

Elevation: lowest point: Asal −509 ft. (−155 m.); highest point: Mousa Alli 6,653 ft. (2,028 m.)

Natural resources: geothermal areas

People
Population: 447,439 (July 1999 est.)

Population growth rate: 1.5%

Infant mortality rate: 100.24 deaths/1,000 live births

Life expectancy at birth: total population: 50.54 years; male: 49.48 years; female: 53.67 years

Major ethnic groups: Somali 60%, Afar 35%

Major religions: Muslim 94%, Christian 6%

Major languages: French (official), Arabic (official), Somali, Afar

Government
Official name: Republic of Djibouti

Government type: republic

National capital: Djibouti

Independence: June 27, 1977 (from France)

Legal system: based on French civil law system, traditional practices, and Islamic law

Economy
Industries: limited to a few small-scale enter-
prises, such as dairy products and mineral-
water bottling
Agricultural products: fruits, vegetables; goats,
sheep, camels
Currency: 1 Djiboutian franc (DF) = 100 centimes

Economy
Industries: soap, coconut oil, tourism, copra, furniture, cement blocks, shoes
Agricultural products: bananas, citrus, mangoes,
root crops, coconuts; forestry and fisheries
potential not exploited
Currency: 1 East Caribbean dollar (EC$) = 100
cents

Dominica

Geography
Location: Caribbean, island between the
Caribbean Sea and the North Atlantic Ocean,
about one-half of the way from Puerto Rico
to Trinidad and Tobago
Area: 290 sq. mi. (750 sq. km.); more than four
times the size of Washington, D.C.
Climate: tropical; moderated by northeast trade
winds; heavy
rainfall
Terrain: rugged mountains of volcanic
origin
Elevation: lowest point: Caribbean Sea 0 ft.
(0 m.); highest point: Morne Diablatins
4,747 ft. (1,447 m.)
Natural resources: timber

People
Population: 64,881 (July 1999 est.)
Population growth rate: –1.41%
Infant mortality rate: 8.75 deaths/1,000 live
births
Life expectancy at birth: total population:
78.01 years; male: 75.15 years; female:
81.01 years
Major ethnic groups: black, Carib Indians
Major religions: Roman Catholic 77%, Protestant
15%
Major languages: English (official), French
patois

Government
Official name: Commonwealth of Dominica
Government type: parliamentary democracy
National capital: Roseau
Independence: November 3, 1978 (from U.K.)
Legal system: based on English common law

Dominican Republic

Geography
Location: Caribbean, eastern two-thirds of the
island of Hispaniola, between the Caribbean
Sea and the North Atlantic Ocean, east of
Haiti
Area: 18,815 sq. mi. (48,730 sq. km.); slightly
more than twice the size of New Hampshire
Climate: tropical maritime; little seasonal temperature variation; seasonal variation in rainfall
Terrain: rugged highlands and mountains with
fertile valleys interspersed
Elevation; lowest point: Lago Enriquillo –151 ft.
(–46 m.); highest point: Pico Duarte 10,417 ft.
(3,175 m.)
Natural resources: nickel, bauxite, gold, silver

People
Population: 8,129,734 (July 1999 est.)
Population growth rate: 1.62%
Infant mortality rate: 42.52 deaths/1,000 live
births
Life expectancy at birth: total population:
70.07 years; male: 67.86 years; female:
72.4 years
Major ethnic groups: white 16%, black 11%,
mixed 73%
Major religions: Roman Catholic 95%
Major languages: Spanish

Government
Official name: Dominican Republic
Government type: republic
National capital: Santo Domingo
Independence: February 27, 1844 (from Haiti)
Legal system: based on French civil codes

Economy

Industries: tourism, sugar processing, ferro-nickel and gold mining, textiles, cement, tobacco

Agricultural products: sugarcane, coffee, cotton, cocoa, tobacco, rice, beans, potatoes, corn, bananas; cattle, pigs, dairy products, meat, eggs

Currency: 1 Dominican peso (RD$) = 100 centavos

Ecuador

Geography

Location: Western South America, bordering the Pacific Ocean at the Equator, between Colombia and Peru

Area (including Galapagos Islands): 109,483 sq. mi. (283,560 sq. km.); slightly smaller than Nevada

Climate: tropical along coast becoming cooler inland

Terrain: coastal plain, inter-Andean central highlands (sierra), and flat to rolling eastern jungle

Elevation: lowest point: Pacific Ocean 0 ft. (0 m.); highest point: Chimborazo 20,561 ft. (6,267 m.)

Natural resources: petroleum, fish, timber

People

Population: 12,562,496 (July 1999 est.)

Population growth rate: 1.78%

Infant mortality rate: 30.69 deaths/1,000 live births

Life expectancy at birth: total population: 72.16 years; male: 69.54 years; female: 74.9 years

Major ethnic groups: mestizo (mixed Indian and Spanish) 55%, Indian 25%, Spanish 10%, black 10%

Major religions: Roman Catholic 95%

Major languages: Spanish (official), Indian languages (especially Quechua)

Government

Official name: Republic of Ecuador

Government type: republic

National capital: Quito

Independence: May 24, 1822 (from Spain)

Legal system: based on civil law system, has not accepted compulsory ICJ jurisdiction

Economy

Industries: petroleum, food processing, textiles, metal work, paper products, wood products, chemicals, plastics, fishing, lumber

Agricultural products: bananas, coffee, cocoa, rice, potatoes, manioc, plantains, sugarcane; cattle, sheep, pigs, beef, pork, dairy products; balsa wood; fish, shrimp

Currency: 1 sucre (S/) = 100 centavos

Egypt

Geography

Location: Northern Africa, bordering the Mediterranean Sea, between Libya and the Gaza Strip

Area: 386,660 sq. mi. (1,001,450 sq. km.); slightly more than three times the size of New Mexico

Climate: desert; hot, dry summers with moderate winters

Terrain: vast desert plateau interrupted by Nile valley and delta

Elevation: lowest point: Qattara Depression −436 ft. (−133 m.); highest point: Mount Catherine 8,625 ft. (2,629 m.)

Natural resources: petroleum, natural gas, iron ore, phosphates, manganese, limestone, gypsum, talc, asbestos, lead, zinc

People

Population: 67,273,906 (July 1999 est.)

Population growth rate: 1.28%

Infant mortality rate: 67.46 deaths/1,000 live births

Life expectancy at birth: total population: 62.39 years; male: 60.39 years; female: 64.49 years

Major ethnic groups: Eastern Hamitic stock (Egyptians, Bedouins, and Berbers) 99%, Greek, Nubian, Armenian

Major religions: Muslim (mostly Sunni) 94%,
Coptic Christian and other 6%
Major languages: Arabic (official), English and
French widely understood by educated classes

Government

Official name: Arab Republic of Egypt
Government type: republic
National capital: Cairo
Independence: February 28, 1922 (from U.K.)
Legal system: based on English common law,
Islamic law, and Napoleonic codes

Economy

Industries: textiles, food processing, tourism,
chemicals, petroleum, construction, cement,
metals
Agricultural products: cotton, rice, corn, wheat,
beans, fruits, vegetables; cattle, water buffalo,
sheep, goats; annual fish catch about 140,000
metric tons
Currency: 1 Egyptian pound (£E) = 100
piasters

El Salvador

Geography

Location: Central America, bordering the North
Pacific Ocean, between Guatemala and
Honduras
Area: 8,124 sq. mi. (21,040 sq. km.); slightly
smaller than Massachusetts
Climate: tropical; rainy season (May to October);
dry season (November to April)
Terrain: mostly mountains with narrow coastal
belt and central plateau
Elevation: lowest point: Pacific Ocean 0 ft.
(0 m.); highest point: Cerro El Pital 8,957 ft.
(2,730 m.)
Natural resources: hydropower, geothermal
power, petroleum

People

Population: 5,839,079 (July 1999 est.)
Population growth rate: 1.53%
Infant mortality rate: 28.38 deaths/1,000 live
births
Life expectancy at birth: total population: 70.02
years; male: 66.7 years; female: 73.5 years

Major ethnic groups: mestizo 94%, Amerindian
5%
Major religions: Roman Catholic 75% and
Protestant
Major languages: Spanish, Nahua (among some
Amerindians)

Government

Official name: Republic of El Salvador
Government type: republic
National capital: San Salvador
Independence: September 15, 1821 (from Spain)
Legal system: based on civil and Roman law, with
traces of common law

Economy

Industries: food processing, beverages, petroleum, chemicals, fertilizer, textiles, furniture,
light metals
Agricultural products: coffee, sugarcane, corn,
rice, beans, oilseed, cotton, sorghum; beef,
dairy products; shrimp
Currency: 1 Salvadoran colon (C) = 100
centavos

Equatorial Guinea

Geography

Location: Western Africa, bordering the Bight of
Biafra, between Cameroon and Gabon
Area: 10,830 sq. mi. (28,050 sq. km.); slightly
smaller than Maryland
Climate: tropical; always hot, humid
Terrain: coastal plains rise to interior hills;
islands are volcanic
Elevation: lowest point: Atlantic Ocean 0 ft.
(0 m.); highest point: Mount Malabo 9,869 ft.
(3,008 m.)
Natural resources: timber, petroleum, small
unexploited deposits of gold, manganese,
uranium

People

Population: 465,746 (July 1999 est.)
Population growth rate: 2.55%
Infant mortality rate: 91.18 deaths/1,000 live
births
Life expectancy at birth: total population: 54.39
years; male: 52.03 years; female: 56.83 years

Major ethnic groups: Bioko (primarily Bubi, some Fernandinos), Rio Muni (primarily Fang)

Major religions: nominally Christian and predominantly Roman Catholic, pagan practices

Major languages: Spanish (official), French (official), pidgin English, Fang, Bubi, Ibo

Government

Official name: Republic of Equatorial Guinea

Government type: republic in transition to multiparty democracy

National capital: Malabo

Independence: October 12, 1968 (from Spain)

Legal system: partly based on Spanish civil law and tribal custom

Economy

Industries: fishing, sawmilling

Agricultural products: coffee, cocoa, rice, yams, cassava (tapioca), bananas, palm oil nuts, manioc; livestock; timber

Currency: 1 Communauté Financière Africaine franc (CFAF) = 100 centimes

Eritrea

Geography

Location: Eastern Africa, bordering the Red Sea, between Djibouti and Sudan

Area: 46,842 sq. mi. (121,320 sq. km.); slightly larger than Pennsylvania

Climate: hot, dry desert strip along Red Sea coast; cooler and wetter in the central highlands (up to 61 cm of rainfall annually); semi-arid in western hills and lowlands; rainfall heaviest during June-September except on coastal desert

Terrain: dominated by extension of Ethiopian north-south trending highlands, descending on the east to a coastal desert plain, on the northwest to hilly terrain and on the southwest to flat-to-rolling plains

Elevation: lowest point: Kobar Sink –246 ft. (–75 m.); highest point: Soira 9,885 ft. (3,013 m.)

Natural resources: gold, potash, zinc, copper, salt, probably oil and natural gas (petroleum geologists are prospecting for it), fish

People

Population: 3,984,723 (July 1999 est.)

Population growth rate: 3.88%

Infant mortality rate: 76.84 deaths/1,000 live births

Life expectancy at birth: total population: 55.74 years; male: 53.61 years; female: 57.95 years

Major ethnic groups: ethnic Tigrinya 50%, Tigre and Kunama 40%, Afar 4%, Saho (Red Sea coast dwellers) 3%

Major religions: Muslim, Coptic Christian, Roman Catholic, Protestant

Major languages: Afar, Amharic, Arabic, Tigre and Kunama, Tigrinya

Government

Official name: State of Eritrea

Government type: transitional government

National capital: Asmara (formerly Asmera)

Independence: May 27, 1993 (from Ethiopia; formerly the Eritrea Autonomous Region)

Economy

Industries: food processing, beverages, clothing and textiles

Agricultural products: sorghum, lentils, vegetables, maize, cotton, tobacco, coffee, sisal (for making rope); livestock (including goats); fish

Currency: 1 nafka = 100 cents

Estonia

Geography

Location: Eastern Europe, bordering the Baltic Sea and Gulf of Finland, between Latvia and Russia

Area: 17,462 sq. mi. (45,226 sq. km.); slightly smaller than New Hampshire and Vermont combined

Climate: maritime, wet, moderate winters, cool summers

Terrain: marshy, lowlands
Elevation: lowest point: Baltic Sea o ft. (o m.); highest point: Suur Munamagi 1,043 ft. (318 m.)
Natural resources: shale oil (kukersite), peat, phosphorite, amber, cambrian blue clay

People
Population: 1,408,523 (July 1999 est.)
Population growth rate: −0.82%
Infant mortality rate: 13.83 deaths/1,000 live births
Life expectancy at birth: total population: 68.65 years; male: 62.61 years; female: 75 years
Major ethnic groups: Estonian 64.2%, Russian 28.7
Major religions: Evangelical Lutheran, Russian Orthodox, Estonian Orthodox,
Major languages: Estonian (official), Russian, Ukrainian

Government
Official name: Republic of Estonia
Government type: parliamentary democracy
National capital: Tallinn
Independence: September 6, 1991 (from Soviet Union)
Legal system: based on civil law system; no judicial review of legislative acts

Economy
Industries: oil shale, shipbuilding, phosphates, electric motors, excavators, cement, furniture, clothing, textiles, paper, shoes, apparel
Agricultural products: potatoes, fruits, vegetables; livestock and dairy products; fish
Currency: 1 Estonian kroon (EEK) = 100 cents

Ethiopia

Geography
Location: Eastern Africa, west of Somalia
Area: 435,184 sq. mi. (1,127,127 sq. km.); slightly less than twice the size of Texas
Climate: tropical monsoon with wide topographic-induced variation
Terrain: high plateau with central mountain range divided by Great Rift Valley

Elevation: lowest point: Denakil −410 ft. (−125 m.); highest point: Ras Dashen Terara 15,157 ft. (4,620 m.)
Natural resources: small reserves of gold, platinum, copper, potash, natural gas

People
Population: 58,680,383 (July 1999 est.)
Population growth rate: 2.16%
Infant mortality rate: 124.57 deaths/1,000 live births
Life expectancy at birth: total population: 40.46 years; male: 39.22 years; female: 41.73 years
Major ethnic groups: Oromo 40%, Amhara and Tigrean 32%, Sidamo 9%, Shankella 6%, Somali 6%, Afar 4%, Gurage 2%
Major religions: Muslim 45–50%, Ethiopian Orthodox 35–40%, animist 12%
Major languages: Amharic (official), Tigrinya, Orominga, Guaraginga, Somali, Arabic

Government
Official name: Federal Democratic Republic of Ethiopia
Government type: federal republic
National capital: Addis Ababa
Independence: oldest independent country in Africa and one of the oldest in the world—at least 2,000 years
Legal system: (currently transitional)

Economy
Industries: food processing, beverages, textiles, chemicals, metals processing, cement
Agricultural products: cereals, pulses, coffee, oilseed, sugarcane, potatoes, other vegetables; hides, cattle, sheep, goats
Currency: 1 birr (Br) = 100 cents

Falkland Islands; (Islas Malvinas)

Geography
Location: Southern South America, islands in the South Atlantic Ocean, east of southern Argentina
Area: 4,700 sq. mi. (12,173 sq. km.); slightly smaller than Connecticut

Climate: cold marine; strong westerly winds, cloudy, humid; rain occurs on more than half of days in year; occasional snow all year, except in January and February, but does not accumulate

Terrain: rocky, hilly, mountainous with some boggy, undulating plains

Elevation: lowest point: Atlantic Ocean 0 ft. (0 m.); highest point: Mount Usborne 2,313 ft. (705 m.)

Natural resources: fish, wildlife

People

Population: 2,758 (July 1999 est.)

Population growth rate: 2.43%

Major ethnic groups: British

Major religions: primarily Anglican

Major languages: English

Government

Official name: Colony of the Falkland Islands

National capital: Stanley

Independence: none (dependent territory of the U.K., also claimed by Argentina)

Legal system: English common law

Economy

Industries: wool and fish processing; sale of stamps and coins

Agricultural products: fodder and vegetable crops; sheep farming, small dairy herds

Currency: 1 Falkland pound (£F) = 100 pence

Faroe Islands

Geography

Location: Northern Europe, island group between the Norwegian Sea and the north Atlantic Ocean, about one-half of the way from Iceland to Norway

Area: 540 sq. mi. (1,399 sq. km.); eight times the size of Washington, D.C.

Climate: mild winters, cool summers; usually overcast; foggy, windy

Terrain: rugged, rocky, some low peaks; cliffs along most of coast

Elevation: lowest point: Atlantic Ocean 0 ft. (0 m.); highest point: Slaettaratindur 2,894 ft. (882 m.)

Natural resources: fish, whales

People

Population: 41,059 (July 1999 est.)

Population growth rate: −2.03%

Infant mortality rate: 10.26 deaths/1,000 live births

Life expectancy at birth: total population: 78.56 years; male: 75.66 years; female: 81.58 years

Major ethnic groups: Scandinavian

Major religions: Evangelical Lutheran

Major languages: Faroese (derived from Old Norse), Danish

Government

Official name: Faroe Islands

National capital: Torshavn

Independence: none (part of the Kingdom of Denmark; self-governing overseas administrative division of Denmark)

Legal system: Danish

Economy

Industries: fishing, shipbuilding, construction, handicrafts

Agricultural products: milk, potatoes, vegetables; sheep; salmon farming; fish

Currency: 1 Danish krone (DKr) = 100 oere

Fiji

Geography

Location: Oceania, island group in the South Pacific Ocean, about two-thirds of the way from Hawaii to New Zealand

Area: 7,054 sq. mi. (18,270 sq. km.); slightly smaller than New Jersey

Climate: tropical marine; only slight seasonal temperature variation

Terrain: mostly mountains of volcanic origin

Elevation: lowest point: Pacific Ocean 0 ft. (0 m.); highest point: Tomanivi 4,344 ft. (1,324 m.)

Natural resources: timber, fish, gold, copper, off-shore oil potential

People

Population: 812,918 (July 1999 est.)

Population growth rate: 1.28%

Infant mortality rate: 16.3 deaths/1,000 live births

Life expectancy at birth: total population: 66.59 years; male: 64.19 years; female: 69.11 years

Major ethnic groups: Fijian 49%, Indian 46%

Major religions: Christian 52% , Hindu 38%

Major languages: English (official), Fijian, Hindustani

Government

Official name: Republic of the Fiji Islands

Government type: republic; note: military coup leader Maj. Gen. Sitiveni Rabuka formally declared Fiji a republic on October 6, 1987

National capital: Suva

Independence: October 10, 1970 (from U.K.)

Legal system: based on British system

Economy

Industries: sugar, tourism, copra, gold, silver, clothing, lumber, small cottage industries

Agricultural products: sugarcane, coconuts, cassava (tapioca), rice, sweet potatoes, bananas; cattle, pigs, horses, goats; fish

Currency: 1 Fijian dollar (F$) = 100 cents

Finland

Geography

Location: Northern Europe, bordering the Baltic Sea, Gulf of Bothnia, and Gulf of Finland, between Sweden and Russia

Area: 130,127 sq. mi. (337,030 sq. km.); slightly smaller than Montana

Climate: cold temperate; potentially sub-arctic, but comparatively mild because of moderating influence of the North Atlantic Current, Baltic Sea, and more than 60,000 lakes

Terrain: mostly low, flat to rolling plains interspersed with lakes and low hills

Elevation: lowest point: Baltic Sea 0 ft. (0 m.); highest point: Haltiatunturi 4,357 ft. (1,328 m.)

Natural resources: timber, copper, zinc, iron ore, silver

People

Population: 5,158,372 (July 1999 est.)

Population growth rate: 0.15%

Infant mortality rate: 3.82 deaths/1,000 live births

Life expectancy at birth: total population: 77.32 years; male: 73.81 years; female: 80.98 years

Major ethnic groups: Finn 93%, Swede 6%, Lapp 0.11%, Gypsy 0.12%, Tatar 0.02%

Major religions: Evangelical Lutheran 89%, Greek Orthodox 1%, none 9%, other 1%

Major languages: Finnish 93.5% (official), Swedish 6.3% (official), small Lapp and Russian-speaking minorities

Government

Official name: Republic of Finland

Government type: republic

National capital: Helsinki

Independence: December 6, 1917 (from Russia)

Legal system: civil law system based on Swedish law; Supreme Court may request legislation interpreting or modifying laws

Economy

Industries: metal products, shipbuilding, pulp and paper, copper refining, foodstuffs, chemicals, textiles, clothing

Agricultural products: cereals, sugar beets, potatoes; dairy cattle; fish

Currency: 1 markka (FMk) or Finmark = 100 pennia

France

Geography

Location: Western Europe, bordering the Bay of Biscay and English Channel, between Belgium and Spain southeast of the U.K.; bordering the Mediterranean Sea, between Italy and Spain

Area: 211,208 sq. mi. (547,030 sq. km.); slightly less than twice the size of Colorado

Climate: generally cool winters and mild summers, but mild winters and hot summers along the Mediterranean

Terrain: mostly flat plains or gently rolling hills in north and west; remainder is mountainous, especially Pyrenees in south, Alps in east

Elevation: lowest point: Rhone River delta –7 ft. (–2 m.); highest point: Mont Blanc 15,771 ft. (4,807 m.)

Natural resources: coal, iron ore, bauxite, fish, timber, zinc, potash

People

Population: 58,978,172 (July 1999 est.)

Population growth rate: 0.27%

Infant mortality rate: 5.62 deaths/1,000 live births

Life expectancy at birth: total population: 78.63 years; male: 74.76 years; female: 82.71 years

Major ethnic groups: Celtic and Latin with Teutonic, Slavic, North African, Indochinese, Basque minorities

Major religions: Roman Catholic 90%, Protestant 2%, Jewish 1%

Major languages: French 100%, rapidly declining regional dialects and languages (Provencal, Breton, Alsatian, Corsican, Catalan, Basque, Flemish)

Government

Official name: French Republic

Government type: republic

National capital: Paris

Independence: 486 (unified by Clovis)

Legal system: civil law system with indigenous concepts; review of administrative but not legislative acts

Economy

Industries: steel, machinery, chemicals, automobiles, metallurgy, aircraft, electronics, mining, textiles, food processing, tourism

Agricultural products: wheat, cereals, sugar beets, potatoes, wine grapes; beef, dairy products; fish

Currency: 1 French franc (F) = 100 centimes

French Guiana

Geography

Location: Northern South America, bordering the North Atlantic Ocean, between Brazil and Suriname

Area: 35,135 sq. mi. (91,000 sq. km.); slightly smaller than Indiana

Climate: tropical; hot, humid; little seasonal temperature variation

Terrain: low-lying coastal plains rising to hills and small mountains

Elevation: lowest point: Atlantic Ocean 0 ft. (0 m.); highest point: Bellevue de l'Inini 2,792 ft. (851 m.)

Natural resources: bauxite, timber, gold (widely scattered), cinnabar, kaolin, fish

People

Population: 167,982 (July 1999 est.)

Population growth rate: 3.19%

Infant mortality rate: 12.93 deaths/1,000 live births

Life expectancy at birth: total population: 76.61 years; male: 73.41 years; female: 79.97 years

Major ethnic groups: black or mulatto 66%, white 12%, East Indian, Chinese, Amerindian 12%

Major religions: Roman Catholic

Major languages: French

Government

Official name: Department of Guiana

National capital: Cayenne

Independence: none (overseas department of France)

Legal system: French legal system

Economy

Industries: construction, shrimp processing, forestry products, rum, gold mining

Agricultural products: rice, corn, manioc, cocoa, vegetables, bananas, sugar; cattle, pigs, poultry

Currency: 1 French franc (F) = 100 centimes

French Polynesia

Geography

Location: Oceania, archipelago in the South Pacific Ocean, about one-half of the way from South America to Australia

Area: 1,609 sq. mi. (4,167 sq. km.); slightly less than one-third the size of Connecticut

Climate: tropical, but moderate

Terrain: mixture of rugged high islands and low islands with reefs

Elevation: lowest point: Pacific Ocean 0 ft. (0 m.); highest point: Mount Orohena 7,352 ft. (2,241 m.)

Natural resources: timber, fish, cobalt

People

Population: 242,073 (July 1999 est.)

Population growth rate: 1.72%

Infant mortality rate: 13.59 deaths/1,000 live births

Life expectancy at birth: total population: 72.33 years; male: 69.93 years; female: 74.85 years

Major ethnic groups: Polynesian 78%, Chinese 12%, local French 6%, metropolitan French 4%

Major religions: Protestant 54%, Roman Catholic 30%

Major languages: French (official), Tahitian (official)

Government

Official name: Territory of French Polynesia

National capital: Papeete

Independence: none (overseas territory of France)

Legal system: based on French system

Economy

Industries: tourism, pearls, agricultural processing, handicrafts

Agricultural products: coconuts, vanilla, vegetables, fruits; poultry, beef, dairy products

Currency: 1 Communauté Financière Africaine franc (CFAF) = 100 centimes

Gabon

Geography

Location: Western Africa, bordering the Atlantic Ocean at the Equator, between Republic of the Congo and Equatorial Guinea

Area: 103,347 sq. mi. (267,670 sq. km.); slightly smaller than Colorado

Climate: tropical; always hot, humid

Terrain: narrow coastal plain; hilly interior; savanna in east and south

Elevation: lowest point: Atlantic Ocean 0 ft. (0 m.); highest point: Mont Iboundji 5,167 ft. (1,575 m.)

Natural resources: petroleum, manganese, uranium, gold, timber, iron ore

People

Population: 1,225,853 (July 1999 est.)

Population growth rate: 1.48%

Infant mortality rate: 83.1 deaths/1,000 live births

Life expectancy at birth: total population: 56.98 years; male: 53.98 years; female: 60.08 years

Major ethnic groups: Bantu tribes including four major tribal groupings (Fang, Eshira, Bapounou, Bateke), other Africans and Europeans 154,000, including 6,000 French and 11,000 persons of dual nationality

Major religions: Christian 55%–75%, Muslim less than 1%, animist

Major languages: French (official), Fang, Myene, Bateke, Bapounou/Eschira, Bandjabi

Government

Official name: Gabonese Republic

Government type: republic; multiparty presidential regime (opposition parties legalized 1990)

National capital: Libreville

Independence: August 17, 1960 (from France)

Legal system: based on French civil law system and customary law; judicial review of legislative acts in Constitutional Chamber of the Supreme Court; compulsory ICJ jurisdiction not accepted

Economy

Industries: food and beverage; textile; lumbering and plywood; cement; petroleum extraction and refining; manganese, uranium, and gold mining; chemicals; ship repair

Agricultural products: cocoa, coffee, sugar, palm oil; rubber; okoume (a tropical softwood); cattle; small fishing operations

Currency: 1 Communauté Financière Africaine franc (CFAF) = 100 centimes

Gambia, The

Geography

Location: Western Africa, bordering the North Atlantic Ocean and Senegal

Area: 4,363 sq. mi. (11,300 sq. km.); slightly less than twice the size of Delaware

Climate: tropical; hot, rainy season (June to November); cooler, dry season (November to May)

Terrain: flood plain of the Gambia River flanked by some low hills

Elevation: lowest point: Atlantic Ocean 0 ft. (0 m.); highest point: unnamed location 174 ft. (53 m.)

Natural resources: fish

People

Population: 1,336,320 (July 1999 est.)

Population growth rate: 3.35%

Infant mortality rate: 75.33 deaths/1,000 live births

Life expectancy at birth: total population: 54.39 years; male: 52.02 years; female: 56.83 years

Major ethnic groups: African 99% (Mandinka 42%, Fula 18%, Wolof 16%, Jola 10%, Serahuli 9%)

Major religions: Muslim 90%, Christian 9%

Major languages: English (official), Mandinka, Wolof, Fula, other indigenous vernaculars

Government

Official name: Republic of The Gambia

Government type: republic under multiparty democratic rule

National capital: Banjul

Independence: February 18, 1965 (from U.K.)

Legal system: based on a composite of English common law, Koranic law, and customary law

Economy

Industries: processing peanuts, fish, and hides; tourism; beverages; agricultural machinery assembly, woodworking, metalworking; clothing

Agricultural products: peanuts, millet, sorghum, rice, corn, cassava (tapioca), palm kernels; cattle, sheep, goats; forest and fishing resources not fully exploited

Currency: 1 dalasi (D) = 100 butut

Gaza Strip

Geography

Location: Middle East, bordering the Mediterranean Sea, between Egypt and Israel

Area: 139 sq. mi. (360 sq. km.); slightly more than twice the size of Washington, D.C.

Climate: temperate, mild winters, dry and warm to hot summers

Terrain: flat to rolling, sand- and dune-covered coastal plain

Elevation: lowest point: Mediterranean Sea 0 ft. (0 m.); highest point: Abu 'Awdah (Joz Abu 'Auda) 344 ft. (105 m.)

Natural resources: negligible

People

Population: 1,112,654 (July 1999 est.) Note: there are approximately 6,000 Israeli settlers in the Gaza Strip (August 1998 est.)

Population growth rate: 4.44%

Infant mortality rate: 22.92 deaths/1,000 live births

Life expectancy at birth: total population: 73.44 years; male: 72.01 years; female: 74.95 years

Major ethnic groups: Palestinian Arab

Major religions: Muslim (predominantly Sunni) 98.7%

Major languages: Arabic, Hebrew

Government

Government note: Under the Israeli-PLO Declaration of Principles on Interim Self-Government Arrangements ("the DOP"), Israel agreed to transfer certain powers and responsibilities to the Palestinian Authority, which includes a Palestinian Legislative Council elected in January 1996, as part of interim self-governing arrangements in the West Bank and Gaza Strip.

Official name: Gaza Strip

Economy

Industries: generally small family businesses that produce textiles, soap, olive-wood carvings, and mother-of-pearl souvenirs; the Israelis have established some small-scale modern industries in an industrial center

Agricultural products: olives, citrus, other fruits, vegetables; beef, dairy products

Currency: 1 new Israeli shekel (NIS) = 100 new agorot

Georgia

Geography

Location: Southwestern Asia, bordering the Black Sea, between Turkey and Russia

Area: 26,911 sq. mi. (69,700 sq. km.); slightly smaller than South Carolina

Climate: warm and pleasant; Mediterranean-like on Black Sea coast

Terrain: largely mountainous with Great Caucasus Mountains in the north and Lesser Caucasus Mountains in the south; Kolkhida Lowland opens to the Black Sea in the west; Mtkvari River Basin in the east; good soils in river valley flood plains, foothills of Kolkhida Lowland

Elevation: lowest point: Black Sea 0 ft. (0 m.); highest point: Mt'a Mqinvartsveri (Gora Kazbek) 16,561 ft. (5,048 m.)

Natural resources: forests, hydropower, manganese deposits, iron ore, copper, minor coal and oil deposits; coastal climate and soils allow for important tea and citrus growth

People

Population: 5,066,499 (July 1999 est.)

Population growth rate: –0.74%

Infant mortality rate: 52.01 deaths/1,000 live births

Life expectancy at birth: total population: 64.63 years; male: 61.13 years; female: 68.32 years

Major ethnic groups: Georgian 70.1%, Armenian 8.1%, Russian 6.3%, Azeri 5.7%, Ossetian 3%, Abkhaz 1.8%

Major religions: Christian Orthodox 75% (Georgian Orthodox 65%, Russian Orthodox 10%), Muslim 11%, Armenian Apostolic 8%

Major languages: Armenian 7%, Azeri 6%, Georgian 71% (official), Russian 9%

Government

Official name: Georgia

Government type: republic

National capital: T'bilisi

Independence: April 9, 1991 (from Soviet Union)

Legal system: based on civil law system

Economy

Industries: steel, aircraft, machine tools, foundry equipment, electric locomotives, tower cranes, electric welding equipment, machinery for food preparation and meat packing, electric motors, process control equipment, trucks, tractors, textiles, shoes, chemicals, wood products, wine

Agricultural products: citrus, grapes, tea, vegetables, potatoes; small livestock sector

Currency: lari introduced September 1995 replacing the coupon

Germany

Geography

Location: Central Europe, bordering the Baltic Sea and the North Sea, between the Netherlands and Poland, south of Denmark

Area: 137,803 sq. ft. (356,910 sq. km.); slightly smaller than Montana

Climate: temperate and marine; cool, cloudy, wet winters and summers; occasional warm, tropical foehn wind; high relative humidity

Terrain: lowlands in north, uplands in center, Bavarian Alps in south

Elevation: lowest point: Freepsum Lake –7 ft. (–2 m.); highest point: Zugspitze 9,718 ft. (2,962 m.)

Natural resources: iron ore, coal, potash, timber, lignite, uranium, copper, natural gas, salt, nickel

People

Population: 82,087,361 (July 1999 est.)

Population growth rate: 0.01%

Infant mortality rate: 5.14 deaths/1,000 live births

Life expectancy at birth: total population: 77.17 years; male: 74.01 years; female: 80.5 years

Major ethnic groups: German 91.5%, Turkish 2.4%

Major religions: Protestant 38%, Roman Catholic 34%

Major languages: German

Government

Official name: Federal Republic of Germany

Government type: federal republic

National capital: Berlin

Independence: January 18, 1871 (German Empire unification); unification of West Germany and East Germany took place October 3, 1990

Legal system: civil law system with indigenous concepts; judicial review of legislative acts in the Federal Constitutional Court

Economy

Industries: among world's largest and most technologically advanced producers of iron, steel, coal, cement, chemicals, machinery, vehicles, machine tools, electronics, food and beverages; eastern: metal fabrication, chemicals, brown coal, shipbuilding, machine building, food and beverages, textiles, petroleum refining

Agricultural products: western: potatoes, wheat, barley, sugar beets, fruit, cabbage; cattle, pigs, poultry; eastern: wheat, rye, barley, potatoes, sugar beets, fruit; pork, beef, chicken, milk, hides

Currency: 1 deutsche mark (DM) = 100 pfennige

Ghana

Geography

Location: Western Africa, bordering the Gulf of Guinea, between Côte d'Ivoire and Togo

Area: 92,100 sq. mi. (238,540 sq. km.); slightly smaller than Oregon

Climate: tropical; warm and comparatively dry along southeast coast; hot and humid in southwest; hot and dry in north

Terrain: mostly low plains with dissected plateau in south-central area

Elevation: lowest point: Atlantic Ocean 0 ft. (0 m.); highest point: Mount Afadjato 2,887 ft. (880 m.)

Natural resources: gold, timber, industrial diamonds, bauxite, manganese, fish, rubber

People

Population: 18,887,626 (July 1999 est.)

Population growth rate: 2.05%

Infant mortality rate: 76.15 deaths/1,000 live births

Life expectancy at birth: total population: 57.14 years; male: 53.08 years; female: 59.27 years

Major ethnic groups: black African 99.8% (major tribes: Akan 44%, Moshi-Dagomba 16%, Ewe 13%, Ga 8%)

Major religions: indigenous beliefs 38%, Muslim 30%, Christian 24%

Major languages: English (official), African languages (including Akan, Moshi-Dagomba, Ewe, and Ga)

Government

Official name: Republic of Ghana

Government type: constitutional democracy
National capital: Accra
Independence: March 6, 1957 (from U.K.)
Legal system: based on English common law and customary law

Economy
Industries: mining, lumbering, light manufacturing, aluminum smelting, food processing
Agricultural products: cocoa, rice, coffee, cassava (tapioca), peanuts, corn, shea nuts, bananas; timber
Currency: 1 new cedi (C) = 100 pesewas

Gibraltar

Geography
Location: Southwestern Europe, bordering the Strait of Gibraltar, which links the Mediterranean Sea and the North Atlantic Ocean, on the southern coast of Spain
Area: 3 sq. mi. (6.5 sq. km.); about 11 times the size of The Mall in Washington, D.C.
Climate: Mediterranean with mild winters and warm summers
Terrain: a narrow coastal lowland borders the Rock of Gibraltar
Elevation: lowest point: Mediterranean Sea 0 ft. (0 m.); highest point: Rock of Gibraltar 1,398 ft. (426 m.)
Natural resources: negligible

People
Population: 29,165 (July 1999 est.)
Population growth rate: 0.39%
Infant mortality rate: 6.47 deaths/1,000 live births
Life expectancy at birth: total population: 78.37 years; male: 75.1 years; female: 81.81 years
Major ethnic groups: Italian, English, Maltese, Portuguese, Spanish
Major religions: Roman Catholic 74%, Protestant 11%
Major languages: English (used in schools and for official purposes), Spanish

Government
Official name: Gibraltar

National capital: Gibraltar
Independence: none (dependent territory of the U.K.)
Legal system: English law

Economy
Industries: tourism, banking and finance, shipbuilding and repairing; support two large U.K. naval and air bases; tobacco, mineral waters, beer, canned fish
Agricultural products: none
Currency: 1 Gibraltar pound (£G) = 100 pence

Greece

Geography
Location: Southern Europe, bordering the Aegean Sea, Ionian Sea, and the Mediterranean Sea, between Albania and Turkey
Area: 50,942 sq. mi. (131,940 sq. km.); slightly smaller than Alabama
Climate: temperate; mild, wet winters; hot, dry summers
Terrain: mostly mountains with ranges extending into sea as peninsulas or chains of islands
Elevation: : lowest point: Mediterranean Sea 0 ft. (0 m.); highest point: Mount Olympus 9,570 ft. (2,917 m.)
Natural resources: bauxite, lignite, magnesite, petroleum, marble

People
Population: 10,707,135 (July 1999 est.)
Population growth rate: 0.41%
Infant mortality rate: 7.13 deaths/1,000 live births
Life expectancy at birth: total population: 78.43 years; male: 75.87 years; female: 81.18 years
Major ethnic groups: Greek 98%, other 2%
Major religions: Greek Orthodox 98%, Muslim 1.3%, other 0.7%
Major languages: Greek (official), English, French

Government

Official name: Hellenic Republic

Government type: parliamentary republic

National capital: Athens

Independence: 1829 (from the Ottoman Empire)

Legal system: based on codified Roman law; judiciary divided into civil, criminal, and administrative courts

Economy

Industries: tourism; food and tobacco processing, textiles; chemicals, metal products; mining, petroleum

Agricultural products: wheat, corn, barley, sugar beets, olives, tomatoes, wine, tobacco, potatoes; meat, dairy products

Currency: 1 drachma (Dr) = 100 lepta

Greenland

Geography

Location: Northern North America, island between the Arctic Ocean and the North Atlantic Ocean, northeast of Canada

Area: 839,999 sq. mi. (2,175,600 sq. km.) slightly more than three times the size of Texas

Climate: arctic to subarctic; cool summers, cold winters

Terrain: flat to gradually sloping icecap covers all but a narrow, mountainous, barren, rocky coast

Elevation: lowest point: Atlantic Ocean 0 ft. (0 m.); highest point: Gunnbjorn 12,139 ft. (3,700 m.)

Natural resources: zinc, lead, iron ore, coal, molybdenum, gold, platinum, uranium, fish, seals, whales

People

Population: 59,827 (July 1999 est.)

Population growth rate: 0.84%

Infant mortality rate: 20.06 deaths/1,000 live births

Life expectancy at birth: total population: 70.01 years; male: 65.98 years; female: 74.24 years

Major ethnic groups: Greenlander 87% (Eskimos and Greenland-born whites), Danish and others 13%

Major religions: Evangelical Lutheran

Major languages: Eskimo dialects, Danish, Greenlandic (an Inuit dialect)

Government

Official name: Greenland

National capital: Nuuk (Godthab)

Independence: none (part of the Kingdom of Denmark; self-governing overseas administrative division of Denmark since 1979)

Legal system: Danish

Economy

Industries: fish processing (mainly shrimp), handicrafts, furs, small shipyards

Agricultural products: forage crops, small garden vegetables; sheep, fish

Currency: 1 Danish krone (DKr) = 100 oere

Grenada

Geography

Location: Caribbean, island between the Caribbean Sea and Atlantic Ocean, north of Trinidad and Tobago

Area: 131 sq. mi. (340 sq. km.); twice the size of Washington, D.C.

Climate: tropical; tempered by northeast trade winds

Terrain: volcanic in origin with central mountains

Elevation: lowest point: Caribbean Sea 0 ft. (0 m.); highest point: Mount Saint Catherine 2,756 ft. (840 m.)

Natural resources: timber, tropical fruit, deepwater harbors

People

Population: 97,008 (July 1999 est.)

Population growth rate: 0.87%

Infant mortality rate: 11.13 deaths/1,000 live births
Life expectancy at birth: total population: 71.6 years; male: 68.97 years; female: 74.29 years
Major ethnic groups: black
Major religions: Roman Catholic 53%, Anglican 13.8%, other Protestant sects 33.2%
Major languages: English (official), French patois

Government

Official name: Grenada
Government type: parliamentary democracy
National capital: Saint George's
Independence: February 7, 1974 (from U.K.)
Legal system: based on English common law

Economy

Industries: food and beverages, textiles, light assembly operations, tourism, construction
Agricultural products: bananas, cocoa, nutmeg, mace, citrus, avocados, root crops, sugarcane, corn, vegetables
Currency: 1 East Caribbean dollar (EC$) = 100 cents

Guadeloupe

Geography

Location: Caribbean, islands in the eastern Caribbean Sea, southeast of Puerto Rico
Area: 687 sq. mi. (1,780 sq. km.); 10 times the size of Washington, D.C.
Climate: subtropical tempered by trade winds; moderately high humidity
Terrain: Basse-Terre is volcanic in origin with interior mountains; Grande-Terre is low limestone formation; most of the seven other islands are volcanic in origin
Elevation: lowest point: Caribbean Sea 0 ft. (0 m.); highest point: Soufriere 4,813 ft. (1,467 m.)
Natural resources: cultivable land, beaches and climate that foster tourism

People

Population: 420,943 (July 1999 est.)
Population growth rate: 1.06%

Infant mortality rate: 8.54 deaths/1,000 live births
Life expectancy at birth: total population: 78.01 years; male: 74.98 years; female: 81.18 years
Major ethnic groups: black or mulatto 90%, white 5%
Major religions: Roman Catholic 95%, Hindu and pagan African 4%
Major languages: French (official) 99%, Creole patois

Government

Official name: Department of Guadeloupe
National capital: Basse-Terre
Independence: none (overseas department of France)
Legal system: French legal system

Economy

Industries: construction, cement, rum, sugar, tourism
Agricultural products: bananas, sugarcane, tropical fruits and vegetables; cattle, pigs, goats
Currency: 1 French franc (F) = 100 centimes

Guam

Geography

Location: Oceania, island in the North Pacific Ocean, about three-quarters of the way from Hawaii to the Philippines
Area: 209 sq. mi. (541.3 sq. km.); three times the size of Washington, D.C.
Climate: tropical marine; generally warm and humid, moderated by northeast trade winds; dry season from January to June, rainy season from July to December; little seasonal temperature variation
Terrain: volcanic origin, surrounded by coral reefs; relatively flat coralline limestone plateau (source of most fresh water) with steep coastal cliffs and narrow coastal plains in north, low-rising hills in center, mountains in south
Elevation: lowest point: Pacific Ocean 0 ft. (0 m.); highest point: Mount Lamlam 1,332 ft. (406 m.)

Natural resources: fishing (largely undeveloped), tourism

People

Population: 151,716 (July 1999 est.)

Population growth rate: 1.67%

Infant mortality rate: 7.81 deaths/1,000 live births

Life expectancy at birth: total population: 77.78 years; male: 74.6 years; female: 81.31 years

Major ethnic groups: Chamorro 47%, Filipino 25%, white 10%, Chinese, Japanese, Korean, and other 18%

Major religions: Roman Catholic 98%, other 2%

Major languages: English, Chamorro, Japanese

Government

Official name: Territory of Guam

National capital: Hagatna (Agana)

Independence: none (territory of the U.S.)

Legal system: modeled on U.S.; U.S. federal laws apply

Economy

Industries: U.S. military, tourism, construction, transshipment services, concrete products, printing and publishing, food processing, textiles

Agricultural products: fruits, copra, vegetables; eggs, pork, poultry, beef

Currency: 1 U.S. dollar (US$) = 100 cents

Guatemala

Geography

Location: Central America, bordering the Caribbean Sea, between Honduras and Belize and bordering the North Pacific Ocean, between El Salvador and Mexico

Area: 42,042 sq. mi. (108,890 sq. km.); slightly smaller than Tennessee

Climate: tropical; hot, humid in lowlands; cooler in highlands

Terrain: mostly mountains with narrow coastal plains and rolling limestone plateau (Peten)

Elevation: lowest point: Pacific Ocean 0 ft. (0 m.); highest point: Volcan Tajumulco 13,815 ft. (4,211 m.)

Natural resources: petroleum, nickel, rare woods, fish, chicle

People

Population: 12,335,580 (July 1999 est.)

Population growth rate: 2.68%

Infant mortality rate: 46.15 deaths/1,000 live births

Life expectancy at birth: total population: 66.45 years; male: 63.78 years; female: 69.24 years

Major ethnic groups: Mestizo (mixed Amerindian-Spanish—in local Spanish called Ladino) 56%, Amerindian or predominantly Amerindian 44%

Major religions: Roman Catholic, Protestant, traditional Mayan

Major languages: Spanish 60%, Amerindian languages 40% (23 Amerindian languages, including Quiche, Cakchiquel, Kekchi)

Government

Official name: Republic of Guatemala

Government type: republic

National capital: Guatemala

Independence: September 15, 1821 (from Spain)

Legal system: civil law system; judicial review of legislative acts

Economy

Industries: sugar, textiles and clothing, furniture, chemicals, petroleum, metals, rubber, tourism

Agricultural products: sugarcane, corn, bananas, coffee, beans, cardamom; cattle, sheep, pigs, chickens

Currency: 1 quetzal (Q) = 100 centavos

Guernsey

Geography

Location: Western Europe, islands in the English Channel, northwest of France

Area: 75 sq. mi. (194 sq. km.); slightly larger than Washington, D.C.

Climate: temperate with mild winters and cool summers; about 50% of days are overcast

Terrain: mostly level with low hills in south-west

Elevation: lowest point: Atlantic Ocean 0 ft. (0 m.); highest point: unnamed location on Sark 374 ft. (114 m.)

Natural resources: cropland

People

Population: 65,386 (July 1999 est.)

Population growth rate: 1.27%

Infant mortality rate: 8.42 deaths/1,000 live births

Life expectancy at birth: total population: 78.72 years; male: 75.78 years; female: 81.77 years

Major ethnic groups: U.K. and Norman-French descent

Major religions: Anglican, Roman Catholic, Presbyterian, Baptist, Congregational, Methodist

Major languages: English, French, Norman-French dialect spoken in country districts

Government

Official name: Bailiwick of Guernsey

National capital: Saint Peter Port

Independence: none (British crown dependency)

Legal system: English law and local statute; justice is administered by the Royal Court

Economy

Industries: tourism, banking

Agricultural products: tomatoes, greenhouse flowers, sweet peppers, eggplant, other vegetables, fruit; Guernsey cattle

Currency: 1 Guernsey (£G) pound = 100 pence

Guinea

Geography

Location: Western Africa, bordering the North Atlantic Ocean, between Guinea-Bissau and Sierra Leone

Area: 94,927 sq. mi. (245,860 sq. km.); slightly smaller than Oregon

Climate: generally hot and humid; monsoonal-type rainy season (June to November) with southwesterly winds; dry season (December to May) with northeasterly harmattan winds

Terrain: generally flat coastal plain, hilly to mountainous interior

Elevation: lowest point: Atlantic Ocean 0 ft. (0 m.); highest point: Mont Nimba 5,748 ft. (1,752 m.)

Natural resources: bauxite, iron ore, diamonds, gold, uranium, hydropower, fish

People

Population: 7,538,953 (July 1999 est.)

Population growth rate: 0.82%

Infant mortality rate: 126.32 deaths/1,000 live births

Life expectancy at birth: total population: 46.5 years; male: 44.02 years; female: 49.06 years

Major ethnic groups: Peuhl 40%, Malinke 30%, Soussou 20%, smaller tribes 10%

Major religions: Muslim 85%, Christian 8%, indigenous beliefs 7%

Major languages: French (official), each tribe has its own language

Government

Official name: Republic of Guinea

Government type: republic

National capital: Conakry

Independence: October 2, 1958 (from France)

Legal system: based on French civil law system, customary law, and decree; legal codes currently being revised

Economy

Industries: bauxite, gold, diamonds; alumina refining; light manufacturing and agricultural processing industries

Agricultural products: rice, coffee, pineapples, palm kernels, cassava (tapioca), bananas, sweet potatoes; cattle, sheep, goats; timber

Currency: 1 Guinean franc (FG) = 100 centimes

Guinea-Bissau

Geography

Location: Western Africa, bordering the North Atlantic Ocean, between Guinea and Senegal

Area: 13,946 sq. mi. (36,120 sq. km.); slightly less than three times the size of Connecticut

Climate: tropical; generally hot and humid; monsoonal-type rainy season (June to November) with southwesterly winds; dry season (December to May) with northeasterly harmattan winds

Terrain: mostly low coastal plain rising to savanna in east

Elevation: lowest point: Atlantic Ocean o ft. (o m.); highest point: unnamed location in the northeast corner of the country 984 ft. (300 m.)

Natural resources: fish, timber, phosphates, bauxite, unexploited deposits of petroleum

People

Population: 1,234,555 (July 1999 est.)

Population growth rate: 2.31%

Infant mortality rate: 109.5 deaths/1,000 live births

Life expectancy at birth: total population: 49.57 years; male: 47.91 years; female: 51.28 years

Major ethnic groups: African 99% (Balanta 30%, Fula 20%, Manjaca 14%, Mandinga 13%, Papel 7%)

Major religions: indigenous beliefs 50%, Muslim 45%, Christian 5%

Major languages: Portuguese (official), Crioulo, African languages

Government

Official name: Republic of Guinea-Bissau

Government type: republic, multiparty since mid-1991

National capital: Bissau

Independence: September 24, 1973 (unilaterally declared by Guinea-Bissau); September 10, 1974 (recognized by Portugal)

Economy

Industries: agricultural products processing, beer, soft drinks

Agricultural products: rice, corn, beans, cassava (tapioca), cashew nuts, peanuts, palm kernels, cotton; fishing and forest potential not fully exploited

Currency: 1 Communauté Financière Africaine franc (CFAF) = 100 centimes

Guyana

Geography

Location: Northern South America, bordering the North Atlantic Ocean, between Suriname and Venezuela

Area: 83,000 sq. mi. (214,970 sq. km.); slightly smaller than Idaho

Climate: tropical; hot, humid, moderated by northeast trade winds; two rainy seasons (May to mid-August, mid-November to mid-January)

Terrain: mostly rolling highlands; low coastal plain; savanna in south

Elevation: lowest point: Atlantic Ocean o ft. (o m.); highest point: Mount Roraima 9,301 ft. (2,835 m.)

Natural resources: bauxite, gold, diamonds, hardwood timber, shrimp, fish

People

Population: 705,156 (July 1999 est.)

Population growth rate: -0.32%

Infant mortality rate: 48.64 deaths/1,000 live births

Life expectancy at birth: total population: 61.82 years; male: 59.15 years; female: 64.61 years

Major ethnic groups: East Indian 49%, black 32%, mixed 12%, Amerindian 6%

Major religions: Christian 57%, Hindu 33%, Muslim 9%

Major languages: English, Amerindian dialects

Government

Official name: Co-operative Republic of Guyana

Government type: republic

National capital: Georgetown
Independence: May 26, 1966 (from U.K.)
Legal system: based on English common law with certain admixtures of Roman-Dutch law

Economy

Industries: bauxite, sugar, rice milling, timber, fishing (shrimp), textiles, gold mining
Agricultural products: sugar, rice, wheat, vegetable oils; beef, pork, poultry, dairy products; development potential exists for fishing and forestry
Currency: 1 Guyanese dollar (G$) = 100 cents

Haiti

Geography

Location: Caribbean, western one-third of the island of Hispaniola, between the Caribbean Sea and the North
Atlantic Ocean, west of the Dominican Republic
Area: 10,714 sq. mi. (27,750 sq. km.); slightly smaller than Maryland
Climate: tropical; semiarid where mountains in east cut off trade winds
Terrain: mostly rough and mountainous
Elevation: lowest point: Caribbean Sea 0 ft. (0 m.); highest point: Chaine de la Selle 8,793 ft. (2,680 m.)
Natural resources: none

People

Population: 6,884,264 (July 1999 est.)
Population growth rate: 1.53%
Infant mortality rate: 97.64 deaths/1,000 live births
Life expectancy at birth: total population: 51.65 years; male: 49.53 years; female: 53.88 years
Major ethnic groups: black 95%, mulatto plus white 5%
Major religions: Roman Catholic 80%, Protestant 16%; note: roughly one-half of the population also practices Voodoo
Major languages: French (official) 20%, Creole

Government

Official name: Republic of Haiti

Government type: republic
National capital: Port-au-Prince
Independence: January 1, 1804 (from France)
Legal system: based on Roman civil law system

Economy

Industries: sugar refining, flour milling, textiles, cement, tourism, light assembly industries based on imported parts
Agricultural products: coffee, mangoes, sugarcane, rice, corn, sorghum; wood
Currency: 1 gourde (G) = 100 centimes

Holy See (Vatican City)

Geography

Location: Southern Europe, an enclave of Rome (Italy)
Area: 0.2 sq. mi. (0.44 sq. km.); about 0.7 times the size of The Mall in Washington, D.C.
Climate: temperate; mild, rainy winters (September to mid-May) with hot, dry summers (May to September)
Terrain: low hills
Elevation: lowest point: unnamed location 62 ft. (19 m.); highest point: unnamed location 246 ft. (75 m.)
Natural resources: none

People

Population: 860 (July 1999 est.)
Population growth rate: 1.15%
Major ethnic groups: Italians, Swiss
Major religions: Roman Catholic
Major languages: Italian, Latin, various other languages

Government

Official name: The Holy See (State of the Vatican City)
Government type: monarchical-sacerdotal state
National capital: Vatican City
Independence: February 11, 1929 (from Italy)

Economy

Industries: printing and production of a small amount of mosaics and staff uniforms; worldwide banking and financial activities
Currency: 1 Vatican lira (VLit) = 100 centesimi

Honduras

Geography

Location: Central America, bordering the Caribbean Sea, between Guatemala and Nicaragua and bordering the North Pacific Ocean, between El Salvador and Nicaragua

Area: 43,278 sq. mi. (112,090 sq. km.); slightly larger than Tennessee

Climate: subtropical in lowlands, temperate in mountains

Terrain: mostly mountains in interior, narrow coastal plains

Elevation: lowest point: Caribbean Sea 0 ft. (0 m.); highest point: Cerro Las Minas 9,416 ft. (2,870 m.)

Natural resources: timber, gold, silver, copper, lead, zinc, iron ore, antimony, coal, fish

People

Population: 5,997,327 (July 1999 est.)

Population growth rate: 2.24%

Infant mortality rate: 40.84 deaths/1,000 live births

Life expectancy at birth: total population: 64.68 years; male: 63.16 years; female: 66.27 years

Major ethnic groups: mestizo (mixed Amerindian and European) 90%, Amerindian 7%, black 2%, white 1%

Major religions: Roman Catholic 97%, Protestant minority

Major languages: Spanish, Amerindian dialects

Government

Official name: Republic of Honduras

Government type: republic

National capital: Tegucigalpa

Independence: September 15, 1821 (from Spain)

Legal system: rooted in Roman and Spanish civil law; some influence of English common law

Economy

Industries: sugar, coffee, textiles, clothing, wood products

Agricultural products: bananas, coffee, citrus; beef; timber; shrimp

Currency: 1 lempira (L) = 100 centavos

Hong Kong

Geography

Location: Eastern Asia, bordering the South China Sea and China

Area: 422 sq. mi. (1,092 sq. km.); six times the size of Washington, D.C.

Climate: tropical monsoon; cool and humid in winter, hot and rainy from spring through summer, warm and sunny in fall

Terrain: hilly to mountainous with steep slopes; lowlands in north

Elevation: lowest point: South China Sea 0 ft. (0 m.); highest point: Tai Mo Shan 3,143 ft. (958 m.)

Natural resources: outstanding deepwater harbor, feldspar

People

Population: 6,847,125 (July 1999 est.)

Population growth rate: 2.24%

Infant mortality rate: 5.2 deaths/1,000 live births

Life expectancy at birth: total population: 78.91 years; male: 76.15 years; female: 81.85 years

Major ethnic groups: Chinese 95%, other 5%

Major religions: eclectic mixture of local religions 90%, Christian 10%

Major languages: Chinese (Cantonese), English

Government

Official name: Hong Kong Special Administrative Region

National capital: Victoria

Independence: none (special administrative region of China)

Legal system: based on English common law

Economy

Industries: textiles, clothing, tourism, electronics, plastics, toys, watches, clocks

Agricultural products: fresh vegetables; poultry
Currency: 1 Hong Kong dollar (HK$) = 100 cents

Hungary

Geography

Location: Central Europe, northwest of Romania

Area: 35,919 sq. mi. (93,030 sq. km.); slightly smaller than Indiana

Climate: temperate; cold, cloudy, humid winters; warm summers

Terrain: mostly flat to rolling plains; hills and low mountains on the Slovakian border

Elevation: lowest point: Tisza River 256 ft. (78 m.); highest point: Kekes 3,327 ft. (1,014 m.)

Natural resources: bauxite, coal, natural gas, fertile soils

People

Population: 10,186,372 (July 1999 est.)

Population growth rate: -0.2%

Infant mortality rate: 9.46 deaths/1,000 live births

Life expectancy at birth: total population: 71.18 years; male: 66.85 years; female: 75.74 years

Major ethnic groups: Hungarian 89.9%, Gypsy 4%, German 2.6%, Serb 2%, Slovak 0.8%, Romanian 0.7%

Major religions: Roman Catholic 67.5%, Calvinist 20%, Lutheran 5%, atheist and other 7.5%

Major languages: Hungarian 98.2%, other 1.8%

Government

Official name: Republic of Hungary

Government type: republic

National capital: Budapest

Independence: 1001 (unification by King Stephen I)

Legal system: in process of revision, moving toward rule of law based on Western model

Economy

Industries: mining, metallurgy, construction materials, processed foods, textiles, chemicals (especially pharmaceuticals), motor vehicles

Agricultural products: wheat, corn, sunflower seed, potatoes, sugar beets; pigs, cattle, poultry, dairy products

Currency: 1 forint (Ft) = 100 filler

Iceland

Geography

Location: Northern Europe, island between the Greenland Sea and the North Atlantic Ocean, northwest of the U.K.

Area: 39,768 sq. mi. (103,000 sq. km.); slightly smaller than Kentucky

Climate: temperate; moderated by North Atlantic Current; mild, windy winters; damp, cool summers

Terrain: mostly plateau interspersed with mountain peaks, ice fields; coast deeply indented by bays and fiords

Elevation: lowest point: Atlantic Ocean 0 ft. (0 m.); highest point; Hvannadalshnukur 6,952 ft. (2,119 m.)

Natural resources: fish, hydropower, geothermal power, diatomite

People

Population: 272,512 (July 1999 est.)

Population growth rate: 0.57%

Infant mortality rate: 5.22 deaths/1,000 live births

Life expectancy at birth: total population: 78.96 years; male: 76.85 years; female: 81.19 years

Major ethnic groups: homogeneous mixture of descendants of Norwegians and Celts

Major religions: Evangelical Lutheran 96%, other Protestant and Roman Catholic 3%

Major languages: Icelandic

Government

Official name: Republic of Iceland

Government type: constitutional republic

National capital: Reykjavik

Independence: June 17, 1944 (from Denmark)

Legal system: civil law system based on Danish law, does not accept compulsory ICJ jurisdiction

Economy

Industries: fish processing; aluminum smelting, ferrosilicon production, geothermal power; tourism

Agricultural products: potatoes, turnips; cattle, sheep; fish

Currency: 1 Icelandic krona (IKr) = 100 aurar

India

Geography

Location: Southern Asia, bordering the Arabian Sea and the Bay of Bengal, between Burma and Pakistan

Area: 1,269,338 sq. mi. (3,287,590 sq. km.); slightly more than one-third the size of the U.S.

Climate: varies from tropical monsoon in south to temperate in north

Terrain: upland plain (Deccan Plateau) in south, flat to rolling plain along the Ganges, deserts in west, Himalayas in north

Elevation: lowest point: Indian Ocean 0 ft. (0 m.); highest point: Kanchenjunga 28,208 ft. (8,598 m.)

Natural resources: coal (fourth-largest reserves in the world), iron ore, manganese, mica, bauxite, titanium ore, chromite, natural gas, diamonds, petroleum, limestone

People

Population: 1,000,848,550 (July 1999 est.)

Population growth rate: 1.68%

Infant mortality rate: 60.81 deaths/1,000 live births

Life expectancy at birth: total population: 63.4 years; male: 62.54 years; female: 64.29 years

Major ethnic groups: Indo-Aryan 72%, Dravidian 25%, Mongoloid

Major religions: Hindu 80%, Muslim 14%, Christian 2.4%, Sikh 2%

Major languages: English enjoys associate status but is the most important language for national, political, and commercial communication, Hindi is the national language and primary tongue of 30% of the people, Bengali (official), Telugu (official), Marathi (official), Tamil (official), Urdu (official), Gujarati (official), Malayalam (official), Kannada (official), Oriya (official), Punjabi (official), Assamese (official), Kashmiri (official), Sindhi (official), Sanskrit (official), Hindustani a popular variant of Hindu/Urdu, is spoken widely throughout northern India. (Note: 24 languages each spoken by a million or more persons; numerous other languages and dialects, for the most part mutually unintelligible)

Government

Official name: Republic of India

Government type: federal republic

National capital: New Delhi

Independence: August 15, 1947 (from U.K.)

Legal system: based on English common law; limited judicial review of legislative acts

Economy

Industries: textiles, chemicals, food processing, steel, transportation equipment, cement, mining, petroleum, machinery

Agricultural products: rice, wheat, oilseed, cotton, jute, tea, sugarcane, potatoes; cattle, water buffalo, sheep, goats, poultry; fish

Currency: 1 Indian rupee (Re) = 100 paise

Indonesia

Geography

Location: Southeastern Asia, archipelago between the Indian Ocean and the Pacific Ocean

Area: 741,096 sq. mi. (1,919,440 sq. km.); slightly less than three times the size of Texas

Climate: tropical; hot, humid; more moderate in highlands

Terrain: mostly coastal lowlands; larger islands have interior mountains

Elevation: lowest point: Indian Ocean 0 ft. (0 m.); highest point: Puncak Jaya 16,502 ft. (5,030 m.)

Natural resources: petroleum, tin, natural gas, nickel, timber, bauxite, copper, fertile soils, coal, gold, silver

People

Population: 216,108,345 (July 1999 est.)
Population growth rate: 1.46%
Infant mortality rate: 57.3 deaths/1,000 live births
Life expectancy at birth: total population: 62.92 years; male: 60.67 years; female: 65.29 years
Major ethnic groups: Javanese 45%, Sundanese 14%, Madurese 7.5%, coastal Malays 7.5%, other 26%
Major religions: Muslim 87%, Protestant 6%, Roman Catholic 3%
Major languages: Bahasa Indonesia (official, modified form of Malay), English, Dutch, local dialects, the most widely spoken of which is Japanese

Government

Official name: Republic of Indonesia
Government type: republic
National capital: Jakarta
Independence: August 17, 1945 (proclaimed independence; on December 27, 1949, Indonesia became legally independent from the Netherlands)
Legal system: based on Roman-Dutch law, substantially modified by indigenous concepts and by new criminal procedures code, has not accepted compulsory ICJ jurisdiction

Economy

Industries: petroleum and natural gas, textiles, mining, cement, chemical fertilizers, plywood, food, rubber; tourism
Agricultural products: rice, cassava (tapioca), peanuts, rubber, cocoa, coffee, palm oil, copra, other tropical products; poultry, beef, pork, eggs
Currency: Indonesian rupiah (Rp)

Iran

Geography

Location: Middle East, bordering the Gulf of Oman, the Persian Gulf, and the Caspian Sea, between Iraq and Pakistan

Area: 636,293 sq. mi. (1,648,000 sq. km.); slightly larger than Alaska
Climate: mostly arid or semiarid, subtropical along Caspian coast
Terrain: rugged, mountainous rim; high, central basin with deserts, mountains; small, discontinuous plains along both coasts
Elevation: lowest point: Caspian Sea −92 ft. (−28 m.); highest point: Qolleh-ye Damavand 18,605 ft. (5,671 m.)
Natural resources: petroleum, natural gas, coal, chromium, copper, iron ore, lead, manganese, zinc, sulfur

People

Population: 65,179,752 (July 1999 est.)
Population growth rate: 1.07%
Infant mortality rate: 29.73 deaths/1,000 live births
Life expectancy at birth: total population: 69.76 years; male: 68.43 years; female: 71.16 years
Major ethnic groups: Persian 51%, Azerbaijani 24%, Gilaki and Mazandarani 8%, Kurd 7%, Arab 3%, Lur 2%, Baloch 2%, Turkmen 2%
Major religions: Shi'a Muslim 89%, Sunni Muslim 10%
Major languages: Persian and Persian dialects 58%, Turkic and Turkic dialects 26%, Kurdish 9%

Government

Official name: Islamic Republic of Iran
Government type: theocratic republic
National capital: Tehran
Independence: April 1, 1979 (Islamic Republic of Iran proclaimed)
Legal system: the Constitution codifies Islamic principles of government

Economy

Industries: petroleum, petrochemicals, textiles, cement and other construction materials, food processing (particularly sugar refining and vegetable oil production), metal fabricating, armaments

Agricultural products: wheat, rice, other grains, sugar beets, fruits, nuts, cotton; dairy products, wool; caviar

Currency: 10 Iranian rials (IR) = 1 toman (Note: domestic figures are generally given in terms of the toman)

Iraq

Geography

Location: Middle East, bordering the Persian Gulf, between Iran and Kuwait

Area: 168,753 sq. mi. (437,072 sq. km.); slightly more than twice the size of Idaho

Climate: mostly desert; mild to cool winters with dry, hot, cloudless summers; northern mountainous regions along Iranian and Turkish borders experience cold winters with occasionally heavy snows that melt in early spring, sometimes causing extensive flooding in central and southern Iraq

Terrain: mostly broad plains; reedy marshes along Iranian border in south with large flooded areas; mountains along borders with Iran and Turkey

Elevation: lowest point: Persian Gulf 0 ft. (0 m.); highest point Gundah Zhur 11,837 ft. (3,608 m.)

Natural resources: petroleum, natural gas, phosphates, sulfur

People

Population: 22,427,150 (July 1999 est.)

Population growth rate: 3.19%

Infant mortality rate: 62.41 deaths/1,000 live births

Life expectancy at birth: total population: 66.52 years; male: 65.54 years; female: 67.56 years

Major ethnic groups: Arab 75%–80%, Kurdish 15%–20%,

Major religions: Muslim 97% (Shi'a 60%–65%, Sunni 32%–37%)

Major languages: Arabic, Kurdish (official in Kurdish regions), Assyrian, Armenian

Government

Official name: Republic of Iraq

Government type: republic

National capital: Baghdad

Independence: October 3, 1932 (from League of Nations mandate under British administration)

Legal system: based on Islamic law in special religious courts, civil law system elsewhere; has not accepted compulsory ICJ jurisdiction

Economy

Industries: petroleum, chemicals, textiles, construction materials, food processing

Agricultural products: wheat, barley, rice, vegetables, dates, other fruit, cotton; cattle, sheep

Currency: 1 Iraqi dinar (ID) = 1,000 fils

Ireland

Geography

Location: Western Europe, occupying five-sixths of the island of Ireland in the North Atlantic Ocean, west of Great Britain

Area: 27,135 sq. mi. (70,280 sq. km.); slightly larger than West Virginia

Climate: temperate maritime; modified by North Atlantic Current; mild winters, cool summers; consistently humid; overcast about half the time

Terrain: mostly level to rolling interior plain surrounded by rugged hills and low mountains; sea cliffs on west coast

Elevation: lowest point: Atlantic Ocean 0 ft. (0 m.); highest point: Carrauntoohill 3,415 ft. (1,041 m.)

Natural resources: zinc, lead, natural gas, barite, copper, gypsum, limestone, dolomite, peat, silver

People

Population: 3,632,944 (July 1999 est.)

Population growth rate: 0.38%

Infant mortality rate: 5.94 deaths/1,000 live
  births
Life expectancy at birth: total population:
  76.39 years; male: 73.64 years; female:
  79.32 years
Major ethnic groups: Celtic, English
Major religions: Roman Catholic 93%, Anglican
  3%, none 1%, unknown 2%, other 1%
Major languages: Irish (Gaelic), spoken mainly
  in areas located along the western seaboard,
  English is the language generally used

Government

Official name: Ireland
Government type: republic
National capital: Dublin
Independence: December 6, 1921 (from U.K.)
Legal system: based on English common law,
  substantially modified by indigenous concepts;
  judicial review of legislative acts in Supreme
  Court; has not accepted compulsory ICJ
  jurisdiction

Economy

Industries: food products, brewing, textiles,
  clothing, chemicals, pharmaceuticals,
  machinery, transportation equipment, glass
  and crystal
Agricultural products: turnips, barley, potatoes, sugar beets, wheat; meat and dairy
  products
Currency: 1 Irish pound (£Ir) = 100 pence

Israel

Geography

Location: Middle East, bordering the
  Mediterranean Sea, between Egypt and
  Lebanon
Area: 8,019 sq. mi. (20,770 sq. km.); slightly
  smaller than New Jersey
Climate: temperate; hot and dry in southern and
  eastern desert areas
Terrain: Negev desert in the south; low coastal
  plain; central mountains; Jordan Rift Valley
Elevation: lowest point: Dead Sea –1,339 ft.
  (–408 m.); highest point: Har Meron 3,963 ft.
  (1,208 m.)

Natural resources: copper, phosphates, bro-
  mide, potash, clay, sand, sulfur, asphalt, manganese, small amounts of natural gas and
  crude oil

People

Population: 5,749,760 (July 1999 est.) [Note:
  this figure includes about 166,000 Israeli set-
  tlers in the West bank, about 19,000 in the
  Israeli-occupied Golan Heights, 6,000 in the
  Gaza Strip, and about 176,000 in East
  Jerusalem (August 1998 est.)]
Population growth rate: 1.81%
Infant mortality rate: 7.78 deaths/1,000 live
  births
Life expectancy at birth: total population:
  78.61 years; male: 76.71 years; female:
  80.61 years
Major ethnic groups: Jewish 82%, non-Jewish
  18% (mostly Arab)
Major religions: Judaism 82%, Islam 14%
Major languages: Hebrew (official), Arabic used
  officially for Arab minority

Government

Official name: State of Israel
Government type: republic
National capital: Jerusalem
Note: Israel proclaimed Jerusalem as its
  capital in 1950, but the U.S., like nearly all
  other countries, maintains its Embassy in
  Tel Aviv
Independence: May 14, 1948 (from League of
  Nations mandate under British adminis-
  tration)
Legal system: mixture of English common law,
  British Mandate regulations, and, in personal
  matters, Jewish, Christian, and Muslim legal
  systems; has not, since 1985, accepted com-
  pulsory ICJ jurisdiction

Economy

Industries: food processing, diamond cutting
  and polishing, textiles and apparel, chemicals, metal products, military equipment,
  transport equipment, electrical equipment,
  potash mining, high-technology electronics,
  tourism

Agricultural products: citrus and other fruits, vegetables, cotton; beef, poultry, dairy products

Currency: 1 new Israeli shekel (NIS) = 100 new agorot

Italy

Geography

Location: Southern Europe, a peninsula extending into the central Mediterranean Sea, northeast of Tunisia

Area: 116,305 sq. mi. (301,230 sq. km.); slightly larger than Arizona

Climate: predominantly Mediterranean; Alpine in far north; hot, dry in south

Terrain: mostly rugged and mountainous; some plains, coastal lowlands

Elevation: lowest point: Mediterranean Sea 0 ft. (0 m.); highest point: Mont Blanc 15,771 ft. (4,807 m.)

Natural resources: mercury, potash, marble, sulfur, dwindling natural gas and crude oil reserves, fish, coal

People

Population: 56,735,130 (July 1999 est.)

Population growth rate: -0.08%

Infant mortality rate: 6.3 deaths/1,000 live births

Life expectancy at birth: total population: 75.51 years; male: 75.4 years; female: 81.82 years

Major ethnic groups: Italian (includes small clusters of German-, French-, and Slovene-Italians in the north and Albanian-Italians and Greek-Italians in the south)

Major religions: Roman Catholic 98%

Major languages: Italian, German, French, Slovene

Government

Official name: Italian Republic

Government type: republic

National capital: Rome

Independence: March 17, 1861 (Kingdom of Italy proclaimed)

Legal system: based on civil law system, with ecclesiastical law influence; appeals treated as trials de novo

Economy

Industries: tourism, machinery, iron and steel, chemicals, food processing, textiles, motor vehicles, clothing, footwear, ceramics

Agricultural products: fruits, vegetables, grapes, potatoes, sugar beets, soybeans, grain, olives; meat and dairy products; fish

Currency: 1 Italian lira (Lit) = 100 centesimi

Jamaica

Geography

Location: Caribbean, island in the Caribbean Sea, south of Cuba

Area: 4,243 sq. mi. (10,990 sq. km.); slightly smaller than Connecticut

Climate: tropical; hot, humid; temperate interior

Terrain: mostly mountains with narrow, discontinuous coastal plain

Elevation: lowest point: Caribbean Sea 0 ft. (0 m.); highest point: Blue Mountain Peak 7,401 ft. (2,256 m.)

Natural resources: bauxite, gypsum, limestone

People

Population: 2,652,443 (July 1999 est.)

Population growth rate: 0.64%

Infant mortality rate: 13.93 deaths/1,000 live births

Life expectancy at birth: total population: 75.62 years; male: 73.22 years; female: 78.13 years

Major ethnic groups: black 90.4%, East Indian 1.3%, white 0.2%, Chinese 0.2%, mixed 7.3%

Major religions: Protestant 61.3%, Roman Catholic 4%, other, including some spiritual cults 34.7%

Major languages: English, Creole

Government

Official name: Jamaica

Government type: parliamentary democracy
National capital: Kingston
Independence: August 6, 1962 (from U.K.)
Legal system: based on English common law

Economy
Industries: tourism, bauxite, textiles, food processing, light manufactures
Agricultural products: sugarcane, bananas, coffee, citrus, potatoes, vegetables; poultry, goats, milk
Currency: 1 Jamaican dollar (J$) = 100 cents

Japan

Geography
Location: Eastern Asia, island chain between the North Pacific Ocean and the Sea of Japan, east of the Korean Peninsula
Area: 145,882 sq. mi. (377,835 sq. km.); slightly smaller than California
Climate: varies from tropical in south to cool temperate in north
Terrain: mostly rugged and mountainous
Elevation: lowest point: Hachiro-gata −13 ft. (−4 m.); highest point: Fujiyama 12,388 ft. (3,776 m.)
Natural resources: negligible mineral resources, fish

People
Population: 126,182,077 (July 1999 est.)
Population growth rate: 0.2%
Infant mortality rate: 4.07 deaths/1,000 live births
Life expectancy at birth: total population: 80.11 years; male: 77.02 years; female: 83.35 years
Major ethnic groups: Japanese 99.4%, other 0.6% (mostly Korean)
Major religions: observe both Shinto and Buddhist 84%, other 16%
Major languages: Japanese

Government
Official name: Japan
Government type: constitutional monarchy
National capital: Tokyo

Independence: 660 BC (traditional founding by Emperor Jimmu)
Legal system: modeled after European civil law system with English-American influence; judicial review of legislative acts in the Supreme Court

Economy
Industries: among world's largest and technologically advanced producers of steel and nonferrous metallurgy, heavy electrical equipment, construction and mining equipment, motor vehicles and parts, electronic and telecommunication equipment, machine tools, automated production systems, locomotives and railroad rolling stock, ships, chemicals; textiles, processed foods
Agricultural products: rice, sugar beets, vegetables, fruit; pork, poultry, dairy products, eggs; fish
Currency: Yen (¥)

Jersey

Geography
Location: Western Europe, island in the English Channel, northwest of France
Area: 45 sq. mi. (116 sq. km.); about 0.7 times the size of Washington, D.C.
Climate: temperate; mild winters and cool summers
Terrain: gently rolling plain with low, rugged hills along north coast
Elevation: lowest point: Atlantic Ocean 0 ft. (0 m.); highest point: unnamed location 469 ft. (143 m.)
Natural resources: agricultural land

People
Population: 89,721 (July 1999 est.)
Population growth rate: 0.63%
Infant mortality rate: 2.76 deaths/1,000 live births
Life expectancy at birth: total population: 78.83 years; male: 76.08 years; female: 81.87 years
Major ethnic groups: U.K. and Norman-French descent

Major religions: Anglican, Roman Catholic, Baptist, Congregational New Church, Methodist, Presbyterian

Major languages: English (official), French (official), Norman-French dialect spoken in country districts

Government

Official name: Bailiwick of Jersey

National capital: Saint Helier

Independence: none (British crown dependency)

Legal system: English law and local statute

Economy

Industries: tourism, banking and finance, dairy

Agricultural products: potatoes, cauliflowers, tomatoes; meat, dairy products

Currency: 1 Jersey pound (£J) = 100 pence ›

Jordan

Geography

Location: Middle East, northwest of Saudi Arabia

Area: 34,445 sq. mi. (89,213 sq. km.); slightly smaller than Indiana

Climate: mostly arid desert; rainy season in west (November to April)

Terrain: mostly desert plateau in east, highland area in west; Great Rift Valley separates East and West Banks of the Jordan River

Elevation: lowest point: Dead Sea –1,339 ft. (–408 m.); highest point: Jabal Ram 5,755 ft. (1,754 m.)

Natural resources: phosphates, potash, shale oil

People

Population: 4,561,147 (July 1999 est.)

Population growth rate: 3.05%

Infant mortality rate: 32.7 deaths/1,000 live births

Life expectancy at birth: total population: 73.06 years; male: 71.15 years; female: 75.08 years

Major ethnic groups: Arab 98%

Major religions: Sunni Muslim 96%, Christian 4%

Major languages: Arabic (official)

Government

Official name: Hashemite Kingdom of Jordan

Government type: constitutional monarchy

National capital: Amman

Independence: May 25, 1946 (from League of Nations mandate under British administration)

Legal system: based on Islamic law and French codes; judicial review of legislative acts in a specially provided High Tribunal; has not accepted compulsory ICJ jurisdiction

Economy

Industries: phosphate mining, petroleum refining, cement, potash, light manufacturing

Agricultural products: wheat, barley, citrus, tomatoes, melons, olives; sheep, goats, poultry

Currency: 1 Jordanian dinar (JD) = 1,000 fils

Kazakhstan

Geography

Location: Central Asia, northwest of China

Area: 1,049,150 sq. mi. (2,717,300 sq. km.) slightly less than four times the size of Texas

Climate: continental, cold winters and hot summers, arid and semiarid

Terrain: extends from the Volga to the Altai Mountains and from the plains in western Siberia to oasis and desert in Central Asia

Elevation: lowest point: Vpadina Kaundy –433 ft. (–132 m.); highest point: Zhengis Shingy (Pik Khan-Tengri) 22,949 ft. (6,995 m.)

Natural resources: major deposits of petroleum, natural gas, coal, iron ore, manganese, chrome ore, nickel, cobalt, copper, molybdenum, lead, zinc, bauxite, gold, uranium

People

Population: 16,824,825 (July 1999 est.)

Population growth rate: -0.09%

Infant mortality rate: 58.82 deaths/1,000 live births

Life expectancy at birth: total population: 63.39 years; male: 57.92 years; female: 69.13 years

Major ethnic groups: Kazakh (Qazaq) 46%, Russian 34.7%, Ukrainian 4.9%, German 3.1%, Uzbek 2.3%, Tatar 1.9%

Major religions: Muslim 47%, Russian Orthodox 44%, Protestant 2%

Major languages: Kazakh (Qazaq) official language spoken by over 40% of population, Russian official language spoken by two-thirds of population and used in everyday business

Government

Official name: Republic of Kazakhstan

Government type: republic

National capital: Astana (Akmola)

Note: the government has recently moved from Almaty to Astana

Independence: December 16, 1991 (from the Soviet Union)

Legal system: based on civil law system

Economy

Industries: oil, coal, iron ore, manganese, chromite, lead, zinc, copper, titanium, bauxite, gold, silver, phosphates, sulfur, iron and steel, nonferrous metal, tractors and other agricultural machinery, electric motors, construction materials; much of industrial capacity is shut down and/or is in need of repair

Agricultural products: grain, mostly spring wheat, cotton; wool, meat

Currency: 1 Kazakhstani tenge = 100 tiyn

Kenya

Geography

Location: Eastern Africa, bordering the Indian Ocean, between Somalia and Tanzania

Area: 224,961 sq. mi. (582,650 sq. km.); slightly more than twice the size of Nevada

Climate: varies from tropical along coast to arid in interior

Terrain: low plains rise to central highlands bisected by Great Rift Valley; fertile plateau in west

Elevation: lowest point: Indian Ocean 0 ft. (0 m.); highest point: Mount Kenya 17,057 ft. (5,199 m.)

Natural resources: gold, limestone, soda ash, salt barytes, rubies, fluorspar, garnets, wildlife

People

Population: 28,808,658 (July 1999 est.)

Population growth rate: 1.59%

Infant mortality rate: 59.07 deaths/1,000 live births

Life expectancy at birth: total population: 47.02 years; male: 46.56 years; female: 47.49 years

Major ethnic groups: Kikuyu 22%, Luhya 14%, Luo 13%, Kalenjin 12%, Kamba 11%, Kisii 6%, Meru 6%, other African 15%

Major religions: Protestant (including Anglican) 38%, Roman Catholic 28%, indigenous beliefs 26%, Muslim 6%

Major languages: English (official), Swahili (official), numerous indigenous languages

Government

Official name: Republic of Kenya

Government type: republic

National capital: Nairobi

Independence: December 12, 1963 (from U.K.)

Legal system: based on English common law, tribal law, and Islamic law; judicial review in High Court

Economy

Industries: small-scale consumer goods (plastic, furniture, batteries, textiles, soap, cigarettes, flour), processing agricultural products; oil refining, cement; tourism

Agricultural products: coffee, tea, corn, wheat, sugarcane, fruit, vegetables; dairy products, beef, pork, poultry, eggs

Currency: 1 Kenyan shilling (KSh) = 100 cents

Kiribati

Geography

Location: Oceania, group of islands in the Pacific Ocean, straddling the equator, about one-half of the way from Hawaii to Australia

Area: 277 sq. mi. (717 sq. km.); four times the size of Washington, D.C.

Climate: tropical; marine, hot and humid, moderated by trade winds

Terrain: mostly low-lying coral atolls surrounded by extensive reefs

Elevation: lowest point: Pacific Ocean 0 ft. (0 m.); highest point: unnamed location on Banaba 266 ft. (81 m.)

Natural resources: phosphate (production discontinued in 1979)

People

Population: 85,501 (July 1999 est.)

Population growth rate: 1.78%

Infant mortality rate: 48.22 deaths/1,000 live births

Life expectancy at birth: total population: 62.88 years; male: 61.02 years; female: 64.98 years

Major ethnic groups: Micronesian

Major religions: Roman Catholic 53%, Protestant (Congregational) 41%, Seventh-Day Adventist, Baha'i, Church of God, Mormon 6%

Major languages: English (official), Gilbertese

Government

Official name: Republic of Kiribati

Government type: republic

National capital: Tarawa

Independence: July 12, 1979 (from U.K.)

Economy

Industries: fishing, handicrafts

Agricultural products: copra, taro, breadfruit, sweet potatoes, vegetables; fish

Currency: 1 Australian dollar ($A) = 100 cents

Korea, North

Geography

Location: Eastern Asia, northern half of the Korean Peninsula bordering the Korea Bay and the Sea of Japan, between China and South Korea

Area: 46,540 sq. mi. (120,540 sq. km.); slightly smaller than Mississippi

Climate: temperate with rainfall concentrated in summer

Terrain: mostly hills and mountains separated by deep, narrow valleys; coastal plains wide in west, discontinuous in east

Elevation: extremes: lowest point: Sea of Japan 0 ft. (0 m.); highest point: Paektu-san 9,003 ft. (2,744 m.)

Natural resources: coal, lead, tungsten, zinc, graphite, magnesite, iron ore, copper, gold, pyrites, salt, fluorspar, hydropower

People

Population: 21,386,109 (July 1999 est.)

Population growth rate: 1.45%

Infant mortality rate: 25.52 deaths/1,000 live births

Life expectancy at birth: total population: 70.07 years; male: 67.41 years; female: 72.86 years

Major ethnic groups: racially homogenous; there is a small Chinese community and a few ethnic Japanese

Major religions: Buddhism and Confucianism, some Christianity and syncretic Chondogyo

Major languages: Korean

Government

Official name: Democratic People's Republic of Korea; Note: the North Koreans generally use the term "Choson" to refer to their country

Government type: Communist state; one-man dictatorship

National capital: P'yongyang

Independence: September 9, 1948 Democratic People's Republic of Korea

Legal system: based on German civil law system with Japanese influences and Communist legal theory; no judicial review of legislative acts; has not accepted compulsory ICJ jurisdiction

Economy

Industries: military products; machine building, electric power, chemicals; mining (coal, iron ore, magnesite, graphite, copper, zinc, lead, and precious metals), metallurgy; textiles, food processing

Agricultural products: rice, corn, potatoes, soybeans, pulses; cattle, pigs, pork, eggs

Currency: 1 North Korean won (Wn) = 100 chon

Korea, South

Geography

Location: Eastern Asia, southern half of the Korean Peninsula bordering the Sea of Japan and the Yellow Sea

Area: 38,023 sq. mi. (98,480 sq. km.); slightly larger than Indiana

Climate: temperate, with rainfall heavier in summer than winter

Terrain: mostly hills and mountains; wide coastal plains in west and south

Elevation: lowest point: Sea of Japan 0 ft. (0 m.); highest point: Halla-san 6,398 ft. (1,950 m.)

Natural resources: coal, tungsten, graphite, molybdenum, lead, hydropower

People

Population: 46,884,800 (July 1999 est.)

Population growth rate: 1%

Infant mortality rate: 7.57 deaths/1,000 live births

Life expectancy at birth: total population: 74.3 years; male: 70.75 years; female: 78.32 years

Major ethnic groups: racially homogenous; there is a small (≈ 20,000) Chinese community

Major religions: Christianity 49%, Buddhism 47%, Confucianism 3%, pervasive folk religion (shamanism), Chondogyo (Religion of the Heavenly Way)

Major languages: Korean

Government

Official name: Republic of Korea

Government type: republic

National capital: Seoul

Independence: August 15, 1945; note: date of liberation from Japanese colonial rule

Legal system: combines elements of continental European civil law systems, Anglo-American law, and Chinese classical thought

Economy

Industries: electronics, automobile production, chemicals, shipbuilding, steel, textiles, clothing, footwear, food processing

Agricultural products: rice, root crops, barley, vegetables, fruit; cattle, pigs, chickens, milk, eggs; fish catch of 2.9 million metric tons, seventh largest in world

Currency: 1 South Korean won (W) = 100 chun (theoretical)

Kuwait

Geography

Location: Middle East, bordering the Persian Gulf, between Iraq and Saudi Arabia

Area: 6,880 sq. mi. (17,820 sq. km.) slightly smaller than New Jersey

Climate: dry desert; intensely hot summers; short, cool winters

Terrain: flat to slightly undulating desert plain

Elevation: lowest point: Persian Gulf 0 ft. (0 m.); highest point: unnamed location 1,004 ft. (306 m.)

Natural resources: petroleum, fish, shrimp, natural gas

People

Population: 1,991,115 (Note: includes 1,220,935 non-nationals)

Population growth rate: 3.88% (Note: this rate reflects the continued post-Gulf crisis return of expatriates)

Infant mortality rate: 10.26 deaths/1,000 live births

Life expectancy at birth: total population: 77.15 years; male: 75.11 years; female: 79.3 years

Major ethnic groups: Kuwaiti 45%, other Arab 35%, South Asian 9%, Iranian 4%

Major religions: Muslim 85% (Sunni 45%, Shi'a 40%), Christian, Hindu, Parsi

Major languages: Arabic (official)

Government

Official name: State of Kuwait

Government type: nominal constitutional monarchy

National capital: Kuwait

Independence: June 19, 1961 (from U.K.)

Legal system: civil law system with Islamic law significant in personal matters

Economy

Industries: petroleum, petrochemicals, desalination, food processing, construction materials, salt, construction

Agricultural products: practically no crops; extensive fishing in territorial waters

Currency: 1 Kuwaiti dinar (KD) = 1,000 fils

Kyrgyzstan

Geography

Location: Central Asia, west of China

Area: 76,641 sq. mi. (198,500 sq. km.); slightly smaller than South Dakota

Climate: dry continental to polar in high Tien Shan; subtropical in southwest (Fergana Valley); temperate in northern foothill zone

Terrain: peaks of Tien Shan and associated valleys and basins encompass entire nation

Elevation: lowest point: Kara-Darya 433 ft. (132 m.); highest point: Jengish Chokusu (Pik Pobedy) 24,406 ft. (7,439 m.)

Natural resources: abundant hydroelectric potential; significant deposits of gold and rare earth metals; locally exploitable coal, oil, and natural gas; other deposits of nepheline, mercury, bismuth, lead, and zinc

People

Population: 4,546,055 (July 1999 est.)

Population growth rate: 0.68%

Infant mortality rate: 75.92 deaths/1,000 live births

Life expectancy at birth: total population: 63.57 years; male: 59.25 years; female: 68.1 years

Major ethnic groups: Kirghiz 52.4%, Russian 18%, Uzbek 12.9%, Ukrainian 2.5%, German 2.4%

Major religions: Muslim 75%, Russian Orthodox 20%

Major languages: Kirghiz (Kyrgyz)-official language, Russian-official language

Government

Official name: Kyrgyz Republic

Government type: republic

National capital: Bishkek

Independence: August 31, 1991 (from Soviet Union)

Legal system: based on civil law system

Economy

Industries: small machinery, textiles, food processing, cement, shoes, sawn logs, refrigerators, furniture, electric motors, gold, rare earth metals

Agricultural products: wool, tobacco, cotton, potatoes, vegetables, grapes, fruits and berries; sheep, goats, cattle

Currency: 1 Kyrgyzstani som (KGS) = 100 tyiyn

Laos

Geography

Location: Southeastern Asia, northeast of Thailand, west of Vietnam

Area: 91,428 sq. mi. (236,800 sq. km.); slightly larger than Utah

Climate: tropical monsoon; rainy season (May to November); dry season (December to April)

Terrain: mostly rugged mountains; some plains and plateaus

Elevation: lowest point: Mekong River 230 ft. (70 m.); highest point: Phou Bia 9,242 ft. (2,817 m.)

Natural resources: timber, hydropower, gypsum, tin, gold, gemstones

People

Population: 5,407,453 (July 1999 est.)

Population growth rate: 2.74%

Infant mortality rate: 89.32 deaths/1,000 live births

Life expectancy at birth: total population: 54.21 years; male: 52.63 years; female: 55.87 years

Major ethnic groups: Lao Loum (lowland) 68%, Lao Theung (upland) 22%, Lao Soung (highland) including the Hmong ("Meo") and the Yao (Mien) 9%

Major religions: Buddhist 60%, animist and other 40%

Major languages: Lao (official), French, English, and various ethnic languages

Government

Official name: Lao People's Democratic Republic

Government type: Communist state

National capital: Vientiane

Independence: July 19, 1949 (from France)

Legal system: based on traditional customs, French legal norms and procedures, and Socialist practice

Economy

Industries: tin and gypsum mining, timber, electric power, agricultural processing, construction, garments

Agricultural products: sweet potatoes, vegetables, corn, coffee, sugarcane, cotton; water buffalo, pigs, cattle, poultry; tobacco

Currency: 1 new kip (NK) = 100 at

Latvia

Geography

Location: Eastern Europe, bordering the Baltic Sea, between Estonia and Lithuania

Area: 24,749 sq. mi. (64,100 sq. km.); slightly larger than West Virginia

Climate: maritime; wet, moderate winters

Terrain: low plain

Elevation: lowest point: Baltic Sea 0 ft. (0 m.); highest point: Gaizinkalns 1,024 ft. (312 m.)

Natural resources: minimal; amber, peat, limestone, dolomite

People

Population: 2,353,874 (July 1999 est.)

Population growth rate: −1.25%

Infant mortality rate: 17.19 deaths/1,000 live births

Life expectancy at birth: total population: 67.3 years; male: 61.24 years; female: 73.66 years

Major ethnic groups: Latvian 56.5%, Russian 30.4%, Byelorussian 4.3%, Ukrainian 2.8%, Polish 2.6%

Major religions: Lutheran, Roman Catholic, Russian Orthodox

Major languages: Lettish (official), Lithuanian, Russian

Government

Official name: Republic of Latvia

Government type: parliamentary democracy

National capital: Riga

Independence: September 6, 1991 (from Soviet Union)

Legal system: based on civil law system

Economy

Industries: buses, vans, street and railroad cars, synthetic fibers, agricultural machinery, fertilizers, washing machines, radios, electronics, pharmaceuticals, processed foods, textiles; dependent on imports for energy, raw materials, and intermediate products

Agricultural products: grain, sugar beets, potatoes, vegetables; meat, milk, eggs; fish

Currency: 1 Latvian lat (LVL) = 100 santims; introduced March 1993

Lebanon

Geography

Location: Middle East, bordering the Mediterranean Sea, between Israel and Syria

Area: 4,015 sq. mi. (10,400 sq. km.); about 0.7 times the size of Connecticut

Climate: Mediterranean; mild to cool, wet winters with hot, dry summers; Lebanon mountains experience heavy winter snows

Terrain: narrow coastal plain; Al Biqa' (Bekaa Valley) separates Lebanon and Anti-Lebanon Mountains

Elevation: lowest point: Mediterranean Sea 0 ft. (0 m.); highest point: Jabal al Makmal 10,128 ft. (3,087 m.)

Natural resources: limestone, iron ore, salt, water-surplus state in a water-deficit region

People

Population: 3,562,699 (July 1999 est.)

Population growth rate: 1.61%

Infant mortality rate: 30.53 deaths/1,000 live births

Life expectancy at birth: total population: 70.93 years; male: 68.34 years; female: 73.66 years

Major ethnic groups: Arab 95%, Armenian 4%

Major religions: Islam 70%, Christian 30%

Major languages: Arabic (official), French

Government

Official name: Lebanese Republic

Government type: republic

National capital: Beirut

Independence: November 22, 1943 (from League of Nations mandate under French administration)

Legal system: mixture of Ottoman law, canon law, Napoleonic code, and civil law; no judicial review of legislative acts; has not accepted compulsory ICJ jurisdiction

Economy

Industries: banking; food processing; jewelry; cement; textiles; mineral and chemical products; wood and furniture products; oil refining; metal fabricating

Agricultural products: citrus, vegetables, potatoes, olives, tobacco, hemp (hashish); sheep, goats

Currency: 1 Lebanese pound (£L) = 100 piasters

Lesotho

Geography

Location: Southern Africa, an enclave of South Africa

Area: 11,718 sq. mi. (30,350 sq. km.); slightly smaller than Maryland

Climate: temperate; cool to cold, dry winters; hot, wet summers

Terrain: mostly highland with plateaus, hills, and mountains

Elevation: lowest point: junction of the Orange and Makhaleng Rivers 4,593 ft. (1,400 m.); highest point: Mount Thabana Ntlenyana 11,424 ft. (3,482 m.)

Natural resources: water, agricultural and grazing land, some diamonds and other minerals

People

Population: 2,128,950 (July 1999 est.)

Population growth rate: 1.8%

Infant mortality rate: 77.58 deaths/1,000 live births

Life expectancy at birth: total population: 52.99 years; male: 51.37 years; female: 54.65 years

Major ethnic groups: Sotho 99.7%

Major religions: Christian 80%, indigenous beliefs

Major languages: Sesotho (southern Sotho), English (official), Zulu, Xhosa

Government

Official name: Kingdom of Lesotho

Government type: parliamentary constitutional monarchy

National capital: Maseru

Independence: October 4, 1966 (from U.K.)

Legal system: based on English common law and Roman-Dutch law; judicial review of legislative acts in High Court and Court of Appeal; has not accepted compulsory ICJ jurisdiction

Economy

Industries: food, beverages, textiles, handicrafts; construction; tourism

Agricultural products: corn, wheat, pulses, sorghum, barley; livestock
Currency: 1 loti (L) = 100 lisente

Liberia

Geography

Location: Western Africa, bordering the North Atlantic Ocean, between Cote d'Ivoire and Sierra Leone

Area: 43,000 sq. mi. (111,370 sq. km.); slightly larger than Tennessee

Climate: tropical; hot, humid; dry winters with hot days and cool to cold nights; wet, cloudy summers with frequent heavy showers

Terrain: mostly flat to rolling coastal plains rising to rolling plateau and low mountains in northeast

Elevation: lowest point: Atlantic Ocean 0 ft. (0 m.); highest point: Mount Wuteve 4,528 ft. (1,380 m.)

Natural resources: iron ore, timber, diamonds, gold

People

Population: 2,923,725 (July 199 est.)

Population growth rate: 5.76%

Infant mortality rate: 100.63 deaths/1,000 live births

Life expectancy at birth: total population: 59.88 years; male: 57.2 years; female: 62.64 years

Major ethnic groups: indigenous African tribes 95% (including Kpelle, Bassa, Gio, Kru, Grebo, Mano, Krahn, Gola, Gbandi, Loma, Kissi, Vai, and Bella), Americo-Liberians 2.5% (descendants of immigrants from the U.S. who had been slaves)

Major religions: traditional 70%, Muslim 20%, Christian 10%

Major languages: English 20% (official), about 20 tribal languages

Government

Official name: Republic of Liberia
Government type: republic
National capital: Monrovia

Independence: July 26, 1847

Legal system: dual system of statutory law based on Anglo-American common law for the modern sector and customary law based on unwritten tribal practices for indigenous sector

Economy

Industries: rubber processing, food processing, construction materials, furniture, palm oil processing, iron ore, diamonds

Agricultural products: rubber, coffee, cocoa, rice, cassava (tapioca), palm oil, sugarcane, bananas; sheep, goats; timber

Currency: 1 Liberian dollar (L$) = 100 cents

Libya

Geography

Location: Northern Africa, bordering the Mediterranean Sea, between Egypt and Tunisia

Area: 679,358 sq. mi. (1,759,540 sq. km.); slightly larger than Alaska

Climate: Mediterranean along coast; dry, extreme desert interior

Terrain: mostly barren, flat to undulating plains, plateaus, depressions

Elevation: lowest point: Sabkhat Ghuzayyil −154 ft. (−47 m.); highest point: Bikku Bitti 7,438 ft. (2,267 m.)

Natural resources: petroleum, natural gas, gypsum

People

Population: 4,992,838 (July 1999 est.)

Population growth rate: 2.4%

Infant mortality rate: 28.15 deaths/1,000 live births

Life expectancy at birth: total population: 75.73 years; male: 73.81 years; female: 77.74 years

Major ethnic groups: Berber and Arab 97%

Major religions: Sunni Muslim 97%

Major languages: Arabic, Italian

Government

Official name: Socialist People's Libyan Arab Jamahiriya

Government type: Jamahiriya (a state of the masses) in theory, governed by the populace through local councils; in fact, a military dictatorship

National capital: Tripoli

Independence: December 24, 1951 (from Italy)

Legal system: based on Italian civil law system and Islamic law; separate religious courts; no constitutional provision for judicial review of legislative acts; has not accepted compulsory ICJ jurisdiction

Economy

Industries: petroleum, food processing, textiles, handicrafts, cement

Agricultural products: wheat, barley, olives, dates, citrus, vegetables, peanuts; meat, eggs

Currency: 1 Libyan dinar (LD) = 1,000 dirhams

Liechtenstein

Geography

Location: Central Europe, between Austria and Switzerland

Area: 62 sq. mi. (160 sq. km.); about 0.9 times the size of Washington, D.C.

Climate: continental; cold, cloudy winters with frequent snow or rain; cool to moderately warm, cloudy, humid summers

Terrain: mostly mountainous (Alps) with Rhine Valley in western third

Elevation: lowest point: Ruggeller Riet 1,411 ft. (430 m.); highest point: Grauspitz 8,527 ft. (2,599 m.)

Natural resources: hydroelectric potential

People

Population: 32,057 (July 199 est.)

Population growth rate: 1.08%

Infant mortality rate: 5.23 deaths/1,000 live births

Life expectancy at birth: total population: 78.11 years; male: 75.64 years; female: 80.69 years

Major ethnic groups: Alemannic 87.5%, Italian, Turkish, and other 12.5%

Major religions: Roman Catholic 80%, Protestant 7.4%

Major languages: German (official), Alemannic dialect

Government

Official name: Principality of Liechtenstein

Government type: hereditary constitutional monarchy

National capital: Vaduz

Independence: January 23, 1719 (Imperial Principality of Liechtenstein established)

Legal system: local civil and penal codes

Economy

Industries: electronics, metal manufacturing, textiles, ceramics, pharmaceuticals, food products, precision instruments, tourism

Agricultural products: wheat, barley, maize, potatoes; livestock, dairy products

Currency: 1 Swiss franc, franken, or franco (SwF) = 100 centimes

Lithuania

Geography

Location: Eastern Europe, bordering the Baltic Sea, between Latvia and Russia

Area: 25,174 sq. mi. (65,200 sq. km.); slightly larger than West Virginia

Climate: transitional, between maritime and continental; wet, moderate winters and summers

Terrain: lowland, many scattered small lakes, fertile soil

Elevation: lowest point: Baltic Sea 0 ft. (0 m.); highest point: Juozapines/Kalnas 958 ft. (292 m.)

Natural resources: peat

People

Population: 3,584,966 (July 1999 est.)

Population growth rate: -0.4%

Infant mortality rate: 14.71 deaths/1,000 live births

Life expectancy at birth: total population: 68.96 years; male: 62.91 years; female: 75.31 years

Major ethnic groups: Lithuanian 80.6%, Russian 8.7%, Polish 7%, Byelorussian 1.6%

Major religions: primarily Roman Catholic, others include Lutheran, Russian Orthodox, Protestant, evangelical Christian Baptist, Islam, Judaism

Major languages: Lithuanian (official), Polish, Russian

Government

Official name: Republic of Lithuania
Government type: parliamentary democracy
National capital: Vilnius
Independence: September 6, 1991 (from Soviet Union)
Legal system: based on civil law system; no judicial review of legislative acts

Economy

Industries: metal-cutting machine tools, electric motors, television sets, refrigerators and freezers, petroleum refining, shipbuilding (small ships), furniture making, textiles, food processing, fertilizers, agricultural machinery, optical equipment, electronic components, computers, amber

Agricultural products: grain, potatoes, sugar beets, vegetables; meat, milk, eggs; fish; flax fiber

Currency: 1 Lithuanian litas = 100 centas

Luxembourg

Geography

Location: Western Europe, between France and Germany
Area: 998 sq. mi. (2,586 sq. km.); slightly smaller than Rhode Island
Climate: modified continental with mild winters, cool summers
Terrain: mostly gently rolling uplands with broad, shallow valleys; uplands to slightly mountainous in the north; steep slope down to Moselle floodplain in the southeast
Elevation: lowest point: Moselle River 436 ft. (133 m.); highest point: Burgplatz 1,834 ft. (559 m.)
Natural resources: iron ore (no longer exploited)

People

Population: 429,080 (July 1999 est.)
Population growth rate: 0.88%
Infant mortality rate: 4.99 deaths/1,000 live births
Life expectancy at birth: total population: 77.65 years; male: 74.58 years; female: 80.83 years
Major ethnic groups: Celtic base (with French and German blend), Portuguese, Italian, and European (guest and worker residents)
Major religions: Roman Catholic 97%, Protestant and Jewish 3%
Major languages: Luxembourgian, German, French, English

Government

Official name: Grand Duchy of Luxembourg
Government type: constitutional monarchy
National capital: Luxembourg
Independence: 1839 (from the Netherlands)
Legal system: based on civil law system

Economy

Industries: banking, iron and steel, food processing, chemicals, metal products, engineering, tires, glass, aluminum
Agricultural products: barley, oats, potatoes, wheat, fruits, wine grapes; livestock products
Currency: 1 Luxembourg franc (LuxF) = 100 centimes

Macau

Geography

Location: Eastern Asia, bordering the South China Sea and China
Area: 8 sq. mi. (21 sq. km.); about 0.1 times the size of Washington, D.C.
Climate: subtropical; marine with cool winters, warm summers
Terrain: generally flat
Elevation: lowest point: South China Sea 0 ft. (0 m.); highest point: Coloane Alto 571 ft. (174 m.)
Natural resources: negilible

People

Population: 437,312 (July 1999 est.)

Population growth rate: 1.86%

Infant mortality rate: 4.23 deaths/1,000 live births

Life expectancy at birth: total population: 81.88 years; male: 78.79 years; female: 85.13 years

Major ethnic groups: Chinese 95%, Portuguese 3%

Major religions: Buddhist 50%, Roman Catholic 15%, other 35%

Major languages: Portuguese, Chinese (Cantonese)

Government

Official name: Macau Special Administrative Region

National capital: Macau

Independence: none (special administrative region of China)

Legal system: Portuguese civil law system

Economy

Industries: clothing, textiles, toys, electronics, footwear, tourism

Agricultural products: rice, vegetables

Currency: 1 pataca (P) = 100 avos

Macedonia, The Former Yugoslav Republic of

Geography

Location: Southeastern Europe, north of Greece

Area: 9,781 sq. mi. (25,333 sq. km.); slightly larger than Vermont

Climate: hot, dry summers and autumns and relatively cold winters with heavy snowfall

Terrain: mountainous territory covered with deep basins and valleys; there are three large lakes, each divided by a frontier line; country bisected by the Vardar River

Elevation: lowest point: Vardar River 164 ft. (50 m.); highest point: Korab 9,032 ft. (2,753 m.)

Natural resources: chromium, lead, zinc, manganese, tungsten, nickel, low-grade iron ore, asbestos, sulfur, timber

People

Population: 2,022,604 (July 1999 est.)

Population growth rate: 0.64%

Infant mortality rate: 18.68 deaths/1,000 live births

Life expectancy at birth: total population: 73.05 years; male: 70.93 years; female: 75.34 years

Major ethnic groups: Macedonian 65%, Albanian 22%, Turkish 4%, Serb 2%, Gypsies 3%

Major religions: Eastern Orthodox 67%, Muslim 30%

Major languages: Macedonian 70%, Albanian 21%, Turkish 3%, Serbo-Croatian 3%

Government

Official name: The Former Yugoslav Republic of Macedonia

Government type: emerging democracy

National capital: Skopje

Independence: September 17, 1991 (from Yugoslavia)

Legal system: based on civil law system; judicial review of legislative acts

Economy

Industries: coal, metallic chromium, lead, zinc, ferronickel, textiles, wood products, tobacco

Agricultural products: rice, tobacco, wheat, corn, millet, cotton, sesame, mulberry leaves, citrus, vegetables; beef, pork, poultry, mutton

Currency: 1 Macedonian denar (MKD) = 100 deni

Madagascar

Geography

Location: Southern Africa, island in the Indian Ocean, east of Mozambique

Area: 226,656 sq. mi. (587,040 sq. km.); slightly less than twice the size of Arizona

Climate: tropical along coast, temperate inland, arid in south

Terrain: narrow coastal plain, high plateau and mountains in center

Elevation: lowest point: Indian Ocean o ft. (o m.); highest point: Maromokotro 9,436 ft. (2,876 m.)

Natural resources: graphite, chromite, coal, bauxite, salt, quartz, tar sands, semiprecious stones, mica, fish

People

Population: 14,873,387 (July 1999 est.)

Population growth rate: 2.8%

Infant mortality rate: 89.1 deaths/1,000 live births

Life expectancy at birth: total population: 53.24 years; male: 52.01 years; female: 54.51 years

Major ethnic groups: Malayo-Indonesian (Merina and related Betsileo), Cotiers (mixed African, Malayo-Indonesian, and Arab ancestry), French, Indian, Creole, Comoran

Major religions: indigenous beliefs 52%, Christian 41%, Muslim 7%

Major languages: French (official), Malagasy (official)

Government

Official name: Republic of Madagascar

Government type: republic

National capital: Antananarivo

Independence: June 26, 1960 (from France)

Legal system: based on French civil law system and traditional Malagasy law

Economy

Industries: meat processing, soap, breweries, tanneries, sugar, textiles, glassware, cement, automobile assembly plant, paper, petroleum, tourism

Agricultural products: coffee, vanilla, sugarcane, cloves, cocoa, rice, cassava (tapioca), beans, bananas, peanuts; livestock products

Currency: 1 Malagasy franc (FMG) = 100 centimes

Malawi

Geography

Location: Southern Africa, east of Zambia

Area: 45,745 sq. mi. (118,480 sq. km.); slightly smaller than Pennsylvania

Climate: tropical; rainy season (November to May); dry season (May to November)

Terrain: narrow elongated plateau with rolling plains, rounded hills, some mountains

Elevation: lowest point: junction of the Shire River and international boundary with Mozambique 121 ft. (37 m.); highest point: Mount Mlanje Sapitwa 9,849 ft. (3,002 m.)

Natural resources: limestone, unexploited deposits of uranium, coal, and bauxite

People

Population: 10,000,416 (July 1999 est.)

Population growth rate: 1.57%

Infant mortality rate: 132.14 deaths/1,000 live births

Life expectancy at birth: total population: 36.3 years; male: 36.49 years; female: 36.2 years

Major ethnic groups: Chewa, Nyanja, Tumbuko, Yao, Lomwe, Sena, Tonga, Ngoni, Ngonde, Asian, European

Major religions: Protestant 55%, Roman Catholic 20%, Muslim 20%, traditional indigenous beliefs

Major languages: English (official), Chichewa (official), other languages important regionally

Government

Official name: Republic of Malawi

Government type: multiparty democracy

National capital: Lilongwe

Independence: July 6, 1964 (from U.K.)

Legal system: based on English common law and customary law; judicial review of legislative acts in the Supreme Court of Appeal; has not accepted compulsory ICJ jurisdiction

Economy

Industries: tea, tobacco, sugar, sawmill products, cement, consumer goods

Agricultural products: tobacco, sugarcane, cotton, tea, corn, potatoes, cassava (tapioca), sorghum, pulses; cattle, goats

Currency: 1 Malawian kwacha (MK) = 100 tambala

Malaysia

Geography

Location: Southeastern Asia, peninsula and northern one-third of the island of Borneo, bordering Indonesia and the South China Sea, south of Vietnam

Area: 127,316 sq. mi. (329,750 sq. km.); slightly larger than New Mexico

Climate: tropical; annual southwest (April to October) and northeast (October to February) monsoons

Terrain: coastal plains rising to hills and mountains

Elevation: lowest point: Indian Ocean 0 ft. (0 m.); highest point: Mount Kinabalu 13,451 ft. (4,100 m.)

Natural resources: tin, petroleum, timber, copper, iron ore, natural gas, bauxite

People

Population: 21,376,066 (July 1999 est.)

Population growth rate: 2.08%

Infant mortality rate: 21.68 deaths/1,000 live births

Life expectancy at birth: total population: 70.67 years; male: 67.62 years; female: 73.9 years

Major ethnic groups: Malay and other indigenous 58%, Chinese 26%, Indian 7%

Major religions: Muslim 38%, Christian 17%; Sarawak-tribal religion 35%, Buddhist and Confucianist 24%, Muslim 20%, Christian 16%

Major languages: Peninsular Malaysia-Malay (official), English, Chinese dialects, numerous tribal languages

Government

Official name: Malaysia

Government type: constitutional monarchy

National capital: Kuala Lumpur

Independence: August 31, 1957 (from U.K.)

Legal system: based on English common law; judicial review of legislative acts in the Supreme Court at request of supreme head of the federation; has not accepted compulsory ICJ jurisdiction

Economy

Industries: Peninsular Malaysia—rubber and oil palm processing and manufacturing, light manufacturing industry, electronics, tin mining and smelting, logging and processing timber; Sabah—logging, petroleum production; Sarawak—agriculture processing, petroleum production and refining, logging

Agricultural products: Peninsular Malaysia—natural rubber, palm oil, rice; Sabah—-subsistence crops, rubber, timber, coconut, rice; Sarawak—rubber, pepper; timber

Currency: 1 ringgit (M$) = 100 sen

Maldives

Geography

Location: Southern Asia, group of atolls in the Indian Ocean, south-southwest of India

Area: 116 sq. mi. (300 sq. km.); about 1.7 times the size of Washington, D.C.

Climate: tropical; hot, humid; dry, northeast monsoon (November to March); rainy, southwest monsoon (June to August)

Terrain: flat, with white sandy beaches

Elevation: lowest point: Indian Ocean 0 ft. (0 m.); highest point: unnamed location on Wilingili 79 ft. (24 m.)

Natural resources: fish

People

Population: 300,220 (July 1999 est.)

Population growth rate: 3.37%

Infant mortality rate: 38.14 deaths/1,000 live births

Life expectancy at birth: total population: 68.29 years; male: 66.53 years; female: 70.15 years

Major ethnic groups: Sinhalese, Dravidian, Arab, African

Major religions: Sunni Muslim

Major languages: Maldivian Divehi (dialect of Sinhala, script derived from Arabic), English spoken by most government officials

Government

Official name: Republic of Maldives
Government type: republic
National capital: Male (Maale)
Independence: July 26, 1965 (from U.K.)
Legal system: based on Islamic law with admixtures of English common law primarily in commercial matters; has not accepted compulsory ICJ jurisdiction

Economy

Industries: fish processing, tourism, shipping, boat building, coconut processing, garments, woven mats, rope, handicrafts, coral and sand mining
Agricultural products: coconuts, corn, sweet potatoes; fishing
Currency: 1 rufiyaa (Rf) = 100 laari

Mali

Geography

Location: Western Africa, southwest of Algeria
Area: 478,764 sq. mi. (1,240,000 sq. km.); slightly less than twice the size of Texas
Climate: subtropical to arid; hot and dry February to June; rainy, humid, and mild June to November; cool and dry November to February
Terrain: mostly flat to rolling northern plains covered by sand; savanna in south, rugged hills in northeast
Elevation: lowest point: Senegal River 75 ft. (23 m.); highest point: Hombori Tondo 3,789 ft. (1,155 m.)
Natural resources: gold, phosphates, kaolin, salt, limestone, uranium, bauxite, iron ore, manganese, tin, and copper deposits are known but not exploited

People

Population: 10,429,124 (July 1999 est.)
Population growth rate: 3.01%
Infant mortality rate: 119.44 deaths/1,000 live births
Life expectancy at birth: total population: 47.5 years; male: 46.09 years; female: 48.96 years

Major ethnic groups: Mande 50% (Bambara, Malinke, Sarakole), Peul 17%, Voltaic 12%, Songhai 6%, Tuareg and Moor 10%
Major religions: Muslim 90%, indigenous beliefs 9%
Major languages: French (official), Bambara 80%, numerous African languages

Government

Official name: Republic of Mali
Government type: republic
National capital: Bamako
Independence: September 22, 1960 (from France)
Legal system: based on French civil law system and customary law; judicial review of legislative acts in Constitutional Court; has not accepted compulsory ICJ jurisdiction

Economy

Industries: minor local consumer goods production and food processing; construction; phosphate and gold mining
Agricultural products: cotton, millet, rice, corn, vegetables, peanuts; cattle, sheep, goats
Currency: 1 Communauté Financière Africaine franc (CFAF) = 100 centimes

Malta

Geography

Location: Southern Europe, islands in the Mediterranean Sea, south of Sicily (Italy)
Area: 124 sq. mi. (320 sq. km.); slightly less than twice the size of Washington, D.C.
Climate: Mediterranean with mild, rainy winters and hot, dry summers
Terrain: mostly low, rocky, flat to dissected plains; many coastal cliffs
Elevation: lowest point: Mediterranean Sea 0 ft. (0 m.); highest point: Dingli Cliffs 804 ft. (245 m.)
Natural resources: limestone, salt

People

Population: 381,603 (July 1999 est.)
Population growth rate: 0.49%
Infant mortality rate: 7.42 deaths/1,000 live births

Life expectancy at birth: total population: 77.76 years; male: 75.43 years; female: 80.23 years

Major ethnic groups: Maltese (descendants of ancient Carthaginians and Phoenicians, with strong elements of Italian and other Mediterranean stock)

Major religions: Roman Catholic 98%

Major languages: Maltese (official), English (official)

Government

Official name: Republic of Malta

Government type: parliamentary democracy

National capital: Valletta

Independence: September 21, 1964 (from U.K.)

Legal system: based on English common law and Roman civil law

Economy

Industries: tourism; electronics, ship building and repair, construction; food and beverages, textiles, footwear, clothing, tobacco

Agricultural products: potatoes, cauliflower, grapes, wheat, barley, tomatoes, citrus, cut flowers, green peppers; pork, milk, poultry, eggs

Currency: 1 Maltese lira (LM) = 100 cents

Man, Isle of

Geography

Location: Western Europe, island in the Irish Sea, between Great Britain and Ireland

Area: 227 sq. mi. (588 sq. km.); slightly more than three times the size of Washington, D.C.

Climate: cool summers and mild winters; humid; overcast about half the time

Terrain: hills in north and south bisected by central valley

Elevation: lowest point: Irish Sea 0 ft. (0 m.); highest point: Snaefell 2,034 ft. (620 m.)

Natural resources: lead, iron ore

People

Population: 75,686 (July 1999 est.)

Population growth rate: 0.71%

Infant mortality rate: 2.45 deaths/1,000 live births

Life expectancy at birth: total population: 77.79 years; male: 74.28 years; female: 81.47 years

Major ethnic groups: Manx (Norse-Celtic descent), Briton

Major religions: Anglican, Roman Catholic, Methodist, Baptist, Presbyterian, Society of Friends

Major languages: English, Manx Gaelic

Government

Official name: Isle of Man

National capital: Douglas

Independence: none (British crown dependency)

Legal system: English law and local statute

Economy

Industries: financial services, light manufacturing, tourism

Agricultural products: cereals, vegetables; cattle, sheep, pigs, poultry

Currency: 1 Manx pound (£M) = 100 pence

Marshall Islands

Geography

Location: Oceania, group of atolls and reefs in the North Pacific Ocean, about one-half of the way from Hawaii to Papua New Guinea

Area: 70.0 sq. mi. (181.3 sq. km.); about the size of Washington, D.C.

Climate: wet season from May to November; hot and humid; islands border typhoon belt

Terrain: low coral limestone and sand islands

Elevation: lowest point: Pacific Ocean 0 ft. (0 m.); highest point: unnamed location on Likiep 33 ft. (10 m.)

Natural resources: phosphate deposits, marine products, deep seabed minerals

People

Population: 65,507 (July 1999 est.)

Population growth rate: 3.86%

Infant mortality rate: 43.38 deaths/1,000 live births

Life expectancy at birth: total population: 64.81 years; male: 63.21 years; female: 66.5 years

Major ethnic groups: Micronesian

Major religions: Christian (mostly Protestant)

Major languages: English (universally spoken and is the official language), two major Marshallese dialects from the Malayo-Polynesian family, Japanese

Government

Official name: Republic of the Marshall Islands

Government type: constitutional government in free association with the U.S.; the Compact of Free Association entered into force October 21, 1986

National capital: Majuro

Independence: October 21, 1986 (from the U.S.-administered UN trusteeship)

Legal system: based on adapted Trust Territory laws, acts of the legislature, municipal, common, and customary laws

Economy

Industries: copra, fish, tourism, craft items from shell, wood, and pearls, offshore banking (embryonic)

Agricultural products: coconuts, cacao, taro, breadfruit, fruits; pigs, chickens

Currency: 1 U.S. dollar (US$) = 100 cents

Martinique

Geography

Location: Caribbean, island in the Caribbean Sea, north of Trinidad and Tobago

Area: 425 sq. mi. (1,100 sq. km.); slightly more than six times the size of Washington, D.C.

Climate: tropical; moderated by trade winds; rainy season (June to October); vulnerable to devastating cyclones ((hurricanes) every eight year on average; average temperature 63.1 degrees F (17.3 degrees C); humid

Terrain: mountainous with indented coastline; dormant volcano

Elevation: lowest point: Caribbean Sea 0 ft. (0 m.); highest point: Montagne Pelee 4,583 ft. (1,397 m.)

Natural resources: coastal scenery and beaches, cultivable land

People

Population: 411,539 (July 1999 est.)

Population growth rate: 1.03%

Infant mortality rate: 6.76 deaths/1,000 live births

Life expectancy at birth: total population: 79.27 years; male: 76.47 years; female: 82.13 years

Major ethnic groups: African and African-white-Indian mixture 90%, white 5%, East Indian, Lebanese, Chinese less than 5%

Major religions: Roman Catholic 95%, Hindu and pagan African 5%

Major languages: French, Creole patois

Government

Official name: Department of Martinique

National capital: Fort-de-France

Independence: none (overseas department of France)

Legal system: French legal system

Economy

Industries: construction, rum, cement, oil refining, sugar, tourism

Agricultural products: pineapples, avocados, bananas, flowers, vegetables, sugarcane for rum

Currency: 1 French franc (F) = 100 centimes

Mauritania

Geography

Location: Northern Africa, bordering the North Atlantic Ocean, between Senegal and Western Sahara

Area: 397,953 sq. mi. (1,030,700 sq. km.); slightly larger than three times the size of New Mexico

Climate: desert; constantly hot, dry, dusty

Terrain: mostly barren, flat plains of the Sahara; some central hills

Elevation: lowest point: Sebkha de Ndrhamcha
   −10 ft. (−3 m.); highest point: Kediet Ijill
   2,986 ft. (910 m.)
Natural resources: iron ore, gypsum, fish, copper, phosphate

People
Population: 2,581,738 (July 1999 est.)
Population growth rate: 2.99%
Infant mortality rate: 76.46 deaths/1,000 live
   births
Life expectancy at birth: total population:
   50.48 years; male: 47.39 years; female:
   53.65 years
Major ethnic groups: mixed Maur/black 40%,
   Maur 30%, black 30%
Major religions: Muslim 100%
Major languages: Hasaniya Arabic (official),
   Pular, Soninke, Wolof (official), French

Government
Official name: Islamic Republic of Mauritania
Government type: republic
National capital: Nouakchott
Independence: November 28, 1960 (from
   France)
Legal system: three-tier system: Islamic (Shari'a)
   courts, special courts, and state security courts
   (in the process of being eliminated)

Economy
Industries: fish processing, mining of iron ore
   and gypsum
Agricultural products: dates, millet, sorghum,
   root crops; cattle, sheep; fish products
Currency: 1 ouguiya (UM) = 5 khoums

Mauritius

Geography
Location: Southern Africa, island in the Indian
   Ocean, east of Madagascar
Area: 718 sq. mi. (1,860 sq. km.); almost 11 times
   the size of Washington, D.C.
Climate: tropical, modified by southeast trade
   winds; warm, dry winter (May to November);
   hot, wet, humid summer (November to May)

Terrain: small coastal plain rising to discontinuous mountains encircling central
   plateau
Elevation: lowest point: Indian Ocean 0 ft.
   (0 m.); highest point: Piton de la Petite
   Riviere Noire 2,717 ft. (828 m.)
Natural resources: arable land, fish

People
Population: 1,182,212 (July 1999 est.)
Population growth rate: 1.18%
Infant mortality rate: 16.2 deaths/1,000 live
   births
Life expectancy at birth: total population:
   71.09 years; male: 67.21 years; female:
   74.96 years
Major ethnic groups: Indo-Mauritian 68%,
   Creole 27%, Sino-Mauritian 3%, Franco-
   Mauritian 2%
Major religions: Hindu 52%, Christian 28.3%
   (Roman Catholic 26%, Protestant 2.3%),
   Muslim 16.6%
Major languages: English (official), Creole,
   French, Hindi, Urdu, Hakka, Bojpoori

Government
Official name: Republic of Mauritius
Government type: parliamentary democracy
National capital: Port Louis
Independence: March 12, 1968 (from U.K.)
Legal system: based on French civil law system
   with elements of English common law in
   certain areas

Economy
Industries: food processing (largely sugar
   milling), textiles, apparel, chemicals, metal
   products, transport equipment, nonelectrical
   machinery, tourism
Agricultural products: sugarcane, tea, corn,
   potatoes, bananas, pulses; cattle, goats;
   fish
Currency: 1 Mauritian rupee (MauR) = 100
   cents

Mayotte

Geography
Location: Southern Africa, island in the Mozambique Channel, about one-half of the way from northern Madagascar to northern Mozambique

Area: 145 sq. mi. (375 sq. km.); slightly more than twice the size of Washington, D.C.

Climate: tropical; marine; hot, humid, rainy season during northeastern monsoon (November to May); dry season is cooler (May to November)

Terrain: generally undulating, with deep ravines and ancient volcanic peaks

Elevation: lowest point: Indian Ocean 0 ft. (0 m.); highest point: Benara 2,165 ft. (660 m.)

Natural resources: negligible

People
Population: 149,336 (July 1999 est.)

Population growth rate: 5%

Infant mortality rate: 69.06 deaths/1,000 live births

Life expectancy at birth: total population: 60.02 years; male: 57.61 years; female: 62.15 years

Major religions: Muslim 99%, Christian (mostly Roman Catholic)

Major languages: Mahorian (a Swahili dialect), French

Government
Official name: Territorial Collectivity of Mayotte

National capital: Mamoutzou

Independence: none (territorial collectivity of France)

Legal system: French law

Economy
Industries: newly created lobster and shrimp industry

Agricultural products: vanilla, ylang-ylang (perfume essence), coffee, copra

Currency: 1 French franc (F) = 100 centimes

Mexico

Geography
Location: North America, bordering the Caribbean Sea and the Gulf of Mexico, between Belize and the U.S. and bordering the North Pacific Ocean, between Guatemala and the U.S.

Area: 761,602 sq. mi. (1,972,550 sq. km.); slightly less than three times the size of Texas

Climate: varies from tropical to desert

Terrain: high, rugged mountains, low coastal plains, high plateaus, and desert

Elevation: lowest point: Laguna Salada –33 ft. (–10 m.); highest point: Volcan Pico de Orizaba 18,701 ft. (5,700 m.)

Natural resources: petroleum, silver, copper, gold, lead, zinc, natural gas, timber

People
Population: 100,294,036 (July 1999 est.)

Population growth rate: 1.73%

Infant mortality rate: 24.62 deaths/1,000 live births

Life expectancy at birth: total population: 72 years; male: 68.98 years; female: 75.17 years

Major ethnic groups: mestizo (Amerindian-Spanish) 60%, Amerindian or predominantly Amerindian 30%, white 9%

Major religions: nominally Roman Catholic 89%, Protestant 6%

Major languages: Spanish, various Mayan, Nahuatl, and other regional indigenous languages

Government
Official name: United Mexican States

Government type: federal republic operating under a centralized government

National capital: Mexico

Independence: September 16, 1810 (from Spain)

Legal system: mixture of U.S. constitutional theory and civil law system; judicial review of legislative acts

Economy

Industries: food and beverages, tobacco, chemicals, iron and steel, petroleum, mining, textiles, clothing, motor vehicles, consumer durables, tourism

Agricultural products: corn, wheat, soybeans, rice, beans, cotton, coffee, fruit, tomatoes; beef, poultry, dairy products; wood products

Currency: 1 New Mexican peso (Mex$) = 100 centavos

Micronesia, Federated States of

Geography

Location: Oceania, island group in the North Pacific Ocean, about three-quarters of the way from Hawaii to Indonesia

Area: 271 sq. mi. (702 sq. km.); four times the size of Washington, D.C.

Climate: tropical; heavy year-round rainfall, especially in the eastern islands; located on southern edge of the typhoon belt with occasionally severe damage

Terrain: islands vary geologically from high mountainous islands to low, coral atolls; volcanic outcroppings on Pohnpei, Kosrae, and Truk

Elevation: lowest point: Pacific Ocean 0 ft. (0 m.); highest point: Totolom 2,595 ft. (791 m.)

Natural resources: forests, marine products, deep-seabed minerals

People

Population: 131,500 (July 1999 est.)

Population growth rate: 3.3%

Infant mortality rate: 33.99 deaths/1,000 live births

Life expectancy at birth: total population: 68.48 years; male: 66.52 years; female: 70.48 years

Major ethnic groups: nine ethnic Micronesian and Polynesian groups

Major religions: Roman Catholic 50%, Protestant 47%

Major languages: English (official and common language), Trukese, Pohnpeian, Yapese, Kosrean

Government

Official name: Federated States of Micronesia

Government type: constitutional government in free association with the U.S.; the Compact of Free Association entered into force November 3, 1986

National capital: Palikir

Independence: November 3, 1986 (from the U.S.-administered UN Trusteeship)

Legal system: based on adapted Trust Territory laws, acts of the legislature, municipal, common, and customary laws

Economy

Industries: tourism, construction, fish processing, craft items from shell, wood, and pearls

Agricultural products: black pepper, tropical fruits and vegetables, coconuts, cassava (tapioca), sweet potatoes; pigs, chickens

Currency: 1 U.S. dollar (US$) = 100 cents

Moldova

Geography

Location: Eastern Europe, northeast of Romania

Area: 13,012 sq. mi. (33,700 sq. km.); slightly more than twice the size of Hawaii

Climate: moderate winters, warm summers

Terrain: rolling steppe, gradual slope south to Black Sea

Elevation: lowest point: Nistru River 7 ft. (2 m.); highest point: Mount Balaneshty 1,411 ft. (430 m.)

Natural resources: lignite, phosphorites, gypsum

People

Population: 4,460,838 (July 1999 est.)

Population growth rate: 0.1%

Infant mortality rate: 43.52 deaths/1,000 live births

Life expectancy at birth: total population:
64.39 years; male: 59.76 years; female:
69.24 years

Major ethnic groups: Moldavian/Romanian
64.5%, Ukrainian 13.8%, Russian 13%, Gagauz
3.5%, Bulgarian 2%, Jewish 1.5%

Major religions: Eastern Orthodox 98.5%, Jewish
1.5%

Major languages: Moldovan (official, virtually the
same as the Romanian language), Russian,
Gagauz (a Turkish dialect)

Government

Official name: Republic of Moldova
Government type: republic
National capital: Chisinau
Independence: August 27, 1991 (from Soviet
Union)
Legal system: based on civil law system;
Constitutional Court reviews legality of legis-
lative acts and governmental decisions of
resolution

Economy

Industries: food processing, agricultural machinery, foundry equipment, refrigerators and
freezers, washing machines, hosiery, sugar,
vegetable oil, shoes, textiles

Agricultural products: vegetables, fruits, wine,
grain, sugar beets, sunflower seed, tobacco;
meat, milk

Currency: Moldovan leu (MLD)

Monaco

Geography

Location: Western Europe, bordering the
Mediterranean Sea, on the southern coast of
France, near the border with Italy

Area: 0.8 sq. mi. (1.95 sq. km.); about three
times the size of The Mall in Washington,
D.C.

Climate: Mediterranean with mild, wet winters
and hot, dry summers

Terrain: hilly, rugged, rocky

Elevation: extremes: lowestt point: Mediterranean Sea 0 ft. (0 m.); highest point: Mont
Agel 459 ft. (140 m.)

Natural resources: none

People

Population: 32,149 (July 1999 est.)
Population growth rate: 0.31%
Infant mortality rate: 6.47 deaths/1,000 live
births

Life expectancy at birth: total population:
78.58 years; male: 75 years; female:
82.35 years

Major ethnic groups: French 47%, Monegasque
16%, Italian 16%

Major religions: Roman Catholic 95%

Major languages: French (official), English,
Italian, Monegasque

Government

Official name: Principality of Monaco
Government type: constitutional monarchy
National capital: Monaco
Independence: 1419 (rule by the House of
Grimaldi)
Legal system: based on French law; has not
accepted compulsory ICJ jurisdiction

Economy

Industries: negligible
Agricultural products: none
Currency: 1 French franc (F) = 100 centimes

Mongolia

Geography

Location: Northern Asia, between China and
Russia

Area: 604,247 sq. mi. (1,565,000 sq. km.);
slightly smaller than Alaska

Climate: desert; continental (large daily and seasonal temperature ranges)

Terrain: vast semidesert and desert plains;
mountains in west and southwest; Gobi Desert
in southeast

Elevation: lowest point: Hoh Nuur 1,699 ft.
(518 m.); highest point: Tavan Bogd Uul
14,350 ft. (4,374 m.)

Natural resources: oil, coal, copper, molybdenum, tungsten, phosphates, tin, nickel, zinc,
wolfram, fluorspar, gold

People

Population: 2,617,379 (July 1999 est.)

Population growth rate: 1.45%

Infant mortality rate: 64.63 deaths/1,000 live births

Life expectancy at birth: total population: 61.81 years; male: 59.71 years; female: 64.02 years

Major ethnic groups: Mongol 90%, Kazakh 4%, Chinese 2%, Russian 2%

Major religions: predominantly Tibetan Buddhist, Muslim 4%

Major languages: Khalkha Mongol 90%, Turkic, Russian, Chinese

Government

Official name: Mongolia

Government type: republic

National capital: Ulaanbaatar

Independence: March 13, 1921 (from China)

Legal system: blend of Russian, Chinese, and Turkish systems of law; no constitutional provision for judicial review of legislative acts; has not accepted compulsory ICJ jurisdiction

Economy

Industries: copper, construction materials, mining (particularly coal); food and beverage, processing of animal products

Agricultural products: wheat, barley, potatoes, forage crops; sheep, goats, cattle, camels, horses

Currency: 1 tughrik (Tug) = 100 mongos

Montserrat

Geography

Location: Caribbean, island in the Caribbean Sea, southeast of Puerto Rico

Area: 39 sq. mi. (100 sq. km.); about 0.6 times the size of Washington, D.C.

Climate: tropical; little daily or seasonal temperature variation

Terrain: volcanic islands, mostly mountainous, with small coastal lowland

Elevation: lowest point: Caribbean Sea 0 ft. (0 m.); highest point: Chances Peak 2,999 ft. (914 m.)

Natural resources: negligible

People

Population: 112,853 (July 1999 est.) Note—demographic figures include an estimated 8,000 refugees who fled the island following the resumption of volcanic activity in July 1995

Population growth rate: 0.21%

Infant mortality rate: 12 deaths/1,000 live births

Life expectancy at birth: total population: 75.56 years; male: 73.79 years; female: 77.37 years

Major ethnic groups: black, white

Major religions: Anglican, Methodist, Roman Catholic, Pentecostal, Seventh-Day Adventist

Major languages: English

Government

Official name: Montserrat

National capital: Plymouth (abandoned in 1997 due to volcanic activity)

Independence: none (dependent territory of the U.K.)

Legal system: English common law and statute law

Economy

Industries: tourism, rum, textiles, electronic appliances

Agricultural products: cabbages, carrots, cucumbers, tomatoes, onions, peppers; livestock products

Currency: 1 East Caribbean dollar (EC$) = 100 cents

Morocco

Geography

Location: Northern Africa, bordering the North Atlantic Ocean and the Mediterranean Sea, between Algeria and Western Sahara

Area: 172,413 sq. mi. (446,550 sq. km.); slightly
larger than California
Climate: Mediterranean, becoming more
extreme in the interior
Terrain: northern coast and interior are mountainous with large areas of bordering
plateaus, intermontane valleys, and rich
coastal plains
Elevation: lowest point: Sebkha Tah −180 ft.
(−55 m.); highest point: Jebel Toubkal
13,665 ft. (4,165 m.)
Natural resources: phosphates, iron ore, manganese, lead, zinc, fish, salt

People

Population: 29,661,636 (July 1999 est.)
Population growth rate: 1.84%
Infant mortality rate: 50.96 deaths/1,000 live
births
Life expectancy at birth: total population:
68.87 years; male: 66.85 years; female:
70.99 years
Major ethnic groups: Arab-Berber 99.1%, Jewish
0.2%, other 0.7%
Major religions: Muslim 98.7%, Christian 1.1%,
Jewish 0.2%
Major languages: Arabic (official), Berber
dialects, French (often the language of busi-
ness, government, and diplomacy)

Government

Official name: Kingdom of Morocco
Government type: constitutional monarchy
National capital: Rabat
Independence: March 2, 1956 (from France)
Legal system: based on Islamic law and French
and Spanish civil law system; judicial review of
legislative acts in Constitutional Chamber of
Supreme Court

Economy

Industries: phosphate rock mining and processing, food processing, leather goods, textiles,
construction, tourism
Agricultural products: barley, wheat, citrus, wine,
vegetables, olives; livestock
Currency: 1 Moroccan dirham (DH) = 100 centimes

Mozambique

Geography

Location: Southern Africa, bordering the
Mozambique Channel, between South Africa
and Tanzania
Area: 309,494 sq. mi. (801,590 sq. km.); slightly
less than twice the size of California
Climate: tropical to subtropical
Terrain: mostly coastal lowlands, uplands in
center, high plateaus in northwest, mountains
in west
Elevation: lowest point: Indian Ocean 0 ft.
(0 m.); highest point: Monte Binga 7,992 ft.
(2,436 m.)
Natural resources: coal, titanium, natural gas

People

Population: 19,124,335 (July 1999 est.)
Population growth rate: 2.54%
Infant mortality rate: 117.56 deaths/1,000 live
births
Life expectancy at birth: total population:
45.89 years; male: 44.73 years; female:
47.09 years
Major ethnic groups: indigenous tribal groups
99.66% (Shangaan, Chokwe, Manyika, Sena,
Makua, and others)
Major religions: indigenous beliefs 50%,
Christian 30%, Muslim 20%
Major languages: Portuguese (official), indige-
nous dialects

Government

Official name: Republic of Mozambique
Government type: republic
National capital: Maputo
Independence: June 25, 1975 (from Portugal)
Legal system: based on Portuguese civil law sys-
tem and customary law

Economy

Industries: food, beverages, chemicals (fertilizer,
soap, paints), petroleum products, textiles,
cement, glass, asbestos, tobacco
Agricultural products: cotton, cashew nuts,
sugarcane, tea, cassava (tapioca), corn, rice,
tropical fruits; beef, poultry

Currency: 1 metical (Mt) = 100 centavos

Namibia

Geography

Location: Southern Africa, bordering the South Atlantic Ocean, between Angola and South Africa

Area: 318,694 sq. mi. (825,418 sq. km.); slightly more than half the size of Alaska

Climate: desert; hot, dry; rainfall sparse and erratic

Terrain: mostly high plateau; Namib Desert along coast; Kalahari Desert in east

Elevation: lowest point: Atlantic Ocean 0 ft. (0 m.); highest point: Konigstein 8,550 ft. (2,606 m.)

Natural resources: diamonds, copper, uranium, gold, lead, tin, lithium, cadmium, zinc, salt, vanadium, natural gas, fish; suspected deposits of oil, natural gas, coal, iron ore

People

Population: 1,648,270 (July 1999 est.)

Population growth rate: 1.57%

Infant mortality rate: 66.94 deaths/1,000 live births

Life expectancy at birth: total population: 41.26 years; male: 41.64 years; female: 40.87 years

Major ethnic groups: black 86%, white 6.6%, mixed 7.4% (Note—about 50% of the population belong to the Ovambo tribe and 9% to the Kavangos tribe); other ethnic groups are: Herero 7%, Damara 7%, Nama 5%, Caprivian 4%, Bushmen 3%, Baster 2%, Tswana 0.5%

Major religions: Christian 80% to 90% (Lutheran 50% at least, other Christian denominations 30%), native religions 10% to 20%

Major languages: English 7% (official), Afrikaans common language of most of the population and about 60% of the white population, German 32%, indigenous languages: Oshivambo, Herero, Nama

Government

Official name: Republic of Namibia

Government type: republic

National capital: Windhoek

Independence: March 21, 1990 (from South African mandate)

Legal system: based on Roman-Dutch law and 1990 constitution

Economy

Industries: meat packing, fish processing, dairy products; mining (diamond, lead, zinc, tin, silver, tungsten, uranium, copper)

Agricultural products: millet, sorghum, peanuts; livestock; fish

Currency: 1 Namibian dollar (N$) = 100 cents

Nauru

Geography

Location: Oceania, island in the South Pacific Ocean, south of the Marshall Islands

Area: 8 sq. mi. (21 sq. km.); about 0.1 times the size of Washington, D.C.

Climate: tropical; monsoonal; rainy season (November to February)

Terrain: sandy beach rises to fertile ring around raised coral reefs with phosphate plateau in center

Elevation: lowest point: Pacific Ocean 0 ft. (0 m.); highest point: unnamed location along plateau rim 200 ft. (61 m.)

Natural resources: phosphates

People

Population: 10,605 (July 1999 est.)

Population growth rate: 0%

Major ethnic groups: Nauruan 58%, other Pacific Islander 26%, Chinese 8%, European 8%

Major religions: Christian (two-thirds Protestant, one-third Roman Catholic)

Major languages: Nauruan (official, a distinct Pacific Island language), English widely understood, spoken, and used for most government and commercial purposes

Government

Official name: Republic of Nauru

Government type: republic

National capital: no official capital; government offices in Yaren District

Independence: January 31, 1968 (from the Australia-, New Zealand-, and U.K.-administered UN trusteeship)

Legal system: acts of the Nauru Parliament and British common law

Economy

Industries: phosphate mining, financial services, coconut products

Agricultural products: coconuts predominate

Currency: 1 Australian dollar ($A) = 100 cents

Nepal

Geography

Location: Southern Asia, between China and India

Area: 54,363 sq. mi. (140,800 sq. km.); slightly larger than Arkansas

Climate: varies from cool summers and severe winters in north to subtropical summers and mild winters in south

Terrain: Terai or flat river plain of the Ganges in south, central hill region, rugged Himalayas in north

Elevation: lowest point: Kanchan Kalan 230 ft. (70 m.); highest point: Mount Everest 29,028 ft. (8,848 m.)

Natural resources: quartz, water, timber, hydropower potential, scenic beauty, small deposits of lignite, copper, cobalt, iron ore

People

Population: 24,302,653 (July 1999 est.)

Population growth rate: 2.51%

Infant mortality rate: 73.58 deaths/1,000 live births

Life expectancy at birth: total population: 58.42 years; male: 58.47 years; female: 58.36 years

Major ethnic groups: Newars, Indians, Tibetans, Gurungs, Magars, Tamangs, Bhotias, Rais, Limbus, Sherpas

Major religions: Hindu 90%, Buddhist 5%, Muslim 3%

Major languages: Nepali (official), 20 other languages divided into numerous dialects

Government

Official name: Kingdom of Nepal

Government type: parliamentary democracy as of May 12, 1991

National capital: Kathmandu

Independence: 1768 (unified by Prithvi Narayan Shah)

Legal system: based on Hindu legal concepts and English common law

Economy

Industries: tourism, carpet, textiles; small rice, jute, sugar, and oilseed mills; cigarette; cement and brick production

Agricultural products: rice, corn, wheat, sugarcane, root crops; milk, water buffalo meat

Currency: 1 Nepalese rupee (NR) = 100 paisa

Netherlands

Geography

Location: Western Europe, bordering the North Sea, between Belgium and Germany

Area: 16,033 sq. mi. (41,526 sq. km.); slightly less than twice the size of New Jersey

Climate: temperate; marine; cool summers and mild winters

Terrain: mostly coastal lowland and reclaimed land (polders); some hills in southeast

Elevation: lowest point: Prins Alexanderpolder −23 ft. (−7 m.); highest point: Vaalserberg 1,053 ft. (321 m.)

Natural resources: natural gas, petroleum, fertile soil

People

Population: 15,807,641 (July 1999 est.)

Population growth rate: 0.47%

Infant mortality rate: 5.11 deaths/1,000 live births

Life expectancy at birth: total population: 78.15 years; male: 75.28 years; female: 81.17 years

Major ethnic groups: Dutch 96%, Moroccans, Turks
Major religions: Roman Catholic 34%, Protestant 25%, Muslim 3%
Major languages: Dutch

Government
Official name: Kingdom of the Netherlands
Government type: constitutional monarchy
National capital: Amsterdam; The Hague is the seat of government
Independence: 1579 (from Spain)
Legal system: civil law system incorporating French penal theory; constitution does not permit judicial review of acts of the States General

Economy
Industries: agroindustries, metal and engineering products, electrical machinery and equipment, chemicals, petroleum, fishing, construction, microelectronics
Agricultural products: grains, potatoes, sugar beets, fruits, vegetables; livestock
Currency: 1 Netherlands guilder, gulden, or florin (f.) = 100 cents

Netherlands Antilles

Geography
Location: Caribbean, two island groups in the Caribbean Sea—one includes Curacao and Bonaire north of Venezuela and the other is east of the Virgin Islands
Area: 371 sq. mi. (960 sq. km.); more than five times the size of Washington, D.C.
Climate: tropical; ameliorated by northeast trade winds
Terrain: generally hilly, volcanic interiors
Elevation: lowest point: Caribbean Sea 0 ft. (0 m.); highest point: Mount Scenery 2,828 ft. (862 m.)
Natural resources: phosphates (Curacao only), salt (Bonaire only)

People
Population: 207,827 (July 1999 est.)

Population growth rate: 1.01%
Infant mortality rate: 12.59 deaths/1,000 live births
Life expectancy at birth: total population: 74.25 years; male: 72.19 years; female: 76.41 years
Major ethnic groups: mixed black 85%, Carib Amerindian, white, East Asian
Major religions: Roman Catholic, Protestant, Jewish, Seventh-Day Adventist
Major languages: Dutch (official), Papiamento, a Spanish-Portuguese-Dutch-English dialect predominates, English widely spoken, Spanish

Government
Official name: Netherlands Antilles
Government type: parliamentary
National capital: Willemstad
Independence: none (part of the Kingdom of the Netherlands)
Legal system: based on Dutch civil law system, with some English common law influence

Economy
Industries: tourism (Curacao, Sint Maarten, and Bonaire), petroleum refining (Curacao), petroleum transshipment facilities (Curacao and Bonaire), light manufacturing (Curacao)
Agricultural products: aloes, sorghum, peanuts, vegetables, tropical fruit
Currency: 1 Netherlands Antillean guilder, gulden, or florin (NAf.) = 100 cents

New Caledonia

Geography
Location: Oceania, islands in the South Pacific Ocean, east of Australia
Area: 7,359 sq. mi. (19,060 sq. km.); slightly smaller than New Jersey
Climate: tropical; modified by southeast trade winds; hot, humid
Terrain: coastal plains with interior mountains

Elevation: lowest point: Pacific Ocean 0 ft.
(0 m.); highest point: Mont Panie 5,341 ft.
(1,628 m.)
Natural resources: nickel, chrome, iron, cobalt,
manganese, silver, gold, lead, copper

People

Population: 197,361 (July 1999 est.)
Population growth rate: 1.59%
Infant mortality rate: 12.15 deaths/1,000 live
births
Life expectancy at birth: total population:
75.35 years; male: 72.1 years; female:
78.77 years
Major ethnic groups: Melanesian 42.5%,
European 37.1%, Wallisian 8.4%, Polynesian
3.8%, Indonesian 3.6%, Vietnamese 1.6%
Major religions: Roman Catholic 60%,
Protestant 30%
Major languages: French, 28 Melanesian-
Polynesian dialects

Government

Official name: Territory of New Caledonia and
Dependencies
National capital: Noumea
Independence: none (overseas territory of
France)
Legal system: the 1988 Matignon Accords grant
substantial autonomy to the islands; formerly
under French law

Economy

Industries: nickel mining and smelting
Agricultural products: vegetables; beef, other
livestock products
Currency: 1 CFP franc (CFPF) = 100 centimes

New Zealand

Geography

Location: Oceania, islands in the South Pacific
Ocean, southeast of Australia
Area: 103,737 sq. mi. (268,680 sq. km.); about
the size of Colorado
Climate: temperate with sharp regional
contrasts
Terrain: predominately mountainous with some
large coastal plains

Elevation: lowest point: Pacific Ocean 0 ft.
(0 m.); highest point: Mount Cook 12,349 ft.
(3,764 m.)
Natural resources: natural gas, iron ore, sand,
coal, timber, hydropower, gold, limestone

People

Population: 3,662,265 (July 1999 est.)
Population growth rate: 1.04%
Infant mortality rate: 6.22 deaths/1,000 live
births
Life expectancy at birth: total population:
78.82 years; male: 74.55 years; female:
81.27 years
Major ethnic groups: New Zealand European
74.5%, Maori 9.7%, other European 4.6%,
Pacific Islander 3.8%, Asian and others
7.4%
Major religions: Anglican 24%, Presbyterian
18%, Roman Catholic 15%, Methodist 5%,
Baptist 2%, other Protestant 3%
Major languages: English (official), Maori

Government

Official name: New Zealand
Government type: parliamentary democracy
National capital: Wellington
Independence: September 26, 1907 (from
U.K.)
Legal system: based on English law, with special
land legislation and land courts for Maoris

Economy

Industries: food processing, wood and paper
products, textiles, machinery, transportation
equipment, banking and insurance, tourism,
mining
Agricultural products: wheat, barley, potatoes,
pulses, fruits, vegetables; wool, meat, dairy
products; fish
Currency: 1 New Zealand dollar (NZ$) = 100
cents

Nicaragua

Geography

Location: Central America, bordering both the
Caribbean Sea and the North Pacific Ocean,
between Costa Rica and Honduras

Area: 49,998 sq. mi. (129,494 sq. km.); slightly
smaller than New York State

Climate: tropical in lowlands, cooler in highlands

Terrain: extensive Atlantic coastal plains rising
to central interior mountains; narrow Pacific
coastal plain interrupted by volcanoes

Elevation: lowest point: Pacific Ocean 0 ft.
(0 m.); highest point: Mogoton 7,999 ft.
(2,438 m.)

Natural resources: gold, silver, copper, tungsten,
lead, zinc, timber, fish

People

Population: 4,717,132 (July 1999 est.)

Population growth rate: 2.84%

Infant mortality rate: 40.47 deaths/1,000 live
births

Life expectancy at birth: total population:
67.08 years; male: 64.7 years; female:
69.56 years

Major ethnic groups: mestizo (mixed Amerindian
and white) 69%, white 17%, black 9%,
Amerindian 5%

Major religions: Roman Catholic 95%, Protestant
5%

Major languages: Spanish (official), English- and
Amerindian-speaking minorities on Atlantic
coast

Government

Official name: Republic of Nicaragua

Government type: republic

National capital: Managua

Independence: September 15, 1821 (from Spain)

Legal system: civil law system; Supreme Court
may review administrative acts

Economy

Industries: food processing, chemicals, metal
products, textiles, clothing, petroleum refining
and distribution, beverages, footwear

Agricultural products: coffee, bananas, sugarcane, cotton, rice, corn, cassava (tapioca), citrus, beans; beef, veal, pork, poultry, dairy
products

Currency: 1 gold cordoba (C$) = 100 centavos

Niger

Geography

Location: Western Africa, southeast of
Algeria

Area: 489,189 sq. mi. (1,267,000 sq. km.);
slightly less than twice the size of Texas

Climate: desert; mostly hot, dry, dusty; tropical
in extreme south

Terrain: predominately desert plains and sand
dunes; flat to rolling plains in south; hills in
north

Elevation: lowest point: Niger River 656 ft.
(200 m.); highest point: Mont Greboun
6,378 ft. (1,944 m.)

Natural resources: uranium, coal, iron ore, tin,
phosphates, gold, petroleum

People

Population: 9,962,242 (July 1999 est.)

Population growth rate: 2.95%

Infant mortality rate: 112.79 deaths/1,000 live
births

Life expectancy at birth: total population:
41.96 years; male: 42.22 years; female:
41.7 years

Major ethnic groups: Hausa 56%, Djerma 22%,
Fula 8.5%, Tuareg 8%, Beri Beri (Kanouri)
4.3%, Arab, Toubou, and Gourmantche 1.2%

Major religions: Muslim 80%, remainder indigenous beliefs and Christians

Major languages: French (official), Hausa,
Djerma

Government

Official name: Republic of Niger

Government type: republic

National capital: Niamey

Independence: August 3, 1960 (from France)

Legal system: based on French civil law system
and customary law

Economy

Industries: cement, brick, textiles, food processing, chemicals, slaughterhouses, and a few

other small light industries; uranium mining

Agricultural products: cowpeas, cotton, peanuts, millet, sorghum, cassava (tapioca), rice; cattle, sheep, goats, camels, donkeys, horses, poultry

Currency: 1 Communauté Financière Africaine franc (CFAF) = 100 centimes

Nigeria

Geography

Location: Western Africa, bordering the Gulf of Guinea, between Benin and Cameroon

Area: 356,668 sq. mi. (923,770 sq. km.); slightly more than twice the size of California

Climate: varies; equatorial in south, tropical in center, arid in north

Terrain: southern lowlands merge into central hills and plateaus; mountains in southeast, plains in north

Elevation: lowest point: Atlantic Ocean o ft. (o m.); highest point: Chappal Waddi 7,936 ft. (2,419 m.)

Natural resources: petroleum, tin, columbite, iron ore, coal, limestone, lead, zinc, natural gas

People

Population: 113,828,587 (July 1999 est.)

Population growth rate: 2.92%

Infant mortality rate: 69.46 deaths/1,000 live births

Life expectancy at birth: total population: 53.3 years; male: 52.55 years; female: 54.06 years

Major ethnic groups: Hausa, Fulani, Yoruba, Ibo, Kanuri, Ibibio, Tiv, Ijaw

Major religions: Muslim 50%, Christian 40%, indigenous beliefs 10%

Major languages: English (official), Hausa, Yoruba, Ibo, Fulani

Government

Official name: Federal Republic of Nigeria

Government type: military government

National capital: Abuja

Independence: October 1, 1960 (from U.K.)

Legal system: based on English common law, Islamic law, and tribal law

Economy

Industries: crude oil, coal, tin, columbite, palm oil, peanuts, cotton, rubber, wood, hides and skins, textiles, cement and other construction materials, food products, footwear, chemicals, fertilizer, printing, ceramics, steel

Agricultural products: cocoa, peanuts, palm oil, corn, rice, sorghum, millet, cassava (tapioca), yams, rubber; cattle, sheep, goats, pigs; fishing and forest resources extensively exploited

Currency: 1 naira (N) = 100 kobo

Niue

Geography

Location: Oceania, island in the South Pacific Ocean, east of Tonga

Area: 100 sq. mi. (260 sq. km.); 1.5 times the size of Washington, D.C.

Climate: tropical; modified by southeast trade winds

Terrain: steep limestone cliffs along coast, central plateau

Elevation: lowest point: Pacific Ocean o ft. (o m.); highest point: unnamed location near Mutalau settlement 223 ft. (68 m.)

Natural resources: fish, arable land

People

Population: 2,103 (July 1999 est.)

Population growth rate: 0.5%

Major ethnic groups: Polynesian

Major religions: Ekalesia Niue (Niuean Church) 75%-a Protestant church closely related to the London Missionary Society, Latter-Day Saints 10%, other 15%

Major languages: Polynesian closely related to Tongan and Samoan, English

Government

Official name: Niue

Government type: self-governing parliamentary democracy

National capital: Alofi

Independence: on October 19, 1974, Niue became a self-governing parliamentary government in free association with New Zealand
Legal system: English common law

Economy
Industries: tourism, handicrafts, food processing
Agricultural products: coconuts, passion fruit, honey, limes, taro, yams, cassava (tapioca), sweet potatoes; pigs, poultry, beef cattle
Currency: 1 New Zealand dollar (NZ$) = 100 cents

Norfolk Island

Geography
Location: Oceania, island in the South Pacific Ocean, east of Australia
Area: 13 sq. mi. (34.6 sq. km.); about 0.2 times the size of Washington, D.C.
Climate: subtropical, mild, little seasonal temperature variation
Terrain: volcanic formation with mostly rolling plains
Elevation: lowest point: Pacific Ocean 0 ft. (0 m.); highest point: Mount Bates 1,047 ft. (319 m.)
Natural resources: fish

People
Population: 1,905 (July 1999 est.)
Population growth rate: -0.71%
Major ethnic groups: descendants of the Bounty mutineers, Australian, New Zealander, Polynesians
Major religions: Anglican 39%, Roman Catholic 11.7%, Uniting Church in Australia 16.4%, Seventh-Day Adventist 4.4%
Major languages: English (official), Norfolk (a mixture of 18th century English and ancient Tahitian)

Government
Official name: Territory of Norfolk Island
National capital: Kingston (administrative center); Burnt Pine (commercial center)
Independence: none (territory of Australia)

Legal system: based on the laws of Australia, local ordinances and acts; English common law applies in matters not covered by either Australian or Norfolk Island law

Economy
Industries: tourism
Agricultural products: Norfolk Island pine seed, Kentia palm seed, cereals, vegetables, fruit; cattle, poultry
Currency: 1 Australian dollar ($A) = 100 cents

Northern Mariana Islands

Geography
Location: Oceania, islands in the North Pacific Ocean, about three-quarters of the way from Hawaii to the Philippines
Area: 184 sq. mi. (477 sq. km.); 2.5 times the size of Washington, D.C.
Climate: tropical marine; moderated by northeast trade winds, little seasonal temperature variation; dry season December to June, rainy season July to October
Terrain: southern islands are limestone with level terraces and fringing coral reefs; northern islands are volcanic
Elevation: lowest point: Pacific Ocean 0 ft. (0 m.); highest point: unnamed location on Agrihan 3,166 ft. (965 m.)
Natural resources: arable land, fish

People
Population: 69,398
Population growth rate: 3.99%
Infant mortality rate: 6.8 deaths/1,000 live births
Life expectancy at birth: total population: 75.36 years; male: 72.19 years; female: 78.72 years
Major ethnic groups: Chamorro, Carolinians and other Micronesians, Caucasian, Japanese, Chinese, Korean
Major religions: Christian (Roman Catholic majority, although traditional beliefs and taboos may still be found)

Major languages: English, Chamorro, Carolinian; Note—86% of population speaks a language other than English at home

Government

Official name: Commonwealth of the Northern Mariana Islands

Government type: commonwealth; self-governing with locally elected governor, lieutenant governor, and legislature

National capital: Saipan

Independence: none (commonwealth in political union with the U.S.)

Legal system: based on U.S. system except for customs, wages, immigration laws, and taxation

Economy

Industries: tourism, construction, garments, handicrafts

Agricultural products: coconuts, fruits, vegetables; cattle

Currency: 1 U.S. dollar (US$) = 100 cents

Norway

Geography

Location: Northern Europe, bordering the North Sea and the North Atlantic Ocean, west of Sweden

Area: 125,181 sq. mi. (324,220 sq. km.); slightly larger than New Mexico

Climate: temperate along coast, modified by North Atlantic Current; colder interior; rainy year-round on west coast

Terrain: glaciated; mostly high plateaus and rugged mountains broken by fertile valleys; small, scattered plains; coastline deeply indented by fjords; arctic tundra in north

Elevation: lowest point: Norwegian Sea 0 ft. (0 m.); highest point: Glittertinden 8,110 ft. (2,472 m.)

Natural resources: petroleum, copper, natural gas, pyrites, nickel, iron ore, zinc, lead, fish, timber, hydropower

People

Population: 4,438,547 (July 1999 est.)

Population growth rate: 0.4%

Infant mortality rate: 4.96 deaths/1,000 live births

Life expectancy at birth: total population: 78.36 years; male: 75.55 years; female: 81.35 years

Major ethnic groups: Germanic (Nordic, Alpine, Baltic), Lapps (Sami) 20,000

Major religions: Evangelical Lutheran 87.8% (state church), other Protestant and Roman Catholic 3.8%, none 3.2%, unknown 5.2%

Major languages: Norwegian (official); Note—small Lapp- and Finnish-speaking minorities

Government

Official name: Kingdom of Norway

Government type: constitutional monarchy

National capital: Oslo

Independence: October 26, 1905 (from Sweden)

Legal system: mixture of customary law, civil law system, and common law traditions; Supreme Court renders advisory opinions to legislature when asked

Economy

Industries: petroleum and gas, food processing, shipbuilding, pulp and paper products, metals, chemicals, timber, mining, textiles, fishing

Agricultural products: oats, other grains; beef, milk (livestock output exceeds value of crops); fish

Currency: 1 Norwegian krone (NKr) = 100 oere

Oman

Geography

Location: Middle East, bordering the Arabian Sea, Gulf of Oman, and Persian Gulf, between Yemen and United Arab Emirates

Area: 82,031 sq. mi. (212,460 sq. km.); slightly smaller than Kansas

Climate: dry desert; hot, humid along coast; hot, dry interior; strong southwest summer monsoon (May to September) in far south

Terrain: vast central desert plain, rugged mountains in north and south

Elevation: lowest point: Arabian Sea 0 ft. (0 m.); highest point: Jabal ash Sham 9,777 ft. (2,980 m.)

Natural resources: petroleum, copper, asbestos, some marble, limestone, chromium, gypsum, natural gas

People

Population: 2,446,645 (July 1999 est.)

Population growth rate: 3.45%

Infant mortality rate: 25.55 deaths/1,000 live births

Life expectancy at birth: total population: 71.3 years; male: 69.31 years; female: 73.39 years

Major ethnic groups: Arab, Baluchi, South Asian (Indian, Pakistani, Sri Lankan, Bangladeshi), African

Major religions: Ibadhi Muslim 75%, Sunni Muslim, Shi'a Muslim, Hindu

Major languages: Arabic (official), English, Baluchi, Urdu, Indian dialects

Government

Official name: Sultanate of Oman

Government type: monarchy

National capital: Muscat

Independence: 1650 (expulsion of the Portuguese)

Legal system: based on English common law and Islamic law; ultimate appeal to the sultan; has not accepted compulsory ICJ jurisdiction

Economy

Industries: crude oil production and refining, natural gas production, construction, cement, copper

Agricultural products: dates, limes, bananas, alfalfa, vegetables; camels, cattle; fish

Currency: 1 Omani rial (RO) = 1,000 baiza

Pakistan

Geography

Location: Southern Asia, bordering the Arabian Sea, between India on the east and Iran and Afghanistan on the west and China in the north

Area: 310,401 sq. mi. (803,940 sq. km.); slightly less than twice the size of Cali-fornia

Climate: mostly hot, dry desert; temperate in northwest; arctic in north

Terrain: flat Indus plain in east; mountains in north and northwest; Balochistan plateau in west

Elevation: lowest point: Indian Ocean 0 ft. (0 m.); highest point: K2 (Mt. Godwin-Austen) 28,251 ft. (8,611 m.)

Natural resources: land, extensive natural gas reserves, limited petroleum, poor quality coal, iron ore, copper, salt, limestone

People

Population: 138,123,359 (July 1999 est.)

Population growth rate: 2.18%

Infant mortality rate: 91.86 deaths/1,000 live births

Life expectancy at birth: total population: 59.38 years; male: 58.49 years; female: 60.3 years

Major ethnic groups: Punjabi, Sindhi, Pashtun (Pathan), Baloch, Muhajir

Major religions: Muslim 97% (Sunni 77%, Shi'a 20%)

Major languages: Punjabi 48%, Sindhi 12%, Siraiki (a Punjabi variant) 10%, Pashtu 8%, Urdu (official) 8%, Balochi 3%, Hindko 2%, Brahui 1%, English (official and lingua franca of Pakistani elite and most government ministries)

Government

Official name: Islamic Republic of Pakistan

Government type: federal republic

National capital: Islamabad

Independence: August 14, 1947 (from U.K.)

Legal system: based on English common law with provisions to accommodate Pakistan's status as an Islamic state

Economy

Industries: textiles, food processing, beverages, construction materials, clothing, paper products, shrimp

Agricultural products: cotton, wheat, rice, sugarcane, fruits, vegetables; milk, beef, mutton, eggs

Currency: 1 Pakistani rupee (PRe) = 100 paisa

Palau

Geography

Location: Oceania, group of islands in the North Pacific Ocean, southeast of the Philippines

Area: 177 sq. mi. (458 sq. km.); slightly more than 2.5 times the size of Washington, D.C.

Climate: wet season May to November; hot and humid

Terrain: varying geologically from the high, mountainous main island of Babelthuap to low, coral islands usually fringed by large barrier reefs

Elevation: lowest point: Pacific Ocean 0 ft. (0 m.); highest point: Mount Ngerchelchauus 794 ft. (242 m.)

Natural resources: forests, minerals (especially gold), marine products, deep-seabed minerals

People

Population: 18,467 (July 1999 est.)

Population growth rate: 1.94%

Infant mortality rate: 18.5 deaths/1,000 live births

Life expectancy at birth: total population: 67.75 years; male: 64.69 years; female: 70.98 years

Major ethnic groups: Palauans are a composite of Polynesian, Malayan, and Melanesian races

Major religions: Christian, Modekngei religion (one-third of the population observes this religion which is indigenous to Palau)

Major languages: English (official in all of Palau's 16 states), Sonsorolese (official in the state of Sonsoral), Angaur and Japanese (in the state of Anguar), Tobi (in the state of Tobi), Palauan (in the other 13 states)

Government

Official name: Republic of Palau

Government type: constitutional government in free association with the U.S.; the Compact of Free Association entered into force 1 October 1994

National capital: Koror (Note: a new capital is being built about 20 km. northeast in eastern Babelthuap)

Independence: October 1, 1994 (from the U.S.-administered UN Trusteeship)

Legal system: based on Trust Territory laws, acts of the legislature, municipal, common, and customary laws

Economy

Industries: tourism, craft items (from shell, wood, pearls), some commercial fishing and agriculture

Agricultural products: coconuts, copra, cassava (tapioca), sweet potatoes

Currency: 1 U.S. dollar (US$) = 100 cents

Panama

Geography

Location: Central America, bordering both the Caribbean Sea and the North Pacific Ocean, between Colombia and Costa Rica

Area: 30,193 sq. mi. (78,200 sq. km.); slightly smaller than South Carolina

Climate: tropical; hot, humid, cloudy; prolonged rainy season (May to January), short dry season (January to May)

Terrain: interior mostly steep, rugged mountains and dissected, upland plains; coastal areas largely plains and rolling hills

Elevation: lowest point: Pacific Ocean 0 ft. (0 m.); highest point: Volcan de Chiriqui 11,401 ft. (3,475 m.)

Natural resources: copper, mahogany forests, shrimp

Nations *(cont.)*

People

Population: 2,778,526 (July 1999 est.)

Population growth rate: 1.53%

Infant mortality rate: 23.35 deaths/1,000 live births

Life expectancy at birth: total population: 74.66 years; male: 71.91 years; female: 77.51 years

Major ethnic groups: mestizo (mixed Amerindian and white) 70%, Amerindian and mixed (West Indian) 14%, white 10%, Amerindian 6%

Major religions: Roman Catholic 85%, Protestant 15%

Major languages: Spanish (official), English 14%

Government

Official name: Republic of Panama

Government type: constitutional republic

National capital: Panama

Independence: November 3, 1903 (from Colombia; became independent from Spain November 28 , 1821)

Legal system: based on civil law system; judicial review of legislative acts in the Supreme Court of Justice

Economy

Industries: construction, petroleum refining, brewing, cement and other construction materials, sugar milling

Agricultural products: bananas, rice, corn, coffee, sugarcane, vegetables; livestock; fishing (shrimp)

Currency: 1 balboa (B) = 100 centesimos

Papua New Guinea

Geography

Location: Southeastern Asia, group of islands including the eastern half of the island of New Guinea between the Coral Sea and the South Pacific Ocean, east of Indonesia

Area: 178,703 sq. mi. (462,840 sq. km.); slightly larger than California

Climate: tropical; northwest monsoon (December to March), southeast monsoon (May to October); slight seasonal temperature variation

Terrain: mostly mountains with coastal lowlands and rolling foothills

Elevation: lowest point: Pacific Ocean 0 ft. (0 m.); highest point: Mount Wilhelm 14,793 ft. (4,509 m.)

Natural resources: gold, copper, silver, natural gas, timber, oil, fisheries

People

Population: 4,705,126 (July 1999 est.)

Population growth rate: 2.26%

Infant mortality rate: 55.58 deaths/1,000 live births

Life expectancy at birth: total population: 58.47 years; male: 57.58 years; female: 59.4 years

Major ethnic groups: Melanesian, Papuan, Negrito, Micronesian, Polynesian

Major religions: Roman Catholic 22%, Lutheran 16%, Presbyterian/Methodist/London Missionary Society 8%, Anglican 5%, Evangelical Alliance 4%, Seventh-Day Adventist 1%, other Protestant sects 10%, indigenous beliefs 34%

Major languages: English spoken by 1%–2%, pidgin English widespread, Motu spoken in Papua region; Note— 715 indigenous languages

Government

Official name: Independent State of Papua New Guinea

Government type: parliamentary democracy

National capital: Port Moresby

Independence: September 16, 1975 (from the Australian-administered UN trusteeship)

Legal system: based on English common law

Economy

Industries: copra crushing, palm oil processing, plywood production, wood chip production;

mining of gold, silver, and copper; crude oil production; construction, tourism

Agricultural products: coffee, cocoa, coconuts, palm kernels, tea, rubber, sweet potatoes, fruit, vegetables; poultry, pork

Currency: 1 kina (K) = 100 toea

Paraguay

Geography

Location: Central South America, northeast of Argentina

Area: 157,046 sq. mi. (406,750 sq. km.); slightly smaller than California

Climate: subtropical; substantial rainfall in the eastern portions, becoming semiarid in the far west

Terrain: grassy plains and wooded hills east of Rio Paraguay; Gran Chaco region west of Rio Paraguay mostly low, marshy plain near the river, and dry forest and thorny scrub elsewhere

Elevation: lowest point: junction of Rio Paraguay and Rio Parana 151 ft. (46 m.); highest point: Cerro San Rafael 2,789 ft. (850 m.)

Natural resources: hydropower, timber, iron ore, manganese, limestone

People

Population: 5,434,095 (July 1999 est.)

Population growth rate: 2.65%

Infant mortality rate: 36.35 deaths/1,000 live births

Life expectancy at birth: total population: 72.43 years; male: 70.47 years; female: 74.49 years

Major ethnic groups: mestizo (mixed Spanish and Amerindian) 95%, white plus Amerindian 5%

Major religions: Roman Catholic 90%, Mennonite and other Protestant denominations

Major languages: Spanish (official), Guarani

Government

Official name: Republic of Paraguay

Government type: republic

National capital: Asuncion

Independence: May 14, 1811 (from Spain)

Legal system: based on Argentine codes, Roman law, and French codes; judicial review of legislative acts in Supreme Court of Justice

Economy

Industries: meat packing, oilseed crushing, milling, brewing, textiles, other light consumer goods, cement, construction

Agricultural products: cotton, sugarcane, soybeans, corn, wheat, tobacco, cassava (tapioca), fruits, vegetables; beef, pork, eggs, milk; timber

Currency: 1 guarani (G) = 100 centimos

Peru

Geography

Location: Western South America, bordering the South Pacific Ocean, between Chile and Ecuador

Area: 496,223 sq. mi. (1,285,220 sq. km.); slightly smaller than Alaska

Climate: varies from tropical in east to dry desert in west

Terrain: western coastal plain (costa), high and rugged Andes in center (sierra), eastern lowland jungle of Amazon Basin (selva)

Elevation: lowest point: Pacific Ocean 0 ft. (0 m.); highest point: Nevado Huascaran 22,204 ft. (6,768 m.)

Natural resources: copper, silver, gold, petroleum, timber, fish, iron ore, coal, phosphate, potash

People

Population: 26,624,582 (July 1999 est.)

Population growth rate: 1.93%

Infant mortality rate: 38.97 deaths/1,000 live births

Life expectancy at birth: total population: 70.38 years; male: 68.08 years; female: 72.78 years

Major ethnic groups: Amerindian 45%, mestizo (mixed Amerindian and white) 37%, white 15%

Major religions: Roman Catholic

Major languages: Spanish (official), Quechua (official), Aymara

Government

Official name: Republic of Peru
Government type: republic
National capital: Lima
Independence: July 28, 1821 (from Spain)
Legal system: based on civil law system; has not accepted compulsory ICJ jurisdiction

Economy

Industries: mining of metals, petroleum, fishing, textiles, clothing, food processing, cement, auto assembly, steel, shipbuilding, metal fabrication
Agricultural products: coffee, cotton, sugarcane, rice, wheat, potatoes, plantains, coca; poultry, red meats, dairy products, wool; fish
Currency: 1 nuevo sol (S/.) = 100 centimos

Philippines

Geography

Location: Southeastern Asia, archipelago between the Philippine Sea and the South China Sea, east of Vietnam
Area: 115,830 sq. mi. (300,000 sq. km.); slightly larger than Arizona
Climate: tropical marine; northeast monsoon (November to April); southwest monsoon (May to October)
Terrain: mostly mountains with narrow to extensive coastal lowlands
Elevation: lowest point: Philippine Sea 0 ft. (0 m.); highest point: Mount Apo 9,691 ft. (2,954 m.)
Natural resources: timber, petroleum, nickel, cobalt

People

Population: 79,345,812 (July 1999 est.)
Population growth rate: 2.04%
Infant mortality rate: 33.89 deaths/1,000 live births
Life expectancy at birth: total population: 66.58 years; male: 63.79 years; female: 69.5 years
Major ethnic groups: Christian Malay 91.5%, Muslim Malay 4%, Chinese 1.5%

Major religions: Roman Catholic 83%, Protestant 9%, Muslim 5%
Major languages: Pilipino (official, based on Tagalog), English (official)

Government

Official name: Republic of the Philippines
Government type: republic
National capital: Manila
Independence: July 4, 1946 (from U.S.)
Legal system: based on Spanish and Anglo-American law

Economy

Industries: textiles, pharmaceuticals, chemicals, wood products, food processing, electronics assembly, petroleum refining, fishing
Agricultural products: rice, coconuts, corn, sugarcane, bananas, pineapples, mangoes; pork, eggs, beef; fish catch of 2 million metric tons annually
Currency: 1 Philippine peso (P) = 100 centavos

Pitcairn Islands

Geography

Location: Oceania, islands in the South Pacific Ocean, about one-half of the way from Peru to New Zealand
Area: 18 sq. mi. (47 sq. km.); about 0.3 times the size of Washington, D.C.
Climate: tropical, hot, humid, modified by southeast trade winds; rainy season (November to March)
Terrain: rugged volcanic formation; rocky coastline with cliffs
Elevation: lowest point: Pacific Ocean 0 ft. (0 m.); highest point: Pawala Valley Ridge 1,138 ft. (347 m.)
Natural resources: miro trees (used for handicrafts), fish; Note—manganese, iron, copper, gold, silver, and zinc have been discovered offshore

People

Population: 49 (July 1999 est.)
Population growth rate: −2.04%

Major ethnic groups: descendants of the Bounty
mutineers and their Tahitian wives
Major religions: Seventh-Day Adventist 100%
Major languages: English (official), Tahitian/
English dialect

Government

Official name: Pitcairn, Henderson, Ducie, and
Oeno Islands
National capital: Adamstown
Independence: none (dependent territory of the
U.K.)
Legal system: local island by-laws

Economy

Industries: postage stamps, handicrafts
Agricultural products: wide variety of fruits and
vegetables
Currency: 1 New Zealand dollar (NZ$) = 100
cents

Poland

Geography

Location: Central Europe, east of Germany
Area: 120,727 sq. mi. (312,683 sq. km.); slightly
smaller than New Mexico
Climate: temperate with cold, cloudy, moderately
severe winters with frequent precipitation;
mild summers with frequent showers and
thundershowers
Terrain: mostly flat plain; mountains along
southern border
Elevation: lowest point: Raczki Elblaskie –6 ft.
(–2 m.); highest point: Rysy 8,199 ft.
(2,499 m.)
Natural resources: coal, sulfur, copper, natural
gas, silver, lead, salt

People

Population: 38,608,929 (July 1999 est.)
Population growth rate: 0.05%
Infant mortality rate: 12.76 deaths/1,000 live
births
Life expectancy at birth: total population:
73.06 years; male: 68.93 years; female:
77.41 years
Major ethnic groups: Polish 97.6%, German
1.3%

Major religions: Roman Catholic 95%
Major languages: Polish

Government

Official name: Republic of Poland
Government type: democratic state
National capital: Warsaw
Independence: November 11, 1918 (independent
republic proclaimed)
Legal system: mixture of Continental
(Napoleonic) civil law and holdover communist legal theory; changes being gradually
introduced as part of broader democratization
process; limited judicial review of legislative
acts although under the new constitution, the
Constitutional Tribunal ruling will become
final as of October 1999; court decisions can
be appealed to the European Court of Justice
in Strasbourg

Economy

Industries: machine building, iron and steel, coal
mining, chemicals, shipbuilding, food processing, glass, beverages, textiles
Agricultural products: potatoes, milk, cheese,
fruits, vegetables, wheat; poultry and eggs;
pork, beef
Currency: 1 zloty (Zl) = 100 groszy

Portugal

Geography

Location: Southwestern Europe, bordering the
North Atlantic Ocean, west of Spain
Area: 35,672 sq. mi. (92,391 sq. km.); slightly
smaller than Indiana
Climate: maritime temperate; cool and rainy in
north, warmer and drier in south
Terrain: mountainous north of the Tagus, rolling
plains in south
Elevation: lowest point: Atlantic
Ocean 0 ft. (0 m.); highest point: Ponta do Pico
in Azores 7,713 ft. (2,351 m.)
Natural resources: fish, forests (cork), tungsten,
iron ore, uranium ore, marble

People

Population: 9,918,040 (July 1999 est.)
Population growth rate: -0.13%

Infant mortality rate: 6.73 deaths/1,000 live
births
Life expectancy at birth: total population:
75.88 years; male: 72.51 years; female:
79.46 years
Major ethnic groups: homogeneous
Mediterranean stock in mainland, Azores,
Madeira Islands; citizens
of black African descent who immigrated to
mainland during decolonization number less
than 100,000
Major religions: Roman Catholic 97%, Protestant denominations 1%, other 2%
Major languages: Portuguese

Government

Official name: Portuguese Republic
Government type: parliamentary democracy
National capital: Lisbon
Independence: 1140 (independent republic pro-
claimed October 5, 1910)
Legal system: civil law system; the Constitutional
Tribunal reviews the constitutionality of legis-
lation

Economy

Industries: textiles and footwear; wood pulp,
paper, and cork; metalworking; oil refining;
chemicals; fish canning; wine; tourism
Agricultural products: grain, potatoes, olives,
grapes; sheep, cattle, goats, poultry, meat,
dairy products
Currency: 1 Portuguese escudo (Esc) = 100 centavos

Puerto Rico

Geography

Location: Caribbean, island between the
Caribbean Sea and the North Atlantic Ocean,
east of the Dominican Republic
Area: 3,515 sq. mi. (9,104 sq. km.); slightly
less than three times the size of Rhode
Island
Climate: tropical marine, mild; little seasonal
temperature variation

Terrain: mostly mountains with coastal plain belt
in north; mountains precipitous to sea on west
coast; sandy beaches along most coastal areas
Elevation: lowest point: Caribbean Sea 0 ft.
(0 m.); highest point: Cerro de Punta 4,390 ft.
(1,338 m.)
Natural resources: some copper and nickel;
potential for onshore and offshore oil

People

Population: 3,887,652 (July 1999 est.)
Population growth rate: 0.59%
Infant mortality rate: 10.79 deaths/1,000 live
births
Life expectancy at birth: total population:
75.06 years; male: 70.95 years; female:
79.41 years
Major ethnic groups: Hispanic
Major religions: Roman Catholic 85%, Prot-
estant denominations and other 15%
Major languages: Spanish, English

Government

Official name: Commonwealth of Puerto Rico
Government type: commonwealth
National capital: San Juan
Independence: none (commonwealth associated
with the U.S.)
Legal system: based on Spanish civil code

Economy

Industries: pharmaceuticals, electronics, apparel,
food products; tourism
Agricultural products: livestock products, chickens; sugarcane, coffee, pineapples, plantains,
bananas
Currency: 1 U.S. dollar (US$) = 100 cents

Qatar

Geography

Location: Middle East, peninsula bordering the
Persian Gulf and Saudi Arabia
Area: 4,416 sq. mi. (11,437 sq. km.); slightly
smaller than Connecticut
Climate: desert; hot, dry; humid and sultry in
summer

Terrain: mostly flat and barren desert covered with loose sand and gravel

Elevation: lowest point: Persian Gulf o ft. (o m.); highest point: Qurayn Aba al Bawl 338 ft. (103 m.)

Natural resources: petroleum, natural gas, fish

People

Population: 723,542 (July 1999 est.) Note— includes 516,508 non-nationals)

Population growth rate: 3.62%

Infant mortality rate: 17.25 deaths/1,000 live births

Life expectancy at birth: total population: 74.23 years; male: 71.7 years; female: 76.89 years

Major ethnic groups: Arab 40%, Pakistani 18%, Indian 18%, Iranian 10%, other 14%

Major religions: Muslim 95%

Major languages: Arabic (official), English commonly used as a second language

Government

Official name: State of Qatar

Government type: traditional monarchy

National capital: Doha

Independence: September 3, 1971 (from U.K.)

Legal system: discretionary system of law controlled by the amir, although civil codes are being implemented; Islamic law is significant in personal matters

Economy

Industries: crude oil production and refining, fertilizers, petrochemicals, steel reinforcing bars, cement

Agricultural products: fruits, vegetables; poultry, dairy products, beef; fish

Currency: 1 Qatari riyal (QR) = 100 dirhams

Reunion

Geography

Location: Southern Africa, island in the Indian Ocean, east of Madagascar

Area: 969 sq. mi. (2,510 sq. km.); slightly smaller than Rhode Island

Climate: tropical, but temperature moderates with elevation; cool and dry from May to November, hot and rainy from November to April

Terrain: mostly rugged and mountainous; fertile lowlands along coast

Elevation: extremes: lowest point: Indian Ocean o ft. (o m.); highest point: Piton des Neiges 10,069 ft. (3,069 m.)

Natural resources: fish, arable land

People

Population: 717,723 (July 1999 est.)

Population growth rate: 1.75%

Infant mortality rate: 6.9 deaths/1,000 live births

Life expectancy at birth: total population: 75.73 years; male: 72.69 years; female: 78.93 years

Major ethnic groups: French, African, Malagasy, Chinese, Pakistani, Indian

Major religions: Roman Catholic 94%, Hindu, Islam, Buddhist

Major languages: French (official), Creole widely used

Government

Official name: Department of Reunion

National capital: Saint-Denis

Independence: none (overseas department of France)

Legal system: French law

Economy

Industries: sugar, rum, cigarettes, handicraft items, flower oil extraction

Agricultural products: sugarcane, vanilla, tobacco, tropical fruits, vegetables, corn

Currency: 1 French franc (F) = 100 centimes

Romania

Geography

Location: Southeastern Europe, bordering the Black Sea, between Bulgaria and Ukraine

Area: 91,699 sq. mi. (237,500 sq. km.); slightly smaller than Oregon

Climate: temperate; cold, cloudy winters with frequent snow and fog; sunny summers with frequent showers and thunderstorms

Terrain: central Transylvanian Basin is separated from the Plain of Moldavia on the east by the Carpathian Mountains and separated from the Walachian Plain on the south by the Transylvanian Alps

Elevation: lowest point: Black Sea 0 ft. (0 m.); highest point: Moldoveanu 8,346 ft. (2,544 m.)

Natural resources: petroleum (reserves declining), timber, natural gas, coal, iron ore, salt

People

Population: 22,334,312 (July 1999 est.)

Population growth rate: -0.23%

Infant mortality rate: 18.12 deaths/1,000 live births

Life expectancy at birth: total population: 70.83 years; male: 67.05 years; female: 74.81 years

Major ethnic groups: Romanian 89.1%, Hungarian 8.9%, Ukrainian, Serb, Croat, Russian, Turk, Gypsy 1.6%, and German 0.4%

Major religions: Romanian Orthodox 70%, Roman Catholic 6%, Protestant 6%

Major languages: Romanian, Hungarian, German

Government

Official name: Romania

Government type: republic

National capital: Bucharest

Independence: 1881 (from Turkey; republic proclaimed December 30, 1947)

Legal system: based on the Constitution of France's Fifth Republic

Economy

Industries: mining, timber, construction materials, metallurgy, chemicals, machine building, food processing, petroleum production and refining

Agricultural products: wheat, corn, sugar beets, sunflower seed, potatoes, grapes; milk, eggs, meat

Currency: 1 leu (L) = 100 bani

Russia

Geography

Location: Northern Asia (that part west of the Urals is sometimes included with Europe), bordering the Arctic Ocean, between Europe and the North Pacific Ocean

Area: 6,592,735 sq. mi. (17,075,200 sq. km.); slightly less than 1.8 times the size of the U.S.

Climate: ranges from steppes in the south through humid continental in much of European Russia; subarctic in Siberia to tundra climate in the polar north; winters vary from cool along Black Sea coast to frigid in Siberia; summers vary from warm in the steppes to cool along Arctic coast

Terrain: broad plain with low hills west of Urals; vast coniferous forest and tundra in Siberia; uplands and mountains along southern border regions

Elevation: lowest point: Caspian Sea −92 ft. (−8 m.); highest point: Mount El'brus 18,481 ft. (5,633 m.)

Natural resources: wide natural resource base including major deposits of oil, natural gas, coal, and many strategic minerals, timber note: formidable obstacles of climate, terrain, and distance hinder exploitation of natural resources

People

Population: 146,393,569 (July 1999 est.)

Population growth rate: −0.33%

Infant mortality rate: 23 deaths/1,000 live births

Life expectancy at birth: total population: 65.12 years; male: 58.83 years; female: 71.72 years

Major ethnic groups: Russian 81.5%, Tatar 3.8%, Ukrainian 3%

Major religions: Russian Orthodox, Muslim

Major languages: Russian, other

Government

Official name: Russian Federation

Government type: federation
National capital: Moscow
Independence: August 24, 1991 (from Soviet Union)
Legal system: based on civil law system; judicial review of legislative acts

Economy

Industries: complete range of mining and extractive industries producing coal, oil, gas, chemicals, and metals; all forms of machine building from rolling mills to high-performance aircraft and space vehicles; shipbuilding; road and rail transportation equipment; communications equipment; agricultural machinery, tractors, and construction equipment; electric power generating and transmitting equipment; medical and scientific instruments; consumer durables, textiles, foodstuffs, handicrafts

Agricultural products: grain, sugar beets, sunflower seed, vegetables, fruits; meat, milk

Currency: 1 ruble (R) = 100 kopeks

Rwanda

Geography

Location: Central Africa, east of Democratic Republic of the Congo

Area: 10,170 sq. mi. (26,340 sq. km.); slightly smaller than Maryland

Climate: temperate; two rainy seasons (February to April, November to January); mild in mountains with frost and snow possible

Terrain: mostly grassy uplands and hills; relief is mountainous with altitude declining from west to east

Elevation: lowest point: Rusizi River 3,117 ft. (950 m.); highest point: Volcan Karisimbi 14,826 ft. (4,519 m.)

Natural resources: gold, cassiterite (tin ore), wolframite (tungsten ore), natural gas, hydropower

People

Population: 8,154,933 (July 1999 est.)
Population growth rate: 2.43%

Infant mortality rate: 112.86 deaths/1,000 live births

Life expectancy at birth: total population: 41.31 years; male: 40.84 years; female: 41.8 years

Major ethnic groups: Hutu 80%, Tutsi 19%, Twa (Pygmoid) 1%

Major religions: Roman Catholic 65%, Protestant 9%, Muslim 1%, indigenous beliefs and other 25%

Major languages: Kinyarwanda (official) universal Bantu vernacular, French (official), English (official), Kiswahili (Swahili) used in commercial centers

Government

Official name: Rwandese Republic

Government type: republic; presidential, multiparty system

National capital: Kigali

Independence: July 1, 1962 (from Belgium-administered UN trusteeship)

Legal system: based on German and Belgian civil law systems and customary law; judicial review of legislative acts in the Supreme Court; has not accepted compulsory ICJ jurisdiction

Economy

Industries: mining of cassiterite (tin ore) and wolframite (tungsten ore), tin, cement, processing of agricultural products, small-scale beverage production, soap, furniture, shoes, plastic goods, textiles, cigarettes

Agricultural products: coffee, tea, pyrethrum (insecticide made from chrysanthemums), bananas, beans, sorghum, potatoes; livestock

Currency: 1 Rwandan franc (RF) = 100 centimes

Saint Helena

Geography

Location: islands in the South Atlantic Ocean, about mid-way between South America and Africa

Area: 158 sq. mi. (410 sq. km.); slightly more than two times the size of Washington, D.C.

Climate: Saint Helena—tropical; marine; mild, tempered by trade winds; Tristan da Cunha—temperate; marine, mild, tempered by trade winds (tends to be cooler than Saint Helena)

Terrain: Saint Helena—rugged, volcanic; small scattered plateaus and plains

Elevation: lowest point: Atlantic Ocean 0 ft. (0 m.); highest point: Queen Mary's Peak 6,758 ft. (2,060 m.)

Natural resources: fish

People

Population: 7,145 (July 1999 est.)

Population growth rate: 0.74%

Infant mortality rate: 28.98 deaths/1,000 live births

Life expectancy at birth: total population: 75.88 years; male: 72.78 years; female: 79.13 years

Major ethnic groups: African descent, white

Major religions: Anglican (majority), Baptist, Seventh-Day Adventist, Roman Catholic

Major languages: English

Government

Official name: Saint Helena

National capital: Jamestown

Independence: none (dependent territory of the U.K.)

Economy

Industries: crafts (furniture, lacework, fancy woodwork), fishing

Agricultural products: maize, potatoes, vegetables; timber production being developed; fishing, including crawfishing on Tristan da Cunha

Currency: 1 Saint Helenian pound (£S) = 100 pence

Saint Kitts and Nevis

Geography

Location: Caribbean, islands in the Caribbean Sea, about one-third of the way from Puerto Rico to Trinidad and Tobago

Area: 104 sq. mi. (269 sq. km.); 1.5 times the size of Washington, D.C.

Climate: subtropical tempered by constant sea breezes; little seasonal temperature variation; rainy season (May to November)

Terrain: volcanic with mountainous interiors

Elevation: lowest point: Caribbean Sea 0 ft. (0 m.); highest point: Mount Liamuiga 3,793 ft. (1,156 m.)

Natural resources: negligible

People

Population: 42,838 (July 1999 est.)

Population growth rate: 1.34%

Infant mortality rate: 17.39 deaths/1,000 live births

Life expectancy at birth: total population: 67.94 years; male: 64.87 years; female: 71.21 years

Major ethnic groups: black

Major religions: Anglican, other Protestant sects, Roman Catholic

Major languages: English

Government

Official name: Federation of Saint Kitts and Nevis

Government type: constitutional monarchy

National capital: Basseterre

Independence: September 19, 1983 (from U.K.)

Legal system: based on English common law

Economy

Industries: sugar processing, tourism, cotton, salt, copra, clothing, footwear, beverages

Agricultural products: sugarcane, rice, yams, vegetables, bananas; fishing potential not fully exploited

Currency: 1 East Caribbean dollar (EC$) = 100 cents

Saint Lucia

Geography

Location: Caribbean, island between the Caribbean Sea and North Atlantic Ocean, north of Trinidad and Tobago

Area: 239 sq. mi. (620 sq. km.); 3.5 times the size of Washington, D.C.

Climate: tropical, moderated by northeast trade winds; dry season from January to April, rainy season from May to August

Terrain: volcanic and mountainous with some broad, fertile valleys

Elevation: extremes: lowest point: Caribbean Sea 0 ft. (0 m.); highest point: Mount Gimie 3,117 ft. (950 m.)

Natural resources: forests, sandy beaches, minerals (pumice), mineral springs, geothermal potential

People

Population: 154,020 (July 1999 est.)

Population growth rate: 1.09%

Infant mortality rate: 16.55 deaths/1,000 live births

Life expectancy at birth: total population: 71.81 years; male: 68.14 years; female: 75.74 years

Major ethnic groups: black 90%, mixed 6%, East Indian 3%, white 1%

Major religions: Roman Catholic 90%, Protestant 7%, Anglican 3%

Major languages: English (official), French patois

Government

Official name: Saint Lucia

Government type: parliamentary democracy

National capital: Castries

Independence: February 22, 1979 (from U.K.)

Legal system: based on English common law

Economy

Industries: clothing, assembly of electronic components, beverages, corrugated cardboard boxes, tourism, lime processing, coconut processing

Agricultural products: bananas, coconuts, vegetables, citrus, root crops, cocoa

Currency: 1 East Caribbean dollar (EC$) = 100 cents

Saint Pierre and Miquelon

Geography

Location: Northern North America, islands in the North Atlantic Ocean, south of Newfoundland (Canada)

Area: 93 sq. mi. (242 sq. km.); 1.5 times the size of Washington, D.C.

Climate: cold and wet, with much mist and fog; spring and autumn are windy

Terrain: mostly barren rock

Elevation: extremes: lowest point: Atlantic Ocean 0 ft. (0 m.); highest point: Morne de la Grande Montagne 787 ft. (240 m.)

Natural resources: fish, deepwater ports

People

Population: 6,966 (July 1999 est.)

Population growth rate: 0.75%

Infant mortality rate: 8.12 deaths/1,000 live births

Life expectancy at birth: total population: 77.13 years; male: 75.58 years; female: 79 years

Major ethnic groups: Basques and Bretons (French fishermen)

Major religions: Roman Catholic 99%

Major languages: French

Government

Official name: Territorial Collectivity of Saint Pierre and

National capital: Saint-Pierre

Independence: none (territorial collectivity of France; has been under French control since 1763)

Legal system: French law with special adaptations for local conditions, such as housing and taxation

Economy

Industries: fish processing and supply base for fishing fleets; tourism

Agricultural products: vegetables; cattle, sheep, pigs; fish

Currency: 1 French franc (F) = 100 centimes

Saint Vincent and the Grenadines

Geography

Location: Caribbean, islands in the Caribbean Sea, north of Trinidad and Tobago

Area: 131 sq. mi. (340 sq. km.); twice the size of Washington, D.C.

Climate: tropical; little seasonal temperature variation; rainy season (May to November)

Terrain: volcanic, mountainous
Elevation: lowest point: Caribbean Sea 0 ft.
  (0 m.); highest point: Soufriere 4,049 ft.
  (1,234 m.)
Natural resources: negligible

People

Population: 120,519 (July 1999 est.)
Population growth rate: 0.57%
Infant mortality rate: 15.16 deaths/1,000 live
  births
Life expectancy at birth: total population:
  73.8 years; male: 72.29 years; female:
  75.36 years
Major ethnic groups: black, white, East Indian,
  Carib Amerindian
Major religions: Anglican, Methodist, Roman
  Catholic, Seventh-Day Adventist
Major languages: English, French patois

Government

Official name: Saint Vincent and the
  Grenadines
Government type: constitutional monarchy
National capital: Kingstown
Independence: 27, October 1979 (from
  U.K.)
Legal system: based on English common
  law

Economy

Industries: food processing, cement, furniture,
  clothing, starch
Agricultural products: bananas, coconuts, sweet
  potatoes, spices; small numbers of cattle,
  sheep, pigs, goats; small fish catch used locally
Currency: 1 East Caribbean dollar (EC$) = 100
  cents

Samoa

Geography

Location: Oceania, group of islands in the South
  Pacific Ocean, about one-half of the way from
  Hawaii to New Zealand
Area: 1,104 sq. mi. (2,860 sq. km.); slightly
  smaller than Rhode Island

Climate: tropical; rainy season (October to
  March), dry season (May to October)
Terrain: narrow coastal plain with volcanic,
  rocky, rugged mountains in interior
Elevation: lowest point: Pacific Ocean 0 ft.
  (0 m.); highest point: Mauga Silisili 6,092 ft.
  (1,857 m.)
Natural resources: hardwood forests, fish

People

Population: 229,979 (July 1999 est.)
Population growth rate: 2.3%
Infant mortality rate: 30.5 deaths/1,000 live
  births
Life expectancy at birth: total population:
  69.82 years; male: 67.43 years; female:
  72.33 years
Major ethnic groups: Samoan 92.6%,
  Euronesians 7% (persons of European and
  Polynesian blood)
Major religions: Christian 99.7%
Major languages: Samoan (Polynesian), English

Government

Official name: Independent State of Samoa
Government type: constitutional monarchy under
  native chief
National capital: Apia
Independence: January 1, 1962 (from New
  Zealand-administered UN trusteeship)
Legal system: based on English common law
  and local customs; judicial review of legislative
  acts with respect to fundamental rights of the
  citizen

Economy

Industries: timber, tourism, food processing,
  fishing
Agricultural products: coconuts, bananas, taro,
  yams
Currency: 1 tala (WS$) = 100 sene

San Marino

Geography

Location: Southern Europe, an enclave in central
  Italy

Area: 23 sq. mi. (60 sq. km.); about 0.3 times the size of Washington, D.C.

Climate: Mediterranean; mild to cool winters; warm, sunny summers

Terrain: rugged mountains

Elevation: lowest point: Fiume Ausa 180 ft. (55 m.); highest point: Monte Titano 2,457 ft. (749 m.)

Natural resources: building stone

People

Population: 25,061 (July 1999 est.)

Population growth rate: 0.64%

Infant mortality rate: 5.39 deaths/1,000 live births

Life expectancy at birth: total population: 81.47 years; male: 77.59 years; female: 85.35 years

Major ethnic groups: Sammarinese, Italian

Major religions: Roman Catholic

Major languages: Italian

Government

Official name: Republic of San Marino

Government type: republic

National capital: San Marino

Independence: 301 AD (by tradition)

Legal system: based on civil law system with Italian law influences

Economy

Industries: tourism, textiles, electronics, ceramics, cement, wine

Agricultural products: wheat, grapes, maize, olives; cattle, pigs, horses, meat, cheese, hides

Currency: 1 Italian lire (Lit) = 100 centesimi; note-also mints its own coins

São Tomé and Príncipe

Geography

Location: Western Africa, island in the Gulf of Guinea, straddling the Equator, west of Gabon

Area: 371 sq. mi. (960 sq. km.); more than five times the size of Washington, D.C.

Climate: tropical; hot, humid; one rainy season (October to May)

Terrain: volcanic, mountainous

Elevation: extremes: lowest point: Atlantic Ocean 0 ft. (0 m.); highest point: Pico de São Tomé 6,640 ft. (2,024 m.)

Natural resources: fish

People

Population: 154,878 (July 1999 est.)

Population growth rate: 3.14%

Infant mortality rate: 52.93 deaths/1,000 live births

Life expectancy at birth: total population: 64.71 years; male: 63.18 years; female: 66.28 years

Major ethnic groups: mestiço, angolares (descendants of Angolan slaves), forros (descendants of freed slaves), servicais (contract laborers from Angola, Mozambique, and Cape Verde), tongas (children of servicais born on the islands), Europeans (primarily Portuguese)

Major religions: Roman Catholic, Evangelical Protestant, Seventh-Day Adventist

Major languages: Portuguese (official)

Government

Official name: Democratic Republic of São Tomé and Príncipe

Government type: republic

National capital: São Tomé

Independence: July 12, 1975 (from Portugal)

Legal system: based on Portuguese legal system and customary law

Economy

Industries: light construction, textiles, soap, beer; fish processing; timber

Agricultural products: cocoa, coconuts, palm kernels, copra, cinnamon, pepper, coffee, bananas, papaya, beans; poultry; fish

Currency: 1 dobra (Db) = 100 centimos

Saudi Arabia

Geography

Location: Middle East, bordering the Persian Gulf and the Red Sea, north of Yemen

Area: 756,981 sq. mi. (1,960,582 sq. km.); slightly more than one-fifth the size of the U.S.

Climate: harsh, dry desert with great extremes of temperature

Terrain: mostly uninhabited, sandy desert

Elevation: lowest point: Persian Gulf 0 ft. (0 m.); highest point: Jabal Sawda' 10,279 ft. (3,133 m.)

Natural resources: petroleum, natural gas, iron ore, gold, copper

People

Population: 21,504,613 (July 1999 est.) (Note: includes 5,244,058 non-nationals)

Population growth rate: 3.39%

Infant mortality rate: 38.8 deaths/1,000 live births

Life expectancy at birth: total population: 70.55 years; male: 68.67 years; female: 72.53 years

Major ethnic groups: Arab 90%, Afro-Asian 10%

Major religions: Muslim 100%

Major languages: Arabic

Government

Official name: Kingdom of Saudi Arabia

Government type: monarchy

National capital: Riyadh

Independence: September 23, 1932 (unification)

Legal system: based on Islamic law, several secular codes have been introduced; commercial disputes handled by special committees; has not accepted compulsory ICJ jurisdiction

Economy

Industries: crude oil production, petroleum refining, basic petrochemicals, cement, two small steel-rolling mills, construction, fertilizer, plastics

Agricultural products: wheat, barley, tomatoes, melons, dates, citrus; mutton, chickens, eggs, milk

Currency: 1 Saudi riyal (SR) = 100 halalah

Senegal

Geography

Location: Western Africa, bordering the North Atlantic Ocean, between Guinea-Bissau and Mauritania

Area: 75,749 sq. mi. (196,190 sq. km.); slightly smaller than South Dakota

Climate: tropical; hot, humid; rainy season (May to November) has strong southeast winds; dry season (December to April) dominated by hot, dry, harmattan wind

Terrain: generally low, rolling plains rising to foothills in southeast

Elevation: lowest point: Atlantic Ocean 0 ft. (0 m.); highest point: unnamed location in the Futa Jaldon foothills 1,906 ft. (581 m.)

Natural resources: fish, phosphates, iron ore

People

Population: 10,051,930 (July 1999 est.)

Population growth rate: 3.32%

Infant mortality rate: 59.81 deaths/1,000 live births

Life expectancy at birth: total population: 57.83 years; male: 54.95 years; female: 60.78 years

Major ethnic groups: Wolof 36%, Fulani 17%, Serer 17%, Toucouleur 9%, Diola 9%, Mandingo 9%, European and Lebanese 1%

Major religions: Muslim 92%, indigenous beliefs 6%, Christian 2% (mostly Roman Catholic)

Major languages: French (official), Wolof, Pulaar, Diola, Mandingo

Government

Official name: Republic of Senegal

Government type: republic under multiparty democratic rule

National capital: Dakar

Independence: April 4, 1960 from France; complete independence was achieved upon dissolution of federation with Mali on August 20, 1960 (The Gambia and Senegal signed an agreement on December 12, 1981 that called for the creation of a loose confederation to be known as Senegambia, but the agreement was dissolved on September 30, 1989)

Legal system: based on French civil law system; judicial review of legislative acts in

Constitutional Court; the Council of State audits the government's accounting office

Economy

Industries: agricultural and fish processing, phosphate mining, fertilizer production, petroleum refining, construction materials

Agricultural products: peanuts, millet, corn, sorghum, rice, cotton, tomatoes, green vegetables; cattle, poultry, pigs; fish

Currency: 1 Communauté Financière Africaine franc (CFAF) = 100 centimes

Serbia and Montenegro

Geography

Location: Southeastern Europe, bordering the Adriatic Sea, between Albania and Bosnia and Herzegovina

Area: 39,517 sq. mi. (102,350 sq. km.); slightly smaller than Kentucky (Serbia is slightly larger than Maine; Montenegro is slightly smaller than Connecticut)

Climate: in the north, continental climate (cold winter and hot, humid summers with well distributed rainfall); central portion, continental and Mediterranean climate; to the south, Adriatic climate along the coast, hot, dry summers and autumns and relatively cold winters with heavy snowfall inland

Terrain: extremely varied; to the north, rich fertile plains; to the east, limestone ranges and basins; to the southeast, ancient mountains and hills; to the southwest, extremely high shoreline with no islands off the coast

Elevation: lowest point: Adriatic Sea 0 ft. (0 m.); highest point: Daravica 8,714 ft. (2,656 m.)

Natural resources: oil, gas, coal, antimony, copper, lead, zinc, nickel, gold, pyrite, chrome

People

Population: 11,206,847 (Montenegro 680,369; Serbia 10,526,478) (July 1999 est.)

Population growth rate: Montenegro 0.07%; Serbia 0.02%

Infant mortality rate: Montenegro 10.99 deaths/1,000 live births; Serbia 16.49 deaths/1,000 live births

Life expectancy at birth: total population: Montenegro 76.32 years; Serbia 73.45 years; male: Montenegro 72.87 years; Serbia 71.03 years; female: Montenegro 80.07 years; Serbia 76.05 years

Major ethnic groups: Serbs 63%, Albanians 14%, Montenegrins 6%, Hungarians 4%, other 13%

Major religions: Orthodox 65%, Muslim 19%, Roman Catholic 4%, Protestant 1%, other 11%

Major languages: Serbo-Croatian 95%, Albanian 5%

Government

Official name: Serbia and Montenegro (Note: Serbia and Montenegro has proclaimed itself the "Federal Republic of Yugoslavia," but the U.S. view is that the Socialist Federal Republic of Yugoslavia [SFRY] has dissolved and that none of the successor republics represents its continuation.)

Government type: republic

National capital: Belgrade (Serbia), Podgorica (Montenegro)

Independence: April 11, 1992 (Federal Republic of Yugoslavia formed as self-proclaimed successor to the Socialist Federal Republic of Yugoslavia-SFRY)

Legal system: based on civil law system

Economy

Industries: machine building (aircraft, trucks, and automobiles; tanks and weapons; electrical equipment; agricultural machinery); metallurgy (steel, aluminum, copper, lead, zinc, chromium, antimony, bismuth, cadmium); mining (coal, bauxite, nonferrous ore, iron ore, limestone); consumer goods (textiles, footwear, foodstuffs, appliances); electronics, petroleum products, chemicals, and pharmaceuticals

Agricultural products: cereals, fruits, vegetables, tobacco, olives; cattle, sheep, goats

Currency: 1 Yugoslav new dinar (YD) = 100 paras

Seychelles

Geography

Location: Eastern Africa, group of islands in the Indian Ocean, northeast of Madagascar

Area: 176 sq. mi. (455 sq. km.); 2.5 times the size of Washington, D.C.

Climate: tropical marine; humid; cooler season during southeast monsoon (late May to September); warmer season during northwest monsoon (March to May)

Terrain: Mahe Group is granitic, narrow coastal strip, rocky, hilly; others are coral, flat, elevated reefs

Elevation: extremes: lowest point: Indian Ocean 0 ft. (0 m.); highest point: Morne Seychellois 2,969 ft. (905 m.)

Natural resources: fish, copra, cinnamon trees

People

Population: 79,164 (July 1999 est.)

Population growth rate: 0.65%

Infant mortality rate: 16.65 deaths/1,000 live births

Life expectancy at birth: total population: 70.95 years; male: 66.61 years; female: 75.42 years

Major ethnic groups: Seychellois (mixture of Asians, Africans, Europeans)

Major religions: Roman Catholic 90%, Anglican 8%

Major languages: English (official), French (official), Creole

Government

Official name: Republic of Seychelles

Government type: republic

National capital: Victoria

Independence: June 29, 1976 (from U.K.)

Legal system: based on English common law, French civil law, and customary law

Economy

Industries: fishing; tourism; processing of coconuts and vanilla, coir (coconut fiber) rope, boat building, printing, furniture; beverages

Agricultural products: coconuts, cinnamon, vanilla, sweet potatoes, cassava (tapioca), bananas; broiler chickens; tuna fishing (expansion under way)

Currency: 1 Seychelles rupee (SRe) = 100 cents

Sierra Leone

Geography

Location: Western Africa, bordering the North Atlantic Ocean, between Guinea and Liberia

Area: 27,699 sq. mi. (71,740 sq. km.); slightly smaller than South Carolina

Climate: tropical; hot, humid; summer rainy season (May to December); winter dry season (December to April)

Terrain: coastal belt of mangrove swamps, wooded hill country, upland plateau, mountains in east

Elevation: lowest point: Atlantic Ocean 0 ft. (0 m.); highest point: Loma Mansa (Bintimani) 6,391 ft. (1,948 m.)

Natural resources: diamonds, titanium ore, bauxite, iron ore, gold, chromite

People

Population: 5,296,651 (July 1999 est.)

Population growth rate: 4.34%

Infant mortality rate: 126.23 deaths/1,000 live births

Life expectancy at birth: total population: 49.13 years; male: 46.07 years; female: 52.27 years

Major ethnic groups: 20 native African tribes 90% (Temne 30%, Mende 30%, other 30%), Creole 10% (descendants of freed Jamaican slaves who were settled in the Freetown area in the late-eighteenth century), refugees from Liberia's recent civil war, small numbers of Europeans, Lebanese, Pakistanis and Indians

Major religions: Muslim 60%, indigenous beliefs 30%, Christian 10%

Major languages: English (official, regular use limited to literate minority), Mende (principal vernacular in the south), Temne (principal vernacular in the north), Krio (English-based Creole, spoken by the descendents of freed Jamaican slaves who were settled in the Freetown area, a lingua franca and a first language for 10% of the population but understood by 95%)

Government

Official name: Republic of Sierra Leone
Government type: constitutional democracy
National capital: Freetown
Independence: April 27, 1961 (from U.K.)
Legal system: based on English law and customary laws indigenous to local tribes; has not accepted compulsory ICJ jurisdiction

Economy

Industries: mining (diamonds); small-scale manufacturing (beverages, textiles, cigarettes, footwear); petroleum refining
Agricultural products: rice, coffee, cocoa, palm kernels, palm oil, peanuts; poultry, cattle, sheep, pigs; fish
Currency: 1 leone (Le) = 100 cents

Singapore

Geography

Location: Southeastern Asia, islands between Malaysia and Indonesia
Area: 250 sq. mi. (647.5 sq. km.); slightly more than 3.5 times the size of Washington, D.C.
Climate: tropical; hot, humid, rainy; no pronounced rainy or dry seasons; thunderstorms occur on 40% of all days (67% of days in April)
Terrain: lowland; gently undulating central plateau contains water catchment area and nature preserve
Elevation: lowest point: Singapore Strait 0 ft. (0 m.); highest point: Bukit Timah 166 (m166 m.)
Natural resources: fish, deepwater ports

People

Population: 3,531,600 (July 1999 est.)
Population growth rate: 1.15%

Infant mortality rate: 3.84 deaths/1,000 live births
Life expectancy at birth: total population: 78.84 years; male: 75.79 years; female: 82.14 years
Major ethnic groups: Chinese 76.4%, Malay 14.9%, Indian 6.4%
Major religions: Buddhist (Chinese), Muslim (Malays), Christian, Hindu, Sikh, Taoist, Confucianist
Major languages: Chinese (official), Malay (official and national), Tamil (official), English (official)

Government

Official name: Republic of Singapore
Government type: republic within Commonwealth
National capital: Singapore
Independence: August 9, 1965 (from Malaysia)
Legal system: based on English common law

Economy

Industries: electronics, financial services, oil drilling equipment, petroleum refining, rubber processing and rubber products, processed food and beverages, ship repair, entrepot trade, biotechnology
Agricultural products: rubber, copra, fruit, vegetables; poultry
Currency: 1 Singapore dollar (S$) = 100 cents

Slovakia

Geography

Location: Central Europe, south of Poland
Area: 18,859 sq. mi. (48,845 sq. km.); about twice the size of New Hampshire
Climate: temperate; cool summers; cold, cloudy, humid winters
Terrain: rugged mountains in the central and northern part and lowlands in the south
Elevation: lowest point: Bodrok River 308 ft. (94 m.); highest point: Gerlachovka 8,711 ft. (2,655 m.)
Natural resources: brown coal and lignite; small amounts of iron ore, copper and manganese ore; salt

People
Population: 5,396,193 (July 1999 est.)
Population growth rate: 0.04%
Infant mortality rate: 9.48 deaths/1,000 live
births
Life expectancy at birth: total population:
73.46 years; male: 69.71 years; female:
77.4 years
Major ethnic groups: Slovak 85.7%, Hungarian
10.7%, Gypsy 1.5% (the 1992 census figures
underreport the Gypsy/Romany community,
which could reach 500,000 or more), Czech 1%
Major religions: Roman Catholic 60.3%, atheist
9.7%, Protestant 8.4%, Orthodox 4.1%
Major languages: Slovak (official), Hungarian

Government
Official name: Slovak Republic
Government type: parliamentary democracy
National capital: Bratislava
Independence: January 1, 1993 (from
Czechoslovakia)
Legal system: civil law system based on Austro-
Hungarian codes; legal code modified to com-
ply with the obligations of Organization on
Security and Cooperation in Europe (OSCE)
and to expunge Marxist-Leninist legal theory

Economy
Industries: metal and metal products; food and
beverages; electricity, gas, coke, oil, and
nuclear fuel; chemicals and manmade fibers;
machinery; paper and printing; earthenware
and ceramics; transport vehicles; textiles; electrical and optical apparatus; rubber products
Agricultural products: grains, potatoes, sugar
beets, hops, fruit; hogs, cattle, poultry; forest
products
Currency: 1 koruna (Sk) = 100 halierov

Slovenia

Geography
Location: Southeastern Europe, eastern Alps bor-
dering the Adriatic Sea, between Austria and
Croatia

Area: 7,821 sq. mi. (20,256 sq. km.); slightly
smaller than New Jersey
Climate: Mediterranean climate on the coast,
continental climate with mild to hot summers
and cold winters in the plateaus and valleys to
the east
Terrain: a short coastal strip on the Adriatic, an
alpine mountain region adjacent to Italy,
mixed mountain and valleys with numerous
rivers to the east
Elevation: lowest point: Adriatic Sea 0 ft. (0 m.);
highest point: Triglav 9,396 ft. (2,864 m.)
Natural resources: lignite coal, lead, zinc, mercury, uranium, silver

People
Population: 1,970,570 (July 1999 est.)
Population growth rate: −0.04%
Infant mortality rate: 5.28 deaths/1,000 live
births
Life expectancy at birth: total population:
75.36 years; male: 71.71 years; female:
79.21 years
Major ethnic groups: Slovene 91%, Croat 3%,
Serb 2%, Muslim 1%
Major religions: Roman Catholic 70.8% (includ-
ing 2% Uniate), Lutheran 1%, Muslim 1%,
atheist 4.3%
Major languages: Slovenian 91%, Serbo-
Croatian 6%

Government
Official name: Republic of Slovenia
Government type: parliamentary democratic
republic
National capital: Ljubljana
Independence: June 25, 1991 (from Yugoslavia)
Legal system: based on civil law system

Economy
Industries: ferrous metallurgy and rolling mill
products, aluminum reduction and rolled
products, lead and zinc smelting, electronics
(including military electronics), trucks, electric
power equipment, wood products, textiles,
chemicals, machine tools

Agricultural products: potatoes, hops, wheat, sugar beets, corn, grapes; cattle, sheep, poultry

Currency: 1 tolar (SIT) = 100 stotins

Solomon Islands

Geography

Location: Oceania, group of islands in the South Pacific Ocean, east of Papua New Guinea

Area: 10,985 sq. mi. (28,450 sq. km.); slightly smaller than Maryland

Climate: tropical monsoon; few extremes of temperature and weather

Terrain: mostly rugged mountains with some low coral atolls

Elevation: lowest point: Pacific Ocean 0 ft. (0 m.); highest point: Mount Makarakomburu 8,028 ft. (2,447 m.)

Natural resources: fish, forests, gold, bauxite, phosphates, lead, zinc, nickel

People

Population: 455,429 (July 1999 est.)

Population growth rate: 3.18%

Infant mortality rate: 23 deaths/1,000 live births

Life expectancy at birth: total population: 72.09 years; male: 69.55 years; female: 74.75 years

Major ethnic groups: Melanesian 93%, Polynesian 4%, Micronesian 1.5%

Major religions: Anglican 34%, Roman Catholic 19%, Baptist 17%, United (Methodist/Presbyterian) 11%, Seventh-Day Adventist 10%, other Protestant 5%, traditional beliefs 4%

Major languages: Melanesian pidgin in much of the country, English spoken by 1% of population; Note—120 indigenous languages

Government

Official name: Solomon Islands

Government type: parliamentary democracy

National capital: Honiara

Independence: July 7, 1978 (from U.K.)

Legal system: English common law

Economy

Industries: copra, fish (tuna)

Agricultural products: cocoa, beans, coconuts, palm kernels, rice, potatoes, vegetables, fruit; cattle, pigs; timber; fish

Currency: 1 Solomon Islands dollar (SI$) = 100 cents

Somalia

Geography

Location: Eastern Africa, bordering the Gulf of Aden and the Indian Ocean, east of Ethiopia

Area: 246,201 sq. mi. (637,660 sq. km.); slightly smaller than Texas

Climate: principally desert; December to February—northeast monsoon, moderate —temperatures in north and very hot in south; May to October—southwest monsoon, torrid in the north and hot in the south, irregular rainfall, hot and humid periods (tangambili) between monsoons

Terrain: mostly flat to undulating plateau rising to hills in north

Elevation: lowest point: Indian Ocean 0 ft. (0 m.); highest point: Shimbiris 8,038 ft. (2,450 m.)

Natural resources: uranium and largely unexploited reserves of iron ore, tin, gypsum, bauxite, copper, salt

People

Population: 7,140,643 (July 1999 est.)

Population growth rate: 4.13%

Infant mortality rate: 125.77 deaths/1,000 live births

Life expectancy at birth: total population: 46.23 years; male: 44.66 years; female: 47.85 years

Major ethnic groups: Somali 85%, Bantu, Arabs 30,000

Major religions: Sunni Muslim

Major languages: Somali (official), Arabic, Italian

Government

Official name: Somalia

Government type: none

National capital: Mogadishu

Independence: July 1, 1960 (from a merger of British Somaliland, which became independent from the U.K. on June 26, 1960, and Italian Somaliland, which became independent from the Italian-administered UN trusteeship on July 1, 1960, to form the Somali Republic)

Economy

Industries: a few small industries, including sugar refining, textiles, petroleum refining (mostly shut down)

Agricultural products: bananas, sorghum, corn, sugarcane, mangoes, sesame seeds, beans; cattle, sheep, goats; fishing potential largely unexploited

Currency: 1 Somali shilling (So. Sh.) = 100 cents

South Africa

Geography

Location: Southern Africa, at the southern tip of the continent of Africa

Area: 471,008 sq. mi. (1,219,912 sq. km.); slightly less than twice the size of Texas

Climate: mostly semiarid; subtropical along east coast; sunny days, cool nights

Terrain: vast interior plateau rimmed by rugged hills and narrow coastal plain

Elevation: lowest point: Atlantic Ocean 0 ft. (0 m.); highest point: Njesuthi 11,181 ft. (3,408 m.)

Natural resources: gold, chromium, antimony, coal, iron ore, manganese, nickel, phosphates, tin, uranium, gem diamonds, platinum, copper, vanadium, salt, natural gas

People

Population: 43,426,386 (July 1999 est.)

Population growth rate: 1.32%

Infant mortality rate: 51.99 deaths/1,000 live births

Life expectancy at birth: total population: 54.76 years; male: 52.68 years; female: 56.9 years

Major ethnic groups: black 75.2%, white 13.6%, Colored 8.6%, Indian 2.6%

Major religions: Christian 68% (includes most whites and Coloreds, about 60% of blacks and about 40% of Indians), Muslim 2%, Hindu 1.5% (60% of Indians), traditional and animistic 28.5%

Major languages: 11 official languages, including Afrikaans, English, Ndebele, Pedi, Sotho, Swazi, Tsonga, Tswana, Venda, Xhosa, Zulu

Government

Official name: Republic of South Africa

Government type: republic

National capital: Pretoria (administrative); Cape Town (legislative); Bloemfontein (judicial)

Independence: May 31, 1910 (from U.K.)

Legal system: based on Roman-Dutch law and English common law

Economy

Industries: mining (world's largest producer of platinum, gold, chromium), automobile assembly, metalworking, machinery, textile, iron and steel, chemical, fertilizer, foodstuffs

Agricultural products: corn, wheat, sugarcane, fruits, vegetables, beef, poultry, mutton, wool, dairy products

Currency: 1 rand (R) = 100 cents

Spain

Geography

Location: Southwestern Europe, bordering the Bay of Biscay, Mediterranean Sea, North Atlantic Ocean, and Pyrenees Mountains, southwest of France

Area: 194,884 sq. mi. (504,750 sq. km.); slightly more than twice the size of Oregon

Climate: temperate; clear, hot summers in interior, more moderate and cloudy along coast; cloudy, cold winters in interior, partly cloudy and cool along coast

Terrain: large, flat to dissected plateau surrounded by rugged hills; Pyrenees in north

Elevation: lowest point: Atlantic Ocean 0 ft. (0 m.); highest point: Pico de Teide on Canary Islands 12,198 ft. (3,718 m.)

Natural resources: coal, lignite, iron ore, uranium, mercury, pyrites, fluorspar, gypsum, zinc, lead, tungsten, copper, kaolin, potash, hydropower

People

Population: 39,167,744 (July 1999 est.)

Population growth rate: 0.1%

Infant mortality rate: 6.41 deaths/1,000 live births

Life expectancy at birth: total population: 77.71 years; male: 73.97 years; female: 81.71 years

Major ethnic groups: composite of Mediterranean and Nordic types

Major religions: Roman Catholic 99%

Major languages: Castilian Spanish 74%, Catalan 17%, Galician 7%, Basque 2%

Government

Official name: Kingdom of Spain

Government type: parliamentary monarchy

National capital: Madrid

Independence: 1492 (expulsion of the Moors and unification)

Legal system: civil law system, with regional applications

Economy

Industries: textiles and apparel (including footwear), food and beverages, metals and metal manufactures, chemicals, shipbuilding, automobiles, machine tools, tourism

Agricultural products: grain, vegetables, olives, wine grapes, sugar beets, citrus; beef, pork, poultry, dairy products; fish

Currency: 1 peseta (Pta) = 100 centimos

Sri Lanka

Geography

Location: Southern Asia, island in the Indian Ocean, south of India

Area: 25,332 sq. mi. (65,610 sq. km.); slightly larger than West Virginia

Climate: tropical monsoon; northeast monsoon (December to March); southwest monsoon (June to October)

Terrain: mostly low, flat to rolling plain; mountains in south-central interior

Elevation: lowest point: Indian Ocean 0 ft. (0 m.); highest point: Pidurutalagala 8,281 ft. (2,524 m.)

Natural resources: limestone, graphite, mineral sands, gems, phosphates, clay

People

Population: 19,144,875 (July 1999 est.)

Population growth rate: 1.1%

Infant mortality rate: 16.12 deaths/1,000 live births

Life expectancy at birth: total population: 72.67 years; male: 69.89 years; female: 75.59 years

Major ethnic groups: Sinhalese 74%, Tamil 18%, Moor 7%, Burgher, Malay, and Vedda 1%

Major religions: Buddhist 69%, Hindu 15%, Christian 8%, Muslim 8%

Major languages: Sinhala (official and national language) 74%, Tamil (national language) 18%; Note—English is commonly used in government and is spoken by about 10% of the population

Government

Official name: Democratic Socialist Republic of Sri Lanka

Government type: republic

National capital: Colombo

Independence: February 4, 1948 (from U.K.)

Legal system: a highly complex mixture of English common law, Roman-Dutch, Muslim, Sinhalese, and customary law

Economy

Industries: processing of rubber, tea, coconuts, and other agricultural commodities; clothing, cement, petroleum refining, textiles, tobacco

Agricultural products: rice, sugarcane, grains, pulses, oilseed, roots, spices, tea, rubber, coconuts; milk, eggs, hides, meat

Currency: 1 Sri Lankan rupee (SLRe) = 100 cents

Sudan

Geography

Location: Northern Africa, bordering the Red
Sea, between Egypt and Eritrea

Area: 967,493 sq. mi. (2,505,810 sq. km.);
slightly more than one-quarter the size of the
U.S.

Climate: tropical in south; arid desert in north;
rainy season (April to October)

Terrain: generally flat, featureless plain; mountains in east and west

Elevation: lowest point: Red Sea 0 ft. (0 m.);
highest point: Kinyeti 10,456 ft. (3,187 m.)

Natural resources: petroleum; small reserves of
iron ore, copper, chromium ore, zinc, tungsten, mica, silver, gold

People

Population: 34,475,690 (July 1999 est.)

Population growth rate: 2.71%

Infant mortality rate: 72.94 deaths/1,000 live
births

Life expectancy at birth: total population:
56.4 years; male: 55.41 years; female:
57.44 years

Major ethnic groups: black 52%, Arab 39%,
Beja 6%

Major religions: Sunni Muslim 70% (in north),
indigenous beliefs 25%, Christian 5% (mostly
in south and Khartoum)

Major languages: Arabic (official), Nubian, Ta
Bedawie, diverse dialects of Nilotic, Nilo-
Hamitic, Sudanic languages

Government

Official name: Republic of the Sudan

Government type: transitional—previously ruling
military junta; presidential and National
Assembly elections held in March 1996; new
constitution drafted by Presidential
Committee, went before public in national ref-
erendum in May-June 1998

National capital: Khartoum

Independence: January 1, 1956 (from Egypt and
U.K.)

Legal system: based on English common law
and Islamic law; as of January 20, 1991, the
now defunct Revolutionary Command
Council imposed Islamic law in the northern
states; Islamic law applies to all residents
of the northern states regardless of their religion; some separate religious courts

Economy

Industries: cotton ginning, textiles, cement, edi-
ble oils, sugar, soap distilling, shoes, petroleum refining

Agricultural products: cotton, groundnuts,
sorghum, millet, wheat, gum arabic, sesame;
sheep

Currency: 1 Sudanese pound (£Sd) = 100
piastres

Suriname

Geography

Location: Northern South America, bordering
the North Atlantic
Ocean, between French Guiana and Guyana

Area: 63,039 sq. mi. (163,270 sq. km.); slightly
larger than Georgia

Climate: tropical; moderated by trade winds

Terrain: mostly rolling hills; narrow coastal plain
with swamps

Elevation: lowest point: unnamed location in
the coastal plain –6 ft. (–2 m.); highest
point: Wilhelmina Gebergte 4,219 ft.
(1,286 m.)

Natural resources: timber, hydropower potential,
fish, kaolin, shrimp, bauxite, gold, and small
amounts of nickel, copper, platinum, iron
ore

People

Population: 431,156 (July 1999 est.)

Population growth rate: 0.71%

Infant mortality rate: 26.52 deaths/1,000 live
births

Life expectancy at birth: total population:
70.89 years; male: 68.32 years; female:
73.59 years

Major ethnic groups: Hindustani (also known locally as "East Indians") 37%, Creole (mixed white and black) 31%, Javanese 15.3%, "Maroons" (their African ancestors were brought to the country in the 17th and 18th centuries as slaves and escaped to the interior) 10.3%, Amerindian 2.6%, Chinese 1.7%, white 1%

Major religions: Hindu 27.4%, Muslim 19.6%, Roman Catholic 22.8%, Protestant 25.2% (predominantly Moravian), indigenous beliefs 5%

Major languages: Dutch (official), English (widely spoken), Sranang Tongo (Surinamese, sometimes called Taki-Taki, is native language of Creoles and much of the younger population and is lingua franca among others), Hindustani (a dialect of Hindi), Javanese

Government

Official name: Republic of Suriname
Government type: republic
National capital: Paramaribo
Independence: November 25, 1975 (from Netherlands)
Legal system: based on Dutch legal system incorporating French penal theory

Economy

Industries: bauxite and gold mining, alumina and aluminum produc-tion, lumbering, food processing, fishing
Agricultural products: paddy rice, bananas, palm kernels, coconuts, plantains, peanuts; beef, chicken; forest products and shrimp of increasing importance
Currency: 1 Surinamese guilder, gulden, or florin (Sf.) = 100 cents

Svalbard

Geography

Location: Northern Europe, islands between the Arctic Ocean, Barents Sea, Greenland Sea, and Norwegian Sea, north of Norway
Area: 23,957 sq. mi. (62,049 sq. km.); slightly smaller than West Virginia

Climate: arctic, tempered by warm North Atlantic Current; cool summers, cold winters; North Atlantic Current flows along west and north coasts of Spitsbergen, keeping water open and navigable most of the year
Terrain: wild, rugged mountains; much of high land ice covered; west coast clear of ice about one-half of the year; fjords along west and north coasts
Elevation: lowest point: Arctic Ocean 0 ft. (0 m.); highest point: Newtontoppen 5,633 ft. (1,717 m.)
Natural resources: coal, copper, iron ore, phosphate, zinc, wildlife, fish

People

Population: 2,503 (July 1999 est.)
Population growth rate: −3.55%
Major ethnic groups: Russian and Ukrainian 62%, Norwegian 38%
Major languages: Russian, Norwegian

Government

Official name: Svalbard (sometimes referred to as Spitzbergen)
National capital: Longyearbyen
Independence: none (territory of Norway)

Economy

Industries: Coal mining.
Agricultural products: none
Currency: 1 Norwegian krone (NKr) = 100 oere

Swaziland

Geography

Location: Southern Africa, between Mozambique and South Africa
Area: 6,703 sq. mi. (17,360 sq. km.); slightly smaller than New Jersey
Climate: varies from tropical to near temperate
Terrain: mostly mountains and hills; some moderately sloping plains
Elevation: lowest point: Great Usutu River 69 ft. (21 m.); highest point: Emlembe 6,109 ft. (1,862 m.)

Natural resources: asbestos, coal, clay, cassiterite, hydropower, forests, small gold and diamond deposits, quarry stone, and talc

People
Population: 985,335 (July 1999 est.)
Population growth rate: 1.91%
Infant mortality rate: 101.87 deaths/1,000 live births
Life expectancy at birth: total population: 38.11 years; male: 36.86 years; female: 39.4 years
Major ethnic groups: African 97%, European 3%
Major religions: Christian 60%, indigenous beliefs 40%
Major languages: English (official, government business conducted in English), siSwati (official)

Government
Official name: Kingdom of Swaziland
Government type: monarchy; independent member of Commonwealth
National capital: Mbabane (administrative); Lobamba (legislative)
Independence: September 6, 1968 (from U.K.)
Legal system: based on South African Roman-Dutch law in statutory courts and Swazi traditional law and custom in traditional courts; has not accepted compulsory ICJ jurisdiction

Economy
Industries: mining (coal and asbestos), wood pulp, sugar, soft drink concentrates
Agricultural products: sugarcane, cotton, maize, tobacco, rice, citrus, pineapples, corn, sorghum, peanuts; cattle, goats, sheep
Currency: 1 lilangeni (E) = 100 cents

Sweden

Geography
Location: Northern Europe, bordering the Baltic Sea, Gulf of Bothnia, Kattegat, and Skagerrak, between Finland and Norway

Area: 173,731 sq. mi. (449,964 sq. km.); slightly larger than California
Climate: temperate in south with cold, cloudy winters and cool, partly cloudy summers; sub-arctic in north
Terrain: mostly flat or gently rolling lowlands; mountains in west
Elevation: lowest point: Baltic Sea 0 ft. (0 m.); highest point: Kebnekaise 6,926 ft. (2,111 m.)
Natural resources: zinc, iron ore, lead, copper, silver, timber, uranium, hydropower potential

People
Population: 8,911,296 (July 1999 est.)
Population growth rate: 0.29%
Infant mortality rate: 3.91 deaths/1,000 live births
Life expectancy at birth: total population: 79.29 years; male: 76.61 years; female: 82.11 years
Major ethnic groups: white, Lapp (Sami), foreign-born or first-generation immigrants 12% (Finns, Yugoslavs, Danes, Norwegians, Greeks, Turks)
Major religions: Evangelical Lutheran 94%, Roman Catholic 1.5%, Pentecostal 1%
Major languages: Swedish (Note: small Lapp- and Finnish-speaking minorities exist)

Government
Official name: Kingdom of Sweden
Government type: constitutional monarchy
National capital: Stockholm
Independence: June 6, 1523, Gustav Vasa was elected king; June 6, 1809, a constitutional monarchy was established
Legal system: civil law system influenced by customary law

Economy
Industries: iron and steel, precision equipment (bearings, radio and telephone parts, armaments), wood pulp and paper products, processed foods, motor vehicles

Agricultural products: grains, sugar beets, potatoes; meat, milk
Currency: 1 Swedish krona (SKr) = 100 oere

Switzerland

Geography
Location: Central Europe, east of France, north
of Italy
Area: 15,942 sq. mi. (41,290 sq. km.); slightly
less than twice the size of New Jersey
Climate: temperate, but varies with altitude; cold,
cloudy, rainy/snowy winters; cool to warm,
cloudy, humid summers with occasional
showers
Terrain: mostly mountains (Alps in south, Jura
in northwest) with a central plateau of rolling
hills, plains, and large lakes
Elevation: lowest point: Lake Maggiore 640 ft.
(195 m.); highest point: Dufourspitze 15,203 ft.
(4,634 m.)
Natural resources: hydropower potential, timber,
salt

People
Population: 7,275,467 (July 1999 est.)
Population growth rate: 0.2%
Infant mortality rate: 4.87 deaths/1,000 live
births
Life expectancy at birth: total population:
78.99 years; male: 75.83 years; female:
82.32 years
Major ethnic groups: German 65%, French 18%,
Italian 10%, Romansch 1%, other 6% (Note:
Swiss nationals are German 74%, French
20%, Italian 4%, Romansch 1%)
Major religions: Roman Catholic 46.1%,
Protestant 40%
Major languages: German 63.7%, French 19.2%,
Italian 7.6%, Romansch 0.6%

Government
Official name: Swiss Confederation
Government type: federal republic
National capital: Bern
Independence: August 1, 1291
Legal system: civil law system influenced by cus-
tomary law; judicial review of legislative acts,
except with respect to federal decrees of gen-
eral obligatory character

Economy
Industries: machinery, chemicals, watches, textiles, precision instruments
Agricultural products: grains, fruits, vegetables;
meat, eggs
Currency: 1 Swiss franc, franken, or franco (SFR)
= 100 centimes, rappen, or centesimi

Syria

Geography
Location: Middle East, bordering the
Mediterranean Sea, between Lebanon and
Turkey
Area: 71,498 sq. mi. (185,180 sq. km.); slightly
larger than North Dakota
Climate: mostly desert; hot, dry, sunny
summers (June to August) and mild, rainy
winters (December to February) along coast;
cold weather with snow or sleet periodically
hitting Damascus
Terrain: primarily semiarid and desert plateau; narrow coastal plain; mountains in
west
Elevation: lowest point: unnamed location
near Lake Tiberias −656 ft. (−200 m.);
highest point: Mount Hermon 9,232 ft.
(2,814 m.)
Natural resources: petroleum, phosphates,
chrome and manganese ores, asphalt, iron ore,
rock salt, marble, gypsum

People
Population: 17,213,871 (July 1999 est.)
Population growth rate: 3.15%
Infant mortality rate: 36.42 deaths/1,000 live
births
Life expectancy at birth: total population:
68.09 years; male: 66.75 years; female:
69.48 years
Major ethnic groups: Arab 90.3%, Kurds,
Armenians
Major religions: Sunni Muslim 74%, Alawite,
Druze, and other Muslim sects 16%, Christian
(various sects) 10%

Major languages: Arabic (official); Kurdish, Armenian, Aramaic, Circassian widely understood

Government

Official name: Syrian Arab Republic

Government type: republic under military regime since March 1963

National capital: Damascus

Independence: April 17,1946 (from League of Nations mandate under French administration)

Legal system: based on Islamic law and civil law system; special religious courts

Economy

Industries: petroleum, textiles, food processing, beverages, tobacco, phosphate rock mining

Agricultural products: wheat, barley, cotton, lentils, chickpeas; beef, lamb, eggs, poultry, milk

Currency: 1 Syrian pound (£S) = 100 piastres

Taiwan

Geography

Location: Eastern Asia, islands bordering the East China Sea, Philippine Sea, South China Sea, and Taiwan Strait, north of the Philippines, off the southeastern coast of China

Area: 13,892 sq. mi. (35,980 sq. km.); slightly smaller than Maryland and Delaware combined

Climate: tropical; marine; rainy season during southwest monsoon (June to August); cloudiness is persistent and extensive all year

Terrain: eastern two-thirds mostly rugged mountains; flat to gently rolling plains in west

Elevation: lowest point: South China Sea o ft. (o m.); highest point: Yu Shan 13,113 ft. (3,997 m.)

Natural resources: small deposits of coal, natural gas, limestone, marble, and asbestos

People

Population: 22,113,250 (July 1999 est.)

Population growth rate: 0.94%

Infant mortality rate: 6.34 deaths/1,000 live births

Life expectancy at birth: total population: 76.82 years; male: 73.82 years; female: 80.05 years

Major ethnic groups: Taiwanese (including Hakka) 84%, mainland Chinese 14%, aborigine 2%

Major religions: mixture of Buddhist, Confucian, and Taoist 93%, Christian 4.5%

Major languages: Mandarin Chinese (official), Taiwanese (Min), Hakka dialects

Government

Official name: Taiwan

Government type: multiparty democratic regime headed by popularly elected president

National capital: Taipei

Independence: constitution adopted January 1, 1947 (status in relation to China still in dispute)

Legal system: based on civil law system

Economy

Industries: electronics, petroleum refining, chemicals, textiles, iron and steel, machinery, cement, food processing

Agricultural products: rice, corn, vegetables, fruit, tea; pigs, poultry, beef, milk; fish

Currency: 1 New Taiwan dollar (NT$) = 100 cents

Tajikistan

Geography

Location: Central Asia, west of China

Area: 88,722 sq. mi. (143,100 sq. km.); slightly smaller than Wisconsin

Climate: mid-latitude continental, hot summers, mild winters; semiarid to polar in Pamir Mountains

Terrain: Pamirs and Alay Mountains dominate landscape; western Fergana Valley in north, Kofarnihon and Vakhsh Valleys in southwest

Elevation: lowest point: Syrdariya 984 ft. (300 m.); highest point: Qullai Kommunizm 24,590 ft. (7,495 m.)

Natural resources: significant hydropower potential, some petroleum, uranium, mercury, brown coal, lead, zinc, antimony, tungsten

People

Population: 6,102,854 (July 1999 est.)

Population growth rate: 1.3%

Infant mortality rate: 112.14 deaths/1,000 live births

Life expectancy at birth: total population: 64.48 years; male: 61.35 years; female: 67.77 years

Major ethnic groups: Tajik 64.9%, Uzbek 25%, Russian 3.5% (declining because of emigration)

Major religions: Sunni Muslim 80%, Shi'a Muslim 5%

Major languages: Tajik (official), Russian widely used in government and business

Government

Official name: Republic of Tajikistan

Government type: republic

National capital: Dushanbe

Independence: September 9, 1991 (from Soviet Union)

Legal system: based on civil law system; no judicial review of legislative acts

Economy

Industries: aluminum, zinc, lead, chemicals and fertilizers, cement, vegetable oil, metal-cutting machine tools, refrigerators and freezers

Agricultural products: cotton, grain, fruits, grapes, vegetables; cattle, sheep, goats

Currency: Tajikistani ruble (TJR) = 100 tanga

Tanzania

Geography

Location: Eastern Africa, bordering the Indian Ocean, between Kenya and Mozambique

Area: 364,899 sq. mi.(945,090 sq. km.), slightly larger than twice the size of California

Climate: varies from tropical along coast to temperate in highlands

Terrain: plains along coast; central plateau; highlands in north, south

Elevation: lowest point: Indian Ocean 0 ft. (0 m.); highest point: Kilimanjaro 19,340 ft. (5,895 m.)

Natural resources: hydropower potential, tin, phosphates, iron ore, coal, diamonds, gemstones, gold, natural gas, nickel

People

Population: 31,270,820 (July 1999 est.)

Population growth rate: 2.14%

Infant mortality rate: 96.94 deaths/1,000 live births

Life expectancy at birth: total population: 46.37 years; male: 44.22 years; female: 48.59 years

Major ethnic groups: mainland-native African 99% (95% Bantu from more than 130 tribes), other 1% (Asian, European, Arab). Zanzibar: Arab, native African, mixed Arab-native African

Major religions: Christian 45%, Muslim 35%, indigenous beliefs 20%. Zanzibar: more than 99% Muslim

Major languages: Kiswahili or Swahili (official), Kiunguju (name for Swahili in Zanzibar), English (official, primary language of commerce, administration, and higher education), Arabic (widely spoken in Zanzibar), many local languages

Government

Official name: United Republic of Tanzania

Government type: republic

National capital: Dar es Salaam (some government offices have been transferred to Dodoma, which is planned as the new national capital; the National Assembly now meets there on regular basis)

Independence: April 26, 1964; Tanganyika became independent December 9, 1961 (from U.K.-administered UN trusteeship); Zanzibar became independent December 19, 1963

(from U.K.); Tanganyika united with Zanzibar April 26, 1964 to form the United Republic of Tanganyika and Zanzibar; renamed United Republic of Tanzania October 29, 1964

Legal system: based on English common law; judicial review of legislative acts limited to matters of interpretation

Economy

Industries: primarily agricultural processing (sugar, beer, cigarettes, sisal twine), diamond and gold mining, oil refining, shoes, cement, textiles, wood products, fertilizer, salt

Agricultural products: coffee, sisal, tea, cotton, pyrethrum (insecticide made from chrysanthemums), cashews, tobacco, cloves (Zanzibar), corn, wheat, cassava (tapioca), bananas, fruits, vegetables; cattle, sheep, goats

Currency: 1 Tanzanian shilling (TSh) = 100 cents

Thailand

Geography

Location: Southeastern Asia, border-
ing the Andaman Sea and the Gulf of Thailand, southeast of Burma

Area: 198,455 sq. mi. (514,000 sq. km.); slightly more than twice the size of Wyoming

Climate: tropical; rainy, warm, cloudy southwest monsoon (mid-May to September); dry, cool northeast monsoon (November to mid-March); southern isthmus always hot and humid

Terrain: central plain; Khorat Plateau in the east; mountains elsewhere

Elevation: lowest point: Gulf of Thailand 0 ft. (0 m.); highest point: Doi Inthanon 8,451 ft. (2,576 m.)

Natural resources: tin, rubber, natural gas, tungsten, tantalum, timber, lead, fish, gypsum, lignite, fluorite

People

Population: 60,609,046 (July 1999 est.)

Population growth rate: 0.93%

Infant mortality rate: 29.54 deaths/1,000 live births

Life expectancy at birth: total population: 69.21 years; male: 65.58 years; female: 72.01 years

Major ethnic groups: Thai 75%, Chinese 14%

Major religions: Buddhism 95%, Muslim 3.8%

Major languages: Thai, English (secondary language of the elite), ethnic and regional dialects

Government

Official name: Kingdom of Thailand

Government type: constitutional monarchy

National capital: Bangkok

Independence: 1238 (traditional founding date; never colonized)

Legal system: based on civil law system, with influences of common law; has not accepted compulsory ICJ jurisdiction

Economy

Industries: tourism; textiles and garments, agricultural processing, beverages, tobacco, cement, light manufacturing, such as jewelry; electric appliances and components, computers and parts, integrated circuits, furniture, plastics; world's second-largest tungsten producer and third-largest tin producer

Agricultural products: rice, cassava (tapioca), rubber, corn, sugarcane, coconuts, soybeans

Currency: 1 baht (B) = 100 satang

Togo

Geography

Location: Western Africa, bordering the Bight of Benin, between Benin and Ghana

Area: 21,927 sq. mi. (56,790 sq. km.); slightly smaller than West Virginia

Climate: tropical; hot, humid in south; semiarid in north

Terrain: gently rolling savanna in north; central
hills; southern plateau; low coastal plain with
extensive lagoons and marshes
Elevation: lowest point: Atlantic Ocean 0 ft.
(0 m.); highest point: Pic Agou 3,235 ft.
(986 m.)
Natural resources: phosphates, limestone,
marble

People

Population: 5,081,413 (July 1999 est.)
Population growth rate: 3.51%
Infant mortality rate: 77.55 deaths/1,000 live
births
Life expectancy at birth: total population:
59.25 years; male: 56.93 years; female:
61.64 years
Major ethnic groups: native African 99% (37
tribes; largest and most important are Ewe,
Mina, and Kabre)
Major religions: indigenous beliefs 70%,
Christian 20%, Muslim 10%
Major languages: French (official and the
language of commerce), Ewe and Mina (the
two major African languages in the south),
Kabye (sometimes spelled Kabiye) and
Dagomba (the two major African languages
in the north)

Government

Official name: Togolese Republic
Government type: republic under transition to
multiparty democratic rule
National capital: Lome
Independence: April 27, 1960 (from French-
administered UN trusteeship)
Legal system: French-based court system

Economy

Industries: phosphate mining, agricultural
processing, cement; handicrafts, textiles,
beverages
Agricultural products: coffee, cocoa, cotton,
yams, cassava (tapioca), corn, beans, rice, millet, sorghum; meat; fish
Currency: 1 Communauté Financière Africaine
franc (CFAF) = 100 centimes

Tonga

Geography

Location: Oceania, archipelago in the South
Pacific Ocean, about two-thirds of the way
from Hawaii to New Zealand
Area: 289 sq. mi. (748 sq. km.); four times the
size of Washington, D.C.
Climate: tropical; modified by trade winds; warm
season (December to May), cool season (May
to December)
Terrain: most islands have limestone base
formed from uplifted coral formation;
others have limestone overlying volcanic
base
Elevation: lowest point: Pacific Ocean 0 ft.
(0 m.); highest point: unnamed location on
Kao Island 3,389 ft. (1,033 m.)
Natural resources: fish, fertile soil

People

Population: 109,082 (July 1999 est.)
Population growth rate: 0.8%
Infant mortality rate: 37.93 deaths/1,000 live
births
Life expectancy at birth: total population:
69.78 years; male: 67.73 years; female:
72.22 years
Major ethnic groups: Polynesian, Europeans
about 300
Major religions: Christian
Major languages: Tongan, English

Government

Official name: Kingdom of Tonga
Government type: hereditary constitutional
monarchy
National capital: Nuku'alofa
Independence: June 4, 1970 (emancipation from
U.K. protectorate)
Legal system: based on English law

Economy

Industries: tourism, fishing
Agricultural products: coconuts, copra, bananas,
vanilla beans, cocoa, coffee, ginger, black pepper; fish
Currency: 1 pa'anga (T$) = 100 seniti

Trinidad and Tobago

Geography

Location: Caribbean, islands between the Caribbean Sea and the Atlantic Ocean, northeast of Venezuela

Area: 1,981 sq. mi. (5,130 sq. km.); slightly smaller than Delaware

Climate: tropical; rainy season (June to December)

Terrain: mostly plains with some hills and low mountains

Elevation: lowest point: Caribbean Sea 0 ft. (0 m.); highest point: El Cerro del Aripo 3,084 ft. (940 m.)

Natural resources: petroleum, natural gas, asphalt

People

Population: 1,102,096 (July 1999 est.)

Population growth rate: –1.35%

Infant mortality rate: 18.56 deaths/1,000 live births

Life expectancy at birth: total population: 70.66 years; male: 68.19 years; female: 73.19 years

Major ethnic groups: black 40%, East Indian (a local term-primarily immigrants from northern India) 40.3%, mixed 14%, white 1%, Chinese 1%

Major religions: Roman Catholic 32.2%, Hindu 24.3%, Anglican 14.4%, other Protestant 14%, Muslim 6%

Major languages: English (official), Hindi, French, Spanish

Government

Official name: Republic of Trinidad and Tobago

Government type: parliamentary democracy

National capital: Port-of-Spain

Independence: August 31, 1962 (from U.K.)

Legal system: based on English common law; judicial review of legislative acts in the Supreme Court

Economy

Industries: petroleum, chemicals, tourism, food processing, cement, beverage, cotton textiles

Agricultural products: cocoa, sugarcane, rice, citrus, coffee, vegetables; poultry

Currency: 1 Trinidad and Tobago dollar (TT$) = 100 cents

Tunisia

Geography

Location: Northern Africa, bordering the Mediterranean Sea, between Algeria and Libya

Area: 63,170 sq. mi. (163,610) sq. km.; slightly larger than Georgia

Climate: temperate in north with mild, rainy winters and hot, dry summers; desert in south

Terrain: mountains in north; hot, dry central plain; semiarid south merges into the Sahara

Elevation: lowest point: Shatt al Gharsah –56 ft. (–17 m.); highest point: Jabal ash Shanabi 5,066 ft. (1,544 m.)

Natural resources: petroleum, phosphates, iron ore, lead, zinc, salt

People

Population: 9,513,603 (July 1999 est.)

Population growth rate: 1.39%

Infant mortality rate: 31.38 deaths/1,000 live births

Life expectancy at birth: total population: 73.35 years; male: 71.95 years; female: 74.86 years

Major ethnic groups: Arab 98%, European 1%

Major religions: Muslim 98%, Christian 1%

Major languages: Arabic (official and one of the languages of commerce), French (commerce)

Government

Official name: Republic of Tunisia

Government type: republic

National capital: Tunis

Independence: March 20, 1956 (from France)

Legal system: based on French civil law system and Islamic law; some judicial review of legislative acts in the Supreme Court in joint session

Economy

Industries: petroleum, mining (particularly phosphate and iron ore), tourism, textiles, footwear, food, beverages

Agricultural products: olives, dates, oranges, almonds, grain, sugar beets, grapes; poultry, beef, dairy products

Currency: 1 Tunisian dinar (TD) = 1,000 millimes

Turkey

Geography

Location: southwestern Asia (that part west of the Bosporus is sometimes included with Europe), bordering the Black Sea, between Bulgaria and Georgia, and bordering the Aegean Sea and the Mediterranean Sea, between Greece and Syria

Area: 301,382 sq. mi. (780,580 sq. km.); slightly larger than Texas

Climate: temperate; hot, dry summers with mild, wet winters; harsher in interior

Terrain: mostly mountains; narrow coastal plain; high central plateau (Anatolia)

Elevation: extremes: lowest point: Mediterranean Sea 0 ft. (0 m.); highest point: Mount Ararat 16,949 ft. (5,166 m.)

Natural resources: antimony, coal, chromium, mercury, copper, borate, sulfur, iron ore

People

Population: 65,599,206 (July 1999 est.)

Population growth rate: 1.57%

Infant mortality rate: 35.81 deaths/1,000 live births

Life expectancy at birth: total population: 73.29 years; male: 70.81 years; female: 75.88 years

Major ethnic groups: Turkish 80%, Kurdish 20%

Major religions: Muslim 99.8% (mostly Sunni)

Major languages: Turkish (official), Kurdish, Arabic

Government

Official name: Republic of Turkey

Government type: republican parliamentary democracy

National capital: Ankara

Independence: October 29, 1923 (successor state to the Ottoman Empire)

Legal system: derived from various European continental legal systems

Economy

Industries: textiles, food processing, mining (coal, chromite, copper, boron), steel, petroleum, construction, lumber, paper

Agricultural products: tobacco, cotton, grain, olives, sugar beets, pulses, citrus; livestock

Currency: Turkish lira (TL)

Turkmenistan

Geography

Location: Central Asia, bordering the Caspian Sea, between Iran and Kazakhstan

Area: 188,455 sq. mi. (488,100 sq. km.); slightly larger than California

Climate: subtropical desert

Terrain: flat-to-rolling sandy desert with dunes rising to mountains in the south; low mountains along border with Iran; borders Caspian Sea in west

Elevation: lowest point: Sarygamysh Koli −361 ft. (−110 m.); highest point: Ayrybaba 10,298 ft. (3,139 m.)

Natural resources: petroleum, natural gas, coal, sulfur, salt

People

Population: 4,366,383 (July 1999 est.)

Population growth rate: 1.58%

Infant mortality rate: 73.1 deaths/1,000 live births

Life expectancy at birth: total population: 61.11 years; male: 57.48 years; female: 64.91 years

Major ethnic groups: Turkmen 77%, Uzbek 9.2%, Russian 6.7%, Kazakh 2%

Major religions: Muslim 89%, Eastern Orthodox 9%

Major languages: Turkmen 72%, Russian 12%, Uzbek 9%

Government

Official name: Turkmenistan
Government type: republic
National capital: Ashgabat
Independence: October 27,1991 (from the Soviet Union)
Legal system: based on civil law system

Economy

Industries: natural gas, oil, petroleum products, textiles, food processing
Agricultural products: cotton, grain; livestock
Currency: 1 Tukmen manat (TMM) = 100 tenesi

Turks and Caicos Islands

Geography

Location: Caribbean, two island groups in the North Atlantic Ocean, southeast of The Bahamas
Area: 166 sq. mi. (430 sq. km.); 2.5 times the size of Washington, D.C.
Climate: tropical; marine; moderated by trade winds; sunny and relatively dry
Terrain: low, flat limestone; extensive marshes and mangrove swamps
Elevation: lowest point: Caribbean Sea 0 ft. (0 m.); highest point: Blue Hills 161 ft. (49 m.)
Natural resources: spiny lobster, conch

People

Population: 16,863 (July 1999 est.)
Population growth rate: 3.65%
Infant mortality rate: 21.11 deaths/1,000 live births
Life expectancy at birth: total population: 72.35 years; male: 70.4 years; female: 74.4 years
Major ethnic groups: black
Major religions: Baptist 41.2%, Methodist 18.9%, Anglican 18.3%, Seventh-Day Adventist 1.7%

Major languages: English (official)

Government

Official name: Turks and Caicos Islands
National capital: Grand Turk
Independence: none (dependent territory of the U.K.)
Legal system: based on laws of England and Wales with a small number adopted from Jamaica and The Bahamas

Economy

Industries: tourism, offshore financial services
Agricultural products: corn, beans, cassava, citrus fruits; fish
Currency: 1 U.S. dollar (US$) = 100 cents

Tuvalu

Geography

Location: Oceania, island group consisting of nine coral atolls in the South Pacific Ocean, about one-half of the way from Hawaii to Australia
Area: 10 sq. mi. (26 sq. km.); 0.1 times the size of Washington, D.C.
Climate: tropical; moderated by easterly trade winds (March to November); westerly gales and heavy rain (November to March)
Terrain: very low-lying and narrow coral atolls
Elevation: lowest point: Pacific Ocean 0 ft. (0 m.); highest point: unnamed location 16 ft. (5 m.)
Natural resources: fish

People

Population: 10,588 (July 1999 est.)
Population growth rate: 1.34%
Infant mortality rate: 25.53 deaths/1,000 live births
Life expectancy at birth: total population: 64.15 years; male: 63.01 years; female: 65.34 years
Major ethnic groups: Polynesian 96%
Major religions: Church of Tuvalu (Congregationalist) 97%, Seventh-Day Adventist 1.4%, Baha'i 1%

Major languages: Tuvaluan, English

Government

Official name: Tuvalu

Government type: constitutional monarchy with a parliamentary democracy; began debating republic status in 1992

National capital: Funafuti

Independence: October 1, 1978 (from U.K.)

Economy

Industries: fishing, tourism, copra

Agricultural products: coconuts; fish

Currency: 1 Tuvaluan dollar ($T) or 1 Australian dollar ($A) = 100 cents

Uganda

Geography

Location: Eastern Africa, west of Kenya

Area: 91,135 sq. mi. (236,040 sq. km.); slightly smaller than Oregon

Climate: tropical; generally rainy with two dry seasons (December to February, June to August); semiarid in northeast

Terrain: mostly plateau with rim of mountains

Elevation: lowest point: Lake Albert 2,037 ft. (621 m.); highest point: Margherita (Mount Stanley) 16,765 ft. (5,110 m.)

Natural resources: copper, cobalt, limestone, salt

People

Population: 22,804,973 (July 1999 est.)

Population growth rate: 2.83%

Infant mortality rate: 90.68 deaths/1,000 live births

Life expectancy at birth: total population: 43.06 years; male: 42.2 years; female: 43.94 years

Major ethnic groups: Baganda 17%, Karamojong 12%, Basogo 8%, Iteso 8%, Langi 6%, Rwanda 6%, Bagisu 5%, Acholi 4%, Lugbara 4%, Bunyoro 3%, Batobo 3%

Major religions: Roman Catholic 33%, Protestant 33%, Muslim 16%, indigenous beliefs 18%

Major languages: English (official national language, taught in grade schools, used in courts of law and by most newspapers and some radio broadcasts), Ganda or Luganda (most widely used of the Niger-Congo languages, preferred for native language publications and may be taught in school), other Niger-Congo languages, Nilo-Saharan languages, Swahili, Arabic

Government

Official name: Republic of Uganda

Government type: republic

National capital: Kampala

Independence: October 9, 1962 (from U.K.)

Legal system: in 1995, the government restored the legal system to one based on English common law and customary law and reinstituted a normal judicial system

Economy

Industries: sugar, brewing, tobacco, cotton textiles, cement

Agricultural products: coffee, tea, cotton, tobacco, cassava (tapioca), potatoes, corn, millet, pulses; beef, goat meat, milk, poultry

Currency: 1 Ugandan shilling (USh) = 100 cents

Ukraine

Geography

Location: Eastern Europe, bordering the Black Sea, between Poland and Russia

Area: 233,089 sq. mi. (603,700 sq. km.); slightly smaller than Texas

Climate: temperate continental; Mediterranean only on the southern Crimean coast; precipitation disproportionately distributed, highest in west and north, lesser in east and southeast; winters vary from cool along the Black Sea to cold farther inland; summers are warm across the greater part of the country, hot in the south

Terrain: most of Ukraine consists of fertile plains (steppes) and plateaus, mountains being found only in the west (the Carpathians), and in the Crimean Peninsula in the extreme south

Elevation: lowest point: Black Sea 0 ft. (0 m.); highest point: Hora Hoverla 6,762 ft. (2,061 m.)

Natural resources: iron ore, coal, manganese, natural gas, oil, salt, sulfur, graphite, titanium, magnesium, kaolin, nickel, mercury, timber

People

Population: 49,811,174 (July 1999 est.)
Population growth rate: −0.62%
Infant mortality rate: 21.73 deaths/1,000 live births
Life expectancy at birth: total population: 65.91 years; male: 60.23 years; female: 71.87 years
Major ethnic groups: Ukrainian 73%, Russian 22%, Jewish 1%
Major religions: Ukrainian Orthodox-Moscow Patriarchate, Ukrainian Orthodox-Kiev Patriarchate, Ukrainian Autocephalous Orthodox, Ukrainian Catholic (Uniate), Protestant, Jewish
Major languages: Ukrainian, Russian, Romanian, Polish, Hungarian

Government

Official name: Ukraine
Government type: republic
National capital: Kiev
Independence: December 1, 1991 (from Soviet Union)
Legal system: based on civil law system; judicial review of legislative acts

Economy

Industries: coal, electric power, ferrous and non-ferrous metals, machinery and transport equipment, chemicals, food-processing (especially sugar)
Agricultural products: grain, sugar beets, sunflower seeds, vegetables; meat, milk
Currency: 1 hryvnia = 100,000 karbovantsi

United Arab Emirates

Geography

Location: Middle East, bordering the Gulf of Oman and the Persian Gulf, between Oman and Saudi Arabia

Area: 32,000 sq. mi. (82,880 sq. km.); slightly smaller than Maine
Climate: desert; cooler in eastern mountains
Terrain: flat, barren coastal plain merging into rolling sand dunes of vast desert wasteland; mountains in east
Elevation: lowest point: Persian Gulf 0 ft. (0 m.); highest point: Jabal Yibir 5,010 ft. (1,527 m.)
Natural resources: petroleum, natural gas

People

Population: 2,344,402 (July 1999 est.)
Population growth rate: 1.78%
Infant mortality rate: 14.1 deaths/1,000 live births
Life expectancy at birth: total population: 75.24 years; male: 73.83 years; female: 76.72 years
Major ethnic groups: Emiri 19%, other Arab and Iranian 23%, South Asian 50%, other expatriates (includes Westerners and East Asians) 8%
Major religions: Muslim 96% (Shi'a 16%), Christian, Hindu
Major languages: Arabic (official), Persian, English, Hindi, Urdu

Government

Official name: United Arab Emirates
Government type: federation with specified powers delegated to the U.A.E. federal government and other powers reserved to member emirates
National capital: Abu Dhabi
Independence: December 2, 1971 (from U.K.)
Legal system: federal court system introduced in 1971; all emirates except Dubayy (Dubai) and Ra's al Khaymah have joined the federal system; all emirates have secular and Islamic law for civil, criminal, and high courts

Economy

Industries: petroleum, fishing, petrochemicals, construction materials, some boat building, handicrafts, pearling

Agricultural products: dates, vegetables, water-
melons; poultry, eggs, dairy products; fish
Currency: 1 Emirian dirham (Dh) = 100 fils

United Kingdom

Geography
Location: Western Europe, islands including the
northern one-sixth of the island of Ireland
between the North Atlantic Ocean and the
North Sea, northwest of France
Area: 244,820 sq. mi. (244,820 sq. km.); slightly
smaller than Oregon
Climate: temperate; moderated by prevailing
southwest winds over the North Atlantic
Current; more than one-half of the days are
overcast
Terrain: mostly rugged hills and low mountains; level to rolling plains in east and southeast
Elevation: lowest point: Fenland –13 ft. (–4 m.);
highest point: Ben Nevis 4,406 ft. (1,343 m.)
Natural resources: coal, petroleum, natural gas,
tin, limestone, iron ore, salt, clay, chalk, gypsum, lead, silica

People
Population: 59,113,439 (July 1999 est.)
Population growth rate: 0.24%
Infant mortality rate: 5.78 deaths/1,000 live
births
Life expectancy at birth: total population:
77.37 years; male: 74.73 years; female:
80.15 years
Major ethnic groups: English 81.5%, Scottish
9.6%, Irish 2.4%, Welsh 1.9%, Ulster 1.8%,
Major religions: Anglican 27 million, Roman
Catholic 9 million, Muslim 1 million,
Presbyterian 800,000, Methodist 760,000,
Sikh 400,000, Hindu 350,000, Jewish
300,000
Major languages: English, Welsh (about 26% of
the population of Wales), Scottish form of
Gaelic (about 60,000 in Scotland)

Government
Official name: United Kingdom of Great Britain
and Northern Ireland

Government type: constitutional monarchy
National capital: London
Independence: England has existed as
a unified entity since the 10th century; the union
between England and Wales was enacted
under the Statute of Rhuddlan in 1284; in the
Act of Union of 1707, England and Scotland
agreed to permanent union as Great Britain;
the legislative union of Great Britain and
Ireland was implemented in 1801 adopting the
name the United Kingdom of Great Britain
and Ireland; the Anglo-Irish treaty of 1921 for-
malized a partition of Ireland; six northern
Irish counties remained part of the United
Kingdom as Northern Ireland and the current
name of the country, the United Kingdom of
Great Britain and Northern Ireland, was
adopted in 1927
Legal system: common law tradition with early
Roman and modern continental influences; no
judicial review of Acts of Parliament

Economy
Industries: production machinery including
machine tools, electric power equipment,
automation equipment, railroad equipment,
shipbuilding, aircraft, motor vehicles and
parts, electronics and communications
equipment, metals, chemicals, coal, petroleum, paper and paper products, food
processing, textiles, clothing, and other
consumer goods
Agricultural products: cereals, oilseed, potatoes,
vegetables; cattle, sheep, poultry; fish
Currency: 1 British pound (£) = 100 pence

United States

Geography
Location: North America, bordering both the
North Atlantic Ocean and the North Pacific
Ocean, between Canada and Mexico
Area: 3,717,792 sq. mi. (9,629,091 sq. km.);
about one-half the size of Russia
Climate: mostly temperate, but tropical in
Hawaii and Florida and arctic in Alaska,
semiarid in the great plains west of the
Mississippi River and arid in the Great Basin

of the southwest; low winter temperatures in the northwest are ameliorated occasionally in January and February by warm chinook winds from the eastern slopes of the Rocky Mountains

Terrain: vast central plain, mountains in west, hills and low mountains in east; rugged mountains and broad river valleys in Alaska; rugged, volcanic topography in Hawaii

Elevation: lowest point: Death Valley −282 ft. (−86 m.); highest point: Mount McKinley 20,321 ft. (6,194 m.)

Natural resources: coal, copper, lead, molybdenum, phosphates, uranium, bauxite, gold, iron, mercury, nickel, potash, silver, tungsten, zinc, petroleum, natural gas, timber

People

Population: 281,421,906 (April 2000 est.)

Population growth rate: 0.85%

Infant mortality rate: 6.33 deaths/1,000 live births

Life expectancy at birth: total population: 76.23 years; male: 72.95 years; female: 79.67 years

Major ethnic groups: white 83.4%, black 12.4%, Asian 3.3%, Amerindian 0.8%

Major religions: Protestant 56%, Roman Catholic 28%, Jewish 2%, other 4%, none 10%

Major languages: English, Spanish (spoken by a sizable minority)

Government

Official name: United States of America

Government type: federal republic; strong democratic tradition

National capital: Washington, D.C.

Independence: July 4, 1776 (from England)

Legal system: based on English common law; judicial review of legislative acts

Economy

Industries: leading industrial power in the world, highly diversified and technologically advanced; petroleum, steel, motor vehicles, aerospace, telecommunications, chemicals, electronics, food processing, consumer goods, lumber, mining

Agricultural products: wheat, other grains, corn, fruits, vegetables, cotton; beef, pork, poultry, dairy products; forest products; fish

Currency: 1 U.S. dollar (US$) = 100 cents

Uruguay

Geography

Location: Southern South America, bordering the South Atlantic Ocean, between Argentina and Brazil

Area: 68,039 sq. mi. (176,220 sq. km.); slightly smaller than Washington State

Climate: warm temperate; freezing temperatures almost unknown

Terrain: mostly rolling plains and low hills; fertile coastal lowland

Elevation: extremes: lowest point: Atlantic Ocean 0 ft. (0 m.); highest point: Cerro Catedral 1,686 ft. (514 m.)

Natural resources: fertile soil, hydropower, minor minerals, fisheries

People

Population: 3,308,523 (July 1999 est.)

Population growth rate: 0.73%

Infant mortality rate: 13.49 deaths/1,000 live births

Life expectancy at birth: total population: 75.83 years; male: 72.69 years; female: 79.15 years

Major ethnic groups: white 88%, mestizo 8%, black 4%, Amerindian, practically nonexistent

Major religions: Roman Catholic 66% (less than one-half of the adult population attends church regularly), Protestant 2%, Jewish 2%

Major languages: Spanish, Portunol, or Brazilero (Portuguese-Spanish mix)

Government

Official name: Oriental Republic of Uruguay

Government type: republic

National capital: Montevideo
Independence: August 25, 1825 (from Brazil)
Legal system: based on Spanish civil law system

Economy

Industries: meat processing, wool and hides, sugar, textiles, footwear, leather apparel, tires, cement, petroleum refining, wine
Agricultural products: wheat, rice, corn, sorghum; livestock; fishing
Currency: 1 Uruguayan peso ($Ur) = 100 centesimos

Uzbekistan

Geography

Location: Central Asia, north of Afghanistan
Area: 172,741 sq. mi. (447,400 sq. km.); slightly larger than California
Climate: mostly mid-latitude desert; long, hot summers, mild winters; semiarid grassland in east
Terrain: mostly flat-to-rolling sandy desert with dunes; broad, flat intensely irrigated river valleys along course of Amu Darya, Sirdaryo, and Zarafshon; Fergana Valley in east surrounded by mountainous Tajikistan and Kyrgyzstan; shrinking Aral Sea in west
Elevation: lowest point: Sariqarnish Kuli −39 ft. (−12 m.); highest point: Adelunga Toghi 14,111 ft. (4,301 m.)
Natural resources: natural gas, petroleum, coal, gold, uranium, silver, copper, lead and zinc, tungsten, molybdenum

People

Population: 24,102,473 (July 1999 est.)
Population growth rate: 1.32%
Infant mortality rate: 71.85 deaths/1,000 live births
Life expectancy at birth: total population: 63.91 years; male: 60.29 years; female: 67.71 years
Major ethnic groups: Uzbek 80%, Russian 5.5%, Tajik 5%, Kazakh 3%, Karakalpak 2.5%, Tatar 1.5%
Major religions: Muslim 88% (mostly Sunnis), Eastern Orthodox 9%

Major languages: Uzbek 74.3%, Russian 14.2%, Tajik 4.4%

Government

Official name: Republic of Uzbekistan
Government type: republic; effectively authoritarian presidential rule, with little power outside the executive branch and executive power concentrated in the presidency
National capital: Tashkent (Toshkent)
Independence: August 31, 1991 (from Soviet Union)
Legal system: evolution of Soviet civil law; still lacks independent judicial system

Economy

Industries: textiles, food processing, machine building, metallurgy, natural gas
Agricultural products: cotton, vegetables, fruits, grain; livestock
Currency: 1 Som = 100 tiyin

Vanuatu

Geography

Location: Oceania, group of islands in the South Pacific Ocean, about three-quarters of the way from Hawaii to Australia
Area: 5,699 sq. mi. (14,760 sq. km.); slightly larger than Connecticut
Climate: tropical; moderated by southeast trade winds
Terrain: mostly mountains of volcanic origin; narrow coastal plains
Elevation: lowest point: Pacific Ocean 0 ft. (0 m.); highest point: Mount Tabwemasana 6,158 ft. (1,877 m.)
Natural resources: manganese, hardwood forests, fish

People

Population: 189,036 (July 1999 est.)
Population growth rate: 2.02%
Infant mortality rate: 59.58 deaths/1,000 live births
Life expectancy at birth: total population: 61.44 years; male: 59.41 years; female: 63.57 years

Major ethnic groups: indigenous Melanesian 94%, French 4%, Vietnamese, Chinese, Pacific Islanders

Major religions: Presbyterian 36.7%, Anglican 15%, Catholic 15%, indigenous beliefs 7.6%, Seventh-Day Adventist 6.2%, Church of Christ 3.8%

Major languages: English (official), French (official), pidgin (known as Bislama or Bichelama)

Government

Official name: Republic of Vanuatu

Government type: republic

National capital: Port-Vila

Independence: July 30, 1980 (from France and U.K.)

Legal system: unified system being created from former dual French and British systems

Economy

Industries: food and fish freezing, wood processing, meat canning

Agricultural products: copra, coconuts, cocoa, coffee, taro, yams, coconuts, fruits, vegetables; fish, beef

Currency: 1 vatu (VT) = 100 centimes

Venezuela

Geography

Location: Northern South America, bordering the Caribbean Sea and the North Atlantic Ocean, between Colombia and Guyana

Area: 352,143 sq. mi. (912,050 sq. km.); slightly more than twice the size of California

Climate: tropical; hot, humid; more moderate in highlands

Terrain: Andes Mountains and Maracaibo Lowlands in northwest; central plains (llanos); Guiana Highlands in southeast

Elevation: lowest point: Caribbean Sea 0 ft. (0 m.); highest point: Pico Bolivar (La Columna) 16,427 ft. (5,007 m.)

Natural resources: petroleum, natural gas, iron ore, gold, bauxite, other minerals, hydropower, diamonds

People

Population: 23,203,466 (July 1999 est.)

Population growth rate: 1.71%

Infant mortality rate: 26.51 deaths/1,000 live births

Life expectancy at birth: total population: 72.95 years; male: 69.97 years; female: 76.16 years

Major ethnic groups: mestizo 67%, white 21%, black 10%, Amerindian 2%

Major religions: nominally Roman Catholic 96%, Protestant 2%

Major languages: Spanish (official), native dialects spoken by about 200,000 Amerindians in the remote interior

Government

Official name: Republic of Venezuela

Government type: republic

National capital: Caracas

Independence: July 5, 1811 (from Spain)

Legal system: based on Napoleonic code; judicial review of legislative acts in Cassation Court only

Economy

Industries: petroleum, iron ore mining, construction materials, food processing, textiles, steel, aluminum, motor vehicle assembly

Agricultural products: corn, sorghum, sugarcane, rice, bananas, vegetables, coffee; beef, pork, milk, eggs; fish

Currency: 1 bolivar (Bs) = 100 centimos

Vietnam

Geography

Location: Southeastern Asia, bordering the Gulf of Thailand, Gulf of Tonkin, and South China Sea, alongside China, Laos, and Cambodia

Area: 127,243 sq. mi. (329,560 sq. km.); slightly larger than New Mexico

Climate: tropical in south; monsoonal in north with hot, rainy season (mid-May to mid-September) and warm, dry season (mid-October to mid-March)

Terrain: low, flat delta in south and north; central highlands; hilly, mountainous in far north and northwest

Elevation: lowest point: South China Sea 0 ft. (0 m.); highest point: Ngoc Linh 10,312 ft. (3,143 m.)

Natural resources: phosphates, coal, manganese, bauxite, chromate, offshore oil and gas deposits, forests

People

Population: 77,311,210 (July 1999 est.)

Population growth rate: 1.37%

Infant mortality rate: 38.84 deaths/1,000 live births

Life expectancy at birth: total population: 68.1 years; male: 65.71 years; female: 70.64 years

Major ethnic groups: Vietnamese 85–90%, Chinese 3%, Muong, Tai, Meo, Khmer, Man, Cham

Major religions: Buddhist, Taoist, Roman Catholic, indigenous beliefs, Islam, Protestant, Cao Dai, Hoa Hao

Major languages: Vietnamese (official), Chinese, English, French, Khmer, tribal languages (Mon-Khmer and Malayo-Polynesian)

Government

Official name: Socialist Republic of Vietnam

Government type: Communist state

National capital: Hanoi

Independence: September 2, 1945 (from France)

Legal system: based on communist legal theory and French civil law system

Economy

Industries: food processing, garments, shoes, machine building, mining, cement, chemical fertilizer, glass, tires, oil

Agricultural products: paddy rice, corn, potatoes, rubber, soybeans, coffee, tea, bananas; poultry, pigs; fish

Currency: 1 new dong (D) = 100 xu

Virgin Islands, British

Geography

Location: Caribbean, between the Caribbean Sea and the North Atlantic Ocean, east of Puerto Rico

Area: 58 sq. mi. (150 sq. km.) comparative area: about 0.9 times the size of Washington, D.C.

Climate: subtropical; humid; temperatures moderated by trade winds

Terrain: coral islands relatively flat; volcanic islands steep, hilly

Elevation: lowest point: Caribbean Sea 0 ft. (0 m.); highest point: Mount Sage 1709 ft. (521 m.)

Natural resources: negligible

People

Population: 19,156 (July 1999 est.)

Population growth rate: 1.19%

Infant mortality rate: 10.07 deaths/1,000 live births

Life expectancy at birth: total population: 77.74 years; male: 74.04 years; female: 81.67 years

Major ethnic groups: black 90%, white, Asian

Major religions: Protestant 86%, Roman Catholic 6%

Major languages: English (official)

Government

Official name: British Virgin Islands

Government type: dependent territory of the U.K.

National capital: Road Town

Independence: none (dependent territory of the U.K.)

Legal system: English law

Economy

Industries: tourism, light industry, construction, rum, concrete block, offshore financial center

Agricultural products: fruits, vegetables; livestock, poultry; fish

Currency: 1 U.S. dollar (US$) = 100 cents

Virgin Islands, U.S.

Geography

Location: Caribbean, islands between the Caribbean Sea and the North Atlantic Ocean, east of Puerto Rico

Area: 136 sq. mi. (352 sq. km.); twice the size of Washington, D.C.

Climate: subtropical, tempered by easterly trade winds, relatively low humidity, little seasonal temperature variation; rainy season May to November

Terrain: mostly hilly to rugged and mountainous with little level land

Elevation: lowest point: Caribbean Sea 0 ft. (0 m.); highest point: Crown Mountain 1,555 ft. (474 m.)

Natural resources: sun, sand, sea, surf

People

Population: 119,827 (July 1999 est.)

Population growth rate: 1.19%

Infant mortality rate: 10.07 deaths/1,000 live births

Life expectancy at birth: total population: 77.74 years; male: 74.04 years; female: 81.67 years

Major ethnic groups: black 80%, white 15%

Major religions: Baptist 42%, Roman Catholic 34%, Episcopalian 17%

Major languages: English (official), Spanish, Creole

Government

Official name: Virgin Islands of the United States

National capital: Charlotte Amalie

Legal system: based on U.S. laws

Economy

Industries: tourism, petroleum refining, watch assembly, rum distilling, construction, pharmaceuticals, textiles, electronics

Agricultural products: truck garden products, fruit, vegetables, sorghum; Senepol cattle

Currency: 1 U.S. dollar (US$) = 100 cents

Wallis and Futuna

Geography

Location: Oceania, islands in the South Pacific Ocean, about two-thirds of the way from Hawaii to New Zealand

Area: 106 sq. mi. (274 sq. km.); 1.5 times the size of Washington, D.C.

Climate: tropical; hot, rainy season (November to April); cool, dry season (May to October); rains 2,500–3,000 mm per year (80% humidity); average temperature 79.9 degrees F (26.6 degrees C)

Terrain: volcanic origin; low hills

Elevation: lowest point: Pacific Ocean 0 ft. (0 m.); highest point: Mount Singavi 2,510 ft. (765 m.)

Natural resources: negligible

People

Population: 15,129 (July 1999 est.)

Population growth rate: 1.04%

Major ethnic groups: Polynesian

Major religions: Roman Catholic 100%

Major languages: French, Wallisian (indigenous Polynesian language)

Government

Official name: Territory of the Wallis and Futuna Islands

Dependency status: overseas territory of France

National capital: Mata-Utu (on Ile Uvea)

Independence: none (overseas territory of France)

Legal system: French legal system

Economy

Industries: copra, handicrafts, fishing, lumber

Agricultural products: breadfruit, yams, taro, bananas; pigs, goats

Currency: 1 CFP franc (CFPF) = 100 centimes

West Bank

Geography

Location: Middle East, west of Jordan

Area: 2,263 sq. mi. (5,860) sq. km.; slightly smaller than Delaware

Climate: temperate, temperature and precipitation vary with altitude, warm to hot summers, cool to mild winters

Terrain: mostly rugged dissected upland, some vegetation in west, but barren in east

Elevation: lowest point: Dead Sea −1339 ft. (−408 m.); highest point: Tall Asur 3,353 ft. (1,022 m.)

Natural resources: negligible

People

Population: 1,611,109; Note—in addition, there are 155,000 Israeli settlers in the West Bank and 164,000 in East Jerusalem (July 1999 est.)

Population growth rate: 3.14%

Infant mortality rate: 25.22 deaths/1,000 live births

Life expectancy at birth: total population: 72.83 years; male: 70.96 years; female: 74.79 years

Major ethnic groups: Palestinian Arab and other 83%, Jewish 17%

Major religions: Muslim 75% (predominantly Sunni), Jewish 17%, Christian and other 8%

Major languages: Arabic, Hebrew (spoken by Israeli settlers and many Palestinians), English (widely understood)

Government

Official name: West Bank

Status: Former territory of Jordan now occupied by Israel; negotiations between Israel and the Palestinians are being conducted

National capital: none

Economy

Industries: generally small family businesses that produce cement, textiles, soap, olive-wood carvings, and mother-of-pearl souvenirs; the Israelis have established some small-scale, modern industries in the settlements and industrial centers

Agricultural products: olives, citrus and other fruits, vegetables; beef, dairy products

Currency: 1 new Israeli shekel (NIS) = 100 new agorot; 1 Jordanian dinar (JD) = 1,000 fils

Western Sahara

Geography

Location: Northern Africa, bordering the North Atlantic Ocean, between Mauritania and Morocco

Area: 102,703 sq. mi. (266,000 sq. km.); about the size of Colorado

Climate: hot, dry desert; rain is rare; cold off-shore air currents produce fog and heavy dew

Terrain: mostly low, flat desert with large areas of rocky or sandy surfaces rising to small mountains in south and northeast

Elevation: lowest point: Sebjet Tah −180 ft. (−55 m.); highest point: unnamed location 1,519 ft. (463 m.)

Natural resources: phosphates, iron ore

People

Population: 239,333 (July 1999 est.)

Population growth rate: 2.34%

Infant mortality rate: 139.67 deaths/1,000 live births

Life expectancy at birth: total population: 49.1 years; male: 47.98 years; female: 50.57 years

Major ethnic groups: Arab, Berber

Major religions: Muslim

Major languages: Hassaniya Arabic, Moroccan Arabic

Government

Official name: Western Sahara

Government type: legal status of territory and question of sovereignty unresolved; territory contested by Morocco and Polisario Front (Popular Front for the Liberation of the Saguia el Hamra and Rio de Oro)

National capital: none

Economy

Industries: phosphate mining, handicrafts

Agricultural products: fruits and vegetables (grown in the few oases); camels, sheep, goats (kept by the nomads)

Currency: 1 Moroccan dirham (DH) = 100 centimes

Yemen

Geography

Location: Middle East, bordering the Arabian
Sea, Gulf of Aden, and Red Sea, between
Oman and Saudi Arabia

Area: 203,849 sq. mi. (527,970 sq. km.); slightly
larger than twice the size of Wyoming

Climate: mostly desert; hot and humid along
west coast; temperate in western mountains
affected by seasonal monsoon; extraordinarily
hot, dry, harsh desert in east

Terrain: narrow coastal plain backed by flat-
topped hills and rugged mountains; dissected upland desert plains in center slope
into the desert interior of the Arabian
Peninsula

Elevation: lowest point: Arabian Sea 0 ft. (0 m.);
highest point: Jabal an Nabi Shu'ayb 12,336 ft.
(3,760 m.)

Natural resources: petroleum, fish, rock salt,
marble, small deposits of coal, gold, lead,
nickel, and copper, fertile soil in west

People

Population: 16,942,230 (July 1999 est.)

Population growth rate: 3.34%

Infant mortality rate: 69.82 deaths/1,000 live
births

Life expectancy at birth: total population:
59.98 years; male: 58.17 years; female:
61.88 years

Major ethnic groups: predominantly Arab; Afro-
Arab concentrations in western coastal locations; South Asians in southern regions; small
European communities in major metropolitan
areas

Major religions: Muslim including Shaf'i (Sunni)
and Zaydi (Shi'a), small numbers of Jewish,
Christian, and Hindu

Major languages: Arabic

Government

Official name: Republic of Yemen

Government type: republic

National capital: Sanaa

Independence: May 22, 1990 Republic of Yemen
was established with the merger of the Yemen
Arab Republic (Yemen [Sanaa] or North
Yemen) and the Marxist-dominated People's
Democratic Republic of Yemen (Yemen [Aden]
or South Yemen)

Legal system: based on Islamic law, Turkish law,
English common law, and local tribal customary law

Economy

Industries: crude oil production and petroleum
refining; small-scale production of cotton textiles and leather goods; food processing; handicrafts; small aluminum products factory;
cement

Agricultural products: grain, fruits, vegetables,
qat (mildly narcotic shrub), coffee, cotton;
dairy products, poultry, meat; fish

Currency: Yemeni rial (YRl) (new currency)

Zambia

Geography

Location: Southern Africa, east of Angola

Area: 290,583 sq. mi. (752,610 sq. km.); slightly
larger than Texas

Climate: tropical; modified by altitude; rainy season (October to April)

Terrain: mostly high plateau with some hills and
mountains

Elevation: lowest point: Zambezi
river 1,079 ft. (329 m.); highest point: in Mafinga
Hills 7,549 ft. (2,301 m.)

Natural resources: copper, cobalt, zinc, lead, coal,
emeralds, gold, silver, uranium, hydropower
potential

People

Population: 9,663,535 (July 1999 est.)

Population growth rate: 2.12%

Infant mortality rate: 91.85 deaths/1,000 live
births

Life expectancy at birth: total population:
36.96 years; male: 36.72 years; female:
37.21 years

Major ethnic groups: African 98.7%, European 1.1%

Major religions: Christian 50–75%, Muslim and Hindu 24–49%, indigenous beliefs 1%

Major languages: English (official), major vernaculars—Bemba, Kaonda, Lozi, Lunda, Luvale, Nyanja, Tonga, and about 70 other indigenous languages

Government

Official name: Republic of Zambia

Government type: republic

National capital: Lusaka

Independence: October 24, 1964 (from U.K.)

Legal system: based on English common law and customary law; judicial review of legislative acts in an ad hoc constitutional council

Economy

Industries: copper mining and processing, construction, foodstuffs, beverages, chemicals, textiles, fertilizer

Agricultural products: corn, sorghum, rice, peanuts, sunflower seed, tobacco, cotton, sugarcane, cassava (tapioca); cattle, goats, pigs, poultry, beef, pork, poultry, milk, eggs, hides

Currency: 1 Zambian kwacha (ZK) = 100 ngwee

Zimbabwe

Geography

Location: Southern Africa, northeast of Botswana

Area: 150,803 sq. mi. (390,580 sq. km.); slightly larger than Montana

Climate: tropical; moderated by altitude; rainy season (November to March)

Terrain: mostly high plateau with higher central plateau (high veld); mountains in east

Elevation: lowest point: junction of the Lundi and Savi rivers 531 ft. (162 m.); highest point: Inyangani 8,504 ft. (2,592 m.)

Natural resources: coal, chromium ore, asbestos, gold, nickel, copper, iron ore, vanadium, lithium, tin, platinum group metals

People

Population: 11,163,160 (July 1999 est.)

Population growth rate: 1.02%

Infant mortality rate: 61.21 deaths/1,000 live births

Life expectancy at birth: total population: 38.86 years; male: 38.77 years; female: 38.94 years

Major ethnic groups: African 98% (Shona 71%, Ndebele 16%, other 11%), white 1%, mixed and Asian 1%

Major religions: syncretic (part Christian, part indigenous beliefs) 50%, Christian 25%, indigenous beliefs 24%, Muslim

Major languages: English (official), Shona, Sindebele (sometimes called Ndebele), numerous but minor tribal dialects

Government

Official name: Republic of Zimbabwe

Government type: parliamentary democracy

National capital: Harare

Independence: April 18, 1980 (from U.K.)

Legal system: mixture of Roman-Dutch and English common law

Economy

Industries: mining (coal, clay, numerous metallic and nonmetallic ores), copper, steel, nickel, tin, wood products, cement, chemicals, fertilizer, clothing and footwear, foodstuffs, beverages

Agricultural products: corn, cotton, tobacco, wheat, coffee, sugarcane, peanuts; cattle, sheep, goats, pigs

Currency: 1 Zimbabwean dollar (Z$) = 100 cents

⊙ Central Intelligence Agency. "The World Fact Book 1999," www.cia.gov/cia/publications/factbok/index.html

Rank	Nation/Territory	Population	Rank	Nation/Territory	Population
1	China	1,261,832,482	47	Saudi Arabia	22,023,506
2	India	1,014,003,817	48	Malaysia	21,793,293
3	United States	281,421,906	49	Korea, Democratic	
4	Indonesia	224,784,210		People's Republic of	21,687,550
5	Brazil	172,860,370	50	Ghana	19,533,560
6	Russia	146,001,176	51	Australia	19,164,620
7	Pakistan	141,553,775	52	Sri Lanka	19,238,757
8	Bangladesh	129,194,224	53	Mozambique	19,104,696
9	Japan	126,549,976	54	Yemen	17,479,206
10	Nigeria	123,337,822	55	Kazakhstan	16,733,227
11	Mexico	100,349,766	56	Syria	16,305,659
12	Germany	82,797,408	57	Côte d'Ivoire	15,980,950
13	Philippines	81,159,644	58	Netherlands	15,892,237
14	Vietnam	78,773,873	59	Madagascar	15,506,472
15	Egypt	68,359,979	60	Cameroon	15,421,937
16	Turkey	65,666,677	61	Chile	15,153,797
17	Iran	65,619,636	62	Ecuador	12,920,092
18	Ethiopia	64,227,452	63	Guatemala	12,639,939
19	Thailand	61,230,874	64	Cambodia	12,212,306
20	United Kingdom	59,508,382	65	Burkina Faso	11,946,065
21	France	59,329,691	66	Zimbabwe	11,342,521
22	Italy	57,634,327	67	Cuba	11,141,997
23	Congo, Democratic		68	Mali	10,685,948
	Republic of the	51,964,999	69	Greece	10,601,527
24	Ukraine	49,153,027	70	Malawi	10,385,849
25	Korea, Republic of	47,470,969	71	Belarus	10,366,719
26	South Africa	43,421,021	72	Czech Republic	10,272,179
27	Burma	41,734,853	73	Belgium	10,241,506
28	Spain	39,996,671	74	Angola	10,145,267
29	Colombia	39,685,655	75	Hungary	10,138,844
30	Argentina	36,955,182	76	Niger	10,075,511
31	Poland	38,646,023	77	Portugal	10,048,232
32	Tanzania	35,306,126	78	Senegal	9,987,494
33	Sudan	35,079,814	79	Serbia	9,981,929
34	Canada	31,278,097	80	Tunisia	9,593,402
35	Algeria	31,193,917	81	Zambia	9,582,418
36	Kenya	30,339,770	82	Sweden	8,873,052
37	Morocco	30,122,350	83	Chad	8,424,504
38	Peru	27,012,899	84	Bolivia	8,152,620
39	Afghanistan	25,888,797	85	Austria	8,131,111
40	Uzbekistan	24,755,519	86	Dominican Republic	8,442,533
41	Nepal	24,702,119	87	Bulgaria	7,796,694
42	Venezuela	23,542,649	88	Azerbaijan	7,748,163
43	Uganda	23,317,560	89	Guinea	7,466,200
44	Iraq	22,675,617	90	Switzerland	7,276,372
45	Romania	22,411,121	92	Rwanda	7,229,129
46	Taiwan	22,191,087	93	Somalia	7,253,137

94	Hong Kong S.A.R.	7,115,620	144	Bhutan	2,005,222
95	Haiti	6,867,995	145	Kuwait	1,973,572
96	Tajikistan	6,440,732	146	Slovenia	1,927,593
97	Benin	6,395,919	147	Namibia	1,771,327
98	Honduras	6,249,598	148	Botswana	1,574,470
99	El Salvador	6,122,515	149	Estonia	1,431,471
100	Burundi	6,054,714	150	Gambia, The	1,367,124
101	Israel	5,842,454	151	Guinea-Bissau	1,285,715
102	Paraguay	5,585,282	152	Gabon	1,208,436
103	Laos	5,497,459	153	Mauritius	1,179,368
104	Slovakia	5,407,956	154	Trinidad and Tobago	1,175,523
105	Denmark	5,336,394	155	Gaza Strip	1,132,063
106	Sierra Leone	5,232,624	156	Swaziland	1,083,289
107	Finland	5,167,486	157	Fiji	832,494
108	Libya	5,115,450	158	Cyprus	758,363
109	Togo	5,081,502	159	Qatar	744,483
110	Georgia	5,019,538	160	Reunion	720,934
111	Jordan	4,998,564	161	Guyana	697,286
112	Papua New Guinea	4,926,984	162	Montenegro	680,158
113	Nicaragua	4,812,591	163	Bahrain	634,137
114	Kyrgyzstan	4,685,230	164	Comoros	578,400
115	Turkmenistan	4,518,268	165	Equatorial Guinea	474,214
116	Norway	4,481,162	166	Solomon Islands	466,194
117	Moldova	4,430,654	167	Djibouti	451,442
118	Croatia	4,282,216	168	Macau	445,594
119	Singapore	4,151,720	169	Luxembourg	437,389
120	Eritrea	4,135,933	170	Suriname	431,303
121	Puerto Rico	3,915,798	171	Guadeloupe	426,493
122	Bosnia and Herzegovina	3,835,777	172	Martinique	414,516
123	New Zealand	3,819,762	173	Cape Verde	401,343
124	Ireland	3,797,257	174	Malta	391,670
125	Costa Rica	3,710,558	175	Brunei	336,376
126	Lithuania	3,620,756	176	Maldives	301,475
127	Lebanon	3,578,036	177	Bahamas, The	294,982
128	Central African Republic	3,512,751	178	Iceland	276,365
129	Albania	3,490,435	179	Barbados	274,059
130	Armenia	3,344,336	180	Belize	249,183
131	Uruguay	3,334,074	181	French Polynesia	249,110
132	Liberia	3,164,156	182	Western Sahara	244,943
133	Panama	2,808,268	183	Netherlands Antilles	210,134
134	Congo, Republic of the	2,830,961	184	New Caledonia	201,816
135	Mauritania	2,667,859	185	Vanuatu	189,618
136	Jamaica	2,652,689	186	Samoa	179,466
137	Mongolia	2,616,383	187	French Guiana	172,605
138	Oman	2,533,389	188	São Tomé and Príncipe	159,883
139	Latvia	2,404,926	189	Mayotte	155,911
140	United Arab Emirates	2,369,153	190	Guam	154,623
141	Lesotho	2,143,141	191	Saint Lucia	156,260
142	Macedonia, The Former Yugoslavian Republic of	2,041,467	192	Micronesia, Federated States of	133,144
143	West Bank	2,020,298	193	Virgin Islands	120,917

Rank	Nation/Territory	Population	Rank	Nation/Territory	Population
194	Saint Vincent and the Grenadines	115,461	212	Saint Kitts and Nevis	38,819
195	Tonga	102,321	213	Cayman Islands	34,736
196	Kiribati	91,985	214	Liechtenstein	32,204
197	Grenada	89,312	215	Monaco	31,693
198	Jersey	88,915	216	Gibraltar	27,578
199	Seychelles	79,326	217	San Marino	26,937
200	Isle of Man	73,112	218	Cook Islands	20,407
201	Northern Mariana Islands	71,912	219	Virgin Islands, British	20,353
202	Dominica	71,540	220	Palau	18,766
203	Aruba	69,539	221	Turks and Caicos Islands	17,502
204	Marshall Islands	68,126	222	Wallis and Futuna	15,283
205	Andorra	66,824	223	Nauru	11,845
206	Antigua and Barbuda	66,464	224	Anguilla	11,797
207	American Samoa	65,446	225	Tuvalu	10,383
208	Guernsey	64,080	226	Saint Helena	7,212
209	Bermuda	63,033	227	Saint Pierre and Miquelon	6,896
210	Greenland	56,309	228	Montserrat	6,409
211	Faroe Islands	45,296	229	Falkland Islands	2,805
			230	Norfolk Island	2,179

⊙ United States Bureau of the Census. "IDB Data Access," www.census.gov/ipc/www.idbacc.html
United Nations Population Information Network. "U.N Population Division Department of Economic and Social Affairs," www.undp.org/popin

Urban Areas: Population Over 2 Million

(in millions as of 1996)

Rank	Urban Area	Country	Pop.	Rank	Urban Area	Country	Pop.
1	Tokyo	Japan	27.2	19	Tianjin	China	9.6
2	Mexico City	Mexico	16.9	20	Paris	France	9.6
3	São Paulo	Brazil	16.8	21	Moscow	Russia	9.3
4	New York	United States	16.4	22	Dhaka	Bangladesh	9.0
5	Bombay	India	15.7	23	Jakarta	Indonesia	8.8
6	Shanghai	China	13.7	24	Istanbul	Turkey	8.2
7	Los Angeles	United States	12.6	25	London	United Kingdom	7.6
8	Calcutta	India	12.1	26	Teheran	Iran	6.9
9	Buenos Aires	Argentina	11.9	27	Chicago	United States	6.9
10	Seoul	South Korea	11.8	28	Lima	Peru	6.8
11	Beijing	China	11.4	29	Bangkok	Thailand	6.7
12	Lagos	Nigeria	10.9	30	Essen	Germany	6.5
13	Osaka	Japan	10.6	31	Bogota	Columbia	6.2
14	Delhi	India	10.3	32	Madras	India	6.1
15	Rio de Janeiro	Brazil	10.3	33	Hong Kong	China	5.9
16	Karachi	Pakistan	10.1	34	Hyderabad	India	5.7
17	Cairo	Egypt	9.9	35	Shenyang	China	5.2
18	Metro Manila	Philippines	9.6	36	Lahore	Pakistan	5.2

37	Saint Petersburg	Russia	5.1	83	Monterrey	Mexico	3.1
38	Santiago	Chile	5.0	84	Pune	India	3.1
39	Bangalore	India	5.0	85	Nanjing	China	3.0
40	Harbin	China	4.7	86	Xian	China	3.0
41	Guangzhou	China	4.6	87	Caracas	Venezuela	3.0
42	Hangzhou	China	4.6	88	Cologne	Germany	3.0
43	Chengdu	China	4.5	89	Naples	Italy	3.0
44	Changchun	China	4.4	90	Bandung	Indonesia	3.0
45	Baghdad	Iraq	4.4	91	Ankara	Turkey	2.9
46	Toronto	Canada	4.4	92	Abidjan	Côte d'Ivoire	2.9
47	Kinshasa	Democratic Republic of the Congo	4.4	93	Salvador	Brazil	2.9
				94	Handan	China	2.9
48	Wuhan	China	4.3	95	Boston	United States	2.9
49	Philadelphia	United States	4.3	96	Kiev	Ukraine	2.8
50	Milan	Italy	4.2	97	Barcelona	Spain	2.8
51	Pusan	South Korea	4.1	98	Cape Town	South Africa	2.8
52	Madrid	Spain	4.1	99	San Diego	United States	2.8
53	Yangon	Myanmar	4.0	100	Kitakyushu	Japan	2.8
54	San Francisco	United States	3.9	101	Riyadh	Saudi Arabia	2.8
55	Belo Horizonte	Brazil	3.9	102	Fortaleza	Brazil	2.7
56	Algiers	Algeria	3.8	103	Taipei	China	2.7
57	Ahmedabad	India	3.8	104	Dalian	China	2.7
58	Washington, D.C.	United States	3.7	105	Rome	Italy	2.7
59	Detroit	United States	3.7	106	Hamburg	Germany	2.6
60	Jinan	China	3.7	107	Stuttgart	Germany	2.6
61	Dallas	United States	3.7	108	Chittagong	Bangladesh	2.6
62	Alexandria	Egypt	3.7	109	Addis Ababa	Ethiopia	2.6
63	Frankfurt	Germany	3.6	110	Pyongyang	North Korea	2.5
64	Sydney	Australia	3.6	111	Atlanta	United States	2.5
65	Ho Chi Min	Vietnam	3.6	112	Taegu	South Korea	2.5
66	Chongqing	China	3.6	113	Inch'on	South Korea	2.4
67	Guadalajara	Mexico	3.5	114	Phoenix	United States	2.4
68	Katowice	Poland	3.4	115	Maputo	Mozambique	2.4
69	Porto Alegre	Brazil	3.4	116	Khartoum	Sudan	2.3
70	Medellin	Colombia	3.4	117	Tashkent	Uzbekistan	2.3
71	Singapore	Singapore	3.4	118	Guatemala City	Guatemala	2.3
72	Qingdao	China	3.4	119	Curitiba	Brazil	2.3
73	Montreal	Canada	3.3	120	Surabaja	Indonesia	2.3
74	Berlin	Germany	3.3	121	Kanpur	India	2.3
75	Santo Domingo	Dominican Republic	3.3	122	Birmingham	United Kingdom	2.3
76	Nagoya	Japan	3.3	123	Minneapolis	United States	2.3
77	Houston	United States	3.2	124	Munich	Germany	2.3
78	Casablanca	Morocco	3.2	125	Manchester	United Kingdom	2.2
79	Recife	Brazil	3.1	126	Havana	Cuba	2.2
80	Melbourne	Australia	3.1	127	Warsaw	Poland	2.2
81	Athens	Greece	3.1	128	Johannesburg	South Africa	2.2
82	Dusseldorf	Germany	3.1	129	Luanda	Angola	2.2
				130	Lucknow	India	2.2
				131	Kabul	Afghanistan	2.2
				132	Taiyuan	China	2.1
				133	Izmir	Turkey	2.1

Urban Areas: Population Over 2 Million *(cont.)*

Rank	Urban Area	Country	Pop.	Rank	Urban Area	Country	Pop.
134	Miami	United States	2.1	141	Saint Louis	United States	2.0
135	Bucharest	Romania	2.1	142	Budapest	Hungary	2.0
136	Damascus	Syria	2.1	143	Tel-Aviv-Yafo	Israel	2.0
137	Mashhad	Iran	2.1	144	Guiyang	China	2.0
138	Vienna	Austria	2.1	145	Surat	India	2.0
139	Esfahan	Iran	2.1	146	Baltimore	United States	2.0
140	Zhengzhou	China	2.0	147	Seattle	United States	2.0

⊙ United Nations Population Division. www.un.org/esa/population/unpop.htm
United Nations Population Division. "United Nations Population Division Population Information Network," www.undp.org/popin

WORLD: *History*

Chronology

c. 6000 BC	Farming begins in Tigris-Euphrates and Nile River Valleys
c. 4000 BC	Farming begins in Yellow River Valley
c. 3500 BC	Sumerian city-states emerge
3300 BC	Rulers divide Nile Valley into Upper and Lower Egypt by this time
c. 3100 BC	Egypt unified into single kingdom
c. 2800	Indus River Valley civilization begins
2180 BC	Egypt's Middle Kingdom established
c. 2000 BC	Stonehenge built in England
c. 1760 BC	Hammurabi rules in Babylon
c. 1700 BC	Hebrew monotheism emerges
c. 1650 BC	Minoan civilization, based on Crete, expands
c. 1600 BC	Shang dynasty introduces writing in China
c. 1500 BC	Olmecs settle in Mexico.
c. 1450 BC	Earthquake destroys Minoan civilization
1299 BC	Egyptian pharoah Ramses I fights Hittites at Kadesh
c. 1250 BC	Moses leads Jews from Egypt to promised land of Palestine
c. 1200 BC	Trojan War
1122 BC	Zhou dynasty established in China
1000 BC	David begins reign as king of the Jews, defeats Philistines before his death in 961
c. 814 BC	Carthage founded by Phoenicians
776 BC	1st Olympic Games are staged at Olympia, Greece
753 BC	Traditional founding date of Rome
725 BC	Kushite kingdom of Nubia conquers Egypt
c. 600 BC	Zoroaster announces Zoroastrianism, a religion emphasizing spirits of good and evil
c. 545 BC	Cyrus the Great solidifies power and founds Persian Empire
509 BC	Rome forces out Etruscan kings, Roman Republic founded
492 BC	Persian Wars, a 40-year series of Persian military expeditions against the Greeks, begin
431 BC	Athens and Sparta oppose each other in Peloponnesian War
405 BC	Peloponnesian War concludes with Athens' defeat at Aegospotami
371 BC	Thebes and Athens defeat Sparta

336 BC	Alexander the Great of Macedon conquers Greece
333 BC	Alexander defeats Darius at Issus
323 BC	Alexander dies; in less than 20 years his empire has been divided several times
241 BC	Rome defeats Carthage in 1st Punic War
218 BC	Hannibal leads Cathaginian forces across the Alps in 2d Punic War
214 BC	Earliest version of the Great Wall amalgamated in China
201 BC	Roman general Scipio defeats Hannibal at Zama, ending 2nd Punic War
146 BC	3rd Punic War ends with destruction of Carthage, which becomes Roman province
136 BC	China's Emperor Wudi makes Confucianism the basis of government administration
c. 60 BC	China's Han dynasty extends control to central Asia
44 BC	Julius Caesar assassinated in Roman Senate by opponents of his dictatorship
27 BC	Augustus Caesar becomes emperor
c. 4 BC	Jesus born in Bethlehem, Palestine
c. 50 AD	Buddhist monks reach China
70	Jews revolt; Romans destroy temple in Jerusalem, end of Hebrew state
79	Roman city of Pompeii buried in volcanic ash from Vesuvius eruption
c. 100	Paper invented in China
265	China reunited under Western Jin dynasty, ending Three Kingdoms period
285	Emperor Diocletian divides Roman Empire into Eastern and Western realms
c. 300	Axum (Ethiopia) adopts Christianity
313	Eastern Roman Emperor Constantine grants freedom to all religions; Christians gain major influence by 330
410	Visigoths, led by Alaric, sack Rome
452	Attila the Hun's invasion of Gaul stopped
476	Western Roman Empire begins to decline
486	Clovis defeats Romans in Gaul and establishes Merovingian dynasty
534	Byzantine Emperor Justinian conquers North Africa and Italy (554)
550	Northern India's Gupta dynasty falls
551	Buddhism introduced into Japan
589	Sui dynasty reunifies China
618	Tang dynasty founded in China
622	Mohammed flees from Mecca to Medina in episode known as the Hejira
632	Death of Mohammed leads to struggle over succession; Islam divided
638	Umayyad dynasty founded in Jerusalem
652	Koran completed in final form
688	Islam's Dome of the Rock begun in Jerusalem
710	Nara era begins in Japan
711	Moorish invasion of Spain starts
732	Charles Martel halts Muslim invasion of France
750	Al Mansur establishes Abbasid caliphate
774	Charlemagne conquers Italy, beginning major expansion of his empire
800	Charlemagne crowned Holy Roman Emperor in Rome
843	Treaty of Verdun divides Charlemagne's empire into three parts
865	Byzantine (Eastern Orthodox) and Roman Catholic forms of Christianity separate
955	Otto I, Holy Roman Emperor since 936, defeats Magyars at Lechfeld
960	Northern Song dynasty established in China
987	Quetzalcoatl, ruler of Mexico's Toltecs, abdicates
c. 1000	Viking invasions of Europe peak; Leif Ericson sails to North America; Norse colony set up in Newfoundland
1031	Umayyad dynasty falls in Spain
1055	Muslims driven from Portugal by Ferdinand of Castile

1066	William of Normandy becomes king of England after defeating King Harold at Battle of Hastings
1071	Ottoman Empire established
1096	1st Crusade begins; crusaders take Jerusalem from Arabs
c. 1100	Cambodia's Khmer empire achieves height of power
1204	4th Crusade takes Constantinople and founds Latin Empire of the East
1206	Genghis Khan begins reign as Mongol leader, assembling vast empire before his death in 1227
1215	England's King John is pressured to sign Magna Carta, curbing royal power
1234	Mongols absorb China's Chin Empire
1244	Turks capture Jerusalem; 7th Crusade (1248-50) is unable to retake city
1260	Kublai Khan becomes leader of the Mongols, establishes Yuan dynasty in China (1280)
1270	Louis IX of France dies in Tunis leading the 9th Crusade
1271	Marco Polo begins expedition to China
1273	1st Mongol invasion of Japan fails
1325	Aztec capital of Tenochtitlan established in Mexico
1327	England's King Edward II deposed and killed
1337	Hundred Years' War between England and France begins over claims to England's throne
1348	Black Death begins to ravage Europe
1368	Rebellion against Mongol rule leads to founding of Ming dynasty in China
1378	Papacy splits, Great Schism results in popes installed at Rome and Avignon, France
1391	Tamerlane extends his power into Central Asia with defeat of Mongols' Golden Horde
1399	England's Richard II deposed; Henry IV ascends the throne
1421	Beijing becomes capital of China's Ming dynasty
1431	French heroine Joan of Arc burned at the stake
1434	Medici family begins 60-year control of Florence
1453	Fall of Constantinople to Ottomans ends Byzantine Empire
1472	Russia's Ivan the Great takes the title of tsar
1479	Spain's Ferdinand and Isabella unite their kingdoms of Aragon and Castile
1482	Agreement with the papacy permits Spain to put the church and Inquisition under royal control
1488	Explorer Bartolomeu Diaz sails around Africa's Cape of Good Hope
1492	Christopher Columbus reaches the New World (Hispaniola); Spain captures Granada, completing reconquest of Spain from Moors
1498	Vasco da Gama lands in India after sailing around Cape of Good Hope
1500	Portugal claims Brazil
1517	Martin Luther writes 95 theses
1519	Hernan Cortes begins conquest of the Aztecs in Mexico; Ferdinand Magellan starts voyage that circumnavigates the world
c. 1519	Nanak establishes Sikhism as a religion
1520	Luther, excommunicated in 1520, addresses the Diet of Worms
1540	Jesuit order founded by Ignatius de Loyola
1541	Puritan theocracy founded by John Calvin at Geneva, Switzerland
1546	Catholic Counter Reformation, supported by Holy Roman Emperor Charles V, opposes German Protestant princes
1563	Church of England (Anglican Church) established
1580	Philip II unites Spain and Portugal
1587	Japan expels Portuguese missionaries

1588	England defeats the Spanish Armada
1598	France's Henry IV grants Protestant Huguenots equal rights with Catholics in Edict of Nantes
1603	Tokugawa (Edo) period begins in Japan
1618	Thirty Years War starts in Europe
1619	Mayflower lands Pilgrims on Cape Cod, Massachusetts
1642	English Civil War starts
1648	Peace of Westphalia ends Thirty Years War; Fronde uprisings try unsuccessfully to challenge royal power in France
1649	Charles I of England executed; Oliver Cromwell governs England through Commonwealth
1660	England restores monarchy with Charles II as king
1661	France's Louis XIV begins ruling in his own right
1673	Jacques Marquette and Louis Joliet explore Mississippi River for France
1676	King Philip's War ends with defeat of Indians after decimating New England
1685	Louis XIV revokes Edict of Nantes, resulting in Huguenot emigration from France
1687	Austro-Hungarian forces defeat Turks at Mohacs, halting Turks expansion into Europe
1688	In Glorious Revolution, England deposes Catholic-supporting James II and replaces him with his Protestant daughter Mary
1713	Treaty of Utrecht, ending War of the Spanish Succession, keeps France and Spain separate
1725	Peter the Great of Russia dies
1726	Spiritual movement called the Great Awakening begins in American colonies
1741	Russia's Vitus Bering explores Alaska
1754	French and Indian War begins in North America, with Britain and France vying for control of the continent
1756	Seven Years War starts in Europe
1763	Britain's supremacy over France in North American and India confirmed by Treaty of Paris
1764	Stamp Act inspires protests in American colonies
1765	Egypt declares independence from Ottoman Empire
1768	James Cook begins exploration of Australia
1770	Boston Massacre increases American resentment of British
1773	Boston Tea Party protests British tax on tea in American colonies
1774	1st Continental Congress meets
1775	Battle of Lexington and Concord opens Revolutionary War
1776	American independence declared; Declaration of Independence signed
1783	Treaty of Paris formalizes American independence. Russia occupies Crimea
1788	U.S. Constitution ratified
1789	French Revolution begins
1792	France becomes a republic; Louis XVI executed in 1793
1793	Eli Whitney invents cotton gin, immensely speeding cotton production
1798	Britain's Admiral Nelson defeats French at Battle of the Nile
1804	Napoleon takes the title of emperor
1807	British abolish slave trade
1811	Venezuela and Paraguay gain independence from Spain
1812	United States and Britain begin War of 1812. Napoleon invades Russia, resulting in huge losses
1814	Napoleon forced to abdicate and goes into exile. Washington, D.C. burned by British
1815	Napoleon returns to power but is defeated at Battle of Waterloo and exiled again. War of 1812 ends with American victory over British at Battle of New Orleans
1818	U.S.-Canadian border agreed upon
1819	Missouri Compromise establishes line between free and slave states
1820	Mexico and Peru gain independence from Spain

1821	Brazil becomes independent of Portugal
1822	Through Monroe Doctrine, United States warns European powers to stay out of colonial affairs in the Americas
1830	French depose Charles X, replacing him with Louis Philippe
1831	Nat Turner's Rebellion, a U.S. slave uprising, results in about 60 white and 100 slave deaths
1836	Americans annihilated at Alamo during Texas Rebellion
1837	Queen Victoria ascends British throne
1839	Opium Wars start in China
1845	Potato Famine beings in Ireland, resulting in starvation and widespread emigration
1849	California gold rush follows discovery of gold at Sutter's Mill in 1848
1850	Compromise of 1850 attempts to resolve U.S. slavery questions
1852	Napoleon III takes power in France as emperor
1856	Crimean War ends
1858	Last of Indian Mutinies are suppressed by British in India
1861	Civil War begins with Confederate shelling of Ft. Sumter
1865	Civil War ends with Confederate surrender at Appomattox; Lincoln assassinated
1866	Prussia defeats Austria in Austro-Prussian War
1867	British North America Act forms Dominion of Canada. Shogunate abolished in Japan; Emperor Meiji ascends throne
1869	Suez Canal opens
1870	Empire falls after Prussia's defeat of France in Franco-Prussian War
1876	Battle of the Little Bighorn. Alexander Graham Bell patents telephone
1878	Thomas Edison patents his light bulb
1881	Germany signs alliance with Russia and Austria
1884	Treaty of Berlin states the rights of European powers in Africa
1885	Canadian-Pacific Railway completed
1894	Dreyfus Affair surfaces in France
1895	After military victories, Japan wins concessions from China
1898	Spanish-American War results in U.S. territorial gains
1899	Boxer Rebellion in China brings foreign intervention
1902	Boer War ends in southern Africa
1903	Wilbur and Orville Wright make 1st airplane flight
1904	Revolution in Russia brings few reforms
1906	San Francisco earthquake and fire destroy much of the city
1908	Henry Ford markets 1st Model T
1910	Union of South Africa formed
1911	Mexican dictator Porfirio Diaz overthrown. Sun Yat-sen establishes republic in China
1914	World War I begins after Austrian Archduke Ferdinand is assassinated. Panama Canal opens
1917	Russian Revolution overthrows tsar
1918	World War I ends with defeat of Germany
1919	Treaty of Versailles. League of Nations is established
1923	Modernization of Turkey begins under Kemal Ataturk
1927	Charles Lindbergh makes 1st non-stop solo flight across Atlantic Ocean
1928	Chiang Kai-shek becomes president of China
1929	Stock market crash on Wall St. leads to business depression
1931	Japan occupies Manchuria

1933	Adolf Hitler and Nazis come to power in Germany. Franklin Roosevelt inaugurates New Deal programs in United States
1935	Italy invades Ethiopia. Nuremberg Laws deprive Jews of all citizenship rights in Germany
1937	Japan starts war against China
1938	Germany annexes Austria
1939	World War II starts with Germany's invasion of Poland
1940	Germany overruns France
1941	Japanese bombing of Pearl Harbor brings United States into World War II
1944	Normandy invasion initiates final phase of war against Germany
1945	Germany surrenders; United States drops two atomic bombs on Japan to end war in Pacific; United Nations founded
1947	Marshall Plan devised to rebuild post-war Europe. India gains independence from Britain
1948	Israel becomes independent. Berlin Airlift carries supplies to blockaded city
1949	Mao Zedong and communists set up People's Republic of China. North Atlantic Treaty Organization (NATO) established
1950	Korean War opens as North Korea invades South Korea
1954	Egypt declared a republic with Nasser as prime minister
1955	Warsaw Pact of Soviet Union and its satellites formed to oppose NATO. Vietnam divided into North and South by Geneva Conference
1956	Soviet troops intervene in Hungary to crush nationalist uprising. Egypt nationalizes Suez Canal, triggering war with Britain, France, and Israel
1957	Treaty of Rome establishes European Common Market
1958	Russians build Berlin Wall. U.S.-supported Bay of Pigs invasion fails in Cuba
1962	Soviets back down during Cuban Missile Crisis
1963	U.S. President Kennedy is assassinated and is succeeded by Lyndon Johnson
1964	Gulf of Tonkin Resolution authorizes U.S. action in Vietnam
1967	Israel defeats Arab coalition in Six Day War
1968	China's Cultural Revolution comes to an end. Martin Luther King assassinated
1969	American astronauts walk on the moon
1973	Arab forces oppose Israel in Yom Kippur War. Last U.S. troops leave Vietnam. Military coup in Chile
1974	U.S. President Nixon resigns in wake of Watergate scandal
1975	Communist regimes take power in Vietnam and Cambodia
1978	Leaders of Egypt and Israel meet at Camp David. Spain returns to constitutional monarchy
1979	Soviet Union invades Afghanistan
1982	Britain defeats Argentina in Falklands War
1986	Soviet Union starts reforms of glasnost and perestroika
1987	Iran-Contra Affair tarnishes Reagan administration
1988	Long Iran-Iraq war halted by truce. Soviets withdraw from Afghanistan
1989	Communist governments fall in Soviet Union and Eastern Europe. United States invades Panama to topple General Noriega's government. China kills pro-democracy demonstrators in Beijing's Tiananmen Square
1990	Iraq invades Kuwait, provoking international opposition. Germany reunifies. Yugoslavia's republics begin to declare independence. Maastricht Treaty proposes European monetary union
1991	Iraq defeated by U.S.-led international force. Most former Soviet republics reassemble in looser Commonwealth of Independent States
1992	South Africa decides to end white-minority rule. Brutal civil wars continue in former Yugoslavia
1993	North American Free Trade Agreement (NAFTA) signed. South Africa moves toward a multi-racial society. Israel and Palestinians sign peace agreement

1994	Nelson Mandela elected as South Africa's 1st black president. Civil war breaks out in Rwanda. Russia faces internal unrest
1995	Israeli prime minister Itzhak Rabin is assassinated
1996	Bosnia, Croatia, and Serbia reach agreement on peace
1997	Hong Kong comes under Chinese rule, ending British control. Rebellion in Zaire results in toppling of long-time leader Mobutu Sese Seko; nation takes new name as Democratic Republic of Congo
1998	Irish factions agree on basic framework for peace. Serbian province of Kosovo is the scene of massacres of ethnic Albanians
1999	U.S. President Clinton acquitted during impeachment trial. Conflict between Russians and Chechnyans escalates
2000	United Nations report on AIDS released; disease has killed 19 million people worldwide, another 34 million infected with AIDS virus, HIV
2001	Muslim extremists hijack four passenger jets on U.S. east coast and use them to destroy New York's World Trade Center towers and a section of the Pentagon

⊙ *Atlas of World History.* Chicago: Rand McNally, 1995.
 Beeching, Cyril Leslie. *A Dictionary of Dates,* 2d ed. New York: Oxford University Press, 1997.
 McKay, John P., Bennett Hill, John Buckler, and Patricia Buckley Ebrey. *A History of World Societies,* 2 vols. Boston: Houghton Mifflin, 2000.

Dynasties of China

Dynasty	Dates	Dynasty	Dates
Qin	221–207 BC	Western Wei	535–557
Western Han	207 BC–AD 9	Northern Chou	557–581
Xin	9–25	Sui	581–618
Eastern Han	25–220	Tang	618–907
The Three Kingdoms		**The Five Dynasties**	
Wei	220–266	Later Liang	907–923
Shu Han	221–263	Later Tang	923–937
Wu	222–280	Later Jin	937–947
Western Jin	266–316	Later Han	947–951
Southern Dynasties		Later Zhou	951–960
Eastern Jin	317–420		
Liu Sung	420–479	**The Border Empires**	
Southern Ch'i	479–502	Liao	907–1125
Liang	502–557	Chin	1115–1234
Ch'en	557–589	Northern Song	960–1127
Northern Dynasties		Southern Song	1127–1279
Northern Wei	386–535	Yuan	1206–1368
Eastern Wei	534–550	Ming	1368–1644
Northern Ch'i	550–577	Qing	1644–1912

⊙ Ebrey, Patricia Buckley, ed. *Chinese Civilization: A Sourcebook,* 2nd ed. New York: Free Press/Macmillan, 1993.
 Paludan, Ann. *Chronicle of the Chinese Emperors: The Reign-By-Reign Record of the Rulers of Imperial China.* New York: Thames and Hudson, 1998.
 Pei, Ming L., ed. "China the Beautiful," www.chinapage.org/history1.html

House	Monarch	Reign	House	Monarch	Reign
Wessex (West Saxon)			**York**		
	Egbert	802–839		Edward IV	1461–1483
	Ethelwulf	839–856		Edward V	1483
	Ethelbald	856–860		Richard III	1483–1485
	Ethelbert	860–866	**Tudor**		
	Ethelred I	866–871			
	Alfred the Great	871–899		Henry VII	1485–1509
	Edward the Elder	899–924		Henry VIII	1509–1547
	Athelstan	925–939		Edward VI	1547–1553
	Edmund I	939–946		Jane (Lady Jane Grey)	1553
	Edred	946–955		Mary I	1553–1558
	Edwy	955–957		Elizabeth I	1558–1603
	Edgar	959–975	**Stuart**		
	Edward the Martyr	975–978			
	Ethelred II (the Unready)	978–1016		James I	1603–1625
	Edmund II (Ironside)	1016		Charles I	1625–1649
Danish			**Commonwealth**		
	Canute (Cnut)	1016–1035		Long Parliament	1649–1660
	Harold I	1035–1040	**Protectorate**		
	Hardecanute	1040–1042		Oliver Cromwell	1653–1658
West Saxon (restored)				Richard Cromwell	1658–1660
	Edward II (the Confessor)	1042–1066	**Stuart**		
	Harold II	1066			
Normandy				Charles II	1660–1685
	William I (the Conqueror)	1066–1087		James II	1685–1688
	William II	1087–1100		interregnum	1688–1689
	Henry I	1100–1135		William III and	
	Stephen	1135–1154		Mary II	1689–1694
Plantagenet (Anjou)				Anne	1702–1714
	Henry II	1154–1189	**Hanover**		
	Richard I			George I	1714–1727
	(the Lion-heart)	1189–1199		George II	1727–1760
	John	1199–1216		George III	1760–1820
	Harold I	1035–1040		George IV	1820–1830
	Henry III	1216–1272		William IV	1830–1837
	Edward I	1272–1307	**Saxe-Coburg-Gotha**		
	Edward II	1307–1327		Victoria	1837–1901
	Edward III	1327–1377		Edward VII	1901–1910
	Richard II	1377–1399	**Windsor**		
Lancaster				George V	1910–1936
	Henry IV	1399–1413		Edward VIII	1936
	Henry V	1413–1422		George VI	1936–1952
	Henry VI	1422–1461		Elizabeth II	1952–

⊙ Davies, Norman. *The Isles: A History*. New York: Oxford University Press, 2000.

Fraser, Antonia. *The Lives of the Kings and Queens of England*, rev. ed. Berkeley: University of California Press, 1998.

Morgan, Kenneth O. *The Oxford Illustrated History of Britain*. Oxford: Oxford University Press, 1984.

Kings and Emperors of France

House	Monarch	Reign
Carolingian		
	Pepin (the Short)	751–768
	Carloman	768–771
	Charles (Charlemagne)	768–814
	Louis I (the Pious)	814–840
	Charles II (the Bald)	840–877
	Louis II (the Stammerer)	877–879
	Louis III	879–882
	Carloman	879–884
	Charles III (the Fat)	885–888
Robertian		
	Eudes	888–898
Carolingian		
	Charles III (the Simple)	893–923
Robertian		
	Robert I	922–923
	Rudolf	923–936
Carolingian		
	Louis IV	936–954
	Lothair	954–986
	Louis V	986–987
Capetian		
	Hugh Capet	987–996
	Robert II	996–1031
	Hugh	1017–1025
	Henry I	1031–1060
	Philip I	1060–1108
	Louis VI (the Fat)	1108–1137
	Philip	1129–1131
	Louis VII	1137–1180
	Philip II	1180–1223
	Louis VIII	1223–1226
	Louis IX (St.)	1226–1270
	Philip III	1270–1285
	Philip IV (the Fair)	1285–1314
	Louis X (the Stubborn)	1314–1316
	John I	1316
	Philip V (the Tall)	1316–1322
	Charles IV (the Fair)	1322–1328
Valois		
	Philip VI	1328–1350
	John II (the Good)	1350–1364

House	Monarch	Reign
	Charles V (the Wise)	1364–1380
	Charles VI (the Mad)	1380–1422
	Charles VII (the Victorious)	1422–1461
	Louis XI	1461–1498
	Charles VIII	1483–1498
Orléans		
	Louis XII	1498–1515
Angoulême		
	Francis I	1515–1547
	Henry II	1547–1559
	Francis II	1559–1560
	Charles IX	1560–1574
	Henry III	1574–1589
Bourbon		
	Henry IV	1589–1610
	Louis XIII	1610–1643
	Louis XIV	1643–1715
	Louis XV	1715–1774
	Louis XVI	1774–1792
	Louis XVII	1793–1795
First Republic		
	National Convention	1792–1795
	Directory	1795–1799
	Consulate	1799–1804
Bonaparte		
	Napoleon I	1804–1814
	Napoleon I	1815
	Napoleon II	1815
Bourbon		
	Louis XVIII	1814–1824
	Charles X	1824–1830
Orléans		
	Louis Philippe I	1830–1848
Second Republic		
	Louis Napoleon Bonaparte	1848–1852
Bonaparte		
	Napoleon III	1852–1870

⊙ James, E. *The Franks*. New York: Basil Blackwell, 1988.
McKitterick, R. *The Frankish Kingdoms and the Early Carolingians, 751–987*. New York: Longman, 1983.
Price, R. *A Concise History of France*. Cambridge: Cambridge University Press, 1993.

Dynasties of Japan

Dynasty	Dates	Dynasty	Dates
Yamato	40 BC–AD 70	Northern Court	1331–1392
Asuka	552–710	Muromachi	1392–1573
Nara	710–784	Tokugawa	1600–1868
Early Heian	794–857	Kamakura Shogunate	1185–1195
Late Heian or Fujiwara	858–1185	Hojo Regency	1203–1333
Kamakura	1185–1336	Ashikaga Shogunate	1338–1358
Southern Court	1336–1392	Tokugawa Shogunate	1603–1868

⊙ Collcott, M., M. Jansen, and I. Kumakura, *Cultural Atlas of Japan.* New York: Facts on File, 1988.
Morton, W. Scott. *Japan: Its History and Culture,* 3rd ed. New York: McGraw-Hill, 1994.

Holy Roman Emperors

House	Monarch	Reign	House	Monarch	Reign
Carolingian			Hohenstaufen		
	Charles (Charlemagne)	800–814		Conrad III	1138–1152
	Louis I (the Pious)	814–840		Henry	1147–1150
	Lothair I	840–855		Fredrick I (Barbarosa)	1152–1190
	Louis II	855–875		Henry VI	1190–1197
	Charles II (the Bald)	875–877		Philip of Swabia	1198–1208
	Charles III (the Fat)	881–887	Welf		
	Arnulf of Carinthia	887–899		Otto IV	1198–1218
	Louis III (the Child)	900–911			
Franconia			Hohenstaufen		
	Conrad I	911–918		Fredrick II	1212–1250
				Henry	1220–1235
Saxony				[Henry Raspe of	
	Henry I (the Fowler)	919–936		Thuringia	1246–1247]
	Otto I (the Great)	936–973		[William of Holland	1247–1256]
	Otto II	973–983		Conrad IV	1250–1254
	Otto III	983–1002		[Richard of Cornwall	1257–1272]
	St. Henry II	1002–1024	Habsburg		
				Rudolf I	1273–1291
Salian			Nassau		
	Conrad II	1024–1039		Adolf	1292–1298
	Henry III	1039–1056			
	Henry IV	1056–1105	Habsburg		
	[Rudolf of Swabia	1077–1080]		Albert I of Austria	1298–1308
	[Herman of Salm	1081–1088]	Luxemburg		
	Conrad	1087–1098		Henry VII	1308–1313
	Henry V	1105–1125			
Suplinburg			Wittelsbach		
	Lothair II of Saxony	1125–1137		Louis IV of Bavaria	1314–1347
				[Frederick of Austria	1314–1330]

Holy Roman Emperors *(cont.)*

House	Monarch	Reign	House	Monarch	Reign
Luxemburg				Maximilian II	1564–1576
	Charles IV	1346–1378		Rudolf II	1576–1612
	[Günther of Schwarzburg	1349]		Matthias	1612–1619
	Wenceslas	1378–1400		Ferdinand II	1619–1637
				Ferdinand III	1637–1657
Wittelsbach				Leopold I	1658–1705
	Rupert of the Palatinate	1400–1410		Joseph I	1705–1711
Luxemburg				Charles VI	1711–1740
	Sigismund	1410–1437	Wittelsbach		
	[Jobst of Moravia	1410–1411]		Charles VII of Bavaria	1742–1745
Habsburg			Habsburg-Lorraine		
	Albert II of Austria	1438–1439		Francis I of Lorraine	1745–1765
	Frederick III	1440–1493		Joseph II	1765–1790
	Maximilian I	1493–1558		Leopold II	1790–1792
	Charles V	1519–1558		Francis II	1792–1806
	Ferdinand I	1558–1564			

⊙ Bartlett, R. *The Making of Europe: Conquest, Colonization, and Cultural Change, 950–1350.* Princeton, N.J.: Princeton University Press, 1993.

Scott, H., ed. *The European Nobilities in the Seventeenth and Eighteenth Centuries.* New York: Addison-Wesley, 1995.

Roman Emperors from Augustus to Constantine

Dynasty	Emperor	Reign	Dynasty	Emperor	Reign
Julio-Claudians				Lucius Verus	
	Augustus	27 BC–AD 14		(co-emperor)	161–169
	Tiberius	AD 14–37		Commodus	180–192
	Gaius (Caligula)	37–41		Pertinax	193
	Claudius	41–54		Didius Julianus	193
	Nero	54–68	Severi		
	Galba	68–69		Septimius Severus	193–211
	Otho	69		Caracalla	211–217
	Vitellius	69		Macrinus	217–218
Flavians				Elagabalus	218–222
	Vespasian	69–79		Severus	
	Titus	79–81		Alexander	222–235
	Domitian	81–96	The Soldier-Emperors		
Antonines				Maximinus the Thracian	235–238
	Nerva	96–98		Gordian I and Gordian II	238
	Trajan	97–117		Balbinus and Pupienus	
	Hadrian	117–138		Maximus	238
	Antoninus Pius	138–161		Gordian III	238–244
	Marcus Aurelius	161–180		Philip I the Arab	244–249

Philip II	247–249		Carinus	283–285
Decius	249–251		Numerian	283–284
Trebonianus Gallus	251–253			

Diocletian and the Tetrarchy

Aemilian	253		Diocletian	284–305
Valerian	253–260		Maximian	286–305
Gallienus	253–268		Constantius	292–306
Claudius II Gothicus	268–270		Galerius	293–311
Aurelian	270–275		Licinius	311–323
Tacitus	275–276			

Dynasty of Constantine

Florian	276		Constantine	306–337
Probus	276–282			
Carus	282–283			

⊙ Louisiana State University. "List of Roman Emperors to AD 235," http://skross.hist.lsu.edu/
  emperors.htm

  Oxford University Press. *Oxford Illustrated Encyclopedia: Index and Ready Reference.* New York: Oxford
  University Press, 1993.

  University of Illinois at Urbana-Champaign. "The Roman Achievement," www.classics.uiuc.edu/
  RomanCiv/Overheads/Emperors.htm

Czars and Czarinas of Russia

House	Monarch	Reign	House	Monarch	Reign
Rurik			**Shuiskii**		
	Daniel	1263–1303		Basil IV Shuiskii	1606–1610
	Yurii	1303–1325	**Romanov**		
	Ivan I (Kalita)	1325–1340		Michael Romanov	1613–1645
	Simeon (the Proud)	1340–1353		Alexis	1645–1676
	Ivan II (the Gentle)	1353–1359		Theodore III	1676–1682
Grand Princes of Moscow-Vladimir				Ivan V	1682–1696
	Dimitri Donskoi	1359–1389		Peter I (the Great)	1682–1725
	Basil I	1389–1425		Catherine I	1725–1727
	Basil II (the Blind)	1425–1462		Peter II	1727–1730
	Ivan III (the Great)	1462–1505		Anne	1730–1740
	Ivan the Younger	1471–1490		Ivan VI	1740–1741
	Basil III	1505–1533		Elizabeth	1741–1762
Czars of Russia			**Holstein-Gottorp-Romanov**		
	Ivan IV (the Terrible)	1533–1584		Peter III	1762
	Theodore I	1584–1598		Catherine II (the Great)	1762–1796
Godunov				Paul I	1796–1801
	Boris Godunov	1598–1605		Alexander I	1801–1825
	Theodore II	1605		Nicholas I	1825–1855
	Dimitri	1605–1606		Alexander II	1855–1881
				Alexander III	1881–1894
				Nicholas II	1894–1917

⊙ Dukes, Paul. *A History of Russia: Medieval, Modern, Contemporary* c. 882–1996, 3d ed. Durham, N.C.:
  Duke University Press, 1998.

  Lawrence, John. *A History of Russia: A Brilliant Chronicle of Russian History from Its Ancient Beginnings to
  the Present Day,* 7th ed., rev. New York: Meridian, 1993.

Rulers of Spain

House	Monarch	Reign	House	Monarch	Reign
House of Habsburg			**Provisional Government:**		1868–1870
	Charles I	1516–1556			
	Philip II	1556–1598	**House of Savoy**		
	Philip III	1598–1621		Amadeus I	1870–1873
	Philip IV	1621–1665			
	Charles II	1665–1700	**First Republic**		1873–1874
House of Bourbon					
	Philip V	1700–1724	**House of Bourbon**		
	Louis I	1724		Alfonso XII	1874–1885
	Philip V (second reign)	1724–1746		Alfonso XIII	1886–1931
	Ferdinand VI	1746–1759			
	Charles III	1759–1788	**Second Republic**		1931–1939
	Charles IV	1788–1808			
	Ferdinand VII	1808	**Spanish State** (Francisco Franco)		1939–1975
House of Bonaparte					
	Joseph Napoleon	1808–1813	**House of Bourbon**		
House of Bourbon				Juan Carlos I	1975–
	Ferdinand VII (second reign)	1813–1833			
	Isabel II	1833–1868			

⊙ Oxford University Press. Oxford Illustrated Encyclopedia: Index and Ready Reference. New York: Oxford University Press, 1993.
Wetterau, Bruce. World History. New York: Henry Holt, 1994.

WORLD: *Religion*

Major World Religions

Religion	Approximate Number of Adherents	Religion	Approximate Number of Adherents
Christianity	2,000,000,000	Spiritism	14,000,000
Islam	1,200,000,000	Babi and Baha'i	6,000,000
Hinduism	880,000,000	Jainism	4,000,000
Buddhism	350,000,000	Shinto	4,000,000
Chinese traditional religion (including Confucianism and Taoism)	200,000,000	Cao Dai	3,000,000
		Tenrikyo	2,400,000
Primal (or tribal) indigenous religion (including animism, shamanism, and paganism)	190,000,000	Neo-Paganism	1,000,000
		Unitarian Universalism	800,000
		Scientology	750,000
Yoruba	20,000,000	Rastafarianism	700,000
Juche	19,000,000	Zoroastrianism	150,000
Sikhism	18,000,000	Nonreligion (including secularism, atheism, and agnosticism)	900,000,000
Judaism	16,000,000		

⊙ Adherents.com. "List of World's Major Religions," www.adherents.com/Religions_By_Adherents.html
Bach, Marcus. *Major Religions of the World.* Marina Del Rey, Calif.: DeVorss, 1984.

Major U.S. Religions and Their Principal Denominations

Religion and Denomination	Approximate Number of Adherents	Religion and Denomination	Approximate Number of Adherents
Christianity		**Judaism**	3,200,000
Protestant	105,500,000	Conservative	1,600,000
Baptist	34,000,000	Reform	900,000
Methodist	14,000,000	Orthodox	700,000
Lutheran	9,000,000		
Presbyterian	5,000,000		
Pentecostal	3,200,000	**Islam**	1,000,000
Episcopalian	3,000,000	Black Muslim	460,000
Mormon (Latter-Day Saints)	3,000,000		
United Church of Christ	1,700,000	Unitarian Universalism	500,000
Church of Christ	1,600,000		
Jehovah's Witnesses	1,300,000	Buddhism	400,000
Mennonites	180,000		
Society of Friends (Quakers)	140,000	Hinduism	230,000
Amish Mennonites	50,000		
Anglican Orthodox (Church of England)	6,000	Baha'i	64,000
		Native American traditional religion	50,000
Roman Catholic	50,000,000	Scientology	45,000

⊙ Adherents.com. "List of World's Major Religions," www.adherents.com/Religions_By_Adherents.html
Bach, Marcus. Major Religions of the World. Marina Del Rey, Calif.: DeVorss, 1984.

Major Religious Holidays and Festivals

Religion	Holiday/Festival	Date*
Baha'i	Ayyam-i-Ha (Days of Ha)	February 25–March 1
	Feast of Ridvan	April 21–May 2
	Declaration of the Bab	May 23
	Ascension of Baha'u'llah	May 29
	Martyrdom of the Bab	July 9
	Birth of the Bab	October 20
	Birth of Baha'u'llah	November 12
	Ascension of Abdu'l-Baha	November 28
Buddhism	Magha Puja (Full Moon Day)	full moon of March or April*
	Songkran (Pi Mai)	April 12–14
	Vesak (Buddha Day)	full moon of May or June*
	Obon (Festival of the Dead)	July 13–15 or August 13–15 (regional)
	Loi Krathong	full moon of November*
Christianity (in U.S.)	Feast of the Epiphany	January 6
	Candlemas	February 2

movable date on Gregorian calendar

Religion	Holiday/Festival	Date*
	Shrove Tuesday	day before Ash Wednesday*
	Ash Wednesday (1st day of Lent)	between February 4 and March 10*
	Palm Sunday	Sunday before Easter*
	Maundy Thursday	day before Good Friday*
	Good Friday	Friday before Easter*
	Easter Sunday	between March 22 and April 25*
	Pentecost	seventh Sunday after Easter*
	All Saints' Day	November 1
	Christmas	December 25
Confucianism	Qing Ming (Ching Ming)	106 days after winter solstice Festival (April)*
	Chongmyo Taeje	first Sunday in May*
	Birth of Confucius	September 28
Hinduism	Vasant Panchami	waxing moon of January or February*
	Holi	waxing moon of February or March*
	Ram Navami (birth of Rama)	waxing moon of March or April*
	Naag Panchami	waxing moon of July or August*
	Janmashtami (birth of	new moon of August or Krishna) September*
	Ganesh Chathurthi	waxing moon of August or September*
	Durga Puja	waxing moon of September or October*
	Dhan Teras	2 days before Dewali*
	Dewali (Festival of Lights)	waning moon of October or November*
	Pongal	3 days in December and/or January*
	Kumbh Mela (Pitcher Fair)	once every 12 years*
Islam	Nawruz (New Year)	first day of 1st lunar month (usu. March 21)*
	Ashura	first 10 days of 1st lunar month*
	Data Ganj Baksh	18th and 19th days of 2nd lunar Death Festival month*
	Mawlid al-Nabi (birth of Prophet)	12th day of 3rd lunar month*
	Ramadan	all days of 9th lunar month (late autumn)*
	'Id al-Fitr (end of Ramadan fast)	first day of 10th lunar month*
	Hajj (Pilgrimage to Mecca)	8th–13th days of 12th lunar month*
	'Id al-Adha (Feast of Sacrifice)	10th–12th days of 12th lunar month*
Jainism	Mahavir Jayanti	waxing moon of March or April*
	Paryushana	8–10 days in August and/or September*
Judaism	Rosh Hashanah (New Year)	2 days in September and/or October*
	Yom Kippur	between September 15 and
	(Day of Atonement)	October 13*
	Sukkot (Feast of Booths)	8–9 days in September and/or October*

*movable date on Gregorian calendar

	Shemini Atzeret	8th day of Sukkot*
	Simhat Torah	first 2 days following Sukkot*
	Hanukkah (Chanukah)	8 days in November and/or December*
	Purim	between February 25 and March 25*
	Passover	7–8 days in March and/or April*
	Shavuot	50th day after Passover*
Rastafarianism	Haile Selassie's Coronation Day	around November 15*
Shinto	Hari-Kuyo (Broken Needles)	February 8 (or December 8)
	Rice-Planting Festival at Osaka	June 14
	Bettara-Ichi (Pickle Market)	October 19
	Tori-no-Ichi (Eagle Market)	various days in November*
	Shichi-Go-San	November 15
Sikhism	Hola Mohalla	the day after the Hindu Holi festival*
	Vaisakh	first day of month of Vaisakha (April or May)*
	Guru Parab	full moon of October or November*
Taoism	Tam Kung Festival	8th day of 4th lunar month (usu. May)*
	Birth of Lu Pan	13th day of 6th lunar month (usu. July)*
	Festival of Hungry Ghosts	full moon of July or August*
	Festival of the Nine Imperial Gods	9 days in September and/or October*
Yoruba	Awoojoh (thanksgiving feast)	observed at any time of year
Zoroastrianism	Farvardegan Days	March 11–20 (or 10 days in July or August)
	Jamshed Navaroz (New Year)	March 21
	Khordad Sal	March 21 (or July 13 or August 15)
	Zarthastno Diso	April 30 (or May 29 or June 1)

⊙ Hartford Seminary Library. "Religious Holidays," www.library.hartsem.edu/guides/holidays/htm
Henderson, Helene, and Sue Ellen Thompson. *Holidays, Festivals, and Celebrations of the World Dictionary*, Second Edition. Detroit, Mich.: Omnigraphics, 1997.

Books of the Bible

Hebrew Bible (Old Testament)

Genesis	1 Kings	Ecclesiastes	Amos
Exodus	2 Kings	Song of Songs (Song of	Obadiah
Leviticus	1 Chronicles	Solomon)	Jonah
Numbers	2 Chronicles	Isaiah	Micah
Deuteronomy	Ezra	Jeremiah	Nahum
Joshua	Nehemiah	Lamentations	Habakkuk
Judges	Esther	Ezekiel	Zephaniah
Ruth	Job	Daniel	Haggai
1 Samuel	Psalms	Hosea	Zechariah
2 Samuel	Proverbs	Joel	Malachi

New Testament

Matthew	2 Corinthians	1 Timothy	2 Peter
Mark	Galatians	2 Timothy	1 John
Luke	Ephesians	Titus	2 John
John	Philippians	Philemon	3 John
Acts	Colossians	Hebrews	Jude
Romans	1 Thessalonians	James	Revelation
1 Corinthians	2 Thessalonians	1 Peter	

⊙ American Bible Society. www.americanbible.org/
New Revised Standard Version Bible with Apocrypha. New York: Oxford University Press, 1991.

Other Books of the Bible

Hebrew Bible Apocrypha

Of the numerous apocryphal works associated with the Old Testament, the most familiar are those that comprise the body of books known (primarily by Protestants) as the Apocrypha ("Hidden Books"). Protestants have rejected the authority of these works since the Reformation of the 16th century, but often include them as a separate section of the Bible. Roman Catholics and Greek Orthodox Christians embrace the holiness of a number of these books (usually 12 to 16 of them), which, when so considered, are called the Deuterocanonical Books ("Second-Level Books"). In addition, there are the works known collectively as the Pseudepigrapha ("False Writings"). These books, although associated with the Hebrew Bible, are regarded as strictly noncanonical.

Note: Because there is no universal agreement on which books belong to the Apocrypha, which books are recognized as authoritative, or even by which titles the books properly go, any classification of the apocryphal works is subject to dispute.

The Apocrypha (incorporating the Deuterocanonical Books)

1 Esdras	Ecclesiasticus (Sirach)	Song of the Three Holy
2 Esdras	Wisdom of Solomon	Children
1 Maccabees	1 Baruch (with Epistle of	Prayer of Azariah
2 Maccabees	Jeremiah)	Susanna
3 Maccabees	Prayer of Manasseh	Bel and the Dragon
Tobit	Additions to Book of	Additions to Book of Esther
Judith	Daniel	Psalm 151

The Pseudepigrapha (selected works)

Jubilees	2 Enoch	2 Baruch
Letter of Aristeas	Testament of the Twelve	3 Baruch
Books of Adam and Eve	Patriarchs	4 Esdras
Martyrdom of Isaiah	Sybilline Oracles	Psalms of Solomon
1 Enoch	Assumption of Moses	4 Maccabees (Story of Ahiqar)

New Testament Apocrypha

The extracanonical Christian writings associated with the New Testament are typically classified in accordance with the four major genres of New Testament literature: gospels, acts, epistles (letters), and apocalypses. Lacking a widely accepted definitive list of contents, this body of works includes the following books:

Gospels
Protoevangelium of James
Infancy Gospel of Thomas
Gospel of Peter
Gospel of Nicodemus
Gospel of the Nazoreans
Gospel of the Ebionites
Gospel of the Hebrews
Gospel of the Egyptians
Gospel of Thomas
Gospel of Philip
Gospel of Mary

Acts
Acts of John
Acts of Peter
Acts of Paul
Acts of Andrew
Acts of Thomas
Acts of Andrew and Matthias
Acts of Philip
Acts of Thaddaeus
Acts of Peter and Paul
Acts of Peter and Andrew
Martyrdom of Matthew
Slavonic Act of Peter
Acts of Peter and the Twelve Apostles

Epistles
3 Corinthians (Letter of Paul)
Epistle to the Laodiceans
Letters of Paul and Seneca
Didache (Teachings of the Twelve Apostles)
Letters of Jesus and Abgar
Epistle of Barnabas
Epistle to Diognetus
Letter of Lentulus
Letters of Ignatius
Letters of Clement to the Corinthians
Epistle of Titus

Apocalypses
Apocalypse of Peter
Coptic Apocalypse of Peter
Apocalypse of Paul
1 Apocalypse of James
2 Apocalypse of James
Apocryphon of John
Sophia of Jesus Christ
Letter of Peter to Philip
Apocalypse of Mary
Apocalypse of Bartholomew
Apocalypse of Thomas

⊙ Christian Classics Ethereal Library at Calvin College. "World Wide Study Bible," www.ccel.org/wwsb/ *New Revised Standard Version Bible with Apocrypha.* New York: Oxford University Press, 1991.

Roman Catholic Popes

Note: Where indicated, "antipope" identifies an individual whose election to the papacy has been contested, and therefore declared noncanonical.

Pope	Reign	Pope	Reign
St. Peter	c.32–c.64	St. Hyginus	c.138–c.142
St. Linus	c.66–c.78	St. Pius I	c.142–c.155
St. Anacletus (Cletus)	c.79–c.91	St. Anicetus	c.155–c.166
St. Clement I	c.91–c.101	St. Soter	c.166–c.174
St. Evaristus	c.100–c.109	St. Eleutherius (Eleutherus)	c.174–189
St. Alexander I	c.109–c.116	St. Victor I	189–198
St. Sixtus I (Xystus I)	c.116–c.125	St. Zephyrinus	199–217
St. Telesphorus	c.125–c.136	St. Callistus I (Calixtus I)	217–222

Pope	Reign		Pope	Reign	
St. Hippolytus	217–235	antipope	St. Agapitus I (Agapetus I)	535–536	
St. Urban I	222–230		St. Silverius	536–537	
St. Pontain	230–235		Vigilius	537–555	
St. Anterus	235–236		Pelagius I	556–561	
St. Fabian	236–250		John III	561–574	
St. Cornelius	251–253		Benedict I	575–579	
Novatian	251–258	antipope	Pelagius II	579–590	
St. Lucius I	253–254		St. Gregory I (the Great)	590–604	
St. Stephen I	254–257		Sabinian	604–606	
St. Sixtus II (St. Xystus II)	257–258		Boniface III	607	
St. Dionysius	260–268		St. Boniface IV	608–615	
St. Felix I	269–274		St. Deusdedit (Adeodatus I)	615–618	
St. Eutychian	275–283		Boniface V	619–625	
St. Caius (Gaius)	283–296		Honorius I	625–638	
St. Marcellinus	296–304		Severinus	640	
St. Marcellus I	306–308		John IV	640–642	
St. Eusebius	c.310		Theodore I	642–649	
St. Miltiades (Melchiades)	311–314		St. Martin I	649–653	
St. Sylvester I (St. Silvester I)	314–335		St. Eugene I	654–657	
St. Mark	336		St. Vitalian	657–672	
St. Julius I	337–352		Adeodatus II	672–676	
Liberius	352–366		Donus	676–678	
St. Felix II	355–365	antipope	St. Agatho	678–681	
St. Damasus I	366–384		St. Leo II	682–683	
Ursinus	366–367	antipope	St. Benedict II	684–685	
St. Siricius	384–399		John V	685–686	
St. Anastasius I	399–401		Conon	686–687	
St. Innocent I	401–417		Theodore	687	antipope
St. Zosimus	417–418		Paschal	687	antipope
Eulalius	418–419	antipope	St. Sergius I	687–701	
St. Boniface I	418–422		John VI	701–705	
St. Celestine I	422–432		John VII	705–707	
St. Sixtus III (Xystus III)	432–440		Sisinnius	708	
St. Leo I (the Great)	440–461		Constantine	708–715	
St. Hilarus (Hilary)	461–468		St. Gregory II	715–731	
St. Simplicius	468–483		St. Gregory III	731–741	
St. Felix III (or II)	483–492		St. Zacharius (St. Zachary)	741–752	
St. Gelasius I	492–496		Stephen (II)	752	(died before consecration)
Anastasius II	496–498				
St. Symmachus	498–514		Stephen II (or III)	752–757	
Lawrence	498–499; 501–506	antipope	St. Paul I	757–767	
			Constantine	767–768	antipope
St. Hormisdas	514–523		Philip	768	antipope
St. John I	523–526		Stephen III (or IV)	768–772	
St. Felix IV (or III)	526–530		Adrian I (Hadrian I)	772–795	
Dioscorus	530	antipope (or pope)	St. Leo III	795–816	
			Stephen IV (or V)	816–817	
Boniface II	530–532		St. Paschal I	817–824	
John II	533–535		Eugene II	824–827	

Valentine	827		Benedict IX	1032–1044	
Gregory IV	827–844		Sylvester III (Silvester III)	1045	
John	844	antipope	Benedict IX	1045	
Sergius II	844–847		Gregory VI	1045–1046	
St. Leo IV	847–855		Clement II	1046–1047	
Benedict III	855–858		Benedict IX	1047–1048	
Anastasius Bibliothecarius	855	antipope	Damasus II	1048	
St. Nicholas I (the Great)	858–867		St. Leo IX	1049–1054	
Adrian II (Hadrian II)	867–872		Victor II	1055–1057	
John VIII	872–882		Stephen IX (or X)	1057–1058	
Marinus I	882–884		Benedict X	1058–1059 antipope	
St. Adrian III (St. Hadrian III)	884–885		Nicholas II	1058–1061	
Stephen V (or VI)	885–891		Alexander II	1061–1073	
Formosus	891–896		Honorius (II)	1061–1064 antipope	
Boniface VI	896		St. Gregory VII	1073–1085	
Stephen VI (or VII)	896–897		Clement III (Guibert)	1080; 1084–1100 antipope	
Romanus	897		Blessed Victor III	1086–1087	
Theodore II	897		Blessed Urban II	1088–1099	
John IX	898–900		Paschal II	1099–1118	
Benedict IV	900–903		Theoderic	1100–1101 antipope	
Leo V	903		Albert (Adalbert)	1101 antipope	
Christopher	903–904	antipope	Sylvester IV (Silvester IV)	1105–1111 antipope	
Sergius III	904–911		Gelasius II	1118–1119	
Anastasius III	911–913		Gregory (VIII)	1118–1121 antipope	
Lando	913–914		Callistus II (Calixtus II)	1119–1124	
John X	914–928		Honorius II	1124–1130	
Leo VI	928		Celestine (II)	1124 antipope	
Stephen VII (or VIII)	928–931		Innocent II	1130–1143	
John XI	931–935		Anacletus II	1130–1138 antipope	
Leo VII	936–939		Victor IV*	1138 antipope	
Stephen VIII (or IX)	939–942		Celestine II	1143–1144	
Marinus II	942–946		Lucius II	1144–1145	
Agapitus II (Agapetus II)	946–955		Blessed Eugene III	1145–1153	
John XII	955–964		Anastasius IV	1153–1154	
Leo VIII	963–965		Adrian IV (Hadrian IV)	1154–1159	
Benedict V	964		Alexander III	1159–1181	
John XIII	965–972		Victor IV (*not the same)	1159–1164 antipope	
Benedict VI	973–974		Paschal III	1164–1168 antipope	
Boniface VII	974	antipope	Calistus III (Calixtus III)	1168–1178 antipope	
Benedict VII	974–983		Innocent (III)	1179–1180 antipope	
John XIV	983–984		Lucius III	1181–1185	
Boniface VII	984–985	antipope	Urban III	1185–1187	
John XV	985–996		Gregory VIII	1187	
Gregory V	996–999		Clement III	1187–1191	
John XVI	997–998	antipope	Celestine III	1191–1198	
Sylvester II (Silvester II)	999–1003		Innocent III	1198–1216	
John XVII	1003		Honorius III	1216–1227	
John XVIII	1003–1009		Gregory IX	1227–1241	
Sergius IV	1009–1012		Celestine IV	1241	
Benedict VIII	1012–1024		Innocent IV	1243–1254	
Gregory (VI)	1012	antipope	Alexander IV	1254–1261	
John XIX	1024–1032		Urban IV	1261–1264	

Roman Catholic Popes *(cont.)*

Pope	Reign	Pope	Reign
Clement IV	1265–1268	Paul III	1534–1549
Blessed Gregory X	1271–1276	Julius III	1550–1555
Blessed Innocent V	1276	Marcellus II	1555
Adrian V (Hadrian V)	1276	Paul IV	1555–1559
John XXI	1276–1277	Pius IV	1559–1565
Nicholas III	1277–1280	St. Pius V	1566–1572
Martin IV	1281–1285	Gregory XIII	1572–1585
Honorius IV	1285–1287	Sixtus V	1585–1590
Nicholas IV	1288–1292	Urban VII	1590
St. Celestine V	1294	Gregory XIV	1590–1591
Boniface VIII	1294–1303	Innocent IX	1591
Blessed Benedict XI	1303–1304	Clement VIII	1592–1605
Clement V	1305–1314	Leo XI	1605
John XXII	1316–1334	Paul V	1605–1621
Nicholas (V)	1328–1330 *antipope*	Gregory XV	1621–1623
Benedict XII	1334–1342	Urban VIII	1623–1644
Clement VI	1342–1352	Innocent X	1644–1655
Innocent VI	1352–1362	Alexander VII	1655–1667
Blessed Urban V	1362–1370	Clement IX	1667–1669
Gregory XI	1370–1378	Clement X	1670–1676
Urban VI	1378–1389	Blessed Innocent XI	1676–1689
Clement (VII)	1378–1394 *antipope*	Alexander VIII	1689–1691
Boniface IX	1389–1404	Innocent XII	1691–1700
Benedict (XIII)	1394–1417 *antipope*	Clement XI	1700–1721
Innocent VII	1404–1406	Innocent XIII	1721–1724
Gregory XII	1406–1415	Benedict XIII	1724–1730
Alexander V	1409–1415 *antipope*	Clement XII	1730–1740
John (XXIII)	1410–1429 *antipope*	Benedict XIV	1740–1758
Martin V	1417–1431	Clement XIII	1758–1769
Clement (VIII)	1423–1429 *antipope*	Clement XIV	1769–1774
Benedict (XIV)	1425–c.1430 *antipope*	Pius VI	1775–1799
Eugene IV	1431–1447	Pius VII	1800–1823
Felix V	1439–1449 *antipope*	Leo XII	1823–1829
Nicholas V	1447–1455	Pius VIII	1829–1830
Callistus III (Calixtus III)	1455–1458	Gregory XVI	1831–1846
Pius II	1458–1464	Pius IX	1846–1878
Paul II	1464–1471	Leo XIII	1878–1903
Sixtus IV	1471–1484	St. Pius X	1903–1914
Innocent VIII	1484–1492	Benedict XV	1914–1922
Alexander VI	1492–1503	Pius XI	1922–1939
Pius III	1503	Pius XII	1939–1958
Julius II	1503–1513	John XXIII	1958–1963
Leo X	1513–1521	Paul VI	1963–1978
Adrian VI (Hadrian VI)	1522–1523	John Paul I	1978
Clement VII	1523–1534	John Paul II	1978–

⊙ Kelly, J. N. D. *The Oxford Dictionary of Popes.* New York: Oxford University Press, 1989.
New Advent. "Catholic Encyclopedia: The List of Popes," www.newadvent.org/cathen/12272b.htm

Note: Any one group may claim the patronage of several saints. What follows is a selection of those saints who are typically associated with the groups listed, along with the traditionally observed date of each saint's Memorial/Feast Day.

Patron of	*Saint*	*Day*
Abandoned Children	Jerome Emiliani	Feb. 8
Accountants	Matthew	Sep. 21
Actors	Genesius	Aug. 25
Advertisers	Bernadine of Siena	May 20
Air Travelers	Joseph of Cupertino	Sep. 18
Altar Servers	John Berchmans	Nov. 26
Anesthetists	Rene Goupil	Oct. 19
Animals	Francis of Assisi	Oct. 4
Archaeologists	Damasus I	Dec. 11
Archers	Sebastian	Jan. 20
Architects	Barbara	Dec. 4
Armies	Maurice	Sep. 22
Art & Artists	Catherine of Bologna	Mar. 9
Astronauts	Joseph of Cupertino	Sep. 18
Astronomers	Dominic	Aug. 8
Athletes	Sebastian	Jan. 20
Authors	Francis de Sales	Jan. 24
Babies	Nicholas of Tolentino	Sep. 10
Bakers	Elizabeth of Hungary	Nov. 17
Bankers	Matthew	Sep. 21
Barbers	Martin de Porres	Nov. 3
Basket Makers	Anthony the Abbot	Jan. 17
Beekeepers	Ambrose	Dec. 7
Beggars	Giles	Sep. 1
Birds	Gall	Oct. 16
Blacksmiths	Dunstan	May 19
Blind	Raphael the Archangel	Sep. 29
Bookbinders	Celestine V	May 19
Bookkeepers	Matthew	Sep. 21
Booksellers	John of God	Mar. 8
Boys	Dominic Savio	Mar. 9
Brewers	Augustine of Hippo	Aug. 28
Bricklayers	Stephen	Dec. 26
Brides	Nicholas of Myra	Dec. 6
Broadcasters	Gabriel the Archangel	Sep. 29
Builders	Vincent Ferrer	Apr. 5
Businessmen	Homobonus	Nov. 13
Businesswomen	Margaret of Clitherow	Mar. 26
Butchers	Adrian of Nicomedia	Sep. 8
Cab Drivers	Fiacre	Sep. 1
Cancer Victims	Peregrine Laziosi	May 1
Candle Makers	Ambrose	Dec. 7
Carpenters	Joseph	Mar. 19/May 1

Patron of	Saint	Day
Cattle Breeders	Mark the Evangelist	Apr. 25
Chaplains	John of Capistrano	Oct. 23
Charities	Vincent de Paul	Sep. 27
Childbirth	Gerard Majella	Oct. 16
Children	Nicholas of Myra	Dec. 6
Childless Women	Anne (Mother of Mary)	July 26
Choirs	Dominic Savio	Mar. 9
Church	Joseph	Mar. 19/May 1
Civil Servants	Thomas More	June 22
Clerics	Thomas a Becket	Dec. 29
Colleges	Thomas Aquinas	Jan. 28
Comedians	Vitus	June 15
Cooks	Martha	July 29
Court Clerks	Thomas More	June 22
Craftspeople	Eligius (Eloi)	Dec. 1
Criminals	Dismas	Mar. 25
Cripples	Giles	Sep. 1
Dairy Workers	Brigid of Ireland	Feb. 1
Dancers	Vitus	June 15
Deaf	Francis de Sales	Jan. 24
Dentists	Apollonia	Feb. 9
Desperate Cases	Jude	Oct. 28
Domestic Workers	Zita	Apr. 27
Doubters	Joseph	Mar. 19/May 1
Drought Relief	Herbert	Mar. 20
Dyers	Maurice	Sep. 22
Dying	Joseph	Mar. 19/May 1
Ecologists	Francis of Assisi	Oct. 4
Editors	John Bosco	Jan. 31
Education, Public	Martin de Porres	Nov. 3
Embroiderers	Clare of Assisi	Aug. 11
Emigrants	Frances Xavier Cabrini	Nov. 13
Falsely Accused	Raymond Nonnatus	Aug. 31
Farmers	Isidore the Farmer	May 15
Farm Workers	Benedict	July 11
Fathers	Joseph	Mar. 19/May 1
Firefighters	Florian	May 4
Fire Prevention	Catherine of Siena	Apr. 29
Fishermen	Andrew	Nov. 30
Florists	Therese of Lisieux	Oct. 1
Foundlings	Holy Innocents	Dec. 28
Funeral Directors	Joseph of Arimathea	Mar. 17
Gardeners	Adelard	Jan. 2
Garment Workers	Homobonus	Nov. 13
Geese	Martin of Tours	Nov. 11
Girls	Agnes of Rome	Jan. 21
Glassworkers	Luke	Oct. 18

Gravediggers	Anthony the Abbot	Jan. 17
Grocers	Michael the Archangel	Sep. 29/May 8
Hairdressers	Martin de Porres	Nov. 3
Harvest	Anthony of Padua	June 13
Health Inspectors	Raphael the Archangel	Sep. 29
Heart Patients	John of God	Mar. 8
Highways	John the Baptist	June 24
Horse Riders	Martin of Tours	Nov. 11
Horses	Hippolytus of Rome	Aug. 13
Hospitals	Camillus de Lellis	July 14
Hotelkeepers	Amand	Feb. 6
Housewives	Martha	July 29
Hunters	Hubert	Nov. 3
Immigrants	Frances Xavier Cabrini	Nov. 13
Impossible Cases	Rita Cascia	May 22
Infertile Women	Anthony of Padua	June 13
Invalids	Roch	Aug. 16
Jewelers	Eligius (Eloi)	Dec. 1
Journalists	Francis de Sales	Jan. 24
Judges & Jurists	John of Capistrano	Oct. 23
Juvenile Delinquents	Dominic Savio	Mar. 9
Laborers	Isidore the Farmer	May 15
Lacemakers	Luke	Oct. 18
Lawyers	Thomas More	June 22
Learning	Ambrose	Dec. 7
Leatherworkers	Crispin & Crispinian	Oct. 25
Lecturers	Justin	June 1
Lepers	Giles	Sep. 1
Librarians	Jerome	Sep. 30
Lighthouse Keepers	Venerius	May 4
Lost Articles	Anthony of Padua	June 13
Lovers	Valentine	Feb. 14
Maids	Zita	Apr. 27
Mariners	Nicholas of Tolentino	Sep. 10
Married Women	Monica	Aug. 27
Mentally Ill	Dymphna	May 15
Merchants	Francis of Assisi	Oct. 4
Messengers	Gabriel the Archangel	Sep. 29
Metalworkers	Eligius (Eloi)	Dec. 1
Midwives	Raymond Nonnatus	Aug. 31
Migrants	Frances Xavier Cabrini	Nov. 13
Milliners	James the Greater	July 25
Miners	Anne (Mother of Mary)	July 26
Missionary Priests	Vincent Pallotti	Jan. 22
Missions	Therese of Lisieux	Oct. 1
Motorists	Frances of Rome	Mar. 9
Mothers	Monica	Aug. 27
Mountain Climbers	Bernard of Montjoux	May 28
Munitions Workers	Erasmus (Elmo)	June 2
Musicians	Cecilia	Nov. 22
Navigators	Francis of Paola	Apr. 2

Patron of	Saint	Day
Notaries	Mark	Apr. 25
Nurses	Agatha	Feb. 5
Nursing Mothers	Basilissa	May 20
Orators	John Chrysostom	Sep. 13
Orphans	Jerome Emiliani	Feb. 8
Painters	Luke	Oct. 18
Pallbearers	Joseph of Arimathea	Mar. 17
Paratroopers	Michael the Archangel	Sep. 29
Pawnbrokers	Nicholas of Myra	Dec. 6
Pets	Anthony the Abbot	Jan. 17
Pharmacists	Cosmas & Damian	Sep. 26
Philatelists	Gabriel the Archangel	Sep. 29
Philosophers	Catherine of Alexandria	Nov. 25
Physicians	Luke	Oct. 18
Plasterers	Bartholomew	Aug. 24
Poets	Columba	June 9
Police Officers	Michael the Archangel	Sep. 29
Poor	Anthony of Padua	June 13
Postal Workers	Gabriel the Archangel	Sep. 29
Preachers	Catherine of Alexandria	Nov. 25
Pregnant Women	Gerard Majella	Oct. 16
Priests	John Vianney	Aug. 4
Printers	Genesius	Aug. 25
Prisoners	Dismas	Mar. 25
Prison Guards	Adrian of Nicomedia	Sep. 8
Radio Workers	Gabriel the Archangel	Sep. 29
Rape Victims	Maria Goretti	July 6
Rheumatism	James the Greater	July 25
Rulers	Ferdinand III of Castile	May 30
Sailors	Erasmus (Elmo)	June 2
Scholars	Brigid of Ireland	Feb. 1
Schools	Thomas Aquinas	Jan. 28
Scientists	Albert the Great	Nov. 15
Scripture Scholars	Jerome	Sep. 30
Sculptors	Claude	Feb. 15
Secretaries	Genesius	Aug. 25
Security Guards	Matthew	Sep. 21
Senior Citizens	Anthony of Padua	June 13
Servants	Martha	July 29
Shepherds	Cuthman	Feb. 8
Shoemakers	Crispin & Crispinian	Oct. 25
Sick	John of God	Mar. 8
Silversmiths	Andronicus	Oct. 11

Skaters	Lidwina (Lydwina)	Apr. 14
Skiers	Bernard of Montjoux	May 28
Sleepwalkers	Dymphna	May 15
Snakebite Victims	Hilary of Poitiers	Jan. 13
Social Justice	Joseph	Mar. 19/May 1
Social Workers	Louise de Marillac	Mar. 15
Soldiers	Martin of Tours	Nov. 11
Souls in Purgatory	Nicholas of Tolentino	Sep. 10
Spinners	Parasceva	Oct. 14
Stenographers	Cassian	Dec. 3
Stonemasons	Stephen	Dec. 26
Storms, Safety in	Vitus	June 15
Stroke Victims	Andrew Avellino	Nov. 10
Students	Thomas Aquinas	Jan. 28
Surgeons	Cosmas & Damian	Sep. 26
Surveyors	Thomas	July 3
Swimmers	Adjutor	Apr. 30
Tailors	Homobonus	Nov. 13
Tax Collectors	Matthew	Sep. 21
Taxi Drivers	Fiacre	Sep. 1
Teachers	John Baptist de la Salle	Apr. 7
Television	Clare of Assisi	Aug. 11
Theologians	Alphonsus	Aug. 1
Throat Ailments	Blaise	Feb. 3
Toothaches	Apollonia	Feb. 9
Tradespeople	Homobonus	Nov. 13
Travelers	Raphael the Archangel	Sep. 29
Undertakers	Dismas	Mar. 25
Universities	Contardo Ferrini	Oct. 17
Unmarried Men	Benezet	Apr. 14
Unmarried Women	Nicholas of Myra	Dec. 6
Veterinarians	Eligius (Eloi)	Dec. 1
Vintners	Morand	June 3
Vocations	Alphonsus	Aug. 1
Waitpersons	Martha	July 29
Weavers	Parasceva	Oct. 14
Widows	Paula	Jan. 26
Winegrowers	Vincent of Saragossa	Jan. 22
Women in Labor	Anne (Mother of Mary)	July 26
Workers	Joseph	Mar. 19/May 1
Writers	Francis de Sales	Jan. 24
Youth	Aloysius Gonzaga	June 2

⊙ Adels, Jill Haak. *The Wisdom of the Saints: An Anthology*. New York: Oxford University Press, 1989.
   Catholic Community Forum. "Patron Saints Index," www.catholic-forum.com/saints/indexsnt.htm
   Catholic Online Saints. "Patron Saints," http://saints.catholic.org/patron.html

Deities of Classical Mythology

Greek

Name	Realm, Position or Symbolism	Name	Realm, Position or Symbolism
Adonis	god of the cycle of vegetation; personification of beautiful youth	Hermes	messenger of the gods
		Hestia	goddess of the hearth
Aeolus	god of the winds	Hygeia	goddess of health
Amphitrite	goddess of the oceans	Hymen	god of marriage
Aphrodite	goddess of love and beauty	Hypnos	god of sleep
Apollo	god of youth, music, poetry, archery, and prophecy	Irene (or Eirene)	goddess of peace
Ares	god of war	Iris	goddess of the rainbow
Artemis	goddess of the hunt and the moon	Masyas	satyr flayed to death after losing flute-playing contest to Apollo
Asclepius	god of medicine and healing	Metis	personification of prudence; first wife of Zeus
Athena	goddess of wisdom		
Carpo	goddess of summer fruit	Morpheus	god of dreams
Chaos	personification of confusion	Muses	9 sisters; goddesses of arts/ sciences:
Chloris	goddess of flowers		
Cronus	ruler of the Titans, after deposing his father, Uranus	Calliope	chief of the Muses
		Clio	muse of history
Demeter	goddess of grains and harvest	Erato	muse of erotic poetry
Dionysus	god of wine	Euterpe	muse of lyric poetry
Enyo	goddess of war	Melpomene	muse of tragedy
Eos	goddess of the dawn	Polyhymnia	muse of sacred poetry
Eris	goddess of discord	Terpsichore	muse of dance
Eros	god of love	Thalia	muse of comedy
Fates (or Moirai)	3 goddesses of human destiny (Atropos, Clotho, Lachesis)	Urania	muse of astronomy
		Nemesis	goddess of vengeance
Graces (or Charities)	personification of charm, grace, and beauty; 3 daughters of Zeus (Aglaia, Euphrosyne, Thalia)	Nereids	sea nymphs
		Nereus	old sea god; father of the Nereids
		Nike	goddess of victory
Hades (or Pluto)	god of the underworld	Nymphs	female spirits of nature
		Nyx	goddess of night
Hebe	cupbearer of the gods	Pan	god of shepherds, flocks, forests, and pastures
Hecate	goddess of dark places		
Helios	god of the sun	Persephone	queen of the underworld; goddess of spring
Hephaestus	god of fire and the forge		
Hera	queen of the goddesses; wife and sister of Zeus	Pleiades	seven daughters of Atlas; changed into cluster of stars by Zeus
Heracles	superhuman hero; performed 12 labors to win immortality	Plutus	god of wealth
		Poseidon	god of the oceans
Hermaphro-ditus	a male-female deity, having been joined as one with the nymph Salmacis	Priapus	god of fertility
		Psyche	female personification of the soul
		Rhea	wife of Cronus; mother of Zeus

Satyrs	gods of woodlands	Titans	children of Uranus, who helped, then defeated, Cronus
Selene	goddess of the moon		
Sirens	sea nymphs and enchantresses	Triton	trumpeter of the sea; son of Poseidon
Thanatos	god of death		
Themis	personification of order and justice; daughter of Uranus and Gaia	Tyche	goddess of fortune
		Uranus	god of heaven; father of the Titans
		Zeus	chief god of Olympus

Roman

Name	Realm, Position or Symbolism	Name	Realm, Position or Symbolism
Aesculapius	god of medicine and healing	Lemures	spirits of the dead
Apollo	god of youth, music, poetry, archery, and prophecy	Libitina	goddess of the underworld
		Lucina	goddess of childbirth
Aurora	goddess of the dawn	Luna	goddess of the moon
Bacchus (or Liber)	god of wine	Mars	god of war
		Mercury	messenger of the gods
Bellona	goddess of war	Minerva	goddess of wisdom
Ceres	goddess of grains and harvest	Mors	god of death
Coelus	god of heaven	Neptune	god of the oceans
Cupid (or Amor)	god of love	Nox	goddess of night
		Orcus (or Pluto)	god of the underworld
Diana	goddess of the hunt and the moon		
Discordia	goddess of discord	Picus	god who could predict the future
Fauna	goddess of fields	Pomona	goddess of fruit trees and their fruit
Faunus (or Inuus)	god of shepherds and flocks		
Flora	goddess of flowers	Proserpina (Persipina)	queen of the underworld; goddess of spring
Fortuna	goddess of fortune	Psyche	female personification of the soul
Graces (or Gratiae)	personification of charm, grace, and beauty; 3 daughters of Jupiter (Aglaia, Euphrosyne, Thalia)		
		Salacia	goddess of the oceans
		Saturn	god of agriculture (equivalent of Greeks' Cronus)
Hercules	superhuman hero; performed 12 labors to win immortality		
		Sol	god of the sun
Janus	god of beginnings, especially of the year and the seasons	Somnus	god of sleep
		Silvanus (Sylvanus)	god of forests and uncultivated land
Juno	queen of the goddesses; wife of Jupiter		
		Tartarus	primeval god of the underworld
Jupiter (or Jove)	chief of all gods	Terminus	guardian of boundaries
		Trivia	goddess of dark places
Juturna	goddess of springs of water	Venus	goddess of love and beauty
Juventas	goddess of youth	Vesta	goddess of the hearth
Juventus	god of youth	Victoria	goddess of victory
Lares and Penates	household gods who watch over homes and cities	Voluptas	goddess of pleasure
		Vulcan	god of fire and the forge

⊙ Hamilton, Edith. *Mythology*. Boston: Little, Brown, 1950.
  Morford, Mark P. O., and Robert J. Lenardon. *Classical Mythology*, Sixth Edition. New York: Oxford University Press, 1999.
  ThinkQuest. "Mythology," http://library.thinkquest.org/25535/

U.S. Presidents

President	Party	Life Dates	Term	Vice President
George Washington	Federalist	1732–1799	1789–1797	John Adams
John Adams	Federalist	1735–1826	1797–1801	Thomas Jefferson
Thomas Jefferson	Democratic- Republican	1743–1826	1801–1809	Aaron Burr; George Clinton
James Madison	Democratic--Republican	1751–1836	1809–1817	George Clinton; Elbridge Gerry
James Monroe	Democratic- Republican	1758–1831	1817–1825	Daniel D. Tompkins
John Quincy Adams	Democratic- Republican	1767–1848	1825–1829	John C. Calhoun
Andrew Jackson	Democratic	1767–1845	1829–1837	John C. Calhoun; Martin Van Buren
Martin Van Buren	Democratic	1782–1862	1837–1841	Richard M. Johnson
William Henry Harrison	Whig	1773–1841	1841	John Tyler
John Tyler	Whig	1790–1862	1841–1845	
James Knox Polk	Democratic	1795–1849	1845–1849	George M. Dallas
Zachary Taylor	Whig	1784–1850	1849–1850	Millard Fillmore
Millard Fillmore	Whig	1800–1874	1850–1853	
Franklin Pierce	Democratic	1804–1809	1853–1857	William R. King
James Buchanan	Democratic	1791–1868	1857–1861	John C. Breckinridge
Abraham Lincoln	Republican	1809–1865	1861–1865	Hannibal Hamlin; Andrew Johnson
Andrew Johnson	Union	1808–1875	1865–1869	
Ulysses Simpson Grant (b. Hiram Ulysses Grant)	Republican	1822–1885	1869–1877	Schuyler Colfax; Henry Wilson
Rutherford Birchard Hayes	Republican	1822–1893	1877–1881	William A. Wheeler
James Abram Garfield	Republican	1831–1881	1881	Chester A. Arthur
Chester Alan Arthur	Republican	1829–1886	1881–1885	
Stephen Grover Cleveland	Democratic	1837–1908	1885–1889	Thomas A. Hendricks
Benjamin Harrison	Republican	1833–1901	1889–1893	Levi P. Morton
[Stephen] Grover Cleveland	Democratic	1837–1908	1893–1897	Adlai E. Stevenson
William McKinley	Republican	1843–1901	1897–1901	Garret A. Hobart; Theodore Roosevelt
Theodore Roosevelt	Republican	1858–1919	1901–1909	Charles W. Fairbanks
William Howard Taft	Republican	1857–1930	1909–1913	James S. Sherman
[Thomas] Woodrow Wilson	Democratic	1856–1924	1913–1921	Thomas R. Marshall
Warren Gamaliel Harding	Republican	1865–1923	1921–1923	Calvin Coolidge
[John] Calvin Coolidge	Republican	1872–1933	1923–1929	Charles G. Dawes
Herbert Clark Hoover	Republican	1874–1964	1929–1933	Charles Curtis
Franklin Delano Roosevelt	Democratic	1882–1945	1933–1945	John N. Garner; Henry A. Wallace; Harry S. Truman

Harry S. Truman	Democratic	1884–1972	1945–1953	Alben W. Barkley
Dwight David Eisenhower	Republican	1890–1969	1953–1961	Richard M. Nixon
John Fitzgerald Kennedy	Democratic	1917–1963	1961–1963	Lyndon B. Johnson
Lyndon Baines Johnson	Democratic	1908–1973	1963–1969	Hubert H. Humphrey
Richard Milhous Nixon	Republican	1913–1994	1969–1974	Spiro T. Agnew; Gerald R. Ford
Gerald Rudolph Ford (b. Leslie Lynch King)	Republican	1913–	1974–1977	Nelson A. Rockefeller
James Earl Carter, Jr.	Democratic	1924–	1977–1981	Walter F. Mondale
Ronald Wilson Reagan	Republican	1911–	1981–1989	George Bush
George Herbert Walker Bush	Republican	1924–	1989–1993	J. Danforth Quayle
William Jefferson Clinton (b. William Jefferson Blythe)	Democratic	1946–	1993–2001	Albert A. Gore, Jr.
George W. Bush	Republican	1946–	2001–	Richard B. Cheney

⊙ The White House. "Presidents of the United States,"
     www.whitehouse.gov/WH/glimpse/presidents/html/presidents/html
     Patrick, John J. et al. *The Oxford Guide to the U.S. Government.* New York: Oxford University Press,
     2001.

First Ladies of the United States

First Lady	Life Dates	President	Term	Notes
Martha Dandridge Custis Washington	1731–1802	George Washington	1789–1797	
Abigail Smith Adams	1744–1818	John Adams	1797–1801	
Martha Jefferson Randolph	1772–1836	Thomas Jefferson	1801–1809	Jefferson's elder daughter
Dolley Payne Todd Madison	1768–1849	James Madison	1809–1817	
Elizabeth Kortright Monroe	1763–1830	James Monroe	1817–1825	
Louisa Catherine Johnson Adams	1775–1852	John Quincy Adams	1825–1829	
Emily Donelson	1809–1836	Andrew Jackson	1829–1836	Jackson's niece
Sarah Yorke Jackson	1805–1887	Andrew Jackson	1836–1837	Jackson's daughter-in-law
Angelica Singleton Van Buren	1816–1878	Martin Van Buren	1838–1841	Van Buren's daughter-in-law
Anna Symmes Harrison	1775–1864	William Henry Harrison	1841	
Letitia Christian Tyler	1790–1842	John Tyler	1841–1842	
Julia Gardiner Tyler	1820–1889	John Tyler	1844–1845	
Sarah Childress Polk	1803–1891	James K. Polk	1845–1849	
Margaret Smith Taylor	1788–1852	Zachary Taylor	1849–1850	nickname: Peggy
Abigail Powers Fillmore	1798–1853	Millard Fillmore	1850–1853	
Jane Appleton Pierce	1806–1863	Franklin Pierce	1853–1857	
Harriet Rebecca Lane	1830–1903	James Buchanan	1857–1861	Buchanan's niece
Mary Ann Todd Lincoln	1818–1882	Abraham Lincoln	1861–1865	
Eliza McCardle Johnson	1810–1876	Andrew Johnson	1865–1869	
Julia Dent Grant	1826–1902	Ulysses S. Grant	1869–1877	

First Lady	Life Dates	President	Term	Notes
Lucy Webb Hayes	1831–1889	Rutherford B. Hayes	1877–1881	nickname: "Lemon ade Lucy" (for White House temperance policy)
Lucretia Rudolph Garfield	1832–1918	James Garfield	1881	nickname: Crete
Mary Arthur McElroy	1836–1916	Chester Alan Arthur	1881–1885	Arthur's sister
Rose Elizabeth Cleveland	1846–1918	Grover Cleveland	1885–1886	Cleveland's sister; served until his 1886 marriage
Frances Folsom Cleveland	1864–1947	Grover Cleveland	1886–1889	nickname: Frankie
Caroline Lavinia Scott Harrison	1832–1892	Benjamin Harrison	1889–1892	nickname: Carrie
Ida Saxton McKinley	1847–1907	William McKinley	1897–1901	
Edith Kermit Carow Roosevelt	1861–1948	Theodore Roosevelt	1901–1909	nickname: Edie
Helen Herron Taft	1861–1943	William Howard Taft	1909–1913	nickname: Nellie
Ellen Axson Wilson	1860–1914	Woodrow Wilson	1913–1914	nickname: Ellie
Edith Bolling Galt Wilson	1872–1961	Woodrow Wilson	1915–1921	
Florence Kling de Wolfe Harding	1860–1924	Warren G. Harding	1921–1923	nickname: Flossie
Grace Goodhue Coolidge	1879–1957	Calvin Coolidge	1923–1929	
Lou Henry Hoover	1874–1944	Herbert Hoover	1929–1933	
Anna Eleanor Roosevelt Roosevelt	1884–1962	Franklin D. Roosevelt	1933–1945	
Elizabeth Virginia Wallace Truman	1885–1982	Harry S. Truman	1945–1953	nickname: Bess
Mamie Geneva Doud Eisenhower	1896–1979	Dwight D. Eisenhower	1953–1961	
Jacqueline Lee Bouvier Kennedy	1929–1994	John Fitzgerald Kennedy	1961–1963	nickname: Jackie
Claudia Alta Taylor Johnson	1912–	Lyndon B. Johnson	1963–1969	nickname: Lady Bird
Thelma Catharine Ryan Nixon	1912–93	Richard M. Nixon	1969–1974	nickname: Pat
Elizabeth Ann Bloomer Warren Ford	1918–	Gerald R. Ford	1974–1977	nickname: Betty
Eleanor Rosalynn Smith Carter	1927–	Jimmy Carter	1977–1981	
Anne Francis Robbins Davis Reagan	1921–	Ronald Reagan	1981–1989	nickname: Nancy
Barbara Pierce Bush	1925–	George Bush	1989–1993	
Hillary Diane Rodham Clinton	1947–	Bill Clinton	1993–2001	
Laura Welch Bush	1946–	George W. Bush	2001–	

⊙ The First Ladies Library. "The First Ladies Library," www.firstladies.org/
The White House. "The First Ladies," www.whitehouse.gov/WH/glimpse/firstladies/html/firstladies.html.

U.S. Vice Presidents

Name	Party	Life Dates	Term	President
John Adams	Federalist	1735–1826	1789–97	George Washington
Thomas Jefferson	Democratic-Republican	1743–1826	1797–1801	John Adams
Aaron Burr	Democratic-Republican	1756–1836	1801–05	Thomas Jefferson
George Clinton	Democratic-Republican	1739–1812	1805–12	Thomas Jefferson; James Madison
Elbridge Gerry	Democratic-Republican	1744–1814	1813–14	James Madison
Daniel D. Tompkins	Democratic-Republican	1774–1825	1817–25	James Monroe
John Caldwell Calhoun	Democratic-Republican	1782–1850	1825–32	John Quincy Adams; Andrew Jackson
Martin Van Buren	Democratic	1782–1862	1833–37	Andrew Jackson
Richard Mentor Johnson	Democratic	1780–1850	1837–41	Martin Van Buren
John Tyler	Whig	1790–1862	1841	William Henry Harrison
George Miflin Dallas	Democratic	1792–1864	1845–49	James K. Polk
Millard Filmore	Whig	1800–74	1849–50	Zachary Taylor
William Rufus DeVane King	Democratic	1786–1853	1853	Franklin Pierce
John Cabel Breckinridge	Democratic	1821–75	1857–61	James Buchanan
Hannibal Hamlin	Republican	1809–91	1861–65	Abraham Lincoln
Andrew Johnson	Union	1808–75	1865	Abraham Lincoln
Schuyler Colfax	Republican	1823–85	1869–73	Ulysses S. Grant
Henry Wilson	Republican	1812–75	1873–75	Ulysses S. Grant
William Alnom Wheeler	Republican	1819–87	1877–81	Rutherford B. Hayes
Chester Alan Arthur	Republican	1829–86	1881	James Garfield
Thomas Andrews Hendricks	Democratic	1819–85	1885	[S.] Grover Cleveland
Levi Parsons Morton	Republican	1824–1920	1889–93	Benjamin Harrison
Adlai Ewing Stevenson	Democratic	1835–1914	1893–97	[S.] Grover Cleveland
Garret Augustus Hobart	Republican	1844–99	1897–99	William McKinley
Theodore Roosevelt	Republican	1858–1919	1901	William McKinley
Charles Warren Fairbanks	Republican	1852–1918	1905–09	Theodore Roosevelt
James Schoolcraft Sherman	Republican	1855–1912	1909–12	William H. Taft
Thomas Riley Marshall	Democratic	1854–1925	1913–21	[T.] Woodrow Wilson
[John] Calvin Coolidge	Republican	1872–1933	1921–23	Warren Harding
Charles Gates Davies	Republican	1865–1951	1925–29	[J.] Calvin Coolidge
Charles Curtis	Republican	1860–1936	1929–33	Herbert Hoover
John Nance Garner	Democratic	1868–1967	1933–41	Franklin D. Roosevelt
Henry A. Wallace	Democratic	1888–1965	1941–45	Franklin D. Roosevelt
Harry S. Truman	Democratic	1884–1972	1945	Franklin D. Roosevelt
Alben W. Barkley (b. Willie Alben Barkley)	Democratic	1877–1956	1949–53	Harry S. Truman
Richard Milhous Nixon	Republican	1913–94	1953–61	Dwight D. Eisenhower
Lyndon Baines Johnson	Democratic	1908–73	1961–63	John F. Kennedy

Name	Party	Life Dates	Term	President
Hubert Horatio Humphrey	Democratic-Farmer Labor	1911–78	1965–69	Lyndon B. Johnson
Spiro Theodore Agnew	Republican	1918–96	1969–73	Richard M. Nixon
Gerald Randolph Ford	Republican	1913–	1973–74	Richard M. Nixon
Nelson Adlrich Rockefeller	Republican	1908–79	1974–77	Gerald R. Ford
Walter Frederick Mondale	Democratic	1928–	1977–81	James E. Carter, Jr.
George Herbert Walker Bush	Republican	1924–	1981–89	Ronald W. Reagan
James Danforth Quayle	Republican	1947–	1989–93	George H. Bush
Albert A. Gore, Jr.	Democratic	1948–	1993–00	William J. Clinton
Richard B. Cheney	Republican	1941–	2001–	George W. Bush

⊙ Southwick, Leslie H. *Presidential Also-Rans and Running Mates.* Jefferson, N.C.: McFarland & Co., 1998.
Witcover, Jules. *Crapshoot: Rolling the Dice on the Vice Presidency.* New York: Crown, 1992.

Cabinet Departments

Department	Year Created	Main Agencies
Department of Agriculture (USDA)	1862	Forest Service; Natural Resources Conservation Service; Farm Service Agency; Foreign Agricultural Service; Rural Utilities Service; Rural Housing Service; Rural Business-Cooperative Service; Food and Nutrition Service; Food Safety and Inspection Service; Agricultural Research Service; Cooperative State Research, Education, and Extension Service; Economic Research Service, National Agricultural Statistics Service; Agricultural Marketing Service; Animal and Plant Health Inspection Service; Grain Inspection, Packers and Stockyards Administration; Rural Community Development
Department of Commerce (DOC)	1913	National Oceanic and Atmospheric Administration; International Trade Administration; Bureau of Export Administration; Economics and Statistics Administration; Technology Administration; Patent and Trademark Office; Minority Business Development Agency; Economic Development Administration; National Telecommunications and Information Administration; Bureau of the Census; National Institute of Standards and Technology; National Technical Information Service; Bureau of Economic Analysis

Department of Defense (DOD)	1949	Department of the Army; Department of the Navy; Department of the Air Force, Joint Chiefs of Staff; National Guard; Advanced Research Projects Agency; American Forces Information Service; American Forces Press Service; Ballistic Missile Defense Organization; Defense Contract and Audit Agency; Defense Finance and Accounting Service; Defense Information Systems Agency; Defense Intelligence Agency; Defense Logistics Agency; Defense Special Weapons Agency; Defense Technical Information Center; National Imagery and Mapping Agency; National Security Agency; On-Site Inspection Agency
Department of Education	1979	Office of Elementary and Secondary Education; Office of Post-Secondary Education; Office of Special Education and Rehabilitative Services; Office of Bilingual Education and Minority Languages Affairs; Office of Vocational and Adult Education; Office for Civil Rights; Office of Educational Research and Improvement
Department of Energy (DOE)	1977	Environment, Safety and Health; Defense Nuclear Facilities Safety Board; Office of Environmental Management; Office of Economic Impact and Diversity; Office of Worker and Community Transition; Energy Efficiency and Renewable Energy; Fossil Energy; Energy Information Administration; Office of Non-Proliferation and National Security; Office of Civilian Radioactive Waste Management; Office of Fissile Materials Disposition; Office of Energy Research; Office of Nuclear Energy, Science and Technology; Power Marketing Administrations: Southeastern, Alaska, Southwestern, Western; Bonneville
Department of Health and Human Services (HHS)	1953	Administration for Children and Families; Food and Drug Administration; Administration on Aging; Health Care and Financing Administration; Agency for Health Care Policy and Research; Centers for Disease Control and Prevention; Agency for Toxic Substances and Disease Registry; Health Resources and Services Administration; Indian Health Service, National Institutes of Health; Substance Abuse and Mental Health Services Administration; Program Support Center
Department of Housing and Urban Development (HUD)	1965	Office of Small and Disadvantaged Business Utilization; Federal Housing Enterprise Over-sight; Office of Community Planning and Development; Federal Housing Finance Board; Office of Public and Indian Housing; Office of Lead Hazard Control; Government National Mortgage Association (Ginnie Mae)

Department	Year Created	Main Agencies
Department of the Interior (DOI)	1849	U.S. Fish and Wildlife Service; National Park Service; National Biological Service; Bureau of Indian Affairs; Bureau of Land Management; Minerals Management Service; Office of Surface Mining Reclamation and Enforcement; U.S. Geological Survey; Bureau of Reclamation
Department of Justice (DOJ)	1870	Foreign Claims Settlement Commission; Office of Information and Privacy; Community-Oriented Policing Services; Civil Division, Civil Rights Division; Criminal Division; Antitrust Division; Tax Division; Environment and Natural Resources Division; Community Relations Service; Drug Enforcement Agency; Executive Office for U.S. Attorneys; Immigration and Naturalization Service; Federal Bureau of Investigation; Federal Bureau of Prisons; U.S. Marshals Service; U.S. National Central Bureau-Interpol; Office of Justice Programs
Department of Labor (DOL)	1913	Office of Small Business Programs; Occupational Safety and Health Administration; Employment and Training Administration; Mine Safety and Health Administration; Pension and Welfare Benefits Administration; Veterans' Employment and Training Service; Employment Standards Administration; Bureau of Labor Statistics; Women's Bureau; Bureau of International Labor Affairs; Employees' Compensation Appeal Board
Department of State	1789	African Affairs; East Asian and Pacific Affairs; European and Canadian Affairs; Inter-American Affairs; Near Eastern Affairs; South Asian Affairs; International Organization Affairs; Economic and Business Affairs; Political-Military Affairs; Office of Foreign Missions; Foreign Service Institute; Consular Affairs; Diplomatic Security; Finance and Management Policy; Democracy, Human Rights and Labor; International Narcotics and Law Enforcement Affairs; Oceans and International Environmental and Scientific Affairs; Population, Refugees, and Migration
Department of Transportation (DOT)	1966	U.S. Coast Guard; Federal Aviation Administration; Federal Highway Administration; Federal Railroad Administration; National Highway Traffic Safety Administration; Federal Transit Administration; Saint Lawrence Seaway Development Corporation; Maritime Administration; Research and Special Programs Administration; Bureau of Transportation Statistics; Transportation Administrative Service Center; Surface Transportation Board

Department of the Treasury	1789	Office of the Comptroller of the Currency; Office of Thrift Supervision; Bureau of Alcohol, Tobacco and Firearms; U.S. Secret Service; Federal Law Enforcement Training Center; Internal Revenue Service; U.S. Mint; Bureau of Engraving and Printing; U.S. Customs Service; Bureau of the Public Debt
Department of Veterans Affairs	1930	Center for Minority Veterans; Center for Women Veterans; National Center for Veteran Analysis and Statistics; National Cemetery Administration; Veterans Benefits Administration; Veterans Health Administration

⊙   The White House. "The President's Cabinet," www.whitehouse.gov/WH/Cabinet/html/ cabinet_links.html

Independent Federal Agencies and Commissions

Agency/Commission	Year Created	Mission
Advisory Council on Historic Preservation	1966	to influence federal policy, programs, and deci sions as they affect historic resources in communities and on public lands nationwide
Arms Control and Disarmament Agency	1961	to strengthen the national security of the United States by formulating, advocating, negotiating, implementing, and verifying effective arms control, nonproliferation, and disarmament policies, strategies, and agreements
Central Intelligence Agency	1947	to provide accurate, evidence-based, comprehensive, and timely foreign intelligence related to national security, and to conduct counter-intelligence activities, special activities, and other functions related to foreign intelligence and national security as directed by the President
Consumer Product Safety Commission	1972	to protect the public against unreasonable risks of injuries and deaths associated with consumer products; to develop voluntary standards with industry; to issue and enforce mandatory standards; to obtain recalls of defective products; to conduct research and inform and educate consumers
Corporation for National Service	1993	to work with community organizations to provide opportunities for Americans of all ages to serve their community and country through such organizations as AmeriCorps, Learn & Serve America, and the National Senior Service Corps
Commodity Futures Trading Commission	1974	to regulate U.S. commodity futures and option markets; to protect market participants against manipulation, abusive trade practices, and fraud, and to enable markets to provide a mechanism for price discovery and a means of offsetting price risk

Agency/Commission	Year Created	Mission
Environmental Protection Agency	1970	to solve urgent environmental problems and to protect the public health
Farm Credit Administration	1933	to regulate and examine banks, associations, and related entities that collectively comprise the Farm Credit System, including the Federal Agricultural Mortgage Corporation
Federal Communications Commission	1934	to encourage competition in all communications markets and to protect the public interest; to develop and implement policy concerning interstate and international communications by radio, television, wire, satellite, and cable
Federal Deposit Insurance Corporation	1933	to insure deposits of banks and saving associations; to promote the safety and soundness of insured depository institutions and the U.S. financial system; to maintain stability and public confidence in the nation's banking system; to provide financial and economic information and analyses
Federal Election Commission	1975	to govern the financing of federal elections; to disclose campaign finance information; to enforce the limits, prohibitions, and other provisions of the election law; to administer the public funding of presidential elections
Federal Emergency Management Agency	1979	to reduce loss of life and property and protect our nation's critical infrastructure from all types of hazards through a comprehensive, risk-based, emergency management program of mitigation, preparedness, response, and recovery
Federal Housing Finance Board	1989	to regulate the Federal Home Loan Bank and to oversee residential mortgage lending banks
Federal Trade Commission	1914	to enforce a variety of federal antitrust and consumer protection laws to ensure that markets function competitively; to eliminate unfair or deceptive acts or practices toward consumers
General Services Administration	1949	to provide workspace, supplies, services, and solutions, at the best value, for Federal employees
Institute of Museum and Library Services	1996	to improve museum, library, and information services; to consolidate federal programs of support for museums; to support public libraries
U.S. Merit Systems Protection Board	1978	to regulate federal merit-based system of employment, principally by hearing and deciding appeals from federal employees of removals and other major personnel

		actions; to review significant actions and regulations of the Office of Personnel Management; to hear and decide on other types of civil service cases; and to conduct studies of the merit systems
National Aeronautics and Space Administration	1958	to plan, direct, and conduct aeronautical and space activities; to arrange for participation by the scientific community in planning scientific measurements and observations to be made through use of aeronautical and space vehicles; to provide for the widest practicable and appropriate dissemination of information concerning its activities the results thereof
National Archives and Records Administration	1985	to preserve the nation's history and to oversee the management of all federal records
National Endowment for the Arts	1965	to nurture the expression of human creativity; to support the cultivation of community spirit; to foster the recognition and appreciation of the excellence and diversity of the nation's artistic accomplishments
National Endowment for the Humanities	1965	to provide grants to individuals and organizations for research in the humanities, educational opportunities for teachers, preservation of texts and materials, translations of important works, museum exhibitions, television and radio programs, and public discussion and study
National Partnership for Reinventing Government	1993	to reinvent government to work better, cost less, and get results most important to Americans
National Science Foundation	1950	to promote the progress of science; to advance the national health, prosperity, and welfare; to secure the national defense
National Security Agency	1952	to be responsible for the centralized coordination, direction, and performance of highly specialized technical functions in support of U.S. government activities to protect U.S. information systems and produce foreign intelligence information; a separate organized agency within the Department of Defense
National Technology Transfer Center	1980	to strengthen U.S. industrial competitiveness by identifying industry's needs and matching those needs with technologies and commercialization services required to bring new products or services to market
Nuclear Regulatory Commission	1974	to ensure adequate protection of the public health and safety, the common defense and security, and the environment in the use of nuclear materials in the United States
Peace Corps	1961	to serve the cause of peace by living, working, and teaching in underdeveloped countries

Agency/Commission	Year Created	Mission
President's Commission to Study Capital Budgeting	1997	to develop a report that addresses: capital budgeting practices by other governments and the private sector and their pertinence for the federal government; the appropriate definition of capital for federal budgeting; the role of depreciation in capital budgeting; and the effect of a federal capital budget on budgetary choices, implications for macroeconomic stability, and potential mechanisms for budgetary discipline
President's Council on Physical Fitness	1963	to foster improvements in existing programs and promote additional efforts to enhance the physical fitness of Americans; to coordinate, stimulate, and improve the functions of federal agencies with respect to physical fitness; to enlist the active support and assistance of individuals and groups in a vigorous effort to promote and improve physical fitness in the United States
President's Council on Sustainable Development	1993	to advise the president on sustainable development and to develop bold, new approaches to achieve economic, environmental, and equity goals
President's Interagency Council on Women	1995	to make sure that all the effort and good ideas of the United Nations Fourth World Conference on Women in Beijing are implemented; to implement the Platform for Action adopted at the conference; to further women's progress through outreaching and public education
Railroad Retirement Board	1934	to administer comprehensive retirement-survivor and unemployment-sickness benefit programs for U.S. railroad workers and their families; to administer certain benefit payments and railroad workers' Medicare coverage
Securities and Exchange Commission	1934	to administer federal securities laws that protect investors in securities markets that operate fairly and to ensure that investors have access to disclosure of all material information concerning publicly traded securities; to regulate firms engaged in the purchase or sale of securities, people who provide investment advice, and investment companies
Selective Service System	1940	to provide manpower to the armed forces in an emergency; to run an Alternative Service Program for men classified as conscientious objectors during a draft
Small Business Administration	1953	to provide financial, technical, and management assistance to help Americans start, run, and grow their businesses through loans, loan guarantees, and disaster loans

Smithsonian Institution	1846	to hold artifacts and specients in trust for "the increase and diffusion of knowledge"; to act as a center for research dedicated to public education, national service, and scholarship in the arts, sciences, and history
Social Security Administration	1935	to provide for the material needs of individuals and families; to protect the aged and disabled against the expenses of illnesses that could otherwise exhaust their savings; to keep families together; to give children the opportunity to grow up in health and security
United States Advisory Commission on Public Diplomacy	1948	to assess public diplomacy policies and programs of the United States Information Agency, other U.S. foreign affairs agencies, and U.S. missions abroad
United States Agency for International Development	1961	to provide economic development and humanitarian assistance to advance U.S. economic and political interests overseas
United States Chemical Safety and and Hazard Investigation Board	1990	to work in concert with industry, labor, government, and communities to help prevent chemical accidents
United States Information Agency	1948	to support U.S. foreign policy and national interests abroad; to inform foreign citizens about America and its foreign policy by conducting international educational and cultural exchanges, broadcasting, and information programs
United States International Trade Commission	1916	to provide objective trade expertise to both the legislative and executive branches of government; to determine the impact of imports on U.S. industries; to direct actions against certain unfair trade practices; to investigate and publish reports on U.S. industries and the global trends that affect them; to update and publish the Harmonized Tariff Schedule of the United States
United States Office of Government Ethics	1978	to prevent conflicts of interest on the part of government employees and to resolve them when they do occur; to foster high ethical standards for government employees and to strengthen the public's confidence that government business is conducted with impartiality and integrity
United States Postal Service	1789	to provide postal services to bind the nation together through the personal, educational, literary, and business correspondence of the people; to provide prompt, reliable, and efficient services to patrons in all areas
United States Trade and Development Agency	1981	to help U.S. companies compete for infrastructure and industrial project business opportunities in middle-income and developing countries
Voice of America	1942	to represent the United States to the people of the world via radio by broadcasting news reliably, authoritatively, and accurately in a comprehensive and objective

Agency/Commission	Year Created	Mission
Voice of America *(cont.)*		manner and by projecting a comprehensive, well-balanced picture of American thought and institutions; part of the U.S. Information Agency
White House Fellows	1964	to provide gifted and highly motivated young Americans with some first-hand experience in the process of governing the nation and a sense of personal involvement in the leadership of society
Women's History Commission	1998	to consider how best to acknowledge and celebrate the roles and accomplishments of women in American history

⊙ The White House. "Federal Agencies and Commissions," www.whitehouse.gov/WH/ Independent_Agencies/html/independent_links.html

Lobbyist Groups

Lobbyist groups are required to register with the federal government and to report semi-annually to the government on their lobbying activities. The following table lists some of the larger lobbying groups.

Group	Mission
American Association of Retired Persons (AARP)	to inform, educate, and serve as an advocate for the important issues regarding aging Americans
American Bar Association (ABA)	to uphold the Constitution and the honor of the legal profession and to serve as a legislative and judicial advocate for uniformity in laws
American Civil Liberties Union (ACLU)	to achieve, through litigation, legislation, and education, the preservation of the Bill of Rights and individual rights
American Medical Association (AMA)	to uphold the standards of the medical profession and to promote research and education in the healthcare field
American Public Health Association (APHA)	to provide health professionals with the latest information in the field and to serve as an advocate for issues, such as funding for health programs and for pollution control, that affect personal and environmental health
Association of American Universities (AAU)	to provide an environment for the formation of national policy on academic issues and for the discussion of institutional issues
Christian Coalition	to encourage Christians, particularly those who are conservatives, to be pro-active in government through social and political action
Common Cause	to hold government accountable; to promote openness and honesty in government; to protest against corruption in government

Concord Coalition	to serve as a watchdog of the federal budget and to ensure that Social Security, Medicare, and Medicaid are secure
Family Research Council (FRC)	to promote traditional family and Judeo-Christian values
Federation of American Scientists (FAS)	to bring the scientific perspective to the legislative arena; to end the arms race and avoid the use of nuclear weapons
Greenpeace	to expose crimes against the environment and to work to find solutions
Judicial Watch	to watch over government and judicial systems and to promote political and legal reform
League of Conservation Voters	to make Congress more aware of voters' environmental concerns and to inform the public about legislators' voting records on the environment
League of Women Voters (LWV)	to encourage informed and active participation of citizens in government and to influence public policy through education and advocacy
National Association for the Advancement of Colored People (NAACP)	to ensure the political, educational, social, and economic equality of minority groups
National Education Association (NEA)	to advance the cause of public education and to make public schools as effective as possible
National Gay and Lesbian Task Force (NGLTF)	to promote the civil rights of lesbians, gays, bisexuals, and transgenders and to work for social change
National Organization for Women (NOW)	to push for social change that will achieve equality for all women
National Priorities Project	to offer citizen and community groups tools and resources to shape federal budget and policy priorities that promote social and economic justice
National Rifle Association (NRA)	to uphold the Second Amendment right to keep and bear arms; to assure that firearms are used lawfully, effectively, responsibly, and safely
Public Citizen	to work for the consumer for safer drugs and medical devices, cleaner and safer energy sources, a cleaner environment, fair trade, and a more open, democratic government
Sierra Club	to preserve America's natural resources
The Wilderness Society	to preserve wilderness and wildlife; to protect America's prime forest, parks, rivers, deserts, and shorelands; to foster an American land ethic

⊙ Hrebenar, Ronald J. *Interest Group Politics in America.* Armonk, N.Y.: M.E. Sharpe, 1997.
   Government Publishing Office. *Congress and Pressure Groups: Lobbying in a Modern Democracy.*
   Washington, D.C.: U.S. GPO, 1986.

Afghanistan: Consulate of the Islamic State of
  Afghanistan
369 Lexington Avenue, 19th Floor
New York, NY 10017
(212) 972-2277

Albania: Embassy of the Republic of Albania
2100 S Street, NW
Washington, D.C. 20008
(202) 223-4942

Algeria: Embassy of the Democratic and Popular
  Republic of Algeria
2137 Wyoming Avenue, NW
Washington, D.C. 20008
(202) 265-2800

Andorra: Embassy of Spain
2375 Pennsylvania Avenue, NW
Washington, D.C. 20037
(202) 728-2330
  or
Andorran Mission to the United Nations:
  212-750-8064

Angola: Embassy of Angola
1819 L Street, NW, Suite 400
Washington, D.C. 20036
(202) 452-1042/3

Anguilla: See United Kingdom
  or
U.S. Embassy, Bridgetown, Barbados
(246) 431-0225
  or
U.S. Consulate, English Harbour, Antigua
(268) 463-6531

Antigua and Barbuda: Embassy of Antigua and
  Barbuda
3216 New Mexico Avenue, NW
Washington, D.C. 20016
(202) 362-5122

Argentina: Consul Section of the Argentine
  Embassy
1718 Connecticut Avenue, NW
Washington, D.C. 20009
(202) 797-8826
Consulates: CA (213) 954-9155
  FL (305) 373-7794

GA (404) 880-0805
IL (312) 819-2620
NY (212) 603-0400
TX (713) 871-8335

Armenia: Embassy of the Republic of Armenia
2225 R Street NW
Washington, D.C. 20008
(202) 319-1976
  or
Consulate General
50 North La Cienega Blvd.,
  Suite 210
Los Angeles, CA 90211
(310) 657-6102

Australia: Embassy of Australia
1601 Massachusetts Avenue, NW
Washington, D.C. 20036
(202) 797-3000
Consulates: CA (213) 469-4300
  or (415) 362-6160
  MI (808) 524-5050
  NY (212) 245-4000
  TX (713) 629-9131

Austria: Embassy of Austria
3524 International Court, NW
Washington, D.C. 20008
(202) 895-6767
Consulates: CA (310) 444-9310
  IL (312) 222-1515
  NY (212) 737-6400

Azerbaijan: Embassy of the Republic of
  Azerbaijan
927 15th Street, NW, Suite 700
Washington, D.C. 20035
(202) 842-0001

Azores: See Portugal

Bahamas: Embassy of the Commonwealth of the
  Bahamas
2220 Massachusetts Avenue, NW
Washington, D.C. 20008
(202) 319-2660
Consulates: FL (305) 373-6295
  NY (212) 421-6420

Bahrain: Embassy of the State of Bahrain
3502 International Drive, NW
Washington, D.C. 20008
(202) 342-0741
  or
Permanent Mission to the United Nations:
  (212) 223-6200

Bangladesh: Embassy of the People's Republic
  of Bangladesh
2201 Wisconsin Avenue, NW
Washington, D.C. 20007
(202) 342-8373

Barbados: Embassy of Barbados
2144 Wyoming Avenue, NW
Washington, D.C. 20008
(202) 939-9200
  or
Consulate General:
  (212) 867-8435

Belarus: Embassy of the Republic of Belarus
1619 New Hampshire Avenue, NW
Washington, D.C. 20009
(202) 986-1606
  or
Consulate General: (212) 682-5392

Belgium: Embassy of Belgium
3330 Garfield Street, NW
Washington, D.C. 20008
(202) 333-6900
Consulates: CA (213) 857-1244
  GA (404) 659-2150
  IL (312) 263-6624
  NY (212) 586-5110

Belize: Embassy of Belize
2535 Massachusetts Avenue, NW
Washington, D.C. 20008
(202) 332-9636
Belize Mission: (212) 599-0233

Benin: Embassy of the Republic of Benin
2737 Cathedral Avenue, NW
Washington, D.C. 10008
(202) 232-6656

Bermuda. See United Kingdom

Bhutan: Tourism Authority of Bhutan in Bhutan
011-975-2-23251/2

Bolivia: Embassy of Bolivia (Consular Section)
3014 Massachusetts Avenue, NW
Washington, D.C. 20008
(202) 483-4410
Consulates: FL (305) 358-3450
  NY (212) 687-0530
  CA (415) 495-5173

Bosnia and Herzegovina: Embassy of the
  Republic of Bosnia and Herzegovina
2109 E Street NW
Washington, D.C. 20037
(202) 833-3612
  or
Consulate General: (212) 751-9015

Botswana: Embassy of the Republic of Botswana
3400 International Drive, NW,
  Suite 7M
Washington, D.C. 20008
(202) 244-4990/1
Consulates: CA (213) 626-8484
  TX (713) 622-1900

Brazil: Embassy of Brazil (Consular Section)
3009 Whitehaven Street
Washington, D.C. 20008
(202) 238-2820 or 2831
Consulates: CA (213) 651-2664 or
  (415) 981-8170
  FL (305) 285-6200
  IL (312) 464-0244
  MA (617) 542-4000
  NY (212) 757-3080
  PR (809) 754-7983
  TX (713) 961-3063

British Virgin Islands: U.S. Embassy,
  Bridgetown, Barbados
(246) 431-0225
  or
U.S. Consulate, English Harbour, Antigua
(268) 463-6531

Brunei: Embassy of the State of Brunei
  Darussalam
2600 Virginia Avenue, NW,
  Suite 300
Washington, D.C. 20037
(202) 342-0159
  or
Brunei Permanent Mission to the United
  Nations: (212) 838-1600

Bulgaria: Embassy of the Republic of Bulgaria
1621 22nd Street, NW
Washington, D.C. 20008
(202) 387-7969

Burkina Faso: Embassy of Burkina Faso
2340 Massachusetts Avenue, NW
Washington, D.C. 20008
(202) 332-5577
Consulates: GA (404) 378-7278
  CA (213) 824-5100
  LA (504) 945-3152

Burma: See Myanmar

Burundi: Embassy of the Republic of Burundi
2233 Wisconsin Avenue, NW,
  Suite 212
Washington, D.C. 20007
(202) 342-2574
  or
Permanent Mission to the United Nations:
  212-687-1180

Cambodia: Royal Embassy of Cambodia
4500 16th Street NW
Washington, D.C. 20011
(202) 726-7742

Cameroon: Embassy of the Republic of
  Cameroon
2349 Massachusetts Avenue, NW
Washington, D.C. 20008
(202) 265-8790/94

Canada: Embassy of Canada
501 Pennsylvania Avenue, NW
Washington, D.C. 20001
(202) 682-1740
Consulates: CA (213) 346-2700
  MI (313) 567-2085
  NY (212) 596-1700 or
  (716) 852-1252
  WA (206) 443-1377

Cape Verde: Embassy of the Republic of Cape
  Verde
3415 Massachusetts Avenue, NW
Washington, D.C. 20007
(202) 965-6820

Cayman Islands: See United Kingdom
  or
U.S. Embassy, Kingston, Jamaica
(876) 949-4850
  or
U.S. Consulate, English Harbour, Antigua
(268) 463-6531

Central African Republic: Embassy of the
  Central African Republic
1618 22nd Street, NW
Washington, D.C. 20008
No operating public telephone; communicate
  by mail

Chad: Embassy of the Republic of Chad
2002 R Street, NW
Washington, D.C. 20009
(202) 462-4009

Chile: Embassy of Chile
1732 Massachusetts Avenue, NW
Washington, D.C. 20036
(202) 785-1746
Consulates: CA (310) 785-0113
  or (415)982-7662
  FL (305) 373-8623
  IL (312) 654-8780
  PA (215) 829-9520
  NY (212) 980-3366
  TX (713) 621-5853
  PR (809) 725-6365

China: Embassy of the People's Republic of
  China
2300 Connecticut Ave., NW
Washington, D.C. 20008
(202) 328-2500/2
Consulates: IL (312) 803-0098
  TX (713) 524-4311
  CA (213) 807-8018 or
  (415) 563-4857
  NY (212) 330-7409

Colombia: Embassy of Colombia
2118 Leroy Place, NW
Washington, D.C. 20008
(202) 387-8338
Consulates: CA (213) 382-1137 or
  (415) 495-7191
  FL (315) 448-5558

GA (404) 237-1045
IL (312) 923-1196
LA (504) 525-5580
MA (617) 536-6222
MN (612) 933-2408
MO (314) 991-3636
OH (216) 943-1200
NY (212) 949-9898
PR (809) 754-6885
TX (713) 527-8919
WV (304) 234-8561

Comoros Islands: Mission of the Federal and
Islamic Republic of the Comoros
336 East 45th Street, 2nd Floor
New York, NY 10017
(212) 972-8010

Congo, Republic of the: Embassy of the
Republic of the Congo
4891 Colorado Avenue, NW
Washington, D.C. 20011
726-0825
or
Permanent Mission to the UN:
(212) 744-7840

Congo, Democratic Republic of: Embassy of
the Democratic Republic of Congo
1800 New Hampshire Avenue, NW
Washington, D.C. 20009
(202) 234-7690

Costa Rica: Embassy of Costa Rica
2114 S Street, NW
Washington, D.C. 20008
(202) 328-6628
Consulates: CA (415) 392-8488
GA (404) 951-7025
FL (305) 371-7485
IL (312) 263-2772
LA (504) 887-8131
NY (212) 425-2620
TX (713) 266-1527

Côte d'Ivoire: Embassy of the Republic of Côte
d'Ivoire
2424 Massachusetts Avenue, NW
Washington, D.C. 20008
(202) 797-0300
or
Consulate: (415) 391-0176

Croatia: Embassy of the Republic of Croatia
2343 Massachusetts Avenue, NW
Washington, D.C. 20008
(202) 588-5899
Consulates: OH (216) 951-4246
NY (212) 599-3066

Cuba: Cuba Interests Section
2639 16th Street, NW
Washington, D.C. 20009
(202) 797-8509 or 8518

Curacao: See Netherlands Antilles

Cyprus: Embassy of the Republic of Cyprus
2211 R Street, NW
Washington, D.C. 20008
(202) 462-5772
or
Consulate General
13 East 40th Street
New York, NY 10016
(212) 686-6016
Other consulates:
AR (602) 264-9701
CA (310) 397-0771 or
(510) 547-5689
GA (404) 941-3764
IN (219) 481-6897
LA (504) 388-8701
MA (617) 497-0219
MI (513) 582-1411
OH (330) 296-8191
OR (503) 248-0500
PA (215) 928-4290
TX (713) 928-2264,
VA (804) 481-3538
WA (206) 827-1700

Czech Republic: Embassy of the Czech Republic
3900 Spring of Freedom Street, NW
Washington, D.C. 20008
(202) 274-9173
Consulates: CA (310) 473-0889
NY (212) 717-5643

Denmark: Royal Danish Embassy
3200 Whitehaven Street, NW
Washington, D.C. 20008
(202) 234-4300
Consulates: CA (310) 443-2090
IL (312) 787-8780
NY (212) 223-4545

Djibouti: Embassy of the Republic of Djibouti
1156 15th Street, NW, Suite 515
Washington, D.C. 20005
(202) 331-0202
or
Djibouti Mission to the United Nations: (212) 753-3163

Dominica: Embassy of the Commonwealth of Dominica
3216 New Mexico Avenue, NW
Washington, D.C. 20015
(202) 364-6781

Dominican Republic: Embassy of the Dominican Republic
1715 22nd Street, NW
Washington, D.C. 20008
(202) 332-6280
Consulates: CA (415) 982-5144
FL (305) 358-3220
IL (312) 486-8400
LA (504) 522-1843
MA (617) 482-8121
NY (212) 768-2480
PA (215) 923-3006
PR (787) 833-4756
TX (713) 266-0165

Ecuador: Embassy of Ecuador
2535 15th Street, NW
Washington, D.C. 20009
(202) 234-7200
Consulates: IL (312) 329-0266
TX (713) 622-1787
CA (213) 628-3014 or
(415) 957-5921
FL (305) 461-2363
NJ (201) 985-1707
LA (504) 523-3229
NY (212) 808-0170

Egypt: Embassy of the Arab Republic of Egypt
3521 International Court, NW
Washington, D.C. 20008
(202) 895-5400
Consulates: CA (415) 346-9700
IL (312) 828-9162
NY (212) 759-7120
TX (713) 961-4915

El Salvador: Consulate General of El Salvador
1010 16th Street, NW, 3rd Floor
Washington, D.C. 20036
(202) 331-4032
Consulates: CA (213) 383-5776
(415) 781-7924, or
(714) 542-3250)
FL (305) 371-8850
IL (312) 322-1393
LA (504) 522-4266
MA (617) 577-9111
NY (212) 889-3608
TX (713) 270-6239 or
(214) 637-1018

England: See United Kingdom

Equatorial Guinea: Embassy of the Republic of Equatorial Guinea
1511 K Street, NW
Washington, D.C. 20005
(202) 393-0525

Eritrea: Embassy of Eritrea
1708 New Hampshire Avenue, NW
Washington, D.C. 20009
(202) 319-1991

Estonia: Embassy of Estonia
2131 Massachusetts Avenue, NW
Washington, D.C. 20008
(202) 588-0101
or
Consulate General of Estonia
630 Fifth Avenue, Suite 2415
New York, NY 10111
(212) 247-7634 or 1450

Ethiopia: Embassy of Ethiopia
2134 Kalorama Road, NW
Washington, D.C. 20008
(202) 234-2281/2

Fiji: Embassy of Fiji
2233 Wisconsin Avenue, NW, #240
Washington, D.C. 20007
(202) 337-8320

Finland: Embassy of Finland
3301 Massachusetts Avenue, NW
Washington, D.C. 20008

(202) 298-5800
Consulates: CA (310) 203-9903
NY (212) 750-4400

Former Yugoslav Republic of Macedonia:
Embassy of the Former Yugoslav Republic
of Macedonia
3050 K Street, NW, Suite 210
Washington, D.C. 20007
(202) 337-3063 or
Consulate General: (212) 317-1727

France: Consulate General of France
4101 Reservoir Road, NW
Washington, D.C. 20007
(202) 944-6000
Other Consulates:
CA (310) 235-3200 or
(415) 397-4330
FL (305) 372-9798
GA (404) 522-4226
IL (312) 787-5359
LA (504) 523-5772
MA (617) 542-7374
NY (212) 606-3644
TX (713) 528-2181

French Guiana: See France

French Polynesia: See France

Gabon: Embassy of the Gabonese Republic
2035 20th Street, NW
Washington, D.C. 20009
(202) 797-1000
or
Permanent Mission of the Gabonese Republic
to the United Nations: (212) 686-6720

Galapagos Islands: See Ecuador
Gambia: Embassy of the Gambia
1155 15th Street, NW, Suite 1000
Washington, D.C. 20005
(202) 785-1399
or
Permanent Mission of The Gambia to the
United Nations:
(212) 949-6640

Georgia: Embassy of the Republic of Georgia
1615 New Hampshire Avenue, NW, Suite 300
Washington, D.C. 20009
(202) 347-3415

Germany: Embassy of the Federal Republic of
Germany
4645 Reservoir Road, NW
Washington, D.C. 20007
(202) 298-4000
Consulates: CA (415) 775-1061 or
(213) 930-2703
FL (305) 358-0290
GA (404) 659-4760
IL (312) 580-1199
MA (617) 536-4414
MI (313) 962-6526
NY (212) 308-8700
TX (713) 627-7770
WA (206) 682-4312

Ghana: Embassy of Ghana
3512 International Drive, NW
Washington, D.C. 20008
(202) 686-4520
or
Consulate General:
(212) 832-1300

Gilbert Islands: See Kiribati

Greece: Embassy of Greece
2221 Massachusetts Avenue, NW
Washington, D.C. 20008
(202) 939-5818
Consulates: CA (310) 826-5555 or
(415) 775-2102/4
GA (404) 261-3313
IL (312) 335-3915 or 17
LA (504) 523-1167
MA (617) 543-0100
NY (212) 988-5500
TX (713) 840-7522

Greenland: See Denmark

Grenada: Consulate General of Grenada
1701 New Hampshire Ave., NW
Washington, D.C. 20009
(202) 265-2561
or
Permanent Mission of Grenada to the United
Nations:
(212) 599-0301

Guadeloupe: See France

Guatemala: Embassy of Guatemala
2220 R Street, NW
Washington, D.C. 20008-4081
(202) 745-4952
Consulates: CA (213) 365-9251 or
  (415) 788-5651
  FL (305) 443-4828
  IL (312) 332-3170
  NY (212) 686-3837
  TX (713) 953-9531

Guinea: Embassy of the Republic of
  Guinea
2112 Leroy Place, NW
Washington, D.C. 20008
(202) 483-9420

Guinea-Bissau: Embassy of the Republic of
  Guinea-Bissau
918 16th Street, NW, Mezzanine Suite
Washington, D.C. 20006
(202) 872-4222

Guyana: Embassy of Guyana
2490 Tracy Place, NW
Washington, D.C. 20008
(202) 265-6900/03

Haiti: Embassy of the Republic of Haiti
2311 Massachusetts Avenue, NW
Washington, D.C. 20008
(202) 332-4090
Consulates: FL (305) 859-2003
  MA (617) 266-3660
  NY (212) 697-9767
  PR (809) 764-1392
  IL (312) 922-4004

Holy See (Vatican): Apostolic Nunciature of the
  Holy See
3339 Massachusetts Avenue, NW
Washington, D.C. 20008
(202) 333-7121
  or
Embassy of Italy: (202) 328-5500

Honduras: Embassy of Honduras
3007 Tilden Street, NW
Washington, D.C. 20008
(202) 966-7702

Consulates: CA (213) 383-9244 or
  (415) 392-0076
  FL (304) 447-8927
  IL (312) 951-6382
  LA (504) 522-3118
  NY (212) 269-3611
  TX (713) 622-4572

Hong Kong: Embassy of the People's Republic
  of China
2300 Connecticut Avenue, NW
Washington, D.C. 20008
(202) 328-2500

Hungary: Embassy of the Republic of
  Hungary
3910 Shoemaker Street, NW
Washington, D.C. 20008
(202) 362-6730
Consulates: NY (212) 752-0661
  CA (310) 473-9344

Iceland: Embassy of Iceland
1156 15th Street, NW, Suite 1200
Washington, D.C. 20005
(202) 265-6653/5
  or
Consulate General: (212) 593-2700

India: Embassy of India
2536 Massachusetts Avenue, NW
Washington, D.C. 20008
(202) 939-9806
Consulates: IL (312) 515-0405
  TX (713) 626-2355
  NY (212) 774-0600
  CA (415) 668-0683

Indonesia: Embassy of the Republic of
  Indonesia
2020 Massachusetts Avenue, NW
Washington, D.C. 20036
(202) 775-5200
Consulates: CA (213) 383-5126 or
  (415) 474-9571
  IL (312-) 345-9300
  NY (212) 879-0600
  TX (713) 785-1691

Iran: Embassy of Pakistan
Iranian Interests Section
2209 Wisconsin Avenue NW
Washington, D.C. 20007
(202) 965-4990

Iraq: Iraqi Interests Section
1801 P Street, NW
Washington, D.C. 20036
(202) 483-7500

Ireland: Embassy of Ireland
2234 Massachusetts Avenue, NW
Washington, D.C. 20008
(202) 462-3939
Consulates: CA (415) 392-4214
   IL (312) 337-1868
   MA (617) 267-9330
   NY (212) 319-2555

Israel: Embassy of Israel
3514 International Drive, NW
Washington, D.C. 20008
(202) 364-5500
Consulates: CA (213) 852-5500 or
   (415) 398-8885
   FL (305) 358-8111
   GA (404) 875-7851
   IL (312) 565-3300
   MA (617) 542-0041
   NY (212) 499-5300
   PA (215) 546-5556
   TX (713) 627-3780

Italy: Embassy of Italy
1601 Fuller Street, NW
Washington, D.C. 20009
(202) 328-5500
Consulates: CA (310) 820-0622 or
   (415) 931-4924
   FL (305) 374-6322
   TX (713) 850-7520
   IL (312) 467-1550
   MA (617) 542-0483/4
   MI (313) 963-8560
   NJ (201) 643-1448
   NY (212) 737-9100
   PA (215) 592-7329

Jamaica: Embassy of Jamaica
1520 New Hampshire Avenue, NW
Washington, D.C. 20036
(202) 452-0660
Consulates: CA (310) 559-3822 or
   (510) 266-0072
   FL (305) 374-8431
   IL (312) 663-0023
   NY (212) 935-9000
   MA (617) 266-8604
   WA (206) 872-8950

Japan: Embassy of Japan
2520 Massachusetts Avenue NW
Washington, D.C. 20008
(202) 939-6700
Consulates: AK (907) 279-8428
   CA (213) 617-6700 or
   (415) 777-3533
   FL (305) 530-9090
   GA (404) 892-2700
   HI (808) 536-2226
   IL (312) 280-0400
   LA (504) 529-2101
   MA (617) 973-9772
   MI (313) 567-0120
   MO (816) 471-0111
   NY (212) 371-8222 or
   (503) 221-1811
   TX (713) 652-2977
   WA (206) 682-9107
   CNMI (670) 234-8764
   Guam (671) 646-1290

Jordan: Embassy of the Hashemite Kingdom of
Jordan
3504 International Drive, NW
Washington, D.C. 20008
(202) 966-2664

Kazakhstan: Embassy of the Republic of
Kazakhstan
1401 16th Street, NW
Washington, D.C. 20036
(202) 232-5488

Kenya: Embassy of Kenya
2249 R. Street, NW
Washington, D.C. 20008
(202) 387-6101
   or
Consulate General: (212) 486-1300

Korea, South: Embassy of the Republic of Korea
(Consular Division)
2320 Massachusetts Avenue, NW
Washington, D.C. 20008
(202) 939-5600 or 63
Consulates: CA (213) 385-9300 or (415) 921-2251/3
FL (305) 372-1555
GA (404) 522-1611/3
HI (808) 595-6109
IL (312) 822-9485
MA (617) 348-3660
NY (212) 752-1700
TX (713) 961-0186
WA (206) 441-1011/4
Guam (671) 472-6109

Korea, North: Permanent Representative to the
Democratic Republic of Korea to the United
Nations
515 East 72nd Street, 38-F
New York, NY 10021
(212) 972-3106

Kuwait: Embassy of the State of Kuwait
2940 Tilden Street, NW
Washington, D.C. 20008
(202) 966-0702
or
Consulate: (212) 973-4318

Kyrgyz Republic: Embassy of the Kyrgyz
Republic
1732 Wisconsin Avenue, NW
Washington, D.C. 20007
(202) 338-5141

Laos: Embassy of the Lao People's Democratic
Republic
2222 S Street, NW
Washington, D.C. 20008
(202) 332-6416

Latvia: Embassy of Latvia
4325 17th Street, NW
Washington, D.C. 20011
(202) 726-8213

Lebanon: Embassy of Lebanon
2560 28th Street, NW
Washington, D.C. 20008

(202) 939-6300
Consulates: CA (213) 467-1253
MI (313) 567-0233
NY (212) 744-7905

Lesotho: Embassy of the Kingdom of Lesotho
2511 Massachusetts Avenue, NW
Washington, D.C. 20008
(202) 797-5533

Liberia: Embassy of the Republic of Liberia
5201 16th Street, NW
Washington, D.C. 20011
(202) 723-0437
Consulates: CA (213) 277-7692
GA (404) 753-4754
IL (312) 643-8635
LA (504) 523-7784
MI (313) 342-3900
NY (212) 687-1025

Libya: Passport Services
U.S. Department of State
1111 19th Street, NW
Washington, D.C. 20524
Attn.: CA/PPT/PAS

Liechtenstein: Embassy of Switzerland
2900 Cathedral Avenue, NW
Washington, D.C. 20008
(202) 745-7900

Lithuania: Embassy of Lithuania
2622 Sixteenth Street, NW
Washington, D.C. 20009
(202) 234-5860
or
Consulate General: (212) 354-7849

Luxembourg: Embassy of Luxembourg
2200 Massachusetts Avenue, NW
Washington, D.C. 20008
(202) 265-4171
Consulates: CA (415) 788-0816
NY (212) 888-6664

Macau: Embassy of Portugal
2125 Kalorama Road, NW
Washington, D.C. 20008
(202) 328-8610

Macedonia: See Former Yugoslav Republic of
   Macedonia

Madagascar: Embassy of the Democratic
   Republic of Madagascar
   2374 Massachusetts Avenue, NW
   Washington, D.C. 20008
   (202) 265-5525/6
   Consulates: CA 800-856-2721
      PA (215) 893-3067
      NY (212) 986-9411

Madeira Islands: See Portugal

Malawi: Embassy of Malawi
   2408 Massachusetts Avenue, NW
   Washington, D.C. 20008
   (202) 797-1007
   or
   Mission to the United Nations:
      (212) 949-0180

Malaysia: Embassy of Malaysia
   2401 Massachusetts Avenue, NW
   Washington, D.C. 20008
   (202) 328-2700
   Consulates: CA (213) 892-1238
      NY (212) 490-2722

Maldives: Mission to the United Nations
   (212) 599-6195

Mali: Embassy of the Republic of Mali
   2130 R Street, NW
   Washington, D.C. 20008
   (202) 332-2249

Malta: Embassy of Malta
   2017 Connecticut Avenue, NW
   Washington, D.C. 20008
   (202) 462-3611/2
   Consulates: CA (415) 468-4321
      MI (313) 525-9777
      MO (816) 833-0033
      MN (612) 228-0935
      NY (212) 725-2345
      PA (610) 664-7475
      TX (713) 428-7800 or
      (214) 777-4463

Marshall Islands: Embassy of Marshall
   Islands
   2433 Massachusetts Avenue, NW
   Washington, D.C. 20008
   (202) 234-5414

   or
   Permanent Mission to the United Nations:
      (212) 983-3040
   Consulate General: (808) 545-7767

Martinique: See France

Mauritania: Embassy of the Islamic Republic of
   Mauritania
   2129 Leroy Place, NW
   Washington, D.C. 20008
   (202) 232-5700
   or
   Permanent Mission to the United Nations:
      (212) 986-7963

Mauritius: Embassy of Mauritius
   4301 Connecticut Avenue, NW, Suite 441
   Washington, D.C. 20008
   244-1491/2
   Consulates: GA (404) 892-8733
      CA (818) 788-3720

Mexico: Embassy of Mexico
   1911 Pennsylvania Avenue, NW
   Washington, D.C. 20006
   (202) 736-1000
   Consulates: AZ (602) 242-7398
      CA (213) 351-6800 or
      (619) 231-8414
      CO (303) 331-1110
      FL (305) 716-4977
      GA (404) 266-1913
      IL (312) 855-1380
      LA (504) 522-3596
      NY (212) 689-0460
      PR (809) 764-0258
      TX (210) 227-1085,
      (214) 630-7231, or (713) 542-2300

Micronesia: Embassy of the Federated States of
   Micronesia
   1725 N Street, NW
   Washington, D.C. 20038
   (202) 223-4383
   Consulates: HI (808) 836-4775
      Guam (671) 646-9154

Moldova: Embassy of the Republic of
   Moldova
   2101 S Street, NW
   Washington, D.C. 20008
   (202) 667-1131

Monaco: See France
or
Consulate General of Monaco
565 Fifth Avenue
New York, NY 10017
(212) 759-5227
Consulates: CA (213) 655-8970
  IL (312) 642-1242
  LA (504) 522-5700
  NY (212) 759-5227
  PR (809) 721-4215

Mongolia: Embassy of Mongolia
2833 M Street, NW
Washington, D.C. 20007
(202) 333-7117
or
United Nations Mission of Mongolia: (212)
861-9460

Montserrat: See United Kingdom
or
U.S. Embassy, Bridgetown, Barbados
(246) 431-0225
or
U.S. Consulate, English Harbour, Antigua
(268) 463-6531

Morocco: Embassy of the Kingdom of Morocco
1601 21st Street, NW
Washington, D.C. 20009
(202) 462-7979/82
or
Consulate General: (212) 758-2625

Mozambique: Embassy of the Republic of
Mozambique
1990 M Street, NW, Suite 570
Washington, D.C. 20036
(202) 293-7146

Myanmar (formerly Burma): Embassy of the
Union of Myanmar
2300 S Street, NW
Washington, D.C. 20008
(202) 332-9044/5

Namibia: Embassy of the Republic of Namibia
1605 New Hampshire Avenue, NW
Washington, D.C. 20009
(202) 986-0540

Nauru: Consulate of the Republic of Nauru in
Guam
Ada Professional Building
Marine Drive, 1st Floor
Agana, Guam 96910
(671) 649-7106/7

Nepal: Royal Nepalese Embassy
2131 Leroy Place, NW
Washington, D.C. 20008
(202) 667-4550
or
Consulate General: (212) 370-4188

Netherlands: Embassy of the Netherlands
4200 Linnean Avenue, NW
Washington, D.C. 20008
(202) 244-5300
Consulates: CA (310) 268-1598
  IL (312) 856-0110
  NY (212) 246-1429
  TX (713) 622-8000

Netherlands Antilles: Embassy of the
Netherlands
4200 Linnean Avenue, NW
Washington, D.C. 20008
(202) 244-5300

New Zealand: Embassy of New Zealand
37 Observatory Circle, NW
Washington, D.C. 20008
(202) 328-4800
or
Consulate General: (213) 477-8241

Nicaragua: Consulate of Nicaragua
1627 New Hampshire Avenue, NW
Washington, D.C. 20009
(202) 939-6531 or 6570
Consulates: CA (213) 252-1170 or
  (415) 765-6821
  FL (305) 220-6900
  LA (504) 523-1507
  NY (212) 983-1981
  TX (713) 272-9628

Niger: Embassy of the Republic of Niger
2204 R Street, NW
Washington, D.C. 20008
(202) 483-4224

Nigeria: Embassy of the Federal Republic of
Nigeria
2201 M Street, NW
Washington, D.C. 20037
(202) 822-1500 or 1522
or
Consulate General: (212) 715-7200

Northern Ireland: See United Kingdom

Norway: Royal Embassy of Norway
2720 34th Street, NW
Washington, D.C. 20008
(202) 333-6000
Consulates: CA (415) 986-0766/68
MN (612) 332-3338
NY (212) 421-7333
TX (713) 521-2900

Oman: Embassy of the Sultanate of Oman
2535 Belmond Road, NW
Washington, D.C. 20008
(202) 387-1980/2

Pakistan: Embassy of the Islamic Republic of
Pakistan (Consular Section)
2315 Massachusetts Avenue, NW
Washington, D.C. 20008
(202) 939-6200
Consulates: CA (310) 441-5114
NY (212) 879-5800

Palau: Representative Office
1150 18th Street, NW, Suite 750
Washington, D.C. 20036
(202) 452-6814

Panama: Embassy of the Republic of Panama
2862 McGill Terrace, NW
Washington, D.C. 20008
(202) 483-1407
Consulates: CA (415) 391-4268
FL (305) 371-7031 or
(813) 831-6685
LA (504) 525-3458
NY (212) 840-2450
PA (215) 574-2994
TX (713) 622-4451

Papua New Guinea: Embassy of Papua New
Guinea
1615 New Hampshire Avenue, NW, Suite 300
Washington, D.C. 20009
(202) 745-3680

Paraguay: Embassy of Paraguay
2400 Massachusetts Avenue, NW
Washington, D.C. 20008
(202) 483-6960

Peru: Consulate General of Peru
1625 Massachusetts Avenue, NW, 6th Floor
Washington, D.C. 20036
(202) 462-1084
Other Consulates:
CA (213) 383-9896 or
(415) 362-5185
FL (305) 374-1407
IL (312) 374-1407
NY (212) 644-2850
PR (809) 763-769
TX (713) 781-5000

Philippines: Embassy of the Philippines
1600 Massachusetts Avenue, NW
Washington, D.C. 20036
(202) 467-9300
Consulates: CA (213) 387-5321 or
(415) 433-6666
HI (808) 595-6316
IL (312) 332-6458
NY (212) 764-1330
Guam (671) 646-4620

Poland: Embassy of the Republic of Poland
(Consular Division)
2224 Wyoming Avenue, NW
Washington, D.C. 20009
(202) 232-4517
Consulates: IL (312) 337-8166
CA (310) 442-8500
NY (212) 889-8360

Portugal: Embassy of Portugal
2310 Tracy Place, NW
Washington, D.C. 20008
(202) 332-3007
Consulates: CA (415) 346-3400
MA (617) 536-8740 or
(508) 997-6151
NJ (201) 622-7300
NY (212) 246-4580
RI (401) 272-2003

Qatar: Embassy of the State of Qatar
4200 Wisconsin Ave, NW.
Suite 200
Washington, D.C. 20016
(202) 274-1600

Reunion: See France

Romania: Embassy of Romania
1607 23rd Street, NW
Washington, D.C. 20008
(202) 332-4847
Consulates: NY (212) 682-9120
CA (310) 444-0043

Russia: Embassy of Russia (Consular
Division)
2641 Tunlaw Road, NW
Washington, D.C. 20007
(202) 939-8907
Consulates: NY (212) 348-0926
CA (415) 928-6878
WA (206) 728-1910

Rwanda: Embassy of the Republic of Rwanda
1714 New Hampshire Avenue, NW
Washington, D.C. 20009
(202) 232-2882
or
Permanent Mission to the United Nations:
(212) 696-0644/45/46
Consulates: IL (708) 205-1188
CO (303) 321-2400

Saint Kitts and Nevis: Embassy of Saint Kitts
and Nevis
OECS Building
3216 New Mexico Avenue, NW
Washington, D.C. 20016
(202) 686-2636
or
Permanent Mission to the United Nations:
(212) 535-1234

Saint Lucia: Embassy of Saint Lucia
3216 New Mexico Avenue, NW
Washington, D.C. 20016
(202) 364-6792
or
Permanent Mission to the United Nations:
(212) 697-9360

Saint Martin (Saint Maarten): See Netherlands
Antilles

Saint Pierre: Embassy of France
(202) 944-6000

Saint Vincent and the Grenadines: Embassy
of Saint Vincent and the Grenadines
3216 New Mexico Avenue, NW
Washington, D.C. 20016
(202) 364-6730

Samoa: Samoa Mission to the United
Nations
820 Second Avenue, Suite 800
New York, NY 10017
Consulates: HI (808) 677-7197

San Marino: Honorary Consulate of the
Republic of San Marino
1899 L St., NW, Suite 500
Washington, D.C. 20036
(202) 223-3517
Other Consulates: MI (313) 528-1190
NY (516) 242-2212

São Tomé and Príncipe: Permanent Mission
of São Tomé and Príncipe to the United
Nations
400 Park Avenue, 7th Floor
New York, NY 10022
(212) 317-0533

Saudi Arabia: Royal Embassy of Saudi
Arabia
601 New Hampshire Avenue, NW
Washington, D.C. 20037
(202) 333-2740
Consulates: CA (310) 479-6000
NY (212) 752-2740
TX (713) 785-5577

Scotland: See United Kingdom

Senegal: Embassy of the Republic of Senegal
2112 Wyoming Avenue, NW
Washington, D.C. 20008
(202) 234-0540

Serbia and Montenegro: Embassy of the
Former Federal Republic of Yugoslavia
(Serbia & Montenegro)
2410 California Street, NW
Washington, D.C. 20008
(202) 462-6566

Seychelles: Permanent Mission of the
Seychelles to the United Nations
820 Second Avenue, Suite 203
New York, NY 10017
(212) 687-9766

Sierra Leone: Embassy of Sierra Leone
1701 19th Street, NW
Washington, D.C. 20009
(202) 939-9261

Singapore: Embassy of the Republic of
Singapore
3501 International Place, NW
Washington, D.C. 20008
(202) 537-3100

Slovak Republic: Embassy of the Slovak
Republic
2201 Wisconsin Avenue, NW,
Suite 250
Washington, D.C. 20007
(202) 965-5160, Extension 270

Slovenia: Embassy of the Republic of
Slovenia
1525 New Hampshire Avenue, NW
Washington, D.C. 20036
(202) 667-5363
or
Consulate General: (212) 370-3006

Solomon Islands: British Embassy
(202) 986-0205
or
Solomon Islands Mission to the United
Nations
800 Second Avenue, 4th Floor
New York, NY 10017
(212) 599-6192

Somalia: no embassy, consulate, or mission in
the United States

South Africa: Embassy of South Africa
3051 Massachusetts Avenue, NW
Washington, D.C. 20008
(202) 232-4400
Consulates: CA (310) 657-9200
IL (312) 939-7929
NY (212) 213-4880

Spain: Embassy of Spain
2375 Pennsylvania Avenue, NW
Washington, D.C. 20037

(202) 452-0100 and 728-2330
Consulates: CA (415) 922-2995 or
(213) 938-0158
FL (305) 446-5511
IL (312) 782-4588
LA (504) 525-4951
MA (617) 536-2506
NY (212) 355-4080
PR (809) 758-6090
TX (713) 783-6200

Sri Lanka: Embassy of Sri Lanka
2148 Wyoming Avenue, NW
Washington, D.C. 20008
(202) 483-4025
Consulates: CA (805) 323-8975 or
(504) 362-3232
HI (808) 373-2040
NJ (201) 627-7855
NY (212) 986-7040

Sudan: Embassy of the Republic of the
Sudan
2210 Massachusetts Avenue, NW
Washington, D.C. 20008
(202) 338-8565/70
or
Consulate General: (212) 573-6033 or 6035

Suriname: Embassy of the Republic of
Suriname
4301 Connecticut Avenue, NW, Suite 460
Washington, D.C. 20008
(202) 244-7488
or
Consulate: FL (305) 593-2163

Swaziland: Embassy of the Kingdom of
Swaziland
3400 International Drive, NW, Suite 3M
Washington, D.C. 20008
(202) 362-6683

Sweden: Embassy of Sweden
1501 M Street, NW
Washington, D.C. 20005-1702
(202) 467-2600
Consulates: CA (310) 445-4008
FL (954) 467-3507
IL (312) 781-6262
NY (212) 583-2550

Switzerland: Embassy of Switzerland
2900 Cathedral Avenue, NW
Washington, D.C. 20008
(202) 745-7900
Consulates: CA (310) 575-1145 or
(415) 788-2272
GA (404) 870-2000
IL (312) 915-0061
NY (212) 758-2560
TX (713) 650-0000

Syria: Embassy of the Syrian Arab Republic
2215 Wyoming Avenue, NW
Washington, D.C. 20008
(202) 232-6313

Tahiti: See France

Taiwan: Taipei Economic and Cultural
Representative Office
4201 Wisconsin Avenue, NW
Washington, D.C. 20016-2137
(202) 895-1800
Other Offices: GA (404) 872-0123,
MA (617) 737-2050
IL (312) 616-0100
Guam (671) 472-5865
HI (808) 595-6347
TX (713) 626-7445
MO (816) 531-1298
CA (213) 389-1215 or
(415) 362-7680
FL (305) 443-8917
NY (212) 486-0088
WA (206) 441-4586

Tajikistan: Embassy of Russia (Consular
Division)
(202) 939-8907

Tanzania: Embassy of the United Republic of
Tanzania
2139 R Street, NW
Washington, D.C. 20008
(202) 939-6125
or
Tanzanian Permanent Mission to the United
Nations:
(212) 972-9160

Thailand: Royal Thai Embassy
1024 Wisconsin Avenue, NW
Washington, D.C. 20007
(202) 944-3608
Consulates: CA (213) 962-9574/77
IL (312) 236-2447
NY (212) 754-1770

Togo: Embassy of the Republic of Togo
2208 Massachusetts Avenue, NW
Washington, D.C. 20008
(202) 234-4212/3

Tonga: Consulate General of Tonga
360 Post Street, Suite 604
San Francisco, CA 94108
(415) 781-0365

Trinidad and Tobago: Embassy of the
Republic of Trinidad and Tobago
1708 Massachusetts Avenue, NW
Washington, D.C. 20036
(202) 467-6490
Consulates: NY (212) 682-7272
MI (305) 374-2199

Tunisia: Embassy of Tunisia
1515 Massachusetts Avenue, NW
Washington, D.C. 20005
(202) 862-1850
Consulates: CA (415) 922-9222
NY (212) 272-6962

Turkey: Embassy of the Republic of Turkey
1714 Massachusetts Avenue, NW
Washington, D.C. 20036
(202) 659-8200
Consulates: CA (213) 937-0118
IL (312) 263-0644
NY (212) 949-0160
TX (713) 622-5849

Turkmenistan: Embassy of Turkmenistan
2207 Massachusetts Avenue, NW
Washington, D.C. 20008
(202) 588-1500

Turks and Caicos: See United Kingdom
or
U.S. Embassy, Nassau, Bahamas
(242) 322-1181 or 328-2206

Tuvalu: See United Kingdom

Uganda: Embassy of the Republic of Uganda
5909 16th Street, NW
Washington, D.C. 20011
(202) 726-7100/02
or
Permanent Mission to the United Nations: (212) 949-0110

Ukraine: Embassy of Ukraine
3350 M Street, NW
Washington, D.C. 20007
(202) 333-0606 or 7507/09
Consulates: IL (312) 642-4388
NY (212) 371-5690

United Arab Emirates: Embassy of the United Arab Emirates
1255 22nd Street, NW, Suite 700
Washington, D.C. 20037
(202) 955-7999

United Kingdom: British Embassy (Consular Section)
19 Observatory Circle, NW
Washington, D.C. 20008
(202) 986-0205
Consulates: CA (415) 922-9222
NY (212) 272-6962

Uruguay: Embassy of Uruguay
2715 M Street, NW, 3rd Floor
Washington, D.C. 20007
(202) 331-1313
Consulates: CA (213) 394-5777
FL (305) 358-9350
LA (504) 525-8354
NY (212) 753-8191/2

Uzbekistan: Embassy of the Republic of Uzbekistan
1746 Massachusetts Avenue, NW
Washington, D.C. 20036
(202) 293-6803
or
Uzbekistan Consulate: (212) 754-6178 or 7403

Vanuatu: See United Kingdom
or
Vanuatu Mission to the United Nations: (212) 593-0144

Venezuela: Embassy the Republic of Venezuela
1099 30th Street NW
Washington, D.C. 20007
(202) 342-2214
Consulates: CA (415) 512-8340
FL (305) 577-3834
IL (312) 236-9655
LA (504) 522-3284
MA (617) 266-9355
NY (212) 826-1660
PR (809) 766-4250/1
TX (713) 961-5141

Vietnam: Embassy of Vietnam
1233 20th Street NW, Suite 400
Washington, D.C. 20036
(202) 861-2293 or 0694

Virgin Islands, British: See United Kingdom

Wales: See United Kingdom

Western Samoa: See Samoa

West Indies, British: See United Kingdom

West Indies, French: See France

Yemen: Embassy of the Republic of Yemen
2600 Virginia Avenue, NW, Suite 705
Washington, D.C. 20037
(202) 965-4760
or
Yemen Mission to the United Nations: (212) 355-1730

Zambia: Embassy of the Republic of Zambia
2419 Massachusetts Avenue, NW
Washington, D.C. 20008
(202) 265-9717/19

Zimbabwe: Embassy of Zimbabwe
1608 New Hampshire Avenue, NW
Washington, D.C. 20009
(202) 332-7100

⊙ Central Intelligence Agency. "World Fact Book 2000," www.cia.gov/publications/factbook/fields/diplomatic_representation_in_the_us.html

Congress: The House of Representatives and the Senate

"All legislative Powers herein granted shall be vested in a Congress of the United States, which shall consist of a Senate and a House of Representatives." (U.S. Constitution, 1787)

Although the first Congress in 1789 consisted of 20 senators and 59 representatives, today there are 100 senators—2 from each state—and 435 representatives. The number of representatives from each state is determined by the population of the state. There is a resident commissioner from Puerto Rico, who is elected for a 4-year term, and delegates from American Samoa, the District of Columbia, Guam, and the Virgin Islands, who are elected for two-year terms.

A representative must reside in the state from which he or she is elected, be at least 25 years old, and have been a citizen of the United States for at least seven years. A senator must reside in the state from which he or she is elected, be at least 30 years old, and have been a citizen of the United States for at least nine years.

The Senate and the House have equal responsibility for declaring war, maintaining the armed forces, assessing taxes, borrowing money, minting currency, regulating commerce, and making all laws necessary for the operation of the government. The Senate holds exclusive authority to advise and consent on treaties and nominations. In cases of impeachment, the House votes to impeach and the Senate conducts the impeachment trial.

⊙ GPO. *History of the House of Representatives*. Washington, D.C.: U.S. GPO, 1994.
United States House of Representatives. "Historical Facts-Historical Highlights-Office of the Clerk," www.clerkweb.house.gov/histrecs/househis/index.htm
United States Senate. "Learning about the Senate," www.senate.gov/learning

House Committees and Subcommittees

Standing Committees	*Subcommittees*
Agriculture	General Farm Commodities, Resource Conservation, and Credit; Livestock and Horticulture; Risk Management, Research, and Specialty Crops; Department Operations, Oversight, Nutrition, and Forestry
Appropriations	Agriculture, Rural Development, Food and Drug Administration, and Related Agencies; Commerce, Justice, State, and Judiciary; Defense; District of Columbia; Energy and Water Development; Foreign Operations, Export Financing, and Related Programs; Interior; Labor, Health and Human Services, and Education; Legislative; Military Construction; Transportation; Treasury, Postal Service, and General Government; VA, HUD, and Independent Agencies
Armed Services	Military Procurement; Military Research and Development; Military Readiness; Military Installations and Facilities
Budget Education and the Workforce	Employer-Employee Relations; Workforce Protections; Early Childhood, Youth, and Families; Oversight and Investigations
Energy and Commerce	Telecommunications, Trade, and Consumer Protection; Finance and Hazardous Materials; Health and Environment; Energy and Power; Oversight and Investigations
Financial Services	Housing and Community Opportunity; Financial Institutions and Consumer Credit; Domestic and International Monetary Policy; Capital Markets, Securities, and Government Sponsored Enterprises; General Oversight

Government Reform	National Security, International Affairs, and Criminal Justice; Civil Service; Human Resources; Postal Service; Government Management, Information, and Technology; District of Columbia; National Economic Growth, Natural Resources, and Regulatory Affairs; Census
House Administration	
International Relations	International Economic Policy and Trade; Asia and the Pacific; International Operations and Human Rights; The Western Hemisphere; Africa
Judiciary	Courts and Intellectual Property; Crime; Immigration and Claims; The Constitution; Commercial and Administrative Law
Resources	National Parks and Public Lands; Fisheries, Conservation, Wildlife, and Oceans; Energy and Mineral Resources; Water and Power; Forests and Forest Health
Rules	Rules and Organization of the House; Legislative and Budget Process
Science	Basic Research; Energy and Environment; Space and Aeronautics; Technology
Small Business	Empowerment; Government Programs and Oversight; Regulatory Reform and Paperwork Reduction; Tax, Finance, and Exports; Rural Enterprises, Business Opportunities, and Special Small Business Problems
Standards of Official Conduct	
Transportation and Infrastructure	Aviation; Coast Guard and Maritime Transportation; Public Buildings and Economic Development; Railroads; Surface Transportation; Water Resources and Environment
Veterans' Affairs	Health; Benefits; Oversight and Investigations
Ways and Means	Trade; Oversight; Health; Social Security; Human Resources

Select Committees

Permanent Select Committee on Intelligence	Human Intelligence, Analysis, and Counterintelligence; Technical and Tactical Intelligence

Select Committee on U.S. National Security and Military/Commercial Concerns with the People's Republic of China

Joint Committees

Joint Economic Committee   Joint Committee on Printing

Joint Committee on the Library   Joint Committee on Taxation

⊙ U.S. House of Representatives. "House Committee Information," www.clerkweb.house.gov/mbrcmtee/members/commem.htm

Congress	Speaker	Party	State	Date Elected	President
1	Frederick A. C. Muhlenberg	—	Pennsylvania	Apr. 1, 1789	Washington
2	Jonathan Trumbull	—	Connecticut	Oct. 24, 1791	Washington
3	Frederick A. C. Muhlenberg	—	Pennsylvania	Dec. 2, 1793	Washington
4, 5	Jonathan Dayton	—	New Jersey	Dec. 7, 1795	Washington
6	Theodore Sedgwick	—	Massachusetts	Dec. 2, 1799	J. Adams
7, 8, 9	Nathaniel Macon	Republican	North Carolina	Dec. 7, 1801	Jefferson
10, 11	Joseph B. Varnum	Republican	Massachusetts	Oct. 26, 1807	Jefferson
12	Henry Clay	Republican	Kentucky	Nov. 4, 1811	Madison
13	Henry Clay	Republican	Kentucky	May 24, 1813	Madison
13	Langdon Cheves	Republican	South Carolina	Jan. 19, 1814	Madison
14, 15	Henry Clay	Republican	Kentucky	Dec. 4, 1815	Madison
16	Henry Clay	Republican	Kentucky	Dec. 6, 1819	Monroe
16	John W. Taylor	Republican	New York	Nov. 15, 1820	Monroe
17	Philip P. Barbour	Republican	Virginia	Dec. 4, 1821	Monroe
18	Henry Clay	Republican	Kentucky	Dec. 1, 1823	Monroe
19	John W. Taylor	Republican	New York	Dec. 5, 1825	Monroe
20, 21,	Andrew Stevenson	Jacksonian	Virginia	Dec. 3, 1827	J. Q. Adams
22, 23	Andrew Stevenson	Jacksonian	Virginia	Dec. 2, 1833	Jackson
23	John Bell	Whig	Tennessee	June 2, 1834	Jackson
24, 25	James K. Polk	Republican	Tennessee	Dec. 7, 1835	Jackson
26	Robert M. T. Hunter	States Rights Whig	Virginia	Dec. 16, 1839	Van Buren
27	John White	Whig	Kentucky	May 31, 1841	Van Buren
28	John W. Jones	Democrat	Virginia	Dec. 4, 1843	Tyler
29	John W. Davis	Democrat	Indiana	Dec. 1, 1845	Tyler
30	Robert C. Winthrop	Whig	Massachusetts	Dec. 6, 1847	Polk
31	Howell Cobb	Democrat	Georgia	Dec. 22, 1849	Taylor
32, 33	Linn Boyd	Democrat	Kentucky	Dec. 1, 1851	Fillmore
34	Nathaniel P. Banks	American	Massachusetts	Feb. 2, 1856	Pierce
35	James L. Orr	Democrat	South Carolina	Dec. 7, 1857	Pierce
36	William Pennington	Republican	New Jersey	Feb. 1, 1860	Buchanan
37	Galusha A. Grow	Republican	Pennsylvania	July 4, 1861	Lincoln
38, 39	Schuyler Colfax	Republican	Indiana	Dec. 7, 1863	Lincoln
40	Schuyler Colfax	Republican	Indiana	Mar. 4, 1867	Johnson
40	Theodore M. Pomeroy	Republican	New York	Mar. 3, 1869	Grant

Congress	Speaker	Party	State	Date	President
41, 42, 43	James G. Blaine	Republican	Maine	Mar. 4, 1869	Grant
44	Michael C. Kerr	Democrat	Indiana	Dec. 6, 1875	Grant
44	Samuel J. Randall	Democrat	Pennsylvania	Dec. 4, 1876	Grant
45, 46	Samuel J. Randall	Democrat	Pennsylvania	Oct. 15, 1877	Grant
47	J. Warren Keifer	Republican	Ohio	Dec. 5, 1881	Hayes
48, 49, 50	John G. Carlisle	Democrat	Kentucky	Dec. 3, 1883	Arthur
51	Thomas B. Reed	Republican	Maine	Dec. 2, 1889	Cleveland
52	Charles F. Crisp	Democrat	Georgia	Dec. 8, 1891	Harrison, B.
54, 55	Thomas B. Reed	Republican	Maine	Dec. 2, 1895	Cleveland
56, 57	David B. Henderson	Republican	Iowa	Dec. 4, 1899	McKinley
58, 59, 60, 61	Joseph G. Cannon	Republican	Illinois	Nov. 9, 1903	Roosevelt, T.
62, 63, 64, 65	Champ Clark	Democrat	Missouri	Apr. 4, 1911	Taft
66, 67, 68	Frederick H. Gillett	Republican	Massachusetts	May 19, 1919	Wilson
69, 70, 71	Nicholas Longworth	Republican	Ohio	Dec. 7, 1925	Coolidge
72	John N. Garner	Democrat	Texas	Dec. 7, 1931	Hoover
73	Henry T. Rainey	Democrat	Illinois	Mar. 9, 1933	Hoover
74	Joseph W. Byrns	Democrat	Tennessee	Jan. 3, 1935	F. D. Roosevelt
74	William B. Bankhead	Democrat	Alabama	June 4, 1936	F. D. Roosevelt
75, 76	William B. Bankhead	Democrat	Alabama	Jan. 5, 1937	F. D. Roosevelt
77, 78, 79	Sam T. Rayburn	Democrat	Texas	Jan. 3, 1941	F. D. Roosevelt
80	Joseph W. Martin	Republican	Massachusetts	Jan. 3, 1947	Truman
81, 82	Sam T. Rayburn	Democrat	Texas	Jan. 3, 1949	Truman
83	Joseph W. Martin	Republican	Massachusetts	Jan. 3, 1953	Truman
84, 85, 86, 87	Sam T. Rayburn	Democrat	Texas	Jan. 5, 1955	Eisenhower
88, 89, 90, 91	John W. McCormack	Democrat	Massachusetts	Jan. 9, 1963	Johnson
92, 93, 94	Carl Albert	Democrat	Oklahoma	Jan. 21, 1971	Nixon
95, 96, 97, 98, 99	Thomas P. O'Neill, Jr.	Democrat	Massachusetts	Jan. 4, 1977	Ford
100	James C. Wright, Jr.	Democrat	Texas	Jan. 6, 1987	Reagan
101	James C. Wright, Jr.	Democrat	Texas	Jan. 3, 1989	Bush
101	Thomas S. Foley	Democrat	Washington	June 6, 1989	Bush
102, 103	Thomas S. Foley	Democrat	Washington	Jan. 3, 1991	Bush
104, 105	Newt Gingrich	Republican	Georgia	Jan. 4, 1995	Clinton
106, 107	John Dennis Hastert	Republican	Illinois	Jan. 6, 1999	Clinton

◉ United States House of Representatives. "Historical Facts-Historical Highlights-Office of the Clerk," http://clerkweb.house.gov/histrecs/househis/lead.htm

House of Representatives Membership by State

(valid through the 2000 election)

State	No. of Representatives	State	No. of Representatives
Alabama	7	Nevada	2
Alaska	1	New Hampshire	2
Arizona	6	New Jersey	13
Arkansas	4	New Mexico	3
California	52	New York	31
Colorado	6	North Carolina	12
Connecticut	6	North Dakota	1
Delaware	1	Ohio	19
Florida	23	Oklahoma	6
Georgia	11	Oregon	5
Hawaii	2	Pennsylvania	21
Idaho	2	Rhode Island	2
Illinois	20	South Carolina	6
Indiana	10	South Dakota	1
Iowa	5	Tennessee	9
Kansas	4	Texas	30
Kentucky	6	Utah	3
Louisiana	7	Vermont	1
Maine	2	Virginia	11
Maryland	8	Washington	9
Massachusetts	10	West Virginia	3
Michigan	16	Wisconsin	9
Minnesota	8	Wyoming	1
Mississippi	5	District of Columbia	1
Missouri	9	Puerto Rico	1
Montana	1	U.S. Virgin Islands	1
Nebraska	3		

⊙ United States House of Representatives. "Historical Facts-Historical Highlights-Office of the Clerk," www.clerkweb.house.gov/histrecs/househis/index.html

Wawro, Gregory. *Legislative Entrepreneurship in the U.S. House of Representatives*. Ann Arbor: University of Michigan Press, 2000.

Women Representatives

Name	State	Party	Years of Service
Corinne Claiborne (Lindy) Boggs	North Carolina	Republican	1917–19; 1941–43
Jeannette Rankin	Montana	Republican	1917–19; 1941–43
Alice Mary Robertson	Oklahoma	Republican	1921–23
Winnifred Sprague Mason Huck	Illinois	Republican	1922–23
Mae Ella Nolan	California	Republican	1923–25
Florence Prag Kahn	California	Republican	1925–37
Mary Teresa Norton	New Jersey	Democrat	1925–51
Edith Nourse Rogers	Massachusetts	Republican	1925–60

Katherine Gudger Langley	Kentucky	Republican	1927–31
Pearl Peden Oldfield	Arkansas	Democrat	1929–31
Ruth Hanna McCormick	Illinois	Republican	1929–31
Ruth Bryan Owen	Florida	Democrat	1929–33
Ruth Sears Baker Pratt	New York	Republican	1929–33
Effiegene Locke Wingo	Arkansas	Democrat	1930–33
Willa McCord Blake Eslick	Tennessee	Democrat	1932–33
Kathryn Ellen O'Loughlin (McCarthy)	Kansas	Democrat	1933–35
Virginia Ellis Jenckes	Indiana	Democrat	1933–39
Isabella Selmes Greenway	Arizona	Democrat	1933–37
Marian Williams Clarke	New York	Republican	1933–35
Caroline Love Goodwin O'Day	New York	Democrat	1935–43
Nan Wood Honeyman	Oregon	Democrat	1937–39
Elizabeth Hawley Gasque	South Carolina	Democrat	1938–39
Jessie Sumner	Illinois	Republican	1939–47
Clara Gooding McMillan	South Carolina	Democrat	1939–41
Frances Payne Bolton	Ohio	Republican	1940–69
Margaret Chase Smith	Maine	Republican	1940–49
Florence Reville Gibbs	Georgia	Democrat	1940–41
Katharine Edgar Byron	Maryland	Democrat	1941–43
Veronica Grace Boland	Pennsylvania	Democrat	1942–43
Clare Boothe Luce	Connecticut	Republican	1943–47
Winifred Claire Stanley	New York	Republican	1943–45
Willa Lybrand Fulmer	South Carolina	Democrat	1944–45
Emily Taft Douglas	Illinois	Democrat	1945–47
Helen Gahagan Douglas	California	Democrat	1945–51
Chase Going Woodhouse	Connecticut	Democrat	1945–47; 1949–51
Helen Douglas Mankin	Goergia	Democrat	1946–47
Eliza Jane Pratt	North Carolina	Democrat	1946–47
Georgia Lee Lusk	New Mexico	Democrat	1947–49
Katharine Price Collier St. George	New York	Republican	1947–65
Reva Zilpha Beck Bosone	Utah	Democrat	1949–53
Cecil Murray Harden	Indiana	Republican	1949–59
Edna Flannery Kelly	New York	Democrat	1949–69
Marguerite Stitt Church	Illinois	Republican	1951–63
Ruth Thompson	Michigan	Republican	1951–57
Maude Elizabeth Kee	West Virginia	Democrat	1951–65
Vera Daerr Buchanan	Pennsylvania	Democrat	1951–55
Gracie Bowers Pfost	Idaho	Democrat	1953–63
Leonor Kretzer Sullivan	Missouri	Democrat	1953–77
Mary Elizabeth Pruett Farrington (Delegate)	Hawaii	Republican	1954–57
Iris Faircloth Blitch	Georgia	Democrat	1955–63
Edith Starrett Green	Oregon	Democrat	1955–74
Martha Wright Griffiths	Michigan	Democrat	1955–74
Coya Gjesdal Knutson	Florida, Minnesota	Democrat	1955–59
Kathryn Elizabeth Granahan	Pennsylvania	Democrat	1956–63
Florence Price Dwyer	New Jersey	Republican	1957–73
Catherine Dean May	Washington	Republican	1959–71
Edna Oakes Simpson	Illinois	Republican	1959–61

Women Representatives *(cont.)*

Name	State	Party	Years of Service
Jessica McCullough Weis	New York	Republican	1959–63
Julia Butler Hansen	Washington	Democrat	1960–74
Catherine Dorris Norrell	Arkansas	Democrat	1961–63
Louise Goff Reece	Tennessee	Republican	1961–63
Corinne Boyd Riley	South Carolina	Democrat	1962–63
Charlotte Thompson Reid	Illinois	Republican	1963–71
Irene Bailey Baker	Tennessee	Republican	1964–65
Patsy Takemoto Mink	Hawaii	Democrat	1965–77; 1990–
Lera Millard Thomas	Texas	Democrat	1966–67
Nargaret M. Heckler	Massachusetts	Republican	1967–83
Shirley Anita Chisholm	New York	Democrat	1969–83
Bella Savitzky Abzug	New York	Democrat	1971–77
Ella Tambussi Grasso	Connecticut	Democrat	1971–75
Louise Day Hicks	Massachusetts	Democrat	1971–73
Elizabeth Bullock Andrews	Alabama	Democrat	1972–73
Yvonne Brathwaite Burke	California	Democrat	1973–79
Marjorie Sewell Holt	Maryland	Republican	1973–87
Elizabeth Holtzman	New York	Democrat	1973–81
Barbara Charline Jordan	Texas	Democrat	1973–79
Patricia Scott Schroeder	Colorado	Democrat	1973–97
Corinne Claiborne (Lindy) Boggs	Louisiana	Democrat	1973–91
Cardiss Collins	Illinois	Democrat	1973–97
Millicent Hammond Fenwick	New Jersey	Republican	1975–83
Martha Elizabeth Keys	Kansas	Democrat	1975–89
Marilyn Laird Lloyd	Tennessee	Democrat	1975–95
Helen Stevenson Meyner	New Jersey	Democrat	1975–79
Virginia Dodd Smith	Nebraska	Republican	1975–91
Gladys Noon Spellman	Maryland	Democrat	1975–81
Shirley Neil Pettis	California	Republican	1975–79
Barbara Ann Mikulski	Maryland	Democrat	1977–87
Mary Rose Oakar	Ohio	Democrat	1977–93
Beverly Barton Butcher Byron	Maryland	Democrat	1979–93
Geraldine Anne Ferraro	New York	Democrat	1979–85
Olympia Jean Snowe	Maine	Republican	1979–95
Bobbi Fiedler	California	Republican	1981–87
Lynn Morley Martin	Illinois	Republican	1981–91
Margaret Scafati Roukema	New Jersey	Republican	1981–
Claudene Schneider	Rhode Island	Republican	1981–91
Barbara Bailey Kennelly	Connecticut	Democrat	1982–99
Jean Spencer Ashbrook	Ohio	Republican	1982–83
Katie Beatrice Hall	Indiana	Democrat	1982–85
Barbara Boxer	California	Democrat	1983–93
Nancy Lee Johnson	Connecticut	Republican	1983–
Marcia Carolyn (Marcy) Kaptur	Ohio	Democrat	1983–
Barbara Farrell Vucanovich	Nevada	Republican	1983–97
Sala Burton	California	Democrat	1983–87
Helen Delich Bentley	Maryland	Republican	1985–95

Jan Meyers	Kansas	Republican	195–97
Catherine S. Long	Louisiana	Democrat	1985–87
Constance A. Morella	Maryland	Republican	1987–
Elizabeth J. Patterson	South Carolina	Democrat	1987–93
Patricia Fukuda Saiki	Hawaii	Republican	1987–91
Louise M. Slaughter	New York	Democrat	1987–
Nancy Pelosi	California	Democrat	1987–
Nita M. Lowey	New York	Democrat	1989–
Jolene Unsoeld	Washington	Democrat	1989–95
Jill Long	Indiana	Democrat	1989–95
Ileana Ros-Lehtinen	Florida	Republican	1989–
Susan Molinari	New York	Republican	1990–97
Barbara-Rose Collins	Mississippi	Democrat	1991–97
Rosa DeLauro	Connecticut	Democrat	1991–
Joan Kelly Horn	Missouri	Democrat	1991–93
Eleanor Holmes Norton (Delegate)	District of Columbia	Democrat	1991–
Maxine Waters	California	Democrat	1991–
Eva Clayton	North Carolina	Democrat	1992–
Corrine Brown	Florida	Democrat	1993–
Leslie Byrne	Virginia	Democrat	1993–95
Maria Cantwell	Washington	Democrat	1993–95
Pat Danner	Missouri	Democrat	1993–
Jennifer Dunn	Washington	Republican	1993–
Karan English	Arizona	Democrat	1993–95
Anna G. Eshoo	California	Democrat	1993–
Tillie Fowler	Florida	Republican	1993–
Elizabeth Furse	Oregon	Democrat	1993–99
Jane Harman	California	Democrat	1993–99
Eddie Bernice Johnson	Texas	Democrat	1993–
Blanche Lambert Lincoln	Arkansas	Democrat	1993–97
Carolyn B. Maloney	New York	Democrat	1993–
Marjorie Margolies-Mezvinsky	Pennsylvania	Democrat	1993–95
Cynthia McKinney	Georgia	Democrat	1993–
Carrie P. Meek	Florida	Democrat	1993–
Deborah Pryce	Ohio	Republican	1993–
Lucille Roybal-Allard	California	Democrat	1993–
Lynn Schenk	California	Democrat	1993–95
Karen Shepherd	Utah	Democrat	1993–95
Karen Thurman	Florida	Democrat	1993–
Nydia M. Velazquez	New York	Democrat	1993–
Lynn Woolsey	California	Democrat	1993
Helen Chenoweth	Idaho	Republican	1995–
Barbara Cubin	Wyoming	Republican	1995–
Sheila Jackson-Lee	Texas	Democrat	1995–
Sue Kelly	New York	Republican	1995–
Zoe Lofgren	California	Democrat	1995–
Karen McCarthy	Missouri	Democrat	1995–
Sue Myrick	North Carolina	Republican	1995–
Lynn Rivers	Mississippi	Democrat	1995–

Women Representatives (cont.)

Name	State	Party	Years of Service
Andrea Seastrand	California	Republican	1995–97
Linda Smith	Washington	Republican	1995–99
Enid Greene (Waldholtz)	Utah	Republican	1995–97
Juanita Millender-McDonald	California	Democrat	1997–
JoAnn Emerson	Missouri	Republican	1997–
Julia Carson	Indiana	Democrat	1997–
Donna M. Christian-Green (Delegate)	Virginia	Democrat	1997–
Diana DeGette	Colorado	Democrat	1997–
Kay Granger	Texas	Republican	1997–
Darlene Hooley	Oregon	Democrat	1997–
Carolyn Cheeks Kilpatrick	Mississippi	Democrat	1997–
Carolyn McCarthy	New York	Democrat	1997–
Anne Northup	Kentucky	Republican	1997–
Loretta Sanchez	California	Democrat	1997–
Debbie Stabenow	Mississippi	Democrat	1997–
Ellen Tauscher	California	Democrat	1997–
Mary Bono	California	Republican	1998–
Lois Capps	California	Democrat	1998–
Barbara Lee	California	Democrat	1998–
Heather Wilson	New Mexico	Republican	1998–
Janice Schakowsky	Illinois	Democrat	1998–
Shelly Capito	West Virginia	Republican	2000–
Jo Ann Davis	Virginia	Democrat	2000–
Susan Davis	California	Democrat	2000–
Melissa Hart	Pennsylvania	Republican	2000–
Betty McCollum	Maryland	Democrat	2000–
Hilda Solis	California	Democrat	2000–

⊙ United States House of Representatives. "Women in Congress," http://bioguide.congress.gov/congresswomen/index.asp

Young, Lisa. *Feminists and Party Politics.* Vancouver: University of British Columbia Press, 2000.

Foerstel, Karen. *Climbing the Hill: Gender Conflict in Congress.* Wesport, Conn.: Praeger, 1996.

Senate Committees and Subcommittees

Standing Committees	Subcommittees
Agriculture, Nutrition, and Forestry	Forestry, Conservation, and Rural Revitalization; Marketing, Inspection, and Product Promotion; Production and Price Competitiveness; Research, Nutrition, and General Legislation
Appropriations	Agriculture, Rural Development, and Related Agencies; Commerce, Justice, State, and Judiciary; Defense; District of Columbia; Energy and Water Development; Interior; Labor, Health, and Human Services; Education; Legislative Branch; Military Construction; Transportation; Treasury and General Government; Va-Hud-Independent Agencies

Armed Services	Acquisitions and Technology; Airland Forces; Personnel; Readiness; Sea Power; Strategic Forces
Banking, Housing, and Urban Affairs	Financial Institutions and Regulatory Relief; Financial Services and Technology; Housing Opportunity and Community Development; International Finance; Securities
Budget	
Commerce, Science, and Transportation	Aviation; Communications; Consumer Affairs, Foreign Commerce and Tourism; Manufacturing and Competitiveness; Oceans and Fisheries; Science, Technology, and Space; Surface Transportation and Merchant Marine
Energy and Natural Resources	Energy Research, Development, Production, and Regulation; Forests and Public Land Management; Parks, Historic Preservation and Recreation; Water and Power
Environment and Public Works	Clean Air Wetlands, Private Property, and Nuclear Safety; Drinking Water, Fisheries, and Wildlife; Superfund, Waste Control, and Risk Assessment; Transportation and Infrastructure
Finance	Health Care; International Trade; Long-Term Growth, Debt, and Deficit Reduction; Social Security and Family Policy; Taxation and IRS Oversight
Foreign Relations	African Affairs; East Asian and Pacific Affairs; European Affairs; International Economic Policy, Export, and Trade Promotion; International Operations; Near Eastern and South Asian Affairs; Western Hemisphere, Peace Corps, Narcotics, and Terrorism
Governmental Affairs	International Security Proliferation and Federal Services; Oversight of Government Management, Restructuring, and the District of Columbia; Permanent Subcommittee on Investigations
Judiciary	Administration Oversight and the Courts; Antitrust, Business Rights, and Competition; Constitution, Federalism and Property Rights; Immigration; Technology, Terrorism, and Government Information; Youth Violence
Health, Education, Labor, and Pensions	Aging; Children and Families; Employment and Training; Public Health and Safety
Rules and Administration	
Small Business	
Veterans' Affairs	

Select and Special Committees

Senate Select Committee on Intelligence	Joint Committees of Congress
Senate Select Committee on Ethics	Joint Economic Committee
Senate Select Committee on Indian Affairs	Joint Committee on Taxation
Senate Special Committee on Aging	Joint Committee on the Library of Congress

⊙ U.S. Senate. "Senate Committees," www.senage.gov/committees/index.cfm
   Congressional Research Service. *The Committee System in the U.S. Congress.* Washington, D.C.:
   Congressional Research Service, Library of Congress, 1994.

Congress	Majority Leader	Minority Leader	President
66th 1920–21	Henry Cabot Lodge [R]	Oscar W. Underwood [D]	Wilson (D)
67th 1921–23	Henry Cabot Lodge [R]	Oscar W. Underwood [D]	Harding (R)
68th 1923–25	Henry Cabot Lodge [R]		
	Charles Curtis [R]	Joseph T. Robinson [D]	Harding (R)
			Coolidge (R)
69th 1925–27	Charles Curtis [R]	Joseph T. Robinson [D]	Coolidge (R)
70th 1927–29	Charles Curtis [R]	Joseph T. Robinson [D]	Coolidge (R)
71st 1929–31	James E. Watson [R]	Joseph T. Robinson [D]	Hoover (R)
72nd 1931–33	James E. Watson [R]	Joseph T. Robinson [D]	Hoover (R)
73rd 1933–35	Joseph T. Robinson [D]	Charles L. McNary [R]	Roosevelt (D)
74th 1935–37	Joseph T. Robinson [D]	Charles L. McNary [R]	Roosevelt (D)
75th 1937–39	Joseph T. Robinson [D]		
	Alben Barkley [D]	Charles L. McNary [R]	Roosevelt (D)
76th 1939–41	Alben Barkley [D]	Charles L. McNary [R]	Roosevelt (D)
77th 1941–43	Alben Barkley [D]	Charles L. McNary [R]	Roosevelt (D)
78th 1943–45	Alben Barkley [D]	W. H. White, Jr. [R]	Roosevelt (D)
79th 1945–47	Alben Barkley [D]	W. H. White, Jr. [R]	Roosevelt (D)
			Truman (D)
80th 1947–49	W. H. White, Jr. [R]	Alben Barkley [D]	Truman (D)
81st 1949–51	Scott W. Lucas [D]	Kenneth S. Wherry [R]	Truman (D)
82nd 1951–53	E. W. McFarland [D]	Kenneth S. Wherry [R]	
		Styles Bridges [R]	Truman (D)
83rd 1953–55	Robert A. Taft [R]		
	William F. Knowland [R]	Lyndon Johnson [D]	Eisenhower (R)
84th 1955–57	L. B. Johnson [D]	William F. Knowland [R]	Eisenhower (R)
85th 1957–59	L. B. Johnson [D]	William F. Knowland [R]	Eisenhower (R)
86th 1959–61	L. B. Johnson [D]	Everett Dirksen [R]	Eisenhower (R)
87th 1961–63	Mike Mansfield [D]	Everett Dirksen [R]	Kennedy (D)
88th 1963–65	Mike Mansfield [D]	Everett Dirksen [R]	Kennedy (D)
			Johnson (D)
89th 1965–67	Mike Mansfield [D]	Everett Dirksen [R]	Johnson (D)
90th 1967–69	Mike Mansfield [D]	Everett Dirksen {R}	Nixon (R)
91st 1969–71	Mike Mansfield [D]	Everett Dirksen [R]	
		Hugh D. Scott, Jr. [R]	Nixon (R)
92nd 1971–73	Mike Mansfield [D]	Hugh D. Scott, Jr. [R]	Nixon (R)
93rd 1973–75	Mike Mansfield [D]	Hugh D. Scott, Jr. [R]	Nixon (R)
			Ford (R)
94th 1975–77	Mike Mansfield [D]	Hugh D. Scott, Jr. [R]	Ford (R)
95th 1977–79	Robert C. Byrd [D]	Howard H. Baker, Jr. [R]	Carter (D)
96th 1979–81	Robert C. Byrd [D]	Howard H. Baker, Jr. [R]	Carter (D)
97th 1981–83	Howard H. Baker, Jr. [R]	Robert C. Byrd [D]	Reagan (R)
98th 1983–85	Howard H. Baker, Jr. [R]	Robert C. Byrd [D]	Reagan (R)
99th 1985–87	Bob Dole [R]	Robert C. Byrd [D]	Reagan (R)
100th 1987–89	Robert C. Byrd [D]	Bob Dole [R]	Reagan (R)
101st 1989–91	George J. Mitchell [D]	Bob Dole [R]	Bush (R)
102nd 1991–93	George J. Mitchell [D]	Bob Dole [R]	Bush (R)
103rd 1993–95	George J. Mitchell [D]	Bob Dole [R]	Clinton (D)

104th 1995–97	Bob Dole [R]		
	Trent Lott [R]	Thomas A. Daschle [D]	Clinton (D)
105th 1997–99	Trent Lott [R]	Thomas A. Daschle [D]	Clinton (D)
106th 1999–2001	Trent Lott [R]	Thomas A. Daschle [D]	Clinton (D)
107th 2001	Trent Lott [R]	Thomas A Daschle [D]	Bush (R)
107th 2001–03	Thomas A. Daschle [D]	Trent Lott [R]	Bush (R)

⊙ Congressional Quarterly. *First Among Equals: Outstanding Senate Leaders of the Twentieth Century.* Washington, D.C: Congressional Quarterly, 1991.

U.S. Congress, Senate. *Majority and Minority Leaders of the Senate.* Washington, D.C.: U.S. Congress, Senate Doc. 100-29.

United States Senate. www.senate.gov/learning

Women Senators

Name	State	Party	Years of Service
Rebecca Latimer Felton	Georgia	Democrat	1922
Hattie Wyatt Caraway	Arkansas	Democrat	1931–45
Rose McConnell Long	Louisiana	Democrat	1936–37
Dixie Bibb Graves	Alabama	Democrat	1937–38
Gladys Pyle	South Dakota	Republican	1938–39
Vera Cahlahan Bushfield	South Dakota	Republican	1948
Margaret Chase-Smith	Maine	Republican	1949–73
Eva Kelley Bowring	Nebraska	Republican	1954
Maurice Brown Neuberger	Oregon	Democrat	1960–67
Elaine S. Edwards	Louisiana	Democrat	1972
Muriel Humphrey	Minnesota	Democrat	1978
Maryon Allen	Alabama	Democrat	1978
Nancy Landon Kassebaum	Kansas	Republican	1978–97
Paula Hawkins	Florida	Republican	1981–87
Barbara Mikulski	Maryland	Democrat	1987–
Jocelyn Burdick	North Dakota	Democrat	1992
Dianne Feinstein	California	Democrat	1993–
Barbara Boxer	California	Democrat	1993–
Carol Moseley-Braun	Illinois	Democrat	1993–99
Patty Murray	Washington	Democrat	1993–
Kay Bailey Hutchison	Texas	Republican	1993–
Olympia Jean Snowe	Maine	Republican	1995–
Shelia Frahm	Kansas	Republican	1996
Mary Landrieu	Louisiana	Democrat	1997–
Susan Collins	Maine	Republican	1997–
Blanche Lincoln	Arkansas	Democrat	1999–
Hillary Rodham Clinton	New York	Democrat	2001–
Deborah Stabenow	Michigan	Democrat	2001–
Maria E. Cantwell	Washington	Democrat	2001–
Jean Carnahan	Missouri	Democrat	2001–

⊙ Schenken, Suzanne O'Dea, and Ann Richards. *From Suffrage to the Senate: An Encyclopedia of American Women in Politics.* Santa Barbara, Calif.: ABC-CLIO, 1999.

Rinehart, Sue Tolleson. *Gender Consciousness and Politics.* New York: Routledge, 1992.

United States Senate. "Learning About the Senate," www.senate.gov/learning/stat–14.html

Year	Candidate	Parties	Electoral Vote	Popular Vote/Notes
1789	**George Washington**	Federalist	69	Adams becomes V.P.
	John Adams	Federalist	34	
1792	**George Washington**	Federalist	132	
	John Adams	Federalist	77	
	George Clinton		50	
	Thomas Jefferson		4	
1796	**John Adams**	Federalist	71	Jefferson becomes V.P.
	Thomas Jefferson	Democratic-Republican	68	
1800	**Thomas Jefferson**	Democratic-Republican	73	House of Representatives breaks
	Aaron Burr	Democratic-Republican	73	the tie: Jefferson 10, Burr 4
	John Adams	Federalist	65	
1804	**Thomas Jefferson**	Democratic-Republican	162	
	Charles Pickney	Federalist		
1808	**James Madison**	Democratic-Republican	122	
	Charles C. Pinckney	Federalist	47	
1812	**James Madison**	Democratic-Republican	128	
	DeWitt Clinton	Federalist	89	
1816	**James Monroe**	Democratic-Republican	183	
	Rufus King	Federalist	34	
1820	**James Monroe**	Democratic-Republican	231	
	John Quincy Adams	National-Republican	1	
1824	**John Quincy Adams**	Coalition	84	Adams 108,740
	Andrew Jackson	Democratic-Republican	99	Jackson 153,544; House vote: Adams: 13, Jackson 7
1828	**Andrew Jackson**	Democrat	178	Jackson 647,286
	John Quincy Adams	National-Republican	83	Adams 508,064
1832	**Andrew Jackson**	Democrat	219	Jackson 687,502
	Henry Clay	National-Republican	49	Clay 530,189
1836	**Martin Van Buren**	Democrat	179	Van Buren 726,678
	William Henry Harrison	Whig	73	Harrison 735,651
1840	**William Henry Harrison**	Whig	234	Harrison 1,275,016,
	Martin Van Buren	Democrat	60	Van Buren 1,129,102
1844	**James K. Polk**	Democrat	170	Polk 1,337,243
	Henry Clay	Whig	105	Clay 1,299,062
1848	**Zachary Taylor**	Whig	163	Taylor 1,360,099
	Lewis Cass	Democrat	127	Cass 1,220,544
1852	**Franklin Pierce**	Democrat	254	Pierce 1,601,274
	Winfield Scott	Whig	42	Scott 1,386,580

1856	**James Buchanan**	Democrat	174	Buchanan 1,838,169
	John C. Fremont	Republican	114	Fremont 1,341,264
1860	**Abraham Lincoln**	Republican	180	Lincoln 1,866,452
	John C. Breckinridge	Democrat	72	Breckinridge 847,953
1864	**Abraham Lincoln**	Republican	212	Lincoln 2,213,665
	George B. McClellan	Democrat	21	McClellan 1,805,237
1868	**Ulysses S. Grant**	Republican	214	Grant 3,012,833
	Horatio Seymour	Democrat	80	Seymour 2,703,249
1872	**Ulysses S. Grant**	Republican	286	Grant 3,597,132
	Horace Greeley	Democrat-Liberal Republican	0	Greeley 2,843,125; the House does not count 3 electoral votes for Greeley
1876	**Rutherford B. Hayes**	Republican	185	Hayes 4,036,289
	Samuel J. Tilden	Democrat	184	Tilden 4,300,590
1880	**James Garfield**	Republican	214	Garfield 4,454,416
	Winfield S. Hancock	Democrat	155	Hancock 4,444,952
1884	**Grover Cleveland**	Democrat	219	Cleveland 4,874,986
	James G. Blaine	Republican	182	Blaine 4,851,981
1888	**Benjamin Harrison**	Republican	233	Harrison 5,439,853
	Grover Cleveland	Democrat	168	Cleveland 5,540,309
1892	**Grover Cleveland**	Democrat	277	Cleveland 5,556,918
	Benjamin Harrison	Republican	145	Harrison 5,176,108
1896	**William McKinley**	Republican	271	McKinley 7,104,779
	William Jennings Bryan	Democrat-Populist	176	Bryan 6,502,925
1900	**William McKinley**	Republican	292	McKinley 7,207,923
	William Jennings Bryan	Democrat-Populist	155	Bryan 6,358,133
1904	**Theodore Roosevelt**	Republican	336	Roosevelt 7,623,486
	Alton B. Parker	Democrat	140	Parker 5,077,911
1908	**William Howard Taft**	Republican	321	Taft 7,678,908
	William Jennings Bryan	Democrat	162	Bryan 6,409,104
1912	**Woodrow Wilson**	Democrat	435	Wilson 6,293,454
	Theodore Roosevelt	Progressive	88	Roosevelt 3,484,980
	William Howard Taft	Republican	8	Taft 3,483,922
1916	**Woodrow Wilson**	Democrat	277	Wilson 9,120,606
	Charles Evans Hughes	Republican	254	Hughes 8,538,221
1920	**Warren G. Harding**	Republican	404	Harding 16,152,200
	James M. Cox	Democrat	127	Cox 9,147,353
1924	**Calvin Coolidge**	Republican	382	Coolidge 15,725,016
	John W. Davis	Democrat	136	Davis 8,386,503
1928	**Herbert Hoover**	Republican	444	Hoover 21,391,381
	Alfred E. Smith	Democrat	87	Smith 15,016,443
1932	**Franklin D. Roosevelt**	Democrat	472	Roosevelt 22,821,579
	Herbert Hoover	Republican	59	Hoover 15,761,841

Year	Candidate	Parties	Electoral Vote	Popular Vote/Notes
1936	Franklin D. Roosevelt	Democrat	523	Roosevelt 27,751,597
	Alfred M. Landon	Republican	8	Landon 16,679,583
1940	Franklin D. Roosevelt	Democrat	449	Roosevelt 27,244,160
	Wendell L. Wilkie	Republican	82	Wilkie 22,305,198
1944	Franklin D. Roosevelt	Democrat	432	Roosevelt 25,602,504
	Thomas E. Dewey	Republican	99	Dewey 22,006,285
1948	Harry S Truman	Democrat	303	Truman 24,105,695
	Thomas E. Dewey	Republican	189	Dewey 21,969,170
1952	Dwight D. Eisenhower	Republican	442	Eisenhower 33,778,963
	Adlai Stevenson	Democrat	89	Stevenson 27,314,992
1956	Dwight D. Eisenhower	Republican	457	Eisenhower 35,581,003
	Adlai Stevenson	Democrat	73	Stevenson 25,738,765
1960	John F. Kennedy	Democrat	203	Kennedy 34,227,096
	Richard M. Nixon	Republican	219	Nixon 34,107,646
1964	Lyndon B. Johnson	Democrat	486	Johnson 42,825,463
	Barry M. Goldwater	Republican	52	Goldwater 27,146,969
1968	Richard M. Nixon	Republican	301	Nixon 31,170,470
	Hubert H. Humphrey	Democrat	191	Humphrey 30,898,055
1972	Richard M. Nixon	Republican	520	Nixon 46,740,323
	George McGovern	Democrat	17	McGovern 28,901,598
1976	Jimmy Carter	Democrat	297	Carter 40,825,839
	Gerald R. Ford	Republican	240	Ford 39,147,770
1980	Ronald Reagan	Republican	538	Reagan 43,901,812
	Jimmy Carter	Democrat	49	Carter 35,483,820
1984	Ronald Reagan	Republican	525	Reagan 54,455,000
	Walter Mondale	Democrat	13	Mondale 37,577,000
1988	George Bush	Republican	426	Bush 47,946,000
	Michael S. Dukakis	Democrat	111	Dukakis 41,016,000
1992	Bill Clinton	Democrat	370	Clinton 44,908,254
	George Bush	Republican	168	Bush 39,102,343
	Ross Perot	Independent	0	Perot 7,866,284
1996	Bill Clinton	Democrat	379	Clinton 45,590,703
	Robert Dole	Republican	159	Dole 37,816,307
	Ross Perot	Independent	0	Perot 7,866,284
2000	George W. Bush	Republican	271	Bush 49,820,518
	Albert A. Gore, Jr.	Democrat	267	Gore 50,158,094

⊙ Schantz, Harvey L., ed. *The American Presidential Elections: Progress, Policy, and Political Change.* Albany: State University of New York, 1996.

Campbell, James E. *The American Campaign: U.S. Presidential Campaigns and the National Vote.* College Station: Texas A&M University Press, 2000.

The Electoral College

The Electoral College was established by the Founders as a compromise between election of the president by Congress and election by popular vote. The electors are a popularly elected body chosen by the states and the District of Columbia on the Tuesday after the first Monday in November. The Electoral College consists of 538 electors. Each state's allotment of electors is equal to the number of House members to which it is entitled plus its two Senators. The District of Columbia received three electors.

In most states, each political party nominates electors, and the state's voters select them when they vote for a presidential candidate. The states prepare a list of the slate of electors for the candidate who receives the most popular votes on a Certificate of Ascertainment.

The electors meet in each state on the first Monday after the second Wednesday in December. A majority of 270 electoral votes is required to elect the president and vice president. No constitutional provision or federal law requires electors to vote in accordance with the popular vote in their state.

The electors prepare six original Certificates of Vote. Each Certificate of Vote lists all persons voted for as President and the number of electors voting for each person and separately lists all persons voted for as Vice President and the number of electors voting for each person.

If no presidential candidate wins a majority of electoral votes, the 12th Amendment to the Constitution provides for the presidential election to be decided by the House of Representatives. The House would select the president by majority vote, choosing from the three candidates who received the greatest number of electoral votes. The vote would be taken by state, with each state delegation having one vote. Similarly, the Senate would elect a vice president.

Electoral Votes per State (as of 2000 census results)

State	Votes	State	Votes	State	Votes
Alabama	9	Kentucky	8	North Dakota	3
Alaska	3	Louisiana	9	Ohio	20
Arizona	10	Maine	4	Oklahoma	7
Arkansas	6	Maryland	10	Oregon	7
California	55	Massachusetts	12	Pennsylvania	21
Colorado	9	Michigan	17	Rhode Island	4
Connecticut	7	Minnesota	10	South Carolina	8
Delaware	3	Mississippi	6	South Dakota	3
District of Columbia	3	Missouri	11	Tennessee	11
Florida	27	Montana	3	Texas	34
Georgia	15	Nebraska	5	Utah	5
Hawaii	4	Nevada	5	Vermont	3
Idaho	4	New Hampshire	4	Virginia	13
Illinois	21	New Jersey	15	Washington	11
Indiana	11	New Mexico	5	West Virginia	5
Iowa	7	New York	31	Wisconsin	10
Kansas	6	North Carolina	15	Wyoming	3

⊙ Berns, Walter, ed. *After the People Vote: A Guide to the Electoral College.* Washington, D.C.: AEI Press, 1992.

National Archives and Records Administration. "Office of the Federal Register," www.nara.gov/fedreg/elctcoll/proced.html

Major Political Parties in U.S. History

American Party (Know-Nothings): Founded during the early 1850s by nativists who wished to restrict immigration to the United States because they feared that jobs would be taken away from Americans and that Americans would be forced to pay more taxes to support the immigrants. When asked about their party, members would respond, "I know nothing." The party, split over the question of slavery, was short-lived.

Anti-Masonic Party: Founded in 1827 as a protest against Masonic principles when it was alleged that a member of the Masons was murdered because he had threatened to make the group's secret rites public. More successful at the state level, the party was eventually folded into the Whig Party.

Communist Party of the U.S.A.: Founded in 1919 by the most radical members of the Socialist Party. Supported by the Soviet Union, it advocated the overthrow of American capitalism. Although it exerted some influence on U.S. politics during the 1930s, the party was virtually powerless after the 1950s.

Democratic Party: Founded in 1793, first as the Democratic-Republican Party, by Thomas Jefferson to promote his philosophy of state and individual rights and his belief that government involved all citizens rather than a select few. By the election of 1828, the party's name had been shortened to Democratic Party. During the administration of Pres. Franklin D. Roosevelt, and because of the Great Depression of the 1930s, the party's platform was directed more toward the involvement of the federal government, especially regarding social welfare issues.

Farmer-Labor Party: Founded in 1920 to promote the interests of farmers and of labor. Not very successful on the national front, the party had a significant influence on state politics in Minnesota. By 1944, it had merged with the Democratic Party in Minnesota.

Federalist Party: Founded in 1794 in support of the U.S. Constitution, its interpretation and direction, and of a strong central government. The party's major leaders were George Washington, Alexander Hamilton, and John Adams. The party declined during the early 1800s.

Free-Soil Party: Founded in 1848 in the belief that allowing slavery in new territories would lessen the amount of land available for homesteading. The party was weakened by the Compromise of 1850 and ceased to exist after the election of 1852.

Green Party: Founded in 1984 in response to the Green Party of Germany and focusing on issues of environmentalism, social justice, and peace. The party nominated consumer activist Ralph Nader as its presidential candidate in 2000.

Greenback Party: Founded around 1875 to protest the U.S. government's plan to stop the circulation of greenbacks, paper money printed to finance the Civil War, and return to a hard-currency economy. The party later broadened its platform to include support of current labor issues but by 1884 the movement had failed.

Liberal-Republican Party: Founded in 1872 in Missouri by dissident Republicans to oppose Pres. Ulysses S. Grant's renomination. The party's presidential nominee, Horace Greeley, ran on a platform that included civil service reform. It disbanded after the 1872 elections when Grant was returned to office.

Loco-Focos or Equal Rights Party: Founded in 1835 by some New York Democrats who were disenchanted with the conservative politics of the controlling Tammany political machine and who advocated free banking in order to prevent bribery of officials. By 1839, Loco-Focos had returned to the Democratic fold.

Populist (People's) Party: Founded in 1892 by down-and-out farmers, who still felt the effects of an earlier depression. They advocated currency, transportation, banking, taxation, election, and civil service reforms. Although they made a significant showing in the 1892 presidential election, the party disbanded in 1896.

Progressive Party: Initially founded in 1911 by Republicans who felt that President Taft's administration was too conservative. The party was seized by Theodore Roosevelt in 1912, enabling him to run unsuccessfully for the presidency as the "Bull Moose" Party's candidate after he lost the Republican nomination. Resurrected in 1924 by Robert LaFollette, the party presented a platform of government, agriculture, and labor reform. A new Progressive Party nominated presidential candidate Henry Wallace in the 1948 election.

Reform Party: Founded in 1997 as a grassroots outgrowth of Ross Perot's presidential campaigns of 1992 and 1996 and his United We Stand, America movement. Advocating the restoration of "integrity, accountability and fiscal responsibility to government and its leadership," the party platform includes campaign reform, a balanced budget, and a new tax system.

Republican Party: Founded in 1854 in answer to the waning influence of the Whig Party and in opposition to slavery in new U.S. territories. Abraham Lincoln, the first Republican president, based his election campaign on this issue. By 1896, the Republican Party often favored conservatism as well as a lack of government involvement in business The party defended the gold standard in the late 1800s and was dubbed the "Grand Old Party" (GOP), a moniker by which it is still known today.

Socialist Party: Founded in 1898 as the Socialist Democratic Party of America. One of its founders, Eugene V. Debs, was often its presidential candidate. Opposed to U.S. entry into World War I, the Socialists, after 1920, campaigned for the abolishment of capitalism.

States' Rights Party or Dixiecrats: Founded in 1948 by some Democrats, among them South Carolina's governor Strom Thurmond, who were disgruntled over the civil rights section of the Democratic platform at the Democratic National Convention.

Whig Party: Founded in 1836 as an outgrowth of the National Republicans with the purpose of opposing Andrew Jackson. Led by Henry Clay and Daniel Webster, the party was successful in having two of its candidates become president—William Henry Harrison and Zachary Taylor. A split over the slavery question caused the decline of the party in the mid-1850s.

⊙ Congressional Quarterly. *Congressional Quarterly's Guide to U.S. Elections.* 3d ed. Washington, D.C.: Congressional Quarterly Inc., 1994.

Martí, José. *Political Parties and Elections in the United States: An Encyclopedia.* Philadelphia: Temple University Press, 1989.

University of Pennsylvania Library. "U.S. Political Parties and Elections," www.library.upenn.edu/ vanpelt/guides/elections.html

When in the course of human events it becomes necessary for one people to dissolve the political bands which have connected them with another and to assume, among the powers of the earth, the separate and equal station to which the laws of nature and of nature's God entitle them, a decent respect to the opinions of mankind requires that they should declare the causes which impel them to the separation.

We hold these truths to be self-evident, that all men are created equal; that they are endowed by their Creator with certain unalienable rights; that among these are life, liberty, and the pursuit of happiness. That, to secure these rights, governments are instituted among men, deriving their just powers from the consent of the governed; that, whenever any form of government becomes destructive of these ends, it is the right of the people to alter or to abolish it, and to institute a new government, laying its foundation on such principles, and organizing its powers in such form, as to them shall seem most likely to effect their safety and happiness. Prudence, indeed, will dictate that governments long established should not be changed for light and transient causes; and, accordingly, all experience hath shown that mankind are more disposed to suffer, while evils are sufferable, than to right themselves by abolishing the forms to which they are accustomed. But when a long train of abuses and usurpations, pursuing invariably the same object, evinces a design to reduce them under absolute despotism, it is their right, it is their duty, to throw off such government and to provide new guards for their future security. Such has been the patient sufferance of these colonies, and such is now the necessity which constrains them to alter their former systems of government. The history of the present King of Great Britain is a history of repeated injuries and usurpations, all having, in direct object, the establishment of an absolute tyranny over these States. To prove this, let facts be submitted to a candid world:

He has refused his assent to laws the most wholesome and necessary for the public good.

He has forbidden his governors to pass laws of immediate and pressing importance, unless suspended in their operation till his assent should be obtained; and, when so suspended, he has utterly neglected to attend to them.

He has refused to pass other laws for the accommodation of large districts of people, unless those people would relinquish the right of representation in the legislature; a right inestimable to them and formidable to tyrants only.

He has called together legislative bodies at places unusual, uncomfortable, and distant from the depository of their public records, for the sole purpose of fatiguing them into compliance with his measures.

He has dissolved representative houses, repeatedly for opposing, with manly firmness, his invasions on the rights of the people.

He has refused, for a long time after such dissolutions, to cause others to be elected; whereby the legislative powers, incapable of annihilation, have returned to the people at large for their exercise; the state remaining, in the meantime, exposed to all the danger of invasion from without and convulsions within.

He has endeavored to prevent the population of these States; for that purpose, obstructing the laws for naturalization of foreigners, refusing to pass others to encourage their migration hither, and raising the conditions of new appropriations of lands.

He has obstructed the administration of justice by refusing his assent to laws for establishing judiciary powers.

He has made judges dependent on his will alone for the tenure of their offices and the amount and payment of their salaries.

He has erected a multitude of new offices and sent hither swarms of officers to harass our people and eat out their substance.

He has kept among us, in time of peace, standing armies, without the consent of our legislatures.

He has affected to render the military independent of, and superior to, the civil power.

He has combined with others to subject us to a jurisdiction foreign to our Constitution and unacknowledged by our laws, giving his assent to their acts of pretended legislation—For quartering large bodies of armed troops among us; For protecting them by a mock trial from punishment for any murders which they should commit on the inhabitants of these States; For cutting off our trade with all parts of the world; For imposing taxes on us without our consent; For depriving us, in many cases, of the benefit of trial by jury; For transporting us beyond seas to be tried for pretended offences; For abolishing the free system of English laws in a neighboring province, establishing therein an arbitrary government, and enlarging its boundaries, so as to render it at once an example and fit instrument for introducing the same absolute rule into these colonies; For taking away our charters, abolishing our most valuable laws, and altering, fundamentally, the powers of our governments; For suspending our own legislatures and declaring themselves invested with power to legislate for us in all cases whatsoever.

He has abdicated government here by declaring us out of his protection and waging war against us.

He has plundered our seas, ravaged our coasts, burnt our towns, and destroyed the lives of our people.

He is, at this time, transporting large armies of foreign mercenaries to complete the works of death, desolation, and tyranny already begun with circumstances of cruelty and perfidy scarcely paralleled in the most barbarous ages, and totally unworthy the head of a civilized nation.

He has constrained our fellow citizens, taken captive on the high seas, to bear arms against their country, to become the executioners of their friends and brethren, or to fall themselves by their hands.

He has excited domestic insurrections amongst us and has endeavored to bring on the inhabitants of our frontiers, the merciless Indian savages, whose known rule of warfare is an undistinguished destruction of all ages, sexes, and conditions.

In every stage of these oppressions, we have petitioned for redress in the most humble terms; our repeated petitions have been answered only by repeated injury. A prince whose character is thus marked by every act which may define a tyrant is unfit to be the ruler of a free people. Nor have we been wanting in attention to our British brethren. We have warned them, from time to time, of attempts made by their legislature to extend an unwarrantable jurisdiction over us. We have reminded them of the circumstances of our emigration and settlement here. We have appealed to their native justice and magnanimity, and we have conjured them, by the ties of our common kindred, to disavow these usurpations, which would inevitably interrupt our connections and correspondence. They, too, have been deaf to the voice of justice and consanguinity. We must, therefore, acquiesce in the necessity which denounces our separation, and hold them, as we hold the rest of mankind, enemies in war, in peace, friends.

We, therefore, the representatives of the United States of America, in general Congress assembled, appealing to the Supreme Judge of the world for the rectitude of our intentions, do, in the name and by the authority of the good people of these colonies, solemnly publish and declare, that these united colonies are, and of right ought to be, free and independent states: that they are absolved from all allegiance to the British Crown, and that all political connection between them and the state of

The Declaration of Independence *(cont.)*

Great Britain is, and ought to be, totally dissolved; and that, as free and independent states, they have full power to levy war, conclude peace, contract alliances, establish commerce, and to do all other acts and things which independent states may of right do. And, for the support of this declaration, with a firm reliance on the protection of Divine Providence, we mutually pledge to each other our lives, our fortunes, and our sacred honor.

John Hancock

New Hampshire
Josiah Bartlett
William Whipple
Matthew Thorton

Massachusetts Bay
Samuel Adams
John Adams
Robert Treat Paine
Elbridge Gerry

Rhode Island
Stephen Hopkins
William Ellery

North Carolina
William Hooper
Joseph Huges
John Penn

Connecticut
Robert Sherman
Samuel Huntingdon
William Williams
Oliver Wolcott

New York
William Floyd
Philip Livingston
Francis Lewis
Lewis Morris

New Jersey
Richard Stockton
John Witherspoon
Francis Hopkinson
John Hart
Abraham Clark

Pennsylvania
Robert Morris
Benjamin Rush
Benjamin Franklin
John Morton
George Clymer
James Smith
George Taylor
James Wilson
George Ross

Delaware
Caesar Rodney
George Read
Thomas McKean

South Carolina
Edward Routledge
Thomas Heyward, Jr.
Arthur Middleton

Maryland
Samuel Chase
William Paca
Thomas Stone
Charles Carroll of Carrollton

Virginia
George Wythe
Richard Henry Lee
Thomas Jefferson
Benjamin Harrison
Thomas Nelson, Jr.
Francis Lightfoot Lee
Carter Braxton

Georgia
Button Gwinnett
Lyman Hall
George Walton

⊙ National Archives and Records Administration. "The Declaration of Independence," www.nara.gov/exhall/charters/declaration/decmain.html

Jayne, Allen. *Jefferson's Declaration of Independence: Origins, Philosophy, and Theology.* Lexington: University Press of Kentucky, 1998.

The Constitution

We the people of the United States, in order to form a more perfect union, establish justice, insure domestic tranquillity, provide for the common defense, promote the general welfare, and secure the blessings of liberty to ourselves and our posterity, do ordain and establish this Constitution for the United States of America.

Article I

Section 1.

All legislative powers herein granted shall be vested in a Congress of the United States, which shall consist of a Senate and House of Representatives.

Section 2.

1. The House of Representatives shall be composed of members chosen every second year by the people of the several States, and the electors in each State shall have the qualifications requisite for electors of the most numerous branch of the State legislature.

2. No person shall be a representative who shall not have attained to the age of twenty-five years, and been seven years a citizen of the United States, and who shall not, when elected, be an inhabitant of that State in which he shall be chosen.

3. Representatives and direct taxes shall be apportioned among the several States which may be included within this Union, according to their respective numbers, which shall be determined by adding to the whole number of free persons, including those bound to service for a term of years, and excluding Indians not taxed, three fifths of all other persons. The actual enumeration shall be made within three years after the first meeting of the Congress of the United States, and within every subsequent term of ten years, in such manner as they shall by law direct. The number of representatives shall not exceed one for every thirty thousand, but each State shall have at least one representative; and until such enumeration shall be made, the State of New Hampshire shall be entitled to choose three, Massachusetts eight, Rhode Island and Providence Plantations one, Connecticut five, New York six, New Jersey four, Pennsylvania eight, Delaware one, Maryland six, Virginia ten, North Carolina five, South Carolina five, and Georgia three.

4. When vacancies happen in the representation from any State, the executive authority thereof shall issue writs of election to fill such vacancies.

5. The House of Representatives shall choose their speaker and other officers; and shall have the sole power of impeachment.

Section 3.

1. The Senate of the United States shall be composed of two senators from each State, chosen by the legislature thereof, for six years; and each senator shall have one vote.

2. Immediately after they shall be assembled in consequence of the first election, they shall be divided as equally as may be into three classes. The seats of the senators of the first class shall be vacated at the expiration of the second year, of the second class at the expiration of the fourth year, and of the third class at the expiration of the sixth year, so that one third may be chosen every second year; and if vacancies happen by resignation, or otherwise, during the recess of the legislature of any State, the executive thereof may make temporary appointments until the next meeting of the legislature, which shall then fill such vacancies.

3. No person shall be a senator who shall not have attained to the age of thirty years, and been nine years a citizen of the United States, and who shall not, when elected, be an inhabitant of that State for which he shall be chosen.

4. The Vice President of the United States shall be President of the Senate, but shall have no vote, unless they be equally divided.

5. The Senate shall choose their other officers, and also a president pro tempore, in the absence of the Vice President, or when he shall exercise the office of the President of the United States.

6. The Senate shall have the sole power to try all impeachments. When sitting for that purpose, they shall be on oath or affirmation. When the President of the United States is tried, the chief justice shall preside: and no person shall be convicted without the concurrence of two thirds of the members present.

7. Judgment in cases of impeachment shall not extend further than to removal from office, and disqualification to hold and enjoy any office of honor, trust or profit under the United States: but the party convicted shall nevertheless be liable and subject to indictment, trial, judgment and punishment, according to law.

Section 4.

1. The times, places, and manner of holding elections for senators and representatives, shall be prescribed in each State by the legislature thereof; but the Congress may at any time by law make or alter such regulations, except as to the places of choosing senators.

2. The Congress shall assemble at least once in every year, and such meeting shall be on the first Monday in December, unless they shall by law appoint a different day.

Section 5.

1. Each House shall be the judge of the elections, returns and qualifications of its own members, and a majority of each shall constitute a quorum to do business; but a smaller number may adjourn from day to day, and may be authorized to compel the attendance of absent members, in such manner, and under such penalties as each House may provide.

2. Each House may determine the rules of its proceedings, punish its members for disorderly behavior, and, with the concurrence of two thirds, expel a member.

3. Each House shall keep a journal of its proceedings, and from time to time publish the same, excepting such parts as may in their judgment require secrecy; and the yeas and nays of the members of either House on any question shall, at the desire of one fifth of those present, be entered on the journal.

4. Neither House, during the session of Congress, shall, without the consent of the other, adjourn for more than three days, nor to any other place than that in which the two Houses shall be sitting.

Section 6.

1. The senators and representatives shall receive a compensation for their services, to be ascertained by law, and paid out of the Treasury of the United States. They shall in all cases, except treason, felony, and breach of the peace, be privileged from arrest during their attendance at the session of their respective Houses, and in going to and returning from the same; and for any speech or debate in either House, they shall not be questioned in any other place.

2. No senator or representative shall, during the time for which he was elected, be appointed to any civil office under the authority of the United States, which shall have been created, or the emoluments whereof shall have been increased, during such time; and no person holding any office under the United States shall be a member of either House during his continuance in office.

Section 7.

1. All bills for raising revenue shall originate in the House of Representatives; but the Senate may propose or concur with amendments as on other bills.

2. Every bill which shall have passed the House of Representatives and the Senate, shall, before it become a law, be presented to the President of the United States; If he approves he shall sign it, but if not he shall return it, with his objections, to that House in which it shall have originated, who shall enter the objections at large on their journal, and proceed to reconsider it. If after such reconsideration two thirds of that House shall agree to pass the bill, it shall be

sent, together with the objections, to the other House, by which it shall likewise be reconsidered, and if approved by two thirds of that House, it shall become a law. But in all such cases the votes of both Houses shall be determined by yeas and nays, and the names of the persons voting for and against the bill shall be entered on the journal of each House respectively. If any bill shall not be returned by the President within ten days (Sundays excepted) after it shall have been presented to him, the same shall be a law, in like manner as if he had signed it, unless the Congress by their adjournment prevent its return, in which case it shall not be a law.

3. Every order, resolution, or vote to which the concurrence of the Senate and the House of Representatives may be necessary (except on a question of adjournment) shall be presented to the President of the United States; and before the same shall take effect, shall be approved by him, or being disapproved by him, shall be repassed by two thirds of the Senate and House of Representatives, according to the rules and limitations prescribed in the case of a bill.

Section 8.

The Congress shall have the power

1. To lay and collect taxes, duties, imposts, and excises, to pay the debts and provide for the common defense and general welfare of the United States; but all duties, imposts, and excises shall be uniform throughout the United States;

2. To borrow money on the credit of the United States;

3. To regulate commerce with foreign nations, and among the several States, and with the Indian tribes;

4. To establish a uniform rule of naturalization, and uniform laws on the subject of bankruptcies throughout the United States;

5. To coin money, regulate the value thereof, and of foreign coin, and fix the standard of weights and measures;

6. To provide for the punishment of counterfeiting the securities and current coin of the United States;

7. To establish post offices and post roads;

8. To promote the progress of science and useful arts, by securing for limited times to authors and inventors the exclusive right to their respective writings and discoveries;

9. To constitute tribunals inferior to the Supreme Court;

10. To define and punish piracies and felonies committed on the high seas, and offenses against the law of nations;

11. To declare war, grant letters of marque and reprisal, and make rules concerning captures on land and water;

12. To raise and support armies, but no appropriation of money to that use shall be for a longer term than two years;

13. To provide and maintain a navy;

14. To make rules for the government and regulation of the land and naval forces;

15. To provide for calling forth the militia to execute the laws of the Union, suppress insurrections and repel invasions;

16. To provide for organizing, arming, and disciplining the militia, and for governing such part of them as may be employed in the service of the United States, reserving to the States respectively, the appointment of the officers, and the authority of training the militia according to the discipline prescribed by Congress;

17. To exercise exclusive legislation in all cases whatsoever, over such district (not exceeding ten miles square) as may, by cession of particular States, and the acceptance of Congress, become the seat of the government of the United States, and to exercise like authority over all places purchased by the consent of the legislature of the State in which the same shall be, for the erection of forts, magazines, arsenals, dockyards, and other needful buildings; and

18. To make all laws which shall be necessary and proper for carrying into execution the foregoing powers, and all other powers vested by this Constitution in the government of the United States, or any department or officer thereof.

Section 9.

1. The migration or importation of such persons as any of the States now existing shall think proper to admit, shall not be prohibited by the Congress prior to the year one thousand eight hundred

and eight, but a tax or duty may be imposed on such importation, not exceeding ten dollars for each person.

2. The privilege of the writ of habeas corpus shall not be suspended, unless when in cases of rebellion or invasion the public safety may require it.

3. No bill of attainder or ex post facto law shall be passed.

4. No capitation, or other direct, tax shall be laid, unless in proportion to the census or enumeration hereinbefore directed to be taken.

5. No tax or duty shall be laid on articles exported from any State.

6. No preference shall be given by any regulation of commerce or revenue to the ports of one State over those of another: nor shall vessels bound to, or from, one State be obliged to enter, clear, or pay duties in another.

7. No money shall be drawn from the treasury, but in consequence of appropriations made by law; and a regular statement and account of the receipts and expenditures of all public money shall be published from time to time.

8. No title of nobility shall be granted by the United States: and no person holding any office of profit or trust under them, shall, without the consent of the Congress, accept of any present, emolument, office, or title, of any kind whatever, from any king, prince, or foreign State.

Section 10.

1. No State shall enter into any treaty, alliance, or confederation; grant letters of marque and reprisal; coin money; emit bills of credit; make any thing but gold and silver coin a tender in payment of debts; pass any bill of attainder, ex post facto law, or law impairing the obligation of contracts, or grant any title of nobility.

2. No State shall, without the consent of the Congress, lay any imposts or duties on imports or exports, except what may be absolutely necessary for executing its inspection laws: and the net produce of all duties and imposts laid by any State on imports or exports, shall be for the use of the treasury of the United States; and all such laws shall be subject to the revision and control of the Congress.

3. No State shall, without the consent of the Congress, lay any duty of tonnage, keep troops, or ships of war in time of peace, enter into any agreement or compact with another State, or with a foreign power, or engage in war, unless actually invaded, or in such imminent danger as will not admit of delay.

Article II

Section 1.

1. The executive power shall be vested in a President of the United States of America. He shall hold his office during the term of four years, and, together with the Vice President, chosen for the same term, be elected, as follows:

2. Each State shall appoint, in such manner as the legislature thereof may direct, a number of electors, equal to the whole number of senators and representatives to which the State may be entitled in the Congress: but no senator or representative, or person holding any office of trust or profit under the United States, shall be appointed an elector.

The electors shall meet in their respective States, and vote by ballot for two persons, of whom one at least shall not be an inhabitant of the same State with themselves. And they shall make a list of all the persons voted for, and of the number of votes for each; which list they shall sign and certify, and transmit sealed to the seat of the government of the United States, directed to the president of the Senate. The president of the Senate shall, in the presence of the Senate and House of Representatives, open all the certificates, and the votes shall then be counted. The person having the greatest number of votes shall be the President, if such number be a majority of the whole number of electors appointed; and if there be more than one who have such majority, and have an equal number of votes, then the House of Representatives shall immediately choose by ballot one of them for President; and if no person have a majority, then from the five highest on the list the said House shall in like manner choose the President. But in choosing the President, the votes shall be taken by States, the representation from each State having one vote; a quorum for this purpose shall consist of a member or members from two thirds of the States, and a majority of all the States shall be necessary to a choice. In every case after the choice of the President, the person having the greatest number of votes of the electors shall be the Vice President. But if there should remain two or more who have equal votes, the Senate shall chose from them by ballot the Vice President.

3. The Congress may determine the time of choosing the electors, and the day on which they shall give their votes; which day shall be the same throughout the United States.

4. No person except a natural born citizen, or a citizen of the United States, at the time of the adoption of this Constitution, shall be eligible to the office of President; neither shall any person be eligible to the office who shall not have attained to the age of thirty-five years, and been fourteen years a resident within the United States.

5. In case of the removal of the President from office, or of his death, resignation, or inability to discharge the powers and duties of the said office, the same shall devolve on the Vice President, and the Congress may by law provide for the case of removal, death, resignation or inability, both of the President and Vice President, declaring what officer shall then act as President, and such officer shall act accordingly until the disability be removed, or a President shall be elected.

6. The President shall, at stated times, receive for his services a compensation which shall neither be increased nor diminished during the period for which he shall have been elected, and he shall not receive within that period any other emolument from the United States, or any of them.

7. Before he enter on the execution of his office, he shall take the following oath or affirmation:—"I do solemnly swear (or affirm) that I will faithfully execute the office of President of the United States, and will to the best of my ability, preserve, protect and defend the Constitution of the United States."

Section 2.

1. The President shall be commander in chief of the army and navy of the United States, and of the militia of the several States, when called into the actual service of the United States; he may require the opinion in writing, of the principal officer in each of the executive departments, upon any subject relating to the duties of their respective offices, and he shall have power to grant reprieves and pardons for offenses against the United States, except in cases of impeachment.

2. He shall have power, by and with the advice and consent of the Senate, to make treaties, provided two thirds of the senators present concur; and he shall nominate, and by and with the advice and consent of the Senate, shall appoint ambassadors, other public ministers and consuls, judges of the Supreme Court, and all other officers of the United States, whose appointments are not herein otherwise provided for, and which shall be established by law; but the Congress may by law vest the appointment of such inferior officers, as they think proper, in the President alone, in the courts of laws, or in the heads of departments.

3. The President shall have power to fill up all vacancies that may happen during the recess of the Senate, by granting commissions which shall expire at the end of their next session.

Section 3.

He shall from time to time give to the Congress information of the state of the Union, and recommend to their consideration such measures as he shall judge necessary and expedient; he may, on extraordinary occasions, convene both Houses, or either of them, and in case of disagreement between them with respect to the time of adjournment, he may adjourn them to such time as he shall think proper; he shall receive ambassadors and other public ministers; he shall take care that the laws be faithfully executed, and shall commission all the officers of the United States.

Section 4.

The President, Vice President, and all civil officers of the United States, shall be removed from office on impeachment for, and conviction of, treason, bribery, or other high crimes and misdemeanors.

Article III

Section 1.

The judicial power of the United States shall be vested in one Supreme Court, and in such inferior courts as the Congress may from time to time ordain and establish. The judges, both of the Supreme and inferior courts, shall hold their offices during good behavior, and shall, at stated times, receive for their services, a compensation, which shall not be diminished during their continuance in office.

Section 2.

1. The judicial power shall extend to all cases, in law and equity, arising under this Constitution, the laws of the United States, and treaties made, or which shall be made, under their authority;—to all cases affecting ambassadors, other public ministers and consuls;—to all cases of admiralty and maritime jurisdiction;—to controversies to which the United States shall be a party;—to controversies between two or more States;—between a State and citizens of another State;—between citizens of different States;—between citizens of the same State claiming lands under grants of different States, and between a State, or the citizens thereof, and foreign States, citizens or subjects.

2. In all cases affecting ambassadors, other public ministers and consuls, and those in which a State shall be party, the Supreme Court shall have original jurisdiction. In all the other cases before mentioned, the Supreme Court shall have appellate jurisdiction, both as to law and fact, with such exceptions, and under such regulations as the Congress shall make.

3. The trial of all crimes, except in cases of impeachment, shall be by jury; and such trial shall be held in the State where the said crimes shall have been committed; but when not committed within any State, the trial shall be at such place or places as the Congress may by law have directed.

Section 3.

1. Treason against the United States shall consist only in levying war against them, or in adhering to their enemies, giving them aid and comfort. No person shall be convicted of treason unless on the testimony of two witnesses to the same overt act, or on confession in open court.

2. The Congress shall have power to declare the punishment of treason, but no attainder of treason shall work corruption of blood, or forfeiture except during the life of the person attainted.

Article IV

Section 1.

Full faith and credit shall be given in each State to the public acts, records, and judicial proceedings of every other State. And the Congress may by general laws prescribe the manner in which such acts, records and proceedings shall be proved, and the effect thereof.

Section 2.

1. The citizens of each State shall be entitled to all privileges and immunities of citizens in the several States.

2. A person charged in any State with treason, felony, or other crime, who shall flee from justice, and be found in another State, shall on demand of the executive authority of the State from which he fled, be delivered up to be removed to the State having jurisdiction of the crime.

3. No person held to service or labor in one State under the laws thereof, escaping into another, shall, in consequence of any law or regulation therein, be discharged from such service or labor, but shall be delivered up on claim of the party to whom such service or labor may be due.

Section 3.

1. New States may be admitted by the Congress into this Union; but no new State shall be formed or erected within the jurisdiction of any other State; nor any State be formed by the junction of two or more States, or parts of States, without the consent of the legislatures of the States concerned as well as of the Congress.

2. The Congress shall have power to dispose of and make all needful rules and regulations respecting the territory or other property belonging to the United States; and nothing in this Constitution shall be so construed as to prejudice any claims of the United States, or of any particular State.

Section 4.

The United States shall guarantee to every State in this Union a republican form of government, and shall protect each of them against invasion; and on application of the legislature, or of the executive (when the legislature cannot be convened) against domestic violence.

Article V

The Congress, whenever two thirds of both Houses shall deem it necessary, shall propose amendments to this Constitution, or, on the application of the legislatures of two thirds of the several States, shall call a convention for proposing amendments, which in either case, shall be valid to all intents and purposes, as part of this Constitution, when ratified by the legislatures of three fourths of the several States, or by conventions in three fourths thereof, as the one or the other mode of ratification may be proposed by the Congress; Provided that no amendment which may be made prior to the year one thousand eight hundred and eight shall in any manner affect the first and fourth clauses in the ninth section of the first article; and that no State, without its consent, shall be deprived of its equal suffrage in the Senate.

Article VI

1. All debts contracted and engagements entered into, before the adoption of this Constitution, shall be as valid against the United States under this Constitution, as under the Confederation.

2. This Constitution, and the laws of the United States which shall be made in pursuance thereof; and all treaties made, or which shall be made, under the authority of the United States, shall be the supreme law of the land; and the judges in every State shall be bound thereby, any thing in the Constitution or laws of any State to the contrary notwithstanding.

3. The senators and representatives before mentioned, and the members of the several State legislatures, and all executive and judicial officers, both of the United States and of the several States, shall be bound by oath or affirmation to support this Constitution; but no religious test shall ever be required as a qualification to any office or public trust under the United States.

Article VII

The ratification of the conventions of nine States shall be sufficient for the establishment of this Constitution between the States so ratifying the same.

Done in Convention by the unanimous consent of the States present the seventeenth day of September in the year of our Lord one thousand seven hundred and eighty-seven, and of the independence of the United States of America the twelfth. In witness whereof we have hereunto subscribed our names.

Articles in addition to, and amendment of, the Constitution of the United States of America, proposed by Congress, and ratified by the legislatures of the several States, pursuant to the fifth article of the original Constitution.

George Washington
President and deputy from Virginia

New Hampshire
John Langdon
Nicholas Gilman

New York
Alexander Hamilton
Rufus King
William Paterson
Jonathan Dayton

Massachusetts
Nathaniel Gorman
David Bearley

New Jersey
William Livingston

Connecticut
William Samuel Johnson
Roger Sherman

Pennsylvania
Benjamin Franklin
Thomas Mifflin
Robert Morris
George Clymer
Thomas FitzSimons
Jared Ingersoll
James Wilson
Gouverner Morris

Virginia
John Blair
James Madison, Jr.

Georgia
William Few
Abraham Baldwin

North Carolina
William Blount
Richard Dobbs Spaight
Hugh Williamson

Delaware
George Reed
Gunning Beford, Jr.
John Dickinson
Richard Bassett
Jacob Broom

South Carolina
John Rutledge
Charles Cotesworth Pinckney
Charles Pinckney
Pierce Butler

Maryland
James McHenry
Daniel of St. Thomas Jenifer
Daniel Carroll

Amendment I [First ten amendments ratified December 15, 1791]

Congress shall make no law respecting an establishment of religion, or prohibiting the free exercise thereof; or abridging the freedom of speech, or of the press; or the right of the people peaceably to assemble, and to petition the government for a redress of grievances.

Amendment II

A well regulated militia, being necessary to the security of a free State, the right of the people to keep and bear arms, shall not be infringed.

Amendment III

No soldier shall, in time of peace be quartered in any house, without the consent of the owner, nor in time of war, but in a manner to be prescribed by law.

Amendment IV

The right of the people to be secure in their persons, houses, papers, and effects, against unreasonable searches and seizures, shall not be violated, and no warrants shall issue, but upon probable cause, supported by oath or affirmation, and particularly describing the place to be searched, and the persons or things to be seized.

Amendment V

No person shall be held to answer for a capital or otherwise infamous crime, unless on a present-ment or indictment of a grand jury, except in cases arising in the land or naval forces, or in the militia, when in actual service in time of war or public danger; nor shall any person be subject for the same offense to be twice put in jeopardy of life or limb; nor shall be compelled in any criminal case to be a witness against himself, nor be deprived of life, liberty, or property, without due process of law; nor shall private property be taken for public use, without just compensation.

Amendment VI

In all criminal prosecutions, the accused shall enjoy the right to a speedy and public trial, by an impartial jury of the State and district wherein the crime shall have been committed, which district shall have been previously ascertained by law, and to be informed of the nature and cause of the accu-sation; to be confronted with the witnesses against him; to have compulsory process for obtaining wit-nesses in his favor, and to have the assistance of counsel for his defense.

Amendment VII

In suits at common law, where the value in controversy shall exceed twenty dollars, the right of trial by jury shall be preserved, and no fact tried by a jury shall be otherwise reexamined in any court of the United States, than according to the rules of the common law.

Amendment VIII

Excessive bail shall not be required, nor excessive fines imposed, nor cruel and unusual punish-ments inflicted.

Amendment IX

The enumeration in the Constitution of certain rights shall not be construed to deny or disparage others retained by the people.

Amendment X

The powers not delegated to the United States by the Constitution, nor prohibited by it to the States, are reserved to the States respectively, or to the people.

Amendment XI [January 8, 1798]

The judicial power of the United States shall not be construed to extend to any suit in law or equity, commenced or prosecuted against one of the United States by citizens of another State, or by citizens or subjects of any foreign State.

Amendment XII [September 25, 1804]

The electors shall meet in their respective States, and vote by ballot for President and Vice President, one of whom, at least, shall not be an inhabitant of the same State with themselves; they shall name in their ballots the person voted for as President, and in distinct ballots, the person voted for as Vice President, and they shall make distinct lists of all persons voted for as President and of all persons voted for as Vice President, and of the number of votes for each, which lists they shall sign and certify, and transmit sealed to the seat of the government of the United States, directed to the President of the Senate;—The President of the Senate shall, in the presence of the Senate and House of Representatives, open all the certificates and the votes shall then be counted;—The person having the greatest number of votes for President, shall be the President, if such number be a majority of the whole number of electors appointed; and if no person have such majority, then from the persons hav-ing the highest numbers not exceeding three on the list of those voted for as President, the House of Representatives shall choose immediately, by ballot, the President. But in choosing the President, the votes shall be taken by States, the representation from each State having one vote; a quorum for this purpose shall consist of a member or members from two thirds of the States, and a majority of all the

States shall be necessary to a choice. And if the House of Representatives shall not choose a President whenever the right of choice shall devolve upon them, before the fourth day of March next following, then the Vice President shall act as President, as in the case of the death or other constitutional disability of the President. The person having the greatest number of votes as Vice President shall be the Vice President, if such number be a majority of the whole number of electors appointed, and if no person have a majority, then from the two highest numbers on the list, the Senate shall choose the Vice President; a quorum for the purpose shall consist of two thirds of the whole number of Senators, and a majority of the whole number shall be necessary to a choice. But no person constitutionally ineligible to the office of President shall be eligible to that of Vice President of the United States.

Amendment XIII [December 18, 1865]

Section 1.

Neither slavery nor involuntary servitude, except as a punishment for crime whereof the party shall have been duly convicted, shall exist within the United States, or any place subject to their jurisdiction.

Section 2.

Congress shall have power to enforce this article by appropriate legislation.

Amendment XIV [July 28, 1868]

Section 1.

All persons born or naturalized in the United States, and subject to the jurisdiction thereof, are citizens of the United States and of the State wherein they reside. No State shall make or enforce any law which shall abridge the privileges or immunities of citizens of the United States; nor shall any State deprive any person of life, liberty, or property, without due process of law; nor deny to any person within its jurisdiction the equal protection of the laws.

Section 2.

Representatives shall be apportioned among the several States according to their respective numbers, counting the whole number of persons in each State, excluding Indians not taxed. But when the right to vote at any election for the choice of electors for President and Vice President of the United States, representatives in Congress, the executive and judicial officers of a State, or the members of the legislature thereof, is denied to any of the male inhabitants of such State, being twenty-one years of age, and citizens of the United States, or in any way abridged, except for participating in rebellion, or other crime, the basis of representation therein shall be reduced in the proportion which the number of such male citizens shall bear to the whole number of male citizens twenty-one years of age in such State.

Section 3.

No person shall be a senator or representative in Congress, or elector of President and Vice President, or hold any office, civil or military, under the United States, or under any State, who having previously taken an oath, as a member of Congress, or as an officer of the United States, or as a member of any State legislature, or as an executive or judicial officer of any State, to support the Constitution of the United States, shall have engaged in insurrection or rebellion against the same, or given aid or comfort to the enemies thereof. But Congress may by a vote of two thirds of each House, remove such disability.

Section 4.

The validity of the public debt of the United States, authorized by law, including debts incurred for payment of pensions and bounties for services in suppressing insurrection or rebellion; shall not be questioned. But neither the United States nor any State shall assume or pay any debt or obligation incurred in aid of insurrection or rebellion against the United States, or any claim for the loss or emancipation of any slave; but all such debts, obligations, and claims shall be held illegal and void.

Section 5.

The Congress shall have the power to enforce, by appropriate legislation, the provisions of this article.

Amendment XV [March 30, 1870]

Section 1.

The right of citizens of the United States to vote shall not be denied or abridged by the United States or by any State on account of race, color, or previous condition of servitude.

Section 2.

The Congress shall have power to enforce this article by appropriate legislation.

Amendment XVI [February 25, 1913]

The Congress shall have power to lay and collect taxes on incomes, from whatever source derived, without apportionment among the several States, and without regard to any census or enumeration.

Amendment XVII [May 31, 1913]

The Senate of the United States shall be composed of two senators from each State, elected by the people thereof, for six years; and each senator shall have one vote. The electors in each State shall have the qualifications requisite for electors of the most numerous branch of the State legislature.

When vacancies happen in the representation of any State in the Senate, the executive authority of such State shall issue writs of election to fill such vacancies: Provided, That the legislature of any State may empower the executive thereof to make temporary appointments until the people fill the vacancies by election as the legislature may direct.

This amendment shall not be so construed as to affect the election or term of any senator chosen before it becomes valid as part of the Constitution.

Amendment XVIII [January 29, 1919]

After one year from the ratification of this article, the manufacture, sale, or transportation of intoxicating liquors within, the importation thereof into, or the exportation thereof from the United States and all territory subject to the jurisdiction thereof for beverage purposes is thereby prohibited.

The Congress and the several States shall have concurrent power to enforce this article by appropriate legislation.

This article shall be inoperative unless it shall have been ratified as an amendment to the Constitution by the legislatures of the several States, as provided in the Constitution, within seven years from the date of the submission hereof to the States by Congress.

Amendment XIX [August 26, 1920]

The right of citizens of the United States to vote shall not be denied or abridged by the United States or by any State on account of sex.

Congress shall have the power to enforce this article by appropriate legislation.

Amendment XX [January 23, 1933]

Section 1.

The terms of the President and Vice President shall end at noon on the 20th day of January and the terms of Senators and Representatives at noon on the 3d day of January, of the years in which such terms would have ended if this article had not been ratified; and the terms of their successors shall then begin.

Section 2.

The Congress shall assemble at least once in every year, and such meeting shall begin at noon on the 3d day of January, unless they shall by law appoint a different day.

Section 3.

If, at the time fixed for the beginning of the term of President, the President-elect shall have died, the Vice President-elect shall become President. If a President shall not have been chosen before the time fixed for the beginning of his term, or if the President-elect shall have failed to qualify, then the Vice President-elect shall act as President until a President shall have qualified; and the Congress may by law provide for the case wherein neither a President-elect nor a Vice President-elect shall have qualified, declaring who shall then act as President, or the manner in which one who is to act shall be selected, and such person shall act accordingly until a President or Vice President shall have qualified.

Section 4.

The Congress may by law provide for the case of the death of any of the persons from whom the House of Representatives may choose a President whenever the right of choice shall have devolved upon them, and for the case of the death of any of the persons from whom the Senate may choose a Vice President whenever the right of choice shall have devolved upon them.

Section 5.

Sections 1 and 2 shall take effect on the 15th day of October following the ratification of this article.

Section 6.

This article shall be inoperative unless it shall have been ratified as an amendment to the Constitution by the legislatures of three-fourths of the several States within seven years from the date of its submission.

Amendment XXI [December 5, 1933]

Section 1.

The Eighteenth Article of amendment to the Constitution of the United States is hereby repealed.

Section 2.

The transportation or importation into any State, Territory, or possession of the United States for delivery or use therein of intoxicating liquors in violation of the laws thereof, is hereby prohibited.

Section 3.

This article shall be inoperative unless it shall have been ratified as an amendment to the Constitution by conventions in the several States, as provided in the Constitution, within seven years from the date of the submission thereof to the States by the Congress.

Amendment XXII [March 1, 1951]

No person shall be elected to the office of the President more than twice, and no person who has held the office of President, or acted as President, for more than two years of a term to which some other person was elected President shall be elected to the office of the President more than once.

But this article shall not apply to any person holding the office of President when this article was proposed by the Congress, and shall not prevent any person who may be holding the office of President, or acting as President, during the term within which this article becomes operative from holding the office of President or acting as President during the remainder of such term.

This article shall be inoperative unless it shall have been ratified as an amendment to the Constitution by the legislatures of three-fourths of the several States within seven years from the date of its submission to the States by the Congress.

Amendment XXIII [March 29, 1961]

Section 1.

The District constituting the seat of Government of the United States shall appoint in such manner as the Congress may direct.

A number of electors of President and Vice President equal to the whole number of Senators and Representatives in Congress to which the District would be entitled if it were a State, but in no event more than the least populous State; they shall be in addition to those appointed by the States, but they shall be considered, for the purposes of the election of President and Vice President, to be electors appointed by a State; and they shall meet in the District and perform such duties as provided by the twelfth article of amendment.

Section 2.

The Congress shall have power to enforce this article by appropriate legislation.

Amendment XXIV [January 23, 1964]

Section 1.

The right of citizens of the United States to vote in any primary or other election for President or Vice President, for electors for President or Vice President, or for Senator or Representative in Congress, shall not be denied or abridged by the United States or any State by reason of failure to pay any poll tax or other tax.

Section 2.

The Congress shall have power to enforce this article by appropriate legislation.

Amendment XXV [February 10, 1967]

Section 1.

In case of the removal of the President from office or of his death or resignation, the Vice President shall become President.

Section 2.

Whenever there is a vacancy in the office of the Vice President, the President shall nominate a Vice President who shall take office upon confirmation by a majority of both Houses of Congress.

Section 3.

Whenever the President transmits to the President pro tempore of the Senate and the Speaker of the House of Representatives his written declaration that he is unable to discharge the powers and duties of his office, and until he transmits to them a written declaration to the contrary, such powers and duties shall be discharged by the Vice President as Acting President.

Section 4.

Whenever the Vice President and a majority of either the principal officers of the executive departments or of such other body as Congress may by law provide, transmit to the President pro tempore of the Senate and the Speaker of the House of Representatives their written declaration that the President is unable to discharge the powers and duties of his office, the Vice President shall immediately assume the powers and duties of the office as Acting President.

Thereafter, when the President transmits to the President pro tempore of the Senate and the Speaker of the House of Representatives his written declaration that no inability exists, he shall resume the powers and duties of his office unless the Vice President and a majority of either the principal officers of the executive departments or of such other body as Congress may by law provide, transmit within four days to the President pro tempore of the Senate and the Speaker of the House of Representatives their written declaration that the President is unable to discharge the powers and duties of his office. Thereupon Congress shall decide the issue, assembling within forty-eight hours for that purpose if not in session.

If the Congress, within twenty-one days after receipt of the latter written declaration, or, if Congress is not in session, within twenty-one days after Congress is required to assemble, determines by two-thirds vote of both Houses that the President is unable to discharge the powers and duties of his office, the Vice President shall continue to discharge the same as Acting President; otherwise, the President shall resume the powers and duties of his office.

Amendment XXVI [June 30, 1971]

Section 1.

The right of citizens of the United States who are eighteen years of age or older to vote shall not be denied or abridged by the United States or by any State on account of age.

Section 2.

The Congress shall have power to enforce this article by appropriate legislation.

Amendment XXVII [May 7, 1992]

Section 1.

No law, varying the compensation for the services of the Senators and Representatives, shall take effect, until an election of Representatives shall have intervened.

⊙ Brinkley, Alan. *American History, A Survey*. 10th ed. New York: McGraw Hill, 1999.
National Archives and Records Administration. "The Constitution of the United States," www.nara.gov/ exhall/charters/constitution/conmain.html
Mayer, David N. *The Constitutional Thought of Thomas Jefferson*. Charlottesville: University Press of Virginia, 1994.

The Gettysburg Address

Four score and seven years ago our fathers brought forth on this continent, a new nation, conceived in Liberty, and dedicated to the proposition that all men are created equal.

Now we are engaged in a great civil war, testing whether that nation, or any nation so conceived and so dedicated, can long endure. We are met on a great battle-field of that war. We have come to dedicate a portion of that field, as a final resting place for those who here gave their lives that that nation might live. It is altogether fitting and proper that we should do this.

But, in a larger sense, we can not dedicate—we can not consecrate—we can not hallow—this ground. The brave men, living and dead, who struggled here, have consecrated it, far above our poor power to add or detract. The world will little note, nor long remember what we say here, but I can never forget what they did here. It is for us the living, rather, to be dedicated here to the unfinished work which they who fought here have thus far so nobly advanced. It is rather for us to be here dedicated to the great task remaining before us—that from these honored dead we take increased devotion to that cause for which they gave the last full measure of devotion—that we here highly resolve that these dead shall not have died in vain—that this nation, under God, shall have a new birth of freedom—and that government of the people, by the people, for the people, shall not perish from the earth.

⊙ Brinkley, Alan. *American History: A Survey*. 10th ed. New York: McGraw Hill, 1999.
Wills, Garry. *Lincoln at Gettysburg*. New York: Simon & Schuster, 1992.

Time Period	Event
25,000 BC	Approximate date of earliest human settlement in the Americas
c.5000 BC	Beginning of Athapaskan migration
c.3000 BC	Inupiat and Aleut migrations
2500 BC	Date of the Serpent Mound located in the Ohio Valley
1000 BC	Leif Eriksson sails to Newfoundland
c.AD 500	Height of Mayan culture (Mexico)
AD 650	Earliest evidence of bow and arrow, flint hoes, and Northern Flint corn in the Northeast
1000	Cultivation of tobacco throughout North America
1050–1250	Peak of Cahokia Culture (Illinois)
c.1200	High point of Mississippian and Anasazi cultures
1300	Athapaskans reach Southwest
1325	Aztec city Tenochititlán founded
1451	Founding of the Iroquois Confederacy
1492	Christopher Columbus reaches Caribbean
1497	John Cabot explores east coast of North America
1513	Juan Ponce de Leon lands in Florida
1519	Hernan Cortés arrives in Mexico; imprisons Aztec emperor Montezuma, who later dies in battle
1519–22	Ferdinand Magellan circumnavigates the world
1535	Jacques Cartier begins exploring the St. Lawrence River
1539–40	Expeditions of Hernando de Soto and Francisco de Coronado
1565	Spanish found St. Augustine; French Huguenot colony of Ft. Caroline in Florida is destroyed by Spanish; Spanish missions introduce Roman Catholicism to Florida
1584–87	Sir Walter Raleigh establishes colony on Roanoke Island
1586	Sir Francis Drake destroys Spanish settlements in Florida and the West Indies
1598	Juan de Onate leads Spain into New Mexico; Spanish missions are established in New Mexico
1607	Settlement of Jamestown, Virginia
1608	Samuel Champlain founds Quebec
1609	Henry Hudson discovers the Hudson River; Spanish found Santa Fe (first Spanish settlement in New Mexico); Church of England is established by law in Virginia
1612	Introduction of tobacco cultivation in Virginia
1619	First Africans are sold as slaves in Virginia
1620	Pilgrims settle Plymouth
1621	William Bradford is elected governor of the Plymouth Colony; Treaty between Plymouth and Massasoit, Wampanoag chief
1625	Puritans settle Massachusetts Bay; Jesuit missionaries arrive in New France
1650–96	Parliament enacts the Navigation Acts
1656	First Quakers arrive in Boston

Time Period	Event
1661	Algonquian New Testament becomes the first Bible printed in North America
1664	English conquer New Amsterdam
1665	New Jersey colony founded
1669	South Carolina founded
1675	King Philip's War
1676	Bacon's Rebellion
1681	Settlement of Philadelphia; Exploration of the Mississippi River by Sieur de La Salle
1683	Earliest Mennonites settle in Pennsylvania
1692	Salem witch trials
1696	Introduction of rice cultivation in South Carolina
1700s	Plains Indians begin using horses
1702	St. Augustine burned by South Carolinians
1705	Virginia Slave Code established
1716	Spanish build missions in Texas
1732	Benjamin Franklin begins publication of *Poor Richard's Almanac*
1733	Molasses Act; Georgia settled
1738	George Whitefield begins preaching in the colonies
1740s	Indigo production starts in South Carolina
1740	Naturalization Act
1741	Vitus Bering explores Alaska
1745	British take Louisburg, Canada, from France
1754–63	French and Indian War
1759	John Winthrop publishes *Two Lectures on Comets*
1760s	Height of the Great Awakening
1763	Pontiac's Rebellion; Paxton Boys Massacre; Proclamation of 1763
1764	Sugar Act
1765	Stamp Act
1767	Townshend Acts
1767–68	Daniel Boone explores Kentucky; Spanish begin settling California; Boston Massacre
1773	Boston Tea Party
1774	First Continental Congress meets
1775	Daniel Boone crosses Cumberland Gap to Kentucky's bluegrass region; Battles of Lexington and Concord and Bunker Hill; George Washington named commander-in-chief of Continental Army
1776	Declaration of Independence; Washington occupies Boston; Battles of Long Island, Trenton, and Princeton; San Francisco founded; Thomas Paine publishes *Common Sense*
1777	Battle of Saratoga
1777–78	Continental Army winters over at Valley Forge
1778	British capture Savannah and Charleston

1781	Ratification of the Articles of Confederation; General Cornwallis surrenders at Yorktown
1783	Treaty of Paris; Britain recognizes U.S. independence
1784	Russians settle Aleutian Islands of Alaska
1785	Land Ordinance of 1785
1787	Shays' Rebellion; Constitutional Convention; Northwest Ordinance; first American steamboat is launched on the Delaware River by John Fitch
1789	Washington inaugurated as president; Annapolis Convention; Bill of Rights
1790	First U.S. ship reaches Hawaii; Samuel Slater opens his first mill in Rhode Island
1793	Eli Whitney invents the cotton gin
1794	Whiskey Rebellion
1795	Ratification of Jay's Treaty
1798	XYZ Affair; Alien and Sedition Acts are passed
1803	Louisiana Purchase
1804–6	Louis and Clark expedition
1806	Zebulon Pike explores the Great Plains to the Rocky Mountains
1807	Robert Fulton builds his first successful steamboat, the *Clermont*
1808	Congress bars importation of slaves
1811	Battle of Tippecanoe
1812	War of 1812
1814	Francis Scott Key writes "The Star Spangled Banner"
1815	Battle of New Orleans; Stephen Decatur's Algerian expedition
1817	Rush-Bagot Agreement with Great Britain
1818	1st Seminole War
1820	Missouri Compromise
1821	Mexico achieves independence from Spain
1823	Monroe Doctrine
1825	Baltimore and Ohio railroad begins operation; Erie Canal opens
1830	Indian Removal Act; Joseph Smith founds Mormon Church
1830s	Height of the Second Great Awakening
1831	Nat Turner's slave uprising
1835	Texas Revolt against Mexico
1836	Battles of the Alamo and San Jacinto
1843–44	John C. Fremont maps trails to Oregon and California
1844	First successful telegraph transmission
1845	U.S. annexes Texas as slave state
1846	Beginning of Mexican-American War; Wilmot Proviso; Oregon Treaty; Elias Howe invents the sewing machine
1848	Women's Rights Convention at Seneca Falls, N.Y.; treaty of Guadalupe Hidalgo ends Mexican-American War
1849	California Gold Rush
1850	Compromise of 1850; California admitted as a free state
1851	Publication of Harriet Beecher Stowe's *Uncle Tom's Cabin*

Time Period	Event
1853	Commodore Matthew Perry opens Japan to U.S. trade; Washington Territory established
1854	Kansas-Nebraska Act; Henry David Thoreau publishes *Walden*
1856	John Brown's raid; caning of Sen. Charles Sumner
1857	Dred Scott case
1858	Lincoln-Douglas debates
1860	Abraham Lincoln elected president; Pony Express established
1861	Civil War begins; First Battle of Bull Run
1862	Battles of the *Monitor* and the *Merrimack*, Shiloh, Antietam, and Fredericksburg; Pacific Railway Act; Homestead Act
1863	Emancipation Proclamation; Battles of Chancellorsville, Gettysburg, and Vicksburg
1864	Sherman's march to the sea
1865	Freedmen's Bureau established; Lee surrenders at Appomattox; Lincoln assassinated
1865–66	Enactment of Black Codes in the South
1865–67	Great Sioux War
1867	Reconstruction Acts passed; U.S. purchases Alaska from Russia
1868	House of Representatives impeaches Andrew Johnson; Senate acquits him in 1871
1871	Chicago fire
1871–86	Apache Wars in New Mexico
1874	Invention of barbed wire
1876	Battle of Little Big Horn; Rutherford B. Hayes wins disputed presidential election; Alexander Graham Bell invents telephone
1879	Carlisle Indian School founded; Thomas Edison invents light bulb
1881	President Garfield assassinated; Tuskegee Institute founded
1882	Chinese Exclusion Act
1886	American Federation of Labor founded; Haymarket bombing
1887	Dawes Severalty (Allotment) Act; Interstate Commerce Act
1889	Jane Addams founds Hull House
1890	Wounded Knee Massacre; National American Women's Suffrage Association founded; Sherman Antitrust Act
1894	Pullman Strike
1896	*Plessy* v. *Ferguson* upholds "separate but equal" doctrine; William Jennings Bryan's "Cross of Gold" speech
1898	Spanish-American War; U.S. acquires overseas territories from Spain; annexes Hawaii
1901	Pres. McKinley assassinated, V.P. Theodore Roosevelt succeeds as president
1903	U.S. secures canal rights in Panama; W.E.B. Du Bois publishes *The Souls of Black Folk*; Wright brothers launch the first successful manned flight in Kittyhawk, N.C.
1905	Albert Einstein develops his theory of relativity
1907	"Gentlemen's Agreement" with Japan
1908	Henry Ford produces first Model T automobile
1909	W.E.B. Du Bois helps found National Association for the Advancement of Colored People (NAACP)

1914	World War I begins; Panama Canal opens; Clayton Anti-Trust Act
1914	Keating-Owen Act bars child-labor products from interstate commerce
1916–17	Mexican Border Campaign
1917	U.S. declares war on the Central Powers; 18th Amendment passes, prohibiting the manufacture and sale of alcoholic beverages
1918	U.S. troops fight in France; armistice ends World War I; Wilson announces his Fourteen Points; Sedition Act passed; Eugene Debs imprisoned
1919	Senate rejects the Treaty of Versailles; Red Scare and Palmer Raids begin; Chicago race riot
1919–30	Harlem Renaissance
1920	19th Amendment guarantees women's right to vote
1921	Congress establishes first immigration quotas
1921–22	Washington Armament Conference
1923	Pres. Warren Harding dies; exposure of Teapot Dome and other Harding administration scandals
1924	Congress extends citizenship to all Indians
1925	Scopes Monkey trial in Dayton, Tenn.
1927	Execution of Sacco and Vanzetti; Charles Lindbergh's solo flight from New York to Paris
1929	New York Stock Exchange crashes
1930s	Great Depression
1932	Bonus March on Washington
1933	First New Deal
1934	Indian Reorganization Act
1935	Social Security Act passed
1937	Franklin D. Roosevelt's Court Packing plan thwarted
1938	Formation of Congress of Industrial Organizations
1939	World War II begins
1940	Selective Service and Raining Act passed
1941	Japan attacks Pearl Harbor; United States enters World War II
1942	Internment of Japanese Americans; Congress of Racial Equality (CORE) established
1943	Race riots in Detroit and Los Angeles
1945	Yalta Conference; Roosevelt dies and V.P. Harry Truman becomes president; Germany surrenders; first atomic bomb detonated at Alamogordo, N.M.; U.S. drops atomic bombs on Hiroshima and Nagasaki; Japan surrenders; union membership reaches 14.8 million
1946	United Mine Workers' strike; Richard Evelyn Byrd leads an expedition to the South Pole
1947	Marshall Plan proposed; Truman Doctrine; HUAC hearings in Hollywood; Jackie Robinson becomes the first African-American major league baseball player; Taft-Hartley (Labor-Management Relations) Act
1948	Military desegregation ordered by Harry Truman
1948–49	Berlin Airlift
1949	Truman announces Fair Deal; NATO founded
1950	Korean War starts
1951	Gen. MacArthur dismissed by Pres. Truman
1952	Dwight D. Eisenhower elected president
1953	Armistice agreement in Korea

Time Period	Event
1954	Supreme Court *Brown* v. *Board of Education* desegregation decision; United States explodes first hydrogen bomb; Army-McCarthy Hearings; first atomic-powered ship, USS *Nautilus*, launched
1955	Merger of AFL and CIO; Jonas Salk develops polio vaccine
1956	Montgomery, Alabama, bus boycott ends successfully
1957	Pres. Eisenhower sends the National Guard to desegregate Little Rock High School
1960	John F. Kennedy elected president; founding of the Student-Nonviolent Coordinating Committee (SNCC)
1962	Cuban Missile Crisis
1963	Pres. Kennedy assassinated; V.P. Lyndon B. Johnson succeeds
1964	Civil Rights Act; U.S. role in Vietnam expands after Gulf of Tonkin Resolution; Economic Opportunity Act
1965	Malcolm X assassinated
1966	Formation of National Organization of Women (NOW) and of Black Panthers
1968	Vietnam War protests grow; Martin Luther King, Jr. and Robert Kennedy assassinated
1969	American Neil Armstrong becomes first man to walk on the moon
1970	Shooting of Kent State student protesters against Vietnam War
1972	Pres. Nixon visits China
1973	Signing of the Vietnam cease-fire; OPEC forms; Supreme Court issues *Roe* v. *Wade* abortion decision; American Indian Movement occupies Wounded Knee; Watergate hearings
1974	House Judiciary Committee votes to impeach Pres. Nixon; Nixon resigns; Gerald Ford pardons Nixon
1980	Ronald Reagan elected president
1982	Equal Rights Amendment (ERA) dies
1983	U.S. leads international force to occupy Grenada to halt Communist influence
1986	Space shuttle *Challenger* explodes, killing all aboard
1987	Iran-Contra hearings
1989	United States invades Panama, overthrows regime of Gen. Noriega; tanker *Exxon Valdez* causes the largest oil spill in U.S. history in the Gulf of Alaska
1990–91	Persian Gulf War
1991	Hewlett-Packard introduces a handheld lightweight computer
1993	Congress approves North American Free Trade Agreement (NAFTA)
1997	Congress and Pres. Bill Clinton agree to balance budget
1998	House of Representatives impeaches Clinton for perjury and obstruction of justice
1999	Senate fails to convict Clinton of impeachment charges
2001	United States launches a "campaign against terrorism" after Muslim extremists destroy New York's World Trade Center and part of the Pentagon, killing thousands.

⊙ Brinkley, Alan. *American History: A Survey.* 10th ed. New York: McGraw Hill, 1999.
Divine, Robert A., et al. *America Past and Present.* 5th ed. New York: Longman, 1998.
Goldfield, David, et al. *The American Journey: A History of the United States.* Paramus, N.J.: Prentice Hall, 1997.

Legal Terms

Acquittal: A release, absolution, or discharge of an obligation or liability. In criminal law, the finding of not guilty

Affidavit: A voluntary, written, or printed declaration of facts, confirmed by oath of the party making it before a person with authority to administer the oath

Allegation: A statement of the issues in a written document (a pleading) which a person is prepared to prove in court

Appeal: A proceeding brought to a higher court to review a lower court's decision for the purpose of reversing a judgment or granting a new trial

Arraignment: The hearing at which the accused is brought before the court to plead to the criminal charge in the indictment

Arrest: To take into custody by legal authority

Bail: Money or other security (such as a bail bond) provided to the court to temporarily allow a person's release from jail and assure their appearance in court. "Bail" and "Bond" are often used interchangeably. (Applies mainly to state courts.)

Bail bond: An obligation signed by the accused to secure his or her presence at the trial. This obligation means that the accused may lose money by not properly appearing for the trial. Often referred to simply as "bond."

Bankruptcy: Refers to statutes and judicial proceedings involving persons or businesses that cannot pay their debts and seek the assistance of the court in getting a fresh start

Burden of proof: In the law of evidence, the necessity or duty of affirmatively proving a fact or facts in dispute on an issue raised between the parties in a lawsuit

Capital crime: A crime punishable by death

Contempt of court: Willful disobedience of a judge's command or of an official court order

Conviction: A judgment of guilt against a criminal defendant

Cross-examination: The questioning of a witness produced by the other side in order to discredit or clarify testimony

Defendant: The person defending or denying a suit

Dismissal: The termination of a lawsuit without a complete trial; denial of a motion

Double jeopardy: Putting a person on trial more than once for the same crime. It is forbidden by the 5th Amendment to the United States Constitution

Due process of law: The right of all persons to receive the guarantees and safeguards of the law and the judicial process

Equal Protection of the Law: The guarantee in the 14th Amendment to the U.S. Constitution that all persons be treated equally by the law

Exhibit: A document or other item introduced as evidence during a trial or hearing

Exonerate: Removal of a charge, responsibility, or duty

File: To place a paper in the official custody of the clerk of court/court administrator to enter into the files or records of a case

Finding: Formal conclusion by a judge or regulatory agency on issues of fact. Also, a conclusion by a jury regarding a fact

Grand Jury: A jury that receives complaints and accusations in criminal matters and issues a formal indictment if appropriate

Habeas corpus: A legal writ that causes a person to be brought before the court to discover whether the individual is lawfully detained

Hostile witness: A witness whose testimony is not favorable to the party who calls him or her as a witness. A hostile witness may be asked leading questions and may be cross-examined by the party who calls him or her to the stand

Impeachment: The raising of criminal charges against a public official for wrongdoing while in office

Indictment: A written accusation by a grand jury charging a person with a crime

Jurisdiction: The power or authority of a court to hear and try a case; the geographic area in which a court has power or the types of cases it has power to hear

Jury: A certain number of citizens (frequently six or twelve) selected according to law and sworn to try a question of fact or indict a person for public offense

Lawsuit: An action or proceeding in a civil court; term used for a suit or action between two private parties in a court of law

Miranda warning: Requirement that police tell a suspect in their custody that he or she has the right to remain silent and has the right to the presence and advice of a lawyer

Objection: The process by which one party takes exception to some statement or procedure

Overrule: A judge's decision not to allow an objection. Also, a decision by a higher court finding that a lower court decision was in error

Pardon: An act of grace from governing power which mitigates punishment and restores rights and privileges forfeited on account of the offense

Parole: Supervised release of a prisoner from imprisonment on certain prescribed conditions which entitle him or her to serve the remainder of his or her sentence outside the prison if all the conditions are satisfactorily complied with

Plaintiff: A person who brings an action; the party who complains or sues in a civil action

Plea: The first pleading by a criminal defendant, the defendant's declaration in open court that he or she is guilty or not guilty

Probation: An alternative to imprisonment allowing a person found guilty of an offense to stay in the community, usually under conditions and under the supervision of a probation officer

Prosecutor: A trial lawyer who represents the government in a criminal case, or the interests of the state in civil matters

Reasonable doubt: An accused person is entitled to acquittal if, in the minds of the jury, his or her guilt has not been proved beyond a "reasonable doubt;" that state of minds of jurors in which they cannot say they feel an abiding conviction as to the truth of the charge

Remand: To send a dispute back to the court where it was originally heard. Usually it is an appellate court that remands a case for proceedings in the trial court consistent with the appellate court's ruling

Restitution: Act of restoring anything to its rightful owner; the act of restoring someone to an economic position he enjoyed before he suffered a loss

Search warrant: A written order issued by a judge that directs a law enforcement officer to search a specific area for a particular piece of evidence

Sentence: The punishment ordered by a court for a defendant convicted of a crime

Settlement: An agreement between the parties disposing of a lawsuit

Summons: Instrument used to commence a civil action or special proceeding; formal notification of a defendant that a civil action or special proceeding has begun against him or her and that he or she is required to appear in court to answer the complaint

Testimony: Verbal evidence given by a witness under oath

United States Attorney: A federal district attorney appointed by the President to prosecute for all offenses committed against the United States

Verdict: The opinion of a jury, or a judge where there is no jury, on a question of fact; used by the court in formulating the final judgment

Warrant: Most commonly, a court order authorizing law enforcement officers to make an arrest or conduct a search

Witness: One who personally sees or perceives a thing; one who testifies as to what he has seen, heard, or otherwise observed

Writ: A judicial order directing a person to do something

⊙ Oran, Daniel, and Mark Tosti. *Oran's Dictionary of the Law.* 3d ed. Albany, N.Y.:Delmar, 1999.
United States Judiciary. www.id.uscourts.gov/glossary.htm

Chief Justices of the United States

Name	Life Dates	Appointed by	Years Served
John Jay	1745–1829	Washington	1789–1795
John *Rutledge	1739–1800	Washington	1795
Oliver Ellsworth	1745–1807	Washington	1796–1800
John Marshall	1755–1835	J. Adams	1801–1835
Roger Brooke Taney	1777–1864	Jackson	1836–1864
Salmon Portland Chase	1808–1873	Lincoln	1864–1873
Morrison Remick Waite	1816–1888	Grant	1874–1888
Melville Weston Fuller	1833–1910	Cleveland	1888–1910
Edward Douglass *White Jr.	1845–1921	Taft	1910–1921
William Howard Taft	1857–1930	Harding	1921–1930
Charles Evans *Hughes	1862–1948	Hoover	1930–1941
Harlan Fiske *Stone	1872–1946	F. D. Roosevelt	1941–1946
Frederick Moore Vinson	1890–1953	Truman	1946–1953
Earl Warren	1891–1974	Eisenhower	1953–1969
Warren Earl Burger	1907–1995	Nixon	1969–1986
William Hubbs *Rehnquist	1924–	Reagan	1986–

*also served as Associate Justice

⊙ Choper, Jesse H, ed. *Supreme Court and Its Justices.* Chicago: American Bar Association, 2000.
Brinkley, Allan. *American History, A Survey.* 10th ed. New York: McGraw Hill, 1999.

Associate Justices of the Supreme Court

Name	Life Dates	Appointed by	Years Served	Chief Justice(s)
Henry Baldwin	1780–1844	Jackson	1830–1844	Marshall; Taney
Philip Pendleton Barbour	1783–1841	Jackson	1836–1841	Taney
Hugo Lafayette Black	1886–1971	F. D. Roosevelt	1937–1971	Hughes; Stone; Vinson; Warren; Burger
Harry Andrew Blackmun	1908–1999	Nixon	1970–1994	Burger; Rehnquist
John Blair	1732–1800	Washington	1789–1796	Jay
Samuel Milford Blatchford	1820–1893	Arthur	1882–1893	Waite; Fuller
Joseph P. Bradley	1813–1892	Grant	1870–1892	Chase; Waite; Fuller
Louis Dembitz Brandeis	1856–1941	Wilson	1916–1939	White; Taft; Hughes
William Joseph Brennan Jr.	1906–1997	Eisenhower	1956–1990	Warren; Burger; Rehnquist
David Josiah Brewer	1837–1910	Harrison	1889–1910	Fuller
Stephen Gerald Breyer	1938–	Clinton	1994–	Rehnquist
Henry Billings Brown	1836–1913	Harrison	1890–1906	Fuller
Harold Hitz Burton	1888–1964	Truman	1945–1958	Stone; Vinson; Warren
Pierce Butler	1866–1939	Harding	1922–1939	Taft; Hughes
James Francis Byrnes	1879–1972	F. D. Roosevelt	1941–1942	Stone
John Archibald Campbell	1811–1889	Pierce	1853–1861	Taney
Benjamin Nathan Cardozo	1870–1938	Hoover	1932–1938	Hughes
John Catron	1786–1865	Jackson	1837–1865	Taney; Chase
Samuel Chase	1741–1811	Washington	1796–1811	Ellsworth; Marshall
Tom Campbell Clark	1899–1977	Truman	1949–1967	Vinson; Warren
John Hessin Clarke	1857–1945	Wilson	1916–1922	White; Taft
Nathan Clifford	1803–1881	Buchanan	1858–1881	Taney; Chase; Waite
Benjamin R. Curtis	1809–1874	Fillmore	1851–1857	Taney
William Cushing	1732–1810	Washington	1789–1810	Jay; Ellsworth; Marshall
Peter Vivian Daniel	1784–1860	Van Buren	1841–1860	Taney
David Davis	1815–1886	Lincoln	1862–1877	Taney; Chase; Waite
William Rufus Day	1849–1923	T. Roosevelt	1903–1922	Fuller; White; Taft
William Orville Douglas	1898–1980	F. D. Roosevelt	1939–1975	Hughes; Stone; Vinson; Warren; Burger
Gabriel Duvall	1752–1844	Madison	1811–1835	Marshall
Stephen Johnson Field	1816–1899	Lincoln	1863–1897	Taney; Chase; Waite; Fuller
Abe Fortas	1910–1982	Johnson	1965–1969	Warren
Felix Frankfurter	1882–1965	F. D. Roosevelt	1939–1962	Hughes; Stone; Vinson; Warren
Ruth Bader Ginsburg	1933–	Clinton	1993–	Rehnquist
Arthur Joseph Goldberg	1908–1990	Kennedy	1962–1965	Warren
Horace Gray	1828–1902	Arthur	1881–1902	Waite; Fuller
Robert Cooper Grier	1794–1870	Polk	1846–1870	Taney; Chase
John Marshall Harlan	1833–1911	Hayes	1877–1911	Waite; Fuller; White

UNITED STATES: Courts and Law

John Marshall Harlan	1899–1971	Eisenhower	1955–1971	Warren; Burger
Oliver Wendell Holmes Jr.	1841–1935	T. Roosevelt	1902–1932	Fuller; White; Taft; Hughes
Charles Evans Hughes *	1862–1948	Taft	1910–1916	Fuller; White
Ward Hunt	1810–1886	Grant	1872–1882	Chase; Waite
James Iredell	1751–1799	Washington	1790–1799	Jay; Ellsworth
Howell Edmunds Jackson	1832–1895	Harrison	1893–1895	Fuller
Robert Houghwout Jackson	1892–1954	F. D. Roosevelt	1941–1954	Stone; Vinson; Warren
Thomas Johnson	1732–1819	Washington	1791–1793	Jay
William Johnson	1771–1834	Jefferson	1803–1834	Marshall
Anthony McLeod Kennedy	1936–	Reagan	1988–	Rehnquist
Joseph Rucker Lamar	1857–1916	Taft	1911–1916	White
Lucius Quintus Cincinnatus Lamar	1825–1893	Cleveland	1888–1893	Waite; Fuller
Henry Brockholst Livingston	1757–1823	Jefferson	1806–1823	Marshall
Horace Harmon Lurton	1844–1914	Taft	1909–1914	Fuller; White
Thurgood Marshall	1908–1993	Johnson	1967–1991	Warren; Burger; Rehnquist
Stanley Matthews	1824–1889	Garfield	1881–1889	Waite; Fuller
Joseph McKenna	1843–1926	McKinley	1898–1925	Fuller; White; Taft
John McKinley	1780–1852	Van Buren	1837–1852	Taney
John McLean	1785–1861	Jackson	1829–1861	Marshall; Taney
James Clark McReynolds	1862–1946	Wilson	1914–1941	White; Taft; Hughes
Samuel Freeman Miller	1816–1890	Lincoln	1862–1890	Taney; Chase; Waite; Fuller
Sherman Minton	1890–1965	Truman	1949–1956	Vinson; Warren
William Henry Moody	1853–1917	T. Roosevelt	1906–1910	Fuller
Alfred Moore	1755–1810	Adams	1799–1804	Ellsworth; Marshall
Frank Murphy	1890–1949	F. D. Roosevelt	1940–1949	Hughes; Stone; Vinson
Samuel Nelson	1792–1873	Tyler	1845–1872	Taney; Chase
Sandra Day O'Connor	1930–	Reagan	1981–	Burger; Rehnquist
William Paterson	1745–1806	Washington	1793–1806	Jay; Ellsworth; Marshall
Rufus Wheeler Peckham Jr.	1838–1909	Cleveland	1895–1909	Fuller
Mahlon Pitney	1858–1924	Taft	1912–1922	White; Taft
Lewis Franklin Powell Jr.	1907–1998	Nixon	1971–1987	Burger; Rehnquist
Stanley Forman Reed	1884–1980	F. D. Roosevelt	1938–1957	Hughes; Stone; Vinson; Warren
William Hubbs Rehnquist *	1924–	Nixon	1971–1986	Burger
Owen Josephus Roberts	1875–1955	Hoover	1930–1945	Hughes; Stone
John Rutledge *	1739–1800	Washington	1789–1791	Jay
Wiley Blout Rutledge Jr.	1894–1949	F. D. Roosevelt	1943–1949	Stone; Vinson
Edward Terry Sanford	1865–1930	Harding	1923–1930	Taft
Antonin Scalia	1936–	Reagan	1986–	Rehnquist
George Shiras Jr.	1832–1924	Harrison	1892–1903	Fuller
David H. Souter	1939–	Bush	1990–	Rehnquist

Name	Life Dates	Appointed by	Years Served	Chief Justice(s)
John Paul Stevens	1920–	Ford	1975–	Burger; Rehnquist
Potter Stewart	1915–1985	Eisenhower	1958–1981	Warren; Burger
Joseph Story	1779–1845	Madison	1811–1845	Marshall; Taney
Harlan Fiske Stone*	1872–1946	Coolidge	1925–1941	Taft; Hughes
William Strong	1808–1895	Grant	1870–1880	Chase; Waite
George Sutherland	1862–1942	Harding	1922–1938	Taft; Hughes
Noah Haynes Swayne	1804–1884	Lincoln	1862–1881	Taney; Chase; Waite
Clarence Thomas	1948–	Bush	1991–	Rehnquist
Smith Thompson	1768–1843	Monroe	1823–1843	Marshall; Taney
Thomas Todd	1765–1826	Jefferson	1807–1826	Marshall
Robert Trimble	1776–1828	J. Q. Adams	1826–1828	Marshall
Willis Van Devanter	1859–1941	Taft	1910–1937	White; Taft; Hughes
Bushrod Washington	1762–1829	Adams	1798–1829	Ellsworth; Marshall
James Moore Wayne	c.1790–1867	Jackson	1835–1867	Marshall; Taney; Chase
Byron Raymond White	1917–	Kennedy	1962–1993	Warren; Burger; Rehnquist
Edward D. White*	1845–1921	Cleveland	1894–1910	Fuller
Charles Evans Whittaker	1901–1973	Eisenhower	1957–1962	Warren
James Wilson	1742–1798	Washington	1789–1798	Jay; Ellsworth
Levi Woodbury	1789–1851	Polk	1846–1851	Taney
William Burnham Woods	1824–1887	Hayes	1880–1887	Waite

* also served as Chief Justice

⊙ Choper, Jesse H, ed. *Supreme Court and Its Justices.* Chicago: American Bar Association, 2000.
  Brinkley, Allan. *American History, A Survey.* 10th ed. New York: McGraw Hill, 1999.

Landmark Supreme Court Cases

Baker v. Carr **(1962)** Supreme Court held that the federal courts have jurisdiction to review state apportionment cases; led to implementation of "one person, one vote" principle.

Bank of Augusta v. Earle **(1839)** Corporate-law case that set the stage for the emergence of national corporations by holding that an out-of-state corporation had legal status in other states.

Barron v. Baltimore **(1833)** Limited federal power by declaring that the first eight constitutional amendments applied only to the federal government and did not protect individual rights from actions of state governments.

Brown v. Board of Education of Topeka **(1954)** Found that segregated educational facilities violated the 14th Amendment's equal protection clause; overturned Plessy v. Ferguson (1896).

Charles River Bridge v. Warren Bridge **(1837)** Held that state legislatures could regulate private property; the dissenters stated that the rights of private property were absolute.

Cherokee Nation v. Georgia **(1831)** Held that a Native American tribe was neither a state in the Union nor a foreign nation within the meaning of the Constitution and, therefore, could not maintain an action in the federal courts. Tribes were described as "domestic dependent nations" under the sovereignty and dominion of the U.S.

Civil Rights Cases (1883) Limited the application of the 14th amendment to state action; the amendment did not prevent discrimination by private individuals or businesses, a doctrine that remained influential for 80 years.

Cruzan v. *Director, Missouri Department of Health* (1990) Established the right of a state to regulate the "right to die."

Dartmouth College v. *Woodward* (1819) Established that the contract clause of the Constitution was intended as a protection for private property; ruling was based on the validity of Dartmouth College's colonial charter.

In re Debs (1895) Upheld the federal government's right to use court injunctions to resolve conflicts with striking unions; the Court held that labor leader Eugene V. Debs' use of a strike violated the Sherman Antitrust Act by hindering interstate commerce.

Dennis v. *U.S.* (1951) Greatly restricted freedom of speech by narrowing the definition of the "clear and present danger" test.

Dred Scott v. *Sandford* (1857) Ruled that African Americans were not citizens and could not bring suit in federal court; intended to answer the question of slavery's legality, the opinion declared the Missouri Compromise unconstitutional and heightened tensions before the Civil War.

Edwards v. *Aguillard* (1987) Invalidated Louisiana's creation-science law as violating the 1st Amendment prohibition of establishing religion.

Engel v. *Vitale* (1962) School-prayer case that struck down a New York law allowing a prayer on the basis that such prayer was barred by the 1st Amendment prohibition against the establishment of religion.

Fletcher v. *Peck* (1810) Held that a Georgia law violated the Constitution's contract clause; established the Court's right of judicial review over the laws of the states.

Frontiero v. *Richardson* (1973) Established that gender discrimination, like racial discrimination, was unconstitutional.

Furman v. *Georgia* (1972) Found the death penalty, when imposed without specific guidelines or limits on juries' decisions, to be cruel and unusual punishment; *Gregg* v. *Georgia* (1976) upheld statutes that guide judge and jury when imposing the death penalty.

In re Gault (1967) Held that "due process" provisions should be applied to juvenile courts, an extension of constitutional protections.

Gibbons v. *Ogden* (1824) Highlighted the power of the federal government over the states, holding that the Constitution's commerce clause gave the federal government broad regulatory powers (the case upheld the federal government's right to grant a ferry-service contract in competition with a service that had been granted a monopoly by a state government).

Gideon v. *Wainwright* (1963) Expanded defendants' (including indigent defendants') rights to legal counsel in virtually all criminal cases in both state and federal courts, extending the principles laid out in *Powell* v. *Alabama* (1932).

Hammer v. *Dagenhart* (1918) Overturned the Keating-Owen Child Labor Act (1916), holding that child labor involved manufacturing and was therefore a state concern.

Heart of Atlanta Motel v. *U.S.* (1964) Held racial discrimination in public accommodation to be unlawful; upheld the Civil Rights Act of 1964 barring such discrimination and Congressional authority to pass such laws; *Katzenbach* v. *McClung* (1964) applied the same standard to ban discrimination in restaurants.

Immigration and Naturalization Service v. *Cardoza-Fonseca* **(1987)** Granted immigrants political asylum if a refugee had a well-founded fear of prosecution in his or her country of origin.

Immigration and Naturalization Service v. *Chadha* **(1983)** Barred the "legislative veto" that Congress had used to restrict executive power.

Korematsu v. *U.S.* **(1944)** Japanese-internment case during World War II, in which the Court upheld the right of military authorities to evacuate persons of Japanese ancestry from the West Coast; reversed by writ of error filed in 1983.

Lemon v. *Kurtzman* **(1971)** Ensured the First Amendment separation of church and state by promulgating a three-prong test to determine establishment: a law must have a secular legislative purpose, its primary effect must be one that neither advances nor inhibits religions, and it must not foster an excessive entanglement with religion.

Lochner v. *New York* **(1905)** Set the precedent for an era of judicial activism when the Court declared a state labor regulation unconstitutional.

Mapp v. *Ohio* **(1961)** Forced the states to apply the 4th Amendment's protection against unreasonable searches to state courts.

Marbury v. *Madison* **(1803)** Established the power of judicial review, the federal courts' authority to find laws unconstitutional.

Martin v. *Hunter's Lessee* **(1816)** Held that states do not share sovereignty equally with the federal government; the case upheld federal supremacy.

McCulloch v. *Maryland* **(1819)** Case involving the Bank of the United States, in which the Court held that Maryland's tax on federal banks violated the concept of the federal government's supremacy, as set forth in the Constitution's Article I, Section 8, the necessary-and-proper clause; established the principle that the federal government had implied powers.

Ex parte Merryman **(1861)** Confronted President Lincoln's declaration of martial law during the Civil War; the issue remained open until *Ex Parte Milligan* (1866).

Ex parte Milligan **(1866)** Case brought by a civilian convicted in a military court in a non-combat area during the Civil War, in which the Court ruled that Milligan should not have been tried by the military and that military courts should not try civilians outside a war zone.

Minor v. *Happersett* **(1875)** Denied the claim of Virginia Minor that the right to vote was guaranteed by the Constitution's 14th Amendment; woman suffrage supporters thereafter concluded that a constitutional amendment was needed to obtain the vote.

Miranda v. *Arizona* **(1966)** Established that suspects have to be informed of the right to remain silent and the right to counsel under the 5th Amendment.

Muller v. *Oregon* **(1908)** Upheld, because of women's physical differences from men, an Oregon law regulating women's work hours; indicated the Court's acceptance of protective labor legislation for women, but not for men.

National Association for the Advancement of Colored People v. *Alabama* **(1958)** Case in which the Court reversed the contempt conviction of the NAACP for refusing to provide membership lists on the basis of the 1st Amendment's guarantee of freedom of association and the 14th Amendment's extension of that guarantee to the states.

National Labor Relations Board v. *Jones & Laughlin Steel Corp.* **(1937)** Upheld the National Labor Relations Act, a piece of New Deal Legislation that guaranteed the right of workers involved in interstate commerce to organize; the ruling averted the constitutional crisis raised by President F. D. Roosevelt's court-packing plan.

New York Times v. _Sullivan_ **(1964)** Case in which the Court established a higher standard of libel for public figures because the public's right to public debate overrode the individual's rights.

Plessy v. _Ferguson_ **(1896)** Upheld the constitutionality of the "separate but equal" philosophy that served as the basis for racial segregation in the South for the first half of the 20th century; overturned by _Brown_ v. _Board of Education of Topeka_ (1954).

Powell v. _Alabama_ **(1932)** Case in which the Court held that defendants were guaranteed a fair trial, including the right to counsel, under the due process clause of the 14th Amendment; one of the "Scottsboro Boys" cases.

Regents of the University of California v. _Bakke_ **(1978)** Affirmative action case in which the Court held that state universities could consider race as one of several factors in selecting students for admission, but could not establish racial quotas.

Roe v. _Wade_ **(1973)** Upheld a woman's unrestricted right to an abortion during the first three months of pregnancy, an extension of the right to sexual privacy established by Griswold v. Connecticut (1965).

Roth v. _U.S._ **(1970)** Declared that obscenity was unprotected by the free-speech guarantee of the First Amendment on the ground that it is "utterly without redeeming social importance."

Schenck v. _U.S._ **(1919)** Upheld the WWI-era Espionage Act and laid out the "clear and present danger" test to determine the limits of First Amendment protection of political speech.

Standard Oil Company of New Jersey v. _U.S._ **(1911)** Held that the Sherman Antitrust Act applied only when trusts "unreasonably" hindered competition; this "rule of reason" became the test for the legality of a monopoly.

Texas v. _Johnson_ **(1989)** Defined flag burning as "symbolic" speech that was protected under the 1st Amendment; Congress then passed the Flag Protection Act, which the Court invalidated in _U.S._ v. _Eichman_ **(1990)**.

_U.S._ v. _Darby Lumber Co._ **(1941)** Interpreted the commerce powers of Congress broadly in upholding minimum-wage and maximum-hour laws, overturning _Hammer_ v. _Dagenhart_ (1918).

_U.S._ v. _Wong Kim Ark_ **(1898)** Upheld the principle, based on the 14th Amendment, that anyone born in the United States is a citizen, overturning a California law barring citizenship to those of Chinese descent.

Webster v. _Reproductive Health Services_ **(1989)** Case in which the Court declared constitutional a Missouri law limiting the use of public money and facilities for abortion; the decision indicated that the Court was open to revisions of _Roe_ v. _Wade_ (1973).

West Virginia State Board of Education v. _Barnette_ **(1943)** Jehovah's Witness case that upheld a refusal to salute the American flag as a protected right to free expression under the 1st Amendment; overturned _Minersville School District_ v. _Gobitis_ **(1940)**.

Youngstown Sheet & Tube Co. v. _Sawyer_ **(1952)** Rejected the claim of President Truman of authority to take control of private companies for national security reasons because Congress held the authority to intervene in labor disputes and the power to seize private property.

⊙ Brinkley, Allan. _American History, A Survey._ 10th ed. New York: McGraw Hill, 1999.
  U.S. Supreme Court Reports. _The Decisions of the United States Supreme Court._ Charlottesville, Va.: U.S. Supreme Court Reports, 1997.
  Virginia Foundation for the Humanities and Public Policy. _The Bill of Rights, the Courts & Law: The Landmark Cases That Have Shaped American Society._ Charlottesville, Va.: Virginia Foundation for the Humanities and Public Policy, 1999.

Structure of the Federal Courts

Supreme Court

The Supreme Court, the highest court in the federal judiciary, consists of the Chief Justice of the United States and eight associate justices. As decreed by the Constitution, the Supreme Court hears a limited number of cases, usually those that involve questions about interpretation of the Constitution or federal law.

Trial Courts

Congress established two levels of courts beneath the Supreme Court, the trial and the appellate courts. The trial courts consist of the U.S. District Courts, the Bankruptcy Courts, the U.S. Court of International Trade, and the U.S. Court of Federal Claims. There are ninety-four federal judicial districts, with at least one in each state, the District of Columbia, and Puerto Rico. The U.S. Court of International Trade addresses cases involving trade and customs issues, while the U.S. Court of Federal Claims has jurisdiction over most claims for money damages and other claims against the United States.

Appellate Courts

The appellate courts consist of twelve regional Circuit Courts of Appeals, and one U.S. Court of Appeals for the Federal Circuit. Each of the twelve appellate courts can hear cases appealed from the Federal Trial Courts. The Court of Appeals for the Federal Circuit hears appeals in special cases, such as those involving patent law and cases decided by the Court of International Trade and the Court of Federal Claims.

Other Federal Courts

Beneath the Appellate and Trial Courts are the Military Courts, the Court of Veterans Appeals, the U.S. Tax Court, and various federal administrative agencies and boards.

⊙ The U.S. Federal Judiciary. "Understanding the Federal Courts," www.uscourts.gov/about.html
   Federal Judiciary Center. *The Federal Courts and What They Do.* Washington, D.C.: Federal Judiciary
      Center, 1997.
   Federal Judiciary Center. *Understanding the Federal Courts.* Washington, D.C.: Federal Judiciary Center,
      1999.

Types of Crime

The Federal Bureau of Investigation collects crime data from local law-enforcement agencies under the following definitions.

Aggravated Assault: An unlawful attack by one person upon another for the purpose of inflicting severe or aggravated bodily injury. This type of assault is usually accompanied by the use of a weapon or by means likely to produce death or great bodily harm.

Arson: Any willful or malicious burning or attempt to burn, with or without intent to defraud, a dwelling house, public building, motor vehicle or aircraft, personal property of another, etc.

Assault (simple): To knowingly or recklessly cause or attempt to cause physical harm to another, but without use of a weapon

Burglary: Unlawful entry of a structure to commit a felony or a theft

Disorderly Conduct: Any unlawful breach of the peace

Driving under the Influence: Driving or operating any vehicle while drunk or under the influence of liquor or narcotics

Drug Abuse Violations: Violations of state and local laws relating to the unlawful possession, sale, use, growing, manufacturing, and making of narcotic drugs, including opium or cocaine and their derivatives (morphine, heroin, codeine); marijuana; synthetic narcotics (Demerol, methadone); and dangerous non-narcotic drugs (barbiturates, Benzedrine)

Drunkenness: Offenses relating to drunkenness or intoxication, not including "driving under the influence"

Embezzlement: The misappropriation or misapplication of money or property entrusted to one's care, custody, or control

Forgery and Counterfeiting: Making, altering, uttering, or possessing, with intent to defraud; anything false that resembles that which is true (e.g. a document or monetary note)

Fraud: Converting or obtaining money or property by false pretense, including confidence games and the use of bad checks

Gambling: Promoting, permitting, or engaging in illegal gambling

Hate Crime: Also called bias crime, a criminal offense committed against a person, property, or society that is motivated, in whole or in part, by the offender's bias against a race, religion, ethnic/national origin group, or sexual-orientation group

Larceny-Theft: Unlawful taking of property from the possession or constructive possession of another; includes shoplifting, pocket picking, purse snatching, thefts from motor vehicles, thefts of motor vehicle parts and accessories, and bicycle thefts

Liquor Law Violations: Violations of laws or ordinances prohibiting the manufacture, sale, transporting, furnishing, or possessing of intoxicating liquor

Manslaughter by Negligence: The death of a person through another person or organization's act of gross negligence

Motor Vehicle Theft: Theft or attempted theft of a motor vehicle

Murder and Non-negligent Manslaughter: Willful (non-negligent) killing of one human being by another

Non-forcible Rape: Unlawful but unforced sexual conduct; includes the crimes of incest and statutory rape

Offenses against the Family and Children: Nonsupport, neglect, desertion, or abuse of family and children

Prostitution and Commercialized Vice: Sex offenses of a commercialized nature, such as prostitution, procuring, or transporting women for immoral purposes

Rape: Carnal knowledge of a person, forcibly and against that person's will; in non-forcible rape, the victim is incapable of giving consent because of a temporary or permanent mental or physical incapacity or because of his/her youth

Robbery: Taking or attempting to take anything of value from the care, custody, or control of a person or persons by force or threat of force or violence and/or by putting the victim in fear

Sex Offenses: Statutory rape and offenses against chastity, common decency, morals, and the like, including voyeurism, forcible sodomy, and forcible fondling

Stolen Property: Buying, Receiving, Possessing: Knowingly buying, receiving, and possessing stolen property

Vandalism: Willful or malicious destruction, injury, disfigurement, or defacement of any public or private property, real or personal, without consent of the owner or persons having custody or control

Types of Crime *(cont.)*

Weapons Law Violations: Violation of laws or ordinances dealing with regulatory weapons offenses, including unlawful manufacturing, selling, or possession of deadly weapons; carrying deadly weapons, concealed or openly; and furnishing deadly weapons to minors

⊙ Federal Bureau of Investigation. "Uniform Crime Reporting Handbook," www.fbi.gov/ucr/Cius_98/98crime/98cius05.pdf
  Federal Bureau of Investigation. "Uniform Crime Reports," www.fbi.gov/ucr.htm

Patents and Copyrights

The United States Patent and Trademark Office was established under Article 1, section 8 of the United States Constitution. Its main purpose is to "promote the progress of science and the useful arts by securing for limited times to inventors the exclusive right to their respective discoveries."
The office itself is part of the Department of Commerce and since 1991 it has operated as a private business, providing patents, trademarks, and patent information for fees that are used to fund day-to-day operations.

A large part of the duties of the Patent Office is the issuing of trademarks and copyrights. Copyright is a form of protection given to authors of "original works" that include literary, dramatic, musical, artistic, and other intellectual works. Copyright law allows the owner of the copyright to authorize others to reproduce the work, produce derivative works, to distribute copies of the work, perform or display the work publicly, and in the case of sound recordings to perform them publicly by means of digital audio transmission. If the owner of the copyright does not authorize any of the above activities, it is illegal for anyone to violate that authorization and produce the work. There are, however, limitations on copyright law that can allow for specific exemptions from copyright liability.

Copyright protection, unlike the indefinite protection a patent can offer, cannot extend indefinitely. In this case, a work that is created on or after January 1, 1978, is protected from the moment of creation and is given protection through the author's life and an additional 70 years after the author's death. For works created and registered before 1978, there are different rules that sustain copyright for 95 years.

Patent law is a complex procedure that categorizes different kinds of inventions into various groups. Different offices examine each application to ascertain if the product is, in fact, original. The law then protects the item and its creator(s) from fraudulent claims of ownership. A patent lawyer is well versed the laws protecting patented items.

To obtain more information or to register for copyright, the Library of Congress may be contacted by telephone (202-707-3000) or fax (202-707-2600), or regular mail:

Library of Congress
Copyright Office
Publications Section, LM-455
101 Independence Avenue, SE
Washington, D.C. 20559-6000

The United States Patent and Trademark office can be reached by telephone (800-786-9199 or 703-308-4375) or regular mail:

Commissioner for Patents and Trademarks
United States Patent and Trademark Office
Washington, D.C. 20231

⊙ Library of Congress. "U.S. Copyright Office Home Page," www.loc.gov/copyright
  United States Patent and Trademark Office. www.uspto.gov

UNITED STATES: *Military*

Branches of the Armed Forces

The Department of Defense is a Cabinet-level organization charged with deterring war and preserving America's national security. Its major branches are the Departments of the Air Force, Army, and Navy. The Marine Corps is a separate armed service within the Department of the Navy. The Coast Guard reports to the Department of the Navy in wartime; normally it is under the jurisdiction of the Department of Transportation.

Military operations are coordinated by the Joint Chiefs of Staff, the chairman of which is the principal military advisor to the president. Field operations are directed by one or more of the nine Unified Combatant Commands.

⊙ U.S. Department of Defense. "DOD at a Glance," www.defenselink.mil/pubs/almanac/

Military Branches: Structure and Strength

Conventional Force Structure Summary, Fiscal Year 2000

Force	Number	Troop Strength
Army		
Active Corps	4	Active: 480,000
Divisions (Active/National Guard)	10/8	Nat'l Guard: 350,000
Active Armored Cavalry Regiments	2	Reserve: 205,000
Enhanced Separate Brigades (National Guard)	15	
Separate Brigades (National Guard)	3	
Navy		
Aircraft Carriers	12	
Air Wings (Active/Reserve)	10/1	Active: 371,300
Amphibious Ready Groups	12	Reserve: 89,600
Attack Submarines	55	
Ballistic Missile Submarines	18	
Logistics Force Ships/Support Force	59	
Mine Warfare Ships (Active/Reserve)	11/5	
Surface Combatants (Active/Reserve)	108/8	
Air Force		
Active Fighter Wings	12+	Active: 354,400
Reserve Fighter Wings	7+	Air Nat'l Guard: 160,700
Reserve Air Defense Squadrons	4	Reserve: 73,900
Bombers (Total Inventory)*	190	
Marine Corps		
Marine Expeditionary Forces	3	Active: 172,000
Divisions (Active/Reserve)	3/1	Reserve: 39,500
Air Wings (Active/Reserve)	3/1	
Force Service Support Groups (Active/Reserve)	3/1	

*Reflects intended reduction of 18 B–52 aircraft.

⊙ Annual Report of the Secretary of Defense (FY 2000). "Chapter 5," www.dtic.mil/execsec/adr2000/chap5.html

Annual Report of the Secretary of Defense (FY 2000). "Appendix C-1," www.dtic.mil.execsec/adr2000/toc.html

(As of May 31, 1999)

Pay grades are levels of compensation that have been standardized across the services. O = commissioned Officer. W = Warrant officer. E = Enlisted personnel. Some E-level pay grades encompass two ranks.

Pay Grade	Army Title	No.	Air Force Title	No.	Navy Title	No.	Marine Corps Title	No.	Total No.
O-10	General	10	General	11	General	9	General	4	34
O-9	Lieutenant General	45	Lieutenant General	36	Vice Admiral	24	Lieutenant General	11	116
O-8	Major General	98	Major General	87	Rear Admiral, Upper Half	73	Major General	25	283
O-7	General	154	General	139	Rear Admiral, Lower Half; Commodore	112		40	445
O-6	Colonel	3,558	Colonel	3,999	Captain	3,254	Colonel	620	11,431
O-5	Lieutenant Colonel	9,091	Lieutenant Colonel	10,409	Commander	7,217	Lieutenant Colonel	1,755	28,472
O-4	Major	14,348	Major	15,859	Lieutenant Commander	10,110	Major	3,393	43,710
O-3	Captain	20,341	Captain	26,216	Lieutenant	17,136	Captain	4,848	68,541
O-2	1st Lieutenant	10,843	1st Lieutenant	7,176	Lieutenant, JG	8,006	1st Lieutenant	3,073	29,098
O-1	2nd Lieutenant	7,917	2nd Lieutenant	5,707	Ensign	6,232	2nd Lieutenant	2,430	22,286
W-5	Master Warrant Officer 5	357	Warrant Officer 5	96					453
W-4	Chief Warrant Officer 4	1,427	—	—	Chief Warrant Officer	415	Warrant Officer 4	265	2,107
W-3	Chief Warrant Officer 3	3,074	—	—	Chief Warrant Officer	498	Warrant Officer 3	452	4,024
W-2	Chief Warrant Officer 2	5,073	—	—	Chief Warrant Officer	756	Warrant Officer 2	692	6,521
W-1	Chief Warrant Officer 1	1,823	—	—	—	—	Warrant Officer 1	431	2,254
Total Officers		78,159		69,639		53,842		18,135	219,775

Grade	Army		Air Force		Navy		Marines		Total
E-9	Sergeant Major; Command Master Sergeant	3,220	Chief Master Sergeant; 1st Sergeant	2,960	Master Chief Petty Officer	2,908	Master Gunnery Sergeant; Sergeant/Sergeant Major	1,287	10,375
E-8	Master Sergeant; 1st Sergeant	10,609	Sr. Master Sergeant; 1st Sergeant	5,955	Sr. Chief Petty Officer	6,094	Master Sergeant; 1st Sergeant	3,491	26,149
E-7	Sergeant 1st Class	38,136	Master Sergeant	28,901	Chief Petty Officer	23,338	Gunnery Sergeant	8,646	99,021
E-6	Staff Sergeant	54,720	Technical Sergeant	39,396	Petty Officer 1st Class	54,572	Staff Sergeant	14,959	163,647
E-5	Sergeant	69,871	Staff Sergeant	70,925	Petty Officer 2nd Class	67,983	Sergeant	23,241	232,020
E-4	Specialist Corporal	110,021	Senior Airman; Sergeant	65,280	Petty Officer 3rd Class	63,402	Corporal	30,328	269,031
E-3	Private 1st Class	52,112	Airman 1st Class	46,274	Seaman	47,791	Lance Corporal	40,453	186,630
E-2	Private 2	33,320	Airman	16,180	Seaman Apprentice	23,976	Private 1st Class	20,378	93,854
E-1	Private	14,464	Airman Basic	10,866	Seaman Recruit	16,503	Private	9,811	53,644
Total Enlisted		386,473		286,737		308,567		152,594	1,134,371
Cadets & Midshipmen		3,125		3,840		4,096		—	11,061
Grand Total		467,757		360,216		366,505		170,729	1,365,207

⊙ U.S. Department of Defense. "Active Duty Military Personnel By Rank/Grade," www.defenselink.mil/pubs/almanac/

Historical Conflicts: Statistics

Conflict (a)	Number Serving	Battle Deaths	Other Deaths (b)	Wounded, not Fatal (c)
Revolutionary War, 1775–83				
Total	184,000–250,000 (est.)	4,435		6,188
Army		4,044		6,004
Navy		342		114
Marines		49		70
War of 1812, 1812–15				
Total	286,730	2,260		4,505
Army		1,950		4,000
Navy		265		439
Marines		45		66
Mexican War, 1846–48				
Total	78,718	1,733	11,550	4,152
Army		1,721	11,550	4,102
Navy		1		3
Marines		11		47
Civil War, 1861–65				
Union Forces				
Total	2,213,363	140,414	224,097	281,881
Army	2,128,948	138,154	221,374	280,040
Navy		2,112	2,411	1,710
Marines	84,415	148	312	131
Confederate Forces				
Total	600,000–1,500,000 (est.)	74,524	59,297	
Spanish-American War, 1898				
Total	306,760	385	2,061	1,662
Army	280,564	369	2,061	1,594
Navy	22,875	10		47
Marines	3,321	6		21
World War I, 1917–18				
Total	4,734,991	53,402	63,114	204,002
Army (inc. Air Corps)	4,057,101	50,510	55,868	193,663
Navy	599,051	431	6,856	819
Marines	78,839	2,461	390	9,520

World War II, 1941–46 (d)

Total	16,112,566	291,557	113,842	671,846
Army	11,260,000 (inc. Air Corps)	234,874	83,400	565,861
Navy	4,183,466	36,950	25,664	37,778
Marines	669,100	19,733	4,778	68,207

Korean Conflict, 1950–53

Total	5,720,000	33,651	3,262	103,284
Army	2,834,000	27,709	2,452	77,596
Navy	1,177,000	475	173	1,576
Marines	424,000	4,269	339	23,744
Air Force	1,285,000	1,198	298	368

Vietnam Conflict, 1964–73

Total	8,744,000	47,378	10,799	153,303
Army	4,368,000	30,922	7,273	96,802
Navy	1,842,000	1,631	931	4,178
Marines	794,000	13,084	1,753	51,392
Air Force	1,740,000	1,741	842	931

(a) Data prior to World War I are based on incomplete records in many cases. Casualty data are confined to dead and wounded and, therefore, exclude personnel captured or missing in action who were subsequently returned to military control.

(b) For example, disease, accident, etc.

(c) Marine Corps data for World War II, the Spanish-American War, and prior wars represent the number of individuals wounded, whereas all other data in this column represent the total number (incidence) of wounds.

(d) Data are for the period December 1, 1941, through December 31, 1946, when hostilities were officially terminated by Presidential Proclamation, but few battle deaths or wounds not mortal were incurred after the Japanese acceptance of the Allied peace terms on August 14, 1945. Number serving from December 1, 1941, through August 31, 1945: Total–14,903,213; Army–10,420,000; Navy–3,883,520; and Marine Corps–599,693.

⊙ U.S. Department of Defense. "Principal Wars in Which the United States Participated, U.S. Military Personnel Serving and Casualties," http://web1.whs.osd.mil/mmid/m01/SMS223R.HTM

Recent Conflicts: Statistics

Military Operation/Incident	Casualty Type	Army	Navy	Air Force	Marine Corps	Total
Iranian Hostage Rescue Mission April 25, 1980	Nonhostile	0	0	5	3	8
Lebanon Peacekeeping August 25, 1982– February 26, 1984						
	Hostile	3	19	0	234	256
	Nonhostile	5	2	0	2	9
	Total	8	21	0	236	265

Recent Conflicts: Statistics

Military Operation/Incident	Casualty Type	Army	Navy	Air Force	Marine Corps	Total
Urgent Fury, Grenada, 1983						
	Hostile	11	4	0	3	18
	Nonhostile	1				1
	Total	12	4	0	3	19
Just Cause, Panama, 1989						
	Hostile	18	4	0	1	23
Persian Gulf War, 1990–91						
Desert Shield	Nonhostile	21	36	9	18	84
Desert Storm	Hostile	98	6	20	24	148
	Nonhostile	105	14	6	26	151
	Total	203	20	26	50	299
Desert Shield/Storm						
	Total	224	56	35	68	383
Restore Hope/UNOSOM, Somalia 1992–94						
	Hostile	27	0	0	2	29
	Nonhostile	4	0	8	2	14
	Total	31	0	8	4	43
Uphold Democracy, Haiti 1994–96						
	Nonhostile	3	0	0	1	4

Note: "Nonhostile" casualties are those not directly caused by enemy action.

⊙ U.S. Army. "Worldwide U.S. Active Duty Military Deaths, Selected Military Operations," http://web1.whs.osd.mil/mmid/casualty/table13.htm

Veterans' and Retirees' Organizations

American Gulf War Veterans Association
P.O. Box 85
Versailles, MO 65084
800-231-7631
www.gulfwarvets.com
webmaster@golfwarvets.com

American Legion*
Indianapolis Office
700 North Pennsylvania Street
P.O. Box 1055
Indianapolis, IN 46206
Phone: (317) 630-1200
Fax: (317) 630-1223
www.legion.org
pr@legion.org

Washington Office
1608 K Street, NW
Washington, D.C. 20006
Phone: (202) 861-2700
Fax: (202) 861-2728
www.legion.org

AMVETS*

4647 Forbes Boulevard
Lanham, MD 20706-4380
(877) 726-8387 (877-7AMVETS)
www.amvets.org

Disabled American Veterans*

P.O. Box 14301
Cincinnati, OH 45250-0301
www.dav.org

American Military Retirees Association

22 U.S. Oval, Suite 1200
Plattsburgh, NY 12903
(518) 563-9479
www.amra1973.org
infoamra1973@westelcom.com

Korean War Veterans Association

P.O. Box 10806
Arlington, VA 22210
(703) 522-9629
www.kwva.org

Military Order of the Purple Heart*

5413-B Backlick Road
Springfield, VA 22151-3960
(703) 642-5360
www.purpleheart.org
info@purpleheart.org

Military Order of the World Wars*

435 North Lee Street
Alexandria, VA 22314
(703) 683-4911
www.militaryorder.org

National Association for Black Veterans*

P.O. Box 11432
Milwaukee, WI 53211-0432
800-842-4597
www.execpc.com/~nabvets

National Association for Uniformed Services

5535 Hempstead Way
Springfield, VA 22151
(703) 750-1342
www.naus.org

National Veterans Legal Services Program, Inc.*

2001 S Street, NW, Suite 610
Washington, D.C. 20009
Phone (202) 265-8305, Ext. 105
www.nvlsp.org
nvlsp@nvlsp.org

National Veterans Organization of America

7700 Alabama Street
P.O. Box 640064
El Paso, TX 79904-0064
(915) 759-8387
www.nvo.org

The Retired Enlisted Association*

1111 S. Abilene Court
Aurora, CO 80012
800-338-9337
(303) 752-0660
www.trea.org

The Retired Officers Association (TROA)

201 N. Washington Street
Alexandria, VA 22314
800-245-TROA
www.troa.org

United Armed Forces Association

P.O. Box 20672
Waco, TX 76702
888-457-7667

Veterans News and Information Service

38620 Pleasant Avenue, #B
Sandy, OR 97055-9348
www.vnis.org

Veterans of Foreign Wars of the United States*

406 West 34th Street
Kansas City, MO 64111
(816) 756-3390
www.vfw.org
info@vfw.org

Veterans' and Retirees' Organizations *(cont.)*

Veterans Resource Network Association

P.O. Box 3011
Frazer, PA 19355-9778
877-848-VRNA (8762)
www.vrna.org

Vietnam Veterans of America*

8605 Cameron Street, Suite 400
Silver Spring, MD 20910-3710
Phone: (301) 585-4000
Fax: (301) 585-0519
www.vva.org
communications@vva.org

*These organizations have been chartered by Congress and/or recognized by the Veterans Administration to
represent veterans' claims.

⊙ Veterans Administration. "Veterans Service Organizations," www.va.gov/vso.view.asp
Military.com. "Veteran and Retiree Organizations," http://military.com/UnReg/Association/
?aType=veterans

Service Academies

Army:

United States Military Academy
Attn: Public Affairs Office
Taylor Hall, Bldg. 600
West Point, NY 10996-1788
(914) 938-4261 www.usma.edu

Navy:

United States Naval Academy
Attn: Public Affairs Officer
121 Blake Road
Annapolis, MD 21402-5000
(410) 267-2291 www.nadn.navy.mil

Air Force:

United States Air Force Academy
Attn: Public Affairs Officer
2304 Cadet Drive, Suite 320
U.S. Air Force Academy, CO 80840-5016
(719) 472-2990 www.usafa.af.mil

Coast Guard:

United States Coast Guard Academy*
Attn: Public Affairs Officer
15 Mohegan Avenue
New London, CT 06320-4195
(203) 444-8270 www.cga.edu

United States Merchant Marine Academy**

Attn: Public Affairs Officer
300 Steamboat Road
Kings Point, NY 11024
(516) 773-5000 www.usmma.edu

*The Coast Guard reports to the Department of the Navy in wartime; normally it is under the jurisdiction of
the Department of Transportation.
**The Merchant Marine Academy works closely with the U.S. armed forces, but is not a Defense Department
organization.

⊙ U.S. Department of Defense. "Military Service Academies," www.defenselink.mil/faq/pis/20.html

Largest Islands

Island	Area sq. mi. (sq. km.)	Location
Kodiak Island	5,363 (13,890)	Alaska, in Gulf of Alaska
Hawaii	4,021 (10,414)	Hawaii
Prince of Wales Island	2,587 (6,700)	Alaska, Alexander Archipelago
Chichagof Island	2,062 (5,340)	Alaska, Alexander Archipelago
St. Lawrence Island	1,712 (4,434)	Alaska, in Bering Sea
Admiralty Island	1,650 (4,273)	Alaska, Alexander Archipelago
Nunivak Island	1,625 (4,209)	Alaska, in Bering Sea
Baranof Island	1,600 (4,144)	Alaska, Alexander Archipelago
Unimak	1,600 (4,144)	Alaska, Aleutian Islands
Long Island	1,401 (3,628)	New York
Revillagigedo Island	1,145 (2,965)	Alaska, Alexander Archipelago
Kupreanof Island	1,084 (2,807)	Alaska, Alexander Archipelago
Unalaska	1,064 (2,755)	Alaska, Aleutian Islands
Nelson Island	843 (2,183)	Alaska
Kuiu Island	750 (1,942)	Alaska
Maui	727 (1,883)	Hawaii
Afognak	721 (1,867)	Alaska
Umnak	675 (1,748)	Alaska, Aleutian Islands
Oahu	597 (1,546)	Hawaii
Kauai	555 (1,437)	Hawaii
Atka Island	422 (1,093)	Alaska, Aleutian Islands
Attu Island	338 (875)	Alaska, Aleutian Islands
Montague Island	315 (816)	Alaska
Adak Island	289 (748)	Alaska, Aleutian Islands
Dall Island	260 (673)	Alaska, Alexander Archipelago
Molokai	260 (673)	Hawaii
Wrangell Island	217 (562)	Alaska
Mitkof Island	213 (551)	Alaska
Isle Royale	209 (541)	Michigan, in Lake Superior
Tanaga Island	209 (541)	Alaska, Aleutian Islands
Zarembo Island	180 (466)	Alaska
Whidbey Island	172 (445)	Washington, in Puget Sound
Lanai	141 (365)	Hawaii
Drummond Island	134 (347)	Michigan, in Lake Huron
Marsh Island	117 (303)	Louisiana

Largest Islands *(cont.)*

Island	Area sq. mi. (sq. km.)	Location
Martha's Vineyard	108 (279)	Massachusetts
Mount Desert Island	106 (274)	Maine, part of Acadia National Park
Santa Cruz Island	96 (248)	California, Santa Barbara Islands
Niihau	70 (181)	Hawaii
Nantucket	57 (148)	Massachusetts
Padre Island	46 (119)	Texas
Kahoolawe	45 (117)	Hawaii
Antelope Island	39 (101)	Utah, in Great Salt Lake
Rhode Island	39 (101)	Rhode Island, in Narragansett Bay
Madeline Island	24 (62)	Wisconsin, in Lake Superior
Manhattan	23 (60)	New York

⊙ Wright, John W., ed. *The New York Times Almanac, Millennium Edition.* New York: Penguin, 1999.

North American Deserts

Desert	Type	Location	Area sq. mi. (sq. km.)	Sub-deserts
Great Basin	Cold	Nevada; parts of Idaho, Oregon, California, and Utah	189,000 (489,500)	Black Rock, Escalante, Great Sandy, Red, Sevier, Smoke Creek
Chihuahuan	Hot	Mexico; parts of southern New Mexico, southeast Arizona, and west Texas	175,000 (450,000)	Trans-Pecos
Sonoran	Hot	Southwest Arizona, southeast California, Baja Peninsula, northwest Mexico	120,000 (310,800)	Arizona Upland, Borrego, Colorado, Magdalena, Vizcaino, Yuha, Yuma
Mojave	Hot	between the Great Basin and Sonoran deserts; southern California, southern Nevada, northwest Arizona	25,000 (64,750)	Northern Mojave, Southern Mojave, Death Valley

⊙ Desert USA, "Desert Life in the American Southwest," www.desertusa.com/life.html

UNITED STATES: *Geography*

Highest Mountains

Mountain	Height ft. (m.)	State	Mountain	Height ft. (m.)	State
Mount McKinley	20,320 (6,193)	Alaska	Mount Shavano	14,229 (4,337)	Colorado
Mount St. Elias	18,008 (5,488)	Alaska	Crestone Needle	14,197 (4,327)	Colorado
Mount Foraker	17,400 (5,303)	Alaska	Mount Belford	14,197 (4,327)	Colorado
Mount Bona	16,500 (5,029)	Alaska	Mount Princeton	14,197 (4,327)	Colorado
Mount Blackburn	16,390 (4,995)	Alaska	Mount Yale	14,196 (4,327)	Colorado
Mount Sanford	16,237 (4,949)	Alaska	Mount Bross	14,172 (4,319)	Colorado
Mount Vancouver	15,979 (4,870)	Alaska	Kit Carson Mountain	14,165 (4,317)	Colorado
South Buttress	15,885 (4,841)	Alaska	Mount Wrangell	14,163 (4,316)	Alaska
Mount Churchill	15,638 (4,766)	Alaska	Mount Sill	14,163 (4,316)	California
Mount Fairweather	15,300 (4,663)	Alaska	Mount Shasta	14,162 (4,316)	California
Mount Hubbard	14,950 (4,556)	Alaska	El Diente Peak	14,159 (4,315)	Colorado
Mount Bear	14,831 (4,520)	Alaska	Point Success	14,158 (4,315)	Washington
East Buttress	14,730 (4,489)	Alaska	Maroon Peak	14,156 (4,314)	Colorado
Mount Hunter	14,537 (4,430)	Alaska	Tabeguache Mountain	14,155 (4,314)	Colorado
Browne Tower	14,530 (4,428)	Alaska			
Mount Alverstone	14,500 (4,419)	Alaska	Mount Oxford	14,153 (4,313)	Colorado
Mount Whitney	14,494 (4,417)	California	Mount Sill	14,153 (4,313)	California
University Peak	14,470 (4,410)	Alaska	Mount Sneffels	14,150 (4,312)	Colorado
Mount Elbert	14,433 (4,399)	Colorado	Mount Democrat	14,148 (4,312)	Colorado
Mount Massive	14,421 (4,395)	Colorado	Capitol Peak	14,130 (4,306)	Colorado
Mount Harvard	14,420 (4,395)	Colorado	Liberty Cap	14,112 (4,301)	Washington
Mount Rainier	14,410 (4,392)	Washington	Pikes Peak	14,110 (4,300)	Colorado
Mount Williamson	14,370 (4,380)	California	Snowmass Mountain	14,092 (4,295)	Colorado
La Plata Peak	14,361 (4,377)	Colorado			
Blanca Peak	14,345 (4,372)	Colorado	Mount Russell	14,088 (4,294)	California
Uncompahgre Peak	14,309 (4,361)	Colorado	Mount Eolus	14,083 (4,292)	Colorado
Crestone Peak	14,294 (4,356)	Colorado	Windom Peak	14,082 (4,292)	Colorado
Mount Lincoln	14,286 (4,354)	Colorado	Mount Columbia	14,073 (4,289)	Colorado
Grays Peak	14,270 (4,349)	Colorado	Mount Augusta	14,070 (4,288)	Alaska
Mount Antero	14,269 (4,349)	Colorado	Missouri Mountain	14,067 (4,287)	Colorado
Torreys Peak	14,267 (4,348)	Colorado	Humboldt Peak	14,064 (4,286)	Colorado
Castle Peak	14,265 (4,348)	Colorado	Mount Bierstadt	14,060 (4,285)	Colorado
Quandary Peak	14,265 (4,348)	Colorado	Sunlight Peak	14,059 (4,285)	Colorado
Mount Evans	14,264 (4,347)	Colorado	Split Mountain	14,058 (4,284)	California
Longs Peak	14,255 (4,345)	Colorado	Handies Peak	14,048 (4,281)	Colorado
Mount Wilson	14,246 (4,342)	Colorado	Culebra Peak	14,047 (4,281)	Colorado
White Mountain	14,246 (4,342)	California	Mount Lindsey	14,042 (4,280)	Colorado
North Palisade	14,242 (4,341)	California	Ellingwood Point	14,042 (4,280)	Colorado
Mount Cameron	14,238 (4,339)	Colorado	Middle Palisade	14,040 (4,279)	California
			Little Bear Peak	14,037 (4,278)	Colorado

Highest Mountains *(cont.)*

Mountain	Height ft. (m.)	State	Mountain	Height ft. (m.)	State
Mount Sherman	14,036 (4,278)	Colorado	North Maroon Peak	14,014 (4,271)	Colorado
Redcloud Peak	14,034 (4,277)	Colorado	San Luis Peak	14,014 (4,271)	Colorado
Mount Langley	14,027 (4,275)	California	Middle Palisade	14,012 (4,270)	California
Conundrum Peak	14,022 (4,274)	Colorado	Mount Muir	14,012 (4,270)	California
Mount Tyndall	14,019 (4,273)	California	Mount of the Holy Cross	14,005 (4,268)	Colorado
Pyramid Peak	14,018 (4,272)	Colorado			
Wilson Peak	14,017 (4,272)	Colorado	Huron Peak	14,003 (4,268)	Colorado
Wetterhorn Peak	14,015 (4,271)	Colorado	Thunderbolt Peak	14,003 (4,268)	California
			Sunshine Peak	14,001 (4,267)	Colorado

Other Notable Mountains

Mountain	Height ft. (m.)	State	Mountain	Height ft. (m.)	State
Grand Teton	13,766 (4,195)	Wyoming	Mount Rushmore	5,600 (1,706)	South Dakota
Mount Mitchell	6,684 (2,037)	North Carolina	Mount Marcy	5,344 (1,628)	New York
Mount Washington	6,288 (1,916)	New Hampshire	Mount Katahdin	5,268 (1,605)	Maine

⊙ *The World Almanac and Book of Facts, 2000: Millennium Collector's Edition.* Mahwah, N.J.: World Almanac Books, 1999.

Largest Lakes

Lake	Area sq. mi. (sq. km.)	Location
Superior	31,800 (82,362)	Michigan; Wisconsin; Minnesota; Ontario, Canada
Huron	23,000 (59,570)	Michigan; Canada
Michigan	22,400 (58,000)	Michigan; Indiana; Illinois; Wisconsin
Erie	9,910 (25,666)	New York; Pennsylvania; Ohio; Michigan; Canada
Ontario	7,600 (19,684)	New York; Canada
Great Salt Lake	2,000 (5,180)	Utah
Lake of the Woods	1,695 (4,390)	Minnesota; Canada
Iliamna	1,033 (2,675)	Alaska
Okeechobee	730 (1,890)	Florida
Pontchartrain	630 (1,632)	Louisiana
Becharof	458 (1,186)	Alaska
Red Lake	451 (1,168)	Minnesota
St. Clair	450 (1,150)	Michigan; Canada
Champlain	430 (1,114)	New York; Vermont; Canada
Salton Sea	360 (932)	California

UNITED STATES: *Geography*

Mead	227 (588)	Arizona; Nevada
Winnebago	215 (557)	Wisconsin
Tahoe	192 (497)	California; Nevada
Yellowstone	137 (355)	Wyoming
Moosehead	117 (303)	Maine
Owasco	110 (284)	New York

⊙ *The World Almanac and Book of Facts, 2000: Millennium Collector's Edition.* Mahwah, N.J.: World Almanac Books, 1999.

Longest Rivers

River	Length mi. (km.)	Location
Mississippi	3,860 (7,148)	Minnesota-Wisconsin-Iowa-Illinois-Missouri-Kentucky-Tennessee-Arkansas-Mississippi-Louisiana
Missouri	2,466 (4,567)	Montana-North Dakota-South Dakota-Nebraska-Iowa-Missouri-Kansas-Missouri
Yukon	1,979 (3,665)	Canada-Alaska
Rio Grande	1,885 (3,491)	Colorado-New Mexico-Texas-Mexico
Arkansas	1,450 (2,685)	Colorado-Kansas-Oklahoma-Arkansas
Colorado	1,450 (2,685)	Colorado-Utah-Arizona-Nevada-California-Mexico
Columbia	1,214 (2,248)	British Columbia-Washington-Oregon
Snake	1,038 (1,922)	Wyoming-Idaho-Oregon-Washington
Red	1,018 (1,885)	New Mexico-Texas-Oklahoma-Arkansas-Louisiana
Ohio	975 (1,805)	Pennsylvania-Ohio-West Virginia-Kentucky-Indiana-Illinois
Canadian	906 (1,678)	Colorado-New Mexico-Texas-Oklahoma
Brazos	840 (1,555)	Texas
Colorado	840 (1,555)	Texas
Saint Lawrence	800 (1,287)*	Canada-New York
Kansas (Kaw)	743 (1,376)	Kansas
Green	730 (1,351)	Wyoming-Utah
Dakota (James)	710 (1,314)	North Dakota-South Dakota
Yellowstone	691 (1,279)	Wyoming-Montana
White	690 (1,277)	Arkansas
Cumberland	687 (1,272)	Kentucky-Tennessee-Kentucky
North Platte	680 (1,259)	Colorado-Wyoming-Nebraska
Tennessee	652 (1,207)	Tennessee-Alabama-Tennessee-Kentucky
Milk	625 (1,157)	Montana-Canada-Montana
Ouachita	605 (1,120)	Arkansas-Louisiana
Kuskokwim	600 (1,111)	Alaska
Little Missouri	560 (1,037)	Wyoming-Montana-South Dakota-North Dakota
Trinity	550 (1,018)	Texas
Smoky Hill	540 (1,000)	Colorado-Kansas
Cimarron	500 (926)	New Mexico-Kansas-Oklahoma

River	Length mi. (km.)	Location
Gila	500 (926)	New Mexico-Arizona
Koyukuk	500 (926)	Alaska
Osage	500 (926)	Missouri
Pecos	500 (926)	New Mexico-Texas
Washita	500 (926)	Texas-Oklahoma
Pearl	490 (907)	Mississippi-Louisiana
Tanana	475 (879)	Alaska
Wabash	475 (879)	Ohio-Indiana-Illinois
Neosho (Grand)	460 (851)	Kansas-Oklahoma
Porcupine	448 (829)	Canada-Alaska
Susquehanna	444 (822)	New York-Pennsylvania-Maryland
North Canadian	440 (814)	Oklahoma
Chattahoochee	436 (807)	Georgia-Alabama-Florida
Niobrara	431 (798)	Wyoming-Nebraska
Wisconsin	430 (796)	Wisconsin
Saint Francis	425 (787)	Missouri-Arkansas
South Platte	424 (785)	Colorado-Nebraska
Republican	422 (781)	Colorado-Nebraska-Kansas
Salmon	420 (777)	Idaho
Roanoke	410 (759)	Virginia-North Carolina
Tombigbee	409 (757)	Mississippi-Alabama
Connecticut	407 (753)	New Hampshire-Vermont-Massachusetts-Connecticut
Noatak	400 (740)	Alaska
Wateree-Catawba	395 (731)	North Carolina-South Carolina
Colville	375 (694)	Alaska
Powder	375 (694)	Wyoming-Montana
Green	360 (666)	Kentucky
Sabine	360 (666)	Texas-Louisiana
San Juan	360 (666)	Colorado-New Mexico-Colorado-Utah
Red River of the North	355 (657)	Minnesota-North Dakota-Canada
San Joaquin	350 (648)	California
James	340 (629)	Virginia
Stikine	335 (620)	Canada-Alaska
Allegheny	325 (601)	Pennsylvania-New York-Pennsylvania
Licking	320 (592)	Kentucky
New	320 (592)	Virginia-West Virginia
Sacramento	320 (592)	California
Alabama	315 (583)	Alabama
Platte	310 (574)	Nebraska
Hudson	306 (566)	New York
Clark Fork	300 (555)	Montana-Idaho
Platte	300 (555)	Iowa-Missouri
Willamette	300 (555)	Oregon

Potomac	287 (531)	West Virginia-Virginia-Maryland-Washington, D.C.
Coosa	286 (529)	Alabama
Delaware	280 (518)	New York-Pennsylvania-New Jersey-Delaware
Illinois	273 (505)	Illinois
Ocmulgee	255 (472)	Georgia
Pee Dee	233 (431)	North Carolina-South Carolina
Yadkin	202 (374)	North Carolina
Santee	143 (264)	South Carolina
Altamaha	137 (253)	Georgia
Pend Oreille	100 (185)	Idaho-Washington-Canada

* not including waterway provided by the Great Lakes

⊙ *The World Almanac and Book of Facts, 2000: Millennium Collector's Edition.* Mahwah, N.J.: World Almanac Books, 1999.

UNITED STATES: *States and Cities*

Date and Order of Admittance

State	Date Admitted	Order	State	Date Admitted	Order
Alabama	Dec. 14, 1819	22	Montana	Nov. 8, 1889	41
Alaska	Jan. 3, 1959	49	Nebraska	Mar. 1, 1867	37
Arizona	Feb. 14, 1912	48	Nevada	Oct. 31, 1864	36
Arkansas	June 15, 1836	25	New Hampshire	June 21, 1788	9
California	Sep. 9, 1850	31	New Jersey	Dec. 18, 1787	3
Colorado	Aug. 1, 1876	38	New Mexico	Jan. 6, 1912	47
Connecticut	Jan. 9, 1788	5	New York	July 26, 1788	11
Delaware	Dec. 7, 1787	1	North Carolina	Nov. 21, 1789	12
Florida	Mar. 3, 1845	27	North Dakota	Nov. 2, 1889	39
Georgia	Jan. 2, 1788	4	Ohio	Mar. 1, 1803	17
Hawaii	Aug. 21, 1959	50	Oklahoma	Nov. 16, 1907	46
Idaho	July 3, 1890	43	Oregon	Feb. 14, 1859	33
Illinois	Dec. 3, 1818	21	Pennsylvania	Dec. 12, 1787	2
Indiana	Dec. 11, 1816	19	Rhode Island	May 29, 1790	13
Iowa	Dec. 28, 1846	29	South Carolina	May 23, 1788	8
Kansas	Jan. 29, 1861	34	South Dakota	Nov. 2, 1889	40
Kentucky	June 1, 1792	15	Tennessee	June 1, 1796	16
Louisiana	Apr. 30, 1812	18	Texas	Dec. 29, 1845	28
Maine	Mar. 15, 1820	23	Utah	Jan. 4, 1896	45
Maryland	Apr. 28, 1788	7	Vermont	Mar. 4, 1791	14
Massachusetts	Feb. 6, 1788	6	Virginia	June 25, 1788	10
Michigan	Jan. 26, 1837	26	Washington	Nov. 11, 1889	42
Minnesota	May 11, 1858	32	West Virginia	June 20, 1863	35
Mississippi	Dec. 10, 1817	20	Wisconsin	May 29, 1848	30
Missouri	Aug. 10, 1821	24	Wyoming	July 10, 1890	44

Capitals and Area

State	Capital	Total Area (land and water) sq. mi. (sq. km.)	Area Rank
Alabama	Montgomery	52,423 (277,317)	30
Alaska	Juneau	656,424 (1,700,130)	1
Arizona	Phoenix	114,006 (295,274)	6
Arkansas	Little Rock	53,182 (137,740)	29
California	Sacramento	163,707 (423,999)	3
Colorado	Denver	104,100 (296,618)	8
Connecticut	Hartford	5,544 (14,359)	48
Delaware	Dover	2,489 (6,446)	49
Florida	Tallahassee	65,758 (170,312)	22
Georgia	Atlanta	59,441 (153,951)	24
Hawaii	Honolulu	10,931 (28,311)	43
Idaho	Boise	83,574 (216,456)	14
Illinois	Springfield	57,918 (150,007)	25
Indiana	Indianapolis	36,420 (94,327)	38
Iowa	Des Moines	56,276 (145,754)	26
Kansas	Topeka	82,282 (213,109)	15
Kentucky	Frankfort	40,411 (104,664)	37
Louisiana	Baton Rouge	51,844 (134,275)	31
Maine	Augusta	35,387 (91,652)	39
Maryland	Annapolis	12,407 (32,134)	42
Massachusetts	Boston	10,555 (27,337)	44
Michigan	Lansing	96,810 (250,737)	11
Minnesota	St. Paul	86,943 (225,181)	12
Mississippi	Jackson	48,934 (126,739)	32
Missouri	Jefferson City	69,709 (180,546)	21
Montana	Helena	147,046 (380,847)	4
Nebraska	Lincoln	77,358 (200,356)	16
Nevada	Carson City	110,567 (286,367)	7
New Hampshire	Concord	9,351 (24,219)	46
New Jersey	Trenton	8,722 (22,590)	47
New Mexico	Santa Fe	123,598 (320,117)	5
New York	Albany	54,475 (140,090)	27
North Carolina	Raleigh	53,821 (139,396)	28
North Dakota	Bismarck	70,704 (183,122)	19
Ohio	Columbus	44,828 (116,104)	34
Oklahoma	Oklahoma City	69,903 (181,048)	20
Oregon	Salem	98,386 (254,819)	9
Pennsylvania	Harrisburg	46,058 (119,290)	33
Rhode Island	Providence	1,545 (4,001)	50
South Carolina	Columbia	32,007 (82,898)	40
South Dakota	Pierre	77,122 (199,745)	17
Tennessee	Nashville	42,146 (109,158)	36

Texas	Austin	268,601 (695,673)	2
Utah	Salt Lake City	84,904 (219,900)	13
Vermont	Montpelier	9,615 (24,903)	45
Virginia	Richmond	42,769 (110,771)	35
Washington	Olympia	71,303 (184,674)	18
West Virginia	Charleston	24,231 (62,758)	41
Wisconsin	Madison	65,503 (169,652)	23
Wyoming	Cheyenne	97,818 (253,347)	10

State Flowers, Birds, and Trees

State	*Flower*	*Bird*	*Tree*
Alabama	Camellia	Yellowhammer	Southern Pine
Alaska	Forget-Me-Not	Willow Ptarmigan	Sitka Spruce
Arizona	Saguaro Blossom	Cactus Wren	Paloverde
Arkansas	Apple Blossom	Mockingbird	Pine
California	Golden Poppy	California Valley Quail	California Redwood
Colorado	Rocky Mtn. Columbine	Lark Bunting	Colorado Blue Spruce
Connecticut	Mountain Laurel	American Robin	White Oak
Delaware	Peach Blossom	Blue Hen Chicken	American Holly
Florida	Orange Blossom	Mockingbird	Sabal Palm
Georgia	Cherokee Rose	Brown Thrasher	Live Oak
Hawaii	Red Hibiscus	Nene (Hawaiian Goose)	Kukui (Candlenut)
Idaho	Syringa (Mock Orange)	Mountain Bluebird	White Pine
Illinois	Native Violet	Cardinal	White Oak
Indiana	Peony	Cardinal	Tulip Poplar
Iowa	Wild Rose	Eastern Goldfinch	Oak
Kansas	Sunflower	Western Meadowlark	Cottonwood
Kentucky	Goldenrod	Cardinal	Tulip Poplar
Louisiana	Magnolia Bloom	Brown Pelican	Bald Cypress
Maine	White Pine Cone & Tassel	Chickadee	Eastern White Pine
Maryland	Black-eyed Susan	Baltimore Oriole	White Oak
Massachusetts	Mayflower	Chickadee	American Elm
Michigan	Apple Blossom	Robin	White Pine
Minnesota	Pink & White Lady's Slipper	Common Loon	Red (Norway)Pine
Mississippi	Magnolia Bloom	Mockingbird	Magnolia
Missouri	Hawthorn Blossom	Eastern Bluebird	Dogwood
Montana	Bitterroot	Western Meadowlark	Ponderosa Pine
Nebraska	Goldenrod	Western Meadowlark	Cottonwood
Nevada	Sagebrush	Mountain Bluebird	Single-leaf Piñon Pine
New Hampshire	Purple Lilac	Purple Finch	White Birch
New Jersey	Purple Violet	Eastern Goldfinch	Red Oak
New Mexico	Yucca	Roadrunner	Piñon

State Flower, Birds, and Trees *(cont.)*

State	Flower	Bird	Tree
New York	Rose	Bluebird	Sugar Maple
North Carolina	Dogwood Blossom	Cardinal	Pine
North Dakota	Wild Prairie Rose	Western Meadowlark	American Elm
Ohio	Scarlet Carnation	Cardinal	Buckeye
Oklahoma	Mistletoe	Scissor-tailed Flycatcher	Redbud
Oregon	Oregon Grape	Western Meadowlark	Douglas Fir
Pennsylvania	Mountain Laurel	Ruffed Grouse	Hemlock
Rhode Island	Violet	Rhode Island Red Hen	Red Maple
South Carolina	Carolina Yellow Jessamine	Carolina Wren	Palmetto
South Dakota	Pasqueflower	Chinese Ring-necked Pheasant	Black Hills Spruce
Tennessee	Iris	Mockingbird	Tulip Poplar
Texas	Bluebonnet	Mockingbird	Pecan
Utah	Sego Lily	Seagull	Blue Spruce
Vermont	Red Clover	Hermit Thrush	Sugar Maple
Virginia	Dogwood Blossom	Cardinal	Dogwood
Washington	Western Rhododendron	Willow Goldfinch	Western Hemlock
West Virginia	Big Rhododendron	Cardinal	Sugar Maple
Wisconsin	Wood Violet	Robin	Sugar Maple
Wyoming	Indian Paintbrush	Meadowlark	Cottonwood

State Mottoes and Nicknames

State	Motto	Nickname
Alabama	We Dare Defend Our Rights	Yellowhammer State; Heart of Dixie
Alaska	North to the Future	The Last Frontier
Arizona	*Diat Deus* (God Enriches)	Grand Canyon State
Arkansas	*Regnat Populus* (The People Rule)	Land of Opportunity
California	*Eureka* (I Have Found It)	Golden State
Colorado	*Nil Sine Numine* (Nothing Without Providence)	Centennial State
Connecticut	*Qui Transtulit Sustinet* (He Who Transplanted Still Sustains)	Constitution State
Delaware	Liberty and Independence	First State; Diamond State
Florida	In God We Trust	Sunshine State
Georgia	Wisdom, Justice, and Moderation	Peach State
Hawaii	The Life of the Land Is Perpetuated in Righteousness	Aloha State
Idaho	*Esto Perpetua* (May It Endure Forever)	Gem State
Illinois	State Sovereignty—National Union	Land of Lincoln; Prairie State
Indiana	Crossroads of America	Hoosier State
Iowa	Our Liberties We Prize and Our Rights We Will Maintain	Hawkeye State

Kansas	*Ad Astra Per Aspera*	Sunflower State
	(To the Stars with Difficulty)	
Kentucky	United We Stand, Divided We Fall	Bluegrass State
Louisiana	Union, Justice, and Confidence	Pelican State
Maine	*Dirigo* (I Direct)	Pine Tree State
Maryland	*Fatti Maschii, Parole Femine*	Old Line State; Free State
	(Manly Deeds, Womanly Words)	
Massachusetts	*Ense Petit Placidam sub Libertate Quietem*	Bay State
	(By the Sword We Seek Peace,	
	But Peace Only Under Liberty)	
Michigan	*Si Quaeris Peninsulam Amoenam Circimspice*	Great Lake State; Wolverine State
	(If You Seek a Pleasant Peninsula,	
	Look About You)	
Minnesota	*L'etoile du Nord*	North Star State; Gopher State
	(The Star of the North)	
Mississippi	*Virtute et Armis* (By Valor and Arms)	Magnolia State
Missouri	*Salus Populi Suprema Lex Esto*	Show-Me State
	(The Welfare of the People Shall Be	
	the Supreme Law)	
Montana	*Oro y Plata* (Gold and Silver)	Big Sky Country; Treasure State
Nebraska	Equality Before the Law	Cornhusker State
Nevada	All for Our Country	Silver State; Sagebrush State
New Hampshire	Live Free or Die	Granite State
New Jersey	Liberty and Prosperity	Garden State
New Mexico	*Crescit Eundo* (It Grows As It Goes)	Land of Enchantment
New York	*Excelsior* (Ever Upward)	Empire State
North Carolina	*Esse Quam Videri* (To Be Rather Than to Seem)	Tarheel State; Old North State
North Dakota	Liberty and Union, Now and Forever, One	Peace Garden State; Flickertail State
	and Inseparable	
Ohio	With God, All Things Are Possible	Buckeye State
Oklahoma	*Labor Omnia Vincit* (Labor Conquers All Things)	Sooner State
Oregon	She Flies with Her Own Wings	Beaver State
Pennsylvania	Virtue, Liberty, and Independence	Keystone State
Rhode Island	Hope	Little Rhody; Ocean State
South Carolina	*Sum Spiro Spero* (While I Breathe, I Hope)	Palmetto State
South Dakota	Under God, the People Rule	Mount Rushmore State;
		Coyote State; Sunshine State
Tennessee	Agriculture and Commerce	Volunteer State
Texas	Friendship	Lone Star State
Utah	Industry	Beehive State
Vermont	Freedom and Unity	Green Mountain State
Virginia	*Sic Semper Tyrannis* (Thus Always to Tyrants)	Old Dominion
Washington	*Alki* (Bye and Bye)	Evergreen State
West Virginia	*Montani Semper Liberi*	Mountain State
	(Mountaineers Are Always Free)	
Wisconsin	Forward	Badger State
Wyoming	Equal Rights	Equality State

State	Resources	Industries/Products	Noted Physical Features	Attractions
Alabama	coal; marble; salt; iron ore; natural gas; petroleum; timber	poultry and cattle; peanuts and pecans; fishing; cotton; paper and plastic products; lumber; chemicals; textiles; metals; food; clothing	Black Belt; Cumberland Plateau; Appalachian foothills; underground caves; swamplands; beaches	Huntsville Space and Rocket Center; Motorsports Hall of Fame and Museum; home of Jefferson Davis; Mobile Bay's exhibition of World War II ships and aircraft; 17th-century plantations
Alaska	oil; natural gas; fish; timber; coal; gold; silver; copper; zinc; uranium; platinum	oil; natural gas; fish and seafood processing; lumber; tourism	Mt. McKinley; Arctic Slope; glaciers	Mount McKinley; Iditarod race; glaciers; Inside Passage; Glacier Bay National Park and Preserve; Denali National Park
Arizona	copper; gold; silver	cattle; grain; tourism	mountains; Grand Canyon; Painted Desert; Sonoran Desert; Canyon Diablo	The Grand Canyon of the Colorado; Painted Desert; Petrified Forest National Park; Meteor Crater; Sedona; Hoover Dam; rodeos
Arkansas	bauxite; coal; oil; natural gas; iron ore; zinc; lead; sandstone; timber	cotton; rice; soybeans; wheat; steel; aluminum; chemicals; plastics; paper, food, and wood products; tourism	mountains; wilderness; Mississippi Delta; Ozark Plateaus	Hot Springs National Park; Ozark Mountains; Crater of Diamonds; Eureka Springs
California	timber; gold; petroleum; borax	fruits; vegetables; flowers; film; wine; computers; telecommunications; mining; tourism	mountains; Mt. Whitney; desert; Mojave Desert; seashore; Death Valley; Yosemite National Park; redwood forests	Hollywood; Disneyland; Sea World; Alcatraz; San Diego Zoo; Yosemite, Sequoia, King's Canyon, Redwood, and Joshua Tree national parks; Death Valley; Golden Gate Bridge; Spanish missions; Napa Valley

State				
Colorado	gold; molybdenum; vanadium; tungsten; uranium; coal; oil; natural gas; marble; granite; sand; gravel	vegetables; cattle; pigs; chemicals; high technology equipment; heavy machinery; skiing; tourism	Rocky Mountains; high plains	Rocky Mountain and Mesa Verde national parks; Grand Mesa National Forest; winter sports
Connecticut	sand, gravel, stone, clay	insurance; banking; aircraft engine and helicopter manufacturing; chemicals; submarine construction; dairy and tobacco farming; gambling; tourism	seashore; Berkshire foothills	Mystic Seaport; Mystic Aquarium; Peabody Museum; American Shakespeare Festival Theater; Goodspeed Opera House; Eugene O'Neill Memorial Theater; Long Island Sound beaches; Foxwoods Resort and Casino; Mark Twain House
Delaware	sand; gravel; magnesium	soybeans; corn; poultry; dairy farming; fishing; chemicals; food, rubber, plastic, and paper products; tourism	seashore; piedmont plateau; Delmarva Peninsula	Winterthur Museum and Garden; Rehoboth Beach; fishing
Florida	phosphate; oil; natural gas; limestone; clay; sand; gravel; titanium	citrus fruits; cattle; lumber; telecommunications; aerospace; tourism	seashore; peninsula; Florida Keys; Everglades; Lake Okeechobee	Everglades National Park; Florida Keys; Kennedy Space Center; Walt Disney World; Sea World; St. Augustine; water sports; Miami Beach
Georgia	clay; stone; kaolin; bauxite; coal; iron ore; barite	tobacco; peanuts; cattle; cotton; fruits; food products; textiles	Okefenokee Swamp; Blue Ridge Mountains	Andersonville Confederate Cemetery; Okefenokee Swamp; beaches; Sea Island; Savannah's historic riverfront district
Hawaii	limestone	sugarcane; fruits; flowers; coffee; tourism	seashore; volcanoes (Mauna Loa, Kilauea); islands	water sports; Pearl Harbor; volcanoes; Waikiki Beach; Diamond Head

State	Resources	Industries/Products	Noted Physical Features	Attractions
Idaho	silver; lead; zinc; gold; tungsten; copper; timber	mining; logging; cattle; sheep; potatoes and other vegetables; technology	mountains; Hells Canyon	Hells Canyon; Craters of the Moon; Sun Valley; winter sports; Shoshone Falls
Illinois	coal; oil; lead; zinc	corn; soybeans; livestock; food products; iron; steel; clay; mining; publishing	prairies; plains	Chicago sites (Museum of Science and Industry; Sears tower); Lincoln Heritage Trail
Indiana	coal; oil; gypsum; sandstone; sand; gravel	soybeans; corn; oil refining; steel; plastics; furniture; automobile parts;	plains; dunes along Lake Michigan shores	Wyandotte Cave; Indianapolis 500; Lincoln Log Cabin Historical Site
Iowa	cement; stone; clay; coal; gypsum; limestone; sand; gravel	cattle; pigs; corn; oats; banking; insurance; farm equipment; food products; mining	Mississippi River; Missouri River watershed	Herbert Hoover Presidential Library; Effigy Mounds National Monument; Amana Colony
Kansas	oil; natural gas; coal; lead; zinc	cattle; pigs; wheat; hay; food products; aircraft	Prairies; Osage plains	Dwight D. Eisenhower Presidential Library; Fort Leavenworth; Dodge City; U.S. Cavalry Museum
Kentucky	coal; timber; natural gas; oil; crushed stone	farming; heavy machinery; transportation equipment; textiles; whiskey; horse breeding; tourism	Appalachian Mountains; Bluegrass; Western Coal Field	Kentucky Derby; Fort Knox; Mammoth Cave National Park; Cumberland Gap
Louisiana	oil; natural gas; fish; timber	oil refining; wood products; sugarcane; vegetables; cotton; food products; tourism	Mississippi Delta; Lake Pontchartrain; Gulf Coast	Mardi Gras; French Quarter of New Orleans; jazz; Louisiana Hayride

State				
Maine	fish; timber; sand; gravel; zinc; clay; lead	blueberries; potatoes; fishing; lumber; dairy farming; tourism	seashore; Mount Katahdin; wilderness	Acadia National Park; Bar Harbor; Freeport/L.L. Bean; cool summers; hunting; fishing
Maryland	coal; fish; timber	technical and scientific research; fishing (crab, oyster, clam); dairy, poultry, and vegetable farming; food products; tourism	Chesapeake Bay; Chincoteague Island; Assateague Island; Appalachian foothills	U.S. Naval Academy; Ocean City; Baltimore's Inner Harbor; the Preakness at Pimlico Track; Fort McHenry
Massachusetts	stone; gravel; clay	technology; textiles; shoes; telecommunications; cranberries; tourism	seashore; Cape Cod; Martha's Vineyard; Nantucket Island; Berkshire Mountains	Freedom Trail; Quincy Market; Faneuil Hall; Tanglewood; John F. Kennedy Library; Cape Cod National Seashore; Provincetown; Lexington and Concord; water sports; Plymouth Rock and Plantation
Michigan	iron; copper; timber; fish	automobiles; furniture; food products; dairy farming; flowers; tourism	Great Lakes; Upper Peninsula; Lower Peninsula; Straits of Mackinac	Great Lakes; Erie Canal; Mackinac Island; Soo Canals; Dezwann Windmill and Tulip Festival; Greenfield Village; Henry Ford Museum: Kellogg's Cereal City U.S.A.
Minnesota	iron; taconite; timber	dairy farming; wheat; soybeans; corn; oats; logging; mining; technology; computers; health care and equipment; food products; paper; tourism	Great Lakes Storm Belt; Lake Superior	water sports; camping; Mayo Clinic; St. Paul Winter Carnival
Mississippi	oil; natural gas; sand; gravel; clay; salt; fish	cotton; textiles; clothing; chemicals; shipbuilding; lumber; shrimp; tourism	Black Prairie Belt; Mississippi delta; Pontotoc Ridge	John C. Stennis Space Center; Natchez Trace Parkway; Vicksburg and other Civil War sites; Gulf Islands National Seashore; antebellum homes

State	Resources	Industries/Products	Noted Physical Features	Attractions
Missouri	lead; iron; crushed stone; fire clay; limestone; portland cement; zinc	soybeans; wheat; oats; corn; cattle; mining; aircraft and electronic equipment; paper products, food and dairy products; beer; greeting cards; automobile parts; chemicals	plains; prairies; Mississippi River; Missouri River	Branson country music theaters; Lake of the Ozark; Mark Twain Area historic sites; Harry S. Truman Library and Museum; St. Louis's Gateway Arch
Montana	coal; gold; copper; silver; oil; timber	wheat; barley; sugar beets; lumber; paper products	Rocky Mountains; Great Plains; glaciers	Rocky Mountains; Glacier and Yellowstone national parks; Badlands; hunting and fishing; Little Bighorn Battlefield National Monument and Custer National Cemetery
Nebraska	oil; natural gas; sand; gravel; limestone	corn; wheat; cattle; food products; tourism	Great Plains	Chimney Rock; Scotts Bluff National Monument
Nevada	gold; silver; copper; stone; clay; oil; gypsum; limestone; barite	gambling; food products; electronic equipment; mining; cattle; sheep; glass products; entertainment; tourism	mountains; Mojave Desert	gambling casinos (Las Vegas, Reno); Hoover Dam; Virginia City; Lake Tahoe; Great Basin National Park
New Hampshire	timber; granite	lumber; wood and paper products; livestock; dairy and fruit farming; electrical equipment; heavy machinery; precision instruments; tourism	White Mountains	autumn foliage; White Mountains attractions (The Flume; Mt. Washington; Franconia Notch); winter sports; Portsmouth; Lake Winnipesaukee

State	Natural resources	Industries/agriculture	Geographic features	Places of interest
New Jersey	zinc; limonite; magnetite; sand; gravel	vegetables; fruit; cattle; chemicals; pharmaceuticals; printing; publishing; shipping; gambling casinos tourism	seashore; Palisades; Piedmont Plateau; Appalachian Highlands coastal plain	Beaches (127 total mi.); Cape May historic district; Delaware Water Gap; Atlantic City; Pine Barrens Wilderness Area
New Mexico	oil; natural gas; coal; uranium; copper; molybdenum; timber	cattle and sheep; grain; mining; defense installations; tourism	Rocky Mountains; Great Plains	Carlsbad Caverns National Park; White Sands National Monument; Chaco Culture National Historic Park; Palace of the Governors; Indian reservations; Acoma Pueblo
New York	timber; wollastonite; zinc; lead; aluminum; talc; salt	dairy and poultry farming; financial, information, and media services; textiles and apparel; photographic and ophthalmic supplies; glass; electrical equipment; transportation equipment; tourism	Adirondack Mountains; Appalachian Mountains; Finger Lakes; Lake Champlain; Great Lakes; Catskill Mountains	New York City sites (United Nations; Statue of Liberty); National Baseball Hall of Fame and Museum; Adirondack Mountains; Fort Ticonderoga; West Point; Seneca Falls; winter and summer sports; Franklin D. Roosevelt National Historic Site; Niagara Falls; Corning Glass Center; Lake Placid; Saranac Lake
North Carolina	timber; fish; rock	corn; tobacco and tobacco products; soybeans; furniture; textiles; paper; electronics; telecommunications; tourism	Great Smoky Mountains; Blue Ridge Mountains; Mount Mitchell; Cape Hatteras; seashore	Wright Brothers National Memorial; Blue Ridge and Great Smoky Mountains; Blue Ridge Parkway; Biltmore House and Gardens; Roanoke Island; Cape Hatteras and Cape Lookout National Seashores; Outer Banks
North Dakota	coal; oil; lignite; limestone; clay	wheat; barley; oats; rye; cattle farming; mining; tourism	Badlands; Black Hills; Great Plains; Red River Valley; Rolling Drift Prairie	Badlands; International Peace Garden; hunting; fishing; Fort Abraham Lincoln State Park and Museum; Bonanzaville

State	Resources	Industries/Products	Noted Physical Features	Attractions
Ohio	coal; oil; natural gas; stone; clay; salt	automotive products; iron and steel; glass; tires; chemicals; mining	Lake Erie; Allegheny Plateau	Professional Football Hall of Fame; birthplaces of presidents William Henry Harrison, Ulysses S. Grant, James A. Garfield, Rutherford B. Hayes, William McKinley, Warren G. Harding; Mound City Group National Monuments
Oklahoma	oil; natural gas; coal; gypsum; pumice; bentonite; helium; stone; sand; gravel; feldspar	cattle; sheep; hogs; cotton; wheat; peanuts; mining; milling; aircraft; machinery; metal products	mountains; plains; Black Mesa; Arkansas River basin	Cowboy Hall of Fame; Ouachita National Forest; Will Rogers Memorial; Fort Sill; Cherokee Heritage Center
Oregon	timber; mercury; nickel; uranium; stone; sand; gravel; clay; limestone; talc; fish	fruits and vegetables; cattle; sheep; lumber; tourism	Coastal range of rugged mountains; Willamette River Valley	Crater Lake National Park; Hells Canyon; Bonneville Hatchery; John Day Fossil Beds National Monument
Pennsylvania	coal; oil; natural gas; copper; lead; zinc; nickel; cement; limestone; timber	mining; iron; steel; stone products; cattle; food products; chemicals; wood products; tourism	Lake Erie; Cumberland Valley; Pocono Mountains; Delaware Water Gap; Allegheny Mountains	Philadelphia sites (Independence Hall; Liberty Bell); Valley Forge National Historic Park; Brandywine; Pennsylvania Dutch country; Gettysburg National Military Park
Rhode Island	sand; gravel; fish	textiles; electronics; fishing; lobsters; tourism	Block Island; Narragansett Basin	Newport mansions; Block Island; Slater Mill Historic Site
South Carolina	kaolin; vermiculite; barite; sand; gravel; clay; timber	tobacco; soybeans; fruit; textiles; furniture; chemicals; paper and wood products; tourism	Blue Ridge Mountains; Whitewater Falls; coastal plain	Historic Charleston; Cypress Gardens; Myrtle Beach and other coast beaches; Hilton Head Island; Fort Sumter National Monument

State	Minerals/Resources	Industries/Products	Physical Features	Places of Interest
South Dakota	gold; silver; lignite; oil; manganese; sand; gravel; granite	livestock; flaxseed; rye; oats; sunflower seeds; hay; wheat; sorghum; meat packing and other food products; machinery and equipment	Black Hills; Great Plains; Prairie Plains	Mount Rushmore; Badlands; Jewel Cave National Monument; Wind Cave National Park; Spirit Mound; Black Hills Passion Play
Tennessee	coal; oil; natural gas; zinc; aluminum; phosphate; marble; hydroelectric power	tobacco; cotton; music; chemicals; food products; textiles; paper products; tourism	Blue Ridge Mountains; Great Smoky Mountains; Cumberland Plateau; Mississippi Alluvial Plain	Grand Old Opry; Graceland; Great Smoky Mountains National Park; Cumberland Gap National Park; Natchez Trace Parkway; The Hermitage (Andrew Jackson's home)
Texas	oil; natural gas; sulfur; helium; salt; iron; gypsum; uranium	cotton; cattle; oil refining; transportation equipment; food processing; textiles; clothing; lumber; tourism	Great Plains; Guadalupe Mountains; Big Bend; Rio Grande; coastal plains; Rocky Mountains; Great Plains Gulf of Mexico	Houston Space Center; The Alamo; Big Bend; Guadalupe Mountains National Parks; Padre Island National Seashore; San Antonio Missions National Historic Park rodeos
Utah	copper; beryllium; gold; silver; lead; uranium	cattle; steel; food products; electrical equipment; tourism	Bryce Canyon; Great Salt Lake; Great Basin; Bonneville Salt Flats; Rocky Mountains	Temple Square, Mormon Church headquarters; Bryce Canyon, Zion, Capitol Reef, Canyonlands, and Arches national parks; Flaming Gorge National Recreation Area; Dinosaur National Monument
Vermont	granite; marble; asbestos; timber	quarrying; dairy farming; lumber; machinery and tools; stone and marble products; food processing; tourism	Green Mountains	foliage; winter and summer sports; Rock of Ages Quarry
Virginia	coal; timber; kyanite; pyrites; titanium; limestone	tobacco products; government services; shipbuilding; chemicals; food products; lumber; stone products; shellfish; tourism	Blue Ridge Mountains; Piedmont Plateau; coastal plains	Colonial Williamsburg; Monticello; Mount Vernon (estate of George Washington); Civil War battlefields, including Yorktown; Jamestown; plantations; Blue Ridge Mountains (Blue Ridge Parkway); estate of Robert E. Lee; Virginia Beach

State	Resources	Industries/Products	Noted Physical Features	Attractions
Washington	timber; fish; zinc; lead; magnesium; gold; coal; sand; gravel; hydroelectric power	wheat; livestock; vegetables; flowers; fruit; fish; lumber; paper products; aircraft; fish products; transportation equipment; computer software; biotechnology; technological research; shipbuilding; tourism	Mt. Rainier; Mt. St. Helens; Cascade Mountains; Olympic Mountains; Puget Sound lowlands; Columbia basin	Seattle Center; Space Needle; Mt. Rainier, Olympic and North Cascades National Parks; Bonneville and Grand Coulee dams; rodeos
West Virginia	coal; timber; oil; natural gas; salt; barite	dairy and fruit farming; lumber; iron; steel; chemicals; glass, clay, and stone products	Allegheny Mountains	Allegheny Mountains; Seneca Rocks; Harpers Ferry National Historic Park; Mammoth Mound; White Sulphur and Berkeley Springs Mineral Water Spas
Wisconsin	iron ore; lead; zinc; copper; timber; fish	dairy products; livestock; machinery; paper; food products; automobiles; lumber; leather good; breweries; tourism	Lake Winnebago; Lake Michigan; Lake Superior	Water activities; The Wisconsin Dells; Great Lakes; Little Norway; Frank Lloyd Wright's house, Taliesin
Wyoming	oil; natural gas; coal; bentonite; trona; uranium; agate; jade	mining; petroleum, coal, and uranium processing; cattle and sheep farming; food products; hay; wheat; lumber products; wool; tourism	Rocky Mountains foothills; Great Plains; desert; Continental Divide; Black Hills; Devil's Tower; Big Horn and Great Divide Basins; desert	Devil's Tower National Monument; Yellowstone and Grand Teton National Parks; Jackson Hole Wildlife Preserve; Periodic Spring; Cheyenne Frontier Days; Buffalo Bill Historical Center; dude ranches

U.S. Territories and Possessions

American Samoa

Geography

Location: Oceania, group of islands in the South Pacific Ocean, about one-half of the way from Hawaii to New Zealand

Area: 77 mi. (199 sq. km.); slightly larger than Washington, D.C.

Climate: tropical marine, moderated by southeast trade winds; annual rainfall averages 124 inches; rainy season from November to April, dry season from May to October; little seasonal temperature variation

Terrain: five volcanic islands with rugged peaks and limited coastal plains, two coral atolls (Rose Island, Swains Island)

Elevation: lowest point: Pacific Ocean 0 ft. (0 m.); highest point: Lata 373 ft. (966 m.)

Natural resources: pumice, pumicite

People

Population: 67,084 (2000 census figure)

Population growth rate: 2.42%

Infant mortality rate: 10.36 deaths/1,000 live births

Life expectancy at birth: total population: 75.32 years; male: 70.89 years; female: 80.02 years

Major ethnic groups: Samoan (Polynesian) 89%, Caucasian 2%, Tongan 4%, other 5%

Major religions: Christian Congregationalist 50%, Roman Catholic 20%, Protestant denominations and other 30%

Major languages: Samoan (closely related to Hawaiian and other Polynesian languages), English; Note—most people are bilingual

Government

Official name: Territory of American Samoa

Government type: unincorporated and unorganized territory of the U.S.; administered by the U.S. Department of Interior, Office of Territorial and International Affairs

National capital: Pago Pago

Economy

Industries: tuna canneries (largely dependent on foreign fishing vessels), meat canning, handicrafts

Agricultural products: bananas, coconuts, vegetables, taro, breadfruit, yams, copra, pineapples, papayas; dairy farming

Currency: 1 U.S. dollar (US$) = 100 cents

Guam

Geography

Location: Oceania, island in the North Pacific Ocean, about three-quarters of the way from Hawaii to the Philippines

Area: 209 sq. mi. (541.3 sq. km.); three times the size of Washington, D.C.

Climate: tropical marine; generally warm and humid, moderated by northeast trade winds; dry season from January to June, rainy season from July to December; little seasonal temperature variation

Terrain: volcanic origin, surrounded by coral reefs; relatively flat coralline limestone plateau (source of most fresh water) with steep coastal cliffs and narrow coastal plains in north, low-rising hills in center, mountains in south

Elevation: lowest point: Pacific Ocean 0 ft. (0 m.); highest point: Mount Lamlam 1,332 ft. (406 m.)

Natural resources: fishing (largely undeveloped), tourism

People

Population: 157,557 (2000 census figure)

Population growth rate: 2.09%

Infant mortality rate: 6.71 deaths/1,000 live births

Life expectancy at birth: total population: 77.94 years; male: 75.66 years; female: 80.55 years

Major ethnic groups: Chamorro 47%, Filipino 25%, white 10%, Chinese, Japanese, Korean, and other 18%

Major religions: Roman Catholic 85%, other 15%

Major languages: English, Chamorro, Japanese

Government

Official name: Territory of Guam

Dependency status: organized, unincorporated territory of the U.S. with policy relations between Guam and the U.S. under the jurisdiction of the Office of Insular Affairs, U.S. Department of the Interior

National capital: Hagatna (Agana)

Legal system: modeled on U.S.; U.S. federal laws apply

Economy

Industries: U.S. military, tourism, construction, transshipment services, concrete products, printing and publishing, food processing, textiles

Agricultural products: fruits, copra, vegetables; eggs, pork, poultry, beef

Currency: 1 U.S. dollar (US$) = 100 cents

Northern Mariana Islands

Geography

Location: Oceania, islands in the North Pacific Ocean, about three-quarters of the way from Hawaii to the Philippines

Area: 184 sq. mi. (477 sq. km.); 2.5 times the size of Washington, D.C.

Climate: tropical marine; moderated by northeast trade winds; little seasonal temperature variation; dry season December to June, rainy season July to October

Terrain: southern islands are limestone with level terraces and fringing coral reefs; northern islands are volcanic

Elevation: lowest point: Pacific Ocean 0 ft. (0 m.); highest point: unnamed location on Agrihan 3,166 ft. (965 m.)

Natural resources: arable land, fish

People

Population: 74,612 (2000 census figure)

Population growth rate: 3.62%

Infant mortality rate: 5.7 deaths/1,000 live births

Life expectancy at birth: total population: 75.74 years; male: 72.65 years; female: 79.02 years

Major ethnic groups: Chamorro, Carolinians and other Micronesians, Caucasian, Japanese, Chinese, Korean

Major religions: Christian (Roman Catholic majority, although traditional beliefs and taboos may still be found)

Major languages: English, Chamorro, Carolinian; note: 86% of population speaks a language other than English at home

Government

Official name: Commonwealth of the Northern Mariana Islands

Dependency status: commonwealth in political union with the U.S.

Government type: commonwealth; self-governing with locally elected governor, lieutenant governor, and legislature

National capital: Saipan

Legal system: based on U.S. system except for customs, wages, immigration laws, and taxation

Economy

Industries: tourism, construction, garments, handicrafts

Agricultural products: coconuts, fruits, vegetables; cattle

Currency: 1 U.S. dollar (US$) = 100 cents

Puerto Rico

Geography

Location: Caribbean, island between the Caribbean Sea and the North Atlantic Ocean, east of the Dominican Republic

Area: 3,515 sq. mi. (9,104 sq. km.); slightly less than three times the size of Rhode Island

Climate: tropical marine, mild; little seasonal temperature variation

Terrain: mostly mountains with coastal plain belt in north; mountains precipitous to sea on west coast; sandy beaches along most coastal areas

Elevation: lowest point: Caribbean Sea 0 ft. (0 m.); highest point: Cerro de Punta 4,390 ft. (1,338 m.)

Natural resources: some copper and nickel; potential for onshore and offshore oil

People

Population: 3,937,316 (2000 census figure)

Population growth rate: 0.54%

Infant mortality rate: 9.51 deaths/1,000 live births

Life expectancy at birth: total population: 75.76 years; male: 71.28 years; female: 80.48 years

Major ethnic groups: Hispanic

Major religions: Roman Catholic 85%, Protestant denominations and other 15%

Major languages: Spanish, English

Government

Official name: Commonwealth of Puerto Rico

Dependency status: commonwealth associated with the U.S.

Government type: commonwealth

National capital: San Juan

Legal system: based on Spanish civil code

Economy

Industries: pharmaceuticals, electronics, apparel, food products; tourism

Agricultural products: livestock products, chickens; sugarcane, coffee, pineapples, plantains, bananas

Currency: 1 U.S. dollar (US$) = 100 cents

Virgin Islands

Geography

Location: Caribbean, islands between the Caribbean Sea and the North Atlantic Ocean, east of Puerto Rico

Area: 136 sq. mi. (352 sq. km.); twice the size of Washington, D.C.

Climate: subtropical, tempered by easterly trade winds, relatively low humidity, little seasonal temperature variation; rainy season May to November

Terrain: mostly hilly to rugged and mountainous with little level land

Elevation: lowest point: Caribbean Sea 0 ft. (0 m.); highest point: Crown Mountain 1,555 ft. (474 m.)

Natural resources: sun, sand, sea, surf

People

Population: 122,211 (2000 census figure)

Population growth rate: 1.06%

Infant mortality rate: 9.43 deaths/1,000 live births

Life expectancy at birth: total population: 78.27 years; male: 74.38 years; female: 82.39 years

Major ethnic groups: black 80%, white 15%

Major religions: Baptist 42%, Roman Catholic 34%, Episcopalian 17%

Major languages: English (official), Spanish, Creole

Government

Official name: Virgin Islands of the United States

Dependency status: organized, unincorporated territory of the U.S.;

National capital: Charlotte Amalie

Legal system: based on U.S. laws

Economy

Industries: tourism, petroleum refining, watch assembly, rum distilling, construction, pharmaceuticals, textiles, electronics

Agricultural products: truck garden products, fruit, vegetables, sorghum; Senepol cattle

Currency: 1 U.S. dollar (US$) = 100 cents

The following U.S. territories are uninhabited:

Baker Island, Howland Island, Jarvis Island, Johnston Atoll, Kingman Reef, Midway Islands, Navassa Island, Palmyra Atoll, Wake Island

⊙ Central Intelligence Agency. "*The World Factbook 2000* Country Listing," www.odci.gov/cia/publications/factbook/index.html

Rank	City	Population (July 1, 1999, est.)	Change in Population (1990–99)	Percent Change (1990–99)
1	New York City, NY	7,428,162	105,598	+1.4
2	Los Angeles, CA	3,633,591	148,092	+4.2
3	Chicago, IL	2,799,050	15,390	+.6
4	Houston, TX	1,845,967	148,094	+8.7
5	Philadelphia, PA	1,417,601	–167,976	–10.6
6	San Diego, CA	1,238,974	127,943	+11.5
7	Phoenix, AZ	1,211,466	222,483	+22.5
8	San Antonio, TX	1,147,213	149,779	+15.0
9	Dallas, TX	1,076,214	69,568	+6.9
10	Detroit, MI	965,084	–62,862	–6.1
11	San Jose, CA	867,675	84,351	+10.8
12	San Francisco, CA	746,777	22,818	+3.2
13	Indianapolis, IN	738,907	7,181	+1.0
14	Jacksonville, FL	695,877	60,835	+9.6
15	Columbus, OH	671,247	34,924	+5.5
16	Baltimore, MD	632,681	–103,333	–14.0
17	El Paso, TX	612,770	97,118	+18.8
18	Memphis, TN	606,109	–12,785	–2.1
19	Austin, TX	587,873	93,583	+18.9
20	Milwaukee, WI	572,424	–55,876	–8.9
21	Boston, MA	555,249	–19,040	–3.3
22	Seattle, WA	537,150	20,818	+4.0
23	Charlotte, NC	520,829	93,845	+22.0
24	Washington, DC	519,000	–87,900	–14.5
25	Nashville-Davidson, TN	506,385	18,197	+3.7
26	Portland, OR	503,637	17,554	+3.6
27	Fort Worth, TX	502,369	54,188	+12.1
28	Cleveland, OH	501,662	–3,788	–.7
29	Denver, CO	499,775	32,226	+6.9
30	Oklahoma City, OK	475,322	30,717	+6.9
31	Tucson, AZ	466,591	49,452	+11.9
32	New Orleans, LA	460,913	–36,025	–7.2
33	Kansas City, MO	437,764	2,643	+.6
34	Long Beach, CA	435,027	5,157	+1.2
35	Virginia Beach, VA	433,461	40,372	+10.3
36	Albuquerque, NM	420,578	33,590	+8.7
37	Las Vegas, NV	418,658	158,824	+61.1
38	Sacramento, CA	406,899	11,799	+3.0
39	Fresno, CA	404,141	48,697	+13.7

40	Atlanta, GA	401,726	7,966	+2.0
41	Honolulu, HI	395,327	18,390	+4.9
42	Omaha, NE	386,742	28,935	+8.1
43	Tulsa, OK	381,579	14,412	+3.9
44	Miami, FL	369,253	9,463	+2.6
45	Mesa, AZ	368,811	78,599	+27.1
46	Oakland, CA	365,210	−34,676	−8.7
47	Minneapolis, MN	353,395	−14,889	−4.0
48	Colorado Springs, CO	350,199	67,087	+23.7
49	Pittsburgh, PA	336,882	−33,257	−9.0
50	Wichita, KS	335,562	26,910	+8.7
51	St. Louis, MO	333,960	−62,725	−15.8
52	Cincinnati, OH	330,914	−33,639	−9.2
53	Arlington, TX	311,962	49,963	+19.1
54	Santa Ana, CA	309,290	14,981	+5.1
55	Toledo, OH	307,946	−24,886	−7.5
56	Anaheim, CA	300,650	34,025	+12.8
57	Buffalo, NY	295,619	−32,312	−9.9
58	Tampa, FL	290,973	10,147	3.6
59	Corpus Christi, TX	281,791	23,352	+9.0
60	Riverside, CA	265,721	39,139	+17.3
61	Newark, NJ	263,087	−12,204	−4.4
62	Raleigh, NC	261,205	40,780	+18.5
63	Anchorage, AK	257,808	31,470	+13.9
64	St. Paul, MN	256,213	−16,022	−5.9
65	Louisville, KY	253,128	−16,710	−6.2
66	Aurora, CO	252,956	31,101	+14.0
67	Birmingham, AL	249,459	−16,481	−6.2
68	Stockton, CA	245,020	33,525	+15.9
69	Lexington-Fayette, KY	243,785	18,419	+8.2
70	St. Petersburg, FL	234,647	−5,721	−2.4
71	Plano, TX	232,904	104,397	+81.2
72	Jersey City, NJ	230,458	1,983	+.9
73	Norfolk, VA	225,875	−35,375	−13.5
74	Bakersfield, CA	222,352	38,393	+20.9
75	Lincoln, NE	215,928	23,206	+12.0
76	Rochester, NY	214,470	−16,402	−7.1
77	Hialeah, FL	212,547	24,642	+13.1
78	Akron, OH	211,822	−11,360	−5.1
79	Madison, WI	210,674	19,858	+10.4
80	Baton Rouge, LA	210,667	−11,675	−5.3
81	Fremont, CA	208,620	35,261	+20.3
82	Chesapeake, VA	202,759	50,777	+33.4
83	Glendale, AZ	201,456	50,589	+33.5
84	Mobile, AL	200,206	1,789	+.9

Rank	City	Population (July 1, 1998, est.)	Change in Population (1990–98)	Percent Change (1990–98)
85	Scottsdale, AZ	199,943	69,857	+53.7
86	Huntington Beach, CA	199,618	16,719	+9.1
87	Greensboro, NC	199,562	7,971	+4.2
88	Fort Wayne, IN	196,708	–6,287	–3.1
89	Montgomery, AL	195,690	4,859	+2.5
90	Garland, TX	193,272	12,428	+6.9
91	Yonkers, NY	191,458	3,273	+1.7
92	Des Moines, IA	190,958	–2,375	–1.2
93	Lubbock, TX	190,002	3,232	+1.7
94	Richmond, VA	189,700	–13,013	–6.4
95	San Bernardino, CA	188,924	17,715	+10.3
96	Modesto, CA	188,253	21,823	+13.1
97	Shreveport, LA	187,393	–11,009	–5.5
98	Glendale, CA	186,903	6,843	+3.8
99	Augusta, GA	186,206	29	0.0
100	Grand Rapids, MI	185,009	–4,664	–2.5

⊙U. S. Bureau of the Census. "Population Estimates for Cities With Populations of 100,000 and Greater, "www.census.gov/population/estimates/metro-city/SC100K-T1.txt

100 Largest Metropolitan Areas

Rank	Metro Area	Population (July 1, 1999, est.)
2	Los Angeles-Riverside-Orange Coun	395,953
1	New York-Northern New Jersey-Long Island, NY-NJ-CT-PA	20,196,649
2	Los Angeles-Riverside- Orange County, CA	16,036,587
3	Chicago-Gary-Kenosha, IL-IN-WI	8,885,919
4	Washington-Baltimore, DC-MD-VA-WV	7,359,004
5	San Francisco-Oakland-San Jose, CA	6,873,645
6	Philadelphia-Wilmington-Atlantic City, PA-NJ-DE-MD	5,999,034
7	Boston-Worcester-Lawrence, MA-NH-ME-CT	5,667,225
8	Detroit-Ann Arbor-Flint, MI	5,469,312
9	Dallas-Fort Worth, TX	4,909,523
10	Houston-Galveston-Brazoria, TX	4,493,741
11	Atlanta, GA	3,857,097
12	Miami-Fort Lauderdale, FL	3,711,102
13	Seattle-Tacoma-Bremerton, WA	3,465,760
14	Phoenix-Mesa, AZ	3,013,696
15	Cleveland-Akron, OH	2,910,616
16	Minneapolis-St.Paul, MN-WI	2,872,109

17	San Diego, CA	2,820,844
18	St. Louis, MO-IL	2,569,029
19	Denver-Boulder-Greeley, CO	2,417,908
20	Pittsburgh, PA	2,331,336
21	Tampa-St. Petersburg-Clearwater, FL	2,278,169
22	Portland-Salem, OR-WA	2,180,996
23	Cincinnati-Hamilton, OH-KY-IN	1,960,995
24	Kansas City, MO-KS	1,755,899
25	Sacramento-Yolo, CA	1,741,002
26	Milwaukee-Racine, WI	1,648,199
27	San Antonio, TX	1,564,949
28	Norfolk-Virginia Beach-Newport News, VA-NC	1,562,635
29	Indianapolis, IN	1,536,665
30	Orlando, FL	1,535,044
31	Columbus, OH	1,489,487
32	Charlotte-Gastonia-Rock Hill, NC-SC	1,417,217
33	Las Vegas, NV-AZ	1,381,086
34	New Orleans, LA	1,305,479
35	Salt Lake City-Ogden, UT	1,275,076
36	Greensboro—Winston-Salem—High Point, NC	1,179,384
37	Nashville, TN	1,171,755
38	Hartford, CT	1,147,504
39	Austin-San Marcos, TX	1,146,050
40	Buffalo-Niagara Falls, NY	1,142,121
41	Providence-Fall River-Warwick, RI-MA	1,125,639
42	Raleigh-Durham-Chapel Hill, NC	1,105,535
43	Memphis, TN-AR-MS	1,105,058
44	Rochester, NY	1,079,073
45	Jacksonville, FL	1,056,332
46	Grand Rapids-Muskegon-Holland, MI	1,052,092
47	West Palm Beach-Boca Raton, FL	1,049,420
48	Oklahoma City, OK	1,046,283
49	Louisville, KY-IN	1,005,849
50	Richmond-Petersburg, VA	961,416
51	Dayton-Springfield, OH	958,698
52	Greenville-Spartanburg-Anderson, SC	929,565
53	Birmingham, AL	915,077
54	Fresno, CA	879,829
55	Albany-Schenectady-Troy, NY	869,474
56	Honolulu, HI	864,571
57	Tucson, AZ	803,618
58	Tulsa, OK	786,117
59	Syracuse, NY	732,920
60	El Paso, TX	701,908
61	Omaha, NE-IA	698,875
62	Albuquerque, NM	678,820

Rank	Metro Area	Population (July 1, 1999, est.)
63	Knoxville, TN	672,087
64	Bakersfield, CA	642,495
65	Harrisburg-Lebanon-Carlisle, PA	618,375
66	Allentown-Bethlehem-Easton, PA	618,350
67	Scranton—Wilkes-Barre—Hazelton, PA	611,492
68	Toledo, OH	608,976
69	Youngstown-Warren, OH	589,236
70	Baton Rouge, LA	578,946
71	Springfield, MA	573,940
72	Stockton-Lodi, CA	563,183
73	Little Rock, North Little Rock, AR	559,074
74	Charleston-North Charleston, SC	552,803
75	Sarasota-Bradenton, FL	550,077
76	Wichita, KS	548,714
77	Mobile, AL	535,472
78	McAllen-Edinburg-Mission, TX	534,907
79	Columbia, SC	516,251
80	Colorado Springs, CO	499,994
81	Fort Wayne, IN	484,320
82	Daytona Beach, FL	474,711
83	Melbourne-Titusville-Palm Bay, FL	470,365
84	Johnson City-Kingsport-Bristol, TN-VA	462,769
85	Augusta-Aiken, GA-SC	460,826
86	Lancaster, PA	460,035
87	Lakeland-Winter Haven, FL	457,347
88	Lexington, KY	455,617
89	Chattanooga, TN-GA	452,034
90	Lansing-East Lansing, MI	450,789
91	Kalamazoo-Battle Creek, MI	447,164
92	Des Moines, IA	443,496
93	Modesto, CA	436,790
94	Jackson, MS	432,647
95	Madison, WI	428,563
96	Spokane, WA	409,736
97	Boise City, ID	407,844
98	Pensacola, FL	403,384
99	Canton-Massillon, OH	402,460
100	Saginaw-Bay City—Midland, MI	400,753

⊙ U.S. Bureau of the Census. "Metro Area and Central City Population Estimates for July 1, 1999,"
www.census.gov/population/estimates/metro-city/ma99-05.txt

U.S. Bureau of the Census. "Metro Area Rankings in Population Size for July 1, 1999,"
www.census.gov/population/estimates/metro-city/ma99-04.txt

UNITED STATES: *Population*

Population Estimates: Current, Historical, and Projected

Current

Oct. 16, 2000 est.: 275,950,532

Historical

1790:	3,929,214	1900:	76,212,168
1800:	5,308,483	1910:	92,228,496
1810:	7,239,881	1920:	106,021,537
1820:	9,638,453	1930:	123,202,624
1830:	12,860,702	1940:	132,164,569
1840:	17,063,353	1950:	151,325,798
1850:	23,191,876	1960:	179,323,175
1860:	31,443,321	1970:	203,302,031
1870:	38,558,371	1980:	226,542,199
1880:	50,189,209	1990:	248,709,873
1890:	62,979,766		

Projected

2010:	299,862,000	2040:	377,350,000
2020:	324,927,000	2050:	403,687,000
2030:	351,070,000	2100:	570,954,000

⊙ The United States Bureau of the Census. "Annual Projections of the Total Resident Population as of July
1: Middle, Lowest, and Highest, and Zero International Migration Series, 1999–2100,"
www.census.gov/population/projections/nation/summary/np-t1.txt
———. "Historical National Population Estimates: July 1, 1900 to July 1, 1999," www.census.gov/popula-
tion/estimates/nation/popclockest.txt
———. "Population: 1790 to 1990," www.census.gov/population/censusdata/table-16.pdf

State Population (inc. District of Columbia), 1999

State	Population (est.)	Rank	State	Population (est.)	Rank
Alabama	4,369,862	23	Iowa	2,869,413	30
Alaska	619,500	48	Kansas	2,654,052	32
Arizona	4,778,332	20	Kentucky	3,960,825	25
Arkansas	2,551,373	33	Louisiana	4,372,035	22
California	33,145,121	1	Maine	1,253,040	39
Colorado	4,056,133	24	Maryland	5,171,634	19
Connecticut	3,282,031	29	Massachusetts	6,175,169	13
Delaware	753,538	45	Michigan	9,863,775	8
District of Columbia	519,000	50	Minnesota	4,775,508	21
Florida	15,111,244	4	Mississippi	2,768,619	31
Georgia	7,788,240	10	Missouri	5,468,338	17
Hawaii	1,185,497	42	Montana	882,779	44
Idaho	1,251,700	40	Nebraska	1,666,028	38
Illinois	12,128,370	5	Nevada	1,809,253	35
Indiana	5,942,901	14	New Hampshire	1,201,134	41

State Population (inc. District of Columbia), 1999 *(cont.)*

State	Population (est.)	Rank	State	Population (est.)	Rank
New Jersey	8,143,412	9	South Dakota	733,133	46
New Mexico	1,739,844	37	Tennessee	5,483,535	16
New York	18,1196,601	3	Texas	20,044,141	2
North Carolina	7,650,789	11	Utah	2,129,836	34
North Dakota	633,666	47	Vermont	593,740	49
Ohio	11,256,654	7	Virginia	6,872,912	12
Oklahoma	3,358,044	27	Washington	5,756,361	15
Oregon	3,316,154	28	West Virginia	1,806,928	36
Pennsylvania	11,994,016	6	Wisconsin	5,250,446	18
Rhode Island	990,819	43	Wyoming	479,602	51
South Carolina	3,885,736	26			

⊙ The United States Bureau of the Census. "State Population Estimates and Demographic Components of Population Change: July 1, 1998 to July 1, 1999," www.census.gov/population/estimates/state/st-99-1.txt

Racial Percentages by State (incl. District of Columbia), 1999

State	% White (est.)	% Black (est.)	% American Indian and Alaskan Native (est.)	% Asian and Pacific Islander (est.)
United States	82.5	12.7	.9	3.9
Alabama	73.0	26.1	.3	.7
Alaska	75.2	3.9	16.4	4.5
Arizona	88.7	3.7	5.5	2.1
Arkansas	82.6	16.1	.5	.7
California	79.4	7.5	.9	12.2
Colorado	92.3	4.3	.9	2.5
Connecticut	87.8	9.4	.2	2.6
Delaware	77.7	19.8	.5	2.1
District of Columbia	35.2	61.4	.3	3.1
Florida	82.3	15.4	.4	1.9
Georgia	69.0	28.7	.2	2.1
Hawaii	33.0	2.8	.6	63.6
Idaho	96.9	.6	1.3	1.2
Illinois	81.1	15.3	.2	3.4
Indiana	90.4	8.4	.3	1.0
Iowa	96.4	2.0	.3	1.3
Kansas	91.4	5.9	.9	1.8
Kentucky	91.9	7.3	.1	.7
Louisiana	65.9	32.4	.4	1.3
Maine	98.3	.5	.5	.8
Maryland	67.5	28.1	.3	4.0
Massachusetts	89.4	6.6	.2	3.8

Michigan	83.4	14.3	.6	1.7
Minnesota	92.9	3.1	1.2	2.7
Mississippi	62.4	36.5	.4	.7
Missouri	87.2	11.3	.4	1.1
Montana	92.5	.4	6.5	.6
Nebraska	93.6	4.1	.9	1.4
Nevada	85.6	7.7	1.8	4.9
New Hampshire	97.8	.8	.2	1.2
New Jersey	79.3	14.7	.3	5.8
New Mexico	86.3	2.6	9.5	1.5
New York	76.2	17.7	.4	5.6
North Carolina	75.3	22.0	1.3	1.4
North Dakota	93.7	.6	4.8	.8
Ohio	87.0	11.6	.2	1.2
Oklahoma	83.0	7.8	7.8	1.3
Oregon	93.4	1.9	1.4	3.3
Pennsylvania	88.4	9.8	.2	1.7
Rhode Island	92.1	5.1	.5	2.3
South Carolina	69.1	29.8	.2	.9
South Dakota	90.4	.7	8.2	.7
Tennessee	82.1	16.6	.2	1.0
Texas	84.3	12.3	.5	2.9
Utah	95.1	.9	1.4	2.6
Vermont	98.4	.5	.2	.8
Virginia	75.8	20.1	.3	3.8
Washington	88.7	3.5	1.8	6.0
West Virginia	96.3	3.1	.1	.5
Wisconsin	91.9	5.6	.9	1.6
Wyoming	96.0	.9	2.3	.9

⊙ The United States Bureau of the Census. "States Ranked by White Population, July 1, 1999," www.census.gov/population/estimates/state/rank/white.txt
———. "States Ranked by Black Population, July 1, 1999," www.census.gov/population/estimates/state/rank/black.txt
———. "States Ranked by American Indian and Alaska Native Population, July 1, 1999," www.census.gov/population/estimates/state/rank/aiea.txt
———. "States Ranked by Asian and Pacific Islander Population, July 1, 1999," www.census.gov/population/estimates/state/rank/api.txt

100 Most Populous Native American Tribes

Name	Population (1990)	Name	Population (1990)
Cherokee	369,035	Apache	53,330
Navajo	225,298	Iroquois	52,557
Sioux	107,321	Lumbee	50,888
Chippewa	105,988	Creek	45,872
Choctaw	86,231	Blackfoot	37,992
Pueblo	55,330	Canadian and Latin American	27,179

100 Most Populous Native American Tribes

Name	Population (1990)	Name	Population (1990)
Chickasaw	21,522	Karok	3,077
Tohono O'odham	16,876	Laddo	2,984
Potawatomi	16,719	Yokuts	2,967
Seminole	15,564	Haliwa	2,946
Pima	15,074	Gros Ventres	2,875
Tlingit	14,417	Luiseno	2,798
Alaskan Athabaskans	14,198	Ponca	2,788
Cheyenne	11,809	Milmac	2,726
Comanche	11,437	Warm Springs	2,685
Paiute	11,369	Narragansett	2,564
Osage	10,430	Quinault	2,513
Puget Sound Salish	10,384	Passamaquoddy	2,466
Yaqui	9,838	Penobscot	2,407
Delaware	9,800	Hoopa	2,390
Shoshone	9,506	Wampanoag	2,334
Kiowa	9,460	Maidu	2,334
Crow	9,394	Shoshone Paiute	2,320
Cree	8,467	Wintu	2,319
Menominee	8,064	Salish and Kootenai	2,293
Ottawa	7,885	Diegueno	2,249
Houma	7,809	Stolkbridge	2,219
Ute	7,658	Tsimshian	2,157
Yakima	7,577	Mission Indians	2,056
Yuman	7,319	Spokane	2,042
Colville	7,057	Haida	1,936
Arapaho	6,918	Otoe-Missouria	1,762
Shawnee	6,640	Pit River	1,753
Winnebago	6,591	Siletz	1,726
Assiniboine	5,521	Algonquian	1,700
Pomo	4,898	Mono	1,697
Salish	4,830	Arikara	1,671
Sac and Fox	4,774	Shinnecock	1,670
Miami	4,580	Makah	1,661
Yurok	4,444	Colorado River	1,645
Omaha	4,363	Fort Berthold	1,643
Nez Perce	4,003	Juaneno	1,605
Eastern Tribes	3,853	Iowa	1,555
Kickapoo	3,576	Abenaki	1,549
Fort Hall	3,450	Hidatsa	1,539
Miwok	3,438	Nantikoke	1,529
Pawnee	3,387	Klallam	1,522
Chumash	3,208	Washo	1,489
Lummi	3,125	Gila River	1,484
Klamath	3,113	Quapaw	1,438

⊙ The United States Bureau of the Census. *Characteristics of American Indians by Tribe and Language* "Table 1: American Indian Population by Selected Tribes: 1990," www.census.gov/prod/3/98pubs/CP-3-7-1.PDF

United States Immigrants by Decade

Decade	Number of Immigrants	Decade	Number of Immigrants
1820–1998 (H1)	64,599,082	1911–1920	5,735,811
1821–1830	143,439	1921–1930	4,107,209
1831–1840	599,125	1931–1940	528,431
1841–1850	1,713,251	1941–1950	1,035,039
1851–1860	2,598,214	1951–1960	2,515,479
1861–1870	2,314,824	1961–1970	3,321,677
1871–1880	2,812,191	1971–1980	4,493,314
1881–1890	5,246,613	1981–1990	7,338,062
1891–1900	3,687,564	1991–1998	7,605,068
1901–1910	8,795,386		

⊙ The United States Department of Justice Immigration and Naturalization Service. *1998 Statistical Yearbook of the Immigration and Naturalization Service: Immigrants, Fiscal Year 1998.* "Table 1: Immigration to the U.S.: Fiscal Years: 1820–1998," www.ins.usdoj.gov/graphics/aboutins/statistics/imm98.pdf

United States Immigrants by Region and Country of Origin (Fiscal Year 1998)

Region	Number of Legal Immigrants	Region	Number of Legal Immigrants
Total	660,477	North America	252,996
Africa	40,660	Oceania	3,935
Asia	219,696	South America	45,394
Europe	90,793	Unknown	7,003

Country (Top 20)	Number of Legal Immigrants	Country (Top 20)	Number of Legal Immigrants
Mexico	131,575	Haiti	13,449
China (People's Republic)	36,884	Pakistan	13,094
India	36,482	Colombia	11,836
Philippines	34,466	Russia	11,529
Dominican Republic	20,387	Canada	10,190
Vietnam	17,649	Peru	10,154
Cuba	17,375	United Kingdom	9,011
Jamaica	15,146	Bangladesh	8,621
El Salvador	14,590	Poland	8,469
Korea	14,268	Iran	7,883

⊙ The United States Department of Justice Immigration and Naturalization Service. *U.S. DOJ Immigration and Naturalization Service Annual Report: Legal Immigration, Fiscal Year 1998.* "Table 2: Immigrants Admitted by Region and Selected Country of Birth: Fiscal Years 1995–1998," www.ins.usdoj.gov/graphics/publicaffairs/newsrels/98legal.pdf

Common Medical Tests

Name	Purpose	Procedure	Requirements	Other
Blood Pressure	To test for hypertension	Blood pressure is measured with a rubber cuff wrapped around your upper arm. The cuff is inflated to measure blood pressure.	To ensure accuracy, try to avoid caffeine, nicotine, and certain medications (such as non-steroidal anti-inflammatory drugs and cold medications) before being tested.	The American Heart Association recommends getting blood pressure checked at least every two years.
Bone Mineral Density Test	To test for osteoporosis	A scanner uses a small amount of radiation to measure bone density.	Bone density can be measured at the spine, hip, wrist, or heel. Your doctor will determine the best test for you.	
Breast Self-Exam	To screen for breast cancer	Feel for any unusual lumps, dimpling, or thickening and look for discharge from the nipple or any other abnormalities.		The American Cancer Society recommends monthly self-exams for women 20 and older. The best time to examine your breasts is about a week after your period begins, or if you have reached menopause, choose the same time to do it each month.
Clinical Breast Exam	To screen for breast cancer	The doctor palpates the breasts to check for any unusual lumps, dimpling, or thickening, and looks for discharge from the nipple or any other abnormalities.		The American Cancer Society recommends a clinical breast exam every three years for women age 20–39 and every year for women 40 and older.

Test	Purpose	Procedure	Preparation	Recommendation
Cholesterol	To test for hypercholesterolemia, which poses an increased risk of coronary heart disease	The test requires a quick blood sample drawn from your finger or arm.	Avoid any medications that influence cholesterol levels prior to testing. (Ask your doctor for a list of such medications.) An overnight fast is required if testing for a full lipid profile.	According to the National Heart, Lung, and Blood Institute, adults age 20 and older should have both their total and HDL cholesterol measured at least once every five years.
Colorectal Cancer	To screen for colorectal cancer	*Sigmoidoscopy:* a soft, bendable tube the thickness of the index finger is gently inserted into the rectal opening and advanced into the rectum and the lower colon to examine their linings. *Colonoscopy:* a visual exam of the interior lining of the large intestine using a colonoscope, a flexible fiber-optic tube.	Thorough cleansing of the bowel is mandatory. Your health care provider may ask you to abstain from all solid foods 2 or 3 days before the test, ingest laxatives, or have an enema.	The American Cancer Society recommends men and women age 50 and older follow this schedule for colorectal cancer testing: sigmoidoscopy every five years, or colonoscopy every ten years, or double contrast barium enema every five to ten years.
Digital Rectal Exam	To test for colorectal cancer	The doctor inserts a gloved, lubricated finger into the rectum to feel for any type of growth or abnormality.		The American Cancer Society recommends men and women age 50 and older have a digital rectal exam with their chosen colorectal exam schedule (see above).
Dental Exam	To screen for tooth decay and gum disease	Your dentist performs a visual examination of your teeth and gums.		

Name	Purpose	Procedure	Requirements	Other
Eye Exam	To test general eye health, including tests for glaucoma, macular degeneration, cataracts, and diabetic retinopathy	Your ophthalmologist may have you read letters at a distance, examine your retinas with special viewing machinery, and measure your eyeball's elasticity with a puff of compressed air.		The American Academy of Ophthalmology recommends the following schedule for eye exams. Under 40: a single comprehensive exam if your vision is normal; every three to five years for African Americans and others at higher risk for glaucoma. Ages 40–64: every two to four years, even if you have no symptoms. Age 65 and older: every one to two years, even if you have no symptoms.
Fasting Plasma Glucose	To test for diabetes	A blood sample is taken after an eight-hour overnight fast.		The American Diabetes Association recommends that all adults over 45 get tested for Type II (adult onset) diabetes every three years.
Fecal Occult Blood	To screen for colorectal cancer	You will collect stool samples for three days in a row before the test, or your doctor will collect a sample during a rectal exam.	Eat a high-fiber diet for 48 to 72 hours before the test. Avoid red meat, poultry, aspirin, large amounts of vitamin C, iron supplements, and certain fruits and vegetables (get a complete list from your doctor), all of which can interfere with test results. You may also need to stop certain medications for two days prior to the test.	The American Cancer Society recommends yearly testing for men and women age 50 and older.

FSH (follicle-stimulating hormone)	To screen for ovarian failure, which leads to menopause	A blood sample is taken and tested by your doctor.	
HIV Test	To screen for human immunodeficiency virus (HIV) antibodies	A blood sample is taken and tested by your doctor.	The Centers for Disease Control and Prevention (CDC) recommends HIV testing if: *You have used intravenous drugs or had a partner who did; *You have had another sexually transmitted disease; *You have had unprotected sex with anyone whose HIV status you weren't sure of; *You are pregnant or plan to conceive.
Mammogram	To screen for breast cancer and non-cancerous breast disease	A low-dose X ray of the breast is taken and examined by your doctor.	On the day of your mammogram, do not wear any powder, cream, or deodorant on your upper body. Most experts recommend annual mammograms for women 40 and over.
Pap Test	To screen for cervical cancer	The doctor inserts a speculum into the vagina and collects a tissue sample from the cervix. The procedure takes five to ten minutes and can be done during a pelvic exam.	For the greatest accuracy, have the test done 12 to 14 days after the first day of your period. If you douche within 24 hours before the test, or are menstruating, the results may be distorted. The College of American Pathologists recommends that women who are sexually active or who have reached 18 years of age get annual Pap tests.
Pelvic Exam	To screen for cervical and ovarian cancers and pre-cancerous cells	The physician performs a speculum exam to view the vagina and cervix. A bimanual is also performed to check the uterus and ovaries for any palpable mass. Pap tests are often performed during a pelvic exam.	The American Cancer Society recommends annual pelvic exams for women 18 and older, and for younger women who are sexually active.

Name	Purpose	Procedure	Requirements	Other
PSA	To screen for prostate cancer with a prostate-specific antigen (PSA)	A blood sample is taken and tested by your doctor.	The sample is collected in the morning, if possible.	The American Cancer Society recommends that the PSA test be offered annually, beginning at age 50, to men who have at least a 10-year life expectancy.
Skin Self-Exam	To screen for skin cancer	Look for any changes in moles or freckles, as well as any new spots that are asymmetrical, more than one color, the size of a pencil eraser or larger, or have uneven borders.		The American Academy of Dermatology recommends self-exams every month.
Clinical Skin Exam	To screen for skin cancer	The doctor will examine your entire body, including back, buttocks, genitals, soles of the feet, scalp, and underarms.		The American Academy of Dermatology recommends yearly skin exams by a dermatologist.
Testicular Self-Exam	To screen for testicular cancer	Look for any change in the size, shape, or consistency of the testes, as well as any hard lumps or smooth, rounded masses, which might feel like a grain of uncooked rice or a hard pea.		Testicular cancer often produces no symptoms, so many doctors recommend monthly self-exams.
Thyroid Stimulating Hormone (TSH)	To test for hypothyroidism and hyperthyroidism	A blood sample is taken and tested by your doctor.		The American College of Obstetrics and Gynecology recommends that women 65 and older get tested every three to five years.

⊙ Merck.com. "Common Medical Tests," www.merck.com/pubs/mmanual_home/appndxs/app3.htm
MSN. "The Yale University School of Medicine Patient's Guide to Medical Tests," http://content.health.msn.com/yale_books
Thrive Online. "Medical Tests Not to Miss," www.thriveonline.com/health/medicaltests/index.html

Diseases: Common Types

Infectious diseases are communicable illnesses caused by pathogens that invade a host. Pathogens include bacteria, viruses, fungi, and parasites (protozoans, flatworms, and roundworms). The table lists some well-known examples in these categories.

Bacterial	Viral	Fungal	Parasites (Protozoans, Flatworms, Roundworms)
e. coli infection	common colds	athlete's foot	malaria
cholera	mumps	yeast infection	giardiasis
tetanus	measles	ringworm	schistosomiasis
gonorrhea	hepatitis		trichinosis
meningococcal diseases	herpes simplex		
ulcer	HIV		
pneumonia	yellow fever		
toxic shock syndrome	viral hemorrhagic fever		
strep throat	West Nile encephalitis		
urinary tract infections	chickenpox (varicella)		
syphilis	influenza		
salmonella			

Noninfectious diseases include malignancies (cancer) of all kinds, hereditary and congenital disorders, degenerative disorders, immunological diseases, and deficiency diseases.

Hereditary and Congenital Disorders	Degenerative Disorders	Immunological Diseases	Deficiency Diseases
hemophilia	Parkinson's disease	allergies	scurvy
sickle-cell anemia	arthritis	lupus	malnutrition
birth defects	Alzheimer's disease		osteoporosis
asthma			rickets

⊙ OnHealth.com. "Disease Categories," http://onhealth.webmd.com/conditions/condctr/index.asp
  Thrive Online. "Index of Illnesses and Conditions," www.thriveonline.com/health/library/
    lookitup.ills.html
  Centers for Disease Control. "Health Topics A-Z," www.cdc.gov/health/diseases.htm

Diseases: Common Symptoms

Name	Type	Symptoms
Acne vulgaris	bacterial	Blackheads (black spots the size of a pinhead); whiteheads (white spots similar to blackheads); pustules (small pus-filled lesions); cysts (larger and firm swellings) and abscesses (swollen and inflamed areas with pus) with severe acne; redness and inflammation around eruptions

Name	*Type*	*Symptoms*
AIDS (acquired immune deficiency syndrome)	viral	Initial HIV infection may produce no symptoms; fatigue; unexplained weight loss; night sweats; fever; diarrhea; recurrent respiratory and skin infections; swollen lymph glands throughout the body; genital changes; enlarged spleen; mouth sores
Alcoholism	genetic; lifestyle-related	Frequent blackouts; memory loss; delirium tremens (tremors, hallucinations, confusion, sweating, rapid heartbeat)—these occur most often with alcohol withdrawal; liver disease
Alzheimer's disease	unknown; there may be a genetic predisposition.	Forgetfulness of recent events; increasing difficulty performing intellectual tasks, such as accustomed work, balancing a checkbook or maintaining a household; personality changes, including poor impulse control and poor judgment
Asthma	environmental; may be genetic	Difficulty breathing; bluish skin; exhaustion; grunting respiration; inability to speak; mental changes, including restlessness or confusion
Bronchitis	viral	Cough that produces little or no sputum initially, but does later on; low fever (usually less than 101°F or 38.3°C); burning chest discomfort or feeling of pressure behind the breastbone; wheezing or uncomfortable breathing (sometimes)
Chickenpox (varicella)	viral	The following are usually mild in children, severe in adults: fever; abdominal pain or a general ill feeling that lasts 1 or 2 days; skin eruptions that appear almost anywhere on the body, including the scalp, penis, and inside the mouth, nose, throat, or vagina. They may be scattered over large areas, and they occur least on the arms and legs. Blisters collapse within 24 hours and form scabs. New crops of blisters erupt every 3 to 4 days; adults have additional symptoms that resemble influenza
Common cold	viral	Runny or stuffy nose. Nasal discharge is watery at first, then becomes thick and greenish yellow; sore throat; hoarseness; cough that produces little or no sputum; low fever; fatigue; watering eyes; appetite loss
Depression	genetic; lifestyle-related; environmental	Loss of interest in life; listlessness and fatigue; insomnia; excessive or disturbed sleeping; social isolation; feeling not useful or needed; appetite loss or overeating; constipation; loss of sex drive; difficulty making decisions; concentration difficulty;

		unexplained crying bouts; intense guilt feelings over minor or imaginary misdeeds; irritability; restlessness; thoughts of suicide; various pains, such as headache or chest pain, without evidence of disease
Diabetes mellitus (non–insulin dependent)	strong genetic predisposition; may be lifestyle-related	Fatigue; excess thirst; increased appetite; frequent urination; decreased resistance to infection, especially urinary-tract infections and yeast infections of the skin, mouth, or vagina
Ear infection (otitis media)	various (viral, bacterial, allergic reaction)	Irritability; earache; feeling of fullness in the ear; hearing loss; fever; discharge or leakage from the ear; diarrhea, vomiting (sometimes); pulling at the ear (small children)
Eczema	allergy	Itching (sometimes severe); small blisters with oozing; thickening and scaling from chronic inflammation
Gingivitis	lifestyle and environmental, sometimes caused by blood disorders	Gums that are swollen, tender, red, and soft around the teeth; gums that bleed easily; bad breath; fever (rarely); no pain
Glaucoma	unknown; may be genetic	Loss of peripheral vision in small areas; blurred vision on one side toward the nose
Hepatitis	viral	Flu-like symptoms, such as fever, fatigue, nausea, vomiting, diarrhea, and loss of appetite; jaundice (yellow eyes and skin) caused by a buildup of bile in the blood; dark urine from bile spilling into the urine; light, "clay-colored," or whitish stools
Herpes	viral	Usually found around the mouth, but sometimes on the genitals. The blisters are grouped together and each is surrounded by a red ring. They fill with fluid, then dry up and disappear. If the eye is infected: eye pain and redness; feeling that something is in the eye; sensitivity to light; tearing
Influenza	viral	Chills and moderate to high fever; muscle aches, including backache; cough, usually with little or no sputum; sore throat; hoarseness; runny nose; headache; fatigue
Lyme disease	viral	Early stages: Muscle aches and pains; fatigue and lethargy; chills and fever
		Middle stages: Stiff neck with headache; backache; nausea and vomiting; sore throat; enlargement of the spleen and lymph glands; migrating joint pain, eventually accompanied by redness and warmth; cardiac symptoms; migrating arthritis
		Late stages: Neurological disease; chronic arthritis

Name	Type	Symptoms
Osteoporosis	various causes (nutrient deficiency; genetic; lifestyle-related)	Compression fractures; deformed spinal column with humps; loss of height; fractures occurring with minor injury, especially of the hip or arm
Sinusitis	various causes, most often bacterial	Nasal congestion with green-yellow (sometimes blood-tinged) discharge; feeling of pressure inside the head; headache that is worse in the morning or when bending forward. With chronic sinusitis, the headache may occur daily for weeks at a time. Cheek pain that may resemble a toothache; post-nasal drip; cough (sometimes) that is usually non-productive; tiredness; lack of energy; disturbed sleep (sometimes); fever (sometimes); eye pain
Strep throat	bacterial	Rapid onset of throat pain; throat pain that is worse when swallowing; appetite loss; headache; fever; general ill feeling; ear pain when swallowing (sometimes); tender, swollen glands in the neck; bright-red tonsils that may have specks of pus
Ulcer (Peptic)	believed to be bacterial	Appetite and weight loss (with duodenal, may be weight gain, as person eats more to ease discomfort); recurrent vomiting; blood in the stool; anemia; a burning, boring, or gnawing feeling that lasts 30 minutes to 3 hours (often interpreted as heartburn, indigestion, or hunger).

⊙ OnHealth.com. "Disease Categories," onhealth.webmd.com/conditions/condctr/index.asp
Thrive Online. "Index of Illnesses and Conditions," www.thriveonline.com/health/library/
   lookitup.ills.html
Encarta.com. "Human Disease," encarta.msn.com/find/Concise.asp?z=1&pg=2&ti=761566075

First Aid

The information below provides general guidelines for some first aid techniques. The guidelines offered are not intended to replace the formal training in CPR, artificial respiration, or other first aid offered by the American Red Cross or the American Heart Association. In any serious emergency, the first step is always to call emergency medical services.

Adult CPR

Cardiopulmonary Resuscitation (CPR) involves three basic steps, defined by the American Heart Association as:

Airway (ensure a clear airway)

Breathing (restore breathing using artificial respiration)

Circulation (restore heartbeat)

1. Check for consciousness: If the victim appears to be unconscious, tap or gently shake him/her and ask if she is OK. If she does not respond, instruct someone else to call emergency medical services, or shout for help.

2. Make sure the person is on his or her back on a firm surface.

3. Open airway and check for breathing: Tilt the victim's head back by gently lifting the chin while pushing the forehead. Look, listen, and feel for the victim's breath. [fig. 1]

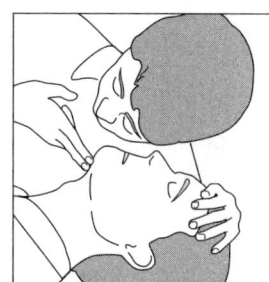

Fig. 1

4. If no breath, check to be sure nothing is obstructing the throat. If necessary, clear the obstruction using the method below (see Adult Choking) and again check for breathing.

5. If no breath, pinch the nostrils shut, open the mouth, and fit your mouth firmly over the victim's mouth. Give 2 full breaths. [fig. 2]

6. Feel for a pulse at the side of the neck.

7. If no pulse, position yourself beside the victim's chest. Use two fingers to find the bottom of the center of the breastbone. Position the heel of your other hand above the two fingers on the breastbone; then place the heel of the second hand over the heel of the first. [fig. 3]

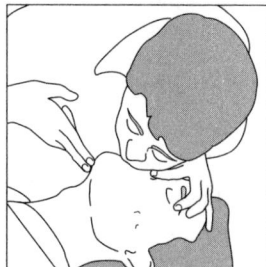

Fig. 2

8. Position your shoulders directly over your hands and lock your arms straight. Give 15 compressions in 10 seconds, depressing the breastbone 1.5–2 inches.

9. Return to Step 5 above and administer another 2 breaths.

10. Continue alternating compressions and breathing until victim revives or help arrives.

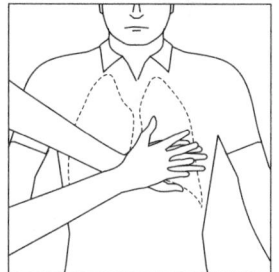

Fig. 3

Adult Choking

1. First ask the victim if he/she can cough or speak.*

2. If the victim cannot cough or speak, stand behind him, reach around to his front, and locate his bottom rib.

3. At the level of the bottom rib, move your hand across the abdomen until it is above the navel. Make a fist and place it in that spot with the thumb-side against the abdomen. Cover the fist with your other hand. [fig. 1]

4. Quickly pull your fist into the victim's abdomen with an upward thrust to dislodge the object obstructing his breathing.

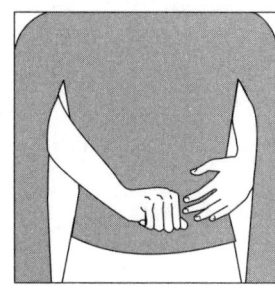

Fig. 1

*If the victim is lying down, turn him face-up, straddle his hips, and locate the correct hand position using the method above. Place your hands one on top of the other and move so your shoulders are directly above the victim's abdomen. Give a sharp forward thrust to dislodge the object and immediately clear the object from the victim's mouth. If the victim does not begin breathing, call emergency medical services and begin artificial respiration. (See Adult CPR above)

External Bleeding

1. If bleeding is heavy, call emergency medical services.
2. Wash hands and put on sterile gloves if available.
3. Remove loose debris from wound.
4. Put a barrier such as layers of sterile dressing or clean cloth between you and the wound and press dressing firmly. If further dressing is required, do not remove first dressing but apply a fresh layer over the soaked dressing.
5. If no bones are broken, raise wound above heart level.

Insect Stings

If a person is stung:

1. Have someone stay with the person to make sure they do not have an allergic reaction.*
2. Wash the area with soap and water.
3. Remove the stinger by wiping a piece of gauze over the area or by scraping a fingernail over the area. Do not squeeze the area or use tweezers as this causes more venom to go into the skin.
4. Apply ice to reduce swelling.
5. Do not scratch the sting. This will cause the sting to swell more and increase the chance of infection.

*Allergic reactions to bee stings can be deadly. People with allergies to stings should always carry an insect sting allergy kit and wear a medical ID bracelet stating their allergy. Signs of an allergic reaction to insect stings include swelling that moves to other parts of the body, especially the face or neck; difficulty breathing; wheezing; dizziness; or a drop in blood pressure. Call for emergency medical care if any of these signs is present.

⊙ American Red Cross and Kathleen A. Handal. *The American Red Cross First Aid & Safety Handbook.* Boston: Little, Brown, 1992.
World Publishing Systems. "First Aid Online," www.wps.com.au/business/firstaid/firstaid.htm

Common Over-the-Counter Drugs and Uses

Generic Name	Brand Names	Purpose
acetaminophen	Excedrin; Tylenol	analgesic
aluminum hydroxide	Alternagel	antacid
aspirin (acetylsalicylic acid)	Bayer; Bufferin	analgesic
bisacodyl	Dulcolax	stimulant laxative
brompheniramine	Dimetane	antihistamine
caffeine	No-Doz; Vivarin	stimulant
calcium carbonate	Tums; Rolaids	antacid
chlorpheniramine		antihistamine
cimetidine	Tagamet HB	anti-ulcer
clotrimazole	Lotrimin	anti-fungal
codeine	Robitussin A-C	cough suppressant
dexbrompheniramine		antihistamine
dextromethorphan	Robitussin Pediatric Cough; Sucrets; Vicks Formula 44	cough suppressant (anti-tussive)

dimenhydrinate	Dramamine; Calm-X	motion sickness
diphenhydramine	Benadryl; Sominex; Unisom; Nytol	antihistamine; motion sickness; sleep aid
doxylamine		antihistamine; sleep aid
famotidine	Pepcid AC; Mylanta AR	anti-ulcer
guaifenesin	Robitussin	expectorant
ibuprofen	Advil; Nuprin; Motrin-IB	anti-inflammatory
ketoprofen	Orudis KT; Actron	analgesic
lidocaine	Xylocaine	anesthetic
loperamide	Immodium; Kaopectate	anti-diarrhea
magnesium salts	Phillips' Milk of Magnesia	antacid; laxative
meclizine	Dramamine II	motion sickness
miconazole nitrate	Monistat	anti-fungal
naphazoline	Clear Eyes	ophthalmic decongestant
naproxen sodium	Aleve	anti-inflammatory
oxymetazoline hydrochloride	Afrin	decongestant
phenolphthalein	Ex-Lax	stimulant laxative
phenylephrine hydrochloride	Dristan; Sinex	decongestant
pink bismuth	Pepto Bismol	anti-diarrhea; anti-emetic
polymyxin B	Neosporin	topical antibiotic
pramoxine	Anusol	anti-hemorrhoid
pseudoephedrine hydrochloride	Chlor-Trimeton; Dimetapp; Drixoral; Sudafed; Triaminic	decongestant
ranitidine	Zantac 75	anti-ulcer
simethicone	Maalox; Mylanta; Gas-X	anti-flatulent
sodium bicarbonate	Alka-Seltzer	antacid
tetrahydrozoline	Visine Allergy Relief	ophthalmic decongestant
tolnaftate	Tinactin	anti-fungal
undecylenate	Desenex	anti-fungal

⊙ Merck.com. "Over-the-Counter Drugs," www.merck.com/pubs/mmanual_home/sec2/13.htm
Eckerd.com. "Healthcare," 146.235.6.106/storefront/Healthcare/otc/table1_2.asp
National Women's Health Information Center. "Drug Interactions," www.4woman.gov/faq/drug.html

Common Prescription Drugs and Uses

Generic Name	Brand Names	Purpose
albuterol	Proventil	orally inhaled bronchodilator
alclometasone	Alclovate	topical steroid
amlodipine	Norvasc	calcium channel blocker
amoxicillin/ clavulanic acid	Augmentin	antibiotic
ampicillin		antibiotic
atenolol	Tenormin	beta-blocker
atorvastatin	Lipitor	lipid lowering agent
azithromycin	Zithromax	antibiotic
beclomethasone	Vanceril	orally inhaled steroid
benazepril	Lotensin	anti-hypertensive
budesonide	Rhinocort	nasally inhaled steroid
bupropion	Wellbutrin/Wellbutrin SR	antidepressant
captoril	Capotril	antihypertensive

Generic Name	Brand Names	Purpose
carvedilol	Coreg	beta-blocker
celecoxib	Celebrex	NSAID (non-steroidal anti-inflammatory drug)
cephalexin	Keflex	antibiotic
cetirizine	Zyrtec	antihistamine
cholestipol	Cholestid	lipid lowering agent
cimetidine	Tagamet	anti-ulcer
desonide	Tridesilon	topical steroid
desoximetasone	Topicort	topical steroid
doxepin	Sinequan	antidepressant
enalapril	Vasotec	anti-hypertensive
erythromycin		antibiotic
estradiol	Estrace	estrogen replacement
estrogen conjugated	Premarin	estrogen replacement
estrogens progesterone	Premphase; Prempro	estrogen replacement
estropipate	Ogen; Ortho EST	estrogen replacement
ethinyl estradiol/norethindrone	Ortho-Novum; Loestrin	oral contraceptive
ethinyl estradiol/norgestimate	Ortho Tri-Cyclen	oral contraceptive
fexophenadine	Allegra	antihistamine
fluocinonide	Derma-Smoothe	topical steroid
fluoxetine	Prozac	antidepressant (SSRI)
fluticasone	Flonase; Flovent	nasally inhaled steroid
fluvoxamine	Luvox	antidepressant
hydrocortisone 2.5%		topical steroid
hydrocortisone valerate	Westcort	topical steroid
ibuprofen	Motrin	NSAID (non-steroidal anti-inflammatory drug)
insulin		diabetes treatment
labetalol	Normodyne; Trandate	alpha- and beta-blocker
lansoprazole	Prevacid	anti-ulcer
lisinopril	Zestril	anti-hypertensive
loratadine	Claritin	antihistamine
losartan	Cozaar	A2 blocker
metronidazole		antibiotic
mometasone	Nasonex	nasally inhaled steroid
nabumetone	Relafen	NSAID (non-steroidal anti-inflammatory drug)
naproxen	Naprosyn	NSAID (non-steroidal anti-inflammatory drug)
nefazodone	Serzone	antidepressant
omeprazole	Prilosec	anti-ulcer
paroxetine	Paxil	antidepressant (SSRI)
penicillin VK		antibiotic
phenelzine	Nardil	antidepressant (MAO inhibitor)
pirbuterol	Maxair	orally inhaled bronchodilator
pravastatin	Pravachol	lipid lowering agent

prioxicam	Feldene	NSAID (non-steroidal anti-inflammatory drug)
quinapril	Accupril	anti-hypertensive
ranitidine	Zantac	anti-ulcer
salmeterol	Serevent	orally inhaled bronchodilator
salsalate	Disalcid	NSAID (non-steroidal anti-inflammatory drug)
sertaline	Zoloft	antidepressant (SSRI)
sildenafil citrate	Viagra	impotence treatment
sulfamethoxazole/trimethoprin		antibiotic
sulindac	Clinoril	NSAID (non-steroidal anti-inflammatory drug)
tetracycline		antibiotic
tranylcypromine	Parnate	antidepressant (MAO inhibitor)
triamcinolone	Azmacort	orally inhaled steroid
valsartan	Diovan	A2 blocker
venlafaxine	Effexor	antidepressant
verapamil	Calan	calcium channel blocker

*Brand names not provided for drugs generally referred to by generic name.

⊙ Minnesota Council of Health Plans. "Prescription Drug Guide," www.mnhealthplans.org/prescrip_guide.html

Thrive Online Medical Library. "Index to Prescription and Non-Prescription Drugs," www.thriveonline.com/medical/library/treatments.html

Recommended Childhood Vaccines

	Birth	2 mos.	4 mos.	6 mos.	12 mos.	15 mos.	24 mos.	4–6 yrs.	11–12 yrs.
Hepatitis B	Hep B	Hep B		Hep B					
Diphtheria, Tetanus, Pertussis		DTaP	DTaP	DTaP		DTaP		DTaP	+Td*
H. influenzae type b	Hib	Hib	Hib	Hib					
Pneumococcal†		PCV7	PCV7	PCV7	PCV7				
Polio	IPV	IPV	IPV						
Measles, Mumps, Rubella					MMR			MMR	
Varicella					Var			Var	
Hepatitis A							Hep A		

* +Td stands for tetanus and diphtheria.

†Pneumococcal vaccine was added to the recommended vaccine schedule on June 6, 2000. Ask your doctor for more information.

Recommended Childhood Vaccines

Initial doses of all these immunizations need to be given before children are 2 years old in order for them to be protected during their most vulnerable period.

Recommended ages above are guidelines; acceptable ages can range from 2 to 12 months beyond the one given. Consult your doctor.

The hepatitis B, MMR, and varicella vaccines may be given at 11–12 years of age if previously recommended doses were missed or given earlier than the recommended ages.

All children and adolescents (through 18 years of age) who have not been immunized against hepatitis B may begin the series during any medical visit. Special efforts should be made to immunize children who were born in or whose parents were born in areas of the world with moderate or high endemicity of hepatitis B virus infection.

The fourth dose of diphtheria and tetanus toxoids and acellular pertussis vaccine may be administered as early as 12 months of age, provided 6 months have elapsed since the third dose and the child is unlikely to return at age 15–18 months. Tetanus and diphtheria toxoids vaccine is recommended at 11–12 years of age if at least 5 years have elapsed since the last dose of DTP, DTaP, or DT. Subsequent routine +Td boosters are recommended every 10 years.

The second dose of measles, mumps, and rubella (MMR) vaccine is recommended routinely at 4–6 years of age but may be administered during any visit, provided at least 4 weeks have elapsed since receipt of the first dose and that both doses are administered beginning at or after 12 months of age. Those who have not previously received the second dose should complete the schedule by the 11- to 12-year-old visit.

Varicella (chickenpox) vaccine is recommended at any medical visit on or after the first birthday for susceptible children (for example, those who lack a reliable history of chickenpox as judged by a health care professional and who have not been immunized). Susceptible persons 13 years of age or older should receive two doses, given at least 4 weeks apart.

⊙ OnHealth.com. "Recommended Childhood Vaccination Schedule," http://onhealth.webmd.com/baby/in-depth/item/item,92164_1_1.asp
American Academy of Pediatrics. "Recommended Childhood Immunization Schedule," www.aap.org/family/parents/immunize.html

Sunburn Index

Sunburn (UV) Index	Level	Description
0–2	Minimal	Minimal danger for the average person; most can stay in the sun for up to 1 hour during peak times (10am–4pm) without burning. Fair-skinned people should always protect skin with a sunscreen that has a sun protection factor (SPF) of at least 15.
3–4	Low	Low risk of harm from unprotected sun exposure. Fair-skinned people may burn in less than 20 minutes.

5–6	Moderate	Moderate risk of harm from unprotected sun exposure. Fair-skinned people may burn in less than 15 minutes.
7–9	High	High risk of harm from unprotected sun exposure. Fair-skinned people may burn in less than 10 minutes.
10+	Very High	High risk of harm from unprotected sun exposure. Fair-skinned people may burn in less than 10 minutes.

To protect yourself from the sun:

- Always use a sunscreen and lip balm with an SPF of at least 15.
- Wear sunglasses that block 99–100 percent of UV radiation.
- Seek shade.

⊙ U.S. Environmental Protection Agency. "SunWise School Program," www.epa.gov/sunwise1

THE SCIENCES: *Health, Nutrition, Fitness*

Life Expectancy in the United States (1997 avg.)

Life expectancy in the United States varies by gender and race. Once a person has reached age 65 the estimate is adjusted because the original estimate factors in premature deaths due to accidents and diseases.

	At Birth	At Age 65
All Americans	76.5	+17.7
All Males	73.6	+15.9
All Females	79.4	+19.2

⊙ Centers for Disease Control and Prevention. "National Center for Health Statistics," www.cdc.gov/nchs/fastats/lifexpec.htm

Causes of Death

Heart disease, cancer, and stroke continue to be the top three causes of death in the United States. Leading causes of death differ by age, race, and gender. The estimated causes (for all groups combined) and ranking for 1998:

Heart disease	724,859	Pneumonia and influenza	91,871
Cancer	541,532	Diabetes	64,751
Stroke	158,448	Suicide	30,575
Lung disease	112,584	Kidney disease	26,182
Accidents	97,835	Liver disease and cirrhosis	25,192

⊙ Centers for Disease Control. *National Vital Statistics Report* 48, no. 11, 1998. www.cdc.gov/nchs/fastats/deaths.htm.

Height and Weight Standards

The tables below show the desirable weight ranges, in pounds, for various heights and body-frame types for men and women between the ages of 25–59. Shoes with 1-inch heels and clothing weighing 5 lbs. for men and 3 lbs. for women are factored into the target ranges.

Height & Weight Table for Men

Height (Feet/Inches)	Small Frame	Medium Frame	Large Frame
5'2"	128–134	131–141	138–150
5'3"	130–136	133–143	140–153
5'4"	132–138	135–145	142–156
5'5"	134–140	137–148	144–160
5'6"	136–142	139–151	146–164
5'7"	138–145	142–154	149–168
5'8"	140–148	145–157	152–172
5'9"	142–151	148–160	155–176
5'10"	144–154	151–163	158–180
5'11"	146–157	154–166	161–184
6'0"	149–160	157–170	164–188
6'1"	152–164	160–174	168–192
6'2"	155–168	164–178	172–197
6'3"	158–172	167–182	176–202
6'4"	162–176	171–187	181–207

Height & Weight Table for Women

Height (Feet/Inches)	Small Frame	Medium Frame	Large Frame
4'10"	102–111	109–121	118–131
4'11"	103–113	111–123	120–134
5'0"	104–115	113–126	122–137
5'1"	106–118	115–129	125–140
5'2"	108–121	118–132	128–143
5'3"	111–124	121–135	131–147
5'4"	114–127	124–138	134–151
5'5"	117–130	127–141	137–155
5'6"	120–133	130–144	140–159
5'7"	123–136	133–147	143–163
5'8"	126–139	136–150	146–167
5'9"	129–142	139–153	149–170
5'10"	132–145	142–156	152–173
5'11"	135–148	145–159	155–176
6'0"	138–151	148–162	158–179

⊙ Metropolitan Life Insurance Company. www.metlife.com

THE SCIENCES: *Health, Nutrition, Fitness*

Food Guide Pyramid

In 1992, the U.S. Food and Drug Administration and the Department of Health and Human Services created the Food Pyramid, containing six food groups. In the pyramid, foods that should be eaten more often are placed at the base, and those that should be eaten less frequently are at the top.

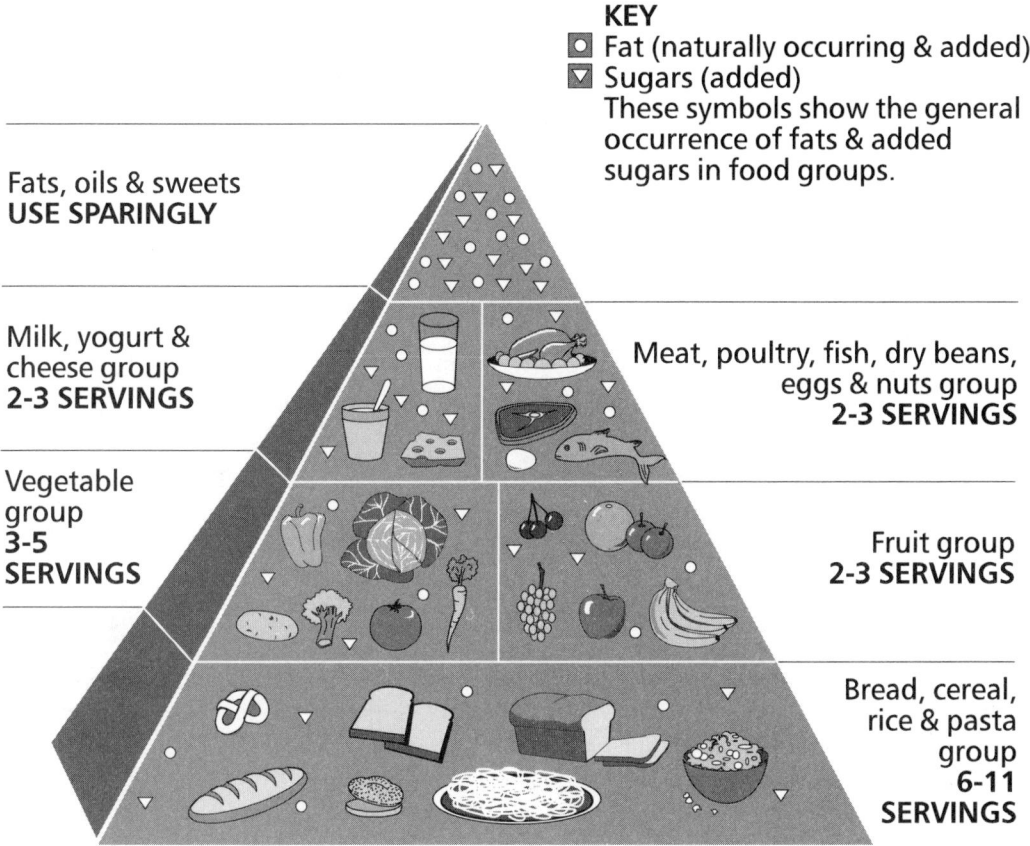

KEY
▣ Fat (naturally occurring & added)
▽ Sugars (added)
These symbols show the general occurrence of fats & added sugars in food groups.

Fats, oils & sweets
USE SPARINGLY

Milk, yogurt & cheese group
2-3 SERVINGS

Meat, poultry, fish, dry beans, eggs & nuts group
2-3 SERVINGS

Vegetable group
3-5 SERVINGS

Fruit group
2-3 SERVINGS

Bread, cereal, rice & pasta group
6-11 SERVINGS

Breads, cereal, rice, and pasta are at the bottom of the pyramid. The USDA recommends six to eleven servings of these foods daily. The next level recommends two to three servings of fruits and three to five servings of vegetables. The third level includes two to three servings of dairy, and two to three servings of meat or other proteins. Fats, oils, and sweets should be eaten sparingly.

What Is a Serving?

- Grains and starches: one slice bread; one ounce ready-to-eat cereal; one-half cup cooked cereal, rice, or pasta
- Vegetables: one cup raw leafy greens; three-quarters cup vegetable juice; one-half cup other chopped vegetables

Food Guide Pyramid *(cont.)*

- Fruits: one medium apple, banana, or orange; one melon wedge; one-half cup chopped fruits or berries; three-quarters cup fruit juice
- Dairy: one cup milk or yogurt; 1.5 ounces cheese
- Meat: two to three ounces cooked, lean meat, poultry or fish; one egg; one-half cup cooked beans; two tablespoons seeds or nuts

Recommended Daily Servings

	Children, Women, Older Adults	Teen Girls, Active Women, Most Men	Teen Boys, Active Men
Milk & Milk Products	2–4	2–4	2–4
Meat & Meat Alternatives	2	2	2
Vegetables	3	4	5
Fruits	2	3	4
Breads and Cereals	6	9	11
Total Fat, in grams*	36–53	49–73	62–93
Calories	about 1,600	about 2,200	about 2,800

*Fat should comprise 20–30% of calories consumed; 1 gram fat = 9 calories

⊙ U.S. Department of Agriculture. "Center for Nutrition Policy Promotion," www.usda.gov/cnpp/

Recommended Daily Allowances

The U.S. Department of Agriculture first developed the Recommended Daily Allowances (RDA) more than 50 years ago to provide a measure of "the levels of intake of essential nutrients that, on the basis of scientific knowledge, are judged by the Food and Nutrition Board to be adequate to meet the known nutrient needs of practically all healthy persons."

Since the RDA's inception, scientific knowledge about nutrition has changed significantly. A simple measure as defined above is no longer adequate. Contemporary nutrition concerns itself not only with preventing diseases caused by nutritional deficiency, but aims to reduce the risk of chronic diseases such as osteoporosis, cancer, and heart disease.

The USDA is in the process of revising its guidelines and will eventually replace the RDA with a new measurement standard, the Dietary Reference Intake (DRI). The DRI will comprise three levels of evaluation, including an average, a minimum, and a maximum recommended amount for each nutrient. Until the new standards are fully in place, a combination of the two will continue to be used, as reflected in the tables below.

THE SCIENCES: *Health, Nutrition, Fitness*

1989 Recommended Daily Allowances (RDA)

(ages)	Children 0–3	4–10	Males 11–24	25–50	51+	Females 11–24	25–50	51+	Pregnant
Protein (g)	13–16	24–28	45–59	63	63	44–46	50	50	60
Vitamin A (µg)	375–400	500–700	1,000	1,000	1,000	800	800	800	800
Vitamin E (µg)	3–6	7	10	10	10	8	8	8	10
Vitamin K (µg)	5–15	20–30	45–70	80	80	45–60	65	65	65
Vitamin C (mg)	30–40	45	50–60	60	60	50–60	60	60	70
Thiamin (mg)	0.3–0.7	0.9–1.0	1.3–1.5	1.5	1.2	1.1	1.1	1.0	1.5
Riboflavin (mg)	0.4–0.8	1.1–1.2	1.5–1.8	1.7	1.4	1.3	1.3	1.2	1.6
Niacin (mg)	5–9	12–13	17–20	19	15	15	15	13	17
Vitamin B6 (mg)	0.3–1.0	1.1–1.4	1.7–2.0	2.0	2.0	1.4–1.6	1.6	1.6	2.2
Folate (µg)	25–50	75–100	150–200	200	200	150–180	180	180	400
Vitamin B12 (µg)	0.3–0.7	1.0–1.4	2.0	2.0	2.0	2.0	2.0	2.0	2.2
Iron (µg)	6–10	10	10–12	10	10	15	15	10	30
Zinc (mg)	5–10	10	15	15	15	12	12	12	15
Iodine (µg)	40–70	90–120	150	150	150	150	150	150	175
Selenium (µg)	10–20	20–30	40–70	70	70	45–55	55	55	65

1997 Dietary Reference Intake (DRI)

(ages)	Children 0–3	4–10	Males 11–24	25–50	51+	Females 11–24	25–50	51+	Pregnant
Vitamin D (mg)	5	5	5	5	10	5	5	10	*
Calcium (mg)	210–500	800	1,300	1,000	1,200	1,300	1,000	1,200	*
Phosphorus (mg)	100–460	500	1,250	700	700	1,250	700	700	*
Magnesium (mg)	30–80	130	240–410	400–420	420	240–360	310–320	320	+40
Fluoride (mg)	0.01–0.7	1.1	2.0–3.2	3.8	3.8	2.0–2.9	3.1	3.1	*

* values are the same as for other women of comparable age

⊙ U.S. Department of Agriculture. "Recommended Dietary Intakes," www.nal.usda.gov/fnic/dga/rda.pdf
Food and Nutrition Board, Institute of Medicine. "Frequently Asked Questions about the DRIs,"
www.nas.edu/IOM/IOMhome.nsf/pages/FNB+FAQ+DRI

Vitamins and Minerals

Vitamins

Name	Organs and systems affected	Other health benefits
A (Beta Carotene)	body tissues, skin, mucous membranes, eyesight, bones, and teeth	reduces risk of lung and certain oral cancers
B1 (Thiamin)	metabolism, nervous system, muscles, heart	stabilizes appetite and aids in digestion of carbohydrates
B2 (Riboflavin)	vision, skin, nails, hair	metabolizes carbohydrates, fats, and proteins; helps form antibodies and red blood cells
B3 (Niacin)	skin, tongue, digestive system	reduces cholesterol and high blood pressure; improves circulation; metabolizes protein, sugar, and fat; prevents pellagra
B6 (Pyridoxine)	skin, central nervous system	helps break down amino acids and form antibodies; metabolizes fats and carbohydrates; helps remove excess fluid and maintain proper balance of sodium and phosphorus
B12 (Cobalamin)	nervous system and growth	assists in formation and regeneration of red blood cells; metabolizes carbohydrate, fats, and protein; aids calcium absorption
Pantothenic Acid	central nervous system, adrenal glands	aids in stress reduction, cell building, fighting infection; releases energy from carbohydrates, fats, and protein; helps body to utilize vitamins
Biotin	hair	aids in utilization of protein, folic acid, pantothenic acid, and vitamin B12
Folic Acid	formation of red blood cells	synthesizes DNA and RNA for cell growth and reproduction; aids in amino acid metabolism
Inositol	hair and formation of lecithin	assists in breakdown of fats and cholesterol reduction
Choline	liver, kidneys, gallbladder	facilitates nerve transmission, memory, fat and cholesterol control
PABA (Paraaminobenzoic Acid)	hair	aids in production of folic acid and red blood cells and in assimilation of pantothenic acid; has sun screen properties
C (Ascorbic Acid)	teeth, gums, bones, blood vessels	aids in healing wounds, resisting infection and preventing common colds and cancer; helps to synthesize collagen

THE SCIENCES: *Health, Nutrition, Fitness*

D	bones, teeth, nervous system, heart	improves absorption and utilization of calcium and phosphorus; antioxidant
E	cells, capillary walls	retards cellular aging; alleviates fatigue; prevents and dissolves blood clots; helps prevent sterility, muscular dystrophy, heart conditions; antioxidant
K	blood	assists in blood clotting

Minerals

Name	Organs and systems affected	Other health benefits
Calcium	bones and teeth	regulates heart rhythm, eases insomnia, nutrient absorption and blood clotting; maintains nerve and muscle function; lowers blood pressure and cholesterol levels; reduces risk of colon cancer
Chromium	digestive system	assists insulin in metabolizing sugar and stabilizing blood sugar levels; cleans arteries; transports amino acids; controls appetite
Copper		facilitates absorption and utilization of iron, oxidation of vitamin C and formation of elastin for muscles; helps red blood cell and bone formation
Fluorine	bones and teeth	
Iodine	thyroid gland	assists metabolism; regulates energy; burns excess fat
Iron		supports the making of hemoglobin and myoglobin; increases resistance to stress and disease; promotes good skin tone; prevents fatigue
Magnesium		helps metabolize calcium and vitamin C; regulates neuromuscular activity of heart and maintains heart rhythm; converts blood sugar to energy
Manganese		aids digestion, blood breakdown of amino acids, metabolism of vitamins B1 and E; triggers breakdown of fats and cholesterol; nourishes nerves and brain; enables normal skeletal development; maintains sex hormone production; antioxidant
Phosphorus	bones and teeth, kidneys, muscles, and heart	
Potassium	blood pressure, skin, heart, brain	preserves proper alkalinity of body fluids; stimulates kidneys to eliminate body wastes

Vitamins and Minerals (cont.)

Minerals (cont.)

Name	Organs and systems affected	Other health benefits
Selenium	cell membranes	prevents free-radical generation; decreases risk of breast, colon, lung, and prostate cancer; preserves tissue elasticity; slows aging process; aids in treatment of dandruff; antioxidant
Zinc		synthesizes protein; heals wounds; aids in development of reproductive organs, prostate functions and male hormone activity; governs contraction of muscles; stabilizes blood and maintains body's alkaline balance; aids in normal tissue function and the digestion and metabolism of phosphorus; antioxidant

⊙ Feinstein, Alice, ed. *Prevention's Healing With Vitamins.* Emmaus, Penn.: Rodale, 1998.
  Murray, Michael T. *The Encyclopedia of Nutritional Supplements.* Rocklin, Calif.: Prima, 1996.

Diet Types

Diabetic: Ten to 20% of calories should come from protein, no more than 30% from fats, and the rest from carbohydrates. Eat frequently to stabilize blood-sugar levels.

Gout: To avoid purines, generally found in meat, poultry, fish, and shellfish, restrict to no more than seven ounces per day. An increased intake of carbohydrates is recommended.

Healthy Heart: Avoid foods high in fat, saturated fat, and cholesterol. No more than 30% of calories consumed should contain fat.

High-Calcium: To combat or halt osteoporosis, consume three to four calcium-rich foods per day, as well as calcium supplements.

High-Fiber: To treat some conditions of the intestinal tract, obtain more fiber from foods such as beans, lentils, whole-grain breads and cereals, fruits, and vegetables.

Lactose-Restricted: Avoid food that contains milk or other dairy products unless they are lactose-reduced. A lactase enzyme pill may assist in lactose toleration.

Low-Sodium: To combat hypertension, substitute herbs and low-sodium spices for table salt and avoid processed foods.

Low-Fiber: To treat some intestinal problems in order to decrease the amount of solid waste products, reduce intake of nuts, seeds, and raw fruits and vegetables.

Reactive Hypoglycemia: Consume three regular meals and several snacks per day and severely restrict sugar intake.

Vegetarian: Meat, fish, and poultry—and sometimes dairy products—are excluded. Nutritional supplements may be necessary.

⊙ Applegate, Elizabeth. *Eat Your Way to a Healthy Heart.* Paramus, N.J.: Prentice Hall, 1999.
  Colbin, Annemarie. *Food and Our Bones: The Natural Way to Prevent Osteoporosis.* New York: Plume, 1998.
  International Food Information Council. "Coping with Lactose Intolerance," http://ificinfo.health.org/insight/fi1112c.htm

Food Additives

Food additives play a vital role in today's food supply. Because most Americans do not grow their own food, additives extend the shelf life of groceries, making it possible to obtain safe, wholesome, and tasty foods year-round.

Additives are used for five main reasons: to maintain product consistency, to improve or maintain nutritional value, to maintain palatability and wholesomeness, to provide leavening and control acidity/alkalinity, or to enhance flavor and color.

Some additives come from natural sources while others are man-made. Salt, baking soda, vanilla, and yeast are some of the most common. All food additives are regulated by federal authorities and various international organizations to ensure that foods are safe to eat and are accurately labeled.

Glossary of Terms

Anticaking and Free-Flow Agents prevent lumping, clustering, or caking in crystalline and finely divided powders; absorb water.

Antimicrobal Agents prevent the growth of microorganisms such as yeast, mold, and bacteria.

Antioxidants retard the oxidation of unsaturated fats and oils, colorings, and flavorings.

Bleaching or Maturing Agents are added to flour during or after milling to improve the color and baking qualities.

Chelating Agents trap trace amounts of metal atoms that would otherwise cause food to discolor or go rancid.

Colors provide or enhance the color of food.

Curing Agents impart color and flavor to foods, increase shelf stability.

Dough Conditioners modify the starch and/or protein (gluten) fractions of flour.

Drying Agents absorb moisture to maintain a "dry" environment for the food or ingredient.

Emulsifiers keep oil and water mixed together.

Enzymes are proteins that catalyze (speed up) reactions.

Firming Agents act on pectins to help them resist the softening that may accompany food processing (canning).

Flavor Enhancers accentuate the natural flavor of foods; usually used when very little of a natural ingredient is present.

Flavoring Agents add flavor or aroma or replace flavors lost in processing.

Formulation Aids help to produce the desired texture of the food.

Fumigants are used to control pests (insects, molds, etc.).

Humectants help foods to retain moisture.

Leavening Agents produce carbon dioxide (usually in baked products) to give a characteristic texture.

Lubricants are added to food-contact surfaces to prevent food from sticking.

Non-Nutritive Sweeteners provide the sweetness of sugar with less than 2% of the calories.

Nutrient Supplements provide essential nutrients for human metabolism.

Nutritive Sweeteners sweeten food, but add more than 2% of the calories of a sugar-sweetened product.

Oxidizing and Reducing Agents cause chemical changes (oxidize or reduce) to help make the product more acceptable, easier to process, or more stable.

pH Control Substances affect the acidity/alkalinity of a product or ingredient.

Processing Aids enhance the ability of a food ingredient to be processed into a desired end product.

Propellants and Aerating Agents provide force for the expulsion of a product or add "air" to a product.

Sequestrants combine with metal ions to prevent the metal from entering into unwanted reactions.

Solvents are used to separate one substance from another.

Food Additives *(cont.)*

Stabilizers and Thickeners increase the viscosity of a solution to improve body, consistency, and prevent emulsions from separating.

Surface Active Agents modify the surface properties (surface tension) of liquid food ingredients to enhance characteristics such as whipping, foaming or anti-foaming, wetting, and dispersing.

Synergists interact with other food ingredients to produce an effect that is greater than the additive effect of the two ingredients alone.

Texturizers alter the viscosity and "feel" of food.

Thickening Agents absorb some of the liquid that is present in food, thereby making the food thicker.

⊙ U.S. Food and Drug Administration. "Food Additives," http://vm.cfsan.fda.gov/~lrd/foodaddi.html

Food Labels

The definitions of terms on food labels are set by the U.S. Food and Drug Administration. Common terms are defined below.

Extra lean: In meat, poultry, and seafood, per serving: 5 g fat, 2 g saturated fat, and 95 mg cholesterol

Free: Must contain only trivial amounts of fat, saturated fat, cholesterol, sodium, sugars, or calories per serving. "Calorie free" means fewer than five calories; "sugar free" or "fat free" means less than 0.5 g.

Fresh: For food that is raw, has never been frozen or heated (other than blanched), and contains no preservatives

Healthy: Must be low in fat and contain limited amounts of cholesterol and sodium. A single-item food must provide at least 10% of vitamins A or C, iron, calcium, protein, or fiber and no more than 360 mg of sodium. A meal-type product must provide 10% of two or three of these vitamins or minerals or of protein or fiber and no more than 480 mg of sodium.

Lean: In meat, poultry, and seafood, per serving: 10 g fat, 4.5 g saturated fat, 95 mg cholesterol

Less: Contains 25% less of a nutrient or of calories than the reference food. For example, pretzels that have 25% less fat than potato chips could carry a "less" claim.

Good source: Contains 10 to 19% of the Daily Value for a particular nutrient

High: Contains 20 percent or more of the Daily Value for a particular nutrient

Light: Contains one-third fewer calories or half the fat of the reference food. "Light in sodium" may be used when the sodium content has been reduced by at least 50%. Also used to describe such properties as texture and color.

Low: Must not exceed dietary guidelines for fat, saturated fat, cholesterol, sodium, or calories per serving. Low-fat: 3 g; low-saturated fat: 1 g; low-sodium: 140 mg; very low sodium: 35 mg; low-cholesterol: 20 mg (and 2 g of saturated fat); low-calorie: 40 calories.

More: Contains a nutrient that is at least 10 percent of the Daily Value more than the reference food

Not a significant source: Used when food contains less the following amounts, per serving: 5 calories from fat, 0.5 g of saturated fat, 2 mg of cholesterol, 1g of dietary fiber, 1 g of sugars, and two percent of the RDA for vitamins/minerals

Percent fat free: Must accurately reflect the amount of fat present in 100 g of the food. If a food contains less than 0.5 g of fat per 100 g, the claim may be "100 percent fat free."

Reduced: Contains at least 25% less of a nutrient or of calories than the regular product

⊙ U.S. Food and Drug Administration. "A Food Labeling Guide," http://vm.cfsan.fda.gov/~dms/flg-toc.html

Poisoning

Children and adults can be poisoned by medicines and household products, lead, and carbon monoxide.

Protect your family by:

- Locking away dangerous substances like medicines, vitamins, beauty products, cleaning supplies, and pesticides, even if they are in child-resistant packaging.
- Keeping syrup of ipecac (which is available in drug stores) on hand in case of poisoning. Use it only after instructed to do so by a doctor or poison control center.

Emergency Action for Poisoning

If poison is inhaled, open all doors and windows and get the victim into the fresh air as quickly as possible. If the victim has stopped breathing, start artificial respiration.

If poison is on the skin, remove the victim's clothing and rinse the skin with water for at least 15 minutes and then wash the skin with soap and water and rinse again.

If poison is in the eye, rinse the eye by pouring lukewarm water into the eye for at least 15 minutes, with the victim blinking as often as possible. It is important that the eyelid not be forced open.

If poison is swallowed and the victim is awake, give water—nothing else—and call the poison center or doctor. If instructed to do so by a doctor or poison control personnel, administer syrup of ipecac.

After the emergency actions, call your area's poison control center:

Alabama
Alabama Poison Center
408-A Paul Bryant Drive
Tuscaloosa, AL 35401
800-462-0800 [AL only]; (205) 345-0600
Regional Poison Control Center
The Children's Hospital of Alabama
1600 - 7th Avenue South
Birmingham, AL 35233-1711
(205) 939-9201; (205) 939-9202;
800-292-6678 [AL only];
(205) 933-4050

Alaska
Anchorage Poison Control Center
3200 Providence Drive
Anchorage, AK 95519-6604
800-478-3193; (907) 261-3193

Arizona
Arizona Poison and Drug Information Center
Arizona Health Sciences Center
1501 N. Campbell Avenue, Rm. 1156
Tucson, AZ 85724
800-362-0101 [AZ only]; (520) 626-6016

Samaritan Regional Poison Center
1111 E. McDowell Road, Ancillary - 1
Phoenix, AZ 85006
(602) 253-3334; 800-362-0101 [AZ only]

Arkansas
Arkansas Poison and Drug Information Center
College of Pharmacy
University of Arkansas for Medical Sciences
4301 West Markham-Slot 522
Little Rock, AR 72205
800-376-4766

California
California Poison Control System, Central Office
University of California, San Francisco
School of Pharmacy, Box 1262
San Francisco, CA 94143
800-876-4766 [All of CA]

Colorado
Rocky Mountain Poison and Drug Center
8802 E. 9th Avenue
Denver, CO 80220-6800
(303) 629-1123

Connecticut
Connecticut Poison Control Center
University of Connecticut Health Center
263 Farmington Avenue
Farmington, CT 06030
800-343-2722 [CT only]; (203) 679-3056

Delaware
The Poison Control Center
3600 Sciences Center, Suite 220
Philadelphia, PA 19104-2641
(215) 386-2100; 800-722-7112

District of Columbia
National Capital Poison Center
3201 New Mexico Avenue, NW, Suite 310
Washington, DC 20016
(202) 625-3333; (202) 362-8563 [TTY]

Florida
Florida Poison Information Center
University Medical Center
University of Florida Health Science Center
655 West 8th Street
Jacksonville, FL 32209
(904) 549-4465; 800-282-3171 [FL only]
Florida Poison Information Center
University of Miami/Jackson Memorial
 Hospital
1611 NW 12th Avenue
Urgent Care Center Bldg., Rm. 219
Miami, FL 33136
800-282-3171 [FL only]
*The Florida Poison Information and Toxicology
 Resource Center*
Tampa General Hospital
P.O. Box 1289
Tampa, FL 33601
(813) 256-4444 [Tampa only];
800-282-3171 [FL only]

Georgia
Georgia Poison Center
Hughes Spalding Children's Hospital
Grady Health Systems
80 Butler Street, SE
PO Box 26066
Atlanta, GA 30335-3801
800-282-5846 [GA only];
(404) 616-9000

Hawaii
Hawaii Poison Center
1500 S. Beretania Street, Rm. 113
Honolulu, HI 96826
(808) 941-4411

Idaho
Idaho Poison Center
3092 Elder Street
Boise, ID 83720-0036
(208) 334-4570; 800-632-8000
[ID only]

Illinois
Illinois Poison Center
222 South Riverside Plaza, Suite 1900
Chicago, IL 60606
800-942-5969

Indiana
Indiana Poison Center
Methodist Hospital of Indiana
I-65 and 21st Street
P.O. Box 1367
Indianapolis, IN 46206-1367
800-382-9097 [IN only]; (317) 929-2323

Iowa
St. Luke's Poison Center
St. Luke's Regional Medical Center
2720 Stone Park Boulevard
Sioux City, IA 51104
(712) 277-2222; 800-352-2222
*Mid-Iowa Poison and Drug Information
 Center*
Variety Club Poison and Drug Information
 Center
Iowa Methodist Medical Center
1200 Pleasant Street
Des Moines, IA 50309
(515) 241-6254; 800-362-2327 [IA only]
Poison Control Center
The University of Iowa Hospitals and
 Clinics
Pharmacy Department
200 Hawkins Drive
Iowa City, IA 52242
800-272-6477

Kansas
Mid-America Poison Control Center
University of Kansas Medical Center
3901 Rainbow Blvd., Room B-400
Kansas City, KS 66160-7231
(913) 588-6633; 800-332-6633 [KS only]

Kentucky
*Kentucky Regional Poison Center of Kosair
   Children's Hospital*
Medical Towers South, Suite 572
P.O. Box 35070
Louisville, KY 40232-5070
(502) 589-8222; 800-722-5725 [KY only]

Louisiana
Louisiana Drug and Poison Information Center
Northeast Louisiana University
Sugar Hall
Monroe, LA 71209-6430
800-256-9822 [LA only]; (318) 362-5393

Maine
Maine Poison Control Center
Maine Medical Center
Department of Emergency Medicine
22 Bramhall Street
Portland, ME 04102
(207) 871-2950; 800-442-6305 [ME only]

Maryland
Maryland Poison Center
University of Maryland School of
   Pharmacy
20 N. Pine Street
Baltimore, MD 21201
(410) 528-7701; 800-492-2414 [MD only]

Massachusetts
Massachusetts Poison Control System
300 Longwood Avenue
Boston, MA 02115
(617) 232-2120; 800-682-9211

Michigan
Blodgett Regional Poison Center
1840 Wealthy SE
Grand Rapids, MI 49506-2968
800-POISON1; 800-356-3232 [TTY]
Poison Control Center
Children's Hospital of Michigan
Harper Professional Office Bldg.

4160 John Road, Suite 425
Detroit, MI 48201
(313) 745-5711; 800-764-7661
Marquette General Hospital
420 W. Magnetic Street
Marquette, MI 49855
(906) 225-3497; 800-562-9781

Minnesota
Hennepin Regional Poison Center
Hennepin County Medical Center
701 Park Avenue
Minneapolis, MN 55415
(612) 347-3141; (612) 337-7387 [Petline];
   (612) 337-7474 [TDD]
Minnesota Regional Poison Center
8100 34th Avenue S.
P.O. Box 1309
Minneapolis, MN 55440-1309
(612) 221-2113

Mississippi
Mississippi Regional Poison Control Center
University of Mississippi Medical Center
2500 North State Street
Jackson, MS 39216-4505
(601) 354-7660

Missouri
*Cardinal Glennon Children's Hospital Regional
   Poison Center*
1465 S. Grand Boulevard
St. Louis, MO 63104
(314) 772-5200; 800-366-8888;
800-392-9111
Children's Mercy Hospital
2401 Gillham Road
Kansas City, MO 64108
(816) 234-3430

Montana
Rocky Mountain Poison and Drug Center
8802 E. 9th Avenue
Denver, CO 80220-6800
(303) 629-1123
Nebraska
The Poison Center
8301 Dodge Street
Omaha, NE 68114
(402) 390-5555 [Omaha]; 800-955-9119
   [NE & WY]

Nevada

Rocky Mountain Poison and Drug Center
8802 E. 9th Avenue
Denver, CO 80220-6800
(303) 629-1123;
800-332-3073 [COLO WATTS];
800-525-5042 [MONT WATTS];
800-446-6179 [NEV WATTS];
(303) 739-1127 [TTY]

New Hampshire

New Hampshire Poison Information Center
Dartmouth-Hitchcock Medical Center
One Medical Center Drive
Lebanon, NH 03756
(603) 650-8000; (603) 650-5000
[11pm-8am]; 800-562-8236 [NH only]

New Jersey

*New Jersey Poison Information and Education
  System*
201 Lyons Avenue
Newark, NJ 07112
800-POISON1 [800-764-7661]

New Mexico

New Mexico Poison and Drug Information Center
University of New Mexico
Health Sciences Library, Room 125
Albuquerque, NM 87131-1076
(505) 843-2551; 800-432-6866 [NM only]

New York

Central New York Poison Control Center
SUNY Health Science Center
750 E. Adams Street
Syracuse, NY 13210
(315) 476-4766; 800-252-5655
Finger Lakes Regional Poison Center
University of Rochester Medical Center
601 Elmwood Avenue, Box 321,
Rm. G-3275
Rochester, NY 14642
(716) 275-5151; 800-333-0542
Hudson Valley Regional Poison Center
Phelps Memorial Hospital Center
701 North Broadway
North Tarrytown, NY 10591
800-336-6997; (914) 366-3030
Long Island Regional Poison Control Center

Winthrop University Hospital
259 First Street
Mineola, NY 11501
(516) 542-2323
New York City Poison Control Center
NYC Department of Health
455 First Avenue, Rm. 123
New York, NY 10016
(212) 340-4494; (212) POISONS;
(212) 689-9014 [TDD]
*Western New York Regional Poison Control
  Center*
Children's Hospital of Buffalo
219 Bryant Street
Buffalo, NY 14222
(716) 878-7654, also extensions 7655, 7856,
  7857

North Carolina

Carolinas Poison Center
1000 Blythe Boulevard
P.O. Box 32861
Charlotte, NC 28232-2861
(704) 355-4000; 800-84-TOXIN
[800-848-6946]
*Catawba Memorial Hospital Poison Control
  Center*
Pharmacy Department
810 Fairgrove Church Road
Hickory, NC 28602
(704) 322-6649
Duke Poison Control Center
North Carolina Regional Center
Box 3007
Duke University
Durham, NC 27710
(919) 684-8111; 800-672-1697 [NC only]
Triad Poison Center
1200 N. Elm Street
Greensboro, NC 27401-1020
(910) 574-8105; 800-953-4001 [NC only]

North Dakota

North Dakota Poison Information Center
MeritCare Medical Center
720 4th Street North
Fargo, ND 58122
(701) 234-5575; 800-732-2200
[ND, MN, SD only]

Ohio

Akron Regional Poison Center
1 Perkins Square
Akron, OH 44308
(216) 379-8562; 800-362-9922
[OH only]; (216) 379-8446 [TTY]
Bethesda Poison Control Center
2951 Maple Avenue
Zanesville, OH 43701
(614) 454-4221
Central Ohio Poison Center
700 Children's Drive
Columbus, OH 43205-2696
(614) 228-1323; 800-682-7625;
(614) 228-2272 [TTY]; (614) 461-2012
Cincinnati Drug & Poison Information and Regional Poison Control System
P.O. Box 670144
Cincinnati, OH 45267-0144
(513) 558-5111; 800-872-5111 [OH only]; 800-253-7955 [TTY]
Greater Cleveland Poison Control Center
11100 Euclid Avenue
Cleveland, OH 44106
(216) 231-4455
Medical College of Ohio Poison and Drug Information Center
3000 Arlington Avenue
Toledo, OH 43614
(419) 381-3897; 800-589-3897
[419 area code only]
Northeast Ohio Poison Education/Information Center
1320 Timken Mercy Drive NW
Canton, OH 44708
800-456-8662 [OH only]

Oklahoma

Oklahoma Poison Control Center
940 N.E. 13th Street, Rm. 3N118
Oklahoma, OK 73104
(405) 271-5454; 800-522-4611
[OK only]

Oregon

Oregon Poison Center
Oregon Health Sciences University
3181 SW Sam Jackson Park Road, CB550
Portland, OR 97201
(503) 494-8968; 800-452-7165
[OR only]

Pennsylvania

Central Pennsylvania Poison Center
University Hospital
Milton S. Hershey Medical Center
Hershey, PA 17033-0850
800-521-6110; (717) 531-6111
The Poison Control Center
3600 Sciences Center, Suite 220
Philadelphia, PA 19104-2641
(215) 386-2100
Pittsburgh Poison Center
3705 Fifth Avenue
Pittsburgh, PA 15213
(412) 681-6669; 800-722-7112

Rhode Island

Rhode Island Poison Center
593 Eddy Street
Providence, RI 02903
(401) 444-5727

South Carolina

Palmetto Poison Center
College of Pharmacy
University of South Carolina
Columbia, SC 29208
(803) 765-7359; 800-922-1117
[SC only]; (706) 724-5050;
(803) 777-1117

South Dakota

McKennan Poison Control Center
Box 5045
800 E. 21st Street
Sioux Falls, SD 57117-5045
(605) 336-3894; 800-952-0123;
800-843-0505

Tennessee

Middle Tennessee Poison Center
The Center for Clinical Toxicology
Vanderbilt University Medical Center
1161 21st Avenue South
501 Oxford House
Nashville, TN 37232-4632
(615) 936-2034 [local]; 800-288-9999
[regional]; (615) 322-0157 [TDD]
Southern Poison Center, Inc.
847 Monroe Avenue, Suite 230
Memphis, TN 38163
(901) 528-6048; 800-228-9999
[TN only]

Texas

Central Texas Poison Center
Scott & White Memorial Clinic & Hospital
2401 S. 31st Street
Temple, TX 76508
(817) 774-2005; 800-POISON1
[800-764-7661] [TX only]
North Texas Poison Center
Texas Poison Center Network at Parkland
Memorial Hospital
5201 Harry Hines Boulevard
P.O. Box 35926
Dallas, TX 75235
800-POISON1 [800-764-7661] [TX only]
South Texas Poison Center
7703 Floyd Curl Drive
San Antonio, TX 78284-7834
800-POISON1 [800-764-7661] [TX only]
Texas Poison Control Network
P.O. Box 1110, 1501 S. Coulter
Amarillo, TX 79175
800-POISON1 [800-764-7661] [TX only]
Texas Poison Control Network
Southeast Texas Poison Center
The University of Texas Medical Branch
301 University Avenue
Galveston, TX 77555-1175
(409)-765-1420 [Galveston]; (713) 654-1701
[Houston]; 800-POISON [800-764-7661]
[TX only]
West Texas Regional Poison Center
4815 Alameda Avenue
El Paso, TX 79905
800-POISON1 [800-764-7661] [TX only]

Utah

Utah Poison Control Center
410 Chipeta Way, Suite 230
Salt Lake City, UT 84108
(801) 581-2151; 800-456-7707 [UT only]

Vermont

Vermont Poison Center
Fletcher Allen Health Care
111 Colchester Avenue
Burlington, VT 05401
(802) 658-3456

Virginia

Blue Ridge Poison Center
University of Virginia
Blue Ridge Hospital
Box 67
Charlottesville, VA 22901
(804) 924-5543; 800-451-1428
Virginia Poison Center
401 N. 12th Street
Virginia Commonwealth University
Richmond, VA 23298-0522
(804) 828-9123 [Richmond];
800-552-6337 [VA only]

Washington

Washington Poison Center
155 N.E. 100th Street, Suite 400
Seattle, WA 98125
(206) 526-2121; 800-732-6985 [WA only];
(206) 517-2394 [TDD]; (206) 517-2394
[TDD; WA only]

West Virginia

West Virginia Poison Center
3110 MacCorkle Avenue, SE
Charleston, WV 25304
800-642-3625 [WV only]; (304) 348-4211

Wisconsin

Poison Center of Eastern Wisconsin
Children's Hospital of Wisconsin
P.O. Box 1997
Milwaukee, WI 53201
(414) 266-2222; 800-815-8855 [WI only]
University of Wisconsin Hospital Regional
Poison Center
E5/238 CSC
600 Highland Avenue
Madison, WI 53792
(608) 262-3702; 800-815-8855 [WI only]

Wyoming

The Poison Center
8301 Dodge Street
Omaha, NE 68114
(402) 390-5555 [Omaha NE];
800-955-9119 [NE & WY]

⊙ American Association of Poison Control Centers. www.aapcc.org/
 Kids Health. "U.S. Poison Control Centers," www.kidshealth.org/parent/firstaid_safe/home/
  poison_control_center.html
 U.S. Department of Housing and Urban Development. "Are Your Children Safe from Poisons?"
  www.hud.gov/poison.html

World Time Zones

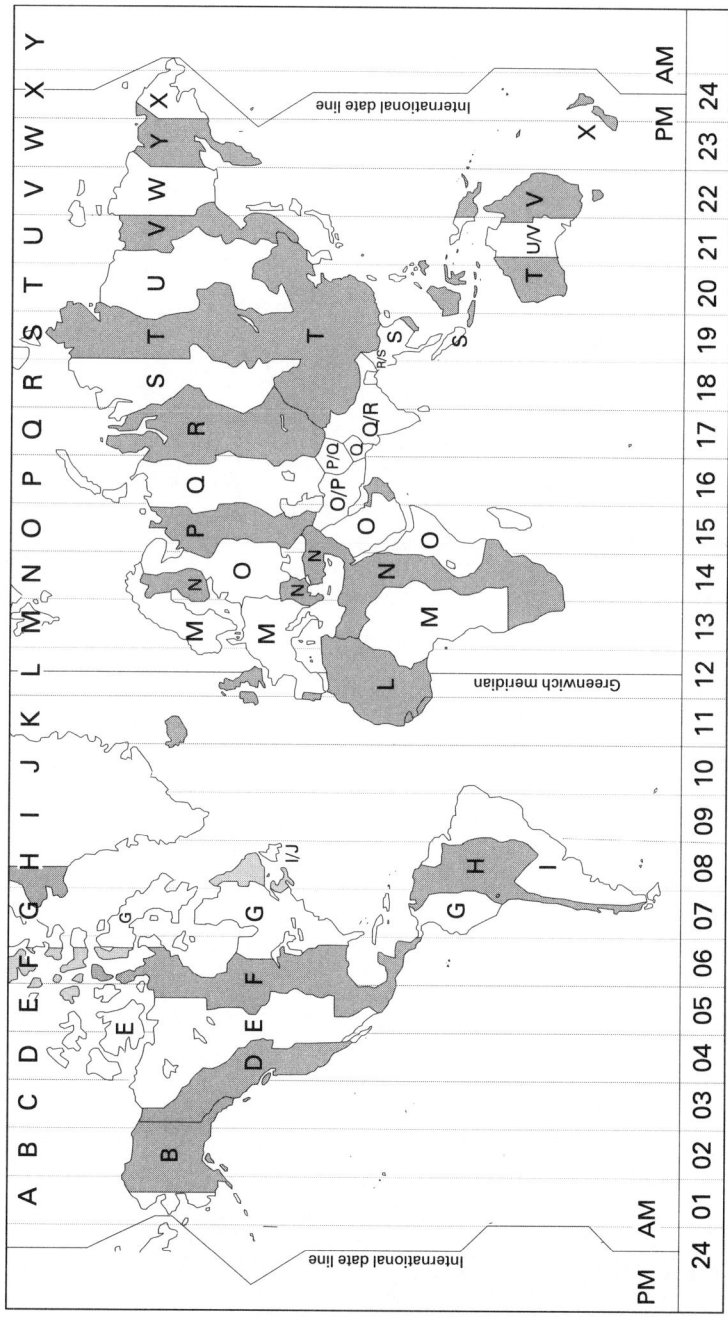

U.S. Naval Observatory. "World Time Zone Map," http://aa.usno.navy.mil/AA/faq/docs/world_tzones.html

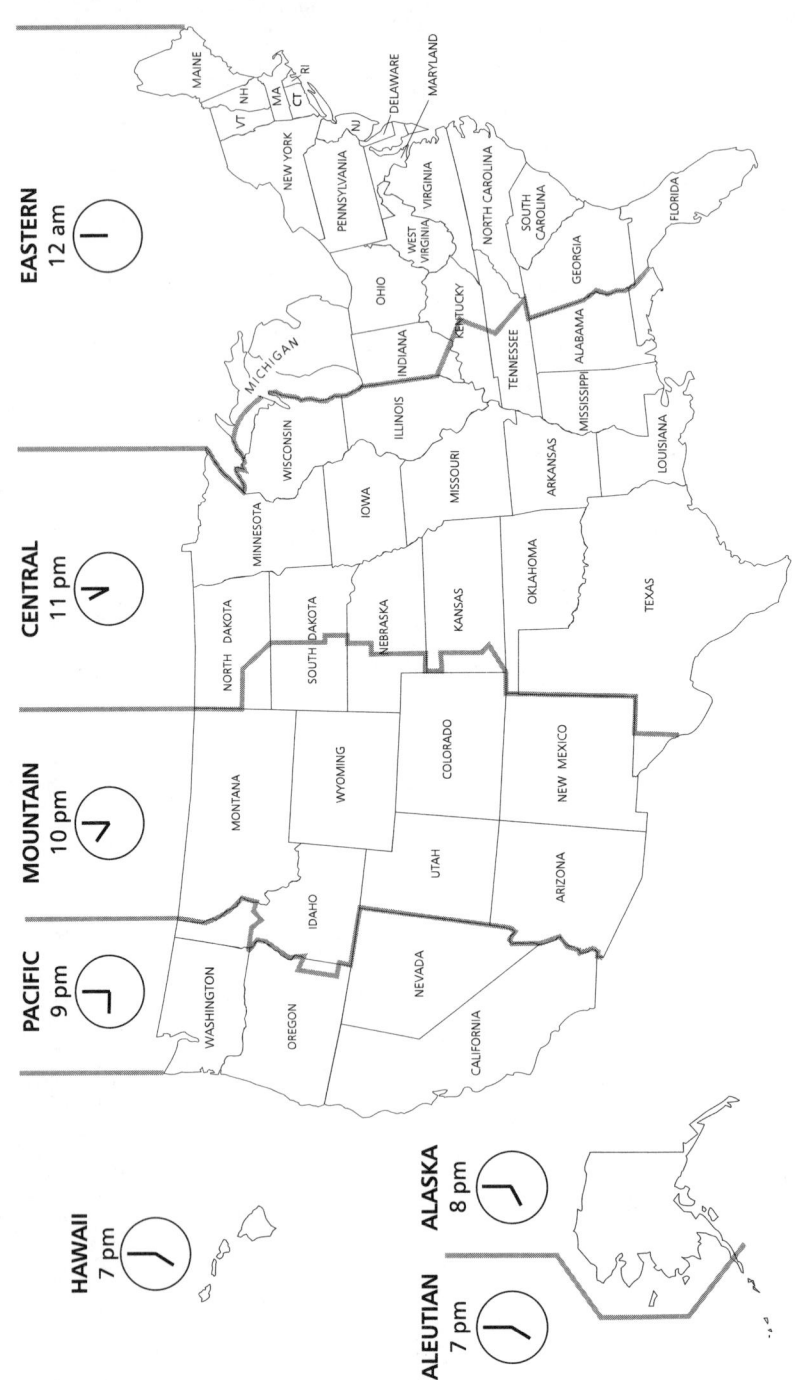

⊙ Intrasearch.com. "Standard Time Zones for the US," www.intrasearch.com/tzone.htm
World Time Zones, "USA Time Zones Map," www.worldtimezone.com/time-usa2.htm

A perpetual calendar lets you find the day of the week for any date in any year, past, present, or future. Since January 1 may fall on any of the seven days of the week, a perpetual calendar requires 14 different calendars to cover all possibilities, including leap and non–leap years.

To use the perpetual calendar, find the year desired in the table below. The number next to each year corresponds to one of the 14 calendars on the following pages. For example, calendar 9 (a leap year in which January 1 fell on a Monday) was in use during 1776, meaning that July 4 of that year was a Thursday. Calendar 9 was used again in 1816 and 1844 and was last used in 1996. Calendar 4 will be used in 2002.

1775	1	1815	1	1855	2	1895	3	1935	3	1975	4	2015	5
1776	9	1816	9	1856	10	1896	11	1936	11	1976	12	2016	13
1777	4	1817	4	1857	5	1897	6	1937	6	1977	7	2017	1
1778	5	1818	5	1858	6	1898	7	1938	7	1978	1	2018	2
1779	6	1819	6	1859	7	1899	1	1939	1	1979	2	2019	3
1780	14	1820	14	1860	8	1900	2	1940	9	1980	10	2020	11
1781	2	1821	2	1861	3	1901	3	1941	4	1981	5	2021	6
1782	3	1822	3	1862	4	1902	4	1942	5	1982	6	2022	7
1783	4	1823	4	1863	5	1903	5	1943	6	1983	7	2023	1
1784	12	1824	12	1864	13	1904	13	1944	14	1984	8	2024	9
1785	7	1825	7	1865	1	1905	1	1945	2	1985	3	2025	4
1786	1	1826	1	1866	2	1906	2	1946	3	1986	4	2026	5
1787	2	1827	2	1867	3	1907	3	1947	4	1987	5	2027	6
1788	10	1828	10	1868	11	1908	11	1948	12	1988	13	2028	14
1789	5	1829	5	1869	6	1909	6	1949	7	1989	1	2029	2
1790	6	1830	6	1870	7	1910	7	1950	1	1990	2	2030	3
1791	7	1831	7	1871	1	1911	1	1951	2	1991	3	2031	4
1792	8	1832	8	1872	9	1912	9	1952	10	1992	11	2032	12
1793	3	1833	3	1873	4	1913	4	1953	5	1993	6	2033	7
1794	4	1834	4	1874	5	1914	5	1954	6	1994	7	2034	1
1795	5	1835	5	1875	6	1915	6	1955	7	1995	1	2035	2
1796	13	1836	13	1876	14	1916	14	1956	8	1996	9	2036	10
1797	1	1837	1	1877	2	1917	2	1957	3	1997	4	2037	5
1798	2	1838	2	1878	3	1918	3	1958	4	1998	5	2038	6
1799	3	1839	3	1879	4	1919	4	1959	5	1999	6	2039	7
1800	4	1840	11	1880	12	1920	12	1960	13	2000	14	2040	8
1801	5	1841	6	1881	7	1921	7	1961	1	2001	2	2041	3
1802	6	1842	7	1882	1	1922	1	1962	2	2002	3	2042	4
1803	7	1843	1	1883	2	1923	2	1963	3	2003	4	2043	5
1804	8	1844	9	1884	10	1924	10	1964	11	2004	12	2044	13
1805	3	1845	4	1885	5	1925	5	1965	6	2005	7	2045	1
1806	4	1846	5	1886	6	1926	6	1966	7	2006	1	2046	2
1807	5	1847	6	1887	7	1927	7	1967	1	2007	2	2047	3
1808	13	1848	14	1888	8	1928	8	1968	9	2008	10	2048	11
1809	1	1849	2	1889	3	1929	3	1969	4	2009	5	2049	6
1810	2	1850	3	1890	4	1930	4	1970	5	2010	6	2050	7
1811	3	1851	4	1891	5	1931	5	1971	6	2011	7	2051	1
1812	11	1852	12	1892	13	1932	13	1972	14	2012	8	2052	9
1813	6	1853	7	1893	1	1933	1	1973	2	2013	3	2053	4
1814	7	1854	1	1894	2	1934	2	1974	3	2014	4	2054	5

1

January
S	M	T	W	T	F	S
	1	2	3	4	5	6	7
8	9	10	11	12	13	14
15	16	17	18	19	20	21
22	23	24	25	26	27	28
29	30	31				

February
S	M	T	W	T	F	S
				1	2	3	4
5	6	7	8	9	10	11
12	13	14	15	16	17	18
19	20	21	22	23	24	25
26	27	28				

March
S	M	T	W	T	F	S
				1	2	3	4
5	6	7	8	9	10	11
12	13	14	15	16	17	18
19	20	21	22	23	24	25
26	27	28	29	30	31	

April
S	M	T	W	T	F	S
						1
2	3	4	5	6	7	8
9	10	11	12	13	14	15
16	17	18	19	20	21	22
23	24	25	26	27	28	29
30						

May
S	M	T	W	T	F	S
	1	2	3	4	5	6
7	8	9	10	11	12	13
14	15	16	17	18	19	20
21	22	23	24	25	26	27
28	29	30	31			

June
S	M	T	W	T	F	S
					1	2	3
4	5	6	7	8	9	10
11	12	13	14	15	16	17
18	19	20	21	22	23	24
25	26	27	28	29	30	

July
S	M	T	W	T	F	S
						1
2	3	4	5	6	7	8
9	10	11	12	13	14	15
16	17	18	19	20	21	22
23	24	25	26	27	28	29
30	31					

August
S	M	T	W	T	F	S
			1	2	3	4	5
6	7	8	9	10	11	12
13	14	15	16	17	18	19
20	21	22	23	24	25	26
27	28	29	30	31		

September
S	M	T	W	T	F	S
						1	2
3	4	5	6	7	8	9
10	11	12	13	14	15	16
17	18	19	20	21	22	23
24	25	26	27	28	29	30

October
S	M	T	W	T	F	S
1	2	3	4	5	6	7
8	9	10	11	12	13	14
15	16	17	18	19	20	21
22	23	24	25	26	27	28
29	30	31				

November
S	M	T	W	T	F	S
				1	2	3	4
5	6	7	8	9	10	11
12	13	14	15	16	17	18
19	20	21	22	23	24	25
26	27	28	29	30		

December
S	M	T	W	T	F	S
						1	2
3	4	5	6	7	8	9
10	11	12	13	14	15	16
17	18	19	20	21	22	23
24	25	26	27	28	29	30
31						

2

January
S	M	T	W	T	F	S
	1	2	3	4	5	6
7	8	9	10	11	12	13
14	15	16	17	18	19	20
21	22	23	24	25	26	27
28	29	30	31			

February
S	M	T	W	T	F	S
					1	2	3
4	5	6	7	8	9	10
11	12	13	14	15	16	17
18	19	20	21	22	23	24
25	26	27	28			

March
S	M	T	W	T	F	S
					1	2	3
4	5	6	7	8	9	10
11	12	13	14	15	16	17
18	19	20	21	22	23	24
25	26	27	28	29	30	31

April
S	M	T	W	T	F	S
1	2	3	4	5	6	7
8	9	10	11	12	13	14
15	16	17	18	19	20	21
22	23	24	25	26	27	28
29	30					

May
S	M	T	W	T	F	S
		1	2	3	4	5
6	7	8	9	10	11	12
13	14	15	16	17	18	19
20	21	22	23	24	25	26
27	28	29	30	31		

June
S	M	T	W	T	F	S
						1	2
3	4	5	6	7	8	9
10	11	12	13	14	15	16
17	18	19	20	21	22	23
24	25	26	27	28	29	30

July
S	M	T	W	T	F	S
1	2	3	4	5	6	7
8	9	10	11	12	13	14
15	16	17	18	19	20	21
22	23	24	25	26	27	28
29	30	31				

August
S	M	T	W	T	F	S
			1	2	3	4
5	6	7	8	9	10	11
12	13	14	15	16	17	18
19	20	21	22	23	24	25
26	27	28	29	30	31	

September
S	M	T	W	T	F	S
						1
2	3	4	5	6	7	8
9	10	11	12	13	14	15
16	17	18	19	20	21	22
23	24	25	26	27	28	29
30						

October
S	M	T	W	T	F	S
	1	2	3	4	5	6
7	8	9	10	11	12	13
14	15	16	17	18	19	20
21	22	23	24	25	26	27
28	29	30	31			

November
S	M	T	W	T	F	S
				1	2	3
4	5	6	7	8	9	10
11	12	13	14	15	16	17
18	19	20	21	22	23	24
25	26	27	28	29	30	

December
S	M	T	W	T	F	S
						1
2	3	4	5	6	7	8
9	10	11	12	13	14	15
16	17	18	19	20	21	22
23	24	25	26	27	28	29
30	31					

Calendar 3

January
S	M	T	W	T	F	S
		1	2	3	4	5
6	7	8	9	10	11	12
13	14	15	16	17	18	19
20	21	22	23	24	25	26
27	28	29	30	31		

February
S	M	T	W	T	F	S
					1	2
3	4	5	6	7	8	9
10	11	12	13	14	15	16
17	18	19	20	21	22	23
24	25	26	27	28		

March
S	M	T	W	T	F	S
					1	2
3	4	5	6	7	8	9
10	11	12	13	14	15	16
17	18	19	20	21	22	23
24	25	26	27	28	29	30
31						

April
S	M	T	W	T	F	S
	1	2	3	4	5	6
7	8	9	10	11	12	13
14	15	16	17	18	19	20
21	22	23	24	25	26	27
28	29	30				

May
S	M	T	W	T	F	S
			1	2	3	4
5	6	7	8	9	10	11
12	13	14	15	16	17	18
19	20	21	22	23	24	25
26	27	28	29	30	31	

June
S	M	T	W	T	F	S
						1
2	3	4	5	6	7	8
9	10	11	12	13	14	15
16	17	18	19	20	21	22
23	24	25	26	27	28	29
30						

July
S	M	T	W	T	F	S
	1	2	3	4	5	6
7	8	9	10	11	12	13
14	15	16	17	18	19	20
21	22	23	24	25	26	27
28	29	30	31			

August
S	M	T	W	T	F	S
				1	2	3
4	5	6	7	8	9	10
11	12	13	14	15	16	17
18	19	20	21	22	23	24
25	26	27	28	29	30	31

September
S	M	T	W	T	F	S
1	2	3	4	5	6	7
8	9	10	11	12	13	14
15	16	17	18	19	20	21
22	23	24	25	26	27	28
29	30					

October
S	M	T	W	T	F	S
		1	2	3	4	5
6	7	8	9	10	11	12
13	14	15	16	17	18	19
20	21	22	23	24	25	26
27	28	29	30	31		

November
S	M	T	W	T	F	S
					1	2
3	4	5	6	7	8	9
10	11	12	13	14	15	16
17	18	19	20	21	22	23
24	25	26	27	28	29	30

December
S	M	T	W	T	F	S
1	2	3	4	5	6	7
8	9	10	11	12	13	14
15	16	17	18	19	20	21
22	23	24	25	26	27	28
29	30	31				

3

Calendar 4

January
S	M	T	W	T	F	S
			1	2	3	4
5	6	7	8	9	10	11
12	13	14	15	16	17	18
19	20	21	22	23	24	25
26	27	28	29	30	31	

February
S	M	T	W	T	F	S
						1
2	3	4	5	6	7	8
9	10	11	12	13	14	15
16	17	18	19	20	21	22
23	24	25	26	27	28	

March
S	M	T	W	T	F	S
						1
2	3	4	5	6	7	8
9	10	11	12	13	14	15
16	17	18	19	20	21	22
23	24	25	26	27	28	29
30	31					

April
S	M	T	W	T	F	S
		1	2	3	4	5
6	7	8	9	10	11	12
13	14	15	16	17	18	19
20	21	22	23	24	25	26
27	28	29	30			

May
S	M	T	W	T	F	S
				1	2	3
4	5	6	7	8	9	10
11	12	13	14	15	16	17
18	19	20	21	22	23	24
25	26	27	28	29	30	31

June
S	M	T	W	T	F	S
1	2	3	4	5	6	7
8	9	10	11	12	13	14
15	16	17	18	19	20	21
22	23	24	25	26	27	28
29	30					

July
S	M	T	W	T	F	S
		1	2	3	4	5
6	7	8	9	10	11	12
13	14	15	16	17	18	19
20	21	22	23	24	25	26
27	28	29	30	31		

August
S	M	T	W	T	F	S
					1	2
3	4	5	6	7	8	9
10	11	12	13	14	15	16
17	18	19	20	21	22	23
24	25	26	27	28	29	30
31						

4

September
S	M	T	W	T	F	S
	1	2	3	4	5	6
7	8	9	10	11	12	13
14	15	16	17	18	19	20
21	22	23	24	25	26	27
28	29	30				

October
S	M	T	W	T	F	S
			1	2	3	4
5	6	7	8	9	10	11
12	13	14	15	16	17	18
19	20	21	22	23	24	25
26	27	28	29	30	31	

November
S	M	T	W	T	F	S
						1
2	3	4	5	6	7	8
9	10	11	12	13	14	15
16	17	18	19	20	21	22
23	24	25	26	27	28	29
30						

December
S	M	T	W	T	F	S
	1	2	3	4	5	6
7	8	9	10	11	12	13
14	15	16	17	18	19	20
21	22	23	24	25	26	27
28	29	30	31			

5

January
S	M	T	W	T	F	S
				1	2	3
4	5	6	7	8	9	10
11	12	13	14	15	16	17
18	19	20	21	22	23	24
25	26	27	28	29	30	31

February
S	M	T	W	T	F	S
1	2	3	4	5	6	7
8	9	10	11	12	13	14
15	16	17	18	19	20	21
22	23	24	25	26	27	28

March
S	M	T	W	T	F	S
1	2	3	4	5	6	7
8	9	10	11	12	13	14
15	16	17	18	19	20	21
22	23	24	25	26	27	28
29	30	31				

April
S	M	T	W	T	F	S
			1	2	3	4
5	6	7	8	9	10	11
12	13	14	15	16	17	18
19	20	21	22	23	24	25
26	27	28	29	30		

May
S	M	T	W	T	F	S
					1	2
3	4	5	6	7	8	9
10	11	12	13	14	15	16
17	18	19	20	21	22	23
24	25	26	27	28	29	30
31						

June
S	M	T	W	T	F	S
	1	2	3	4	5	6
7	8	9	10	11	12	13
14	15	16	17	18	19	20
21	22	23	24	25	26	27
28	29	30				

July
S	M	T	W	T	F	S
			1	2	3	4
5	6	7	8	9	10	11
12	13	14	15	16	17	18
19	20	21	22	23	24	25
26	27	28	29	30	31	

August
S	M	T	W	T	F	S
						1
2	3	4	5	6	7	8
9	10	11	12	13	14	15
16	17	18	19	20	21	22
23	24	25	26	27	28	29
30	31					

September
S	M	T	W	T	F	S
		1	2	3	4	5
6	7	8	9	10	11	12
13	14	15	16	17	18	19
20	21	22	23	24	25	26
27	28	29	30			

October
S	M	T	W	T	F	S
				1	2	3
4	5	6	7	8	9	10
11	12	13	14	15	16	17
18	19	20	21	22	23	24
25	26	27	28	29	30	31

November
S	M	T	W	T	F	S
1	2	3	4	5	6	7
8	9	10	11	12	13	14
15	16	17	18	19	20	21
22	23	24	25	26	27	28
29	30					

December
S	M	T	W	T	F	S
		1	2	3	4	5
6	7	8	9	10	11	12
13	14	15	16	17	18	19
20	21	22	23	24	25	26
27	28	29	30	31		

6

January
S	M	T	W	T	F	S
					1	2
3	4	5	6	7	8	9
10	11	12	13	14	15	16
17	18	19	20	21	22	23
24	25	26	27	28	29	30
31						

February
S	M	T	W	T	F	S
	1	2	3	4	5	6
7	8	9	10	11	12	13
14	15	16	17	18	19	20
21	22	23	24	25	26	27
28						

March
S	M	T	W	T	F	S
	1	2	3	4	5	6
7	8	9	10	11	12	13
14	15	16	17	18	19	20
21	22	23	24	25	26	27
28	29	30	31			

April
S	M	T	W	T	F	S
					1	2	3
4	5	6	7	8	9	10
11	12	13	14	15	16	17
18	19	20	21	22	23	24
25	26	27	28	29	30	

May
S	M	T	W	T	F	S
						1
2	3	4	5	6	7	8
9	10	11	12	13	14	15
16	17	18	19	20	21	22
23	24	25	26	27	28	29
30	31					

June
S	M	T	W	T	F	S
	1	2	3	4	5
6	7	8	9	10	11	12
13	14	15	16	17	18	19
20	21	22	23	24	25	26
27	28	29	30			

July
S	M	T	W	T	F	S
				1	2	3
4	5	6	7	8	9	10
11	12	13	14	15	16	17
18	19	20	21	22	23	24
25	26	27	28	29	30	31

August
S	M	T	W	T	F	S
1	2	3	4	5	6	7
8	9	10	11	12	13	14
15	16	17	18	19	20	21
22	23	24	25	26	27	28
29	30	31				

September
S	M	T	W	T	F	S
			1	2	3	4
5	6	7	8	9	10	11
12	13	14	15	16	17	18
19	20	21	22	23	24	25
26	27	28	29	30		

October
S	M	T	W	T	F	S
					1	2
3	4	5	6	7	8	9
10	11	12	13	14	15	16
17	18	19	20	21	22	23
24	25	26	27	28	29	30
31						

November
S	M	T	W	T	F	S
	1	2	3	4	5	6
7	8	9	10	11	12	13
14	15	16	17	18	19	20
21	22	23	24	25	26	27
28	29	30				

December
S	M	T	W	T	F	S
			1	2	3	4
5	6	7	8	9	10	11
12	13	14	15	16	17	18
19	20	21	22	23	24	25
26	27	28	29	30	31	

Year 7

January
S	M	T	W	T	F	S
						1
2	3	4	5	6	7	8
9	10	11	12	13	14	15
16	17	18	19	20	21	22
23	24	25	26	27	28	29
30	31					

February
S	M	T	W	T	F	S
		1	2	3	4	5
6	7	8	9	10	11	12
13	14	15	16	17	18	19
20	21	22	23	24	25	26
27	28					

March
S	M	T	W	T	F	S
		1	2	3	4	5
6	7	8	9	10	11	12
13	14	15	16	17	18	19
20	21	22	23	24	25	26
27	28	29	30	31		

April
S	M	T	W	T	F	S
					1	2
3	4	5	6	7	8	9
10	11	12	13	14	15	16
17	18	19	20	21	22	23
24	25	26	27	28	29	30

May
S	M	T	W	T	F	S
1	2	3	4	5	6	7
8	9	10	11	12	13	14
15	16	17	18	19	20	21
22	23	24	25	26	27	28
29	30	31				

June
S	M	T	W	T	F	S
			1	2	3	4
5	6	7	8	9	10	11
12	13	14	15	16	17	18
19	20	21	22	23	24	25
26	27	28	29	30		

July
S	M	T	W	T	F	S
					1	2
3	4	5	6	7	8	9
10	11	12	13	14	15	16
17	18	19	20	21	22	23
24	25	26	27	28	29	30
31						

August
S	M	T	W	T	F	S
	1	2	3	4	5	6
7	8	9	10	11	12	13
14	15	16	17	18	19	20
21	22	23	24	25	26	27
28	29	30	31			

September
S	M	T	W	T	F	S
					1	2	3
4	5	6	7	8	9	10
11	12	13	14	15	16	17
18	19	20	21	22	23	24
25	26	27	28	29	30	

October
S	M	T	W	T	F	S
						1
2	3	4	5	6	7	8
9	10	11	12	13	14	15
16	17	18	19	20	21	22
23	24	25	26	27	28	29
30	31					

November
S	M	T	W	T	F	S
		1	2	3	4	5
6	7	8	9	10	11	12
13	14	15	16	17	18	19
20	21	22	23	24	25	26
27	28	29	30			

December
S	M	T	W	T	F	S
				1	2	3
4	5	6	7	8	9	10
11	12	13	14	15	16	17
18	19	20	21	22	23	24
25	26	27	28	29	30	31

Year 8

January
S	M	T	W	T	F	S
1	2	3	4	5	6	7
8	9	10	11	12	13	14
15	16	17	18	19	20	21
22	23	24	25	26	27	28
29	30	31				

February
S	M	T	W	T	F	S
			1	2	3	4
5	6	7	8	9	10	11
12	13	14	15	16	17	18
19	20	21	22	23	24	25
26	27	28	29			

March
S	M	T	W	T	F	S
			1	2	3	
4	5	6	7	8	9	10
11	12	13	14	15	16	17
18	19	20	21	22	23	24
25	26	27	28	29	30	31

April
S	M	T	W	T	F	S
1	2	3	4	5	6	7
8	9	10	11	12	13	14
15	16	17	18	19	20	21
22	23	24	25	26	27	28
29	30					

May
S	M	T	W	T	F	S
	1	2	3	4	5	
6	7	8	9	10	11	12
13	14	15	16	17	18	19
20	21	22	23	24	25	26
27	28	29	30	31		

June
S	M	T	W	T	F	S
					1	2
3	4	5	6	7	8	9
10	11	12	13	14	15	16
17	18	19	20	21	22	23
24	25	26	27	28	29	30

July
S	M	T	W	T	F	S
1	2	3	4	5	6	7
8	9	10	11	12	13	14
15	16	17	18	19	20	21
22	23	24	25	26	27	28
29	30	31				

August
S	M	T	W	T	F	S
			1	2	3	4
5	6	7	8	9	10	11
12	13	14	15	16	17	18
19	20	21	22	23	24	25
26	27	28	29	30	31	

September
S	M	T	W	T	F	S
						1
2	3	4	5	6	7	8
9	10	11	12	13	14	15
16	17	18	19	20	21	22
23	24	25	26	27	28	29
30						

October
S	M	T	W	T	F	S
	1	2	3	4	5	6
7	8	9	10	11	12	13
14	15	16	17	18	19	20
21	22	23	24	25	26	27
28	29	30	31			

November
S	M	T	W	T	F	S
				1	2	3
4	5	6	7	8	9	10
11	12	13	14	15	16	17
18	19	20	21	22	23	24
25	26	27	28	29	30	

December
S	M	T	W	T	F	S
						1
2	3	4	5	6	7	8
9	10	11	12	13	14	15
16	17	18	19	20	21	22
23	24	25	26	27	28	29
30	31					

9

January
S	M	T	W	T	F	S
	1	2	3	4	5	6
7	8	9	10	11	12	13
14	15	16	17	18	19	20
21	22	23	24	25	26	27
28	29	30	31			

February
S	M	T	W	T	F	S
					1	2	3
4	5	6	7	8	9	10
11	12	13	14	15	16	17
18	19	20	21	22	23	24
25	26	27	28	29		

March
S	M	T	W	T	F	S
					1	2
3	4	5	6	7	8	9
10	11	12	13	14	15	16
17	18	19	20	21	22	23
24	25	26	27	28	29	30
31						

April
S	M	T	W	T	F	S
1	2	3	4	5	6
7	8	9	10	11	12	13
14	15	16	17	18	19	20
21	22	23	24	25	26	27
28	29	30				

May
S	M	T	W	T	F	S
		1	2	3	4
5	6	7	8	9	10	11
12	13	14	15	16	17	18
19	20	21	22	23	24	25
26	27	28	29	30	31	

June
S	M	T	W	T	F	S
						1
2	3	4	5	6	7	8
9	10	11	12	13	14	15
16	17	18	19	20	21	22
23	24	25	26	27	28	29
30						

July
S	M	T	W	T	F	S
1	2	3	4	5	6
7	8	9	10	11	12	13
14	15	16	17	18	19	20
21	22	23	24	25	26	27
28	29	30	31			

August
S	M	T	W	T	F	S
				1	2	3
4	5	6	7	8	9	10
11	12	13	14	15	16	17
18	19	20	21	22	23	24
25	26	27	28	29	30	31

September
S	M	T	W	T	F	S
1	2	3	4	5	6	7
8	9	10	11	12	13	14
15	16	17	18	19	20	21
22	23	24	25	26	27	28
29	30					

October
S	M	T	W	T	F	S
	1	2	3	4	5
6	7	8	9	10	11	12
13	14	15	16	17	18	19
20	21	22	23	24	25	26
27	28	29	30	31		

November
S	M	T	W	T	F	S
					1	2
3	4	5	6	7	8	9
10	11	12	13	14	15	16
17	18	19	20	21	22	23
24	25	26	27	28	29	30

December
S	M	T	W	T	F	S
1	2	3	4	5	6	7
8	9	10	11	12	13	14
15	16	17	18	19	20	21
22	23	24	25	26	27	28
29	30	31				

10

January
S	M	T	W	T	F	S
		1	2	3	4	5
6	7	8	9	10	11	12
13	14	15	16	17	18	19
20	21	22	23	24	25	26
27	28	29	30	31		

February
S	M	T	W	T	F	S
					1	2
3	4	5	6	7	8	9
10	11	12	13	14	15	16
17	18	19	20	21	22	23
24	25	26	27	28	29	

March
S	M	T	W	T	F	S
						1
2	3	4	5	6	7	8
9	10	11	12	13	14	15
16	17	18	19	20	21	22
23	24	25	26	27	28	29
30	31					

April
S	M	T	W	T	F	S
		1	2	3	4	5
6	7	8	9	10	11	12
13	14	15	16	17	18	19
20	21	22	23	24	25	26
27	28	29	30			

May
S	M	T	W	T	F	S
				1	2	3
4	5	6	7	8	9	10
11	12	13	14	15	16	17
18	19	20	21	22	23	24
25	26	27	28	29	30	31

June
S	M	T	W	T	F	S
1	2	3	4	5	6	7
8	9	10	11	12	13	14
15	16	17	18	19	20	21
22	23	24	25	26	27	28
29	30					

July
S	M	T	W	T	F	S
		1	2	3	4	5
6	7	8	9	10	11	12
13	14	15	16	17	18	19
20	21	22	23	24	25	26
27	28	29	30	31		

August
S	M	T	W	T	F	S
					1	2
3	4	5	6	7	8	9
10	11	12	13	14	15	16
17	18	19	20	21	22	23
24	25	26	27	28	29	30
31						

September
S	M	T	W	T	F	S
	1	2	3	4	5	6
7	8	9	10	11	12	13
14	15	16	17	18	19	20
21	22	23	24	25	26	27
28	29	30				

October
S	M	T	W	T	F	S
		1	2	3	4
5	6	7	8	9	10	11
12	13	14	15	16	17	18
19	20	21	22	23	24	25
26	27	28	29	30	31	

November
S	M	T	W	T	F	S
						1
2	3	4	5	6	7	8
9	10	11	12	13	14	15
16	17	18	19	20	21	22
23	24	25	26	27	28	29
30						

December
S	M	T	W	T	F	S
1	2	3	4	5	6
7	8	9	10	11	12	13
14	15	16	17	18	19	20
21	22	23	24	25	26	27
28	29	30	31			

Year 1

January
S	M	T	W	T	F	S
			1	2	3	4
5	6	7	8	9	10	11
12	13	14	15	16	17	18
19	20	21	22	23	24	25
26	27	28	29	30	31	

February
S	M	T	W	T	F	S
						1
2	3	4	5	6	7	8
9	10	11	12	13	14	15
16	17	18	19	20	21	22
23	24	25	26	27	28	29

March
S	M	T	W	T	F	S
1	2	3	4	5	6	7
8	9	10	11	12	13	14
15	16	17	18	19	20	21
22	23	24	25	26	27	28
29	30	31				

April
S	M	T	W	T	F	S
			1	2	3	4
5	6	7	8	9	10	11
12	13	14	15	16	17	18
19	20	21	22	23	24	25
26	27	28	29	30		

May
S	M	T	W	T	F	S
					1	2
3	4	5	6	7	8	9
10	11	12	13	14	15	16
17	18	19	20	21	22	23
24	25	26	27	28	29	30
31						

June
S	M	T	W	T	F	S
	1	2	3	4	5	6
7	8	9	10	11	12	13
14	15	16	17	18	19	20
21	22	23	24	25	26	27
28	29	30				

July
S	M	T	W	T	F	S
			1	2	3	4
5	6	7	8	9	10	11
12	13	14	15	16	17	18
19	20	21	22	23	24	25
26	27	28	29	30	31	

August
S	M	T	W	T	F	S
						1
2	3	4	5	6	7	8
9	10	11	12	13	14	15
16	17	18	19	20	21	22
23	24	25	26	27	28	29
30	31					

September
S	M	T	W	T	F	S
		1	2	3	4	5
6	7	8	9	10	11	12
13	14	15	16	17	18	19
20	21	22	23	24	25	26
27	28	29	30			

October
S	M	T	W	T	F	S
				1	2	3
4	5	6	7	8	9	10
11	12	13	14	15	16	17
18	19	20	21	22	23	24
25	26	27	28	29	30	31

November
S	M	T	W	T	F	S
1	2	3	4	5	6	7
8	9	10	11	12	13	14
15	16	17	18	19	20	21
22	23	24	25	26	27	28
29	30					

December
S	M	T	W	T	F	S
		1	2	3	4	5
6	7	8	9	10	11	12
13	14	15	16	17	18	19
20	21	22	23	24	25	26
27	28	29	30	31		

11

Year 2

January
S	M	T	W	T	F	S
					1	2	3
4	5	6	7	8	9	10
11	12	13	14	15	16	17
18	19	20	21	22	23	24
25	26	27	28	29	30	31

February
S	M	T	W	T	F	S
1	2	3	4	5	6	7
8	9	10	11	12	13	14
15	16	17	18	19	20	21
22	23	24	25	26	27	28
29						

March
S	M	T	W	T	F	S
	1	2	3	4	5	6
7	8	9	10	11	12	13
14	15	16	17	18	19	20
21	22	23	24	25	26	27
28	29	30	31			

April
S	M	T	W	T	F	S
					1	2	3
4	5	6	7	8	9	10
11	12	13	14	15	16	17
18	19	20	21	22	23	24
25	26	27	28	29	30	

May
S	M	T	W	T	F	S
						1
2	3	4	5	6	7	8
9	10	11	12	13	14	15
16	17	18	19	20	21	22
23	24	25	26	27	28	29
30	31					

June
S	M	T	W	T	F	S
		1	2	3	4	5
6	7	8	9	10	11	12
13	14	15	16	17	18	19
20	21	22	23	24	25	26
27	28	29	30			

July
S	M	T	W	T	F	S
				1	2	3
4	5	6	7	8	9	10
11	12	13	14	15	16	17
18	19	20	21	22	23	24
25	26	27	28	29	30	31

August
S	M	T	W	T	F	S
1	2	3	4	5	6	7
8	9	10	11	12	13	14
15	16	17	18	19	20	21
22	23	24	25	26	27	28
29	30	31				

September
S	M	T	W	T	F	S
			1	2	3	4
5	6	7	8	9	10	11
12	13	14	15	16	17	18
19	20	21	22	23	24	25
26	27	28	29	30		

October
S	M	T	W	T	F	S
					1	2
3	4	5	6	7	8	9
10	11	12	13	14	15	16
17	18	19	20	21	22	23
24	25	26	27	28	29	30
31						

November
S	M	T	W	T	F	S
	1	2	3	4	5	6
7	8	9	10	11	12	13
14	15	16	17	18	19	20
21	22	23	24	25	26	27
28	29	30				

December
S	M	T	W	T	F	S
			1	2	3	4
5	6	7	8	9	10	11
12	13	14	15	16	17	18
19	20	21	22	23	24	25
26	27	28	29	30	31	

12

13

January
S	M	T	W	T	F	S
					1	2
3	4	5	6	7	8	9
10	11	12	13	14	15	16
17	18	19	20	21	22	23
24	25	26	27	28	29	30
31						

February
S	M	T	W	T	F	S
	1	2	3	4	5	6
7	8	9	10	11	12	13
14	15	16	17	18	19	20
21	22	23	24	25	26	27
28	29					

March
S	M	T	W	T	F	S
		1	2	3	4	5
6	7	8	9	10	11	12
13	14	15	16	17	18	19
20	21	22	23	24	25	26
27	28	29	30	31		

April
S	M	T	W	T	F	S
					1	2
3	4	5	6	7	8	9
10	11	12	13	14	15	16
17	18	19	20	21	22	23
24	25	26	27	28	29	30

May
S	M	T	W	T	F	S
1	2	3	4	5	6	7
8	9	10	11	12	13	14
15	16	17	18	19	20	21
22	23	24	25	26	27	28
29	30	31				

June
S	M	T	W	T	F	S
				1	2	3	4
5	6	7	8	9	10	11
12	13	14	15	16	17	18
19	20	21	22	23	24	25
26	27	28	29	30		

July
S	M	T	W	T	F	S
					1	2
3	4	5	6	7	8	9
10	11	12	13	14	15	16
17	18	19	20	21	22	23
24	25	26	27	28	29	30
31						

August
S	M	T	W	T	F	S
1	2	3	4	5	6
7	8	9	10	11	12	13
14	15	16	17	18	19	20
21	22	23	24	25	26	27
28	29	30	31			

September
S	M	T	W	T	F	S
				1	2	3
4	5	6	7	8	9	10
11	12	13	14	15	16	17
18	19	20	21	22	23	24
25	26	27	28	29	30	

October
S	M	T	W	T	F	S
						1
2	3	4	5	6	7	8
9	10	11	12	13	14	15
16	17	18	19	20	21	22
23	24	25	26	27	28	29
30	31					

November
S	M	T	W	T	F	S
	1	2	3	4	5
6	7	8	9	10	11	12
13	14	15	16	17	18	19
20	21	22	23	24	25	26
27	28	29	30			

December
S	M	T	W	T	F	S
				1	2	3
4	5	6	7	8	9	10
11	12	13	14	15	16	17
18	19	20	21	22	23	24
25	26	27	28	29	30	31

14

January
S	M	T	W	T	F	S
						1
2	3	4	5	6	7	8
9	10	11	12	13	14	15
16	17	18	19	20	21	22
23	24	25	26	27	28	29
30	31					

February
S	M	T	W	T	F	S
	1	2	3	4	5
6	7	8	9	10	11	12
13	14	15	16	17	18	19
20	21	22	23	24	25	26
27	28	29				

March
S	M	T	W	T	F	S
			1	2	3	4
5	6	7	8	9	10	11
12	13	14	15	16	17	18
19	20	21	22	23	24	25
26	27	28	29	30	31	

April
S	M	T	W	T	F	S
						1
2	3	4	5	6	7	8
9	10	11	12	13	14	15
16	17	18	19	20	21	22
23	24	25	26	27	28	29
30						

May
S	M	T	W	T	F	S
	1	2	3	4	5	6
7	8	9	10	11	12	13
14	15	16	17	18	19	20
21	22	23	24	25	26	27
28	29	30	31			

June
S	M	T	W	T	F	S
					1	2	3
4	5	6	7	8	9	10
11	12	13	14	15	16	17
18	19	20	21	22	23	24
25	26	27	28	29	30	

July
S	M	T	W	T	F	S
						1
2	3	4	5	6	7	8
9	10	11	12	13	14	15
16	17	18	19	20	21	22
23	24	25	26	27	28	29
30	31					

August
S	M	T	W	T	F	S
		1	2	3	4	5
6	7	8	9	10	11	12
13	14	15	16	17	18	19
20	21	22	23	24	25	26
27	28	29	30	31		

September
S	M	T	W	T	F	S
					1	2
3	4	5	6	7	8	9
10	11	12	13	14	15	16
17	18	19	20	21	22	23
24	25	26	27	28	29	30

October
S	M	T	W	T	F	S
1	2	3	4	5	6	7
8	9	10	11	12	13	14
15	16	17	18	19	20	21
22	23	24	25	26	27	28
29	30	31				

November
S	M	T	W	T	F	S
			1	2	3	4
5	6	7	8	9	10	11
12	13	14	15	16	17	18
19	20	21	22	23	24	25
26	27	28	29	30		

December
S	M	T	W	T	F	S
					1	2
3	4	5	6	7	8	9
10	11	12	13	14	15	16
17	18	19	20	21	22	23
24	25	26	27	28	29	30
31						

National Holidays: U.S.

Holiday	Date
New Year's Day	January 1 (observed Friday or Monday if it falls on a weekend)
Martin Luther King Jr. Day	third Monday in January
President's Day	third Monday in February
Memorial Day	last Monday in May
Independence Day	July 4
Labor Day	first Monday in September
Columbus Day	second Monday in October
Veterans' Day	November 11
Thanksgiving	fourth Thursday in November
Christmas Day	December 25

⊙ United States Office of Personnel Management. "Federal Holidays," www.opm.gov/fedhol/
Dallas Tour Planner Online. "US Holidays," www.dallascvb.com/tourplanner/USHolidays.htm

Major Holidays in Selected Countries (excluding U.S.)

Holiday	Nation	Date
Bank Holiday	Japan, Scotland	January 2
Second Day of New Year	Russia	January 2
Bank Holiday	Japan	January 3
Coming of Age Day	Japan	second Monday in January
Republic Day	India	January 26
Australia Day	Australia	January 26 (if this holiday falls on a Saturday or Sunday, it is observed the following Monday)
Anniversary of the Constitution	Mexico	February 5
Waitangi Day	New Zealand	February 6
National Foundation Day	Japan	February 11
Defenders of the Motherland Day	Russia	February 23
Carnival Week	Brazil	five days before Ash Wednesday
Independence Movement Day	South Korea	March 1
St. Patrick's Day	Northern Ireland	March 17
Human Rights Day	South Africa	March 21
Emancipation Day	Puerto Rico	March 22
Liberation Day	Italy	April 25
ANZAC Day	Australia, New Zealand	April 25 (if this holiday falls on a Saturday or Sunday, it is observed the following Monday)
Sinai Liberation Day	Egypt	April 25

Holiday	Nation	Date
Freedom Day	South Africa	April 27
Queen's Day	Netherlands	April 30
May Day	Italy, Sweden	May 1
Labo(u)r Day	Belgium, Brazil, Canada, Egypt, France, Germany, Mexico, Philippines	May 1
Workers Day	South Africa	May 1
International Labour Day	China, Russia	May 1–2
Constitution Memorial Day	Japan	May 3
May Day Bank Holiday	U.K.	first Monday in May
Youth Day	China	May 4
Holiday for a Nation	Japan	May 4
Cinco de Mayo	Mexico	May 5
Liberation Day	Netherlands	May 5
WWII Victory Day	France	May 8
WWII Victory Day	Russia	May 9
Victoria Day	Canada	last Monday before May 25
Bank Holiday	U.K.	last Monday in May
Children's Day	China	June 1
Anniversary of the Republic	Italy	Sunday nearest June 2
Queen's Birthday	New Zealand	first Monday in June
Independence Day	Russia	June 12
Independence Day	Philippines	June 12
Evacuation Day	Egypt	June 18
Midsummer Day	Sweden	Saturday after June 19
Anniversary of the Founding of the Communist Party	China	July 1
Canada Day	Canada	July 1
Bastille Day	France	July 14
Constitution Day	South Korea	July 17
National Holiday	Belgium	July 21
Revolution Day	Egypt	July 23
Constitution Day	Puerto Rico	July 25
Summer Bank Holiday	Scotland	first Monday in August
Anniversary of the Founding of the Chinese PLA	China	August 1
Independence Day	India	August 15
Independence Day	Indonesia	August 17

Victory Day	Turkey	August 30
National Heroes Day	Philippines	August 31
Summer Bank Holiday	U.K.	last Monday in August
National Day	Vietnam	September 2
Independence Day	Brazil	September 7
Independence Day	Mexico	September 16
National Day	China	October 1–2
Mahatma Gandhi's Birthday	India	October 2
Day of German Unity	Germany	October 3
National Foundation Day	South Korea	October 3
Armed Forces Day	Egypt	October 6
Thanksgiving Day	Canada	second Monday in October
Spanish National Day	Spain	October 12
Suez Victory Day	Egypt	October 24
Republic Day	Turkey	October 29
Labour Day	New Zealand	fourth Monday in October
National Culture Day	Japan	November 3
World War I Victory Anniversary Day	Italy	Sunday nearest November 4
Day of Accord and Reconciliation	Russia	November 7
Armistice Day	France	November 11
Proclamation of the Republic	Brazil	November 15
Discovery of Puerto Rico Day	Puerto Rico	November 19
Anniversary of the Mexican Revolution	Mexico	November 20
Labor Thanksgiving Day	Japan	November 23
Day of the Constitution	Spain	December 6
Constitution Day	Russia	December 12
Independence Day	Kenya	December 12
Day of Reconciliation	South Africa	December 16
Emperor's Birthday	Japan	December 23
Victory Day	Egypt	December 23
St. Stephen's Day	Italy	December 26
Boxing Day	Australia, Canada, Germany, Netherlands, Sweden, U.K.	December 26
Bank Holiday	Japan	December 31

⊙ Holiday Festival. "National Holidays," www.holidayfestival.com/Ctr.html
Tyzo.com. "World Holidays Database," www.tyzo.com/tools/holidays.html.
Earthcalendar.net. "Earth Calendar 2000," http://www.earthcalendar.net/

Aries

Dates:	Mar. 21–Apr. 19
Element:	fire
Type:	masculine
Quality:	cardinal
Symbol:	ram
Gemstone:	diamond
Metal:	iron
Color:	red
Ruled by:	Mars
Motto:	"I am"
Rules:	head

Taurus

Dates:	Apr. 20–May 20
Element:	earth
Type:	feminine
Quality:	fixed
Symbol:	bull
Gemstone:	emerald
Metal:	copper
Colors:	pink or blue
Ruled by:	Venus
Motto:	"I have"
Rules:	throat

Cancer

Dates:	June 21–July 22
Element:	water
Type:	feminine
Quality:	cardinal
Symbol:	crab
Gemstone:	moonstone
Metal:	silver
Color:	silver
Ruled by:	Moon
Motto:	"I feel"
Rules:	breast, stomach

Leo

Dates:	July 23–Aug. 22
Element:	fire
Type:	masculine
Quality:	fixed
Symbol:	lion
Gemstone:	ruby
Metal:	gold
Colors:	yellow or orange
Ruled by:	Sun
Motto:	"I will"
Rules:	heart, spine

Gemini

Dates:	May 21–June 20
Element:	air
Type:	masculine
Quality:	mutable
Symbols:	Castor & Pollux (twins)
Gemstone:	beryl
Metal:	mercury
Color:	orange
Ruled by:	Mercury
Motto:	"I think"
Rules:	nervous system, hands, shoulders, arms, lungs

Virgo

Dates:	Aug. 23–Sep. 22
Element:	earth
Type:	feminine
Quality:	mutable
Symbol:	virgin
Gemstone:	agate
Metal:	nickel
Colors:	green, brown, or blue
Ruled by:	Mercury
Motto:	"I analyze"
Rules:	intestinal tract

Libra

Dates:	Sep. 23–Oct. 22
Element:	air
Type:	masculine
Quality:	cardinal
Symbol:	scale of justice
Gemstone:	opal
Metal:	bronze
Colors:	pink or blue
Ruled by:	Venus
Motto:	"we balance"
Rules:	kidneys, lower back

Capricorn

Dates:	Dec. 22–Jan. 19
Element:	earth
Type:	feminine
Quality:	cardinal
Symbol:	goat with dolphin's tail
Gemstone:	garnet
Metal:	lead
Color:	brown
Ruled by:	Saturn
Motto:	"I use"
Rules:	knees, bones, skin

Scorpio

Dates:	Oct. 23–Nov. 21
Element:	water
Type:	feminine
Quality:	fixed
Symbols:	scorpion, eagle, or phoenix
Gemstone:	topaz
Metal:	steel
Color:	red
Ruled by:	Mars or Pluto
Motto:	"I create"
Rules:	generative system

Aquarius

Dates:	Jan. 20–Feb. 18
Element:	air
Type:	masculine
Quality:	fixed
Symbol:	water bearer
Gemstone:	amethyst
Metal:	aluminum
Color:	bright blue
Ruled by:	Uranus
Motto:	"I know"
Rules:	circulation, ankles

Sagittarius

Dates:	Nov. 22–Dec. 21
Element:	fire
Type:	masculine
Quality:	mutable
Symbol:	centaur
Gemstone:	turquoise
Metal:	tin
Colors:	purple or dark blue
Ruled by:	Jupiter
Motto:	"I perceive"
Rules:	hips, thighs

Pisces

Dates:	Feb. 19–Mar. 20
Element:	water
Type:	feminine
Quality:	mutable
Symbol:	two fish
Gemstone:	aquamarine
Metal:	platinum
Color:	green
Ruled by:	Neptune or Jupiter
Motto:	"I believe"
Rules:	feet

⊙ Zodiachouse.com. "The Signs," http://zodiachouse.com/signs.html
Astrology For Beginners. "The Signs," http://astro4begin.terrashare.com/

Birthstones and Flowers

Month	Birthstone(s)	Flower(s)
January	Garnet	Carnation, Snowdrop
February	Amethyst	Violet
March	Aquamarine, Bloodstone	Daffodil, Jonquil
April	Diamond	Sweet Pea
May	Emerald	Lily of the Valley, Hawthorn
June	Pearl, Moonstone, Alexandrite	Rose
July	Ruby	Larkspur, Delphinium
August	Peridot, Sardonyx	Gladiolus
September	Sapphire	Aster
October	Opal, Tourmaline	Calendula, Marigold
November	Yellow Topaz, Citrine	Chrysanthemum
December	Blue Topaz, Turquoise, Blue Zircon, Lapis Lazuli	Narcissus, Holly

⊙ Infoplease.com. "Birthstones," www.infoplease.com/ipa/A0002118.html
  The Gift Chick.com. "Birthstone and Flower Guide," www.thegiftchick.com/birthstones.htm

Wedding Anniversary Gifts

Year	Gift(s)	Year	Gift(s)
1	Paper	14	Ivory
2	Cotton	15	Crystal
3	Leather	20	China
4	Linen; Fruit and Flowers	25	Silver
5	Wood	30	Pearl
6	Iron, Sugar	35	Coral, Jade
7	Wool, Copper	40	Ruby
8	Bronze, Rubber	45	Sapphire
9	Pottery, Willow	50	Gold
10	Tin, Aluminum	55	Emerald
11	Steel	60	Diamond
12	Silk	75	Diamond, Gold
13	Lace		

⊙ Infoplease.com. "Traditional Wedding Anniversary Gift List,"
  www.infoplease.com/ipa/A0763772.html

THE SCIENCES: *Climate, Weather, Environment*

Meteorology Symbols

WINDSPEED AND DIRECTIONS (in knots)

| NE 2 KT | NE 6 KT | NE 10 KT | NE 15 KT | NNE 45 KT | N 50 KT | N 65 KT |

FRONTS

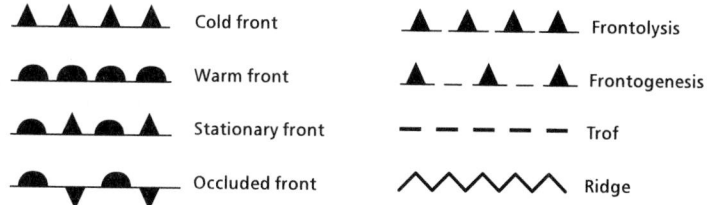

▲▲▲▲ Cold front	▲ ▲ ▲ ▲ Frontolysis
●●●● Warm front	▲ _ ▲ _ ▲ Frontogenesis
●▲●▲ Stationary front	– – – – – Trof
Occluded front	/\/\/\ Ridge

COMMON WEATHER SYMBOLS

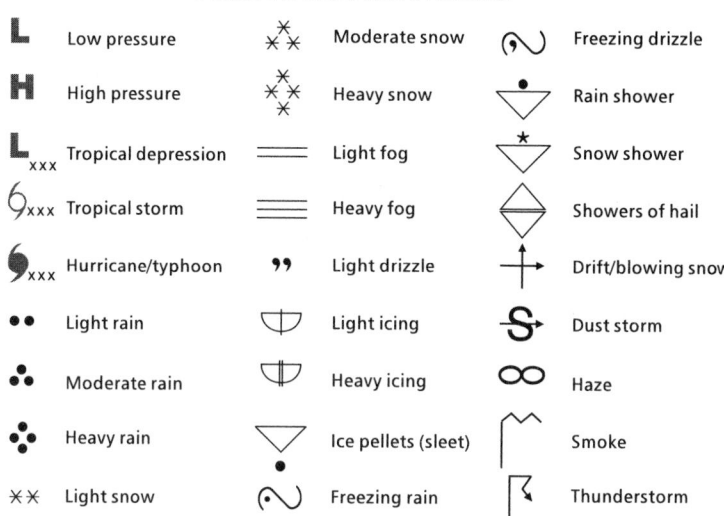

L	Low pressure	✳✳	Moderate snow		Freezing drizzle
H	High pressure	✳✳✳	Heavy snow		Rain shower
Lxxx	Tropical depression	=	Light fog		Snow shower
6xxx	Tropical storm	≡	Heavy fog		Showers of hail
6xxx	Hurricane/typhoon	❞	Light drizzle		Drift/blowing snow
••	Light rain		Light icing	**S**	Dust storm
••	Moderate rain		Heavy icing	∞	Haze
••••	Heavy rain		Ice pellets (sleet)		Smoke
✳✳	Light snow		Freezing rain		Thunderstorm

⊙ National Oceanographic and Atmospheric Administration. "Key Terms and Symbols,"
www.mpc.ncep.noaa.gov/product_description/keyterm.html
University of Wisconsin–Stout Meteorology Physics Department. "Common Weather Symbols,"
http://physics.uwstout.edu/WX/reference/symbols/commonsymb.htm

Climate Types

Type	Region	Description
Wet equatorial climate	Within about 12° latitude of the Equator	High temperatures around 86° F (30° C), with plentiful precipitation 59–394 inches (150–1,000 cm), heavy cloud cover, and high humidity, with very little annual temperature variation
Tropical monsoon and trade-wind littoral climates	Between 15° and 30° latitude	Small annual temperature ranges, high temperatures, and plentiful precipitation. A short dry season, usually in the "winter" season
Tropical wet-dry climate	Between 15° and 30° latitude	This climate has distinct wet and dry seasons, with most of the precipitation occurring in "summer."

Type	Region	Description
Tropical and subtropical desert climate	Between 15° and 30° latitude	Arid
Tropical and subtropical steppe climate	the periphery of tropical and subtropical desert climate	Semiarid
Mid-latitude steppe and desert climate	This climate extends to 50° latitude, and cool steppes reach nearly 60° N	Extreme temperature variations and little precipitation
Humid subtropical climate	These climates are found on the eastern sides of the continents between 20° and 35° N and S latitude.	A relatively uniform distribution of precipitation throughout the year.
Mediterranean climate	Between about 30° and 45° latitude on the western sides of the continents	Hot, dry summers and cool, wet winters.
Marine west coast climate	Poleward of the Mediterranean climate region on the western sides of the continents, between 35° and 60° N and S latitude	Precipitation is plentiful and frequent. Few extremes of temperature.
Humid continental climate	The humid continental subgroup occupies a region between 30° and 60° N in central and eastern North America and Asia in the major zone of conflict between polar and tropical air masses.	Large seasonal temperature contrasts with hot summers and cold winters. Precipitation is plentiful throughout the year.
Continental subarctic climate	North of the humid continental climate, from about 50° to 70° N, in a broad swath extending from Alaska to Newfoundland in North America and from northern Scandinavia to Siberia in Eurasia, lie the continental subarctic climates.	These are regions dominated by the winter season, a long, bitterly cold period with short, clear days, and relatively little precipitation.
Tundra climate	Tundra climates occur between 60° and 75° of latitude, mostly along the Arctic coast of North America and Eurasia and on the coastal margins of Greenland.	Mean annual temperatures are below freezing and annual ranges are large. Summers are generally mild and days are long, but they are often cloudy. The snow cover of winter melts in the warmer season. Winters are long and cold and precipitation generally consists of dry snow.

Snow and ice climate	This climate occurs poleward of 65° N and S latitude over the ice caps of Greenland and Antarctica and over the permanently frozen portion of the Arctic Ocean.	Winters are frigid, with mean monthly temperatures from −4°F to −85° F (−20° C to −65° C). Daily temperature variations are very small, because at such high latitudes the Sun's elevation varies little over the daylight period. Precipitation is meager in the cold, stable air with the largest amounts occurring on the coastal margins. Precipitation is usually in the form of snow and ice pellets, with strong winds, and blizzards. High winds also occur in the outer portions of the Greenland and Antarctic EF climates.
Highland climates	The major highland regions of the world (the Cascades, Sierra Nevada, and Rockies of North America, the Andes of South America, the Himalayas and adjacent ranges and the Tibetan Highlands [or Plateau] of Asia, the eastern highlands of Africa, and the central portions of Borneo and New Guinea)	Highland climates tend to resemble cooler, wetter versions of the climates of nearby lowlands in terms of their annual temperature ranges and seasonality of precipitation.

⊙ Encyclopedia Britannica. "Climate," www.britannica.com/bcom/eb/article/printable/4/0,5722,109114,00.html

Wind Chill and Heat Index

The wind chill index combines the temperature and wind speed to tell you how cold the wind makes the temperature "feel."

Air Temperature (°Fahrenheit)

Wind Speed (MPH)	30	25	20	15	10	5	0	−5	−10	−15	−20	−25
5	25	19	13	7	1	−5	−11	−16	−22	−28	−34	−40
10	21	15	9	3	−4	−10	−16	−22	−28	−35	−41	−47
15	19	13	6	0	−7	−13	−19	−26	−32	−39	−45	−51
20	17	11	4	−2	−9	−15	−22	−29	−35	−42	−48	−55
25	16	9	3	−4	−11	−17	−24	−31	−37	−44	−51	−58
30	15	8	1	−5	−12	−19	−26	−33	−39	−46	−53	−60
35	14	7	0	−7	−14	−21	−27	−34	−41	−48	−55	−62
40	13	6	−1	−8	−15	−22	−29	−36	−43	−50	−57	−64
45	12	5	−2	−9	−16	−23	−30	−37	−44	−51	−58	−65
50	12	4	−3	−10	−17	−24	−31	−38	−45	−52	−60	−67
55	11	4	−3	−11	−18	−25	−32	−39	−46	−54	−61	−68
60	10	3	−4	−11	−19	−26	−33	−40	−48	−55	−62	−69

◑ Cold   ◔ Very Cold   ◯ Bitter Cold   ◯ Frostbite occurs in 15 minutes or less.

Wind Chill and Heat Index *(cont.)*

The heat index is an accurate measure of how hot it feels when the effects of humidity are added to high temperature. Heat index is shown either as a function of Temperature/Dewpoint or as a function of Temperature/Relative Humidity (RH).

Relative Humidity (Percent)

Air Temperature (×Fahrenheit)	0	5	10	15	20	25	30	35	40	45	50	55	60	65	70	75	80	85	90	95	100
140	125																				
135	120	128																			
130	117	122	131																		
125	111	116	123	131	141																
120	107	111	116	123	130	139	148														
115	103	107	111	115	120	127	135	143	151												
110	99	102	105	108	112	117	123	130	137	143	151										
105	95	97	100	102	105	109	113	118	123	129	135	142	149								
100	91	93	95	97	99	101	104	107	110	115	120	126	132	139	144						
95	87	88	90	91	93	94	96	98	101	104	107	110	114	119	124	130	136				
90	83	84	85	86	87	88	90	91	93	95	96	98	100	102	106	109	113	118	122		
85	78	79	80	81	82	83	84	85	86	87	88	89	90	91	93	95	97	99	102	105	108
80	73	74	75	76	77	77	78	79	79	80	81	81	82	83	84	85	86	87	88	89	91
75	69	69	70	71	72	72	73	73	74	74	75	75	76	76	77	77	78	78	79	79	80
70	64	64	65	65	66	66	67	67	68	68	69	69	70	70	70	71	71	71	71	71	72

● Extreme Danger   ● Danger   ● Extreme Caution   ○ Caution

USA Today. "Windchill," www.usatoday.com/weather/windchill.htm
National Oceanographic and Atmospheric Administration. "Heat Index Table," www.nws.noaa.gov/er/lwx/wxcalc/heatindx.htm
USA Today. "Heat Index," www.usatoday.com/weather/wheat3.htm

Clouds

Name	Height	Description	Indicates
Cirrus	High (45,000 to 16,500 feet)	Wispy and thin	Fair weather
Stratus	Low (6,500 to 0 feet)	Cover most of the sky with an even, gray color similar to a fog	Light rain
Cumulonimbus	Low (6,500 to 0 feet)	Tall, dense, shaped like a block or anvil	Violent weather, such as hail and lightning. Signal thunderstorms and can spawn tornadoes
Nimbostratus	Middle (23,000 to 6,500 feet)	Dark and low	Light rain

Cirrostratus	Troposphere	Halo	Precipitation is likely within 15 to 25 hours if winds steady from NE E to S, or sooner if winds SE to S. Other wind directions bring overcast skies.
Cumulus	Low (6,500 to 0 feet)	Have the appearance of floating cotton and have a lifetime of 5–40 minutes. Known for their flat bases and distinct outlines	Fair weather
Altocumulus	Middle (23,000 to 6,500 feet)	Parallel bands or rounded masses	The presence of altocumulus clouds on a warm and humid summer morning is commonly followed by thunderstorms later in the day.
Stratocumulus	Low (6,500 to 0 feet)	Vary in color from dark gray to light gray and may appear as rounded masses, rolls, etc., with breaks of clear sky in between	Light precipitation

⊙ Annenberg/CPB. "Weather," www.learner.org/exhibits/weather/watercycle.html
Cloud Types: Common Cloud Classifications. www.gfdl.gov/~io/WEATHER/clouds.html

Storms and Storm Warnings

These terms are used by the U.S. National Weather Service to describe potentially dangerous weather patterns and effects.

Type	Description
Tornado	A violently rotating column of air, pendant to a cumulonimbus, with circulation reaching the ground
Hurricane	A tropical cyclone with winds of 74 mph or greater that occurs especially in the western Atlantic, that is usually accompanied by rain, thunder, and lightning, and that sometimes moves into temperate latitudes
Severe Thunderstorm	A thunderstorm that produces a tornado, and/or winds of at least 50 kt (58 mph), and/or hail. Structural damage may imply the occurrence of a severe thunderstorm.
Flood	The filling with water of a normally dry area of land caused by an increased water level in a watercourse (stream, river, drainage ditch) or by the ponding of rainwater
Flash Flood	A flood that is caused by heavy or excessive rainfall in a short period of time, generally less than 6 hours. These conditions are often produced by slow-moving thunderstorms that train one behind the other or tropical systems that make landfall.
Winter Storm	Severe winter conditions, such as accumulations of heavy snow and/or ice of 4" or more possible within the next 24 hours

⊙ National Weather Service. "Storm Warnings," http://iwin.nws.noaa.gov/iwin/nationalwarnings.html

Beaufort Wind Scale

The Beaufort wind scale is used for estimating wind speed when there is no standard instrumentation available.

Beaufort number	Wind Speed [knots]	Wind Speed [mph]	Wind Speed [m/s]	Sea Wave Height [feet]	Sea Wave Height [meters]	Description	Effects observed on sea	Effects observed on land
0	< 1	< 1	0.0–0.2	~0	~0	Calm	Sea like mirror	Calm; smoke rises vertically
1	1–3	1–3	0.3–1.5	0.25	0.1	Light air	Ripples with appearance of scales; no foam crests	Direction of wind shown by smoke drift but not by wind vanes
2	4–6	4–7	1.6–3.3	0.5–1.0	0.2–0.3	Light breeze	Small wavelets; crests of glassy appearance, not breaking	Wind felt on face; leaves rustle; vanes moved by wind
3	7–10	8–12	3.4–5.4	2.0–3.0	0.6–1.0	Gentle breeze	Large wavelets; crests begin to break; scattered whitecaps	Leaves and small twigs in constant motion; wind extends light flag
4	11–16	13–18	5.5–7.9	3.5–5.0	1.0–1.5	Moderate breeze	Small waves, becoming longer; numerous whitecaps	Raises dust and loose paper; small branches are moved
5	17–21	19–24	8.0–10.7	6.0–8.0	2 – 2.5	Fresh breeze	Moderate waves, taking longer form; many whitecaps; some spray	Small trees in leaf begin to sway; crested wavelets form on inland waters
6	22–27	25–31	10.8–13.8	9.5–13.0	3.0–4.0	Strong breeze	Larger waves forming; whitecaps everywhere; more spray	Large branches in motion; whistling heard in telegraph wires; umbrellas used with difficulty
7	28–33	32–38	13.9–17.1	13.5–19.0	4.0–5.5	Near gale	Sea heaps up; white foam from breaking waves begin to be blown in streaks	Whole trees in motion; inconvenience felt when walking against the wind

THE SCIENCES: *Climate, Weather, Environment*

Force					Name	Sea conditions	Land conditions
8	34–40	39–46	17.2–20.7	18.0–25.0	5.5–7.5	Gale	Moderately high waves of greater length; edges of crests begin to break into spindrift; foam is blown in well-marked streaks	Breaks twigs off trees; generally impedes progress
9	41–47	47–54	20.8–24.4	23.0–32.0	7.0–10.0	Strong gale	High waves; sea begins to roll; dense streaks of foam; spray may reduce visibility	Slight structural damage occurs
10	48–55	55–63	24.5–28.4	29.0–41.0	9.0–12.5	Storm	Very high waves with overhanging crests; sea takes white appearance as foam is blown in very dense streaks; rolling is heavy and visibility reduced	Trees uprooted; considerable structural damage occurs
11	56–63	64–72	28.5–32.6	37.0–52.0	11.5–16.0	Violent storm	Exceptionally high waves; sea covered with white foam patches; visibility still more reduced	Accompanied by widespread damage
12	64 +	73 +	32.7 +	45 +	14 +	Hurricane	Air filled with foam; sea completely white with driving spray; visibility greatly reduced	Accompanied by widespread damage

⊙ National Weather Service. "Beaufort Wind Scale," www.nws.noaa.gov/er/cae/beaufort.htm

The Saffir-Simpson scale measures hurricane intensity on the basis of observed damage and top windspeeds.

Category	Windspeed	Effect
1	74–95 mph (64–82 kts) Minimal	No real damage to building structures. Damage primarily to unanchored mobile homes, shrubbery, and trees. Some damage to poorly constructed signs. Also, some coastal road flooding and minor pier damage.
2	96–110 mph (83–95 kts) Moderate	Some roofing material, door, and window damage of buildings. Considerable damage to shrubbery and trees with some trees blown down. Considerable damage to mobile homes, poorly constructed signs, and piers. Coastal and low-lying escape routes flood 2–4 hours before arrival of the hurricane center. Small craft in unprotected anchorages break moorings.
3	111–130 mph (96–113 kts) Extensive	Some structural damage to small residences and utility buildings with a minor amount of curtainwall failures. Damage to shrubbery and trees with foliage blown off trees and large trees blown down. Mobile homes and poorly constructed signs are destroyed. Low-lying escape routes are cut by rising water 3-5 hours before arrival of the hurricane center. Flooding near the coast destroys smaller structures with larger structures damaged by battering of floating debris. Terrain continuously lower than 5 ft. above mean sea level may be flooded inland 8 miles or more. Evacuation of low-lying residences within several blocks of the shoreline may be required.
4	131–155 mph (114–135 kts) Extreme	More extensive curtainwall failures with some complete roof structure failures on small residences. Shrubs, trees, and all signs are blown down. Complete destruction of mobile homes. Extensive damage to doors and windows. Low-lying escape routes may be cut by rising water 3-5 hours before arrival of the hurricane center. Major damage to lower floors of structures near the shore. Terrain lower than 10 ft. above sea level may be flooded, requiring massive evacuation of residential areas as far inland as 6 miles.
5	156 mph + (135 kts) Catastrophic	Complete roof failure on many residences and industrial buildings. Some complete building failures with small utility buildings blown over or away. All shrubs, trees, and signs blown down. Complete destruction of mobile homes. Severe and extensive window and door damage. Low-lying escape routes are cut by rising water 3–5 hours before arrival of the hurricane center. Major damage to lower floors of all structures located less than 15 ft. above sea level and within 500 yards of the shoreline. Massive evacuation of residential areas on low ground 5–10 miles of the shoreline may be required.

⊙ National Hurricane Center. "The Saffir-Simpson Hurricane Scale," www.nhc.noaa.gov/aboutsshs.html

Hurricanes

Following are the 25 most intense hurricanes that have struck the continental United States since 1900.

Ranking	Hurricane	Year	Category	Pressure (Millibars)	Pressure (Inches of Mercury)
1	FL (Keys)	1935	5	892	26.35
2	Camille (MS/SE LA/VA)	1969	5	909	26.84
3	Andrew (SE FL/SE LA)	1992	4	922	27.23
4	FL (Keys)/S TX	1919	4	927	27.37
5	FL (Lake Okeechobee)	1928	4	929	27.43
6	Donna (FL/Eastern U.S.)	1960	4	930	27.46
7	TX (Galveston)	1900	4	931	27.49
8	LA (Grand Isle)	1909	4	931	27.49
9	LA (New Orleans)	1915	4	931	27.49
10	Carla (N & Cent. TX)	1961	4	931	27.49
11	Hugo (SC)	1989	4	934	27.58
12	FL (Miami)/MS/AL/NW FL	1926	4	935	27.61
13	Hazel (SC/NC)	1954	4	938	27.70
14	SE FL/SE LA/MS	1947	4	940	27.76
15	N TX	1932	4	941	27.79
16	Gloria (Eastern U.S.)	1985	3	942	27.82
17	Opal (NW FL/AL)	1995	3	942	27.82
18	Audrey (SW LA/N TX)	1957	4	945	27.91
19	TX (Galveston)	1915	4	945	27.91
20	Celia (S TX)	1970	3	945	27.91
21	Allen (S TX)	1980	3	945	27.91
22	New England	1938	3	946	27.94
23	Frederic (AL/MS)	1979	3	946	27.94
24	NE U.S.	1944	3	947	27.97
25	SC/NC	1906	3	947	27.97

⊙ NOAA Atlantic Oceanographic and Meterological Laboratory. "Hurricane FAQ," www.aoml.noaa.gov/hrd/tcfaq/tcfaqE.html#E10

Hurricane Names

Names of tropical storms are selected by a committee of the World Meteorological Association. The lists are recycled every six years. A name is retired if it becomes associated with a particularly deadly or destructive storm.

Atlantic Hurricanes

Year 2001	Year 2002	Year 2003	Year 2004	Year 2005
Allison	Arthur	Ana	Alex	Arlene
Barry	Bertha	Bill	Bonnie	Brett
Chantal	Cristobal	Claudette	Charley	Cindy
Dean	Dolly	Danny	Danielle	Dennis
Erin	Edouard	Erika	Earl	Emily
Felix	Fay	Fabian	Frances	Franklin
Gabrielle	Gustav	Grace	Gaston	Gert
Humberto	Hanna	Henri	Hermione	Harvey
Iris	Isidore	Isabel	Ivan	Irene
Jerry	Josephine	Juan	Jeanne	Jose
Karen	Kyle	Kate	Karl	Katrina
Lorenzo	Lili	Larry	Lisa	Lee
Michelle	Marco	Mindy	Matthew	Maria
Noel	Nana	Nicholas	Nicole	Nate
Olga	Omar	Odette	Otto	Ophelia
Pablo	Paloma	Peter	Paula	Philippe
Rebekah	Rene	Rose	Richard	Rita
Sebastien	Sally	Sam	Shary	Stan
Tanya	Teddy	Teresa	Tomas	Tammy
Van	Vicky	Victor	Virginie	Vince
Wendy	Wilfred	Wanda	Walter	Wilma

Eastern North Pacific Hurricanes

Year 2001	Year 2002	Year 2003	Year 2004	Year 2005
Adolph	Alma	Andres	Agatha	Adrian
Barbara	Boris	Blanca	Blas	Beatris
Cosme	Cristina	Carlos	Celia	Calvin
Dalila	Douglas	Dolores	Darby	Dora
Erick	Elida	Enrique	Estelle	Eugene
Flossie	Fausto	Felicia	Frank	Fernanda
Gil	Genevieve	Guillermo	Georgette	Greg
Henriette	Hernan	Hilda	Howard	Hilary
Israel	Iselle	Ignacio	Isis	Irwin
Juliette	Julio	Jimena	Javier	Jova
Kiko	Kenna	Kevin	Kay	Kenneth
Lorena	Lowell	Linda	Lester	Lidia
Manuel	Marie	Marty	Madeline	Max
Narda	Norbert	Nora	Newton	Norma
Octave	Odile	Olaf	Orlene	Otis

Priscilla	Polo	Patricia	Paine	Pilar
Raymond	Rachel	Rick	Roslyn	Ramon
Sonia	Simon	Sandra	Seymour	Selma
Tico	Trudy	Terry	Tina	Todd
Velma	Vance	Vivian	Virgil	Veronica
Wallis	Winnie	Waldo	Winifred	Wiley
Xina	Xavier	Xina	Xavier	Xina
York	Yolanda	York	Yolanda	York
Zelda	Zeke	Zelda	Zeke	Zelda

⊙ NOAA. "Hurricane Names," www.nhc.noaa.gov/aboutnames.html

Tornado Intensity Scale

The TORRO Tornado Intensity Scale was devised in 1972 by Dr. G. Terence Meaden, of Bradford-on-Avon, Wiltshire (United Kingdom), in order to categorize windspeeds in tornadoes. The scale is directly related to—and is a natural extension of—the Beaufort Scale. The scale allows for the rating of a tornado's windspeed by various means, namely by

- *viewing the damage caused*
- *engineering analysis of the damage caused*
- *Doppler radar*
- *photogrammetric analysis*
- *direct measurement*

TORRO Intensity	Description of Tornado & Windspeeds	Description of Damage
T0	**Light Tornado** 39–54 miles/hour (17–24 meters/sec)	Loose light litter raised from ground-level in spirals. Tents, marquees seriously disturbed; most exposed tiles, slates on roofs dislodged. Twigs snapped; trail visible through crops.
T1	**Mild Tornado** 55–72 miles/hour (25–32 meters/sec)	Deckchairs, small plants, heavy litter made airborne; minor damage to sheds. More serious dislodging of tiles, slates, chimney pots. Wooden fences flattened. Slight damage to hedges and trees.
T2	**Moderate Tornado** 73–92 miles/hour (33–41 meters/sec)	Heavy mobile homes displaced, light caravans blown over, garden sheds destroyed, garage roofs torn away, much damage to tiled roofs and chimney stacks. General damage to trees, some big branches twisted or snapped off, small trees uprooted.
T3	**Strong Tornado** 93–114 miles/hour (42–51 meters/sec)	Mobile homes overturned/badly damaged; light caravans destroyed; garages, outbuildings destroyed; house roof timbers considerably exposed. Some bigger trees snapped or uprooted.

Tornado Intensity Scale

TORRO Intensity	Description of Tornado & Windspeeds	Description of Damage
T4	**Severe Tornado** 115–136 miles/hour (52–61 meters/sec)	Mobile homes destroyed; some sheds airborne for considerable distances; entire roofs removed from some houses or prefabricated buildings; roof timbers of stronger brick or stone houses completely exposed; possible collapse of gable ends. Numerous trees uprooted or snapped.
T5	**Intense Tornado** 137–160 miles/hour (62–72 meters/sec)	Motor cars levitated; more serious building damage than T4, yet house walls usually remaining; weak/old buildings may collapse completely.
T6	**Moderately Devastating Tornado** 161–186 miles/hour (73–83 meters/sec)	Heavy motor vehicles levitated; strong houses lose entire roofs and perhaps also a wall; more of the weaker buildings collapse.
T7	**Strongly Devastating Tornado** 187–212 miles/hour (84–95 meters/sec)	Frame house completely demolished; some walls of stone or brick houses beaten down or collapse; steel-framed warehouse-type buildings may buckle slightly. Locomotives thrown over. Noticeable de-barking of any standing trees by flying debris.
T8	**Severely Devastating Tornado** 213–240 miles/hour (96–107 meters/sec)	Frame houses and their contents dispersed over big distances; most other stone or brick houses irreparably damaged; steel-framed buildings buckled; motor cars hurled great distances.
T9	**Intensely Devastating Tornado** 241–269 miles/hour (108–120 meters/sec)	Many steel-framed buildings badly damaged; locomotives or trains hurled some distance. Complete debarking of any standing tree trunks.
T10	**Super Tornado** 270–299 miles/hour (121–134 meters/sec)	Entire frame houses and similar buildings lifted bodily from foundations and carried some distances. Steel-reinforced concrete buildings may be severely damaged.

Tornado intensities are grouped more generally thus:

T0, T1, T2, T3 - weak tornadoes

T4, T5, T6, T7 - strong tornadoes

T8, T9, T10 - violent tornadoes

⊙ Tornado Storm and Research Organisation. "The TORRO Tornado Intensity Scale," www.torro.org.uk/tnintens.htm

10 Deadliest Tornadoes

Most of the world's tornadoes—about 75%—occur in the United States. The following are the deadliest tornadoes ever recorded in American history.

State	Date	Dead	Injured
MO-IL-IN	Mar. 18, 1925	695	2,027
LA-MS	May 7, 1840	317	109
MO-IL	May 27, 1896	255	1,000
MS	Apr. 5, 1936	216	700
GA	Apr. 6, 1936	203	1,600
TX-OK-KS	Apr. 9, 1947	181	970
LA-MS	Apr. 24, 1908	143	770
WI	June 12, 1899	117	220
MI	June 8, 1953	115	844
TX	May 11, 1953	114	597

⊙ Disaster Relief. "Tornadoes of the Twentieth Century," www.disasterrelief.org/Disasters/000104tornadocentury/
Weather.com. "Tornadoes!," www.weather.com/weather_center/tornado/inside/about.html

Earthquake Intensity Scales

Richter Scale	Mercalli Scale	Description
0–4.3	I	Mild; not felt
0–4.3	II	Mild; felt by a few, usually those at rest
0–4.3	III	Mild; noticeable to persons indoors, especially on upper floors
4.3–4.8	IV	Moderate; felt indoors by many, a few outside; dishes, windows, and doors rattle, walls make cracking sound; sensation like truck hitting building
4.3–4.8	V	Moderate; felt by nearly everyone; broken dishes and windows
4.8–6.2	VI	Intermediate; felt by all; heavy furniture moved; plaster falls
4.8–6.2	VII	Intermediate; considerable damage to poorly built, badly designed buildings; some chimneys broken
6.2–7.3	VIII	Severe; considerable damage in ordinary substantial buildings; heavy furniture overturned
6.2–7.3	IX	Severe; considerable damage to specially designed buildings; buildings shifted off foundations
6.2–7.3	X	Severe; well-built wooden structures and masonry and frame structures destroyed; rails bent
7.3–8.9	XI	Catastrophic; most structures and bridges destroyed; rails greatly bent
7.3–8.9	XII	Catastrophic; total damage

⊙ U.S. Geologic Survey Earthquake Hazards Program. "Magnitude and Intensity," http://neic.usgs.gov/neis/general/handouts/magnitude_intensity.html

10 Strongest U.S. Earthquakes

Location	Date	Magnitude	Casualties	Damage (US$)
Prince William Sound, Alaska	Mar. 28, 1964	9.2 Mw	125	$311 million
Andreanof Islands, Alaska	Mar. 9, 1957	8.8 Mw	0	$5 million
Rat Islands, Alaska	Feb. 4, 1965	8.7 Mw	0	$10,00 from resulting flooding
East of Shumagin Islands, Alaska	Nov. 10, 1938	8.3 Mw	0	0
Lituya Bay, Alaska	July 10, 1958	8.3 Mw	3	unknown
Yakutat Bay, Alaska	Sept. 10, 1899	8.2 Mw	0	0
Near Cape Yakataga, Alaska	Sept. 4, 1899	8.2 Mw	0	0
Andreanof Islands, Alaska	May 7, 1986	8.0 Mw	0	0
New Madrid, Missouri	Feb. 7, 1812	7.9 Mw	unknown	unknown
Fort Tejon, California	Jan. 9, 1857	7.9 Mw	2	unknown

⊙ U. S. Geological Survey Earthquake Hazards Program. "Fifteen Largest Earthquakes,"
   http://neic.usgs.gov/neis/eqlists/10maps_usa.html

10 Strongest World Earthquakes

Location	Date	Magnitude	Casualties	Damage (US$)
Chile	May 22, 1960	9.5 Mw	2,000	$550 million
Alaska	Mar. 28, 1964	9.2 Mw	125	$311 million
Russia	Nov. 4, 1952	9.0 Mw	0	$1 million in Alaska from resulting tsunami
Ecuador	Jan. 31, 1906	8.8 Mw	500–1,500	unknown
Alaska	Mar. 9, 1957	8.8 Mw	0	$5 million in Hawaii from resulting tsunami
Kuril Islands	Nov. 6, 1958	8.7 Mw	0	0
Alaska	Feb. 4, 1965	8.7 Mw	0	~$10,000 from resulting flooding
India	Aug. 8, 1950	8.6 Mw	1,526	$25 million
Chile	Nov. 11, 1922	8.5 Mw	100	$5–25 million
Indonesia	Feb. 1, 1938	8.5 Mw	unknown	unknown

⊙ U. S. Geological Survey. "Ten Largest Earthquakes in the World Since 1900,"
   http://neis.usgs.gov/neis/eqlists/10mpas_world.html

THE SCIENCES: *Climate, Weather, Environment*

Endangered U.S. Animals and Birds

Lead Regions

1   Far West: CA, HI, ID, NV, OR, WA

2   Southwest: AZ, NM, OK, TX

3   Midwest: IL, IN, IA, MI, MN, OH, WI

4   South: AL, AR, FL, GA, KY, LA, MS, NC, PR, SC, TN

5   East: CT, DE, ME, MD, MA, NH, NJ, NY, PA, RI, VT, VA, WV

6   West: CO, KS, MO, MT, NE, ND, UT, SD, WY

7   Alaska: AK

8   Similarity of appearance to a listed species is a regulatory designation to facilitate the enforcement and further the policy of the Endangered Species Act. It is used when a species is so closely similar to a listed species that enforcement personnel would have substantial difficulty in attempting to differentiate between the listed and unlisted species.

N   National Marine Fisheries Service has jurisdiction for the species.

Lead Region	Common Name (Scientific Name)
Mammals	
3	Bat, gray (Myotis grisescens)
1	Bat, Hawaiian hoary (Lasiurus cinereus semotus)
3	Bat, Indiana (Myotis sodalis)
2	Bat, lesser (=Sanborn's) long-nosed (Leptonycteris curasoae yerbabuenae)
1	Bat, little Mariana fruit (Pteropus tokudae)
1	Bat, Mariana fruit (Pteropus mariannus mariannus)
2	Bat, Mexican long-nosed (Leptonycteris nivalis)
2	Bat, Ozark big-eared (Corynorhinus [=Plecotus] townsendii ingens)
5	Bat, Virginia big-eared (Corynorhinus [=Plecotus] townsendii virginianus)
1	Caribou, woodland (Rangifer tarandus caribou)
1	Deer, Columbian white-tailed (Odocoileus virginianus leucurus)
4	Deer, key (Odocoileus virginianus clavium)
6	Ferret, black-footed (Mustela nigripes)
1	Fox, San Joaquin kit (Vulpes macrotis mutica)
2	Jaguar (Panthera onca)
2	Jaguarundi, Gulf Coast (Herpailurus [=Felis] yagouaroundi cacomitli)
2	Jaguarundi, Sinaloan (Herpailurus [=Felis] yagouaroundi tolteca)
1	Kangaroo rat, Fresno (Dipodomys nitratoides exilis)
1	Kangaroo rat, giant (Dipodomys ingens)
1	Kangaroo rat, Morro Bay (Dipodomys heermanni morroensis)
1	Kangaroo rat, Stephens' (Dipodomys stephensi [incl. D. cascus])
1	Kangaroo rat, Tipton (Dipodomys nitratoides nitratoides)
1	Kangaroo rat, San Bernardino Merriam's (Dipodomys merriami parvus)
4	Manatee, West Indian (Trichechus manatus)
1	Mountain beaver, Point Arena (Aplodontia rufa nigra)
4	Mouse, Alabama beach (Peromyscus polionotus ammobates)
4	Mouse, Anastasia Island beach (Peromyscus polionotus phasma)
4	Mouse, Choctawhatchee beach (Peromyscus polionotus allophrys)

Lead Region	Common Name (Scientific Name)
4	Mouse, Key Largo cotton (Peromyscus gossypinus allapaticola)
1	Mouse, Pacific pocket (Perognathus longimembris pacificus)
4	Mouse, Perdido Key beach (Peromyscus polionotus trissyllepsis)
1	Mouse, salt marsh harvest (Reithrodontomys raviventris)
4	Mouse, St. Andrew beach (Peromyscus polionotus peninsularis)
2	Ocelot (Leopardus [=Felis] pardalis)
4	Panther, Florida (Puma [=Felis] concolor coryi)
2	Pronghorn, Sonoran (Antilocapra americana sonoriensis)
5	Puma, eastern (=eastern cougar) (Puma [=Felis] concolor couguar)
4	Rabbit, Lower Keys (Sylvilagus palustris hefneri)
4	Rice rat, silver (Oryzomys palustris natator)
N	Sea-lion, Steller (=northern), western pop. (Eumetopias jubatus)
N	Seal, Caribbean monk (Monachus tropicalis)
N	Seal, Hawaiian monk (Monachus schauinslandi)
1	Sheep, bighorn (Peninsular Ranges pop. in CA) (Ovis canadensis)
4	Squirrel, Carolina northern flying (Glaucomys sabrinus coloratus)
5	Squirrel, Delmarva Peninsula fox (Sciurus niger cinereus)
2	Squirrel, Mount Graham red (Tamiasciurus hudsonicus grahamensis)
5	Squirrel, Virginia northern flying (Glaucomys sabrinus fuscus)
1	Vole, Amargosa (Microtus californicus scirpensis)
4	Vole, Florida salt marsh (Microtus pennsylvanicus dukecampbelli)
2	Vole, Hualapai Mexican (Microtus mexicanus hualpaiensis)
N	Whale, blue (Balaenoptera musculus)
N	Whale, bowhead (Balaena mysticetus)
N	Whale, finback (Balaenoptera physalus)
N	Whale, humpback (Megaptera novaeangliae)
N	Whale, right (Balaena glacialis [incl. australis])
N	Whale, Sei (Balaenoptera borealis)
N	Whale, sperm (Physeter catodon [=macrocephalus])
3	Wolf, gray (Canis lupus)
4	Wolf, red (Canis rufus)
4	Woodrat, Key Largo (Neotoma floridana smalli)

Birds

Lead Region	Common Name (Scientific Name)
1	`Akepa, Hawaii (honeycreeper) (Loxops coccineus coccineus)
1	`Akepa, Maui (honeycreeper) (Loxops coccineus ochraceus)
1	`Akialoa, Kauai (honeycreeper) (Hemignathus procerus)
1	`Akiapola`au (honeycreeper) (Hemignathus munroi)
4	Blackbird, yellow-shouldered (Agelaius xanthomus)
2	Bobwhite, masked (quail) (Colinus virginianus ridgwayi)
1	Broadbill, Guam (Myiagra freycineti)
1	Condor, California (Gymnogyps californianus)
1	Coot, Hawaiian (=`alae-ke`oke`o) (Fulica americana alai)
4	Crane, Mississippi sandhill (Grus canadensis pulla)
2	Crane, whooping (Grus americana)

I	Creeper, Hawaii (Oreomystis mana)
I	Creeper, Molokai (=kakawahie) (Paroreomyza flammea)
I	Creeper, Oahu (=alauwahio) (Paroreomyza maculata)
I	Crow, Hawaiian (=`alala) (Corvus hawaiiensis)
I	Crow, Mariana (Corvus kubaryi)
7	Curlew, Eskimo (Numenius borealis)
I	Duck, Hawaiian (=koloa) (Anas wyvilliana)
I	Duck, Laysan (Anas laysanensis)
I	Falcon, American peregrine (Falco peregrinus anatum)
2	Falcon, northern aplomado (Falco femoralis septentrionalis)
8	Falcon, peregrine (Falco peregrinus)
I	Finch, Laysan (honeycreeper) (Telespyza cantans)
I	Finch, Nihoa (honeycreeper) (Telespyza ultima)
2	Flycatcher, Southwestern willow (Empidonax traillii extimus)
I	Goose, Hawaiian (=nene) (Branta [=Nesochen] sandvicensis)
I	Hawk, Hawaiian (=io) (Buteo solitarius)
4	Hawk, Puerto Rican broad-winged (Buteo platypterus brunnescens)
4	Hawk, Puerto Rican sharp-shinned (Accipiter striatus venator)
I	Honeycreeper, crested (=`akohekohe) (Palmeria dolei)
I	Kingfisher, Guam Micronesian (Halcyon cinnamomina cinnamomina)
4	Kite, Everglade snail (Rostrhamus sociabilis plumbeus)
I	Mallard, Mariana (Anas oustaleti)
I	Megapode, Micronesian (=La Perouse's) (Megapodius laperouse)
I	Millerbird, Nihoa (old world warbler) (Acrocephalus familiaris kingi)
I	Moorhen (=gallinule), Hawaiian common (Gallinula chloropus sandvicensis)
I	Moorhen (=gallinule), Mariana common (Gallinula chloropus guami)
4	Nightjar, Puerto Rican (=whip-poor-will) (Caprimulgus noctitherus)
I	Nukupu`u (honeycreeper) (Hemignathus lucidus)
I	`O`o, Kauai (=`o`o `a`a) (honeyeater) (Moho braccatus)
I	`O`u (honeycreeper) (Psittirostra psittacea)
I	Palila (honeycreeper) (Loxioides bailleui)
4	Parrot, Puerto Rican (Amazona vittata)
I	Parrotbill, Maui (honeycreeper) (Pseudonestor xanthophrys)
I	Pelican, brown (Pelecanus occidentalis)
I	Petrel, Hawaiian dark-rumped (Pterodroma phaeopygia sandwichensis)
4	Pigeon, Puerto Rican plain (Columba inornata wetmorei)
3	Plover, piping (Charadrius melodus)
I	Po`ouli (honeycreeper) (Melamprosops phaeosoma)
2	Prairie-chicken, Attwater's greater (Tympanuchus cupido attwateri)
2	Pygmy-owl, cactus ferruginous (Glaucidium brasilianum cactorum)
I	Rail, California clapper (Rallus longirostris obsoletus)
I	Rail, Guam (Rallus owstoni)
I	Rail, light-footed clapper (Rallus longirostris levipes)
2	Rail, Yuma clapper (Rallus longirostris yumanensis)
I	Shrike, San Clemente loggerhead (Lanius ludovicianus mearnsi)
4	Sparrow, Cape Sable seaside (Ammodramus maritimus mirabilis)
4	Sparrow, Florida grasshopper (Ammodramus savannarum floridanus)
I	Stilt, Hawaiian (=ae`o) (Himantopus mexicanus knudseni)

Lead Region	Common Name (Scientific Name)
4	Stork, wood (Mycteria americana)
1	Swiftlet, Mariana gray (=vanikoro) (Aerodramus vanikorensis bartschi)
1	Tern, California least (Sterna antillarum browni)
3	Tern, least (Sterna antillarum)
5	Tern, roseate (Sterna dougallii dougallii)
1	Thrush, large Kauai (Myadestes myadestinus)
1	Thrush, Molokai (=oloma`o) (Myadestes lanaiensis rutha)
1	Thrush, small Kauai (=puaiohi) (Myadestes palmeri)
2	Vireo, black-capped (Vireo atricapillus)
1	Vireo, least Bell's (Vireo bellii pusillus)
4	Warbler, Bachman's (Vermivora bachmanii)
2	Warbler, golden-cheeked (Dendroica chrysoparia)
3	Warbler, Kirtland's (Dendroica kirtlandii)
1	Warbler, nightingale reed (Acrocephalus luscinia)
1	White-eye, bridled (Zosterops conspicillatus conspicillatus)
4	Woodpecker, ivory-billed (Campephilus principalis)
4	Woodpecker, red-cockaded (Picoides borealis)

Reptiles

Lead Region	Common Name (Scientific Name)
8	Alligator, American (Alligator mississippiensis)
4	Anole, Culebra Island giant (Anolis roosevelti)
4	Boa, Puerto Rican (Epicrates inornatus)
4	Boa, Virgin Islands tree (Epicrates monensis granti)
4	Crocodile, American (Crocodylus acutus)
4	Gecko, Monito (Sphaerodactylus micropithecus)
1	Lizard, blunt-nosed leopard (Gambelia silus)
4	Lizard, St. Croix ground (Ameiva polops)
4	Sea turtle, green (Chelonia mydas)
4	Sea turtle, hawksbill (Eretmochelys imbricata)
2	Sea turtle, Kemp's (=Atlantic) ridley (Lepidochelys kempii)
4	Sea turtle, leatherback (Dermochelys coriacea)
1	Snake, San Francisco garter (Thamnophis sirtalis tetrataenia)
4	Turtle, Alabama redbelly (Pseudemys alabamensis)
5	Turtle, Plymouth redbelly (Pseudemys rubriventris bangsi)

Amphibians

Lead Region	Common Name (Scientific Name)
2	Salamander, Barton Springs (Eurycea sosorum)
1	Salamander, desert slender (Batrachoseps aridus)
1	Salamander, Santa Cruz long-toed (Ambystoma macrodactylum croceum)
5	Salamander, Shenandoah (Plethodon shenandoah)
2	Salamander, Sonoran tiger (Ambystoma tigrinum stebbinsi)
2	Salamander, Texas blind (Typhlomolge rathbuni)
1	Toad, arroyo (Bufo microscaphus californicus)
2	Toad, Houston (Bufo houstonensis)
6	Toad, Wyoming (Bufo hemiophrys baxteri)

⊙ U.S. Fish and Wildlife Service, Division of Endangered Species. "Endangered Species List," www.fws.gov

Pollution

The United States Environmental Protection Agency (EPA) is the federal body responsible for regulating pollution and for protecting human health and the environment. Learn more about the EPA at www.epa.gov.

Air

Pollutant	Health Effect	Environmental Effect
Carbon Monoxide	Reduces ability of blood to bring oxygen to body cells and tissues; cells and tissues need oxygen to work. Carbon monoxide may be particularly hazardous to people who have heart or circulatory (blood vessel) problems and people who have damaged lungs or breathing passages	
Lead	Brain and other nervous system damage; children are at special risk. Some lead-containing chemicals cause cancer in animals. Lead causes digestive and other health problems.	Lead can harm wildlife
Ground Level Ozone	Breathing problems, reduced lung function, asthma, irritates eyes, stuffy nose, reduced resistance to colds and other infections, may speed up aging of lung tissue	Ozone can damage plants and trees; smog can cause reduced visibility
Nitrogen Oxides (NOx)	Lung damage, illnesses of breathing passages and lungs (respiratory system)	Nitrogen dioxide is an ingredient of acid rain (acid aerosols), which can damage trees and lakes. Acid aerosols can reduce visibility.
Particulate Matter	Nose and throat irritation, lung damage, bronchitis, early death	Particulates are the main source of haze that reduces visibility
Sulfur Oxides (SOx)	Breathing problems, may cause permanent damage to lungs	SO_2 is an ingredient in acid rain (acid aerosols), which can damage trees and lakes. Acid aerosols can also reduce visibility.
Volatile Organic Compounds (VOCs)	In addition to ozone (smog) effects, many VOCs can cause serious health problems such as cancer and other effects.	In addition to ozone (smog) effects, some VOCs such as formaldehyde and ethylene may harm plants.

Water

Pollutant	Health Effect
Contaminated Sediment	Metals, PAHs, and organics listed above are toxic to various plants and animals, including people. These contaminants tend to biomagnify as they travel up the food chain. All have been linked to health problems in people.
Disinfection Byproducts	Acute and chronic gastrointestinal illness, cancer, liver toxicity, and reproductive and developmental disorders
Dredged Materials	Acute and chronic gastrointestinal illness, cancer, liver toxicity, and reproductive and developmental disorders
Microbial Pathogens	Acute and chronic gastrointestinal illness, cancer, liver toxicity, and reproductive and developmental disorders

Land

Pollutant	Health Effect
Arsenic	Skin damage; circulatory system problems; increased risk of cancer
Barium	Increase in blood pressure
Benzene	Anemia; decrease in blood platelets; increased risk of cancer
Cadmium	Kidney damage
Cyanide	Nerve damage or thyroid problems
Lead	Infants and children: Delays in physical or mental development. Adults: Kidney problems; high blood pressure
Mercury	Kidney damage
Polychlorinated Biphenyls (PCBs)	Skin changes; thymus gland problems; immune deficiencies; reproductive or nervous system difficulties; increased risk of cancer
Toluene	Nervous system, kidney, or liver problems
Trichloroethylene (TCE)	Liver problems; increased risk of cancer

⊙ United States Environmental Protection Agency. "Water Pollutants," www.epa.gov/ebtpages/pwaterpollu-tants.html

United States Environmental Protection Agency. "Air Pollutants," www.epa.gov/ebtpages/pairpollu-tants.html

United States Environmental Protection Agency. "Soil Pollutants," www.epa.gov/ebtpages/psoilcontami-nants.html

THE SCIENCES: *Mathematics*

Mathematical Terms

Area	the number of square units that can fit inside a figure
Circumference	distance around the circle
Composite number	a number with more than two factors
Diameter	distance across a circle, passing through its center; equals two times the radius
Factor	any number that can divide evenly into a given number; for example, 2 and 3 are factors of 6
Hypotenuse	the longest side of a right triangle
Integer	the set of whole numbers and their additive inverses
Irrational number	real numbers that cannot be expressed as the quotient of two integers
Mean	the average
Median	the middle number when the data are listed in size order
Mode	the piece of data that appears most often
Perimeter	the distance around a figure
Pi (π)	the ratio of the measure of the circumference and diameter of a circle; estimated value is 3.14
Prime Number	a number with only two factors, itself and 1
Radius	the distance from the center of circle to any point on the circle; one-half of the diameter
Rational number	a number that can be expressed as the quotient of two integers
Reciprocal	a fraction that is the result of switching a fraction's numerator and denominator; the multiplicative inverse of a fraction
Volume	the number of cubic units that can fit inside a three-dimensional figure

⊙ Heddens, James W., and William R. Speer. *Today's Mathematics.* 7th ed. New York: Macmillan, 1992.

Mathematical Symbols

Below are some of the more common symbols and expressions used in mathematics, geometry, and statistics.

+	1. plus	≥	is greater than or equal to	x^3	x cubed
	2. positive (number or charge)	%	percent	x^n	x to the power n
		∞	infinity	π	pi
−	1. minus	∝	varies as	r	radius of circle
	2. negative (number or charge)	:	is to, the ratio of	n!	n factorial
		∈	is an element of (a set)	∫	the integral of
±	plus or minus	∉	is not an element of (a set)	∠	angle
× or ·	multiplied by			∟	right angle
÷	divided by	Ø	empty set	△	triangle
=	is equal to	∩	intersection	∥	is parallel to
≠	is not equal to	∪	union	⊥	is perpendicular to
≈	approximately equal to	⊂	is a subset of	°	degree
≡	is equivalent to	⇒	implies	′	1. minute (of an arc)
<	is less than	√	square root		2. foot, feet
≤	is less than or equal to	∛	cube root	″	1. second (of an arc)
>	is greater than	x^2	x squared		2. inch, inches

Roman Numerals

Roman Numeral	Arabic numeral		Roman Numeral	Arabic numeral
I	1		XLV	45
II	2		L	50
III	3		LX	60
IIII or IV	4		LXX	70
V	5		LXXX	80
VI	6		XC	90
VII	7		C	100
VIII	8		CL	150
IX	9		CC	200
X	10		CCL	250
XI	11		CCC	300
XII	12		CCCL	350
XIII	13		CD	400
XIV	14		CDL	450
XV	15		D	500
XVI	16		DC	600
XVII	17		DCC	700
XVIII	18		DCCC	800
XIX	19		CM	900
XX	20		M	1,000
XXV	25		MD	1,500
XXX	30		MM	2,000
XXXV	35		MMD	2,500
XL	40		MMM	3,000

⊙ Roman Numerals 101. "Starting Off," www.cod.edu/people/faculty/lawrence/romaindx.htm

Common Mathematical Procedures

Addition of fractions with like denominators	$\frac{1}{8} + \frac{6}{8} = \frac{7}{8}$	Add numerators; keep denominators
Addition of fractions with unlike denominators	$\frac{3}{4} + \frac{1}{8} = \frac{6}{8} + \frac{1}{8} = \frac{7}{8}$	Rewrite the fractions with common denominators, then add as usual
Addition of mixed numbers	$1\frac{5}{8} + 3\frac{1}{8} = 4\frac{6}{8}$	Add the whole number part, then add the fraction part

THE SCIENCES: Mathematics

Subtraction of fractions with like denominators	$\dfrac{6}{8} - \dfrac{1}{8} = \dfrac{5}{8}$	Subtract the numerators and keep the denominators
Subtraction of fractions with unlike denominators	$\dfrac{3}{4} - \dfrac{3}{8} = \dfrac{6}{8} - \dfrac{3}{8} = \dfrac{3}{8}$	Rewrite the fractions with common denominators, then subtract as usual
Multiplying fractions	$\dfrac{1}{2} \times \dfrac{3}{4} = \dfrac{3}{8}$	Multiply the numerators, then multiply the denominators
Dividing fractions	$\dfrac{1}{7} \div \dfrac{1}{2} = \dfrac{1}{7} \times 2 = \dfrac{2}{7}$	Multiply the first fraction by the reciprocal of the second fraction
Proportions	$\dfrac{2}{10} \times \dfrac{1}{5}$ $2 \times 5 = 1 \times 10$ $10 = 10$	When two ratios form a proportion, then the cross products are equal
Finding the part of a whole when the percentage is known	50% of 84 is _____ $50 \div 100 = .50$ $.50 \times 84 = 42$	Divide the percentage by 100, then multiply the result by the whole
Finding the whole when the percentage is known	20% of _____ is 12 $20 \div 100 = .20$ $12 \div .20 = 60$	Divide the percentage by 100, then divide the result into the part
Finding the percentage of a number	_____% of 80 is 20 $20 \div 80 = .25$ $.25 \times 100 = 25\%$	Divide the part by the whole, then multiply the result by 100
Combining like terms	$5x^2 + 4x^2 = 9x^2$ $11y^6 - 7y^6 = 4y^6$	Add or subtract the coefficients; the base and exponents remain the same

⊙ Occhiogrosso, Marilyn, et al. *Integrated Mathematics Integrated Course.* New York: Amsco, 1995.

Areas and Volumes

Figure	Diagram	To calculate volume	Figure	Diagram	To calculate volume
Square		s^2	Cube		s^3
Rectangle		$l \times w$	Rectangular prism		$l \times w \times h$
Parallelogram		$b \times h$	Triangular prism		$\frac{1}{2}(l \times w \times h)$
Triangle		$\frac{1}{2}\,b \times h$	Cylinder		$r^2 \times \pi \times h$
Trapezoid		$\frac{1}{2}\,(b_1 + b_2)h$	Pyramid		$\frac{1}{3}(l \times w \times h)$
			Cone		$\frac{1}{3}(r^2 \times \pi \times h)$
Circle		$r^2(\pi)$	Sphere		$\frac{4}{3} \times \pi \times r^2$

⊙ The Math Forum. "Area and Volume Formulas," http://forum.swarthmore/edu/dr.math

THE SCIENCES: *Mathematics*

The Solar System

Planets

Name	Orbits (Designation)	Distance from Sun 000 mi. / 000 km.	Radius mi. / km.	Rotate (days)	Period (days)	Discoverer	Date
Sun	—	—	431,520 / 696,000	25.4	—	Known in antiquity	
Mercury	Sun (I)	36,000 / 57,910	1,600 / 2,440	58.7	87.97	Known in antiquity	
Venus	Sun (II)	67,000 / 108,200	3,350 / 6,052	243*	224.70	Known in antiquity	
Earth	Sun (III)	93,000 / 149,600	3,960 / 6,378	0.99	365.26	Known in antiquity	
Mars	Sun (IV)	141,000 / 227,940	2,100 / 3,397	1.03	686.98	Known in antiquity	
Jupiter	Sun (V)	483,000 / 778,570	44,320 / 71,492	0.41	4,331.59	Known in antiquity	
Saturn	Sun (VI)	886,000 / 1,433,525	37,250 / 60,268	0.45	10,747	Known in antiquity	
Uranus	Sun (VII)	1,782,000 / 2,872,450	16,000 / 25,559	0.72*	30,589	Herschel	1781
Neptune	Sun (VIII)	2,793,000 / 4,495,100	15,500 / 24,764	0.67	59,800	Adams, LeVerrier, Galle, and d'Arrest	1846
Pluto	Sun (IX)	3,670,000 / 5,869,660	750 / 1,195	6.39*	90,588	Tombaugh	1930

Planetary Satellites

Planet (No. of Satellites)	Satellite Name	Distance 000 mi. / 000 km.	Radius mi. / km.	Period (days)	Discoverer	Date
Earth (1)	Moon	238 / 384	1,077 / 1,737	27.32	Known in antiquity	
Mars (2)	Phobos	6 / 9	8 × 7 × 6 / 13 × 11 × 9	0.32	Hall	1877
	Deimos	14 / 23	5 × 4 × 3 / 8 × 6 × 5	1.26	Hall	1877
Jupiter (16)	Metis	79 / 128	12 / 20	0.29	Synnott**	1979
	Adrastea	80 / 129	8 × 6 × 5 / 13 × 10 × 8	0.30	Jewitt, Danielson	1979

Notes: * Retrograde motion
** Identified from photographs returned from *Voyager 2*
*** Identified from photographs returned from *Voyager 1*

Planet (No. of Satellites)	Satellite Name	Distance 000 mi. / 000 km.	Radius mi. / km.	Period (days)	Discoverer	Date
Jupiter (cont.)	Amalthea	112 / 181	81 × 45 × 42 / 131 × 73 × 67	0.50	Barnard	1892
	Thebe	138 / 222	34 × 28 / 55 × 45	0.67	Synnott***	1979
	Io	262 / 422	1,129 / 1,821	1.77	Galileo	1610
	Europa	416 / 671	970 / 1,565	3.55	Galileo	1610
	Ganymede	663 / 1,070	1,633 / 2,634	7.15	Galileo	1610
	Callisto	1,167 / 1,883	1,490 / 2,403	16.69	Galileo	1610
	Leda	6,878 / 11,094	3 / 5	238.72	Kowal	1974
	Himalia	7,118 / 11,480	58 / 85	250.57	Perrine	1904
	Lysithea	7,266 / 11,720	7 / 12	259.22	Nicholson	1938
	Elara	7,277 / 11,737	25 / 40	259.65	Perrine	1905
	Ananke	13,144 / 21,200	6 / 10	631*	Nicholson	1951
	Carme	14,012 / 22,600	9 / 15	692*	Nicholson	1938
	Pasiphae	14,570 / 23,500	11 / 18	735*	Melotte	1908
	Sinope	14,694 / 23,700	9 / 14	758*	Nicholson	1914
Saturn (18)	Pan	83 / 134	6 / 10	0.58	Showalter**	1990
	Atlas	86 / 138	12 × 11 × 9 / 19 × 17 × 14	0.60	Terrile***	1980
	Prometheus	86 / 139	46 × 31 × 21 / 74 × 50 × 34	0.61	Collins***	1980
	Pandora	88 / 142	34 × 27 × 19 / 55 × 44 × 31	0.63	Collins***	1980
	Epimetheus	94 / 151	43 × 34 × 34 / 69 × 55 × 55	0.69	Fountain, Larson, Reitsema, Smith***	1980
	Janus	94 / 151	60 × 59 × 48 / 97 × 95 × 77	0.69	Dollfus	1966
	Mimas	115 / 186	130 × 122 × 118 / 209 × 196 × 190	94	Herschel	1789
	Enceladus	148 / 238	159 × 153 × 152 / 256 × 247 × 245	1.37	Herschel	1789
	Tethys	183 / 295	332 × 327 × 326 / 536 × 528 × 526	1.89	Cassini	1684

Telesto	183 / 295	9 × 8 × 5 / 15 × 13 × 8	1.89	Fountain, Larson, Reitsema, Smith***	1980
Calypso	183 / 295	9 × 5 × 5 / 15 × 8 × 8	1.89	Pascu, Seidelman, Baum, Currie	1980
Dione	234 / 377	347 / 560	2.74	Cassini	1684
Helene	234 / 377	11 × 10 × 9 / 18 × 16 × 15	2.74	Laques, Lecacheux	1980
Rhea	327 / 527	474 / 764	4.52	Cassini	1672
Titan	758 / 1,222	1,597 / 2,575	15.95	Huygens	1655
Hyperion	918 / 1,481	115 × 87 × 70 / 185 × 140 × 113	21.28	Bond, Lassell	1848
Iapetus	2,208 / 3,561	445 / 718	79.33	Cassini	1671
Phoebe	8,030 / 12,952	71 × 68 × 65 / 115 × 110 × 105	550.48*	Pickering	1898
Uranus (17)					
Cordelia	31 / 50	8 / 13	0.34	Terrile**	1986
Ophelia	33 / 54	9 / 15	0.38	Terrile**	1986
Bianca	37 / 59	13 / 21	0.43	Voyager 2 photos	1986
Cressida	38 / 62	19 / 31	0.46	Synnott**	1986
Desdemona	39 / 63	17 / 27	0.47	Synnott**	1986
Juliet	40 / 64	26 / 42	0.49	Synnott**	1986
Portia	41 / 66	33 / 54	0.51	Synnott**	1986
Rosalind	43 / 70	17 / 27	0.56	Synnott**	1986
Belinda	47 / 75	20 / 33	0.62	Synnott**	1986
Puck	53 / 86	48 / 77	0.76	Synnott**	1985
Miranda	80 / 129	149 × 145 × 144 / 240 × 234 × 233	1.41	Kuiper	1948
Ariel	118 / 191	360 × 358 × 358 / 581 × 578 × 578	2.52	Lassell	1851

Notes: * Retrograde motion
** Identified from photographs returned from *Voyager 2*
*** Identified from photographs returned from *Voyager 1*

Planet (No. of Satellites)	Satellite Name	Distance 000 mi. / 000 km.	Radius mi. / km.	Period (days)	Discoverer	Date
Uranus (cont.)	Umbriel	165 / 266	363 / 585	4.14	Lassell	1851
	Titania	270 / 436	489 / 789	8.71	Herschel	1787
	Oberon	362 / 584	472 / 761	13.46	Herschel	1787
	Caliban	4,445 / 7,169	19 / 30	579.38*	Gladman, Nicholson, Burns, Kavelaars	1997
	Sycorax	7,549 / 12,175	37 / 60	1289*	Gladman, Nicholson, Burns, Kavelaars	1997
Neptune (8)	Naiad	30 / 48	18 / 29	0.29	Terrile**	1989
	Thalassa	31 / 50	25 / 40	0.31	Terrile**	1989
	Despina	33 / 53	46 / 74	0.33	Synnott**	1989
	Galatea	38 / 62	49 / 79	0.43	Synnott**	1989
	Larissa	46 / 74	$65 \times 55 \times 56$ / $104 \times 89 \times 90$	0.55	Reitsema, Tholen, Hubbard, Lebofsky**	1989
	Proteus	73 / 118	$135 \times 129 \times 125$ / $218 \times 208 \times 201$	1.12	Synnott**	1989
	Triton	220 / 355	839 / 1,353	5.88*	Lassell	1846
	Nereid	3,418 / 5,513	105 / 170	360.14	Kuiper	1949
Pluto (1)	Charon	12 / 20	368 / 593	6.39	Christy	1978

Notes: * Retrograde motion
** Identified from photographs returned from *Voyager 2*
*** Identified from photographs returned from *Voyager 1*

⊙ Encrenaz, Thérèse. *The Solar System*. Berlin, New York: Springer, 1995.
National Space Science Data Center. "Planetary Fact Sheet," http://nssdc.gsfc.nasa.gov/planetary/planetfact.html

Phases of the Moon

The moon is visible from Earth as a disk that reflects light from the sun. Only one hemisphere of the moon is illuminated, and as it orbits Earth the illuminated face moves in and out of view. This results in what are known as the phases of the moon. When the moon is on the far side of Earth, directly opposite the sun, the whole of its illuminated face can be seen as a circle—a full moon. As the moon circles around and the illuminated portion moves out of view, it is said to be waning; when it is between Earth and the sun and none of the illuminated face is visible, it is a new moon; and as it returns to full visibility it is said to be waxing.

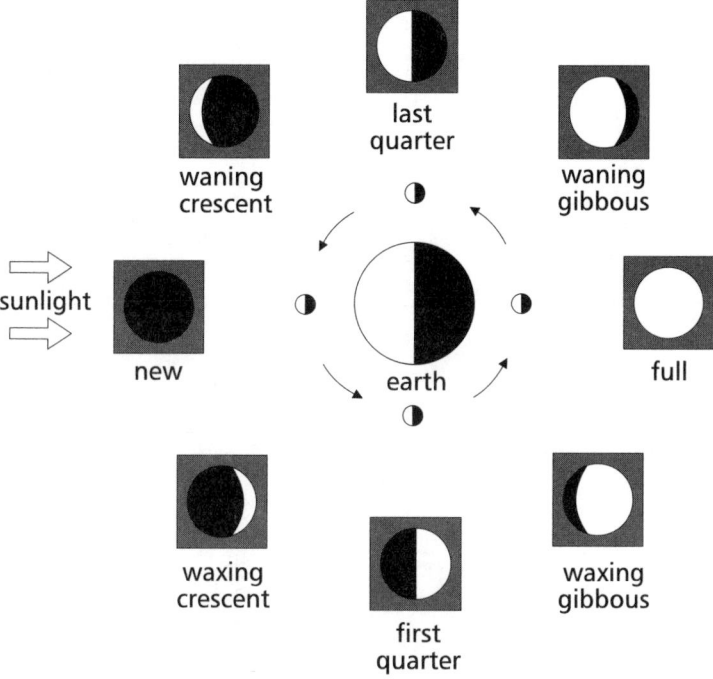

⊙ U.S. Naval Observatory. "Phases of the Moon," http://aa.usno.navy.mil/AA/data/docs/MoonPhase.html

Future Total Solar Eclipses

Date	*Duration*	*Where Visible*
Dec. 4, 2002	2 min. 4 sec.	Southern Africa, Australia
Nov. 23, 2003	1 min. 57 sec.	Antarctica
Mar. 29, 2006	4 min. 7 sec.	Africa, Turkey, Russia
Aug. 1, 2008	2 min. 27 sec.	Greenland, northern Russia, China
July 22, 2009	6 min. 39 sec.	India, Himalayan region, China
July 11, 2010	5 min. 20 sec.	South Pacific, southern Chile, Argentina
Nov. 13, 2012	4 min. 2 sec.	Northern Australia
Mar. 20, 2015	2 min. 47 sec.	North Atlantic
Mar. 9, 2016	4 min. 9 sec.	Indonesia, North Pacific
Aug. 21, 2017	2 min. 40 sec.	United States
July 2, 2019	4 min. 33 sec.	South Pacific, Chile, Argentina

Future Total Solar Eclipses *(cont.)*

Date	Duration	Where Visible
Dec. 14, 2020	2 min. 10 sec.	Chile, Argentina
Dec. 4, 2021	1 min. 54 sec.	Antarctica
Apr. 8, 2024	4 min. 38 sec.	Mexico, United States, Canada
Aug. 12, 2026	2 min. 18 sec.	Greenland, Iceland, Spain
Aug. 2, 2027	6 min. 23 sec.	North Africa, Saudi Arabia
July 22, 2028	5 min. 10 sec.	Australia, New Zealand
Nov. 25, 2030	3 min. 44 sec.	Southern Africa, Australia

⊙ Espenak, Fred. "Eclipse Predictions by Fred Espenak, NASA/GSFC," http://sunearth.gsfc.nasa.gov/eclipse/SEcat/SE2001-2100.html

Harrington, Philip S. *Eclipse! The What, Where, When, Why, and How Guide to Watching Solar and Lunar Eclipses.* New York: Wiley, 1997.

U.S. Naval Observatory. "Upcoming and Recent Eclipses of the Sun and Moon," http://riemann.usno.navy.mil/AA/data/docs/UpcomingEclipses.html

Galaxies

Name	Type	Distance[1]	Diameter[1]
Milky Way*	Spiral	—	110
Small Magellanic Cloud (SMC)*	Irregular	18	20
Large Magellanic Cloud (LMC)*	Irregular	160	30
Ursa Minor*	Dwarf elliptical	222	7.8
Sculptor system*	Dwarf elliptical	280	7.5
Fornax system*	Dwarf elliptical	612	20
NGC 6822*	Irregular	2,150	5.5
NGC 205*	Elliptical	2,220	14
M32 / NGC 221*	Elliptical	2,220	6.8
M31 / NGC 224* (Andromeda)	Spiral	2,220	170
M33 / NGC 598* (Triangulum)	Spiral	2,720	59
Maffei I	Elliptical	3,300	unknown
M82	Irregular	10,000	23
M81 (Ursa Major group)	Spiral	10,500	100
M51 (Whirlpool)	Spiral	13,000	65
Centaurus A	Elliptical	16,000	30
M101 (Pinwheel)	Spiral	20,000	200
M83	Spiral	27,000	100
M104 (Sombrero)	Spiral	40,000	30
M87 (Virgo A)	Elliptical	50,000	40

[1]Distances and diameters are given in thousands of light-years and are approximate.
M refers to the Messier Catalog number.
NGC refers to the New General Catalogue number.
* Indicates a member of the Local Group

⊙ Friedman, Herbert. *The Astronomer's Universe: Stars, Galaxies, and Cosmos.* New York: Norton, 1990.

Sandage, Allan, and John Bedke. *The Carnegie Atlas of Galaxies.* Washington, D.C.: Carnegie Institution of Washington, 1994.

Wray, James D. *A Color Atlas of Galaxies.* Cambridge: Cambridge University Press, 1988.

Stars: 10 Closest to the Sun

Rank	Star	Distance in light-years	Magnitude
1	Proxima Centauri	4.2	11.3
2	Alpha Centauri A	4.3	.33
3	Alpha Centauri B	4.3	1.70
4	Barnard's Star	5.96	9.5
5	Wolf 359	7.6	13.5
6	Lalande 21185	8.11	7.5
7	UV Ceti A	8.55	12.52
8	UV Ceti B	8.55	13.02
9	Alpha Sirius	8.7	−1.47
10	Beta Sirius	8.7	8.3

⊙ Royal Observatory Greenwich. "The 30 Closest Stars," www.rog.nmm.ac.uk/leaflets/closeststars/closest-stars.html

Speer, Gordon. "Table of the Earth's Nearest Stars," www.essex1.com/people/speer/stars.html

Constellations

Constellation	Common Name(s)	When Visible*
Andromeda		autumn (Nov.)
Aquarius	Water bearer	autumn (Oct.)
Aquila	Eagle	summer (Sep.)
Ara	Altar	summer (July)
Aries	Ram	winter (Dec.)
Boötes	Herdsman	spring (June)
Cancer	Crab	spring (Mar.)
Canis major	Greater dog	winter (Feb.)
Canis minor	Lesser dog	spring (Mar.)
Capricornus	Goat	autumn (Sep.)
Cassiopeia		all year (Nov.)
Centaurus	Centaur	spring (May)
Cepheus		all year (Oct.)
Cetus	Sea monster	winter (Dec.)
Crater	Cup	spring (Apr.)
Crux	Southern cross	spring (May)
Cygnus	Swan, Northern cross	summer (Sep.)
Draco		all year (July)
Eridanus	River	winter (Dec.)
Gemini	Twins	winter (Feb.)
Hercules		summer (July)
Hydra	Sea serpent	spring (Apr.)
Leo	Lion	spring (Apr.)
Libra	Balance	summer (June)

Constellations *(cont.)*

Constellation	Common Name(s)	When Visible*
Lynx		spring (Mar.)
Lyra	Harp	summer (Aug.)
Ophiuchus	Serpent bearer	summer (July)
Orion	Hunter	winter (Jan.)
Pegasus		autumn (Oct.)
Perseus		winter (Dec.)
Pisces	Fishes	autumn (Nov.)
Sagittarius	Archer	summer (Aug.)
Scorpius	Scorpion	summer (July)
Taurus	Bull	winter (Jan.)
Ursa major	Big dipper, Great bear, Plough	all year (Apr.)
Ursa minor	Little dipper, Little bear	all year (June)
Virgo	Maiden, Virgin	spring (May)

*Visibility information is for the northern hemisphere; month in parentheses is the best time for observation.

⊙ Bakich, Michael Eli. *The Cambridge Guide to the Constellations.* New York: Cambridge University Press, 1995.
"The Constellations and Their Stars," www.astro.wisc.edu/~dolan/constellations/

Potentially Hazardous Asteroids*

Asteroids are listed in order of date of close-approach to Earth.

Asteroid Name or Designation	Earth Close-Approach Date	AU**	Asteroid Name or Designation	Earth Close-Approach Date	AU**
1998 VD35	Jan. 2, 2001	0.098	3362 Khufu	Dec. 25, 2002	0.150
1994 WR12	Jan. 17, 2001	0.135	6489 Golevka	May 20, 2003	0.092
1998 WT	Feb. 26, 2001	0.148	1998 FH12	June 27, 2003	0.049
1998 SF36	Mar. 28, 2001	0.043	1994 PM	Aug. 16, 2003	0.025
4034 1986 PA	Apr. 3, 2001	0.147	1998 VS	Sep. 11, 2003	0.158
1998 HD14	Aug. 26, 2001	0.076	1998 FG2	Oct. 22, 2003	0.035
1998 WT24	Dec. 16, 2001	0.012	1989 UQ	Oct. 24, 2003	0.150
3362 Khufu	Dec. 29, 2001	0.160	1990 OS	Nov. 10, 2003	0.030
4660 Nereus	Jan. 22, 2002	0.029	1996 GT	Nov. 12, 2003	0.048
3361 Orpheus	Jan. 27, 2002	0.170	1998 UT18	Nov. 28, 2003	0.066
5604 1992 FE	June 22, 2002	0.077	1996 JG	Nov. 30, 2003	0.142
2101 Adonis	June 29, 2002	0.161	3362 Khufu	Dec. 20, 2003	0.195
1998 WT	Oct. 17, 2002	0.103	6239 Minos	Feb. 2, 2004	0.056
1997 XF11	Oct. 31, 2002	0.064	1993 KH	June 14, 2004	0.132

*Asteroids approaching within 0.2 Astronomical Units (18.58 million mi./30 million km.) of the Earth
**AU=Astronomical Unit (92.9 million mi./150 million km. Earth is about one AU from the Sun.)

THE SCIENCES: *Astronomy*

1998 SF36	June 25, 2004	0.014		1996 SK	Apr. 18, 2012	0.175
4179 Toutatis	Sep. 29, 2004	0.010		4183 Cuno	May 20, 2012	0.122
1999 LF6	Oct. 18, 2004	0.071		1999 BJ8	June 16, 2012	0.177
1998 WT24	Nov. 12, 2004	0.096		1994 PM	Aug. 12, 2012	0.095
7753 1988 XB	Nov. 21, 2004	0.073		4581 Asclepius	Aug. 16, 2012	0.108
1998 DV9	Jan. 11, 2005	0.078		4769 Castalia	Aug. 28, 2012	0.114
1998 WT	Mar. 7, 2005	0.072		1998 QC1	Sep. 15, 2012	0.161
1992 UY4	Aug. 8, 2005	0.040		4179 Toutatis	Dec. 12, 2012	0.046
1862 Apollo	Nov. 6, 2005	0.075		1998 WT24	Dec. 23, 2012	0.178
3361 Orpheus	Jan. 11, 2006	0.160		4034 1986 PA	Apr. 1, 2013	0.153
1999 A010	Mar. 18, 2006	0.090		7753 1988 XB	July 10, 2013	0.118
4450 Pan	Sep. 8, 2006	0.146		6037 1988 EG	Aug. 12, 2013	0.185
7341 1991 VK	Jan. 21, 2007	0.068		1998 ML14	Aug. 24, 2013	0.056
1998 VO	May 7, 2007	0.063		4581 Asclepius	Aug. 25, 2013	0.119
1862 Apollo	May 8, 2007	0.071		1998 UT18	Nov. 21, 2013	0.172
1999 AQ10	Oct. 1, 2007	0.138		1996 RG3	Nov. 25, 2013	0.159
2340 Hathor	Oct. 22, 2007	0.060		3361 Orpheus	Dec. 7, 2013	0.103
11500 1989 UR	Nov. 24, 2007	0.071		1995 SA	Apr. 2, 2014	0.191
3200 Phaethon	Dec. 10, 2007	0.121		2340 Hathor	Oct. 21, 2014	0.048
4450 Pan	Feb. 19, 2008	0.041		1998 HD14	Apr. 14, 2015	0.195
6037 1988 EG	Mar. 7, 2008	0.167		1566 Icarus	June 16, 2015	0.054
1620 Geographo	Mar. 17, 2008	0.125		1994 AW1	July 15, 2015	0.065
1991 DG	Aug. 2, 2008	0.175		7822 1991 CS	Sep. 4, 2015	0.160
1991 VH	Aug. 15, 2008	0.046		1998 WT24	Dec. 11, 2015	0.028
1998 VO	Oct. 29, 2008	0.080		7822 1991 CS	Feb. 23, 2016	0.168
4179 Toutatis	Nov. 9, 2008	0.050		1998 HD14	Apr. 9, 2016	0.155
1993 KH	Nov. 22, 2008	0.099		1997 XF11	June 10, 2016	0.180
2000 AF6	Dec. 13, 2008	0.074		1998 HL3	July 6, 2016	0.195
1998 CS1	Jan. 17, 2009	0.028		1999 AQ10	Oct. 18, 2016	0.144
1999 AQ10	Feb. 18, 2009	0.012		1998 VN	Nov. 16, 2016	0.087
14402 1991 DB	Mar. 15, 2009	0.113		2102 Tantalus	Dec. 30, 2016	0.137
1998 OR2	Mar. 19, 2009	0.123		5604 1992 FE	Feb. 24, 2017	0.034
1996 FG3	May 6, 2009	0.156		6063 Jason	May 27, 2017	0.099
1991 JW	May 23, 2009	0.081		1998 FW4	Sep. 26, 2017	0.029
1994 CC	June 10, 2009	0.017		1989 UQ	Oct. 16, 2017	0.156
8566 1996 EN	Aug. 28, 2009	0.194		1989 UP	Nov. 2, 2017	0.055
1999 AP10	Oct. 20, 2009	0.076		3361 Orpheus	Nov. 25, 2017	0.061
3361 Orpheus	Dec. 25, 2009	0.138		3200 Phaethon	Dec. 16, 2017	0.069
4486 Mithra	Mar. 12, 2010	0.189		1999 AQ10	Jan. 29, 2018	0.139
6239 Minos	Aug. 10, 2010	0.099		1981 Midas	Mar. 21, 2018	0.090
1989 UQ	Oct. 21, 2010	0.153		1998 WT24	Nov. 11, 2018	0.134
1991 JW	Nov. 28, 2010	0.095		4953 1990 MU	Nov. 29, 2018	0.107
2000 AZ93	Jan. 11, 2011	0.047		2340 Hathor	Jan. 13, 2019	0.144
1998 FH12	June 23, 2011	0.135		4581 Asclepius	Mar. 22, 2019	0.138
1998 SC15	Oct. 18, 2011	0.121		1998 SC15	Apr. 16, 2019	0.141
1996 FG3	Nov. 23, 2011	0.101		12538 1998 OH	May 16, 2019	0.187
1996 FG3	Nov. 23, 2011	0.101		5604 1992 FE	June 18, 2019	0.132

Potentially Hazardous Asteroids* *(cont.)*

Asteroid Name or Designation	Earth Close-Approach Date	AU**	Asteroid Name or Designation	Earth Close-Approach Date	AU**
11500 1989 UR	June 21, 2019	0.187	4581 Asclepius	Mar. 25, 2020	0.071
1620 Geographos	Aug. 31, 2019	0.137	1991 DG	Apr. 6, 2020	0.085
1998 HL1	Oct. 25, 2019	0.042	1997 BQ	May 21, 2020	0.041
1993 KH	Nov. 8, 2019	0.101	8014 1990 MF	July 23, 2020	0.055

*Asteroids approaching within 0.2 Astronomical Units (18.58 million mi./30 million km.) of the Earth
**AU=Astronomical Unit (92.9 million mi./150 million km. Earth is about one AU from the Sun.)

⊙ Remo, John L, ed. *Near-Earth Objects: The United Nations International Conference.* New York: New York Academy of Sciences, 1997.
Williams, David R. "Near Earth Object Fact Sheet," http://nssdc.gsfc.nasa.gov/planetary/factsheet/neofact.html

Astronomical Units and Constants

Name	Symbol	Metric Equivalent
Astronomical unit	AU	1.496×10^{11} m
Earth mass	$M_\oplus$	5.974×10^{24} kg
Gravitational Constant	G	6.673×10^{-11} N·m²/s²
Light-year	ly	9.461×10^{15} m
Parsec	pc	3.086×10^{16} m [3.26 ly]
Solar luminosity	$L_\odot$	3.846×10^{26} Watts
Solar mass	$M_\odot$	1.99×10^{30} kg
Solar Temperature	$T_\odot$	5.780×10^3 K

⊙ Dolan, C. "Physical Constants and Astronomical Data," www.astro.wisc.edu/~dolan/constants.html
NASA Astronomical Data Center. "Units and Constants," http://adc.gsfc.nasa.gov/adc/quick_ref/ref_units.html#astroconst
Smith, S. "Some Non-SI Units," http://alpha.lasalle.edu/~smithsc/Astronomy/Units/astro_units.html

THE SCIENCES: *Chemistry*

Types of Chemistry

Organic Chemistry

Organic chemistry is the study of compounds containing carbon (known as organic molecules) and of their interactions. Because silicon is very similar to carbon, it and its compounds have also come to be included in the definition of organic chemistry.

The most common and basic of organic compounds, hydrocarbons, are made up of only carbon and hydrogen. The simplest example of a hydrocarbon is methane, which consists of one carbon atom surrounded by four hydrogen atoms. Some other elements common in organic molecules are oxygen, sulfur, chlorine, and nitrogen.

Much of the complexity and abundance of the compounds studied in organic chemistry is the result of a unique property of carbon: its atoms can bond with each other to form long chains, and can also link with each other to form circular agglomerations. This allows carbon to form myriad different molecules, which themselves can be transformed into entirely new compounds by the addition of one atom of a different atom. Thus there are millions of different organic compounds in the world. Some of the major types of organic compounds are alkanes, alkenes, alkynes, aromatic hydrocarbons, alcohols, isomers, ethers, aldehydes, ketones, carboxcylic acids, and esters.

Biochemistry

Biochemistry differs from organic chemistry in that it is concerned primarily with the molecular basis of life processes. It studies the organic molecules such as lipids, proteins, and carbohydrates that make up living cells, and their interactions with other fundamental compounds in living organisms, such as vitamins and hormones. Biochemistry uses concepts and methods drawn from both the biological and the physical sciences to study the many and highly complex chemical interactions involved in the creation and maintenance of living organisms. Processes examined by biochemists include protein synthesis, hormone production and activity, the transformation of food into energy, and the transmission of genetic information.

Acids and Bases

One of the more fundamental categorizations in chemistry is the grouping of substances into acids and bases. Acids are commonly defined as compounds that when dissolved in water release one or more hydrogen atoms as positively charged hydrogen ions. Acids share various identifying properties: they have a sour taste, corrode metals, and turn certain blue dyes (such as that used in litmus paper) red. Bases, when dissolved in water, release hydroxide ions (OH-). They are bitter to the taste, slippery to the touch when in water, and turn red dyes blue. The release of hydrogen or hydroxide ions is called dissociation; the stronger an acid or base, the more completely it dissociates in water. This commonly used definition of acids and bases is known as the Arrhenius definition.

When acids and bases come into contact, they react vigorously and exchange one or more hydrogen ions. In the process, they neutralize each other and produce water and salts that have characteristics entirely different from those of both acids and bases.

The level of acidity or alkalinity (basicity), of a substance can be quantified by measuring the amount of hydrogen ions it releases or consumes when in solution. This measurement yields a scale known as the pH scale, which runs from 0 to 14, with the neutral 7 (pure water) in the center—the pH is defined as the negative log of the concentration of hydrogen ions in the solution. A pH below 7 is considered acidic, and one above 7 alkaline.

Approximate pH of Some Common Substances

Substance	Hydrogen ions*	pH	Substance	Hydrogen ions*	pH
Hydrochloric acid (HCl)	1×10^0	0	Milk	1×10^{-6}	6
			Pure water	1×10^{-7}	7
Stomach acid	1×10^{-1}	1	Egg whites	1×10^{-8}	8
Lemon juice	1×10^{-2}	2	Baking soda	1×10^{-9}	9
Vinegar	1×10^{-3}	3	Ammonia	1×10^{-10}	10
Root beer	1×10^{-4}	4	Drain cleaner	1×10^{-12}	12
Unpolluted rainwater	1×10^{-5}	5	Sodium hydroxide (NaOH)	1×10^{-13}	13

*Moles per liter

⊙ McQuarrie, Donald A., and Peter A. Rock. *General Chemistry, Third Edition.* New York: W. H. Freeman, 1991.

Stine, William, et al. *Applied Chemistry, Third Edition.* Lexington, Mass.: D.C. Heath, 1994.

Virginia Tech Chemistry Department. "A Brief Introduction to Organic Chemistry," www.chem.vt.edu/RVGS/notes/ACT-notes.html

Key: Atomic number, Chemical symbol, Atomic weight

H	
1.00794	

Period 1

1 IA	18 VIIIA
1 **H** 1.00794	2 **He** 4.00260

Period 2

1 IA	2 IIA	13 IIIA	14 IVA	15 VA	16 VIA	17 VIIA	18 VIIIA
3 **Li** 6.941	4 **Be** 9.01218	5 **B** 10.811	6 **C** 12.011	7 **N** 14.0067	8 **O** 15.9994	9 **F** 18.99840	10 **Ne** 20.1797

Period 3

1 IA	2 IIA	13 IIIA	14 IVA	15 VA	16 VIA	17 VIIA	18 VIIIA
11 **Na** 22.98977	12 **Mg** 24.3050	13 **Al** 26.98154	14 **Si** 28.0855	15 **P** 30.97376	16 **S** 32.066	17 **Cl** 35.4527	18 **Ar** 39.948

Period 4

1 IA	2 IIA	3 IIIB	4 IVB	5 VB	6 VIB	7 VIIB	8 VIIIB	9 VIIIB	10 VIIIB	11 IB	12 IIB	13 IIIA	14 IVA	15 VA	16 VIA	17 VIIA	18 VIIIA
19 **K** 39.0983	20 **Ca** 40.078	21 **Sc** 44.95591	22 **Ti** 47.88	23 **V** 50.9415	24 **Cr** 51.996	25 **Mn** 54.9380	26 **Fe** 55.847	27 **Co** 58.9320	28 **Ni** 58.6934	29 **Cu** 63.546	30 **Zn** 65.39	31 **Ga** 69.723	32 **Ge** 72.61	33 **As** 74.92159	34 **Se** 78.96	35 **Br** 79.904	36 **Kr** 83.80

Period 5

1 IA	2 IIA	3 IIIB	4 IVB	5 VB	6 VIB	7 VIIB	8 VIIIB	9 VIIIB	10 VIIIB	11 IB	12 IIB	13 IIIA	14 IVA	15 VA	16 VIA	17 VIIA	18 VIIIA
37 **Rb** 85.4678	38 **Sr** 87.62	39 **Y** 88.90585	40 **Zr** 91.224	41 **Nb** 92.90638	42 **Mo** 95.94	43 **Tc**** 98.9072	44 **Ru** 101.07	45 **Rh** 102.90550	46 **Pd** 106.42	47 **Ag** 107.8682	48 **Cd** 112.411	49 **In** 114.82	50 **Sn** 118.710	51 **Sb** 121.76	52 **Te** 121.757	53 **I** 126.9447	54 **Xe** 131.29

Period 6

1 IA	2 IIA	3 IIIB	4 IVB	5 VB	6 VIB	7 VIIB	8 VIIIB	9 VIIIB	10 VIIIB	11 IB	12 IIB	13 IIIA	14 IVA	15 VA	16 VIA	17 VIIA	18 VIIIA
55 **Cs** 139.90543	56 **Ba** 137.327	57 ***La** 138.9055	72 **Hf** 178.49	73 **Ta** 180.9479	74 **W** 183.85	75 **Re** 186.207	76 **Os** 190.2	77 **Ir** 192.22	78 **Pt** 195.08	79 **Au** 196.96654	80 **Hg** 200.59	81 **Tl** 204.3833	82 **Pb** 207.2	83 **Bi** 208.98037	84 **Po**** 208.9824	85 **At**** 209.9871	86 **Rn**** 222.0176

Period 7

1 IA	2 IIA	3 IIIB	4 IVB	5 VB	6 VIB	7 VIIB	8 VIIIB	9 VIIIB	10 VIIIB	11 IB	12 IIB	14 IVA
87 **Fr**** 223.0197	88 **Ra**** 226.0254	89 **†Ac**** 227.0278	104 **Rf**** 261.11	105 **Db**** 262.114	106 **Sg**** 263.118	107 **Bh**** 262.12	108 **Hs**** 262.12 (265)	109 **Mt**** (266)	110 **Uun**** (269)	111 **Uuu**** (272)	112 **Uub**** (277)	114 **Uuq** (285)

* Lanthanide series

58 **Ce** 140.115	59 **Pr** 140.90765	60 **Nd** 144.24	61 **Pm**** 144.9127	62 **Sm** 150.36	63 **Eu** 151.965	64 **Gd** 157.25	65 **Tb** 158.92534	66 **Dy** 162.50	67 **Ho** 164.93032	68 **Er** 167.26	69 **Tm** 168.93421	70 **Yb** 173.04	71 **Lu** 174.967

† Actinide series

90 **Th**** 222.0081	91 **Pa**** 223.0359	92 **U** 238.0289	93 **Np**** 237.0482	94 **Pu**** 244.0642	95 **Am**** 243.0614	96 **Cm**** 247.0703	97 **Bk**** 247.0703	98 **Cf**** 251.0796	99 **Es**** 252.083	100 **Fm**** 257.0951	101 **Md**** 258.10	102 **No**** 259.1009	103 **Lr**** 262.11

**All the isotopes of this element are radioactive. With the exception of uranium and thorium, the atomic weight shown represents the relative atomic weight of the longest lived isotope. The numbers in parenthesis are the mass numbers of the longest lived isotope.

⊙ Levi, Primo. *The Periodic Table.* New York: Random House, 1996.

Stwertka, Albert, and Eve Stwertka. *A Guide to the Elements.* 2nd ed. New York: Oxford University Press, 2001.

Wilson, Bruce. "Numbering the Columns of the Periodic Table," www.carolina.com/tips/97oct/1097d.htm

Winter, Mark. "WebElementsTM Periodic Table," www.webelements.com/

THE SCIENCES: *Chemistry*

Element Name	Symbol	Number	Atomic Weight* (amu)	Discoverer	Date
Actinium	Ac	89	[227]	Debierne	1899
Aluminum	Al	13	26.98154	Oersted	1825
Americium	Am	95	[243]	Seaborg et al.	1944
Antimony	Sb	51	121.75	Known in antiquity	
Argon	Ar	18	39.948	Ramsay, Rayleigh	1894
Arsenic	As	33	74.9216	Known in antiquity	
Astatine	At	85	[210]	Corson et al.	1940
Barium	Ba	56	137.34	Davy	1808
Berkelium	Bk	97	[247]	Seaborg et al.	1949
Beryllium	Be	4	9.012182	Vacquelin	1798
Bismuth	Bi	83	208.98038	Known in antiquity	
Bohrium	Bh	107	[262]	Armbruster et al.	1981
Boron	B	5	10.811	Davy, Gay-Lussac	1808
Bromine	Br	35	79.904	Balard	1826
Cadmium	Cd	48	112.411	Stromeyer	1817
Calcium	Ca	20	40.078	Davy	1808
Californium	Cf	98	[251]	Seaborg et al.	1950
Carbon	C	6	12.0107	Known in antiquity	
Cerium	Ce	58	140.116	Hisinger, Klaproth	1803
Cesium	Cs	55	132.9054	Bunsen, Kirchoff	1860
Chlorine	Cl	17	35.4527	Scheele	1774
Chromium	Cr	24	51.9961	Vauquelin	1797
Cobalt	Co	27	58.9332	Brandt	1735
Copper	Cu	29	63.546	Known in antiquity	
Curium	Cm	96	[247]	Seaborg et al.	1944
Dubnium	Db	105	[262]	Ghiorso et al.	1970
Dysprosium	Dy	66	162.5	Boisbaudran	1886
Einsteinium	Es	99	[252]	Ghiorso et al.	1952
Erbium	Er	68	167.26	Mosander	1843
Europium	Eu	63	151.964	Demarcay	1901
Fermium	Fm	100	[257]	Ghiorso et al.	1953
Fluorine	F	9	18.998403	Moissan	1886
Francium	Fr	87	[223]	Perey	1939
Gadolinium	Gd	64	157.25	Marignac	1880
Gallium	Ga	31	69.723	Boisbaudran	1875
Germanium	Ge	32	72.61	Winkler	1886
Gold	Au	79	196.96655	Known in antiquity	
Hafnium	Hf	72	178.49	Coster, von Hevesy	1923
Hassium	Hs	108	[265]	Armbruster et al.	1984
Helium	He	2	4.0026	A. Ramsay	1895
Holmium	Ho	67	164.9304	Soret, Delafontaine	1878
Hydrogen	H	1	1.00794	Cavendish	1766
Indium	In	49	114.818	Reich, Richter	1863
Iodine	I	53	126.90447	Courtois	1811
Iridium	Ir	77	192.217	Tennant	1803
Iron	Fe	26	55.847	Known in antiquity	

Element Name	Symbol	Number	Atomic Weight* (amu)	Discoverer	Date
Krypton	Kr	36	83.8	Ramsay, Travers	1898
Lanthanum	La	57	138.9055	Mosander	1839
Lawrencium	Lr	103	[262]	Ghiorso et al.	1961
Lead	Pb	82	207.2	Known in antiquity	
Lithium	Li	3	6.941	Arfvedson	1817
Lutetium	Lu	71	174.967	Urbain	1907
Magnesium	Mg	12	24.305	Davy	1808
Manganese	Mn	25	54.938049	Gahn	1774
Meitnerium	Mt	109	[265]	Münzenberg et al.	1982
Mendelevium	Md	101	[258]	Seaborg et al.	1955
Mercury	Hg	80	200.59	Known in antiquity	
Molybdenum	Mo	42	95.94	Scheele	1778
Neodymium	Nd	60	144.24	von Welsbach	1885
Neon	Ne	10	20.1797	Ramsay, Travers	1898
Neptunium	Np	93	[237]	McMillan, Abelson	1940
Nickel	Ni	28	58.6934	Cronstedt	1751
Niobium	Nb	41	92.90638	Hatchett	1801
Nitrogen	N	7	14.00674	Rutherford	1772
Nobelium	No	102	[259]	Seaborg et al.	1958
Osmium	Os	76	190.23	Tennant	1803
Oxygen	O	8	15.9994	Priestly, Scheele	1774
Palladium	Pd	46	106.42	Wollaston	1803
Phosphorus	P	15	30.973762	Brand	1669
Platinum	Pt	78	195.078	Ulloa	1735
Plutonium	Pu	94	[244]	Seaborg et al.	1940
Polonium	Po	84	[209]	Curie	1898
Potassium	K	19	39.0983	Davy	1807
Praseodymium	Pr	59	140.90765	von Welsbach	1885
Promethium	Pm	61	[145]	Marinsky et al.	1945
Protactinium	Pa	91	231.03587	Hahn, Meitner	1918
Radium	Ra	88	[22]	P. & M. Curie	1898
Radon	Rn	86	[222]	Dorn	1900
Rhenium	Re	75	186.207	Noddack, Tacke, Berg	1925
Rhodium	Rh	45	102.9055	Wollaston	1803
Rubidium	Rb	37	85.4678	Bunsen, Kirchhoff	1861
Ruthenium	Ru	44	101.07	Klaus	1844
Rutherfordium	Rf	104	[261]	Ghiorso et al.	1969
Samarium	Sm	62	150.36	Boisbaudran	1879
Scandium	Sc	21	44.95591	Nilson	1879
Seaborgium	Sg	106	[263]	Ghiorso et al.	1974
Selenium	Se	34	78.96	Berzelius	1817
Silicon	Si	14	28.0855	Berzelius	1824
Silver	Ag	47	107.8682	Known in antiquity	
Sodium	Na	11	22.98977	Davy	1807
Strontium	Sr	38	87.62	Crawford	1790
Sulfur	S	16	32.06	Known in antiquity	
Tantalum	Ta	73	180.9479	Ekeberg	1802

Technetium	Tc	43	[97]	Perrier, Segre	1937
Tellurium	Te	52	127.6	Reichenstein	1782
Terbium	Tb	65	158.9254	Mosander	1843
Thallium	Tl	81	204.3833	Crookes	1861
Thorium	Th	90	232.0381	Berzelius	1828
Thulium	Tm	69	168.93421	Cleve	1879
Tin	Sn	50	118.69	Known in antiquity	
Titanium	Ti	22	47.90	Gregor	1791
Tungsten	W	74	183.85	F. & J. de Elhuyar	1783
Ununbium	Uub	112	[27]	Armbruster et al.	1996
Ununnilium	Uun	110	[269]	Armbruster et al.	1994
Ununquadium	Uuq	114	[285]	Joint Institute for Nuclear Research, Dubna (unconfirmed)	1999
Unununium	Uuu	111	[27]	Armbruster et al.	1994
Uranium	U	92	238.0289	Klaproth	1789
Vanadium	V	23	50.9415	Sefstrom	1830
Xenon	Xe	54	131.29	A. Ramsay, Travers	1898
Ytterbium	Yb	70	173.04	Marignac	1878
Yttrium	Y	39	88.9059	Gadolin	1794
Zinc	Zn	30	65.38	Marggraf	1746
Zirconium	Zr	40	91.224	Klaproth	1789

* Brackets indicate mass of most stable isotope

⊙ Bentor, Yinon. "An Online, Interactive Periodic Table of the Elements," www.chemicalelements.com/index.html

Los Alamos National Laboratory, CST Division. "Elements with Their Symbol and Atomic Number," http://pearl1.lanl.gov/periodic/list1.html

Lide, David. CRC Handbook of Chemistry and Physics. Boca Raton, Fl.: CRC Press, 1992.

Stwertka, Albert, and Eve Stwertka. A Guide to the Elements. 2nd ed. New York: Oxford University Press, 2001.

Radioisotopes

Isotopes are atoms of a chemical element whose nuclei have the same number of protons but a different number of neutrons. An element's isotopes have nearly identical chemical properties, but differ in certain observable physical properties—their spectral line emission may be different, or they may be radioactive.

Radioisotopes are isotopes that decay by spontaneously emitting particles. The two most important types of decay are:

Alpha decay, the emission of a positively charged particle consisting of two protons bound to two neutrons. An alpha emission thus reduces the isotope's atomic number by two and its mass number by four.

Beta decay, the emission of a charged particle, an electron or a positron, along with a neutrino or an antineutrino. Electron emission changes a neutron into a proton; positron emission changes a proton into a neutron. Both change the isotope's atomic number but not its mass number.

By changing an isotope's atomic number, decay creates a different element. The time it takes for half of an isotope to decay into another isotope is called its half-life. The sequence of emissions results in a consistent chain of isotopes called a decay series, which ends with a stable isotope (one that does not decay). Only four decay series occur naturally.

Radioisotopes *(cont.)*

Alpha and beta radiation (and the gamma radiation that accompanies decay) can be dangerous, but can also be harnessed for useful purposes.

⊙ Firestone, Richard B. *Table of Isotopes*. New York: Wiley, 1999.
  The Regulation and Use of Radioisotopes in Today's World. Washington, D.C.: U.S. Nuclear Regulatory Commission, 1996.

Elementary Particles

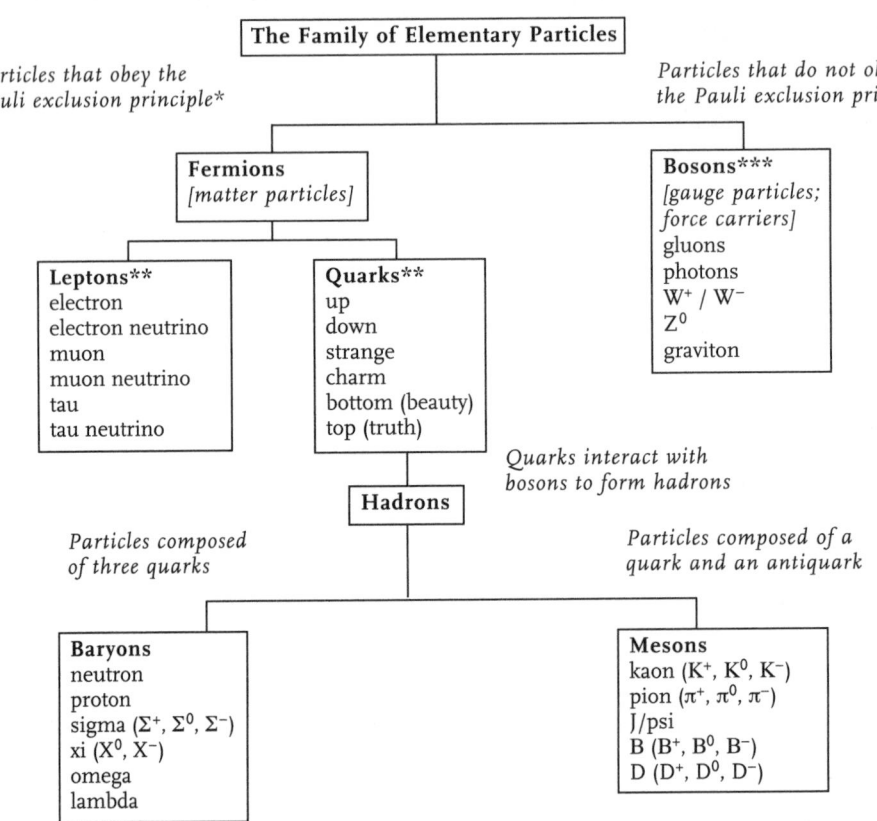

*Pauli's principle states that no two electrons in an atom can exist in the same quantum state.
**Each lepton and quark has an antiparticle, a particle with a number of opposite properties
***Each gauge boson carries a force that interacts with quarks to form hadrons. The gluon carries the strong nuclear force of protons and neutrons, the photon carries the electromagnetic force, the W and Z bosons carry the weak force that affects neutrinos, and the graviton carries the gravitational force.

⊙ Hughes, I. S. *Elementary Particles*. 3d ed. Cambridge: Cambridge University Press, 1991.
  Griffiths, David. *Introduction to Elementary Particles*. New York: Wiley, 1987.
  Nave, C. R. "Hyperphysics: Particle Concepts," http://hyperphysics.phy-astr.gsu.edu/hbase/particles/parcon.html

THE SCIENCES: *Chemistry*

Basic Taxonomic Classifications

The living world is categorized by biologists into hierarchically arranged groups, starting with the most closely related organisms (a species) and expanding outward to include organisms of more distant relatedness (e.g., a family is a group of genera, and each genus is a group of species). In descending order of size, the classifications are as follows—group names for the honeybee are given alongside as examples:

Species	*mellifera*
Genus	*Apis*
Family	Apidae (bees)
Order	Hymenoptera (wasps, ants, and bees)
Class	Insecta (all insects)
Phylum	Arthropoda (spiders, crustaceans, etc.)
Kingdom	Animalia

To refer to a specific organism, biologists use the genus and species names together, genus first and capitalized, species second and lowercased; in writing, these are always italicized. Certain conventions are followed in assigning names to categories of organisms. For example, order names usually end in "-era," and family names in "-ae." Classifications can be refined further if a main classification group shows variation within it that is great enough to merit further subdivision, but the groups being subdivided would not properly fall into the next major category. Families can contain subfamilies—the family Rosaceae contains several subfamilies, including Pomoideae (apples, pears, and loquats), and Rosoideae (roses). Species are sometimes subdivided into groups that are clearly distinct, but not differentiated enough to be separate species (one of the principal criteria for distinguishing species is the inability of matings between different species to produce viable offspring).

Genetics

Genetics is the science of the study of genes—the molecules (DNA) that are arranged like strings of beads on the chromosomes within living cells. Genetics is a fundamental branch of biology because it deals with the units of inheritance that are passed from parent to offspring during reproduction and that thus carry and develop the characteristics of a species or population.

There are many branches of genetics. Molecular genetics studies the nature and replication of DNA during the formation of eggs and sperm, and during cell division that occurs within an organism as it grows.

Developmental genetics studies the "expression" of the genes, or the process by which the DNA makes proteins that influence individual development.

Mendelian genetics, named for Gregor Mendel, who discovered important genetic principles in the late 19th century, studies the patterns of inheritance of particular traits, such as eye color or height. It focuses on the effects of particular genes by using abnormalities due to "mutation" or altered DNA.

Population genetics studies the frequencies or proportions of occurrence of genes in populations of organisms. For example, it examines how successful traits become more common as the genes that influence them spread in a population.

Quantitative genetics is related to population genetics. It studies how traits of organisms change through human-induced "artificial selection"—for example, in the breeding of farm animals and crops.

Advances in genetics are regularly featured in the news, as the techniques of biotechnology result in new strains of plants and animals. The human genome (the complete set of chromosomes containing all the DNA instructions that create an organism) is on the verge of translation, and cloning (the creation of a genetically identical individual from an adult's cell) methods are now sophisticated enough to produce healthy mammals.

Cell Biology

As its name suggests, cell biology is the science that studies the cells of organisms. This field was born when scientists discovered that the bodies of plants and animals are composed of microscopic units, named "cells." Later, as microscopes improved, it was found that the cells contain even smaller structures, now called "organelles," including such things as the mitochondria, chloroplasts, nucleus (with chromosomes), and many other smaller structures. At this stage cell biology was called "cytology."

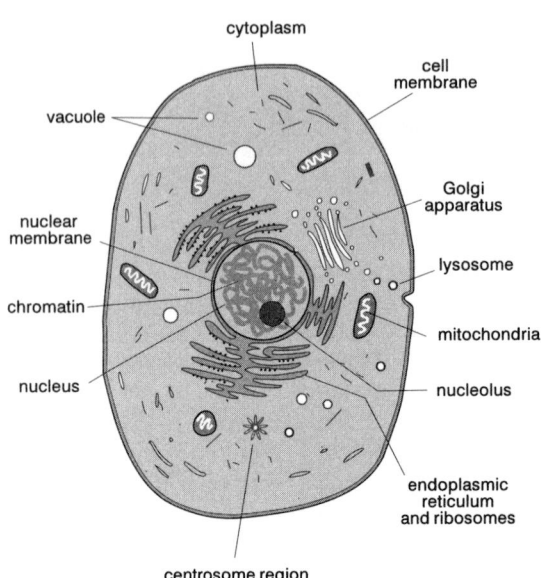

Modern cell biology takes advantage of progress in molecular biology and biochemistry to study dynamic processes within and between cells in minute detail. For example, it is possible to study the individual molecules (polymers) that form, move, and interact as the mitotic spindles pull apart chromosomes during mitosis, or cell division.

Cell biology examines the structure and function of many different kinds of cells: nerve cells and their special properties for transmitting signals; brain cells as they function in storage of memory and integration of behavior; cells of other organs, such as the liver or kidney with their special functions of concentrating wastes or secreting hormones. Cell biologists also study the fascinating movements of animal cells during the growth of embryos, and the membranes cells have that allow chemical communication among them and with the outside world.

Microbiology

Microbiology is the study of microscopic organisms. The term derives from "microbe," a word coined in the late 19th century to refer to these life forms that are invisible to the naked eye. Microorganisms, as they are now called, form a group of very diverse organisms, ranging from viruses and bacteria to protozoans, molds, and algae, and microbiology is accordingly divided into various specialties such as bacteriology, virology, and so on.

Because microorganisms inhabit almost all the organic and inorganic realms of the Earth, they are closely involved with the life processes of many other life forms. Some microorganisms are largely responsible for the decay of dead organic matter, others are often the causes of disease, yet others inhabit the mammalian gastrointestinal tract and aid in digestion.

⊙ Berg, Paul, and Maxine Singer. *Dealing with Genes: The Language of Heredity.* Mill Valley, Calif.: University Science Books, 1992.

Campbell, Neil. *Biology,* Fifth Edition. Menlo Park, Calif.: Benjamin Cummings, 1999.

Margulis, Lynn, and Karlene V. Schwartz. *Five Kingdoms: An Illustrated Guide to the Phyla of Life on Earth,* Third Edition. New York: W. H. Freeman, 1998.

BRAIN

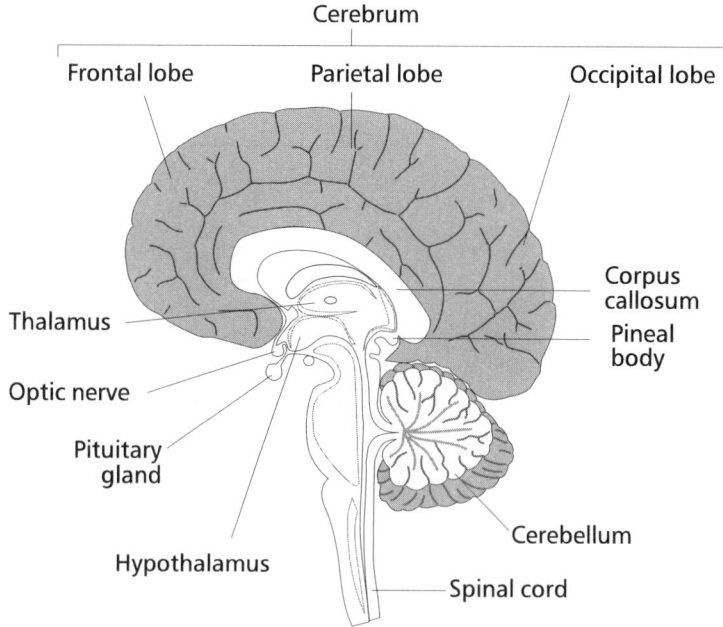

HEART

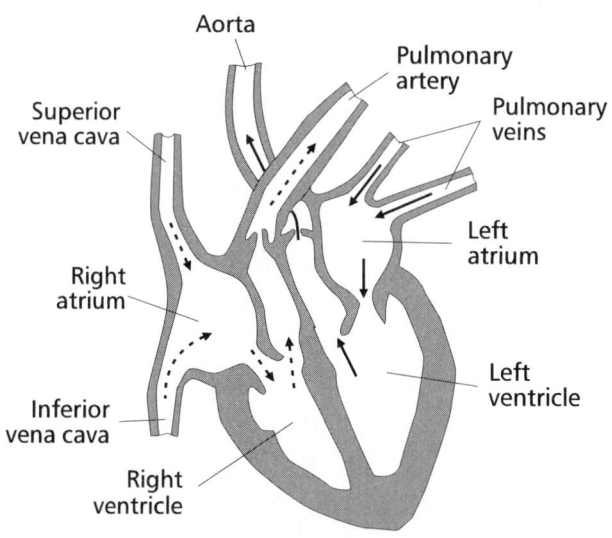

REPRODUCTIVE SYSTEM

FEMALE

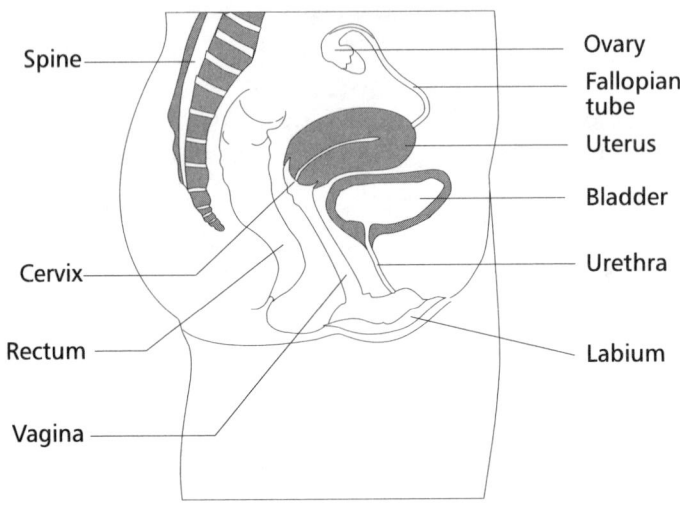

Spine

Ovary

Fallopian tube

Uterus

Bladder

Urethra

Cervix

Rectum

Labium

Vagina

MALE

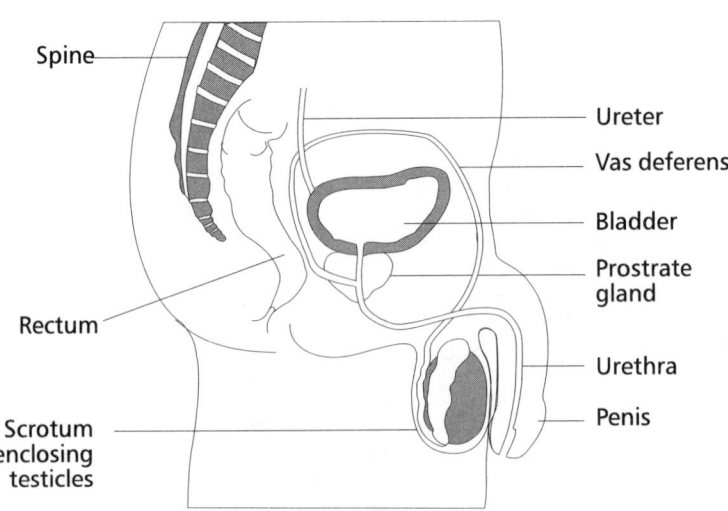

Spine

Ureter

Vas deferens

Bladder

Prostrate gland

Rectum

Urethra

Penis

Scrotum enclosing testicles

NOSE, MOUTH, AND THROAT

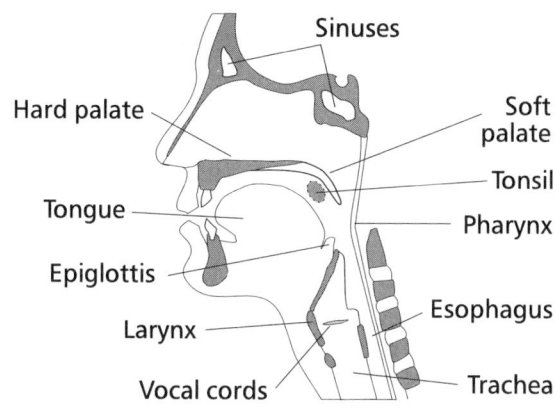

Sinuses

Hard palate

Soft palate

Tongue

Tonsil

Pharynx

Epiglottis

Esophagus

Larynx

Vocal cords

Trachea

THE ALIMENTARY CANAL

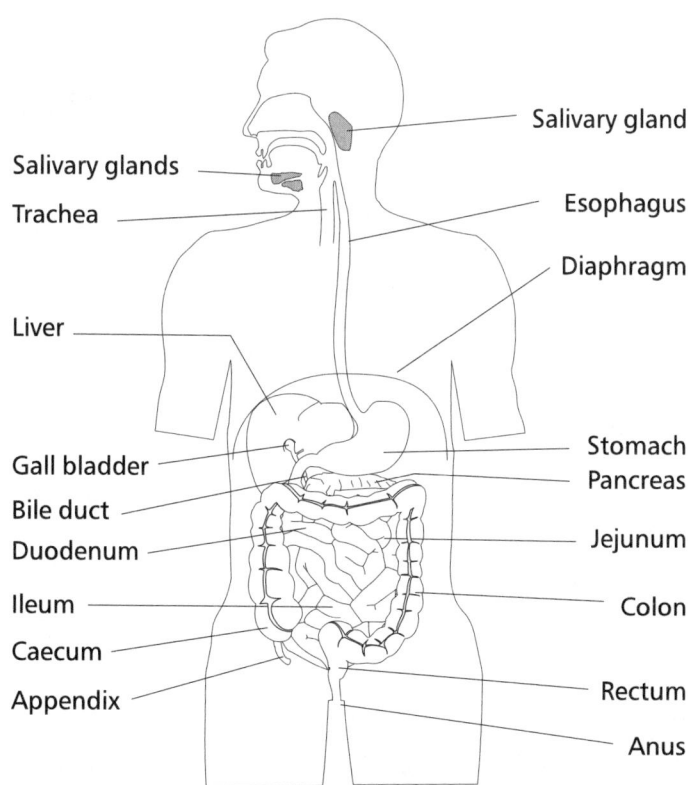

Salivary gland

Salivary glands

Trachea

Esophagus

Diaphragm

Liver

Gall bladder

Stomach

Pancreas

Bile duct

Duodenum

Jejunum

Ileum

Colon

Caecum

Appendix

Rectum

Anus

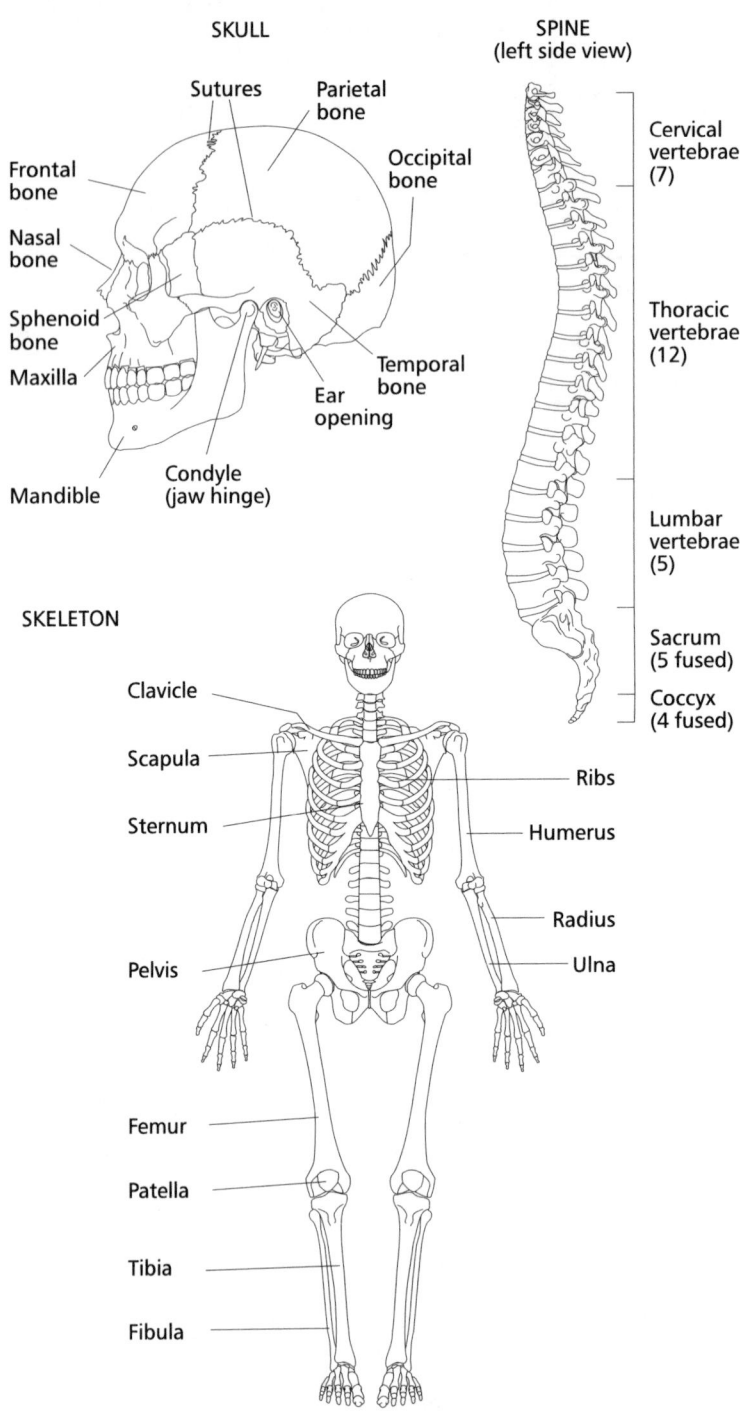

SKULL

Sutures

Parietal bone

Occipital bone

Frontal bone

Nasal bone

Sphenoid bone

Maxilla

Temporal bone

Ear opening

Mandible

Condyle (jaw hinge)

SPINE
(left side view)

Cervical vertebrae (7)

Thoracic vertebrae (12)

Lumbar vertebrae (5)

Sacrum (5 fused)

Coccyx (4 fused)

SKELETON

Clavicle

Scapula

Sternum

Ribs

Humerus

Radius

Ulna

Pelvis

Femur

Patella

Tibia

Fibula

EYE

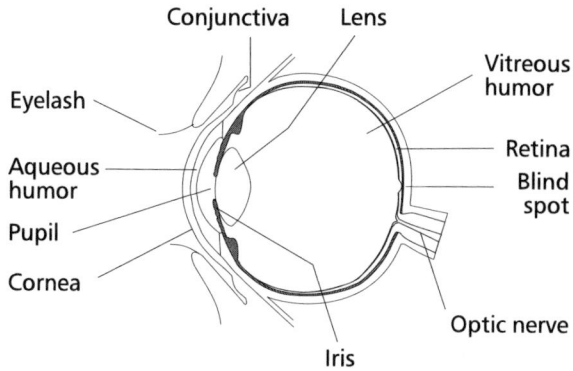

Conjunctiva Lens

Eyelash

Aqueous humor

Pupil

Cornea

Iris

Vitreous humor

Retina

Blind spot

Optic nerve

EAR

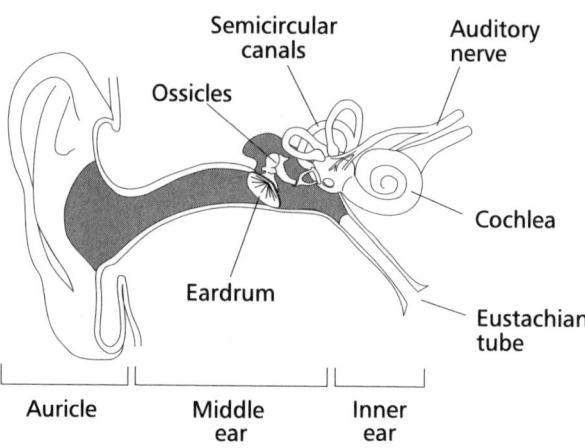

Semicircular canals Auditory nerve

Ossicles

Eardrum

Cochlea

Eustachian tube

Auricle Middle ear Inner ear

TEETH

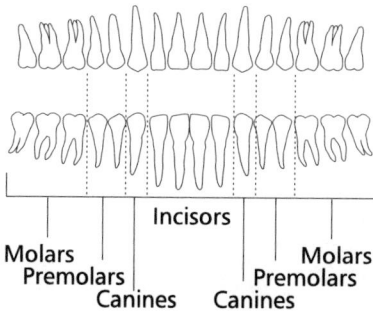

Incisors

Molars
Premolars
Canines

Canines
Premolars
Molars

Minerals and Mineral Commodities*

Mineral	Properties	Uses	Mining Centers**
Aluminum*	Light; nonmagnetic; malleable; ductile	Automobiles; product packaging; building materials	Australia, Guinea, Jamaica, Brazil, India
Asbestos	Insulator; fire resistant	Insulation; roofing	Russia, Canada, China, Brazil
Beryl	Many colors; hard	Main source of beryllium; gemstones (emerald, aquamarine)	Colombia, Brazil, Russia, South Africa, Austria
Bismuth	Expands when solidifying; diamagnetic	Electronics	Mexico, Peru, Bolivia, China
Borax	Dissolves in water	Antiseptic; water softener; detergent	Southwest United States
Boron*	Variable conductivity of electricity; transmits infrared light	Glass production; detergents; fire retardants	United States, Russia, Turkey, Argentina, Chile
Calcite	Fluorescent; main component of many kinds of rock	Agriculture; ore of calcium; chalk; base for cement; many other industrial uses	Iceland, Mexico, United States, many others
Chromite	Resistant to corrosion; hard	Ore of chromium; used in making stainless steel	South Africa, Kazakhstan, India, Turkey, Finland
Cobalt*	Brittle; hard; resistant to corrosion	Aircraft metal alloys; magnetic alloys	Zambia, Canada, Australia, Russia, Cuba
Copper	Highly conductive of electricity; malleable; ductile	Electrical wire and machinery; coins; cooking utensils	Chile, United States, Canada, Russia, Australia
Corundum	Very hard; stable; easily synthesized; many colors; insoluble in acids	Abrasives; gemstones (ruby, sapphire)	Myanmar, Sri Lanka, Tanzania, Thailand, United States
Diamond	Hardest, best heat conductor, highest melting point, and highest refractive index of known natural materials	Jewelry; abrasives; thermal insulation; optics; electronics	South Africa, Australia, Botswana, Russia, Brazil, Canada

Fluorite	Fluorescent; many colors (but colorless when pure)	Main source of fluorine; steel manufacture; optics	England, Switzerland, Mexico, United States
Gold	Highly conductive of electricity; malleable; ductile; very stable	Jewelry and ornaments; coins; photography; dentistry	South Africa, United States, Australia, China, Russia
Graphite	Conductive of electricity; soft; smudges	Pencil leads; lubricant; electrical applications	New York, Alabama, Finland, Italy, England, Quebec
Gypsum	Flexible crystals	Primary ingredient of plaster; cement; sheetrock; decorative (alabaster); dentistry	United States, Thailand, Iran, China, Canada, others
Iodine*	Volatile at room temperature	Food supplementation; colorants; pharmaceuticals	Chile, Japan, United States, China
Iron*	Conductive of heat; corrodes easily; brittle; can be magnetized	Main ingredient of steel; building materials; automobiles; containers	China, Brazil, Australia, Russia, United States
Lead*	Heavy; malleable; soft	Batteries; paint pigments; glasswork; radioactive shielding	Australia, United States, China, Peru, Canada
Magnesium*	Light; strong; ignites when heated in air	Aluminum alloys; iron and steel production; cathodes	United States, Canada, China, Russia, Norway
Manganese*	Hard; brittle	Steel production	South Africa, China, Gabon, Brazil, Ukraine
Mercury*	Liquid at room temperature; poisonous	Thermometers; amalgams for extracting metals from ores	Kyrgyzstan, Spain, Algeria
Molybdenum*	High melting point; very hard	Iron and steel production	United States, China, Chile, Canada, Mexico
Nickel*	Hard; takes high polish; ductile; malleable	Stainless steel production; batteries	Russia, Canada, Australia, New Caledonia
Nitrogen*	Colorless; odorless; inert gas	Ammonia; fertilizers; plastics and resins production	China, United States, India, Russia
Platinum	Ductile; malleable; heavy; does not tarnish	Jewelry; catalysts; dentistry	South Africa, Russia, Canada, United States

THE SCIENCES: *Earth Science*

Minerals and Mineral Commodities* *(cont.)*

Mineral	Properties	Uses	Mining Centers**
Potash*	Alkaline	Fertilizers; soaps	Canada, Russia, Belarus, Germany, Israel
Quartz	Piezoelectric (generates electrical charge when subjected to pressure)	Electronics; optical equipment; timepieces	Brazil, Germany, Madagascar (all sources of lascas, used for synthesizing quartz crystal)
Salt	Lowers freezing point of water; enhances food flavors; preserves organic material	Highway deicing; food; water treatment	United States, China, Germany, Canada, India
Silicon*	Resistant to most acids; conductive of heat	Iron and steel production; aluminum production; semiconductors	China, United States, Norway, Russia, Brazil
Silver*	Ductile; conductive of electricity	Jewelry; tableware; photography; coins; dentistry	Mexico, Peru, United States, Australia, Canada
Sulfur	Odorless; brittle; insoluble in water	Sulfuric acid; fertilizers; petroleum refining	United States, Canada, China, Russia, Japan
Talc	Very soft; smooth and slippery; high luster; low conductivity	Ceramics; paper production; paints; roofing; cosmetics	China, United States, Japan, South Korea, India
Tin*	Malleable; crystalline structure; corrosion resistant	Containers; roofing; electrical applications	China, Indonesia, Peru, Brazil, Bolivia, Australia
Titanium*	Light and strong; corrosion resistant; burns in air	Aerospace industry; armor; sporting goods; paint (as titanium dioxide)	Japan, Russia, Kazakhstan, China, Ukraine
Tungsten*	Highest melting point of metals; corrosion resistant	Industrial cutting blades; light bulb filaments	China, Russia, Austria, North Korea, Portugal
Uraninite	Highly radioactive	Primary ore of uranium	France, Czech Republic, Germany, South Africa, Canada
Yttrium*	Lustrous; fine bits can ignite in air	Color television phosphors; fluorescent lights; laser crystals	China, Russia, India, Brazil

THE SCIENCES: *Earth Science*

| Zinc* | Fairly conductive of electricity; burns in air | Galvanizing of steel; brass and bronze production | China, Australia, Canada, Peru, United States |
| Zirconium* | Very heat and corrosion resistant; strong | Ceramics; abrasives; sandblasting | Australia, South Africa, Ukraine |

*Mineral commodities listed are not minerals but are chemical elements or compounds recovered from minerals.
**Countries listed in order of production, larger to smaller

⊙ Skinner, Brian J. *Earth Resources,* Third Edition. Englewood Cliffs, N.J.: Prentice-Hall, 1986.
United States Geological Survey. "Mineral Commodity Summaries 2000,"
http://minerals.usgs.gov/minerals/pubs/mcs/2000/mcs2000.pdf

Geology

Layers of the Earth

The interior of the Earth has three distinct compositional layers. The thin outermost layer, called the crust, varies in thickness between averages of 5 kilometers (under the oceans) and 31 kilometers (under the continents). It is composed of various kinds of solid rock and sits atop the mantle, the Earth's middle layer. The mantle is about 2,900 kilometers thick. It is made up primarily of silicate rock at temperatures that vary between 1000°C nearest the crust and 5000°C in the deepest regions. At these temperatures, the rock has little strength and can flow very slowly (centimeters per year) like a very viscous liquid. The innermost layer, the core, has a radius of about 3,480 kilometers, and is made up primarily of iron and nickel. It has two distinct layers as well: the outer one is liquid, and the inner is a rigid mass of superhot iron that spins faster than the rest of the Earth around its axis. It is believed that whirlpool-like currents in the outer core give rise to the Earth's magnetic field.

Plate Tectonics

The Earth's outer layer is not a solid shell, but is broken up into many irregular segments known as plates, which extend through the top 100 km. of the earth's surface, known as the lithosphere. The nine largest plates are the Pacific, North American, South American, Eurasian, Indo-Australian, Antarctic, African, Nazca, and Cocos. The convection movements of the Earth's mantle appear to create local areas of circulation in the upper mantle called convection cells, which cause a boundary layer of hot, malleable rock called the asthenosphere to flow slowly. The asthenosphere carries the plates of the lithosphere along in a constant motion. These pull apart in some places, collide in others, and in some slide past each other. This movement is known as plate tectonics, and gives rise to many geological phenomena such as earthquakes (caused by sudden movement of plates past each other), mountain ranges (caused by the buckling up of one plate as another pushes under it), and mid-ocean ridges, underwater mountain ranges formed where plates pull apart and hot magma (highly heated rock) wells up from the mantle.

The movement of plate tectonics means that the continents carried on the plates have not always been arranged as we know them. Some 250 million years ago, Earth's landmasses were all joined into the supercontinent known as Pangea. In the Triassic period, about 200 million years ago, Pangea had divided into the northern mass of Laurasia and southern Gondwanaland. The component plates of these two supercontinents slowly continued to drift apart until the continents reached today's configuration. This drifting continues.

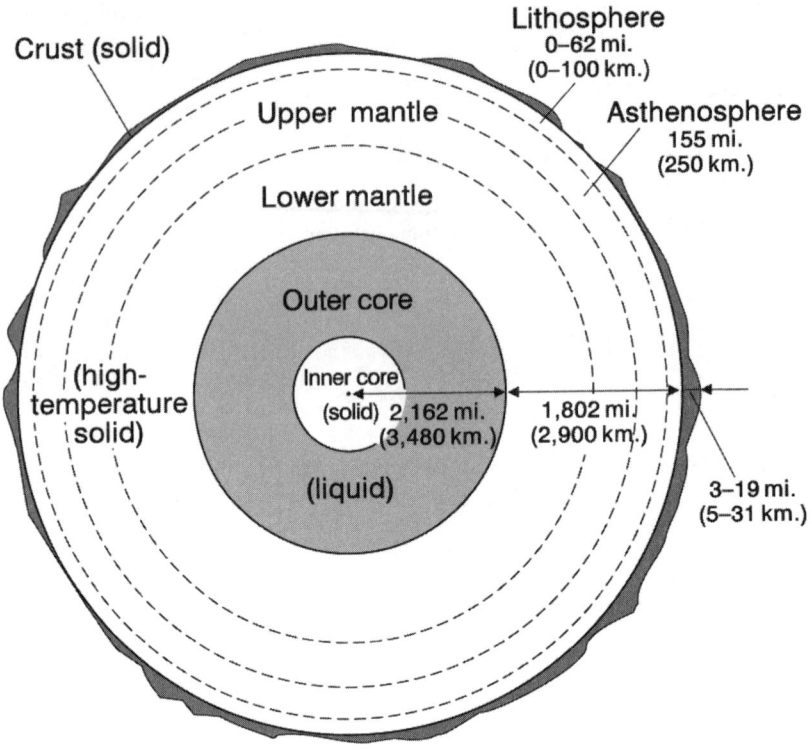

Crust (solid)

Lithosphere
0–62 mi.
(0–100 km.)

Upper mantle

Asthenosphere
155 mi.
(250 km.)

Lower mantle

Outer core

(high-
temperature
solid)

Inner core
(solid) 2,162 mi.
(3,480 km.)

1,802 mi.
(2,900 km.)

3–19 mi.
(5–31 km.)

(liquid)

Types of Rock

There are three main types of rock: igneous, sedimentary, and metamorphic. Igneous rock is formed when molten rock (magma) rises through the crust and cools into solid form; it may cool beneath the crust's surface (intrusive) or above the surface (extrusive). Fine-grained extrusive rock such as basalt results when hot mantle rocks are brought close to the crust and a partial melting occurs. This cools too quickly for large crystals to form. Intrusive rock such as granite forms when pockets of magma cool slowly while trapped underground, giving crystals of quartz, feldspar, and other minerals a chance to grow large.

Sedimentary rock is formed when particles of rock weathered from granite and other rocky masses accumulate and eventually are compacted and cemented together into a new rocky mass. Some examples of sedimentary rock are sandstone, breccia, shale, and limestone.

When sedimentary or igneous rock is subjected to extreme pressure, high temperature, and hot water underground, its mineral constituents are changed, and it transforms into what is known as metamorphic rock. Some examples of metamorphic rock are slate, schist, marble, and gneiss.

⊙ Chernicoff, Stanley. *Essentials of Geology,* Second Edition. Boston: Houghton Mifflin, 2000.
Encyclopedia of Geology. London: Fitzroy Dearborn, 1999.
Kious, Jacqueline, and Robert I. Tilling. *This Dynamic Earth: The Story of Plate Tectonics.* Washington, D.C.: U.S. Government Printing Office, 1996. (also online at http://pubs.usgs.gov/publications/text/dynamic.html)

Layers of the Earth's Atmosphere

Layer	Altitude mi (km)*	Temp. °F (°C)	Primary Gases	Properties
Troposphere	0<->5 (0<->10)	63 <-> -71 (17<-> -57)	N2 (78%), O2 (21%), Ar (1%), CO2 (.04%), water vapor	Temp. decreases with altitude; vertical circulation; weather and clouds
Stratosphere	5<->30 (10<->45)	-71<-> 65 (-57<-> 18)	Same proportions as troposphere, but at much lower densities	Temp. increases with altitude; horizontal circulation
Ozone layer	15 (25)	-71 <-> 65 (-57<-> 18)	O3 (10ppm—about 90% of all O3 in atmosphere)	Absorbs ultraviolet solar radiation
Mesosphere	30<->50 (45<->95)	65 <-> -225 (18<-> -143)	O2, He, H, N2	Temp. decreases with altitude
Thermosphere	50<->400 (95<->640)	-225 <-> 3,600 (-143<-> 2,000)	O2, He, H, N2	Temp. increases with altitude
Ionosphere (D, E, F layers)	55<->375 (90<->600)	-225 <-> 3,600 (-143<-> 2,000)	O2, He, H, N2	Auroras, radio waves, absorbs X rays
Exosphere	>400 (>640)	>3,600 (>2,000)	H, He	Temp. constant

*Atmospheric layers are continuous, and the general boundaries between them can vary in altitude depending on latitude and various other factors; altitudes given are therefore approximate. The symbol <->, used for altitude and temperature, indicates "greater than, and less than" the two numbers given.

⊙ Houghton, John T. *The Physics of Atmospheres, Second Edition.* Cambridge: Cambridge University Press, 1986.
NASA Atmospheric Chemistry Data and Resources. "Atmospheric Structure." http://daac.gsfc.nasa.gov/CAMPAIGN_DOCS/ATM_CHEM/atmospheric_structure.html
University of Oulu (Finland). "Atmosphere (Earth's)." www.oulu.fi/~spaceweb/textbook/atmosphere.html

THE SCIENCES: *Physics*

Laws of Physics

Physics is the science that is concerned with the fundamental structure of matter and with the interactions among the basic forces and materials that make up the universe. The various areas of study within the vast field of physics address topics ranging from the elementary particles that make up atoms to the movements of galaxies.

Scholars have studied the phenomena of the natural world for many centuries, and in 1687 Sir Isaac Newton formulated the basic laws of motion that serve as the foundation for modern physics. (Newton was the first to publish practical formulations of the laws, but they had been observed decades earlier by Galileo.)

Newton's First Law: If a body is at rest or moving at a constant speed, it will remain at rest or moving at that speed unless it is acted upon by external forces. This is also known as the law of inertia, which is a property of all bodies with mass—the tendency of things to remain in their current state of motion.

Newton's Second Law: When force is applied to an object, the acceleration induced is directly proportional to the force, and inversely proportional to its mass. Specifically,

$$F = ma,$$

where F is the force applied to a body with mass m, inducing acceleration a. All the basic equations of dynamics can be derived from this fundamental law through calculus.

Newton's Third Law: Every action has an equal and opposite reaction. For example, just as the Earth pulls on all objects with its gravitational field, it is equally true that each object pulls up on the Earth in exactly the opposite direction with its own gravitational field. A fourth fundamental law of physics, formulated by Newton, is the law of gravitation. This law states that bodies attract each other with forces proportional to their mass: bodies with masses m_1 and m_2, that are at distance r from one another, will exert on each other attractive forces proportional to $m_1 m_2 / r_2$. The proportionality is given by the gravitational constant G, which is universal. The law of gravity is expressed as $F = G\ m_1 m_2 / r_2$.

Heat

All matter in the universe has a certain amount of energy stored in it. Some of that energy is stored in the natural vibration of the component atoms. Heat is the transfer of that energy from one body to another, from the warmer (more energetic) to the colder (less energetic). Heat transfer usually means that the warmer substance decreases in temperature and the cooler one's temperature increases. It is, however, possible for materials to absorb or release heat without changing temperature: this happens in the instant at which the substance is changing from one state to another, such as when ice melts into water. The three laws of thermodynamics govern the mechanics of heat and its transfer to and from other forms of energy.

Light

Light, as the term is commonly used, is electromagnetic radiation visible to the human eye—wavelengths shorter or longer than those in the visual spectrum are not visible to us, but are also light and are known as ultraviolet (shorter) and infrared (longer). The fundamental unit of light is the photon, but depending on the properties being observed, light can behave either like a wave or like a particle.

Light moves at a very high speed (its 299,792,458 meters per second in a vacuum is one of the funda- mental physical constants), and it is the only form of energy that is always moving. As soon as it stops (i.e., is absorbed by matter), it ceases to be light and becomes some other form of energy, such as heat. Another, very useful, property of light is that it can carry large amounts of information, only a small amount of which can be detected and processed by the human eye and brain.

Mechanics

Mechanics is the study of the motion of bodies, and how that motion may exert forces on other bodies in a system. Newtonian (or classical) mechanics is based on Newton's three basic laws, which hold for most motion on Earth. Celestial mechanics studies the motion and interaction of moons, planets, stars, and other celestial bodies; these motions can differ somewhat from the predictions of classical mechanics, which are corrected by the theory of relativity. A third type of mechanics, quantum mechanics, examines motion at the atomic and subatomic level, a realm in which classical mechanics has limited use.

Electricity

Electricity is energy that is stored and transmitted by electrons, which by definition carry a negative charge. Many metals allow the free flow of electrons through their molecules, and we thus describe these as conductive and use them for electric motors and other applications. However, electricity may move through many media. The most striking example is lightning. Lightning results when the accu- mulation of highly charged electrons causes a strong electric charge differential to accumulate between clouds and the ground. When that difference is large enough, the air's resistance to the flow of elec- trons is overcome and the electrons flow freely from one point to another in the form of lightning.

Sound

Sound can be defined as the transfer of energy via vibrations through a solid, a fluid, or a gaseous medium. Sound moves through any given medium as a wave, which propagates at different speeds through different materials, depending on specific properties of the materials such as density and equi- librium pressure. For example, sound travels much farther and faster through steel (5,000 meters per second) and seawater (1,490 meters per second) than through air (331.29 meters per second). Some of the basic parameters of sound are velocity, frequency (pitch), and intensity.

Nuclear Physics

Nuclear physics is the study of the particles that make up the nucleus of the atom, and the forces with which they interact. These particles are bound together by very powerful nuclear forces that are about one million times stronger than forces involved in other atomic structures. The extremely high energy of these bonds requires a special branch of physics, quantum theory, for the study of nuclear behavior. One of the principal methods for studying nuclear structures is the bombardment of nuclear material with streams of particles such as protons and electrons, followed by analysis of the reactions of the nuclear particles to these collisions.

⊙ Encyclopaedia Britannica Online. "Physics," www.eb.com:180/bol/topic?eu=61378&sctn=1
    Holton, Gerald J., and Stephen G. Brush. *Physics, the Human Adventure: From Copernicus to Einstein and Beyond.* New Brunswick, N.J.: Rutgers University Press , 2001.
    Lerner, Rita G., and George L. Trigg, eds. *Encyclopedia of Physics,* Second Edition. New York: VCH, 1991.

THE SCIENCES: *Technology*

Automobiles: Chronology

1670	A steam-powered cart is built in China.
1769	Nicolas-Joseph Cugnot builds a steam-powered, three-wheeled tractor to transport artillery for the French Army.
1801	In England, Richard Trevithick builds the first steam-powered passenger vehicle.
1802	In England, a steam-powered automobile travels from Cornwall to London, a journey of over 100 miles.
1830s	London's first omnibus service transports passengers in steam-powered carriages.
1860	In France, the first one-cylinder internal-combustion engine is patented; it uses kerosene for fuel.
1864	In Australia, a two-cylinder gasoline engine is introduced.
1865	In Germany, Karl Benz builds a three-wheeled, gas-powered motor vehicle.
1876	In Germany, Nikolaus August Otto builds the first four-stroke gas engine.
1887	In Germany, Gottlieb Daimler and Wilhelm Maybech manufacture their first automobile.
1888	In Scotland, John Dunlop invents the pneumatic tire.
1890	Daimler and Maybech start the Daimler Motor Company.
1893	In the United States, brothers Charles Edgar Duryea and James Frank Duryea build their first one-cylinder, four-horsepower automobile.
1893	In the United States, engineer Henry Ford builds his first internal-combustion engine.
1894	A French company, Panhard-Levassor, begins producing automobiles using the Daimler patent; Panhard-Levassor is the first manufacturer to use gears and a clutch.
1899	In Italy, FIAT begins manufacturing cars.
1899	Electric cars make up 38 percent of American automobile market; an electric car sets a speed record of 65.79 miles per hour.
1901	The 1901 Mercedes reaches a speed of 53 miles per hour.
1902	The Locomobile is the first automobile in the United States to use a four-cylinder, water-cooled, front-mounted engine.
1902	In France, Louis Renault develops the drum brake.
1903	Henry Ford starts the Ford Motor Company and introduces its first car, the Model A.
1904	Approximately eight percent of roads in the United States are surfaced.
1907	Ford Motor Company's share of the American automobile market is 35 percent.
1908	Ford Motor Company introduces the Model T; it sells for $825.
1911	The electric starter replaces the hand-cranked engine starter.
1913	Approximately 80 percent of the world's automobiles are manufactured in the United States.
1914	Ford Motor Company begins using the assembly-line method of automobile production.
1915	Production of Ford's Model T exceeds 500,000; it now sells for $440.
1919	In the United States, a gasoline tax is imposed to fund highway construction.
1920	In the United States, Deusenberg develops four-wheel hydraulic brakes.
1920	More than 8 million Americans own cars.
1930s	Franklin D. Roosevelt proposes a federal interstate highway system.

1936	Mercedes introduces the first diesel-powered car.
1938	In Germany, a prototype of the Volkswagen Beetle is introduced.
1939	In the United States, air conditioning becomes available in some automobiles.
1947	In the United States, Goodyear develops the tubeless tire.
1949	The Volkswagen Beetle is introduced in the United States, prompting some American manufacturers to begin producing smaller cars.
1950s	In Germany, Mercedes-Benz develops fuel injection.
1956	In the United States, the Interstate Highway Act provides funding for approximately 43,000 miles of interstate highways.
1956	The first Japanese passenger vehicles are introduced in the United States.
1958	In the United States, aluminum car engines are developed.
1966	In England, the electronic fuel-injection system is introduced.
1970s	To reduce exhaust emissions, catalytic converters are introduced.
1970s	The energy crisis prompts more consumers to purchase fuel-efficient compact cars; Japanese imports become increasingly popular.
1980	Japan is the world's leading automobile manufacturer.
1980s	In Australia, a solar-powered vehicle travels 1,846 miles in six days.
1980s	Japanese automobile manufacturers open plants in the United States.
1999	53.2 million passenger vehicles are produced this year; approximately 16.8 million of them are sold in North America.

⊙ Microsoft® Encarta® Online Encyclopedia 2000. "Automobile," www.encarta.msn.com
The History Channel. "Automobiles," www.historychannel.com
Wetterau, Bruce. *The New York Public Library Book of Chronologies.* New York: Simon & Schuster, 1990.

Boats: Chronology

c.6000 BC	In Africa, wooden dugout boats are built.
c.5000 BC	Earliest evidence of wood-plank construction of boats
c.4500 BC	In Mesopotamia, boats are made of wood frames covered with bark or animal skins.
c.4000 BC	In China, flat bamboo rafts are built.
c.3300 BC	Early Egyptian boats have one square sail and one row of oarsmen. As Egyptians begin navigating the Mediterranean Sea, they develop long, narrow warships with two rows of oarsmen; they also develop rounder ships to transport cargo.
c.3000 BC	Earliest evidence of rudders
c.700 BC	In Greece, the trireme (a warship with three levels of oarsmen) is invented.
800s AD	In northern Europe, lapstrake boat construction is developed; in lapstrake construction, overlapping wood planks are attached to the boat frame with lashings or nails.
800s	Byzantines build carvel-planked ships; in carvel-plank construction, wood planks are nailed to the frame edge-to-edge instead of overlapping.
1200s	Most Mediterranean sailing ships now have two masts.
1300s	Italians build ships with three decks.
1400s	Chinese junks are the most sophisticated and most seaworthy ships in the world.
c.1540	The galleon, powered solely by sail, is introduced.
1783	In France, the first steam-powered paddleboat is built.

1814	The first steam-powered warship is built.
1838	The British ship Archimedes is the first propeller-driven steamship.
1838	The ship Sirius is the first large passenger ship to cross the Atlantic Ocean using only steam power; it crosses the Atlantic in 18 days.
1840s	The iron hull is developed.
1843	The Great Britain is the first propeller-powered ship to cross the Atlantic Ocean.
1853	The Monumental City, a paddle wheeler, is the first steamship to cross the Pacific Ocean, traveling from San Francisco to Sydney, Australia.
1857	The British steamship Great Eastern is built; constructed of iron, it weighs 18,000 tons and is 693 feet long.
1861	In the United States, the first tanker (Elizabeth Watts) is built; it carries oil in wooden barrels from Pennsylvania to London.
1869	The clipper ship Cutty Sark is introduced.
1880s	Boat builders begin using internal-combustion inboard engines.
1884	In England, Sir Charles Parsons introduces the steam turbine.
1891	The aluminum boat is introduced in Europe.
1910s	Boat builders begin using outboard motors.
1918	Alexander Graham Bell and Casey Baldwin invent the hydrofoil, which reaches a speed of 70 miles per hour; the hydrofoil has fins on its hull that create hydrodynamic pressure, allowing the boat to be lifted out of the water when in motion.
1918	In the United States, boat builders begin using plywood construction; plywood boats are either paneled or molded.
1922	The United States Navy builds its first aircraft carrier.
1952	The ocean liner United States crosses the Atlantic Ocean in 3 days, 10 hours.
1959	The first hovercraft crosses the English Channel in two hours; the hovercraft travels on a cushion of air, not coming into contact with water when in motion.
1970s	The surface-piercing propeller is introduced.

⊙ Microsoft® Encarta® Online Encyclopedia 2000. "Boats and Boatbuilding," www.encarta.msn.com
Mount, Ellis, and Barbara A. List. *Milestones in Science and Technology*. Phoenix: Oryx, 1994.
Wetterau, Bruce. *The New York Public Library Book of Chronologies*. New York: Simon & Schuster, 1990.

Boats: Rules of the Sea

Maritime law refers to the body of laws that govern navigation, shipping, and recreational boating. Most maritime law deals with legal issues surrounding the private shipping industry. Today's maritime law is derived from laws created by ancient Greeks, Egyptians, and Phoenicians. English admiralty courts were in place by the 14th century. Maritime law includes the following components:

Maritime liens: Covers liens against ships, cargo, or freight. In maritime law, a ship can be named as a defendant in legal cases (proceeding in rem), and the ship can be "arrested" and held in custody until its owner satisfies a condition, such as paying bail.

Carriage of goods: Covers the transport of cargo or passengers

Charter parties: Covers contracts between ship owners and those who charter their ships

Limitation of liability: Covers the extent to which ship owners are liable in claims against them

Collision liability: Covers responsibility for damage and losses caused by collisions

Salvage and general average: Covers possession of, and awards for the return of, salvaged property

Marine insurance: Covers insurance of ships as well as liability insurance

The Law of the Sea refers to the maritime issues of public international law. The Convention on the Law of the Sea is a United Nations agreement that establishes rules governing the use of oceans and their resources. It was signed by 119 nations on December 10, 1982.

The Rules of the Road at Sea refer to a set of international traffic regulations for oceans. These rules cover lights, sounds, collision avoidance, and other regulations.

⊙ United Nations. "Oceans and Law of the Sea," www.un.org/Depts/los/index.htm
  Encyclopedia Britannica. "Maritime Law," www.britannica.com/bcom/eb/article/
  0,5716,115491+1_108706,00.html
  Maritime Legal Resources. "Maritime Law in Detail," www.marlegal.com/law.html

Computers: Bits and Bytes

Binary Code uses two symbols, 0 and 1, to represent numbers. Binary numbering is used in computer technology because it is compact and reliable, and can easily represent two states such as "on-off," or "start-stop."

A bit is short for "binary digit." Bits are the smallest units of computer data, having a binary value of either 0 or 1. A byte consists of 8 adjacent bits. Bytes are the basic unit of information in computer storage and processing and are the smallest operable units of storage in computer technology.

Computer Data Information and Storage Units

Common Computer Storage Capacities	Number of Bytes
Nibble	one-half (four bits)
Byte	8
Kilobytes (KB)	1024
Megabytes (MB)	1,048,576
Gigabytes (GB)	about 1 billion
Terabytes (TB)	about 1 trillion

⊙ Britannica.com. "Bit," www.britannica.com/bcom/eb/article/3/0,5716,82463+1+80319,00.html
  Britannica.com. "Byte," "Binary Number System," www.britannica.com/bcom/eb/article/2/
  0,5716,2002+1+1994,00.html

Computers: ASCII

The American Standard Code for Information Interchange (ASCII) is a code used to represent textual information, such as letters, numbers, and punctuation, as well as non-input device commands such as control characters. It is the most common code format for representing text files in computers and on the Internet and is used for information exchange between computers.

ASCII was originally developed by the American National Standards Institute. In an ASCII file, each character is represented with a 7-digit binary number, making 128 possible characters defined. Since digital computers use 8-digit binary code (bytes), ASCII code is commonly embedded in an 8-bit field, known as extended ASCII. 256 characters are defined in extended ASCII.

While different operating systems use different code for text file representation, conversion programs allow different operating systems to change from one file format to another.

Computers: ASCII (cont.)

Operating System Text File Codes

Operating System	Code
UNIX	ASCII
DOS	ASCII
Windows 98 and Windows 2000	ASCII
Macintosh	ASCII modified for use with Macintosh operating systems
Windows NT	Unicode
IBM	ASCII modified for use with IBM system 390 computers, known as the IBM extended character set

⊙ Britannica.com. "ASCII," www.britannica.com/bcom/eb/article/9/0,5716,1609+1+1602,00.html
  Whatis.com. "ASCII," www.whatis.com/WhatIs_Definition_Page/0,4152,211600,00.html

Computers: Languages and Uses

Computer languages are used to communicate instructions to a computer. Similar to natural languages, such as English, programming languages have a vocabulary, syntax, and grammar. Computer languages differ from natural languages because they are logical and have no ambiguity. There are many types of computer languages that are used for different purposes.

Programming languages can be classified as either low-level languages or high-level languages. Low-level programming languages, or machine languages, are the most basic type of programming languages and can be understood directly by a computer. Machine languages differ depending on the manufacturer and model of computer. High-level languages are programming languages that must first be translated into a machine language before they can be understood and processed by a computer. Examples of high-level languages are C, C++, PASCAL, and FORTRAN. Assembly languages are intermediate languages that are very close to machine language and do not have the level of linguistic sophistication exhibited by other high-level languages, but must still be translated into machine language.

Some programming languages are written to address a particular kind of computing problem or for use on a specific type of computer system. Although these languages were designed to address specific categories of computer problems, they are highly portable, meaning that they may be used to program many types of computers. Other languages, such as machine languages, are designed for use by one specific model of computer system, or even by one specific computer in certain research applications. The most commonly used programming languages are highly portable and are used to solve diverse types of computing problems. Languages like C, PASCAL, and BASIC fall into this category.

High-level languages are commonly classified as procedure-oriented, functional, object-oriented, or logic languages. The most common high-level languages today are procedure-oriented languages. Object-oriented languages, such as C++ and Java, use self-contained collections of instructions, called objects, which can be re-used in other programs.

THE SCIENCES: *Technology*

Major Computer Programming Languages

Language	Description and Use
Machine Language	Low-level basic programming languages, expressed in binary digits, which are understood directly by a computer and are used to represent operation codes and memory addresses. Machine languages differ depending on the manufacturer and model of computer.
Assembly Language	Low-level language expressed in alphanumeric characters. Used to minimize the time it takes to run a program. Also used when some part of the computer has to be controlled directly, such as individual dots on a monitor or the flow of individual characters to a printer.
FORTRAN (FORmula TRANslation)	A high-level procedural language commonly used for scientific applications
COBOL (Common Business-Oriented Language)	A high-level procedural language commonly used for business applications
BASIC (Beginner's All-Purpose Instruction Code)	A high-level, procedural language that is easy to learn and understand
PASCAL	A high-level procedural language designed for instructional purposes in 1967 by Nicholas Wirth. Most serious programmers now use C, C++, or Java instead of PASCAL.
Smalltalk	A high-level object-oriented language developed in the early 1970s by Alan Kay at Xerox for a variety of business purposes. C++ and Java have replaced Smalltalk as the most popular object-oriented programming languages.
Visual Basic (VB)	An object-oriented language developed at Microsoft. VB is easy to learn and understand, and is used for a variety of programming purposes.
C	A high-level procedural language. It is a compiled, structured programming language used for a variety of purposes.
C++	A high-level language that is an object-oriented version of C invented by Bjarne Stroustrup in the 1980s.
JAVA	A high-level object-oriented language similar to C++ but it allows programmers to build small application modules, called "applets," for use as part of a Web page. Applets make it possible for a Web page user to interact with the page.

⊙ Britannica.com. "Computer Programming Language," www.britannica.com/bcom/eb/article/0/
0,5716,25460+1+25054,00.html
Microsoft® Encarta® Online Encyclopedia 2000. "Programming Language," www.encarta.msn.com/
find/Concise.asp?z=1&pg=2&ti=761575695.

Aviation: Chronology

Year	Inventions and Aircraft Evolution	Company and/or Inventor	Statistics (military, Commercial, Etc.)
1781	ornithopter (flapping-wing machine resembling a glider)	Karl Friedrich Meerwein (Germany)	Limited testing and documentation of first flying machine

Year	Inventions and Aircraft Evolution	Company and/or Inventor	Statistics (military, Commercial, Etc.)
1783	hot-air balloon	Joseph and Etienne Montgolfier (France)	First manned flight of hot-air balloon
early 1800s	hydrogen balloon		Same construction as hot-air balloon, but filled with hydrogen gas; specialized warfare vehicle for spying
early 1800s	blimp		First non-rigid structure with aerodynamic shape
early 1800s	dirigible		First rigid structure with aerodynamic shape
1852	glider	George Cayley (England)	First glider trials
1900	luftschiff (airship based on the design of the dirigible)	Count Ferdinand von Zeppelin (Germany)	First experimental flight of a luftschiff
1903	aeroplane (biplane)	Wilbur and Orville Wright (USA)	First manned flight of a motorized airplane
1909	monoplane	Louis Bleriot (France)	First aerial crossing of the English Channel
1910–15	LZ-5 (luftschiff/airship)	Deutsche-Luftschiffahrts AG (Germany)	First well-financed commercial air transportation company operated the LZ-5; 1,588 flights; 34,228 passengers
1913	four-engine plane	Sikorsky	First four-engine plane
1914	twin-engine seaplane	Glenn Curtiss (USA)	First commercial airplane service in the world, flying between Tampa and St. Petersburg, Florida
during WWI	zeppelin (luftschiff/airship)	Zeppelin Company (Germany)	88 constructed for military purposes; first sustained distant aerial warfare, which included the bombing of London; 45 mph

1919	Curtiss NC-4 flying boat	Curtiss Company (USA)	First aerial crossing of the Atlantic
mid-1920s	Graf Zeppelin	Zeppelin Company (Germany)	First around-the-world air voyage; continued commercial flights into the mid-1930s
1927	Vega (radial-engined airplane with a stressed wooden skin)	Lockheed Aircraft Company / John Northrup (USA)	Model for modern commercial aircraft; 110–135 mph
1928	trimotor airplane (with strongest yet-used radial engines)	Ford (USA)	Commercial flight
1930	Monomail (all-metal airplane with retractable landing gear)	Boeing (USA)	
1933	Boeing-247 (twin-engine)	Boeing (USA)	Advanced model for modern commercial aircraft; safer than trimotors
1935	Martin M-130—The China Clipper (four-engine flying boat with a 130-foot wingspan)	Martin Company (USA)	First airmail flight between California and Manila; passengers added in 1936
1936	DC-3 (twin-engine)	Douglas Company (USA)	First airliner to operate at a profit; 21-passenger transcontinental routes; 175 mph; unrivaled master airliner for several years; used for military cargo as the C-47 in the U.S.
1940	Stratoliner	Boeing Company (USA)	First plane with an airtight cabin, capable of flying at 14,000 at 200 mph; could navigate above weather and mountains, choosing routes of shortest possible distance; used for military flights during WWII
1940	DC-4	Douglas Company (USA)	DC-3 transformed into a four-engine size; 200 mph; unpressurized cabin; main transatlantic aircraft used during WWII in the form of the U.S. Army's C-54 troop transport

Year	Inventions and Aircraft Evolution	Company and/or Inventor	Statistics (military, Commercial, Etc.)
1940	Constellation	Lockheed Company (USA)	280 mph; main commercial competitor of DC-4
1945–55	multiple advances in aircraft technology		Rapid growth in air traffic calls forth advanced aircraft technology to extend routes and enlarge markets
1953	DC-7	Douglas Company (USA)	First plane to fly 3,000 miles; 300 mph
1957			Number of passengers crossing Atlantic by air was greater than by sea
1958	Boeing 707	Boeing Company (USA)	The jet engine replaces the piston engine; 550 mph
1969	Concorde	British Aircraft Corp. (U.K.) and Sud-Aviation (France)	Concorde becomes first airplane to break sound barrier
1970	Boeing 747 (jumbo jet)	Boeing Company (USA)	Becomes longest, widest plane with greatest passenger capacity (416–524), and greatest maximum take-off weight (875,000 pounds); 565 mph
1970s	Gossamer Albatross (human-powered aircraft)	Paul MacCready (USA)	First human-powered aerial crossing of the English Channel
1970s	Solar Challenger (solar-powered aircraft)	Paul MacCready (USA)	First solar-powered aerial crossing of the English Channel
1976	Concorde	British Airways and Air France	First commercial passenger flight of supersonic jet

⊙ Encyclopaedia Britannica. "History of Transportation, Aviation: the ultimate ubiquity," www.britannica.com/bcom/eb/article/2/0,5716,120012+24+110734,00.html
The Boeing Company. "Product Line Family Overview," www.boeing.com/commercial/productline/index.html.
The Unofficial Concorde Home Page. "Concorde Jet History," www.concorde-jet.com/

Type of Aircraft	Wing Span	Overall Length	Max. Takeoff Weight (000 lbs.)	Avg. Cruise Speed (mph)	Seating Cap.	Cargo Space (cu. ft.)	Use
717	93 ft. 3 in.	124 ft.	121	504	106	935	Commercial short-range, high-frequency passenger airliner
737-200	93 ft.	100 ft. 2 in.	115.5	575	95–130	875	Commercial passenger airliner
737-200C	93 ft.	100 ft. 2 in.	115.5	575	95–130	875–2,605	Commercial convertible passenger or freight airliners
737-200C Advanced	93 ft.	100 ft. 2 in.	128.1	575	95–130	875–2,635	
737-300	94 ft. 9 in.	101 ft. 9 in.	138.5	495	128–149	1,068	Commercial passenger airliners
737-400	94 ft. 9 in.	109 ft. 7 in.	138.5	495	147–168	1,373	
737-500	94 ft. 9 in.	119 ft. 7 in.	133.5	495	110–132	822	
747 Passenger	211 ft. 5 in.	231 ft. 10 in.	875	565	416–524	6,025	Commercial passenger airliners
747 Domestic	195 ft. 8 in.	231 ft. 10 in.	833	565	568	6,025	
747 Freighter	211 ft. 5 in.	231 ft. 10 in.	875	565	N/A	27,467	Commercial cargo airliner (largest in service)
747 Combi	211 ft. 5 in.	231 ft. 10 in.	875	565	410	10,422	Commercial long-range passenger and freight combination airliner
757-200	124 ft. 10 in.	155 ft. 3 in.	272.5	530	192–239	1,670	Commercial passenger airliners
757-300	124 ft. 10 in.	178 ft. 7 in.	255	530	238–289	2,370	
757-200 Freighter	124 ft. 10 in.	155 ft. 3 in.	255	530	N/A	8,430	Commercial cargo airliner
767-200	156 ft. 1 in.	159 ft. 2 in.	395	530	181–285	2,875	Commercial long-range passenger airliners

Type of Aircraft	Wing Span	Overall Length	Max. Takeoff Weight (ooo lbs.)	Avg. Cruise Speed (mph)	Seating Cap.	Cargo Space (cu. ft.)	Use
767-300	156 ft. 1 in.	180 ft. 3 in.	412	530	218–269	3,770	Commercial long-range cargo airliner
767-300 Freighter	156 ft. 1 in.	180 ft. 3 in.	412	530	N/A	16,034	
777-200	199 ft. 11 in.	209 ft. 1 in.	545	560	320–440	5,656	Commercial long-range passenger airliners
777-200ER	199 ft. 11 in.	209 ft. 1 in.	656	560	320–440	5,656	
777-300	199 ft. 11 in.	242 ft. 4 in.	660	560	386–440	7,552	
MD-11 Passenger	169 ft. 5 in.	200 ft. 8 in.	630.5	588	285–410	6,850	Commercial long-range passenger airliners
MD-11 Combi	169 ft. 5 in.	200 ft. 8 in.	630.5	588	181–285	6,850–10,440	Commercial long-range convertible and combination airliner for passengers and cargo
MD-11 Convertible	169 ft. 5 in.	200 ft. 8 in.	630.5	588	350–410	6,850–21,358	Commercial long-range cargo airliner
MD-11 Freighter	169 ft. 5 in.	200 ft. 8 in.	630.5	588	N/A	22,380	
MD-81	107 ft. 8 in.	147 ft. 8 in.	140	504	144–172	1,253	Commercial passenger airliners
MD-82	107 ft. 8 in.	147 ft. 8 in.	149.5	504	144–172	1,253	
MD-83	107 ft. 8 in.	147 ft. 8 in.	160	504	144–172	1,103	
MD-88	107 ft. 8 in.	130 ft. 4 in.	140	504	144–172	938	
MD-90-30	107 ft. 8 in.	152 ft. 6 in.	156	504	152–172	1,300	Commercial passenger airliners
MD-90-30ER	107 ft. 8 in.	152 ft. 6 in.	166	504	152–172	1,183	
DC-8	N/A	N/A	N/A	N/A	258	N/A	Commercial passenger airliner

Model							Description
DC-9-10	89.4 ft.	104.4 ft.	90.7	561	80–90	600	Commercial passenger airliners designed for short runways and short- to medium-range routes
DC-9-21	93.3 ft.	104.4 ft.	98	557	80–90	600	
DC-9-30	93.3 ft.	119.3 ft.	110	570	80–90	895	
DC-9-40	93.3 ft.	125.6 ft.	114	561	80–90	1,019	
DC-9-50	93.3 ft.	133.5 ft.	121	558	80–90	1,034	
DC-10 Series 10	155 ft. 4 in.	182 ft. 3 in.	430	600	250–380	4,618	Commercial passenger airliners
DC-10 Series 15	155 ft. 4 in.	180 ft. 8 in.	455	600	250–380	4,618	
DC-10 Series 30	165 ft. 4 in.	180 ft. 8 in.	572	600	250–380	4,618	
DC-10 Series 40	165 ft. 4 in.	180 ft. 7 in.	555	600	250–380	4,618	
DC-10 Series 10	155 ft. 4 in.	182 ft. 3 in.	430	600	250–380	4,618	Commercial convertible all-passenger or all-cargo airliners
DC-10 Series 30	165 ft. 4 in.	180 ft. 8 in.	572	600	250–380	4,618	
DC-10 Series 40	165 ft. 4 in.	180 ft. 7 in.	555	600	250–380	4,618	
DC-10 Series 30F	165 ft. 4 in.	180 ft. 8 in.	572	600	N/A	N/A	Commercial cargo-only airliner; military variant is the U.S. Air Force KC-10 tanker/cargo aircraft

⊙ The Boeing Company. "Product Line Family Overview," www.boeing.com/commercial/productline/index.html

Launch/ Flight Date(s)	Project/Vehicle	Astronaut(s) Cosmonaut(s)	Country	Accomplishments and Mission Description
3/25/61	Sputnik 5	Simulated cosmonaut Ivan Ivanovich; Zvezdochka (dog)	USSR	First dog in space; first simulated person in space
4/12/61	Vostok 1	Yury A. Gagarin	USSR	First person in space; single orbit around the Earth
5/5/61	Mercury/Freedom 7	Alan B. Shepard, Jr.	U.S.	First person in space from U.S.
2/20/62	Mercury/Friendship 7	John Glenn	U.S.	First person to circle Earth; 3 orbits
6/16/63	Vostok VI	Valentina Tereshkova	USSR	First woman in space
3/18/65	Voskhod 2	Pavel I Belyayev; Alexei A. Leonov	USSR	First space walk
6/3–7/65	Gemini 4	Edward H. White II; James A. McDevitt	U.S.	First space walk by U.S.
12/4/65	Gemini 7	Frank Borman; James A. Lovell, Jr.	U.S.	Set endurance record for longest space flight of 14 days
4/23/67	Soyuz 1	V. M. Komarov	USSR	Largest; most complex spacecraft launched up to that time; cosmonaut killed in failure of parachute recovery system
7/16–24/69	Apollo/Apollo 11	Neil A. Armstrong; Edwin E. Aldrin; Michael Collins	U.S.	First astronauts to walk on the moon; Lunar Module landed on moon; took core samples and collected data
4/11–17/70	Apollo/Apollo 13	James A. Lovell, Jr.; Fred W. Haise, Jr.; John L. Sweigert, Jr.	U.S.	Near-disastrous mission: ruptured oxygen tank forced emergency return to Earth
7/26/71	Apollo 15	David R. Scott; James B. Irwin; Alfred M. Worden	U.S.	First extensive exploration of Moon's surface by crew members in a Lunar Roving Vehicle
12/7–19/72	Apollo/Apollo 17	Eugene Cernan; Ronald B. Evans; Harrison H. Schmitt	U.S.	Last men to walk on the moon (so far)

Date	Mission	Crew	Country	Notes
5/25–6/22/73	*Skylab/Skylab* II	Charles Conrad, Jr.; Paul J. Weitz; Joseph P. Kerwin	U.S.	*Skylab* is repaired after damage during initial launch; crew able to exit and reenter *Skylab* for work in space through Airlock Module; mission more than doubled the previous American space endurance record
11/16/73–2/8/74	*Skylab/Skylab* IV	Gerald P. Carr; William R. Pogue; Edward G. Gibson	U.S.	Longest *Skylab* mission and U.S. space flight: over 84 days with 1,214 orbits of Earth
7/15–24/75	Apollo-Soyuz Test Project: *Apollo* 18, *Soyuz* 19	U.S.: Thomas P. Stafford; Vance D. Brand; Donald K. Slayton USSR: Alexei Leonov; Valeri Kubasov	U.S., USSR	First joint international meeting in space; crafts remained linked for 2 days; final flight of the *Apollo* spacecraft
4/12/81	*Space Shuttle/Columbia*	John W. Young; Robert L. Crippen	U.S.	First reusable space craft; first to use liquid- and solid-propellant rocket engines
6/18/83	*Space Shuttle/Challenger*	Robert L. Crippen; Frederick H. Hauck; John M. Fabian; Sally K. Ride; Norman E. Thagard	U.S.	First U.S. female astronaut in space (Ride)
8/30/83	*Space Shuttle/Challenger*	Richard H. Truly; Daniel C. Brandenstein; Dale A. Gardner; Guion S. Bluford; William E. Thornton	U.S.	First African-American astronaut in space (Bluford)
1/28/86	*Space Shuttle/Challenger*	Francis R. Scobee; Michael J. Smith; Judith A. Resnik; Ellison S. Onizuka; Ronald E. McNair; Gregory B. Jarvis; Sharon Christa McAuliffe	U.S.	Destroyed during launch with all crew aboard; first U.S. civilian astronaut in space (schoolteacher McAuliffe) aboard

Launch/ Flight Date(s)	Project/Vehicle	Astronaut(s) Cosmonaut(s)	Country	Accomplishments and Mission Description
3/13/86	Soyuz to Mir	Leonid Kizim; Vladimir Solovyev	USSR	First occupants of space station Mir (core of a large, permanent, multi-manned orbiting complex designed to accommodate various expansion modules for crew living quarters and research facilities)
4/24–29/90	Space Shuttle/ Discovery	Loren J. Shriver; Charles F. Bolden, Jr.; Steven A. Hawley; Bruce McCandless; Kathryn D. Sullivan	U.S.	Deployed Hubble Space Telescope
1/94	Mir project	Valery Polyakov	USSR	Mission length record: 438 days
10/29–11/7/98	Space Shuttle/ Discovery	Curtis L. Brown; Steven W. Lindsey; Stephen K. Robinson; Scott F. Parazynski; Pedro Duque; Chiaki Mukai; John Glenn	U.S.	Glenn (77) becomes the oldest person to go into space; medical links between aging and spaceflight studied
7/25–28/99	Space Shuttle/ Columbia	Eileen M. Collins; Jeffrey S. Ashby; Steven A. Hawley; Catherine G. Coleman; Michel Tognini	U.S.	First female commander (Collins) of a U.S. space-flight

⊙ Encyclopaedia Britannica. "Space Exploration," www.britannica.com/bcom/eb/article/6/0,5716,120716+1+111026,00.html
 NASA. "Astronaut Information," www.hq.nasa.gov/office/pao.History/apollo/welcome.html#chart
 NASA. "Human Spaceflight Programs History," www.hq.nasa.gov/office/pao/History/humansp.html

Launch Date	Mission Name or Vehicle	Country	Mission Description
10/4/57	Sputnik 1	USSR	First satellite ever launched
1/31/58	Explorer 1	U.S.	First satellite launched by U.S.
1/4/59	Luna 1	USSR	First space craft to reach escape velocity; passed Moon and orbited Sun
10/7/59	Luna 3	USSR	First photographs of another celestial body: far side of the Moon
3/7/62	OSO: Orbiting Solar Observatory	U.S.	Satellite pointed toward the sun to record and transmit scientific data
8/27/62	Mariner 2	U.S.	Gathered temperature and atmospheric density measurements of Venus
12/7/68	OAO: Orbiting Astronomical Observatory	U.S.	Satellite equipped to map entire electromagnetic spectrum and record other astronomical data
2/24/69	Mariner 6	U.S.	Obtained photographs, atmosphere analyses, and thermal maps of Mars
8/17/70	Venera 7	USSR	Instrumented capsule dropped by parachute into Venusian atmosphere yielded useful data from surface of Venus
11/10/70	Luna 17	USSR	Automated television-equipped roving vehicle landed on the Moon
3/3/72	Pioneer 10	U.S.	First spacecraft to fly by Jupiter; returned physical data and photographs
5/14/73	Skylab	U.S.	First U.S. space station launched
11/3/73	Mariner 10	U.S.	Used Venusian gravity to increase velocity to fly by Mercury; obtained first close-up photographs of Mercury
8/20/77	Viking 1	U.S.	First landing on Mars; transmitted detailed color images of planet's landscape back to Earth; conducted in situ analyses of Martian soil and atmosphere
8/20/77	Voyager 1	U.S.	Fly-by of Jupiter in 1979 and Saturn in 1980; revealed features of their moons, magnetic fields, and ring systems

Launch Date	Mission Name or Vehicle	Country	Mission Description
9/5/77	*Voyager 2*	U.S.	Fly-bys of Jupiter and Saturn, and then passed Uranus in 1986; passed by Neptune's clouds in 1989, provided data and images of Neptune
9/29/77	*Salyut 2*	USSR	Second generation of Soviet space station; two docking ports; increased length of time crews could live and work on board the station, reaching a record 211 days; visited by guest cosmonauts from Communist-bloc nations, France, and India
1/83	IRAS: *Infrared Astronomy Satellite*	U.S. w/ U.K., Netherlands	Study of infrared sources beyond the limits of the solar system
2/20/86	*Mir*	USSR	Space station satellite with six docking ports; core of a large, permanent, multi-manned orbiting complex designed to accommodate various expansion modules for crew living quarters and research facilities
3/31/87	*Kvant 1* to *Mir*	USSR	Astrophysics observatory module docked at *Mir* complex
5/4/89	*Magellan*	U.S.	Placed in orbit around Venus for scientific studies
11/89	*Kvant 2* to *Mir*	USSR	Delivered equipment for producing oxygen, recycling water supplies, and an airlock for cosmonaut spacewalks to perform outside maintenance work
4/24/90	HST: *Hubble Space Telescope*	U.S.	Deployed by the *Space Shuttle*; largest and most powerful observatory placed in Earth's orbit
4/96	*Priroda* to *Mir*	Russia	Sent to study Earth's environmental health and ecology
12/4/96	*Mars Pathfinder*	U.S.	Landed on Mars and collected surface data

⊙ NASA. "Space Program History," www.hq.nasa.gov/office/pao/History
Encyclopaedia Britannica. "Space Exploration," www.britannica.com/bcom/eb/article/6/0,5716,120716+1+111026,00.html

Space Flight: Moon Walkers

Astronaut	Mission	Moon Landing Date
Neil A. Armstrong	*Apollo* 11	July 20, 1969
Edwin E. Aldrin	*Apollo* 11	July 20, 1969
Charles P. Conrad, Jr.	*Apollo* 12	Nov. 19, 1969
Alan L. Bean	*Apollo* 12	Nov. 19, 1969
Alan B. Shepard, Jr.	*Apollo* 14	Feb. 5, 1971
Edgar D. Mitchell	*Apollo* 14	Feb. 5, 1971
David R. Scott	*Apollo* 15	July 30, 1971
James B. Irwin	*Apollo* 15	July 30, 1971
John W. Young	*Apollo* 16	Apr. 21, 1972
Charles M. Duke, Jr.	*Apollo* 16	Apr. 21, 1972
Eugene A. Cernan	*Apollo* 17	Dec. 11, 1972
Harrison Schmitt	*Apollo* 17	Dec. 11, 1972

⊙ NASA. "The Apollo Missions," www.hq.nasa.gov/office/pao/History/apollo/welcome.html#chart

Railroads: Chronology

100 BC	Roads paved with stone blocks that had grooves cut in them built in Greece; wagons with wheels the width of the grooves were pulled over the roads by horses
1500s	Tramroads with wooden rails built in Europe to facilitate hauling of coal, ore, or stone from mines
early 1700s	Iron replaces wood on tramroads, spreads from Europe to Northern America
1705	Steam-powered pump invented to remove water from mines
1767	First cast-iron rails, produced in England
1803	First steam-pumping engine mounted on a car with wheels set to operate on rails of cast-iron tramroad at Pen-y-Darren, Wales
1804	First steam locomotive hauls freight and passengers over Pen-y-Darren tram line
1820	First wrought-iron rails introduced in England
1825	First railroad line, the Stockton & Darlington, travels 9 miles; designed to carry goods and passengers on regular schedules (England)
1828	First cornerstone on the Baltimore & Ohio Railroad laid (U.S.)
1846	Pennsylvania Railroad incorporated (U.S.)
1853	New York Central Railroad organized (U.S.)
1859	First Pullman sleeping car (U.S.)
1864	U.S. Post Office first tests a railway mail car
1869	Union Pacific and Central Pacific meet at Promitory, Utah; becomes first transcontinental route in U.S.
1889	Great Northern Railway Company organized (U.S.)

Railroads: Chronology *(cont.)*

1895	Electric traction introduced on short sections of U.S. railroads
1917	One million miles of rail routes worldwide, about one-quarter of them in the U.S.
1918	U.S. government takes over railroads for purpose of increasing wartime efficiency
1925	Installation of centralized traffic control (CTC) increases track capacity
1935	First diesel-powered train in U.S.
1950–90	Soviet Union Railway adds a second Trans-Siberian line, the Baikal-Amur Magistral
1950–90	China doubles route length of its national system to 33,500 miles
1959–64	Tokyo-Osaka railway expands with the Shinkansen electric line (320 miles of track, 130 mph) (Japan)
1970	Great Northern, Northern Pacific, and the Chicago, Burlington & Quincy merge to form the Burlington Northern (U.S.)
1975	Japanese Shinkansen line extends to Kyushu island via underwater tunnel; 664 mile route; 171 mph max. speed
1983	France's first high-speed Train à Grande Vitesse (TGV) completed; 168 mph
1990s	High speed railways built extensively in France, Gremany, Italy, Spain
1990s	High speed railways planned in South Korea, Taiwan, China, Canada, U.S.
1990s	India continues new trunk route construction
1991	World's last steam locomotive factory switches to electric locomotive manufacture (China)
1994	Trans-Channel Tunnel opens between France and Britain; 30 miles long
1996	Union Pacific and Southern Pacific merge

⊙ National Railroad Museum. "Railroad History," www.NationalRRMuseum.org/
Encyclopaedia Britannica. "Railroad," www.britannica.com
Microsoft® Encarta® Online Encyclopedia 2000. "Automobile," www.encarta.msn.com

Subways: Chronology

1860	Work begins on London's Metropolitan Railway, using the cut-and-cover construction method; this method involves digging a trench in the street above the railway, constructing a brick tunnel over the tracks, and then restoring the surface of the street.
1863	The world's first subway system, London's Metropolitan Railway, opens, carrying 9,500,000 passengers in its first year of service.
1866	Work begins on what will become London's "tube" line; to avoid causing disruption to the streets above, twin tunnels are excavated in a layer of clay approximately 60 feet below ground.
1870	In New York, in a 312-foot tunnel under Broadway, a subway car is operated by pneumatic pressure created by a giant fan; operation ceases in 1873.
1890	London's "tube" line opens; while earlier trains were steam-powered, all trains on the line now run on electric power.

1896	In Budapest, an electric subway begins operation.
1898	Boston's subway begins operation; it is the first subway system in the United States.
1898	Work begins on the Métro subway in Paris, using a variation of the cut-and-cover construction method that causes less disruption of street traffic.
1900	The Métro begins operation in Paris with 6.25 miles of track.
1902	Berlin's subway begins operation.
1904	The first section of the New York City subway opens.
1908	Philadelphia's subway begins operation.
1913	The Buenos Aires subway begins operation.
1919	Madrid's subway begins operation.
1927	Tokyo's subway begins operation.
1931	Kyoto's subway begins operation.
1933	Osaka's subway begins operation.
1935	Moscow's subway begins operation.
1943	Chicago's subway begins operation.
1954	Toronto's subway begins operation; it is the first subway system in Canada.
1955	Cleveland's subway begins operation.
1966	Montreal's subway begins operation.
1969	Mexico City's subway begins operation; this system is modeled after the Métro in Paris.
1971	The Victoria Line of the London Underground is completed; it is the first line to use automatic trains.
1976	San Francisco's BART (Bay Area Rapid Transit) system, the first completely automatic subway system, is completed.
1976	The Washington, D.C., Metro begins operation.
1979	Atlanta's subway begins operation.
1983	Baltimore's subway begins operation.
1984	Miami's subway begins operation.
1993	The Los Angeles subway begins operation.
2000	Moscow's subway system has the largest ridership, approximately 3.2 billion annually.
2000	With 256 miles of track, the London Underground has more track than any other subway system in the world.
2000	New York's subway system has more cars (6,273) and more stations (463) than any other system in the world.

⊙ Encyclopedia Britannica. "Subway," www.britannica.com
London Transport. "The Early Years," www.londontransport.co.uk/tube/ciu_about.html
New York City Transit. "About New York City Transit," www.mta.nyc.ny.us/nyct/facts/ffist.htm

Span Type	Function	Record Holders		
		Name	Location	Length
Beam	Most common bridge form. Carries vertical loads by bending. As the beam bridge bends, it undergoes horizontal compression on the top. At the same time, the bottom of the beam is subjected to horizontal tension. The supports carry the loads from the beam by compression vertically to the foundations.	Lake Ponchartrain Causeway (#2)	Metairie-Lewisburg, La., U.S.	23.9 mi. (38,462 m.)
Arch	Carries loads primarily by compression, which exerts both vertical and horizontal forces on the foundation. Arch foundations must therefore prevent both vertical settling and horizontal sliding.	New River Gorge	Fayette County, West Virginia, U.S.	0.32 mi. (518 m.)
Suspension	Carries vertical loads through curved cables in tension. These loads are transferred both to the towers, which carry them by vertical compression to the ground, and to the anchorages, which must resist the inward and sometimes vertical pull of the cables. The suspension bridge can be viewed as an upside-down arch in tension, with only the towers in compression.	Akashi-Kaikyo	Kobe, Akashi-Awaji Island, Japan	1.28 mi. (1,991 m.)
Cantilever	A beam is said to be cantilevered when it projects outward, supported only at one end. A cantilevered bridge is generally made with three spans, of which the outer spans are both anchored down at the shore and cantilever out over the channel to be crossed. The central span rests on the cantilevered arms extending from the outer spans. Towers carry the tension and compressions forces of the spans to central or far foundations.	Quebec	Quebec City, Quebec, Canada	0.34 mi. (549 m.)
Cable-stay	Carries the vertical main-span loads by nearly straight diagonal cables in tension. The towers transfer the cable forces to the foundations through vertical compression. The tensile forces in the cables also put the deck into horizontal compression.	Tatara Ohashi	Shikoku-Honshu, Japan	0.55 mi. (890 m.)

⊙ Nova Online. "Super Bridge," www.pbs.org/wgbh/nova/bridge/build.html
Encyclopaedia Britannica. "The Elements of Bridge Design," www.britannica.com/bcom/eb/article/3/0,5716,127643+2+117290,00.html

THE SCIENCES: *Inventors and Discoverers*

Inventor/Discoverer	Dates	Nationality	Major Invention/Discovery
Acheson, Edward Goodrich	1856–1931	American	carborundum (1891)
Alexanderson, Ernst F. W.	1878–1975	American	high-frequency alternator (1906)
Alvarez, Luis Walter	1911–1988	American	radio distance & direction finder (1945)
Ampere, André-Marie	1775–1836	French	discovered electrodynamics
Appleton, Edward Victor	1892–1965	English	discovered ionospheric reflection of radio waves (1924)
Archimedes	c.287–c.212 BC	Greek	Archimedes screw
Aristarchus	c.310–230 BC	Greek	theory that Earth moves around Sun
Arkwright, Richard	1732–1792	English	water frame for spinning cotton (1769)
Armstrong, Edwin Howard	1890–1954	American	radio frequency-modulation system (1933)
Aspdin, Joseph	1779–1855	English	Portland cement (1824)
Babbage, Charles	1791–1871	English	laid groundwork for computer
Babcock, George Herman	1832–1893	American	co-invented water tube steam boiler (1867) [see Wilcox]
Bacon, Roger	c.1220–c.1292	British	spectacles with corrective lenses
Baekeland, Leo Hendrik	1863–1944	American	plastic Bakelite (1909)
Baird, John Logie	1888–1946	Scottish	first TV picture of moving objects (1926)
Bardeen, John	1908–1991	American	co-invented transistor (1947) [see Brattain; Shockley]
Beckman, Arnold O.	1900–	American	pH meter (1935)
Becquerel, Antoine-Henri	1852–1908	French	radioactivity (1896)
Begun, S. Joseph	1905–1995	American	magnetic recording (1934)
Bell, Alexander Graham	1847–1922	American	telephone (1876)
Bennett, Willard Harrison	1903–1987	American	radio frequency mass spectrometer (1950)
Benz, Carl Friedrich	1844–1929	German	first gas-powered automobile (1885)
Berliner, Emile	1851–1929	American	phonograph record disc (1887)
Bernoulli, Daniel	1700–1782	Swiss	related fluid flow to pressure (1738)
Berthollet, Claude-Louis	1748–1822	French	chlorine bleach (1785)
Bessemer, Henry	1813–1898	British	steel manufacturing (1856)
Binnig, Gerd Karl	1947–	German	co-invented scanning tunneling microscope (1981) [see Rohrer]
Bird, Forrest M.	1921–	American	respirator (1958) & pediatric ventilator (1970)
Birdseye, Clarence	1886–1956	American	frozen foods (1924)
Black, Harold Stephen	1898–1983	American	negative feedback principle
Black, Joseph	1728–1799	Scottish	discovered carbon dioxide (1756)
Blumberg, Baruch Samuel	1925–	American	co-invented vaccine for viral hepatitis (1971) [see Millman]

Inventor/Discoverer	Dates	Nationality	Major Invention/Discovery
Boyle, Robert	1627–1691	English-born Irish	formulated Boyle's law (1662)
Brandt, George	1694–1768	Swedish	discovered cobalt (1730)
Brattain, Walter H.	1902–1987	American	co-invented transistor (1947) [see Bardeen; Shockley]
Brown, Rachel Fuller	1898–1980	American	co-invented antifungal antibiotic (1954) [see Hazen]
Brown, Robert	1773–1858	Scottish	discovered Brownian motion (1827) and nucleus of living cell (1831)
Burbank, Luther	1849–1926	American	developed types of potatoes and peaches and many other crops
Burroughs, William Seward	1855–1898	American	adding machine (1885)
Burton, William Meriam	1865–1954	American	efficient manufacture of gasoline (1913)
Bushnell, David	1742–1824	American	submarine (hand-powered) (1775)
Campbell, Donald L.	1904–	American	co-invented fluid catalytic cracking (1942) [see Martin]
Carlson, Chester F.	1906–1968	American	xerography (1938)
Carothers, Wallace Hume	1896–1937	American	nylon (1934)
Carrel, Alexis	1873–1944	French	method of suturing blood vessels
Carrier, Willis Haviland	1876–1950	American	air conditioning (1911)
Cartwright, Edmund	1743–1823	English	power loom (1785)
Carver, George Washington	c.1861–1943	American	developed peanut, sweet potato, and soybean products
Cavendish, Henry	1731–1810	English	discovered hydrogen (1766)
Celsius, Anders	1701–1744	Swedish	Celsius temperature scale (1742)
Colt, Samuel	1814–1862	American	revolver (1835)
Colton, Frank B.	1923–	American	Enovid—first oral contraceptive (1960)
Coolidge, William D.	1873–1975	American	X-ray tube (1916)
Copernicus, Nicolas	1473–1543	Polish	Sun-centered solar system theory
Cottrell, Frederick G.	1877–1948	American	electrostatic precipitator (1906)
Cray, Seymour R.	1925–1996	American	supercomputer (1976)
Crompton, Samuel	1753–1827	English	spinning mule (1779)
Curie, Marie	1867–1934	French	discovered polonium and radium (1898)
Curie, Pierre	1859–1906	French	discovered piezoelectricity (1880)
da Vinci, Leonardo	1452–1519	Italian	theories about anatomy, mechanics, flying, others
Daimler, Gottlieb	1834–1900	German	gasoline engine (1885)
Damadian, Raymond V.	1936–	American	magnetic resonance imaging scanner (MRI) (1977)

Darby, Abraham	c.1678–1717	English	high-quality iron (1709)
Davy, Humphry	1778–1829	English	discovered potassium and sodium (1806–07), miner's safety lamp (1825)
Dean, Mark	1957–	American	co-inventor of improved computer architecture (1984) [see Moeller]
Deere, John	1804–1886	American	better plow (1838)
Deforest, Lee	1873–1961	American	vacuum tube amplifier (1906)
Dennard, Robert	1932–	American	random access memory (RAM) (1968)
Diesel, Rudolf	1858–1913	German	internal combustion diesel engine (1896)
Djerassi, Carl	1923–	American	oral contraceptives
Dow, Herbert Henry	1866–1930	American	bromine extraction from brine (1889)
Draper, Charles Stark	1901–1987	American	gyroscopic gunsight
Drew, Richard	1886–1956	American	transparent adhesive tape (1930)
Dunlop, John Boyd	1840–1921	English	pneumatic tire (1888)
Eastman, George	1854–1932	American	Kodak camera (1888), transparent film (1889)
Edgerton, Harold E.	1903–1990	American	flash tube (1931), stroboscopic photography
Edison, Thomas Alva	1847–1931	American	electric light bulb (1879); phonograph (1877), 1,091 other patents
Einstein, Albert	1879–1955	German/ American	theories of relativity (special, 1905; general, 1916)
Einthoven, Willem	1860–1927	Dutch	electrocardiograph (1903)
Elion, Gertrude Belle	1918–1999	American	drugs to fight various cancers
Engelbart, Douglas	1925–	American	computer mouse (1963–64)
Ericsson, John	1803–1889	Swedish/ American	screw propeller for ships (1836)
Faggin, Federico	1941–(1969)	American	co-invented computer microprocessor [see Hoff; Mazor]
Fahrenheit, Daniel Gabriel	1686–1736	German	mercury thermometer (1714), Fahrenheit temperature scale
Faraday, Michael	1791–1867	English	electromagnetic induction (1831)
Farnsworth, Philo Taylor	1906–1971	American	electronic television (1927)
Fergason, James	1934–	American	liquid-crystal display (1969)
Fermi, Enrico	1901–1954	American	nuclear reactor (1942)
Fitch, John	1743–1798	American	first American steamboat (1787)
Fleming, Alexander	1881–1955	Scottish	penicillin (1928)
Fleming, John Ambrose	1849–1945	English	two-electrode radio rectifier (1904)
Flemming, Walther	1843–1905	German	discovered mitotic cell division (1879)
Ford, Henry	1863–1947	American	assembly line (1913)
Forrester, Jay Wright	1918–	American	random-access magnetic core memory (1949)

Inventor/Discoverer	Dates	Nationality	Major Invention/Discovery
Franklin, Benjamin	1706–1790	American	Franklin stove (1740)
Fulton, Robert	1765–1815	American	first steamboat to carry people and freight (1807)
Galileo	1564–1642	Italian	experimental scientific method
Galle, Johann Gottfried	1812–1910	German	discovered planet Neptune (1846)
Galvani, Luigi	1737–1798	Italian	discovered bioelectric forces in animal tissues
Geiger, Johannes	1882–1945	German	Geiger counter (1928)
Gerbert of Aurillac	c.945–1003	French	mechanical clock
Germer, Edmund	1901–	German/ American	fluorescent lamp, mercury- vapor lamp
Ginsburg, Charles P.	1920–1992	American	videotape recorder (1956)
Glauber, Johann Rudolf	1604–1668	German/Dutch	many chemical compounds
Goddard, Robert Hutchings	1882–1945	American	liquid-propelled rocket engine (1926)
Goodyear, Charles	1800–1860	American	vulcanization of rubber (1839)
Graham, Thomas	1805–1869	Scottish	described colloids (1860s) and osmosis
Greatbatch, Wilson	1919–	American	cardiac pacemaker
Guericke, Otto von	1602–1686	German	air pump (1650)
Gutenberg, Johannes	c.1400–68	German	printing—developed movable type
Hadley, John	1682–1744	English	reflecting quadrant (1730)
Hall, Charles Martin	1863–1914	American	electrolytic aluminum manufacture (1886)
Hall, Robert N.	1919–	American	magnetron for microwave oven; CD-player laser (1962)
Halley, Edmond	1656–1742	English	theory that comets orbit the Sun
Hargreaves, James	c.1702–1778	English	spinning jenny (1764)
Harrison, John	1693–1776	English	accurate chronometer (1730–63)
Harvey, William	1578–1657	English	blood circulation (1628)
Hazen, Elizabeth Lee	1885–1975	American	co-invented antifungal antibiotic (1954) [see Brown]
Herschel, William	1738–1822	English	discovered planet Uranus (1781)
Hertz, Heinrich	1857–1894	German	discovered radio waves
Hewlett, William R.	1913–	American	audio oscillator
Higonnet, René Alphonse	1902–1983	French	co-invented Lithomat photo-typesetter (1949) [see Moyroud]
Hillier, James	1915–	American	electron microscope (1937)
Hipparchus	c.190– after 127 BC	Greek	first star catalog
Hoe, Richard March	1812–1886	American	rotary printing press (1847)

Hoff, Marcian	1937–	American	co-invented computer microprocessor (1969) [see Faggin; Mazor]
Hollerith, Herman	1860–1929	American	statistics-tabulating machine (1884)
Hopper, Grace	1906–1992	American	improved data processing, computer languages
Houdry, Eugene	1892–1962	French	catalytic converter (1962)
Howe, Elias	1819–1867	American	sewing machine (1846)
Hubble, Edwin Powell	1889–1953	American	discovered external spiral galaxies (1923)
Hunt, Walter	1796–1859	American	safety pin (1849)
Huygens, Christiaan	1629–1695	Dutch	pendulum clock (1656)
Jacquard, Joseph Marie	1752–1834	French	automated loom (1801)
Jarvik, Robert K.	1946–	American	artificial heart
Jenner, Edward	1749–1823	English	smallpox vaccination (1796)
Julian, Percy Lavon	1899–1975	American	cortisone synthesis
Kay, John	1704–1764	English	flying shuttle for weaving (1733)
Keck, Donald B.	1941–	American	co-invented optical fiber (1970) [see Maurer; Schultz]
Kekule von Stradonitz, Friedrich	1829–1896	German	principles of molecular structure
Kettering, Charles Franklin	1876–1958	American	electrical ignition
Kilby, Jack S.	1923–	American	miniaturized integrated circuits (1958)
Koch, Robert	1843–1910	German	discovered several disease-causing bacteria
Kolff, Willem J.	1911–	Dutch	artificial kidney dialysis
Kwolek, Stephanie Louise	1923–	American	para-aramid fibers, Kevlar
Laënnec, René T. H.	1781–1826	French	stethoscope
Land, Edwin Herbert	1909–1991	American	Polaroid camera (1947)
Langmuir, Irving	1881–1957	American	long-life incandescent electric light
Lawrence, Ernest Orlando	1901–1958	American	cyclotron (1930)
Lear, William Powell	1902–1978	American	car radio, car eight-track tape player, aircraft autopilot
Leeuwenhoek, Antonie van	1632–1723	Dutch	discovered protozoa and bacteria (1674)
Leibniz, Gottfried Wilhelm	1646–1716	German	integral and differential calculus (c. 1675)
Lilienthal, Otto	1848–1896	German	glider
Lippershey, Hans	c.1570–1619	Dutch	telescope (1608)
Lumière, Auguste	1862–1954	French	co-invented cinématograph (1895) [see Lumière]
Lumière, Louis	1864–1948	French	co-invented cinématograph (1895) [see Lumière]
Maiman, Theodore Harold	1927–	American	first laser (1960)
Malpighi, Marcello	1628–1694	Italian	capillary blood vessels (1661)
Marconi, Guglielmo	1874–1937	Italian	wireless telegraph/radio (1896)

Inventor/Discoverer	Dates	Nationality	Major Invention/Discovery
Martin, Homer Z.	1910–1993	American	co-invented fluid catalytic cracking (1942) [see Campbell]
Maurer, Robert D.	1924–	American	co-invented optical fiber (1970) [see Keck; Schultz]
Maxim, Hiram Stevens	1840–1916	American/ English	Maxim machine gun (1884)
Mazor, Stanley	1941–	American	co-invented computer microprocessor (1969) [see Faggin; Hoff]
McCormick, Cyrus Hall	1809–1884	American	mechanical reaper (1831)
Meikle, Andrew	1719–1811	Scottish	threshing machine (1788)
Mercator, Gerardus	1512–1594	Flemish	Mercator projection in mapmaking (1569)
Mergenthaler, Ottmar	1854–1899	American	Linotype typesetter (1886)
Mestral, George de	1907–1990	Swiss	Velcro (1955)
Millman, Irving	1923–	American	co-invented vaccine for viral hepatitis (1971) [see Blumberg]
Moeller, Dennis	1950–	American	co-inventor of improved computer architecture (1984) [see Dean]
Monier, Joseph	1823–1906	French	reinforced concrete (1867)
Morse, Samuel F. B.	1791–1872	American	electric telegraph (1832–35), Morse Code (1838)
Moyer, Andrew J.	1899–1959	American	mass production of penicillin
Moyroud, Louis Marius	1914–	French	co-invented Lithomat phototypesetter (1949) [see Higonnet]
Mullis, Kary B.	1944–	American	polymerase chain reaction (1983)
Murphree, Eger V.	1891–1962	American	co-invented fluid catalytic cracking (1942) [see Tyson]
Newcomen, Thomas	1663–1729	English	atmospheric steam engine (1705)
Newton, Isaac	1642–1727	British	laws of motion and gravity, infinitesimal calculus
Nieuwland, Julius Arthur	1878–1936	American	first synthetic rubber—neoprene (1931)
Nobel, Alfred Bernhard	1833–1896	Swedish	dynamite (1867)
Noyce, Robert N.	1927–1990	American	integrated circuit (1959)
Oersted (or Ørsted), Hans	1777–1851	Danish	discovered electromagnetism (1820)
Ohm, Georg Simon	1789–1854	German	related current voltage and resistance (1827)
Olsen, Kenneth H.	1926–	American	magnetic core memory
Otis, Elisha Graves	1811–1861	American	safety elevator (1852)
Otto, Nikolaus August	1832–1891	German	four-stroke internal combustion engine (1861)
Oughtred, William	1574–1660	English	slide rule (c.1632)

Papin, Denis	1647–1712	French/ English	pressure cooker (1679)
Parker, Louis W.	1906–1993	American	television receiver
Parkes, Alexander	1813–1890	English	synthetic plastic (1855), cold vulcanization (1841)
Parsons, Charles Algernon	1854–1931	English	steam turbine (1884)
Parsons, John T.	1913–	American	numerical control of machines
Pascal, Blaise	1623–1662	French	mechanical calculating machine (1642–44), law of pressure, syringe
Pasteur, Louis	1822–1895	French	pasteurization
Plunkett, Roy J.	1910–1994	American	Teflon (1949)
Poulsen, Valdemar	1869–1942	Danish	magnetic recording (1898), generation of radio waves (1903)
Priestley, Joseph	1733–1804	English	independently discovered oxygen (1774)
Ptolemy	act. 127–145	Greek	theory that Earth is center of universe
Pythagoras	c.580–c.500 BC	Greek	theory of numbers
Raman, Chandrasekhara V.	1888–1970	Indian	discovered Raman effect—light diffusion (1928)
Ritter, Johann Wilhelm	1776–1810	German	ultraviolet light (1801)
Roebuck, John	1718–1794	British	manufactured sulfuric acid (1746)
Roemer (or Rømer), Ole	1644–1710	Danish	calculated speed of light (1676)
Roentgen, Wilhelm Conrad	1845–1923	German	X-ray tube (1895)
Rohrer, Heinrich	1933–	Swiss	co-invented scanning tunneling microscope (1981) [see Binnig]
Rubin, Benjamin A.	1917–	American	vaccination needle (1965)
Rutherford, Daniel	1749–1819	Scottish	discovered nitrogen (1772)
Rutherford, Ernest	1871–1937	English	discovered alpha and beta rays in radioactivity
Sarett, Lewis Hastings	1917–1999	American	cortisone (1944)
Savery, Thomas	1650–1715	English	first practical steam engine (1698)
Schawlow, Arthur L.	1921–1999	American	co-invented laser (1958) [see Townes]
Scheele, Carl Wilhelm	1742–1786	Swedish	discovered oxygen (1772)
Schick, Jacob	1877–1937	American	electric razor (1928)
Schultz, Peter C.	1942–	American	co-invented optical fiber (1970) [see Keck; Maurer]
Semon, Waldo Lonsbury	1898–1999	American	vinyl (1926)
Sheehan, John C.	1915–1992	American	synthetic penicillin (1957)
Shockley, William Bradford	1910–1989	American	co-invented transistor (1947) [see Bardeen; Brattain]
Sholes, Christopher L.	1819–1890	American	typewriter (1868)
Siemens, Charles William	1823–1883	German/ English	regenerative open-heart steel furnace (1861)
Sikorsky, Igor	1889–1972	American	helicopter (1909/1939)
Singer, Isaac Merrit	1811–1875	American	domestic sewing machine (1851)

Inventor/Discoverer	Dates	Nationality	Major Invention/Discovery
Sobrero, Ascanio	1812–1888	Italian	discovered nitroglycerine (1846)
Spencer, Percy LeBaron	1894–1970	American	microwave oven (1945)
Sperry, Elmer Ambrose	1860–1930	American	gyroscopic compass (1908) and stabilizers
Stanley, William, Jr.	1858–1916	American	transformer (1885)
Steinmetz, Charles Proteus	1865–1923	American	theory of alternating current
Stibitz, George Robert	1904–1995	American	digital computer (1940)
Sturgeon, William	1783–1850	English	first useful electromagnet (1825)
Szilard, Leo	1898–1964	American	nuclear reactor (1942)
Taylor, Frederick Winslow	1856–1915	American	time and motion studies for industrial management (1881)
Tesla, Nikola	1856–1943	Serbian/ American	induction motor (1883), Tesla coil (1891)
Theiler, Max	1899–1972	American	yellow fever vaccine (1937)
Thompson, John Taliaferro	1860–1940	American	Thompson submachine gun (1920)
Thomson, Joseph John	1856–1940	English	discovered electron (1897)
Timken, Henry	1831–1909	American	tapered roller bearing (1898)
Torricelli, Evangelista	1608–1647	Italian	barometer (1643)
Townes, Charles Hard	1915–	American	co-invented laser (1958) [see Schawlow]
Trevithick, Richard	1771–1833	British	first railroad locomotive (1801)
Tull, Jethro	1674–1741	English	drill for sowing seeds (1701)
Tyson, Charles W.	1914–1978	American	co-invented fluid catalytic cracking (1942) [see Murphree]
Villard, Paul	1860–1934	French	discovered gamma rays in radioactivity (1900)
Volta, Alessandro	1745–1827	Italian	electric battery (1800)
Wang, An	1920–1990	American	magnetic memory core (1948)
Watt, James	1736–1819	Scottish	steam engine separate condenser (1765)
Westinghouse, George	1846–1914	American	air brakes (1869)
Whitney, Eli	1765–1825	American	cotton gin (1793)
Wilcox, Stephen	1830–1893	American	co-invented water tube steam boiler (1867) [see Babcock]
Wright, Orville	1871–1948	American	airplane (1903)
Wright, Wilbur	1867–1912	American	airplane (1903)
Zeppelin, Ferdinand Graf von	1838–1917	German	dirigible airships
Zworykin, Vladimir Kosma	1889–1982	American	cathode ray tube (1929)

⊙ National Inventors Hall of Fame. "Inventure Place," www.invent.org/

Novelists and Short-Story Writers

The following list spans time periods and nationalities. In addition to works whose literary merit has been recognized by scholars, the list highlights best-selling authors and writers who have influenced the development of specific genres.

Name	Dates	Nationality	Selected Works
Abe, Kobo	1924–1993	Japanese	*The Woman in the Dunes* (1962); *The Box Man* (1973)
Achebe, Chinua	1930–	Nigerian	*Things Fall Apart* (1958)
Agee, James	1909–1955	American	*A Death in the Family* (1957)
Amis, Kingsley	1922–1995	English	*Lucky Jim* (1954)
Anderson, Sherwood	1876–1941	American	Stories: *Winesburg, Ohio* (1919)
Asimov, Isaac	1920–1992	Russian-born American	*Foundation and Empire* (1952); Stories: *I, Robot* (1950)
Atwood, Margaret	1939–	Canadian	*The Circle Game* (1966); *The Handmaid's Tale* (1985); *The Blind Assassin* (2000)
Austen, Jane	1775–1817	English	*Sense and Sensibility* (1811); *Pride and Prejudice* (1813); *Emma* (1816); *Persuasion* (1818)
Baldwin, James	1924–1987	American	*Another Country* (1962)
Balzac, Honoré de	1799–1850	French	*The Human Comedy* (1842–53); *Cousin Bette* (1846)
Barth, John	1930–	American	*The Floating Opera* (1956); *The Sot-Weed Factor* (1960); *Giles Goat-Boy* (1966)
Bellow, Saul	1915–	American	*The Adventures of Augie March* (1953); *Seize the Day* (1956); *Herzog* (1964)
Benét, Stephen Vincent	1898–1943	American	Stories: "The King of the Cats" (1929); "The Devil and Daniel Webster" (1937)
Bierce, Ambrose	1842–1914	American	Stories: *An Occurrence at Owl Creek Bridge* (1891); *The Eyes of the Panther* (1891)
Blackwood, Algernon Henry	1869–1951	English	Stories: *The Willows* (1907); *The Wendigo* (1910)
Böll, Heinrich	1917–1985	German	*Group Portrait with Lady* (1971); *The Lost Honor of Katharina Blum* (1974)
Borges, Jorge Luis	1899–1986	Argentine	Stories: *Fictions* (1944); *The Aleph* (1949); *The Maker* (1960)

Novelists and Short-Story Writers *(cont.)*

Name	Dates	Nationality	Selected Works
Bowles, Paul	1910–	American	*The Sheltering Sky* (1948). Stories: "A Distant Episode" (1945); "Pages from Cold Point" (1947)
Bradbury, Ray	1920–	American	*The Martian Chronicles* (1950); *Fahrenheit 451* (1953)
Breton, André	1896–1966	French	*The Communicating Vessels* (1932); *Mad Love* (1937)
Brontë, Charlotte	1816–1855	English	*Jane Eyre* (1847)
Brontë, Emily	1818–1848	English	*Wuthering Heights* (1847)
Bukowski, Charles	1920–1994	American	*Post Office* (1971); *Factotum* (1975); *Hollywood* (1989)
Burgess, Anthony	1917–1993	English	*A Clockwork Orange* (1962)
Burroughs, William S.	1914–1997	American	*Naked Lunch* (1962); *The Soft Machine* (1961)
Cain, James M.	1892–1977	American	*The Postman Always Rings Twice* (1934); *Double Indemnity* (1936)
Caldwell, Erskine	1903–1987	American	*Tobacco Road* (1932); *God's Little Acre* (1933)
Camus, Albert	1913–1960	French	*The Stranger* (1942); *The Plague* (1947)
Capote, Truman	1924–1984	American	*The Grass Harp* (1951); *Breakfast at Tiffany's* (1958). Non-fiction: *In Cold Blood* (1965)
Cather, Willa	1873–1947	American	*O Pioneers!* (1913); *My Ántonia* (1918)
Cervantes Saavedra, Miguel de	1547–1616	Spanish	*Don Quixote* (1605–15)
Chandler, Raymond	1888–1959	American	*The Big Sleep* (1939); *The Lady in the Lake* (1943)
Cheever, John	1912–1982	American	*The Wapshot Chronicle* (1957); *Falconer* (1977)
Christie, Agatha	1891–1976	English	*Murder on the Orient Express* (1934); *And Then There Were None* (1940)
Clarke, Arthur C.	1917–	English	*2001: A Space Odyssey* (1968)
Clavell, James	1924–1994	Australian-born American	*Tai-Pan* (1966);) *Shogun* (1975
Cocteau, Jean	1889–1963	French	*Thomas the Imposter* (1923); *Les Enfants terribles* (1929)
Colette [Sidonie-Gabrielle Colette]	1873–1954	French	*Gigi* (1944)
Conrad, Joseph	1857–1924	English	*Lord Jim* (1900); *Heart of Darkness* (1902)
Cooper, James Fenimore	1789–1851	American	*The Last of the Mohicans* (1826); *The Deerslayer* (1841)

Crane, Stephen	1871–1900	American	*The Red Badge of Courage* (1895)
Crichton, [John] Michael	1942–	American	*The Andromeda Strain* (1969); *Jurassic Park* (1990)
Davies, Robertson	1913–1995	Canadian	*What's Bred in the Bone* (1985)
Defoe, Daniel	1660–1731	English	*Robinson Crusoe* (1719); *Moll Flanders* (1722)
Dickens, Charles	1812–1870	English	*The Pickwick Papers* (1836–37); *A Christmas Carol* (1843); *A Tale of Two Cities* (1859); *Great Expectations* (1861)
Dinesen, Isak [Karen Blixen]	1885–1962	Danish	Stories: *Seven Gothic Tales* (1934); *Winter's Tales* (1942); Memoir: *Out of Africa* (1937)
Doctorow, E. L.	1931–	American	*Ragtime* (1975); *Billy Bathgate* (1989)
Dos Passos, John	1896–1970	American	*U.S.A.* (trilogy; 1930–36)
Dostoyevsky, Fyodor Mikhaylovich	1821–1881	Russian	*Crime and Punishment* (1866); *The Idiot* (1869); *The Brothers Karamazov* (1880)
Doyle, Sir Arthur Conan	1859–1930	English	*A Study in Scarlet* (1887); *The Adventures of Sherlock Holmes* (1892)
Dreiser, Theodore	1871–1945	American	*Sister Carrie* (1900); *An American Tragedy* (1925)
Du Maurier, Daphne	1907–1989	English	*Rebecca* (1938)
Dumas, Alexandre père	1802–1870	French	*The Count of Monte Cristo* (1844–45); *The Three Musketeers* (1844)
Eco, Umberto	1932–	Italian	*The Name of the Rose* (1980); *Foucault's Pendulum* (1989)
Eliot, George [Mary Ann Evans]	1819–1880	English	*Silas Marner* (1861); *Middlemarch* (1871–72)
Ellison, Harlan	1934–	American	Stories: "Repent, Harlequin!" Said the Ticktockman (1965); *A Boy and His Dog* (1969)
Ellison, Ralph	1914–1994	American	*Invisible Man* (1952)
Faulkner, William	1897–1962	American	*As I Lay Dying* (1930); *Sanctuary* (1931); *Light in August* (1932); *Absalom, Absalom!* (1936)
Fielding, Henry	1707–1754	English	*Tom Jones* (1749)
Finney, Jack	1911–1995	American	*Invasion of the Body Snatchers* (1955)
Fitzgerald, F. Scott	1896–1940	American	*The Great Gatsby* (1925); *Tender Is the Night* (1934)
Flaubert, Gustave	1821–1880	French	*Madame Bovary* (1857); *A Sentimental Education* (1869)
Ford, Ford Madox	1873–1939	English	*The Good Soldier* (1915)
Forster, E. M.	1879–1970	English	*Howard's End* (1910); *A Passage to India* (1924)

Name	Dates	Nationality	Selected Works
Fowles, John	1926–	English	*The Collector* (1963); *The French Lieutenant's Woman* (1969)
Fuentes, Carlos	1928–	Mexican	*The Old Gringo* (1986)
Galsworthy, John	1867–1933	English	*The Forsyte Saga* (1922)
García Márquez, Gabriel	1928–	Colombian	*One Hundred Years of Solitude* (1967); *Love in the Time of Cholera* (1988)
Gide, André	1868–1951	French	*The Immoralist* (1902); *The Counterfeiters* (1926)
Gogol, Nikolai	1809–1852	Russian	*Dead Souls* (1842). Stories: "Diary of a Madman" (1935); "The Overcoat" (1842)
Golding, William	1911–1993	English	*Lord of the Flies* (1954)
Goldsmith, Oliver	1730–1774	English	*The Vicar of Wakefield* (1766)
Gordimer, Nadine	1923–	South African	*The Lying Days* (1953); *The Conversationist* (1974); *The House Gun* (1998)
Gorky, Maxim	1868–1936	Russian	*Mother* (1906). Stories: "Chelkash" (1895); "Twenty-Six Men and a Girl" (1899)
Grass, Günther	1927–	German	*The Tin Drum* (1959)
Graves, Robert	1895–1985	English	*I, Claudius* (1934)
Greene, Graham	1904–1991	English	*The End of the Affair* (1951); *The Quiet American* (1957); *Our Man in Havana* (1958)
Grisham, John	1955–	American	*The Firm* (1991); *The Client* (1993)
Hammett, [Samuel] Dashiell	1894–1961	American	*The Maltese Falcon* (1930); *The Glass Key* (1931); *The Thin Man* (1934)
Hardy, Thomas	1840–1928	English	*Far from the Madding Crowd* (1874); *The Return of the Native* (1878); *Tess of the D'Urbevilles* (1891); *Jude the Obscure* (1896)
Hawthorne, Nathaniel	1804–1864	American	*The Scarlet Letter* (1850); *The House of the Seven Gables* (1851); *The Blithedale Romance* (1852)
Heller, Joseph	1923–2000	American	*Catch-22* (1961)
Hemingway, Ernest	1899–1961	American	*The Sun Also Rises* (1926); *A Farewell to Arms* (1929); *For Whom the Bell Tolls* (1940); *The Old Man and the Sea* (1952).
Henry, O. [William Sydney Porter]	1862–1910	American	Stories: "The Gift of the Magi" (1905); "The Ransom of Red Chief" (1910)

Hesse, Hermann	1877–1962	German	*Siddhartha* (1922); *Steppenwolf* (1927)
Highsmith, Patricia	1921–1995	American	*Strangers on a Train* (1949); *The Talented Mr. Ripley* (1955)
Hilton, James	1900–1954	English-born American	*Goodbye, Mr. Chips* (1934)
Himes, Chester	1909–1984	American	*If He Hollers Let Him Go* (1945); *Cotton Comes to Harlem* (1965)
Howells, William Dean	1837–1920	American	*The Rise of Silas Lapham* (1885)
Hugo, Victor Marie	1802–1885	French	*The Hunchback of Notre Dame* (1831); *Les Misérables* (1862)
Hurston, Zora Neale	1903–1960	American	*Their Eyes Were Watching God* (1937)
Huxley, Aldous	1894–1963	English	*Crome Yellow* (1921); *Antic Hay* (1923); *Brave New World* (1932)
Irving, John	1942–	American	*The World According to Garp* (1978); *A Prayer for Owen Meany* (1989)
Irving, Washington	1783–1859	American	Stories: *The Sketch Book* (1819–20)
James, Henry	1843–1916	American	*The American* (1877); *Portrait of a Lady* (1881); *The Ambassadors* (1903)
Jong, Erica	1942–	American	*Fear of Flying* (1973)
Joyce, James	1882–1941	Irish	*Portrait of the Artist as a Young Man* (1916); *Ulysses* (1922); Stories: *Dubliners* (1914)
Kafka, Franz	1883–1924	German	*Metamorphosis* (1915); *Amerika* (1927)
Keneally, Thomas	1935–	Australian	*The Chant of Jimmie Blacksmith* (1972); *Schindler's List* (1982)
Kerouac, Jack	1922–1969	American	*On the Road* (1957)
Kesey, Ken	1935–	American	*One Flew Over the Cuckoo's Nest* (1962)
King, Stephen	1947–	American	*Carrie* (1974); *The Shining* (1977); *The Tommyknockers* (1987)
Knowles, John	1926–	American	*A Separate Peace* (1959)
Krantz, Judith	1927–	American	*Scruples* (1978); *Princess Daisy* (1980); *I'll Take Manhattan* (1986)
L'Amour, Louis	1908–1988	American	*How the West Was Won* (1963)
Laclos, Pierre Choderlos de	1741–1803	French	*Les Liaisons dangereuses* (1782)
Lampedusa, Tomasi di	1896–1957	Italian	*The Leopard* (1958)
Lawrence, D. H.	1885–1930	English	*Sons and Lovers* (1913); *Lady Chatterly's Lover* (1928)

Novelists and Short-Story Writers *(cont.)*

Name	Dates	Nationality	Selected Works
Le Carré, John	1931–	English	*The Spy Who Came in from the Cold* (1963); *Tinker, Tailor, Soldier, Spy* (1974)
Le Guin, Ursula K.	1929–	American	*The Left Hand of Darkness* (1969); *The Dispossessed* (1974)
Lee, Harper	1926–	American	*To Kill a Mockingbird* (1960)
Lessing, Doris	1919–	English	*Children of Violence* (5 vols.; 1952–69); *The Golden Notebook* (1962)
Levin, Ira	1929–	American	*A Kiss Before Dying* (1953); *Rosemary's Baby* (1967)
Lewis, [Harry] Sinclair Lewis	1885–1951	American	*Babbitt* (1922); *Arrowsmith* (1925); *Elmer Gantry* (1927)
London, Jack	1876–1916	American	*The Call of the Wild* (1903); *White Fang* (1906)
Mahfouz, Naguib	1911–	Egyptian	*New Cairo* (1946); *The Palace of Desire* (1957); *Wedding Song* (1987)
Mailer, Norman	1923–	American	*The Naked and the Dead* (1948); *The Executioner's Song* (1979)
Malamud, Bernard	1914–1986	American	*The Natural* (1952); *The Assistant* (1957)
Mann, Thomas	1875–1955	German	*Buddenbrooks* (1900); *The Magic Mountain* (1924); *Doctor Faustus* (1947)
Mansfield, Katherine	1888–1923	New Zealander	Stories: "Prelude" (1918); "The Garden Party" (1922)
Maugham, William Somerset	1874–1965	English	*The Moon and Sixpence* (1916); *The Razor's Edge* (1944)
Maupin, Armistead	1944–	American	*Tales of the City* (1978)
McCarthy, Mary	1912–1989	American	*The Group* (1963). Autobiography: *Memories of a Catholic Girlhood* (1957)
McCullers, Carson	1917–1967	American	*The Heart is a Lonely Hunter* (1940); *The Ballad of the Sad Café* (1951)
McCullough, Colleen	1937–	Australian	*The Thorn Birds* (1977)
Melville, Herman	1819–1891	American	*Typee* (1846); *Moby Dick* (1851). Stories: "Bartleby the Scrivener" (1853)
Michener, James	1907–1997	American	*Hawaii* (1959); *Chesapeake* (1978)
Miller, Henry	1891–1980	American	*Tropic of Cancer* (1934); *Tropic of Capricorn* (1939)

Mishima, Yukio	1925–1970	Japanese	*The Sailor Who Fell From Grace with the Sea* (1963)
Mitchell, Joseph	1908–1996	American	Stories: *Up in the Old Hotel* (1992)
Mitchell, Margaret	1900–1949	American	*Gone with the Wind* (1936)
Morrison, Toni	1931–	American	*Song of Solomon* (1977); *Beloved* (1987); *Jazz* (1992)
Murasaki, Lady Shikibu	c.978–c.1014	Japanese	*The Tale of Genji* (c.1010)
Murdoch, Iris	1919–1999	English	*A Severed Head* (1961); *The Good Apprentice* (1985)
Nabokov, Vladimir Vladimirovich	1889–1977	Russian-born American	*Lolita* (1955); *Pnin* (1957); *Pale Fire* (1962)
Naipaul, V. S.	1932–	Trinidadian	*A Bend in the River* (1979); *Way in the World* (1994)
Natsume, Soseki	1867–1916	Japanese	*I Am a Cat* (1905–6); *The Wayfayer* (1912-13)
Nin, Anaïs	1903–1977	French-born American	*Cities of the Interior* (5 vols.; 1959); *Seduction of the Minotaur* (1961)
Noma, Hiroshi	1915–1991	Japanese	*Zone of Emptiness* (1952)
O'Connor, [Mary] Flannery	1925–1964	American	*Wise Blood* (1949); *The Violent Bear It Away* (1955)
O'Hara, John	1905–1970	American	*Appointment in Samarra* (1934); *Butterfield 8* (1935)
Oates, Joyce Carol	1938–	American	*Do With Me What You Will* (1973); *Bellefleur* (1980)
Orwell, George	1903–1950	English	*Animal Farm* (1945); *1984* (1949)
Page, Thomas Nelson	1853–1922	American	*In Ole Virgina, Marse Chan, and Other Stories* (1887)
Parker, Dorothy	1893–1967	American	Stories: "Lady with a Lamp" (1932); "The Waltz" (1933)
Pasternak, Boris Leonidovich	1890–1960	Russian	*Doctor Zhivago* (1957)
Paton, Alan Stewart	1903–1988	South African	*Cry the Beloved Country* (1948)
Petronius, Gaius	d. AD 66	Roman	*The Satyricon* (c.50)
Poe, Edgar Allan	1809–1849	American	Stories: "The Fall of the House of Usher" (1839); "The Tell-Tale Heart" (1843); "The Pit and the Pendulum" (1843); "The Cask of Amontillado" (1846)
Porter, Katherine Anne	1890–1980	American	*Ship of Fools* (1962). Stories: "Pale Horse, Pale Rider" (1939); "Noon Wine" (1939)
Potok, Chaim	1929–	American	*The Chosen* (1967); *The Promise* (1969)
Proust, Marcel	1871–1922	French	*Remembrance of Things Past* (7 vols.; 1913–27)
Puig, Manuel	1932–1990	Argentinian	*The Kiss of the Spider Woman* (1976)
Pushkin, Alexander Sergeevich	1789–1837	Russian	*Eugene Onegin* (1831); *The Captain's Daughter* (1836)

Name	Dates	Nationality	Selected Works
Rabelais, François	c.1494–1553	French	*Gargantua and Pantagruel* (1532–64)
Rand, Ayn	1905–1982	Russian-born American	*The Fountainhead* (1943); *Atlas Shrugged* (1957)
Réage, Pauline	1908–1998	French	*The Story of O* (1955)
Remarque, Erich Maria	1898–1970	German	*All Quiet on the Western Front* (1929)
Rice, Anne	1941–	American	*Interview with the Vampire* (1976); *Cry to Heaven* (1982); *The Vampire Lestat* (1985)
Robbins, Tom	1936–	American	*Another Roadside Attraction* (1971); *Even Cowgirls Get the Blues* (1976)
Roth, Philip	1933–	American	*Goodbye, Columbus* (1959); *Portnoy's Complaint* (1969); *The Human Stain* (2000)
Rushdie, Salman	1947–	Indian	*Midnight's Children* (1980); *The Satanic Verses* (1989)
Sagan, Francoise	1935–	French	*Bonjour tristesse* (1954)
Saki [Hector Hugh Munro]	1870–1916	Scottish	*The Unbearable Bassington* (1912). Stories: "Tobermory" (1911); "The Open Window" (1914)
Salinger, J. D.	1919–	American	*The Catcher in the Rye* (1951); *Franny and Zooey* (1961)
Sand, George [Amandine Lucie Aurore Dupin]	1804–1876	French	*The Devil's Pool* (1846); *The Country Waif* (1848)
Sandburg, Carl	1878–1967	American	*Remembrance Rock* (1948); Stories: *Rootabaga Stories* (1922)
Saroyan, William	1908–1981	American	*The Human Comedy* (1943). Stories: *The Daring Young Man on the Flying Trapeze* (1934)
Sartre, Jean-Paul	1905–1980	French	*Nausea* (1938)
Scott, Sir Walter	1771–1832	Scottish	*Rob Roy* (1817); *Ivanhoe* (1819)
Shelley, Mary Wollstonecraft	1791–1851	English	*Frankenstein* (1818)
Shute, Nevil	1899–1960	Australian	*A Town Like Alice* (1950); *On the Beach* (1957)
Sinclair, Upton	1878–1968	American	*The Jungle* (1906)
Singer, Isaac Bashevis	1904–1991	Polish-born American	*The Magician of Lublin* (1960); *Enemies, a Love Story* (1972). Stories: "The Spinoza of Market Street" (1944); "Gimpel the Fool" (1945)
Smiley, Jane	1949–	American	*A Thousand Acres* (1991); *Horse Heaven* (2000)
Solzhenitsyn, Aleksandr I.	1918–	Russian	*One Day in the Life of Ivan Denisovich* (1962); *The Cancer Ward* (1968)

Southern, Terry	1926–1995	American	*Candy* (1958); *Blue Movie* (1970)
Spark, Muriel	1918–	Scottish-born English	*Memento Mori* (1959); *The Girls of Slender Means* (1963)
Stein, Gertrude	1874–1946	American	*The Making of Americans* (1906–11). Autobiography: *The Autobiography of Alice B. Toklas* (1933)
Steinbeck, John Ernst	1902–1968	American	*The Grapes of Wrath* (1939); *Of Mice and Men* (1937); *Cannery Row* (1945)
Stendhal [Marie-Henri Beyle]	1788–1842	French	*The Charterhouse of Parma* (1839)
Sterne, Laurence	1713–1768	Irish-born English	*Tristam Shandy* (1759–67)
Stevenson, Robert Louis	1850–1894	Scottish	*Treasure Island* (1883); *The Strange Case of Dr. Jekyll and Mr. Hyde* (1886)
Stoker, Bram	1847–1912	Irish	*Dracula* (1897)
Stowe, Harriet Beecher	1811–1896	American	*Uncle Tom's Cabin* (1852)
Styron, William	1925–	American	*The Confessions of Nat Turner* (1967); *Sophie's Choice* (1979)
Swift, Jonathan	1667–1745	Irish	*Gulliver's Travels* (1726)
Tanizaki, Jun'ichiro	1886–1965	Japanese	*The Secret History of the Lord Musashi* (1935); *Seven Japanese Tales* (1963)
Thackeray, William Makepeace	1811–1863	English	*Barry Lyndon* (1844); *Vanity Fair* (1847–48)
Theroux, Paul	1941–	American	*The Family Arsenal* (1976); *The Mosquito Coast* (1981)
Thurber, James	1894–1961	American	Story: "The Secret Life of Walter Mitty" (1939)
Tolstoy, Leo	1828–1910	Russian	*War and Peace* (1863–69); *Anna Karenina* (1875–77). Play: *Redemption* (1911)
Trollope, Anthony	1815–1882	English	*Barchester Towers* (1857); *He Knew He Was Right* (1869)
Ts'ao Hsueh-ch'in	c.1715–1763	Chinese	*Dream of the Red Chamber* (c.1763)
Turgenev, Ivan	1818–1883	Russian	*Fathers and Sons* (1862); Stories: "The Diary of a Superfluous Man" (1850)
Twain, Mark [Samuel Clemens]	1835–1910	American	*Tom Sawyer* (1876); *Huckleberry Finn* (1884)
Updike, John	1932–	American	*Rabbit, Run* (1960); *Gertrude and Claudius* (2000)
Vidal, Gore	1925–	American	*The City and the Pillar* (1948); *Burr* (1974)
Voltaire [Francois-Marie Arouet]	1694–1778	French	*Candide* (1759)
Vonnegut, Kurt, Jr.	1922–	American	*Player Piano* (1952); *Slaughterhouse Five* (1969)

Novelists and Short-Story Writers *(cont.)*

Name	Dates	Nationality	Selected Works
Walker, Alice	1944–	American	*The Color Purple* (1982)
Warren, Robert Penn	1905–1989	American	*All the King's Men* (1946); *World Enough and Time* (1950)
Waugh, Evelyn	1903–1966	English	*Decline and Fall* (1928); *A Handful of Dust* (1934); *Brideshead Revisited* (1945)
Weldon, Faye	1933–	English	*The Life and Loves of a She-Devil* (1983)
Wells, H. G.	1866–1946	English	*The Invisible Man* (1897); *The War of the Worlds* (1898)
Welty, Eudora	1909–	American	*Delta Wedding* (1946); *The Optimist's Daughter* (1972)
West, Nathaniel	1903–1940	American	*Miss Lonelyhearts* (1933); *The Day of the Locust* (1939)
Wharton, Edith	1862–1937	American	*Ethan Frome* (1911); *The Age of Innocence* (1920)
Wodehouse, P. G.	1881–1975	English-born American	*My Man Jeeves* (1919)
Wolfe, Thomas	1900–1938	American	*Look Homeward, Angel* (1929)
Wolfe, Tom	1930–	American	*The Bonfire of the Vanities* (1987)
Woolf, Virginia	1882–1941	English	*Mrs. Dalloway* (1925); *To the Lighthouse* (1927)
Wouk, Herman	1915–	American	*The Caine Mutiny* (1951)
Wright, Richard	1908–1960	American	*Native Son* (1940)
Yourcenar, Marguerite	1903–1987	French-born American	*The Memoirs of Hadrian* (1951)

⊙ Brown, Susan Windisch, ed. *Contemporary Novelists*, 6th ed. Detroit: St. James, 1996.
  Goring, Rosemary, ed. *Larousse Dictionary of Writers*. Edinburgh: Larousse, 1994.
  Riggs, Thomas, ed. *Reference Guide to Short Fiction*, 2nd. ed. Detroit: St. James, 1999.
  Vinson, James, and Daniel Kirkpatrick, eds. *Great Foreign Language Writers*. New York: St. Martin's, 1984.

British Poets Laureate

The first English poet laureate, Ben Jonson, was appointed in 1616, but the royal office did not become official until 1668. English poet laureates are appointed for life.

Laureateship	Poet	Dates	Major Works
1668	John Dryden	1631–1700	"Absalom and Achitophel" (1681); "Mac Flecknoe" (1682)
1689	Thomas Shadwell	1643?–1692	The Virtuoso (1676); *The Squire of Alsatia* (1688)
1692	Nahum Tate	1652–1715	"Absalom and Achitophel" (2nd part 1681); "Dido and Aeneas" (1689)
1715	Nicholas Rowe	1674–1718	*Tamberlane* (1701); *The Fair Penitent* (1703)

1718	Laurence Eusden	1688–1730	[unknown]
1730	Colley Cibber	1671–1757	*She Would and She Would Not* (1702); *The Careless Husband* (1704)
1757	William Whitehead	1715–1785	"The Danger of Writing Verse" (1741); "A Charge to the Poets" (1762)
1785	Thomas Warton	1728–1790	[unknown]
1790	Henry James Pye	1745–1813	[unknown]
1813	Robert Southey	1774–1843	"The Curse of Kehama" (1810); "Roderick: The Last of the Goths" (1814)
1843	William Wordsworth	1770–1850	"Tintern Abbey" (1798); "Ode: Intimations of Immortality" (1807)
1850	Alfred, Lord Tennyson	1809–1892	*Maud and Other Poems* (1855); *Idylls of the King* (1859–85)
1896	Alfred Austin	1835–1913	[unknown]
1913	Robert Bridges	1844–1930	*The Growth of Love* (1890); *Poetical Works* (1898–1905)
1930	John Masefield	1878–1967	*Salt-Water Ballads* (1902); *Collected Poems* (1923)
1968	Cecil Day-Lewis	1904–1972	*The Magnetic Mountain* (1933); *Poems in Wartime* (1940)
1972	Sir John Betjeman	1906–1984	*Collected Poems* (1962); *A Nip in the Air* (1972)
1984	Ted Hughes	1930–1998	*Crow* (1970); *River* (1983)
1998	Andrew Motion	1952–	*The Pleasure Steamers* (1978); *Dangerous Play* (1984)

American Poets Laureate

The official title of this honor is Poet Laureate Consultant in Poetry to the Library of Congress. The Consultant position has been awarded since 1937, but the title of Poet Laureate was not created until 1986. The position is awarded annually by the Library of Congress.

Laureateship	Poet	Dates	Major Works
1986–87	Robert Penn Warren	1905–1989	*Promises: Poems, 1954–56*; *Now and Then: Poems, 1976–1978*
1987–88	Richard Wilbur	1921–	*Poems* (1957); *New and Collected Poems* (1988)
1988–90	Howard Nemerov	1920–1991	*Guide to the Ruins* (1950); *Collected Poems* (1977)
1990–91	Mark Strand	1934–	*Selected Poems* (1980); *Blizzard of One* (1998)
1991–92	Joseph Brodsky	1940–1996	*A Part of Speech* (1980); *Watermark* (1993)
1992–93	Mona Van Duyn	1921–	*To See, To Take* (1970); *Near Changes* (1990)
1993–95	Rita Dove	1952–	*The Yellow House on the Corner* (1980); *Museum* (1983)
1995–97	Robert Haas	1941–	*Praise* (1980); *Human Wishes* (1990)
1997–2000	Robert Pinsky	1940–	*Sadness and Happiness* (1975); *An Explanation of America* (1979)
2000–2001	Stanley Kunitz	1905–	*Selected Poems* (1958); *The Poems of Stanley Kunitz, 1928–1978*
2001–2002	Billy Collins	1941–	*Questions About Angels* (1991); *The Art of Drowning* (1995)

Playwrights

The following list spans time periods and nationalities. In addition to recognized masters, the list features important theatrical innovators and the authors of popular plays.

Name	Dates	Nationality	Major Works
Aeschylus	525–456 BC	Greek	*The Oresteia* (458 BC)
Albee, Edward	1928–	American	*The Zoo Story* (1959); *Who's Afraid of Virginia Woolf?* (1962)
Aristophanes	c.448– c.380 BC	Greek	*The Birds* (414 BC); *Lysistrata* (411 BC); *The Frogs* (405 BC)
Beckett, Samuel	1906–1989	Irish-born French	*Waiting for Godot* (1953); *Endgame* (1957); *Happy Days* (1961)
Brecht, Bertolt	1898–1956	German	*Mother Courage* (1938–39); *The Good Woman of Setzuan* (1938–41); *The Caucasian Chalk Circle* (1943–45); *The Threepenny Opera* (1928); *The Rise and Fall of the City of Mahagonny* (1930)
Büchner, Georg	1813–1837	German	*Danton's Death* (1835); *Wozzeck* (1837)
Calderón de la Barca, Pedro	1600–1681	Spanish	*Life is a Dream* (1635)
Chekhov, Anton Pavlovich	1860–1904	Russian	*The Seagull* (1896); *Three Sisters* (1900); *The Cherry Orchard* (1904)
Corneille, Pierre	1606–1684	French	*Médée* (1635); *Le Cid* (1637)
Coward, Sir Noel	1899–1973	English	*Private Lives* (1930); *Blithe Spirit* (1941); *Present Laughter* (1942)
Dryden, John	1631–1700	English	*All for Love* (1678); *Marriage à la Mode* (1672)
Euripides	484–406 BC	Greek	*Medea* (431 BC); *Hippolytus* (428 BC); *Electra* (413 BC); *The Bacchae* (posthumous)
Fugard, Athol	1932–	South African	*The Blood Knot* (1963); "Master Harold" and the Boys (1982)
García Lorca, Federico	1898–1936	Spanish	*Blood Wedding* (1933); *Yerma* (1934); *The House of Bernarda Alba* (posthumous; 1945)

Giraudoux, Jean	1882–1944	French	*Amphitryon '38* (1939); *Ondine* (1939); *The Madwoman of Chaillot* (1945)
Hellman, Lillian	1905–1984	American	*The Children's Hour* (1934); *The Little Foxes* (1939); *Watch on the Rhine* (1941)
Henley, Beth	1952–	American	*Crimes of the Heart* (1982)
Ibsen, Henrik	1828–1906	Norwegian	*Peer Gynt* (1867); *A Doll's House* (1878–79); *Ghosts* (1881); *The Wild Duck* (1884); *Hedda Gabler* (1890)
Inge, William	1913–1973	American	*Come Back, Little Sheba* (1950); *Picnic* (1953); *The Dark at the Top of the Stairs* (1957)
Ionesco, Eugène	1912–1994	Romanian-born French	*The Bald Soprano* (1948); *The Lesson* (1951); *Rhinoceros* (1958)
Jonson, Ben	1572–1637	English	*Volpone* (1605–06); *The Alchemist* (1610); *Bartholomew Fair* (1614)
Kaiser, Georg	1878–1945	German	*The Burghers of Calais* (1914)
Kaufman, George S.	1889–1961	American	*Dinner at Eight* (1932); *Stage Door* (1936); *You Can't Take it With You* (1936)
Kushner, Tony	1957–	American	*Angels in America, Parts One and Two* (1992, 1993)
Mamet, David	1947–	American	*American Buffalo* (1977); *Speed-the-Plow* (1987)
Marlowe, Christopher	1564–1593	English	*The Tragical History of Doctor Faustus* (1604); *The Jew of Malta* (1633)
McNally, Terrence	1939–	American	*And Things That Go Bump in the Night* (1965); *Love! Valour! Compassion!* (1994); *Master Class* (1996)
Miller, Arthur	1915–	American	*Death of a Salesman* (1949); *The Crucible* (1953)
Molière [Jean Baptiste Poquelin]	1622–1673	French	*The School for Wives* (1662); *Tartuffe* (1664); *Le Misanthrope* (1666)
Molnár, Ferenc	1878–1952	Hungarian	*Liliom* (1909); *The Guardsman* (1910); *The Swan* (1920)

Name	Dates	Nationality	Major Works
O'Casey, Sean	1880–1964	Irish	*Juno and the Paycock* (1924); *The Plough and the Stars* (1926)
O'Neill, Eugene	1888–1953	American	*Anna Christie* (1921); *Mourning Becomes Electra* (1931); *The Iceman Cometh* (1946); *Long Day's Journey into Night* (1956)
Odets, Clifford	1906–1963	American	*Waiting for Lefty* (1935); *Awake and Sing!* (1935)
Osborne, John	1929–1994	English	*The Entertainer* (1957); *Luther* (1961)
Pinter, Harold	1930–	English	*The Birthday Party* (1958); *The Caretaker* (1960); *The Homecoming* (1965)
Pirandello, Luigi	1867–1936	Italian	*Six Characters in Search of an Author* (1921); *Henry IV* (1922)
Plautus	c.251 BC– c.184 BC	Roman	*Pseudolus* (192 BC); *The Menaechmi* (?); *Miles Gloriosus* (?)
Rabe, David	1940–	American	*The Basic Training of Pavlo Hummel* (1969); *Streamers* (1975)
Racine, Jean	1639–1699	French	*Andromaque* (1667); *Bérénice* (1671); *Phèdre* (1677)
Rostand, Edmond	1868–1918	French	*Cyrano de Bergerac* (1898)
Seneca, Lucius Annaeus	c.4 BC– AD 65	Roman	*Medea; Phaedra; Agamemnon* (all undated)
Shakespeare, William	1564–1616	English	*Romeo and Juliet* (1594–95); *A Midsummer's Night Dream* (1595–96); *Hamlet* (1600–1); *Othello* (1604–5); *King Lear* (1605–6); *Macbeth* (1605–6)
Shaw, George Bernard	1856–1950	English	*Arms and the Man* (1894); *Mrs. Warren's Profession* (1893); *Candida* (1895); *Caesar and Cleopatra* (1898); *Man and Superman* (1901–3); *Major Barbara* (1905); *Pygmalion* (1913); *Saint Joan* (1923)

Sheridan, Richard Brinsley	1751–1816	Anglo-Irish	*The Rivals* (1775); *The School for Scandal* (1777); *The Critic* (1779)
Simon, Neil	1927–	American	*Barefoot in the Park* (1963); *The Odd Couple* (1965); *Brighton Beach Memoirs* (1983); *Lost in Yonkers* (1991)
Sophocles	496–406 BC	Greek	*Antigone* (c. 442 BC); *Oedipus Rex* (c. 425 BC); *Oedipus at Colonus* (406 BC)
Soyinka, Wole	1934–	Nigerian	*Three Plays* (1963); *The Road* (1965); *The Forest of a Thousand Daemons* (1968); *Ake* (1981)
Stoppard, Tom	1932–	English	*Rosencrantz and Guildenstern Are Dead* (1967); *The Real Inspector Hound* (1968)
Strindberg, August	1849–1912	Swedish	*The Father* (1887); *Miss Julie* (1888); *A Dream Play* (1902)
Synge, J. M.	1871–1909	Irish	*Riders to the Sea* (1904); *The Playboy of the Western World* (1908)
Vega, Lope de	1562–1635	Spanish	*The Peasant in His Nook* (1611–15); *The King's Best Magistrate* (1620–23)
Wasserstein, Wendy	1950–	American	*The Heidi Chronicles* (1989); *The Sisters Rosenzweig* (1993)
Wilde, Oscar	1854–1900	Irish	*Salome* (1892); *An Ideal Husband* (1895); *The Importance of Being Earnest* (1895)
Wilder, Thornton	1897–1975	American	*Our Town* (1938); *The Skin of Our Teeth* (1942); *The Matchmaker* (1954)
Williams, Tennessee	1911–1983	American	*The Glass Menagerie* (1945); *A Streetcar Named Desire* (1947); *Cat on a Hot Tin Roof* (1955)
Wilson, August	1945–	American	*Ma Rainey's Black Bottom* (1985); *Fences* (1986); *The Piano Lesson* (1990)
Wilson, Lanford	1937–	American	*The Hot L Baltimore* (1973); *Talley's Folly* (1980)

⊙ Billington, Michael, ed. *Contemporary Dramatists,* 5th ed. Detroit: Gale Research, 1993.
Hartnoll, Phyllis, ed. *The Oxford Companion to the Theatre,* 4th ed. Oxford: Oxford University Press, 1993.
Hawkins, Mark-Dady, ed. *International Dictionary of Theatre,* 3 vols. Chicago: St. James, 1992.

With the exception of several foreign language classics, this list emphasizes writers in English and includes award-quality children's and young adult works as well as popular favorites.

Children's and Young Adult Authors

Name	Dates	Nationality	Major Works
Alcott, Louisa May	1832–1888	American	*Little Women* (1868–69)
Anderson, Hans Christian	1805–1875	Danish	*Fairy Tales* (1858–72)
Atwater, Richard and Florence	1892–1948; 1896–1979	Both American	*Mr. Popper's Penguins* (1938)
Bagnold, Enid	1889–1981	English	*National Velvet* (1935)
Baum, Frank [Lyman Baum]	1856–1919	American	*The Wonderful Wizard of Oz* (1900)
Bemelmans, Ludwig	1898–1962	Austrian-born American	*Madeline* (1939)
Blume, Judy	1938–	American	*Are You There God? It's Me, Margaret* (1970); *Super Fudge* (1980)
Bond, Michael	1926–	English	*A Bear Called Paddington* (1958)
Brown, Margaret Wise	1910–1952	American	*Goodnight, Moon* (1947)
Burnett, Frances (Eliza) Hodgson	1849–1924	American	*The Secret Garden* (1911)
Burnford, Sheila	1918–1984	Scottish-born Canadian	*The Incredible Journey* (1961)
Burton, Virginia Lee	1909–1968	American	*Mike Mulligan and His Steam Shovel* (1939)
Carle, Eric	1929–	American	*The Very Hungry Caterpillar* (1969)
Cleary, Beverly	1916–	American	*Henry Huggins* (1950); *Ramona the Pest* (1968)
Dahl, Roald	1916–1990	English	*James and the Giant Peach* (1961); *Charlie and the Chocolate Factory* (1964)
De Brunhoff, Jean	1899–1937	French	*The Story of Babar* (1937)
Dixon, Franklin W. [see Stratemeyer, Edward L.]			
Dodge, Mary Mapes	1831–1905	American	*Hans Brinker and the Silver Skates* (1865)
Eastman, P. D. [Philip Dey]	1909–1986	American	*Are You My Mother?* (1960)
Fitzhugh, Louise	1928–1974	American	*Harriet the Spy* (1964)
Gág, Wanda	1893–1946	American	*Millions of Cats* (1928)
Garis, Howard	1873–1962	American	Creator of the Uncle Wiggily stories, beginning in 1910
Gipson, Fred	1908–1973	American	*Old Yeller* (1956)
Grahame, Kenneth	1859–1932	English	*The Wind in the Willows* (1908)
Gramatky, Hardie	1907–1979	American	*Little Toot* (1939)
Grimm, Wilhem and Jakob	1786–1859; 1785–1863	Both German	Stories: *Grimms' Fairy Tales* (1812–15)
Hamilton, Virginia	1936–	American	*Zeely* (1967); *The House of Dies Drear* (1968)
Harris, Joel Chandler	1848–1908	American	*Uncle Remus: His Songs and Sayings* (1880)

Hinton, S. E.	1950–	American	*The Outsiders* (1967); *That Was Then, This Is Now* (1970); *Rumblefish* (1975)
Hoban, Russell	1925–	American	*Bedtime for Frances* (1960)
Hope, Laura Lee [see Stratemeyer, Edward L.]			
John, Crockett	1906–1975	American	*Harold and the Purple Crayon* (1955)
Juster, Norton	1929–	American	*The Phantom Toll Booth* (1961)
Keats, Ezra Jack	1916–1983	American	*The Snowy Day* (1963); *Whistle for Willie* (1964)
Keene, Carolyn [see Stratemeyer, Edward L.]			
Konigsburg, E. L. (Elaine Loeb)	1930–	American	*From the Mixed-Up Files of Mrs. Basil E. Frankweiler* (1967)
L'Engle, Madeline	1918–	American	*A Wrinkle in Time* (1962)
Lewis, C. S. (Clive Staples)	1898–1963	English	Creator of the *Chronicles of Narnia* series (1950–56)
Lindgen, Astrid	1907–	Swedish	*Pippi Longstocking* (1945)
Lobel, Arnold	1933–1987	American	*Frog and Toad are Friends* (1970)
Lowry, Lois	1937–	American	*A Summer to Die* (1977); *Anastasia at Your Service* (1984)
MacLachlan, Patricia	1938–	American	*Sarah, Plain and Tall* (1985)
Martin, Ann M.	1955–	American	Creator of the *Baby-Sitters Club* series beginning 1986
McCloskey, Robert	1914–	American	*Make Way for Ducklings* (1941)
Milne, A. A. (Alan Alexander)	1882–1956	English	*Winnie the Pooh* (1926); *The House at Pooh Corner* (1928)
Montgomery, L. M. (Lucy Maud)	1874–1942	Canadian	*Anne of Green Gables* (1908)
Norton, Mary	1903–1992	English	*The Borrowers* (1953); *Bed-Knob and Broomstick* (1957)
O'Hara, Mary [Mary O'Hara Alsop]	1885–1980	American	*My Friend Flicka* (1941)
Patterson, Katherine	1932–	American	*Bridge to Terabithia* (1977)
Perrault, Charles	1628–1703	French	Stories: *Tales of Mother Goose* (1697)
Piper, Watty [Mabel Caroline Bragg]	1870–1945	American	*The Little Engine That Could* (1930)
Porter, Eleanor Hodgman	1868–1920	American	*Pollyanna* (1913)
Potter, Beatrix [Helen Beatrix Potter]	1866–1943	English	*The Tale of Peter Rabbit* (1902)
Pyle, Howard	1853–1911	American	*The Merry Adventures of Robin Hood* (1883)
Rawlings, Marjorie Kinnan	1896–1953	American	*The Yearling* (1938)
Rey, H. A. (Hans Augusto)	1898–1977	American	*Curious George* (1941)
Rowling, J. K.	1966–	English	*The Harry Potter* series, beginning with *Harry Potter and the Sorcerer's Stone* (1998)
Scarry, Richard	1919–1994	American	*Richard Scarry's Best Word Book Ever* (1963); *Cars and Trucks and Things That Go* (1974)

Name	Dates	Nationality	Major Works
Sendak, Maurice	1928–	American	*Where the Wild Things Are* (1963)
Seuss, Dr. [Theodore Seuss Geisel]	1904–1991	American	*Horton Hatches the Egg* (1940); *The Cat in the Hat* (1957)
Sewell, Anna	1820–1878	English	*Black Beauty* (1877)
Silverstein, Shel [Shelby]	1932–	American	*The Giving Tree* (1964); *Where the Sidewalk Ends* (1974); *A Light in the Attic* (1981)
Smith, Betty	1904–1972	American	*A Tree Grows in Brooklyn* (1943)
Stine, R. L. (Robert Lawrence)	1943–	American	The *Goosebumps* series, starting with *Welcome to Dead House* (1992)
Stratemeyer, Edward L.	1862–1930	American	The *Bobbsey Twins* series (under the pseudonym Laura Lee Hope) (beg. 1904); The *Hardy Boys* series (under the pseudonym Franklin W. Dixon) (beg. 1927); and *Nancy Drew* series (under the pseudonym Carolyn Keene) (beg. 1930)
Thompson, Kay	1912–1998	American	*Eloise* (1955)
Tolkien, J. R. R.	1892–1973	English	*The Hobbit* (1937); *The Lord of the Rings* (3 vols., 1954–56)
Travers, P. L. (Pamela Lyndon)	1906–1996	Australian-born English	*Mary Poppins* (1934)
Van Allsburg, Chris	1949–	American	*Jumanji* (1981); *The Polar Express* (1985)
Verne, Jules	1828–1905	French	*A Voyage to the Center of the Earth* (1864); *Twenty Thousand Leagues Under the Sea* (1870); *Around the World in Eighty Days* (1873)
White, E. B. (Elwyn Brooks)	1899–1985	American	*Stuart Little* (1945); *Charlotte's Web* (1952)
White, T. H. (Terence Hanbury)	1906–1964	Indian-born English	*The Sword in the Stone* (1938); *The Once and Future King* (1958)
Wilder, Laura Ingalls	1867–1957	American	*Little House on the Prairie* (1935)
Williams, Margery (Winifred)	1888–1944	English-born American	*The Velveteen Rabbit* (1922)
Wyss, J. D. (Johann David)	1743–1818	Swiss	*The Swiss Family Robinson* (1812–13)
Zindel, Paul	1936–	American	*The Pigman* (1968); *My Darling, My Hamburger* (1969)

⊙ Carpenter, Humphrey, and Mari Pritchard, eds. *The Oxford Companion to Children's Literature.* New York: Oxford University Press, 1991.
Pendergast, Sara and Tom, eds. *St. James Guide to Children's Writers*, 5th ed. Detroit: St. James, 1999.
Silvey, Anita, ed. *Children's Books and Their Creators.* Boston: Houghton Mifflin, 1995.

ARTS AND LEISURE: *Journalism*

Top 20 U.S. Newspapers (in Circulation)

Rank	Newspaper	Daily Circulation (as of 9/30/99)	Website
1	Wall Street Journal	1,752,693	www.wsj.com
2	USA Today	1,671,539	www.usatoday.com
3	New York Times	1,086,293	www.nytimes.com
4	Los Angeles Times	1,078,186	www.latimes.com
5	Washington Post	763,305	www.washingtonpost.com
6	New York Daily News	701,831	www.mostnewyork.com
7	Chicago Tribune	657,690	www.chicago.tribune.com
8	Newsday	574,941	www.newsday.com
9	Houston Chronicle	542,414	www.chron.com
10	Dallas Morning News	490,249	www.dallasnews.com
11	Chicago Sun-Times	468,170	www.suntimes.com
12	Boston Globe	462,850	www.boston.com/globe/
13	San Francisco Chronicle	456,742	www.sfgate.com
14	New York Post	438,158	www.nypostonline.com
15	Arizona Republic	433,296	www.azcentral.com
16	Newark Star-Ledger	407,129	www.nj.com
17	Philadelphia Inquirer	399,339	www.phillynews.com
18	Rocky Mountain News	396,114	www.rockymountainnews.com
19	Cleveland Plain Dealer	386,312	www.cleveland.com
20	San Diego Union-Tribune	376,604	www.uniontrib.com

⊙ Detroit Free Press. "100 Largest Newspapers," www.freep.com/jobspage/links/top100.htm

ARTS AND LEISURE: *Art*

Major Painters and Sculptors

The following charts display a selection of 150 of Western civilization's most renowned painters and 50 of its best-known sculptors, each identified by two or three notable works. Reference sources for both tables are provided at the end of the section.

Painters

Artist	Dates	Nationality	Notable Works
Angelico, Fra (Guido di Pietro)	c.1400–1455	Florentine	*Madonna of the Star* (c.1428–33); *The Deposition* (c.1440); *The Annunciation* (c.1451–55)
Bacon, Francis	1909–1992	Irish-born English	*Three Studies for Figures at the Base of a Crucifixion* (1944); *Pope Innocent X* (1953)

Artist	Dates	Nationality	Notable Works
Beardsley, Aubrey Vincent	1872–1898	English	*Illustrations for Morte D'Arthur* (1893); *Salomé* (1894); *Lysistrata* (1896)
Bellini, Giovanni	c.1430–1516	Venetian	*The Agony in the Garden* (1459); *The Feast of the Gods* (1514)
Bellows, George Wesley	1882–1925	American	*Stag at Sharkey's* (1907); *Cliff Dwellers* (1913); *Love of Winter* (1914)
Benton, Thomas Hart	1889–1975	American	*Cotton Pickers* (1928–29); *The Jealous Lover of Lone Green Valley* (1930); *Persephone* (1939)
Bingham, George Caleb	1811–1879	American	*Fur Traders Going Down the Missouri* (1845); *Raftsmen Playing Cards* (1847)
Boccioni, Umberto	1882–1916	Italian	*States of Mind: The Farewells* (1911); *Dynamism of a Soccer Player* (1913)
Bonnard, Pierre	1867–1947	French	*The Circus Rider* (1897); *Nude with a Lamp* (c.1912); *The Rape of Europa* (1919)
Bosch, Hieronymus	c.1450–1516	Dutch	*The Ship of Fools* (1500); *The Temptation of St. Anthony* (c.1506); *The Garden of Earthly Delights* (c.1505–10)
Botticelli, Sandro (Alessandro di Mariano Filipepi)	1445–1510	Florentine	*Adoration of the Magi* (c.1475); *Primavera* (c.1475–78); *The Birth of Venus* (c.1483)
Boucher, François	1703–1770	French	*Miss O'Murphy* (1732); *The Triumph of Venus* (1740); *La Toilette* (1742)
Braque, Georges	1882–1963	French	*Man with a Guitar* (1911); *Clarinet* (1913); *Woman with a Mandolin* (1937)
Bronzino (Agnolo di Cosimo)	1503–1572	Florentine	*Portrait of a Young Man* (1535); *Venus, Cupid, Folly and Time* (1545); *Andrea Doria as Neptune* (c.1550–55)
Bruegel, Pieter, the Elder	c.1525–1569	Flemish	*The Triumph of Death* (1562); *The Tower of Babel* (1563); *The Peasant Wedding* (c.1567)
Burchfield, Charles Ephraim	1893–1967	American	*February Thaw* (1920); *Six O'Clock* (1936); *Over the Dam* (1936)
Caravaggio (Michelangelo Merisi)	c.1573–1610	Italian	*A Basket of Fruit* (1596); *Amore Vincitore* (1598–99); *The Calling of St. Matthew* (1599–1600)

Cassatt, Mary Stevenson	1844–1926	American	*Alexander Cassatt and His Son Robert* (1884–85); *La Toilette* (c.1891); *The Bath* (1892)
Cézanne, Paul	1839–1906	French	*The Card Players* (1890–92); *Still Life With Apples and Oranges* (1895–1900)
Chagall, Marc	1887–1985	Russian-born French	*The Wedding* (1910); *I and the Village* (1911); *Birthday* (1915)
Chardin, Jean-Baptiste Siméon	1699–1779	French	*The Skate (The Ray)* (1729); *Boy Playing With Cards* (1740); *Girl with Racket and Shuttlecock* (1740)
Copley, John Singleton	1738–1815	American	*Henry Pelham (Boy with a Squirrel)* (1765); *Paul Revere* (1768–70); *Watson and the Shark* (1778)
Corot, Jean-Baptiste Camille	1796–1875	French	*View of the Forest of Fontainebleau* (1831); *Morning, the Dance of the Nymphs* (c.1850); *The Letter* (1865)
Courbet, Jean Désiré Gustave	1819–1877	French	*The Meeting* (1854); *The Painter's Studio* (1855); *The Sleepers* (1862)
Cranach, Lucas	1472–1553	German	*Crucifixion* (1503); *Venus and Cupid* (1509); *Nymph of Spring* (1518)
Curry, John Steuart	1897–1946	American	*Baptism in Kansas* (1928); *Tornado Over Kansas* (1929); *Circus Elephants* (1932)
Dali, Salvador	1904–1989	Spanish	*The Persistence of Memory* (1931); *Sleep* (1937); *Crucifixion* (1951)
Daumier, Honoré	1808–1879	French	*The Legislative Paunch* (1833–34); *The Print Collector* (1857–63); *Advice to a Young Artist* (c.1865)
David, Jacques-Louis	1748–1825	French	*The Death of Socrates* (1787); *Marat Assassinated* (1793); *Intervention of the Sabine Women* (1799)
De Chirico, Giorgio	1888–1978	Italian	*The Song of Love* (1914); *The Mystery and Melancholy of a Street* (1914); *Grand Metaphysical Interior* (1917)
Degas, Edgar	1834–1917	French	*The Orchestra of the Opera* (1870); *The Rape* (1868–69); *Dance Class* (1871)
de Kooning, Willem	1904–1997	Dutch-born American	*Woman* (1943); *Woman* (1950–52); *Woman on the Dune* (1967)

Artist	Dates	Nationality	Notable Works
Delacroix, Eugène	1798–1863	French	*The Death of Sardanapalus* (1827); *Liberty Leading the People* (1830)
Derain, André	1880–1954	French	*Henri Matisse* (1905); *Houses of Parliament at Night* (1905–6)
Dix, Otto	1891–1969	German	*Sunrise* (1913); *Sylvia von Harden* (1926); *Metropolis* (1927–28)
Dubuffet, Jean	1901–1985	French	*Corps de Dame: La Juive* (1950); *The Cow with the Subtile Nose* (1954); *Texturology* (1958)
Duchamp, Marcel	1887–1968	French-born American	*Nude Descending a Staircase No. 2* (1912); *Mona Lisa* (with mustache) (1919)
Dufy, Raoul	1877–1953	French	*The Three Umbrellas* (1906); *Open Window at Nice* (1928); *Regatta at Crowes* (1934)
Durand, Asher Brown	1796–1886	American	*The Beeches* (1845); *Kindred Spirits* (1849); *Progress (The Advance of Civilization)* (1853)
Dürer, Albrecht	1471–1528	German	*The Young Hare* (1502); *Adam and Eve* (1507); *Study of Praying Hands* (1508)
Eakins, Thomas	1844–1916	American	*Max Schmitt in a Single Scull* (1871); *The Gross Clinic* (1875); *The Swimming Hole* (1883)
El Greco (Doménikos Theotokópoulos)	1541–1614	Cretan-born Spanish	*Christ Driving the Traders from the Temple* (1600–5); *Vision of St. John the Divine* (1608–14)
Ensor, James Sydney	1860–1949	Belgian	*Red Apples and White Bowl* (1883); *The Entry of Christ into Brussels* (1889); *The Intrigue* (1890)
Ernst, Max	1891–1976	German-born French	*Oedipus Rex* (1922); *Two Children are Threatened by a Nightingale* (1924); *Napoleon in the Desert* (1941)
Fragonard, Jean-Honoré	1732–1806	French	*The Swing* (1769); *Progress of Love* (1771–73); *The Bolt* (1778)
Friedrich, Caspar David	1774–1840	German	*Moonrise Over the Sea* (1822); *Man and Woman Gazing at the Moon* (c.1830–35); *The Stages of Life* (c.1835)
Gainsborough, Thomas	1727–1788	English	*Mr. and Mrs. Robert Andrews* (1748–49); *The Blue Boy* (1770); *Mrs. Sarah Siddons* (1785)

Gauguin, Paul	1848–1903	French	*Four Breton Women* (1886); *By the Sea* (1892); *Tahitian Women with Mango Blossoms* (1899)
Gérard, François	1770–1837	French	*Cupid and Psyche* (1796); *Caroline Murat and her Children* (1808)
Géricault, Théodore	1791–1824	French	*The Charging Chasseur* (1812); *The Raft of the Medusa* (1819); *Madwoman* (1822)
Ghirlandaio, Domenico (Domenico di Tommaso Bigordi)	1449–1494	Florentine	*Old Man with His Grandson* (1480); *Scenes from the Life of St. Francis* (1485); *Adoration of the Magi* (1487)
Giotto (Giotto di Bondone)	c.1266–1337	Florentine	*The Mourning of Christ* (c.1305); *The Presentation of the Virgin* (1305–13); *Madonna in Glory* (1310)
Goya y Lucientes, Francisco José de	1746–1828	Spanish	*Don Manuel Osorio de Zúñiga* (1788); *The Naked Maja* (1800–5); *The Shootings of the Third of May* (1814)
Gris, Juan (José Victoriano González)	1887–1927	Spanish	*Pablo Picasso* (1912); *Guitar and Flowers* (1912); *Fruit Dish and Bottle* (1917)
Grosz, George	1893–1959	German-born American	*To Oskar Panizza* (1917–18); *Ecce Homo* (1921); *Twilight* (1922)
Hals, Frans	1580–1666	Dutch	*The Laughing Cavalier* (1624); *The Gypsy Girl* (1628–30); *Regentesses of the Old Men's Almshouse* (1664)
Henri, Robert	1865–1929	American	*Figures on a Boardwalk* (1892); *Blue-Eyed Man* (1910); *Catharine* (1913)
Hicks, Edward	1780–1849	American	*The Peaceable Kingdom* (1840–45); *The Grave of William Penn* (c.1847); *The Cornell Farm* (1848)
Hockney, David	1937–	English	*A Bigger Splash* (1967); *Nichols Canyon* (1980)
Hogarth, William	1697–1764	English	*The Rake's Progress* (1733–35); *Marriage à la Mode* (1743–45)
Holbein, Hans, the Elder	c.1465–1524	German	*Study of a Bearded Man* (c.1508); *The Martyrdom of Saint Sebastian* (1515–17)
Holbein, Hans, the Younger	c.1497–1543	German	*Body of the Dead Christ in the Tomb* (1521–22); *Erasmus of Rotterdam* (1523); *The Ambassadors* (1533)
Homer, Winslow	1836–1910	American	*Snap the Whip* (1872); *Breezing Up* (1876); *Right and Left* (1909)

Artist	Dates	Nationality	Notable Works
Hopper, Edward	1882–1967	American	*Lighthouse at Two Lights* (1929); *Early Sunday Morning* (1930); *Nighthawks* (1942)
Ingres, Jean-Auguste Dominique	1780–1867	French	*Male Torso* (1800); *La Grande Odalisque* (1814); *Ulysses* (1827)
Johns, Jasper	1930–	American	*Flag* (1954–55); *Dancers on a Plane* (1979); *Perilous Night* (1982)
Kandinsky, Wassily	1866–1944	Russian	*The Summer Landscape* (1909); *Improvisation 31 (Sea Battle)* (1913); *Yellow-Red-Blue* (1925)
Kirchner, Ernst Ludwig	1880–1938	German	*Five Women in the Street* (1913); *Friedrichstrasse, Berlin* (1914)
Klee, Paul	1879–1940	Swiss	*Twittering Machine* (1922); *The Goldfish* (1925); *Cat and Bird* (1928)
Klimt, Gustav	1862–1918	Austrian	*Adele Bloch-Bauer I* (1907); *Danae* (1907–8); *The Kiss* (1907–8)
Kline, Franz Joseph	1910–1962	American	*Chinatown* (1948); *New York, NY* (1953); *Painting No. 2* (1954)
Kokoschka, Oskar	1886–1980	Austrian	*Knight Errant* (1915); *That For Which We Fight* (1943); *Golda Meir, Prime Minister* (1973)
Kollwitz, Käthe Schmidt	1867–1945	German	*Peasants' War* (1902–8); *The War* (1923); *Death* (1934–35)
Leonardo da Vinci	1452–1519	Florentine	*The Annunciation* (c.1472–73); *The Last Supper* (c.1495–97); *Mona Lisa* (c.1503–7)
Leutze, Emanuel Gottlieb	1816–1868	German-born American	*Washington Crossing the Delaware* (1851); *Westward the Course of Empire Takes Its Way* (1860)
Lichtenstein, Roy	1923–1997	American	*Drowning Girl* (1962); *George Washington* (1962); *Statue of Liberty* (1982)
Lippi, Fra Filippo	c.1406–1469	Florentine	*The Annunciation* (1440); *The Nativity* (c.1445); *Madonna and Child with Two Angels* (1464)
Magritte, René	1898–1967	Belgian	*The Human Condition* (1934); *Tomb of the Wrestlers* (1960); *The Blank Signature* (1965)

Manet, Édouard	1832–1883	French	*Luncheon on the Grass* (1862–63); *The Fifer* (1866); *A Bar at the Folies Bergère* (1881–82)
Mantegna, Andrea	1431–1506	Italian	*The Death of the Virgin* (1461); *The Dead Christ* (1490); *Parnassus* (1497)
Marc, Franz	1880–1916	German	*Siberian Dogs in the Snow* (1909–10); *Blue Horses* (1911); *Stables* (1914)
Marsh, Reginald	1898–1954	American	*Pip and Flip* (1932); *High Yaller* (1934); *Twenty Cent Movie* (1936)
Matisse, Henri	1869–1954	French	*Dance* (1909); *The Red Studio* (1911); *Large Composition with Masks* (1953)
Michelangelo Buonarroti	1475–1564	Florentine	Sistine Chapel frescos: *Book of Genesis* (1508–12); *The Last Judgment* (1534–41)
Millet, Jean-François	1814–1875	French	*The Sower* (1850); *The Gleaners* (1857); *The Man with a Hoe* (1863)
Miró, Joan	1893–1983	Spanish	*The Harlequin's Carnival* (1924–25); *The Poetess* (1940); *Woman* (1976)
Modigliani, Amedeo	1884–1920	Italian	*Lunja Czechowska* (1917); *Madame Amédée (Woman with Cigarette)* (1918); *Reclining Nude* (1916)
Monet, Claude	1840–1926	French	*Impression: Sunrise* (1872); *Two Haystacks* (1891); *Waterlilies* (c.1900)
Moreau, Gustave	1826–1898	French	*Orpheus* (1865); *Diomedes Devoured by His Horses* (1865); *Salome* (1876)
Moses, Grandma (Anna Mary Robertson Moses)	1860–1961	American	*Out for the Christmas Tree* (1946); *A Country Wedding* (1951); *Bennington* (1953)
Motherwell, Robert	1915–1991	American	*Personnage* (1945); *Elegy to the Spanish Republic #34* (1953–54); *Reconciliation Elegy* (1978)
Munch, Edvard	1863–1944	Norwegian	*The Scream* (1893); *Vampire* (1895); *The Dance of Life* (1900)
O'Keeffe, Georgia	1887–1986	American	*Red Poppy* (1927); *Summer Days* (1936); *Sky Above White Clouds I* (1962)

Major Painters and Sculptors *(cont.)*

Artist	Dates	Nationality	Notable Works
Parrish, Maxfield	1870–1966	American	*The Dinky Bird* (1904); *Daybreak* (1922); *Stars* (1926)
Peale, Charles Willson	1741–1827	American	*The Staircase Group* (1795); *The Artist in His Museum* (1822)
Peale, Raphaelle	1774–1825	American	*A Dessert* (1814); *Still Life with Cake* (1822); *After the Bath* (1823)
Peale, Rembrandt	1778–1860	American	*George Washington* (1795); *Thomas Jefferson* (1804); *Napoléon Bonaparte* (1810)
Picasso, Pablo	1881–1973	Spanish	*Les Demoiselles d'Avignon* (1907); *Guernica* (1937); *The Charnel House* (1945)
Piero della Francesca	c.1420–1492	Italian	*The Baptism of Christ* (1442); *The Flagellation of Christ* (c.1456)
Pissarro, Camille	1830–1903	French	*The Road to Versailles* (1870); *The Oise Near Pontoise* (1873); *The Pork Butcher* (1883)
Pollock, Jackson (Paul Jackson Pollock)	1912–1956	American	*Blue (Moby Dick)* (1943); *Galaxy* (1947); *Blue Poles No. 11* (1952)
Poussin, Nicolas	1594–1665	French	*The Rape of the Sabine Women* (1636–37); *The Dance to the Music of Time* (c.1640)
Raphael (Raffaello Sanzio)	1483–1520	Italian	*The Three Graces* (1504–5); *The School of Athens* (1509–11); *The Transfiguration* (1518–20)
Rembrandt Harmenszoon van Rijn	1606–1669	Dutch	*The Anatomy Lesson of Dr. Nicholaes Tulp* (1632); *The Night Watch* (1642); *The Staalmeesters* (1662)
Remington, Frederic	1861–1909	American	*The Scout: Friends or Foes?* (1890); *Old Stage Coach of the Plains* (1901); *The Fight for the Waterhole* (1903)
Renoir, Pierre Auguste	1841–1919	French	*A Girl with a Watering Can* (1876); *The Luncheon of the Boating Party* (1881); *The Bathers* (1884–87)
Repin, Ilya Yefimovich	1844–1930	Russian	*Volga Boatmen* (1873); *Modest Mussorgsky* (1881); *Ivan Grozny and His Son Ivan* (1885)
Rivera, Diego	1886–1957	Mexican	murals: National Palace, Mexico City (*History of Mexico*) (1929–36); Detroit Institute of Arts (1932–33)

Rockwell, Norman	1894–1978	American	*Rosie the Riveter* (1943); *Freedom of Speech* (1943); *Freedom from Want* (1943)
Rossetti, Dante Gabriel	1828–1882	English	*Sir Tristram and La Belle Yseult Drinking the Love Potion* (1867); *Astarte Syriaca* (1875–77)
Rothko, Mark (Marcus Rothkowitz)	1903–1970	Russian-born American	*Magenta, Black, Green on Orange* (1949); *Orange and Yellow* (1956); *Black on Grey* (1970)
Rousseau, Henri	1844–1910	French	*Sleeping Gypsy* (1897); *The Ball Players* (1908); *The Dream* (1910)
Rubens, Peter Paul	1577–1640	Flemish	*St. Sebastian* (c.1615); *The Rape of the Daughters of Leucippus* (c.1618); *The Three Graces* (c.1635)
Ryder, Albert Pinkham	1847–1917	American	*The Flying Dutchman* (1887); *Siegfried and the Rhine Maidens* (1888–91); *Death on a Pale Horse* (c.1910)
Sargent, John Singer	1856–1925	American	*El Jaleo* (1882); *The Daughters of Edward Darley Boit* (1888); *Lord Ribblesdale* (1902)
Schiele, Egon	1890–1918	Austrian	*Self Portrait* (1910); *The Embrace* (1917); *Family* (1918)
Seurat, Georges	1859–1891	French	*Bathing at Asnières* (1883–84); *A Sunday Afternoon on the Island of La Grande Jatte* (1884–86)
Sloan, John French	1871–1951	American	*Easter Eve* (1907); *Haymarket* (1907); *Backyards, Greenwich Village* (1914)
Steen, Jan	c.1626–1679	Dutch	*Skittle Players Outside an Inn* (1652); *The Cat Family* (1660); *The Feast of St. Nicholas* (c.1667)
Stella, Joseph	1877–1946	American	*Battle of Lights, Coney Island* (1913); *The Gas Tank* (1918); *Brooklyn Bridge* (1920)
Still, Clyfford	1904–1980	American	*1946-H (Indian Red and Black)* (1946); *Painting* (1951); *1953* (1953)
Stuart, Gilbert Charles	1755–1828	American	*The Skater* (1782); *George Washington* (the "Athenaeum Head") (1796); *James Monroe* (1817)

Artist	Dates	Nationality	Notable Works
Sully, Thomas	1783–1872	American	*The Torn Hat* (1820); *Queen Victoria* (1838); *Andrew Jackson* (1845)
Tanguy, Yves	1900–1955	American	*Mama, Papa is Wounded!* (1927); *Indefinite Divisibility* (1942); *Rose of the Four Winds* (1950)
Tiepolo, Giovanni Battista	1696–1770	Italian	*The Martyrdom of St. Bartholomew* (1722); *The Adoration of the Magi* (1753); *Crucifixion* (1755–60)
Tintoretto (Jacobo Robusti)	c.1518–1594	Italian	*Susannah and the Elders* (c.1550); *Crucifixion* (1564–87); *The Last Supper* (1592–94)
Titian (Tiziano Vecelli)	c.1490–1576	Italian	*Sacred and Profane Love* (1512–15); *Bacchus and Ariadne* (1522–23); *Triple Portrait Mask* (c.1570)
Toulouse-Lautrec, Henri de	1864–1901	French	*At the Moulin Rouge* (1892); *Jane Avril at the Jardin de Paris* (1893); *The Salon in the Rue Des Moulins* (1894)
Trumbell, John	1765–1843	American	*Declaration of Independence* (1786–94); *The Resignation of General Washington* (1824)
Turner, Joseph Mallord William	1775–1851	English	*The Grand Canal, Venice* (1835); *Norham Castle: Sunrise* (c.1835–40); *Dawn After the Wreck* (c.1840)
van der Weyden, Rogier	1400–1464	Flemish	*The Annunciation* (1435); *The Descent from the Cross* (c.1438)
Van Dyck, Sir Anthony	1599–1641	Flemish	*Frans Snyder* (1620); *The Lamentation* (1634); *Charles I of England* (c.1635)
van Eyck, Jan	c.1390–1441	Flemish	*Adam and Eve* (c.1432); *The Arnolfini Marriage* (1434); *Madonna with Canon van der Paele* (1436)
van Gogh, Vincent	1853–1890	Dutch	*Self-Portrait* (1887); *Sunflowers* (1888); *Starry Night* (1889)
Velázquez, Diego Rodríguez de Silva y	1599–1660	Spanish	*Los Borrachos* (*The Triumph of Bacchus*) (c.1628–29); *Las Meninas* (*The Maids of Honor*) (1656)
Vermeer, Jan	1632–1675	Dutch	*A View of Delft* (c.1660); *A Maidservant Pouring Milk* (c.1660); *The Lace Maker* (c.1665)
Veronese, Paolo (Paolo Caliari)	1528–1588	Italian	*Marriage at Cana* (1562–63); *Feast in the House of Levy* (1573); *The Find of Moses* (1570–75)

Warhol, Andy	1928?–1987	American	Campbell Soup Cans (1961–62); Marilyn (1964); Flowers (1964)
Watteau, Jean-Antoine	1684–1721	French	The Embarkation for Cythera (1717); Le Mezzetin (1718); Gersaint's Shopsign (1720)
West, Benjamin	1738–1820	American	The Death of General Wolf (1770); King Lear (1788); Death on a Pale Horse (1788)
Whistler, James Abbott McNeill	1834–1903	American	Wapping (1860–64); Arrangement in Grey and Black ("Whistler's Mother") (1871)
Wood, Grant	1891–1942	American	Woman with Plants (1929); American Gothic (1930); Daughters of Revolution (1932)
Wyeth, Andrew Newell	1917–	American	Christina's World (1948); The Trodden Weed (1951); The Helga Pictures (1971–85)

Sculptors

Artist	Dates	Nationality	Notable Works
Archipenko, Aleksandr Porfiryevich	1887–1964	Ukrainian-born American	Médrano II (1915); Woman Combing Her Hair (1915)
Barlach, Ernst	1870–1939	German	Shepherd in a Storm (1908); The Warrior of the Spirit (1928)
Bernini, Gianlorenzo	1598–1680	Italian	The Goat Amalthea Nursing the Infant Zeus and a Young Satyr (1609); Abduction of Proserpina (1621–22)
Boccioni, Umberto	1882–1916	Italian	Antigraceful (1913); Unique Forms of Continuity in Space (1913)
Borglum, Gutzon	1871–1941	American	The Aviator (1919); Mount Rushmore Memorial (1927–41)
Botero, Fernando	1932–	Colombian	Reclining Nude (1984); Ballerina (1989)
Bourgeois, Louise	1911–	American	Mortise (1950); Spider (1996–97)
Brancusi, Constantin	1876–1957	Romanian-born French	Sleeping Muse (1906); Bird in Space (1919)
Calder, Alexander	1898–1976	American	Cow (1929); Black Camel with Blue Head and Red Tongue (1971)
Cellini, Benvenuto	1500–1571	Florentine	Salt Cellar of Francis I (1539–43); Perseus and Medusa (1545–54)
Degas, Edgar	1834–1917	French	The Little Fourteen-Year-Old Dancer (1880–81); Woman Washing Her Left Leg (c.1890)

Artist	Dates	Nationality	Notable Works
Donatello (Donato di Niccolo de Betto Bardi)	1386–1466	Italian	*David* (c.1430–35); *St. Jerome* (c.1450)
Dubuffet, Jean	1901–1985	French	*Shadow Knight* (1954); *The Amphigoric One* (1954)
Duchamp, Marcel	1887–1968	French-born American	*Bicycle Wheel* (1913); *Boite-en-Valise* (1961)
Epstein, Jacob	1880–1959	American-born English	*An American Soldier* (1917); *Princess Menen* (1949)
Ernst, Max	1891–1976	German-born French	*Head "H"* (1948); *Capricorn* (1948–75)
Flannagan, John Bernard	1895–1942	American	*Christ* (1925); *Gorilla* (1938)
Ghiberti, Lorenzo	1378–1455	Florentine	*Sacrifice of Abraham* (1401); *St. John the Baptist* (1412–16)
Giacometti, Alberto	1901–1966	Swiss	*The Palace at 4 AM* (1932–33); *Walking Man II* (1960)
Girardon, François	1628–1715	French	*Pluto and Persephone (Allegory of Fire)* (1677–99); *Louis XIV* (equestrian) (1683–92)
Greenough, Horatio	1805–1852	American	*George Washington* (1832–41); *The Rescue* (1837–51)
Hoffman, Malvina	1885–1966	American	*Egyptian Dancer, Nyota Inyoka* (1932); *Swami Vivekananda* (1950)
Hosmer, Harriet Goodhue	1830–1908	American	*Puck* (1856); *Zenobia, Queen of Palmyra* (c.1857)
Hyatt, Anna Vaughn (Anna Huntington)	1876–1973	American	*Lion* (1908); *Zebra and Foal* (1939); *Sybil Ludington's Ride* (1960)
Lachaise, Gaston	1882–1935	French-born American	*Floating Woman* (1927); *Standing Woman* (1930–33)
Lewis, Edmonia (Wildfire)	c.1845–19??	American	*Forever Free* (1867); *The Death of Cleopatra* (1876)
Lipchitz, Jacques (Chaim Jacob Lipchitz)	1891–1973	French	*Bas-Relief I* (1918); *Death Mask of Amedeo Modigliani* (1920)
Maillol, Aristide	1861–1944	French	*Modesty* (c.1900); *Torso of a Young Woman* (c.1930); *The Three Nymphs* (1930–38)
Manship, Paul	1885–1966	American	*Dancer and Gazelles* (1916); *Diana and a Hound* (1925)
Marini, Marino	1901–1980	Italian	*Horseman* (1947); *L'Idea del Cavaliere (The Concept of the Rider)* (1952–54)
Mears, Helen Farnsworth	1876–1916	American	*Augustus Saint-Gaudens* (1898); *Aphrodite* (1912)

Michelangelo Buonarroti	1475–1564	Florentine	*Bacchus* (1496–98); *Pietà* (1498–1500); *David* (1501–4)
Moore, Sir Henry	1898–1986	British	*Three Motives Against Wall, No. 1* (1958–59); *Knife Edge Mirror Two Piece* (1977–78)
Nevelson, Louise	1900–1988	Russian-born American	*Mountain Figure* (1946–48); *Gate of Eternity* (1958); *Sky Gate—New York* (1978)
Noguchi, Isamu	1904–1988	American	*Giacometti's Shadow* (1982–83); *Cloud Mountain* (1983)
Oldenburg, Claes	1929–	American	*Glass Case with Pies (Assorted Pies in a Case)* (1962); *Clarinet Bridge* (1992)
Picasso, Pablo	1881–1973	Spanish	*Gorilla* (1926); *Dove* (1954); *Steel Sculpture* (1967)
Remington, Frederic	1861–1909	American	*Bronco Buster* (1895); *Comin' Through the Rye* (1902); *The Mountain Man* (1903)
Rodin, Auguste	1840–1917	French	*The Kiss* (1889); *The Thinker* (1904); *Gustav Mahler* (1909)
Rosso, Medardo	1858–1928	Italian	*Impression of an Omnibus* (1883–84); *Sick Child* (1895); *Boulevard Impression, Paris at Night* (1895)
Saint-Gaudens, Augustus	1848–1907	American	*Charles Stewart Butler and Lawrence Smith Butler* (1880–81); *Diana of the Tower* (1892–99)
Sansovino, Andrea (Andrea Contucci)	c.1467–1529	Italian	*Baptism of Christ* (1502); tombs of Cardinals Ascanio Sforza and Girolamo Basso della Rovere (1509)
Sansovino, Jacopo	1486–1570	Italian	*Doorknocker with Nereid, Triton, and Putti* (c.1550); *Madonna and Child* (c.1550)
Sluter, Claus	c.1340–1406	Dutch	*Memorial to Philip the Bold* (1389–1406); *The Moses Well* (1395–1405)
Smith, David	1906–1965	American	*Sentinel I* (1956); *Cubi XXVI* (1965)
Tatlin, Vladimir	1885–1953	Russian	*Corner Counter-relief* (1914–15); *Model of the Monument to the Third International* (1920)
Verrocchio, Andrea del	1435–1488	Florentine	*Giuliano de' Medici* (c.1475–78); *Putto Poised on a Globe* (c.1480)
Watts, George Frederic	1817–1904	English	*Hugh Lupus* (1876–83); *Physical Energy* (1904)

Major Painters and Sculptors (cont.)

Artist	Dates	Nationality	Notable Works
Whitney, Anne	1821–1915	American	*Africa* (1864); *Roma* (1869); *Harriet Beecher Stowe* (1892)
Whitney, Gertrude	1875–1942	American	*Titanic Memorial* (1914); *Washington Heights War Memorial* (1922); *Peter Stuyvesant* (1939)

⊙ Chilvers, Ian. *The Concise Oxford Dictionary of Art and Artists,* 2d ed. New York: Oxford University Press, 1996.

Curtis, Penelope. *Sculpture 1900–1945.* New York: Oxford University Press, 1999.

Metropolitan Museum of Art, New York. "The Collection," www.metmuseum.org/collections/search.asp

Museum of Modern Art, New York. "Index of Artists," www.moma.org/docs/indexofartists/

Vaughan, William, ed. *Encyclopedia of Artists.* New York: Oxford University Press, 2000.

Tate Gallery/Tate Britain, London. "Tate Collections," www.tate.org.uk/collections/

ARTS AND LEISURE: *Photography*

Photographers

Name	Dates	Nationality	Major Works
Abbott, Berenice	1898–1991	American	Portraiture, documentary photography
Adams, Ansel	1902–1984	American	Landscape photography
Arbus, Diane	1923–1971	American	Portraiture, fashion photography
Atget, Eugène	1857–1927	French	Social documentary
Atkins, Anna	1799–1871	English	Scientific illustration
Avedon, Richard	1923–	American	Portraiture, fashion photography
Beaton, Sir Cecil	1904–1980	English	Portraiture, fashion photography
Bellocq, E. J.	1873–1949	American	Portraiture, social documentary
Bing, Ilse	1899–1998	German-born American	Abstract and surrealist photography
Bourke-White, Margaret	1904–1971	American	Photojournalism
Brady, Matthew	1823–1896	American	Daguerreotype portraiture, documentary photography
Brandt, Bill	1904–1983	German-born English	Photojournalism, social documentary
Brassaï (Gyula Halász)	1899–1984	French	Documentary photography
Cameron, Julia Margaret	1815–1879	English	Portraiture, costume photography
Capa, Robert	1913–1954	Hungarian-born American	Photojournalism
Cartier-Bresson, Henri	1908–	French	Photojournalism
Coburn, Alvin Langdon	1882–1966	American-born English	Portraiture, abstract photography
Cunningham, Imogen	1883–1976	American	Portraiture, botanical photography
Curtis, Edward Sheriff	1868–1952	American	Portraiture, documentary photography

Daguerre, Louis-Jacques-Mandé	1787–1851	French	Invention of the daguerreotype process
Doisneau, Robert	1912–1994	French	Photojournalism, fashion photography
Eisenstaedt, Alfred	1898–1995	German-born American	Photojournalism
Emerson, Peter Henry	1856–1936	English	Documentary photography, naturalist photography
Evans, Walker	1903–1975	American	Documentary photography
Feininger, Andreas	1906–1999	French-born American	Architectural and industrial photography, photojournalism, technique innovation
Fenton, Roger	1819–1869	English	Documentary photography, landscape and still-life photography
Frank, Robert	1924–	Swiss-born American	Industrial photography, fashion photography, cinematography
Friedlander, Lee	1934–	American	Portraiture, social documentary
Gilpin, Laura	1891–1979	American	Landscape photography, documentary photography
Hausmann, Raoul	1886–1971	Austrian	Photomontage, abstract photography
Hawes, Josiah Johnson	1808–1901	American	Daguerreotype portraiture and documentary photography
Henri, Florence	1893–1982	Swiss	Abstract photography
Hine, Lewis Wickes	1874–1940	American	Social documentary
Jackson, William Henry	1843–1942	American	Landscape photography
Käsebier, Gertrude	1852–1934	American	Portraiture
Kertész, André	1894–1985	Hungarian-born American	Photojournalism
Lange, Dorothea	1895–1965	American	Social documentary
Lartigue, Jacques-Henri	1894–1986	French	Documentary photography
Leibovitz, Annie	1949–	American	Celebrity portraiture, advertising photography
Levitt, Helen	1913–	American	Social documentary
Man Ray (Emmanuel Rudnitsky)	1890–1976	American	Surrealist photography
Mapplethorpe, Robert	1946–1989	American	Photomontage, still-life photography, erotic photography
Miller, Lee	1907–1977	American	Surrealist photography, portraiture, documentary photography
Model, Lisette	1901/06–1983	Austrian-born American	Documentary photography
Modotti, Tina	1896–1942	Italian-born American	Social documentary, still-life photography
Moholy-Nagy, László	1895–1946	Hungarian-born American	Abstract photography, art instruction
Morgan, Barbara	1900–1992	American	Dance photography, portraiture, still-life photography
Muybridge, Eadweard	1830–1904	English	Documentary photography, motion studies
Nadar (Gaspard Félix Tournachon)	1820–1910	French	Portraiture, aerial photography

Photographers

Name	Dates	Nationality	Major Works
Newton, Helmut	1920–	German-born American	Fashion photography, celebrity photography
O'Sullivan, Timothy H.	1840–1882	American	Documentary photography
Orkin, Ruth	1921–1985	American	Photojournalism, cinematography
Parks, Gordon	1912–	American	Photojournalism, social documentary
Ritts, Herb	1952–	American	Fashion photography, celebrity photography
Salomon, Erich	1886–1944	German	Photojournalism
Sander, August	1876–1964	German	Documentary photography
Seymour, David	1911–1956	Polish-born American	Photojournalism
Sherman, Cindy	1954–	American	Art photography
Siskind, Aaron	1903–1991	American	Social documentary, abstract photography
Smith, W. Eugene	1918–1978	American	Photojournalism
Southworth, Albert Sands	1811–1894	American	Daguerreotype portraiture and documentary photography
Steichen, Edward	1879–1973	American	Art photography, portraiture
Stieglitz, Alfred	1864–1946	American	Art photography
Strand, Paul	1890–1976	American	Art photography, documentary photography
Sudek, Josef	1896–1976	Czech	Still-life photography, impressionist photography
Talbot, William Henry Fox	1800–1877	English	Calotype innovation, photographic illustration
Ulmann, Doris	1884–1934	American	Social documentary
Van Der Zee, James	1886–1983	American	Documentary photography, portraiture
Vishniac, Roman	1897–1990	Russian-born American	Microphotography, documentary photography
Weegee (Arthur Fellig)	1899–1968	Austrian-born American	Crime photography, documentary photography
Wegman, William	1942/44–	American	Art photography
Weston, Edward	1886–1958	American	Abstract photography
White, Clarence H.	1871–1925	American	Art photography, landscape photography
White, Minor	1908–1976	American	Art photography, abstract photography
Winogrand, Garry	1928–1984	American	Photojournalism

⊙ Capa, Cornell, ed. *The International Center of Photography Encyclopedia of Photography*. New York: Crown, 1986.
Masters of Photography. www.masters-of-photography.com
Artnet.com. "Research Library: Artist Biographies," www.artnet.com/library/bios

50 Great Art Museums

Name	Location	Telephone/Website
Ashmolean Museum of Art	Oxford, England	011-44-1865-27-80-00 www.ashmol.ox.ac.uk
Art Gallery of Ontario	Ontario, Canada	(416) 979-6648 www.ago.on.ca
Art Institute of Chicago	Chicago, IL	(312) 443-3600 www.artic.edu
British Museum	London, England	011-44-207-636-1555 www.thebritishmuseum.ac.uk
Carnegie Museum of Art	Pittsburgh, PA	(412) 622-3131 www.cmoa.org
Capitoline Museum	Rome, Italy	011-39-6-39-96-78-00 www.comune.roma.it/ museicapitolini/pinacoteca
Centre Pompidou	Paris, France	011-33-1-44-78-12-33 www.centrepompidou.fr
Corcoran Gallery of Art	Washington, D.C.	888-CORCORAN www.corcoran.edu
Courtauld Institute Galleries	London, England	011-44-207-848-2526 www.courtauld.edu
Dallas Museum of Art	Dallas, TX	(214) 922-1200 www.dm-art.org
Fine Arts Museum, San Francisco	San Francisco, CA	(415) 863-3300 www.famsf.org
Frick Collection	New York, NY	(212) 288-0070 www.frick.org
Galleria dell'Accademia	Florence, Italy	011-39-55-23-885 www.sbas.firenze.it/accademia
Guggenheim Museum	New York, NY	(212) 423-3500 www.guggenheim.org
Guggenheim Museum, Bilbao	Bilbao, Spain	011-34-9-44-35-90-80 www.guggenheim- bilbao.es/idioma.htm
Hamburger Kunsthalle	Hamburg, Germany	011-49-40-42-85-26-12 www.hamburger-kunsthalle.de
J. Paul Getty Museum	Los Angeles, CA	(310) 440-7300 www.getty.edu/museum
Library of Congress	Washington, D.C.	(202) 707-5000 www.loc.gov
Louvre (Musée de Louvre)	Paris, France	011-33-1-40-20-51-51 www.louvre.fr
Metropolitan Museum of Art	New York, NY	(212) 535-7710 www.metmuseum.org

Name	Location	Telephone/Website
Musée d' Orsay	Paris, France	011-33-1-40-49-48-14 www.musee-orsay.fr
Museo del Prado	Madrid, Spain	011-34-9-13-30-28-00 www.mcu.es/prado
Museum of Contemporary Art	Los Angeles, CA	(213) 621-2766 www.moca-la.org
Museum of Fine Arts, Boston	Boston, MA	(617) 267-9300 www.mfa.org
Museum of Modern Art	New York, NY	(212) 708-9400 www.moma.org
National Archaeological Museum	Athens, Greece	011-30-1-821-7717, 821-7724 www.culture.gr/2/21/214/ 21405m/e21405m1.html
National Building Museum	Washington, D.C.	(202) 272-2448 www.nbm.org
National Gallery, London	London, England	011-44-207-747-2885 www.nationalgallery.org.uk
National Gallery of Art	Washington, D.C.	(202) 737-4215 www.nga.gov
National Museum of American Art	Washington, D.C.	(202) 357-2531 www.nmaa.si.edu
National Museum of Scotland	Edinburgh, Scotland	011-44-31-12-25-75-34 www.museum.scotland.net
National Portrait Gallery	Washington, D.C.	(202) 357-2866 www.npg.si.edu
Norton Simon Museum	Pasadena, CA	(626) 449-6840 www.nortonsimon.org
Peggy Guggenheim Collection	Venice, Italy	011-39-41-240-5411 www.guggenheim.org/venice
Picasso Museum	Paris, France	011-33-1-42-71-25-21 www.musexpo.com/english/ picasso/index.html
Philadelphia Museum of Art	Philadelphia, PA	(215) 736-8100 www.philamuseum.org
Pushkin State Museum of Fine Arts	Moscow, Russia	011-7-09-52-03-95-78 www.museum.ru/gmii
Rijksmuseum	Amsterdam, the Netherlands	011-31-20-674-7047 www.rijksmuseum.nl
Rodin Museum	Paris, France	011-33-1-44-18-61-10 www.musee-rodin.fr
Royal Academy of Art	London, England	011-44-207-300-8000 www.royalacademy.org.uk
San Francisco Museum of Modern Art	San Francisco, CA	(415) 357-4000 www.sfmoma.org/index-r.html

St. Louis Art Museum	Saint Louis, MO	(314) 721-0072
		www.slam.org
State Hermitage Museum	Saint Petersburg, Russia	011-7-81-21-10-90-79
		www.hermitagemuseum.org
Stedelijk Museum of Modern Art	Amsterdam, the Netherlands	011-31-20-573-2911
		www.stedelijk.nl
Tate Gallery	London, England	011-44-207-887-8008
		www.tate.org.uk
Uffizi Gallery	Florence, Italy	011-39-55-23-88-65-16-52
		www.uffizi.firenze.it/welcomeE.html
Van Gogh Museum	Amsterdam, the Netherlands	011-31-20-570-5200
		www.vangoghmuseum.nl
Vatican Museums	Vatican City	011-39-6-69-88-49-47
		www.christusrex.org/www1/ vaticano/0-Musei.html
Victoria and Albert Museum	London, England	011-44-207-942-2000
		www.vam.ac.uk
Whitney Museum of American Art	New York, NY	(212) 570-3676
		www.whitney.org

⊙ International Council of Museums (ICOM). www.icom.org
MuseumSpot. www.museumspot.com
Roberts, Fletcher, et.al., eds. *Traveler's Guide to Art Museum Exhibitions 2000*. New York: Abrams, 1999.
Smithsonian Museums and Research Centers. www.si.edu/info/museums_research.htm

Other Notable Museums

American Museum of the Moving Image
Long Island City, NY
(718) 784-0077
www.ammi.org
Known For: motion picture and television history

American Museum of Natural History
New York, NY
(212) 769-5100
www.anmh.org
Known For: paleontology, zoology

Bronx Zoo
Bronx, NY
(718) 367-1010
http://wcs.org/home/zoos/bronxzoo
Known For: zoology

Children's Museum of Boston
Boston, MA
(617) 426-8855
www.tcmboston.org
Known For: discovery for children

Colonial Williamsburg
Williamsburg, VA
800-HISTORY
www.history.org
Known For: colonial American history

Ellis Island and the Statue of Liberty
New York, NY
(212) 883-1986
www.ellisisland.org
Known For: American immigration museum

Gettysburg
Gettysburg, PA
(717) 334-6274
www.gettysburg.com
Known For: American Civil War battleground

Graceland
Memphis, TN
800-238-2000
www.elvis-presley.com
Known For: Elvis Presley memorabilia

Other Notable Museums *(cont.)*

Henry Ford Museum
Dearborn, MI
(313) 271-2455
www.hfmgv.org
Known For: U.S. automotive history

International Football Hall of Fame
Manchester, England
www.int-foot-fame.com
Known For: soccer hall of fame

Kennedy Space Center
Cape Canaveral, FL
(321) 452-8612
www.kennedyspacecenter.com
Known For: space exploration

Monticello
Charlottesville, VA
(804) 984-9822
www.monticello.org
Known For: Thomas Jefferson home

Mount Vernon
Mount Vernon, VA
(703) 780-2000 www.mountvernon.org
Known For: George Washington home

National Air and Space Museum
Washington, D.C.
(202) 357-2700 www.nasm.si.edu
Known For: historic air- and spacecraft

National Archives
Washington, D.C.
(202) 501-5205 www.nara.gov
Known For: American historical documents

National Baseball Hall of Fame
Cooperstown, NY
(607) 547-7299
www.baseballhalloffame.org
Known For: baseball memorabilia

National Football Hall of Fame
Canton, OH
(330) 456-8270
www.profootballhof.com
Known For: pro football memorabilia

National Museum of the American Indian
New York, NY
(212) 514-3700
www.si.edu/nmai
Known For: American Indian history, culture

Palace of Versailles
Versailles, France
011 33 1 39 51 23 66
www.chateauversailles.org
Known For: French royal history

Rock and Roll Hall of Fame
Cleveland, OH
888-764-ROCK
www.rockhall.com
Known For: rock-and-roll memorabilia

San Diego Zoo
San Diego, CA
(619) 234-3153
www.sandiegozoo.com
Known For: zoology

Theatre Museum
London, England
011 44 207 943 4700
http://theatremuseum.vam.ac.uk
Known For: British theatre history

Tower of London
London, England
011 44 207 709 0765
www.armouries.org.uk
Known For: British history, arms and armor

U.S. Holocaust Memorial Museum
Washington, D.C.
(202) 488-0400
www.ushmm.org
Known For: Holocaust/WWII history

The White House, Washington, D.C.
(202) 456-7041
www.whitehouse.gov
Known For: home of the president, museum

⊙ International Council of Museums (ICOM). www.icom.org
  MuseumSpot. www.museumspot.com
  Smithsonian Museums and Research Centers. www.si.edu/info/museums_research.htm

100 Notable Architects

These architects are among the best known in history. Dates given for major works are completion dates. Architects have been chosen for their influence on the history of architecture, as well as for the fame and importance of their works.

Name	Dates	Nationality	Major Works
Aalto, Alvar	1898–1976	Finnish	Finlandia Conference Center, Helsinki (1975); Baker Dormitory, Massachusetts Institute of Technology, Cambridge (1949)
Adam, Robert	1728–1792	English	Theatre Royal, Drury Lane, London (1776); Apsley House, London (1778)
Alberti, Leone Battista	1404–1472	Italian	Sant' Andra, Mantua (1472); façade of Santa Maria Novella, Florence (1471)
Andrews, John	1933–	Australian	American Express Tower, Sydney (1970); School of Art, Kent State University (1970)
Apollodorus of Damascus	2nd century AD	Roman	Trajan's Baths, Rome (109); Trajan's Forum, Rome (112)
Ashbee, C. R.	1863–1942	English	The Wodehouse, Staffordshire (1901)
Asplund, Erik Gunner	1885–1943	Swedish	Bredenburg Department Store, Stockholm (1935); Goteburg Law Courts Annex (1937)
Barragán, Luis	1902–1987	Mexican	Hotel Pierre Marquez Gardens, Acapulco (1955); Eggerstrom House, Mexico City (1968)
Barry, Charles	1795–1860	English	Houses of Parliament, London (1860)
Bentley, John Francis	1830–1902	English	Westminster Cathedral, London (1903)
Berlage, Hendrick Petrus	1856–1934	Dutch	Municipal Museum, The Hague (1935); Stock Exchange, Amsterdam (1903)
Bernini, Gioanlorezo	1598–1680	Italian	St. Peter's basilica, Rome (1626 renovation); Piazza di San Pietro, Rome (1667)
Borromini, Francesco	1599–1667	Italian	Lateran Tombs, Rome (1655); Villa Falconieri, Frascati (1667)
Bramante, Donate	1444–1514	Italian	S. Maria Presso San Satiro, Milan (1478 renovation); Belvedere Court (1504)
Brunelleschi, Filippo	1377–1446	Italian	Cathedral of Santa Maria del Fiore, Florence (cupola, lantern & tribune morte) (1446)
Burlington, Richard Boyle, 3rd Earl of	1664–1753	English	Wade House, London (1723); Assembly Rooms, York (1732)

Name	Dates	Nationality	Major Works
Burton, Decimus	1800–1881	English	Cornwall Terrace, London (nd); Hyde Park Screen, London (1825)
Butterfield, William	1814–1900	English	Keble College, Oxford (1883); All Saints, (London) 1859
Chambers, William	1732–1790	English	Trent Palace, Middlesex (1777); Theatre Royal, Liverpool (1772)
Cortona, Pietro	1596–1669	Italian	Santi Luci et Marchina, Rome (1650)
Deane, Thomas	1792–1871	Irish	Museum of Natural History, Oxford (1861); Trinity College Library, Dublin (1862)
Fischer von Erlach, Johann	1656–1723	Austrian	Holy Trinity Plague Column, Vienna (1689); Imperial Library, Vienna (1730)
Gandon, James	1743–1823	Irish	County Hall, Nottingham (1772); Emsworth, Dublin (1794)
Gaudi, Antonio	1852–1926	Spanish	Casa Vicens, Barcelona (1880); Casa Mila, Barcelona (1910)
Gibbs, James	1682–1754	Scottish	Alexander Pope Villa, Middlesex (1720); Radcliffe Library, Oxford (1754)
Gehry, Frank	1929–	American	California Aerospace Museum, Santa Monica (1984); Guggenheim Museum, Bilbao (1997)
Goff, Bruce	1904–1982	American	Hopewell Baptist Church, Oklahoma (1950); Nicol House, Kansas City (1967)
Gomez de Mora, Juan	1580–1648	Spanish	Encarnación Church, Madrid (1611–16)
Gropius, Walter	1883–1969	German	Chicago Tribune Building, Chicago (1922); Pan Am Building, New York (1957)
Guimard, Hector	1867–1942	French	Humbert De Romans Auditorium, Paris (1901)
Hansen, Christian	1803–1883	Danish	Mint, Athens (1836); Observatory, Copenhagen (1861)
Hildebrandt, Johann	1668–1745	Austrian	Garden House, Siebenbrunn Palace (1730); Parish Church, Asperdorf (1733)
Hittorff, Jacques	1792–1867	German	Church of St. Vincent De Paul, Paris (1848)
Horta, Victor	1861–1947	Belgian	Horta House, Belgium (1989); Hallet House, Brussels (1903)
Iktinos	c.450–400 BC	Greek	The Parthenon, Athens (437 BC)
Jefferson, Thomas	1742–1826	American	Monticello, Virginia (1782)
Jones, Inigo	1573–1652	English	Whitehall Palace, London (1622); Somerset House, London (1635)

Name	Dates	Nationality	Works
Kahn, Albert	1869–1942	American	General Motors Building, Detroit (1925); Fisher Building, Detroit (1929)
Keyser, Hendrick de	1565–1621	Dutch	Zuiderkerk, Amsterdam, Netherlands (1614)
Krier, Rob	1938–	Austrian	Façade for Hotel, Salzburg, Germany (1988); Apartment Building, Bilbao, Spain (1992)
Kroll, Lucien	1927–	Belgian	Medical Facility Buildings Complex, Belgium (1977)
Latrobe, Benjamin	1764–1820	American	Roman Catholic Cathedral, Baltimore (1818); Capitol Building, Washington, D.C. (1817)
Le Brun, Charles	1619–1690	French	Palais de Versailles (1678)
Le Corbusier [Charles Edouard Jeannert]	1887–1965	French	Villa Planiex, Paris (1927); Museum, Ahmedabad, India (1957)
Loos, Adolf	1870–1933	Czechoslovakian	American bar, Vienna (1907); Muller House, Prague (1930)
Lutyens, Edwin Landeer	1869–1944	English	Munstead Wood, Surrey (1896); Tigbourne Court, Surrey (1899)
Mackintosh, Charles Rennie	1868–1928	Scottish	Glasgow School of Art, Glasgow (1909)
Maki, Fumihiko	1928–	Japanese	Toyota Memorial Hall, Nagoya (1960); National Museum of Modern Art, Kyoto (1986)
Mansart, Francois	1598–1666	French	Chateau de Berry (1623); Hotel du Jars, Paris (1645)
Meier, Richard	1934–	American	High Museum of Art, Atlanta (1983); Getty Center, Los Angeles (1997)
Mendelson, Erich	1887–1953	German-born American	Atomic Energy Commission Labratories, Berkeley (1953)
Michelangelo Buonarrati	1475–1564	Italian	San Lorenzo façade, Florence (1517); St. Peter's basilica, Rome (1564)
Moore, Charles W.	1925–1993	American	Hood Museum of Art, Hanover, NH (1985)
Morgan, Julia	1872–1957	American	Elliott House, Berkeley (1920); Hearst Estate, California (1941)
Nash, John	1752–1835	English	Terraces and facades, Regents Park, London (1827)
Neumann, Johann	1687–1753	German	High Altar, Cathedral of Worms (1749); Schloss Augustusburg (1748)
Neutra, Richard	1892–1970	Austrian-born American	Lincoln Memorial Museum, Gettysburg, PA (1959); Hall of Records, Los Angeles (1961)

Name	Dates	Nationality	Major Works
Niemeyer, Oscar	1907–	Brazilian	City of Brasília (1964); Mondadori Headquarters, Milan (1975)
O'Gorman, Juan	1905–1982	Mexican	Diego Rivera House, Mexico City (1930); Juan O'Gorman House II (1956)
Olmsted, Frederick Law	1822–1903	American	Park System, Rochester, NY (1888); United States Capitol Grounds (1874)
Palladio, Andrea	1508–1580	Italian	Villa of Leonardo Emo, Vincenza, Italy (1567)
Pei, I. M.	1917–	American	Le Grand Louvre, Paris (1983)
Perrault, Claude	1613–1688	French	East Façade of the Louvre, Paris (1670)
Piano, Renzo	1937–	Italian	Centre Pompidou, Paris (1977, with Richard Rogers)
Playfair, William	1790–1857	English	Donaldson Hospital, Edinburgh (1842–54); National Gallery of Scotland (1850–57)
Plečnik, Jože	1872–1957	Yugoslav	Market, Ljubljana (1942); Monastery of the German Knights, Ljubljana (1953)
Pugin, Augustus	1812–1852	English	Manor House, Wiburton (1848); St. Augustine's Church, Kent (1850)
Rastrelli, Bartolomeo	1700–1771	Russian	Fourth Winter Palace, Petrograd (1762)
Renwick, James	1818–1895	American	Smithsonian Institution, Washington, D.C. (1855)
Richardson, Henry Hobson	1838–1886	American	Grace Church, Massachusetts (1869); City Hall, Albany, NY (1882)
Rietveld, Gerrit T.	1888–1964	Dutch	Juliana Hall and Entrance, Utrecht (1956); Van Sloobe House, Heerlen (1964)
Roebling, John	1806–1859	American	Brooklyn Bridge, New York City (1883)
Roebling, Washington Augustus	1837–1926	American	Brooklyn Bridge, New York City (1883 with father, John)
Saarinen, Eliel	1910–1961	Finnish	Railway station, Viborg (1904); City Hall, Lahti (1912)
Sansovino, Jacopo	1486–1570	Italian	Piazza San Marco, Venice (1540)
Schindler, Rudolph	1887–1953	American	Buena Shore Club, Chicago (1918); Tucker House, Hollywood (1950)
Schinkel, Karl Friedrich	1791–1841	German	Schauspielhaus, Berlin (1821)
Scott, H. M. Baillie	1865–1945	English	The Garth, Cobham, Surrey (1900); Oakhams, Kent (1921)
Scott, George Gilbert	1811–1878	English	Exeter College Chapel, Oxford (1860); St. Mary Abbots Church, London (1872)
Shaw, Richard Norman	1831–1913	English	New Scotland Yard, London (1907)

Soane, John	1753–1857	English	St. Peter's Church, Walworth (1824); Holy Trinity Marylebone, London (1827)
Soleri, Paolo	1919–	Italian	Cosanti Foundaion, Scottsdale, AZ (1976); Dome House, Arizona (1949)
Stirling, Sir James	1926–1992	English	House, Isle of Wight (1956); Biennale Bookshop, Venice (1989)
Street, George Edmund	1824–1881	English	Law Courts, London (1882)
Stuart, James	1713–1788	English	Infirmary, Greenwich Hospital (1764); Chapel, Greenwich Hospital (1788)
Sullivan, Louis	1856–1924	American	Guaranty Building, Buffalo (1896); Stock Exchange, Chicago (1894)
Thomson, Alexander	1817–1875	Scottish	New Campus, University of Glasgow (1850); Egyptian Halls, Glasgow (1871)
van der Rohe, Ludwig Mies	1886–1969	German-born American	Wolf House, Germany (1926); Toronto Dominion Center, Canada (1969)
Vasari, Giorgio	1511–1574	Italian	Uffizi Palace, Florence (1580)
Voysey, Charles F.	1857–1941	English	Memorial Manor House, Tonbridge (1920)
Wagner, Otto	1841–1918	Austrian	Synagogue, Budapest (1871); Lupus Sanatorium, Vienna (1913)
Warschavick, Gregori	1896–1972	Brazilian	First Modern House Exhibition, São Paulo (1930); Raul Crespi Beach House (1943)
Webb, Aston	1879–1930	English	Victoria Azzize Courts, Birmingham (1891); Victoria & Albert Museum, London (1909)
Webb, Philip	1831–1915	English	Standen, Sussex (1892); 19 Lincoln's Inn Fields, London (1869)
White, Stanford	1853–1906	American	Boston Public Library (1888); J. Pierpont Morgan Library, New York (1907, with McKim, Mead and White)
Wren, Sir Christopher	1632–1723	English	Royal Hospital, Greenwich (1691); St. Paul's Cathedral. London (1710)
Wright, Frank Lloyd	1867–1959	American	Robie House, Chicago (1909); Falling Water, Bear Run, PA (1936)
Wyatt, James	1764–1813	English	Lee Priory, Kent (1790); Ashbridge Park, Hertfordshire (1813)

⊙ University of Buffalo. "Cyburia-Famous Architects resources page," http://cyburbia.ap.buffalo.edu/cgi-bin/pairc/archtcts
Curl, James Stevens. *Oxford Dictionary of Architecture*. Oxford: Oxford University Press, 1999.

ELEMENTS OF CLASSICAL ORDERS

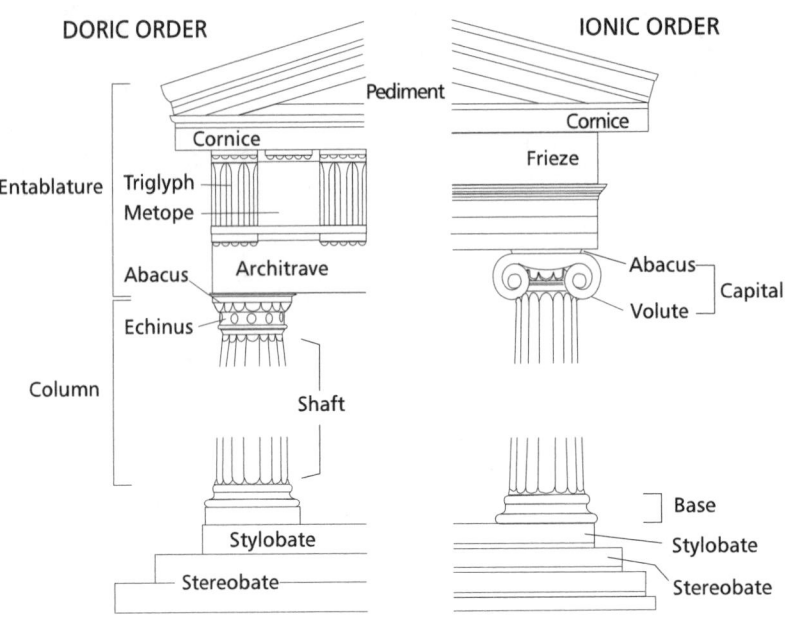

DORIC ORDER

IONIC ORDER

Pediment

Cornice

Cornice

Frieze

Entablature

Triglyph

Metope

Abacus

Architrave

Abacus

Volute

Capital

Echinus

Column

Shaft

Base

Stylobate

Stylobate

Stereobate

Stereobate

TYPES OF COLUMNS

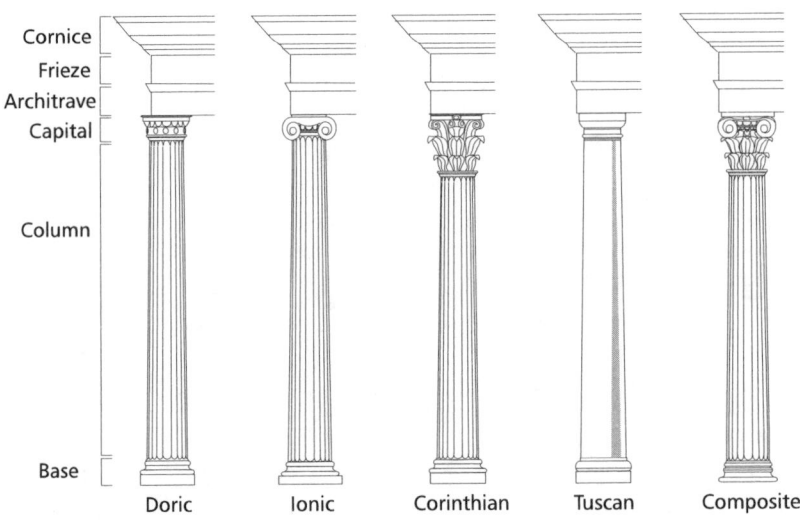

Cornice
Frieze
Architrave
Capital

Column

Base

Doric   Ionic   Corinthian   Tuscan   Composite

Common Music Notation

Treble (G) clef    Alto (C) clef   Bass (F) clef

Flat   Sharp

Dynamics

ppp	pianississimo	very, very quiet
pp	pianissimo	very quiet
p	piano	quiet
mp	mezzopiano	moderately quiet
mf	mezzoforte	moderately loud
f	forte	loud
ff	fortissimo	very loud
fff	fortississimo	very, very loud
sf	sforzando	suddenly very loud

Tempo Indicators

adagio	slow
largo	slow and dignified
andante	flowing, at a walking pace
allegro	quick and bright
allegretto	not as quick as allegro
vivace	fast and lively
presto	very quick
accelerando	getting faster
ritardando (rit.)	holding back
rallentando (rall.)	getting slower
rubato	flexible tempo

Interpretive Indicators

cantabile	singing style
dolce	soft and sweet
expressivo	expressively
legato	smooth
staccato	detached

Crescendo and Diminuendo

Notes

o	Whole note (semibreve)
	Half note (minim)
	Quarter note (crotchet)
	Eighth note (quaver)
	Sixteenth note (semiquaver)
	Thirty-second note (demisemiquaver)

Rests

Staff Line

⊙ Sacher, Jack, ed. *Music A to Z.* New York: Grosset & Dunlap, 1963.
Randel, Don Michael, ed. *The New Harvard Dictionary of Music.* Cambridge, Mass.: Belknap, 1986.

45 Major Orchestras

Orchestra	Year Established
Academy of St. Martin in the Fields (London)	1958
Atlanta Symphony Orchestra	1947
Baltimore Symphony Orchestra	1916
Bamberg Symphony Orchestra	1946
Basle Chamber Orchestra	1926
Bavarian Radio Symphony Orchestra	1960
Berlin Philharmonic Orchestra	1882
Boston Symphony Orchestra	1881
Chicago Symphony Orchestra	1890
Cincinnati Symphony Orchestra	1895
City of Birmingham Symphony Orchestra	1920
Cleveland Orchestra	1918
Czech Philharmonic Orchestra	1896
Dallas Symphony Orchestra	1900
Detroit Symphony Orchestra	1900
Dresden Sächsische Staatskapelle	1548
English Chamber Orchestra	1948
English National Opera Orchestra	1931
Houston Symphony Orchestra	1913
Israel Philharmonic Orchestra	1936
Leipzig Gewandhaus Orchestra	1781
London Philharmonic Orchestra	1932
London Symphony Orchestra	1904
Los Angeles Philharmonic Orchestra	1919
Mariinsky Theater (Kirov) Orchestra	1860
Metropolitan Operas Orchestra	1883
Minnesota Orchestra	1903
National Symphony Orchestra (Washington, D.C.)	1931
New York Philharmonic	1842
Orchestre de la Suisse Romande	1918
Orchestre de Paris	1967
Orchestre symphonique de Montréal	1934
Orpheus Chamber Orchestra	1972
Philadelphia Orchestra	1900
Prague Symphony Orchestra	1934
RAI National Symphony Orchestra	1994
Royal Concertgebouw Orchestra	1888
Royal Opera House Covent Garden Orchestra	1945
Royal Philharmonic Orchestra	1946
Royal Scottish National Orchestra	1894
Saint Louis Symphony Orchestra	1880
San Francisco Symphony Orchestra	1911
Seattle Philharmonic Orchestra	1944
Vienna Philharmonic	1842
Warsaw Philharmonic Orchestra	1946

⊙ Cummings, David, ed. *Random House Encyclopedic Dictionary of Classical Music*. New York: Random House, 1997.

"Orchestral News," ourworld.compuserve.com/homepages/John_Woolard

Sadie, Stanley, ed. *The Norton/Grove Concise Encyclopedia of Music*. New York: Norton, 1994.

125 Major Composers

This section contains composers from different historical eras, countries, and musical genres, both popular and classical. The list includes men and women known for innovation and mastery within their particular musical periods, composers who have experimented with those conventions, and composers whose acclaim comes from the enduring popularity of their work.

Name	Dates	Nationality	Major Works
Adams, John	1947–	American	*Harmonium*; Opera: *Nixon in China*
Adès, Thomas	1971–	English	*Toys for Orchestra*; Opera: *Powder Her Face*

Albeniz, Isaac	1860–1909	Spanish	Rapsodia espanola Op. 70 for Piano and Orchestra; Suite espanola Op. 47 for Piano
Arne, Thomas Augustine	1710–1778	English	Various symphonies; Songs: "Rule Britannia"; "Blow, Blow, Thou Winter Wind"
Auber, Daniel-Francois	1782–1871	French	Operas: *Fra Diavolo*; *Manon Lescaut*
Bach, Johann Sebastian	1685–1750	German	*Art of the Fugue*; *Brandenberg Concertos*; *St. Matthew Passion*
Barber, Samuel	1910–1981	American	Adagio for Strings; Song Cycle: *Knoxville: Summer of 1915*; Opera: *Antony and Cleopatra*
Bartók, Béla	1881–1945	Hungarian	Concerto for Orchestra; Ballet: *Miraculous Mandarin*; Opera: *Bluebeard's Castle*
Beethoven, Ludwig van	1770–1827	German	Sonatas for Piano; Various symphonies; Opera: *Fidelio*
Bellini, Vincenzo	1801–1835	Italian	Operas: *Norma*; *I Puritani*; *La Sonnambula*
Berg, Alban	1885–1935	Austrian	Concerto for Violin; Operas: *Wozzeck*; *Lulu*
Berio, Luciano	1925–	Italian	*Sequences*; *Sinfonia*; Opera: *La vera storia*
Berlin, Irving	1888–1989	Russian-born American	Musicals: *As Thousands Cheer*; *Annie Get Your Gun*; *Call Me Madam*
Berlioz, Hector	1803–1869	French	*Damnation of Faust*; *Symphonie fantastique*; Opera: *Les Troyens*
Bernstein, Leonard	1918–1990	American	*Mass*; Musicals: *On the Town*; *West Side Story*
Bizet, Georges	1838–1875	French	*L'Arlesienne Suites*; Operas: *Carmen*; *The Pearl Fishers*
Blitzstein, Marc	1905–1964	American	Operas: *The Cradle Will Rock, Regina*
Borodin, Alexander	1833–1887	Russian	*Polovtsian Dances*; Opera: *Prince Igor*; Various quartets
Boulez, Pierre	1925–	French	*Le Marteau sans maître*; Sonatas for Piano; *Pli selon pli*
Brahms, Johannes	1833–1897	German	Chamber music; symphonies; Concerto for Violin and Cello; *Variations on a Theme by Haydn*
Britten, Benjamin	1913–1976	English	*Young Person's Guide to the Orchestra*; Operas: *Peter Grimes*; *Billy Budd*
Bruzdowicz, Joanna	1943–	Polish	Operas: *The Penal Colony*; *The Gates of Paradise*; *Tides and Waves*

Name	Dates	Nationality	Major Works
Byrd, William	1543–1623	English	Consort music; Various music for keyboard; Various sacred choral music
Cage, John	1912–1992	American	Music for String Quartet; Sonatas and Interludes for Prepared Piano
Chopin, Frédéric	1810–1849	Polish	Concertos for Piano; Various music for piano (Ballades; Etudes; Nocturnes)
Copland, Aaron	1900–1990	American	*Fanfare for the Common Man*; Ballets: *Appalachian Spring*; *Rodeo*
Corelli, Arcangelo	1653–1713	Italian	Various concerti grossi
Davies, Peter Maxwell	1934–	English	*Strathclyde* Concertos; Opera: *The Lighthouse*
Debussy, Claude	1862–1918	French	Chamber music; *Prelude a l'aprèsmidi d'un faune*; Opera: *Pelleas et Melisande*
Donizetti, Gaetano	1797–1848	Italian	Operas: *Don Pasquale*; *La Fille du Regiment*; *Lucia di Lammermoor*
Dukas, Paul	1865–1935	French	*The Sorcerer's Apprentice*
Dvorák, Antonin	1841–1904	Bohemian	Concerto for Violin; Various symphonies; Opera: *Rusalka*
Edgar, Edward	1857–1934	English	Concerto for Cello; *Enigma Variations*; *Pomp and Circumstance* marches
Fauré, Gabriel	1845–1924	French	Chamber music; *Pavane for Orchestra*; Various songs
Franck, César	1822–1890	French	Organ music; Chamber music; Symphony in D Minor
Gershwin, George	1898–1937	American	*American in Paris*; *Rhapsody in Blue*; Opera: *Porgy and Bess*
Giovanni Pierluigi da Palestrina	c.1525–1594	Italian	Various masses and motets
Glass, Philip	1937–	American	Operas: *Einstein on the Beach*; *The Voyage*; Soundtrack: *Mishima*
Glinka, Mikhail	1804–1857	Russian	Operas: *A Life for the Tsar*; *Russlan and Ludmilla*
Gluck, Christoph Willibald	1714–1787	German	Operas: *Orfeo ed Euridice*; *Iphigénie en Tauride*
Gounod, Charles	1818–1893	French	Operas: *Faust*; *Roméo et Juliette*

Grieg, Edvard	1843–1907	Norwegian	Concerto for Piano; *Peer Gynt Suites*
Guillaume de Machaut	c.1300–1377	French	*Notre Dame Mass*; Various chansons
Handel, George Frideric	1685–1759	German	*Royal Fireworks Music; Water Music;* Oratorio: *Messiah*
Haydn, Franz Joseph	1732–1809	Austrian	Sacred choral music; Various symphonies; Oratorio: *The Creation*
Henze, Hans Werner	1926–	German	Various symphonies; Operas: *The Young Lord; The English Cat*
Hindemith, Paul	1895–1963	German	*Symphonic Metamorphosis of Themes by Weber;* Opera: *Mathis der Maler*
Holst, Gustav	1874–1937	English	*The Planets*
Humperdinck, Engelbert	1854–1921	German	Opera: *Hansel und Gretel*
Ives, Charles	1874–1954	American	Sonatas for piano; Various symphonies; *Three Places in New England*
Janácek, Leos	1854–1928	Czech	Music for piano; Operas: *Jenufa; The Cunning Little Vixen*
Josquin des Prez	c.1450–1521	French	Various masses, motets, chansons
Khachaturian, Aram	1903–1978	Armenian	Ballet: *Gayne;* Soundtracks: *The Battle of Stalingrad; Othello*
Kodály, Zóltan	1882–1967	Hungarian	*Peacock Variations;* Opera: *Háry János*
Lalo, Édouard	1823–1892	French	Concerto in D Minor for Cello; Symphony in G Minor; Symphony espagnole for Violin and Orchestra
Leoncavallo, Ruggero	1858–1919	Italian	Opera: *I Pagliacci*
Ligeti, György	1923–	Hungarian	*Atmosphères;* Opera: *Le grand macabre*
Liszt, Franz	1811–1886	Hungarian	*Annees de Pelerinage* for Piano; *Les Preludes* for Orchestra; *Totentanz* for Piano and Orchestra
Lloyd Webber, Andrew	1948–	English	Musicals: *Jesus Christ, Superstar; Evita; Cats*
Lully, Jean Baptiste	1632–1687	French	Opera: *Atys;* Ballet: *Le Bougeois Gentilhomme*
Mahler, Gustav	1860–1911	Austrian	Various symphonies; *Das Lied von der Erde;* Song Cycle: *Kindertotenlieder*
Marenzio, Luca	?1553–1599	Italian	Madrigals
Massenet, Jules	1842–1912	French	Ballet: *Le Cid;* Operas: *Manon; Thaïs*

Name	Dates	Nationality	Major Works
Mendelssohn, Felix	1809–1847	German	Music for piano; Incidental music for *Midsummer Night's Dream*; Oratorio: *Elijah*
Menotti, Gian Carlo	1911–	Italian-born American	Operas: *Amahl and the Night Visitors*; *The Medium*
Messiaen, Olivier	1908–1992	French	Music for Organ; Music for Piano; *Quatuor pour la fin du temps*
Meyerbeer, Giacomo	1791–1864	German	Operas: *L'Africaine*; *Les Huguenots*
Monteverdi, Claudio	1567–1643	Italian	Various masses; Operas: *La Favola d'Orfeo*; *L'Incoronazione di Poppea*
Mozart, Wolfgang Amadeus	1756–1791	Austrian	Chamber Music; Mass in C Minor ("The Great"); Opera: *Die Zauberflote*
Mussorgsky, Modest	1839–1881	Russian	*Night on Bald Mountain*; *Pictures at an Exhibition*; Opera: *Boris Godounov*
Nielsen, Carl	1865–1931	Danish	Various symphonies
Offenbach, Jacques	1819–1880	French	*Gaite Parisienne*; Opera: *Les Contes d'Hoffmann*
Orlando di Lasso	1532–1594	Franco-Flemish	Various madrigals and motets; *Requiem*
Orff, Carl	1895–1982	German	Oratorio: *Carmina Burana*
Paganini, Niccoló	1782–1840	Italian	Various caprices; Concerto for Violin
Penderecki, Krzystof	1933–	Polish	Various concertos; *Threnody for the Victims of Hiroshima*
Pergolesi, Giovanni Battista	1710–1736	Italian	*Stabat Mater*; Opera: *La Serva padrona*
Ponchielli, Amilcare	1834–1886	Italian	Ballet: *Dance of the Hours*; Opera: *La Gioconda*
Poulenc, Francis	1899–1963	French	Ballet: *Les Biches*; Operas: *Dialogue of the Carmelites*; *Les Mamelles de Tirésias*
Prokofiev, Sergei	1891–1953	Russian	*Peter and the Wolf*; Ballet: *Cinderella*; Opera: *The Love of Three Oranges*
Puccini, Giacomo	1858–1924	Operas	Operas: *La Boheme*; *Madama Butterfly*; *Tosca*
Purcell, Henry	1659–1695	English	*Music for the Funeral of Queen Mary*; Opera: *Dido and Aeneas*

Rachmaninov, Sergei	1873–1943	Russian	Concertos for Piano; Chamber Music; *Rhapsody on a Theme of Paganini*
Ravel, Maurice	1875–1937	French	*Bolero; Rhapsodie espagnole;* Ballet: *Daphnis et Chloé*
Reich, Steve	1936–	American	*Desert Music; Music for 18 Musicians*
Respighi, Ottorino	1879–1936	Italian	*Fountains of Rome; Pines of Rome*
Rimsky-Korsakov, Nikolai	1844–1908	Russian	*Russian Easter Overture; Schherazade;* Ballet: *Coq d'Or*
Rodgers, Richard	1902–1979	American	Musicals: *Pal Joey; Oklahoma!; South Pacific*
Rossini, Gioacchino	1792–1868	Italian	*Stabat Mater;* Operas: *Barber of Seville; La Cenerentola*
Saint-Saëns, Camille	1835–1921	French	*Carnival of the Animals;* Symphony No. 3 ("Organ"); Opera: *Samson et Dalila*
Satie, Erik	1866–1925	French	Music for piano
Scarlatti, Domenico	1685–1757	Italian	Sonatas for keyboard
Schoenberg, Arnold	1874–1951	German	Music for piano; *Verklarte Nacht;* Song Cycle: *Pierrot Lunaire*
Schubert, Franz	1797–1828	Austrian	*Rosamunde;* Song Cycle: *Die Schone Mullerin;* Various symphonies
Schumann, Robert	1810–1856	German	Music for piano; Concerto for Cello; Song Cycle: *Dichterliebe*
Schütz, Heinrich	1585–1672	German	*Symphoniæ sacræ;* three Passions
Scriabin, Alexander	1872–1915	Russian	Music for piano
Sessions, Roger	1896–1985	American	Concerto for Orchestra; Various symphonies
Shostakovich, Dmitri	1906–1975	Russian	Various concertos and symphonies; Music for piano
Sibelius, Jean	1865–1957	Finnish	Concerto for Violin; *Finlandia;* Various symphonies
Smetena, Bedrich	1824–1884	Czech	*Ma Vlast* (including "The Moldau"); Opera: *The Bartered Bride;* Various quartets
Sondheim, Stephen	1930–	American	Musicals: *Company; Sweeney Todd; Passion*
Stockhausen, Karlheinz	1928–	German	*Klavierstucke; Kontakte*
Strauss, Johann, II	1825–1899	Austrian	Various waltzes; Opera: *Die Fledermaus*
Strauss, Richard	1864–1949	German	*Also Sprach Zarathustra; Don Juan;* Opera: *Der Rosenkavalier*

Name	Dates	Nationality	Major Works
Stravinsky, Igor	1882–1971	Russian-born American	Ballets: *The Firebird*; *The Rite of Spring*; Opera: *The Rake's Progress*
Sullivan, Arthur	1842–1900	English	Operas (collab. W. S. Gilbert): *H.M.S. Pinafore*; *The Pirates of Penzance*; *The Mikado*
Szymanowski, Karol	1882–1937	Polish	Concertos for Violin; Various string quartets
Takemitsu, Toru	1930–1996	Japanese	*November Steps*; *River Run*
Tallis, Thomas	c.1505–1585	English	Sacred choral music
Taverner, John	c.1490–1545	English	Festal masses
Tchaikovsky, Pyotr Ilyich	1840–1893	Russian	*Overture for 1812*; Ballets: *The Nutcracker*; *Swan Lake*
Telemann, Georg Philipp	1681–1767	German	Various concertos and oratorios; Chamber Music
Thomson, Virgil	1896–1989	American	Operas: (collab. Gertrude Stein) *Four Saints in Three Acts*; *The Mother of Us All*
Varèse, Edgard	1883–1965	French-born American	*Deserts*; *Ionisation*
Vaughan Williams, Ralph	1872–1958	English	*Fantasia on a theme by Thomas Tallis*; *Fantasia on Greensleeves*
Verdi, Giuseppe	1813–1901	Italian	*Requiem Mass*; Operas: *La Traviata*; *Aida*
Victoria, Tomás Luis de	c.1548–1611	Spanish	Various masses and motets
Vivaldi, Antonio	1678–1741	Italian	*Four Seasons*; *Gloria*; Various concertos
Wagner, Richard	1813–1883	German	Operas: *Tristan und Isolde*; *Der Ring des Nibelungen*; *Parsifal*
Walton, William	1902–1993	English	Soundtracks: *Henry V*; Operas: *Troilus and Cressida*; *The Bear*
Weber, Carl Maria Friedrich von	1786–1826	German	*Invitation to the Dance*; Operas: *Der Freischütz*; *Oberon*
Webern, Anton	1918–1945	Austrian	*Five Orchestral Pieces*; *Music for a String Quartet*
Weill, Kurt	1900–1950	German-born American	Operas: *The Threepenny Opera*; *The Rise and Fall of the City of Mahagonny*; Musicals: *One Touch of Venus*
Zwilich, Ellen Taaffe	1939–	American	Concerto Grosso; Three Movements for Orchestra

⊙ Maxwell Macmillan International. *Baker's Biographical Dictionary of Musicians*. New York: Schirmer, 1992.

Morta, Brian, and Paula Collins, eds. *Contemporary Composers*. Chicago and London: St. James, 1992.

Sadie, Julie Anne, and Rhian Samuel, eds. *The Norton/Grove Dictionary of Women Composers*. New York: Norton, 1995.

50 Notable Conductors

*This list includes conductors of classical and popular orchestral music. It represents a wide range of tempera-
ment and style, differing approaches to musical interpretation, and general historical importance to the development of the field.*

Name	Dates	Nationality
Abbado, Claudio	1933–	Italian
Ashkenazy, Vladimir	1937–	Russian
Barenboim, Daniel	1942–	Argentine-born Israeli
Beecham, Sir Thomas	1879–1961	British
Bernstein, Leonard	1918–1990	American
Böhm, Karl	1894–1981	Austrian
Caldwell, Sarah	1924–	American
Chailly, Riccardo	1953–	Italian
Chung, Myung-Wha	1953–	Korean-born American
Davies, Dennis Russell	1944–	American
De Sabata, Victor	1892–1967	Italian
Dorati, Antal	1906–1988	Hungarian-born American
Dutoit, Charles	1936–	Swiss
Fiedler, Arthur	1894–1979	American
Foss [Fuchs], Lukas	1922–	German-born American
Fricsay, Ferenc	1914–1963	Hungarian-born Austrian
Furtwängler, Wilhelm	1886–1954	German
Gergiev, Valery	1953–	Russian
Groves, Sir Charles	1915–1992	British
Järvi, Neeme	1937–	Estonian
Karajan, Herbert von	1908–1989	German
Kleiber, Carlos	1930–	German-born Austrian
Kleiber, Erich	1890–1956	Austrian
Klemperer, Otto	1885–1973	German
Koussevitzky, Serge	1874–1951	Russian
Kubelik, Rafael	1914–1996	Czech-born Swiss
Leppard, Raymond	1927–	British
Levine, James (Lawrence)	1943–	American
Mahler, Gustav	1860–1911	Austrian
Markevitch, Igor	1912–1983	Russian-born French
Masur, Kurt	1927–	German
Mata, Eduardo	1942–1995	Mexican
Mehta, Zubin	1936–	Indian
Mitropoulos, Dimitri	1896–1960	Greek-born American
Muti, Riccardo	1941–	Italian
Ormandy, Eugene (Blau)	1899–1985	Hungarian-born American
Ozawa, Seiji	1935–	Chinese-born Japanese
Previn, André	1929–	German-born American
Queler, Eve	1936–	American
Rattle, Simon	1955–	British
Salonen, Esa-Pekka	1958–	Finnish
Sargent, Sir (Harold) Malcolm (Watts)	1895–1967	British

50 Notable Conductors *(cont.)*

Name	Dates	Nationality
Schippers, Thomas	1930–1977	American
Solti, Sir Georg (György)	1912–1997	Hungarian-born British
Stokowski, Leopold	1882–1977	British-born American
Szell, George	1897–1970	Hungarian-born American
Tilson Thomas, Michael	1944–	American
Toscanini, Arturo	1867–1957	Italian-born American
Walter, Bruno [B. W. Schlesinger]	1876–1962	German-born American
Zukerman, Pinchas	1948–	Israeli

⊙ Musiker, Ruben, and Naomi Musiker. *Conductors and Composers of Popular Orchestral Music.* Westport, Conn.: Greenwood, 1998.

Slominsky, Nicolas, and Laura Kuhn, eds. *Baker's Biographical Dictionary of 20th Century Classical Musicians.* New York: Schirmer, 1997.

100 Noted Classical Instrumentalists

The following instrumentalists are listed by instrument, in score order.

Name	Dates	Nationality	Instrument
Argerich, Martha	1941–	Argentinian	piano
Arrau, Claudio	1903–1991	Chilean	piano
Ashkenazy, Vladimir	1937–	Russian	piano
Ax, Emmanuel	1949–	American	piano
Backhaus, Wilhelm	1884–1969	German	piano
Barenboim, Daniel	1942–	Argentinian	piano
Bauer, Harold	1873–1951	British	piano
Brendel, Alfred	1931–	Austrian	piano
Casadesus, Robert	1899–1972	French	piano
Cliburn, Van	1934–	American	piano
Cortot, Alfred	1877–1962	French	piano
Firkusny, Rudolf	1912–1994	Czech	piano
Fischer, Edwin	1886–1960	Swiss	piano
Friedman, Ignaz	1882–1948	Polish	piano
Gieseking, Walter	1895–1956	German	piano
Gilels, Emil	1916–1985	Russian	piano
Godowsky, Leopold	1870–1938	Polish	piano
Gould, Glenn	1932–1982	Canadian	piano
Hess, Myra	1890–1965	British	piano
Hofmann, Josef	1876–1957	Polish	piano
Horowitz, Vladimir	1903–1989	Russian	piano
Johannesen, Grant	1921–	American	piano
Kempff, Wilhelm	1895–1991	German	piano
Kissin, Yevgeny	1971–	Russian	piano
Larrocha, Alicia de	1923–	Spanish	piano
Lhevinne, Joseph	1874–1944	Russian	piano
Lipatti, Dinu	1917–1950	Romanian	piano

Liszt, Franz	1811–1886	Hungarian	piano
Michelangeli, Arturo Benedetti	1920–1995	Italian	piano
Oborin, Lev	1907–1974	Russian	piano
Ohlsson, Garrick	1948–	American	piano
Paderewski, Ignacy Jan	1860–1941	Polish	piano
Rachmaninoff, Serge	1873–1943	Russian	piano
Richter, Sviatoslav	1915–1997	Russian	piano
Rubinstein, Artur	1887–1982	Polish	piano
Schnabel, Arthur	1882–1951	Austrian	piano
Serkin, Rudolf	1903–1991	Austrian	piano
Tureck, Roslyn	1914–	American	piano
Watts, André	1946–	American	piano
Kirkpatrick, Ralph	1911–1984	American	harpsichord
Landowska, Wanda	1879–1959	Polish	harpsichord
Valenti, Fernando	1926–1990	American	harpsichord
Grandjany, Marcel	1891–1975	American	harp
Salzedo, Carlos	1885–1961	American	harp
Biggs, E. Power	1906–1977	American	organ
Dupré, Marcel	1886–1971	French	organ
Schweitzer, Albert	1875–1965	Swiss	organ
Auer, Leopold	1845–1930	Russian	violin
Bull, Ole	1810–1880	Norwegian	violin
Chang, Sarah	1980–	American	violin
Elman, Mischa	1891–1967	Russian	violin
Francescatti, Zino	1902–1991	French	violin
Grumiaux, Arthur	1921–1986	Belgian	violin
Heifetz, Jascha	1901–1987	American	violin
Joachim, Joseph	1831–1907	German	violin
Kreisler, Fritz	1875–1962	Austrian	violin
Menuhin, Yehudi	1916–1999	American	violin
Midori	1971–	Japanese	violin
Milstein, Nathan	1904–1992	Russian	violin
Mozart, Leopold	1719–1787	Austrian	violin
Mutter, Anne-Sophie	1963–	German	violin
Oistrakh, David	1908–1974	Russian	violin
Paganini, Niccoló	1782–1840	Italian	violin
Perlman, Itzhak	1945–	Israeli	violin
Ricci, Ruggiero	1918–	American	violin
Salerno-Sonnenberg, Nadja	19??–	Italian	violin
Stern, Isaac	1920–	American	violin
Szigeti, Joseph	1892–1973	Hungarian	violin
Ysaye, Eugene	1858–1931	Belgian	violin
Zimbalist, Efrem	1890–1985	Russian	violin
Aronowitz, Cecil	1916–1978	British	viola
Primrose, William	1903–1982	British	viola
Casals, Pablo	1876–1973	Spanish	violoncello
Du Pré, Jacqueline	1945–1987	British	violoncello
Feuermann, Emmanuel	1902–1942	German	violoncello
Harrell, Lynn	1944–	American	violoncello
Ma, Yo-Yo	1955–	American	violoncello

Name	Dates	Nationality	Instrument
Piatigorsky, Gregor	1903–1976	Russian	violoncello
Popper, David	1843–1913	Czech	violoncello
Rostropovich, Mstislav	1927–	Russian	violoncello
Starker, Janos	1924–	Hungarian	violoncello
Koussevitzky, Serge	1874–1951	Russian	double bass
Giuliani, Mauro	1781–1829	Italian	guitar
Segovia, Andrés	1893–1987	Spanish	guitar
Williams, John	1941–	Australian	guitar
Galway, James	1939–	Irish	flute
Rampal, Jean-Pierre	1922–2000	French	flute
Goossens, Leon	1897–1988	British	oboe
Holliger, Heinz	1939–	Swiss	oboe
Kell, Reginald	1906–1981	British	clarinet
Stoltzman, Richard	1942–	American	clarinet
Camden, Archie	1888–1979	British	bassoon
Weisberg, Arthur	19??–	American	bassoon
Brain, Dennis	1921–1957	British	horn
Tuckwell, Barry	1931–	Australian	horn
André, Maurice	1933–	French	trumpet
Marsalis, Wynton	1961–	American	trumpet
Pryor, Arthur	1870–1942	American	trombone
Phillips, Harvey	1929–	American	tuba

⊙ Cummings, David, ed. *Random House Encyclopedic Dictionary of Classical Music*. New York: Random House, 1997.

Kennedy, Michael, ed. *The Concise Oxford Dictionary of Music*. Oxford and New York: Oxford University Press, 1996.

International Directory of Musicians. "Instrumental soloists, groups and conductors," www.musicbase.org/instrumental.html.

50 Major Classical Singers

Singers on this list represent a broad range of vocal styles and approaches to classical repertory. They range from performers whose popularity has endured for decades to singers whose technical mastery has set the standard for vocal performance.

Name	Dates	Nationality	Range
Bartoli, Cecilia	1966–	Italian	mezzo-soprano
Battle, Kathleen	1948–	American	soprano
Bergonzi, Carlo	1924–	Italian	tenor
Bocelli, Andrea	1958–	Italian	tenor
Caballé, Montserrat	1933–	Spanish	soprano
Callas, Maria	1923–1977	American	soprano
Calvé, Emma	1858–1942	French	soprano
Carreras, José	1946–	Spanish	tenor

Caruso, Enrico	1873–1921	Italian	tenor
Crespin, Régine	1927–	French	soprano
de los Angeles, Victoria	1923–	Spanish	soprano
Domingo, Placido	1941–	Spanish	tenor
Fischer-Dieskau, Dietrich	1925–	German	baritone
Fleming, Renee	1959–	American	soprano
Freni, Mirella	1935–	Italian	soprano
Garden, Mary	1874–1967	Scottish	soprano
Hampson, Thomas	1955–	American	baritone
Hempel, Frieda	1885–1955	German	soprano
Horne, Marilyn	1934–	American	mezzo-soprano
Jurinac, Sena	1921–	Yugoslav	soprano
Lehmann, Lilli	1848–1929	German	soprano
Ludwig, Christa	1928–	German	mezzo-soprano
McCormack, John	1884–1945	Irish	tenor
Melba, Nellie	1861–1931	Australian	soprano
Melchior, Lauritz	1890–1973	Danish	tenor
Milanov, Zinka	1906–1989	Yugoslavian	soprano
Nilsson, Birgit	1918–	Swedish	soprano
Norman, Jessye	1945–	American	soprano
Pavarotti, Luciano	1935–	Italian	tenor
Pears, Peter	1910–1986	English	tenor
Pons, Lily	1898–1976	French	soprano
Ponselle, Rosa	1897–1981	American	soprano
Price, Leontyne	1927–	American	soprano
Ramey, Samuel	1942–	American	bass
Schipa, Tito	1888–1965	Italian	tenor
Schwarzkopf, Elisabeth	1915–	German	soprano
Scotto, Renata	1934–	Italian	soprano
Sembrich, Marcella	1858–1935	Polish	soprano
Sills, Beverly	1929–	American	soprano
Souzay, Gérard	1918–	French	baritone
Stevens, Rïse	1913–	American	mezzo-soprano
Stratas, Teresa	1938–	Canadian	soprano
Sutherland, Joan	1926–	Australian	soprano
Te Kanawa, Kiri	1944–	New Zealander	soprano
Tebaldi, Renata	1922–	Italian	soprano
Terfel, Bryn	1965–	Welsh	baritone
Tetrazzini, Luisa	1871–1940	Italian	soprano
Turner, Eva	1892–1990	English	soprano
Vickers, Jon	1926–	Canadian	tenor
Von Stade, Frederica	1945–	American	mezzo-soprano

⊙ Warrack, John, and Ewan West, eds. *Concise Oxford Dictionary of Opera*. New York: Oxford University Press, 1996.

Anderson, James. *The Harper Dictionary of Opera and Operetta*. New York: HarperCollins, 1989.

Kutsch, K. J., and Leo Rieners. *A Concise Biographical Dictionary of Singers*. New York: Chilton, 1969.

These singers and groups represent a range of music styles and periods. "Popular" refers to musicians who redefined the limits of public taste or captured the spirit of the time, as well as those who had high record sales. The songs following each artist are indicative of the vocal and stylistic range of that singer or group.

[Note: Although line-ups often change, each group listing includes the members most commonly associated with that band. Unless otherwise noted, all singers and groups are from the United States.]

Abba [Anni-Fri "Frida" Lyngstad; Agnetha Fältskog; Bjorn Ulvaeus; Benny Andersson], b. Sweden. *Songs:* "Mamma Mia" (1976); "Take A Chance on Me" (1978)

Andrews Sisters, The [Patti, Maxine, and LaVerne Andrews]. *Songs:* "Boogie Woogie Bugle Boy" (1940); "Don't Sit Under the Apple Tree (With Anyone Else But Me)" (1942)

Armstrong, Louis "Satchmo" (1901–1971). *Songs:* "Ain't Misbehavin'" (1929); "Hello, Dolly" (1964)

Autry, Gene (1907–1998). *Songs:* "Here Comes Santa Claus" (1947); "Rudolph the Red-Nosed Reindeer" (1949)

Baez, Joan [Joan Chandos Baez] (1941–). *Songs:* "The Night They Drove Old Dixie Down" (1971); "Diamonds and Rust" (1975)

Beach Boys, The [original singers: Brian Wilson; Carl Wilson; Dennis Wilson; Mike Love; Al Jardine]. *Songs:* "California Girls" (1965); "Good Vibrations" (1966)

Beatles, The [John Lennon; Paul McCartney; George Harrison; Ringo Starr], b. England. *Songs:* "I Want to Hold Your Hand" (1964); "Hey Jude" (1968)

Bee Gees [Barry Gibb; Maurice Gibb; Robin Gibb], b. England. *Songs:* "Stayin' Alive" (1977); "Night Fever" (1978)

Bennett, Tony [Anthony Dominick Benedetto] (1926–). *Songs:* "Stranger in Paradise" (1953); "I Left My Heart in San Francisco" (1962)

Blondie [Debbie Harry; Chris Stein; Frank Infante; Jimmy Destri; Nigel Harrison; Clem Burke]. *Songs:* "Heart of Glass" (1979); "Call Me" (1980)

Bowie, David [David Robert Jones] (1947–), b. England. *Songs:* "Space Oddity" (1973); "Let's Dance" (1983)

Brown, James (1928–). *Songs:* "I Got You (I Feel Good)" (1965); "Get Up (I Feel Like Being a Sex Machine)" (1970)

Calloway, Cab [Cabell Calloway] (1907–1997). *Songs:* "Minnie the Moocher" (1931); "Jumpin' Jive" (1939)

Campbell, Glen (1936–). *Songs:* "Wichita Lineman" (1968); "Rhinestone Cowboy" (1975)

Cantor, Eddie [Isadore Itzkowitz] (1892–1964). *Songs:* "Yes, We Have No Bananas" (1923); "Makin' Whoopee" (1928)

Carey, Mariah (1970–). *Songs:* "Dreamlover" (1993); "Endless Love" (1994; with Luther Vandross)

Cher [Cherilyn LaPierre] (1946–). *Songs:* "If I Could Turn Back Time" (1989); "Believe" (1998)

Chicago [Peter Cetera; Robert Lamm; James Pankow; Lee Loughnane; Terry Kath; Walt Parazaider; Danny Seraphine]. *Songs:* "Does Anybody Really Know What Time It Is?" (1970); "Hard To Say I'm Sorry" (1982)

Cline, Patsy [Virginia Paterson Hensley] (1932–1963). *Songs:* "Walkin' After Midnight" (1957); "Crazy" (1961)

Cole, Nat "King" (1917–1965). *Songs:* "Mona Lisa" (1949); "Unforgettable" (1952)

Collins, Phil (1951–), b. England. *Songs:* "Against All Odds (Take a Look at Me Now)" (1984); "You'll Be in My Heart" (1999)

Como, Perry (1912–). *Songs:* "Papa Loves Mambo" (1954); "Hot Diggity (Dog Ziggity Boom)" (1956)

Credence Clearwater Revival [John Fogerty; Tom Fogerty; Stu Cook; Doug Clifford]. *Songs:* "Proud Mary" (1969); "Have Your Ever Seen the Rain?" (1971)

Crosby, Bing [Harry Ellis] (1903–1977). *Songs:* "White Christmas" (1942); "Singing on a Star" (1944)

Darin, Bobby (1936–1973). *Songs:* "Splish Splash" (1958); "Mack the Knife" (1959)

Denver, John (1943–1997). *Songs*: "Take Me Home, Country Roads" (1971); "Sunshine on My Shoulders" (1974)

Diamond, Neil (1941–). *Songs*: "Sweet Caroline (Good Times Never Seemed So Good)" (1969); "Cracklin' Rosie" (1970)

Dion, Celine (1968–), b. Canada. *Songs*: "Beauty and the Beast" (1992; with Peabo Bryson); "My Heart Will Go On" (1997)

Doors, The [Jim Morrison; Ray Manzarek; Robby Krieger; John Densmore]. *Songs*: "Light My Fire" (1967); "Riders on the Storm" (1971)

Drifters, The [lead singers: Clyde McPhatter; Ben E. King; Rudy Lewis; Johnny Moore]. *Songs*: "There Goes My Baby" (1959); "Under the Boardwalk" (1964)

Dylan, Bob [Robert Zimmerman] (1941–). *Songs*: "Blowin' in the Wind" (1963); "Like a Rolling Stone" (1965)

Eagles, The [Glenn Frey; Don Henley; Randy Meisner; Bernie Leadon]. *Songs*: "Take It to the Limit" (1976); "Hotel California" (1977)

Estefan, Gloria [Gloria Fajardo] (1957–). *Songs*: [with Miami Sound Machine:] "Rhythm is Gonna Get You" (1987); [solo:] "Turn the Beat Around" (1994)

Eurythmics [Annie Lennox; Dave Stewart], b. England. *Songs*: "Sweet Dreams (Are Made of This)" (1983); "Sisters Are Doing It For Themselves" (1985; with Aretha Franklin)

Fitzgerald, Ella (1918–1996). *Songs*: "A-Tisket, A-Tasket" (1938); Various composers' songbooks

Franklin, Aretha (1942–). *Songs*: "Respect" (1967); "(You Make Me Feel Like) A Natural Woman" (1967)

Garland, Judy [Frances Gumm] (1922–1969). *Songs*: "Over the Rainbow" (1939); "Get Happy" (1951)

Gaye, Marvin [Marvin Pentz Gay, Jr.] (1939–1984). *Songs*: "Ain't No Mountain High Enough" (1967; with Tammi Terrell); "What's Going On" (1971)

Guns N' Roses [W. Axl Rose; Michael "Duff" McKagan; Izzy Stradlin'; Slash; Steven Adler]. *Songs*: "Sweet Child O' Mine" (1988); "Welcome to the Jungle" (1988)

Haley, Bill (1925–1981) and His Comets. Songs: "(We're Gonna) Rock Around the Clock" (1955); "See You Later, Alligator" (1956)

Hall, Daryl [Daryl Franklin Hohl] (1948–) and **John Oates** (1949–). *Songs*: "Kiss On My List" (1981); "I Can't Go For That (No Can Do)" (1981)

Holiday, Billie [Eleanor Gough McKay] (1915–1959). *Songs*: "Strange Fruit" (1939); "God Bless the Child" (1940)

Holly, Buddy (1936–1959) and the Crickets. *Songs*: "Peggy Sue" (1957); "Maybe Baby" (1958)

Horne, Lena (1917–). *Songs*: "Stormy Weather" (1943); "If You Can Dream" (1956)

Houston, Whitney (1963–). *Songs*: "Greatest Love of All" (1986); "It's Not Right But It's Okay" (1999)

Jackson, Janet (1966–). *Songs*: "What Have You Done For Me Lately" (1986); "Rhythm Nation" (1989)

Jackson, Michael (1958–). *Songs*: "Beat It" (1983); "Black or White" (1991)

Joel, Billy (1949–). Songs: "Piano Man" (1974); "Only the Good Die Young" (1978)

John, Elton [Reginald Kenneth Dwight] (1947–), b. England. *Songs*: "Rocket Man" (1972); "Candle in the Wind" (1997)

Jones, Tom [Tom Jones Woodward] (1940–), b. South Wales. *Songs*: "It's Not Unusual" (1965); "She's a Lady" (1972)

Knight, Gladys (1944–) and the Pips [Merald "Bubba" Knight; Edward Patten; Langston George]. *Songs*: "Midnight Train to Georgia" (1973); "That's What Friends Are For" (1985; with Dionne Warwick, Elton John, and Stevie Wonder)

Lee, Peggy [Norma Egstrom] (1920–). *Songs*: "I Got It Bad And That Ain't Good" (1942); "Fever" (1958)

Lennon, John (1940–1980), b. England. *Songs*: "Give Peace a Chance" (1969); "Imagine" (1971)

Lewis, Jerry Lee (1935–). *Songs*: "Great Balls of Fire" (1957); "Breathless" (1958)

Lynn, Loretta (1935–). Songs: "Blue Kentucky Girl" (1965); "Coal Miner's Daughter" (1969)

Madonna [Madonna Louise Ciccone] (1958–). *Songs*: "Material Girl" (1985); "Ray of Light" (1998)

Manilow, Barry [Barry Alan Pincus] (1946–). *Songs:* "I Write the Songs" (1975); "Copacabana (At the Copa)" (1978)

Mathis, Johnny (1935–). *Songs:* "Chances Are" (1957); "Misty" (1959)

Midler, Bette (1945–). *Songs:* "The Rose" (1980); "Wind Beneath My Wings" (1989)

Miracles, The [William "Smokey" Robinson; Emerson Rogers; Bobby Rogers; Ronnie White; Warren "Pete" Moore]. *Songs:* "The Tracks of My Tears" (1965); "I Second That Emotion" (1967)

Moody Blues, The [Justin Hayward; John Lodge; Ray Thomas; Mike Pinder; Graeme Edge], b. England. *Songs:* "Nights in White Satin" (1967); "I'm Just a Singer (In a Rock and Roll Band)" (1973)

Murray, Anne [Morna Anne Murray] (1945–), b. Canada. *Songs:* "Danny's Song" (1973); "You Needed Me" (1978)

Newton-John, Olivia (1948–), b. Australia. *Songs:* "I Honestly Love You" (1974); "Physical" (1981)

Nirvana [Kurt Cobain; Krist Novoselic; Dave Grohl]. *Songs:* "Smells Like Teen Spirit" (1991); "All Apologies" (1993)

Orbison, Roy (1936–1988). *Songs:* "In Dreams" (1963); "Oh, Pretty Woman" (1964)

Parton, Dolly (1946–). *Songs:* "Heartbreaker" (1978); "Islands in the Stream" (1983, with Kenny Rogers)

Peter, Paul and Mary [Peter Yarrow; Paul Stookey; Mary Travers]. *Songs:* "If I Had a Hammer (The Hammer Song)" (1962); "Blowin' in the Wind" (1963)

Pink Floyd [Roger Waters; Syd Barrett; Nick Mason; Rick Wright; Dave Gilmor], b. England. *Songs:* "Money" (1973); "Comfortably Numb" (1979)

Presley, Elvis (1935–1977). *Songs:* "Heartbreak Hotel" (1956); "Burning Love" (1972)

Prince [Prince Roger Nelson; also "The Artist Formerly Known As Prince"] (1958–). *Songs:* "Little Red Corvette" (1982); "Cream" (1991)

Queen [Freddie Mercury (b. Zanzibar); Brian May; John Deacon; Roger Taylor], b. England. *Songs:* "Bohemian Rhapsody" (1976); "Another One Bites the Dust" (1980)

Reddy, Helen (1941–), b. Australia. *Songs:* "I Am Woman" (1972); "Delta Dawn" (1973)

Richie, Lionel (1949–). *Songs:* "All Night Long (All Night)" (1983); "Hello" (1984)

Righteous Brothers, The [Bill Medley; Bobby Hatfield]. *Songs:* "You've Lost That Lovin' Feelin'" (1964); "(You're My) Soul and Inspiration" (1966)

Rogers, Kenny [Kenneth Donald Rogers] (1938–). *Songs:* "The Gambler" (1978); "Coward of the County" (1980)

Rolling Stones, The [Mick Jagger; Keith Richards; Brian Jones; Bill Wyman; Charlie Watts], b. England. *Songs:* "(I Can't Get No) Satisfaction" (1965); "Start Me Up" (1981)

Ronstadt, Linda (1946–). *Songs:* "You're No Good" (1975); "Hurt So Bad" (1980)

Ross, Diana [Diane Earle] (1944–). *Songs:* "Theme From Mahogany (Do You Know Where You're Going To?)" (1975); "I'm Coming Out" (1980)

Simon and Garfunkel [Paul Simon; Art Garfunkel]. *Songs:* "The Sounds of Silence" (1965); "Mrs. Robinson" (1968)

Simon, Carly (1945–). *Songs:* "You're So Vain" (1972); "Nobody Does It Better" (1977)

Simon, Paul (1941–). *Songs:* "50 Ways to Leave Your Lover" (1976); "You Can Call Me Al" (1986)

Sinatra, Frank [Francis Albert Sinatra] (1915–1998). *Songs:* "Young at Heart" (1953); "My Way" (1969)

Sly and the Family Stone [Sylvester "Sly Stone" Stewart; Freddie Stone; Cynthia Robinson; Jerry Martini; Rosie Stone; Larry Graham; Gregg Errico]. *Songs:* "Dance to the Music" (1968); "Everyday People" (1969)

Smith, Bessie (1894–1937). *Songs:* "'Taint Nobody's Bizness If I Do" (1923); "St. Louis Blues" (1925)

Springfield, Dusty [Mary O'Brien] (1939–1999), b. England. *Songs:* "Son of a Preacher Man" (1969); "The Windmills of Your Mind" (1969)

Springsteen, Bruce (1949–). *Songs:* "Born to Run" (1975); "Born in the USA" (1984)

Stewart, Rod [Roderick Stewart] (1945–), b. England. *Songs*: "Tonight's the Night (Gonna Be Alright)" (1976); "Have I Told You Lately" (1993)

Streisand, Barbra [Barbara Joan Streisand] (1942–). *Songs*: "The Way We Were" (1973); "Love Theme from 'A Star is Born' (Evergreen)" (1977)

Summer, Donna [Adrian Donna Gaines] (1948–). *Songs*: "Last Dance" (1978); "Bad Girls" (1979)

Supremes, The [Diana Ross; Mary Wilson; Florence Ballard; Cindy Birdsong]. *Songs*: "Stop! In the Name of Love" (1965); "You Keep Me Hangin' On" (1966)

Taylor, James (1948–). *Songs*: "Fire and Rain" (1970); "How Sweet It Is (To Be Loved by You)" (1975)

Tormé, Mel [Melvin Howard Tormé] (1925–). *Songs*: "The Christmas Song (Chestnuts Roasting on an Open Fire)" (1946); "Careless Hands" (1949)

Turner, Tina (1938–). *Songs*: "What's Love Got to Do With It" (1984); "Typical Male" (1986)

Vallee, Rudy (1901–1986). *Songs*: "My Time is Your Time" (1929); "I'm Just a Vagabond Lover" (1930)

Waller, Thomas "Fats" (1904–1943). *Songs*: "Ain't Misbehavin'" (1929); "Honeysuckle Rose" (1929)

Warwick(e), Dionne [Marie Dionne Warwick] (1940–). *Songs*: "Don't Make Me Over" (1963); "(Theme From) Valley of the Dolls" (1968)

Waters, Ethel (1896–1977). *Songs*: "Heat Wave" (1933); "Cabin in the Sky" (1940)

Who, The [Roger Daltrey, John Entwhistle, Keith Moon, Pete Townsend], b. England. *Songs*: "I Can't Explain" (1965); "Pinball Wizard" (1969)

Wonder, Stevie [Steveland Morris] (1950–). *Songs*: "My Cherie Amour" (1969); "I Just Called to Say I Love You" (1984)

Wynette, Tammy (1942–1998). *Songs*: "Stand By Your Man" (1968); "D-I-V-O-R-C-E" (1968)

⊙ Buckley, Jonathan, and Mark Ellington, eds. *The Rough Guide to Rock*. London: Rough Guides, 1996.
Hardy, Phil, and Dave Laing, eds. *The Faber Companion to 20th-Century Popular Music*. Boston: Faber and Faber, 1990.
Romanowski, Patricia, and Holly George-Warren, eds. *The New Rolling Stone Encyclopedia of Rock & Roll*. New York: Fireside, 1995.

75 Major Jazz Musicians

This section lists jazz musicians of a variety of styles and periods, included here because of their significance to the development of jazz and their mastery of their chosen instrument (many are also composers). They are American unless otherwise noted. Instruments are listed in order of prominence in each musician's work. For selected jazz vocalists, see 100 Popular Singers and Music Groups.

Name	Dates	Instrument
Adderly, Cannonball	1928–1975	alto/soprano sax
Allen, Red	1908–1967	trumpet
Ammons, Gene	1925–1974	tenor sax
Armstrong, Louis	1901–1971	trumpet, vocals
Bailey, Buster	1902–1967	clarinet
Baker, Chet	1929–1988	trumpet, vocals
Basie, Count	1904–1984	piano, organ
Bechet, Sidney	1897–1959	soprano sax, clarinet
Biederbecke, Bix	1903–1931	cornet, piano
Blakey, Art	1919–1990	drums
Blanton, Jimmy	1918–1942	bass
Brown, Clifford	1930–1956	trumpet

Name	Dates	Instrument
Brubeck, Dave	1920–	piano
Carter, Benny	1907–	alto sax, trumpet
Charles, Ray	1930–	piano, alto sax, vocals
Cheatham, Doc	1905–1997	trumpet, vocals
Christian, Charlie	1916–1942	guitar
Clarke, Kenny	1914–1985	drums
Cole, Nat "King"	1917–1965	piano, vocals
Coleman, Ornette	1930–	alto/tenor sax, trumpet, violin
Coltrane, John	1926–1967	tenor/soprano sax
Corea, Chick	1941–	piano, keyboards
Davis, Miles	1926–1991	trumpet, flugelhorn
Desmond, Paul	1924–1977	alto sax
Dolphy, Eric	1928–1964	alto sax, clarinet/bass clarinet, flute
Dorham, Kenny	1924–1972	trumpet
Dorsey, Tommy	1905–1956	trombone
Eldridge, Roy	1911–1989	trumpet, flute, covals, drums
Ellington, Duke	1899–1974	piano
Evans, Bill	1929–1980	piano
Farmer, Art	1928–	trumpet, flugelhorn, flumpet
Getz, Stan	1927–1991	tenor sax
Gillespie, Dizzy	1917–1993	trumpet, vocals, piano
Goodman, Benny	1909–1986	clarinet
Gordon, Dexter	1923–1990	tenor/soprano sax
Grappelli, Stephane	1908–1997 (French)	violin, piano
Hampton, Lionel	1908–	vibraphone, drums, piano, vocals
Hancock, Herbie	1940–	piano, keyboards
Hawkins, Coleman	1904–1969	tenor sax
Henderson, Joe	1937–	tenor/soprano sax, flute
Hines, Earl	1903–1983	piano
Hinton, Milt	1910–	bass
Hodges, Johnny	1906–1970	alto/soprano sax
Hutcherson, Bobby	1941–	vibraphone, marimba
Jackson, Milt	1923–	vibraphone, piano, vocals, guitar
Jacquet, Illinois	1922–	tenor/alto sax, bassoon
Johnson, J. J. (James Louis)	1924–	trombone
Jones, Philly Joe	1923–1985	drums
Kirk, Rahsaan Roland	1936–1977	flugelhorn, tenor sax, manzello, stritch, clarinet, trumpet
Marsalis, Wynton	1961–	trumpet
Mingus, Charles Jr.	1922–1979	bass, piano

Mobley, Hank	1930–1986	tenor sax
Monk, Thelonious Sphere	1917–1982	piano
Montgomery, Wes	1925–1968	guitar
Morgan, Lee	1938–1972	trumpet
Navarro, Fats	1923–1950	trumpet
Oliver, King (Joe)	1885–1938	coronet
Parker, Charlie "Bird"	1920–1955	tenor/alto sax
Peterson, Oscar	1925– (Canadian)	piano
Powell, Bud	1924–1966	piano
Redman, Don	1900–1964	sax, vocals
Reinhardt, Django	1910–1953 (Belgian)	guitar
Roach, Max	1924–	drums
Rollins, Sonny	1930–	tenor sax
Silver, Horace	1928–	piano
Sims, Zoot	1925–1985	tenor/alto/soprano sax, clarinet
Smith, Jimmy	1925–	organ
Smith, Stuff	1909–1967	violin, vocals
Stewart, Slam (Leroy)	1914–1987	bass
Tatum, Art	1909–1956	piano
Tyner, McCoy	1938–	piano
Waller, Fats (Thomas)	1904–1943	piano, organ, vocals
Webster, Ben	1909–1973	tenor sax
Williams, Tony	1945–1997	drums
Young, Lester	1909–1959	tenor sax, clarinet

⊙ Feather, Leonard, and Ira Gitler. *The Biographical Encyclopedia of Jazz.* New York: Oxford University Press, 1999.

ARTS AND LEISURE: *Opera*

100 Major Operas

This list contains operas from a variety of historical periods and spans compositional styles from classical to modern to experimental. The choices often represent the stylistic pinnacles of their composers' musical idioms. Also included are operas whose enduring popularity has ensured them a place in the standard repertory, as well as works of critical importance in the evolution of the art form.

Opera*	Composer	Premiere
L'Africaine,	Giacomo Meyerbeer	1865
Aïda	Giuseppe Verdi	1871
Amahl and the Night Visitors	Gian Carlo Menotti	1951
Antony and Cleopatra	Samuel Barber	1966
Aoki okami (The Dark Blue Wolf)	Saburo Takata	1972
Ariadne auf Naxos	Richard Strauss	1916

Opera*	Composer	Premiere
Armida	Joseph Hayden	1784
Aufstieg und Fall der Stadt Mahagonny	Kurt Weill	1930
Ballad of Baby Doe, The	Douglas Moore	1956
Barbiere di Siviglia, Il	Gioacchino Rossini	1816
Bartered Bride, The	Bedrich Smetana	1866
Béatrice et Bénédict	Hector Berlioz	1862
Beggar's Opera, The	John Gay	1728
Billy Budd	Benjamin Britten	1951
Bluebeard's Castle	Béla Bartók	1918
Bohème, La	Giacomo Puccini	1896
Carmen	Georges Bizet	1875
Cavalleria Rusticana	Pietro Mascagni	1890
Contes d'Hoffmann, Les	Jacques Offenbach	1881
Così fan tutte	Wolfgang Amadeus Mozart	1790
Death in Venice	Benjamin Britten	1973
Devil and Daniel Webster, The	Douglas Moore	1939
Dialogues des Carmélites, Les	Francis Poulenc	1931
Dido and Aeneas	Henry Purcell	1689
Don Giovanni	Wolfgang Amadeus Mozart	1787
Don Pasquale	Gaetano Donizetti	1843
Einstein on the Beach	Philip Glass	1976
Elektra	Richard Strauss	1909
Eugene Onegin	Pyotr Ilyich Tchaikovsky	1879
Fairy Queen, The	Henry Purcell	1692
Faust	Charles Gounod	1859
Favola d'Orfeo, La	Claudio Monteverdi	1607
Fidelio	Ludwig van Beethoven	1814
Fledermaus, Die	Johann Strauss	1874
Fliegende Holländer, Der	Richard Wagner	1843
Four Saints in Three Acts	Virgil Thomson	1934
Gioconda, La	Amilcare Ponchielli	1876
Giulio Cesare in Egitto	George Frideric Handel	1724
Götterdämmerung	Richard Wagner	1876
Guillaume Tell	Gioacchino Rossini	1829
Hamlet	Ambrose Thomas	1868
Hänsel und Gretel	Englebert Humperdinck	1893
Háry János	Zoltán Kodály	1926
Iphigénie en Aulide	Christoph Willibald Gluck	1774
Iphigénie en Tauride	Christoph Willibald Gluck	1779
King Priam	Michael Tippett	1962
Lady Macbeth of Mtsensk	Dmitri Shostakovich	1934
Lakmé	Léo Delibes	1883
Lohengrin	Richard Wagner	1850

Love of Three Oranges, The	Sergei Prokofiev	1921
Lucia di Lammermoor	Gaetano Donizetti	1835
Madama Butterfly	Giacomo Puccini	1904
Maid of Orleans, The	Pyotr Ilyich Tchaikovsky	1887
Makropulos Affair, The	Leos Janácek	1926
Mamelles de Tirésias, Les	Francis Poulenc	1947
Manon	Jules Massenet	1884
Manon Lescaut	Giacomo Puccini	1893
Midsummer's Night Dream, A	Benjamin Britten	1961
Mikado, The	Arthur Sullivan (collab. W. S. Gilbert)	1885
Moses und Aron	Arnold Schoenberg	1954
Nozze di Figaro, Le	Wolfgang Amadeus Mozart	1786
Oberon	Carl Maria von Weber	1826
Orfeo ed Euridice	Christoph Willibald Gluck	1762
Orphée aux Enfers	Jacques Offenbach	1858
Otello	Giuseppe Verdi	1887
Pagliacci, I	Ruggiero Leoncavallo	1892
Parsifal	Richard Wagner	1882
Pêcheurs de Perles, Les	Georges Bizet	1863
Pélleas et Mélisande	Claude Debussy	1902
Peter Grimes	Benjamin Britten	1945
Pilgrim's Progress, The	Ralph Vaughan Williams	1951
Pirates of Penzance, The	Arthur Sullivan (collab. W. S. Gilbert)	1879
Prince Igor	Alexander Borodin	1890
Rake's Progress, The	Igor Stravinsky	1951
Rheingold, Das	Richard Wagner	1869
Rigoletto	Giuseppe Verdi	1851
Ritorno d'Ulisse in Patria, Il	Claudio Monteverdi	1640
Roméo et Juliette	Charles Gounod	1867
Rosenkavalier, Der	Richard Strauss	1911
Rusalka	Antonín Dvorak	1901
Salome	Richard Strauss	1905
Samson et Dalila	Camille Saint-Saëns	1877
Serse	George Frideric Handel	1738
Serva padrona, La	Giovanni Battista Pergolesi	1733
Siegfried	Richard Wagner	1876
Snow Maiden, The	Nikolai Rimsky-Korsakov	1882
Sonnambula, La	Vincenzo Bellini	1835
Tosca	Giacomo Puccini	1900
Traviata, La	Giuseppe Verdi	1853
Tristan und Isolde	Richard Wagner	1865
Troilus and Cressida	William Walton	1954
Trovatore, Il	Giuseppe Verdi	1853
Troyens, Les	Hector Berlioz	1890
Turandot	Giacomo Puccini	1926
Walküre, Die	Richard Wagner	1870

100 Major Operas (cont.)

Opera*	Composer	Premiere
War and Peace	Sergei Prokofiev	1945
Werther	Jules Massenet	1892
Wozzeck	Alban Berg	1925
Yuzuru (The Twilight Heron)	Ikuma Dan	1952
Zauberflöte, Die	Wolfgang Amadeus Mozart	1791

*Most German, French, and Italian titles have been left in the original language. Most Russian, eastern European, and Japanese titles have been translated.

⊙ Boyden, Matthew. *Opera: The Rough Guide*. London: Rough Guides, 1999.
   Larue, C. Steven, ed. *The International Dictionary of Opera*. Detroit & London: St. James, 1993.
   Mondadori, Arnoldo, ed. *The Simon and Schuster Book of the Opera*. New York: Simon & Schuster, 1977.

25 Major Opera-Producing Organizations

Opera Company / House	Location	Premiere
Bayerische Staatsoper	Munich, Germany	1818
Bayreuth Festspiele	Bayreuth, Germany	1876
Bolshoi Theatre	Moscow, Russia	1825
Boston Lyric Opera	Boston, Massachusetts	1976
English National Opera	London, England	1974
Glyndebourne Festival Opera	Glyndebourne, England	1994
Houston Grand Opera	Houston, Texas	1955
Lyric Opera of Chicago	Chicago, Illinois	1954
Metropolitan Opera Association	New York, New York	1883
New National Theatre	Tokyo, Japan	1997
New York City Opera	New York, New York	1944
Opera Australia, Sydney	Sydney, Australia	1996
Opera National de Paris	Paris, France	1875
Opera-Comique	Paris, France	1714
Royal Opera House	London, England	1858
Royal Swedish Opera	Stockholm, Sweden	1773
Salzburger Festspiele	Salzburg, Germany	1927
San Francisco Opera	San Francisco, California	1923
Santa Fe Opera	Santa Fe, New Mexico	1957
Seattle Opera Association	Seattle, Washington	1964
Spoleto Festival USA	Charleston, South Carolina	1977
Teatro alla Scala	Milan, Italy	1778
Teatro Colon	Buenos Aires, Argentina	1908
Teatro dell'Opera	Rome, Italy	1946
Wiener Staatsoper	Vienna, Austria	1869

⊙ Kuhn, Laura. *Baker's Dictionary of Opera*. New York: Schirmer, 2000.
   Orrey, Leslie, ed. *The Encyclopedia of Opera*. New York: Scribner's, 1976.
   Warrack, John, and Ewan West. *The Oxford Dictionary of Opera*. New York: Oxford University Press, 1992.

25 Major Ballets

The following ballets are drawn from a range of historical periods, musical styles, and choreographic idioms. Selections include classical works, groundbreaking modernist experiments, and Broadway musicals.

Ballet	Choreographer	Composer	Premiere
Afternoon of a Faun	Vaslav Nijinsky	Claude Debussy	1912
Apollo (Apollon Musagete)	George Balanchine	Igor Stravinsky	1928
Appalachian Spring	Martha Graham	Aaron Copland	1944
Bayadere, La	Marius Petipa	Ludwig Minkus	1877
Billy the Kid	Eugene Loring	Aaron Copland	1938
Cigne, Le (The Dying Swan)	Michel Fokine	Camille Saint-Saëns (from *Carnival of the Animals*)	1905
Coppelia	Arthur Saint-Léon	Léo Delibes	1870
Daphnis et Chloe	Michel Fokine	Maurice Ravel	1912
Don Quixote	Marius Petipa and Aleksandr Gorsky	Ludwig Minkus	1869
Fall River Legend	Agnes de Mille	Morton Gould	1948
Fancy Free	Jerome Robbins	Leonard Bernstein	1944
Firebird	Michel Fokine	Igor Stravinsky	1911
Giselle	Jean Corralli; Jules Perrot; Marius Petipa	Adolphe Adam	1841
Valse, La	George Balanchine	*Valses Nobles et Sentimentales* (1911, orchestrated 1912); *La Valse* (1920), by Maurice Ravel	1951
Nutcracker, The	Marius Petipa	Peter Ilyich Tchaikovsky	1892
Petrouchka	Michel Fokine	Igor Stravinsky	1911
Rodeo	Agnes de Mille	Aaron Copeland	1942
Romeo and Juliet	Leonid Lavrovsky	Sergei Prokofiev	1940
Sacre du Printemps, Le/ The Rite of Spring	Vaslav Nijinsky	Igor Stravinsky	1913
Slaughter on Tenth Avenue	George Balanchine	Richard Rodgers	1936
Sleeping Beauty, The	Marius Petipa	Peter Ilyich Tchaikovsky	1890
Spectre de la Rose, Le	Michel Fokine	Carl-Maria von Weber (from *Invitation to the Dance*)	1911
Swan Lake	Marius Petipa; Lev Ivanov	Peter Ilyich Tchaikovsky	1895
Sylphides, Les	Michel Fokine	Frederic Chopin	1909
Sylvia où la Nymphe de Diane	Louis Merante	Léo Delibes	1876

⊙ Clarke, Mary, and Clement Crisp. *The Ballet Goer's Guide.* New York: Knopf, 1981.
  Reynolds, Nancy, and Susan Reiner-Torn. *Dance Classics: A Viewer's Guide to the Best-Loved Ballets and Modern Dances.* Pennington, N.J.: a capella books, 1991.

25 Major Dance Companies

Company	Location	Premiere
Adventures in Motion Pictures Company	London, England	1987
Alvin Ailey American Dance Theater	New York, New York	1958
American Ballet Theatre	New York, New York	1939
Ballett Frankfurt	Frankfurt, Germany	1984
Béjart Ballet Lausanne	Lausanne, Switzerland	1987
Bill T. Jones/Arnie Zane Dance Company	New York, New York	1982
Bolshoi Theatre	Moscow, Russia	1776
Dance Theatre of Harlem	New York, New York	1969
Feld Ballet/NY	New York, New York	1990
Garth Fagan Dance	Rochester, New York	1991
The Joffrey Ballet	Chicago, Illinois	1956
José Limón Dance Foundation	New York, New York	1945
Kirov Ballet	St. Petersburg, Russia	1935
Mark Morris Dance Group	New York, New York	1980
Martha Graham Dance Company	New York, New York	1926
Merce Cunningham Dance	New York, New York	1953
New York City Ballet	New York, New York	1948
Paris Opera Ballet	Paris, France	1671
Paul Taylor Dance Company	New York, New York	1954
Pilobolus Dance Theatre	Washington Depot, Connecticut	1971
Royal Ballet	London, England	1956
Royal Winnipeg Ballet	Winnipeg, Canada	1939
Streb/Ringside	New York, New York	1985
Tanztheater Wuppertal	Wuppertal, Germany	1978
White Oak Dance Project	White Oak, Georgia	1990

*This list is composed of currently active companies. Because some companies have changed their names since being founded, "Established" refers to the year of the first appearance of the most current name.

⊙ Gaynor Minden, Inc. "Dance Links," www.dancer.com/dance-links/
Reynolds, Nancy, ed. *The Dance Catalog*. New York: Harmony Books, 1979.

75 Noted Dancers and Choreographers

This section features popular, classical, and experimental dancers, dance teams, and choreographers. The list includes popular performers noted for their consummate skill and technique, as well as artists whose work challenges traditional definitions of dance.

Name	Dates	Nationality	Genre*, Choreographic Achievements
Ailey, Alvin	1931–1990	American	MD/Ch; *Revelations* (1960), *Cry* (1971)
Ashton, Sir Frederick	1906–1988	British	BD/Ch; *Symphonic Variations* (1947), *Ondine* (1958)
Astaire, Adele	1898–1981	American	SD
Astaire, Fred	1899–1987	American	SD/FD

Balanchine, George	1904–1983	Russian-born American	BD/Ch; *Serenade* (1934), *Agon* (1957)
Baryshnikov, Mikhail	1948–	Russian-born American	BD/SD/FD
Bausch, Pina	1940–	German	PMD/Ch/Filmmaker; *Actions for Dancers* (1971), *Palermo, Palermo* (1990)
Béjart, Maurice	1927–	French	BCh; Najinski, *Clown of God* (1971), *Ring Around the Ring* (1991)
Bennett, Michael	1943–1987	American	SD/Ch/Director; *Company* (1970), *A Chorus Line* (1975)
Beriosova, Svetlana	1932–1998	Russian	BD
Bourne, Matthew	1961–	British	BD/Ch; *Highland Fling* (1994), *Swan Lake* (1995)
Caccialanza, Gisella	1915–1998	American	BD
Castle, Vernon	1887–1918	American	Ballroom dance
Castle, Irene	1893–1969	American	Ballroom dance
Charisse, Cyd	1921–	American	FD
Childs, Lucinda	1940–	American	PMD/Ch; *Museum Piece* (1965), *Einstein on the Beach* (1976)
Coles, Charles (Honi)	1911–1992	American	TD
Cunningham, Merce	1919–	American	MD/Ch; *Summerspace* (1958), *CRWDSPCR* (1993)
de Mille, Agnes	1905–1993	American	BD/Ch; *Oklahoma!* (1943), *Fall River Legend* (1948)
Duncan, Isadora	1878–1927	American	MD/Ch; *Dance Idylles* (1901–1904), *Marche Slave* (1917)
Dunham, Katherine	1910–	American	MD/Ch/Ethnographer; *Cabin in the Sky* (1940), *Rites de Passage* (1941)
Fagan, Garth	1940–	Jamaican-born American	MD/Ch; *From Before* (1978), *The Lion King* (1997)
Farrell, Suzanne	1945–	American	BD
Feld, Eliot	1943–	American	BD/Ch; *At Midnight* (1967)
Fokine, Michel	1880–1942	Russian	BCh; *The Firebird* (1910), *Petrouchka* (1911)
Fonteyn, Margot	1919–1991	British	BD
Fosse, Bob	1927–1987	American	SD/FD/Ch; *Pippin* (1972), *Dancin'* (1978)
Glover, Savion	1973–	American	TD/Ch; *Bring in Da Noise, Bring in Da Funk* (1995)
Godunov, Alexander	1950–1995	Russian	BD
Goslar, Lotte	1907–1997	German	MD/Mime
Graham, Martha	1893–1991	American	MD/Ch; *Appalachian Spring* (1944), *Clytemnestra* (1958)
Grisi, Carlotta	1819–1899	Italian	BD
Hawkins, Erick	1909–1994	American	BD
Hines, Gregory	1946–	American	TD

Name	Dates	Nationality	Genre*, Choreographic Achievements
Holm, Hanya	1893–1992	German-born American	MD/Ch; *Trend* (1937), *Kiss Me, Kate* (1948)
Horton, Lester	1906–1953	American	MD/Ch/Teacher; *Aztec Ballet* (1934), *Liberian Suite* (1952)
Humphrey, Doris	1895–1958	American	MD/Ch; *The Shakers* (1930), *With My Red Fires* (1936)
Jamison, Judith	1944–	American	MD
Joffrey, Robert	1930–1988	American	BD/Ch; *Pas de Déesses* (1954), *Astarte* (1967)
Jones, Bill T.	1952–	American	MD/Ch; *Last Summer at Uncle Tom's Cabin/The Promised Land* (1990), *Still/Here* (1994)
Kelly, Gene	1912–1996	American	SD/FD/Ch; *On the Town* (1949), *An American in Paris* (1952)
Kirkland, Gelsey	1952–	American	BD
Limón, José	1908–1972	American	MD/Ch; *The Moor's Pavane* (1949), *A Choreographic Offering* (1962)
Lubovitch, Lar	1943–	American	BD/MD/Ch; *Cavalcade* (1980), *The Red Shoes* (1993)
Makarova, Natalia	1940–	Russian	BD
Markova, Alicia	1910–	British	BD
Massine, Léonide	1895–1979	Russian	BD/Ch; *Parade* (1917), *Gaîté Parisienne* (1938)
Mitchell, Arthur	1934–	American	BD/Ch; *Convergences* (1968), *Tones* (1974)
Monk, Meredith	1943–	American	PD/Ch/Composer/Filmmaker; *Quarry* (1976), *American Archaeology #1: Roosevelt Island* (1994)
Morris, Mark	1956–	American	PD/Ch; *Gloria* (1981), *Nixon in China* (1989)
Nicholas, Fayard & Harold (The Nicholas Brothers)	1917– , 1924–2000	American	TD
Nijinsky, Vaslav	1890–1950	Russian	BD/Ch; *L'Aprés-midi d'un faune* (1912), *Le Sacre du printemps* (1913)
Nureyev, Rudolf	1938–1993	Russian	BD
Otake, Eiko and Koma	1952–, 1948–	Japanese	PD/Ch; *New Moon Stories* (1986), *River* (1995)
Pavlova, Anna	1882–1931	Russian	BD
Perrot, Jules	1810–1892	French	BD/Ch; *Giselle* (1841)
Petipa, Marius	1818–1910	French	BD/Ch; *The Sleeping Beauty* (1890)
Plisetskaya, Maya	1925–	Russian	BD
Primus, Pearl	1920–1994	American	MD/Ch; *Strange Fruit* (1945), *Michael, Row Your Boat Ashore* (1979)

Rainer, Yvonne	1934–	American	PD/Ch/Filmmaker; *The Mind is a Muscle* (1966), *This Is the Story of a Woman Who ...* (1973)
Rivera, Chita	1933–	American	SD
Robbins, Jerome	1918–1998	American	BD/SD/Ch; *Fancy Free* (1944), *West Side Story* (1957)
Robinson, Bill Bojangles	1878–1949	American	TD
Rogers, Ginger	1911–1995	American	SD/FD
Shawn, Ted	1891–1972	American	MD/Ch; *Grecian Suite* (1914), *The Kinetic Molpai* (1935)
Spessivtzeva, Olga	1905–1991	Russian	BD
Stroman, Susan	c.1955–	American	SD/Ch; *Crazy for You* (1992), *Contact* (1999)
St. Denis, Ruth	1879–1968	American	MD/Ch/Teacher; *Radha* (1904), *Death and After-Life in India, Greece, and Egypt* (1916, with Ted Shawn)
Taylor, Paul	1930–	American	MD/Ch; *Diggity* (1978), *Musical Offering* (1986)
Tharp, Twyla	1941–	American	MD/Ch; *Push Comes to Shove* (1976), *Jump Start* (1995)
Toumanova, Tamara	1919–1996	Russian	BD
Tudor, Anthony	1908–1987	British	BD/Ch; *Lilac Garden* (1936), *Pillar of Fire* (1942)
Tune, Tommy	1939–	American	SD/Ch/Director; *The Best Little Whorehouse in Texas* (1978), *Grand Hotel* (1989)
Weidman, Charles	1901–1975	American	MD/Ch; *Flickers* (1940), *... And Daddy Was a Fireman* (1941)
Wigman, Mary	1886–1973	German	MD/Ch; *Vision IV: Witch Dance* (1926), *Totenmal* (1930)
Youskevitch, Igor	1912–1994	Russian	BD

* Key to genres:

BD = Ballet dancer
TD = Tap dancer
MD = Modern dancer
PMD = Postmodern dancer

SD = Stage dancer
FD = Film dancer
Ch = Choreographer
BCh = Ballet Choreographer

⊙ Brenser, Martha, ed. *Fifty Contemporary Choreographers*. London and New York: Routledge, 1999.
  Cohen-Stratyner, Barbara Naomi. *Biographical Dictionary of Dance*. New York: Schirmer, 1982.

ARTS AND LEISURE: *Theater*

125 Significant American Plays and Musicals

The following plays and musicals cover the wide range of popular American theatre for the past two centuries. The shows on this list include long-running favorites, commercial blockbusters, and critically regarded works. Although not every show had its world premiere in the United States, this list charts the evolving theatrical tastes of the nation and pushes the boundaries of those sensibilities.

Title	Author(s)	Premiere	Performances*	Major Awards**
Abie's Irish Rose	Anne Nichols	1922	2,327	
Alison's House	Susan Glaspell	1930	41	PP
Angels in America:				
Millennium Approaches	Tony Kushner	1993	367	PP; NYDC; TA
Perestroika	Tony Kushner	1993	216	TA
Annie	Book: Thomas Meehan Lyrics: Martin Charnin Music: Charles Strouse	1977	2,377	NYDC; TA
Anything Goes	Book: Guy Bolton, P. G. Wodehouse, Howard Lindsay, Russel Crouse Music/Lyrics: Cole Porter	1934	420	
Arsenic and Old Lace	Joseph Kesselring	1941	1,444	
Bat, The	Mary Robert Rinehart / Avery Hopwood	1920	867	
Black Crook, The	Book: Charles M. Barras Music/Lyrics: Various	1866	475	
Boys in the Band, The	Mart Crowley	1968	1,000	
Brighton Beach Memoirs	Neil Simon	1983	1,299	NYDC
Bring in Da Noise, Bring in Da Funk	Created by Savion Glover / Reg E. Gaine / George C. Wolfe Music: Anne Duquesnay / Zane Mark / Darryl Waters	1996	1,135	
Buried Child	Sam Shepherd	1978	152	PP
Cabaret	Book: Joe Masteroff Lyrics: Fred Ebb Music: John Kander	1966	1,165	NYDC; TA
Cabin in the Sky	Book: John Root Lyrics: John Latouche Music: Vernon Duke	1940	156	
Camelot	Book/Lyrics: Alan Jay Lerner Music: Frederick Loewe	1960	873	

Title	Author/Credits	Year	Performances	Awards
Carousel	Book/Lyrics: Oscar Hammerstein II / Music: Richard Rodgers	1945	890	NYDC
Cat on a Hot Tin Roof	Tennessee Williams	1955	694	PP; NYDC
Cats	Book/Lyrics: T. S. Eliot / Music: Andrew Lloyd Webber	1982	7,485	TA
Children's Hour, The	Lillian Hellman	1934	691	
Chorus Line, A	Book: James Kirkwood / Nicholas Dante / Lyrics: Edward Kleban / Music: Marvin Hamlisch	1975	6,137	PP; NYDC; TA
Company	Book: George Furth / Music/Lyrics: Stephen Sondheim	1970	706	NYDC; TA
Contrast, The	Royall Tyler	1787	[in repertory]	
Cradle Will Rock, The	Book/Music/Lyrics: Marc Blitzstein	1938	108	
Craig's Wife	George Kelly	1925	360	PP
Crimes of the Heart	Beth Henley	1981	535	PP; NYDC
Damn Yankees	Book: George Abbott / Douglass Wallop / Music/Lyrics: Richard Adler / Jerry Ross	1955	1,019	TA
Dancin'	Conceived by Bob Fosse	1978	1,774	PP; NYDC; TA
Death of a Salesman	Arthur Miller	1949	742	
Deathtrap	Ira Levin	1978	1,809	
Diary of Anne Frank, The	Frances Goodrich/Albert Hackett	1955	717	PP; NYCDDA; TA
Effect of Gamma Rays on Man-in-the-Moon Marigolds, The	Paul Zindel	1970	819	PP; NYDC
Emperor Jones, The	Eugene O'Neill	1920	204	
Fantasticks, The	Book/Lyrics: Tom Jones / Music: Harvey Schmidt	1960	[still running]	
Fashion, or Life in New York	Anna Cora Mowatt	1845	20	
Fences	August Wilson	1987	526	PP; NYDC; TA
Fiddler on the Roof	Book: Joseph Stein / Lyrics: Sheldon Harnick / Music: Jerry Bock	1964	3,242	NYDC; TA

Title	Author(s)	Premiere	Performances*	Major Awards**
Finian's Rainbow	Book: E. Y. Harburg / Fred Saidy Lyrics: E. Y. Harburg Music: Burton Lane	1947	725	PP
For Colored Girls Who Have Considered Suicide/When the Rainbow Is Enuf	Ntozake Shange	1976	742	
Gin Game, The	D. L. Coburn	1977	517	PP
Glass Menagerie, The	Tennessee Williams	1945	561	NYDC
Glengarry Glen Ross	David Mamet	1984	378	PP; NYDC
Godspell	Conceived by John-Michael Tebelak Music/Lyrics: Stephen Schwartz	1971	2,124	
Grease	Book/Music/Lyrics: Jim Jacobs / Warren Casey	1972	3,388	
Great White Hope, The	Howard Sackler	1968	556	PP; NYDC; TA
Guys and Dolls	Book: Jo Swerling / Abe Burrows Music/Lyrics: Frank Loesser	1950	1,200	NYDC; TA
Gypsy	Book: Arthur Laurents Lyrics: Stephen Sondheim Music: Jules Styne	1959	702	
Hair	Book/Lyrics: Gerome Ragni / James Rado Music: Galt MacDermott	1967	1,836	
Harvey	Mary Chase	1944	1,775	PP
Heidi Chronicles, The	Wendy Wasserstein	1989	621	PP; NYDC; TA
Hello, Dolly!	Book: Michael Stewart Music/Lyrics: Jerry Herman	1964	2,844	NYDC; TA
Hot L Baltimore, The	Lanford Wilson	1973	1,116	NYDC
House of Blue Leaves, The	John Guare	1971	337	NYDC
How I Learned to Drive	Paula Vogel	1997	400	PP; NYDDCA

Title	Credits	Year	Performances	Awards
How to Succeed in Business Without Really Trying	Book: Abe Burrows / Jack Weinstock / Willie Gilbert Music/Lyrics: Frank Loesser	1961	1,417	PP; NYDC; TA
Iceman Cometh, The	Eugene O'Neill	1946	136	
Inherit the Wind	Jerome Lawrence / Robert E. Lee	1955	806	
J.B.	Archibald MacLeish	1958	364	PP; TA
King and I, The	Book/Lyrics: Oscar Hammerstein II Music: Richard Rodgers	1951	1,246	TA
Kiss Me, Kate	Book: Sam and Bella Spewack Music/Lyrics: Cole Porter	1948	1,077	TA
Kiss of the Spider Woman	Book: Terrence McNally Lyrics: Fred Ebb Music: John Kander	1993	906	NYDC; TA
Les Misérables	Book: Alain Boublil / Claude-Michael Schönberg Music: Claude-Michael Schönberg Lyrics: Herbert Kretzmer / James Fenton	1987	[still running]	TA
Life with Father	Book: Howard Lindsay / Russel Crouse	1939	3,224	
Lion King, The	Book: Roger Allers/Irene Mecchi Lyrics: Tim Rice Music: Elton John / Hans Zimmer / Lebo M / Mark Mancina / Jay Rifkin	1997	[still running]	TA
Little Foxes, The	Lillian Hellman	1939	410	
Little Mary Sunshine	Book/Music/Lyrics: Rick Besoyan	1959	1,143	
Little Shop of Horrors	Book/Lyrics: Howard Ashman Music: Alan Menken	1982	2,209	NYDC
Long Day's Journey into Night	Eugene O'Neill	1956	390	PP; NYDC; TA
Lost in Yonkers	Neil Simon	1991	780	PP; TA
Love! Valour! Compassion!	Terrence McNally	1995	249	NYDC; TA
Man of La Mancha	Book: Dale Wasserman Lyrics: Joe Darion Music: Mitch Leigh	1965	2,328	NYDC; TA

Title	Author(s)	Premiere	Performances*	Major Awards**
Man Who Came to Dinner, The	George Kaufmann / Moss Hart	1939	739	
M. Butterfly	David Henry Hwang	1988	777	
Member of the Wedding, The	Carson McCullers	1950	501	NYDC
Mister Roberts	Thomas Heggen / Joshua Logan	1948	1,157	TA
Music Man, The	Book/Music/Lyrics: Meredith Wilson	1957	1,375	NYDC; TA
My Fair Lady	Book/Lyrics: Alan Jay Lerner / Music: Frederick Loewe	1956	2,717	NYDC; TA
New York Idea, The	Langdon Mitchell	1906	66	
No Place to Be Somebody	Charles Gordone	1969	250	PP
Octoroon, The	Dion Boucicault	1859	48	
Odd Couple, The	Neil Simon	1965	964	
Of Thee I Sing	Book: George S. Kaufman / Morrie Ryskind / Lyrics: Ira Gershwin / Music: George Gershwin	1931	444	PP
Oh, Calcutta!	Various contributors	1969	1,314	
Oklahoma!	Book/Lyrics: Oscar Hammerstein II / Music: Richard Rodgers	1943	2,212	
On the Town	Book/Lyrics: Betty Comden / Adolph Green / Music: Leonard Bernstein	1944	463	
One Touch of Venus	Book: S. J. Perelman / Ogden Nash / Lyrics: Ogden Nash / Music: Kurt Weill	1943	567	
Our American Cousin	Tom Taylor	1858	[in repertory]	
Our Town	Thornton Wilder	1938	336	PP
Pal Joey	Book: John O'Hara / Lyrics: Lorenz Hart / Music: Richard Rodgers	1940	374	
Phantom of the Opera, The	Book: Richard Stilgoe / Andrew Lloyd Webber / Lyrics: Charles Hart / Richard Stilgoe / Music: Andrew Lloyd Webber	1988	[still running]	TA

Title	Credits	Year	Performances	Awards
Piano Lesson, The	August Wilson	1990	329	PP; NYDC
Picnic	William Inge	1953	477	PP; NYDC
Pippin	Book: Roger O. Hirson Music/Lyrics: Stephen Schwartz	1972	1,944	
Porgy and Bess	Book/Lyrics: Dubose Heywood / Ira Gershwin Music: George Gershwin	1935	124	
Raisin in the Sun, A	Lorraine Hansberry	1959	530	NYDC
Rent	Book/Music/Lyrics: Jonathan Larson	1996	[still running]	PP; TA
Sherlock Holmes	William Gillette	1899	256	
Show Boat	Book/Lyrics: Oscar Hammerstein II Music: Jerome Kern	1927	575	
Shuffle Along	Book: Flournoy Miller / Aubrey Lyles Lyrics: Noble Sissle Music: Eubie Blake	1921	504	
Skin of Our Teeth, The	Thornton Wilder	1942	359	PP
Soldier's Play, A	Charles Fuller	1981	468	PP; NYDC
Sound of Music, The	Book: Howard Lindsay / Russel Crouse Lyrics: Oscar Hammerstein II Music: Richard Rodgers	1959	1,443	TA
South Pacific	Book: Oscar Hammerstein II/Joshua Logan Lyrics: Oscar Hammerstein II Music: Richard Rodgers	1949	1,925	PP; NYDC; TA
Streamers	David Rabe	1976	478	NYDC
Street Scene	Elmer Rice	1929	601	PP
Streetcar Named Desire, A	Tennessee Williams	1947	855	PP; NYDC
Strike Up the Band	Book: Morrie Ryskind / George S. Kaufman Lyrics: Ira Gershwin Music: George Gershwin	1930	191	
Subject Was Roses, The	Frank D.Gilroy	1964	832	PP; NYDC; TA
Sunday in the Park with George	Book: James Lapine Music/Lyrics: Stephen Sondheim	1984	604	PP; NYDC

Title	Author(s)	Premiere	Performances*	Major Awards**
Sweeney Todd, The Demon Barber of Fleet Street	Book: Hugh Wheeler / Music/Lyrics: Stephen Sondheim	1979	557	NYDC; TA
Tea and Sympathy	Robert Anderson	1953	712	
Teahouse of the August Moon, The	John Patrick	1953	1,027	PP; NYDC; TA
Ten Nights in a Barroom	William W. Pratt	1858	7	
That Championship Season	Jason Miller	1972	844	PP; NYDC; TA
Three Men on a Horse	John Cecil Holm / George Abbott	1935	835	
Three Tall Women	Edward Albee	1994	582	PP; NYDC
Time of Your Life, The	William Saroyan	1939	185	PP; NYDC
Tobacco Road	Jack Kirkland	1933	3,182	
Torch Song Trilogy	Harvey Fierstein	1982	1,222	TA
Uncle Tom's Cabin	George L. Aiken	1853	325	
Waiting For Lefty	Clifford Odets	1935	168	
West Side Story	Book: Arthur Laurents / Lyrics: Stephen Sondheim / Music: Leonard Bernstein	1957	734	
Who's Afraid of Virginia Woolf?	Edward Albee	1962	664	NYDC; TA
Women, The	Clare Boothe Luce	1936	657	
You Can't Take It With You	George S. Kaufman / Moss Hart	1936	837	PP
You're a Good Man, Charlie Brown	Book/Music/Lyrics: Clark Gesner	1967	1,597	

*As of October 15, 2000. Performances in the original New York City run (Broadway, Off-Broadway, etc.), where applicable. In instances where the production transferred from a non-profit theatre to a commercial run, the number of performances in the longer run is given.

**PP=Pulitzer Prize; NYDC=New York Drama Critics Circle Award; TA=Antoinette Perry (Tony) Award for Best Play or Best Musical

⊙ Bordman, Gerald. *The Oxford Companion to American Theatre.* New York: Oxford University Press, 1992.
Brown, Gene. *Show Time.* New York: Macmillan, 1997.
Theatre.com. "Theatre.com New York Theatre Awards." www.theatre.com/awards/

A Contemporary Theatre
700 Union
Seattle, WA 98101-2330
(206) 292-7660

Actors Theatre of Louisville
316 West Main Street
Louisville, KY 40202-2916
(502) 584-1265

Alabama Shakespeare Festival
1 Festival Drive
Montgomery, AL 36117-4605
(334) 271-5300

Alley Theatre
615 Texas Avenue
Houston, TX 77002-2710
(713) 228-9341

Alliance Theatre Company
1280 Peachtree Street NE
Atlanta, GA 30309-3502
(404) 733-4650

American Conservatory Theater
30 Grant Street
San Francisco, CA 94108-3800
(415) 439-2400

The American Place Theatre
111 West 46th Street
New York, NY 10036-8502
(212) 840-2960

American Repertory Theatre
64 Brattle Street
Cambridge, MA 02138-3443
(617) 495-2668

Arena Stage
1101 6th Street NW
Washington, DC 20001-3628
(202) 554-9066

Atlantic Theatre Company
336 West 20th Street
New York, NY 10011-3302
(212) 645-8015

Cleveland Public Theatre
6415 Detroit Avenue
Cleveland, OH 44102-3011
(216) 631-2727

Crossroads Theatre Company
7 Livingston Avenue
New Brunswick, NJ 08901-1903
(732) 249-5581

Denver Center Theatre Company
1050 13th Street
Denver, CO 80204-2157
(303) 893-4000

Ensemble Studio Theatre
549 West 52nd Street
New York, NY 10019-5012
(212) 247-4982

George Street Playhouse
9 Livingston Avenue
New Brunswick, NJ 08901-1903
(732) 846-2895

Goodman Theatre
200 South Columbus Drive
Chicago, IL 60603-6402
(312) 443-3811

Goodspeed Opera House
Box A
East Haddam, CT 06423-0281
(860) 873-8664

The Guthrie Theatre
725 Vineland Place
Minneapolis, MN 55403-1139
(612) 347-1100

Hartford Stage Company
50 Church Street
Hartford, CT 06103-1201
(860) 525-5601

Huntington Theatre Company
264 Huntington Street
Boston, MA 02115-4606
(617) 266-7900

Indiana Repertory Theatre
140 West Washington Street
Indianapolis, IN 46204-3403
(317) 635-5277

Intiman Theatre
P.O. Box 19760
Seattle, WA 98109-6760
(206) 269-1928

La Jolla Playhouse
Box 12039
La Jolla, CA 92039-2039
(619) 550-1070

Lincoln Center Theater
150 West 65th Street
New York, NY 10023-6903
(212) 362-7600

Lond Wharf Theatre
222 Sargent Drive
New Haven, CT 06511-5919
(203) 787-4284

Manhattan Theatre Club
311 West 43rd Street, 8th Floor
New York, NY 10036-6413
(212) 399-3000

Mark Taper Forum
135 North Grand Avenue
Los Angeles, CA 90012-3013
(213) 972-7574

McCarter Theatre Center for the Performing Arts
91 University Place
Princeton, NJ 08540-5121
(609) 683-9100

National Theatre of the Deaf
Box 659
Chester, CT 06412-0659
(860) 526-4971 (voice), 4974 (TTY)

New York Shakespeare Festival
Joseph Papp Public Theatre
425 Lafayette Street
New York, NY 10003-7021
(212) 539-8530

New York Theatre Workshop
79 East 4th Street
New York, NY 10003-8904
(212) 780-9037

Old Globe Theatre
Box 2171
San Diego, CA 92112-2171
(619) 231-1941

Oregon Shakespeare Festival
Box 158
Ashland, OR 97520-0158
(541) 482-2111

Playwrights Horizons
416 West 42nd Street
New York, NY 10036-6809
(212) 564-1235

Roundabout Theatre Company
231 West 39th Street, Suite 1200
New York, NY 10018-3109
(212) 719-9393

Shakespeare & Company
The Mount
Box 865
Lenox, MA 01240-0865
(413) 637-1199

Seattle Repertory Theatre
155 Mercer Street
Seattle, WA 98109-4639
(206) 443-2210

South Coast Repertory
Box 2197
Costa Mesa, CA 92628-2197
(714) 708-5500

Steppenwolf Theatre Company
1650 North Halsted
Chicago, IL 60614-5518
(312) 335-1888

Trinity Repertory Company
201 Washington Street
Providence, RI 02903-3226
(401) 521-1100

Utah Shakespearean Festival
351 West Center Street
Cedar City, UT 84720-2470
(435) 586-7880

The Walnut Street Theatre Company
825 Walnut Street
Philadelphia, PA 19107-5107
(215) 574-3550

Williamstown Theatre Festival
Sep.–May:
100 East 17th Street, 3rd Floor
New York, NY 10003-2160
(212) 228-2286
June–Aug.:
Box 517
Williamstown, MA 01267-0517
(413) 458-3200

Yale Repertory Theatre
Box 208244, Yale Station
New Haven, CT 06520-8244
(203) 432-1560

⊙ Charles, Jill, ed. *Regional Theatre Directory 2000–2001*. Dorset, Vt.: Theatre Directories, 2000.
   Theatre Communications Group. *Theatre Directory 2000–2001*. New York: Theatre Communications Group, 2000.

The following list includes performers of both plays and musicals. It contains not only actors noted for their excellence in creating roles, but also men and women whose colorful off-stage personalities distinguish(ed) their on-stage performances. Actors in this list span a range of historic periods, styles, and approaches to stagecraft.

Name	Dates	Nationality	Famous Roles Played in the U.S.
Adams, Maude	1872–1953	American	Peter Pan, *Peter Pan*; Lady Babbie, *The Little Minister*
Anderson, Judith	1898–1992	Australian-born American	Medea, *Medea*; Lady Macbeth, *Macbeth*
Bancroft, Anne	1931–	American	Gittel Mosca, *Two for the Seesaw*; Annie Sullivan, *The Miracle Worker*
Bankhead, Tallulah	1903–1968	American	Regina, *The Little Foxes*; Sabina, *The Skin of Our Teeth*
Barrymore, Ethel	1879–1959	American	Mme. Trentoni, *Captain Jinks of the Horse Marines*; Miss Moffat, *The Corn is Green*
Barrymore, John	1882–1942	American	Hamlet, *Hamlet*; Richard III, *Richard III*
Barrymore, Lionel	1878–1954	American	Giuseppe, *The Mummy and the Humming Bird*; Colonel Ibbetson, *Peter Ibbetson*
Bernhardt, Sarah	1844–1923	French	Marguerite, *Camille*; Tosca, *Tosca* (non-operatic version)
Booth, Edwin	1833–1893	American	Hamlet, *Hamlet*; Richard III, *Richard III*
Booth, John Wilkes	1838–1865	American	Romeo, *Romeo and Juliet*; Pescara, *The Apostate*
Brynner, Yul	1915–1985	Russian-born American	The King, *The King and I*
Buckley, Betty	1947–	American	Grizabella, *Cats*; Margaret, *Carrie*
Campbell, Mrs. Patrick (Beatrice Stella Tanner)	1865–1940	English	Paula, *The Second Mrs. Tanqueray*; Eliza Doolittle, *Pygmalion*
Channing, Carol	1921–	American	Lorelei Lee, *Gentlemen Prefer Blondes*; Dolly Levi, *Hello, Dolly!*
Cobb, Lee J. (Leo Jacoby)	1911–1976	American	Mr. Carp, *Golden Boy*; Willy Loman, *Death of a Salesman*
Cook, Barbara	1927–	American	Cunegonde, *Candide*; Marion the Librarian, *The Music Man*
Cornell, Katherine	1893–1974	German-born American	Elizabeth Barrett, *The Barretts of Wimpole Street*; Juliet, *Romeo and Juliet*
Cronyn, Hume	1911–	Canadian-born American	Polonius, *Hamlet*; Tobias, *A Delicate Balance*

Name	Nationality	Dates	Famous Roles Played in the U.S.
Davis, Ossie	American	1917–	Jeb, *Jeb*; Purlie, *Purlie Victorious*
Dee, Ruby	American	1923–	Ruth Younger, *A Raisin in the Sun*; Lena, *Boesman and Lena*
Dewhurst, Colleen	American	1926–1991	Mary Follet, *All the Way Home*; Josie Hogan, *A Moon for the Misbegotten*
Duse, Eleonora	Italian	1858–1924	Marguerite, *Camille*; Ellida Wangel, *The Lady from the Sea*
Ferrer, José	American	1912–1992	Cyrano, *Cyrano de Bergerac*; Jim Downs, *The Shrike*
Fiske, Minnie Maddern	American	1865–1932	Tess, *Tess of the D'Urbervilles*; Becky Sharp, *Becky Sharp*
Fontanne, Lynn	English-born American	1887–1983	Katherine, *The Taming of the Shrew*; Clair Zachanassian, *The Visit*
Forrest, Edwin	American	1806–1872	Metamora, *Metamora*; Spartacus, *The Gladiator*
Gielgud, John	English	1904–2000	Hamlet, *Hamlet*; Benedick, *Much Ado About Nothing*
Gillette, William H.	American	1855–1937	Lewis Dumont, *Secret Service*; Sherlock Holmes, *Sherlock Holmes*
Gilpin, Charles	American	1878–1930	William Custis, *Abraham Lincoln*; Brutus Jones, *The Emperor Jones*
Guinness, Alec	English	1914–2000	The Unidentified Guest, *The Cocktail Party*; Dylan Thomas, *Dylan*
Hagen, Uta	German-born American	1919–	Georgie, *The Country Girl*; Martha, *Who's Afraid of Virginia Woolf?*
Harris, Julie	American	1925–	Frankie, *The Member of the Wedding*; Sally Bowles, *I Am a Camera*
Harris, Rosemary	English	1930–	Eleanor of Aquitaine, *The Lion in Winter*; Lady Teazle, *The School for Scandal*
Harrison, Rex	English	1908–1990	Shepherd Henderson, *Bell, Book and Candle*; Henry Higgins, *My Fair Lady*
Hayes, Helen	American	1900–1993	Mary Stuart, *Mary of Scotland*; Queen Victoria, *Victoria Regina*
Holliday, Judy	American	1922–1965	Billie Dawn, *Born Yesterday*; Ella Peterson, *Bells are Ringing*
Jefferson, Joseph	American	1829–1905	Asa Trenchard, *Our American Cousin*; Rip Van Winkle, *Rip Van Winkle*

ARTS AND LEISURE: *Theater*

Name	Nationality	Dates	Roles
Jones, James Earl	American	1931–	Jack Jefferson, *The Great White Hope*; Troy, *Fences*
Lahr, Bert	American	1895–1967	Louis Blore, *DuBarry was a Lady*; Hyacinth Beddoes Laffoon, *The Beauty Part*
Lane, Nathan	American	1956–	Buzz, *Love! Valour! Compassion!*; Pseudolus, *A Funny Thing Happened on the Way to the Forum*;
Langtry, Lillie (Emilie Charlotte Le Breton)	English	1852–1929	Galatea, *Pygmalion and Galatea*; Mrs. Trevelyan, *The Degenerates*
Lansbury, Angela	English	1925–	Mame, *Mame*; Mrs. Lovett, *Sweeney Todd*
Lawrence, Gertrude	English	1898–1952	Amanda Prynne, *Private Lives*; Anna, *The King and I*
Le Gallienne, Eva	English-born American	1899–1991	Masha, *The Three Sisters*; Hedda Gabler, *Hedda Gabler*
Lunt, Alfred	American	1893–1980	Petruchio, *The Taming of the Shrew*; Anton Schill, *The Visit*
LuPone, Patti	American	1949–	Eva Peron, *Evita*; Reno Sweeney, *Anything Goes*
Macready, William Charles	English	1793–1873	Macbeth, *Macbeth*; Rob Roy, *Rob Roy*
March, Frederic	American	1897–1975	Mr. Antrobus, *The Skin of Our Teeth*; James Tyrone, *Long Day's Journey into Night*
Martin, Mary	American	1913–1990	Nellie Forbush, *South Pacific*; Peter Pan, *Peter Pan*
McDonald, Audra	American	1971–	Sharon, *Master Class*; Sarah, *Ragtime*
Merman, Ethel	American	1908–1984	Reno Sweeney, *Anything Goes*; Mama Rose, *Gypsy*
Modjeska, Helena	Polish	1840–1909	Adrienne, *Adrienne Lecouvreur* (non-operatic version); Rosalind, *Twelfth Night*
Morse, Robert	American	1931–	J. Pierpont Finch, *How to Succeed in Business Without Really Trying*; Truman Capote, *Tru*
Mostel, Zero	American	1915–1977	John, *Rhinoceros*; Tevye, *Fiddler on the Roof*
Nazimova, Alla	Russian	1879–1945	Hedda, *Hedda Gabler*; Christine Mannon, *Mourning Becomes Electra*
Olivier, Laurence	English	1907–1989	Antony, *Antony and Cleopatra*; Archie Rice, *The Entertainer*
Page, Geraldine	American	1924–1987	Alma, *Summer and Smoke*; Princess Kosmonopolis, *Sweet Bird of Youth*
Patinkin, Mandy	American	1952–	Che, *Evita*; George Seurat, *Sunday in the Park with George*

Name	Dates	Nationality	Famous Roles Played in the U.S.
Peters, Bernadette	1948–	American	Wicked Witch, *Into the Woods*; Annie Oakley, *Annie Get Your Gun*
Preston, Robert	1918–1987	American	Prof. Harold Hill, *The Music Man*; Henry II, *The Lion in Winter*
Richardson, Ralph	1902–1983	English	Falstaff, *Henry IV, Parts 1 and 2*; General St. Pé, *The Waltz of the Toreadors*
Rivera, Chita (Deolores Conchita Figueroa del Rivero)	1933–	American	Anita, *West Side Story*, The Spider Woman, *Kiss of the Spider Woman*
Robards, Jason, Jr.	1922–	American	Jamie Tyrone in both *Long Day's Journey into Night* and *A Moon for the Misbegotten*
Robeson, Paul	1898–1976	American	Joe, *Show Boat*; Othello, *Othello*
Schildkraut, Joseph	1896–1964	Austrian	Liliom, *Liliom*; Otto Frank, *The Diary of Anne Frank*
Stritch, Elaine	1925–	American	Performed in *Angel in the Wings*; Joanne, *Company*
Tandy, Jessica	1909–1994	English-born American	Blanche duBois, *A Streetcar Named Desire*; Agnes, *A Delicate Balance*
Taylor, Laurette	1884–1946	American	Peg, *Peg o' My Heart*; Amanda Wingfield, *The Glass Menagerie*
Tree, Herbert Beerbohm	1853–1917	English	Svengali, *Trilby*; Professor Higgins, *Pygmalion*
Verdon, Gwen	1926–2000	American	Lola, *Damn Yankees*; Charity, *Sweet Charity*
Vereen, Ben	1946–	American	Judas, *Jesus Christ, Superstar*; Leading Player, *Pippin*
Waters, Ethel	c.1900–1977	American	Petunia, *Cabin in the Sky*; Berenice, *The Member of the Wedding*
Welles, Orson	1915–1985	American	Dr. Faustus, *Dr. Faustus*; Lear, *King Lear*
Wong, B. D.	1962–	American	Song Liling, *M. Butterfly*; Ming, *A Language of Their Own*
Worth, Irene	1916–	American	Miss Alice, *Tiny Alice*; Princess Kosmonopolis, *Sweet Bird of Youth*

⊙ Bordman, Gerald. *The Oxford Companion to American Theatre*. New York: Oxford University Press, 1992. Brown, Dennis. *Actors Talk: Profiles and Stories from the Acting Trade*. New York: Limelight, 1999.

Treasures of American Film

The National Film Preservation Board, in consultation with the Librarian of Congress, chooses up to 25 films each year to be included in the National Film Registry. Congress charges the board with "maintaining and preserving films that are culturally, historically, or aesthetically significant" by publishing the list, obtaining copies of the films for the Library of Congress, and seeking ways to further the conservation of America's film heritage. The films in the National Film Registry, chosen from 1989 to 1999, are:

Adam's Rib (1949)
The Adventures of Robin Hood (1938)
The African Queen (1951)
All About Eve (1950)
All Quiet on the Western Front (1930)
All That Heaven Allows (1955)
American Graffiti (1973)
An American in Paris (1951)
Annie Hall (1977)
The Apartment (1960)
The Awful Truth (1937)
Badlands (1973)
The Band Wagon (1953)
The Bank Dick (1940)
The Battle of San Pietro (1945)
Ben-Hur (1926)
The Best Years of Our Lives (1946)
Big Business (1929)
The Big Parade (1925)
The Big Sleep (1946)
The Birth of a Nation (1915)
The Black Pirate (1926)
Blacksmith Scene (1893)
Blade Runner (1982)
The Blood of Jesus (1941)
Bonnie and Clyde (1967)
Bride of Frankenstein (1935)
The Bridge on the River Kwai (1957)
Bringing Up Baby (1938)
Broken Blossoms (1919)
Cabaret (1972)
Carmen Jones (1954)
Casablanca (1942)
Castro Street (1966)
Cat People (1942)
Chan Is Missing (1982)
The Cheat (1915)
Chinatown (1974)
Chulas Fronteras (1976)
Citizen Kane (1941)
The City (1939)

City Lights (1931)
Civilization (1916)
The Conversation (1974)
Cops (1922)
A Corner in Wheat (1909)
The Cool World (1963)
The Crowd (1928)
Czechoslovakia 1968 (1968)
David Holzman's Diary (1968)
The Day the Earth Stood Still (1951)
Dead Birds (1964)
The Deer Hunter (1978)
Destry Rides Again (1939)
Detour (1946)
Do the Right Thing (1989)
The Docks of New York (1928)
Dodsworth (1936)
Dog Star Man (1964)
Don't Look Back (1967)
Double Indemnity (1944)
Dr. Strangelove (Or, How I Learned to Stop
   Worrying and Love the Bomb) (1964)
Duck Amuck (1953)
Duck Soup (1933)
E.T. The Extra-Terrestrial (1982)
Easy Rider (1969)
Eaux d'Artifice (1953)
El Norte (1983)
The Emperor Jones (1933)
The Exploits of Elaine (1914)
Fantasia (1940)
Fatty's Tintype Tangle (1915)
Flash Gordon Serial (1936)
Footlight Parade (1933)
Force of Evil (1948)
The Forgotten Frontier (1931)
42nd Street (1933)
The Four Horsemen of the Apocalypse (1921)
Frank Film (1973)
Frankenstein (1931)
Freaks (1932)

The Freshman (1925)
From the Manger to the Cross (1912)
Fury (1936)
The General (1927)
Gerald McBoing Boing (1951)
Gertie the Dinosaur (1914)
Gigi (1958)
The Godfather (1972)
The Godfather, Part II (1974)
The Gold Rush (1925)
Gone With the Wind (1939)
The Graduate (1967)
The Grapes of Wrath (1940)
Grass (1925)
The Great Dictator (1940)
The Great Train Robbery (1903)
Greed (1924)
Gun Crazy (1949)
Gunga Din (1939)
Harlan County, U.S.A. (1976)
Harold and Maude (1972)
The Heiress (1949)
Hell's Hinges (1916)
Hindenburg Disaster Newsreel Footage (1937)
High School (1968)
High Noon (1952)
His Girl Friday (1940)
The Hitch-Hiker (1953)
Hospital (1970)
The Hospital (1971)
How Green Was My Valley (1941)
How the West Was Won (1962)
The Hustler (1961)
I Am a Fugitive From a Chain Gang (1932)
The Immigrant (1917)
In the Land of the Head Hunters (a.k.a. In the Land
  of the War Canoes, 1914)
Intolerance (1916)
Invasion of the Body Snatchers (1956)
It Happened One Night (1934)
It's a Wonderful Life (1946)
The Italian (1915)
Jammin' the Blues (1944)
Jazz on a Summer's Day (1959)
The Jazz Singer (1927)
Killer of Sheep (1977)
King: a Filmed Record ... Montgomery to Memphis
  (1970)
King Kong (1933)
The Kiss (1896)

Kiss Me Deadly (1955)
Knute Rockne, All American (1940)
The Lady Eve (1941)
Lambchops (1929)
Lassie Come Home (1943)
The Last of the Mohicans (1920)
The Last Picture Show (1972)
Laura (1944)
Lawrence of Arabia (1962)
The Learning Tree (1969)
Letter From An Unknown Woman (1948)
The Life and Death of 9413—A Hollywood Extra
  (1927)
The Life and Times of Rosie the Riveter (1980)
The Little Fugitive (1953)
Little Miss Marker (1934)
The Lost World (1925)
Louisiana Story (1948)
Love Me Tonight (1932)
M*A*S*H (1970)
Magical Maestro (1952)
The Magnificent Ambersons (1942)
The Maltese Falcon (1941)
The Manchurian Candidate (1962)
Manhatta (1921)
March of Time: Inside Nazi Germany—1938 (1938)
Marty (1955)
Master Hands (1936)
Mean Streets (1973)
Meet Me in St. Louis (1944)
Meshes of the Afternoon (1943)
Midnight Cowboy (1969)
Mildred Pierce (1945)
Modern Times (1936)
Modesta (1956)
Morocco (1930)
Motion Painting No. 1 (1947)
A Movie (1958)
Mr. Smith Goes to Washington (1939)
The Music Box (1932)
My Darling Clementine (1946)
My Man Godfrey (1936)
The Naked Spur (1953)
Nanook of the North (1922)
Nashville (1975)
A Night at the Opera (1935)
The Night of the Hunter (1955)
Night of the Living Dead (1968)
Ninotchka (1939)
North By Northwest (1959)

Nothing But a Man (1964)
On the Waterfront (1954)
One Flew Over the Cuckoo's Nest (1975)
Out of the Past (1947)
The Ox-Bow Incident (1943)
The Outlaw Josey Wales (1976)
Pass the Gravy (1928)
Paths of Glory (1957)
Phantom of the Opera (1925)
The Philadelphia Story (1940)
Pinocchio (1940)
A Place in the Sun (1951)
The Plow That Broke the Plains (1936)
Point of Order (1964)
The Poor Little Rich Girl (1917)
Powers of Ten (1978)
Primary (1960)
The Prisoner of Zenda (1937)
The Producers (1968)
Psycho (1960)
The Public Enemy (1931)
Pull My Daisy (1959)
Raging Bull (1980)
Raiders of the Lost Ark (1981)
Rear Window (1954)
Rebel Without a Cause (1955)
Red River (1948)
Republic Steel Strike Riot Newsreel Footage (1937)
Return of the Secaucus 7 (1980)
Ride the High Country (1962)
Rip Van Winkle (1896)
The River (1937)
Road to Morocco (1942)
Roman Holiday (1953)
Safety Last (1923)
Salesman (1969)
Salt of the Earth (1954)
Scarface (1932)
The Searchers (1956)
Seventh Heaven (1927)
Shadow of a Doubt (1943)
Shadows (1959)
Shane (1953)
She Done Him Wrong (1933)
Sherlock, Jr. (1924)
Shock Corridor (1963)
The Shop Around the Corner (1940)
Show Boat (1936)
Singin' in the Rain (1952)

Sky High (1922)
Snow White (1933)
Snow White and the Seven Dwarfs (1937)
Some Like It Hot (1959)
Stagecoach (1939)
Star Wars (1977)
Steamboat Willie (1928)
A Streetcar Named Desire (1951)
Sullivan's Travels (1941)
Sunrise (1927)
Sunset Boulevard (1950)
Sweet Smell of Success (1957)
Tabu (1931)
Tacoma Narrows Bridge Collapse (1940)
Taxi Driver (1976)
The Ten Commandments (1956)
Tevye (1939)
The Thief of Baghdad (1924)
The Thin Man (1934)
To Be or Not To Be (1942)
To Fly (1976)
To Kill a Mockingbird (1962)
Tootsie (1982)
Top Hat (1935)
Topaz (1943–45)
Touch of Evil (1958)
Trance and Dance in Bali (1936–39)
The Treasure of The Sierra Madre (1948)
Trouble in Paradise (1932)
Tulips Shall Grow (1942)
Twelve O'Clock High (1949)
2001: A Space Odyssey (1968)
Verbena Tragica (1939)
Vertigo (1958)
West Side Story (1961)
Westinghouse Works, 1904 (1904)
What's Opera, Doc? (1957)
Where Are My Children? (1916)
The Wild Bunch (1969)
The Wind (1928)
Wings (1927)
Within Our Gates (1920)
The Wizard of Oz (1939)
Woman of the Year (1942)
A Woman under the Influence (1974)
Woodstock (1970)
Yankee Doodle Dandy (1942)
Zapruder Film (1963)

⊙ Library of Congress, National Film Preservation Board. www.loc.gov/film/
   U.S. Public Law 285. 104th Cong., 2d sess, 11 October 1996.

Classic Foreign-Language Films

The following films in languages other than English are notable for several reasons: they advanced the art of filmmaking, were milestones in the history of censorship, were major films in the directors' careers, or were extremely popular or influential in their day.

Abbreviations: AA = Best Foreign-Language Film Academy Award®; AAN = nomination.

À bout de souffle [Breathless] (France 1959). Director: Jean-Luc Godard

À nous la liberté [Freedom for Us] (France 1931). Director: René Clair

L'âge d'or [The Golden Age] (France 1930). Director: Luis Buñuel

Aguirre, der Zorn Gottes [Aguirre, the Wrath of God] (Peru/Germany/Mexico 1972). Director: Werner Herzog

Alexander Nevsky (USSR 1938). Director: Sergei Eisenstein

Alexis Zorbas [Zorba the Greek] (Greece 1964; Best Picture AAN). Director: Michael Cacoyannis

Amarcord (Italy 1974; AA). Director: Federico Fellini

L'année dernière à Marienbad [Last Year at Marienbad] (France/Italy 1961). Director: Alain Resnais

Apu Trilogy, The [Panther Panchali; Aparajito; The World of Apu] (India 1955–59). Director: Satyajit Ray

Andrei Rublev (USSR 1966). Director: Andrei Tarkovsky

Au revoir les enfants [Goodbye, Children] (France 1987; AAN). Director: Louis Malle

L'Avventura [The Adventure] (Italy 1960). Director: Michelangelo Antonioni

Ba wang bie ji [Farewell My Concubine] (China/Hong Kong 1993; AAN). Director: Kaige Chen

Babettes gæstebud [Babette's Feast] (Denmark 1987; AA). Director: Gabriel Axel

Battleship Potemkin, The (USSR 1925). Director: Sergei Eisenstein

Blechtrommel, Die [The Tin Drum] (West Germany 1978; AA). Director: Volker Schlöndorff

Belle époque [The Age of Beauty] (Spain 1992; AA). Director: Fernando Trueba

Belle et la Bête, La [Beauty and the Beast] (France 1946). Director: Jean Cocteau

Blaue Engel, Der [The Blue Angel] (Germany 1930). Director: Josef von Sternberg

Büchse der Pandora, Die [Pandora's Box] (Germany 1928). Director: G. W. Pabst

Central do Brasil [Central Station] (Brazil 1998; AAN). Director: Walter Salles

Citta Aperta [Open City] (Italy 1945). Director: Roberto Rossellini

Cousin, Cousine (France 1976; AAN). Director: Jean-Charles Tacchella

Cyrano de Bergerac (France 1990; AAN). Director: Jean-Paul Rappeneau

Da hong deng long gao gao gua [Raise the Red Lantern] (China/Hong Kong/Taiwan 1992; AAN). Director: Yimou Zhang

Dolce Vita, La [The Sweet Life] (Italy 1960). Director: Federico Fellini

8 1/2 (Italy 1963; AA). Director: Federico Fellini

Elvira Madigan (Sweden 1967). Director: Bo Widerberg

Enfants du Paradis, Les [Children of Paradise] (France 1944). Director: Marcel Carné

Extase [Ecstasy] (Czechoslovakia 1933). Director: Gustav Machaty

Fanny and Alexander (Sweden 1983; AA). Director: Ingmar Bergman

Giardino dei Finzi-Contini, Il [The Garden of the Finzi-Continis] (Italy/West Germany 1970; AA). Director: Vittorio de Sica

Grande Illusion, La (France 1937; Best Picture AAN). Director: Jean Renoir

Hsi yen [The Wedding Banquet] (Taiwan 1993; AAN). Director: Ang Lee

Indochine (France 1992; AA). Director: Régis Wargnier

Ivan the Terrible (I and II) (USSR 1943–46). Director: Sergei Eisenstein

Ju Dou (China 1990; AAN). Director: Yang Fengliang

Kabinett des Doktor Caligari, Das [The Cabinet of Dr. Caligari] (Germany 1919). Directors: Carl Mayer and Hans Janowitz

Kolya (Czech Republic 1996; AA). Director: Jan Sverák

Ladri di biciclette [The Bicycle Thief] (Italy 1948). Director: Vittorio de Sica

Letzte Mann, Der [The Last Laugh] (Germany 1924). Director: F. W. Murnau

M (Germany 1931). Director: Fritz Lang

Madame de ... (France/Italy 1953). Director: Max Ophüls

Mediterraneo (Italy 1991; AA). Director: Gabriele Salvatores

Metropolis (Germany 1926). Director: Fritz Lang

Napoléon (France 1925). Director: Abel Gance

Nuovo cinema Paradiso (Italy 1988; AA). Director: Giuseppe Tornatore

Orfeu Negro [Black Orpheus] (Brazil/France/Italy 1959; AA). Director: Marcel Camus

Ossessione (Italy 1942). Director: Luchino Visconti

Parapluies de Cherbourg, Les [The Umbrellas of Cherbourg] (France/West Germany 1963; AAN). Director: Jacques Demy

Passion de Jeanne d'Arc, La [The Passion of Joan of Arc] (France 1928). Director: Carl Dreyer

Pelle erobreren [Pelle the Conqueror] (Denmark 1987; AA). Director: Bille August

Popiól i diament [Ashes and Diamonds] (Poland 1958). Director: Andrzej Wajda

Postino, Il [The Postman] (Italy 1994; Best Picture AAN). Director: Michael Radford

Potomok Chingis-Khana [Storm over Asia] (USSR 1928). Director: Vsevolod Pudovkin

Pred dozhdot [Before the Rain] (U.K./France/Macdeonia 1994; AAN). Director: Milcho Manchevski

Quatre cents coups, Les [The 400 Blows] (France 1958). Director: François Truffaut

Rashomon (Japan 1951). Director: Akira Kurosawa

Règle du jeu, La [The Rules of the Game] (France 1939). Director: Jean Renoir

Reise der Hoffnung [Journey of Hope] (Switzerland 1990; AA). Director: Xavier Koller

Salaam Bombay! (India 1988; AAN). Director: Mira Nair

Sang d'un poète, Le [The Blood of a Poet] (France 1930). Director: Jean Cocteau

Shichinin no samurai [Seven Samurai] (Japan 1954). Director: Akira Kurosawa

Sjunde inseglet, Det [The Seventh Seal] (Sweden 1957). Director: Ingmar Bergman

Strada, La (Italy 1954; AA 1956). Director: Federico Fellini

Todo sobre mi madre [All About My Mother] (Spain 1999; AA). Director: Pedro Almodóvar

Tokyo monogatari [Tokyo Story] (Japan 1953). Director: Yasujiro Ozu

Tristana (Spain/France/Italy 1970; AA). Director: Luis Bunuel

Triumph des Willens [The Triumph of the Will] (Germany 1934). Director: Leni Riefenstahl

Ugetsu Monogatari [Tales of Ugetsu] (Japan 1952). Director: Kenji Mizoguchi

Viskningar och rop [Cries and Whispers] (Sweden 1972; Best Picture AAN). Director: Ingmar Bergman

Vita è bella, La [Life Is Beautiful] (Italy 1997; AA; Best Picture AAN). Director: Roberto Benigni

Z (Algeria/France 1969; AA; Best Picture AAN). Director: Costa-Gavras

Zéro de Conduite (France 1933). Director: Jean Vigo

⊙ Canby, Vincent, et al. *The New York Times Guide to the Best 1,000 Movies Ever Made.* New York: Times Books, 1999.

Internet Movie Database. www.imdb.com

Wiley, Mason, and Damien Bona. *Inside Oscar.* 10th ed. New York: Ballantine, 1996.

Wilmington, Michael. *Chicago Tribune.* "The Essentials: Foreign Movies," www.chicagotribune.com/ws/199712essentials/foreign/front3.htm

Included in this list are actors who are known primarily for their work in films. They are not merely popular actors, but respected by audiences, critics, and the film community. Many received multiple awards or nominations in long and distinguished careers, while others shone brightly for only a few years but left indelible impressions.

Name	Dates	Selected Films*
Andrews, Julie (Julia Wells)	1934–	Mary Poppins (1964; AA); The Sound of Music (1965; AAN)
Astaire, Fred (Frederick Austerlitz)	1899–1987	Top Hat (1935); Shall We Dance? (1937)
Bacall, Lauren (Betty Jean Perske)	1924–	To Have and Have Not (1944); The Mirror Has Two Faces (1996; SAAN)
Bancroft, Anne (Anna Maria Italiano)	1931–	The Miracle Worker (1962; AA); The Graduate (1968; AAN)
Bara, Theda (Theodosia Goodman)	1890–1955	A Fool There Was (1916); Cleopatra (1917)
Barrymore, Ethel (Edith Blythe)	1879–1959	None But the Lonely Heart (1944; SAA); The Spiral Staircase (1946; SAAN)
Barrymore, John (John Blythe)	1882–1942	Dr. Jekyll and Mr. Hyde (1920); Dinner at Eight (1933)
Beatty, Warren (Henry Warren Beaty)	1937–	Bonnie and Clyde (1967; AAN); Heaven Can Wait (1978; AAN)
Bergman, Ingrid	1915–1982	Gaslight (1943; AA); Joan of Arc (1948; AAN)
Bogart, Humphrey	1899–1957	Casablanca (1943; AAN); The African Queen (1951; AA)
Borgnine, Ernest (Ermes Effron Borgnino)	1917–	Marty (1955; AA); The Wild Bunch (1969)
Brando, Marlon	1924–	On the Waterfront (1954; AA); The Godfather (1972; AA)
Burstyn, Ellen (Edna Rae Gillooly)	1932–	The Exorcist (1973; AAN); Alice Doesn't Live Here Anymore (1974; AA)
Burton, Richard (Richard Walter Jenkins Jr.)	1925–1984	The Spy Who Came in from the Cold (1965; AAN); Who's Afraid of Virginia Woolf? (1966; AAN)
Cage, Nicolas (Nicholas Kim Coppola)	1964–	Raising Arizona (1987); Leaving Las Vegas (1995; AA)
Cagney, James	1899–1986	Angels with Dirty Faces (1938; AAN); Yankee Doodle Dandy (1942; AA)
Caine, Michael (Maurice Joseph Micklewhite)	1933–	Educating Rita (U.K. 1983; AAN); Hannah and Her Sisters (1986)
Chaney, Lon, Sr. (Leonidas F. Chaney)	1883–1930	The Hunchback of Notre Dame (1923); The Phantom of the Opera (1925)
Chaplin, Charles	1889–1977	The Tramp (1915); The Great Dictator (1940; AAN)
Charisse, Cyd (Tula Ellice Finklea)	1921–	Brigadoon (1954); Silk Stockings (1957)
Cher (Cherilyn Sarkisian LaPierre)	1946–	Mask (1985; AAN); Moonstruck (1987; AA)

Clift, Montgomery	1920–1966	*From Here to Eternity* (1953; AAN); *Judgment at Nuremberg* (1961; SAAN)
Close, Glenn	1947–	*Fatal Attraction* (1987; AAN); *Dangerous Liaisons* (1988; AAN)
Colbert, Claudette (Lily Claudette Chauchoin)	1903–1996	*It Happened One Night* (1934; AA); *Since You Went Away* (1944; AAN)
Connery, Sean (Frank J. Cooper)	1930–	*Doctor No* (1963); *The Untouchables* (1987; SAA)
Cooper, Gary	1901–1961	*Sergeant York* (1941; AA); *High Noon* (1952; AA)
Crawford, Joan (Lucille le Sueur)	1906–1977	*Mildred Pierce* (1945; AA); *Sudden Fear* (1952; AAN)
Crosby, Bing (Harry Lillis Crosby)	1905–1977	*Going My Way* (1944; AA); *The Bells of St. Mary's* (1945; AAN)
Curtis, Tony (Bernard Schwartz)	1925–	*The Defiant Ones* (1958; AAN); *Spartacus* (1960)
Davis, Bette (Ruth Elizabeth Davis)	1908–1989	*Jezebel* (1938; AA); *All About Eve* (1950; AAN)
Day-Lewis, Daniel	1957–	*My Left Foot* (U.K. 1989; AA); *In the Name of the Father* (Ireland/U.K. 1993; AAN)
de Havilland, Olivia	1916–	*To Each His Own* (1946; AA); *The Heiress* (1949; AA)
De Niro, Robert	1943–	*Taxi Driver* (1976; AAN); *Raging Bull* (1980; AA)
Dean, James	1931–1955	*East of Eden* (1955; AAN); *Rebel Without a Cause* (1955)
Dietrich, Marlene (Maria Magdalena von Losch)	1901–1992	*Blonde Venus* (1933); *Touch of Evil* (1958)
Douglas, Kirk (Issur Danielovitch Demsky)	1916–	*Lust for Life* (1956; AAN); *Spartacus* (1960)
Douglas, Michael	1944–	*Fatal Attraction* (1987); *Wall Street* (1987; AA)
Dunaway, Faye	1941–	*Bonnie and Clyde* (1967; AAN); *Network* (1976; AA)
Duvall, Robert	1931–	*The Godfather* (1972; SAAN); *Tender Mercies* (1983; AA)
Eastwood, Clint	1930–	*A Fistful of Dollars* (Italy 1964); *Dirty Harry* (1971)
Fairbanks, Douglas (Douglas Ullman)	1883–1939	*The Mark of Zorro* (1920); *The Thief of Baghdad* (1923)
Ferrer, José (José Vicente Ferrer y Cintrón)	1912–1992	*Cyrano de Bergerac* (1950; AA); *Moulin Rouge* (1952; AAN)
Field, Sally (Sally Mahoney)	1946–	*Norma Rae* (1979; AA); *Places in the Heart* (1984; AA)
Fields, W. C. (William Claude Dukinfield)	1879–1946	*My Little Chickadee* (1940); *Never Give a Sucker an Even Break* (1941)
Fonda, Henry	1905–1982	*The Grapes of Wrath* (1940; AAN); *On Golden Pond* (1981; AA)
Fonda, Jane	1937–	*Coming Home* (1978; AA); *On Golden Pond* (1981; SAAN)
Ford, Harrison	1942–	*Star Wars* (1977); *Blade Runner* (1982)
Foster, Jodie	1962–	*The Accused* (1988; AA); *The Silence of the Lambs* (1991; AA)
Freeman, Morgan	1937–	*Driving Miss Daisy* (1989; AAN); *The Shawshank Redemption* (1994; AAN)
Gable, Clark	1901–1960	*It Happened One Night* (1934; AA); *Gone with the Wind* (1939; AAN)
Garbo, Greta (Greta Gustafson)	1905–1990	*Anna Christie* (1930; AAN); *Queen Christina* (1933)

Name	Dates	Selected Films*
Gardner, Ava	1922–1990	*The Killers* (1946); *Mogambo* (1953; AAN)
Garland, Judy (Frances Gumm)	1922–1969	*The Wizard of Oz* (1939): *A Star is Born* (1954: AAN)
Gish, Lillian (Lillian de Guiche)	1893–1993	*Birth of a Nation* (1914): *Duel in the Sun* (1946): SAAN)
Goddard, Paulette (Marion Levy)	1911–1990	*Modern Times* (1936); *The Diary of a Chambermaid* (1946)
Goldberg, Whoopi (Caryn Johnson)	1949–	*The Color Purple* (1985; AAN); *The Player* (1992)
Grable, Betty	1916–1973	*Moon over Miami* (1941); *How to Marry a Millionaire* (1953)
Grant, Cary (Archibald Leach)	1904–1986	*His Girl Friday* (1940); *None but the Lonely Heart* (1944; AAN)
Guinness, Alec	1914–2000	*The Lavender Hill Mob* (U.K. 1951; AAN); *The Bridge on the River Kwai* (U.K. 1957: AA)
Hackman, Gene	1930–	*The French Connection* (1971; AA); *Unforgiven* (1992; SAA)
Hanks, Tom	1956–	*Philadelphia* (1993; AA); *Saving Private Ryan* (1998: AAN)
Harlow, Jean (Harlean Carpentier)	1911–1937	*Public Enemy* (1931); *Dinner at Eight* (1933)
Harrison, Rex	1908–1990	*Cleopatra* (1963; AAN); *My Fair Lady* (1964; AA)
Hayworth, Rita (Margarita Carmen Cansino)	1918–1987	*Only Angels Have Wings* (1939); *The Lady from Shanghai* (1948)
Hepburn, Audrey (Audrey Hepburn-Ruston)	1929–1993	*Roman Holiday* (1953; AA); *Breakfast at Tiffany's* (1961; AAN)
Hepburn, Katharine	1907–	*Morning Glory* (1933; AA); *On Golden Pond* (1981; AA)
Heston, Charlton (John Charlton Carter)	1924–	*Ben-Hur* (1959; AA); *Planet of the Apes* (1968)
Hoffmann, Dustin	1937–	*Kramer vs. Kramer* (1979; AA); *Rain Man* (1988; AA)
Holden, William (William Beedle)	1918–1981	*Sunset Boulevard* (1950: AAN); *Stalag 17* (1953; AA)
Hopkins, Anthony	1937–	*The Silence of the Lambs* (1991; AA); *The Remains of the Day* (U.K./U.S. 1993; AAN)
Hunter, Holly	1958–	*Broadcast News* (1987; AAN); *The Piano* (1993; AA)
Huston, Anjelica	1952–	*Prizzi's Honor* (1985; SAA); *The Grifters* (1990; AAN)
Jackson, Glenda	1937–	*Women in Love* (U.K. 1970; AA); *A Touch of Class* (1973; AA)
Jackson, Samuel L.	1948–	*Pulp Fiction* (1994; SAAN); *Shaft* (2000)
Jones, Jennifer (Phyllis Isley)	1919–	*The Song of Bernadette* (1943; AA); *Love is a Many-Splendored Thing* (1955; AAN)
Jones, Tommy Lee	1946–	*Coal Miner's Daughter* (1980); *The Fugitive* (1993; SAA)
Karloff, Boris (William Pratt)	1887–1969	*Frankenstein* (1931); *The Mummy* (1932)
Keaton, Buster (Joseph Francis Keaton)	1895–1966	*The Navigator* (1924); *The General* (1927)

Name	Dates	Films
Keaton, Diane (Diane Hall)	1946–	*Annie Hall* (1977; AA); *Reds* (1981; AAN)
Keitel, Harvey	1939–	*The Last Temptation of Christ* (1988); *Bugsy* (1991; SAAN)
Kelly, Gene	1912–1996	*Anchors Aweigh* (1945; AAN); *An American in Paris* (1951)
Kelly, Grace	1928–1982	*Rear Window* (1954); *The Country Girl* (1954; AA)
Kidman, Nicole	1967–	*Dead Calm* (Australia/U.S. 1989); *The Portrait of a Lady* (1996)
Lancaster, Burt	1913–1994	*Elmer Gantry* (1960; AA); *Atlantic City* (1981; AAN)
Lange, Jessica	1949–	*Tootsie* 1982; SAA); *Blue Sky* (1994; AA)
Laughton, Charles	1899–1962	*The Private Life of Henry VIII* (U.K. 1933; AA); *Witness for the Prosecution* (1957; AAN)
Leigh, Vivien (Vivien Mary Hartley)	1913–1967	*Gone with the Wind* (1939; AA); *A Streetcar Named Desire* (1951; AA)
Lemmon, Jack (John Uhler Lemmon III)	1925–	*The Apartment* (1960; AAN); *Save the Tiger* (1973; AA)
Lombard, Carole (Jane Peters)	1908–1942	*My Man Godfrey* (1935; AAN); *Nothing Sacred* (1937)
Loren, Sophia (Sophia Scicoloni)	1934–	*Two Women* (Italy 1961; AA); *Marriage, Italian Style* (Italy 1964; AAN)
Lugosi, Bela (Bela Ferenc Blasko)	1882–1956	*Dracula* (1930); *Son of Frankenstein* (1939)
MacLaine, Shirley (Shirley Mclean Beaty)	1934–	*The Turning Point* (1977; AAN); *Terms of Endearment* (1983; AA)
Malkovich, John	1953–	*Places in the Heart* (1984; SAAN); *In the Line of Fire* (1993; SAAN)
March, Frederic (Frederick McIntyre Bickel)	1897–1975	*Dr. Jekyll and Mr. Hyde* (1932; AA); *The Best Years of Our Lives* (1946; AA)
Marx Brothers, The		*Animal Crackers* (1930); *Horse Feathers* (1932)
Chico (Leonard)	1886–1961	
Harpo (Adolph)	1888–1964	
Groucho (Julius)	1890–1977	
Zeppo (Herbert)	1901–1979	
Mason, James	1909–1984	*A Star is Born* (1954; AAN); *The Verdict* (1982; SAAN)
Matthau, Walter (Walter Matasschanskayasky)	1920–2000	*The Fortune Cookie* (1966; SAA); *The Odd Couple* (1968)
McDaniel, Hattie	1895–1952	*Show Boat* (1935); *Gone with the Wind* (1939; SAA)
Midler, Bette	1945–	*Divine Madness* (1980); *For the Boys* (1991; AAN)
Milland, Ray (Reginald Alfred Truscott-Jones)	1907–1986	*Beau Geste* (1939); *The Lost Weekend* (1945; AA)
Mitchum, Robert	1917–1997	*Night of the Hunter* (1955); *Farewell, My Lovely* (1975)
Monroe, Marilyn (Norma Jean Mortenson)	1926–1962	*Gentlemen Prefer Blondes* (1953); *The Seven Year Itch* (1955)
Montgomery, Robert (Henry Montgomery Jr.)	1904–1981	*Night Must Fall* (1937; AAN); *The Lady in the Lake* (1946)

Name	Dates	Selected Films*
Muni, Paul (Muni Weisenfreund)	1895–1967	*The Story of Louis Pasteur* (1936; AA); *The Last Angry Man* (1959; AAN)
Newman, Paul	1925–	*Hud* (1963; AAN); *The Color of Money* (1986; AA)
Nicholson, Jack	1937–	*One Flew Over the Cuckoo's Nest* (1975; AA); *As Good as It Gets* (1997; AA)
Nolte, Nick	1941–	*The Prince of Tides* (1991; AAN); *Affliction* (1997; AAN)
O'Toole, Peter	1932–	*Lawrence of Arabia* (U.K. 1962; AAN); *Goodbye, Mr. Chips* (1969; AAN)
Olivier, Laurence	1907–1989	*Wuthering Heights* (1939; AAN); *Hamlet* (U.K. 1948; AA)
Pacino, Al	1939–	*The Godfather* (1972; SAAN); *Scent of a Woman* (1992; AA)
Page, Geraldine	1924–1987	*Sweet Bird of Youth* (1962; AAN); *The Trip to Bountiful* (1985; AA)
Peck, Gregory	1916–	*Gentleman's Agreement* (1947; AAN); *To Kill a Mockingbird* (1962; AA)
Penn, Sean	1960–	*Dead Man Walking* (1995; AAN); *Sweet and Lowdown* (1999; AAN)
Perkins, Anthony	1932–1992	*Fear Strikes Out* (1957); *Psycho* (1960)
Pfeiffer, Michelle	1957–	*Dangerous Liaisons* (1988; SAAN); *The Fabulous Baker Boys* (1989; AAN)
Pickford, Mary (Gladys Louise Smith)	1892–1979	*Polyanna* (1919); *Coquette* (1929; AA)
Poitier, Sidney	1927–	*The Blackboard Jungle* (1955); *Lilies of the Field* (1963; AA)
Powell, William	1892–1984	*The Thin Man* (1934; AAN); *Life With Father* (1947; AAN)
Power, Tyrone	1913–1958	*Jesse James* (1939); *The Mark of Zorro* (1940)
Redford, Robert	1936–	*Butch Cassidy and the Sundance Kid* (1969); *The Sting* (1973; AAN)
Redgrave, Vanessa	1937–	*Julia* (1977; SAA); *The Bostonians* (1984; AAN)
Reynolds, Burt	1936–	*Deliverance* (1972); *Boogie Nights* (1997; SAAN)
Robeson, Paul	1898–1976	*Show Boat* (1935); *Song of Freedom* (U.K. 1937)
Rogers, Ginger (Virginia McMath)	1911–1995	*Top Hat* (1935); *Kitty Foyle* (1940; AA)
Rooney, Mickey (Joe Yule Jr.)	1920–	*The Human Comedy* (1943; AAN); *The Black Stallion* (1979; SAAN)
Russell, Rosalind	1908–1976	*Mourning Becomes Electra* (1947; AAN); *Auntie Mame* (1958; AAN)
Sarandon, Susan (Susan Tomaling)	1946–	*Thelma and Louise* (1991; AAN); *Dead Man Walking* (1995; AA)
Scott, George C.	1927–1999	*Anatomy of a Murder* (1959; SAAN); *Patton* (1970; AA)
Sellers, Peter	1925–1980	*The Pink Panther* (1964); *Dr. Strangelove* (1964; AAN)

Name	Dates	Films
Shearer, Norma	1904–1993	*The Divorcee* (1930; AA); *The Barretts of Wimpole Street* (1934; AAN)
Spacek, Sissy (Mary Elizabeth Spacek)	1949–	*Coal Miner's Daughter* (1980; AA); *Crimes of the Heart* (1986; AAN)
Spacey, Kevin (Kevin Spacey Fowler)	1959–	*The Usual Suspects* (1995; SAA); *American Beauty* (1999; AA)
Stanwyck, Barbara (Ruby Stevens)	1907–1990	*Stella Dallas* (1937; AAN); *Double Indemnity* (1944; AAN)
Stewart, James	1908–1997	*The Philadelphia Story* (1940; AA); *It's a Wonderful Life* (1946; AAN)
Streep, Meryl (Mary Louise Streep)	1949–	*Sophie's Choice* (1982; AA); *The Bridges of Madison County* (1995; AAN)
Taylor, Elizabeth	1932–	*Cat on a Hot Tin Roof* (1958; AAN); *Butterfield 8* (1960; AA)
Temple, Shirley	1928–	*Curly Top* (1935); *Heidi* (1937)
Thompson, Emma	1959–	*Howards End* (U.K. 1992; AA); *In the Name of the Father* (Ireland/U.K. 1993; SAAN)
Tracy, Spencer	1900–1967	*Boys' Town* (1938; AA); *Judgment at Nuremberg* (1961; AAN)
Turner, Lana (Julia Jean Mildred Frances Turner)	1920–1995	*The Bad and the Beautiful* (1952); *Peyton Place* (1957; AAN)
Valentino, Rudolph (Rodolpho d'Antonguolla)	1895–1926	*The Sheik* (1921); *Blood and Sand* (1922)
Washington, Denzel	1954–	*Glory* (1989; SAA); *Malcolm X* (1992; AAN)
Wayne, John (Marion Michael Morrison)	1907–1979	*Stagecoach* (1939); *True Grit* (1966; AA)
Weaver, Sigourney (Susan Weaver)	1949–	*Alien* (1979; AAN); *Gorillas in the Mist* (1988; AAN)
Welles, Orson	1915–1985	*Citizen Kane* (1941; AAN); *Touch of Evil* (1958)
West, Mae	1892–1980	*I'm No Angel* (1933); *Myra Breckinridge* (1970)
Williams, Robin	1952–	*Good Morning, Vietnam* (1987; AAN); *Good Will Hunting* (1997; SAA)
Winters, Shelley (Shirley Schrift)	1922–	*A Place in the Sun* (1951; AAN); *The Diary of Anne Frank* (1959; SAA)
Woodward, Joanne	1930–	*The Three Faces of Eve* (1957; AA); *Mr. and Mrs. Bridge* (1991; AAN)
Young, Loretta (Gretchen Michaela Young)	1913–2000	*Ramona* (1936); *The Farmer's Daughter* (1947; AA)

*Abbreviations: AA = Best Actor or Actress Academy Award®. AAN = nomination; SAA = Best Supporting Actor or Actress Academy Award®. SAAN = supporting nomination.

⊙ Internet Movie Database. www.imdb.com
Internet Movie Database. "Academy Awards, USA," http://us.imdb.com/Sections/Awards/Academy_Awards_USA/
Walker, John, ed. *Halliwell's Filmgoer's Companion.* 12th ed. New York: Harper Perennial, 1997.

125 Favorite Television Series

The regularly scheduled, prime-time series included in this list are considered favorites for several reasons: they ran for more than five years, were among the top 20 shows in the Neilsen ratings for at least one season, or were pathbreaking shows that showed the direction of television's future.

Adam-12 (1968–75); police drama

Adventures of Ozzie and Harriet, The (1952–66); situation comedy

Alfred Hitchcock Presents (1955–65); suspense anthology

Alice (1976–85); situation comedy

All in the Family/Archie Bunker's Place (1971–83); situation comedy

Andy Griffith Show, The (1960–68); situation comedy

Baretta (1975–78); police drama

Barney Miller (1975–82); situation comedy

Benson (1979–86); situation comedy

Beverly Hillbillies, The (1962–71); situation comedy

Beverly Hills 90210 (1990–2000); drama

Bewitched (1964–72), situation comedy

Bob Newhart Show, The (1972–78); situation comedy

Bonanza (1959–73); western

Brady Bunch, The (1969–74); situation comedy

Cagney & Lacey (1982–88); police drama

Candid Camera (1948–50; 1953; 1960–67; 1990); humor

Carol Burnett Show, The (1967–79); comedy variety

Charlie's Angels (1976–81); detective drama

Cheers (1982–93); situation comedy

Columbo (1971–77; 1989–90; 1992–93); police drama

Cops (1989–); police documentary

Cosby Show, The (1984–92); situation comedy

Dallas (1978–91); drama

Dean Martin Show, The (1965–74); comedy variety

Death Valley Days (1952–72; 1975); western anthology

Dick Van Dyke Show, The (1961–66); situation comedy

Diff'rent Strokes (1978–86); situation comedy

Different World, A (1987–93); situation comedy

Doris Day Show, The (1968–73); situation comedy

Dragnet (1952–59; 1967–70); police drama

Dukes of Hazzard, The (1979–85); comedy adventure

Dynasty (1981–89); drama

Ed Sullivan Show, The (1948–71); variety

Eight Is Enough (1977–81); comedy/drama

Ellen/These Friends of Mine (1994–98); situation comedy

Emergency (1972–77); medical drama

F.B.I., The (1965–74); police drama

Facts of Life, The (1979–88); situation comedy

Falcon Crest (1981–90); drama

Fall Guy, The (1981–86); adventure

Family Matters (1989–98); situation comedy

Fireside Theatre, The (1949–58; 1963); dramatic anthology

Ford Theater (1949–57); dramatic anthology

Friends (1994–); situation comedy

Fugitive, The (1963–67); adventure

Garry Moore Show, The (1950–51; 1958–67); variety

Gilligan's Island (1964–67); situation comedy

Gomer Pyle, U.S.M.C. (1964–70); situation comedy

Good Times (1974–79); situation comedy

Growing Pains (1985–92); situation comedy

Gunsmoke (1955–75); western

Happy Days (1974–84); situation comedy

Hawaii Five-O (1968–80); police drama

Hee Haw (1969–93); country variety

Hill Street Blues (1981–87); police drama

Hogan's Heroes (1965–71); situation comedy

Home Improvement (1991–99); situation comedy

Honeymooners, The (1952–59); situation comedy

I Dream of Jeannie (1965–70); situation comedy
I Love Lucy (1951–61); situation comedy
Incredible Hulk, The (1978–82); adventure/drama
I've Got a Secret (1952–76); quiz show/audience participation
Jack Benny Show, The (1950–65); comedy
Jackie Gleason Show, The (1962–70); comedy/variety
Jeffersons, The (1975–85); situation comedy
Kate & Allie (1984–89); situation comedy
Knots Landing (1979–93); drama
Kojak (1973–78; 1989–90); police drama
Kraft Television Theatre (1947–58); drama anthology
Lassie (1954–71); adventure
Laverne & Shirley (1976–83); situation comedy
Law & Order (1990–); police/legal drama
Lawrence Welk Show, The (1955–82); music
Leave It to Beaver (1957–63); situation comedy
Little House on the Prairie (1974–83); adventure/drama
Lone Ranger, The (1949–57); western
Love Boat, The (1977–86); situation comedy
M*A*S*H (1972–83); situation comedy
MacGyver (1985–92); adventure
Married … with Children (1987–97); situation comedy
Mary Tyler Moore Show, The (1970–77); situation comedy
Miami Vice (1984–89); police drama
Milton Berle Show, The/Texaco Star Theater (1948–67); comedy/variety
Mission: Impossible (1966–73; 1988–90); adventure
Mork & Mindy (1978–82); situation comedy
Murphy Brown (1988–98); situation comedy
Newhart (1982–90); situation comedy
Night Court (1984–92); situation comedy
Northern Exposure (1990–95); drama
Odd Couple, The (1970–75; 1982–83); situation comedy
One Day at a Time (1974–84); situation comedy

Partridge Family, The (1970–74); situation comedy
Perry Como Show, The (1948–63); musical variety
Perry Mason (1957–66); legal drama
Price is Right, The (1957–86); quiz show/audience participation
Quantum Leap (1989–93); science fiction
Quincy, M.E. (1976–83); police drama
Rawhide (1959–66); western
Red Skelton Show, The/The Red Skelton Hour (1951–71); comedy/variety
Rescue 911 (1989–92); informational
Rockford Files, The (1974–80); detective drama
Roseanne (1988–97); situation comedy
Sanford and Son (1972–77); situation comedy
Seinfeld (1990–98); situation comedy
Simpsons, The (1989–); cartoon
60 Minutes (1968–); newsmagazine
$64,000 Question, The (1955–58); quiz show
Star Trek (1966–69); science fiction
Star Trek: The Next Generation (1987–94); science fiction
Three's Company (1977–84); situation comedy
Trapper John, M.D. (1979–86); medical drama
20/20 (1978–); newsmagazine
Twilight Zone, The (1959–65; 1985–88); science fiction anthology
Twin Peaks (1990–91); drama
Unsolved Mysteries (1988–); mystery anthology
Untouchables, The (1959–63; 1992–94); police drama
Walt Disney (1954–83; 1986–90; 1997–); anthology
Waltons, The (1972–81); drama
What's My Line? (1950–67); quiz show/panel show
Who Wants to Be a Millionaire? (1999–); quiz show
WKRP in Cincinnati (1978–82); situation comedy
X-Files, The (1993–); science fiction
You Bet Your Life/The Groucho Show (1950–61); quiz show
Your Hit Parade (1950–59; 1974); music

⊙ Classic TV Database. www.classic-tv.com/
McNeil, Alex. Total Television. 4th ed. New York: Penguin, 1996.

ARTS AND LEISURE: *Radio*

75 Favorite Radio Programs

These regularly scheduled, nationally syndicated radio programs ran for at least 10 years in national broadcasts or were series noted for their quality or influence on future entertainment. The "golden age" of radio ended when television became the dominant household medium, but some long-running programs can be found on talk radio even today.

Adventures of Ozzie and Harriet, The (1944–54); situation comedy

Aldrich Family, The (1939–53); situation comedy

Amos 'n' Andy (1929–60); situation comedy

Baby Snooks Show (1944–51); situation comedy

Backstage Wife (1935–59); soap opera

Big Sister (1936–52); soap opera

Big Town (1937–52); crime

Blondie (1939–50); situation comedy

Bob Hope Show, The (1935–55); comedy

Breakfast Club, The (1933–68); variety show

Buck Rogers in the 25th Century (1932–36, 1939–47); science fiction

Camel Caravan, The (1933–54); comedy/variety

Charlie McCarthy Show, The (1937–56); comedy

Cities Service Concerts (1927–56); music show

Colgate Sports Newsreel, The (1939–56); talk show

Death Valley Days (1930–45); western anthology

Dr. Laura (1994–); advice

Eddie Cantor Show, The (1931–49); comedy/variety

Father Coughlin (1930–42); religious commentary

Fibber McGee and Molly (1935–57); comedy

Gang Busters (1935–57); crime anthology

Gene Autry's Melody Ranch (1940–56); music/variety/adventure

Goldbergs, The (1929–34, 1937–45, 1949–50); comedy/drama

Grand Central Station (1937–54); drama anthology

Grand Ole Opry (1925–57); country/variety

Green Hornet, The (1930–50); crime

House Party (1945–67); audience participation

Howard Stern Show, The (1991–); talk/comedy

Information, Please (1938–48); quiz show

Jack Armstrong, the All-American Boy (1933–51); adventure

Jack Benny Program, The (1932–58); comedy

Jimmy Fidler (1934–50); gossip

Just Plain Bill (1932–55); soap opera

Kate Smith Hour, The (1931–51); musical/variety

Let's Pretend (1939–54); children's fantasy

Little Orphan Annie (1931–43); adventure

Lone Ranger, The (1934–55); adventure

Lum and Abner (1931–53); comedy

Lux Radio Theatre, The (1934–55); drama anthology

Ma Perkins (1933–60); soap opera

Major Bowes' Original Amateur Hour (1935–46, 1948–52); talent contest

Manhattan Merry-Go-Round (1932–49); popular music

March of Time, The (1931–45); news documentary

Mr. District Attorney (1939–52); crime drama

Mr. Keen, Tracer of Lost Persons (1937–55); detective drama

One Man's Family (1933–59); drama

Our Gal Sunday (1937–59); soap opera

People Are Funny (1942–59); audience participation

People's Platform, The (1938–52); discussion show

Pepper Young's Family (1936–59); soap opera

Perry Mason (1943–55); crime drama

Prairie Home Companion, A (1989–); music/folklore

Queen for a Day (1945–57); audience participation

Quiz Kids, The (1940–53); quiz show

Radio Guild, The (1929–38, 1939–40); drama

Ripley's Believe It or Not (1930–48); strange facts

Red Skelton Show, The (1941–44, 1945–53); variety

Right to Happiness, The (1939–60); soap opera

Romance of Helen Trent, The (1933–60); soap opera

Roy Rogers Show, The (1944–55); western

Rush Limbaugh Show, The (1988–); talk/ politics

Second Mrs. Burton, The (1946–60); soap opera

Shadow, The (1930–54); crime

Sherlock Holmes (1930–36, 1939–50, 1955); mystery

Singing Story Lady, The (1932–45); children's show

Stars Over Hollywood (1941–54); drama anthology

Stella Dallas (1938–55); soap opera

Story of Mary Marlin, The (1935–45, 1951–52); soap opera

Suspense (1942–62); dramatic anthology

Tom Mix Ralston Straight Shooters, The (1933–50); western

Truth or Consequences (1941–57); quiz show

Walter Winchell's Journal (1930–57); news/ gossip

Young Dr. Malone (1939–60); soap opera

Your Hit Parade (1935–59); popular music

⊙ Buxton, Frank, and Bill Owen. *The Big Broadcast, 1920–1950.* New York: Viking, 1972.
Dunning, John. *Tune in Yesterday: The Ultimate Encyclopedia of Old-Time Radio, 1925–1976.* Englewood Cliffs, N.J.: Prentice-Hall, 1976.

ARTS AND LEISURE: *Travel*

World Travel Requirements for U.S. Citizens

Country	Travel Requirements
Afghanistan	Passport; visa; travel warning
Albania	Passport; visa; onward/return transportation ticket
Algeria	Passport; visa; proof of business, hotel reservation, and airline ticket
Andorra	Passport; visa not required for stay of up to 90 days
Angola	Passport; visa; onward/return transportation ticket; sufficient funds; yellow fever and cholera immunizations
Anguilla	Proof of U.S. citizenship; onward/return transportation ticket; sufficient funds
Antigua and Barbuda	Passport or proof of U.S. citizenship
Argentina	Passport; visa not required for stay of up to 90 days
Armenia	Passport; visa; official invitation required for stays longer than 21 days
Aruba	Passport or proof of U.S. citizenship; visa not required for stay of up to 90 days; onward/return transportation ticket; sufficient funds
Australia	Passport; Electronic Travel Authority (ETA)
Austria	Passport; visa not required for stay of up to 90 days
Azerbaijan	Passport; visa
Azores	Passport; visa not required for stay of up to 90 days
Bahamas	Proof of U.S. citizenship; onward/return transportation ticket
Bahrain	Passport; visa; onward/return transportation ticket; sufficient funds; yellow fever immunization if arriving from infected region
Bangladesh	Passport; visa; onward/return transportation ticket; yellow fever immunization if arriving from infected region

Barbados	Passport or proof of U.S. citizenship
Belarus	Passport; visa
Belgium	Passport; visa not required for stay of up to 90 days
Belize	Passport; visa not required for stay of up to 30 days; onward/return transportation ticket; sufficient funds
Benin	Passport; visa; onward/return transportation ticket; yellow fever and cholera immunization
Bermuda	Passport or proof of U.S. citizenship; onward/return transportation ticket
Bhutan	Passport; visa; onward/return transportation ticket; yellow fever immunization recommended
Bolivia	Passport; visa not required for stay of up to 30 days; tourist cards issued on arrival
Bosnia and Herzegovina	Passport; visa
Botswana	Passport; visa not required for stay of up to 90 days; onward/return transportation ticket; sufficient funds
Brazil	Passport; visa; onward/return transportation ticket; yellow fever immunization if arriving from infected region
Brunei	Passport; visa not required for stay of up to 90 days; onward/return transportation ticket; yellow fever immunization if arriving from infected region
Bulgaria	Passport; visa not required for stay of up to 30 days
Burkina Faso	Passport; visa; yellow fever immunization; cholera immunization recommended
Burma (Myanmar)	Passport; visa
Burundi	Passport; visa; onward/return transportation ticket; itinerary from airline or travel agent; yellow fever and cholera immunizations
Cambodia	Passport; visa
Cameroon	Passport; visa; onward/return transportation ticket; sufficient funds; yellow fever and cholera immunizations
Canada	Passport or proof of U.S. citizenship; visa not required for stay of up to 180 days
Cape Verde	Passport; visa; yellow fever immunization if arriving from an infected region
Cayman Islands	Proof of U.S. citizenship; onward/return transportation ticket; sufficient funds
Central African Republic	Passport; visa; onward/return transportation; yellow fever immunization
Chad	Passport; visa; yellow fever immunization
Chile	Passport; visa not required for stay of up to 90 days
China, People's Republic of	Passport; visa; letter of confirmation from Chinese tour agency or relative in China
Colombia	Passport; onward/return transportation ticket
Comoros Islands	Passport; visa; onward/return transportation ticket; anti-malarial suppressants recommended
Congo, Democratic Republic of the	Passport; visa; onward/return transportation ticket; yellow fever immunization
Congo, Republic of the	Passport; visa; onward/return transportation ticket; yellow fever and cholera immunizations

Cook Islands	Passport; visa not required for stay of up to 31 days; onward/return transportation ticket; sufficient funds
Costa Rica	Passport or original U.S. birth certificate; visa not required for stays of up to 90 days; onward/return transportation ticket
Côte d'Ivoire	Passport; visa not required for stay of up to 90 days; onward/return transportation; sufficient funds; yellow fever immunization
Croatia	Passport; visa not required for stay of up to 90 days
Cuba*	Passport; visa
Curaçao	Passport or proof of U.S. citizenship; visa not required for stay of up to 14 days; onward/return transportation ticket; sufficient funds
Cyprus	Passport; visa not required for stay of up to 90 days; onward/return transportation ticket; AIDS test may be required
Czech Republic	Passport; visa not required for stay of up to 30 days; sufficient funds
Denmark	Passport; visa not required for stay of up to 90 days
Djibouti	Passport; visa; onward/return transportation ticket and sufficient funds; yellow fever immunization
Dominica	Proof of U.S. citizenship; onward/return transportation ticket
Dominican Republic	Passport; tourist card
Ecuador	Passport; visa not required for stay of up to 90 days
Egypt	Passport; visa; yellow fever immunization required if arriving from an infected region
El Salvador	Passport; visa
Equatorial Guinea	Passport; sufficient funds; smallpox, yellow fever, and cholera immunization
Eritrea	Passport; visa; onward/return transportation ticket; sufficient funds
Estonia	Passport; visa not required for stay of up to 90 days
Ethiopia	Passport; visa; yellow fever immunization
Fiji	Passport; visa not required for stay of up to 6 months; onward/return transportation ticket; sufficient funds
Finland	Passport; visa not required for stay of up to 90 days
France	Passport; visa not required for stay of up to 90 days
French Guiana	Passport; visa not required for stay of up to 90 days
French Polynesia	Passport; visa not required for stay of up to 30 days
Gabon	Passport; visa; letter from sponsor or hotel; yellow fever immunization
Gambia	Passport; visa
Georgia	Passport; visa; letter of invitation
Germany	Passport; visa not required for stay of up to 90 days; sufficient funds; health insurance
Ghana	Passport; visa; onward/return transportation ticket; yellow fever immunization
Gibraltar	Passport; visa not required for stay of up to 90 days
Greece	Passport; visa not required for stay of up to 90 days; AIDS test may be required
Greenland	Passport; visa not required for stay of up to 90 days
Grenada	Passport recommended; birth certificate and photo ID accepted; visa not required for stay of up to 90 days
Guadeloupe	Passport; proof of U.S. citizenship and photo ID accepted; visa not required for stay of up to 90 days

Guatemala	Passport required for stay of up to 90 days
Guinea	Passport; visa; letter describing purpose; onward/return transportation ticket; yellow fever immunization
Guinea-Bissau	Passport; visa; letter describing purpose; onward/return transportation ticket; sufficient funds
Guyana	Passport; onward/return transportation ticket
Haiti	Passport; visa not required for stay of up to 90 days
Holy See (Vatican City)	Passport required for entry into Italy; visitors dealt with on a case-by-case basis
Honduras	Passport; visa not required for stay of up to 90 days; onward/return transportation ticket
Hong Kong	Passport; visa not required for stay of up to 90 days; onward/return transportation ticket
Hungary	Passport; visa not required for stay of up to 90 days; onward/return transportation sufficient funds
Iceland	Passport; visa not required for stay of up to 90 days
India	Passport; visa; onward/return transportation ticket; yellow fever immunization if arriving from an infected region
Indonesia	Passport; visa not required for stay of up to 60 days; onward/return transportation; sufficient funds
Iran	Passport; visa (diplomatic relations suspended; travel not recommended)
Iraq*	Passport; visa; AIDS test
Ireland	Passport; visa not required for stay of up to 90 days; onward/return transportation ticket
Israel	Passport; onward/return transportation; sufficient funds
Italy	Passport; visa not required for stay of up to 90 days
Jamaica	Passport or U.S. birth certificate and valid driver's license; onward/return transportation ticket; sufficient funds
Japan	Passport; visa not required for stay of up to 90 days; onward/return transportation ticket
Jordan	Passport; visa
Kazakhstan	Passport; visa; letter of invitation from tourist agency or local police
Kenya	Passport; visa not required for stay of up to 30 days; onward/return transportation ticket; yellow fever immunization recommended; anti-malarial pills recommended
Kiribati (Gilbert Islands)	Passport; visa; onward/return transportation ticket; sufficient funds
Korea, Democratic People's Republic of (North Korea)*	Passport; visa
Korea, Republic of (South Korea)	Passport; visa not required for stay of up to 30 days; onward/return transportation ticket; immunization certificate required if arriving from an infected region
Kuwait	Passport; visa; onward/return transportation ticket
Kyrgyz Republic (Kyrgyzstan)	Passport; visa
Laos	Passport; visa; onward/return transportation ticket; sufficient funds

Latvia	Passport; visa not required for stay of up to 90 days
Lebanon	Passport; visa
Lesotho	Passport; onward/return transportation ticket; sufficient funds
Liberia	Passport; visa; onward/return transportation ticket; sufficient funds; yellow fever, cholera, and tetanus immunizations and medical certificate verifying visitor's good health
Libya*	Passport; visa
Liechtenstein	Passport; visa not required for stay of up to 90 days
Lithuania	Passport; visa not required for stay of up to 90 days
Luxembourg	Passport; visa not required for stay of up to 90 days
Macau	Passport; visa not required for stay of up to 60 days
Macedonia, former Yugoslav Republic of	Passport; visa
Madagascar	Passport; visa; onward/return transportation ticket; sufficient funds; yellow fever and cholera immunizations required if arriving from infected region
Malawi	Passport; visa not required for stay of up to 6 months
Malaysia	Passport; visa not required for stay of up to 90 days; yellow fever and cholera immunizations required if arriving from infected region
Maldives	Passport; visa; onward/return transportation ticket, sufficient funds; hotel reservations; yellow fever and cholera immunizations required if arriving from infected region
Mali	Passport; visa; onward/return transportation ticket; yellow fever immunization; cholera immunization recommended
Malta	Passport; visa not required for stay of up to 90 days; onward/return transportation ticket; immunizations required if arriving from an infected region
Marshall Islands, Republic of the	Passport; onward/return transportation ticket; sufficient funds; health certificate required if arriving from an infected area
Martinique	Passport; proof of U.S. citizenship and photo ID accepted; visa not required for stay of up to 90 days
Mauritania	Passport; visa; letter of invitation; onward/return transportation ticket; sufficient funds
Mauritius	Passport; visa not required for stay of up to 90 days; onward/return transportation ticket; sufficient funds; confirmation from hotel
Mexico	Proof of U.S. citizenship; visa not required for stay of up to 90 days; tourist card
Micronesia, Federated States of	Proof of U.S. citizenship; onward/return transportation ticket; sufficient funds; health certificate may be required if arriving from an infected region; typhoid and tetanus immunizations recommended
Moldova	Passport; visa
Monaco	Passport; visa not required for stay of up to 90 days
Mongolia	Passport; visa; onward/return transportation ticket; must register with Civil Registration Information Center Police Department on arrival
Morocco	Passport; visa not required for stay of up to 90 days
Mozambique	Passport; visa; letter detailing itinerary and address in Mozambique; yellow fever and cholera immunizations
Namibia	Passport; visa not required for stay of up to 90 days; onward/return transportation ticket; sufficient funds

Nauru	Passport; visa; onward/return transportation ticket; sponsorship from a resident of Nauru
Nepal	Passport; visa
Netherlands	Passport; visa not required for stay of up to 90 days; onward/return transportation ticket; sufficient funds and health insurance may be required
Netherlands Antilles	Passport or proof of U.S. citizenship; visa not required for stay of up to 14 days; onward/return transportation; sufficient funds may be required
New Zealand	Passport and arrival card; visa not required for stay of up to 90 days; onward/return transportation ticket, visa for next destination, and sufficient funds may be required
Nicaragua	Passport; onward/return transportation ticket
Niger	Passport; visa; onward/return transportation ticket; sufficient funds; yellow fever immunization; cholera immunization recommended if arriving from infected region
Nigeria	Passport; visa; letter of invitation; onward/return transportation ticket; sufficient funds; hotel confirmation; yellow fever immunization
Norway	Passport; visa not required for stay of up to 90 days
Oman	Passport; visa
Pakistan	Passport; visa; onward/return transportation ticket
Palau, The Republic of	Passport or proof of U.S. citizenship; visa not required for stay of up to 30 days; onward/return transportation ticket
Panama	Passport or proof of U.S. citizenship and photo ID; visa or tourist card; onward/return transportation ticket; sufficient funds
Papua, New Guinea	Passport; visa valid for up to 60 days; onward/return transportation ticket; sufficient funds
Paraguay	Passport; visa not required for stay of up to 90 days
Peru	Passport; visa not required for stay of up to 90 days; onward/return transportation ticket
Philippines	Passport; visa not required for stay of up to 21 days; onward/return transportation ticket
Poland	Passport; visa not required for stay of up to 90 days
Portugal	Passport; visa not required for stay of up to 90 days
Qatar	Passport; visa
Reunion	Passport; visa not required for stay of up to 90 days
Romania	Passport; visa not required for stay of up to 30 days
Russia	Passport; original U.S. birth certificate may be required; visa; confirmation from tourist agency in Russia
Rwanda	Passport; visa not required for stay of up to 30 days
Saint Kitts and Nevis	Passport or proof of U.S. citizenship and photo ID; onward/return transportation ticket
Saint Lucia	Passport or proof of U.S. citizenship and photo ID; onward/return transportation ticket
St. Martin	Passport; visa not required for stay of up to 90 days

St. Pierre	Passport or proof of U.S. citizenship and photo ID; visa not required for stay of up to 90 days
Saint Vincent and the Grenadines	Proof of U.S. citizenship and photo ID; onward/return transportation ticket; sufficient funds
Samoa	Passport; visa not required for stay of up to 30 days; onward/return transportation ticket
San Marino	Passport; visa not required for stay of up to 90 days
São Tomé and Príncipe	Passport; visa; letter stating purpose of travel; yellow fever immunization
Saudi Arabia	Passport; tourist visa not available; onward/return transportation ticket; meningitis and cholera immunization highly recommended
Senegal	Passport; visa not required for stay of up to 90 days; onward/return transportation ticket; yellow fever immunization
Serbia and Montenegro	Passport; visa (diplomatic relations suspended; travel not recommended)
Seychelles	Passport; visa issued on arrival for stay of up to 30 days; onward/return transportation ticket; sufficient funds
Sierra Leone	Passport; visa; onward/return transportation ticket; sufficient funds; yellow fever and cholera immunization; malarial suppressants recommended
Singapore	Passport; visa not required for stay of up to 30 days; onward/return transportation ticket; yellow fever and cholera immunizations recommended; AIDS test may be required
Slovak Republic	Passport; visa not required for stay of up to 30 days
Slovenia	Passport; visa not required for stay of up to 90 days
Solomon Islands	Passport; visitors permit; onward/return transportation ticket sufficient funds
Somalia	Passport
South Africa	Passport; visa not required for stay of up to 90 days; onward/return transportation ticket; sufficient funds; yellow fever immunization required if arriving from infected region; malarial suppressants recommended
Spain	Passport; visa not required for stay of up to 90 days
Sri Lanka	Passport; visa not required for stay of up to 30 days; onward/return transportation ticket; sufficient funds; yellow fever and cholera immunizations if arriving from infected area
Sudan	Passport; visa; onward/return transportation ticket; sufficient funds; yellow fever, cholera, and meningitis immunizations recommended; malarial suppressants recommended
Suriname	Passport; visa; onward/return transportation ticket
Swaziland	Passport; visa not required for stay of up to 60 days; yellow fever and cholera immunizations required if arriving from infected area; malarial suppressants recommended
Sweden	Passport; visa not required for stay of up to 90 days
Switzerland	Passport; visa not required for stay of up to 90 days
Syria	Passport; visa
Tahiti	Passport; visa not required for stay of up to 30 days
Taiwan	Passport; visa not required for stay of up to 14 days; onward/return transportation ticket
Tajikistan	Passport; visa

Tanzania	Passport; visa; yellow fever and cholera immunizations recommended if arriving from infected region; malarial suppressants recommended
Thailand	Passport; visa not required for stays of up to 30 days
Togo	Passport; visa; sufficient funds; yellow fever immunization
Tonga	Passport; visa not required for stay of up to 30 days; onward/return transportation ticket
Trinidad and Tobago	Passport; visa not required for stay of up to 90 days
Tunisia	Passport; visa not required for stay of up to 120 days; onward/return transportation ticket
Turkey	Passport; visa
Turkmenistan	Passport; visa; letter of invitation
Turks and Caicos	Proof of U.S. citizenship and photo ID; onward/return transportation ticket; sufficient funds
Tuvalu	Passport; visitor permit; onward/return transportation ticket; sufficient funds
Uganda	Passport; visa; yellow fever immunization; typhoid and malarial suppressants recommended
Ukraine	Passport; visa; invitation and confirmation letter from receiving party
United Arab Emirates	Passport; visa; sufficient funds
United Kingdom (England, Scotland, Wales)	Passport; visa not required for stay of up to 6 months
Uruguay	Passport; visa not required for stay of up to 90 days
Uzbekistan	Passport, visa
Vanuatu	Passport; visa not required for stay of up to 30 days; onward/return transportation ticket
Venezuela	Passport; tourist card
Vietnam	Passport; visa
Virgin Islands, British	Proof of U.S. citizenship and photo ID; onward/return transportation ticket; sufficient funds
West Indies, British	Proof of U.S. citizenship and photo ID; onward/return transportation ticket; sufficient funds
West Indies, French	Passport or proof of U.S. citizenship and photo ID; visa not required for stay of up to 90 days
Yemen, Republic of	Passport; visa; onward/return transportation ticket; letter of invitation; yellow fever, cholera immunizations and malarial suppressants recommended
Zambia	Passport; visa; yellow fever immunization and malarial suppressants recommended
Zimbabwe	Passport; visa; onward/return transportation ticket; sufficient funds; malarial suppressants recommended

* Requires special authorization. Contact Licensing Division, Office of Foreign Assets Control, Department of the Treasury, 1500 Pennsylvania Avenue, NW, Treasury Annex, Washington, DC 20220; (202) 622-2480.

⊙ U.S. Department of State. "Foreign Entry Requirements Page," www.travel.state.gov/foreignentryreqs.html

City	Code	City	Code
Aberdeen, Scotland	ABZ	Delhi, India	DEL
Abingdon, England	ABB	Denver, CO, USA	QDV
Abu Dhabi, United Arab Emirates	AUH	Detroit, MI, USA	DTT
Acapulco, Mexico	ACA	Dominica, Dominica	DOM
Adelaide, Australia	ADL	Dublin, Ireland	DUB
Albuquerque, NM, USA	ABQ	Dusseldorf, Germany	DUS
Amman, Jordan	AMM	Edinburgh, Scotland	EDI
Amsterdam, Netherlands	AMS	Edmonton (Edmonton	
Anchorage, AK, USA	ANC	International), AB, Canada	YEG
Asunción, Paraguay	ASU	Fairbanks, AK, USA	FAI
Athens, Greece	ATH	Frankfurt, Germany	FRA
Atlanta, GA, USA	ATL	Ft. Lauderdale, FL	FLL
Auckland, New Zealand	AKL	Geneva, Switzerland	GVA
Austin, TX, USA	AUS	Glasgow, Scotland	GLA
Baghdad, Iraq	BGT	Gothenburg, Sweden	GOT
Baltimore, MD, USA	BWI	Governors Harbour, Bahamas	GHB
Bangkok, Thailand	BKK	Greenland Kangerlussuaq	SFJ
Barbuda, Antigua and Barbuda	BBQ	Guadalajara, Mexico	GDL
Barcelona, Spain	BCN	Guam	GUM
Basel, Switzerland	BSL	Guangzhou, China	CAN
Beijing, China	PEK	Guatemala City, Guatemala	GUA
Belfast, Northern Ireland	BFS	Guayaquil, Ecuador	GYE
Belgrade, Yugoslavia	BJY	Halifax, NS, Canada	YHZ
Belize City, Belize	BZE	Hamburg, Germany	HAM
Berlin, Germany	BER	Hanoi, Vietnam	HAN
Bogotá, Colombia	BOG	Helsinki, Finland	HEL
Bombay, India	BOM	Hiroshima, Japan	HIW
Boston, MA, USA	BOS	Hong Kong, Hong Kong	HKG
Bridgetown, Barbados	BGI	Honolulu, HI, USA	HNL
Brussels, Belgium	BRU	Houston (Intercontinental), TX, USA	IAH
Bucharest, Romania	OTOP	Indianapolis, IN, USA	IND
Budapest, Hungary	BUD	Istanbul, Turkey	IST
Buenos Aires, Argentina	EZE	Jakarta, Indonesia	CGK
Cairo, Egypt	CAI	Jedda, Saudi Arabia	JED
Calcutta, India	CCU	Jerusalem, Israel	JRS
Calgary, Canada	YYC	Johannesburg, South Africa	JNB
Cancun, Mexico	CUN	Kansas City, KS, USA	KCK
Cape Town, South Africa	CPT	Kathmandu, Nepal	KTM
Caracas, Venezuela	CCS	Kiev, Ukraine	KBP
Charleston, SC, USA	CHS	Kingston, Jamaica	KIN
Charlotte, NC, USA	CLT	Kuala Lumpur, Malaysia	KUL
Chicago, IL, USA	CHI	Larnaca, Cyprus	LCA
Cincinnati, OH, USA	CVG	Las Vegas, NV, USA	LAS
Cleveland, OH, USA	CLE	Lima, Peru	LIM
Columbia, SC, USA	CAE	Lisbon, Portugal	LIS
Copenhagen, Denmark	CPH	Ljubljana, Slovenia	LJU
Dallas/Ft. Worth, TX, USA	DFW	London (Gatwick), England	LGW
Dakar, Senegal	DKR	London (Heathrow), England	LHR

City	Code	City	Code
Los Angeles, CA, USA	QLA	Rio de Janeiro, Brazil	GIG
Lyons, France	LYS	Riyadh, Saudi Arabia	XWM
Madrid, Spain	MAD	Rome (Leonardo Da Vinci/	
Managua, Nicaragua	MGA	Fuimicino), Italy	FCO
Manchester, England	MAN	Salt Lake City, UT, USA	SLC
Manila, Philippines	MNL	San Antonio, TX, USA	SAT
Marseilles, France	MRS	San Diego, CA, USA	SAN
Mazatlan, Mexico	MZT	San Francisco, CA, USA	QSF
Melbourne, Australia	MEL	San Juan, Puerto Rico	SJU
Mexico City, Mexico	MEX	Santiago, Chile	SCL
Miami, FL, USA	MIA	Santo Domino, Dominican Republic	SDQ
Milan (Malpensa), Italy	MXP	São Paulo, Brazil	GRU
Milwaukee, WI, USA	MKE	Sapporo, Japan	CTX
Minneapolis, MN, USA	MSP	Seattle, WA, USA	SEA
Montreal, QC, Canada	YUL	Seoul, Korea	SEL
Moscow (Sheremetyevo), Russia	SVO	Shanghai, China	SHA
Munich, Germany	MUC	Shannon, Ireland	SNN
Nagoya, Japan	NGO	Singapore, Singapore	SIN
Nairobi, Kenya	NBO	Sofia, Bulgaria	SOF
Naples, Italy	NAP	St. Croix, U.S. Virgin Islands	STX
Nassau, Bahamas	NAS	St. Louis, MO, USA	STL
Newark, NJ, USA	EWR	St. Lucia, St. Lucia	SLU
New Orleans, LA, USA	MSY	St. Maarten, Netherlands Antilles	SXM
New York (Kennedy), NY, USA	JFK	St. Petersburg, Russia	LED
New York (La Guardia), NY, USA	LGA	Stockholm, Sweden	ARN
Nice, France	NCE	Stuttgart, Germany	STR
Oostende, Belgium	OST	Sydney, Australia	SYD
Orlando, FL, USA	MCO	Taipei, Taiwan	TPE
Osaka, Japan	KIX	Tallinn, Estonia	TLL
Oslo, Norway	OSL	Tampa, FL, USA	TPA
Ottawa, Canada	YOW	Tehran, Iran	THR
Panama City, Panama	PTY	Tel Aviv, Israel	TLV
Paradise City, Bahamas	PID	Tokyo (Narita), Japan	NRT
Paris (Charles de Gaulle), France	CDG	Toronto, ON, Canada	YYZ
Paris (Orly), France	ORY	Tortola, British Virgin Island	EIS
Perth, Australia	PER	Tulsa, OK, USA	TUL
Philadelphia, PA, USA	PHL	Vancouver, Canada	YVR
Pittsburgh, PA, USA	PIT	Vienna, Austria	VIE
Portland, OR, USA	PDX	Warsaw, Poland	WAW
Prague, Czech Republic	PRG	Washington, D.C. (Dulles), USA	IAD
Puerto Vallarta, Mexico	PVR	Washington, D.C. (National), USA	DCA
Raleigh-Durham, NC, USA	RDU	Xian Xianyang, China	XIY
Reno, NV, USA	RNO	Zurich, Switzerland	ZRH
Reykjavik, Iceland	RKV		

⊙ Airlines of the Web. "Cities with Airports Page," www.flyaow.com/citycode.htm
   Federal Aviation Administration. "Airport Codes Page," www.faa.gov/aircodeinfo.htm

Major Airlines

Airline	Code	Based In	Airline	Code	Based In
Aer Lingus	EI	Ireland	Iberia	IB	Spain
Aeroflot	SU	Russian Federation	Icelandair	FI	Iceland
Aerolinean Argentinas	AR	Argentina	Japan Airlines	JL	Japan
Aeromexico	AM	Mexico	KLM (Royal Dutch	KL	Netherlands
Aeroperu	AP	Peru	Airlines)		
Air Afrique	RK	Côte d'Ivoire	Korean Air	KE	Korea
Air Canada	AC	Canada	Lacsa Airlines	LR	Costa Rica
Air China International	CA	China	Lauda Air	NG	Austria
Air France	AF	France	LOT (Polish Airlines)	LO	Poland
Air India	AI	India	Lufthansa Airlines	LH	Germany
Air Jamaica	JM	Jamaica	Malaysia Airlines	MH	Malaysia
Air Lanka Limited	UL	Sri Lanka	Malev (Hungarian	MA	Hungary
Air New Zealand	NZ	New Zealand	Airlines)		
Air Pacific	FJ	Fiji	MEA (Middle East	ME	Lebanon
Alaska Airlines	AS	United States	Airlines)		
Alitalia	AZ	Italy	Mexicana Airlines	MX	Mexico
All Nippon Airlines	NH	Japan	Midwest Express	YX	United States
Aloha Airlines	AQ	United States	Airlines		
America West Airlines	HP	United States	Northwest Airlines	NW	United States
American Airlines	AA	United States	Philippine Airlines	PR	Philippines
Ansett Australian	AN	Australia	PIA (Pakistan Inter-	PK	Pakistan
Airlines			national Airlines)		
Asiana Airlines	OZ	South Korea	Qantas Airlines	QF	Australia
Austrian Airlines	OS	Austria	Reno Air	QQ	United States
Avianca Airlines	AV	Colombia	Royal Air Maroc	AT	Morocco
Aviateca	GU	Guatemala	Royal Jordanian	RJ	Jordan
Balkan Bulgarian	LZ	Bulgaria	Sabena Airlines	SN	Belgium
AirlinesP9			Saudi Arabian Airlines	SV	Saudi Arabia
British Airways	BA	United Kingdom	Scandinavian Airlines	SK	Sweden and
British Midland	BD	United Kingdom			Denmark
BWIA International	BW	Trinidad & Tobago	Singapore Airlines	SQ	Singapore
Canadian Airlines	CP	Canada	South African Airways	SA	South Africa
Cathay Pacific Airlines	CX	Hong Kong	Southwest Airlines	WN	United States
China Airlines	CI	Taiwan	Swiss Air	SR	Switzerland
Continental Airlines	CO	United States	TACA International	TA	El Salvador and
Copa Airlines	CM	Panama	Airlines		Honduras
Czech Airlines (CSA)	OK	Czech Republic	TAP Air Portugal	TP	Portugal
Delta Air Lines	DL	United States	Thai Airways	TG	Thailand
Egypt Air	MS	Egypt	International		
El Al Israel Airlines	LY	Israel	Tower Air	FF	United States
Emirates Air	EK	United Arab	Turkish Airlines	TK	Turkey
		Emirates	TWA (Trans World	TW	United States
Finnair	AY	Finland	Airlines)		
Garuda Indonesia	GA	Indonesia	United Airlines	UA	United States
Airlines			US Airways	US	United States
Hawaiian Airlines	HA	United States	Varig Brazilian Airlines	RG	Brazil
		(Hawaii)	Virgin Atlantic	VS	Great Britain

⊙ AirportsCheck. "Airline Codes Page," www.virtualsfo.com/yourTravelCenter/flightInformation/ airlineCodes.htm

National Association of Commissioned Travel Agents (NACTA). "International Airline Directory Page," www.nacta.com/intair.htm

Travel-On, Ltd. "Travel Resources: Airline Codes Page," www.tvlon.com/Airlines.htm

	Athens, Greece	Beijing, China	Berlin, Germany	Bombay, India	Brussels, Belgium	Cairo, Egypt	Hong Kong	Jerusalem, Israel	London, England
Athens, Greece	—	4,741	1,119	3,218	1,298	702	5,382	782	1,486
Beijing, China	4,741	—	4,585	2,956	4,656	4,696	1,254	4,433	5,071
Berlin, Germany	1,119	4,585	—	3,916	403	1,802	5,512	1,806	557
Bombay, India	3,218	2,956	3,916	—	4,281	2,709	2,734	2,496	4,477
Brussels, Belgium	1,298	4,656	403	4,281	—	2,000	5,909	2,052	199
Cairo, Egypt	702	4,696	1,802	2,709	2,000	—	5,131	264	2,187
Hong Kong	5,382	1,254	5,512	2,734	5,909	5,131	—	4,873	6,052
Jerusalem, Israel	782	4,433	1,806	2,496	2,052	264	4,873	—	2,246
London, England	1,486	5,071	557	4,477	199	2,187	6,052	2,246	—
Madrid, Spain	1,475	5,742	1,159	4,689	817	2,089	6,623	2,239	783
Manila, Philippines	5,993	1,764	6,141	3,195	6,537	5,709	629	5,455	6,679
Moscow, Russia	1,384	3,608	1,006	3,128	1,404	1,805	4,506	1,660	1,559
Nairobi, Kenya	2,831	5,725	3,948	2,815	4,067	2,182	5,498	2,275	4,228
Paris, France	1,303	5,119	545	4,365	165	2,001	6,057	2,074	213
Rio de Janeiro, Brazil	5,989	10,720	6,161	8,300	5,802	6,096	11,019	6,360	5,708
Rome, Italy	646	5,057	736	3,837	735	1,323	5,836	1,428	897
Seoul, Korea	5,304	598	5,067	3,491	5,424	5,286	1,307	5,024	5,519
Singapore	5,620	2,769	6,162	2,419	6,556	5,127	1,593	4,915	6,739
Sydney, Australia	9,528	5,547	10,005	6,310	10,407	8,959	4,512	8,782	10,562

⊙ Indo.com. "How Far Is It?" www.indo.com/distance/

Madrid, Spain	Manila, Phillippines	Moscow, Russia	Nairobi, Kenya	Paris, France	Rio de Janeiro, Brazil	Rome, Italy	Seoul, Korea	Singapore	Sydney, Australa
1,475	5,993	1,384	2,831	1,303	5,989	646	5,304	5,620	9,528
5,742	1,764	3,608	5,725	5,119	10,720	5,057	598	2,769	5,547
1,159	6,141	1,006	3,948	545	6,161	736	5,067	6,162	10,005
4,689	3,195	3,128	2,815	4,365	8,300	3,837	3,491	2,419	6,310
817	6,537	1,404	4,067	165	5,802	735	5,424	6,556	10,407
2,089	5,709	1,805	2,182	2,001	6,096	1,323	5,286	5,127	8,959
6,623	629	4,506	5,498	6,057	11,019	5,836	1,307	1,593	4,512
2,239	5,455	1,660	2,275	2,074	6,360	1,428	5,024	4,915	8,782
783	6,679	1,559	4,228	213	5,708	897	5,519	6,739	10,562
—	7,252	2,141	3,840	652	5,002	856	6,226	7,072	10,996
7,252	—	5,135	5,858	6,685	11,250	6,460	1,624	1,490	3,888
2,141	5,135	—	3,929	1,550	7,120	1,476	4,117	5,226	9,005
3,840	5,858	3,929	—	4,020	5,521	3,333	6,288	4,633	7,561
652	6,685	1,550	4,020	—	5,639	694	5,587	6,667	10,543
5,002	11,250	7,120	5,521	5,639	—	5,664	11,226	9,764	8,447
856	6,460	1,476	3,333	694	5,664	—	5,584	6,127	10,140
6,226	1,624	4,117	6,288	5,587	11,226	5,584	—	2,900	5,160
7,072	1,490	5,226	4,633	6,667	9,764	6,127	2,900	—	3,925
10,996	3,888	9,005	7,561	10,543	8,447	10,140	5,160	3,925	—

Distances: U.S. Cities (in Miles)

	Atlanta, GA	Baltimore, MD	Boston, MA	Chicago, IL	Cleveland, OH	Dallas, TX	Detroit, MI	Houston, TX	Indianapolis, IN
Atlanta, GA	—	578	938	585	553	717	599	701	426
Baltimore, MD	578	—	360	608	307	1,211	401	1,253	510
Boston, MA	938	360	—	856	552	1,551	618	1,607	809
Chicago, IL	585	608	856	—	312	798	238	937	163
Cleveland, OH	553	307	552	312	—	1,023	96	1,114	263
Dallas, TX	717	1,211	1,551	798	1,023	—	997	224	763
Detroit, MI	599	401	618	238	96	997	—	1,106	240
Houston, TX	701	1,253	1,607	937	1,114	224	1,106	—	866
Indianapolis, IN	426	510	809	163	263	763	240	866	—
Las Vegas, NV	1,748	2,109	2,380	1,525	1,834	1,077	1,762	1,232	1,599
Los Angeles, CA	1,944	2,327	2,606	1,749	2,057	1,251	1,987	1,382	1,818
Memphis, TN	332	793	1,137	481	630	419	625	484	386
Miami, FL	605	955	1,255	1,186	1,086	1,108	1,156	968	1,024
Minneapolis, MN	905	938	1,126	354	632	860	539	1,054	510
New York, NY	748	170	190	719	408	1,373	489	1,421	648
Pittsburgh, PA	522	195	483	413	114	1,069	211	1,139	330
San Francisco, CA	2,145	2,464	2,708	1,863	2,175	1,493	2,095	1,651	1,957
Seattle, WA	2,181	2,335	2,496	1,737	2,028	1,683	1,935	1,891	1,873
St. Louis, MO	467	735	1,042	259	494	544	456	678	234

⊙ Indo.com. "How Far Is It?" www.indo.com/distance/

Las Vegas, NV	Los Angeles, CA	Memphis, TN	Miami, FL	Minneapolis, MN	New York, NY	Pittsburgh, PA	San Francisco, CA	Seattle, WA	St. Louis, MO
1,748	1,944	332	605	905	748	522	2,145	2,181	467
2,109	2,327	793	955	938	170	195	2,464	2,335	735
2,380	2,606	1,137	1,255	1,126	190	483	2,708	2,496	1,042
1,525	1,749	481	1,186	354	719	413	1,863	1,737	259
1,834	2,057	630	1,086	632	408	114	2,175	2,028	494
1,077	1,251	419	1,108	860	1,373	1,069	1,493	1,683	544
1,762	1,987	625	1,156	539	489	211	2,095	1,935	456
1,232	1,382	484	968	1,054	1,421	1,139	1,651	1,891	678
1,599	1,818	386	1,024	510	648	330	1,957	1,873	234
—	231	1,417	2,185	1,298	2,240	1,924	420	868	1,380
231	—	1,615	2,348	1,528	2462	2,145	344	954	1,595
1,417	1,615	—	868	701	956	660	1,813	1,872	244
2,185	2,348	868	—	1,510	1,088	1,011	2,601	2,734	1,062
1,298	1,528	701	1,510	—	1,023	744	1,591	1,396	464
2,240	2,462	956	1,088	1,023	—	318	2,582	2,413	879
1,924	2,145	660	1,011	744	318	—	2,273	2,140	562
420	344	1,813	2,601	1,591	2,582	2,273	—	678	1,750
868	954	1,872	2,734	1,396	2,413	2,140	678	—	1,723
1,380	1,595	244	1,062	464	879	562	1,750	1,723	—

The United States and Major Foreign Destinations

State	Mailing Address	Phone/Fax/Website
Alabama	Alabama Bureau of Tourism and Travel 401 Adams Avenue, Suite 12 Montgomery, AL 36103-49	Phone: (334) 242-4159 or 800-ALABAMA Fax: (334) 242-4554 www.touralabama.org/
Alaska	Alaska Division of Tourism P.O. Box 110801 Juneau, AK 99811-0801	Phone: (907) 465-2012 Fax: (907) 465-3767 www.dced.state.ak.us/tourism/
Arizona	Arizona Office of Tourism 2702 N. 3rd Street, Suite 4015 Phoenix, AZ 85004	Phone: (602) 248-1501 or 800-842-8257 Fax: (602) 240-5432 www.arizonaguide.com/
Arkansas	Arkansas Department of Parks & Tourism One Capitol Mall Little Rock, AR 72201	Phone: (501) 682-7777 or 800-628-8725 Fax: (501) 682-1364 www.arkansas.com/
California	California Division of Tourism 801 K Street, Suite 1600 Sacramento, CA 95814	Phone: (916) 322-2881 Fax: (916) 322-3402 gocalif.ca.gov/
Colorado	Colorado Travel and Tourism Authority 1672 Pennsylvania Street Denver, CO 80203	Phone: (303) 832-6171 or 800-265-6723 www.colorado.com/
Connecticut	Connecticut Office of Travel & Tourism 505 Hudson Street Hartford, CT 06106	Phone: (860) 270-8089 Fax: (860) 270-8077 www.ctbound.org/
Delaware	Delaware Economic Development Office 99 Kings Highway Dover, DE 19901	Phone: (302) 739-4271 Fax: (302) 739-5749 www.state.de.us/tourism/
Florida	Florida Tourism 661 E. Jefferson Street, Suite 300 Tallahassee, FL 32301	Phone: (850) 488-5607 Fax: (850) 224-9783 www.flausa.com/
Georgia	Georgia Dept. of Industry, Trade & Tourism 285 Peachtree Center Avenue, NE Marquis Two Tower, Suite 1000 Atlanta, GA 30303-1230	Phone: (404) 656-3553 Fax: (404) 651-9462 www.georgia.org/
Hawaii	Hawaii Visitors and Convention Bureau 2270 Kalakaua Avenue, #801 Honolulu, HI 96815	Phone: (808) 923-1811 Fax: (808) 924-0290 www.gohawaii.com/

Idaho	Idaho Recreation and Tourism P.O. Box 83720 Boise, ID 83720-0093	Phone: (208) 334-2470 or 800-242-5858 Fax: (208) 334-2631 www.visitid.org/
Illinois	Illinois Bureau of Tourism and Film 100 West Randolph, Suite 3-400 Chicago, IL 60601	Phone: (312)814-4734 Fax: (312) 814-6175 www.enjoyillinois.com/
Indiana	Department of Commerce, Tourism Development Division 1 North Capitol, Suite 700 Indianapolis, IN 46204-2288	Phone: (317) 232-8860 or 888-ENJOY-IN (365-6946) Fax: (317) 233-6887 www.enjoyindiana.com/
Iowa	Iowa Department of Economic Development Division of Tourism 200 E. Grand Avenue Des Moines, IA 50309	Phone: (515) 242-4700 Fax: (515) 242-4809 www.traveliowa.com/
Kansas	Kansas Travel and Tourism 700 SW Harrison Street, Suite 1300 Topeka, KS 66603-3755	Phone: (785) 296-2009 or 800-2KANSAS (252-6727) Fax: (785) 296-6988 www.kansascommerce.com/
Kentucky	Kentucky Department of Travel 500 Mero Street, 22nd Floor Frankfort, KY 40601-1968	Phone: (502) 564-4930 Fax: (502) 564-5695 www.kentuckytourism.com
Louisiana	Louisiana Office of Tourism 1051 N. 3rd Street P.O. Box 94291 Baton Rouge, LA 70804	Phone: (225) 342-8100 Fax: (225) 342-8390 www.louisianatravel.com/
Maine	Maine Office of Tourism 59 State House Station, Augusta, ME 04333-0059	Phone: (207) 287-5711 or (207) 287-3180 Fax: (207) 287-8070 www.visitmaine.com/
Maryland	Maryland Office of Tourism Development 217 East Redwood Street, 9th Floor Baltimore, MD 21202	Phone: (410) 767-6294 or 800-719-5900 Fax: (410) 333-6643 www.mdisfun.org
Massachusetts	Massachusetts Office of Travel & Tourism 10 Park Plaza, Suite 4510 Boston, MA 02116	Phone: (617)973-8500 or 800-447-6277 Fax: (617) 973-8555 www.mass-vacation.com/
Michigan	Travel Michigan Michigan Economic Development Corporation Victor Office Center, 2nd Floor 201 N. Washington Square Lansing, MI 48913	Phone: (517) 373-0670 or 800-78-GREAT (784-7328) Fax: (517) 373-0059 www.michigan.org/

State	Mailing Address	Phone/Fax/Website
Minnesota	Minnesota Office of Tourism 500 Metro Square 121 7th Place East St. Paul, MN 55101	Phone: (651) 296-2755 Fax: (651) 296-7095 www.exploreminnesota.com/
Mississippi	Mississippi Department of Economic and Community Development Division of Tourism Development P.O. Box 849 Jackson, MS 39205	Phone: (601) 359-3297 or 800-WARMEST (927-6378) Fax: (601) 359-5757 www.visitmississippi.org/
Missouri	Missouri Division of Tourism P.O. Box 1055 Jefferson City, MO 65102	Phone: (573) 751-4133 Fax: (573) 751-5160 www.missouritourism.org/
Montana	Montana Travel Promotion 1424 Ninth Avenue Helena, MT 59620	Phone: (406) 444-2654 Fax: (406) 444-1800 www.visitmt.com/
Nebraska	Nebraska Division of Travel & Tourism P.O. Box 98907 Lincoln, NE 68509-8907	Phone: (402) 471-3796 Fax: (402) 471-3026 www.visitnebraska.org
Nevada	Nevada Commission on Tourism 401 North Carson Street Carson City, NV 89701	Phone: (775) 687-4322 or 800-237-0774 Fax: (775) 687-6779 www.travelnevada.com/
New Hampshire	New Hampshire Office of Travel & Tourism Development P.O. Box 1856 Concord, NH 03302-1856	Phone: (603) 271-2665 Fax: (603) 271-6784 www.visitnh.gov/
New Jersey	New Jersey Commerce & Economic Growth Commission Office of Travel & Tourism 20 West State Street, P.O. Box 826 Trenton, NJ 08625-0826	Phone: (609) 633-2377 or (609) 292-2470 Fax: (609) 633-7418 www.state.nj.us/travel/
New Mexico	New Mexico Department of Tourism P.O. Box 20002 Santa Fe, NM 87503	Phone: (505) 827-7400 or 800-545-2040 Fax: (505) 827-7402 www.newmexico.org/
New York	New York State Division of Tourism P.O. Box 2603 Albany, NY 12220-0603	Phone: (518) 474-4116 Fax: (518) 486-6416 www.iloveny.state.ny.us/
North Carolina	North Carolina Travel & Tourism 301 N. Wilmington Street Raleigh, NC 27601	Phone: (919) 733-4171 Fax: (919) 733-8582 www.visitnc.com/

North Dakota	North Dakota Tourism 604 E. Boulevard Avenue Liberty Memorial Building Bismarck, ND 58505-0825	Phone: (701) 328-2525 or 800-HELLOND (435-5663) Fax: (701) 328-4878 www.ndtourism.com/
Ohio	Ohio Division of Travel & Tourism P.O. Box 1001 Columbus, OH 43216-1001	Phone: (614) 466-8844 Fax: (614) 466-6744 www.ohiotourism.com/
Oklahoma	Oklahoma Travel & Tourism Division P.O. Box 52002 Oklahoma City, OK 73152	Phone: (405) 521-4554 or 1-800-652-6552 Fax: (405) 521-3992 www.travelok.com/
Oregon	Oregon Tourism Commission 775 Summer NE Salem, OR 97310	Phone: (503) 986-0000 Fax: (503) 986-0001 www.traveloregon.com/
Pennsylvania	Pennsylvania Tourism Forum Building, Room 404 Harrisburg, PA 17120	Phone: (717) 232-8880 or 800-VISITPA (847-4872) Fax: (717) 787-0687 www.state.pa.us/visit
Rhode Island	Rhode Island Tourism Division One West Exchange Street Providence, RI 02903	Phone: (401) 222-2601 Fax: (401) 222-2102 or (401) 273-8370 www.visitrhodeisland.com
South Carolina	South Carolina Tourism 1205 Pendleton Street, Suite 112 Columbia, SC 29201	Phone: (803) 734-0128 Fax: (803) 734-1163 www.travelsc.com/
South Dakota	South Dakota Department of Tourism 711 East Wells Avenue Pierre, SD 57501-3369	Phone: (605) 773-3301 Fax: (605) 773-3256 www.travelsd.com/
Tennessee	Tennessee Department of Tourist Development 320 Sixth Avenue, North, 5th Floor Nashville, TN 37243	Phone: (615) 741-2159 or 800-836-6200 Fax: (615) 741-7225 www.tourism.state.tn.us/ index.html
Texas	Texas Tourism Division 1700 N. Congress Avenue, Suite 200 Austin, TX 78711-2728	Phone: (512) 462-9191 Fax: (512) 936-0450 www.traveltex.com/
Utah	The Utah Travel Council Council Hall/Capitol Hill Salt Lake City, UT 84114-1396	Phone: (801) 538-1900 or 800-200-1160 Fax: (801) 538-1399 www.utah.com/
Vermont	State of Vermont, Dept. of Tourism & Marketing 6 Baldwin Street, 4th Floor Drawer 33 Montpelier, VT 05633-1301	Phone: (802) 828-3516 Fax: (802) 828-3233 www.travel-vermont.com/

State	Mailing Address	Phone/Fax/Website
Virginia	Virginia Tourism Corporation 901 East Byrd Street Richmond, VA 23219	Phone: (804) 371-8145 Fax: (804) 786-1919 www.virginia.org/
Washington	Washington State Tourism 210 11th Avenue, Suite 101 P.O. Box 42500 Olympia, WA 98504-2500	Phone: (360) 586-2102 Fax: (360) 753-4470 www.tourism.wa.gov/
Washington, D.C.	Washington, D.C. Convention & Visitors Association 212 New York Avenue, N.W., Suite 600 Washington, DC 20005	Phone: (202) 789-7000 Fax: (202) 789-7037 www.washington.org/
West Virginia	West Virginia Division of Tourism 2101 Washington St., E. Charleston, WV 25305	Phone: (304) 558-2288 ext. #343 or 800-CALL WVA (225-5982) Fax: (304) 558-0108 www.state.wv.us/tourism/
Wisconsin	Wisconsin Department of Tourism 201 W. Washington Avenue P.O. Box 7976 Madison, WI 53707-7976	Phone: (608) 266-7621 Fax: (608) 266-3403 or (608) 261-8213 www.travelwisconsin.com/
Wyoming	Wyoming Tourism I-25 at College Drive Cheyenne, WY 82002	Phone: (307) 777-7777 Fax: (307) 777-2878 www.wyomingtourism.org/

Country	Mailing Address	Phone/Fax/Website
Australia	Australian Tourism Industry Association P.O. Box E328 Canberra, ACT 2600	Phone: 011-61-2-6273-1000 Fax: 011-61-2-6273-4999 www.australia.com/
Brazil	Embratur Office (Rio de Janeiro) Rua Uruguaiana, 174 8ffl Andar - Centro Rio de Janeiro / RJ CEP: 20050-092	Phone: 011-55-21-509-6017 (tourist information) or 011-55-21-509-6720 (adminis-tration) Fax: 011-55-21-509-7381 or -7429 www.embratur.gov.br/
Canada	Canadian Tourism Commission 8th Floor West, 235 Queen Street Ottawa, ON K1A 0H6	Phone: (613) 946-1000 www.travelcanada.ca/

Egypt	Egyptian Tourist Authority Misr Travel Tower Abbassia Square, Cairo	Phone: 011-20-2-285-4509 or 284-1970 Fax: 011-20-2-285-4363 www.touregypt.net/
England	British Tourist Authority (USA: New York office) 551 Fifth Avenue, Suite 701 New York, NY 10176-0799	Phone: (212) 986-2200 or 800-462-2748 Fax: (212) 986-1188 www.travelbritain.org/
France	French Government Tourist Office (USA: California office) 9454 Wilshire Blvd, Suite 715 Beverly Hills, CA 90212-2967	Phone: (310) 271-6665 Fax: (310) 276-2835 www.francetourism.com/
India	Government of India Tourist Office (India office) KFC Building, 48 Church Street Bangalore-560 001 Karnataka	Phone: 011-91-80-558-5417 www.tourisminindia.com/
Ireland	Irish Tourist Board (Ireland office) Information Service P.O. Box 273 Dublin 8	Phone: 011-353-1-602-4000 Fax: 011-353-1-602-4100 www.ireland.travel.ie/
Italy	Ente nazionale italiano per il turismo (Italy office) via Marghera no. 2 00185 ROMA	Phone: 011-39-6-49-711 Fax: 011-39-6-446-3379 www.init.it/
Japan	Japan National Tourist Organization (USA:New York office) One Rockefeller Plaza, Suite 1250 New York, NY 10020	Phone: (212) 757-5640 Fax: (212) 307-6754 www.jnto.go.jp/
South Africa	South African Tourism (USA: New York office) 500 Fifth Avenue, Suite 2040 New York, NY 10110	Phone: (212) 730-2929 or 800-822-5368 Fax: (212) 764-1980 www.satour.org
Thailand	Tourism Authority of Thailand (Thailand office) Le Concorde Building 202 Ratchadaphisek Road Huai Khwang Bangkok 10310	Phone: 011-66-2-694-1222 Fax: 011-66-2-694-1372 www.tourismthailand.org/

⊙ Embassy of the United States in Switzerland. "U.S. Tourist Offices Page," www.usembassy.ch/usa/tourist.html

  Tourism Offices Worldwide Directory. www.towd.com

Visitors' and Convention Bureaus in Major World Tourist Destinations

City	Mailing Address	Phone/Fax
Amsterdam	Amsterdam RAI Europaplein 22-30 Postbus 77777 Amsterdam, 1078 GZ Netherlands	Phone: 011-31-20-549-1212 Fax: 011-31-20-646-3042
Bangkok	Tourism Authority of Thailand 372 Bamrung Muang Road Bangkok, 10100 Thailand	Phone: 011-66-2-223-7850 Fax: 011-66-2-226-0303
Barcelona	Barcelona Convention Bureau Tarragona 149-157 Barcelona, 08015 Spain	Phone: 011-34-93-423-1800 Fax: 011-34-93-423-2649
Beijing	Beijing International Convention Center No 8 Beichendong Road Chauyang District Beijing, 100101 China	Phone: 011-86-10-649-10-248 Fax: 011-86-10-649-10-256
Berlin	Berlin Tourismus Marketing AM Karlsbad 11 Berlin, 99 10785 Germany	Phone: 011-30-26-47-48-52 Fax: 011-30-26-47-48-99
Bordeaux	Bordeaux Lac Bordeaux, 33300 France	Phone: 011-33 56 508449 Fax: 011-33 56 431776
Brussels	Belgium Convention and Incentive Bureau Grasmarkt 61 rue du Marche aux Herbes Brussels, B1000 Belgium	Phone: 011-32-2-513-2721 Fax: 011-32-2-513-8803
Budapest	Budapest Convention Centre 1123 Budapest Jagello ut 1-3 Budapest, H-1444 Hungary	Phone: 011-361-166-6756 Fax: 011-361-185-2127
Buenos Aires	Centro Argentino Para La Difusion Y El Formento De Eventos Florida 253 Piso 7 Of. J Buenos Aires, 1349 Argentina	Phone: 011-54-1-394-5496 Fax: 011-54-1-256-22 PIASA AR

Cancun	Cancun Convention and Visitors Bureau Av. Nader Esq Coba S/N Sm.5 Cancun Q.Roo, 77500 Mexico	Phone: 011-52-98-84-65-31 Fax: 011-52-98-87-66-48
Cape Town	Cape Tourism Authority Tourist Information Center Adderley Street Cape Town, 8000 South Africa	Phone: 011-27-21-418-5202 Fax: 011-21-418-5227
Copenhagen	Wonderful Copenhagen Convention and Visitors Bureau Gammel Kongevej 1 Copenhagen V, DK-1610 Denmark	Phone: 011-45-3-325-7400 Fax: 011-45-3-325-7410
Curaçao	Curaçao Convention Bureau Division of Curaçao Tourism Board P.O. Box 3266 Curaçao, Netherlands Antilles	Phone: 011-599-961-6000 Fax: 011-599-961-2305
Florence	Tuscany Convention Bureau Via Borgognissanti #8 Florence, 50123 Italy	Phone: 011-39-55-521-2774 Fax: 011-39-55-528-7263
Frankfurt	Frankfurt Tourist Board Kaiserstrasse 52 Frankfort, D-60329 Germany	Phone: 011-49-69-21-23-03-96 Fax: 011-49-69-21-23-07-76
Hong Kong	Hong Kong Tourist Association 9-11/F Citicorp Centre 18 Whitfield Road North Point Hong Kong, Hong Kong	Phone: 011-852-801-7111 Fax: 011-852-807-6589
Istanbul	Pamfilya Tourism Incorporated Destination Management Ysb Kaya Aldogan Sok 7/1 Zincirlikuyo Istanbul, 80300 Turkey	Phone: 011-212-274-3840 Fax: 011-212-274-3844
Jakarta	Jakarta Convention Bureau Gedung Dinas Pariwisata DKI Jakarta Jalan Kuningan Barat No. 2 Jakarta, 12710 Indonesia	Phone: 011-62-21-520-9691 Fax: 011-62-21-522-9136
Kuala Lumpur	Malaysia Tourism Promotion Board P.O. Box 10328 Kuala Lumpur, 50480 Malaysia	Phone: 011-6-03-293-5188 Fax: 011-6-03-293-5884

Visitors' and Convention Bureaus in Major World Tourist Destinations *(cont.)*

City	Mailing Address	Phone/Fax
London	London Tourist Board and Convention Bureau Glen House Stag Place London, SW1E 5LT England	Phone: 011-44-207-932-2007 Fax: 011-44-207-932-2068
Madrid	Madrid Department of Tourism Mayor 69 Madrid, 28013 Spain	Phone: 011-34-1-588-0002 Fax: 011-34-1-588-2930
Melbourne	Melbourne Convention and Marketing Bureau 114 Flinders Street, Level 5 Melbourne, VIC 3000 Australia	Phone: 011-61-3-96-54-22-88 Fax: 011-61-3-96-54-81-95
Montreal	Greater Montreal Convention and Tourism Bureau 1555 Peel Street, #600 Montreal, PQ H3A 3L8 Canada	Phone: (514) 844-5400 Fax: (514) 844-5757
Nice	Nice Office of Tourism et des Congres BP 4079 Cedex 04 Nice, 06302 France	Phone: 011-33-04-93-92-82-82 Fax: 011-33-04-93-92-82-98
Paris	Paris Convention and Visitors Bureau 127 avenue des Champs Elysees Paris, 75008 France	Phone: 011-33-1-49-52-53-95 Fax: 011-33-1-49-52-53-90
Rio de Janeiro	Rio Convention and Visitors Bureau Rua Visconde de Piraja 547 GR 610/617 Rio de Janeiro, 22415-900 Brazil	Phone: 011-55-21-259-6165 Fax: 011-55-21-511-2592
Singapore	Singapore Convention Bureau #37-00 Raffles City Tower 250 North Bridge Road Singapore, 0617	Phone: 011-65-339-6622
Stockholm	Congrex BV Linnegatan 89A P.O. Box 5619 Stockholm, S-11486 Sweden	Phone: 011-46-8-459-6622 Fax: 011-46-8-662-6095

Tokyo	Tokyo Convention and Visitors Bureau Marunouchi Branch 9th Floor 8-1, Marunouchi 3-chome Chiyoda-ku Tokyo, 100-0005 Japan	Phone: 011-81-3-3212-8728 Fax: 011-81-3-3212-6732
Toronto	Tourism Toronto 207 Queen's Quay West Toronto, ON M5J 1A7 Canada	Phone: (416) 203-3830 Fax: (416) 203-2600
Zurich	Zurich Tourist Association and Convention Bureau Verkehrsverein Zurich Bahnhofbrucke #1 Zurich, CH8023 Switzerland	Phone: 011-41-1-211-4086 Fax: 011-41-1-211-3981

⊙ American Society of Association Executives. "Search the CVB Directory Page," http://info.asaenet.org/convctrs/cvbdir_SQL.cfm

International Association of Convention & Visitor Bureaus. "Official Tourism Organization Around the World Page," www.officialtravelinfo.com/

U.S. Campground Associations

Association	Address/Phone/Fax/Website
American Camping Association	5000 State Road 67 North Martinsville, IN 46151-7902 Phone: (765) 342-8456 Fax: (765) 342-2065 www.acacamps.org
Kampgrounds of America, Inc. (KOA)	P.O. Box 30558 Billings, MT 59114 Phone: (406) 248-7444 Fax: (406) 248-7414 www.koakampgrounds.com
National Association of RV Parks and Campgrounds (ARVC)	113 Park Avenue Falls Church, VA 22046 Phone: (703) 241-8808 Fax: (703) 241-1004 www.gocampingamerica.com
National Recreation Reservation Service (Forest Service and Army Corps of Engineers campgrounds)	Phone: (877) 444-6777 www.reserveusa.com
Northeast Campground Association	P.O. Box 146 Stafford, CT 06075 Phone/Fax: (860) 684-6389 www.campnca.com

Association	Address/Phone/Fax/Website
Tentings Plus of the Northwest	P.O. Box 91 St. Ignatius, MT 59865 Phone: (410) 489-7604 www.tenting-hostels.com
Yogi Bear's Jellystone Park Camp Resorts	Phone: 800-558-2954 www.campjellystone.com

⊙ CampNet America. www.kiz.com/campnet/html/campnet.htm
   Go Camping America! "Camping Directory Page," www.gocampingamerica.com/main.html

U.S. RV Organizations

Association	Address/Phone/Fax/Website
The Escapees RV Club	100 Rainbow Drive Livingston, TX 77351 Phone: 888-757-2582 or (936) 327-8873 Fax: (936) 327-4388 www.escapees.com
Family Motor Coach Association	8291 Clough Pike Cincinnati, OH 45244 Phone: 800-543-3622 or (513) 474-3622 www.fmca.com
The Good Sam Club	P.O. Box 6888 Englewood, CO 80155-6888 Phone: 800-234-3450 www.goodsamclub.com
Life On Wheels Association	P.O. Box 9755 Moscow, ID 83843 www.lifeonwheels.com
Loners of America	P.O. Box 3314 IN Napa, CA 94558-0331 www.napanet.net/~mbost/
Passport America	18315B Landon Road Gulfport, MS 39503 Phone: 800-681-6810 Fax: (228) 831-4616 www.passportamerica.com
United RV Campers Club	6245 Rufe Snow Drive, Suite 280 Fort Worth, TX 76148 Phone: 800-521-6978 www.unitedrvcampers.com

⊙ RV Links. www.rvlinks.org/
   The RV Mall. "RV Organizations Page," www.thervmall.com/rvorg.htm

Park	*Location*
Acadia National Park	Maine
Adams National Historical Park	Massachusetts
Appomattox Court House National Historical Park	Virginia
Arches National Park	Utah
Badlands National Park	South Dakota
Big Bend National Park	Texas
Biscayne National Park	Florida
Black Canyon of the Gunnison National Park	Colorado
Boston National Historical Park	Massachusetts
Bryce Canyon National Park	Utah
Canyonlands National Park	Utah
Capitol Reef National Park	Utah
Carlsbad Caverns National Park	New Mexico
Chaco Culture National Historical Park	New Mexico
Channel Islands National Park	California
Chesapeake & Ohio Canal National Historical Park	Washington, D.C., Maryland, West Virginia
Colonial National Historical Park	Virginia
Crater Lake National Park	Oregon
Cumberland Gap National Historical Park	Kentucky
Dayton Aviation Heritage National Historical Park	Ohio
Death Valley National Park	California, Nevada
Denali National Park & Preserve	Alaska
Dry Tortugas National Park	Florida
Everglades National Park	Florida
Gates of the Arctic National Park & Preserve	Alaska
Glacier Bay National Park & Preserve	Alaska
Glacier National Park	Montana
Grand Canyon National Park	Arizona
Grand Teton National Park	Wyoming
Great Basin National Park	Nevada
Great Smoky Mountain National Park	North Carolina, Tennessee
Guadalupe Mountains National Park	Texas
Haleakala National Park	Hawaii
Harpers Ferry National Historical Park	West Virginia
Hawaii Volcanoes National Park	Hawaii
Hopewell Culture National Historical Park	Ohio
Hot Springs National Park	Arkansas
Independence National Historical Park	Pennsylvania
Inupiat Heritage Center National Historical Park	Alaska
Isle Royale National Park	Michigan
Jean Lafitte National Historic Park & Preserve	Louisiana

Park	Location
Joshua Tree National Park	California
Kalaupapa National Historical Park	Hawaii
Kaloko-Honokohau National Historical Park	Hawaii
Katmai National Park & Preserve	Alaska
Kenai Fjords National Park	Alaska
Keweenaw National Historical Park	Michigan
Klondike Gold Rush National Historical Park	Alaska
Klondike Gold Rush—Seattle Unit National Historical Park	Washington
Kobuk Valley National Park	Alaska
Lake Clark National Park & Preserve	Alaska
Lassen Volcanic National Park	California
Lowell National Historical Park	Massachusetts
Lyndon B. Johnson National Historical Park	Texas
Mammoth Cave National Park	Kentucky
Marsh-Billings-Rockefeller National Historical Park	Vermont
Mesa Verde National Park	Colorado
Minute Man National Historical Park	Massachusetts
Mojave National Preserve	California
Morristown National Historical Park	New Jersey
Mount Rainier National Park	Washington
Natchez National Historical Park	Mississippi
National Park of American Samoa	American Samoa
New Bedford Whaling National Historical Park	Massachusetts
New Orleans Jazz National Historical Park	Louisiana
Nez Perce National Historical Park	Idaho
North Cascades National Park	Washington
Olympic National Park	Washington
Pecos National Historical Park	New Mexico
Petrified Forest National Park	Arizona
Pu`uhonua O Honaunau National Historical Park	Hawaii
Redwood National Park	California
Rocky Mountain National Park	Colorado
Saguaro National Park	Arizona
Salt River Bay National Historic Park & Ecological Preserve	Virgin Islands
San Antonio Missions National Historical Park	Texas
San Francisco Maritime National Historical Park	California
San Juan Island National Historical Park	Washington
Saratoga National Historical Park	New York
Sequoia and Kings Canyon National Park	California

Shenandoah National Park	Virginia		
Sitka National Historical Park	Alaska		
Theodore Roosevelt National Park	North Dakota		
Tumacácori National Historical Park	Arizona		
Valley Forge National Historical Park	Pennsylvania		
Virgin Islands National Park	Virgin Islands		
Voyageurs National Park	Minnesota		
Wind Cave National Park	South Dakota		
Women's Rights National Historical Park	New York		
Wrangell-St. Elias National Park & Preserve	Alaska		
Yellowstone National Park	Idaho, Montana, Wyoming		
Yosemite National Park	California		
Zion National Park	Utah		

⊙ Multicom Publishing, Inc. "Exploring America's National Parks Page,"
  www.americanparks.com
  National Park Services. "Visit Your Parks Park Guide," www.nps.gov/parks.html

U.S. National Forests

Forest	Location	Forest	Location
Allegheny	Pennsylvania	Clearwater	Idaho
Angeles	California	Cleveland	California
Angelina	Texas	Coconino	Arizona
Apache-Sitgreaves	Arizona	Coeur d'Alene	Idaho
Apalachicola	Florida	Colville	Washington
Arapaho	Colorado	Conecuh	Alabama
Ashley	Utah	Coronado	Arizona
Beaverhead	Montana	Croatan	North Carolina
Bienville	Mississippi	Custer	Montana
Bighorn	Wyoming	Daniel Boone	Kentucky
Bitterroot	Montana	Davy Crockett	Texas
Black Hills	South Dakota	Deerlodge	Montana
Boise	Idaho	Delta	Mississippi
Bridger-Teton	Wyoming	Deschutes	Oregon
Caribbean	Puerto Rico	Desoto	Mississippi
Caribou	Idaho	Dixie	Utah
Carson	New Mexico	El Dorado	California
Challis	Idaho	Finger Lakes	New York
Chattahoochee	Georgia	Fishlake	Utah
Chequamegon	Wisconsin	Flathead	Montana
Cherokee	Tennessee	Francis Marion	South Carolina
Chippewa	Minnesota	Fremont	Oregon
Chugach	Alaska	Gallatin	Montana
Cibola	New Mexico	George Washington	Virginia

Forest	Location	Forest	Location
Gifford Pinchot	Washington	Okanogan	Washington
Gila	New Mexico	Olympic	Washington
Grand Mesa	Colorado	Osceola	Florida
Green Mountain	Vermont	Ottawa	Michigan
Gunnison	Colorado	Ouachita	Arkansas
Helena	Montana	Ozark-St. Francis	Arkansas
Hiawatha	Michigan	Pawnee	Colorado
Holly Springs	Mississippi	Payette	Idaho
Homochitto	Mississippi	Pike	Colorado
Hoosier	Indiana	Pisgah	North Carolina
Humboldt	Nevada	Plumas	California
Huron-Manistee	Michigan	Prescott	Arizona
Inyo	California	Rio Grande	Colorado
Jefferson	Virginia	Rogue River	Oregon
Kaibab	Arizona	Roosevelt	Colorado
Kaniksu	Idaho	Routt	Colorado
Kisatchie	Louisiana	Sabine	Texas
Klamath	California	Salmon	Idaho
Kootenai	Montana	Sam Houston	Texas
Lake Tahoe Basin	California	San Bernardino	California
Management Area		San Isabel	Colorado
Lassen	California	San Juan	Colorado
Lewis and Clark	Montana	Santa Fe	New Mexico
Lincoln	New Mexico	Sawtooth	Idaho
Lolo	Montana	Sequoia	California
Los Padres	California	Shasta-Trinity	California
Malheur	Oregon	Shawnee	Illinois
Manti-LaSal	Utah	Shoshone	Wyoming
Mark Twain	Missouri	Sierra	California
Medicine Box	Wyoming	Siskiyou	Oregon
Mendocino	California	Siuslaw	Oregon
Modoc	California	Six Rivers	California
Monongahela	West Virginia	Snoqualmie	Washington
Mount Baker	Washington	St. Joe	Idaho
Mount Hood	Oregon	Stanislaus	California
Nantahala	North Carolina	Sumter	South Carolina
Nebraska	Nebraska	Superior	Minnesota
Nez Perce	Idaho	Tahoe	California
Nicolet	Wisconsin	Talladega	Alabama
Ocala	Florida	Targhee	Idaho
Ochoco	Oregon	Thunder Basin	Wyoming
Oconee	Georgia	Toiyabe	Nevada

Tombigee	Mississippi	Wasatch-Cache	Utah
Tongass	Alaska	Wayne	Ohio
Tonto	Arizona	Wenatchee	Washington
Tuskegg	Alabama	White Mountain	Maine
Uinta	Utah	White Mountain	New Hampshire
Umatilla	Oregon	White River	Colorado
Umpqua	Oregon	Willamette	Oregon
Uncompahgre	Colorado	William B. Bankhead	Alabama
Uwharrie	North Carolina	Winema	Oregon
Wallowa-Whitman	Oregon		

⊙ National Park Services. "Visit Your Parks Park Guide," www.nps.gov/parks.html

U.S. National Monuments and Memorials

Monument/Memorial	Location
Agate Fossil Beds National Monument	Nebraska
Alibates Flint Quarries National Monument	Texas
Aniakchak National Monument & Preserve	Alaska
Arkansas Post National Memorial	Arkansas
Arlington House, The Robert E. Lee Memorial	Virginia
Aztec Ruins National Monument	New Mexico
Bandelier National Monument	New Mexico
Black Canyon of the Gunnison National Monument	Colorado
Booker T. Washington National Monument	Virginia
Buck Island Reef National Monument	Virgin Islands
Cabrillo National Monument	California
Canyon De Chelly National Monument	Arizona
Cape Krusenstern National Monument	Alaska
Capulin Volcano National Monument	New Mexico
Casa Grande Ruins National Monument	Arizona
Castillo de San Marcos National Monument	Florida
Castle Clinton National Monument	New York
Cedar Breaks National Monument	Utah
Chamizal National Memorial	Texas
Chiricahua National Monument	Arizona
Colorado National Monument	Colorado
Congaree Swamp National Monument	South Carolina
Coronado National Memorial	Arizona
Craters of the Moon National Monument	Idaho
Desoto National Memorial	Florida
Devils Postpile National Monument	California
Devils Tower National Monument	Wyoming
Dinosaur National Monument	Colorado

Monument/Memorial	Location
Effigy Mounds National Monument	Iowa
Ellis Island National Monument	New York
El Malpais National Monument	New Mexico
El Morro National Monument	New Mexico
Father Marquette National Memorial	Michigan
Federal Hall National Monument	New York
Florissant Fossil Beds National Monument	Colorado
Fort Caroline National Memorial	Florida
Fort Clatsop National Monument	Oregon
Fort Frederica National Monument	Georgia
Fort Matanzas National Monument	Florida
Fort McHenry National Monument	Maryland
Fort Moultrie National Monument	South Carolina
Fort Pulaski National Monument	Georgia
Fort Stanwix National Monument	New York
Fort Sumter National Monument	South Carolina
Fort Union National Monument	New Mexico
Fossil Butte National Monument	Wyoming
Franklin Delano Roosevelt Memorial	Washington, D.C.
General Grant National Monument	New York
George Washington Birthplace National Monument	Virginia
George Washington Carver National Monument	Missouri
Gila Cliff Dwellings National Monument	New Mexico
Grand Portage National Monument	Minnesota
Great Sand Dunes National Monument	Colorado
Hagerman Fossil Beds National Monument	Idaho
Hamilton Grange National Memorial	New York
Hohokam Pima National Monument	Arizona
Home of Franklin D. Roosevelt National Monument	New York
Homestead National Monument of America	Nebraska
Hovenweep National Monument	Utah
Jefferson National Expansion Memorial	Missouri
Jewel Cave National Monument	South Dakota
John Day Fossil Beds National Monument	Oregon
John D. Rockefeller Jr. Memorial Parkway	Wyoming
Johnstown Flood National Memorial	Pennsylvania
Korean War Veterans Memorial	Washington, D.C.
Lava Beds National Monument	California
Lincoln Boyhood National Memorial	Indiana

Lincoln Memorial	Washington, D.C.
Little Bighorn Battlefield National Monument	Montana
Lyndon Baines Johnson Memorial Grove on the Potomac	Virginia
Montezuma Castle National Monument	Arizona
Mount Rushmore National Monument	South Dakota
Muir Woods National Monument	California
Natural Bridges National Monument	Utah
Navajo National Monument	Arizona
Ocmulgee National Monument	Georgia
Oklahoma City National Memorial	Oklahoma
Oregon Caves National Monument	Oregon
Organ Pipe Cactus National Monument	Arizona
Perry's Victory & International Peace Memorial	Ohio
Petroglyph National Monument	New Mexico
Pinnacles National Monument	California
Pipe Spring National Monument	Arizona
Pipestone National Monument	Minnesota
Port Chicago Naval Magazine National Memorial	California
Poverty Point National Monument	Louisiana
Rainbow Bridge National Monument	Utah
Roger Williams National Memorial	Rhode Island
Russell Cave National Monument	Alabama
Salinas Pueblo Missions National Monument	New Mexico
Scotts Bluff National Monument	Nebraska
Statue of Liberty National Monument	New York
Sunset Crater Volcano National Monument	Arizona
Thaddeus Kosciuszko National Memorial	Pennsylvania
Thomas Jefferson Memorial	Washington, D.C.
Timpanogos Cave National Monument	Utah
Tonto National Monument	Arizona
Tumacacori National Monument	Arizona
Tuzigoot National Monument	Arizona
U.S.S. Arizona Memorial	Hawaii
Vietnam Veterans Memorial	Washington, D.C.
Walnut Canyon National Monument	Arizona
Washington Monument	Washington, D.C.
White Sands National Monument	New Mexico
Wright Brothers National Memorial	North Carolina
Wupatki National Monument	Arizona
Yucca House National Monument	Colorado

⊙ National Park Services. "Visit Your Parks Park Guide," www.nps.gov/parks.html

U.S. National Military Sites

Battlefield/Park/Site	Location
Chickamauga & Chattanooga National Military Park	Georgia
Fredericksburg & Spotsylvania County Battlefields National Military Park	Virginia
Gettysburg National Military Park	Pennsylvania
Guilford Courthouse National Military Park	North Carolina
Horseshoe Bend National Military Park	Alabama
Kings Mountain National Military Park	North Carolina
Pea Ridge National Military Park	Arkansas
Shiloh National Military Park	Tennessee
Vicksburg National Military Park	Mississippi
Antietam National Battlefield	Maryland
Big Hole National Battlefield	Montana
Brices Cross Roads National Battlefield Site	Mississippi
Cowpens National Battlefield	South Carolina
Fort Donelson National Battlefield	Tennessee
Fort Necessity National Battlefield	Pennsylvania
Kennesaw Mountain National Battlefield Park	Georgia
Manassas National Battlefield Park	Virginia
Monocacy National Battlefield	Maryland
Moores Creek National Battlefield	North Carolina
Petersburg National Battlefield	Virginia
Richmond National Battlefield Park	Virginia
Stones River National Battlefield	Tennessee
Tupelo National Battlefield	Mississippi
Wilson's Creek National Battlefield	Missouri

U.S. National Cemeteries

Cemetery	Location
Antietam National Cemetery	Maryland
Battleground National Cemetery	Washington, D.C.
Fort Donelson National Cemetery	Tennessee
Fredericksburg National Cemetery	Virginia
Gettysburg National Cemetery	Pennsylvania
Poplar Grove National Cemetery	Virginia
Shiloh National Cemetery	Tennessee
Stones River National Cemetery	Tennessee
Vicksburg National Cemetery	Mississippi
Yorktown National Cemetery	Virginia

⊙   National Park Services. "Visit Your Parks Park Guide," www.nps.gov/parks.html

U.S. National Seashores, Lakeshores, and Recreation Areas

Seashore/Recreation Area	Location
Amistad National Recreation Area	Texas
Apostle Islands National Lakeshore	Wisconsin
Assateague Island National Seashore	Maryland, Virginia
Big South Fork National River & Recreation Area	Tennessee
Bighorn Canyon National Recreation Area	Montana
Boston Harbor Islands National Recreation Area	Massachusetts
Canaveral National Seashore	Florida
Cape Cod National Seashore	Massachusetts
Cape Hatteras National Seashore	North Carolina
Cape Lookout National Seashore	North Carolina
Chattahoochee River National Recreation Area	Georgia
Chickasaw National Recreation Area	Oklahoma
Cumberland Island National Seashore	Georgia
Curecanti National Recreation Area	Colorado
Cuyahoga Valley National Recreation Area	Ohio
Delaware Water Gap National Recreation Area	New Jersey, Pennsylvania
Fire Island National Seashore	New York
Gateway National Recreation Area	New Jersey, New York
Gauley River National Recreation Area	West Virginia
Glen Canyon National Recreation Area	Arizona, Utah
Golden Gate National Recreation Area	California
Gulf Islands National Seashore	Florida, Mississippi
Indiana Dunes National Lakeshore	Indiana
Lake Chelan National Recreation Area	Washington
Lake Mead National Recreation Area	Arizona
Lake Meredith National Recreation Area	Texas
Lake Roosevelt (formerly Coolee Dam) National Recreation Area	Washington
Mississippi National River & National Recreation Area	Minnesota
Missouri National Recreation River	Nebraska
Padre Island National Seashore	Texas
Pictured Rocks National Lakeshore	Michigan
Point Reyes National Seashore	California
Ross Lake National Recreation Area	Washington
Santa Monica Mountains National Recreation Area	California
Sleeping Bear Dunes National Lakeshore	Michigan
Whiskeytown-Shasta-Trinity National Recreation Area	California

⊙   National Park Services. "Visit Your Parks Park Guide," www.nps.gov/parks.html

U.S. National Preserves, Reserves, Rivers, Islands, and Trails

Preserve/Reserve	Location
Alagnak Wild River	Alaska
Alcatraz Island	California
Aniakchak National Preserve	Alaska
Appalachian National Scenic Trail	Connecticut, Georgia, Maine, Maryland, Massachusetts, New Hampshire, New Jersey, New York, North Carolina, Pennsylvania, Tennessee, Vermont, Virginia, West Virginia
Bering Land Bridge National Preserve	Alaska
Big Cypress National Preserve	Florida
Big South Fork National River & Recreation Area	Tennessee
Big Thicket National Preserve	Texas
Blackstone River Valley National Heritage Corridor	Massachusetts, Rhode Island
Bluestone National Scenic River	West Virginia
Buffalo National River	Arizona
California National Historic Trail	California, Colorado, Kansas, Missouri, Nebraska, Nevada, Oregon, Utah, Wyoming
Cane River Creole National Historic Park and Heritage Area	Louisiana
Chattahoochee National Scenic River	Georgia
City of Rocks National Reserve	Idaho
Delaware and Lehigh National Heritage Corridor	Pennsylvania
Delaware National Scenic River	New Jersey, Pennsylvania
Denali National Park & Preserve	Alaska
Ebey's Landing National Historical Reserve	Washington
Ellis Island	New York
Gates of the Arctic National Park & Preserve	Alaska
Glacier Bay National Park & Preserve	Alaska
Great Egg Harbor National Scenic River	New Jersey
Ice Age National Scenic Trail	Wisconsin
Illinois & Michigan Canal National Heritage Corridor	Illinois
Jean Lafitte National Historic Park & Preserve	Louisiana
Juan Bautista de Anza National Historic Trail	California
Katmai National Park & Preserve	Alaska
Lake Clark National Preserve	Alaska
Lewis & Clark National Trail	Idaho, Illinois, Iowa, Kansas, Missouri, Montana, Nebraska, North Dakota, Oregon, South Dakota, Washington

Little River Canyon National Preserve	Alabama
Lower Saint Croix National Scenic Riverway	Wisconsin
Mississippi National River & Recreation Area	Minnesota
Mojave National Preserve	California
Mormon Pioneer National Historic Trail	Illinois, Iowa, Nebraska, Utah, Wyoming
Natchez Trace National Scenic Trail	Mississippi, Tennessee
New Jersey Coastal Heritage Trail Route	New Jersey
New Jersey Pinelands National Reserve	New Jersey
New River Gorge National River	West Virginia
Niobrara National Scenic River	Nebraska
Noatak National Preserve	Alaska
North Country National Scenic Trail	Michigan, Montana, New York, North Dakota, Ohio, Pennsylvania, Wisconsin
Obed Wild and Scenic River	Tennessee
Oregon National Historic Trail	Idaho, Kansas, Missouri, Nebraska, Oregon, Wyoming
Overmountain Victory National Historic Trail	Georgia, North Carolina, South Carolina, Tennessee, Virginia
Ozark National Scenic River	Missouri
Pony Express National Historic Trail	California, Colorado, Kansas, Missouri, Nevada, Utah, Wyoming
Potomac Heritage National Scenic Trail	Maryland, Pennsylvania, Virginia, Washington, D.C.
Quinebaug and Shetucket Rivers Valley National Heritage Corridor	Connecticut
Rio Grande Wild and Scenic River	Texas
Saint Croix National Scenic River	Wisconsin
Salt River Bay & Ecological Preserve	Virgin Islands
Santa Fe National Historic Trail	New Mexico
Selma To Montgomery National Historic Trail	Alabama
Tallgrass Prairie National Preserve	Kansas
Theodore Roosevelt Island	Virginia
Timucuan Ecological & Historic Preserve	Florida
Upper Delaware Scenic & Recreational River	Pennsylvania
Wrangell–St. Elias National Park & Preserve	Alaska
Yukon Charley Rivers National Preserve	Alaska

⊙ National Park Services. "Visit Your Parks Park Guide," www.nps.gov/parks.html

ARTS AND LEISURE: *Sports and Games*

Major League Baseball Teams

American League

Division	Team	Stadium & Address	Phone/Website
East	Baltimore Orioles	Oriole Park at Camden Yards 333 West Camden Street Baltimore, MD 21201	(410) 685-9800 www.theorioles.com
	Boston Red Sox	Fenway Park 4 Yawkey Way Boston, MA 02215	(617) 267-1700 www.redsox.com
	New York Yankees	Yankee Stadium East 161st Street & River Avenue Bronx, NY 10451	(718) 293-6000 www.yankees.com
	Tampa Bay Devil Rays	Tropicana Field One Tropicana Drive St. Petersburg, FL 33705	(727) 825-3137 www.devilray.com
	Toronto Blue Jays	SkyDome 1 Blue Jays Way Toronto, Ontario M5V1J1	(416) 341-1000 www.bluejays.ca
Central	Chicago White Sox	Comiskey Park 333 West 35th Street Chicago, IL 60616	(312) 674-1000 www.chisox.com
	Cleveland Indians	Jacobs Field 2401 Ontario Street Cleveland, OH 44115	(216) 420-4200 www.indians.com
	Detroit Tigers	Comerica Park 2100 Woodward Avenue Detroit, MI 48201	(313) 962-4000 www.detroittigers.com
	Kansas City Royals	Kauffman Stadium 1 Royal Way Kansas City, MO 64129	(816) 921-8000 www. kcroyals.com
	Minnesota Twins	Hubert H. Humphrey Metrodome 34 Kirby Puckett Place Minneapolis, MN 55415	(612) 375-1366 www.mntwins.com
West	Anaheim Angels	Edison Field 2000 Gene Autry Way Anaheim, CA 92806	(714) 634-2000 www.angelsbaseball.com
	Oakland Athletics	Oakland Coliseum 7677 Oakport Street Oakland, CA 94621	(510) 638-4900 www.oaklandathletics.com
	Seattle Mariners	Safeco Field P.O. Box 4100 Seattle, WA 98134	(206) 346-4000 www.mariners.org
	Texas Rangers	The Ballpark in Arlington 1000 Ballpark Way Arlington, TX 76011	(817) 273-5222 www.texasrangers.com

National League

Division	Team	Stadium & Address	Phone/Website
East	Atlanta Braves	Turner Field 755 Hank Aaron Drive Atlanta, GA 30315	(404) 522-7630 www.atlantabraves.com
	Florida Marlins	Pro Player Stadium 2269 NW 199th Street Miami, FL 33056	(305) 626-7400 www.floridamarlins.com
	Montreal Expos	Olympic Stadium 4549 Avenue Pierre de Coubertin Montreal, Quebec H1V3N7	800-463-9767 www.montrealexpos.com
	New York Mets	Shea Stadium 123-01 Roosevelt Avenue Flushing, NY 11368	(718) 507-6387 www.mets.com
	Philadelphia Phillies	Veterans Stadium 3501 South Broad Street Philadelphia, PA 19148	(215) 463-5000 www.phillies.com
Central	Chicago Cubs	Wrigley Field 1060 West Addison Chicago, IL 60613	(773) 404-2827 www.cubs.com
	Cincinnati Reds	Cinergy Field 100 Cinergy Field Cincinnati, OH 45202	(513) 421-4510 www.cincinnatireds.com
	Houston Astros	Enron Field 501 Crawford Street Houston, TX 77002	(713) 259-8500 www.astros.com
	Milwaukee Brewers	Miller Park Brewers Way Milwaukee, WI 53214	(414) 933-4114 www.milwaukeebrewers.com
	Pittsburgh Pirates	PNC Park P.O. Box 7000 Pittsburgh, PA 15212	(412) 323-5000 www.pirateball.com
	St. Louis Cardinals	Busch Stadium 250 Stadium Plaza St. Louis, MO 63102	(314) 421-3060 www.stlcardinals.com
West	Arizona Diamondbacks	Bank One Ballpark 401 East Jefferson Street Phoenix, AZ 85004	(602) 462-6000 www.azdiamondbacks.com
	Colorado Rockies	Coors Field 2001 Blake Street Denver, CO 80205	(303) 292-0200 www.coloradorockies.com
	Los Angeles Dodgers	Dodger Stadium 1000 Elysian Park Avenue Los Angeles, CA 90012	(323) 224-1500 www.dodgers.com
	San Diego Padres	Qualcomm Stadium 9449 Friars Road San Diego, CA 92108	(619) 881-6500 www.padres.com

Major League Baseball Teams *(cont.)*

Division	Team	Stadium & Address	Phone/Website
West *(cont.)*	San Francisco Giants	Pacific Bell Park 24 Willie Mays Plaza San Francisco, CA 94107	(415) 972-2000 www.sfgiants.com

⊙ ESPN. "Baseball," espn.go.com/mlb/index.html
Major League Baseball. "Franchise Information," www.majorleaguebaseball.com/u/baseball/mlbcom/history/franc_teamcontactinfo.html

Major League Baseball: World Series Championships

The World Series has been an annual event since 1903, with the exception of two years: 1904, when the New York Giants refused to play the Boston Pilgrims, and 1994, when a players' strike cut short the regular season. The best-of-seven-games format has been followed throughout the World Series' history, with the exception of four years (1904, 1919, 1920, 1921), when the champion team had to win five games out of nine.

Note: AL = American League; NL = National League; "Score" shows number of games won; MVP = Most Valuable Player

Year	Winning Team	Losing Team	Score	Series MVP
1903	Boston Pilgrims (AL)	Pittsburgh Pirates (NL)	5–3	—
1905	New York Giants (NL)	Philadelphia Athletics (AL)	4–1	—
1906	Chicago White Sox (AL)	Chicago Cubs (NL)	4–2	—
1907	Chicago Cubs (NL)	Detroit Tigers (AL)	4–0 (1 tie)	—
1908	Chicago Cubs (NL)	Detroit Tigers (AL)	4–1	—
1909	Pittsburgh Pirates (NL)	Detroit Tigers (AL)	4–3	—
1910	Philadelphia Athletics (AL)	Chicago Cubs (NL)	4–1	—
1911	Philadelphia Athletics (AL)	New York Giants (NL)	4–2	—
1912	Boston Red Sox (AL)	New York Giants (NL)	4–3 (1 tie)	—
1913	Philadelphia Athletics (AL)	New York Giants (NL)	4–1	—
1914	Boston Braves (NL)	Philadelphia Athletics (AL)	4–0	—
1915	Boston Red Sox (AL)	Philadelphia Phillies (NL)	4–1	—
1916	Boston Red Sox (AL)	Brooklyn Robins (NL)	4–1	—
1917	Chicago White Sox (AL)	New York Giants (NL)	4–2	—
1918	Boston Red Sox (AL)	Chicago Cubs (NL)	4–2	—
1919	Cincinnati Reds (NL)	Chicago White Sox (AL)	5–3	—
1920	Cleveland Indians (AL)	Brooklyn Robins (NL)	5–2	—
1921	New York Giants (NL)	New York Yankees (AL)	5–3	—
1922	New York Giants (NL)	New York Yankees (AL)	4–0 (1 tie)	—
1923	New York Yankees (AL)	New York Giants (NL)	4–2	—
1924	Washington Senators (AL)	New York Giants (NL)	4–3	—
1925	Pittsburgh Pirates (NL)	Washington Senators (AL)	4–3	—
1926	St. Louis Cardinals (NL)	New York Yankees (AL)	4–3	—
1927	New York Yankees (AL)	Pittsburgh Pirates (NL)	4–0	—
1928	New York Yankees (AL)	St. Louis Cardinals (NL)	4–0	—
1929	Philadelphia Athletics (AL)	Chicago Cubs (NL)	4–1	—

1930	Philadelphia Athletics (AL)	St. Louis Cardinals (NL)	4–2	—
1931	St. Louis Cardinals (NL)	Philadelphia Athletics (AL)	4–3	—
1932	New York Yankees (AL)	Chicago Cubs (NL)	4–0	—
1933	New York Giants (NL)	Washington Senators (AL)	4–1	—
1934	St. Louis Cardinals (NL)	Detroit Tigers (AL)	4–3	—
1935	Detroit Tigers (AL)	Chicago Cubs (NL)	4–2	—
1936	New York Yankees (AL)	New York Giants (NL)	4–2	—
1937	New York Yankees (AL)	New York Giants (NL)	4–1	—
1938	New York Yankees (AL)	Chicago Cubs (NL)	4–0	—
1939	New York Yankees (AL)	Cincinnati Reds (NL)	4–0	—
1940	Cincinnati Reds (NL)	Detroit Tigers (AL)	4–3	—
1941	New York Yankees (AL)	Brooklyn Dodgers (NL)	4–1	—
1942	St. Louis Cardinals (NL)	New York Yankees (AL)	4–1	—
1943	New York Yankees (AL)	St. Louis Cardinals (NL)	4–1	—
1944	St. Louis Cardinals (NL)	St. Louis Browns (AL)	4–2	—
1945	Detroit Tigers (AL)	Chicago Cubs (NL)	4–3	—
1946	St. Louis Cardinals (NL)	Boston Red Sox (AL)	4–3	—
1947	New York Yankees (AL)	Brooklyn Dodgers (NL)	4–3	—
1948	Cleveland Indians (AL)	Boston Braves (NL)	4–2	—
1949	New York Yankees (AL)	Brooklyn Dodgers (NL)	4–1	—
1950	New York Yankees (AL)	Philadelphia Phillies (NL)	4–0	—
1951	New York Yankees (AL)	New York Giants (NL)	4–2	—
1952	New York Yankees (AL)	Brooklyn Dodgers (NL)	4–3	—
1953	New York Yankees (AL)	Brooklyn Dodgers (NL)	4–2	—
1954	New York Giants (NL)	Cleveland Indians (AL)	4–0	—
1955	Brooklyn Dodgers (NL)	New York Yankees (AL)	4–3	Johnny Podres
1956	New York Yankees (AL)	Brooklyn Dodgers (NL)	4–3	Don Larsen
1957	Milwaukee Braves (NL)	New York Yankees (AL)	4–3	Lew Burdette
1958	New York Yankees (AL)	Milwaukee Braves (NL)	4–3	Bob Turley
1959	Los Angeles Dodgers (NL)	Chicago White Sox (AL)	4–2	Larry Sherry
1960	Pittsburgh Pirates (NL)	New York Yankees (AL)	4–3	Bobby Richardson
1961	New York Yankees (AL)	Cincinnati Reds (NL)	4–1	Whitey Ford
1962	New York Yankees (AL)	San Francisco Giants (NL)	4–3	Ralph Terry
1963	Los Angeles Dodgers (NL)	New York Yankees (AL)	4–0	Sandy Koufax
1964	St. Louis Cardinals (NL)	New York Yankees (AL)	4–3	Bob Gibson
1965	Los Angeles Dodgers (NL)	Minnesota Twins (AL)	4–3	Sandy Koufax
1966	Baltimore Orioles (AL)	Los Angeles Dodgers (NL)	4–0	Frank Robinson
1967	St. Louis Cardinals (NL)	Boston Red Sox (AL)	4–3	Bob Gibson
1968	Detroit Tigers (AL)	St. Louis Cardinals (NL)	4–3	Mickey Lolich
1969	New York Mets (NL)	Baltimore Orioles (AL)	4–1	Donn Clendenon
1970	Baltimore Orioles (AL)	Cincinnati Reds (NL)	4–1	Brooks Robinson
1971	Pittsburgh Pirates (NL)	Baltimore Orioles (AL)	4–3	Roberto Clemente
1972	Oakland Athletics (AL)	Cincinnati Reds (NL)	4–3	Gene Tenace
1973	Oakland Athletics (AL)	New York Mets (NL)	4–3	Reggie Jackson
1974	Oakland Athletics (AL)	Los Angeles Dodgers (NL)	4–1	Rollie Fingers
1975	Cincinnati Reds (NL)	Boston Red Sox (AL)	4–3	Pete Rose

Year	Winning Team	Losing Team	Score	Series MVP
1976	Cincinnati Reds (NL)	New York Yankees (AL)	4–0	Johnny Bench
1977	New York Yankees (AL)	Los Angeles Dodgers (NL)	4–2	Reggie Jackson
1978	New York Yankees (AL)	Los Angeles Dodgers (NL)	4–2	Bucky Dent
1979	Pittsburgh Pirates (NL)	Baltimore Orioles (AL)	4–3	Willie Stargell
1980	Philadelphia Phillies (NL)	Kansas City Royals (AL)	4–2	Mike Schmidt
1981	Los Angeles Dodgers (NL)	New York Yankees (AL)	4–2	Ron Cey/ Pedro Guerrero/ Steve Yeager
1982	St. Louis Cardinals (NL)	Milwaukee Brewers (AL)	4–3	Darrell Porter
1983	Baltimore Orioles (AL)	Philadelphia Phillies (NL)	4–1	Rick Dempsey
1984	Detroit Tigers (AL)	San Diego Padres (NL)	4–1	Alan Trammell
1985	Kansas City Royals (AL)	St. Louis Cardinals (NL)	4–3	Bret Saberhagen
1986	New York Mets (NL)	Boston Red Sox (AL)	4–3	Ray Knight
1987	Minnesota Twins (AL)	St. Louis Cardinals (NL)	4–3	Frank Viola
1988	Los Angeles Dodgers (NL)	Oakland Athletics (AL)	4–1	Orel Hershiser
1989	Oakland Athletics (AL)	San Francisco Giants (NL)	4–0	Dave Stewart
1990	Cincinnati Reds (NL)	Oakland Athletics (AL)	4–0	Jose Rijo
1991	Minnesota Twins (AL)	Atlanta Braves (NL)	4–3	Jack Morris
1992	Toronto Blue Jays (AL)	Atlanta Braves (NL)	4–2	Pat Borders
1993	Toronto Blue Jays (AL)	Philadelphia Phillies (NL)	4–1	Paul Molitor
1995	Atlanta Braves (NL) 5	Cleveland Indians (AL)	4–2	Tom Glavine
1996	New York Yankees (AL)	Atlanta Braves (NL)	4–2	John Wetteland
1997	Florida Marlins (NL)	Cleveland Indians (AL)	4–2	Livan Hernandez
1998	New York Yankees (AL)	San Diego Padres (NL)	4–0	Scott Brosius
1999	New York Yankees (AL)	Atlanta Braves (NL)	4–0	Mariano Rivera
2000	New York Yankees (AL)	New York Mets (NL)	4–1	Derek Jeter
2001	Arizona Diamondbacks (NL)	New York Yankees (AL)	4–3	Curt Schilling/ Randy Johnson

⊙ Major League Baseball. "History: World Series," www.majorleaguebaseball.com/u/baseball/ mlbcom/2000/postseason/history.

National Baseball Hall of Fame

Year	Inductees	Year	Inductees	Year	Inductees
1936	Ty Cobb		John McGraw		Charlie Comiskey
	Walter Johnson		Tris Speaker		Candy Cummings
	Christy Mathewson		George Wright		Buck Ewing
	Babe Ruth		Cy Young		Willie Keeler
	Honus Wagner	1938	Pete Alexander		Charley Radbourn
1937	Morgan Bulkeley		Alexander Cartwright		George Sisler
	Ban Johnson		Henry Chadwick		Al Spalding
	Nap Lajoie	1939	Cap Anson		Lou Gehrig
	Connie Mack		Eddie Collins	1942	Rogers Hornsby

1944	Kenesaw Mountain Landis		Bill Terry	1971	Dave Bancroft
1945	Roger Bresnahan	1955	Home Run Baker		Jake Beckley
	Dan Brouthers		Joe DiMaggio		Chick Hafey
	Fred Clarke		Gabby Hartnett		Harry Hooper
	Jimmy Collins		Ted Lyons		Joe Kelley
	Ed Delahanty		Ray Schalk		Rube Marquard
	Hugh Duffy		Dazzy Vance		Satchel Paige
	Hugh Jennings	1956	Joe Cronin		George Weiss
	King Kelly		Hank Greenberg	1972	Yogi Berra
	Jim O'Rourke	1957	Sam Crawford		Josh Gibson
	Wilbert Robinson		Joe McCarthy		Lefty Gómez
1946	Jesse Burkett	1959	Zack Wheat		Will Harridge
	Frank Chance	1961	Max Carey		Sandy Koufax
	Jack Chesbro		Billy Hamilton		Buck Leonard
	Johnny Evers	1962	Bob Feller		Early Wynn
	Clark Griffith		Bill McKechnie		Ross Youngs
	Tommy McCarthy		Jackie Robinson	1973	Roberto Clemente
	Joe McGinnity		Edd Roush		Billy Evans
	Eddie Plank	1963	John Clarkson		Monte Irvin
	Joe Tinker		Elmer Flick		George Kelly
	Rube Waddell		Sam Rice		Warren Spahn
	Ed Walsh		Eppa Rixey		Mickey Welch
1947	Mickey Cochrane	1964	Luke Appling	1974	Cool Papa Bell
	Frankie Frisch		Red Faber		Jim Bottomley
	Lefty Grove		Burleigh Grimes		Jocko Conlan
	Carl Hubbell		Miller Huggins		Whitey Ford
1948	Herb Pennock		Tim Keefe		Mickey Mantle
	Pie Traynor		Heinie Manush		Sam Thompson
1949	Mordecai Brown		John Ward	1975	Earl Averill
	Charlie Gehringer	1965	Pud Galvin		Bucky Harris
	Kid Nichols	1966	Casey Stengel		Billy Herman
1951	Jimmie Foxx		Ted Williams		Judy Johnson
	Mel Ott	1967	Branch Rickey		Ralph Kiner
1952	Harry Heilmann		Red Ruffing	1976	Oscar Charleston
	Paul Waner		Lloyd Waner		Roger Connor
1953	Ed Barrow	1968	Kiki Cuyler		Cal Hubbard
	Chief Bender		Goose Goslin		Bob Lemon
	Tom Connolly		Joe Medwick		Fred Lindstrom
	Dizzy Dean	1969	Roy Campanella		Robin Roberts
	Bill Klem		Stan Coveleski	1977	Ernie Banks
	Al Simmons		Waite Hoyt		Martín Dihigo
	Bobby Wallace		Stan Musial		Pop Lloyd
	Harry Wright	1970	Lou Boudreau		Al López
1954	Bill Dickey		Earle Combs		Amos Rusie
	Rabbit Maranville		Ford Frick		Joe Sewell
			Jesse Haines		

Year	Inductees	Year	Inductees	Year	Inductees
1978	Addie Joss	1986	Bobby Doerr		Vic Willis
	Larry MacPhail		Ernie Lombardi	1996	Jim Bunning
	Eddie Mathews		Willie McCovey		Bill Foster
1979	Warren Giles	1987	Ray Dandridge		Ned Hanlon
	Willie Mays		Catfish Hunter		Earl Weaver
	Hack Wilson		Billy Williams	1997	Nellie Fox
1980	Al Kaline	1988	Willie Stargell		Tommy Lasorda
	Chuck Klein	1989	Al Barlick		Phil Niekro
	Duke Snider		Johnny Bench		Willie Wells
	Tom Yawkey		Red Schoendienst	1998	George Davis
1981	Rube Foster		Carl Yastrzemski		Larry Doby
	Bob Gibson	1990	Joe Morgan		Lee MacPhail
	Johnny Mize		Jim Palmer		Bullet Rogan
1982	Hank Aaron	1991	Rod Carew		Don Sutton
	Happy Chandler		Fergie Jenkins	1999	George Brett
	Travis Jackson		Tony Lazzeri		Orlando Cepeda
	Frank Robinson		Gaylord Perry		Nestor Chylak
1983	Walter Alston		Bill Veeck		Nolan Ryan
	George Kell	1992	Rollie Fingers		Frank Selee
	Juan Marichal		Bill McGowan		Joe Williams
	Brooks Robinson		Hal Newhouser		Robin Yount
1984	Luis Aparicio		Tom Seaver	2000	Sparky Anderson
	Don Drysdale	1993	Reggie Jackson		Carlton Fisk
	Rick Ferrell	1994	Steve Carlton		Bid McPhee
	Harmon Killebrew		Leo Durocher		Tony Pérez
	Pee Wee Reese		Phil Rizzuto		Turkey Stearnes
1985	Lou Brock	1995	Richie Ashburn	2001	Bill Mazeroski
	Enos Slaughter		Leon Day		Kirby Puckett
	Arky Vaughan		William Hulbert		Hilton Smith
	Hoyt Wilhelm		Mike Schmidt		Dave Winfield

⊙ National Baseball Hall of Fame. "Hall of Famers Listed by Induction Year," baseballhalloffame.org/
hofers_and_honorees/lists/induction_year.htm

National Basketball Association Teams

Division	Team	Stadium & Address	Phone/Website
Atlantic	Boston Celtics	FleetCenter One FleetCenter Boston, MA 02114	(617) 931-2222 www.nba.com/celtics

	Miami Heat	American Airlines Arena 601 Biscayne Boulevard Miami, FL 33132	(786) 777-4328 www.nba.com/heat
	New Jersey Nets	Continental Airlines Arena 50 Route 120 North East Rutherford, NJ 07073	800-765-6387 www.nba.com/nets
	New York Knicks	Madison Square Garden Two Pennsylvania Plaza New York, NY 10121	(212) 465-5867 www.nba.com/knicks
	Orlando Magic	TD Waterhouse Centre One Magic Place 600 West Amelia Street Orlando, FL 32801	(407) 896-2442 www.nba.com/magic
	Philadelphia 76ers	First Union Center 3601 South Broad Street Philadelphia, PA 19148	(215) 339-7676 www.nba.com/sixers
	Washington Wizards	MCI Center 601 F Street NW Washington, DC 20004	(202) 661-5050 www.nba.com/wizards
Midwest	Dallas Mavericks	Reunion Arena 777 Sports Street Dallas, Texas 75207	(972) 988-3865 www.nba.com/mavericks
	Denver Nuggets	Pepsi Center 1000 Chopper Circle Denver, CO 80204	(303) 405-1212 www.nba.com/nuggets
	Houston Rockets	The Compaq Center 10 Greenway Plaza East Houston, TX 77046	(713) 627-3865 www.nba.com/rockets
	Minnesota Timberwolves	Target Center 600 First Avenue North Minneapolis, MN 55403	(612) 337-3865 www.nba.com/timberwolves
	San Antonio Spurs	Alamodome 100 Montana Street San Antonio, TX 78203	(210) 554-7700 www.nba.com/spurs
	Utah Jazz	Delta Center 301 West South Temple Salt Lake City, UT 84101	(801) 355-3865 www.nba.com/jazz
	Vancouver Grizzlies	General Motors Place 800 Griffiths Way Vancouver, British Columbia V6B 6G1	(604) 899-4667 www.nba.com/grizzlies
Central	Atlanta Hawks	Philips Arena One CNN Center, South Tower Atlanta, GA 30303	(404) 827-3865 www.nba.com/hawks
	Charlotte Hornets	Charlotte Coliseum 100 Paul Buck Boulevard Charlotte, NC 28217	(704) 357-4700 www.nba.com/hornets

Division	Team	Stadium & Address	Phone/Website
Central *(cont.)*	Chicago Bulls	United Center 1901 West Madison Street Chicago, IL 60612	(312) 455-4000 www.nba.com/bulls
	Cleveland Cavaliers	Gund Arena One Center Court Cleveland, OH 44115	(216) 420-2287 800-332-2287 www.nba.com/cavs
	Detroit Pistons	The Palace of Auburn Hills Two Championship Drive Auburn Hills, MI 48326	(248) 377-0100 www.nba.com/pistons
	Indiana Pacers	Conseco Fieldhouse 125 South Pennsylvania Street Indianapolis, IN 46204	(317) 917-2500 www.nba.com/pacers
	Milwaukee Bucks	Bradley Center 1001 North Fourth Street Milwaukee, WI 53203	(414) 227-0500 www.nba.com/bucks
	Toronto Raptors	Air Canada Centre 40 Bay Street Toronto, Ontario M5J 2X2	(416) 366-3865 www.nba.com/raptors
Pacific	Golden State Warriors	Arena in Oakland 7000 Coliseum Way Oakland, CA 94621	(510) 569-2121 www.nba.com/warriors
	Los Angeles Clippers	Staples Center 1111 South Figueroa Street Los Angeles, CA 90015	(213) 742-7555 www.nba.com/clippers
	Los Angeles Lakers	Staples Center 1111 South Figueroa Street Los Angeles, CA 90015	(310) 673-1300 www.nba.com/lakers
	Phoenix Suns	America West Arena 201 East Jefferson Street Phoenix, AZ 85004	(602) 379-7867 www.nba.com/suns
	Portland Trail Blazers	The Rose Garden One Center Court Portland, OR 97227	(503) 224-4400 www.nba.com/blazers
	Sacramento Kings	ARCO Arena One Sports Parkway Sacramento, CA 95834	(916) 928-6900 www.nba.com/kings
	Seattle SuperSonics	Key Arena 351 Elliott Avenue Seattle, WA 98119	(206) 283-3865 www.nba.com/sonics

⊙ ESPN. "NBA Clubhouses," espn.go.com/nba/clubhouses/index.html
National Basketball Association. "Teams," www.nba.com/teamindex.html

Women's National Basketball Association Teams

Division	Team	Stadium & Address	Phone/Website
Eastern	Charlotte Sting	Charlotte Coliseum 100 Paul Buck Boulevard Charlotte, NC 28217	(704) 424-9622 www.wnba.com/sting
	Cleveland Rockers	Gund Arena One Center Court Cleveland, OH 44115	(216) 263-7625 www.wnba.com/rockers
	Detroit Shock	The Palace of Auburn Hills Two Championship Drive Auburn Hills, MI 48326	(248) 377-0100 www.wnba.com/shock
	Indiana Fever	Conseco Fieldhouse 125 South Pennsylvania Street Indianapolis, IN 46204	(317) 917-2500 www.wnba.com/fever
	Miami Sol	AmericanAirlines Arena 601 Biscayne Boulevard Miami, FL 33132	(786) 777-4765 www.wnba.com/sol
	New York Liberty	Madison Square Garden Two Pennsylvania Plaza New York, NY 10121	(212) 564-9622 www.wnba.com/liberty
	Orlando Miracle	TD Waterhouse Centre One Magic Place 600 West Amelia Street Orlando, FL 32801	(407) 916-9622 www.wnba.com/miracle
	Washington Mystics	MCI Center 601 F Street NW Washington, DC 20004	(202) 661-5050 www.wnba.com/mystics
Western	Houston Comets	The Compaq Center 10 Greenway Plaza East Houston, TX 77046	(713) 627-9622 www.wnba.com/comets
	Los Angeles Sparks	The Great Western Forum 3900 West Manchester Blvd. Inglewood, CA 90385	(310) 426-6031 www.wnba.com/sparks
	Minnesota Lynx	Target Center 600 First Avenue North Minneapolis, MN 55403	(612) 673-8400 www.wnba.com/lynx
	Phoenix Mercury	America West Arena 201 East Jefferson Street Phoenix, AZ 85004	(602) 252-9622 www.wnba.com/mercury
	Portland Fire	The Rose Garden One Center Court Portland, OR 97227	(503) 797-9622 www.wnba.com/fire
	Sacramento Monarchs	ARCO Arena One Sports Parkway Sacramento, CA 95834	(916) 419-9622 www.wnba.com/monarchs

Women's National Basketball Association Teams *(cont.)*

Division	Team	Stadium & Address	Phone/Website
Western *(cont.)*	Seattle Storm	Key Arena 351 Elliott Avenue Seattle, WA 98119	(206) 374-9622 www.wnba.com/storm
	Utah Starzz	Delta Center 301 West South Temple Salt Lake City, UT 84101	(801) 355-3865 www.wnba.com/starzz

⊙ ESPN. "WNBA," espn.go.com/wnba/index.html
Women's National Basketball Association. "Teams," www.wnba.com/teamindex.html

National Basketball Association Championships

The NBA Championship is a best-of-seven-games series.

Note: "Score" shows number of games won; MVP = Most Valuable Player

Year	Winning Team	Losing Team	Score	Series MVP
1947	Philadelphia Warriors	Chicago Stags	4–1	—
1948	Baltimore Bullets	Philadelphia Warriors	4–2	—
1949	Minneapolis Lakers	Washington Capitols	4–2	—
1950	Minneapolis Lakers	Syracuse Nationals	4–2	—
1951	Rochester Royals	New York Knicks	4–3	—
1952	Minneapolis Lakers	New York Knicks	4–3	—
1953	Minneapolis Lakers	New York Knicks	4–1	—
1954	Minneapolis Lakers	Syracuse Nationals	4–3	—
1955	Syracuse Nationals	Fort Wayne Pistons	4–3	—
1956	Philadelphia Warriors	Fort Wayne Pistons	4–1	—
1957	Boston Celtics	St. Louis Hawks	4–3	—
1958	St. Louis Hawks	Boston Celtics	4–2	—
1959	Boston Celtics	Minneapolis Lakers	4–0	—
1960	Boston Celtics	St. Louis Hawks	4–3	—
1961	Boston Celtics	St. Louis Hawks	4–1	—
1962	Boston Celtics	Los Angeles Lakers	4–3	—
1963	Boston Celtics	Los Angeles Lakers	4–2	—
1964	Boston Celtics	San Francisco Warriors	4–1	—
1965	Boston Celtics	Los Angeles Lakers	4–1	—
1966	Boston Celtics	Los Angeles Lakers	4–3	—
1967	Philadelphia 76ers	San Francisco Warriors	4–2	—
1968	Boston Celtics	Los Angeles Lakers	4–2	—
1969	Boston Celtics	Los Angeles Lakers	4–3	Jerry West
1970	New York Knicks	Los Angeles Lakers	4–3	Willis Reed
1971	Milwaukee Bucks	Baltimore Bullets	4–0	Kareem Abdul-Jabbar
1972	Los Angeles Lakers	New York Knicks	4–1	Wilt Chamberlain
1973	New York Knicks	Los Angeles Lakers	4–1	Willis Reed

1974	Boston Celtics	Milwaukee Bucks	4–3	John Havlicek
1975	Golden State Warriors	Washington Bullets	4–0	Rick Barry
1976	Boston Celtics	Phoenix Suns	4–2	Jo Jo White
1977	Portland Trail Blazers	Philadelphia 76ers	4–2	Bill Walton
1978	Washington Bullets	Seattle SuperSonics	4–3	Wes Unseld
1979	Seattle SuperSonics	Washington Bullets	4–1	Dennis Johnson
1980	Los Angeles Lakers	Philadelphia 76ers	4–2	Magic Johnson
1981	Boston Celtics	Houston Rockets	4–2	Cedric Maxwell
1982	Los Angeles Lakers	Philadelphia 76ers	4–2	Magic Johnson
1983	Philadelphia 76ers	Los Angeles Lakers	4–0	Moses Malone
1984	Boston Celtics	Los Angeles Lakers	4–3	Larry Bird
1985	Los Angeles Lakers	Boston Celtics	4–2	Kareem Abdul-Jabbar
1986	Boston Celtics	Houston Rockets	4–2	Larry Bird
1987	Los Angeles Lakers	Boston Celtics	4–2	Magic Johnson
1988	Los Angeles Lakers	Detroit Pistons	4–3	James Worthy
1989	Detroit Pistons	Los Angeles Lakers	4–0	Joe Dumars
1990	Detroit Pistons	Portland Trail Blazers	4–1	Isiah Thomas
1991	Chicago Bulls	Los Angeles Lakers	4–1	Michael Jordan
1992	Chicago Bulls	Portland Trail Blazers	4–2	Michael Jordan
1993	Chicago Bulls	Phoenix Suns	4–2	Michael Jordan
1994	Houston Rockets	New York Knicks	4–3	Hakeem Olajuwon
1995	Houston Rockets	Orlando Magic	4–0	Hakeem Olajuwon
1996	Chicago Bulls	Seattle SuperSonics	4–2	Michael Jordan
1997	Chicago Bulls	Utah Jazz	4–2	Michael Jordan
1998	Chicago Bulls	Utah Jazz	4–2	Michael Jordan
1999	San Antonio Spurs	New York Knicks	4–1	Tim Duncan
2000	Los Angeles Lakers	Indiana Pacers	4–2	Shaquille O'Neal
2001	Los Angeles Lakers	Philadelphia 76ers	4–1	Shaquille O'Neal

⊙ National Basketball Association. "Year-by-Year Finals Champions and MVPs," www.nba.com/history/awards_finalschampsmvp.html

Women's National Basketball Association Championships

In 1997, the inaugural season for the Women's National Basketbal Association (WNBA) ended with a one-game championship. The championship format since then has been a best-of-three-game series.

Note: "Score" shows number of games won; MVP = Most Valuable Player

Year	Winning Team	Losing Team	Score	Series MVP
1997	Houston Comets	New York Liberty	1–0	Cynthia Cooper
1998	Houston Comets	Phoenix Mercury	2–1	Cynthia Cooper
1999	Houston Comets	New York Liberty	2–1	Cynthia Cooper
2000	Houston Comets	New York Liberty	2–0	Cynthia Cooper

⊙ Women's National Basketball Association. "WNBA Championship 2000," www.wnba.com/championship2000/index.html

Basketball Hall of Fame

Year	Inductees	Year	Inductees	Year	Inductees
1959	Forrest "Phog" Allen		Edward A. Wachter		Max Friedman
	Henry Clifford Carlson		David H. Walsh		Edward Gottlieb
	Luther Gulick	1962	Jack McCracken		W. R. Clifford Wells
	Edward J. Hickcox		Frank Morgenweck	1972	John Beckman
	Chuck Hyatt		Harlan "Pat" Page		Bruce Drake
	Matthew "Pat" Kennedy		Barney Sedran		Arthur C. Lonborg
	Angelo "Hank" Luisetti		Lynn W. St. John		Elmer H. Ripley
	Walter E. Meanwell		John "Cat" Thompson		Adolph Schayes
	George L. Mikan	1963	Robert F. Gruenig		John R. Wooden
	Ralph Morgan		William A. Reid	1973	Harry A. Fisher
	James Naismith	1964	John W. Bunn		Maurice Podoloff
	Harold G. Olsen		Harold "Bud" Foster		Ernest J. Schmidt
	John J. Schommer		Nat Holman	1974	Joe Brennan
	Amos Alonzo Stagg		Ned Irish		Emil S. Liston
	Oswald Tower		R. William Jones		Bill Russell
1960	Ernest A. Blood		Ken Loeffler		Robert "Fuzzy" Vandivier
	Victor A. Hanson		John "Honey" Russell		
	George T. Hepbron	1965	Walter A. Brown	1975	Thomas J. Gola
	Frank W. Keaney		Paul "Tony" Hinkle		Edward "Moose" Krause
	Ward L. Lambert		Howard A. Hobson		Harry Litwack
	Ed Macauley		William G. Mokray		Bill Sharman
	Branch McCracken	1966	Everett S. Dean	1976	Elgin Baylor
	Charles "Stretch" Murphy		Joe Lapchick		Charles T. Cooper
	Henry V. Porter	1967	Clair F. Bee		Lauren "Laddie" Gale
	John R. Wooden		Howard G. Cann		William "Skinny" Johnson
1961	Bernhard "Bennie" Borgmann		Amory T. Gill		Frank J. McGuire
			Alvin "Doggie" Julian		
	Forrest S. DeBernardi	1968	Arnold "Red" Auerbach	1977	Paul J. Arizin
	George H. Hoyt				Joe Fulks
	George E. Keogan		Henry "Dutch" Denhart		Clifford O. Hagan
	Bob Kurland		Henry "Hank" Iba		John P. Nucatola
	John J. O'Brien		Adolph F. Rupp		Jim Pollard
	Andy Phillip		Chuck Taylor	1978	Justin "Sam" Barry
	Ernest C. Quigley	1969	Ben Carnevale		Wilt Chamberlain
	John S. Roosma		Robert E. Davies		James E. Enright
	Leonard D. Sachs	1970	Bob Cousy		Eddie Hickey
	Arthur A. Schabinger		Bob Pettit		John B. McLendon, Jr.
	Christian Steinmetz		Abe Saperstein		Ray Meyer
	David Tobey	1971	Edgar A. Diddle		Pete Newell
	Arthur L. Trester		Robert L. Douglas	1979	Lester Harrison
			Paul Endacott		Jerry R. Lucas

Oscar P. Robertson
Everett F. Shelton
J. Dallas Shirley
Jerry A. West
1980 Thomas B. Barlow
Ferenc Hepp
J. Walter Kennedy
Arad A. McCutchan
1981 Everett N. Case
Al Duer
Clarence "Big House"
Gaines
Hal Greer
Slater N. Martin
Frank V. Ramsey, Jr.
Willis Reed, Jr.
1982 Bill Bradley
Dave DeBusschere
Lloyd R. Leith
Dean E. Smith
Jack Twyman
Louis G. Wilke
1983 John Havlicek
Sam Jones
Jack Gardner
Cliff Fagan
Ed Steitz
1984 Senda Berenson
Abbott
W. Harold Anderson
Al Cervi
Marv K. Harshman
Bertha F. Teague
Nate Thurmond
L. Margaret Wade
1986 Billy Cunningham
Tom Heinsohn
William "Red"
Holzman
Zigmund "Red"
Mihalik
Fred R. Taylor
Stanley H. Watts

1987 Rick Barry
Walter Frazier
Bob Houbregs
Pete Maravich
Robert Wanzer
1988 Clyde E. Lovelette
Bobby McDermott
Ralph H. Miller
Wes Unseld
1989 William "Pop" Gates
K. C. Jones
Lenny Wilkens
1990 David Bing
Elvin E. Hayes
Donald Neil Johnston
Vernon "Earl the
Pearl" Monroe
1991 Nate Archibald
Dave Cowens
Harry J. Gallatin
Bob Knight
Larry Fleisher
Larry O'Brien
Borislav Stankovic
1992 Sergei Belov
Lou Carnesecca
Lusia Harris-Stewart
Connie Hawkins
Bob Lanier
Al McGuire
Jack Ramsay
Nera D. White
Phil Woolpert
1993 Walt Bellamy
Julius "Dr. J" Erving
Dan Issel
Ann E. Meyers
Dick McGuire
Calvin J. Murphy
Uljana Semjonova
Bill Walton
1994 Carol Blazejowski
Denny Crum

Chuck Daly
Harry "Buddy"
Jeannette
Cesare Rubini
1995 Kareem Abdul-Jabbar
Anne Donovan
Aleksandr Gomelsky
John Kundla
Vern Mikkelsen
Player Cheryl Miller
Earl Strom
1996 Kresimir Cosic
George Gervin
Gail Goodrich
Nancy Lieberman-
Cline
David Thompson
George Yardley
1997 Alex English
Pete Carril
Joan Crawford
Denise Curry
Antonio Diaz-Miguel
Don Haskins
Bailey Howell
1998 Larry Bird
Jody Conradt
Alex Hannum
Marques Haynes
Aleksandar Nikolic
Arnie Risen
Lenny Wilkens
1999 Wayne Embry
Billie Moore
Kevin McHale
John Thompson
Fred Zollner
2000 Danny Biasone
Bob McAdoo
C. M. Newton
Pat Summitt
Isiah Thomas
Morgan Wootten

⊙ MassLive-Online. "Basketball Hall of Fame: Inductees," www.masslive.com/bballhof/inductees.html

Note: OT = overtime; 3OT = triple overtime

Year	Winning Team (School)	Losing Team (School)	Score
1939	University of Oregon	Ohio State University	46–33
1940	Indiana University	Villanova University	60–42
1941	University of Wisconsin	Washington State University	39–34
1942	Stanford University	Dartmouth College	53–38
1943	University of Wyoming	Georgetown University	46–34
1944	University of Utah	Dartmouth College	42–40 (OT)
1945	Oklahoma State University	New York University	49–45
1946	Oklahoma State University	University of North Carolina	43–40
1947	College of the Holy Cross	University of Oklahoma	58–47
1948	University of Kentucky	Baylor University	58–42
1949	University of Kentucky	Oklahoma State University	46–36
1950	City College of New York	Bradley University	71–68
1951	University of Kentucky	Kansas State University	68–58
1952	University of Kansas	St. John's University (New York)	80–63
1953	Indiana University	University of Kansas	69–68
1954	La Salle University	Bradley University	92–76
1955	University of San Francisco	La Salle University	77–63
1956	University of San Francisco	University of Iowa	83–71
1957	North Carolina	University of Kansas	54–53 (3OT)
1958	University of Kentucky	Seattle University	84–72
1959	University of California	West Virginia University	71–70
1960	Ohio State University	University of California	75–55
1961	University of Cincinnati	Ohio State University	70–75 (OT)
1962	University of Cincinnati	Ohio State University	71–59
1963	Loyola University (Illinois)	University of Cincinnati	60–58 (OT)
1964	University of California at Los Angeles	Duke University	98–83
1965	University of California at Los Angeles	University of Michigan	91–80
1966	University of Texas at El Paso	Kentucky	72–65
1967	University of California at Los Angeles	University of Dayton	79–64
1968	University of California at Los Angeles	University of North Carolina	78–55
1969	University of California at Los Angeles	Purdue University	92–72
1970	University of California at Los Angeles	Jacksonville University	80–69
1971	University of California at Los Angeles	Vacated* (Villanova University)	68–62
1972	University of California at Los Angeles	Florida State University	81–76
1973	University of California at Los Angeles	Memphis State University	87–66
1974	North Carolina State University	Marquette University	76–64
1975	University of California at Los Angeles	University of Kentucky	92–85
1976	Indiana University	University of Michigan	86–68
1977	Marquette University	University of California at Los Angeles	67–59
1978	University of Kentucky	Duke University	94–88
1979	Michigan State University	Indiana State University	75–64

1980	University of Louisville	Vacated* (UCLA)	59–54
1981	Indiana University	University of North Carolina	63–50
1982	University of North Carolina	Georgetown University	63–62
1983	North Carolina State University	University of Houston	54–52
1984	Georgetown University	University of Houston	84–75
1985	Villanova University	Georgetown University	66–64
1986	University of Louisville	Duke University	72–69
1987	Indiana University	Syracuse University	74–73
1988	University of Kansas	University of Oklahoma	83–79
1989	University of Michigan	Seton Hall University	80–79 (OT)
1990	University of Nevada at Las Vegas	Duke University	103–73
1991	Duke University	University of Kansas	72–65
1992	Duke University	University of Michigan	71–51
1993	University of North Carolina	University of Michigan	77–71
1994	University of Arkansas	Duke University	76–72
1995	University of California at Los Angeles	University of Arkansas	89–78
1996	University of Kentucky	Syracuse University	76–67
1997	University of Arizona	University of Kentucky	84–79 (OT)
1998	University of Kentucky	University of Utah	78–69
1999	University of Connecticut	Duke University	77–74
2000	Michigan State University	University of Florida	89–76
2001	Duke University	University of Arizona	82–72

* Student-athletes representing Villanova in 1971 and UCLA in 1980 were declared ineligible subsequent to the tournament. By NCAA rules, the teams' and ineligible student-athletes' records were deleted, and the teams' places in the standings were vacated.

⊙ FinalFour.net. "NCAA Division I Men's Final Four Participants," www.finalfour.net/2000/history/pastff.html

NCAA: Women's Basketball Championships

Note: OT = overtime

Year	Winning Team (School)	Losing Team (School)	Score
1982	Louisiana Tech University	Cheyney State College	76–62
1983	University of Southern California	Louisiana Tech University	69–67
1984	University of Southern California	University of Tennessee	72–61
1985	Old Dominion University	University of Tennessee	70–65
1986	University of Texas	University of Southern California	97–81
1987	University of Tennessee	Louisiana Tech University	67–44
1988	Louisiana Tech University	Auburn University	56–54
1989	University of Tennessee	Auburn University	76–60
1990	Stanford University	Auburn University	88–81
1991	University of Tennessee	University of Virginia	70–67 (OT)
1992	Stanford University	Western Kentucky University	78–62
1993	Texas Tech University	Ohio State University	84–82
1994	University of North Carolina	Louisiana Tech University	60–59

Year	Winning Team (School)	Losing Team (School)	Score
1995	University of Connecticut	University of Tennessee	70–64
1996	University of Tennessee	University of Tennessee	83–65
1997	University of Tennessee	Old Dominion University	68–59
1998	University of Tennessee	Louisiana Tech University	93–75
1999	Purdue University	Duke University	62–45
2000	University of Connecticut	University of Tennessee	71–52
2001	Notre Dame	Purdue	68–66

⊙ FinalFour.net. "Women's Final Four Year-by-Year Results," www.finalfour.net/2000/history/wff-results.html

National Football League Teams

American Football Conference

Division	Team	Stadium & Address	Phone/Website
East	Buffalo Bills	Ralph Wilson Stadium One Bills Drive Orchard Park, NY 14127	(716) 648-1800 www.buffalobills.com
	Indianapolis Colts	RCA Dome 100 South Capital Avenue Indianapolis, IN 46225	(317) 297-2658 www.colts.com
	Miami Dolphins	Pro Player Stadium 2269 NW 199th Street Miami, FL 33056	(305) 620-2578 www.miamidolphins.com
	New England Patriots	Foxboro Stadium 60 Washington Street (Route 1) Foxboro, MA 02035	800-828-7080 www.patriots.com
	New York Jets	Giants Stadium 50 Route 120 East Rutherford, NJ 07073	(201) 560-8200 www.newyorkjets.com
Central	Baltimore Ravens	PSINet Stadium 1101 Russell Street Baltimore, MD 21230	(410) 230-8000 www.ravenszone.net
	Cincinnati Bengals	Paul Brown Stadium One Paul Brown Stadium Cincinnati, OH 45202	(513) 621-3550 www. cincinnatibengals.com
	Cleveland Browns	Cleveland Browns Stadium 1085 West 3rd Street Cleveland, OH 44114	(440) 891-5001 www.clevelandbrowns.com
	Jacksonville Jaguars	ALLTEL Stadium 1 ALLTEL Stadium Place Jacksonville, FL 32202	(904) 633-2000 www.jaguars.com

	Pittsburgh Steelers	Three Rivers Stadium 300 Stadium Circle Pittsburgh, PA 15212	(412) 432-7800 www.steelers.com
	Tennessee Titans	Adelphia Coliseum 460 Great Circle Road Nashville, TN 37228	(615) 565-4000 www.titansonline.com
West	Denver Broncos	Mile High Stadium 1900 Eliot Street Denver, CO 80204	(303) 433-7466 www.denverbroncos.com
	Kansas City Chiefs	Arrowhead Stadium One Arrowhead Drive Kansas City, MO 64129	(816) 920-9300 www.kcchiefs.com
	Oakland Raiders	Network Associates Coliseum 7000 Coliseum Way Oakland, CA 94621	800-949-2626 www.raiders.com
	San Diego Chargers	Qualcomm Stadium 9449 Friars Road San Diego, CA 92108	(619) 525-8266 www. chargers.org
	Seattle Seahawks	Husky Stadium 201 South King Street Seattle, WA 98104	(206) 543-2200 www.seahawks.com

National Football Conference

Division	Team	Stadium & Address	Phone/Website
East	Arizona Cardinals	Sun Devil Stadium Fifth Street Tempe, AZ 85287	(480) 965-8777 www.azcardinals.com
	Dallas Cowboys	Texas Stadium 2401 East Airport Freeway Irving, TX 75062	(214) 953-1500 www.dallascowboys.com
	New York Giants	Giants Stadium 50 Route 120 East Rutherford, NJ 07073	(201) 935-8111 www.giants.com
	Philadelphia Eagles	Veterans Stadium 3501 South Broad Street Philadelphia, PA 19148	(215) 463-5500 www.eaglesnet.com
	Washington Redskins	FedEx Field 1600 Raljon Road Landover, MD 20785	(410) 481-7328 (202) 432-7328 www.redskins.com
Central	Chicago Bears	Soldier Field 425 McFetridge Place Chicago, IL 60605	(847) 295-6600 www.chicagobears.com
	Detroit Lions	Pontiac Silverdome 1200 Featherstone Road Pontiac, MI 48342	800-616-7627 www.detroitlions.com

Division	Team	Stadium & Address	Phone/Website
Central *(cont.)*	Green Bay Packers	Lambeau Field 1265 Lombardi Avenue Green Bay, WI 54304	(920) 496-5700 www.packers.com
	Minnesota Vikings	Hubert H. Humphrey Metrodome 500 11th Avenue South Minneapolis, MN 55415	(612) 828-6500 www.vikings.com
	Tampa Bay Buccaneers	Raymond James Stadium Tampa Bay Road & Dale Mabry Highway Tampa, FL 33607	(813) 879-2827 800-282-0683 www.buccaneers.com
West	Atlanta Falcons	Georgia Dome 2695 East Katella Avenue Atlanta, GA 30313	(770) 965-3115 www.atlantafalcons.com
	Carolina Panthers	Ericsson Stadium 800 South Mint Street Charlotte, NC 28202	(704) 358-7621 www.panthers.com
	New Orleans Saints	Louisiana Superdome Sugar Bowl Drive New Orleans, LA 70112	(504) 731-1700 www.neworleanssaints.com
	St. Louis Rams	Trans World Dome 100 North Broadway St. Louis, MO 63102	(314) 342-5000 www.stlouisrams.com
	San Francisco 49ers	3Com Park Giants Drive & Gilman Avenue San Francisco, CA 94124	(415) 656-4900 www.sf49ers.com

⊙ ESPN. "Football," football.espn.go.com/nfl/index
National Football League. "NFL Teams," www.nfl.com/teams

Football: Super Bowl Championships

Note: MVP = Most Valuable Player

Year	Winning Team	Losing Team	Score	Series MVP
1967 (I)	Green Bay Packers	Kansas City Chiefs	35–10	Bart Starr
1968 (II)	Green Bay Packers	Oakland Raiders	33–14	Bart Starr
1969 (III)	New York Jets	Baltimore Colts	16–7	Joe Namath
1970 (IV)	Kansas City Chiefs	Minnesota Vikings	23–7	Len Dawson
1971 (V)	Baltimore Colts	Dallas Cowboys	16–13	Chuck Howley
1972 (VI)	Dallas Cowboys	Miami Dolphins	24–3	Roger Staubach
1973 (VII)	Miami Dolphins	Washington Redskins	14–7	Jake Scott
1974 (VIII)	Miami Dolphins	Minnesota Vikings	24–7	Larry Csonka
1975 (IX)	Pittsburgh Steelers	Minnesota Vikings	16–6	Franco Harris
1976 (X)	Pittsburgh Steelers	Dallas Cowboys	21–17	Lynn Swann

Year	Winner	Loser	Score	MVP
1977 (XI)	Oakland Raiders	Minnesota Vikings	32–14	Fred Biletnikoff
1978 (XII)	Dallas Cowboys	Denver Broncos	27–10	Harvey Martin, Randy White
1979 (XIII)	Pittsburgh Steelers	Dallas Cowboys	35–31	Terry Bradshaw
1980 (XIV)	Pittsburgh Steelers	Los Angeles Rams	31–19	Terry Bradshaw
1981 (XV)	Oakland Raiders	Philadelphia Eagles	27–10	Jim Plunkett
1982 (XVI)	San Francisco 49ers	Cincinnati Bengals	26–21	Joe Montana
1983 (XVII)	Washington Redskins	Miami Dolphins	27–17	John Riggins
1984 (XVIII)	Los Angeles Raiders	Washington Redskins	38–9	Marcus Allen
1985 (XIX)	San Francisco 49ers	Miami Dolphins	38–16	Joe Montana
1986 (XX)	Chicago Bears	New England Patriots	46–10	Richard Dent
1987 (XXI)	New York Giants	Denver Broncos	39–20	Phil Simms
1988 (XXII)	Washington Redskins	Denver Broncos	42–10	Doug Williams
1989 (XXIII)	San Francisco 49ers	Cincinnati Bengals	20–16	Jerry Rice
1990 (XXIV)	San Francisco 49ers	Denver Broncos	55–10	Joe Montana
1991 (XXV)	New York Giants	Buffalo Bills	20–19	Ottis Anderson
1992 (XXVI)	Washington Redskins	Buffalo Bills	37–24	Mark Rypien
1993 (XXVII)	Dallas Cowboys	Buffalo Bills	52–17	Troy Aikman
1994 (XXVIII)	Dallas Cowboys	Buffalo Bills	30–13	Emmitt Smith
1995 (XXIX)	San Francisco 49ers	San Diego Chargers	49–26	Steve Young
1996 (XXX)	Dallas Cowboys	Pittsburgh Steelers	27–17	Larry Brown
1997 (XXXI)	Green Bay Packers	New England Patriots	35–21	Desmond Howard
1998 (XXXII)	Denver Broncos	Green Bay Packers	31–24	Terrell Davis
1999 (XXXIII)	Denver Broncos	Atlanta Falcons	34–19	John Elway
2000 (XXXIV)	St. Louis Rams	Tennessee Titans	23–16	Kurt Warner
2001 (XXXV)	Baltimore Ravens	New York Giants	34–7	Ray Lewis

◉ FOXSports. "Super Bowl Most Valuable Players," foxsports.com/superbowl34/almanac/mvps.sml
SuperBowl.com. "Super Bowl Recaps," www.superbowl.com/u/xxxv/history

Pro Football Hall of Fame

Year	Inductees	Year	Inductees
1963	Sammy Baugh		Bronko Nagurski
	Bert Bell		Ernie Nevers
	Joe Carr		Jim Thorpe
	Dutch Clark	1964	Jimmy Conzelman
	Harold "Red" Grange		Ed Healey
	George Halas		Clarke Hinkle
	Mel Hein		Link Lyman
	Wilbur "Pete" Henry		Mike Michalske
	Cal Hubbard		Art Rooney
	Don Hutson		George Trafton
	Curly Lambeau	1965	Guy Chamberlin
	Tim Mara		Paddy Driscoll
	George Preston Marshall		Dan Fortmann
	John "Blood" McNally		Otto Graham

Pro Football Hall of Fame (cont.)

Year	Inductees	Year	Inductees
1965 (cont.)	Sid Luckman	1973	Raymond Berry
	Steve Van Buren		Jim Parker
	Bob Waterfield		Joe Schmidt
1966	Bill Dudley	1974	Tony Canadeo
	Joe Guyon		Bill George
	Arnie Herber		Lou Groza
	Walt Kiesling		Dick "Night Train" Lane
	George McAfee	1975	Roosevelt Brown
	Steve Owen		George Connor
	Hugh "Shorty" Ray		Dante Lavelli
	Clyde "Bulldog" Turner		Lenny Moore
1967	Chuck Bednarik	1976	Ray Flaherty
	Charles Bidwill		Len Ford
	Paul Brown		Jim Taylor
	Bobby Layne	1977	Frank Gifford
	Dan Reeves		Forrest Gregg
	Ken Strong		Gale Sayers
	Joe Stydahar		Bart Starr
	Emlen Tunnell		Bill Willis
1968	Cliff Battles	1978	Lance Alworth
	Art Donovan		Weeb Ewbank
	Elroy Hirsch		Alphonse "Tuffy" Leemans
	Wayne Millner		Ray Nitschke
	Marion Motley		Larry Wilson
	Charley Trippi	1979	Dick Butkus
	Alex Wojciechowicz		Yale Lary
1969	Albert Glen "Turk" Edwards		Ron Mix
	Earle "Greasy" Neale		Johnny Unitas
	Leo Nomellini	1980	Herb Adderley
	Joe Perry		David "Deacon" Jones
	Ernie Stautner		Bob Lilly
1970	Jack Christiansen		Jim Otto
	Tom Fears	1981	Morris "Red" Badgro
	Hugh McElhenny		George Blanda
	Pete Pihos		Willie Davis
1971	Jim Brown		Jim Ringo
	Bill Hewitt	1982	Doug Atkins
	Frank "Bruiser" Kinard		Sam Huff
	Vince Lombardi		George Musso
	Andy Robustelli		Merlin Olsen
	Y. A. Tittle	1983	Bobby Bell
	Norm Van Brocklin		Sid Gillman
1972	Lamar Hunt		Sonny Jurgensen
	Gino Marchetti		Bobby Mitchell
	Ollie Matson		Paul Warfield
	Clarence "Ace" Parker	1984	Willie Brown

	Mike McCormack		Chuck Noll
	Charley Taylor		Walter Payton
	Arnie Weinmeister		Bill Walsh
1985	Frank Gatski	1994	Tony Dorsett
	Joe Namath		Bud Grant
	Pete Rozelle		Jimmy Johnson
	O. J. Simpson		Leroy Kelly
	Roger Staubach		Jackie Smith
1986	Paul Hornung		Randy White
	Ken Houston	1995	Jim Finks
	Willie Lanier		Henry Jordan
	Fran Tarkenton		Steve Largent
	Doak Walker		Lee Roy Selmon
1987	Larry Csonka		Kellen Winslow
	Len Dawson	1996	Lou Creekmur
	Joe Greene		Dan Dierdorf
	John Henry Johnson		Joe Gibbs
	Jim Langer		Charlie Joiner
	Don Maynard		Mel Renfro
	Gene Upshaw	1997	Mike Haynes
1988	Fred Biletnikoff		Wellington Mara
	Mike Ditka		Don Shula
	Jack Ham		Mike Webster
	Alan Page	1998	Paul Krause
1989	Mel Blount		Tommy McDonald
	Terry Bradshaw		Anthony Muñoz
	Art Shell		Mike Singletary
	Willie Wood		Dwight Stephenson
1990	Buck Buchanan	1999	Eric Dickerson
	Bob Griese		Tom Mack
	Franco Harris		Ozzie Newsome
	Ted Hendricks		Billy Shaw
	Jack Lambert		Lawrence Taylor
	Tom Landry	2000	Howie Long
	Bob St. Clair		Ronnie Lott
1991	Earl Campbell		Joe Montana
	John Hannah		Dan Rooney
	Stan Jones		Dave Wilcox
	Tex Schramm	2001	Nick Buoniconti
	Jan Stenerud		Marv Levy
1992	Lem Barney		Mike Munchak
	Al Davis		Jackie Slater
	John Mackey		Lynn Swann
	John Riggins		Ron Yary
1993	Dan Fouts		Jack Youngblood
	Larry Little		

⊙ Pro Football Hall of Fame. "Hall of Famers by Class of Induction," www.profootballhof.com/players/
    mainpage.cfm?cont_id=22818

NCAA: Division I-A Football Champions

NCAA Division I-A football teams did not compete in national championship football tournaments until 1998. Prior to that, since 1869, the title of "Champion" was bestowed on teams exclusively by an annual selection process.

Retroactive Poll Champions

Champion teams were selected through a process of polling, historical research, and mathematical ratings.

Year	Teams (Schools)	Year	Teams (Schools)
1869	Princeton University	1899	Harvard University
1870	Princeton University	1900	Yale University
1871	no team selected	1901	University of Michigan
1872	Princeton University	1902	University of Michigan
1873	Princeton University	1903	University of Michigan; Princeton University
1874	Yale University		
1875	Harvard University	1904	University of Michigan; University of Pennsylvania
1876	Yale University		
1877	Yale University	1905	University of Chicago
1878	Princeton University	1906	Princeton University
1879	Princeton University	1907	Yale University
1880	Princeton University; Yale University	1908	Louisiana State University; University of Pennsylvania
1881	Yale University		
1882	Yale University	1909	Yale University
1883	Yale University	1910	Harvard University; University of Pittsburgh
1884	Yale University		
1885	Princeton University	1911	Pennsylvania State University; Princeton University
1886	Yale University		
1887	Yale University	1912	Harvard University; Pennsylvania State University
1888	Yale University		
1889	Princeton University	1913	Harvard University; Army (U.S. Military Academy at West Point); Cornell University
1890	Harvard University		
1891	Yale University		
1892	Yale University	1916	University of Pittsburgh
1893	Princeton University	1917	Georgia Tech University
1894	Yale University	1918	University of Michigan; University of Pittsburgh
1895	University of Pennsylvania		
1896	Lafayette College; Princeton University	1919	Harvard University; University of Illinois; Notre Dame University; Texas A&M University
1897	University of Pennsylvania		
1898	Harvard University	1920	University of California

1921	University of California; Cornell University	1927	University of Illinois; Yale University
1922	University of California; Cornell University; Princeton University	1928	Georgia Tech University
		1929	Notre Dame University
1923	University of Illinois; University of Michigan	1930	University of Alabama; Notre Dame University
1924	Notre Dame University	1931	University of Southern California
1925	University of Alabama	1932	University of Southern California
1926	University of Alabama; Stanford University	1933	University of Michigan
		1934	University of Minnesota
		1935	University of Minnesota

Associated Press Poll Champions

This selection process conducted by the Associated Press initiated a widely circulated poll of sportswriters and broadcasters.

Year	Teams (Schools)	Year	Teams (Schools)
1936	University of Minnesota	1944	Army (U.S. Military Academy at West Point)
1937	University of Pittsburgh		
1938	Texas Christian University	1945	Army (U.S. Military Academy at West Point)
1939	Texas A&M University		
1940	University of Minnesota	1946	Notre Dame University
1941	University of Minnesota	1947	Notre Dame University
1942	Ohio State University	1948	University of Michigan
1943	Notre Dame University	1949	Notre Dame University

Consensus Poll National Champions

Involving numerous jounalistic agencies, this selection process increased the poll's circulation.

Year	Teams (Schools)	Year	Teams (Schools)
1950	University of Oklahoma	1958	Louisiana State University; University of Iowa
1951	University of Tennessee		
1952	Michigan State University	1959	Syracuse University
1953	University of Maryland	1960	University of Minnesota; University of Mississippi
1954	University of California at Los Angeles; Ohio State University	1961	University of Alabama; Ohio State University
1955	University of Oklahoma		
1956	University of Oklahoma	1962	University of Southern California
1957	Ohio State University; Auburn University	1963	University of Texas
		1964	University of Alabama; University of Arkansas; Notre Dame University

Consensus Poll National Champions

Year	Teams (Schools)	Year	Teams (Schools)
1965	Michigan State University; University of Alabama	1980	University of Georgia
1966	Notre Dame University; Michigan State University	1981	Clemson University
		1982	Pennsylvania State University
1967	University of Southern California	1983	University of Miami
1968	Ohio State University	1984	Brigham Young University
1969	University of Texas	1985	University of Oklahoma
1970	University of Nebraska; University of Texas; Ohio State University	1986	Pennsylvania State University
		1987	University of Miami
1971	University of Nebraska	1988	Notre Dame University
1972	University of Southern California	1989	University of Miami
1973	Notre Dame University; University of Alabama	1990	University of Colorado; Georgia Tech University
1974	University of Southern California; University of Oklahoma	1991	University of Washington; University of Miami
		1992	University of Alabama
1975	University of Oklahoma	1993	Florida State University
1976	University of Pittsburgh	1994	University of Nebraska
1977	Notre Dame University	1995	University of Nebraska
1978	University of Alabama; University of Southern California	1996	University of Florida
		1997	University of Michigan; University of Nebraska
1979	University of Alabama		

Bowl Championship Series

Created in 1998, the Bowl Championship Series (BCS) Committee selects two teams to play a national championship game. This selection process is based on four principal criteria: subjective polls of sportswriters and coaches, computer rankings, schedule strength, and number of losses. The two teams with the lowest point total in these four categories play in the championship game.

Year	Teams (Schools)	Year	Teams (Schools)
1998*	University of Tennessee	2000	University of Oklahoma
1999*	Florida State University		

* championship game played in January the following year

⊙ National Collegiate Athletic Association Football. "NCAA Division I-A Past Champions," www.ncaafootball.net/d1_past_champs.html

Heisman Memorial Trophy Winners

The Heisman Memorial Trophy is awarded annually to the outstanding college football player in the United States. In 1935, awarded by the Downtown Athletic Club (DAC) of New York City, it was known as the DAC Trophy. In 1936, the trophy was renamed to honor DAC Athletics Director John W. Heisman, who died that October.

DB = Defensive Back; FB = Full Back; HB = Half Back; QB = Quarter Back; RB = Running Back; TB = Tailback; WR = Wide Receiver

Year	Winner	School	Position
1935	Jay Berwanger	University of Chicago	HB
1936	Larry Kelley	Yale University	End
1937	Clint Frank	Yale University	HB
1938	Davey O'Brien	Texas Christian University	QB
1939	Nile Kinnick	University of Iowa	HB
1940	Tom Harmon	University of Michigan	HB
1941	Bruce Smith	University of Minnesota	HB
1942	Frank Sinkwich	University of Georgia	HB
1943	Angelo Bertelli	Notre Dame University	QB
1944	Les Horvath	Ohio State University	QB/HB
1945	Doc Blanchard	Army	FB
1946	Glenn Davis	Army	HB
1947	Johnny Lujack	Notre Dame University	QB
1948	Doak Walker	Southern Methodist University	HB
1949	Leon Hart	Notre Dame University	End
1950	Vic Janowicz	Ohio State University	HB
1951	Dick Kazmaier	Princeton University	HB
1952	Billy Vessels	University of Oklahoma	HB
1953	Johnny Lattner	Notre Dame University	HB
1954	Alan Ameche	University of Wisconsin	FB
1955	Howard Cassady	Ohio State University	HB
1956	Paul Hornung	Notre Dame University	QB
1957	John David Crow	Texas A&M University	HB
1958	Pete Dawkins	Army	HB
1959	Billy Cannon	Louisiana State University	HB
1960	Joe Bellino	Navy	HB
1961	Ernie Davis	Syracuse University	HB
1962	Terry Baker	Oregon State University	QB
1963	Roger Staubach	Navy	QB
1964	John Huarte	Notre Dame University	QB
1965	Mike Garrett	University of Southern California	HB
1966	Steve Spurrier	University of Florida	QB

Year	Winner	School	Position
1967	Gary Beban	UCLA	QB
1968	O. J. Simpson	University of Southern California	HB
1969	Steve Owens	University of Oklahoma	HB
1970	Jim Plunkett	Stanford University	QB
1971	Pat Sullivan	Auburn University	QB
1972	Johnny Rodgers	University of Nebraska	WR
1973	John Cappelletti	Penn State University	RB
1974	Archie Griffin	Ohio State University	RB
1975	Archie Griffin	Ohio State University	RB
1976	Tony Dorsett	University of Pittsburgh	RB
1977	Earl Campbell	University of Texas	RB
1978	Billy Sims	University of Oklahoma	RB
1979	Charles White	University of Southern California	RB
1980	George Rogers	University of South Carolina	RB
1981	Marcus Allen	University of Southern California	RB
1982	Herschel Walker	University of Georgia	RB
1983	Mike Rozier	University of Nebraska	RB
1984	Doug Flutie	Boston College	QB
1985	Bo Jackson	Auburn University	RB
1986	Vinny Testaverde	University of Miami	QB
1987	Tim Brown	Notre Dame University	WR
1988	Barry Sanders	Oklahoma State University	RB
1989	Andre Ware	University of Houston	QB
1990	Ty Detmer	Brigham Young University	QB
1991	Desmond Howard	University of Michigan	WR
1992	Gino Torretta	University of Miami	QB
1993	Charlie Ward	Florida State University	QB
1994	Rashaan Salaam	University of Colorado	RB
1995	Eddie George	Ohio State University	RB
1996	Danny Wuerffel	University of Florida	QB
1997	Charles Woodson	University of Michigan	DB/Receiver
1998	Ricky Williams	University of Texas	TB
1999	Ron Dayne	University of Wisconsin	TB
2000	Chris Weinke	Florida State University	QB

⊙ College Football Hall of Fame. "Heisman Memorial Trophy," www.collegefootball.org/heisman
Heisman Memorial Trophy Trust. "Winners," www.heisman.com/winners.html

National Hockey League Teams

Eastern Conference

Division	Team	Stadium & Address	Phone/Website
Atlantic	New Jersey Devils	Continental Airlines Arena 50 Route 120 North East Rutherford, NJ 07073	(201) 935-3900 www.newjerseydevils.com
	New York Islanders	Nassau Veterans Memorial Coliseum 1255 Hempstead Turnpike Uniondale, NY 11553	(516) 542-9276 www.newyorkislanders.com
	New York Rangers	Madison Square Garden Two Pennsylvania Plaza New York, NY 10121	(212) 465-6741 www.newyorkrangers.com
	Philadelphia Flyers	First Union Center One Core States Complex Philadelphia, PA 19148	(215) 336-2000 www.philadelphiaflyers.com
	Pittsburgh Penguins	Civic Arena 66 Mario Lemieux Place Pittsburgh, PA 15219	(412) 323-1919 www.pittsburghpenguins.com
Northeast	Boston Bruins	FleetCenter One FleetCenter Boston, MA 02114	(617) 624-1750 www.bostonbruins.com
	Buffalo Sabres	Marine Midland Arena One Seymour H. Knox III Plaza Buffalo, NY 14203	(716) 855-4444 www.sabres.com
	Montréal Canadiens	Le Centre Molson 1260 de La Gauchetiére Street W Montréal, Québec H3B 5E8	(440) 891-5001 www.canadiens.com
	Ottawa Senators	Corel Centre 1000 Palladium Drive Kanata, Ontario K2V 1A5	800-444-7367 www.ottawasenators.com
	Toronto Maple Leafs	Air Canada Centre 40 Bay Street Toronto, Ontario M5J 2X2	(416) 815-5700 www.torontomapleleafs.com
Southeast	Atlanta Thrashers	Philips Arena One Philips Drive Atlanta, GA	(404) 584-7825 www.atlantathrashers.com
	Carolina Hurricanes	Raleigh Entertainment & Sports Arena 5000 Aerial Center Morrisville, NC 27560	888-645-8491 www.caneshockey.com
	Florida Panthers	National Car Rental Center 2555 Panther Parkway Sunrise, FL 33323	(954) 835-8000 www.floridapanthers.com
	Tampa Bay Lightning	Ice Palace 401 Channelside Drive Tampa, FL 33602	(813) 301-2500 www.tampabaylightning.com

National Hockey League Teams *(cont.)*

Division	Team	Stadium & Address	Phone/Website
Southeast *(cont.)*	Washington Capitals	MCI Center 601 F Street NW Washington, DC 20004	(202) 432-7328 www.washingtoncaps.com

Western Conference

Division	Team	Stadium & Address	Phone/Website
Central	Chicago Blackhawks	United Center 1901 West Madison Street Chicago, IL 60612	(312) 455-4500 www.chicagoblackhawks.com
	Columbus Blue Jackets	Nationwide Arena 150 East Wilson Bridge Road Worthington, OH 43085	800-645-2657 www.columbusbluejackets.com
	Detroit Red Wings	Joe Louis Arena 600 Civic Center Drive Detroit, MI 48226	(810) 645-6666 www.detroitredwings.com
	Nashville Predators	Nashville Arena 501 Broadway Nashville, TN 37203	(615) 770-7825 www.nashvillepredators.com
	St. Louis Blues	Kiel Center 1401 Clark Avenue St. Louis, MO 63103	(314) 241-1888 www.stlouisblues.com
Northwest	Calgary Flames	Pengrowth Saddledome at Stampede Park 555 Saddledome Rise SE Calgary, Alberta T2G 2W1	(403) 777-4630 www.calgaryflames.com
	Colorado Avalanche	Pepsi Center 100 Chopper Place Denver, CO 80204	(303) 405-1100 www.coloradoavalanche.com
	Edmonton Oilers	Skyreach Centre 7424-118 Avenue Edmonton, AB T5G 3G8	(403) 414 4000 www.edmontonoilers.com
	Minnesota Wild	Xcel Energy Center 199 West Kellogg Boulevard St. Paul, MN 55102	(651) 222-9453 www.wild.com
	Vancouver Canucks	General Motors Place 800 Griffiths Way Vancouver, British Columbia V6B 6G1	(604) 280-4400 www.orcabay.com/canucks
Pacific	Anaheim Mighty Ducks	Arrowhead Pond of Anaheim 2695 East Katella Avenue Anaheim, CA 92806	(714) 704-2500 www.mightyducks.com
	Dallas Stars	Dr. Pepper Star Center 211 Cowboy Parkway Irving, TX 75063	(214) 467-8277 www.dallasstars.com

Los Angeles Kings	Staples Center 1111 South Figueroa Street Los Angeles, CA 90015	888-546-4752 www.lakings.com
Phoenix Coyotes	Cellular One Ice Den 9375 East Bell Road Scottsdale, AZ 85260	(602) 503-5555 www.nhlcoyotes.com
San Jose Sharks	San Jose Arena 525 West Santa Clara Street San Jose, CA 95113	(408) 287-9200 800-225-2277 www.sj-sharks.com

⊙ ESPN. "Hockey," sports.espn.go.com/nhl/index
National Hockey League. "Teams," www.nhl.com/lineups/team/index.html

National Hockey League:
Stanley Cup Championships

The Stanley Cup is the oldest trophy awarded to professional athletes in North America. Originally presented to amateur Canadian hockey teams (from 1893), it became the property of the National Hockey Association in 1910. In 1926, the Stanley Cup playoffs became an event exclusively for National Hockey League (NHL) teams. Since 1939, the competition has been a best-of-seven-games series. Listed here are the results of the Stanley Cup finals since the 1926–27 season.

Note: "Score" shows number of games won; MVP = Most Valuable Player (awarded the Conn Smyth Trophy)

Year	Winning Team	Losing Team	Score	Series MVP
1927	Ottawa Senators	Boston Bruins	2–0	—
1928	New York Rangers	Montreal Maroons	3–2	—
1929	Boston Bruins	New York Rangers	2–0	—
1930	Montreal Canadiens	Boston Bruins	2–0	—
1931	Montreal Canadiens	Chicago Blackhawks	3–2	—
1932	Toronto Maple Leafs	New York Rangers	3–0	—
1933	New York Rangers	Toronto Maple Leafs	3–1	—
1934	Chicago Blackhawks	Detroit Red Wings	3–1	—
1935	Montreal Maroons	Toronto Maple Leafs	3–0	—
1936	Detroit Red Wings	Toronto Maple Leafs	3–1	—
1937	Detroit Red Wings	New York Rangers	3–2	—
1938	Chicago Blackhawks	Toronto Maple Leafs	3–1	—
1939	Boston Bruins	Toronto Maple Leafs	4–1	—
1940	New York Rangers	Toronto Maple Leafs	4–2	—
1941	Boston Bruins	Detroit Red Wings	4–0	—
1942	Toronto Maple Leafs	Detroit Red Wings	4–3	—
1943	Detroit Red Wings	Boston Bruins	4–0	—
1944	Montreal Canadiens	Chicago Blackhawks	4–0	—
1945	Toronto Maple Leafs	Detroit Red Wings	4–3	—

National Hockey League: Stanley Cup Championships

Year	Winning Team	Losing Team	Score	Series MVP
1946	Montreal Canadiens	Boston Bruins	4–1	—
1947	Toronto Maple Leafs	Montreal Canadiens	4–2	—
1948	Toronto Maple Leafs	Detroit Red Wings	4–0	—
1949	Toronto Maple Leafs	Detroit Red Wings	4–0	—
1950	Detroit Red Wings	New York Rangers	4–3	—
1951	Toronto Maple Leafs	Montreal Canadiens	4–1	—
1952	Detroit Red Wings	Montreal Canadiens	4–0	—
1953	Montreal Canadiens	Boston Bruins	4–1	—
1954	Detroit Red Wings	Montreal Canadiens	4–3	—
1955	Detroit Red Wings	Montreal Canadiens	4–3	—
1956	Montreal Canadiens	Detroit Red Wings	4–1	—
1957	Montreal Canadiens	Boston Bruins	4–1	—
1958	Montreal Canadiens	Boston Bruins	4–2	—
1959	Montreal Canadiens	Toronto Maple Leafs	4–1	—
1960	Montreal Canadiens	Toronto Maple Leafs	4–0	—
1961	Chicago Blackhawks	Detroit Red Wings	4–2	—
1962	Toronto Maple Leafs	Chicago Blackhawks	4–2	—
1963	Toronto Maple Leafs	Detroit Red Wings	4–1	—
1964	Toronto Maple Leafs	Detroit Red Wings	4–3	—
1965	Montreal Canadiens	Chicago Blackhawks	4–3	Jean Beliveau
1966	Montreal Canadiens	Detroit Red Wings	4–2	Roger Crozier
1967	Toronto Maple Leafs	Montreal Canadiens	4–2	Dave Keon
1968	Montreal Canadiens	St. Louis Blues	4–0	Glenn Hall
1969	Montreal Canadiens	St. Louis Blues	4–0	Serge Savard
1970	Boston Bruins	St. Louis Blues	4–0	Bobby Orr
1971	Montreal Canadiens	Chicago Blackhawks	4–3	Ken Dryden
1972	Boston Bruins	New York Rangers	4–2	Bobby Orr
1973	Montreal Canadiens	Chicago Blackhawks	4–2	Yvon Cournoyer
1974	Philadelphia Flyers	Boston Bruins	4–2	Bernie Parent
1975	Philadelphia Flyers	Buffalo Sabres	4–2	Bernie Parent
1976	Montreal Canadiens	Philadelphia Flyers	4–0	Reggie Leach
1977	Montreal Canadiens	Boston Bruins	4–0	Guy Lafleur
1978	Montreal Canadiens	Boston Bruins	4–2	Larry Robinson
1979	Montreal Canadiens	New York Rangers	4–1	Bob Gainey
1980	New York Islanders	Philadelphia Flyers	4–2	Bryan Trottier
1981	New York Islanders	Minnesota North Stars	4–1	Butch Goring
1982	New York Islanders	Vancouver Canucks	4–0	Mike Bossy
1983	New York Islanders	Edmonton Oilers	4–0	Bill Smith

1984	Edmonton Oilers	New York Islanders	4–1	Mark Messier
1985	Edmonton Oilers	Philadelphia Flyers	4–1	Wayne Gretzky
1986	Montreal Canadiens	Calgary Flames	4–1	Patrick Roy
1987	Edmonton Oilers	Philadelphia Flyers	4–3	Ron Hextall
1988	Edmonton Oilers	Boston Bruins	4–0	Wayne Gretzky
1989	Calgary Flames	Montreal Canadiens	4–2	Al MacInnis
1990	Edmonton Oilers	Boston Bruins	4–1	Bill Ranford
1991	Pittsburgh Penguins	Minnesota North Stars	4–2	Mario Lemieux
1992	Pittsburgh Penguins	Chicago Blackhawks	4–0	Mario Lemieux
1993	Montreal Canadiens	Los Angeles Kings	4–1	Patrick Roy
1994	New York Rangers	Vancouver Canucks	4–3	Brian Leetch
1995	New Jersey Devils	Detroit Red Wings	4–0	Claude Lemieux
1996	Colorado Avalanche	Florida Panthers	4–0	Joe Sakic
1997	Detroit Red Wings	Philadelphia Flyers	4–0	Mike Vernon
1998	Detroit Red Wings	Washington Capitals	4–0	Steve Yzerman
1999	Dallas Stars	Buffalo Sabres	4–2	Joe Nieuwendyk
2000	New Jersey Devils	Dallas Stars	4–2	Scott Stevens
2001	Colorado Avalanche	New Jersey Devils	4–3	Patric Roy

⊙ ESPN. "Stanley Cup Finals: Playoff History," espn.go.com/nhl/playoffs00/s/history/index.html
National Hockey League. "Stanley Cup Champions and Finalists," www.nhl.com/hockeyu/history/
cup/champs.html

Hockey Hall of Fame

Year	Inductees	Year	Inductees
1945	Dan Bain		Cyclone Taylor
	Hobey Baker	1950	Scotty Davidson
	Dubbie Bowie		Graham Drinkwater
	Chuck Gardiner		Mike Grant
	Eddie Gerard		Si Griffis
	Frank McGee		Newsy Lalonde
	Howie Morenz		Joe Malone
	Tom Phillips		George Richardson
	Harvey Pulford		Harry Trihey
	Art Ross	1952	Dickie Boon
	Hod Stuart		Bill Cook
	Georges Vezina		Moose Goheen
1947	Dit Clapper		Ernie Johnson
	Aurel Joliat		Mickey MacKay
	Frank Nighbor	1958	Frank Boucher
	Lester Patrick		King Clancy
	Eddie Shore		Sprague Cleghorn

Hockey Hall of Fame

Year	Inductees	Year	Inductees
1958	Alex Connell		Tom Hooper
(cont.)	Red Dutton		Bouse Hutton
	Frank Foyston		Harry Hyland
	Frank Fredrickson		Jack Laviolette
	Herb Gardiner		Fred Maxwell
	George Hay		Billy McGimsie
	Dick Irvin		Reg Noble
	Ching Johnson		Didier Pitre
	Duke Keats		Jack Ruttan
	Hughie Lehman		Sweeney Schriner
	George McNamara		Joe Simpson
	Paddy Moran		Alf Smith
1959	Jack Adams		Barney Stanley
	Cy Denneny		Nels Stewart
	Tiny Thompson		Marty Walsh
1960	George Boucher		Harry "Moose" Watson
	Sylvio Mantha		Harry Westwick
	Jack Walker		Fred Whitcroft
1961	Syl Apps		Phat Wilson
	Charlie Conacher	1963	Ebbie Goodfellow
	George Hainsworth		Joe Primeau
	Hap Day		Earl Seibert
	Joe Hall	1964	Doug Bentley
	Percy LeSueur		Bill Durnan
	Frank Rankin		Babe Siebert
	Maurice Richard		Jack Stewart
	Milt Schmidt	1965	Marty Barry
	Oliver Seibert		Clint Benedict
	Bruce Stuart		Arthur Farrel
1962	Punch Broadbent		Red Horner
	Harry Cameron		Syd Howe
	Rusty Crawford		Jack Marshall
	Jack Darragh		Bill Mosienko
	Jimmy Gardner		Ernie Russell
	Billy Gilmour		Blair Russel
	Shorty Green		Fred Scanlan
	Riley Hern		Frank Brimsek

		1978	Andy Bathgate
	Ted Kennedy		Jacques Plante
	Elmer Lach		Marcel Pronovost
	Ted Lindsay	1979	Harry Howell
	Babe Pratt		Bobby Orr
	Kenny Reardon		Henri Richard
1967	Turk Broda	1980	Harry Lumley
	Neil Colville		Lynn Patrick
	Harry Oliver		Gump Worsley
1968	Bill Cowley	1981	John Bucyk
1969	Sid Abel		Frank Mahovlich
	Bryan Hextall		Allan Stanley
	Red Kelly	1982	Yvan Cournoyer
	Roy Worters		Rod Gilbert
1970	Babe Dye		Norm Ullman
	Bill Gadsby	1983	Ken Dryden
	Tom Johnson		Bobby Hull
1971	Busher Jackson		Stan Mikita
	Gordie Roberts	1984	Phil Esposito
	Terry Sawchuk		Jacques Lemaire
	Cooney Weiland		Bernie Parent
1972	Jean Beliveau	1985	Gerry Cheevers
	Bernie Geoffrion		Bert Olmstead
	Hap Holmes		Jean Ratelle
	Gordie Howe	1986	Leo Boivin
	Hooley Smith		Dave Keon
1973	Doug Harvey		Serge Savard
	Chuck Rayner	1987	Bobby Clarke
	Tommy Smith		Eddie Giacomin
1974	Billy Burch		Jacques Laperriere
	Art Coulter	1988	Tony Esposito
	Tommy Dunderdale		Guy Lafleur
	Dickie Moore		Buddy O'Connor
1975	George Armstrong		Brad Park
	Ace Bailey	1989	Herbie Lewis
	Gordie Drillon		Darryl Sittler
	Glenn Hall		Vladislav Tretiak
	Pierre Pilote	1990	Bill Barber
1976	Johnny Bower		Fernie Flaman
	Bill Quackenbush		Gilbert Perreault
1977	Alex Delvecchio	1991	Mike Bossy
	Tim Horton		

Hockey Hall of Fame *(cont.)*

Year	Inductees	Year	Inductees
1991	Denis Potvin	1996	Bobby Bauer
(cont.)	Bob Pulford		Borje Salming
	Clint Smith	1997	Mario Lemieux
1992	Marcel Dionne		Bryan Trottier
	Woody Dumart	1998	Roy Gordon Conacher
	Bob Gainey		Michel Goulet
	Lanny McDonald		Peter Stastny
1993	Guy Lapointe	1999	Wayne Gretzky
	Edgar Laprade	2000	Walter Bush, Jr.
	Steve Shutt		Joe Mullen
	Billy Smith		Denis Savard
1994	Lionel Conacher	2001	Vlacheslav Fetisov
	Harry Percival Watson		Mike Gartner
1995	Bun Cook		Dale Hawerchuk
	Larry Robinson		Jari Kurri

⊙ Hockey Hall of Fame. "Honoured Players," www.hhof.com/html/hm11500.htm

Tennis: Championships

Although tennis championship games were played from the late 1800s, the tournaments were not officially designated "opens" (open to both professional and amateur tennis players) until 1968 in England, the United States, and France, and until 1969 in Australia.

U.S. Open Singles Champions

Year	Men	Women
1881	Richard Sears	
1882	Richard Sears	
1883	Richard Sears	
1884	Richard Sears	
1885	Richard Sears	
1886	Richard Sears	
1887	Richard Sears	Ellen Hansell
1888	Henry Slocum	Bertha Townsend
1889	Henry Slocum	Bertha Townsend
1890	Oliver Campbell	Ellen Roosevelt
1891	Oliver Campbell	Mabel Cahill
1892	Oliver Campbell	Mabel Cahill
1893	Robert Wrenn	Aline Terry
1894	Robert Wrenn	Helen Helwig

1895	Fred Hovey	Juliette Atkinson
1896	Robert Wrenn	Elisabeth Moore
1897	Robert Wrenn	Juliette Atkinson
1898	Malcolm Whitman	Juliette Atkinson
1899	Malcolm Whitman	Marion Jones
1900	Malcolm Whitman	Myrtle McAteer
1901	William Larned	Elisabeth Moore
1902	William Larned	Marion Jones
1903	Hugh Doherty	Elisabeth Moore
1904	Holcombe Ward	May Sutton
1905	Beals Wright	Elisabeth Moore
1906	William Clothier	Helen Homans
1907	William Larned	Evelyn Sears
1908	William Larned	Maud Barger-Wallach
1909	William Larned	Hazel Hotchkiss
1910	William Larned	Hazel Hotchkiss
1911	William Larned	Hazel Hotchkiss
1912	Maurice McLoughlin	Mary Browne
1913	Maurice McLoughlin	Mary Browne
1914	Richard William	Mary Browne
1915	William Johnston	Molla Bjurstedt
1916	Richard William	Molla Bjurstedt
1917	R. L. Murray	Molla Bjurstedt
1918	R. L. Murray	Molla Bjurstedt
1919	William Johnston	Hazel Hotchkiss Wrightman
1920	Bill Tilden	Molla Bjurstedt Mallory
1921	Bill Tilden	Molla Bjurstedt Mallory
1922	Bill Tilden	Molla Bjurstedt Mallory
1923	Bill Tilden	Helen Wills
1924	Bill Tilden	Helen Wills
1925	Bill Tilden	Helen Wills
1926	Rene Lacoste	Molla Bjurstedt Mallory
1927	Rene Lacoste	Helen Wills
1928	Henri Cochet	Helen Wills
1929	Bill Tilden	Helen Wills
1930	John Doeg	Betty Nuthall
1931	H. Ellsworth Vines	Helen Wills Moody
1932	H. Ellsworth Vines	Helen Jacobs
1933	Fred Perry	Helen Jacobs
1934	Fred Perry	Helen Jacobs
1935	Wilmer Alison	Helen Jacobs
1936	Fred Perry	Alice Marble
1937	Don Budge	Anita Lizana
1938	Don Budge	Alice Marble

U.S. Open Singles Champions

Year	Men	Women
1939	Bobby Riggs	Alice Marble
1940	Don McNeill	Alice Marble
1941	Bobby Riggs	Sarah Palfrey Cooke
1942	F. R. Schroeder, Jr.	Pauline Betz
1943	Joseph Hunt	Pauline Betz
1944	Frank Parker	Pauline Betz
1945	Frank Parker	Sarah Palfrey Cooke
1946	Jack Kramer	Pauline Betz
1947	Jack Kramer	Louise Brough
1948	Pancho Gonzales	Margaret Osborne duPont
1949	Pancho Gonzales	Margaret Osborne duPont
1950	Arthur Larsen	Margaret Osborne duPont
1951	Frank Sedgman	Maureen Connolly
1952	Frank Sedgman	Maureen Connolly
1953	Tony Trabert	Maureen Connolly
1954	Vic Seixas	Doris Hart
1955	Tony Trabert	Doris Hart
1956	Ken Rosewall	Shirley Fry
1957	Malcolm Anderson	Althea Gibson
1958	Ashley Cooper	Althea Gibson
1959	Neale A. Fraser	Maria Bueno
1960	Neale A. Fraser	Darlene Hard
1961	Roy Emerson	Darlene Hard
1962	Rod Laver	Margaret Smith
1963	Rafael Osuna	Maria Bueno
1964	Roy Emerson	Maria Bueno
1965	Manual Santana	Margaret Smith
1966	Fred Stolle	Maria Bueno
1967	John Newcombe	Billie Jean King
1968	Arthur Ashe	Virginia Wade
1969	Rod Laver	Margaret Smith Court
1970	Ken Rosewall	Margaret Smith Court
1971	Stan Smith	Billie Jean King
1972	Ilie Nastase	Billie Jean King
1973	John Newcombe	Margaret Smith Court
1974	Jimmy Connors	Billie Jean King
1975	Manual Orantes	Chris Evert
1976	Jimmy Connors	Chris Evert
1977	Guillermo Vilas	Chris Evert

1978	Jimmy Connors	Chris Evert
1979	John McEnroe	Tracy Austin
1980	John McEnroe	Chris Evert Lloyd
1981	John McEnroe	Tracy Austin
1982	Jimmy Connors	Chris Evert Lloyd
1983	Jimmy Connors	Martina Navratilova
1984	John McEnroe	Martina Navratilova
1985	Ivan Lendl	Hana Mandlikova
1986	Ivan Lendl	Martina Navratilova
1987	Ivan Lendl	Martina Navratilova
1988	Mats Wilander	Steffi Graf
1989	Boris Becker	Steffi Graf
1990	Pete Sampras	Gabriela Sabatini
1991	Stefan Edberg	Monica Seles
1992	Stefan Edberg	Monica Seles
1993	Pete Sampras	Steffi Graf
1994	Andre Agassi	Arantxa Sanchez Vicario
1995	Pete Sampras	Steffi Graf
1996	Pete Sampras	Steffi Graf
1997	Patrick Rafter	Martina Hingis
1998	Patrick Rafter	Lindsay Davenport
1999	Andre Agassi	Serena Williams
2000	Marat Safin	Venus Williams
2001	Lleyton Hewitt	Venus Williams

Wimbledon Singles Champions

Year	Men	Women
1877	Spencer Gore	
1878	P. Frank Hadow	
1879	J. T. Hartley	
1880	J. T. Hartley	
1881	William Renshaw	
1882	William Renshaw	
1883	William Renshaw	
1884	William Renshaw	Maud Watson
1885	William Renshaw	Maud Watson
1886	William Renshaw	Blanche Bingley
1887	Herbert Lawford	Lottie Dod
1888	Ernest Renshaw	Lottie Dod
1889	William Renshaw	Blanche Bingley Hillyard
1890	Willoughby J. Hamilton	Helena Rice
1891	Wilfred Baddeley	Lottie Dod
1892	Wilfred Baddeley	Lottie Dod
1893	Joshua Pim	
1894	Joshua Pim	Blanche Bingley Hillyard

Wimbledon Singles Champions

Year	Men	Women
1895	Wilfred Baddeley	Charlotte Cooper
1896	Harold Mahony	Charlotte Cooper
1897	Reginald Doherty	Blanche Bingley Hillyard
1898	Reginald Doherty	Charlotte Cooper
1899	Reginald Doherty	Blanche Bingley Hillyard
1900	Reginald Doherty	Blanche Bingley Hillyard
1901	Arthur Gore	Charlotte Cooper Sterry
1902	Hugh Doherty	Muriel Robb
1903	Hugh Doherty	Dorothea Douglass
1904	Hugh Doherty	Dorothea Douglass
1905	Hugh Doherty	May Sutton
1906	Hugh Doherty	Dorothea Douglass
1907	Norman Brookes	May Sutton
1908	Arthur Gore	Charlotte Cooper Sterry
1909	Arthur Gore	Dora Boothby
1910	Tony Wilding	Dorothea Douglass Lambert-Chambers
1911	Tony Wilding	Dorothea Douglass Lambert-Chambers
1912	Tony Wilding	Ethel W. Larcombe
1913	Tony Wilding	Dorothea Douglass Lambert-Chambers
1914	Norman Brookes	Dorothea Douglass Lambert-Chambers
1915–18	tournament not played due to World War I	
1919	Gerald Patterson	Suzanne Lenglen
1920	Bill Tilden	Suzanne Lenglen
1921	Bill Tilden	Suzanne Lenglen
1922	Gerald Patterson	Suzanne Lenglen
1923	William Johnston	Suzanne Lenglen
1924	Jean Borotra	Kathleen McKane
1925	Rene Lacoste	Suzanne Lenglen
1926	Jean Borotra	Kathleen McKane
1927	Henri Cochet	Helen Wills
1928	Rene Lacoste	Helen Wills
1929	Henri Cochet	Helen Wills
1930	Bill Tilden	Helen Wills Moody
1931	Sidney Wood	Cilly Aussem
1932	H. Ellsworth Vines	Helen Wills Moody
1933	Jack Crawford	Helen Wills Moody
1934	Fred Perry	Dorothy Round
1935	Fred Perry	Helen Wills Moody

1936	Fred Perry	Helen Jacobs
1937	Don Budge	Dorothy Round
1938	Don Budge	Helen Wills Moody
1939	Bobby Riggs	Alice Marble
1940–45	tournament not played due to World War II	
1946	Yvon Petra	Pauline Betz
1947	Jack Kramer	Margaret Osborne
1948	Bob Falkenburg	Louise Brough
1949	Ted Schroeder	Louise Brough
1950	Budge Patty	Louise Brough
1951	Dick Savitt	Doris Hart
1952	Frank Sedgman	Maureen Connolly
1953	Vic Seizas	Maureen Connolly
1954	Jaroslav Drobny	Maureen Connolly
1955	Tony Trabert	Louise Brough
1956	Lew Hoad	Shirley Fry
1957	Lew Hoad	Althea Gibson
1958	Ashley Cooper	Althea Gibson
1959	Alex Olmedo	Maria Bueno
1960	Neale Fraser	Maria Bueno
1961	Rod Laver	Angela Mortimer
1962	Rod Laver	Karen Hantze-Susman
1963	Chuck McKinley	Margaret Smith
1964	Roy Emerson	Maria Bueno
1965	Roy Emerson	Margaret Smith
1966	Manuel Santana	Billie Jean King
1967	John Newcombe	Billie Jean King
1968	Rod Laver	Billie Jean King
1969	Rod Laver	Ann Haydon-Jones
1970	John Newcombe	Margaret Smith Court
1971	John Newcombe	Evonne Goolagong
1972	Stan Smith	Billie Jean King
1973	Jan Kodes	Billie Jean King
1974	Jimmy Connors	Chris Evert
1975	Arthur Ashe	Billie Jean King
1976	Bjorn Borg	Chris Evert
1977	Bjorn Borg	Virginia Wade
1978	Bjorn Borg	Martina Navratilova
1979	Bjorn Borg	Martina Navratilova
1980	Bjorn Borg	Evonne Goolagong
1981	John McEnroe	Chris Evert Lloyd
1982	Jimmy Connors	Martina Navratilova
1983	John McEnroe	Martina Navratilova

Wimbledon Singles Champions

Year	Men	Women
1984	John McEnroe	Martina Navratilova
1985	Boris Becker	Martina Navratilova
1986	Boris Becker	Martina Navratilova
1987	Pat Cash	Martina Navratilova
1988	Stefan Edberg	Steefi Graf
1989	Boris Becker	Steffi Graf
1990	Stefan Edberg	Martina Navratilova
1991	Michael Stich	Steffi Graf
1992	Andre Agassi	Steffi Graf
1993	Pete Sampras	Steffi Graf
1994	Pete Sampras	Conchita Martinez
1995	Pete Sampras	Steffi Graf
1996	Richard Kralicek	Steffi Graf
1997	Pete Sampras	Martina Hingis
1998	Pete Sampras	Jana Novotna
1999	Pete Sampras	Lindsay Davenport
2000	Pete Sampras	Venus Williams
2001	Goran Ivanisevic	Venus Williams

French Open Singles Champions

Year	Men	Women
1891	J. Briggs	
1892	J. Schoepfer	
1893	L. Riboulet	
1894	Andre Vacherot	
1895	Andre Vacherot	
1896	Andre Vacherot	
1897	Paul Ayme	Cecilia Masson
1898	Paul Ayme	Cecilia Masson
1899	Paul Ayme	Cecilia Masson
1900	Paul Ayme	Cecilia Prevost
1901	Andre Vacherot	P. Girod
1902	Marcel Vacherot	Cecilia Masson
1903	Max Decugis	Cecilia Masson
1904	Max Decugis	Katie Gillou
1905	Maurice Germot	Katie Gillou
1906	Maurice Germot	Katie Fenwick
1907	Max Decugis	C. de Kermel
1908	Max Decugis	Katie Fenwick
1909	Max Decugis	Jeanne Matthey

1910	Maurice Germot	Jeanne Matthey
1911	Andre Gobert	Jeanne Matthey
1912	Max Decugis	Jeanne Matthey
1913	Max Decugis	Marguerite Broquedis
1914	Max Decugis	Marguerite Broquedis
1915–19	tournament not played due to World War I	
1920	Andre Gobert	Suzanne Lenglen
1921	Jean Samzaeuilh	Suzanne Lenglen
1922	Henri Cochet	Suzanne Lenglen
1923	Pierre Blancy	Suzanne Lenglen
1924	Jean Borotra	Didi Vlasto
1925	Rene Lacoste	Suzanne Lenglen
1926	Henri Cochet	Suzanne Lenglen
1927	Rene Lacoste	Kea Bouman
1928	Henri Cochet	Helen Wills
1929	Rene Lacoste	Helen Wills
1930	Henri Cochet	Helen Wills Moody
1931	Jean Borotra	Cilly Aussem
1932	Henri Cochet	Helen Wills Moody
1933	Jack Crawford	Margaret Scriven
1934	Gottfried von Cramm	Margaret Scriven
1935	Fred Perry	Hilda Sperling
1936	Gottfried von Cramm	Hilda Sperling
1937	Henner Henkel	Hilda Sperling
1938	Don Budge	Simone Mathieu
1939	Don McNeill	Simone Mathieu
1940–45	tournament not played due to World War II	
1946	Marcel Bernard	Margaret Osborne
1947	Joseph Asboth	Pat Canning Todd
1948	Frank Parker	Nelly Landry
1949	Frank Parker	Margaret Osborne du Pont
1950	Budge Patty	Doris Hart
1951	Jaroslav Drobny	Shirley Fry
1952	Jaroslav Drobny	Doris Hart
1953	Ken Rosewall	Maureen Connolly
1954	Tony Trabert	Maureen Connolly
1955	Tony Trabert	Angela Mortimer
1956	Lew Hoad	Althea Gibson
1957	Sven Davidson	Shirley Bloomer
1958	Merv Rose	Susi Koermoczi
1959	Nicola Pietrangeli	Christine Truman
1960	Nicola Pietrangeli	Darlene Hard

French Open Singles Champions

Year	Men	Women
1961	Manuel Santana	Ann Haydon
1962	Rod Laver	Margaret Smith
1963	Roy Emerson	Lesley Turner
1964	Manuel Santana	Margaret Smith
1965	Fred Stolle	Lesley Turner
1966	Tony Roche	Ann Haydon
1967	Roy Emerson	Francoise Durr
1968	Ken Rosewall	Nancy Richey
1969	Rod Laver	Margaret Smith Court
1970	Jan Kodes	Margaret Smith Court
1971	Jan Kodes	Evonne Goolagong
1972	Andres Gimano	Billie Jean King
1973	Ilie Nastase	Margaret Smith Court
1974	Bjorn Borg	Chris Evert
1975	Bjorn Borg	Chris Evert
1976	Adriano Panatta	Sue Barker
1977	Guillermo Vilas	Mima Jausovec
1978	Bjorn Borg	Virginia Ruzici
1979	Bjorn Borg	Chris Evert Lloyd
1980	Bjorn Borg	Chris Evert Lloyd
1981	Bjorn Borg	Hana Mandlikova
1982	Mats Wilander	Martina Navratilova
1983	Yannick Noah	Chris Evert Lloyd
1984	Ivan Lendl	Martina Navratilova
1985	Mats Wilander	Chris Evert Lloyd
1986	Ivan Lendl	Chris Evert Lloyd
1987	Ivan Lendl	Steffi Graf
1988	Mats Wilander	Steffi Graf
1989	Michael Chang	Arantxa Sanchez Vicario
1990	Andres Gomez	Monica Seles
1991	Jim Courier	Monica Seles
1992	Jim Courier	Monica Seles
1993	Sergi Bruguera	Steffi Graf
1994	Sergi Bruguera	Arantxa Sanchez Vicario
1995	Thomas Muster	Steffi Graf
1996	Yevgeny Kafelnikov	Steffi Graf
1997	Gustavo Kuerten	Iva Majolif
1998	Carlos Moya	Arantxa Sanchez Vicario
1999	Andre Agassi	Steffi Graf
2000	Gustavo Kuerten	Mary Pierce
2001	Gustavo Kuerten	Jennifer Capriati

Australian Open Singles Champions

Year	Men	Women
1905	Rodney Heath	
1906	Tony Wilding	
1907	Horace Rice	
1908	Fred Alexander	
1909	Tony Wilding	
1910	Rodney Heath	
1911	Norman Brookes	
1912	Cecil Parke	
1913	Ernie Parker	
1914	Arthur O'Hara Wood	
1915	Gordon Lowe	
1916–18	tournament not played due to World War I	
1919	A. R. F. Kingscote	
1920	Arthur O'Hara Wood	
1921	Rhys Gemmell	
1922	James Anderson	Mall Molesworth
1923	Arthur O'Hara Wood	Mall Molesworth
1924	James Anderson	Sylvia Lance
1925	James Anderson	Daphne Akhurst
1926	John Hawkes	Daphne Akhurst
1927	Gerald Patterson	Esna Boyd
1928	Jean Borotra	Daphne Akhurst
1929	John Gregory	Daphne Akhurst
1930	Gar Moon	Daphne Akhurst
1931	Jack Crawford	Coral Buttsworth
1932	Jack Crawford	Coral Buttsworth
1933	Jack Crawford	Joan Hartigan
1934	Fred Perry	Joan Hartigan
1935	Jack Crawford	Dorothy Round
1936	Adroam Qiost	Joan Hartigan
1937	Viv McGrath	Nancye Wynne
1938	Don Budge	Dorothy Bundy
1939	John Bromwich	Emily Westacott
1940	Adrian Quist	Nancye Wynne
1941–45	tournament not played due to World War II	
1946	John Bromwich	Nancye Wynne Bolton
1947	Dinny Pails	Nancye Wynne Bolton
1948	Adrian Quist	Nancye Wynne Bolton
1949	Frank Sedgman	Doris Hart
1950	Frank Sedgman	Louise Brough

Australian Open Singles Champions

Year	Men	Women
1951	Dick Savitt	Nancye Wynne Bolton
1952	Ken McGregor	Thelma Coyne Long
1953	Ken Rosewall	Maureen Connolly
1954	Merv Rose	Thelma Coyne Long
1955	Ken Rosewall	Beryl Pemrose
1956	Lew Hoad	Mary Carter
1957	Ashley Cooper	Shirley Fry
1958	Ashley Cooper	Angela Mortimer
1959	Alex Olmedo	Mary Carter Reitano
1960	Rod Laver	Margaret Smith
1961	Roy Emerson	Margaret Smith
1962	Rod Laver	Margaret Smith
1963	Roy Emerson	Margaret Smith
1964	Roy Emerson	Margaret Smith
1965	Roy Emerson	Margaret Smith
1966	Roy Emerson	Margaret Smith
1967	Roy Emerson	Nancy Richey
1968	Bill Bowrey	Billie Jean King
1969	Rod Laver	Margaret Smith Court
1970	Arthur Ashe	Margaret Smith Court
1971	Ken Rosewall	Margaret Smith Court
1972	Ken Rosewall	Virginia Wade
1973	John Newcombe	Margaret Smith Court
1974	Jimmy Connors	Evonne Goolagong
1975	John Newcombe	Evonne Goolagong
1976	Mark Edmondson	Evonne Goolagong
1977*	Roscoe Tanner	Kerry Reid
1977**	Vitas Gerulaitis	Evonne Goolagong
1978	Guillermo Vilas	Chris O'Neill
1979	Guillermo Vilas	Barbara Jordan
1980	Brian Teacher	Hana Mandlikova
1981	Johan Kriek	Martina Navratukiva
1982	Johan Kriek	Chris Evert Lloyd
1983	Mats Wilander	Martina Navratilova
1984	Mats Wilander	Chris Evert Lloyd
1985	Stefan Edberg	Martina Navratilova
1986	tournament not played	
1987	Stefan Edberg	Hana Mandlikova
1988	Mats Wilander	Steffi Graf
1989	Ivan Lendl	Steffi Graf

1990	Ivan Lendl	Steffi Graf
1991	Boris Becker	Monica Seles
1992	Jim Courier	Monica Seles
1993	Jim Courier	Monica Seles
1994	Pete Sampras	Steffi Graf
1995	Andre Agassi	Mary Pierce
1996	Boris Becker	Monica Seles
1997	Pete Sampras	Martina Hingis
1998	Petr Korda	Martina Hingis
1999	Yevgeny Kafelnikov	Martina Hingis
2000	Andre Agassi	Lindsay Davenport
2001	Andre Agassi	Jennifer Capriati

*January 1977
**December 1977

⊙ CNN/Sports Illustrated. "Tennis," sportsillustrated.cnn.com/tennis/index.html
 ESPN. "Tennis," espn.go.com/tennis/index.html

International Tennis Hall of Fame

Year	Inductees	Year	Inductees
1955	Oliver Campbell	1961	Fred Alexander
	Joseph Clark		Malcolm Chace
	James Dwight		Harold Hackett
	Malcolm Whitman		Frank Hunter
	Richard Sears		Vincent Richards
	Henry Slocum	1962	John Doeg
	Robert Wrenn		Helen Hull Jacobs
1956	May Sutton Bundy		Ellsworth Vines
	William Clothier	1963	Wilmer Allison
	Dwight Davis		Sarah Palfrey Danzig
	William Larned		Julian Myrick
	Holcombe Ward		John Van Ryne
	Beals Wright	1964	George Adee
1957	Mary K. Browne		Don Budge
	Maurice McLoughlin		George Lott
	Hazel Hotchkiss Wightman		Alice Marble
	Richard N. Williams II		Frank Shields
1958	Bill Johnson		Sidney Wood
	Molla Bjurstedt Mallory	1965	Pauline Betz Addie
	R. Lindley Murray		James Van Alen
	Maud Barger-Wallach		Ellen Hansell
1959	Bill Tilden		Don McNeill
	Helen Wills (Moody Roark)		Watson Washburn

Year	Inductees	Year	Inductees
1966	Joe Hunt		Rene Lacoste
	Frank Parker		Dick Savitt
	Theodore Pell	1977	Manuel Alonso
	Ted Schroeder		Norman Brookes
1967	Louise Brough Clapp		Budge Patty
	Margaret Osbourne du Pont		Betty Nuthall Shoemaker
	Bobby Riggs		Gottfried von Cramm
	Bill Talbert	1978	Maria Bueno
1968	Maureen Connolly Brinker		Pierre Etchebaster
	Allison Danzig		Kathleen McKane Godfree
	Pancho Gonzales		Harry Hopman
	Jack Kramer		Suzanne Lenglen
	Eleonora Sears		Anthony Wilding
1969	Karl Behr	1979	Margaret Smith Court
	Charles Garland		Jack Crawford
	Doris Hart		Gladys Heldman
1970	Shirley Fry-Irvin		Al Laney
	Clarence Griffin		Rafael Osuna
	Perry Jones		Frank Sedgman
	Tony Trabert	1980	Lawrence Doherty
1971	Althea Gibson		Reginald Doherty
	Elisabeth Moore		King Gustav V of Sweden
	Arthur Nielsen		Lew Hoad
	Vic Seixas		Ken Rosewall
1972	Bryan Grant	1981	Dorothea Douglass Chambers
	Gardnar Mulloy		W. E. "Slew" Hester
	Elizabeth Ryan		Rod Laver
1973	Darlene Hard		Mary Outerbridge
	Alastair Martin	1982	Roy Emerson
	Gene Mako		William McChesney Martin
1974	Juliette Atkinson	1983	Clarence Clark
	Bob Falkenburg		Lottie Dod
	Fred Hovey		Jaroslav Drobny
	Bertha Townsend Toulmin		Ernest Renshaw
1975	Lawrence Baker, Sr.		William Renshaw
	Fred Perry	1984	John Bromwich
	Ellen Roosevelt		Neale Fraser
1976	Jean Borotra		Adrian Quist
	Jacques Brugnon		Manuel Santana
	Mabel Cahill		Pancho Segura
	Henri Cochet		

1985	Arthur Ashe	1992	Tracy Austin
	David Gray		Philippe Chatrier
	Ann Haydon Jones		Bob Hewitt
	Fred Stolle		Frew McMillan
1986	Dorothy Round Little	1993	Angela Mortimer Barrett
	Chuck McKinley		Lamar Hunt
	John Newcombe	1994	Arthur "Bud" Collins, Jr.
	Nicola Pietrangeli		Hana Mandlikova
	Tony Roche	1995	Chris Evert
	Ted Tinling	1996	Rosemary "Rosie" Casals
1987	Bjorn Borg		Dan Maskell
	Billie Jean Moffitt King	1997	H. W. "Bunny" Austin
	Alex Olmedo		Lesley Turner Bowrey
	Dennis Ralston		Walter Clopton Wingfield
	Stan Smith	1998	Jimmy Connors
1988	Evonne Goolagong Cawley		Herman David
1989	Gerald Patterson	1999	John McEnroe
	Virginia Wade		Ken McGregor
1990	Joseph F. Cullman III	2000	Malcolm Anderson
	Jan Kodes		Robert Kelleher
1991	Ashley Cooper		Martina Navratilova
	Ilie Nastase	2001	Ivan Lendl
	Guillermo Vilas		Mervyn Rose

⊙ International Tennis Hall of Fame. "Hall of Fame Enshrinees," www.tennisfame.org/enshrinees_chrono.html

Men's Professional Golf Association: Championships

The four major championship tournaments of the PGA Tour are listed here.

Masters Tournament

Year	Winner	Year	Winner	Year	Winner
1934	Horton Smith	1948	Claude Harmon	1961	Gary Player
1935	Gene Sarazen	1949	Sam Snead	1962	Arnold Palmer
1936	Horton Smith	1950	Jimmy Demaret	1963	Jack Nicklaus
1937	Byron Nelson	1951	Ben Hogan	1964	Arnold Palmer
1938	Henry Picard	1952	Sam Snead	1965	Jack Nicklaus
1939	Ralph Guldahl	1953	Ben Hogan	1966	Jack Nicklaus
1940	Jimmy Demaret	1954	Sam Snead	1967	Gay Brewer, Jr.
1941	Craig Wood	1955	Cary Middlecoff	1968	Bob Goalby
1942	Byron Nelson	1956	Jack Burke, Jr.	1969	George Archer
1943–45	no tournament played	1957	Doug Ford	1970	Billy Casper
		1958	Arnold Palmer	1971	Charles Coody
1946	Herman Keiser	1959	Art Wall, Jr.	1972	Jack Nicklaus
1947	Jimmy Demaret	1960	Arnold Palmer	1973	Tommy Aaron

Masters Tournament

Year	Winner	Year	Winner	Year	Winner
1974	Gary Player	1984	Ben Crenshaw	1994	Jose Maria Olazabal
1975	Jack Nicklaus	1985	Bernhard Langer	1995	Ben Crenshaw
1976	Ray Floyd	1986	Jack Nicklaus	1996	Nick Faldo
1977	Tom Watson	1987	Larry Mize	1997	Tiger Woods
1978	Gary Player	1988	Sandy Lyle	1998	Mark O'Meara
1979	Fuzzy Zoeller	1989	Nick Faldo	1999	Jose Maria Olazabal
1980	Seve Ballesteros	1990	Nick Faldo	2000	Vijay Singh
1981	Tom Watson	1991	Ian Woosnam	2001	Tiger Woods
1982	Craig Stadler	1992	Fred Couples		
1983	Seve Ballesteros	1993	Bernhard Langer		

PGA Championship

Year	Winner	Year	Winner	Year	Winner
1916	James M. Barnes	1941	Vic Ghezzi	1965	Dave Marr
1917–18	no tournament played	1942	Sam Snead	1966	Al Geiberger
		1943	no tournament played	1967	Don January
1919	James M. Barnes			1968	Julius Boros
1920	Jock Hutchison	1944	Bob Hamilton	1969	Ray Floyd
1921	Walter Hagen	1945	Byron Nelson	1970	Dave Stockton
1922	Gene Sarazen	1946	Ben Hogan	1971	Jack Nicklaus
1923	Gene Sarazen	1947	Jim Ferrier	1972	Gary Player
1924	Walter Hagen	1948	Ben Hogan	1973	Jack Nicklaus
1925	Walter Hagen	1949	Sam Snead	1974	Lee Trevino
1926	Walter Hagen	1950	Chandler Harper	1975	Jack Nicklaus
1927	Walter Hagen	1951	Sam Snead	1976	Dave Stockton
1928	Leo Diegel	1952	Jim Turnesa	1977	Lanny Wadkins
1929	Leo Diegel	1953	Walter Burkemo	1978	John Mahaffey
1930	Tommy Armour	1954	Chick Harbert	1979	David Graham
1931	Tom Creavy	1955	Doug Ford	1980	Jack Nicklaus
1932	Olin Dutra	1956	Jack Burke	1981	Larry Nelson
1933	Gene Sarazen	1957	Lionel Hebert	1982	Raymond Floyd
1934	Paul Runyan	1958	Dow Finsterwald	1983	Hal Sutton
1935	Johnny Revolta	1959	Bob Rosburg	1984	Lee Trevino
1936	Denny Shute	1960	Jay Hebert	1985	Hubert Green
1937	Denny Shute	1961	Jerry Barber	1986	Bob Tway
1938	Paul Runyan	1962	Gary Player	1987	Larry Nelson
1939	Henry Picard	1963	Jack Nicklaus	1988	Jeff Sluman
1940	Byron Nelson	1964	Bobby Nichols	1989	Payne Stewart

Year	Winner	Year	Winner	Year	Winner
1990	Wayne Grady	1994	Nick Price	1998	Vijay Singh
1991	John Daly	1995	Steve Elkington	1999	Tiger Woods
1992	Nick Price	1996	Mark Brooks	2000	Tiger Woods
1993	Paul Azinger	1997	Davis Love III	2001	David Toms

U.S. Open Championship

Year	Winner	Year	Winner	Year	Winner
1895	Horace Rawlins	1930	Bobby Jones	1967	Jack Nicklaus
1896	James Foulis	1931	Billy Burke	1968	Lee Trevino
1897	Joe Lloyd	1932	Gene Sarazen	1969	Orville Moody
1898	Fred Herd	1933	Johnny Goodman	1970	Tony Jacklin
1899	Willie Smith	1934	Olin Dutra	1971	Lee Trevino
1900	Harry Vardon	1935	Sam Parks Jr	1972	Jack Nicklaus
1901	Willie Anderson	1936	Tony Manero	1973	Johnny Miller
1902	Laurie Auchterlonie	1937	Ralph Guldahl	1974	Hale Irwin
1903	Willie Anderson	1938	Ralph Guldahl	1975	Lou Graham
1904	Willie Anderson	1939	Byron Nelson	1976	Jerry Pate
1905	Willie Anderson	1940	Lawson Little	1977	Hubert Green
1906	Alex Smith	1941	Craig Wood	1978	Andy North
1907	Alex Ross	1942–45	no tournament played	1979	Hale Irwin
1908	Fred McLeod			1980	Jack Nicklaus
1909	George Sargent	1946	Lloyd Mangrum	1981	David Graham
1910	Alex Smith	1947	Lew Worsham	1982	Tom Watson
1911	John McDermott	1948	Ben Hogan	1983	Larry Nelson
1912	John McDermott	1949	Cary Middlecoff	1984	Fuzzy Zoeller
1913	Francis Ouimet	1950	Ben Hogan	1985	Andy North
1914	Walter Hagen	1951	Ben Hogan	1986	Ray Floyd
1915	Jerome Travers	1952	Julius Boros	1987	Scott Simpson
1916	Charles Evans Jr.	1953	Ben Hogan	1988	Curtis Strange
1917–18	no tournament played	1954	Ed Furgol	1989	Curtis Strange
		1955	Jack Fleck	1990	Hale Irwin
1919	Walter Hagen	1956	Cary Middlecoff	1991	Payne Stewart
1920	Edward Ray	1957	Dick Mayer	1992	Tom Kite
1921	James Barnes	1958	Tommy Bolt	1993	Lee Janzen
1922	Gene Sarazen	1959	Billy Casper	1994	Ernie Els
1923	Bobby Jones	1960	Arnold Palmer	1995	Corey Pavin
1924	Cyril Walker	1961	Gene Littler	1996	Steve Jones
1925	Willie MacFarlane	1962	Jack Nicklaus	1997	Ernie Els
1926	Bobby Jones	1963	Julius Boros	1998	Lee Janzen
1927	Tommy Armour	1964	Ken Venturi	1999	Payne Stewart
1928	Johnny Farrell	1965	Gary Player	2000	Tiger Woods
1929	Bobby Jones	1966	Billy Casper	2001	Retlef Goosen

British Open Championship

Year	Winner	Year	Winner	Year	Winner
		1898	Harry Vardon		played
1860	Willie Park	1899	Harry Vardon	1946	Sam Snead
1861	Tom Morris, Sr.	1900	J. H. Taylor	1947	Fred Daly
1862	Tom Morris, Sr.	1901	James Braid	1948	Henry Cotton
1863	Willie Park	1902	Alexander Herd	1949	Bobby Locke
1864	Tom Morris, Sr.	1903	Harry Vardon	1950	Bobby Locke
1865	Andrew Strath	1904	Jack White	1951	Max Faulkner
1866	Willie Park	1905	James Braid	1952	Bobby Locke
1867	Tom Morris, Sr.	1906	James Braid	1953	Ben Hogan
1868	Tom Morris, Jr.	1907	Arnaud Massy	1954	Peter Thomson
1869	Tom Morris, Jr.	1908	James Braid	1955	Peter Thomson
1870	Tom Morris, Jr.	1909	J. H. Taylor	1956	Peter Thomson
1871	no tournament	1910	James Braid	1957	Bobby Locke
	played	1911	Harry Vardon	1958	Peter Thomson
1872	Tom Morris, Jr.	1912	Edward Ray	1959	Gary Player
1873	Tom Kidd	1913	J. H. Taylor	1960	Kel Nagle
1874	Mungo Park	1914	Harry Vardon	1961	Arnold Palmer
1875	Willie Park	1915–19	no tournament	1962	Arnold Palmer
1876	Robert Martin		played	1963	Bob Charles
1877	Jamie Anderson	1920	George Duncan	1964	Tony Lema
1878	Jamie Anderson	1921	Jock Hitchison	1965	Peter Thomson
1879	Jamie Anderson	1922	Walter Hagen	1966	Jack Nicklaus
1880	Robert Ferguson	1923	Arthur Havers	1967	Roberto Devicenzo
1881	Robert Ferguson	1924	Walter Hagen	1968	Gary Player
1882	Robert Ferguson	1925	James Barnes	1969	Tony Jacklin
1883	Willie Fernie	1926	Robert Jones, Jr.	1970	Jack Nicklaus
1884	Jack Simpson	1927	Robert Jones, Jr.	1971	Lee Trevino
1885	Bob Martin	1928	Walter Hagen	1972	Lee Trevino
1886	David Brown	1929	Walter Hagen	1973	Tom Weiskopf
1887	Willie Park, Jr.	1930	Robert Jones Jr	1974	Gary Player
1888	Jack Burns	1931	Tommy Armour	1975	Tom Watson
1889	Willie Park, Jr.	1932	Gene Sarazen	1976	Johnny Miller
1890	John Ball	1933	Denny Shute	1977	Tom Watson
1891	Hugh Kirkaldy	1934	Henry Cotton	1978	Jack Nicklaus
1892	Harold Hilton	1935	Alfred Perry	1979	Seve Ballesteros
1893	William Auchterlonie	1936	Alfred Padgham	1980	Tom Watson
1894	J. H. Taylor	1937	Henry Cotton	1981	Bill Rogers
1895	J. H. Taylor	1938	R. A. Whitcombe	1982	Tom Watson
1896	Harry Vardon	1939	Richard Burton	1983	Tom Watson
1897	Harold Hilton	1940–45	no tournament	1984	Seve Ballesteros

1985	Sandy Lyle	1991	Ian Baker-Finch	1997	Justin Leonard
1986	Greg Norman	1992	Nick Faldo	1998	Mark O'Meara
1987	Nick Faldo	1993	Greg Norman	1999	Paul Lawrie
1988	Seve Ballesteros	1994	Nick Price	2000	Tiger Woods
1989	Mark Calcavecchia	1995	John Daly	2001	David Duval
1990	Nick Faldo	1996	Tom Lehman		

⊙ Professional Golf Association. "PGA Tournaments," www.pgatour.com/tournaments/index.html

Ladies' Professional Golf Association: Championships

The four major championship tournaments of the LPGA Tour are listed here.

Nabisco Championship

Formerly Colgate Dinah Shore (1972–81) and Nabisco Dinah Shore (1982–99)

Year	Winner	Year	Winner	Year	Winner
1972	Jane Blalock	1982	Sally Little	1992	Dottie Pepper
1973	Mickey Wright	1983	Amy Alcott	1993	Helen Alfredsson
1974	JoAnn Prentice	1984	Juli Inkster	1994	Donna Andrews
1975	Sandra Palmer	1985	Alice Miller	1995	Nanci Bowen
1976	Judy Rankin	1986	Pat Bradley	1996	Patty Sheehan
1977	Kathy Whitworth	1987	Betsy King	1997	Betsy King
1978	Sandra Post	1988	Amy Alcott	1998	Pat Hurst
1979	Sandra Post	1989	Juli Inkster	1999	Dottie Pepper
1980	Donna Caponi	1990	Betsy King	2000	Karrie Webb
1981	Nancy Lopez	1991	Amy Alcott	2001	Annika Sörenstam

McDonald's LPGA Championship

Formerly LPGA Championship (1955–87) and Mazda LPGA (1987–93)

Year	Winner	Year	Winner	Year	Winner
1955	Beverly Hanson	1971	Kathy Whitworth	1987	Jane Geddes
1956	Marlene Hagge	1972	Kathy Ahern	1988	Sherri Turner
1957	Louise Suggs	1973	Mary Mills	1989	Nancy Lopez
1958	Mickey Wright	1974	Sandra Haynie	1990	Beth Daniel
1959	Betsy Rawls	1975	Kathy Whitworth	1991	Meg Mallon
1960	Mickey Wright	1976	Betty Burfeindt	1992	Betsy King
1961	Mickey Wright	1977	Chako Higuchi	1993	Patty Sheehan
1962	Judy Kimball	1978	Nancy Lopez	1994	Laura Davies
1963	Mickey Wright	1979	Donna Caponi	1995	Kelly Robbins
1964	Mary Mills	1980	Sally Little	1996	Laura Davies
1965	Sandra Haynie	1981	Donna Caponi	1997	Chris Johnson
1966	Gloria Ehret	1982	Jan Stephenson	1998	Se Ri Pak
1967	Kathy Whitworth	1983	Patty Sheehan	1999	Juli Inkster
1968	Sandra Post	1984	Patty Sheehan	2000	Juli Inkster
1969	Betsy Rawls	1985	Nancy Lopez	2001	Karrie Webb
1970	Shirley Englehorn	1986	Pat Bradley		

U.S. Women's Open Championship

Year	Winner	Year	Winner	Year	Winner
1946	Patty Berg	1965	Carol Mann	1984	Hollis Stacy
1947	Betty Jameson	1966	Sandra Spuzich	1985	Kathy Baker
1948	Babe Zaharias	1967	Catherine LaCoste	1986	Jane Geddes
1949	Louise Suggs	1968	Susie Berning	1987	Laura Davies
1950	Babe Zaharias	1969	Donna Caponi	1988	Liselotte Neumann
1951	Betsy Rawls	1970	Donna Caponi	1989	Betsy King
1952	Louise Suggs	1971	JoAnne Carner	1990	Betsy King
1953	Betsy Rawls	1972	Susie Berning	1991	Meg Mallon
1954	Babe Zaharias	1973	Susie Berning	1992	Patty Sheehan
1955	Fay Crocker	1974	Sandra Haynie	1993	Lauri Merten
1956	Kathy Cornelius	1975	Sandra Palmer	1994	Patty Sheehan
1957	Betsy Rawls	1976	JoAnne Carner	1995	Annika Sörenstam
1958	Mickey Wright	1977	Hollis Stacy	1996	Annika Sörenstam
1959	Mickey Wright	1978	Hollis Stacy	1997	Alison Nicholas
1960	Betsy Rawls	1979	Jerilyn Britz	1998	Se Ri Pak
1961	Mickey Wright	1980	Amy Alcott	1999	Juli Inkster
1962	Murle Breer	1981	Pat Bradley	2000	Karrie Webb
1963	Mary Mills	1982	Janet Anderson	2001	Karrie Webb
1964	Mickey Wright	1983	Jan Stephenson		

Du Maurier Classic

Formerly La Canadienne (1973) and Peter Jackson Classic (1974–82)

Year	Winner	Year	Winner	Year	Winner
1973	Jocelyne Bourassa	1983	Hollis Stacy	1993	Brandie Burton
1974	Carole Jo Callison	1984	Juli Inkster	1994	Matha Nause
1975	JoAnne Carner	1985	Pat Bradley	1995	Jenny Lidback
1976	Donna Caponi	1986	Pat Bradley	1996	Laura Davies
1977	Judy Rankin	1987	Jody Rosenthal	1997	Colleen Walker
1978	JoAnne Carner	1988	Sally Little	1998	Brandie Burton
1979	Amy Alcott	1989	Tammie Green	1999	Karrie Webb
1980	Pat Bradley	1990	Cathy Johnston	2000	Meg Mallon
1981	Jan Stephenson	1991	Nancy Scranton		
1982	Sandra Haynie	1992	Sherri Steinhauer		

⊙ Ladies Professional Golf Association. "LPGA Tour: The Majors," www.lpga.com/tour/comptour/majors/majors.html

World Golf Hall of Fame

Year	Inductees	Year	Inductees	Year	Inductees
1951	Betty Jameson (via LPGA Hall of Fame)		Donald Ross	1992	Hale Irwin
1974	Patty Berg	1978	Billy Casper		Chi Chi Rodriguez
	Walter Hagen		Harold Hilton		Richard Tufts
	Ben Hogan		Dorothy Campbell		Harry Cooper
	Robert T. Jones, Jr.		Hurd Howe	1993	Patty Sheehan (via LPGA Hall of Fame)
	Byron Nelson		Bing Crosby		
	Jack Nicklaus		Clifford Roberts	1994	Dinah Shore (via LPGA Hall of Fame)
	Arnold Palmer	1979	Louise Suggs		
	Gary Player		Walter Travis	1995	Betsy King (via LPGA Hall of Fame)
	Francis Quimet	1980	Lawson Little		
	Gene Sarazen		Henry Cotton	1998	Johnny Miller (via PGA Hall of Fame)
	Sam Snead	1981	Lee Trevino		
	Harry Vardon		Ralph Guldahl	1999	Amy Alcott (via LPGA Hall of Fame)
	Babe Didriksen Zaharias	1982	Julius Boros		Seve Ballesteros
1975	Willie Anderson		Kathy Whitworth		Nick Faldo
	Fred Corcoran	1983	Bob Hope		Lloyd Mangrum (via PGA Hall of Fame)
	Joseph C. Dey		Jimmy Demaret		
	Chick Evans	1985	JoAnne Carner	2000	Deane Beman
	Tom Morris Jr.	1986	Cary Middlecoff		Sir Michael Bonallack
	John H. Taylor	1987	Robert Trent Jones, Sr.		Jack Burke
	Glenna C. Vare				Neil Coles
	Joyce Wethered		Betsy Rawls		Beth Daniel (via LPGA Hall of Fame)
1976	Tommy Armour	1988	Tom Watson		
	James Braid		Peter Thomson		Juli Inkster (via LPGA Hall of Fame)
	Tom Morris, Sr.		Bob Harlow		
	Jerome Travers	1989	Raymond Floyd		John Jacob
	Mickey Wright		Nancy Lopez		Judy Rankin (via LPGA Hall of Fame)
1977	John Ball		Roberto De Vicenzo		
	Herb Graffis		Jim Barnes	2001	Greg Norman
	Sandra Haynie (via LPGA Hall of Fame)	1990	William C. Campbell		Payne Stewart
			Paul Runyan		Judy Bell
	Bobby Locke		Gene Littler		Bernard Langer
	Carol Mann (via LPGA Hall of Fame)		Horton Smith		Donna Caponi
		1991	Pat Bradley(via LPGA Hall of Fame)		Karsten Solheim
					Allan Robertson

⊙ World Golf Village. "World Golf Hall of Fame: Inductees," www.wgv.com/wgvf_HallOfFameInductees1.html

Men's Soccer: World Cup Finals

Held every four years since 1930 (except during World War II), the men's World Cup brings soccer teams from all over the globe to compete for the highest title in the world's most popular sport.

Year	Winning Team	Losing Team	Score	Host Nation
1930	Uruguay	Argentina	4–2	Uruguay
1934	Italy	Czechoslovakia	2–1	Italy
1938	Italy	Hungary	4–2	France
1950	Uruguay	Brazil	2–1	Brazil
1954	West Germany	Hungary	3–2	Switzerland
1958	Brazil	Sweden	5–2	Sweden
1962	Brazil	Czechoslovakia	3–1	Chile
1966	England	West Germany	4–2	England
1970	Brazil	Italy	4–1	Mexico
1974	West Germany	Holland	2–1	West Germany
1978	Argentina	Holland	3–1	Argentina
1982	Italy	West Germany	3–1	Spain
1986	Argentina	West Germany	3–2	Mexico
1990	West Germany	Argentina	1–0	Italy
1994	Brazil	Italy	1–0	United States
1998	France	Brazil	3–0	France

Women's Soccer: World Cup Finals

Women's soccer joined the World Cup competition in 1991.

Year	Winning Team	Losing Team	Score	Host Nation
1991	United States	Norway	2–1	China
1995	Norway	Germany	2–0	Sweden
1999	United States	China	5–4	United States

⊙ Fédération Internationale de Football Association (FIFA). "Women's World Cup History," wwc99.fifa.com

Washington Post. "World Cup History," washingtonpost.com/wp-srv/sports/soccer/longterm/worldcup98/history.htm

Olympic Games: Host Cities

Inspired by the Olympic Games of ancient Greece, the modern Olympic Games were established in 1896, when fewer than 250 athletes (all male) competed in 43 athletic events. Featured at the 2000 Summer Olympics in Sydney were some 300 events, in which more than 10,000 athletes (male and female) participated.

Summer Games

Year	Host City	Year	Host City
1896 (I)	Athens, Greece	1948 (XIV)	London, England
1900 (II)	Paris, France	1952 (XV)	Helsinki, Finland
1904 (III)	St. Louis, Missouri, USA	1956 (XVI)	Melbourne, Australia
1908 (IV)	London, England	1960 (XVII)	Rome, Italy
1912 (V)	Stockholm, Sweden	1964 (XVIII)	Tokyo, Japan
1916 (VI)	Games canceled due to World War I	1968 (XIX)	Mexico City, Mexico
		1972 (XX)	Munich, Germany
1920 (VII)	Antwerp, Belgium	1976 (XXI)	Montreal, Quebec, Canada
1924 (VIII)	Paris, France	1980 (XXII)	Moscow, Russia, USSR
1928 (IX)	Amsterdam, The Netherlands	1984 (XXIII)	Los Angeles, California, USA
1932 (X)	Los Angeles, California, USA	1988 (XXIV)	Seoul, South Korea
1936 (XI)	Berlin, Germany	1992 (XXV)	Barcelona, Spain
1940 (XII)	Games canceled due to World War II	1996 (XXVI)	Atlanta, Georgia, USA
		2000 (XXVII)	Sydney, Australia
1944 (XIII)	Games canceled due to World War II	2004 (XXVIII)	Athens, Greece

Winter Games

Year	Host City	Year	Host City
1924 (I)	Chamonix, France	1964 (IX)	Innsbruck, Austria
1928 (II)	St. Moritz, Switzerland	1968 (X)	Grenoble, France
1932 (II)	Lake Placid, New York, USA	1972 (XI)	Sapporo, Japan
1936 (IV)	Garmisch-Partenkirchen, Germany	1976 (XII)	Innsbruck, Austria
		1980 (XIII)	Lake Placid, New York, USA
1940 (—)	Games canceled due to World War II	1984 (XIV)	Sarajevo, Yugoslavia
		1988 (XV)	Calgary, Alberta, Canada
1944 (—)	Games canceled due to World War II	1992 (XVI)	Albertville, France
1948 (V)	St. Moritz, Switzerland	1994 (XVII)	Lillehammer, Norway
1952 (VI)	Oslo, Norway	1998 (XVIII)	Nagano, Japan
1956 (VII)	Cortina D'Ampezzo, Italy	2002 (XIX)	Salt Lake City, Utah, USA
1960 (VIII)	Squaw Valley, California, USA	2006 (XX)	Turin, Italy

⊙ Amateur Athletic Association of Los Angeles. "Olympics Primer," www.aafla.org/
OlympicInformationCenter/OlympicPrimer/OlympicPrimer.htm
International Olympics Committee. "History of the Games," www.museum.olympic.org/e/news/
news_e.html

PRIZES AND AWARDS

Nobel Prize (1901–2000)

The Nobel Prizes were established by the will of Alfred Bernhard Nobel, Swedish manufacturer, inventor, and philanthropist (1833–1896). They are given annually to those persons who have made the most outstanding contributions in the fields of physics, chemistry, physiology or medicine, and economic sciences, as well as to those who have produced the most distinguished literary work of an idealist tendency, and to those who have contributed most toward world peace. Independent award committees select each year's laureates; a committee may bestow joint awards or no award at all, if it so chooses.

Category: Peace

Year	Name/Organization (Country of Origin)	Year	Name/Organization (Country of Origin)
1901	Henri Dunant (Switzerland); Frederick Passy (France)	1925	Sir Austen Chamberlain (U.K.) and Charles G. Dawes (U.S.)
1902	Elie Ducommun and Albert Gobat (Switzerland)	1926	Aristide Briand (France) and Gustav Stresemann (Germany)
1903	Sir William R. Cremer (U.K.)	1927	Ferdinand Buisson (France) and Ludwig Quidde (Germany)
1904	Institut de Droit International (Belgium)		
1905	Bertha von Suttner (Austria)	1928	[no award]
1906	Theodore Roosevelt (U.S.)	1929	Frank B. Kellogg (U.S.)
1907	Ernesto T. Moneta (Italy) and Louis Renault (France)	1930	Lars O. J. Söderblom (Sweden)
1908	Klas P. Arnoldson (Sweden) and Frederik Bajer (Denmark)	1931	Jane Addams and Nicholas M. Butler (U.S.)
1909	Auguste M. F. Beernaert (Belgium) and Baron Paul H. B. B. d'Estournelles de Constant de Rebecque (France)	1932	[no award]
		1933	Sir Norman Angell (U.K.)
		1934	Arthur Henderson (U.K.)
1910	Bureau International Permanent de la Paix (Switzerland)	1935	Karl von Ossietzky (Germany)
		1936	Carlos de S. Lamas (Argentina)
1911	Tobias M. C. Asser (Holland) and Alfred H. Fried (Austria)	1937	Lord Cecil of Chelwood (U.K.)
		1938	Office International Nansen pour les Réfugiés (Switzerland)
1912	Elihu Root (U.S.)		
1913	Henri La Fontaine (Belgium)	1939	[no award]
1914	[no award]	1940	[no award]
1915	[no award]	1941	[no award]
1916	[no award]	1942	[no award]
1917	International Red Cross	1943	[no award]
1918	[no award]	1944	International Red Cross
1919	Woodrow Wilson (U.S.)	1945	Cordell Hull (U.S.)
1920	Léon Bourgeois (France)	1946	Emily G. Balch and John R. Mott (U.S.)
1921	Karl H. Branting (Sweden) and Christian L. Lange (Norway)	1947	American Friends Service Committee (U.S.) and British Society of Friends' Service Council (U.K.)
1922	Fridtjof Nansen (Norway)		
1923	[no award]	1948	[no award]
1924	[no award]	1949	Lord John Boyd Orr (Scotland)
		1950	Ralph J. Bunche (U.S.)

Year		Year	
1951	Léon Jouhaux (France)	1978	Menachem Begin (Israel) and Anwar el-Sadat (Egypt)
1952	Albert Schweitzer (French Equatorial Africa)	1979	Mother Teresa of Calcutta (India)
1953	George C. Marshall (U.S.)	1980	Adolfo Pérez Esquivel (Argentina)
1954	Office of U.N. High Commissioner for Refugees	1981	Office of the United Nations High Commissioner for Refugees
1955	[no award]	1982	Alva Myrdal (Sweden) and Alfonso García Roble (Mexico)
1956	[no award]		
1957	Lester B. Pearson (Canada)	1983	Lech Walesa (Poland)
1958	Rev. Dominique Georges Henri Pire (Belgium)	1984	Bishop Desmond Tutu (South Africa)
		1985	International Physicians for the Prevention of Nuclear War
1959	Philip John Noel-Baker (U.K.)		
1960	Albert John Luthuli (South Africa)	1986	Elie Wiesel (U.S.)
1961	Dag Hammarskjöld (Sweden)	1987	Oscar Arias Sánchez (Costa Rica)
1962	Linus Pauling (U.S.)	1988	U.N. Peacekeeping Forces
1963	Intl. Comm. of Red Cross; League of Red Cross Societies (both Geneva)	1989	Dalai Lama (Tibet)
		1990	Mikhail S. Gorbachev (USSR)
1964	Rev. Dr. Martin Luther King, Jr. (U.S.)	1991	Daw Aung San Suu Kyi (Burma)
1965	UNICEF (United Nations Children's Fund)	1992	Rigoberta Menchú (Guatemala)
		1993	F. W. de Klerk and Nelson Mandela (both South Africa)
1966	[no award]		
1967	[no award]	1994	Yasir Arafat (Palestine) and Yitzhak Rabin (Israel)
1968	René Cassin (France)		
1969	International Labour Organization	1995	Joseph Rotblat and Pugwash Conference on Science and World Affairs (U.K.)
1970	Norman E. Borlaug (U.S.)		
1971	Willy Brandt (West Germany)		
1972	[no award]	1996	Carlos Filipe Ximenes Belo and José Ramos-Horta (East Timor)
1973	Henry A. Kissinger (U.S.); Le Duc Tho (North Vietnam)		
		1997	International Campaign to Ban Landmines and Jody Williams (U.S.)
1974	Eisaku Sato (Japan); Sean MacBride (Ireland)		
		1998	John Hume and David Trimble (both Northern Ireland)
1975	Andrei D. Sakharov (USSR)		
1976	Mairead Corrigan and Betty Williams (both Northern Ireland)	1999	Medecins Sans Frontières
		2000	Kim Dae Jung (South Korea)
1977	Amnesty International	2001	Kofi Annan (Ghana) and United Nations

Category: Literature

Year	Name (Country of Origin)	Year	Name (Country of Origin)
1901	René F. A. Sully Prudhomme (France)	1910	Paul von Heyse (Germany)
1902	Theodor Mommsen (Germany)	1911	Maurice Maeterlinck (Belgium)
1903	Björnstjerne Björnson (Norway)	1912	Gerhart Hauptmann (Germany)
1904	Frédéric Mistral (France) and José Echegaray (Spain)	1913	Rabindranath Tagore (India)
		1914	[no award]
1905	Henryk Sienkiewicz (Poland)	1915	Romain Rolland (France)
1906	Giosuè Carducci (Italy)	1916	Verner von Heidenstam (Sweden)
1907	Rudyard Kipling (U.K.)	1917	Karl Gjellerup (Denmark) and Henrik Pontoppidan (Denmark)
1908	Rudolf Eucken (Germany)		
1909	Selma Lagerlöf (Sweden)	1918	[no award]

Category: Literature

Year	Name (Country of Origin)
1919	Carl Spitteler (Switzerland)
1920	Knut Hamsun (Norway)
1921	Anatole France (France)
1922	Jacinto Benavente (Spain)
1923	William B. Yeats (Ireland)
1924	Wladyslaw Reymont (Poland)
1925	George Bernard Shaw (Ireland)
1926	Grazia Deledda (Italy)
1927	Henri Bergson (France)
1928	Sigrid Undset (Norway)
1929	Thomas Mann (Germany)
1930	Sinclair Lewis (U.S.)
1931	Erik A. Karlfeldt (Sweden)
1932	John Galsworthy (U.K.)
1933	Ivan G. Bunin (Russia)
1934	Luigi Pirandello (Italy)
1935	[no award]
1936	Eugene O'Neill (U.S.)
1937	Roger Martin du Gard (France)
1938	Pearl S. Buck (U.S.)
1939	Frans Eemil Sillanpää (Finland)
1940	[no award]
1941	[no award]
1942	[no award]
1943	[no award]
1944	Johannes V. Jensen (Denmark)
1945	Gabriela Mistral (Chile)
1946	Hermann Hesse (Switzerland)
1947	André Gide (France)
1948	Thomas Stearns Eliot (U.K.)
1949	William Faulkner (U.S.)
1950	Bertrand Russell (U.K.)
1951	Pär Lagerkvist (Sweden)
1952	François Mauriac (France)
1953	Sir Winston Churchill (U.K.)
1954	Ernest Hemingway (U.S.)
1955	Halldór Kiljan Laxness (Iceland)
1956	Juan Ramón Jiménez (Spain)
1957	Albert Camus (France)
1958	Boris Pasternak (USSR) (declined)
1959	Salvatore Quasimodo (Italy)
1960	St. John Perse [Alexis St.-Léger Léger] (France)

Year	Name (Country of Origin)
1961	Ivo Andric (Yugoslavia)
1962	John Steinbeck (U.S.)
1963	Giorgios Seferis [Seferiades] (Greece)
1964	Jean-Paul Sartre (France) (declined)
1965	Mikhail Sholokhov (USSR)
1966	Shmuel Yosef Agnon (Israel) and Nelly Sachs (Sweden)
1967	Miguel Angel Asturias (Guatemala)
1968	Yasunari Kawabata (Japan)
1969	Samuel Beckett (Ireland)
1970	Aleksandr Solzhenitsyn (USSR)
1971	Pablo Neruda (Chile)
1972	Heinrich Böll (Germany)
1973	Patrick White (Australia)
1974	Eyvind Johnson and Harry Martinson (both Sweden)
1975	Eugenio Montale (Italy)
1976	Saul Bellow (U.S.)
1977	Vicente Aleixandre (Spain)
1978	Isaac Bashevis Singer (U.S.)
1979	Odysseus Elytis (Greece)
1980	Czeslaw Milosz (U.S.)
1981	Elias Canetti (Bulgaria)
1982	Gabriel García Márquez (Colombia)
1983	William Golding (U.K.)
1984	Jaroslav Seifert (Czechoslovakia)
1985	Claude Simon (France)
1986	Wole Soyinka (Nigeria)
1987	Joseph Brodsky (U.S.)
1988	Naguib Mahfouz (Egypt)
1989	Camilo José Cela (Spain)
1990	Octavio Paz (Mexico)
1991	Nadine Gordimer (South Africa)
1992	Derek Walcott (Trinidad)
1993	Toni Morrison (U.S.)
1994	Kenzaburo Oe (Japan)
1995	Seamus Heaney (Ireland)
1996	Wislawa Szymborska (Poland)
1997	Dario Fo (Italy)
1998	José Saramago (Portugal)
1999	Gunter Grass (Germany)
2000	Gao Xingjian (China)
2001	Sir V. S. Naipaul (U.K.)

Category: Physics

Year	Name (Country of Origin)
1901	Wilhelm K. Roentgen (Germany)
1902	Hendrik A. Lorentz and Pieter Zeeman (Netherlands)
1903	A. Henri Becquerel (France)
1904	John Strutt [Lord Rayleigh] (U.K.)
1905	Philipp Lenard (Germany)
1906	Sir Joseph Thomson (U.K.)
1907	Albert A. Michelson (U.S.)
1908	Gabriel Lippmann (France)
1909	Guglielmo Marconi (Italy) and Ferdinand Braun (Germany)
1910	Johannes D. van der Waals (Netherlands)
1911	Wilhelm Wien (Germany)
1912	Gustaf Dalén (Sweden)
1913	Heike Kamerlingh-Onnes (Netherlands)
1914	Max von Laue (Germany)
1915	Sir William Bragg and William L. Bragg (U.K.)
1916	[no award]
1917	Charles G. Barkla (U.K.)
1918	Max Planck (Germany)
1919	Johannes Stark (Germany)
1920	Charles E. Guillaume (Switzerland)
1921	Albert Einstein (Germany)
1922	Niels Bohr (Denmark)
1923	Robert A. Millikan (U.S.)
1924	Karl M. G. Siegbahn (Sweden)
1925	James Franck and Gustav Hertz (Germany)
1926	Jean B. Perrin (France)
1927	Arthur H. Compton (U.S.)
1928	Sir Owen Richardson (U.K.)
1929	Prince Louis Victor de Broglie (France)
1930	Sir Chandrasekhara Raman (India)
1931	[no award]
1932	Werner Heisenberg (Germany)
1933	Erwin Schrödinger (Austria) and Paul A. M. Dirac (U.K.)
1934	[no award]
1935	James Chadwick (U.K.)
1936	Victor F. Hess (Austria)
1937	Clinton J. Davisson (U.S.) and George P. Thomson (U.K.)

Year	Name (Country of Origin)
1938	Enrico Fermi (Italy)
1939	Ernest Orlando Lawrence (U.S.)
1940	[no award]
1941	[no award]
1942	[no award]
1943	Otto Stern (U.S.)
1944	Isidor Isaac Rabi (U.S.)
1945	Wolfgang Pauli (Austria)
1946	Percy Williams Bridgman (U.S.)
1947	Sir Edward Appleton (U.K.)
1948	Patrick M. S. Blackett (U.K.)
1949	Hideki Yukawa (Japan)
1950	Cecil Frank Powell (U.K.)
1951	Sir John Douglas Cockcroft (U.K.) and Ernest T. S. Walton (Ireland)
1952	Edward Mills Purcell and Felix Bloch (U.S.)
1953	Fritz Zernike (Netherlands)
1954	Max Born (U.K.)
1955	Polykarp Kusch and Willis E. Lamb, Jr. (U.S.)
1956	William Shockley, Walter H. Brattain, and John Bardeen (all U.S.)
1957	Tsung Dao Lee and Chen Ning Yang (China)
1958	Pavel A. Cherenkov, Ilya M. Frank, and Igor E. Tamm (all USSR)
1959	Emilio Segre and Owen Chamberlain (both U.S.)
1960	Donald A. Glaser (U.S.)
1961	Robert Hofstadter (U.S.)
1962	Lev D. Landau (USSR)
1963	Eugene Paul Wigner, Maria Goeppert Mayer (both U.S.), and J. Hans D. Jensen (Germany)
1964	Charles Hard Townes (U.S.), Nikolai G. Basov, and Aleksandr M. Prochorov (both USSR)
1965	Richard P. Feynman, Julian S. Schwinger (both U.S.), and Shinichiro Tomonaga (Japan)
1966	Alfred Kastler (France)
1967	Hans A. Bethe (U.S.)
1968	Luis Walter Alvarez (U.S.)
1969	Murray Gell-Mann (U.S.)

Category: Physics

Year	Name (Country of Origin)
1970	Hannes Alfvén (Sweden) and Louis Néel (France)
1971	Dennis Gabor (U.K.)
1972	John Bardeen, Leon N. Cooper, and John Robert Schrieffer (all U.S.)
1973	Ivar Giaever (U.S.), Leo Esaki (Japan), and Brian D. Josephson (U.K.)
1974	Antony Hewish (U.K.) and Martin Ryle (U.K.)
1975	James Rainwater (U.S.), Ben Mottelson, and Aage N. Bohr (both Denmark)
1976	Burton Richter and Samuel C. C. Ting (both U.S.)
1977	Philip W. Anderson, John H. Van Vleck (both U.S.), and Nevill F. Mott (U.K.)
1978	Arno A. Penzias and Robert W. Wilson (both U.S.), Piotr L. Kapitsa (USSR)
1979	Steven Weinberg, Sheldon L. Glashow (both U.S.), and Abdus Salam (Pakistan)
1980	James W. Cronin and Val L. Fitch (both U.S.)
1981	Nicolaas Bloembergen, Arthur L. Schawlow (both U.S.), and Kai M. Siegbahn (Sweden)
1982	Kenneth G. Wilson (U.S.)
1983	Subrahmanyam Chandrasekhar and William A. Fowler (both U.S.)
1984	Carlo Rubbia (Italy) and Simon van der Meer (Netherlands)
1985	Klaus von Klitzing (Germany)
1986	Ernst Ruska, Gerd Binnig (both Germany), and Heinrich Rohrer (Switzerland)

Year	Name (Country of Origin)
1987	K. Alex Müller (Switzerland) and J. Georg Bednorz (Germany)
1988	Leon M. Lederman, Melvin Schwartz, and Jack Steinberger (all U.S.)
1989	Norman F. Ramsey (U.S.), Hans G. Dehmelt (U.S.) and Wolfgang Paul (Germany)
1990	Richard E. Taylor (Canada), Jerome I. Friedman, and Dr. Henry W. Kendall (both U.S.)
1991	Pierre-Gilles de Gennes (France)
1992	George Charpak (France)
1993	Joseph H. Taylor and Russell A. Hulse (both U.S.)
1994	Clifford G. Shull (U.S.) and Bertram N. Brockhouse (Canada)
1995	Martin L. Perl and Frederick Reines (both U.S.)
1996	David M. Lee, Robert C. Richardson, and Douglas D. Osheroff (all U.S.)
1997	Steven Chu, William D. Phillips (both U.S.), and Claude Cohen-Tannoudji (France)
1998	Robert B. Laughlin (U.S.), Horst L. Störmer (Germany), and Daniel C. Tsui (U.S.)
1999	Gerardus 't Hooft, Martinus J.G. Veltman (both Netherlands)
2000	Zhores I. Alferov (Russia) and Herbert Kroemer (U.S.); Jack S. Kilby (U.S.)
2001	Eric A. Cornell, Carl E. Wieman (both U.S.), and Wolfgang Ketterle (Germany)

Category: Chemistry

Year	Name (Country of Origin)
1901	Jacobus H. van't Hoff (Netherlands)
1902	Emil Fischer (Germany)
1903	Svante A. Arrhenius (Sweden)
1904	Sir William Ramsay (U.K.)
1905	Adolf von Baeyer (Germany)
1906	Henri Moissan (France)

Year	Name (Country of Origin)
1907	Eduard Buchner (Germany)
1908	Sir Ernest Rutherford (U.K.)
1909	Wilhelm Ostwald (Germany)
1910	Otto Wallach (Germany)
1911	Marie Curie (France)
1912	Victor Grignard (France)

1913	Alfred Werner (Switzerland)
1914	Theodore W. Richards (U.S.)
1915	Richard Willstätter (Germany)
1916	[no award]
1917	[no award]
1918	Fritz Haber (Germany)
1919	[no award]
1920	Walther Nernst (Germany)
1921	Frederick Soddy (U.K.)
1922	Francis W. Aston (U.K.)
1923	Fritz Pregl (Austria)
1924	[no award]
1925	Richard Zsigmondy (Germany)
1926	Theodor Svedberg (Sweden)
1927	Heinrich Wieland (Germany)
1928	Adolf Windaus (Germany)
1929	Sir Arthur Harden (U.K.) and Hans K. A. S. von Euler-Chelpin (Sweden)
1930	Hans Fischer (Germany)
1931	Karl Bosch and Friedrich Bergius (both Germany)
1932	Irving Langmuir (U.S.)
1933	[no award]
1934	Harold C. Urey (U.S.)
1935	Frédéric and Irène Joliot-Curie (both France)
1936	Peter J. W. Debye (Netherlands)
1937	Walter N. Haworth (U.K.); and Paul Karrer (Switzerland)
1938	Richard Kuhn (Germany)
1939	Adolf Butenandt (Germany) and Leopold Ruzicka (Switzerland)
1940	[no award]
1941	[no award]
1942	[no award]
1943	Georg Hevesy De Heves (Hungary)
1944	Otto Hahn (Germany)
1945	Artturi Illmari Virtanen (Finland)
1946	James B. Sumner (U.S.), John H. Northrop and Wendell M. Stanley (all U.S.)
1947	Sir Robert Robinson (U.K.)
1948	Arne Tiselius (Sweden)
1949	William Francis Giauque (U.S.)
1950	Otto Diels and Kurt Alder (both Germany)
1951	Glenn T. Seaborg and Edwin H. McMillan (both U.S.)
1952	Archer John Porter Martin and Richard Laurence Millington Synge (both U.K.)
1953	Hermann Staudinger (Germany)
1954	Linus C. Pauling (U.S.)
1955	Vincent du Vigneaud (U.S.)
1956	Sir Cyril Hinshelwood (U.K.) and Nikolai N. Semenov (USSR)
1957	Sir Alexander Todd (U.K.)
1958	Frederick Sanger (U.K.)
1959	Jaroslav Heyrovsky (Czechoslovakia)
1960	Willard F. Libby (U.S.)
1961	Melvin Calvin (U.S.)
1962	Max F. Perutz and John C. Kendrew (U.K.)
1963	Carl Ziegler (Germany) and Giulio Natta (Italy)
1964	Dorothy Mary Crowfoot Hodgkin (U.K.)
1965	Robert B. Woodward (U.S.)
1966	Robert Sanderson Mulliken (U.S.)
1967	Manfred Eigen (Germany), Ronald G. W. Norrish, and George Porter (both U.K.)
1968	Lars Onsager (U.S.)
1969	Derek H. R. Barton (U.K.) and Odd Hassel (Norway)
1970	Luis F. Leloir (Argentina)
1971	Gerhard Herzberg (Canada)
1972	Christian Boehmer Anfinsen, Stanford Moore, and William Howard Stein (all U.S.)
1973	Ernst Otto Fischer (West Germany) and Geoffrey Wilkinson (U.K.)
1974	Paul J. Flory (U.S.)
1975	John W. Cornforth (Australia) and Vladimir Prelog (Switzerland)
1976	William N. Lipscomb, Jr. (U.S.)
1977	Ilya Prigogine (Belgium)
1978	Peter Mitchell (U.K.)
1979	Herbert C. Brown (U.S.) and Georg Wittig (West Germany)
1980	Paul Berg, Walter Gilbert (both U.S.), and Frederick Sanger (U.K.)
1981	Roald Hoffmann (U.S.) and Kenichi Fukui (Japan)

Category: Chemistry

Year	Name (Country of Origin)
1982	Aaron Klug (U.K.)
1983	Henry Taube (U.S.)
1984	R. Bruce Merrifield (U.S.)
1985	Herbert A. Hauptman and Jerome Karle (both U.S.)
1986	Dudley R. Herschback, Yuan T. Lee (both U.S.), and John C. Polanyi (Canada)
1987	Donald J. Cram, Charles J. Pedersen (both U.S.), and Jean-Marie Lehn (France)
1988	Johann Deisenhofer, Robert Huber, and Hartmut Michel (all West Germany)
1989	Thomas R. Cech and Sidney Altman (both U.S.)
1990	Elias James Corey (U.S.)
1991	Richard R. Ernst (Switzerland)
1992	Rudolph A. Marcus (U.S.)

Year	Name (Country of Origin)
1993	Kary B. Mullis (U.S.) and Michael Smith (Canada)
1994	George A. Olah (U.S.)
1995	F. Sherwood Rowland, Mario Molina (both U.S.), and Paul Crutzen (Netherlands)
1996	Richard E. Smalley, Robert F. Curl, Jr. (both U.S.), and Harold W. Kroto (U.K.)
1997	Paul D. Boyer (U.S.), Jens C. Skou (Denmark), and John E. Walker (U.K.)
1998	Walter Kohn (U.S.) and John A. Pople (U.K.)
1999	Ahmed H. Zewail (Egypt and U.S.)
2000	Alan J. Heeger (U.S.), Alan G. McDiarmid (U.S.), and Hideki Shirakawa (Japan)
2001	William S. Knowles and K. Barry Sharpless (both U.S.), and Ryoji Noyori (Japan)

Category: Physiology or Medicine

Year	Name (Country of Origin)
1901	Emil A. von Behring (Germany)
1902	Sir Ronald Ross (U.K.)
1903	Niels R. Finsen (Denmark)
1904	Ivan P. Pavlov (USSR)
1905	Robert Koch (Germany)
1906	Camillo Golgi (Italy) and Santiago Ramón y Cajal (Spain)
1907	Charles L. A. Laveran (France)
1908	Paul Ehrlich (Germany) and Elie Metchnikoff (USSR)
1909	Theodor Kocher (Switzerland)
1910	Albrecht Kossel (Germany)
1911	Allvar Gullstrand (Sweden)
1912	Alexis Carrel (France)
1913	Charles Richet (France)
1914	Robert Bárány (Austria)
1915	[no award]
1916	[no award]
1917	[no award]
1918	[no award]
1919	Jules Bordet (Belgium)

Year	Name (Country of Origin)
1920	August Krogh (Denmark)
1921	[no award]
1922	Archibald V. Hill (U.K.) and Otto Meyerhof (Germany)
1923	Sir Frederick Banting (Canada) and John J. R. Macleod (Scotland)
1924	Willem Einthoven (Netherlands)
1925	[no award]
1926	Johannes Fibiger (Denmark)
1927	Julius Wagner-Jauregg (Austria)
1928	Charles Nicolle (France)
1929	Christiaan Eijkman (Netherlands) and Sir Frederick Hopkins (U.K.)
1930	Karl Landsteiner (U.S.)
1931	Otto H. Warburg (Germany)
1932	Sir Charles Sherrington (U.K.) and Edgar D. Adrian (U.S.)
1933	Thomas H. Morgan (U.S.)
1934	George H. Whipple, George R. Minot, and William P. Murphy (U.S.)
1935	Hans Spemann (Germany)

1936	Sir Henry Dale (U.K.) and Otto Loewi (Germany)	1964	Konrad E. Bloch (U.S.) and Feodor Lynen (Germany)
1937	Albert Szent-Györgyi von Nagyrapolt (Hungary)	1965	François Jacob, André Lwolff, and Jacques Monod (all France)
1938	Corneille Heymans (Belgium)	1966	Charles Brenton Huggins (U.S.) and Francis Peyton Rous (U.S.)
1939	Gerhard Domagk (Germany)		
1940	[no award]	1967	Haldan K. Hartline, George Wald, and Ragnar Granit (all U.S.)
1941	[no award]		
1942	[no award]	1968	Robert W. Holley, Har Gobind Khorana, and Marshall W. Nirenberg (all U.S.)
1943	Henrik Dam (Denmark) and Edward A. Doisy (U.S.)	1969	Max Delbruck, Alfred D. Hershey, and Salvador E. Luria (all U.S.)
1944	Joseph Erlanger and Herbert Spencer Gasser (both U.S.)	1970	Julius Axelrod (U.S.), Ulf S. von Euler (Sweden), and Sir Bernard Katz (U.K.)
1945	Sir Alexander Fleming, Ernst Boris Chain, and Sir Howard Florey (all U.K.)	1971	Earl W. Sutherland, Jr. (U.S.)
1946	Herman J. Muller (U.S.)	1972	Gerald M. Edelman (U.S.), and Rodney R. Porter (U.K.)
1947	Carl F. and Gerty T. Cori (U.S.) and Bernardo A. Houssay (Argentina)	1973	Karl von Frisch, Konrad Lorenz (both Austria), and Nikolaas Tinbergen (Netherlands)
1948	Paul Mueller (Switzerland)		
1949	Walter Rudolf Hess (Switzerland) and Antonio Caetano de Abreu Freire Egas Moniz (Portugal)	1974	George E. Palade, Christian de Duve (both U.S.), and Albert Claude (Belgium)
1950	Philip S. Hench, Edward C. Kendall (both U.S.), and Tadeus Reichstein (Switzerland)	1975	David Baltimore, Howard M. Temin, and Renato Dulbecco (all U.S.)
1951	Max Theiler (South Africa)	1976	Baruch S. Blumberg and D. Carleton Gajdusek (both U.S.)
1952	Selman A. Waksman (U.S.)		
1953	Fritz A. Lipmann (Germany-U.S.) and Hans Adolph Krebs (Germany-U.K.)	1977	Rosalyn S. Yalow, Roger C. L. Guillemin, and Andrew V. Schally (all U.S.)
1954	John F. Enders, Thomas H. Weller, and Frederick C. Robbins (all U.S.)	1978	Daniel Nathans, Hamilton Smith (both U.S.), and Werner Arber (Switzerland)
1955	Hugo Theorell (Sweden)		
1956	Dickinson W. Richards, Jr., André F. Cournand (both U.S.), and Werner Forssmann (Germany)	1979	Allan McLeod Cormack (U.S.) and Godfrey Newbold Hounsfield (U.K.)
1957	Daniel Bovet (Italy)	1980	Baruj Benacerraf, George D. Snell (both U.S.), and Jean Dausset (France)
1958	Joshua Lederberg, George W. Beadie and Edward L. Tatum (all U.S.)	1981	Roger W. Sperry, David H. Hubel (both U.S.), and Torsten N. Wiesel (Sweden)
1959	Severo Ochoa and Arthur Kornberg (both U.S.)	1982	Sune Bergstrom, Bengt Samuelsson (both Sweden), and John R. Vane (U.K.)
1960	Sir Macfarlane Burnet (Australia) and Peter Brian Medawar (U.K.)	1983	Barbara McClintock (U.S.)
1961	Georg von Bekesy (U.S.)	1984	Cesar Milstein (U.K./Argentina), Georges J. F. Kohler (West Germany), and Niels K. Jerne (U.K./Denmark)
1962	James D. Watson (U.S.), Maurice H. F. Wilkins, and Francis H. C. Crick (both U.K.)		
1963	Alan Lloyd Hodgkin, Andrew Fielding Huxley (both U.K.), and Sir John Carew Eccles (Australia)	1985	Michael S. Brown and Joseph L. Goldstein (both U.S.)
		1986	Rita Levi-Montalcini (dual U.S./Italy) and Stanley Cohen (U.S.)
		1987	Susumu Tonegawa (Japan)

Category: Physiology or Medicine

Year	Name (Country of Origin)	Year	Name (Country of Origin)
1988	Gertrude B. Elion, George H. Hitchings (both U.S.), and Sir James Black (U.K.)	1995	Edward B. Lewis, Eric F. Wieschaus (both U.S.), and Christiane Nüsslein-Volhard (Germany)
1989	J. Michael Bishop and Harold E. Varmus (both U.S.)	1996	Peter C. Doherty (Australia) and Rolf M. Zinkernagel (Switzerland)
1990	Joseph E. Murray and E. Donnall Thomas (both U.S.)	1997	Stanley B. Prusiner (U.S.)
1991	Erwin Neher and Bert Sakmann (both Germany)	1998	Robert F. Furchgott, Louis J. Ignarro, and Ferid Murad (all U.S.)
1992	Edmond H. Fischer and Edwin G. Krebs (both U.S.)	1999	Günter Blobel (U.S.)
1993	Phillip A. Sharp (U.S.) and Richard J. Roberts (U.K.)	2000	Arvid Carlsson (Sweden), Paul Greengard (U.S.), and Eric R. Kandel (U.S.)
1994	Alfred G. Gilman and Martin Rodbell (both U.S.)	2001	Leland H. Hartwell (U.S.), R. Timothy (Tim) Hunt, and Sir Paul M. Nurse (both U.K.)

Category: Economic Science

Year	Name (Country of Origin)	Year	Name (Country of Origin)
1969	Ragnar Frisch (Norway) and Jan Tinbergen (Netherlands)	1986	James M. Buchanan (U.S.)
1970	Paul A. Samuelson (U.S.)	1987	Robert M. Solow (U.S.)
1971	Simon Kuznets (U.S.)	1988	Maurice Allais (France)
1972	Kenneth J. Arrow (U.S.) and Sir John R. Hicks (U.K.)	1989	Trygve Haavelmo (Norway)
1973	Wassily Leontief (U.S.)	1990	Harry M. Markowitz, William F. Sharpe, and Merton H. Miller (all U.S.)
1974	Gunnar Myrdal (Sweden) and Friedrich A. von Hayek (U.K.)	1991	Ronald Coase (U.S.)
1975	Leonid V. Kantorovich (USSR) and Tjalling C. Koopmans (U.S.)	1992	Gary S. Becker (U.S.)
1976	Milton Friedman (U.S.)	1993	Robert W. Fogel and Douglass C. North (both U.S.)
1977	Bertil Ohlin (Sweden) and James E. Meade (U.K.)	1994	John F. Nash, John C. Harsanyi (both U.S.), and Reinhard Selten (Germany)
1978	Herbert A. Simon (U.S.)	1995	Robert E. Lucas, Jr. (U.S.)
1979	Sir Arthur Lewis (U.K.) and Theodore Schultz (U.S.)	1996	James A. Mirrlees (U.K.) and William Vickrey (U.S.)
1980	Lawrence R. Klein (U.S.)	1997	Robert C. Merton and Myron S. Scholes (both U.S.)
1981	James Tobin (U.S.)	1998	Amartya Sen (India)
1982	George J. Stigler (U.S.)	1999	Robert A. Mundell (Canada)
1983	Gerard Debreu (U.S.)	2000	James J. Heckman and Daniel L. McFadden (both U.S.)
1984	Sir Richard Stone (U.K.)	2001	George A. Akerlof, A. Michael Spence, and Joseph E. Stiglitz (all U.S.)
1985	Franco Modigliani (U.S.)		

⊙ The Nobel Foundation. "The Nobel Foundation," www.nobel.se/nobel-foundation/index.html
  The Nobel Foundation. *Les Prix Nobel.* Stockholm: The Nobel Foundation, 1991.
  Schlessinger, Bernard S., and June H. Schlessinger, eds. *The Who's Who of Nobel Prize Winners 1901–1995.* Phoenix: Oryx, 1996.

The Academy Awards (the Oscars) are presented annually by the American Academy of Motion Pictures Arts and Sciences for artistic achievement in motion pictures. There are various explanations for the nickname Oscar, the most popular being that in 1935 it was named after an uncle of Margaret Herrick, the Academy's librarian and future executive director. Winners in each category are listed below by year.

1927–28
Picture: Wings
Actor: Emil Jannings, *The Last Command*
Actress: Jaynor Gaynor, *Seventh Heaven, Street Angel,* and *Sunrise*
Supporting Actor: [no award]
Supporting Actress: [no award]
Director: Frank Borzage, *Seventh Heaven*

1928–29
Picture: Broadway Melody
Actor: Warner Baxter, *In Old Arizona*
Actress: Mary Pickford, *Coquette*
Supporting Actor: [no award]
Supporting Actress: [no award]
Director: Frank Loyd, *The Divine Lady*

1929–30
Picture: All Quiet on the Western Front
Actor: George Arliss, *Disraeli*
Actress: Norma Shearer, *The Divorcée*
Supporting Actor: [no award]
Supporting Actress: [no award]
Director: Lewis Milestone, *All Quiet on the Western Front*

1930–31
Picture: Cimarron
Actor: Lionel Barrymore, *A Free Soul*
Actress: Louise Dressler, *Min and Bill*
Supporting Actor: [no award]
Supporting Actress: [no award]
Director: Norman Taurog, *Skippy*

1931–32
Picture: Grand Hotel
Actor (tie): Wallace Beery, *The Champ*; Frederic March, *Dr. Jekyll and Mr. Hyde*
Actress: Helen Hayes, *The Sins of Madelon Claudet*
Supporting Actor: [no award]
Supporting Actress: [no award]
Director: Frank Borzage, *Bad Girl*

1932–33
Picture: Cavalcade
Actor: Charles Laughton, *The Private Life of Henry VIII*
Actress: Katharine Hepburn, *Morning Glory*
Supporting Actor: [no award]
Supporting Actress: [no award]
Director: Frank Lloyd, *Cavalcade*

1934
Picture: It Happened One Night
Actor: Clark Gable, *It Happened One Night*
Actress: Claudette Colbert, *It Happened One Night*
Supporting Actor: [no award]
Supporting Actress: [no award]
Director: Frank Capra, *It Happened One Night*

1935
Picture: Mutiny on the Bounty
Actor: Victor McLaglen, *The Informer*
Actress: Bette Davis, *Dangerous*
Supporting Actor: [no award]
Supporting Actress: [no award]
Director: John Ford, *The Informer*

1936
Picture: The Great Ziegfeld
Actor: Paul Muni, *The Story of Louis Pasteur*
Actress: Luise Rainer, *The Great Ziegfeld*
Supporting Actor: Walter Brennan, *Come and Get It*
Supporting Actress: Gale Sondergaard, *Antony Adverse*
Director: Frank Capra, *Mr. Deeds Goes to Town*

1937
Picture: The Life of Emile Zola
Actor: Spencer Tracy, *Captains Courageous*
Actress: Luise Rainer, *The Good Earth*
Supporting Actor: Joseph Schildkraut, *The Life of Emile Zola*
Supporting Actress: Alice Brady, *In Old Chicago*
Director: Leo McCarey, *The Awful Truth*

1938
Picture: You Can't Take It With You
Actor: Spency Tracy, *Boy's Town*
Actress: Bette Davis, *Jezebel*
Supporting Actor: Walter Brennan, *Kentucky*
Supporting Actress: Fay Bainter, *Jezebel*
Director: Frank Capra, *You Can't Take It With You*

1939
Picture: Gone With the Wind
Actor: Robert Donat, *Goodbye, Mr. Chips*
Actress: Vivien Leigh, *Gone With the Wind*
Supporting Actor: Thomas Mitchell, *Stagecoach*
Supporting Actress: Hattie McDaniel, *Gone With the Wind*
Director: Victor Fleming, *Gone With the Wind*

1940
Picture: Rebecca
Actor: James Stewart, *The Philadelphia Story*
Actress: Ginger Rogers, *Kitty Foyle*
Supporting Actor: Walter Brennan, *The Westerner*
Supporting Actress: Jane Darwell, *The Grapes of Wrath*
Director: John Ford, *The Grapes of Wrath*

1941
Picture: How Green Was My Valley
Actor: Gary Cooper, *Sergeant York*
Actress: Joan Fontaine, *Suspicion*
Supporting Actor: Donald Crisp, *How Green Was My Valley*
Supporting Actress: Mary Astor, *The Great Lie*
Director: John Ford, *How Green Was My Valley*

1942
Picture: Mrs. Miniver
Actor: James Cagney, *Yankee Doodle Dandy*
Actress: Greer Garson, *Mrs. Miniver*
Supporting Actor: Van Heflin, *Johnny Eager*
Supporting Actress: Teresa Wright, *Mrs. Miniver*
Director: William Wyler, *Mrs. Miniver*

1943
Picture: Casablanca
Actor: Paul Lukas, *Watch on the Rhine*
Actress: Jennifer Jones, *The Song of Bernadette*
Supporting Actor: Charles Coburn, *The More the Merrier*

Supporting Actress: Katina Paxinou, *For Whom the Bell Tolls*
Director: Michael Curtiz, *Casablanca*

1944
Picture: Going My Way
Actor: Bing Crosby, *Going My Way*
Actress: Ingrid Bergman, *Gaslight*
Supporting Actor: Barry Fitzgerald, *Going My Way*
Supporting Actress: Ethel Barrymore, *None but the Lonely Heart*
Director: Leo McCarey, *Going My Way*

1945
Picture: The Lost Weekend
Actor: Ray Milland, *The Lost Weekend*
Actress: Joan Crawford, *Mildred Pierce*
Supporting Actor: James Dunn, *A Tree Grows in Brooklyn*
Supporting Actress: Anne Revere, *National Velvet*
Director: Billy Wilder, *The Lost Weekend*

1946
Picture: The Best Years of Our Lives
Actor: Frederic March, *The Best Years of Our Lives*
Actress: Olivia de Havilland, *To Each His Own*
Supporting Actor: Harold Russell, *The Best Years of Our Lives*
Supporting Actress: Anne Baxter, *The Razor's Edge*
Director: William Wyler, *The Best Years of Our Lives*

1947
Picture: Gentleman's Agreement
Actor: Ronald Coleman, *A Double Life*
Actress: Loretta Young, *The Farmer's Daughter*
Supporting Actor: Edmund Gwenn, *Miracle on 34th Street*
Supporting Actress: Celeste Holm, *Gentleman's Agreement*
Director: Elia Kazan, *Gentleman's Agreement*

1948
Picture: Hamlet
Actor: Laurence Olivier, *Hamlet*
Actress: Jane Wyman, *Johnny Belinda*

Supporting Actor: Walter Huston, *The Treasure of the Sierra Madre*
Supporting Actress: Claire Trevor, *Key Largo*
Director: John Huston, *The Treasure of the Sierra Madre*

1949
Picture: *All the King's Men*
Actor: Broderick Crawford, *All the King's Men*
Actress: Olivia de Havilland, *The Heiress*
Supporting Actor: Dean Jagger, *Twelve O'Clock High*
Supporting Actress: Mercedes McCambridge, *All the King's Men*
Director: Joseph L. Mankiewicz, *A Letter to Three Wives*

1950
Picture: *All About Eve*
Actor: José Ferrer, *Cyrano de Bergerac*
Actress: Judy Holliday, *Born Yesterday*
Supporting Actor: George Sanders, *All About Eve*
Supporting Actress: Josephine Hull, *Harvey*
Director: Joseph L. Mankiewicz, *All About Eve*

1951
Picture: *An American in Paris*
Actor: Humphrey Bogart, *The African Queen*
Actress: Vivien Leigh, *A Streetcar Named Desire*
Supporting Actor: Karl Malden, *A Streetcar Named Desire*
Supporting Actress: Kim Hunter, *A Streetcar Named Desire*
Director: George Stevens, *A Place in the Sun*

1952
Picture: *The Greatest Show on Earth*
Actor: Gary Cooper, *High Noon*
Actress: Shirley Booth, *Come Back, Little Sheba*
Supporting Actor: Anthony Quinn, *Viva Zapata!*
Supporting Actress: Gloria Grahame, *The Bad and the Beautiful*
Director: John Ford, *The Quiet Man*

1953
Picture: *From Here to Eternity*
Actor: William Holden, *Stalag 17*
Actress: Audrey Hepburn, *Roman Holiday*
Supporting Actor: Frank Sinatra, *From Here to Eternity*
Supporting Actress: Donna Reed, *From Here to Eternity*
Director: Fred Zinnemann, *From Here to Eternity*

1954
Picture: *On the Waterfront*
Actor: Marlon Brando, *On the Waterfront*
Actress: Grace Kelly, *The Country Girl*
Supporting Actor: Edmond O'Brien, *The Barefoot Contessa*
Supporting Actress: Eva Marie Saint, *On the Waterfront*
Director: Elia Kazan, *On the Waterfront*

1955
Picture: *Marty*
Actor: Ernest Borgnine, *Marty*
Actress: Anna Magnani, *The Rose Tattoo*
Supporting Actor: Jack Lemmon, *Mr. Roberts*
Supporting Actress: Jo Van Fleet, *East of Eden*
Director: Delbert Mann, *Marty*

1956
Picture: *Around the World in 80 Days*
Actor: Yul Brynner, *The King and I*
Actress: Ingrid Bergman, *Anastasia*
Supporting Actor: Anthony Quinn, *Lust for Life*
Supporting Actress: Dorothy Malone, *Written on the Wind*
Director: George Stevens, *Giant*

1957
Picture: *The Bridge on the River Kwai*
Actor: Alec Guiness, *The Bridge on the River Kwai*
Actress: Joanne Woodward, *The Three Faces of Eve*
Supporting Actor: Red Buttons, *Sayonara*
Supporting Actress: Miyoshi Umeki, *Sayonara*
Director: David Lean, *The Bridge on the River Kwai*

1958
Picture: *Gigi*
Actor: David Niven, *Separate Tables*
Actress: Susan Hayward, *I Want to Live!*
Supporting Actor: Burl Ives, *The Big Country*
Supporting Actress: Wendy Hiller, *Separate Tables*
Director: Vincente Minelli, *Gigi*

1959
Picture: *Ben-Hur*
Actor: Charlton Heston, *Ben-Hur*
Actress: Simone Signoret, *Room at the Top*
Supporting Actor: Hugh Griffith, *Ben-Hur*
Supporting Actress: Shelley Winters, *The Diary of Anne Frank*
Director: William Wyler, *Ben-Hur*

1960

Picture: *The Apartment*
Actor: Burt Lancaster, *Elmer Gantry*
Actress: Elizabeth Taylor, *Butterfield 8*
Supporting Actor: Peter Ustinov, *Spartacus*
Supporting Actress: Shirley Jones, *Elmer Gantry*
Director: Billy Wilder, *The Apartment*

1961

Picture: *West Side Story*
Actor: Maximilian Schell, *Judgment at Nuremberg*
Actress: Sophia Loren, *Two Women*
Supporting Actor: George Chakiris, *West Side Story*
Supporting Actress: Rita Moreno, *West Side Story*
Director: Robert Wise and Jerome Robbins, *West Side Story*

1962

Picture: *Lawrence of Arabia*
Actor: Gregory Peck, *To Kill a Mockingbird*
Actress: Anne Bancroft, *The Miracle Worker*
Supporting Actor: Ed Begley, *Sweet Bird of Youth*
Supporting Actress: Patty Duke, *The Miracle Worker*
Director: David Lean, *Lawrence of Arabia*

1963

Picture: *Tom Jones*
Actor: Sidney Poitier, *Lilies of the Field*
Actress: Patricia Neal, *Hud*
Supporting Actor: Melvyn Douglas, *Hud*
Supporting Actress: Margaret Rutherford, *The V.I.P.'s*
Director: Tony Richardson, *Tom Jones*

1964

Picture: *My Fair Lady*
Actor: Rex Harrison, *My Fair Lady*
Actress: Julie Andrews, *Mary Poppins*
Supporting Actor: Peter Ustinov, *Topkapi*
Supporting Actress: Lila Kedrova, *Zorba the Greek*
Director: George Cukor, *My Fair Lady*

1965

Picture: *The Sound of Music*
Actor: Lee Marvin, *Cat Ballou*
Actress: Julie Christie, *Darling*
Supporting Actor: Martin Balsam, *A Thousand Clowns*
Supporting Actress: Shelley Winters, *A Patch of Blue*
Director: Robert Wise, *The Sound of Music*

1966

Picture: *A Man for All Seasons*
Actor: Paul Scofield, *A Man for All Seasons*
Actress: Elizabeth Taylor, *Who's Afraid of Virginia Woolf?*
Supporting Actor: Walter Matthau, *The Fortune Cookie*
Supporting Actress: Sandy Dennis, *Who's Afraid of Virginia Woolf?*
Director: Fred Zinnemann, *A Man for All Seasons*

1967

Picture: *In the Heat of the Night*
Actor: Rod Steiger, *In the Heat of the Night*
Actress: Katharine Hepburn, *Guess Who's Coming to Dinner?*
Supporting Actor: George Kennedy, *Cool Hand Luke*
Supporting Actress: Estelle Parsons, *Bonnie and Clyde*
Director: Mike Nichols, *The Graduate*

1968

Picture: *Oliver!*
Actor: Cliff Robertson, *Charly*
Actress (tie): Katharine Hepburn, *The Lion in Winter*; Barbra Streisand, *Funny Girl*
Supporting Actor: Jack Albertson, *The Subject Was Roses*
Supporting Actress: Ruth Gordon, *Rosemary's Baby*
Director: Carol Reed, *Oliver!*

1969

Picture: *Midnight Cowboy*
Actor: John Wayne, *True Grit*
Actress: Maggie Smith, *The Prime of Miss Jean Brodie*
Supporting Actor: Gig Young, *They Shoot Horses, Don't They?*
Supporting Actress: Goldie Hawn, *Cactus Flower*
Director: John Schlesinger, *Midnight Cowboy*

1970

Picture: *Patton*
Actor (declined): George C. Scott, *Patton*
Actress: Glenda Jackson, *Women in Love*

Supporting Actor: John Mills, *Ryan's Daughter*
Supporting Actress: Helen Hayes, *Airplane*
Director: Franklin J. Schaffner, *Patton*

1971
Picture: *The French Connection*
Actor: Gene Hackman, *The French Connection*
Actress: Jane Fonda, *Klute*
Supporting Actor: Ben Johnson, *The Last Picture Show*
Supporting Actress: Cloris Leachman, *The Last Picture Show*
Director: William Friedkin, *The French Connection*

1972
Picture: *The Godfather*
Actor: Marlon Brando, *The Godfather*
Actress: Liza Minnelli, *Cabaret*
Supporting Actor: Joel Grey, *Cabaret*
Supporting Actress: Eileen Heckart, *Butterflies Are Free*
Director: Bob Fosse, *Cabaret*

1973
Picture: *The Sting*
Actor: Jack Lemmon, *Save the Tiger*
Actress: Glenda Jackson, *A Touch of Class*
Supporting Actor: John Houseman, *The Paper Chase*
Supporting Actress: Tatum O'Neal, *Paper Moon*
Director: George Roy Hill, *The Sting*

1974
Picture: *The Godfather, Part II*
Actor: Art Carney, *Harry and Tonto*
Actress: Ellen Burstyn, *Alice Doesn't Live Here Anymore*
Supporting Actor: Robert De Niro, *The Godfather, Part II*
Supporting Actress: Ingrid Bergman, *Murder on the Orient Express*
Director: Francis Ford Coppola, *The Godfather, Part II*

1975
Picture: *One Flew Over the Cuckoo's Nest*
Actor: Jack Nicholson, *One Flew Over the Cuckoo's Nest*
Actress: Louise Fletcher, *One Flew Over the Cuckoo's Nest*
Supporting Actor: George Burns, *The Sunshine Boys*
Supporting Actress: Lee Grant, *Shampoo*

Director: Milos Foreman, *One Flew Over the Cuckoo's Nest*

1976
Picture: *Rocky*
Actor: Peter Finch, *Network*
Actress: Faye Dunaway, *Network*
Supporting Actor: Jason Robards, *All the President's Men*
Supporting Actress: Beatrice Straight, *Network*
Director: John G. Avildsen, *Rocky*

1977
Picture: *Annie Hall*
Actor: Richard Dreyfuss, *The Goodbye Girl*
Actress: Diane Keaton, *Annie Hall*
Supporting Actor: Jason Robards, *Julia*
Supporting Actress: Vanessa Redgrave, *Julia*
Director: Woody Allen, *Annie Hall*

1978
Picture: *The Deer Hunter*
Actor: Jon Voight, *Coming Home*
Actress: Jane Fonda, *Coming Home*
Supporting Actor: Christopher Walken, *The Deer Hunter*
Supporting Actress: Maggie Smith, *California Suite*
Director: Michael Cimino, *The Deer Hunter*

1979
Picture: *Kramer vs. Kramer*
Actor: Dustin Hoffman, *Kramer vs. Kramer*
Actress: Sally Field, *Norma Rae*
Supporting Actor: Melvyn Douglas, *Being There*
Supporting Actress: Meryl Streep, *Kramer vs. Kramer*
Director: Robert Benton, *Kramer vs. Kramer*

1980
Picture: *Ordinary People*
Actor: Robert De Niro, *Raging Bull*
Actress: Sissy Spacek, *Coal Miner's Daughter*
Supporting Actor: Timothy Hutton, *Ordinary People*
Supporting Actress: Mary Steenburgen, *Melvin and Howard*
Director: Robert Redford, *Ordinary People*

1981
Picture: *Chariots of Fire*
Actor: Henry Fonda, *On Golden Pond*
Actress: Katharine Hepburn, *On Golden Pond*
Supporting Actor: John Gielgud, *Arthur*
Supporting Actress: Maureen Stapleton, *Reds*
Director: Warren Beatty, *Reds*

1982
Picture: Gandhi
Actor: Ben Kingsley, *Gandhi*
Actress: Meryl Streep, *Sophie's Choice*
Supporting Actor: Louis Gossett, Jr., *An Officer and a Gentleman*
Supporting Actress: Jessica Lange, *Tootsie*
Director: Richard Attenborough, *Gandhi*

1983
Picture: Terms of Endearment
Actor: Robert Duvall, *Tender Mercies*
Actress: Shirley MacLaine, *Terms of Endearment*
Supporting Actor: Jack Nicholson, *Terms of Endearment*
Supporting Actress: Linda Hunt, *The Year of Living Dangerously*
Director: James L. Brooks, *Terms of Endearment*

1984
Picture: Amadeus
Actor: F. Murray Abraham, *Amadeus*
Actress: Sally Field, *Places in the Heart*
Supporting Actor: Haing S. Ngor, *The Killing Fields*
Supporting Actress: Peggy Ashcroft, *A Passage to India*
Director: Milos Foreman, *Amadeus*

1985
Picture: Out of Africa
Actor: William Hurt, *Kiss of the Spider Woman*
Actress: Geraldine Page, *The Trip to Bountiful*
Supporting Actor: Don Ameche, *Cocoon*
Supporting Actress: Anjelica Huston, *Prizzi's Honor*
Director: Sydney Pollack, *Out of Africa*

1986
Picture: Platoon
Actor: Paul Newman, *The Color of Money*
Actress: Marlee Matlin, *Children of a Lesser God*
Supporting Actor: Michael Caine, *Hannah and Her Sisters*
Supporting Actress: Dianne Wiest, *Hannah and Her Sisters*
Director: Oliver Stone, *Platoon*

1987
Picture: The Last Emperor
Actor: Michael Douglas, *Wall Street*
Actress: Cher, *Moonstruck*
Supporting Actor: Sean Connery, *The Untouchables*
Supporting Actress: Olympia Dukakis, *Moonstruck*
Director: Bernardo Bertolucci, *The Last Emperor*

1988
Picture: Rain Man
Actor: Dustin Hoffman, *Rain Man*
Actress: Jodie Foster, *The Accused*
Supporting Actor: Kevin Kline, *A Fish Called Wanda*
Supporting Actress: Geena Davis, *The Accidental Tourist*
Director: Barry Levinson, *Rain Man*

1989
Picture: Driving Miss Daisy
Actor: Daniel Day-Lewis, *My Left Foot*
Actress: Jessica Tandy, *Driving Miss Daisy*
Supporting Actor: Denzel Washington, *Glory*
Supporting Actress: Brenda Fricker, *My Left Foot*
Director: Oliver Stone, *Born on the Fourth of July*

1990
Picture: Dances With Wolves
Actor: Jeremy Irons, *Reversal of Fortune*
Actress: Kathy Bates, *Misery*
Supporting Actor: Joe Pesci, *GoodFellas*
Supporting Actress: Whoopi Goldberg, *Ghost*
Director: Kevin Costner, *Dances With Wolves*

1991
Picture: The Silence of the Lambs
Actor: Anthony Hopkins, *The Silence of the Lambs*
Actress: Jodie Foster, *The Silence of the Lambs*
Supporting Actor: Jack Palance, *City Slickers*
Supporting Actress: Mercedes Ruehl, *The Fisher King*
Director: Jonathan Demme, *The Silence of the Lambs*

1992
Picture: *Unforgiven*
Actor: Al Pacino, *Scent of a Woman*
Actress: Emma Thompson, *Howard's End*
Supporting Actor: Gene Hackman, *Unforgiven*
Supporting Actress: Marisa Tomei, *My Cousin Vinny*
Director: Clint Eastwood, *Unforgiven*

1993
Picture: *Schindler's List*
Actor: Tom Hanks, *Philadelphia*
Actress: Holly Hunter, *The Piano*
Supporting Actor: Tommy Lee Jones, *The Fugitive*
Supporting Actress: Anna Paquin, *The Piano*
Director: Steven Spielberg, *Schindler's List*

1994
Picture: *Forrest Gump*
Actor: Tom Hanks, *Forrest Gump*
Actress: Jessica Lange, *Blue Sky*
Supporting Actor: Martin Landau, *Ed Wood*
Supporting Actress: Dianne Wiest, *Bullets Over Broadway*
Director: Robert Zemeckis, *Forrest Gump*

1995
Picture: *Braveheart*
Actor: Nicolas Cage, *Leaving Las Vegas*
Actress: Susan Sarandon, *Dead Man Walking*
Supporting Actor: Kevin Spacey, *The Usual Suspects*
Supporting Actress: Mira Sorvino, *Mighty Aphrodite*
Director: Mel Gibson, *Braveheart*

1996
Picture: *The English Patient*
Actor: Geoffrey Rush, *Shine*
Actress: Frances McDormand, *Fargo*
Supporting Actor: Cuba Gooding, Jr., *Jerry Maguire*
Supporting Actress: Juliette Binoche, *The English Patient*
Director: Anthony Minghella, *The English Patient*

1997
Picture: *Titanic*
Actor: Jack Nicholson, *As Good As It Gets*
Actress: Helen Hunt, *As Good As It Gets*
Supporting Actor: Robin Williams, *Good Will Hunting*
Supporting Actress: Kim Basinger, *L.A. Confidential*
Director: James Cameron, *Titanic*

1998
Picture: *Shakespeare in Love*
Actor: Roberto Benigni, *Life Is Beautiful*
Actress: Gwyneth Paltrow, *Shakespeare in Love*
Supporting Actor: James Coburn, *Affliction*
Supporting Actress: Judi Dench, *Shakespeare in Love*
Director: Steven Spielberg, *Saving Private Ryan*

1999
Picture: *American Beauty*
Actor: Kevin Spacey, *American Beauty*
Actress: Hilary Swank, *Boys Don't Cry*
Supporting Actor: Michael Caine, *Cider House Rules*
Supporting Actress: Angelina Jolie, *Girl, Interrupted*
Director: Sam Mendes, *American Beauty*

2000
Picture: *Gladiator*
Actor: Russel Crowe, *Gladiator*
Actress: Julia Roberts, *Erin Brockovich*
Supporting Actor: Benicio Del Toro, *Traffic*
Supporting Actress: Marcia Gay Harden, *Pollock*
Director: Steven Soderbergh, *Traffic*

⊙ Harkness, John. *The 1999 Academy Awards Handbook*. New York: Pinnacle, 1999.
Osborne, Robert. *70 Years of the Oscar: The Official History of the Academy Awards*. New York: Abbeville, 1999.
Oscar.com. "History-Past Winners," www.oscar.com/history/pastwinners/pas–index.html

The Pulitzer Prizes were established in 1917 by the will of Joseph Pulitzer (1847–1911), publisher of the New York World, for outstanding achievements in American journalism, letters, music (beginning in 1943), and drama. The prizes are bestowed by an advisory board that has exercised its broad powers to create new award categories and to withhold any award where entries fall below its standards of excellence. Winners in each major category are listed below by year

1917

Editorial Writing: No author named, *New York Tribune*
Novel: [no award]
Drama: [no award]
History: J. J. Jusserand, *With Americans of Past and Present Days*
Biography or Autobiography: Laura E. Richards and Maude Howe Elliott (asst. by Florence Howe Hall), *Julia Ward Howe*
Poetry: [no award]

1918

Editorial Writing: No author named, *Louisville Courier Journal*
Novel: Ernest Poole, *His Family*
Drama: Jesse Lynch Williams, *Why Marry?*
History: James Ford Rhodes, *A History of the Civil War, 1861–1865*
Biography or Autobiography: William Cabell Bruce, *Benjamin Franklin, Self-Revealed*
Poetry: [no award]

1919

Editorial Writing: [no award]
Novel: Booth Tarkington, *The Magnificent Ambersons*
Drama: [no award]
History: [no award]
Biography or Autobiography: Henry Adams, *The Education of Henry Adams*
Poetry: [no award]

1920

Editorial Writing: Harvey E. Newbranch, *Evening World Herald*, Omaha, Nebraska
Novel: [no award]
Drama: Eugene O'Neill, *Beyond the Horizon*
History: Justin H. Smith, *The War with Mexico*
Biography or Autobiography: Albert J. Beveridge, *The Life of John Marshall*
Poetry: [no award]

1921

Editorial Writing: [no award]
Novel: Edith Wharton, *The Age of Innocence*
Drama: Zona Gale, *Miss Lulu Bett*
History: William Sowden Sims and Burton J. Hendrick, *The Victory at Sea*
Biography or Autobiography: Edward Bok, *The Americanization of Edward Bok*
Poetry: [no award]

1922

Editorial Writing: Frank M. O'Brien, *New York Herald*
Novel: Booth Tarkington, *Alice Adams*
Drama: Eugene O'Neill, *Anna Christie*
History: James Truslow Adams, *The Founding of New England*
Biography or Autobiography: Hamlin Garland, *A Daughter of the Middle Border*
Poetry: Edwin Arlington Robinson, *Collected Poems*

1923

Editorial Writing: William Allen White, *Emporia* (Kansas) *Gazette*
Novel: Willa Cather, *One of Ours*
Drama: Owen Davis, *Icebound*
History: Charles Warren, *The Supreme Court in United States History*
Biography or Autobiography: Burton J. Hendrick, *The Life and Letters of Walter H. Page*
Poetry: Edna St. Vincent Millay, *The Ballad of the Harp-Weaver: A Few Figs from Thistles: Eight Sonnets in American Poetry*

1924

Editorial Writing: No author named, *Boston Herald*
Novel: Margaret Wilson, *The Able McLaughlins*
Drama: Hatcher Hughes, *Hell-Bent fer Heaven*

History: Charles Howard McIlwain, *The American Revolution—A Constitutional Interpretation*

Biography or Autobiography: Michael Idvorsky Pupin, *From Immigrant to Inventor*

Poetry: Robert Frost, *New Hampshire: A Poem with Notes and Grace Notes*

1925

Editorial Writing: No author named, *Charleston (South Carolina) News and Courier*

Novel: Edna Ferber, *So Big*

Drama: Sidney Howard, *They Knew What They Wanted*

History: Frederic L. Paxson, *History of the American Frontier*

Biography or Autobiography: M. A. Dewolfe Howe, *Barrett Wendell and His Letters*

Poetry: Edwin Arlington Robinson, *The Man Who Died Twice*

1926

Editorial Writing: Edward M. Kingsbury, *New York Times*

Novel: Sinclair Lewis, *Arrowsmith*

Drama: George Kelly, *Craig's Wife*

History: Edward Channing, *A History of the United States*

Biography or Autobiography: Harvey Cushing, *The Life of Sir William Osler*

Poetry: Amy Lowell, *What's O'Clock*

1927

Editorial Writing: F. Lauriston Bullard, *Boston Herald*

Novel: Louis Bromfield, *Early Autumn*

Drama: Paul Green, *In Abraham's Bosom*

History: Samuel Flagg Bemis, *Pinckney's Treaty*

Biography or Autobiography: Emory Holloway, *Whitman*

Poetry: Leonora Speyer, *Fiddler's Farewell*

1928

Editorial Writing: Grover Cleveland Hall, *Montgomery (Alabama) Advertiser*

Novel: Thornton Wilder, *The Bridge of San Luis Rey*

Drama: Eugene O'Neill, *Strange Interlude*

History: Vernon Louis Parrington, *Main Currents in American Thought*

Biography or Autobiography: Charles Edward Russell, *The American Orchestra and Theodore Thomas*

Poetry: Arlington Robinson, *Tristram*

1929

Editorial Writing: Louis Isaac Jaffe, *Norfolk Virginian-Pilot*

Novel: Julia Peterkin, *Scarlet Sister Mary*

Drama: Elmer L. Rice, *Street Scene*

History: Fred Albert Shannon, *The Organization and Administration of the Union Army, 1861–1865*

Biography or Autobiography: Burton J. Hendrick, *The Training of an American. The Earlier Life of Walter H. Page*

Poetry: Stephen Vincent Benét, *John Brown's Body*

1930

Editorial Writing: [no award]

Novel: Oliver Lafarge, *Laughing Boy*

Drama: Marc Connelly, *The Green Pastures*

History: Claude H. Van Tyne, *The War of Independence*

Biography or Autobiography: Marquis James, *The Raven*

Poetry: Conrad Aiken, *Selected Poems*

1931

Editorial Writing: Charles S. Ryckman, *Fremont (Nebraska) Tribune*

Novel: Margaret Ayer Barnes, *Years of Grace*

Drama: Susan Glaspell, *Alison's House*

History: Bernadotte E. Schmitt, *The Coming of the War: 1914*

Biography or Autobiography: Henry James, *Charles W. Eliot*

Poetry: Robert Frost, *Collected Poems*

1932

Editorial Writing: [no award]

Novel: Pearl S. Buck, *The Good Earth*

Drama: George S. Kaufman, Morrie Ryskind, George and Ira Gershwin, *Of Thee I Sing*

History: John J. Pershing, *My Experiences in the World War*

Biography or Autobiography: Henry F. Pringle, *Theodore Roosevelt*

Poetry: George Dillon, *The Flowering Stone*

1933

Editorial Writing: No author named, *Kansas City* (Missouri) *Star*

Novel: T. S. Stribling, *The Store*

Drama: Maxwell Anderson, *Both Your Houses*

History: Frederick J. Turner, *The Significance of Sections in American History*

Biography or Autobiography: Allan Nevins, *Grover Cleveland*

Poetry: Archibald MacLeish, *Conquistador*

1934

Editorial Writing: E. P. Chase, *Atlantic* (Iowa) *News-Telegraph*

Novel: Caroline Miller, *Lamb in His Bosom*

Drama: Sidney Kingsley, *Men in White*

History: Herbert Agar, *The People's Choice*

Biography or Autobiography: Tyler Dennett, *John Hay*

Poetry: Robert Hillyer, *Collected Verse*

1935

Editorial Writing: [no award]

Novel: Josephine Winslow Johnson, *Now in November*

Drama: Zoë Akins, *The Old Maid*

History: Charles McLean Andrews, *The Colonial Period of American History*

Biography or Autobiography: Douglas S. Freeman, *R. E. Lee*

Poetry: Audrey Wurdemann, *Bright Ambush*

1936

Editorial Writing: Felix Morley, *Washington Post*; and George B. Parker, *Scripps-Howard Newspaper*

Novel: Harold L. Davis, *Honey in the Horn*

Drama: Robert E. Sherwood, *Idiot's Delight*

History: Andrew C. McLaughlin, *A Constitutional History of the United States*

Biography or Autobiography: Ralph Barton Perry, *The Thought and Character of William James*

Poetry: Robert P. Tristram Coffin, *Strange Holiness*

1937

Editorial Writing: John W. Owens, *The Baltimore Sun*

Novel: Margaret Mitchell, *Gone With the Wind*

Drama: Moss Hart and George S. Kaufman, *You Can't Take It With You*

History: Van Wyck Brooks, *The Flowering of New England: 1815–1865*

Biography or Autobiography: Allan Nevins, *Hamilton Fish*

Poetry: Robert Frost, *A Further Range*

1938

Editorial Writing: William Wesley Waymack, *The Register and Tribune*, Des Moines, Iowa

Novel: John Phillips Marquand, *The Late George Apley*

Drama: Thornton Wilder, *Our Town*

History: Paul Herman Buck, *The Road to Reunion 1865–1900*

Biography or Autobiography: Marquis James, *Andrew Jackson*

Poetry: Marya Zaturenska, *Cold Morning Sky*

1939

Editorial Writing: Ronald G. Callert, *The Oregonian*, Portland, Oregon

Novel: Marjorie Kinnan Rawlings, *The Yearling*

Drama: Robert E. Sherwood, *Abe Lincoln in Illinois*

History: Frank Luther Mott, *A History of American Magazines*

Biography or Autobiography: Carl van Doren, *Benjamin Franklin*

Poetry: John Gould Fletcher, *Selected Poems*

1940

Editorial Writing: Bart Howard, *St. Louis Post-Dispatch*

Novel: John Steinbeck, *The Grapes of Wrath*

Drama: William Saroyan, *The Time of Your Life*

History: Carl Sandburg, *Abraham Lincoln: The War Years*

Biography or Autobiography: Ray Stannard Baker, *Woodrow Wilson, Life and Letters*

Poetry: Mark Van Doren, *Collected Poems*

1941

Editorial Writing: Reuben Maury, *New York Daily News*

Novel: [no award]

Drama: Robert E. Sherwood, *There Shall Be No Night*

History: Marcus Lee Hansen, *The Atlantic Migration, 1607–1860*

Biography or Autobiography: Ola Elizabeth Winslow, *Jonathan Edward*

Poetry: Leonard Bacon, *Sunderland Capture*

1942

Editorial Writing: Geoffrey Parsons, *New York Herald Tribune*

Novel: Ellen Glasgow, *In This Our Life*

Drama: [no award]

History: Margaret Leech, *Reveille in Washington, 1860–1865*

Biography or Autobiography: Forrest Wilson, *Crusader in Crinoline*

Poetry: William Rose Benét, *The Dust Which is God*

1943

Editorial Writing: Forrest W. Seymour, *Register and Tribune*, Des Moines, Iowa

Novel: Upton Sinclair, *Dragon's Teeth*

Drama: Thornton Wilder, *The Skin of Our Teeth*

History: Esther Forbes, *Paul Revere and the World He Lived In*

Biography or Autobiography: Samuel Eliot Morison, *Admiral of the Ocean Sea*

Poetry: Robert Frost, *A Witness Tree*

Music: William Schuman, *Secular Cantata No. 2. A Free Song*

1944

Editorial Writing: Henry J. Haskell, *Kansas City* (Missouri) *Star*

Novel: Martin Flavin, *Journey in the Dark*

Drama: [no award]

History: Merle Curti, *The Growth of American Thought*

Biography or Autobiography: Carleton Mabee, *The American Leonardo: The Life of Samuel F. B. Morse*

Poetry: Stephen Vincent Benét, *Western Star*

Music: Howard Hanson, *Symphony No. 4, Opus 34*

1945

Editorial Writing: George W. Potter, *Providence Journal-Bulletin*

Novel: John Hersey, *A Bell for Adano*

Drama: Mary Chase, *Harvey*

History: Stephen Bonsal, *Unfinished Business*

Biography or Autobiography: Russell Blaine Nye, *George Bancroft: Brahmin Rebel*

Poetry: Karl Shapiro, *V-Letter and Other Poems*

Music: Aaron Copeland, *Appalachian Spring*

1946

Editorial Writing: Hodding Carter, *Delta Democrat-Times*, Greenville, Mississippi

Novel: [no award]

Drama: Howard Lindsay and Russel Crouse, *State of the Union*

History: Arthur Meier Schlesinger, Jr., *The Age of Jackson*

Biography or Autobiography: Linnie Marsh Wolfe, *Son of the Wilderness*

Poetry: [no award]

Music: Leo Sowerby, *The Canticle of the Sun*

1947

Editorial Writing: William H. Grimes, *The Wall Street Journal*

Novel: Robert Penn Warren, *All the King's Men*

Drama: [no award]

History: James Phinney Baxter 3rd, *Scientists Against Time*

Biography or Autobiography: William Allen White, *The Autobiography of William Allen White*

Poetry: Robert Lowell, *Lord Weary's Castle*

Music: Charles Ives, *Symphony No. 3*

1948

Editorial Writing: Virginius Dabney, *Richmond Times-Dispatch*

Novel: James Michener, *Tales of the South Pacific*

Drama: Tennessee Williams, *A Streetcar Named Desire*

History: Bernard Devoto, *Across the Wide Missouri*

Biography or Autobiography: Margaret Clapp, *Forgotten First Citizen: John Bigelow*

Poetry: W. H. Auden, *The Age of Anxiety*

Music: Walter Piston, *Symphony No. 3*

1949

Editorial Writing: Herbert Elliston, *Washington Post*; John H. Crider, *Boston Herald*

Novel: James Gould Cozzens, *Guard of Honor*

Drama: Arthur Miller, *Death of a Salesman*

History: Roy Franklin Nichols, *The Disruption of American Democracy*

Biography or Autobiography: Robert E. Sherwood, *Roosevelt and Hopkins*

Poetry: Peter Viereck, *Terror and Decorum*

Music: Virgil Thompson, *Louisiana Story* (soundtrack)

1950

Editorial Writing: Carl M. Saunders, *Jackson* (Mississippi) *Citizen Patriot*

Novel: A. B. Guthrie, Jr., *The Way West*

Drama: Richard Rodgers, Oscar Hammerstein II, and Joshua Logan, *South Pacific*

History: Oliver W. Larkin, *Art and Life in America*

Biography or Autobiography: Samuel Flagg Bemis, *John Quincy Adams and the Foundations of American Foreign Policy*

Poetry: Gwendolyn Brooks, *Annie Allen*

Music: Gian-Carlo Menotti, *The Consul*

1951

Editorial Writing: William Harry Fitzpatrick, *New Orleans States*

Novel: Conrad Richter, *The Town*

Drama: [no award]

History: R. Carlyle Buley, *The Old Northwest, Pioneer Period 1815–1840*

Biography or Autobiography: Margaret Louise Colt, *John C. Calhoun: American Portrait*

Poetry: Carl Sandburg, *Complete Poems*

Music: Douglas S. Moore, *Giants in the Earth*

1952

Editorial Writing: Louis Lacoss, *St. Louis Globe Democrat*

Novel: Herman Wouk, *The Caine Mutiny*

Drama: Joseph Kramm, *The Shrike*

History: Oscar Handlin, *The Uprooted*

Biography or Autobiography: Merlo J. Pusey, *Charles Evans Hughes*

Poetry: Marianne Moore, *Collected Poems*

Music: Gail Kubik, *Symphony Concertante*

1953

Editorial Writing: Vermont Connecticut Royster, *The Wall Street Journal*

Novel: Ernest Hemingway, *The Old Man and the Sea*

Drama: William Inge, *Picnic*

History: George Dangerfield, *The Era of Good Feelings*

Biography or Autobiography: David J. Mays, *Edmund Pendleton 1721–1803*

Poetry: Archibald MacLeish, *Collected Poems 1917–1952*

Music: [no award]

1954

Editorial Writing: Don Murray, *Boston Herald*

Novel: [no award]

Drama: John Patrick, *The Teahouse of the August Moon*

History: Bruce Catton, *A Stillness at Appomattox*

Biography or Autobiography: Charles A. Lindbergh, *The Spirit of St. Louis*

Poetry: Theodore Roethke, *The Waking*

Music: Quincy Porter, *Concerto for Two Pianos and Orchestra*

1955

Editorial Writing: Royce Howes, *Detroit Free Press*

Novel: William Faulkner, *A Fable*

Drama: Tennessee Williams, *Cat on a Hot Tin Roof*

History: Paul Horgan, *Great River: The Rio Grande in North American History*

Biography or Autobiography: William S. White, *The Taft Story*

Poetry: Wallace Stevens, *Collected Poems*

Music: Gian-Carlo Menotti, *The Saint of Bleecker Street*

1956

Editorial Writing: Lauren K. Soth, *Register and Tribune*, Des Moines, Iowa

Novel: Mackinlay Kantor, *Andersonville*

Drama: Albert Hackett and Frances Goodrich, *The Diary of Anne Frank*

History: Richard Hofstadter, *The Age of Reform*

Biography or Autobiography: Talbot Faulkner
Hamlin, *Benjamin Henry Latrobe*
Poetry: Elizabeth Bishop, *Poems – North and
South*
Music: Ernst Toch, *Symphony No. 3*

1957
Editorial Writing: Buford Boone, *Tuscaloosa*
(Alabama) *News*
Novel: [no award]
Drama: Eugene O'Neill, *Long Day's Journey
Into Night*
History: George F. Kennan, *Russia Leaves the
War: Soviet-American Relations, 1917–1920*
Biography or Autobiography: John F. Kennedy,
Profiles in Courage
Poetry: Richard Wilbur, *Things of This World*
Music: Norman Dello Joio, *Meditation on
Ecclesiastics*

1958
Editorial Writing: Harry S. Ashmore, *Arkansas
Gazette*
Novel: James Agee, *A Death in the Family*
Drama: Ketti Frings, *Look Homeward, Angel*
History: Bray Hammond, *Banks and Politics*
Biography or Autobiography: Douglas Southall
Freeman, *George Washington (Volumes I -
VI)*; John Alexander Carroll and Mary Wells
Ashworth, *George Washington (Volume VIII)*
Poetry: Robert Penn Warren, *Promises: Poems
1954-1956*
Music: Samuel Barner, *Vanessa*

1959
Editorial Writing: Ralph McGill, *Atlanta*
(Georgia) *Constitution*
Novel: Robert Lewis Taylor, *The Travels of
Jaimie McPheeters*
Drama: Archibald MacLeish, *J. B.*
History: Leonard D. White and Jean Schneider,
The Republican Era: 1869–1901
Biography or Autobiography: Arthur Walworth,
Woodrow Wilson, American Prophet
Poetry: Stanley Kunitz, *Selected Poems
1928–1958*
Music: John LaMontaine, *Concerto for Piano
and Orchestra*

1960
Editorial Writing: Lenoir Chambers, *Norfolk
Virginian-Pilot*

Novel: Allen Drury, *Advise and Consent*
Drama: Jerome Weidman, George Abbott,
Jerry Bock and Sheldon Harnick, *Fiorello!*
History: Margaret Leech, *In the Days of
McKinley*
Biography or Autobiography: Samuel Eliot
Morison, *John Paul Jones*
Poetry: W. D. Snodgrass, *Heart's Needle*
Music: Elliot Carter, *Second String Quartet*

1961
Editorial Writing: William J. Dorvillier, *San
Juan* (Puerto Rico) *Star*
Novel: Harper Lee, *To Kill a Mockingbird*
Drama: Tad Mosel, *All the Way Home*
History: Herbert Feis, *Between War and Peace:
The Postdam Conference*
Biography or Autobiography: David Donald,
*Charles Sumner and the Coming of the Civil
War*
Poetry: Phyllis McGinley, *Times Three: Selected
Verse From Three Decades*
Music: Walter Piston, *Symphony No. 7*

1962
Editorial Writing: Thomas M. Storke, *Santa
Barbara* (California) *News-Press*
Novel: Edwin O'Connor, *The Edge of Sadness*
Drama: Frank Loesser and Abe Burrows,
*How to Succeed in Business Without Really
Trying*
History: Lawrence H. Gipson, *The Triumphant
Empire: Thunder-Clouds Gather in the West
1763–1766*
Biography or Autobiography: [no award]
Poetry: Alan Dugan, *Poems*
Music: Robert Ward, *The Crucible*

1963
Editorial Writing: Ira B. Harkley, Jr., *Pascagoula*
(Mississippi) *Chronicle*
Novel: William Faulkner, *The Reivers*
Drama: [no award]
History: Constance McLaughlin Green,
Washington, Village and Capital. 1800–1878
Biography or Autobiography: Leon Edel, *Henry
James*
Poetry: William Carlos Williams, *Pictures from
Breughel*
Music: Samuel Barber, *Piano Concerto No. 1*

1964

Editorial Writing: Hazel Brannon Smith, *Lexington* (Mississippi) *Advertiser*

Novel: [no award]

Drama: [no award]

History: Sumner Chilton Powell, *Puritan Village: The Formation of a New England Town*

Biography or Autobiography: Walter Jackson Bate, *John Keats*

Poetry: Louis Simpson, *At the End of the Open Road*

Music: [no award]

1965

Editorial Writing: John R. Harrison, *Gainesville* (Florida) *Sun*

Novel: Shirley Ann Grau, *The Keepers of the House*

Drama: Frank D. Gilroy, *The Subject Was Roses*

History: Irwin Unger, *The Greenback Era*

Biography or Autobiography: Ernest Samuels, *Henry Adams*

Poetry: John Berryman, *77 Dream Songs*

Music: [no award]

1966

Editorial Writing: Robert Lasch, *St. Louis Post-Dispatch*

Novel: Katherine Anne Porter, *Collected Stories*

Drama: [no award]

History: Perry Miller, *The Life of the Mind in America*

Biography or Autobiography: Arthur M. Schlesinger, Jr., *A Thousand Days*

Poetry: Richard Eberhart, *Selected Poems*

Music: Leslie Bassett, *Variations for Orchestra*

1967

Editorial Writing: Eugene Patterson, *Atlanta Constitution*

Novel: Bernard Malamud, *The Fixer*

Drama: Edward Albee, *A Delicate Balance*

History: William H. Goetzmann, *Exploration and Empire: The Explorer and the Scientist in the Winning of the American West*

Biography or Autobiography: Justin Kaplan, *Mr. Clemens and Mark Twain*

Poetry: Anne Sexton, *Live or Die*

Music: Leon Kirchner, *Quarter No. 3*

1968

Editorial Writing: John S. Knight, *Knight Newspapers*

Novel: William Styron, *The Confessions of Nat Turner*

Drama: [no award]

History: Bernard Bailyn, *The Ideological Origins of the American Revolution*

Biography or Autobiography: George E. Kennan, *Memoirs*

Poetry: Anthony Hecht, *The Hard Hours*

Music: George Crumb, *Echoes of Time and the River*

1969

Editorial Writing: Paul Greenberg, *Pine Bluff* (Arkansas) *Commercial*

Novel: N. Scott Momaday, *House Made of Dawn*

Drama: Howard Sackler, *The Great White Hope*

History: Leonard W. Levy, *Origins of the Fifth Amendment*

Biography or Autobiography: Benjamin Lawrence Reid, *The Man from New York: John Quinn and His Friends*

Poetry: George Oppen, *Of Being Numerous*

Music: Karel Husa, *String Quartet No. 3*

1970

Editorial Writing: Philip L. Geyelin, *Washington Post*

Novel: Jean Stafford, *Collected Stories*

Drama: Charles Gordone, *No Place To Be Somebody*

History: Dean Acheson, *Present at the Creation: My Years in the State Department*

Biography or Autobiography: T. Harry Williams, *Huey Long*

Poetry: Richard Howard, *Untitled Subjects*

Music: Charles Wuorinen, *Time's Encomium*

1971

Editorial Writing: Horance G. Davis, Jr., *Gainesville* (Florida) *Sun*

Novel: [no award]

Drama: Paul Zindel, *The Effect of Gamma Rays on Man-in-the-Moon Marigolds*

History: Macgregor Burns, *Roosevelt: The Soldier of Freedom*

Biography or Autobiography: Lawrance Thompson, *Robert Frost: The Years of Triumph, 1915–1938*

Poetry: William S. Merwin, *The Carrier of Ladders*

Music: Mario Davidovsky, *Synchronisms No. 6 for Piano and Electronic Sound*

1972

Editorial Writing: John Strohmeyer, *Bethlehem (Pennsylvania) Globe-Times*

Novel: Wallace Stegner, *Angle of Repose*

Drama: [no award]

History: Carl N. Degler, *Neither Black Nor White*

Biography or Autobiography: Joseph P. Lash, *Eleanor and Franklin*

Poetry: James Wright, *Collected Poems*

Music: Jacob Druckman, *Windows*

1973

Editorial Writing: Roger B. Linscott, *Berkshire Eagle*, Pittsfield, Massachusetts

Novel: Eudora Welty, *The Optimist's Daughter*

Drama: Jason Miller, *That Championship Season*

History: Michael Kammen, *People in Paradox: An Inquiry Concerning the Origins of American Civilization*

Biography or Autobiography: W. A. Swanberg, *Luce and His Empire*

Poetry: Maxine Kumin, *Up Country*

Music: Elliot Carter, *String Quartet No. 3*

1974

Editorial Writing: F. Gilman Spencer, *The Trentonian*, Trenton, New Jersey

Novel: [no award]

Drama: [no award]

History: Daniel J. Boorstein, *The Americans: The Democratic Experience*

Biography or Autobiography: Louis Sheaffer, *O'Neill, Son and Artist*

Poetry: Robert Lowell, *The Dolphin*

Music: Donald Martino, *Notturno*

1975

Editorial Writing: John Daniell Maurice, Charleston (West Virginia) *Daily Mail*

Novel: Michael Shaara, *The Killer Angels*

Drama: Edward Albee, *Seascape*

History: Dumas Malone, *Jefferson and His Time, Vols. I–V*

Biography or Autobiography: Robert Caro, *The Power Broker: Robert Moses and the Fall of New York*

Poetry: Gary Snyder, *Turtle Island*

Music: Dominick Argento, *From the Diary of Virginia Woolf*

1976

Editorial Writing: Philip P. Kerby, *Los Angeles Times*

Novel: Saul Bellow, *Humboldt's Gift*

Drama: James Kirkwood, Nicholas Dante, Edward Kleban, and Marvin Hamlisch, *A Chorus Line*

History: Paul Horgan, *Lamy of Santa Fe*

Biography or Autobiography: R. W. B. Lewis, *Edith Wharton: A Biography*

Poetry: John Ashbery, *Self-Portrait in a Convex Mirror*

Music: Ned Rorem, *Air Music*

1977

Editorial Writing: Warren L. Lerude, Foster Church, and Norman F. Cardoza, (Nevada) *Evening Gazette* and *Nevada State Journal*

Novel: [no award]

Drama: Michael Cristofer, *The Shadow Box*

History: David M. Potter, *The Impending Crisis, 1841–1867*

Biography or Autobiography: John E. Mack, *A Prince of Our Disorder: The Life of T. E. Lawrence*

Poetry: James Merrill, *Divine Comedies*

Music: Richard Wernick, *Visions of Terror and Wonder*

1978

Editorial Writing: Meg Greenfield, *The Washington Post*

Novel: James Alan McPherson, *Elbow Room*

Drama: Donald L. Coburn, *The Gin Game*

History: Alfred D. Chandler, Jr., *The Visible Hand: The Managerial Revolution in American Business*

Biography or Autobiography: Walter Jackson Bate, *Samuel Johnson*

Poetry: Howard Nemerov, *Collected Poems*

Music: Michael Colgrass, *Deja Vu for Percussion Quartet and Orchestra*

1979

Editorial Writing: Edwin M. Yoder, Jr., *The Washington Star*
Novel: John Cheever, *The Stories of John Cheever*
Drama: Sam Shepherd, *Buried Child*
History: Don E. Fehrenbacher, *The Dred Scott Case*
Biography or Autobiography: Leonard Baker, *Days of Sorrow and Pain: Leo Baeck and the Berlin Jews*
Poetry: Robert Penn Warren, *Now and Then*
Music: Joseph Schwantner, *Aftertones of Infinity*

1980

Editorial Writing: Robert L. Bartley, *The Wall Street Journal*
Novel: Norman Mailer, *The Executioner's Song*
Drama: Lanford Wilson, *Talley's Folly*
History: Leon F. Litwack, *Been in the Storm So Long*
Biography or Autobiography: Edmund Morris, *Theodore Roosevelt*
Poetry: Donald Justice, *Selected Poems*
Music: David Del Tredici, *In Memory of a Summer Day*

1981

Editorial Writing: [no award]
Novel: John Kennedy Toole, *A Confederacy of Dunces*
Drama: Beth Henley, *Crimes of the Heart*
History: Lawrence A. Cremin, *American Education: The National Experience, 1783–1876*
Biography or Autobiography: Robert K. Massie, *Peter the Great: His Life and World*
Poetry: James Schuyler, *The Morning of the Poem*
Music: [no award]

1982

Editorial Writing: Jack Rosenthal, *The New York Times*
Novel: John Updike, *Rabbit Is Rich*
Drama: Charles Fuller, *A Soldier's Play*
History: C. Vann Woodward (ed.), *Mary Chesnut's Civil War*
Biography or Autobiography: William McFeely, *Grant: A Biography*
Poetry: Sylvia Plath, *The Collected Poems*
Music: Roger Sessions, *Concerto for Orchestra*

1983

Editorial Writing: No authors named, *The Miami Herald* Editorial Board
Novel: Alice Walker, *The Color Purple*
Drama: Marsha Norman, *'Night, Mother*
History: Rhys L. Isaac, *The Transformation of Virginia, 1740–1790*
Biography or Autobiography: Russell Baker, *Growing Up*
Poetry: Galway Kinnell, *Selected Poems*
Music: Ellen Taaffe Zwilich, *Symphony No. 1 (Three Movements for Orchestra)*

1984

Editorial Writing: Albert Scardino, *The Georgia Gazette*, Savannah
Novel: William Kennedy, *Ironweed*
Drama: David Mamet, *Glengarry Glen Ross*
History: [no award]
Biography or Autobiography: Louis R. Harlan, *Booker T. Washington*
Poetry: Mary Oliver, *American Primitive*
Music: Bernard Rands, *"Canti del Sole" for Tenor and Orchestra*

1985

Editorial Writing: Richard Aregood, *The Philadelphia Daily News*
Novel: Alison Lurie, *Foreign Affairs*
Drama: James Lapine, Stephen Sondheim, *Sunday in the Park With George*
History: Thomas K. McCraw, *Prophets of Regulation*
Biography or Autobiography: Kenneth Silverman, *The Life and Times of Cotton Mather*
Poetry: Carolyn Kizer, *Yin*
Music: Stephen Albert, *Symphony, River Run*

1986

Editorial Writing: Jack Fuller, *Chicago Tribune*
Novel: Larry McMurtry, *Lonesome Dove*
Drama: [no award]
History: Walter A. McDougall, *The Heavens and the Earth*
Biography or Autobiography: Elizabeth Frank, *Louise Bogan: A Portrait*
Poetry: Henry Taylor, *The Flying Change*
Music: George Perle, *Wind Quintet IV*

1987

Editorial Writing: Jonathan Freedman, *The Tribune*, San Diego, California
Novel: Peter Taylor, *A Summons to Memphis*
Drama: August Wilson, *Fences*
History: Bernard Bailyn, *Voyagers to the West*
Biography or Autobiography: David J. Garrow, *Bearing the Cross*
Poetry: Rita Dove, *Thomas and Beulah*
Music: John Harbison, *The Flight into Egypt*

1988

Editorial Writing: Jane Healy, *The Orlando Sentinel*
Novel: Toni Morrison, *Beloved*
Drama: Alfred Uhry, *Driving Miss Daisy*
History: Robert V. Bruce, *The Launching of Modern American Science 1846–1876*
Biography or Autobiography: David Herbert Donald, *Look Homeward: A Life of Thomas Wolfe*
Poetry: William Meredith, *Partial Accounts*
Music: William Bolcom, *12 New Etudes for Piano*

1989

Editorial Writing: Louis Wille, *The Chicago Tribune*
Novel: Anne Tyler, *Breathing Lessons*
Drama: Wendy Wasserstein, *The Heidi Chronicles*
History: James M. McPherson, *Battle Cry of Freedom*
Biography or Autobiography: Richard Ellmann, *Oscar Wilde*
Poetry: Richard Wilbur, *New and Collected Poems*
Music: Roger Reynolds, *Whispers Out of Time*

1990

Editorial Writing: Thomas J. Hylton, *The Pottstown* (Pennsylvania) *Mercury*
Novel: Oscar Hijuelos, *The Mambo Kings Play Songs of Love*
Drama: August Wilson, *The Piano Lesson*
History: Stanley Karnow, *In Our Image*
Biography or Autobiography: Sebastian De Grazia, *Machiavelli in Hell*
Poetry: Charles Simic, *The World Doesn't End*
Music: Mel Powell, *"Duplicates": A Concerto for Two Pianos and Orchestra*

1991

Editorial Writing: Ron Casey, Harold Jackson and Joey Kennedy, *The Birmingham* (Alabama) *News*
Novel: John Updike, *Rabbit at Rest*
Drama: Neil Simon, *Lost in Yonkers*
History: Laurel Thatcher Ulrich, *A Midwife's Tale*
Biography or Autobiography: Steven Naifeh and Gregory White Smith, *Jackson Pollack*
Poetry: Mona Van Duyn, *Near Changes*
Music: Shulamit Ran, *Symphony*

1992

Editorial Writing: Maria Henson, *Lexington* (Kentucky) *Herald-Leader*
Novel: Jane Smiley, *A Thousand Acres*
Drama: Robert Schenkkan, *The Kentucky Cycle*
History: Mark E. Neely, Jr., *The Fate of Liberty: Abraham Lincoln and Civil Liberties*
Biography or Autobiography: Lewis B. Puller, Jr., *Fortunate Son: The Healing of a Vietnam Vet*
Poetry: James Tate, *Selected Poems*
Music: Wayne Peterson, *The Face of the Night, The Heart of the Dark*

1993

Editorial Writing: [no award]
Novel: Robert Olen Butler, *A Good Scent from a Strange Mountain*
Drama: Tony Kushner, *Angels in America: Millennium Approaches*
History: Gordon S. Wood, *The Radicalism of the American Revolution*
Biography or Autobiography: David McCullough, *Truman*
Poetry: Louise Gluck, *The Wild Iris*
Music: Christopher Rouse, *Trombone Concerto*

1994

Editorial Writing: R. Bruce Dold, *Chicago Tribune*
Novel: E. Annie Proulx, *The Shipping News*
Drama: Edward Albee, *Three Tall Women*
History: [no award]
Biography or Autobiography: David Levering Lewis, *W. E. B. Du Bois: Biography of a Race 1868–1919*
Poetry: Yusef Komunyakaa, *Neon Vernacular: New and Selected Poems*
Music: Gunther Schuller, *Of Reminiscences and Reflections*

1995

Editorial Writing: Jeffrey Good, *St. Petersburg* (Florida) *Times*

Novel: Carol Shields, *The Stone Diaries*

Drama: Horton Foote, *The Young Man from Atlanta*

History: Doris Kearns Goodwin, *No Ordinary Time: Franklin and Eleanor Roosevelt: The Home Front in World War II*

Biography or Autobiography: Joan D. Hedrick, *Harriet Beecher Stowe: A Life*

Poetry: Philip Levine, *The Simple Truth*

Music: Morton Gould, *Stringmusic*

1996

Editorial Writing: Robert B. Semple, Jr., *The New York Times*

Novel: Richard Ford, *Independence Day*

Drama: Jonathan Larson, *Rent*

History: Alan Taylor, *William Cooper's Town: Power and Persuasion on the Frontier of the Early American Republic*

Biography or Autobiography: Jack Miles, *God: A Biography*

Poetry: Jorie Graham, *The Dream of the Unified Field*

Music: George Walker, *Lilacs, for voice and orchestra*

1997

Editorial Writing: Michael Gartner, *The Daily Tribune*, Ames, Iowa

Novel: Steven Millhauser, *Martin Dressler: The Tale of an American Dreamer*

Drama: [no award]

History: Jack N. Rakove, *Original Meanings: Politics and Ideas in the Making of the Constitution*

Biography or Autobiography: Frank McCourt, *Angela's Ashes*

Poetry: Lisel Mueller, *Alive Together: New and Selected Poems*

Music: Wynton Marsalis, *Blood on the Fields*

1998

Editorial Writing: Bernard L. Stein, *The Riverdale* (New York) *Press*

Novel: Philip Roth, *American Pastoral*

Drama: Paula Vogel, *How I Learned to Drive*

History: Edward J. Larson, *Summer for the Gods: The Scopes Trial and America's Continuing Debate Over Science and Religion*

Biography or Autobiography: Katharine Graham, *Personal History*

Poetry: Charles Wright, *Black Zodiac*

Music: Aaron Jay Kernis, *String Quartet No. 2, Musica Instrumentalis*

1999

Editorial Writing: *New York Daily News* Editorial Board

Novel: Michael Cunningham, *The Hours*

Drama: Margaret Edson, *Wit*

History: Edwin G. Burrows and Mike Wallace, *Gotham: A History of New York City to 1898*

Biography or Autobiography: A. Scott Berg, *Lindbergh*

Poetry: Mark Strand, *Blizzard of One*

Music: Melinda Wagner, *Concert for Flute, Strings and Percussion*

2000

Editorial Writing: John C. Bersia, *The Orlando Sentinel*

Novel: Jhumpa Lahiri, *Interpreter of Maladies*

Drama: Donald Margulies, *Dinner with Friends*

History: David M. Kennedy, *Freedom from Fear: The American People in Depression and War 1929–1945*

Biography or Autobiography: Stacy Schiff, *Vera (Mrs. Vladimir Nabokov)*

Poetry: C. K. Williams, *Repair*

2001

Editorial Writing: David Moats, *Rutland* (Vermont) *Herald*

Novel: Michael Chabon, *The Amazing Adventures of Kavalier and Clay*

Drama: David Auburn, *Proof*

History: Joseph J. Ellis, *Founding Brothers: The Revolutionary Generation*

Biography or Autobiography: David Levering Lewis, *W. E. B. Du Bois: The Fight for Equality and the American Century, 1919–1963*

Poetry: Stephen Dunn, *Different Hours*

⊙ Bates, J. Douglas. *The Pulitzer Prize: The Inside Story of America's Most Prestigious Award.* New York: Carol Publishing, 1991.

Brennan, Elizabeth A., and Elizabeth C. Clarage. *Who's Who of Pulitzer Prize Winners.* Phoenix: Oryx, 1999.

The Pulitzer Prize Organization. "Pulitzer Prize Archive," www.pulitzer.org/Archive/archive.html

Booker Prize (1969–2000)

The Booker Prize was established in 1968 by Booker McConnell, a multinational company, for achievement in an English-language novel. Contestants are authors from the United Kingdom, the Commonwealth countries, the Republic of Ireland, and South Africa. Authors and titles are listed below by year.

Year	Recipient	Year	Recipient
1969	P. H. Newby, *Something to Answer For*	1985	Keri Hulme, *The Bone People*
1970	Bernice Rubens, *The Elected Member*	1986	Kingsley Amis, *The Old Devils*
1971	V. S. Naipaul, *In a Free State*	1987	Penelope Lively, *Moon Tiger*
1972	John Berger, *G*	1988	Peter Carey, *Oscar and Lucinda*
1973	J. G. Farrell, *The Siege of Krishnapur*; Stanley Middleton, *Holiday*	1989	Kazuo Ishiguro, *The Remains of the Day*
		1990	A. S. Byatt, *Possession*
1974	Nadine Gordimer, *The Conservationist*	1991	Ben Okri, *The Famished Road*
1975	Ruth Prawer Jhabvala, *Heat and Dust*	1992	Michael Ondaatje, *The English Patient*; Barry Unsworth, *Sacred Hunger*
1976	David Storey, *Saville*		
1977	Paul Scott, *Staying On*	1993	Roddy Doyle, *Paddy Clarke Ha Ha Ha*
1978	Iris Murdoch, *The Sea, The Sea*	1994	James Kelman, *How Late It Was, How Late*
1979	Penelope Fitzgerald, *Offshore*		
1980	William Golding, *Rites of Passage*	1995	Pat Barker, *The Ghost Road*
1981	Salman Rushdie, *Midnight's Children*	1996	Graham Swift, *Last Orders*
1982	Thomas Keneally, *Schindler's Ark*	1997	Arundhati Roy, *The God of Small Things*
1983	J. M. Coetzee, *The Life and Times of Michael K.*	1998	Ian McEwan, *Amsterdam*
		1999	J. M. Coetzee, *Disgrace*
1984	Anita Brookner, *Hotel Du Lac*	2000	Margaret Atwood, *The Blind Assassin*

⊙ The Booker Prize. "Previous Winners," www.bookerprize.co.uk/site/fiction/previous/previousfset.html
Booker McConnell Prize Pages. "Winning and Shortlisted Titles by Year," www.utc.edu/~engldept/booker/booker.htm

Templeton Award for Progress in Religion (1973–2001)

The Templeton Award for Progress in Religion was established in 1972 by financier John Marks Templeton (1912–) on the grounds that the Nobel Prizes exclude recognition for advances in spirituality. The Templeton Award is currently the world's largest annual monetary award of $945,000.

Year	Recipient	Year	Recipient
1973	Mother Teresa	1982	Rev. Dr. Billy Graham
1974	Brother Roger	1983	Aleksandr Solzhenitsyn
1975	Sir Sarvepalli Radhakrishnan	1984	The Rev. Michael Bourdeaux
1976	Leon Joseph Cardinal Suenens	1985	Sir Alister Hardy
1977	Chiara Lubich	1986	Rev. Dr. James McCord
1978	Professor Thomas F. Torrance	1987	Rev. Professor Stanley L. Jaki
1979	Rev. Nikkyo Niwano	1988	Dr. Inamullah Khan
1980	Professor Ralph Wendell Burhoe	1989	awarded jointly to The Very Reverend Lord MacLeod and Professor Carl Friedrich von Weizsacker
1981	Dame Cecily Saunders		

Year	Recipient	Year	Recipient
1990	awarded jointly to Baba Amte and Professor L. Charles Birch	1996	William R. "Bill" Bright
1991	The Rt. Hon. Lord Jakobovits	1997	Pandurang Shastri Athavale
1992	Rev. Dr. Kyung-Chik Han	1998	Sir Sigmund Sternberg
1993	Charles W. Colson	1999	Ian G. Barbour
1994	Michael Novak	2000	Freeman Dyson
1995	Paul Charles William Davies	2001	Arthur Peacocke

⊙ Forker, Wilbert, ed. *The Templeton Foundation Prize for Progress in Religion.* Edinburgh: Scottish Academic Press, 1989.

John Templeton Foundation. "The Templeton Prize for Progress in Religion," www.templetonprize.org

The Emmy Awards (1950–2000)

The Emmy Awards were established in 1948 by the National Academy of Television Arts and Sciences for excellence in television performance and production. The award's name is a variation of Immy, a term for an early image orthicon camera tube. While the categories' names have changed with time, they have always included awards for acting achievement and for outstanding programs. Once awarded to programs broadcast within a calendar year, the Emmys are now awarded on the basis of the September-to-August television season. Winners in each major category are listed below by year.

1950
 Best Drama: *Pulitzer Prize Playhouse*
 Best Actor: Alan Young
 Best Actress: Gertude Berg

1951
 Best Comedy: *The Red Skelton Show*
 Best Drama: *Studio One*
 Best Actor: Sid Caesar
 Best Actress: Imogene Coca

1952
 Best Comedy: *I Love Lucy*
 Best Drama: *Robert Montgomery Presents*
 Best Comedy Actor: Jimmy Durante
 Best Comedy Actress: Lucille Ball
 Best Drama Actor: Thomas Mitchell
 Best Drama Actress: Helen Hayes

1953
 Best Comedy: *I Love Lucy*
 Best Drama: *The U.S. Steel Hour*
 Best Actor: Donald O'Connor, *Colgate Comedy Hour*
 Best Actress: Eve Arden, *Our Miss Brooks*

1954
 Best Comedy: *I Love Lucy*
 Best Drama: *The U.S. Steel Hour*
 Best Actor: Danny Thomas, *Make Room for Daddy*
 Best Actress: Loretta Young, *The Loretta Young Show*

1955
 Best Comedy: *The Phil Silvers Show*
 Best Drama: *Producers' Showcase*
 Best Actor: Phil Silvers, *The Phil Silvers Show*
 Best Actress: Lucille Ball, *I Love Lucy*

1956
 Best Comedy: *The Phil Silvers Show*
 Best Drama: *Producer's Showcase*
 Best Comedy Actor: Sid Caesar, *Caesar's Hour*
 Best Comedy Actress: Nanette Fabray, *Caesar's Hour*
 Best Drama Actor: Robert Young, *Father Knows Best*
 Best Drama Actress: Loretta Young, *The Loretta Young Show*

1957

Best Comedy: *The Phil Silvers Show*
Best Drama: *Gunsmoke*
Best Actor: Robert Young, *Father Knows Best*
Best Actress: Jane Wyatt, *Father Knows Best*

1958–1959

Best Comedy: *The Jack Benny Show*
Best Drama: *Playhouse 90, Alcoa-Goodyear Theatre*
Best Comedy Actor: Jack Benny, *The Jack Benny Show*
Best Comedy Actress: Jane Wyatt, *Father Knows Best*
Best Drama Actor: Raymond Burr, *Perry Mason*
Best Drama Actress: Loretta Young, *The Loretta Young Show*

1959–60

Best Comedy: *The Art Carney Special*
Best Drama: *Playhouse 90*
Best Actor: Robert Stack, *The Untouchables*
Best Actress: Jane Wyatt, *Father Knows Best*

1960–61

Best Comedy: *The Jack Benny Show*
Best Drama: *Macbeth, [Hallmark Hall of Fame]*
Best Actor: Raymond Burr, *Perry Mason*
Best Actress: Barbara Stanwyck, *The Barbara Stanwyck Show*

1961–62

Best Comedy: *The Bob Newhart Show*
Best Drama: *The Defenders*
Best Actor: E. G. Marshall, *The Defenders*
Best Actress: Shirley Booth, *Hazel*

1962–63

Best Comedy: *The Dick Van Dyke Show*
Best Drama: *The Defenders*
Best Actor: E. G. Marshall, *The Defenders*
Best Actress: Shirley Booth, *Hazel*

1963–64

Best Comedy: *The Dick Van Dyke Show*
Best Drama: *The Defenders*
Best Actor: Dick Van Dyke, *The Dick Van Dyke Show*
Best Actress: Mary Tyler Moore, *The Dick Van Dyke Show*

1964–65

Best Comedy: *The Dick Van Dyke Show*

Best Drama: *The Magnificent Yankee* (Hallmark Hall of Fame)
Best Comedy Actor: Dick Van Dyke, *The Dick Van Dyke Show*
Best Comedy Actress: Barbra Streisand, *My Name Is Barbra*
Best Drama Actor: Alfred Lunt, *The Magnificent Yankee* (Hallmark Hall of Fame)
Best Drama Actress: Lynne Fontanne, *The Magnificent Yankee* (Hallmark Hall of Fame)

1965–66

Best Comedy: *The Dick Van Dyke Show*
Best Drama: *The Fugitive*
Best Comedy Actor: Dick Van Dyke, *The Dick Van Dyke Show*
Best Comedy Actress: Mary Tyler Moore, *The Dick Van Dyke Show*
Best Drama Actor: Bill Cosby, *I Spy*
Best Drama Actress: Barbara Stanwyck, *The Big Valley*

1966–67

Best Comedy: *The Monkees*
Best Drama: *Mission: Impossible*
Best Comedy Actor: Don Adams, *Get Smart*
Best Comedy Actress: Lucille Ball, *The Lucy Show*
Best Drama Actor: Bill Cosby, *I Spy*
Best Drama Actress: Barbara Bain, *Mission: Impossible*

1967–68

Best Comedy: *Get Smart*
Best Drama: *Mission: Impossible*
Best Comedy Actor: Don Adams, *Get Smart*
Best Comedy Actress: Lucille Ball, *The Lucy Show*
Best Drama Actor: Milburn Stone, *Gunsmoke*
Best Drama Actress: Barbara Bain, *Mission: Impossible*

1968–69

Best Comedy: *Get Smart*
Best Drama: *NET Playhouse*
Best Comedy Actor: Don Adams, *Get Smart*
Best Comedy Actress: Hope Lange, *The Ghost and Mrs. Muir*
Best Drama Actor: Carl Betz, *Judd, For the Defense*
Best Drama Actress: Barbara Bain, *Mission: Impossible*

1969–70

Best Comedy: My World And Welcome To It
Best Drama: Marcus Welby, M.D.
Best Comedy Actor: William Windom, *My World and Welcome To It*
Best Comedy Actress: Hope Lange, *The Ghost and Mrs. Muir*
Best Drama Actor: Robert Young, *Marcus Welby, M.D.*
Best Drama Actress: Susan Hampshire, *The Forsythe Saga*

1970–71

Best Comedy: All in the Family
Best Drama: The Senator: The Bold Ones
Best Comedy Actor: Jack Klugman, *The Odd Couple*
Best Comedy Actress: Jean Stapleton, *All in the Family*
Best Drama Actor: Hal Holbrook, *The Senator: The Bold Ones*
Best Drama Actress: Susan Hampshire, *The First Churchills* (Masterpiece Theatre)

1971–72

Best Comedy: All in the Family
Best Drama: Elizabeth R (Masterpiece Theatre)
Best Comedy Actor: Carroll O'Connor, *All in the Family*
Best Comedy Actress: Jean Stapleton, *All in the Family*
Best Drama Actor: Peter Falk, *Columbo*
Best Drama Actress: Glenda Jackson, *Elizabeth R* (Masterpiece Theatre)

1972–73

Best Comedy: All in the Family
Best Drama: The Waltons
Best Comedy Actor: Jack Klugman, *The Odd Couple*
Best Comedy Actress: Mary Tyler Moore, *The Mary Tyler Moore Show*
Best Drama Actor: Richard Thomas, *The Waltons*
Best Drama Actress: Michael Learned, *The Waltons*

1973–74

Best Comedy: M*A*S*H

Best Drama: Upstairs, Downstairs (Masterpiece Theatre)
Best Comedy Actor: Alan Alda, *M*A*S*H*
Best Comedy Actress: Mary Tyler Moore, *The Mary Tyler Moore Show*
Best Drama Actor: Telly Savalas, *Kojak*
Best Drama Actress: Michael Learned, *The Waltons*

1974–75

Best Comedy: The Mary Tyler Moore Show
Best Drama: Upstairs, Downstairs (Masterpiece Theatre)
Best Comedy Actor: Tony Randall, *The Odd Couple*
Best Comedy Actress: Valerie Harper, *Rhoda*
Best Drama Actor: Robert Blake, *Baretta*
Best Drama Actress: Jean Marsh, *Upstairs, Downstairs* (Masterpiece Theatre)

1975–76

Best Comedy: The Mary Tyler Moore Show
Best Drama: Police Story
Best Comedy Actor: Jack Albertson, *Chico and the Man*
Best Comedy Actress: Mary Tyler Moore, *The Mary Tyler Moore Show*
Best Drama Actor: Peter Falk, *Columbo*
Best Drama Actress: Michael Learned, *The Waltons*

1976–77

Best Comedy: The Mary Tyler Moore Show
Best Drama: Upstairs, Downstairs (Masterpiece Theatre)
Best Comedy Actor: Carroll O'Connor, *All in the Family*
Best Comedy Actress: Beatrice Arthur, *Maude*
Best Drama Actor: James Garner, *The Rockford Files*
Best Drama Actress: Lindsay Wagner, *The Bionic Woman*

1977–78

Best Comedy: All in the Family
Best Drama: The Rockford Files
Best Comedy Actor: Carroll O'Connor, *All in the Family*

Best Comedy Actress: Jean Stapleton, *All in the Family*
Best Drama Actor: Ed Asner, *Lou Grant*
Best Drama Actress: Sada Thompson, *Family*

1978–79
Best Comedy: Taxi
Best Drama: Lou Grant
Best Comedy Actor: Carroll O'Connor, *All in the Family*
Best Comedy Actress: Ruth Gordon, *Taxi*
Best Drama Actor: Ron Leibman, *Kaz*
Best Drama Actress: Mariette Hartley, *The Incredible Hulk*

1979–80
Best Comedy: Taxi
Best Drama: Lou Grant
Best Comedy Actor: Richard Mulligan, *Soap*
Best Comedy Actress: Cathryn Damon, *Soap*
Best Drama Actor: Ed Asner, *Lou Grant*
Best Drama Actress: Barbara Bel Geddes, *Dallas*

1980–81
Best Comedy: Taxi
Best Drama: Hill Street Blues
Best Comedy Actor: Judd Hirsh, *Taxi*
Best Comedy Actress: Isabel Sanford, *The Jeffersons*
Best Drama Actor: Daniel J. Travanti, *Hill Street Blues*
Best Drama Actress: Barbara Babcock, *Hill Street Blues*

1981–82
Best Comedy: Barney Miller
Best Drama: Hill Street Blues
Best Comedy Actor: Alan Alda, *M*A*S*H*
Best Comedy Actress: Carol Kane, *Taxi*
Best Drama Actor: Daniel J. Travanti, *Hill Street Blues*
Best Drama Actress: Michael Learned, *Nurse*

1982–83
Best Comedy: Cheers
Best Drama: Hill Street Blues
Best Comedy Actor: Judd Hirsh, *Taxi*
Best Comedy Actress: Shelley Long, *Cheers*
Best Drama Actor: Ed Flanders, *St. Elsewhere*
Best Drama Actress: Tyne Daly, *Cagney and Lacey*

1983–84
Best Comedy: Cheers
Best Drama: Hill Street Blues
Best Comedy Actor: John Ritter, *Three's Company*
Best Comedy Actress: Jane Curtin, *Kate and Allie*
Best Drama Actor: Tom Selleck, *Magnum, P.I.*
Best Drama Actress: Tyne Daly, *Cagney and Lacey*

1984–85
Best Comedy: The Cosby Show
Best Drama: Cagney and Lacey
Best Comedy Actor: Robert Guillaume, *Benson*
Best Comedy Actress: Jane Curtin, *Kate and Allie*
Best Drama Actor: William Daniels, *St. Elsewhere*
Best Drama Actress: Tyne Daly, *Cagney and Lacey*

1985–86
Best Comedy: The Golden Girls
Best Drama: Cagney and Lacey
Best Comedy Actor: Michael J. Fox, *Family Ties*
Best Comedy Actress: Betty White, *The Golden Girls*
Best Drama Actor: William Daniels, *St. Elsewhere*
Best Drama Actress: Sharon Gless, *Cagney and Lacey*

1986–87
Best Comedy: The Golden Girls
Best Drama: L.A. Law
Best Comedy Actor: Michael J. Fox, *Family Ties*
Best Comedy Actress: Rue McClanahan, *The Golden Girls*
Best Drama Actor: Bruce Willis, *Moonlighting*
Best Drama Actress: Sharon Gless, *Cagney and Lacey*

1987–88
Best Comedy: The Wonder Years
Best Drama: thirtysomething
Best Comedy Actor: Michael J. Fox, *Family Ties*
Best Comedy Actress: Beatrice Arthur, *The Golden Girls*
Best Drama Actor: Richard Kiley, *A Year in the Life*
Best Drama Actress: Tyne Daly, *Cagney and Lacey*

1988–89
Best Comedy: Cheers
Best Drama: L.A. Law
Best Comedy Actor: Richard Mulligan, *Empty Nest*
Best Comedy Actress: Candice Bergen, *Murphy Brown*
Best Drama Actor: Carroll O'Connor, *In the Heat of the Night*
Best Drama Actress: Dana Delany, *China Beach*

1989–90
Best Comedy: Murphy Brown
Best Drama: L.A. Law
Best Comedy Actor: Ted Danson, *Cheers*
Best Comedy Actress: Candice Bergen, *Murphy Brown*
Best Drama Actor: Peter Falk, *Columbo*
Best Drama Actress: Patricia Wettig, *thirtysomething*

1990–91
Best Comedy: Cheers
Best Drama: L.A. Law
Best Comedy Actor: Burt Reynolds, *Evening Shade*
Best Comedy Actress: Kirstie Alley, *Cheers*
Best Drama Actor: James Earl Jones, *Gabriel's Fire*
Best Drama Actress: Patricia Wettig, *thirtysomething*

1991–92
Best Comedy: Murphy Brown
Best Drama: Northern Exposure
Best Comedy Actor: Craig T. Nelson, *Coach*
Best Comedy Actress: Candice Bergen, *Murphy Brown*
Best Drama Actor: Christopher Lloyd, *Avonlea*
Best Drama Actress: Dana Delany, *China Beach*

1992–93
Best Comedy: Seinfeld
Best Drama: Picket Fences
Best Comedy Actor: Ted Danson, *Cheers*
Best Comedy Actress: Roseanne Barr, *Roseanne*
Best Drama Actor: Tom Skerritt, *Picket Fences*
Best Drama Actress: Kathy Baker, *Picket Fences*

1993–94
Best Comedy: Frasier
Best Drama: Picket Fences
Best Comedy Actor: Kelsey Grammer, *Frasier*
Best Comedy Actress: Candice Bergen, *Murphy Brown*
Best Drama Actor: Dennis Franz, *NYPD Blue*
Best Drama Actress: Sela Ward, *Sisters*

1994–95
Best Comedy: Frasier
Best Drama: NYPD Blue
Best Comedy Actor: Kelsey Grammer, *Frasier*
Best Comedy Actress: Candice Bergen, *Murphy Brown*
Best Drama Actor: Mandy Patinkin, *Chicago Hope*
Best Drama Actress: Kathy Baker, *Picket Fences*

1995–96
Best Comedy: Frasier
Best Drama: ER
Best Comedy Actress: John Lithgow, *3rd Rock from the Sun*
Best Comedy Actor: Helen Hunt, *Mad About You*
Best Drama Actor: Dennis Franz, *NYPD Blue*
Best Drama Actress: Kathy Baker, *Picket Fences*

1996–97
Best Comedy: Frasier
Best Drama: Law and Order
Best Comedy Actor: John Lithgow, *3rd Rock From the Sun*
Best Comedy Actress: Helen Hunt, *Mad About You*
Best Drama Actor: Dennis Franz, *NYPD Blue*
Best Drama Actress: Gillian Anderson, *The X-Files*

1997–98
Best Comedy: Frasier
Best Drama: The Practice
Best Comedy Actor: Kelsey Grammer, *Frasier*
Best Comedy Actress: Helen Hunt, *Mad About You*

Best Drama Actor: Andre Braugher, *Homicide: Life on the Street*

Best Drama Actress: Christine Lahti, *Chicago Hope*

1998–99

Best Comedy: *Ally McBeal*

Best Drama: *The Practice*

Best Comedy Actor: John Lithgow, *3rd Rock from the Sun*

Best Comedy Actress: Helen Hunt, *Mad About You*

Best Drama Actor: Dennis Franz, *NYPD Blue*

Best Drama Actress: Edie Falco, *The Sopranos*

1999–2000

Best Comedy: *Will & Grace*

Best Drama: *The West Wing*

Best Comedy Actor: Michael J. Fox, *Spin City*

Best Comedy Actress: Patricia Heaton, *Everybody Loves Raymond*

Best Drama Actor: James Gandolfini, *The Sopranos*

Best Drama Actress: Sela Ward, *Once and Again*

⊙ Academy of Television Arts and Sciences. "Emmy Awards Index," www.emmys.tv/awards/index.htm

O'Neil, Thomas. *The Emmys: Star Wars, Showdowns, and the Supreme Test of TV's Best*. New York: Penguin, 1992.

Antoinette Perry Awards (Tonys) (1947–2001)

The Antoinette Perry Awards (the Tonys) were established by the American Theatre Wing in 1947 for distinguished achievement in American theater produced on Broadway. The award is named after Antoinette Perry (1888–1946), chairman of the board and secretary of the American Theatre Wing. The categories have evolved greatly over time, and categories are opened only if the Nomination Board considers there to be sufficiently excellent nominees in a particular year; the following list of winners reflects such anomalies.

1947

Play: [no award]

Actor: (tie) José Ferrer, *Cyrano de Bergerac*; Frederic March, *Years Ago*

Actress: (tie) Ingrid Bergman, *Joan of Lorraine*; Helen Hayes, *Happy Birthday*

Director: Eliza Kazan, *All My Sons*

Musical: [no award]

Actor: [no award]

Actress: [no award]

Director: [no award]

1948

Play: *Mister Roberts* (Thomas Heggen/Joshua Logan)

Actor: (triple) Henry Fonda, *Mister Roberts*; Paul Kelly, *Command Decision*; Basil Rathbone, *The Heiress*

Actress: (triple) Judith Anderson, *Medea*; Katharine Cornell, *Antony and Cleopatra*; Jessica Tandy, *A Streetcar Named Desire*

Director: [no award]

Musical: [no award]

Actor: Paul Hartman, *Angel in the Wings*

Actress: Grace Hartman, *Angel in the Wings*

Director: [no award]

1949

Play: *Death of a Saleman* (Arthur Miller)

Actor: Rex Harrison, *Anne of the Thousand Days*

Actress: Martita Hunt, *The Madwoman of Chaillot*

Director: Elia Kazan, *Death of a Salesman*

Musical: *Kiss Me, Kate* (Bella and Samuel Spewack/Cole Porter)

Actor: Ray Bolger, *Where's Charley?*

Actress: Nanette Fabray, *Love Life*

Director: [no award]

1950

Play: *The Cocktail Party* (T. S. Eliot)

Actor: Sidney Blackmer, *Come Back, Little Sheba*

Actress: Shirley Booth, *Come Back, Little Sheba*

Featured/Supporting Actor: [no award]

Featured/Supporting Actress: [no award]

Director: [no award]

Musical: *South Pacific* (Joshua Logan, Oscar Hammerstein II, Richard Rodgers)

Actor: Ezio Pinza, *South Pacific*

Actress: Mary Martin, *South Pacific*

Director: Joshua Logan, *South Pacific*

1951

Play: The Rose Tattoo (Tennessee Williams)
Actor: Claude Rains, *Darkness at Noon*
Actress: Uta Hagen, *The Country Girl*
Director: [no award]
Musical: Guys and Dolls (Jo Swerling/Abe Burrows/Frank Loesser)
Actor: Robert Alda, *Guys and Dolls*
Actress: Ethel Merman, *Call Me Madam*
Director: George S. Kaufman, *Guys and Dolls*

1952

Play: The Fourposter (Jan de Hartog)
Actor: José Ferrer, *The Shrike*
Actress: Julie Harris, *I Am a Camera*
Director: [triple] José Ferrer, *The Shrike/The Fourposter/Stalag 17*
Musical: The King and I (Oscar Hammerstein II/Richard Rodgers)
Actor: Phil Silvers, *Top Banana*
Actress: Gertrude Lawrence, *The King and I*
Director: [no award]

1953

Play: The Crucible (Arthur Miller)
Actor: Tom Ewell, *The Seven Year Itch*
Actress: Shirley Booth, *The Time of the Cuckoo*
Director: Joshua Logan, *Picnic*
Musical: Wonderful Town (Joseph Fields/Jerome Chodorov/Betty Comden/Adolph Green/Leonard Bernstein)
Actor: Thomas Mitchell, *Hazel Flagg*
Actress: Rosalind Russell, *Wonderful Town*
Director: [no award]

1954

Play: The Teahouse of the August Moon (John Patrick)
Actor: David Wayne, *The Teahouse of the August Moon*
Actress: Audrey Hepburn, *Ondine*
Director: Alfred Lunt, *Ondine*
Musical: Kismet (Charles Lederer/Luther Davis/Robert Wright/George Forrest/Alexander Borodin)
Actor: Alfred Drake, *Kismet*
Actress: Dolores Gray, *Carnival in Flanders*
Director: [no award]

1955

Play: The Desperate Hours (Joseph Hayes)
Actor: Alfred Lunt, *Quadrille*
Actress: Nancy Kelly, *The Bad Seed*
Director: Robert Montgomery, *The Desperate Hours*
Musical: The Pajama Game (George Abbott/Richard Bissell/Richard Adler/Jerry Ross)
Actor: Walter Slezak, *Fanny*
Actress: Mary Martin, *Peter Pan*
Director: [no award]

1956

Play: The Diary of Anne Frank (Frances Goodrich/Albert Hackett)
Actor: Paul Muni, *Inherit the Wind*
Actress: Julie Harris, *The Lark*
Director: Tyrone Guthrie, *The Matchmaker*
Musical: Damn Yankees (George Abbott/Douglass Wallop/Richard Adler/Jerry Ross)
Actor: Ray Walston, *Damn Yankees*
Actress: Gwen Verdon, *Damn Yankees*
Director: [no award]

1957

Play: Long Day's Journey into Night (Eugene O'Neill)
Actor: Frederic March, *Long Day's Journey into Night*
Actress: Margaret Leighton, *Separate Tables*
Director: [no award]
Musical: My Fair Lady (Alan Jay Lerner/Frederick Loewe)
Actor: Rex Harrison, *My Fair Lady*
Actress: Judy Holliday, *Bells Are Ringing*
Director: Moss Hart, *My Fair Lady*

1958

Play: Sunrise At Campobello (Dore Schary)
Actor: Ralph Bellamy, *Sunrise At Campobello*
Actress: Helen Hayes, *Time Remembered*
Director: Vincent J. Donehue, *Sunrise At Campobello*
Musical: The Music Man (Meredith Wilson)
Actor: Robert Preston, *The Music Man*

Actress: (tie) Thelma Ritter, *New Girl in Town;*
    Gwen Verdon, *New Girl in Town*
Director: [no award]

1959
Play: J.B. (Archibald MacLeish)
Actor: Jason Robards, Jr., *The Disenchanted*
Actress: Gertrude Berg, *A Majority of One*
Director: Elia Kazan, *J.B.*
Musical: Redhead (Herbert and Dorothy
    Fields/Sidney Sheldon/David Shaw/Albert
    Hague)
Actor: Richard Kiley, *Redhead*
Actress: Gwen Verdon, *Redhead*
Director: [no award]

1960
Play: The Miracle Worker (William Gibson)
Actor: Melvyn Douglas, *The Best Man*
Actress: Anne Bancroft, *The Miracle
    Worker*
Director: Arthur Penn, *The Miracle
    Worker*
Musical: (tie) *Fiorello!* (Jerome
    Weidman/George Abbott/Sheldon
    Harnick/Jerry Bock); *The Sound of Music*
    (Howard Lindsay/Russel Crouse/Oscar
    Hammerstein II/Richard Rodgers)
Actor: Jackie Gleason, *Take Me Along*
Actress: Mary Martin, *The Sound of Music*
Director: George Abbott, *Fiorello!*

1961
Play: Becket (Jean Anouilh)
Actor: Zero Mostel, *Rhinoceros*
Actress: Joan Plowright, *A Taste of Honey*
Director: Sir John Gielgud, *Big Fish, Little
    Fish*
Musical: Bye, Bye Birdie (Michael Stewart/Lee
    Adams/Charles Strouse)
Actor: Richard Burton, *Camelot*
Actress: Elizabeth Seal, *Irma La Douce*
Director: Gower Champion, *Bye, Bye Birdie*

1962
Play: A Man for All Seasons (Robert Bolt)
Actor: Paul Scofield, *A Man for All Seasons*
Actress: Margaret Leighton, *The Night of the
    Iguana*
Director: Noel Williams, *A Man for All
    Seasons*

*Musical: How to Succeed in Business Without
    Really Trying* (Abe Burrows/Jack Weinstock/
    Willie Gilbert/Frank Loesser)
Actor: Robert Morse, *How to Succeed in
    Business Without Really Trying*
Actress: (tie) Anna Maria Alberghetti, *Carnival;*
    Diahann Carroll, *No Strings*
Director: Abe Burrows, *How to Succeed in
    Business Without Really Trying*

1963
Play: Who's Afraid of Virginia Woolf? (Edward
    Albee)
Actor: Arthur Hill, *Who's Afraid of Virginia
    Woolf?*
Actress: Uta Hagen, *Who's Afraid of Virginia
    Woolf?*
Director: Alan Schneider, *Who's Afraid of
    Virginia Woolf?*
*Musical: A Funny Thing Happened on the
    Way to the Forum* (Burt Shevelove/
    Larry Gelbart/Stephen Sondheim)
Actor: Zero Mostel, *A Funny Thing Happened
    on the Way to the Forum*
Actress: Vivien Leigh, *Tovarich*
Director: George Abbott, *A Funny Thing
    Happened on the Way to the Forum*

1964
Play: Luther (John Osborne)
Actor: Alec Guiness, *Dylan*
Actress: Sandy Dennis, *Any Wednesday*
Director: Mike Nichols, *Barefoot in the Park*
Musical: Hello, Dolly! (Michael Stewart/Jerry
    Herman)
Actor: Bert Lahr, *Foxy*
Actress: Carol Channing, *Hello, Dolly!*
Director: Gower Champion, *Hello, Dolly!*

1965
Play: The Subject Was Roses (Frank Gilroy)
Actor: Walter Matthau, *The Odd Couple*
Actress: Irene Worth, *Tiny Alice*
Director: Mike Nichols, *Luv* and *The Odd
    Couple*
Musical: Fiddler on the Roof (Joseph
    Stein/Sheldon Harnick/Jerry Bock)
Actor: Zero Mostel, *Fiddler on the Roof*
Actress: Liza Minnelli, *Flora, the Red Menace*
Director: Jerome Robbins, *Fiddler on the
    Roof*

1966

Play: Marat/Sade (Peter Weiss)
Actor: Hal Holbrook, *Mark Twain Tonight!*
Actress: Rosemary Harris, *The Lion in Winter*
Director: Peter Brook, *Marat/Sade*
Musical: Man of LaMancha (Dale
  Wasserman/Joe Darion/Mitch Leigh)
Actor: Richard Kiley, *Man of LaMancha*
Actress: Angela Lansbury, *Mame*
Director: Albert Marre, *Man of LaMancha*

1967

Play: The Homecoming (Harold Pinter)
Actor: Paul Rogers, *The Homecoming*
Actress: Beryl Reid, *The Killing of Sister George*
Director: Peter Hall, *The Homecoming*
Musical: Cabaret (Joe Masteroff/Fred Ebb/John
  Kander)
Actor: Robert Preston, *I Do! I Do!*
Actress: Barbara Harris, *The Apple Tree*
Director: Harold Prince, *Cabaret*

1968

Play: Rosencrantz and Guildenstern Are Dead
  (Tom Stoppard)
Actor: Martin Balsam, *You Know I Can't Hear
  You When the Water's Running*
Actress: Zoe Caldwell, *The Prime of Miss Jean
  Brodie*
Director: Mike Nichols, *Plaza Suite*
Musical: Hallelujah, Baby! (Arthur Laurents,
  Betty Comden/Adolph Green/Jule Styne)
Actor: Robert Goulet, *The Happy Time*
Actress: (tie) Patricia Routledge, *Darling of the
  Day*; Leslie Uggams, *Hallelujah, Baby!*
Director: Gower Champion, *The Happy Time*

1969

Play: The Great White Hope (Howard Sackler)
Actor: James Earl Jones, *The Great White
  Hope*
Actress: Julie Harris, *Forty Carats*
Director: Peter Dews, *Hadrian VII*
Musical: 1776 (Peter Stone/Sherman
  Edwards)
Actor: Jerry Orbach, *Promises, Promises*
Actress: Angela Lansbury, *Dear World*
Director: Peter Hunt, *1776*

1970

Play: Borstal Boy (Frank McMahon)
Actor: Fritz Weaver, *Child's Play*
Actress: Tammy Grimes, *Private Lives*
Director: Joseph Hardy, *Child's Play*
Musical: Applause (Betty Comden/Adolph
  Green/Lee Adams/Charles Strouse)
Actor: Cleavon Little, *Purlie*
Actress: Lauren Bacall, *Applause*
Director: Ron Field, *Applause*

1971

Play: Sleuth (Anthony Shaffer)
Actor: Brian Bedford, *The School for Wives*
Actress: Maureen Stapleton, *The Gingerbread Lady*
Director: Peter Brook, *A Midsummer Night's
  Dream*
Musical: Company (George Furth/Stephen
  Sondheim)
Actor: Hal Linden, *The Rothchilds*
Actress: Helen Gallagher, *No, No, Nanette*
  [revival]
Director: Harold Prince, *Company*

1972

Play: Sticks and Bones (David Rabe)
Actor: Cliff Gorman, *Lenny*
Actress: Sada Thompson, *Twigs*
Director: Mike Nichols, *The Prisoner of Second
  Avenue*
Musical: Two Gentlemen of Verona (John
  Guare/Mel Shapiro/Galt MacDermot)
Actor: Phil Silvers, *A Funny Thing Happened on
  the Way to the Forum*
Actress: Alexis Smith, *Follies*
Director: Harold Prince and Michael Bennett,
  Follies

1973

Play: That Championship Season (Jason Miller)
Actor: Alan Bates, *Butley*
Actress: Julie Harris, *The Last of Mrs. Lincoln*
Director: A. J. Antoon, *That Championship
  Season*
Musical: A Little Night Music (Hugh
  Wheeler/Stephen Sondheim)
Actor: Ben Vereen, *Pippin*
Actress: Glynis Johns, *A Little Night Music*
Director: Bob Fosse, *Pippin*

1974

Play: *The River Niger* (Joseph A. Walker)
Actor: Michael Moriarty, *Find Your Way Home*
Actress: Colleen Dewhurst, *A Moon for the Misbegotten*
Director: José Quintero, *A Moon for the Misbegotten*
Musical: *Raisin* (Robert Nemiroff/Charlotte Zaltzberg/Robert Brittan/Judd Woldin)
Actor: Christopher Plummer, *Cyrano*
Actress: Virginia Capers, *Raisin*
Director: Harold Prince, *Candide*

1975

Play: *Equus* (Peter Shaffer)
Actor: John Kani and Winston Ntshona, *Sizwe Banzi Is Dead* and *The Island*
Actress: Ellen Burstyn, *Same Time, Next Year*
Director: John Dexter, *Equus*
Musical: *The Wiz* (William F. Brown/Charlie Smalls)
Actor: John Cullum, *Shenandoah*
Actress: Angela Lansbury, *Gypsy*
Director: Geoffrey Holder, *The Wiz*

1976

Play: *Travesties* (Tom Stoppard)
Actor: John Wood, *Travesties*
Actress: Irene Worth, *Sweet Bird of Youth*
Director: Ellis Rabb, *The Royal Family*
Musical: *A Chorus Line* (James Kirkwood/Nicholas Dante/Edward Kleban/Marvin Hamlisch)
Actor: George Rose, *My Fair Lady*
Actress: Donna McKechnie, *A Chorus Line*
Director: Michael Bennett, *A Chorus Line*

1977

Play: *The Shadow Box* (Michael Cristofer)
Actor: Al Pacino, *The Basic Training of Pavlo Hummel*
Actress: Julie Harris, *The Belle of Amherst*
Director: Gordon Davidson, *The Shadow Box*
Musical: *Annie* (Thomas Meehan/Martin Charnin/Charles Strouse)
Actor: Barry Bostwick, *The Robber Bridegroom*
Actress: Dorothy Loudon, *Annie*
Director: Gene Saks, *I Love My Wife*

1978

Play: *Da* (Hugh Leonard)
Actor: Barnard Hughes, *Da*
Actress: Jessica Tandy, *The Gin Game*
Director: Melvin Bernhardt, *Da*
Musical: *Ain't Misbehavin'* (Songs by "Fats" Waller)
Actor: John Cullum, *On the Twentieth Century*
Actress: Liza Minnelli, *The Act*
Director: Richard Maltby, Jr., *Ain't Misbehavin'*

1979

Play: *The Elephant Man* (Bernard Pomerance)
Actor: Tom Conti, *Whose Life Is It Anyway?*
Actress: (tie) Constance Cummings, *Wings*; Carole Shelley, *The Elephant Man*
Director: Jack Hofsiss, *The Elephant Man*
Musical: *Sweeney Todd, The Demon Barber of Fleet Street* (Hugh Wheeler/Stephen Sondheim)
Actor: Len Cariou, *Sweeney Todd, The Demon Barber of Fleet Street*
Actress: Angela Lansbury, *Sweeney Todd, The Demon Barber of Fleet Street*
Director: Harold Prince, *Sweeney Todd, The Demon Barber of Fleet Street*

1980

Play: *Children of a Lesser God* (Mark Medoff)
Actor: John Rubinstein, *Children of a Lesser God*
Actress: Phyllis Frelich, *Children of a Lesser God*
Director: Vivian Matalon, *Morning's at Seven*
Musical: *Evita* (Tim Rice/Andrew Lloyd Webber)
Actor: Jim Dale, *Barnum*
Actress: Patti LuPone, *Evita*
Director: Harold Prince, *Evita*

1981

Play: *Amadeus* (Peter Shaffer)
Actor: Ian McKellen, *Amadeus*
Actress: Jane Lapotaire, *Piaf*
Director: Peter Hall, *Amadeus*
Musical: *42nd Street* (Michael Stewart/Mark Bramble/Harry Warren/Al Dubin)
Actor: Kevin Kline, *The Pirates of Penzance*
Actress: Lauren Bacall, *Woman of the Year*
Director: Wilford Leach, *The Pirates of Penzance*

1982

Play: The Life and Adventures of Nicholas Nickleby (David Edgar)
Actor: Roger Rees, *The Life and Adventures of Nicholas Nickleby*
Actress: Zoe Caldwell, *Medea*
Director: Trevor Nunn and John Caird, *The Life and Adventures of Nicholas Nickleby*
Musical: Nine (Arthur Kopit/Maury Yeston)
Actor: Ben Harney, *Dreamgirls*
Actress: Jennifer Holliday, *Dreamgirls*
Director: Tommy Tune, *Nine*

1983

Play: Torch Song Trilogy (Harvey Fierstein)
Actor: Harvey Fierstein, *Torch Song Trilogy*
Actress: Jessica Tandy, *Foxfire*
Director: Gene Saks, *Brighton Beach Memoirs*
Musical: Cats (T. S. Eliot/Andrew Lloyd Webber)
Actor: Tommy Tune, *My One and Only*
Actress: Natalia Makarova, *On Your Toes*
Director: Trevor Nunn, *Cats*

1984

Play: The Real Thing (Tom Stoppard)
Actor: Jeremy Irons, *The Real Thing*
Actress: Glenn Close, *The Real Thing*
Musical: La Cage aux Folles (Harvey Fierstein/Jerry Herman)
Actor: George Hearn, *La Cage aux Folles*
Actress: Chita Rivera, *The Rink*
Director: Arthur Laurents, *La Cage aux Folles*

1985

Play: Biloxi Blues (Neil Simon)
Actor: Derek Jacobi, *Much Ado About Nothing*
Actress: Stockard Channing, *Joe Egg*
Director: Gene Saks, *Biloxi Blues*
Musical: Big River (William Hauptman/Roger Miller)
Actor: [no award]
Actress: [no award]
Director: Des McAnuff, *Big River*

1986

Play: I'm Not Rappaport (Herb Gardner)
Actor: Judd Hirsch, *I'm Not Rappaport*

Actress: Lily Tomlin, *The Search for Signs of Intelligent Life in the Universe*
Director: Jerry Zaks, *The House of Blue Leaves* [revival]
Musical: The Mystery of Edwin Drood (Rupert Holmes)
Actor: George Rose, *The Mystery of Edwin Drood*
Actress: Bernadette Peters, *Song & Dance*
Director: Wilford Leach, *The Mystery of Edwin Drood*

1987

Play: Fences (August Wilson)
Actor: James Earl Jones, *Fences*
Actress: Linda Lavin, *Broadway Bound*
Director: Lloyd Richards, *Fences*
Musical: Les Misérables (Alain Boublil/Herbert Kretzmer/Claude-Michel Schönberg)
Actor: Robert Lindsay, *Me and My Girl*
Actress: Maryann Plunkett, *Me and My Girl*
Director: Trevor Howard and John Caird, *Les Misérables*

1988

Play: M. Butterfly (David Henry Hwang)
Actor: Ron Silver, *Speed the Plow*
Actress: Joan Allen, *Burn This*
Director: John Dexter, *M. Butterfly*
Musical: The Phantom of the Opera (Richard Stigloe/Charles Hart/Andrew Lloyd Webber)
Actor: Michael Crawford, *The Phantom of the Opera*
Actress: Joanna Gleason, *Into the Woods*
Director: Harold Prince, *The Phantom of the Opera*

1989

Play: The Heidi Chronicles (Wendy Wasserstein)
Actor: Philip Bosco, *Lend Me a Tenor*
Actress: Pauline Collins, *Shirley Valentine*
Director: Jerry Zaks, *Lend Me a Tenor*
Musical: Jerome Robbins' Broadway
Actor: Jason Alexander, *Jerome Robbins' Broadway*
Actress: Ruth Brown, *Black and White*
Director: Jerome Robbins, *Jerome Robbins' Broadway*

1990
Play: *The Grapes of Wrath* (Frank Galati)
Actor: Robert Morse, *Tru*
Actress: Maggie Smith, *Lettice and Lovage*
Director: Frank Galati, *The Grapes of Wrath*
Musical: *City of Angels* (Larry Gelbart/David Zippel/Cy Coleman)
Actor: James Naughton, *City of Angels*
Actress: Tyne Daly, *Gypsy*
Director: Tommy Tune, *Grand Hotel*

1991
Play: *Lost in Yonkers* (Neil Simon)
Actor: Nigel Hawthorne, *Shadowlands*
Actress: Mercedes Ruehl, *Lost in Yonkers*
Director: Jerry Zaks, *Six Degrees of Separation*
Musical: *The Will Rogers Follies* (Peter Stone/Betty Comden/Adolph Green/Cy Coleman
Actor: Jonathan Pryce, *Miss Saigon*
Actress: Lea Salonga, *Miss Saigon*
Director: Tommy Tune, *The Will Rogers Follies*

1992
Play: *Dancing at Lughnasa* (Brian Friel)
Actor: Judd Hirsch, *Conversations with My Father*
Actress: Glenn Close, *Death and the Maiden*
Director: Patrick Mason, *Dancing at Lughnasa*
Musical: *Crazy for You* (Ken Ludwig/Ira and George Gershwin)
Actor: Gregory Hines, *Jelly's Last Jam*
Actress: Faith Prince, *Guys and Dolls*
Director: Jerry Zaks, *Guys and Dolls*

1993
Play: *Angels in America - Millennium Approaches* (Tony Kushner)
Actor: Ron Liebman, *Angels in America - Millennium Approaches*
Actress: Madeline Kahn, *The Sisters Rosensweig*
Director: George C. Wolfe, *Angels in America - Millennium Approaches*
Musical: *Kiss of the Spider Woman* (Terrence McNally/Fred Ebb/John Kander)
Actor: Brent Carver, *Kiss of the Spider Woman*
Actress: Chita Rivera, *Kiss of the Spider Woman*
Director: Des McAnuff, *The Who's Tommy*

1994
Play: *Angels in America - Perestroika* (Tony Kushner)
Actor: Stephen Spinella, *Angels in America - Perestroika*
Actress: Diana Rigg, *Medea*
Director: Stephen Daldry, *An Inspector Calls*
Musical: *Passion* (James Lapine/Stephen Sondheim)
Actor: Boyd Gaines, *She Loves Me*
Actress: Donna Murphy, *Passion*
Director: Nicholas Hytner, *Carousel*

1995
Play: *Love! Valour! Compassion!* (Terrence McNally)
Actor: Ralph Fiennes, *Hamlet*
Actress: Cherry Jones, *The Heiress*
Director: Gerald Gutierrez, *The Heiress*
Musical: *Sunset Boulevard* (Christopher Hampton/Don Black/Andrew Lloyd Webber)
Actor: Matthrew Broderick, *How to Succeed in Business Without Really Trying*
Actress: Glenn Close, *Sunset Boulevard*
Director: Harold Prince, *Show Boat*

1996
Play: *Master Class* (Terrence McNally)
Actor: George Grizzard, *A Delicate Balance*
Actress: Zoe Caldwell, *Master Class*
Director: Gerald Gutierrez, *A Delicate Balance*
Musical: *Rent* (Jonathan Larson)
Actor: Nathan Lane, *A Funny Thing Happened on the Way to the Forum*
Actress: Donna Murphy, *The King and I*
Director: George C. Wolfe, *Bring in Da Noise, Bring in Da Funk*

1997
Play: *The Last Night of Ballyhoo* (Alfred Uhry)
Actor: Christopher Plummer, *Barrymore*
Actress: Janet McTeer, *A Doll's House*
Director: Anthony Page, *A Doll's House*
Musical: *Titanic* (Peter Stone/Maury Yeston)
Actor: James Naughton, *Chicago*
Actress: Bebe Neuwirth, *Chicago*
Director: Walter Bobbie, *Chicago*

1998
> *Play:* Art (Yasmina Reza/trans. Christopher Hampton)
> *Actor:* Anthony LaPaglia, *A View from the Bridge*
> *Actress:* Marie Mullen, *The Beauty Queen of Leenane*
> *Director:* Garry Hynes, *The Beauty Queen of Leenane*
> *Musical: The Lion King* (Roger Allers/Irene Mecchi/Tim Rice/Elton John/Hans Zimmer)
> *Actor:* Alan Cumming, *Cabaret*
> *Actress:* Natasha Richardson, *Cabaret*
> *Director:* Julie Taymor, *The Lion King*

1999
> *Play: Side Man*
> *Actor:* Brian Dennehey, *Death of a Salesman*
> *Actress:* Judi Dench, *Amy's View*
> *Director:* Robert Falls, *Death of a Salesman*
> *Musical: Fosse*
> *Actor:* Martin Short, *Little Me*

Actress: Bernadette Peters, *Annie Get Your Gun*
Director: Matthew Bourne, *Swan Lake*

2000
> *Play: Copenhagen*
> *Actor:* Stephen Dillane, *The Real Thing*
> *Actress:* Jennifer Ehle, *The Real Thing*
> *Director:* Michael Blakemore, *Copenhagen*
> *Musical: Contact*
> *Actor:* Brian S. Mitchell, *Kiss Me, Kate*
> *Actress:* Heather Headley, *Aida*
> *Director:* Michael Blakemore, *Kiss Me, Kate*

2001
> *Play: Proof* (David Auburn)
> *Actor:* Richard Easton, *The Invention of Love*
> *Actress:* Mary Louise Parker, *Proof*
> *Director:* Daniel Sullivan, *Proof*
> *Musical: The Producers*
> *Actor:* Nathan Lane, *The Producers*
> *Actress:* Christine Ebersole, *42nd Street*
> *Director:* Susan Stroman, *The Producers*

⊙ The American Theatre Wing's Tony Awards. "Official Website of the American Theatre Wing's Tony Awards," www.tonys.org

Stevenson, Isabelle. *The Tony Award: A Complete Listing with a History of the American Theatre Wing.* New York: Heinemann, 1994.

National Book Awards (1950–2000)

The National Book Award is administered by the National Book Foundation and is considered one of the most prestigious American literary honors, rivaled only by the Pulitzer Prize. The prize was called the American Book Award from 1980 to 1986, then reverted back to its original name in 1987. Winners in each major category are listed below by year.

1950
> *Fiction: The Man With The Golden Arm*, Nelson Algren
> *Nonfiction: Ralph Waldo Emerson*, Ralph L. Rusk
> *Poetry: Paterson: Book III and Selected Poems*, William Carlos Williams

1951
> *Fiction: The Collected Stories of William Faulkner*, William Faulkner
> *Nonfiction: Herman Melville*, Newton Arvin
> *Poetry: The Auroras of Autumn*, Wallace Stevens

1952
> *Fiction: From Here to Eternity*, James Jones
> *Nonfiction: The Sea Around Us*, Rachel Carson
> *Poetry: Collected Poems*, Marianne Moore

1953
> *Fiction: Invisible Man*, Ralph Ellison
> *Nonfiction: The Course of an Empire*, Bernard A. De Voto
> *Poetry: Collected Poems, 1917–1952*, Archibald MacLeish

1954
Fiction: *The Adventures of Augie March*, Saul Bellow
Nonfiction: *The Stillness at Appomattox*, Bruce Catton
Poetry: *Collected Poems*, Conrad Aitken

1955
Fiction: *A Fable*, William Faulkner
Nonfiction: *The Measure of Man*, Joseph Wood Krutch
Poetry: *The Collected Poems of Wallace Stevens*, Wallace Stevens

1956
Fiction: *Ten North Frederick*, John O'Hara
Nonfiction: *An American in Italy*, Herbert Kubly
Poetry: *The Shield of Achilles*, W. H. Auden

1957
Fiction: *The Field of Vision*, Wright Morris
Nonfiction: *Russia Leaves the War*, George F. Kennan
Poetry: *Things of the World*, Richard Wilbur

1958
Fiction: *The Wapshot Chronicle*, John Cheever
Nonfiction: *The Lion and the Throne*, Catherine Drinker Bowen
Poetry: *Promises: Poems, 1954–1956*, Robert Penn Warren

1959
Fiction: *The Magic Barrel*, Bernard Malamud
Nonfiction: *Mistress to an Age: A Life of Madame De Stael*, J. Christopher Herold
Poetry: *Words for the Wind*, Theodore Roethke

1960
Fiction: *Goodbye, Columbus*, Philip Roth
Nonfiction: *James Joyce*, Richard Ellmann
Poetry: *Life Studies*, Robert Lowell

1961
Fiction: *The Waters of Kronos*, Conrad Richter
Nonfiction: *The Rise and Fall of the Third Reich*, William L. Shirer
Poetry: *The Woman at the Washington Zoo*, Randall Jarrell

1962
Fiction: *The Moviegoer*, Walker Percy
Nonfiction: *The City in History: Its Origins, Its Transformations and Its Prospects*, Lewis Mumford
Poetry: *Poems*, Alan Dugan

1963
Fiction: *Morte D'Urban*, J. F. Powers
Nonfiction: *Henry James, Vol. II: The Conquest of London; Henry James, Vol. III: The Middle Years*, Leon Edel
Poetry: *Traveling through the Dark*, William Stafford

1964
Fiction: *The Centaur*, John Updike
History and Biography: *The Rise of the West: A History of the Human Community*, William H. McNeill
Poetry: *Selected Poems*, John Crowe Ransom

1965
Fiction: *Herzog*, Saul Bellow
History and Biography: *The Life of Lenin*, Louis Fischer
Poetry: *The Far Field*, Theodore Roethke

1966
Fiction: *The Collected Stories of Katherine Anne Porter*, Katherine Anne Porter
History and Biography: *A Thousand Days*, Arthur M. Schlesinger, Jr.
Poetry: *Buckdancer's Choice: Poems*, James Dickey

1967
Fiction: *The Fixer*, Bernard Malamud
History and Biography: *The Enlightenment, Vol. I: An Interpretation the Rise of Modern Paganism*, Peter Gay
Poetry: *Nights and Days*, James Merrill

1968
Fiction: *The Eighth Day*, Thornton Wilder
History and Biography: *Memoirs: 1925–1950*, George F. Kennan
Poetry: *The Light Around the Body*, Robert Bly

1969

    Fiction: Steps, Jerzy Kosinski

    History and Biography: White over Black: American Attitudes Toward the Negro, 1550–1812, Winthrop D. Jordan

    Poetry: His Toy, His Dream, His Rest, John Berryman

1970

    Fiction: Them, Joyce Carol Oates

    History and Biography: Huey Long, T. Harry Williams

    Poetry: The Complete Poems, Elizabeth Bishop

1971

    Fiction: Mr. Sammler's Planet, Saul Bellow

    History and Biography: Roosevelt: The Soldier of Freedom, James MacGregor Burns

    Poetry: To See, To Take, Mona Van Duyn

1972

    Biography: Eleanor and Franklin: The Story of Their Relationship, Based on Eleanor Roosevelt's Private Papers, Joseph P. Lash

    Fiction: The Complete Stories of Flannery O'Connor, Flannery O'Connor

    History: Ordeal of the Union, Vols. VII & VIII: The Organized War, 1863–1864; The Organized War to Victory, Allan Nevins

    Poetry: Selected Poems Frank O'Hara—The Collected Poems of Frank O'Hara, Howard Moss

1973

    Biography: George Washington, Vol. IV: Anguish and Farewell, 1793–1799, James Thomas Flexner

    Fiction: Augustus, John Barth; *Chimera*, John Williams

    History: The Children of Pride Isaiah Trunk—Judenrat, Robert Manson Myers

    Poetry: Collected Poems, 1951–1971, A. R. Ammons

1974

    Biography: Macaulay: The Shaping of the Historian (also won History award), John Clive; *Malcolm Lowry: A Biography*, Douglas Day

    Fiction: Gravity's Rainbow, Thomas Pynchon; *A Crown of Feathers and Other Stories*, Isaac Bashevis Singer

    History: The Shaping of the Historian, John Clive

    Poetry: The Fall of America: Poems of These States, Allen Ginsberg; *Driving into the Wreck: Poems 1971–1972*, Adrienne Rich

1975

    Biography: The Life of Emily Dickinson, Richard B. Sewall

    Fiction: Dog Soldiers, Robert Stone; *The Hair of Harold Roux*, Thomas Williams

    History: The Ordeal of Thomas Hutchinson, Bernard Bailyn

    Poetry: Presentation Piece, Marilyn Hacker

1976

    Fiction: Jr, William Gaddis

    History and Biography: The Problem of Slavery in the Age of Revolution, 1770–1823, David Brion Davis

    Poetry: Self-portrait in a Convex Mirror, John Ashbery

1977

    Biography/Autobiography: Norman Thomas: The Last Idealist, W. A. Swanberg

    Fiction: The Spectator Bird, Wallace Stegner

    History: World of Our Fathers, Irving Howe

    Poetry: Collected Poems, 1930–1976, Richard Eberhart

1978

    Biography/Autobiography: Samuel Johnson, W. Jackson Bate

    Fiction: Blood Ties, Mary Lee Settle

    History: The Path Between the Seas: The Creation of the Panama Canal 1870–1914, David McCullough

    Poetry: The Collected Poems of Howard Nemerov, Howard Nemerov

1979

Biography/Autobiography: *Robert Kennedy and His Times*, Arthur M. Schlesinger, Jr.

Fiction: *Going After Cacciato*, Tim O'Brien

History: *Intellectual Life in the Colonial South, 1585–1763*, Richard Beale Davis

Poetry: *Mirabell: Book of Numbers*, James Merrill

1980

Autobiography: *Lauren Bacall by Myself*, Lauren Bacall

Biography: *The Rise of Theodore Roosevelt*, Edmund Morris

Fiction: *Sophie's Choice*, William Styron

History: *The White House Years*, Henry A. Kissinger

Poetry: *Ashes*, Philip Levine

1981

Autobiography/Biography: *Walt Whitman*, Justin Kaplan

Fiction: *Plains Song*, Wright Morris

History: *Christianity, Social Tolerance and Homosexuality*, John Boswell

Poetry: *The Need to Hold Still*, Lisel Mueller

1982

Autobiography/Biography: *Mornings on Horseback*, David McCullough

Fiction: *Rabbit Is Rich*, John Updike

History: *People of the Sacred Mountain: A History of the Northern Cheyenne Chiefs and Warrior Societies, 1830–1879*, Father Peter John Powell

Poetry: *Life Supports: New and Collected Poems*, William Bronk

1983

Autobiography/Biography: *Isak Dinesen: The Life of a Storyteller*, Judith Thurman

Fiction: *The Color Purple*, Alice Walker

History: *Voices of Protest: Huey Long, Father Coughlin and the Great Depression*, Alan Brinkley

Poetry: *Selected Poems*, Galway Kinnell

1984

Fiction: *Victory over Japan: A Book of Stories*, Ellen Gilchrist

Nonfiction: *Andrew Jackson & the Course of American Democracy, 1833–1845*, Robert V. Remini

Poetry: [no award]

1985

Fiction: *White Noise*, Don DeLillo

Nonfiction: *Common Ground: A Turbulent Decade in the Lives of Three American Families*, J. Anthony Lukas

Poetry: [no award]

1986

Fiction: *World's Fair*, E. L. Doctorow

Nonfiction: *Arctic Dreams*, Barry Lopez

Poetry: [no award]

1987

Fiction: *Paco's Story*, Larry Heinemann

Nonfiction: *The Making of the Atom Bomb*, Richard Rhodes

Poetry: [no award]

1988

Fiction: *Paris Trout*, Pete Dexter

Nonfiction: *A Bright Shining Lie: John Paul Vann and America in Vietnam*, Neil Sheehan

Poetry: [no award]

1989

Fiction: *Spartina*, John Casey

Nonfiction: *From Beirut to Jerusalem*, Thomas L. Friedman

Poetry: [no award]

1990

Fiction: *Middle Passage*, Charles Johnson

Nonfiction: *The House of Morgan: An American Banking Dynasty and the Rise of Modern Finance*, Ron Chernow

Poetry: [no award]

1991

Fiction: *Mating*, Norman Rush

Nonfiction: *Freedom*, Orlando Patterson

Poetry: *What Work Is*, Philip Levine

1992

Fiction: *All the Pretty Horses*, Cormac McCarthy

Nonfiction: *Becoming a Man: Half a Life Story*, Paul Monette

Poetry: *New & Selected Poems*, Mary Oliver

1993
Fiction: *The Shipping News*, E. Annie Proulx
Nonfiction: *United States: Essays 1952–1992*, Gore Vidal
Poetry: *Garbage*, A. R. Ammons

1994
Fiction: *A Frolic of His Own*, William Gaddis
Nonfiction: *How We Die: Reflections on Life's Final Chapter*, Sherwin B. Nuland
Poetry: *A Worshipful Company of Fletchers*, James Tate

1995
Fiction: *Sabbath's Theater*, Philip Roth
Nonfiction: *The Haunted Land: Facing Europe's Ghosts After Communism*, Tina Rosenberg
Poetry: *Passing Through: The Later Poems*, Stanley Kunitz

1996
Fiction: *Ship Fever and Other Stories*, Andrea Barrett
Nonfiction: *An American Requiem: God, My Father, and the War that Came Between Us*, James Carroll
Poetry: *Scrambled Eggs & Whiskey*, Hayden Carruth

1997
Fiction: *Cold Mountain*, Charles Frazier
Nonfiction: *American Sphinx: The Character of Thomas Jefferson*, Joseph J. Ellis
Poetry: *Effort at Speech: New & Selected Poems*, William Meredith

1998
Fiction: *Charming Billy*, Alice McDermott
Nonfiction: *Slaves in the Family*, Edward Ball
Poetry: *This Time: New and Selected Poems*, Gerald Stern

1999
Fiction: *Waiting*, Ha Jin
Nonfiction: *Embracing Defeat: Japan in the Wake of WWII*, John W. Dower
Poetry: *Vice: New and Selected Poems*, Ai (née Florence Anthony)

2000
Fiction: *In America*, Susan Sontag
Nonfiction: *In the Heart of the Sea: The Tragedy of the Whaleship Essex*, Nathaniel Philbrick
Poetry: *Blessing the Boats: New and Selected Poems 1988–2000*, Lucille Clifton

⊙ National Book Foundation. *The National Book Awards: 48 Years of Literary Excellence, Winners and Finalists, 1950–1997.* New York: National Book Foundation, 1998.
National Book Foundation. "The National Book Foundation Homepage," www.publishersweekly.com/ NBF/docs/nbf.html

Newbery Medal (1922–2001)

The Newbery Medal was established in 1922 for excellence in American children's books. The award is named after English publisher John Newbery (1713–1767), a pioneer in the field of children's books.

Year	Author/Title	Year	Author/Title
1922	Hendrik Willem van Loon, *The Story of Mankind*	1927	Will James, *Smoky, the Cowhorse*
1923	Hugh Lofting, *The Voyages of Doctor Dolittle*	1928	Dhan Gopal Mukerji, *Gay Neck, the Story of a Pigeon*
1924	Charles Hawes, *The Dark Frigate*	1929	Eric P. Kelly, *The Trumpeter of Krakow*
1925	Charles Finger, *Tales from Silver Lands*	1930	Rachel Field, *Hitty, Her First Hundred Years*
1926	Arthur Bowie Chrisman, *Shen of the Sea*	1931	Elizabeth Coatsworth, *The Cat Who Went to Heaven*

1932	Laura Adams Armer, *Waterless Mountain*	1964	Emily Neville, *It's Like This, Cat*
1933	Elizabeth Lewis, *Young Fu of the Upper Yangtze*	1965	Maia Wojciechowska, *Shadow of a Bull*
1934	Cornelia Meigs, *Invincible Louisa: The Story of the Author of Little Women*	1966	Elizabeth Borton de Trevino, *I, Juan de Pareja*
1935	Monica Shannon, *Dobry*	1967	Irene Hunt, *Up a Road Slowly*
1936	Carol Ryrie Brink, *Caddie Woodlawn*	1968	E. L. Konigsburg, *From the Mixed-Up Files of Mrs. Basil E. Frankweiler*
1937	Ruth Sawyer, *Roller Skates*	1969	Lloyd Alexander, *The High King*
1938	Kate Seredy, *The White Stag*	1970	William H. Armstrong, *Sounder*
1939	Elizabeth Enright, *Thimble Summer*	1971	Betsy Byars, *Summer of the Swans*
1940	James Daughtery, *Daniel Boone*	1972	Robert C. O'Brien, *Mrs. Frisby and the Rats of NIMH*
1941	Armstrong Sperry, *Call It Courage*	1973	Jean Craighead George, *Julie of the Wolves*
1942	Walter Edmonds, *The Matchlock Gun*	1974	Paula Fox, *The Slave Dancer*
1943	Elizabeth Janet Gray, *Adam of the Road*	1975	Virginia Hamilton, *M. C. Higgins, the Great*
1944	Esther Forbes, *Johnny Tremaine*	1976	Susan Cooper, *The Grey King*
1945	Robert Lawson, *Rabbit Hill*	1977	Mildred D. Taylor, *Roll of Thunder, Hear My Cry*
1946	Lois Lenski, *Strawberry Girl*	1978	Katherine Paterson, *Bridge to Terabithia*
1947	Carolyn Sherwin Bailey, *Miss Hickory*	1979	Ellen Raskin, *The Westing Game*
1948	William Pène de Bois, *The Twenty-One Balloons*	1980	Joan W. Blos, *A Gathering of Days: A New England Girl's Journal, 1830–1832*
1949	Marguerite Henry, *King of the Wind*	1981	Katherine Paterson, *Jacob I Have Loved*
1950	Marguerite de Angeli, *The Door in the Wall*	1982	Nancy Willard, *A Visit to Blake's Inn: Poems for Innocent and Experienced Travelers*
1951	Elizabeth Yates, *Amos Fortune, Free Man*	1983	Cynthia Voigt, *Dicey's Song*
1952	Eleanor Estes, *Ginger Pye*	1984	Beverly Cleary, *Dear Mr. Henshaw*
1953	Ann Nolan Clark, *Secret of the Andes*	1985	Robin McKinley, *The Hero and the Crown*
1954	Joseph Krumgold, *And Now Miguel*	1986	Patricia MacLachlan, *Sarah, Plain and Tall*
1955	Meindert DeJong, *The Wheel on the School*	1987	Sid Fleischman, *The Whipping Boy*
1956	Jean Lee Latham, *Carry On, Mr. Bowditch*	1988	Russell Freedman, *Lincoln: A Photobiography*
1957	Virginia Sorenson, *Miracles on Maple Hill*	1989	Paul Fleischman, *Joyful Noise: Poems for Two Voices*
1958	Harold Keith, *Rifles for Watie*	1990	Lois Lowry, *Number the Stars*
1959	Elizabeth George Speare, *The Witch of Blackbird Pond*	1991	Jerry Spinelli, *Maniac Magee*
1960	Joseph Krumgold, *Onion John*	1992	Phyllis Reynolds Naylor, *Shiloh*
1961	Scott O'Dell, *Island of the Blue Dolphins*	1993	Cynthia Rylant, *Missing May*
1962	Elizabeth George Speare, *The Bronze Bow*		
1963	Madeleine L'Engle, *A Wrinkle in Time*		

Newbery Medal (1922–2001) *(cont.)*

Year	Author/Title	Year	Author/Title
1994	Lois Lowry, *The Giver*	1998	Karen Hesse, *Out of the Dust*
1995	Sharon Creech, *Walk Two Moons*	1999	Louis Sachar, *Holes*
1996	Karen Cushman, *The Midwife's Apprentice*	2000	Christopher Paul Curtis, *Bud, Not Buddy*
1997	E. L. Konigsburg, *The View from Saturday*	2001	Richard Peak, *A Year Down Yonder*

⊙ American Library Association. "The Newbery Medal Homepage," www.ala.org/alsc/newbery.html
American Library Association. *The Newbery and Caldecott Awards: A Guide to the Medal and Honor Books.*
Chicago: American Library Association, 1999.

Caldecott Medal (1938–2000)

The Caldecott Medal was established in 1938 by Frederic G. Melcher, chairman of the R. R. Bowker Publishing Company, for excellence in children's picture book illustrations. The medal is named after British illustrator Raymond Caldecott (1846–1886).

Year	Author/Title	Year	Author/Title
1938	Helen Dean Fish (text); Dorothy P. Lathrop (illustrations), *Animals of the Bible, a Picture Book*	1949	Berta and Elmer Hader, *The Big Snow*
1939	Thomas Handforth, *Mei Li*	1950	Leo Politi, *Song of the Swallows*
1940	Ingri and Edgar Parin d'Aulaire, *Abraham Lincoln*	1951	Katherine Milhous, *The Egg Tree*
1941	Robert Lawson, *They Were Strong and Good*	1952	Will, pseud. [William Lipkind] (text); Nicolas, pseud. [Nicholas Mordvinoff] (illustrations), *Finders Keepers*
1942	Robert McCloskey, *Make Way for Ducklings*	1953	Lynd Ward, *The Biggest Bear*
1943	Virginia Lee Burton, *The Little House*	1954	Ludwig Bemelmans, *Madeline's Rescue*
1944	James Thurber (text); Louis Slobodkin (illustrations), *Many Moons*	1955	Marcia Brown, *Cinderella, or the Little Glass Slipper*
1945	Rachel Field (text); Elizabeth Orton Jones (illustrations), *Prayer for a Child*	1956	John Langstaff (text); Feodor Rojankovsky (illustrations), *Frog Went A-Courtin'*
1946	Maude and Miska Petersham, *The Rooster Crows*	1957	Janice Udry (text); Marc Simont (illustrations), *A Tree Is Nice*
1947	Golden MacDonald, pseud. [Margaret Wise Brown] (text); Leonard Weisgard (illustrations), *The Little Island*	1958	Robert McCloskey, *Time of Wonder*
		1959	Barbara Cooney, *Chanticleer and the Fox*
1948	Alvin Tresselt (text); Roger Duvoisin (illustrations), *White Snow, Bright Snow*	1960	Marie Hall Ets and Aurora Labastida (text); Marie Hall Ets (illustrations), *Nine Days to Christmas*
		1961	Ruth Robbins (text); Nicholas Sidjakov (illustrations), *Baboushka and the Three Kings*

1962	Marcia Brown, *Once a Mouse*
1963	Ezra Jack Keats, *The Snowy Day*
1964	Maurice Sendak, *Where the Wild Things Are*
1965	Beatrice Schenk de Regniers (text); Beni Montresor (illustrations), *May I Bring a Friend?*
1966	Sorche Nic Leodhas, pseud. [Leclair Alger] (text); Nonny Hogrogian (illustrations), *Always Room for One More*
1967	Evaline Ness, *Sam, Bangs & Moonshine*
1968	Barbara Emberley (text); Ed Emberley (illustrations), *Drummer Hoff*
1969	Arthur Ransome (text); Uri Shulevitz (illustrations), *The Fool of the World and the Flying Ship*
1970	William Steig, *Sylvester and the Magic Pebble*
1971	Gail E. Haley, *A Story a Story*
1972	Nonny Hogrogian, *One Fine Day*
1973	Arlene Mosel (text); Blair Lent (illustrations), *The Funny Little Woman*
1974	Harve Zemach (text); Margot Zemach (illustrations), *Duffy and the Devil*
1975	Gerald McDermott, *Arrow to the Sun*
1976	Verna Aardema (text); Leo and Diane Dillon (illustrations), *Why Mosquitoes Buzz in People's Ears*
1977	Margaret Musgrove (text); Leo and Diane Dillon (illustrations), *Ashanti to Zulu: African Traditions*
1978	Peter Spier, *Noah's Ark*
1979	Paul Goble, *The Girl Who Loved Wild Horses*
1980	Donald Hall (text); Barbara Cooney (illustrations), *Ox-Cart Man*
1981	Arnold Lobel, *Fables*

1982	Chris van Allsburg, *Jumanji*
1983	Blaise Cendrars (text); Marcia Brown (translation and illustrations), *Shadow*
1984	Alice and Martin Provensen, *The Glorious Flight: Across the Channel with Louis Bleriot*
1985	Margaret Hodges (text); Trina Schart Hyman (illustrations), *Saint George and the Dragon*
1986	Chris Van Allsburg, *The Polar Express*
1987	Arthur Yorinks (text); Richard Egielski (illustrations), *Hey, Al*
1988	Jane Yolen (text); John Schoenherr (illustrations), *Owl Moon*
1989	Karen Ackerman (text); Stephen Gammell (illustrations), *Song and Dance Man*
1990	Ed Young, *Lon Po Po: a Red-Riding Hood Story from China*
1991	David Macaulay, *Black and White*
1992	David Wiesner, *Tuesday*
1993	Emily Arnold McCully, *Mirette on the High Wire*
1994	Allen Say, *Grandfather's Journey*
1995	Eve Bunting (text); David Diaz (illustrations), *Smoky Night*
1996	Peggy Rathmann, *Officer Buckle and Gloria*
1997	David Wisniewski, *Golem*
1998	Paul O. Zelinsky, *Rapunzel*
1999	Jacqueline Briggs (text); Mary Azarian (illustrations), *Snowflake Bentley*
2000	Simms Tarback, *Joseph Had a Little Overcoat*
2001	Judith St. George (text); David Small (illustrations), *So You Want to Be President*

⊙ American Library Association. "The Caldecott Medal Homepage,"http://ala.org/alsc/caldecott.html American Library Association. *The Newbery and Caldecott Awards: A Guide to the Medal and Honor Books.* Chicago: American Library Association, 1999.

The Spingarn Medal was established in 1914 by the National Association for the Advancement of Colored People (NAACP). The award was named for Joel Elias Spingarn (1875–1939), who was then chairman of the NAACP's board of directors. Gold medals are given each year to the African American who reaches the highest achievement in his or her field in the previous year or over a period of time.

Year	Recipient
1915	Ernest E. Just (1883–1941), cell biologist
1916	Charles Young (1864–1922), army officer
1917	Harry T. Burleigh (1866–1949), singer and composer
1918	William Stanley Braithwaite (1878–1962), writer and editor
1919	Archibald H. Grimké (1849–1930), activist and writer
1920	W. E. B. Du Bois (1868–1963), educator and writer
1921	Charles S. Gilpin (1878–1930), actor
1922	Mary B. Talbert (1886–1923), civil rights activist
1923	George Washington Carver (c.1864–1943), botanist
1924	Roland Hayes (1887–1977), singer
1925	James Weldon Johnson (1871–1938), writer and U.S. consul
1926	Carter G. Woodson (1875–1950), historian
1927	Anthony Overton (1865–1946), businessman, judge and newspaper publisher
1928	Charles W. Chesnutt (1858–1932), writer
1929	Mordecai Wyatt Johnson (1890–1976), educator
1930	Henry A. Hunt (1866–1938), educator
1931	Richard Berry Harrison (1864–1935), actor
1932	Robert Russa Moton (1867–1940), educator
1933	Max Yergan (1892–1975), activist and YMCA promoter
1934	William Taylor Burwell Williams (1869–1941), educator
1935	Mary McLeod Bethune (1875–1955), educator
1936	John Hope (1868–1936), educator
1937	Walter White (1893–1955), writer
1938	[no award]
1939	Marian Anderson (1902–1993), singer
1940	Louis T. Wright (1891–1952), civil rights administrator and physician
1941	Richard Wright (1908–1960), writer
1942	A. Philip Randolph (1889–1979), labor leader
1943	William H. Hastie (1904–1976), judge
1944	Charles Drew (1904–1950), physician
1945	Paul Robeson (1898–1976), singer and actor
1946	Thurgood Marshall (1908–1993), Supreme Court Justice
1947	Percy Julian (1899–1975), chemist
1948	Channing H. Tobias (1882–1961), civil rights activist and diplomat
1949	Ralph J. Bunche (1904–1971), diplomat
1950	Charles Hamilton Houston (1895–1950), lawyer
1951	Mabel Keaton Staupers (1890–1989), nurse

1952	Harry T. Moore (1905–1951), civil rights leader
1953	Paul R. Williams (1894–1980), architect
1954	Theodore K. Lawless (1892–1971), physician
1955	Carl Murphy (1889–1967), newspaper editor and publisher
1956	Jackie Robinson (1919–1972), baseball player
1957	Martin Luther King, Jr. (1929–1968), clergyman and reformer
1958	Daisy Bates (1922–), civil rights activist; and the Little Rock Nine (nine students)
1959	Duke Ellington (1899–1974), bandleader and composer
1960	Langston Hughes (1902–1967), writer
1961	Kenneth B. Clark (1914–), psychologist
1962	Robert C. Weaver (1907–), housing administrator and cabinet member
1963	Medgar Wiley Evers (1925–1963), civil rights leader
1964	Roy Wilkins (1901–1981), civil rights leader
1965	Leontyne Price (1927–), singer
1966	John H. Johnson (1918–), publisher
1967	Edward W. Brooke III (1919–), politician
1968	Sammy Davis, Jr. (1925–1990), entertainer
1969	Clarence M. Mitchell, Jr. (1911–1984), civil rights activist and labor secretary of the NAACP
1970	Jacob Lawrence (1917–), painter
1971	Leon Howard Sullivan (1922–), civil rights activist and clergyman
1972	Gordon Parks (1912–), writer and photographer
1973	Wilson C. Riles (1917–), administrator and educator
1974	Damon Keith (1922–), administrator, judge, and lawyer
1975	Hank Aaron (1934–), baseball player
1976	Alvin Ailey (1931–1989), dancer and choreographer
1977	Alexander Haley (1924–1992), writer
1978	Andrew Young, Jr. (1932–), civil rights activist, minister and public official
1979	Rosa L. Parks (1913–), civil rights activist
1980	Rayford W. Logan (1897–1982), historian
1981	Coleman Young (1918–), politician
1982	Benjamin Elijah Mays (1895–1984), clergyman and educator
1983	Lena Horne (1917–), singer
1984	Tom Bradley (1917–1998), politician
1985	Bill Cosby (1937–), actor
1986	Benjamin Hooks (1925–), judge, public official and civil rights reformer
1987	Percy Ellis Sutton (1920–), activist, lawyer and politician
1988	Frederick Douglass Patterson (1901–1988); educator and founder of the United Negro College Fund
1989	Jesse Jackson (1941–), clergyman, civil rights leader, and politician
1990	L. Douglas Wilder (1931–), lawyer and politician
1991	Colin Powell (1937–), general and politician
1992	Barbara Jordan (1936–1996), U.S. representative
1993	Dorothy L. Height (1912–), civil rights activist
1994	Maya Angelou (1928–), poet
1995	John Hope Franklin (1915–) historian

Year	Recipient
1996	A. Leon Higginbotham (1928–), judge
1997	Carl T. Rowan (1925–), journalist
1998	Myrlie Evers-Williams (1933–), civil rights activist, chairwoman of NAACP, 1995–1998
1999	Earl G. Graves, Sr. (1935–), Chairman and CEO of Black Enterprise Magazine
2000	Oprah Winfrey (1954–), host of "The Oprah Winfrey Show," film studio owner

⊙ Douglass, Melvin I. Black Winners: A History of Spingarn Medalists, 1915–1983. New York: T. Gaus, 1984.
Louisville Free Public Library. "The Spingarn Medal," www.lfpl.org/reference/rflksgarn.htm

Pritzker Architecture Prize (1979–2001)

The Pritzker Prize, an annual international award honoring architects whose work offers significant contributions to humanity and the built environment, is considered to be the most prestigious in architecture. It is sponsored by the Hyatt Foundation.

Year	Recipient
1979	Philip Johnson, U.S.
1980	Luis Barragán, Mexico
1981	James Stirling, U.K.
1982	Kevin Roche, U.S.
1983	Ieoh Ming (I. M.) Pei, U.S.
1984	Richard Meier, U.S.
1985	Hans Hollein, Austria
1986	Gottfried Boehm, Germany
1987	Kenzo Tange, Japan
1988	Gordon Bunshaft, U.S., and Oscar Neimeyer, Brazil
1989	Frank O. Gehry, U.S.
1990	Aldo Rossi, Italy
1991	Robert Venturi, U.S.
1992	Alvaro Siza, Portugal
1993	Fumihiko Maki, Japan
1994	Christian de Portzamparc, France
1995	Tadao Ando, Japan
1996	Rafael Moneo, Spain
1997	Sverre Fehn, Norway
1998	Renzo Piano, Italy
1999	Sir Norman Foster, U.K
2000	Rem Koolhaas, Netherlands
2001	Jacques Herzog and Pierre de Meuron, Switzerland

⊙ "The Pritzker Architecture Prize," www.pritzkerprize.com

Labor Unions: Ten Largest AFL-CIO Affiliates

The American Federation of Labor – Committee for Industrial Organization is the biggest labor organization in the United States. Formed in 1955 by the merger of the country's two largest groups of trade unions, it combines the resources of 68 specialized labor groups into a single lobbying force. The table below lists its largest constituent members.

Name	Primary Membership	Members
International Brotherhood of Teamsters (IBT)	Freight, trucking, airline, and other workers	1.5 million
Service Employees International Union (SEIU)	Hospital, home care, nursing home, and public service workers	1.4 million
United Food and Commercial Workers International Union (UFCW)	Retail food, meatpacking, poultry, and food processing workers	1.4 million
American Federation of State, County, and Municipal Employees (AFSCME)	Health care and public employees	1.3 million
American Federation of Teachers (AFT)	Public elementary and high school teachers, other public employees	1 million
United Automobile, Aerospace and Agricultural Implement Workers of America (UAW)	Factory employees of car, plane, and equipment manufacturers	750,000
International Brotherhood of Electrical Workers (IBEW)	Electricians, utility workers, electric-sign makers, broadcast employees	750,000
Communications Workers of America (CWA)	Media and telecommunications workers	740,000
International Association of Machinists and Aerospace Workers (IAM)	Railroad, auto, airplane, and aerospace mechanics	450,000
United Steelworkers of America (USWA)	Steel-manufacturing employees	400,000

⊙ AFL-CIO. "Unions Affiliated with the AFL-CIO," www.aflcio.org/unionand/unions.htm
  Mooney, Green, Gleason, Baker, Gibson & Saindon, P.C. "MGGBGS Labor Union Page,"
    www.mggbgs.com/labor.html

U.S. Stock Markets

Exchange	Founded	Description
American Stock Exchange	1920	This is the world's second largest floor-based exchange. Its 661 regular members that may buy and sell on the floor.
Chicago Mercantile Exchange	1874	Futures and option contracts are traded. These include currencies, interest rates, stock indices, and agricultural futures.
National Association of Securities Dealers Automated Quotation (NASDAQ)	1971	The world's first electronic stock exchange, it was started as a U.S. government project to create the first truly global securities market. It deals mainly in technology and development.
New York Stock Exchange (NYSE)	1790	A not-for-profit organization run by a 25-member board. 1,366 seats are available to member firms for the privilege of buying and selling on the floor.

⊙ NYSE: New York Stock Exchange. www.nyse.com
Chicago Mercantile Exchange. www.cme.com
NASDAQ. www.nasdaq.com
American Stock Exchange. www.amex.com

Consumer Advocacy Organizations

Name	Mission	Phone/Website	Founded
Foundation for Taxpayer and Consumer Rights	Alerts taxpayers to fraud and waste in government	www.consumerwatchdog.org/ftcr	1985
Alliance against Fraud in Marketing	Organization of many groups that research and report about fraud in telemarketing and on the Internet	(202) 835-3323	1988
National Consumer Law Center	Researches and advocates on the needs of low-income consumers	www.consumerlaw.org	1984
American Council on Science and Health	Studies and reports on issues related to food, nutrition, biotechnology, pesticides, and food safety	www.asch.org/about/index.html	1978
Hudson Center for Global Food Issues	Researches and analyzes agricultural and environmental concerns and reports to the public; known for skepticism of conventional wisdom	www.hcgf/	1961

National Community Reinvestment Coalition	Works to end discriminatory banking practices and increase flow of private capital and credit to underserved communities	(202) 628-9800 www.youthlink.net/nrc.org	1990
Quackwatch	Combats health-related frauds, myths, fads, and fallacies	www.quackwatch.com	1969
Consumer Reports	Tests products and informs consumers	www.consumerreports.org	1936
Center for Science in the Public Interest	Researches and advocates on issues of food, nutrition, food safety, and related issues	(202) 332-9110 www.cspinet.org/more/cspi.htm	1971
Consumer Federation of America	Develops and distributes studies of various consumer issues	(202) 387-6121	1968
Citizen Action	Advocate for programs to enable consumers to enjoy a diet that is adequate, safe, and healthy	(202) 776-0595	1975

⊙ Federal Trade Commission. "Consumer Protection," www.ftc.gov/ftc/consumer.htm

WORK AND HOME: *Personal Finance*

Household Budgeting

Making and keeping a household budget is the first step toward financial security. By adhering to spending guidelines, an individual, couple, or family can realize financial goals and plan for retirement. The fundamental principle is simple: expenditures should not exceed income. The only way to maintain this ratio is to set income and spending parameters and stick to them.

Record keeping is the foundation upon which a budget is built. Learning to keep financial records in order will allow you to find the information you need to plan your finances. A file cabinet, envelopes, and some folders are all you need to get started. Make a separate file for each category of bills, for each bank account, and for tax-related receipts. Once the bills are sorted you will be able to figure out the average monthly cost of your utilities, telephone, insurance, etc.

If you are not currently using a budget, chances are you have only a vague idea how much you spend on day-to-day living: groceries, lunches out, movies, and morning coffee. Some people find it helpful to spend a few weeks tracking their cash expenditures in order to have a basis for building a budget. Although it can be tedious, this exercise will enable you to decide if the money that seems to disappear mysteriously from your wallet can be put to better use in another area of your life.

Household Budgeting

Monthly Income and Expense Worksheet

Income

Type	Amount
Monthly Income 1	_____
Monthly Income 2	_____
Interest/Investment Income	_____
Other (rental, additional job)	_____
Total Income	_____

Fixed Expenses

Type	Amount
Rent/Mortgage	_____
Insurance	_____
Automobile Loan	_____
Student Loan	_____
Daily Childcare	_____
Cable TV/Internet Access	_____
Debt Repayment (credit cards)	_____
Other	_____
Other	_____
Total Fixed Expenses	_____

Flexible Expenses

Type	Amount
Groceries	_____
Telephone	_____
Utilities	_____
Gasoline	_____
Entertainment	_____
Additional Childcare	_____
Medical/Dental	_____
Health/Beauty	_____
Clothing	_____
Household/Home Repair	_____
Savings	_____
Vacations	_____
Other	_____
Other	_____
Total Flexible Expenses	_____

Total Income/Expenses   _____ / _____

⊙ Blue, Ron. *Master Your Money*. Nashville, Tenn.: Thomas Nelson, 1993.
Burket, Larry. *The Financial Planning Workbook*. Chicago: Moody, 1991.

Personal Savings

Banks

A bank acts as a middleman between you and the institutions with which you exchange money: employers, service providers, and creditors. It also offers a safe place for storing your money and may let you use that money to earn interest. For basic banking services, however, expect to pay some fees.

Before walking into your local branch and handing over your money, it is a good idea to shop around for a bank that offers accounts tailored to your needs with the lowest fees possible. Unlimited checking is great for people who write a lot of checks, but there is no need to pay extra for a service you are not going to use. Many banks require a minimum balance in order to waive basic fees, but if you have a limited cash flow it is possible to find a bank without such a requirement.

Types of Bank Accounts
Checking accounts

Basic checking	No-frills account with minimal check writing privileges
Unlimited checking	Usually requires a minimum balance for fee waiver
Interest-bearing	With a high balance, interest is earned
Joint checking	Shared between more than one person
ATM / Express	Fees charged for using teller windows to encourage ATM usage
Student / Senior	Special accounts with discounted rates for students and seniors
Money Market	Interest-bearing account with high minimum balance and limited check writing privileges

Savings accounts

Passbook	Interest-bearing account that requires account holder to present a ledger for each transaction
Statement	Interest-bearing account that uses a regular statement, not a passbook, to record transactions
Certificate of Deposit (CD)	Account requiring a minimum amount of time deposited, usually a period of three or six months or more than one year

Stocks

A stock is a small portion of a company that can be bought and sold at a profit or loss. Stocks are publicly traded through an organization called an exchange; various exchanges specialize in specific groupings or types of companies. The exchange determines the value of each stock and rates each company according to its own criteria. Most financial exchanges can be found at InvestorLinks: www.investorlinks.com/exch.html.

Stocks earn money in two ways: through dividends and through capital gains. Dividends are a company's means of distributing profits to its stockholders. Capital gains are profits made when the stock is sold at a higher price than the price at which it was bought.

Stocks are bought and sold through brokers, who charge a fee for their service. Brokers are available through traditional brokerage houses, although a growing number of people are finding brokers online. Online brokers often charge lower fees and require smaller initial investments.

EDGAR, the Securities and Exchange Commission database, is an invaluable resource if you wish to find information on any public company in the U.S. To search the database, register for free as a visitor at www.edgar-online.com.

Types of stock

Income	Regular dividends provide income for shareholders
Growth	Profits are reinvested in the company and the stock experiences long-term growth in value
Cyclical	Prices rise and fall depending upon economic conditions
Defensive	Based in industries that produce necessities of daily life
Penny	Inexpensive shares from small companies
Blue chip	Stable shares from older, more established companies
Value	Low-priced stocks that are expected to rise

To track the performance of stock you have bought, you can read the stock tables in a financial newspaper. Here's what the abbreviations mean:

Stock Table Listings

52 Weeks Hi/Lo	Highest and lowest prices for the past 52 weeks measure volatility and risk
Stock	Name of company, abbreviated
Sym	Trading symbol assigned by the exchange
Div	Dividend anticipated per share
Yld %	Percentage of stock's price paid as dividend
PE	Ration of stock's price to annual earnings of company
Vol 100s	Volume of shares traded the day before, shown in hundreds
Hi-Lo-Close	Previous day's high, low, and closing price
Net Chg	Comparison between the day's closing price and that of the day before

Bonds

Bonds provide a means for a corporation or a government to raise money from the public. Buying bonds makes an individual a lender rather than a part owner. The value of a bond is not tied to the value of the company and the amount of profit is generally a fixed interest rate. For these reasons, bonds usually considered safer than stocks; however, high-risk bonds do exist and care should be taken when evaluating a given bond.

Types of bonds

U.S. Treasury Bonds

Treasury bills (T-bills)	Mature after 13, 26, or 52 weeks
Treasury notes (T-notes)	Mature after 2, 5, or 10 years
Treasury bonds (T-bonds)	Mature after 30 years

U.S. Savings Bonds

Series EE	Bought at half of face value; reach full value as interest is added to principal
Series I	Bought at face value; indexed for inflation
Series HH	Issued only in exchange for other bonds; interest is paid semiannually
Corporate Bonds	Higher-risk than government bonds because of potential default by company
Municipal Bonds	Issued by local government to pay for capital projects

Credit rating agencies evaluate the potential creditworthiness of bond issues. Standard & Poor's (212-438-2400 or www.standardandpoors.com/ratings/index.htm) and Moody's (212-552-1658 or www.moodys.com/ratings/ratdefs.htm#1ttaxable) are two of the best-known agencies. Bonds in the AAA, AA, or A categories are considered to be the safest investments. A rating of BB or lower carries a higher risk.

Mutual Funds

A mutual fund is a diversified investment group run by an investment company. The group pools resources and spreads risks, making it generally safer than individual stock trading. Like all kinds of investments, mutual funds carry some risk; a portfolio may not perform as well as predicted and individual members of the group can lose some of their money.

There are two different types of mutual fund. A closed-end fund performs more like a stock and is traded on an exchange. An open-end fund is the kind most often entered into by average investors.

Mutual funds usually require a smaller initial investment than an individual stock purchase. The earnings structure is similar to that of stocks; namely money is earned both through dividends and through capital gains as the fund sells its stock. In addition, if the securities within a mutual fund increase in value and you sell your shares, you will also realize a capital gain.

To obtain information on mutual funds, you can research them at your public library. Some reports are available online: Morningstar Mutual Funds (www.morningstar.com), Value Line Mutual Fund Survey (www.valueline.com), and Standard & Poor's (www.standardpoor.com). To evaluate the overall cost of investing in a particular mutual fund, the SEC offers an online Mutual Fund Cost Calculator: www.sec.gov/mfcc/mfcc-int.htm.

Before investing in a mutual fund, review the prospectus carefully. A prospectus will disclose the fund's objectives, policies, management team, costs, and performance. Some funds carry sales charges, or loads, and others are no-load funds. Once you invest in a fund, you can track its performance in a newspaper such as the Wall Street Journal according to the table below:

Mutual Fund Listings

Fund name	Company name first, followed by its funds
NAV	Net asset value (dollar value per share)
Net chg.	Change in NAV from previous day
Total return	Percentage of gain or loss on the fund, year to date
Inv Obj.	Investment objective of the fund
Max. Init chrg.	Sales charge fee (load)

Real Estate

An investment in real estate can earn you money in two ways: rental income and capital gains. See "Home Buying" for more information.

Insurance

Some forms of insurance are considered an investment in a family's future. Whole life insurance, in particular, can function in this way. In fact, whole life insurance is considered a "security" subject to federal securities laws and protections, and is sold by prospectus. See "Insurance" for more information.

Education IRAs

An education IRA allows you to contribute up to $500 each year for a child under age 18. Anyone (including the child) can make contributions to the account but these contributions are not tax deductible. Money taken out of the account, including any interest, is tax free as long as it is used to cover educational expenses: books, tuition, fees, supplies, and equipment for college. Room and board are also valid uses if the student is enrolled at least half-time.

The U.S. Department of Education offers online resources to help you plan for sending your children to college: www.ed.gov/thinkcollege/early/tce_home.htm.

⊙ Bryan, Mark, and Julia Cameron. *Money Drunk, Money Sober: 90 Days to Financial Freedom.* New York: Ballantine, 1999.

Morris, Kenneth M., and Virginia B. Morris. *The Wall Street Journal Guide to Understanding Money & Investing.* New York: Simon & Schuster, 1999.

IRA

The Individual Retirement Arrangement (IRA) is a special, tax deductible account designed to help individuals save for retirement. These accounts are available through banks, mutual funds, life insurance companies, and brokerage houses. The funds deposited can be invested in numerous ways in order to earn dividends. These earnings are not taxed until they are distributed; if this falls after retirement, your tax bracket is likely to be lower.

The maximum contribution allowed by law is $2,000 per year. Withdrawals are permitted after the age of 59 1/2 and are required by April 1 of the year after you reach age 70 1/2. Early withdrawals are subject to a penalty of 10% in addition to any regular income tax. Certain types of withdrawals are exempt from this penalty, including those made for higher education, unreimbursed medical expenses in excess of 7.5% of your adjusted gross income, in case of disability, or towards the purchase of a first home.

A special type of IRA, called a Roth IRA, allows for contributions to continue after the age of 70 1/2 and funds can be left in the account indefinitely. Individuals with an income of less than $95,000 and couples with an income of less than $150,000 are eligible.

Employers can set up an IRA for you in the form of a Simplified Employee Pension (SEP). An employer is not limited by the $2,000 annual limit; the maximum allowed is up to 15% of the employee's income up to $30,000.

401(k), 403 (b)

A 401(k) plan allows an employee to contribute a percentage of gross income to an individual retirement account. This money is deducted before any taxes are paid, reducing your taxable income by up to 15%. Some employers match your contributions, in effect increasing your income while reducing your tax burden.

The plan is managed by the company and usually includes a variety of investment options from which you can choose. Whether you wish to invest in stocks, bonds, or a mutual fund is up to you and you can change the plan to suit your changing needs. Costs of managing the plan, including your own investments, are usually absorbed by the company.

If you leave a company before retirement, you will be able to keep some or all of the matching funds, depending upon the company's policy. To avoid penalties, you will have to roll the money over into an individual or company-sponsored IRA. Some companies will allow you to maintain your original investment account but you will not be able to contribute any additional funds. Upon retirement you can cash in the account without penalty.

A 403(b) plan is similar to a 401(k) plan, but it is offered by nonprofit organizations such as hospitals, schools, or social service agencies. In either type of plan, the maximum annual contribution is $9,500 or up to 15% of your income, whichever is less.

Social Security

Social Security is a government-sponsored retirement plan; contributions to Social Security are automatically deducted from the paychecks of every worker in the United States and deposited into a special fund.

Each year that you work, you earn credits toward your retirement based upon your income up to a maximum of 4 credits per year. To be eligible to receive benefits, you must be over the age of 65 and have earned more than 40 credits. If you continue working past age 65, you can still collect benefits, but only within certain income limits. After the age of 70 you can collect benefits with no income limits.

Keep in mind that the average monthly Social Security payment was $500 for an individual in 1999; while these benefits are helpful to retirees, they do not constitute a living wage. Other retirement plans are essential in order to live comfortably after the age of 65.

For more information about Social Security, contact the Social Security Administration: 800-772-1213 or www.ssa.gov.

⊙ Arnone, William J. *Ernst & Young's Retirement Planning Guide*. New York: Wiley, 2000.

Holzer, Bambi, with Elaine Floyd. *Retire Rich: The Baby Boomer's Guide to a Secure Future*. New York: Wiley, 1998.

Howells, John. *Retirement on a Shoestring*. Guilford, Conn: Globe Pequot, 2000.

Rye, David E. *1,001 Ways to Save, Grow, and Invest Your Money*. Franklin Lakes, N.J.: Career Press, 1999.

Insurance

People buy insurance for a variety of reasons, but the most basic reason is protection against future crises. Health insurance can bring an added benefit of facilitating preventive health care. Some types of life insurance also function as a long-term investment. Insurance plans vary significantly, which means that you will need to do some research in order to determine the plan that will suit your needs while giving you the most value for your money.

Health Insurance

Of all kinds of insurance available, health insurance is the most fundamental to everyday life. Without health insurance, routine visits to the doctor are unaffordable for most Americans, let alone the cost of medications, x-rays, lab tests, and so on. Even if you are in good health, it pays to have at least some kind of catastrophic coverage in the event of an accident or sudden illness; one hospital stay can wipe out any assets you have and land you in serious debt.

If you are employed full-time, chances are your employer will offer some type of health insurance and will subsidize the cost. You may be offered several options, or you may have a more limited selection. Generally, employers offer a choice between two basic plan types: fee-for-service or managed care.

Under a *fee-for-service* plan you can go to any doctor you wish, but you will need to pay more out-of-pocket costs. *Managed care* requires you to choose a participating physician from a Health Maintenance Organization (HMO), at a significantly reduced cost. Covered benefits vary greatly from plan to plan and it is essential to review your membership packet carefully. Some services are covered only partially and require that you pay the first portion of expenses (called a deductible).

If you are self-employed you are still eligible for health insurance, but the cost to you is likely to be much greater than if you were under group coverage. In certain fields, professional associations offer group insurance rates to self-employed members.

Life Insurance

The primary reason to buy life insurance is to compensate for lost income to your dependents in the event of your death. There is no benefit to buying life insurance if you are single and have no children or other dependents. The best way to gauge the amount of insurance you need is to multiply your annual income by 10. Proceeds from the policy could be invested at a 10 percent return rate, effectively replacing your income.

Types of Life Insurance

Term	Covers only a specific period of time; usually has lower initial premiums; renewal often brings an increase in premium price
Whole life	More of a long-term investment; premiums are usually level and increase only incrementally
Universal life	Offers the most flexibility; after initial payment you can reduce or increase the amount of death benefit

Companies offering life insurance are rated by numerous organizations: A.M. Best (908-439-2200 or www.ambest.com, Durr & Phelps (312-368-3157 or www.dcro.com), Moody's Investors Service

(212-553-0377 or www.moodys.com), and Standard & Poor's (212-438-2000 or www.standardandpoors.com/ratings).

Property Insurance

Anything you own can be insured, but the type of insurance you buy depends upon whether or not you own your home. *Homeowner's insurance* covers both the value of your home and your possessions in case of fire or natural disaster. The insurance should cover the cost of rebuilding your home, not just the value of your home on the real estate market (which might be significantly lower). Your personal belongings can be covered either at their actual cash value or at full replacement value. *Renter's insurance* covers personal belongings only (usually the landlord's insurance will cover the building itself) either for actual cash value or full replacement value.

⊙ Baldwin, Ben G. *The New Life Insurance Investment Advisor: Achieving Financial Security for You and Your Family Through Today's Insurance Product.* New York: McGraw-Hill, 1994.
Bruel, Brian. *The Complete Idiot's Guide to Buying Insurance and Annuities.* New York: Alpha Books, 1996.
Nader, Ralph, and Wesley J. Smith. *Winning the Insurance Game: The Complete Consumer's Guide to Saving Money.* New York: Doubleday, 1993.

Home Buying

Process

The first element to buying a home is figuring out what you can afford. Generally, the monthly cost of buying and maintaining your home should not exceed 28% of your gross monthly income. Once you calculate your maximum monthly payment, a loan officer or mortgage broker can help you figure out your target price range.

After you've found a home you wish to buy and have agreed upon a price you are willing to pay, you will need to make a written offer to the seller. The offer should be contingent upon a satisfactory inspection (see below) to safeguard against any hidden problems or costs. If the seller agrees, you automatically go into the contract phase of the process and your offer becomes legally binding. Do not make an offer to which you are not willing to commit.

While you should take some time to personally inspect the house, a professional inspector's services are well worth the $300–500 cost. The inspector should be able to detect any major repair work that will need to be done in the foreseeable future, which you may wish to include in the contract as part of your negotiating strategy.

The sales contract is a legally binding agreement between buyer and seller. It will include all pertinent information about the property (i.e., the address, inclusions and exclusions, selling price, mortgage and inspection contingencies, septic system, closing and possession dates).

When setting up your title, you will need to choose the title type that best suits your needs.

Title Types

Joint tenancy	Equal ownership of property; automatic right of succession should the co-owner die
Tenancy-in-common	Equal ownership of property; each party chooses own successor to inherit his/her portion
Community property	Equal right of possession for husband and wife; upon death of one, the other receives half and the rest passes to any other successors
Sole and separate property	No one else has any interest in property; if married, will need additional document to rule out community property interest

Bank Guidelines
Banks and other mortgage lenders will ask you for a great deal of financial information, including your
- Past two years' earned income
- Past two years' dividend / interest income
- Income from other sources (i.e. alimony, child support)
- Current balances and recent statements from checking and savings accounts
- Current market value of all investments, such as stocks, bonds, or mutual funds
- Investments in IRAs or other retirement funds
- Face amount and cash value of life insurance policies
- Value of major property, including automobiles
- Current debt carried, including car loans, credit card balances, or student loans
- Obstacles to mortgage approval include an inadequate down payment; low appraisal value of the property; insufficient income; too many prior debts; and an unsatisfactory credit history. If any of these areas might cause you a problem, speak with your loan officer about them in advance.

Mortgage Types
Mortgages fall into two main categories: fixed-rate and variable-rate. A fixed-rate mortgage is designed for long-term ownership; if you plan to move in and stay there for most of the next 30 years, this is your best option. If you anticipate selling the house within a few years and are hoping to realize a capital gain, you may be able to obtain a variable-rate mortgage at a lower interest rate.

Comparison shopping for the best rate is definitely in order. Many banks advertise their rates in the newspaper and online, but be sure to read the fine print in order to gauge overall costs and fees. A mortgage broker can do some of this legwork for you at additional cost. However, the time you save may well be worth it.

Some government resources for home buyers include Fannie Mae (www.fanniemae.com), Freddie Mac (www.freddiemac.com) and Ginnie Mae (www.ginniemae.com). First-timers might also benefit from consulting with the Mortgage Bankers Association of America (MBA 202-861-6500), an association that will help put you in touch with a real estate loan officer as well as answer any questions you may have.

Online mortgages are available through numerous sites:www.eloan.com; www.homeadvisor. msn.com; www.hsh.com; www.keystroke.com; www.iown.com; www.mortgagelocator.com; www.quickenmortgage.com. If online is your preferred way of doing business, many of these resources will prove invaluable.

Amortization Tables
Amortization is a repayment method in which the amount you borrow is repaid gradually though regular monthly payments of principal and interest. During the first few years, most of each payment is applied toward the interest owed. During the final years of the loan, payment amounts are applied almost exclusively to the remaining principal. The longer the term of your loan, the more interest you will ultimately pay.

Several factors are involved in calculating your schedule of monthly payments, known as an amortization table: amount of loan, interest rate, length of loan, amount of taxes due, and insurance. The final results will show the breakdown of each payment: how much is put towards interest and how much towards the principal.

While your loan officer will calculate your final table, you can obtain reasonably accurate estimates with an online calculator. Go to http://www.getreal-estate.net/javascrp/mamortiz.htm, http://www. commercial-link.com/amortiza.htm, or http://www.aahomeloans.com/amort/ to get started.

⊙ Eilers, Terry. *How to Buy the Home You Want, for the Best Price, in Any Market.* New York: Hyperion, 1997. Johnson, Randy. *How to Save Thousands of Dollars on Your Home Mortgage.* New York: Wiley, 1998. Kibbey, H. L. *First Home Buying Guide: How to Do It Right the First Time!* Lake Oswego, Ore.: Panopoly, 1996.

Home Equity

A home equity loan is commonly referred to as a *second mortgage.* The difference between the amount you owe on your mortgage and the market value of your home is known as equity. Because real estate usually increases in value, after several years you may have more equity in your home than you might think.

Major expenses, especially those that will increase the value of your home such as major renovations, roofing, or adding rooms, can be financed through a home equity loan. However, a common pitfall is to use the equity in your home to pay off other debt, including credit cards. At face value it might seem wise to replace high-interest credit card debt with a lower-interest home equity loan. But if you find yourself unable to make those payments you risk losing your home.

Mortgage brokers and real estate loan officers can help you find a home equity loan (see *Real Estate* for more information).

Automobile

An auto loan can make it possible to drive a new car without having to come up with thousands of dollars in cash. Many loans require only a low down payment, and some require none at all. The lower the down payment the higher a price you will likely pay in the long run, as the interest rates can be quite excessive.

As with mortgages and other forms of major debt, it pays to shop around for the best deal. Setting your sights on a less expensive car might be prudent if you have limited cash available for a down payment. If you take on a heavy auto loan burden and are unable to make the payments, your car is subject to repossession.

Before you even go to look for a car, determine how much you can afford in monthly payments. Many car dealers offer in-house loans and they will have already calculated payments in advance. Unless you know what you can afford, you may wind up with a loan that looks like a good deal but does not really fit your budget.

For basic auto loan information, go to www.carfinance.com or www.1stopauto.com.

Personal

A personal loan, also known as an unsecured loan, should be considered a last resort if you are in need of funds. Because the risk to the lender is high, you will pay around 15% to 18% interest. Many banks offer personal lines of credit to their customers worth $1,000 or more.

Credit Cards

Rare is the person who never uses credit cards, and rarer still is the person who uses credit cards but does not carry long-term debt. Banks and credit companies continuously solicit people who might be suffering from cash-flow crunches, especially college students and recent graduates, with *special low introductory rates* that make the offers nearly impossible to refuse.

Breaking the cycle of credit card debt is essential to long-term financial security. Investments almost never pay more than credit cards cost, so to invest in mutual funds, stocks, or even an IRA before paying off your cards is a losing proposition. In the short-term, try to shop around for the lowest rate and transfer any outstanding balances to low-rate cards. Bankcard Holders of America (BH) is a non-profit consumer organization that will send you a list of low-rate cards for $4. Write to them at 524 Branch Drive, Salem, VA 24153 or call (540) 389-5445.

A refusal to use credit cards can backfire, however, as it is essential to establish a credit rating in order to obtain a mortgage or other loan later in life. A credit card can also provide an easy way to track your spending and document tax-related expenses.

To obtain your credit report, contact one of the three credit bureaus below. Reports are free if you have been denied credit within the past 60 days and cost $8 at all other times:

Equifax
P.O. Box 105873
Atlanta, GA 30348
www.equifax.com
800-682-7654

Experian (formerly TRW) TransUnion
P.O. Box 390
Springfield, PA 19064-0390
www.experian.com
800-888-4213
800-685-1111

If you have trouble managing your credit card debt, you can seek assistance from a number of agencies, including Consumer Credit Counseling Services (800-388-2227) and American Consumer Credit Counseling Service (24 Crescent Street, Waltham, MA, 02453; 800-769-3571; www.consumercredit.com)

⊙ Hammond, Bob. *Life After Debt: Free Yourself from the Burden of Money Worries Once and for All*. Franklin, N.J.: Career Press, 2000.

Mellan, Olivia, with Sherry Christie. *Overcoming Overspending: A Winning Plan for Spenders and Their Partners*. New York: Walker, 1995.

Taxes

Federal Income Taxes

If you are employed full-time, estimated federal taxes are withheld from your paycheck and sent to the Internal Revenue Service (IRS) on your behalf. Self-employed individuals must make quarterly estimated payments to the IRS or face penalties. At the end of the year, you must file a tax return (Form 1040 or 1040EZ) to reconcile the total amount of estimated taxes paid with the actual amount owed.

Income tax is known as a graduated tax, which means that people with higher incomes are taxed at a higher percentage rate than people with lower incomes. The rate at which you are taxed is known as a tax bracket.

You can reduce your tax burden by taking advantages of various deductions offered by the IRS. Some deductions are available to all taxpayers. The standard deduction is taken for each person who files taxes and varies depending upon family status. Dependent deductions are taken for each child supported by the taxpayer. In lieu of the standard deduction, you may choose to itemize certain expenses as permitted by law. These include state and local income taxes; property taxes; housing costs; donations to charities; business-related expenses; medical expenses; and tax-preparation fees. Itemized deductions must be listed on a separate form, known as Schedule A.

State Income Tax Rates

Not all states impose income taxes. Those that do use a system of graduated tax rates based on income levels, similar to that of the federal government. In this table, "Low Income" refers to the lowest annual income required for taxes to be charged; these earners are charged the rate in the "Low Rate" column. "High Income" earners are charged the highest tax rate, as seen in the "High Rate" column.

State	Low Rate (%)	High Rate (%)	Low Income	High Income	Exemption Single	Exemption Married	Exemption per Child
Alabama	2.0	5.0	500	3,000	1,500	3,000	300
Alaska	0	0	0	0	0	0	0
Arizona	2.87	5.04	10,000	150,000	2,100	4,200	2,300
Arkansas	1.0	7.0	2,999	25,000	20***	40***	20***
California	1.0	9.3	5,264	34,548	72***	142***	227***
Colorado	4.75	4.75	Flat rate	Flat rate	0	0	0
Connecticut	3.0	4.5	10,000*	10,000*	12,000	24,000	0
Delaware	2.2	5.95	5,000	60,000	110***	220***	110***
District of Columbia	5.0	9.5	10,000	20,000	1,370	2,740	1,370
Florida	0	0	0	0	0	0	0
Georgia	1.0	6.0	750**	7,000**	2,700	5,400	2,700
Hawaii	1.6	8.75	2,000*	40,000*	1,040	2,080	1,040
Idaho	2.0	8.2	1,000*	20,000*	2,750	5,500	2,750
Illinois	3.0	3.0	Flat rate	Flat rate	2,000	4,000	2,000
Indiana	3.4	3.4	Flat rate	Flat rate	1,000	2,000	1,000
Iowa	0.36	8.98	1,162	52,290	40***	80***	40***
Kansas	3.5	6.45	15,000*	30,000*	2,250	4,500	2,250
Kentucky	2.0	6.0	3,000	8,000	20***	40***	20***
Louisiana	2.0	6.0	10,000*	50,000*	4,500	9,000	1,000
Maine	2.0	8.5	4,150*	16,500*	2,850	5,600	2,850
Maryland	2.0	4.85	1,000	3,000	1,850	3,700	1,850
Massachusetts	5.95	5.95	Flat rate	Flat rate	4,400	8,800	1,000
Michigan	4.3	4.3	Flat rate	Flat rate	2,800	5,600	2,800
Minnesota	5.5	8.0	17,250**	56,680**	2,750	5,500	2,750
Mississippi	3.0	5.0	5,000	10,000	6,000	9,500	1,500
Missouri	1.5	6.0	1,000	9,000	1,200	2,400	1,200
Montana	2.0	11.0	2,000	70,400	1,610	3,220	1,610

State							
Nebraska	2.51	6.68	2,400**	26,500**	91***	182***	91***
Nevada	0	0	0	0	0	0	0
New Hampshire	State income tax limited to dividends and interest income						
New Jersey	1.4	6.37	20,000*	*75,000**	1,000	2,000	1,500
New Mexico	1.7	8.2	5,500**	65,000**	2,750	5,500	2,750
New York	4.0	6.85	8,000*	20,000*	0	0	1,000
North Carolina	6.0	7.75	12,750**	60,000**	2,750	5,500	2,750
North Dakota	2.67	12.0	3,000	50,000	2,750	5,500	2,750
Ohio	0.716	7.228	5,000	200,000	1,050	2,100	1,050
Oklahoma	0.5	6.75	1,000	10,000	1,000	2,000	1,000
Oregon	5.0	9.0	2,350*	5,800*	132***	264***	132***
Pennsylvania	2.8	2.8	Flat rate	Flat rate	0	0	0
Rhode Island	26.0% of federal tax liability				0	0	0
South Carolina	2.5	7.0	2,310	11,550	2,750	5,500	2,750
South Dakota	0	0	0	0	0	0	0
Tennessee	State income tax limited to dividends and interest income						
Texas	0	0	0	0	0	0	0
Utah	2.30	7.0	750*	3,750*	2,063	4,125	2,063
Vermont	24.0% of federal tax liability						
Virginia	2.0	5.75	3,000	17,000	800	1600	800
Washington	0	0	0	0	0	0	0
West Virginia	3.0	6.5	10,000*	60,000*	2,000	4,000	2,000
Wisconsin	4.73	6.75	7,500	15,001	0	0	50***
Wyoming	0	0	0	0	0	0	0

* For joint returns, the taxes are twice the tax imposed on half the income
** For single individual
*** Tax credits

⊙ Federation of Tax Administrators. www.taxadmin.org

State Sales Tax Rates

State	Sales Tax (%)	On Food	On Prescription Drugs	On Non-Prescription Drugs
Alabama	4.0	yes	no	yes
Alaska	0			
Arizona	5.0	no	no	yes
Arkansas	4.625	yes	no	yes
California	6.0	no	no	yes
Colorado	3.0	no	no	yes
Connecticut	6.0	no	no	yes
Delaware	0			
District of Columbia	5.75	no	no	no
Florida	6.0	no	no	no
Georgia	4.0	no	no	yes
Hawaii	4.0	yes	no	yes
Idaho	5.0	yes	no	yes
Illinois	6.25	1.0	1.0	1.0
Indiana	5.0	no	no	yes
Iowa	5.0	no	no	yes
Kansas	4.9	yes	no	yes
Kentucky	6.0	no	no	yes
Louisiana	4.0	3.0	no	yes
Maine	5.5	no	no	yes
Maryland	5.0	no	no	no
Massachusetts	5.0	no	no	yes
Michigan	6.0	no	no	yes
Minnesota	6.5	no	no	no
Mississippi	7.0	yes	no	yes
Missouri	4.225	yes	no	yes
Montana	0			
Nebraska	5.0	no	no	yes
Nevada	6.5	no	no	yes
New Hampshire	0			
New Jersey	6.0	no	no	no
New Mexico	5.0	yes	no	yes
New York	4.0	no	no	no
North Carolina	4.0	yes	no	yes
North Dakota	5.0	no	no	yes
Ohio	5.0	no	no	yes
Oklahoma	4.5	yes	no	yes
Oregon	0			
Pennsylvania	6.0	no	no	no
Rhode Island	7.0	no	no	no
South Carolina	5.0	yes	no	yes
South Dakota	4.0	yes	no	yes

Tennessee	6.0	yes	no	yes
Texas	6.25	no	no	yes
Utah	4.75	yes	no	yes
Vermont	5.0	no	no	no
Virginia	3.5	3.0	no	no
Washington	6.5	no	no	yes
West Virginia	6.0	yes	no	yes
Wisconsin	5.0	no	no	yes
Wyoming	4.0	yes	no	yes

Estate and Gift Taxes

Money that is inherited or received as a gift is subject to federal and state taxes. However, any number of individual gifts of up to $10,000 may be given annually without being subject to federal taxation. In addition, there is a federal tax-free amount of $675,000 in lifetime accumulation gift/estate value. In other words, if when you die your estate assets (after deduction of tax-exempt gifts) are less than $675,000, there should be no federal tax on your estate. This tax-free amount will rise to $1 million by 2006.

Some categories of giving are automatically tax-exempt: gifts to a spouse, to a political organization, to a charity, and gifts that are used to pay tuition or medical expenses.

Federal Estate Taxes as of 2001

Estate Value	Tax Rate	Estate Value	Tax Rate
$675,001–$750,000	37%	$2,000,001–$2,500,000	49%
$750,001–$1,000,000	39%	$2,500,001–$3,000,000	53%
$1,000,001–$1,250,000	41%	$3,000,001–$10,000,000	55%
$1,250,001–$1,500,000	43%	$10,000,001–$17,184,000	60%
$1,500,001–$2,000,000	45%	More than $17,184,000	55%

⊙ Internal Revenue Service. www.irs.gov
Federation of Tax Administrators. www.taxadmin.org
Tyson, Eric, and David J. Silverman. *Taxes for Dummies.* Foster City, Calif.: IDG, 2001.

WORK AND HOME: *In the Home*

Home Safety: Fire Safety Tips

Prevention

- Keep portable space heaters at least three feet from flammable items. Never leave a heater on unattended.
- Never smoke in bed or when sleepy.
- Keep matches and lighters out of the reach of children.
- Teach your children the importance of fire safety.
- Regularly monitor your house for electrical safety. If an appliance ever smokes or sparks, unplug it immediately and have it serviced. Do not overload extension cords.
- Store flammable liquids in metal cabinets. Storage areas should be cool, with adequate airflow.

Home Safety: Fire Safety Tips

Readiness

- Smoke detectors cut the risk of death from fire in half. Install at least one on each floor, including the basement. Test detectors once a month and change batteries once a year. Replace detectors after 10 years, even if they appear to be working. Be sure to purchase smoke detectors certified by Underwriters Laboratories (UL) or Factory Mutual (FM). They should operate on lithium batteries, and should have a hush button.
- Install fire extinguishers on each floor and in the kitchen. Fire extinguishers should be UL or FM listed, and should be of the ABC type (A = wood and paper; B = flammable liquids; C = electrical).
- Post emergency numbers near telephones, but if a fire threatens your home, don't risk your life—evacuate first, and call the authorities from a safe location.
- Make an escape plan: draw a floor plan and identify two routes of escape for each room. Set a meeting place in front of your house.
- Consider installing fire escape ladders on upper floors.
- Test windows and doors for ease of use.
- Keep a bell and a flashlight in each room. Practice ringing the bells and yelling "Fire!"
- Twice a year, have the whole family practice evacuating your home. Learn to stay low to the ground—smoke and gases may be toxic. Practice evacuating while blindfolded—in a real fire, smoke will make it difficult to see. In house fires, people usually have about two minutes to escape.
- Always sleep with the bedroom doors closed. This retards entry of heat and smoke, increasing your escape time.

In the Event of a Fire

- Feel all doors before opening them. If a door is hot, use another route.
- If clothes catch fire, immediately "stop, drop, and roll."
- Do not attempt to save belongings. Remember, you have only about two minutes.
- After evacuating, give first aid as needed. Minor burns should be placed under cool running water. If the burn blisters or chars, see a doctor at once.
- Do not re-enter your house until fire authorities tell you it is safe to do so.

⊙ The Fire Escape Systems Store. "Fire Safety and Protection Tips," www.firesafetytips.com
U.S. Fire Administration. "Fire Safety and Education," www.usfa.fema.gov/safety/sheets.htm

Home Safety: Electrical Safety Tips

Item	Precautions
Wiring	Have house wiring inspected about once every 10 years.
Fuses	Always use the correct fuse. The wrong fuse can allow circuits to overload and cause fires.
Circuits	Do not overload circuits. Most houses are wired at 15 amps, which means each circuit can safely carry about 1,500 watts.

Outlets	Cap unused outlets. Consider installing Ground Fault Circuit Interruptors in kitchens, bathrooms, and other areas with high risk of electric shock exposure. If installed, test them monthly.
Cords	Do not run cords under rugs or blankets, or rest furniture on them. Do not expose them to heat or wetness. Keep cords out of reach of children.
Extension cords	Do not use indoor cords outdoors. Store all cords indoors when not in use, to prevent weather damage.
Appliances	Follow instructions. Watch for overheating, sparking, malfunctioning, etc. Never use any appliance near water or wet surfaces. Buy appliances certified by Underwriters Laboratories or similar reputable third-party agency.

⊙ Mendelson, Cheryl. *Home Comforts.* New York: Scribner, 1999.
National Electrical Safety Foundation. www.electricnet.com/orgs/nesf.htm
National Safety Council. www.nsc.org
Underwriters Laboratories. www.ul.com

Home Safety: Drinking Water

The Centers for Disease Control estimates that each year about 900,000 people fall sick from consuming contaminated water, and up to 900 die. Contaminants include lead, bacteria, arsenic, pesticides, radiation, volatile organic chemicals (VOCs), and trihalomethanes (THMs).

When water stands in pipes, contaminants can become concentrated. Never drink water from a tap until you have let it run for one to two minutes. If you have a well, make sure it uses a lead-free pump.

You may request water analysis results from your water supplier, or hire a private laboratory to test your water supply (at a cost of $50–200). In requests to water suppliers, be sure to list all contaminants that concern you to ensure a complete response. The best water filtration systems combine several filtration methods, such as activated carbon, depth or screen filters, and reverse osmosis or distillation.

Contaminant	Best Filtration Method
bacteria	ultraviolet, screen
lead	distillation, reverse osmosis
nuclear fission products	reverse osmosis, water softeners
particulates	depth filter
pesticides	activated carbon, reverse osmosis
radium	reverse osmosis
radon	activated carbon
uranium	reverse osmosis
volatile organic chemicals	activated carbon, reverse osmosis

⊙ Gabler, Raymond. *Is your water safe to drink?* Mt. Vernon, N.Y.: Consumers Union, 1988.
Steinman, David, and Samuel Epstein. *The Safe Shopper's Bible.* New York: Macmillan, 1995.

Substance	Description	Risk	Sources	Testing	Safety Guidelines	Reduction Methods
Asbestos	Mineral fiber	Lung cancer, mesothelioma, other cancers. Asbestos is only dangerous when its fibers are released into the air and inhaled.	Asbestos is a common building material that was once (pre-1975) widely used in insulation, soundproofing, fireproofing, and texturizing.	Asbestos problems are determined by visual inspection or by air monitoring. Air monitoring technologies are not completely reliable.	There is no safe level for asbestos.	Removal, enclosure, or encapsulation. Asbestos abatement should always be done by professionals.
Carbon Monoxide	Colorless, odorless gas	Fatigue, shortness of breath, dizziness, nausea, heart and brain disorders; asphyxiation and death	Incomplete combustion from improperly ventilated heaters, furnaces, woodburning stoves and fireplaces; car exhaust; tobacco smoke.	Carbon monoxide sensors sound an alarm when hazardous levels are detected.	More than 5 ppm is considered dangerous.	Make sure heaters are used and ventilated correctly. Inspect furnaces, stoves, and fireplaces and perform proper maintenance. Never idle a car in a garage.
Formaldehyde	Colorless water-soluble gas	Eye and lung irritation, neurological disorders	Urea formaldehyde foam (UFF) insulation, formaldehyde-treated wallboard, plywood. Contamination is especially common in mobile homes.	A PF-1 device is placed in the house for a week, then sent to a lab for analysis.	Limit exposure to 0.1 ppm	Improve ventilation, seal or remove the material, or treat it with ammonia (for professionals only).

Lead	Heavy, soft, bluish-gray metal	Lead poisoning has been linked to mental retardation, learning disabilities, kidney ailments, and other health problems.	Lead-based paints, lead pipes, leaded gasoline, industrial pollution.	Annual blood tests for children. Portable X-ray fluorescence test for paint. Professional labs can test drinking water.	A blood lead level of over 15 ug/dl is dangerous for children and pregnant women. Safe levels in paint: 7 mg per square cm; in water: 5 ppb.	aint should be stripped by a professional. Lead painted doors and windows can be replaced. Encapsulation may be a viable option.
Radon	Radioactive gas	Lung cancer	Water supply, soil, basement cracks. Products of radon decay attach to airborne dust particles, which are inhaled.	Test devices are exposed to air, then sent to lab for analysis.	Levels at or above 1 Working Load (WL) or 200 picocuries per liter (pCi/l) are considered dangerous.	Ventilation, crack sealing, covering exposed earth, suction, altering house air pressure, air cleaning.

⊙ Altman, Roberta. *The Complete Book of Home Environmental Hazards*. New York: Facts on File, 1990.
Centers for Disease Control. www.cdc.gov
Lowe's Home Improvement. "Lowe's - Hidden Home Hazards," www.lowes.com/lowes/safety/safehome/safhom10.asp

Common Home Heating Systems

System	Fuel	Description	Comments
Active solar	Solar power	Large panels collect solar energy.	Systems are expensive; practical only in the sunniest, warmest areas.
Electric	Electricity	Electrical resistance units heat the rooms like a toaster.	Clean, efficient; inexpensive to install, no fumes. Produces comfortable, even heat. Utility bills are two to three times more expensive than gas or oil on average.
Electric heat pump	Electricity	A compressor extracts heat from external air and pumps it inside.	Easily overtaxed in cold climates; only suitable for areas with mild winters.
Forced Air	Gas or oil	A blower forces cool air across the hot surface of a heat exchanger. Air then travels through ducts into rooms. Return ducts collect cool air to be reheated.	By far the most common modern heating system. Efficient. Can be adapted for air conditioning. Can be drafty or uneven.
Hot water	Gas or oil	Water is heated in a boiler, then circulated through pipes to radiators.	Common through the 1940s.
Passive solar	Solar power	Newer homes often have more south-facing windows. If these are uncovered during the day and covered at night, some heat is retained.	Not a heating system, and not a stand-alone energy solution, but can considerably reduce conventional heating costs.

⊙ Johnson, Duane. *How a House Works*. *The Family Handyman Series*. Pleasantville, N.Y.: Readers Digest, 1994.

Calculating Heating and Cooling Needs

Winter Heating Zones

To find base BTU/hour for home heating, multiply your zone number (below) by floor space in square feet. For a well-insulated house, multiply total by 0.7; for a poorly insulated house, multiply by 1.5. Adjust capacity further if using a gas or oil furnace: multiply by 1.25 for gas, 1.3 for oil. If the heating system also heats the water supply, multiply by 1.2. Thus, for a well-insulated 2,500 square foot home in northern Virginia heated by a gas system that also heats the water supply:

$$2,500 \times 40 \text{ (zone)} \times 1.7 \text{ (insulation)} \times 1.25 \text{ (gas)} \times 1.2 \text{ (water heater)}$$

$$= 105,000 \text{ BTU/hr.}$$

Zone Heat Factor	Zone Description
90	Alaskan Coast
80	—
70	northern Maine, northern Minnesota, northern North Dakota, High Rockies
60	northern New England, Great Lakes states, northern plains states, Rockies
50	Washington State, eastern Oregon, central Nevada, central Midwest, mid-Atlantic, the Salt Lake basin
40	western Oregon, eastern California through central New Mexico through southern Missouri to northern Kentucky and Virginia
30	California wine country, California Central Valley through northern Texas to Kentucky and Tennessee, inland North Carolina
20	central Texas, the South to the Carolina coast
10	deep Texas, the Gulf Coast
5	southern Florida
0	Hawaii

Summer Cooling Zones

Divide number of square feet by your zone number, then multiply by 12,000.
For a well-insulated house, multiply again by 0.85; for a poorly insulated house, multiply by 1.3. Thus, for the same 2,500 square foot well-insulated house in northern Virginia:

$$2,500 \ / \ 600 \ (\text{zone}) \times 12,000 \times 0.85 \ (\text{insulation})$$

$$= 42,500 \ \text{BTU/hr.}$$

Zone Cooling Factor	Zone Description
700	Hawaii, New England, Great Lakes, northern plains states, Pacific Northwest
600	mid-Atlantic including Virginia and Kentucky, Midwest, mountain states, California coast
500	The South through the Southwest, central and eastern California
400	Gulf Coast
300	southern Texas, southern Florida

⊙ HearthNet. "BTU Calculator," www.hearth.com/calc/btucalc.html
  Spel Group. "Heat Load Calculator," www.spelgroup.com/HLC.hlc.htm

Recycling: Common Recyclable Materials

Always contact your local recycling center for the latest information regarding accepted materials, preparation guidelines, and advice.

Material	Recyclable	Non-recyclable	To Prepare
Paper			
Newsprint	all		Tie with string, then bag or box. Keep stored paper away from damp and sun. Contact recycling center regarding whether to separate slick paper.

Material	Recyclable	Non-recyclable	To Prepare
Mixed Paper	Junk mail, slick paper, paperboard, wrapping paper, stationery, paper bags, phone books	Tissue, paper plates, fax or thermal paper, chemically treated paper, bubble envelopes, foil paper, plastic-coated paperboard	Remove staples, backing, and glue. Tie, bag, or box. Flatten boxes. (Phone books are often disposed of by the phone company.)
Glass and Plastic*			
Glass	Glass bottles	Window glass, glassware, light bulbs, or ceramics	Separate colored from clear glass. Rinse thoroughly and remove caps and neck rings. Contact recycling center regarding whether to remove labels. Do not include broken glass.
1 PETE	All		Rinse lightly and remove caps and collars.
2 HDPE	All		Rinse, remove caps and collars, and flatten. Recycling center may ask you to separate clear and colored.
3 V	All		Rinse, remove caps, collars, and labels, then flatten.
4 LDPE	Shrink wrap, cellophane		Shrink wrap and cellophane use chemicals which are unsuitable for recycling.
5 PP	Varies	Varies	Often not accepted. Contact your local recycling center.
6 PS	Varies	Varies	Often not accepted, but some centers accept polystyrene for conversion to building insulation. Contact the Association of Foam Packaging Recyclers at 800-944-8448.
7 Other		All	Not readily recyclable.
Metal			
Aluminum	Cans		Rinse, remove labels, and crush. Some recycling centers accept foil, TV dinner trays, and other aluminum products. For further information contact the Reynolds Aluminum Recycling Hotline: 800-228-2525.

| Steel | Cans | Aerosol cans, some mixed-material cans | Rinse, remove labels, and crush. Rusty cans are acceptable. Some recycling centers will accept aerosol cans. Contact the Steel Can Recycling Hotline 800-937-1226. |

*Refer to "Recycling: Codes" below for types of plastics associated with codes.

⊙ McVicker, Dee. *Easy Recycling Handbook*. Gilbert, Ariz.: Grassroots Books, 1994.

Recycling: Codes

The symbol [insert symbol] on plastics, metals, and other materials indicates that the material is recyclable. On plastics, the symbol will contain one of the following numbers, indicating the type of plastic.

No.	Abbr.	Material	Description	Examples
1	PETE	polyethylene terephthalate	a clear plastic, denser than water	two-liter carbonated beverage bottles
2	HDPE	high density poly-ethylene	clear or translucent plastic with a dull finish, floats in water	detergent bottles, dairy bottles
3	V	vinyl		some shampoo bottles
4	LDPE	low density poly-ethylene		food wrap
5	PP	polypropylene	a hard, durable plastic	food containers and lids
6	PS	polystyrene	a foamed plastic, trade name Styrofoam™	food containers and foam boxes, hot drink cups
7		Other		

⊙ Gall, Timothy L., and Susan B. Gall. *Consumers' Guide to Product Grades and Terms*. Detroit: Gale Research, 1993.
   SPI's Voluntary Plastic Container Coding System. Washington, D.C.: Society of the Plastics Industry, 1992.

Recycling: Preferred Packaging Materials

The following materials are ranked in order of preference for use in commerical packaging in terms of their reusability.

Rank	Material	Explanation
1	Glass	Inexpensive to produce, reusable
2	Aluminum	Expensive to produce from scratch, but efficient to recycle
3	Paper	The least harmful paper has high post-consumer recycled content and is unbleached.
4	Plastic	Non-biodegradable. Recycling is vital to limit the disposal of plastic in landfills.
5	Multimaterial	Cost-prohibitive to recycle; avoid as much as possible

⊙ Carliss, Jennifer. *Taking out the Trash*. Washington, D.C.: Island, 1992.

Automobile Safety: Air Bags

Air bags reduce the risk of dying in a direct frontal crash by about 30 percent. Almost all adults are safer riding or driving with an airbag than without one. However, airbags can be a source of injury for children and some adults.

The main source of risk is proximity. For maximum safety, a driver's chest should be at least 10 inches from the center of the steering wheel, and a passenger's chest should be at least 10 inches from the dashboard. These margins can almost always be achieved by moving the seats and/or tilting their backs. Seatbelts should be worn, and should fit snugly. Children 12 and under should always ride in the back seat. Under no circumstances should you *ever* place a rear-facing child safety seat in front of an air bag.

If you are unable to seat yourself as recommended, or you have been advised by a doctor that you are at special risk from an air bag, you may apply to the National Highway Traffic Safety Administration (NHTSA) for an air bag on-off switch. You may also apply for a switch if you must accommodate a child 12 or under in your front seat.

⊙ U.S. National Highway Traffic Safety Administration (NHTSA). "Air Bag On-Off Switches: Questions and Answers," www.nhtsa.dot.gov/people/injury/airbags/

Automobile Safety: Child Safety Seats

Age Guidelines

- Children up to one year old should ride in a rear-facing infant's safety seat or convertible seat. The seat must be installed in the rear seat. Never place a rear-facing safety seat in front of an air bag.
- Children over one year old who weigh at least 20 pounds should sit facing forward in a convertible child safety seat.
- Children between 40 and 80 pounds (about 4 to 8 years old) should ride in a booster seat.
- All children aged 12 and under should sit in the back seat, properly restrained.
- A seat that has been in a crash should be replaced immediately. The seat may have sustained damage that is not visible.

Buying Tips

- When buying any safety seat or booster seat, make sure it bears a label reading, "This child restraint system conforms to all applicable U.S. Federal Motor Vehicle Safety Standards."
- High-backed booster seats provide head and neck protection. Five-point harnesses or shields provide full body protection for children up to about 40 pounds. Children 40 to 80 pounds may ride in the seats using the vehicle's lap and shoulder belts.
- Check the seat for ease of installation and use. Try adjusting the harness straps. Make sure the seat can be installed properly in your make and model of car.
- Read the instruction booklet thoroughly and follow all guidelines properly.

⊙ National Highway Traffic Safety Administration. "Child Transportation Safety Tips," www.nhtsa.dot.gov/people/injury/childps/
National Highway Traffic Safety Administration. "A Parent's Guide to Booster Seats," www.nhtsa.dot.gov/people/injury/childps/

Dog Breeds (as recognized by the American Kennel Club)

Herding Dogs

Australian Cattle Dog
Australian Shepherd
Bearded Collie
Belgian Malinois
Belgian Sheepdog
Belgian Tervuren
Border Collie
Bouvier des Flandres
Briard
Canaan Dog
Collie
German Shepherd
Dog
Old English Sheepdog
Puli
Shetland Sheepdog
Welsh Corgi (Cardigan)
Welsh Corgi
(Pembroke)

Hounds

Afghan Hound
Basenji
Basset Hound
Beagle
Black and Tan
Coonhound
Bloodhound
Borzoi
Dachshund
Foxhound
(American)
Foxhound (English)
Greyhound
Harrier
Ibizan Hound
Irish Wolfhound
Norwegian Elkhound
Otterhound
Petit Basset Griffon
Vendeen
Pharaoh Hound
Rhodesian Ridgeback
Saluki
Scottish Deerhound
Whippet

Non-Sporting Dogs

American Eskimo
Dog
Bichon Frise
Boston Terrier
Bulldog
Chinese Shar-pei
Chow Chow
Dalmatian
Finnish Spitz
French Bulldog
Keeshond
Lhasa Apso
Löwchen
Poodle (Standard &
Miniature)
Schipperke
Shiba Inu
Tibetan Spaniel
Tibetan Terrier

Sporting Dogs

American Water
Spaniel
Brittany
Chesapeake Bay
Retriever
Clumber Spaniel
Cocker Spaniel
Curly-Coated Retriever
English Cocker Spaniel
English Setter
English Springer
Spaniel
Field Spaniel
Flat-Coated Retriever
German Shorthaired
Pointer
German Wirehaired
Pointer
Golden Retriever
Gordon Setter
Irish Setter
Irish Water Spaniel
Labrador Retriever
Pointer
Sussex Spaniel
Vizsla
Weimaraner
Welsh Springer
Spaniel
Wirehaired Pointing
Griffon

Terriers

Airedale Terrier
American Staffordshire
Terrier
Australian Terrier
Bedlington Terrier
Border Terrier
Bull Terrier
Cairn Terrier
Dandie Dinmont
Terrier
Fox Terrier (Smooth)
Fox Terrier (Wire)
Irish Terrier
Jack Russell Terrier
Kerry Blue Terrier
Lakeland Terrier
Manchester Terrier
(Standard)
Miniature Bull Terrier
Miniature Schnauzer
Norfolk Terrier
Norwich Terrier
Scottish Terrier
Sealyham Terrier
Skye Terrier
Soft Coated Wheaten
Terrier
Staffordshire Bull
Terrier
Welsh Terrier
West Highland White
Terrier

Dog Breeds (cont.)

Toy Dogs

Affenpinscher
Brussels Griffon
Cavalier King Charles
  Spaniel
Chihuahua
Chinese Crested

English Toy
  Spaniel
Havanese
Italian Greyhound
Japanese Chin
Maltese

Manchester Terrier
  (Toy)
Miniature Pinscher
Papillon
Pekingese
Pomeranian

Poodle (Toy)
Pug
Shih Tzu
Silky Terrier
Yorkshire Terrier

Working Dogs

Akita
Alaskan Malamute
Anatolian Shepherd
Bernese Mountain Dog
Boxer
Bullmastiff

Doberman Pinscher
Giant Schnauzer
Great Dane
Great Pyrenees
Greater Swiss
  Mountain Dog

Komondor
Kuvasz
Mastiff
Newfoundland
Portuguese Water
  Dog

Rottweiler
Saint Bernard
Samoyed
Siberian Husky
Standard Schnauzer

Miscellaneous

Plott Hound

Polish Lowland
  Sheepdog

Spinone Italiano

◉ American Kennel Club. "List of Breeds," www.akc.org/breeds/recbreeds/list.cfm
American Kennel Club Staff. *The Complete Dog Book, 19th Edition.* Foster City, Calif.: IDG, 1997.

Cat Breeds (as recognized by the Cat Fanciers' Association)

Championship Class

Abyssinian
American Curl
American Shorthair
American Wirehair
Balinese
Birman
Bombay
British Shorthair
Burmese

Chartreux
Colorpoint Shorthair
Cornish Rex
Devon Rex
Egyptian Mau
Exotic
Havana Brown
Javanese
Japanese Bobtail

Korat
Maine Coon
Manx
Norwegian Forest Cat
Ocicat
Oriental
Persian
Ragdoll
Russian Blue

Scottish Fold
Selkirk Rex
Siamese
Singapura
Somali
Tonkinese
Turkish Angora
Turkish Van

Provisional Class

European Burmese (*if shown in International Division, may compete with Championship Class*)

Miscellaneous Class

American Bobtail

LaPerm Siberian

Sphynx

◉ Cat Fanciers' Association. "CFA Breeds," www.cfainc.org/breeds.html
Helgren, J. Anne. *Barron's Encyclopedia of Cat Breeds: A Complete Guide to the Domestic Cats of North America.* Hauppauge, N.Y.: Barron's, 1997.

WORK AND HOME: *Communications*

Internet

How to Use

The Internet (a.k.a. the World Wide Web or the Web) is rapidly becoming a major means of communication in the United States. According to AC Nielsen, 64% of Americans age 12 or older used the Internet in the year 2000. Using the Internet requires three components: hardware, software, and a data connection.

Hardware: A personal computer, as well as a modem or networking card. All new personal computers on the market today are technologically capable of accessing the Internet.

Software: A browser program such as Microsoft Internet Explorer or Netscape Communicator. These programs can also be used for basic electronic mail (e-mail), although more sophisticated e-mail programs such as Eudora or Microsoft Outlook allow the user to save and organize messages.

Data connection: Dialup connections, using a modem and an ordinary telephone line, have been the standard until recently. Users contract with an Internet Service Provider (ISP), which provides a telephone number for establishing a connection. Some ISPs offer free access but require that you use an advertising-supported browser program. As new technology develops, faster connections are becoming available in many locations: a cable modem uses the cable television network to access the Internet, and a DSL connection provides high-speed access via telephone lines. Contact your cable and telephone companies to see if this service is available in your area.

Search Engines

Information on the Internet is composed of individual units called Web pages. Many of these pages are linked together into thematically based networks. Because of the decentralized nature of the Internet, no single directory exists for all of these pages. Search engines are programs that can comb through these pages and find information based on keywords.

Portals

Some companies have developed Internet directories based on specific categories of information. Users can follow a series of links to find Web pages that fit into these categories. A portal also contains a search engine to look for information both within the portal and throughout the Internet.

E-mail

Most ISPs include an e-mail account as a basic feature. The ISP provides instructions on how to use e-mail software to send and receive messages. In addition, many Web sites and portals provide free e-mail accounts to users. Web-based e-mail, however, is not as flexible or sophisticated as e-mail software, and these accounts have limited storage space for archiving messages.

⊙ "CNET's Ultimate Guide to Search," www.cnet.com/internet/0-3817-7-1922932.html
"CNET Web Services," http://webservices.cnet.com

Telephone: United States and Canada Area Codes

Code	State/Province	Code	State/Province	Code	State/Province
201	New Jersey	310	California	443	Maryland
202	District of Columbia	312	Illinois	450	Quebec
203	Connecticut	313	Michigan	469	Texas
204	Manitoba	314	Missouri	478	Georgia
205	Alabama	315	New York	480	Arizona
206	Washington	316	Kansas	484	Pennsylvania
207	Maine	317	Indiana	501	Arkansas
208	Idaho	318	Louisiana	502	Kentucky
209	California	319	Iowa	503	Oregon
210	Texas	320	Minnesota	504	Louisiana
212	New York	321	Florida	505	New Mexico
213	California	323	California	506	New Brunswick
214	Texas	330	Ohio	507	Minnesota
215	Pennsylvania	334	Alabama	508	Massachusetts
216	Ohio	336	North Carolina	509	Washington
217	Illinois	337	Louisiana	510	California
218	Minnesota	347	New York	512	Texas
219	Indiana	352	Florida	513	Ohio
225	Louisiana	360	Washington	514	Quebec
228	Mississippi	361	Texas	515	Iowa
229	Georgia	401	Rhode Island	516	New York
231	Michigan	402	Nebraska	517	Michigan
240	Maryland	403	Alberta	518	New York
248	Michigan	404	Georgia	519	Ontario
250	British Columbia	405	Oklahoma	520	Arizona
252	North Carolina	406	Montana	530	California
253	Washington	407	Florida	540	Virginia
254	Texas	408	California	541	Oregon
256	Alabama	409	Texas	559	California
262	Wisconsin	410	Maryland	561	Florida
267	Pennsylvania	412	Pennsylvania	562	California
270	Kentucky	413	Massachusetts	570	Pennsylvania
281	Texas	414	Wisconsin	573	Missouri
301	Maryland	415	California	580	Oklahoma
302	Delaware	416	Ontario	601	Mississippi
303	Colorado	417	Missouri	602	Arizona
304	West Virginia	418	Quebec	603	New Hampshire
305	Florida	419	Ohio	604	British Columbia
306	Saskatchewan	423	Tennessee	605	South Dakota
307	Wyoming	425	Washington	606	Kentucky
308	Nebraska	435	Utah	607	New York
309	Illinois	440	Ohio	608	Wisconsin

WORK AND HOME: *Communications*

609	New Jersey	727	Florida	850	Florida
610	Pennsylvania	732	New Jersey	856	New Jersey
612	Minnesota	734	Michigan	860	Connecticut
613	Ontario	740	Ohio	864	South Carolina
614	Ohio	757	Virginia	865	Tennessee
615	Tennessee	760	California	867	Northwest Territories
616	Michigan	763	Minnesota	870	Arkansas
617	Massachusetts	765	Indiana	901	Tennessee
618	Illinois	770	Georgia	902	Nova Scotia
619	California	773	Illinois	903	Texas
623	Arizona	775	Nevada	904	Florida
626	California	780	Alberta	905	Ontario
630	Illinois	781	Massachusetts	906	Michigan
631	New York	785	Kansas	907	Alaska
650	California	786	Florida	908	New Jersey
651	Minnesota	787	Puerto Rico	909	California
660	Missouri	801	Utah	910	North Carolina
661	California	802	Vermont	912	Georgia
662	Mississippi	803	South Carolina	913	Kansas
678	Georgia	804	Virginia	914	New York
701	North Dakota	805	California	915	Texas
702	Nevada	806	Texas	916	California
703	Virginia	807	Ontario	917	New York
704	North Carolina	808	Hawaii	918	Oklahoma
705	Ontario	810	Michigan	919	North Carolina
706	Georgia	812	Indiana	920	Wisconsin
707	California	813	Florida	925	California
708	Illinois	814	Pennsylvania	931	Tennessee
709	Newfoundland	815	Illinois	937	Ohio
712	Iowa	816	Missouri	940	Texas
713	Texas	817	Texas	941	Florida
714	California	818	California	949	California
715	Wisconsin	819	Quebec	954	Florida
716	New York	828	North Carolina	956	Texas
717	Pennsylvania	830	Texas	970	Colorado
718	New York	831	California	972	Texas
719	Colorado	832	Texas	973	New Jersey
720	Colorado	843	South Carolina	978	Massachusetts
724	Pennsylvania	847	Illinois	979	Texas

⊙ North American Numbering Plan Administration. "Geographic NPAs in Service Sorted by Number,"
   www.nanpa.com/area_codes/geographic_number.html
   North American Numbering Plan Administration. "Area Code Maps," www.nanpa.com/
   number_resource_info/area_code_maps.html
   North American Numbering Plan Administration. "Planned NPAs Not Yet in Service," www.nanpa.com/
   area_codes/npa_planned.html

To call from the United States, dial 011, the international dialing code, the city code, and the telephone number.

International Dialing Code	City Code
Afghanistan 93	
Albania 355	Durres 52
	Elbassan 545
	Tirana 42
Algeria 213	Algiers 2
American Samoa 684	
Andorra 376	
Angola 244	Luanda 2
	Huambo 416
Anguilla 264	
Antarctica 672	
Antigua and Barbuda 1-268 *	
Argentina 54	Buenos Aires 1
	Cordoba 51
	Santa Fe 42
Armenia 374	Aparan 520
	Kotaik 61
	Talin 490
Aruba 297	
Ascension 247	
Australia 61	Canberra 262
	Melbourne 39
	Sydney 2
Austria 43	Linz 70
	Linz Donau 732
	Salzburg 662
	Vienna 1
Azerbaijan 994	Baku 12
Bahamas 1-242 *	
Bahrain 973	
Bangladesh 880	Dhaka 2
	Rangpur 521
Barbados 1-246 *	
Belarus 375	Loev 2347
	Minsk 172
	Mogilev 222
Belgium 32	Antwerp 3
	Brussels 2
	Ghent 9
Belize 501	Belize City 2
	Belmopan 8
	Orange Walk 3
Benin 229	
Bermuda 1-441 *	

International Dialing Code	City Code
Bhutan 975	
Bolivia 591	Cochabamba 42
	La Paz 2
	Santa Cruz 3
Bosnia-	Mostar 88
Herzegovina 387	Sarajevo 71
	Zenica 72
Botswana 267	
Brazil 55	Brasilia 61
	Rio de Janeiro 21
	Salvador 71
	São Paulo 11
British Virgin Islands 1-284 *	
Brunei 673	Behawan 2
	Kuala Belait 3
	Tutong 4
Bulgaria 359	Plovdiv 32
	Sofia 2
	Varna 52
Burkina Faso 226	
Burundi 257	
Cambodia 855	Phnom Penh 23 or 22
Cameroon 237	
Canada 1	Ontario (Ottawa) 613
	Ontario (Toronto Vicinity) 905
	Ontario (Toronto Metro) 416
	Prince Edward Island 902
	Quebec (Montreal) 514
	Quebec (Quebec City) 418
	Quebec (Sherbrooke) 819
	Vancouver 604
Cape Verde Islands 238	
Cayman Islands 1-345 *	
Central African Republic 236	
Chad 235	
Chatham Island 64	
Chile 56	Concepción 41
	Santiago 2
	Valparaiso 32
China 86	Beijing (Peking) 10
	Hangzhou 571
	Fuzhou (Fujian) 591
	Ghuangzhou (Canton) 20
	Shanghai 21
Christmas and Cocos Islands 672	

Colombia 57   Barranquila 53

Bogotá 1

Cali 2

Cartagena 59

Medellín 4

Comoros 269

Congo 242

Congo, Democratic
   Republic of 243   Kinshasa 12

Cook Islands 682

Costa Rica 506

Croatia 385   Dubrovnik 20

Rijeka 51

Split 21

Zagreb 1

Cuba 53   Havana 7

Cyprus, Northern 90392

Cyprus, Republic   Larnaca 4
   of 357   Limassol 5

Nicosia 2

Czech   Brno 5
   Republic 420   Ostrava 69

Prague 2

Denmark 45

Diego Garcia 246

Djibouti 253

Dominica 1-767 *

Dominican Republic 1-809 *

Ecuador 593   Easter Island 56

Guayaquil 4

Quito 2

Egypt 20   Alexandria 3

Asyut 88

Cairo 2

El Salvador 503   La Fontera 503

Los Lagartos 503

Olomega 503

Equatorial Guinea 240

Eritrea 291   Asmara 1

Makale 1

Massawa 1

Estonia 372   Rakvere 32

Tallinn 2 or 372

Tartu 7

Ethiopia 251   Addis Ababa 1

Debre Zeit 1

Dire Dawa 5

Falkland Islands 500

Faroe Islands 298

Fiji Islands 679

Finland 358   Helsinki 9

Turku 2

Vaasa 6

France 33   Bordeaux 556

Marseille 491

Nice 493

Paris 1

French   Basse Pointe 78
   Antilles 596   Grand Bourg 76

Pointe à Pitre 8 or 9

French Guiana 594

French Polynesia 689

Gabon 241

Gambia 220

Georgia 995   Suhumi 881

Tbilisi 32

Germany 49   Berlin 30

Bonn 228

Bremen 421

Cologne (Koln) 221

Dresden 351

Dussledorf 211

Essen 201

Frankfurt 69

Hamburg 40

Munich 89

Ghana 233   Accra 21

Kumasi 51

Takoradi 31

Gibraltar 350

Greece 30   Athens 1

Iraklion (Crete) 81

Thessaloniki 31

Greenland 299

Grenada and Carriacuou 1-473 *

Grenadine Islands 784

Guadeloupe 590

Guam 671

Guantanamo Bay 5399

Guatemala 502   Guatemala City 2

Guinea 224

Guinea-Bissau 245

Guyana 592   Georgetown 2

Linden 4

New Amsterdam 3

Haiti 509

Honduras 504

Hong Kong 852

Hungary 36   Budapest 1

Szolnok 56

Veszprem 88

Iceland 354

India 91   Bombay (Mumbai) 22

Calcutta (Kolkata) 33

New Delhi 11

International Dialing Code	City Code	International Dialing Code	City Code
Indonesia 62	Bandung 22	Lebanon 961	Beirut 1
	Jakarta 21		Tripoli 6
	Medan 61	Lesotho 266	
Iran 98	Tehran 21	Liberia 231	
Iraq 964	Baghdad 1	Libya 218	Benghazi 61
Ireland 353	Cork 21		Tripoli 21
	Donegal 77	Liechtenstein 423	
	Dublin 1	Lithuania 370	Kaunas 7
Israel 972	Haifa 4		Klaipeda 6
	Jerusalem 2		Vilnius 2
	Nazareth 6	Luxembourg 352	
	Tel Aviv 3	Macedonia,	Bitola 97
Italy 39	Bologna 51	Federal Republic	Lozovo 92
	Florence 55	of 389	Skopje 91
	Genoa 10	Madagascar 261	
	Milan 2	Malawi 265	
	Naples 81	Malaysia 60	Ipoh 5
	Rome/Vatican City 6		Johor Bahru 7
	Venice 41		Kuala Lumpur 3
Ivory Coast 225		Maldives 960	
Jamaica 876		Mali 223	
Japan 81	Hiroshima 82	Malta 356	
	Kyoto 75	Mariana Islands 1-670 *	
	Nagasaki 958	Marshall	Ebeye 329
	Tokyo 3	Islands 692	
	Yokohama 45	Martinique 596	
Jordan 962	Amman 6	Mauritania 222	
	Rbid 2	Mauritius 230	
	Zarqa 9	Mayotte 269	
Kazakhstan 7	Alma Ata 327	Mexico 52	Acapulco 74
	Chimkent 325		Cancun 98
	Guryev 312		Guadalajara 3
Kenya 254	Mombasa 11		Merida 99
	Nairobi 2		Mexico City 5
Kiribati 686			Monterrey 8
Korea, North 850		Micronesia,	Kosrae 370
Korea, South 82	Inchon 32	Federated States	Pohnpei 320
	Pusan (Busan) 51	of 691	Truk 330
	Seoul 2		Yap 350
	Taegu (Daegu) 53	Midway Islands 808 *	
Kuwait 965		Miquelon 508	
Kyrgyzstan 7	Bishkek 2	Moldova 373	Benderi 32
	Osh 332	Monaco 33 or 377	
Laos 856		Mongolia 976	Ulan Batar 1
Latvia 371	Daugavpils 54	Montenegro 3818	
	Liepaia 34	Montserrat 664	
	Riga 34		

Morocco 212	Casablanca 2
	Fes 5
	Rabat (5 digits) 77
	Rabat (6 digits) 7
	Tangiers 99
Mozambique 258	
Myanmar	
(Burma) 95	Rangoon 1
Namibia 264	
Nauru 674	
Nepal 977	
Netherlands 31	Amsterdam 20
	Rotterdam 10
	The Hague 70
Netherlands	Bonaire 7
Antilles 599	Curacao 9
	Saba 46
	St. Eustatius 38
	St. Maarten 5
Nevis 809	
New Caledonia 687	
New Zealand 64	Auckland 9
	Christchurch 3
	Hamilton 7
Nicaragua 505	Chinandega 341
	Leon 311
	Managua 2
Niger 227	
Nigeria 234	Kaduna 62
	Lagos 1
	Port Hartcourt 84
Niue 683	
Norfolk Island 672	
North Korea 850	
Norway 47	Bergen 5
	Oslo 22
Oman 968	
Pakistan 92	Islamabad 51
	Karachi 21
	Lahore 42
Palau 680	
Panama 507	
Papua New Guinea 675	
Paraguay 595	Asunción 21
	Concepción 31
	Villarrica 541
Peru 51	Arequipa 54
	Lima 1
Philippines 63	Cebu City 32
	Luzon 455
	Manila 2
	Subic 47

Poland 48	Bialystok 85
	Gdansk 58
	Katowice 32
	Warsaw 22
Portugal 351	Coimbra 39
	Lisbon 1
	Setubal 65
Príncipe 239	
Puerto Rico 1-787 *	
Qatar 974	
Reunion Island 262	
Romania 40	Bacau 34
	Bucharest 1
	Constanta 41
	Iasi 32
Russia 7	Magadan 413
	Moscow 095
	St. Petersburg 812
Rwanda 250	
St. Helena 290	
St. Kitts 1-869 *	
St. Lucia 1-758 *	
St Pierre Et Miquelon 508	
St. Vincent 1-784 *	
Saipan 670	
San Marino 378	
São Tomé 239	
Saudi Arabia 966	Jeddah 2
	Mecca 2
	Medina 4
	Riyadh 1
Senegal	Dakar 8
Republic 221	all others 9
Serbia, Republic of 381	
Seychelles 248	
Sierra Leone 232	Freetown 22
Singapore 65	East 394
	Jurong East 665
	Orchard 834 or 835
Slovakia 421	Bratislava 7
	Presov 91
Slovenia 386	
Solomon Islands 677	
Somalia 252	
South Africa 27	Cape Town 21
	Johannesburg 11
	Pietermaritzburg 331
	Pretoria 12
Spain 34	Barcelona 3
	Madrid 1
	Malaga 5

International Dialing Code	City Code	International Dialing Code	City Code
Sri Lanka 94	Colombo Central 1	Ukraine 380	Kharkov 57
	Kandy 8		Kiev 44
	Kotte 1		Lviv 322
Sudan 249	Atbarah 21	United Arab	Abu Dhabi 2
	Khartoum 11	Emirates 971	Dubai 4
	Port Sudan 31		Sharjah 6
	Wad Medani 51	United	Birmingham 121
Suriname 597		Kingdom 44	Edinburgh 131
Swaziland 268			Liverpool 151
Sweden 46	Gothenburg 31		London (Inner) 207
	Malmo 40		London (Outer) 208
	Stockholm 8		Manchester 161
Switzerland 41	Berne 31		Nottingham 115
	Geneva 22	United States 1	
	Lucerne 41	Uruguay 598	Mercedes 532
	Zurich 1		Montevideo 2
Syria 963	Aleppo 21		San Jose 342
	Damascus 11	U.S. Virgin Islands 340	
	Homs 31	Uzbekistan 7	Karshi 375
Taiwan 886	Changhua 4		Samarkand 3662
	Kaohsiung 7		Tashkent 71 or 712
	Taipei 2	Vanuatu 678	
Tajikistan 7		Vatican City 39	
Tanzania 255		Venezuela 58	Caracas 2
Thailand 66	Bangkok 2		Maracaibo 61
	Chiang Mai 53		Maracay 43
	Nakhonsawan 56		Valencia 4
Togo 228		Vietnam 84	Da Nang City 518
Tonga Islands 676			Hanoi 4
Trinidad and Tobago 868			Ho Chi Minh City 8
Tunisia 216	Tunis 1	Wake Island 1-808 *	
Turkey 90	Ankara 312	Wallis and Futuna Islands 681	
	Istanbul Asya 216	Western Samoa 685	
	Istanbul Avrupa 212	Yemen 967	Aden 2
	Izmir 232		Sanaa 1
Turkmenistan 993			Taiz 4
Turks and Caicos Islands 1-649 *		Yugoslavia 381	Belgrade 11
Tuvalu 688		Zaire (Congo,	
Uganda 256	Entebbe 42	Democratic	
	Jinja 43	Republic of) 243	Kinshasa 12
	Kampala 41	Zambia 260	Lusaka 1
		Zanzibar 259	
		Zimbabwe 263	Harare 4

*Country code can be dialed direct from U.S. without dialing 011.

⊙ AT&T. "City and Country Codes," www.att.com/traveler/tools/codes.html
American Computer Resources. "International Calling Code Directory," www.the-acr.com/codes/cntrycd.htm
Steve Kropla. "International Dialing Codes," www.kropla.com/dialcode.htm

First Class Letters or Letter Packages	Sent within U.S.	Sent to Canada	Sent to Mexico	Sent to other countries
.5 oz.	$0.34	$0.60	$0.60	$0.80
1.0 oz.	$0.34	$0.60	$0.60	$0.80
1.5 oz.	$0.55	$0.85	$0.85	$1.60
2.0 oz.	$0.55	$0.85	$0.85	$1.60
2.5 oz.	$0.76	$1.10	$1.25	$2.40
3.0 oz.	$0.76	$1.10	$1.25	$2.40
3.5 oz.	$0.97	$1.35	$1.65	$3.20
4.0 oz.	$0.97	$1.35	$1.65	$3.20
4.5 oz.	$1.18	$1.60	$2.05	$4.00
5.0 oz.	$1.18	$1.60	$2.05	$4.00
5.5 oz.	$1.39	$1.85	$2.45	$4.80
6.0 oz.	$1.39	$1.85	$2.45	$4.80
6.5 oz.	$1.60	$2.10	$2.85	$5.60
7.0 oz.	$1.60	$2.10	$2.85	$5.60
7.5 oz.	$1.81	$2.35	$3.25	$6.40
8.0 oz.	$1.81	$2.35	$3.25	$6.40
8.5 oz.	$2.02	$3.10	$4.00	$7.55
9.0 oz.	$2.02	$3.10	$4.00	$7.55
9.5 oz.	$2.23	$3.10	$4.00	$7.55
10.0 oz.	$2.23	$3.10	$4.00	$7.55
10.5 oz.	$2.44	$3.10	$4.00	$7.55
11.0 oz.	$2.44	$3.10	$4.00	$7.55
11.5 oz.	$2.65	$3.10	$4.00	$7.55
12.0 oz.	$2.65	$3.10	$4.00	$7.55
12.5 oz.	$2.86	$3.75	$5.15	$8.70
13.0 oz.	$2.86	$3.75	$5.15	$8.70
Postcard	$0.20	$0.50	$0.50	$0.70

Domestic

Priority Mail (70 lbs. or less, 108 in. or less in combined length and girth)
2–3 Days Delivery:

up to 1 lb.	$3.50	up to 5 lbs.	$7.55
up to 2 lbs.	$3.95	over 5 lbs.	rate figured by
up to 3 lbs.	$5.15		weight and zone
up to 4 lbs.	$6.35		

Express Mail (70 lbs. or less, 108 in. or less in combined length and girth)
Next Day Delivery:

up to 8 oz.	$12.25	up to 4 lbs.	$21.70
over 8 oz to 2 lbs.	$16.00	up to 5 lbs.	$24.50
up to 3 lbs.	$18.85	over 5 lbs.	rate figured by
			weight and zone

Bound Printed Matter (advertising, promotional, directory, or editorial material bound by permanent fastenings): rate dependent on weight and zone.

Special Standard Mail (Book Rate; also used for film; printed music, test materials, and educational charts; sound recordings; play scripts; loose-leaf pages and binders consisting of medical information; and computer-readable media): rate dependent on weight

Other Services

Certificate of Mailing (evidence of mailing)	$0.75
Certified Mail (record of delivery kept at post office)	$1.90
Delivery Confirmation (date and time of delivery) Priority Mail	$0.40
Delivery Confirmation (date and time of delivery) Other Mail	$0.50
Signature Confirmation	$1.75
Insured Mail	rate according to value
Money Order (up to $700)	$0.75
Registered Mail	rate according to value
Return Receipt (Express Mail, certified, COD, registered, or mail insured for over $50)	$1.50
Return Receipt for Merchandise	$2.35
Collect on Delivery (COD): rate dependent on amount to be collected	maximum amount $600

International

Global Priority Mail (Expedited airmail in partnership with postal service of destination country) Rates vary according to country. Maximum weight: 4 lbs.

Priority Mail Global Guaranteed (Expedited delivery in partnership with DSL Worldwide Express) Rates vary according to country. Maximum weight: 70 lbs.

Express Mail International Service (Delivery available to more than 170 countries) Rates and weight limits vary according to country.

⊙ U.S. Postal Service. www.usps.gov
  U.S. Postal Service. "International Rate Calculator," http://ircalc.usps.gov
  U.S. Postal Service. "Domestic Rate Calculator," http://postcalc.usps.gov

Postal Abbreviations by State

Alabama	AL	Idaho	ID	Missouri	MO	Pennsylvania	PA
Alaska	AK	Illinois	IL	Montana	MT	Rhode Island	RI
Arizona	AZ	Indiana	IN	Nebraska	NE	South Carolina	SC
Arkansas	AR	Iowa	IA	Nevada	NV	South Dakota	SD
California	CA	Kansas	KS	New Hampshire	NH	Tennessee	TN
Colorado	CO	Kentucky	KY	New Jersey	NJ	Texas	TX
Connecticut	CT	Louisiana	LA	New Mexico	NM	Utah	UT
Delaware	DE	Maine	ME	New York	NY	Vermont	VT
District of		Maryland	MD	North Carolina	NC	Virginia	VA
Columbia	DC	Massachusetts	MA	North Dakota	ND	Washington	WA
Florida	FL	Michigan	MI	Ohio	OH	West Virginia	WV
Georgia	GA	Minnesota	MN	Oklahoma	OK	Wisconsin	WI
Hawaii	HI	Mississippi	MS	Oregon	OR	Wyoming	WY

⊙ Hornor, Edith R., ed. *Almanac of the 50 States: Basic Data Profiles with Comparative Tables 2000*. Palo Alto, Calif.: Information Publications, 2000.

Kane, Joseph Nathan and Gerald. L. Alexander. *Nicknames and Sobriquets of U.S. Cities, States, and Counties*, 3rd ed. Lanham, Md.: Scarecrow Press, 1979.

Other Modes of Communication

Radio: Ham and CB

Ham radio operators are licensed by the government and are prohibited from any commercial activity. Each operator acts as a mini radio station and can broadcast around the world. Legend has it that the term "Ham" comes from the call letters of the first amateur radio broadcasters. Ham radio clubs exist worldwide, and the international amateur broadcast community is full of "Elmers," expert operators who enjoy passing on their skills to newcomers. To get a license you will need to take an inexpensive, volunteer-administered test; once you are licensed you can set up a radio with a simple antenna and start talking.

CB stands for "citizens band," and the CB is the easiest way to get on the radio. Although CB frequencies are regulated by the federal government, a license is not required for operation. Radio types vary from a simple, handheld walkie-talkie to a full "base station" radio system.

Telegraph

The telegraph uses a series of electric signals, organized in code, to send messages. Samuel Morse, inventor of the telegraph, first came up with the idea in the early 1830s, and the first telegraph line was built in 1843. The introduction of the telegraph brought high-speed communication to the United States for the first time and caused the federal government to cease operation of its Pony Express. The end product of a telegraph communication usually came in the form of a telegram, which was then delivered to the recipient. Radio telegraph for communicating with ships at sea was introduced in 1904. Today, communication via telegraph is more or less obsolete except among a select few radio hobbyists.

Telex

For international business communication with countries where telephone and internet communications are unreliable, telex service is available through companies like AT&T (http://www.att.net.au/products/telex.html). Telex provides a secure means of sending and receiving messages nearly everywhere in the world.

Fax

A fax, or facsimile, is a means of sending an image-based copy over a telephone line. A page can be scanned into a fax machine or sent directly from a computer using a modem.

Courier Services

Special delivery of packages and important documents can require the use of a custom service. Packages sent via courier can be easily tracked and delivery is usually guaranteed by the company. Federal Express (1-800-GO-FEDEX or www.fedex.com), Airborne Express (1-800-AIRBORNE or www.airborne.com), and UPS (1-800-PICK-UPS or www.ups.com) are the three best-known services. However, hundreds of companies offer specialized delivery in local areas, nationally, or internationally.

⊙ American Radio Relay League. www.arrl.org

Crenshaw, Gerry. "New Ham Partner," http://web2airmail.net/gerryc/newham.html

Federal Communications Commission. "Amateur Radio Service," www.fcc.gov/wtb/amateur/

Cody, Andrew. "How to Buy a CB Radio," www.iserv.net/~codyspc/cbindex.htm

Deliver-It! Worldwide Transportation Yellow Pages. www.deliver-it.com/

Alphabets

Arabic			Hebrew			Greek			Russian		
ا ا	'alif	'	א	aleph	'	Α α	alpha	a	А а	a
ب ب ب ب	bā	b	ב	beth	b, bh	Β β	beta	b	Б б	b
ت ت ت ت	tā'	t	ג	gimmel	g, gh	Γ γ	gamma	g	В в	v
ث ث ث ث	thā'	th	ד	daleth	d, dh	Δ δ	delta	d	Г г	g
ج ج ج ج	jīm	j	ה	he	h	Ε ε	epsilon	e	Д д	d
ح ح ح ح	ḥā'	ḥ	ו	waw	w	Ζ ζ	zeta	z	Е е	e
خ خ خ خ	khā'	kh	ז	zayin	z	Η η	eta	ē	Ё ё	yo
د د	dāl	d	ח	heth	ḥ	Θ θ	theta	th	Ж ж	zh
ذ ذ	dhāl	dh	ט	teth	ṭ	Ι ι	iota	i	З з	z
ر ر	rā'	r	י	yodh	y	Κ κ	kappa	k	И и	i
ز ز	zay	z	כ ך	kaph	k, kh	Λ λ	lambda	l	Й й	ĭ
س س س س	sīn	s	ל	lamed	l	Μ μ	mu	m	К к	k
ش ش ش ش	shīn	sh	מ ם	mem	m	Ν ν	nu	n	Л л	l
ص ص ص ص	ṣād	ṣ	נ ן	nun	n	Ξ ξ	xi	x	М м	m
ض ض ض ض	ḍād	ḍ	ס	samekh	s	Ο ο	omicron	o	Н н	n
ط ط ط ط	ṭā'	ṭ	ע	'ayin	'	Π π	pi	p	О о	o
ظ ظ ظ ظ	ẓā'	ẓ	פ ף	pe	p, ph	Ρ ρ	rho	r, rh	П п	p
ع ع ع ع	'ayn	'	צ ץ	ṣadhe	ṣ	Σ σ	sigma	s	Р р	r
غ غ غ غ	ghayn	gh	ק	qoph	q	Τ τ	tau	t	С с	s
ف ف ف ف	fā'	f	ר	resh	r	Υ υ	upsilon	u	Т т	t
ق ق ق ق	qāf	q	שׂ	śin	ś	Φ φ	phi	ph	У у	u
ك ك ك ك	kāf	k	שׁ	shin	s	Χ χ	chi	kh	Ф ф	f
ل ل ل ل	lām	l	ת	taw	t, th	Ψ ψ	psi	ps	Х х	kh
م م م م	mīm	m				Ω ω	omega	ō	Ц ц	ts
ن ن ن ن	nūn	n							Ч ч	ch
ه ه ه ه	hā'	h							Ш ш	sh
و و	wāw	w							Щ щ	shch
ي ي ي ي	yā'	y							Ъ ъ	" (hard sign)
									Ы ы	y
									Ь ь	' (soft sign)
									Э э	é
									Ю ю	yu
									Я я	ya

● ▬ A	▬ ● ● ● B	▬ ● ▬ ● C	▬ ● ● D	● E	● ● ▬ ● F
▬ ▬ ● G	● ● ● ● H	● ● I	● ▬ ▬ ▬ J	▬ ● ▬ K	● ▬ ● ● L
▬ ▬ M	▬ ● N	▬ ▬ ▬ O	● ▬ ▬ ● P	▬ ▬ ● ▬ Q	● ▬ ● R
● ● ● S	▬ T	● ● ▬ U	● ● ● ▬ V	● ▬ ▬ W	▬ ● ● ▬ X
▬ ● ▬ ▬ Y	▬ ▬ ● ● Z				

● ▬ ▬ ▬ ▬ 1	● ● ▬ ▬ ▬ 2	● ● ● ▬ ▬ 3	● ● ● ● ▬ 4	● ● ● ● ● 5
▬ ● ● ● ● 6	▬ ▬ ● ● ● 7	▬ ▬ ▬ ● ● 8	▬ ▬ ▬ ▬ ● 9	▬ ▬ ▬ ▬ ▬ 0

▬ ▬ ● ● ▬ ▬ comma	● ▬ ● ▬ ● ▬ full stop	● ● ▬ ▬ ● ● question mark	● ▬ ● ▬ ● ▬ semicolon
▬ ▬ ▬ ● ● ● colon	▬ ● ● ● ● ▬ hyphen	● ▬ ▬ ▬ ▬ ● apostrophe	▬ ● ▬ ▬ ● ▬ parenthesis

The thick arrow represents the right arm, the thin arrow the left arm.

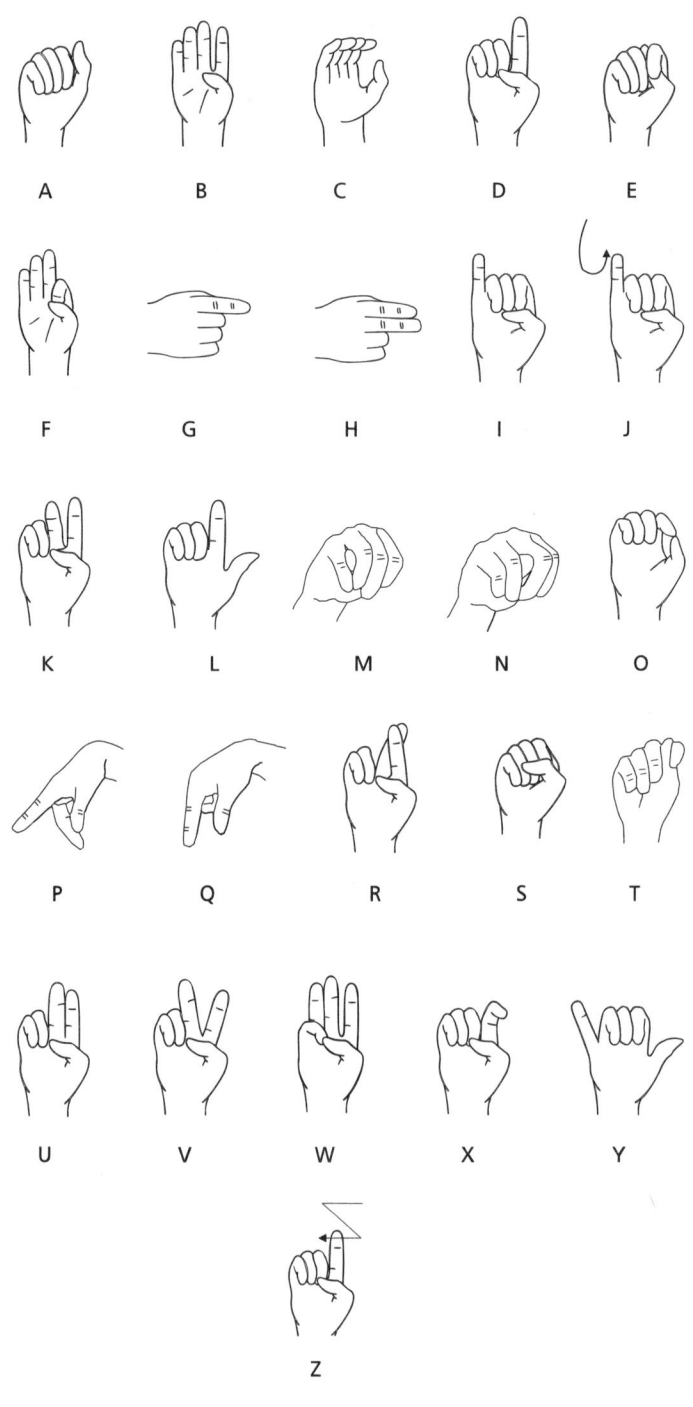

Braille

A   B   C   D   E

F   G   H   I   J

K   L   M   N   O

P   R   Q   S   T

U   V   W   X   Y

Z   and   for   of   the

NATO Alphabet

A	Alpha	J	Juliet	S	Sierra
B	Bravo	K	Kilo	T	Tango
C	Charlie	L	Lima	U	Uniform
D	Delta	M	Mike	V	Victor
E	Echo	N	November	W	Whiskey
F	Foxtrot	O	Oscar	X	X-ray
G	Golf	P	Papa	Y	Yankee
H	Hotel	Q	Quebec	Z	Zulu
I	India	R	Romeo		

WORK AND HOME: *Style and Usage*

Usage

Even the best writers are sometimes troubled by questions of correct usage. A guide to some of the most common questions is provided here, with discussion of the following topics:

singular or plural	group possessive	*you and I* or *you and me*
-s plural or singular	*may* or *might*	collective nouns
comparison of adjectives and adverbs	*I* or *me, we* or *us*	*none* (pronoun)
nouns ending in *-ics*	*we* (with phrase following)	*as* (followed by a pronoun)
	I who, you who, etc.	

singular or plural

1. When subject and complement are different in number (i.e., one is singular, the other plural), the verb normally agrees with the subject, e.g.,

    (Plural subject)
    Their wages were *a mere pittance.*
    Liqueur chocolates are *our specialty.*

    (The Biblical *The wages of sin* is *death* reflects an obsolete idiom in which *wages* took a singular verb.)

    (Singular subject)
    What we need is customers.
    Our specialty is liqueur chocolates.

2. A plural word or phrase used as a name, title, or quotation counts as singular, e.g.,

    Sons and Lovers has always been one of Lawrence's most popular novels.

3. A singular phrase (such as a prepositional phrase following the subject) that happens to end with a plural word should nevertheless be followed by a singular verb, e.g.,

    Everyone except the French wants *(not want) Britain to join.*
    One in six has *(not have)his problem.*

    See also -s plural or singular; nouns ending in –ics.

-s plural or singular

Some nouns, though they have the plural ending -s, are nevertheless usually treated as singular, taking singular verbs and pronouns referring back to them.

1. *News*

2. Diseases:
    measles
    mumps
    rickets
    shingles
    Measles and *rickets* can also be treated as ordinary plural nouns.

3. Games:
    billiards
    dominoes
    checkers
    craps
    quoits
    darts

4. Countries:
    the Bahamas
    the Philippines
    the Netherlands
    the United States

These are treated as singular when considered as a unit, which they commonly are in a political context, or when the complement is singular, e.g.,

The Philippines is *a predominantly agricultural country.*
The United States has *withdrawn its ambassador.*

The Bahamas and *the Philippines* are also the geographical names of the groups of islands that the two nations comprise, and in this use can be treated as plurals, e.g.,

The Bahamas were *settled by British subjects.*

See also nouns ending in -ics.

comparison of adjectives and adverbs

The two ways of forming the comparative and superlative of adjectives and adverbs are:

1. Addition of suffixes *-er* and *-est*. Monosyllabic adjectives and adverbs almost always require these suffixes, e.g., *big* (*bigger, biggest*), *soon* (*sooner, soonest*), and normally so do many adjectives of two syllables, e.g., *narrow* (*narrower, narrowest*), *silly* (*sillier, silliest*).

2. Use of adverbs *more* and *most*. These are used with adjectives of three syllables or more (e.g., *difficult, memorable*), participles (e.g., *bored, boring*), many adjectives of two syllables (e.g., *afraid, awful, childish, harmless, static*), and adverbs ending in *-ly* (e.g., *highly, slowly*).

Adjectives with two syllables sometimes use suffixes and sometimes use adverbs.

There are many that never take the suffixes, e.g.,

antique	*bizarre*
breathless	*constant*
futile	*steadfast*

There is also a large class that is acceptable with either, e.g.,

clever	*pleasant*
handsome	*tranquil*
solemn	*cruel*
common	*polite*

The choice is largely a matter of preference.

nouns ending in -ics

Nouns ending in *-ics* denoting subjects or disciplines are sometimes treated as singular and sometimes as plural. Examples are:

apologetics	*mechanics*
genetics	*politics*
optics	*economics*
classics (as a study)	*metaphysics*
phonetics	*statistics*
linguistics	*electronics*
mathematics	*obstetrics*
physics	*tactics*
dynamics	*ethics*

When used strictly as the name of a discipline they are treated as singular:

Psychometrics is *unable to investigate the nature of intelligence.*

So also when the complement is singular:

Mathematics is *his strong point.*

When used more loosely, to denote a manifestation of qualities, often accompanied by a possessive, they are treated as plural:

His politics were *a mixture of fear, greed, and envy.*
I don't understand the mathematics of it, which are *complicated.*
The acoustics in this hall are *dreadful.*

So also when they denote a set of activities or pattern of behavior, as with words like:

acrobatics	*athletics*
dramatics	*gymnastics*
heroics	*hysterics*

E.g., *The mental gymnastics required to believe this* are *beyond me.*

group possessive

The group possessive is the construction by which the ending -'s of the possessive case can be added to the last word of a noun phrase, which is regarded as a single unit, e.g.,

The king of Spain's daughter
John and Mary's baby
Somebody else's umbrella
A quarter of an hour's drive

Expressions like these are natural and acceptable.

I or *me, we* or *us,* etc.

There is often confusion about which case of a personal pronoun to use when the pronoun stands alone or follows the verb *to be.*

1. When the personal pronoun stands alone, as when it forms the answer to a question, strictly formal usage requires it to have the case it would have if the verb were supplied:

"Who called him?" "I" (in full, *I called him* or *I did*).
"Which of you did he approach?" "Me" (in full, *he approached me*).

Informal usage permits the objective case in both kinds of sentence, but this is not acceptable in formal style. However, the nominative case often sounds stilted. One can avoid the problem by providing a verb, e.g.,

"Who likes cooking?" "I do."
"Who can cook?" "I can."
"Who is here?" "I am."

2. When a personal pronoun follows *it is, it was, it may be, it could have been,* etc., formal usage requires the nominative case:

Nobody could suspect that it was she.
We are given no clues as to what it must have felt like to be he.

Informal usage favors the objective case (not acceptable in formal style):

I thought it might have been him *at the door.*
Don't tell me it's them *again!*

When *who* or *whom* follows, the nominative case is obligatory in formal usage and quite usual informally:

It was I *who painted that sign.*

The informal use of the objective case often sounds incorrect:

It was her *who would get into trouble.*

In constructions that have the form *I am* + noun or noun phrase + *who*, the verb following *who* agrees with the noun (the antecedent of *who*) in number (singular or plural):

I am the sort of person who likes *peace and quiet.*
You are the fourth of my colleagues who has *told me that.*

may or might

There is sometimes confusion about whether to use *may* or *might* with the perfect tense when referring to a past event, e.g., *He may have done* or *He might have done.*

1. If uncertainty about the action or state denoted by the perfect remains—that is, if the truth of the event is still unknown at the time of speaking or writing—then either *may* or *might* is acceptable:

As they all wore so many different clothes of identically the same kind, there may *have been several more or several less.*
For all we knew our complaint went unanswered, although of course they might *have tried to call us while we were out of town.*

2. If there is no longer uncertainty about the event, or the matter was never put to the test, and therefore the event did not in fact occur, use might:

If that had come ten days ago my whole life might *have been different.*
You should not have let him come home alone; he might *have gotten lost.*

It is a common error to use may instead of might in the following circumstances:

If they had not invaded, then eventually we may *have agreed to give them aid.*
I am grateful for his intervention, without which they may *have remained in the refugee camp indefinitely.*
Schoenberg may *never have gone atonal but for the breakup of his marriage.*

In each of these sentences "might" should be substituted for "may."

we (with phrase following)

Expressions consisting of *we* or *us* followed by a qualifying word or phrase, e.g., *we Americans* or *us Americans*, are often misused with the wrong case of the first person plural pronoun. In fact the rules are exactly the same as for *we* or *us* standing alone.

If the expression is the subject, *we* should be used:

(Correct) *We were not always laughing as heartily as we Americans are supposed to do.*
(Incorrect) *We all make mistakes, even us judges.*

If the expression is the object or the complement of a preposition, *us* should be used:

(Correct) *To us Americans, personal liberty is a vital principle.*
(Incorrect) *The president said some nice things about we reporters in the press corps.*

Usage *(cont.)*

I who, you who, etc.

The verb following a personal pronoun (*I, you, he,* etc.) + who should be the same as what would be used with the pronoun as a subject:

> *I, who* have *no savings to speak of, had to pay for the work.*
> *They made me, who* have *no savings at all, pay for the work* (not "who has").

When it is (*it was,* etc.) precedes *I who,* etc., the same rule applies: the verb agrees with the personal pronoun:

> *It's I who* have *done it.*
> *It could have been we who* were *mistaken.*

you and I or you and me

When a personal pronoun is linked by *and* or *or* to a noun or another pronoun, there is often confusion about which case to put the pronoun in. In fact the rule is exactly as it would be for the pronoun standing alone.

1. If the two words linked by *and* or *or* constitute the subject, the pronoun should be in the nominative case, e.g.,

> *Only* she *and her mother cared for the old house.*
> *That's what we would do, that is, John and* I *would.*
> *"Who could go?" "Either you or* he."

The use of the objective case is quite common in informal speech, but it is nonstandard, e.g.,

> *Perhaps only* her *and Mrs. Natwick had stuck to the christened name.*
> *That's how we look at it,* me *and Martha.*
> *Either Mary had to leave or* me.

2. If the two words linked by *and* or *or* constitute the object of the verb, or the complement of a preposition, the objective case should be used:

> *The afternoon would suit* her *and John better.*
> *It was time for Kenneth and* me *to go down to the living room.*

The use of the nominative case is very common informally. It probably arises from an exaggerated fear of the error indicated under 1 above. It remains, however, nonstandard, e.g.,

> *It was this that set Charles and* I *talking of old times.*
> *Why is it that people like you and* I *are so unpopular?*
> *Between you and* I ...

This last expression is very commonly heard. *Between you and me* should always be substituted.

collective nouns

Collective nouns are singular words that denote many individuals, e.g., *audience, government, orchestra, the clergy, the public.*

It is normal for collective nouns, being singular, to be followed by singular verbs and pronouns (*is, has, consists,* and *it* in the examples below):

The government is *determined to beat inflation, as* it has *promised.*
Their family is *huge:* it consists *of five boys and three girls.*
The bourgeoisie is *despised for not being proletarian.*

The singular verb and pronouns are preferable unless the collective is clearly and unmistakably used to refer to separate individuals rather than to a united body, e.g.,

The cabinet has made its *decision.*

but

The cabinet are *sitting at* their *places around the table with the president.*

The singular should always be used if the collective noun is qualified by a singular word like this, that, every, etc.:

This family is *divided.*
Every team has its *chance to win.*

none (pronoun)

The pronoun *none* can be followed either by singular verb and singular pronouns, or by plural ones. Either is acceptable, although the plural tends to be more common.

Singular: *None of them* was *allowed to forget for a moment.*
Plural: *None of the orchestras ever* play *there.*
None of the authors expected their *books to become best-sellers.*

as (followed by a pronoun)

In the following sentences, formal usage requires the nominative case (*I, he, she, we, they*) on the assumption that the pronoun would be the subject if a verb were supplied:

You are just as intelligent as he (in full, "as he is").
He might not have heard the song so often as I (in full, "as I had").

Informal usage permits such constructions as

You are just as intelligent as him.

Formal English uses the objective case (*me, him, her, us, them*) only when the pronoun would be the object if a verb were supplied:

I thought you preferred John to Mary, but I see that you like her just as much as him (meaning "just as much as you like him").

⊙ Kirkpatrick, E.M. *The Oxford Essential Thesaurus.* New York: Berkley, 1998.

Punctuation

Punctuation is an essential element of good writing because it makes the author's meaning clear to the reader. Although precise punctuation styles may vary somewhat among published sources, there are a number of fundamental principles worthy of consideration. Discussed below are the punctuation marks used in English:

comma	question mark	parentheses
semicolon	exclamation point	dash
colon	apostrophe	hyphen
period	quotation marks	

Punctuation *(cont.)*

Comma

The comma is the most frequently used mark of punctuation in the English language. It signals to the reader a pause, which generally clarifies the author's meaning, and establishes a sensible order to the elements of written language. Among the most typical functions of the comma are the following:

1. It can separate the clauses of a compound sentence when there are two independent clauses joined by a conjunction, especially when the clauses are not very short:

> *It never occurred to me to look in the attic, and I'm sure it didn't occur to Rachel either.*
> *The Nelsons wanted to see the Grand Canyon at sunrise, but they overslept that morning.*

2. It can separate the clauses of a compound sentence when there is a series of independent clauses, the last two of which are joined by a conjunction:

> *The bus ride to the campsite was very uncomfortable, the cabins were not ready for us when we got there, the cook had forgotten to start dinner, and the rain was torrential.*

3. It is used to precede or set off, and therefore indicate, a nonrestrictive dependent clause (a clause that could be omitted without changing the meaning of the main clause):

> *I read her autobiography, which was published last July.*
> *They showed up at midnight, after most of the guests had gone home.*
> *The coffee, which is freshly brewed, is in the kitchen.*

4. It can follow an introductory phrase:

> *Having enjoyed the movie so much, he agreed to see it again.*
> *Born and raised in Paris, she had never lost her French accent.*
> *In the beginning, they had very little money to invest.*

5. It can set off words used in direct address:

> *Listen, people, you have no choice in the matter.*
> *Yes, Mrs. Greene, I will be happy to feed your cat.*

6. The comma can separate two or more coordinate adjectives (adjectives that could otherwise be joined with and) that modify one noun:

> *The cruise turned out to be the most entertaining, fun, and relaxing vacation I've ever had.*
> *The horse was tall, lean, and sleek.*

Note that cumulative adjectives (those not able to be joined with *and*) are not separated by a comma:

> *She wore bright yellow rubber boots.*

7. Use a comma to separate three or more items in a series or list:

> *Charlie, Melissa, Stan, and Mark will be this year's soloists in the spring concert.*
> *We need furniture, toys, clothes, books, tools, housewares, and other useful merchandise for the benefit auction.*

Note that the comma between the last two items in a series is sometimes omitted in less precise style:

> *The most popular foods served in the cafeteria are pizza, hamburgers and nachos.*

8. Use a comma to separate and set off the elements in an address or other geographical designation:

My new house is at 1657 Nighthawk Circle, South Kingsbury, Michigan.
We arrived in Pamplona, Spain, on Thursday.

9. Use a comma to set off direct quotations (note the placement or absence of commas with other punctuation):

"Kim forgot her gloves," he said, "but we have a pair she can borrow."
There was a long silence before Jack blurted out, "This must be the world's ugliest painting."
"What are you talking about?" she asked in a puzzled manner.
"Happy New Year!" everyone shouted.

10. A comma is used to set off titles after a person's name:

Katherine Bentley, M.D.
Steven Wells, Esq.

Semicolon

The semicolon has two basic functions:

1. It can separate two main clauses, particularly when these clauses are of equal importance:

The crowds gathered outside the museum hours before the doors were opened; this was one exhibit no one wanted to miss.
She always complained when her relatives stayed for the weekend; even so, she usually was a little sad when they left.

2. It can be used as a comma is used to separate such elements as clauses or items in a series or list, particularly when one or more of the elements already includes a comma:

The path took us through the deep, dark woods; across a small meadow; into a cold, wet cave; and up a hillside overlooking the lake.
Listed for sale in the ad were two bicycles; a battery-powered, leaf-mulching lawn mower; and a maple bookcase.

Colon

The colon has five basic functions:

1. It can introduce something, especially a list of items:

In the basket were three pieces of mail: a postcard, a catalog, and a wedding invitation.
Students should have the following items: backpack, loose-leaf notebook, pens and pencils, pencil sharpener, and ruler.

2. It can separate two clauses in a sentence when the second clause is being used to explain or illustrate the first clause:

We finally understood why she would never go sailing with us: she had a deep fear of the water.
Most of the dogs in our neighborhood are quite large: two of them are St. Bernards.

3. It can introduce a statement or a quotation:

His parents say the most important rule is this: Always tell the truth.
We repeated the final words of his poem: "And such is the plight of fools like me."

4. It can be used to follow the greeting in a formal or business letter:

Dear Ms. Daniels:
Dear Sir or Madam:

5. In the U.S., the colon separates minutes from hours, and seconds from minutes, in showing time of day and measured lengths of time:

Please be at the restaurant before 6:45.
Her best running time so far has been 00:12:35.

Period

The period has two basic functions:
  1. It is used to mark the end of a sentence:

It was reported that there is a shortage of nurses at the hospital. Several of the patients have expressed concern about this problem.

2. It is often used at the end of an abbreviation:

On Fri., Sept. 12, Dr. Brophy noted that the patient's weight was 168 lbs. and that his height was 6 ft. 2 in.

(Note that another period is not added to the end of the sentence when the last word is an abbreviation.)

Question Mark and Exclamation Point

The only sentences that do not end in a period are those that end in either a question mark or an exclamation point.

Question marks are used to mark the end of a sentence that asks a direct question (generally, a question that expects an answer):

Is there any reason for us to bring more than a few dollars?
Who is your science teacher?

Exclamation points are used to mark the end of a sentence that expresses a strong feeling, typically surprise, joy, or anger:

I want you to leave and never come back!
What a beautiful view this is!

Apostrophe

The apostrophe has two basic functions:
  1. It is used to show where a letter or letters are missing in a contraction:

The directions are cont'd [continued] *on the next page.*
We've [we have] *decided that if she can't* [cannot] *go, then we aren't* [are not] *going either.*

2. It can be used to show possession:
  a. The possessive of a singular noun or an irregular plural noun is created by adding an apostrophe and an s:

the pilot's uniform
Mrs. Mendoza's house
a tomato's bright red color
the oxen's yoke

b. The possessive of a regular plural noun is created by adding just an apostrophe:

the pilots' uniforms [referring to more than one pilot]
the Mendozas' house [referring to the Mendoza family]
the tomatoes' bright red color [referring to more than one tomato]

Quotation Marks

Quotation marks have two basic functions:

I. They are used to set off direct quotations (an exact rendering of someone's spoken or written words):

"I think the new library is wonderful," she remarked to David.
We were somewhat lost, so we asked, "Are we anywhere near the art gallery?"
In his letter he had written, "The nights here are quiet and starry. It seems like a hundred years since I've been wakened by the noise of city traffic and squabbling neighbors."

Note that indirect quotes (which often are preceded by *that, if,* or *whether*) are not set off by quotation marks:

He told me that he went to school in Boston.
We asked if we could still get tickets to the game.

2. They can be used to set off words or phrases that have specific technical usage, or to set off meanings of words, or to indicate words that are being used in a special way in a sentence:

The part of the flower that bears the pollen is the "stamen."
When I said "plain," I meant "flat land," not "ordinary."
Oddly enough, in the theater, the statement "break a leg" is meant as an expression of good luck.
What you call "hoagies," we call "grinders" or "submarine sandwiches."
He will never be a responsible adult until he outgrows his "Peter Pan" behavior.

Note that sometimes single quotation marks (the 'stamen.'), rather than double quotation marks as above (the "stamen."), may be used to set off words or phrases. What is most important is to be consistent in such usage.

Parentheses

Parentheses are used, in pairs, to enclose information that gives extra detail or explanation to the regular text. Parentheses are used in two basic ways:

I. They can separate a word or words in a sentence from the rest of the sentence:

On our way to school, we walk past the Turner Farm (the oldest dairy farm in town) and watch the cows being fed.
The stores were filled with holiday shoppers (even more so than last year).

(Note that the period goes outside the parentheses, because the words in the parentheses are only part of the sentence.)

2. They can form a separate complete sentence:

Please bring a dessert to the dinner party. (It can be something very simple.) I look forward to seeing you there.

(Note that the period goes inside the parentheses, because the words in the parentheses are a complete and independent sentence.)

Dash

A dash is used most commonly to replace the usage of parentheses within sentences. If the information being set off is in the middle of the sentence, a pair of dashes is used; if it is at the end of the sentence, just one dash is used:

> *On our way to school, we walk past the Turner Farm—the oldest dairy farm in town—and watch the cows being fed.*
> *The stores were filled with holiday shoppers—even more so than last year.*

Hyphen

A hyphen has three basic functions:

1. It can join two or more words to make a compound, especially when so doing makes the meaning more clear to the reader:

> *We met to discuss long-range planning.*
> *There were six four-month-old piglets at the fair.*
> *That old stove was quite a coal-burner.*

2. It can replace the word "to" when a span or range of data is given:

> *John Adams was president of the United States 1797-1801.*
> *Today we will look for proper nouns in the L-N section of the dictionary.*
> *The ideal weight for that breed of dog would be 75-85 pounds.*

3. It can indicate a word break at the end of a line. The break must always be between syllables:
It is important for any writer to know that there are numerous punctuation principles that are considered standard and proper, but there is also flexibility regarding acceptable punctuation. Having learned the basic "rules" of good punctuation, the writer will be able to adopt a specific and consistent style of punctuation that best suits the material he or she is writing.

⊙ Garner, Bryan A. *A Dictionary of Modern American Usage.* New York: Oxford University Press, 1998.

Confused and Misused Words

adverse/averse Adverse means "unfavorable, opposed," and is usually applied to situations and events, not people, e.g., *The new drug has adverse side effects.* Averse is related in origin and also has the sense of "opposition," but its use is best restricted to describing a person's attitude, e.g., *I would not be averse to the prospect of traveling with you.*

affect/effect Both these words are both verbs and nouns, but only effect is common as a noun, usually meaning "a result, consequence, impression, etc.," e.g., *My father's strictness had no effect on my desire to learn.* As verbs they are used differently. Affect means "to produce an effect upon," e.g., *Smoking during pregnancy can affect a baby's development.* Effect means "to bring about," e.g., *Alterations were effected with some sympathy for the existing fabric.*

aggravate This word is commonly used in informal contexts to mean "to annoy or exasperate," rather than "to make worse or more serious"; this is considered incorrect by many people. An example of correct usage is *The psychological stress aggravates the horse's physical stress.*

all right/alright Although found widely, alright remains nonstandard, even where standard spelling is somewhat cumbersome, e.g., *I wanted to make sure it was all all right.*

all together/altogether These variants are used in different contexts. All together means "all at once" or "all in one place or in one group," e.g., *They came all together* or *We managed to get three bedrooms all together* (i.e., near each other). Altogether means "in total," e.g., *The hotel has twenty rooms altogether.*

amend/emend Amend, meaning "to make improvements or corrections in," is often confused with emend, a more technical word used in the context of textual correction. Examples of each are: *The Constitution was amended to limit presidential terms of office; The poems have been collected, arranged, and emended.*

anticipate Anticipate in the sense "expect, foresee" is well-established in informal use (e.g., *He anticipated a restless night*), but is regarded as incorrect by some people. The formal sense, "deal with or use before the proper time," is illustrated by the sentence *The specialist would find that the thesis he had been planning had already been anticipated.*

anyone/any one Anyone is written as two words only to emphasize a numerical sense, e.g., *Any one of us can do it*. Otherwise it is written as one word (e.g., *Anyone who wants to can come*).

averse See adverse.

born/borne Born is used with reference to birth (e.g., *was born in Detroit*). Borne, meaning "carried," is used in the expression *borne by* followed by the name of the mother (e.g., *was borne by Mary*), as well as in other senses (e.g., *a litter borne by four slaves*).

censor/censure Both these words are both verbs and nouns, but censor is used to mean "to cut unacceptable parts out of a book, movie, etc." or "a person who does this," while censure means "to criticize harshly" or "harsh criticism."

compose/comprise Both these words can be used to mean "to constitute or make up," but compose is preferred in this sense, e.g., *Citizens act as witnesses in the courts and finally may compose the jury.* Comprise is correctly used to mean "to be composed of, consist of," e.g., *Each crew comprises a commander, a gunner, and a driver.*

continual/continuous Continual is used of something that happens very frequently, e.g., *There were continual interruptions*, whereas continuous is used of something that happens without pause, e.g., *There was a dull, continuous background noise.*

deprecate/depreciate Deprecate means "to express disapproval of, to deplore," e.g., *The establishment magazines began by deprecating the film's attitude towards terrorism*, while depreciate (apart from its financial senses) means "to disparage or belittle," e.g., *He was depreciating his own skills out of a strong sense of humility.*

disinterested/uninterested Disinterested is sometimes used in informal contexts to mean "not interested or uninterested," but this is widely regarded as incorrect. The proper meaning is "impartial," e.g., *I for one am making a disinterested search for information.* The use of the noun disinterest to mean "a lack of interest" is also objected to, but it is rarely used in any other sense.

effect See affect.

emend See amend.

enormity The original and preferred meaning is "extreme wickedness," as in *the enormity of the crime.* Enormity is commonly used to mean "enormousness; great size," e.g., *wilting under the enormity of the work,* but this is regarded as incorrect by many. Use the more precise enormousness for this sense.

exceptionable/exceptional Exceptionable means "open to objection," e.g., *There was nothing exceptionable in her behavior,* and is usually found in negative contexts. It is sometimes confused with the much more common word exceptional meaning "unusual, outstanding."

flammable See inflammable.

flaunt/flout These words are often confused because both suggest an element of arrogance or showing off. However, flaunt means "to display ostentatiously," e.g., *He liked to flaunt his wealth,* while flout means "to express contempt for or disobey (laws, convention, etc.)," e.g., *The fine is too low for those who flout the law continuously.*

-fuls/-s full The combining form -ful is used to form nouns meaning "the amount needed to fill," e.g., *cupful, spoonful.* The plural form of such words employs a final -s (*cupfuls, spoonfuls,* etc.). *Three cups full* would denote the individual cups rather than a quantity regarded in terms of a cup used as a measure, and would be used in such contexts as *They brought us three cups full of water.*

fulsome This word means "excessive, cloying, or insincere," but is often imprecisely used to mean "generous," as in the phrase *fulsome praise.*

hoi polloi This phrase, meaning "the common people, the masses," is usually preceded by the word *the,* e.g., *The hoi polloi grew weary and sat on the floor.* Strictly speaking, the *the* is unnecessary because hoi means "the" in Greek. Never use hoi polloi to mean "the elite," a disturbingly common error.

imply See infer.

incredible/incredulous The adjective incredible means "unbelievable" or "not convincing" and can be applied to a situation, statement, policy, or threat to a person, e.g., *I find this testimony incredible.* Incredulous means "disinclined to believe; skeptical" and is usually applied to a person's attitude, e.g., *You shouldn't wonder that I'm incredulous after all your lies.*

infer/imply Infer should be used to mean "to deduce or conclude," as in *We can infer from these studies that....* Its use to mean "to imply or suggest" is widely considered incorrect.

inflammable/flammable/nonflammable Both inflammable and flammable mean "easily set on fire or excited." The opposite is nonflammable. Where there is a danger of inflammable being understood to mean the opposite, i.e., "not easily set on fire," flammable should be used to avoid confusion.

ingenious/ingenuous Ingenious means "clever, skillful, or resourceful," e.g., *an ingenious device,* while ingenuous means "artless" or "frank," e.g., *We were charmed by the ingenuous honesty of the child.*

interment/internment Interment means "the burial of a corpse," while internment means "the confining of a prisoner."

irregardless See regardless.

inveigh/inveigle Inveigh (usually inveigh against) means "to speak or write about (something) with great hostility," while inveigle means "to persuade (someone) to do something by means of deception or flattery."

jibe/jive Jibe has several meanings; one is "to be in accord; to agree." A common error is to use jive for this sense, but as a verb jive really means "to taunt or sneer at," "to talk nonsense," or "to dance, especially to swing, jazz, or rock and roll music."

laudable/laudatory These words are sometimes confused. Laudable is the more common and means "commendable" or "praiseworthy," e.g., *The foundation pursued a laudable program of aid to schools and hospitals.* Laudatory means "expressing praise," e.g., *The proposed legislation enjoyed a laudatory editorial from the local newspaper.*

lay/lie In standard English lay is a transitive verb and lie intransitive. *The intransitive use of lay, as in The park ranger job gave him the opportunity of laying on the grass at lunchtime, is best avoided.* Similarly, the transitive use of lie, as in *Lie it on the table,* is also avoided by careful speakers and writers. In the first example, *laying* should be *lying*; in the second, *lie* should be *lay.* These two verbs are often confused owing to their close similarity in form, including the fact that the past tense of *lie* is *lay.* A mnemonic using the traditional child's prayer *Now I lay me down to sleep ...* serves as a reminder that *lay* is transitive (with direct object *me*).

like The use of like as a conjunction meaning "as" or "as if" (e.g., *I don't have a wealthy set of in-laws like you do* or *They sit up like they're begging for food*) should be avoided in formal writing or speech.

luxuriant/luxurious These words are sometimes confused. Luxuriant means "lush, profuse, or prolific," e.g., *forests of dark luxuriant foliage* or *luxuriant black eyelashes.* Luxurious, a much more common word, means "supplied with luxuries, extremely comfortable," e.g., *a luxurious hotel.*

masterful/masterly These words overlap in meaning and are sometimes confused. Apart from meaning "domineering," masterful also means "masterly" or "very skillful." However, it is generally used in this sense to describe a person, e.g., *He has only a marginal talent that he's masterful at exploiting,* while masterly usually describes an achievement or action, e.g., *This was a masterly use of the backhand volley.*

mutual This word is most properly defined as "reciprocal" (as in *mutual admiration*), but it frequently used to mean "common to two or more people," as in *a mutual friend* or *a mutual interest.* For clarity, use common or joint for this latter sense.

nonflammable See inflammable.

perquisite/prerequisite These words are sometimes confused. Perquisite usually means "an extra benefit or privilege," e.g., *There were no perquisites that came with the job, apart from one or two special privileges.* Prerequisite means "something required as a precondition," e.g., *A general education in the sciences is a prerequisite of professional medical training.*

prescribe/proscribe These words are sometimes confused, but they are nearly opposite in meaning. Prescribe means "to advise the use of" or "impose authoritatively," as in *The teachers would prescribe topics for the students to debate.* Proscribe means "to reject, denounce, or ban": *The superintendent proscribed tabloid newspapers from all school libraries.* (And a dictatorial regime might both prescribe and proscribe literature.)

protagonist The correct meaning of this word is "chief or leading character," e.g., *The choreographer creates movement that displays the protagonist's particular behavior and reactions.* Avoid using it loosely to mean "proponent; advocate or champion of a cause."

refute Strictly speaking, refute means "to prove (a person or statement) to be wrong," e.g., *No amount of empirical research can either confirm or refute the existence of God*. However, it is also sometimes used to mean "to deny or rebut." This usage is incorrect and should be avoided.

regardless/irregardless The latter word, with its illogical negative prefix, is widely heard, perhaps arising under the influence of such perfectly correct terms as "irrespective." It is to be avoided.

Scotch/Scots/Scottish In Scotland the terms Scots and Scottish are preferred to Scotch and they mean the same (e.g., *a Scots/Scottish accent*). Scotch is used in certain compound nouns, such as *Scotch broth, Scotch terrier,* and *Scotch whisky*. Scotsman and Scotswoman are acceptable terms for persons from Scotland, never "Scotchman" or "Scotchwoman."

seasonable/seasonal Seasonable means "usual or suitable for the season" or "opportune," e.g., *Although seasonable, the weather was not suitable for picnics*. Seasonal means "of, depending on, or varying with the season," e.g., *Seasonal changes posed problems for mills situated on larger rivers*.

'til/till See until.

tortuous/torturous Tortuous means "full of twists and turns" or "devious; circuitous," e.g., *Both paths have proved tortuous and are strewn with awkward boulders*. Torturous, an adjective derived from "torture," means "involving torture; excruciating," e.g., *I found the concert a torturous experience because of the loudness of the music*.

triumphal/triumphant The more common of these triumphant, means "victorious" or "exultant," e.g., *Rosie returned triumphant with the file that had been missing*. Triumphal means "used in or celebrating a triumph," e.g., *The last element to be added was the magnificent triumphal arch*.

turbid/turgid Turbid is used of a liquid or color to mean "muddy; not clear," or of literary style, etc., to mean "confused," e.g., *the turbid utterances and twisted language of Carlyle*. Turgid means "swollen, inflated, or enlarged," but is also often used to describe literary style that is pompous or bombastic, e.g., *Communications from corporate headquarters were largely turgid memos filled with bureaucratic lingo*.

until/till/'til Until is more formal than till, and is more usual at the beginning of a sentence, e.g., *Until the 1920s it was quite unusual for women to wear short hair*. 'Til is considered incorrect in standard English and should be avoided.

venal/venial Venal means "corrupt, able to be bribed, or involving bribery," e.g., *Their venal court system can take decades to decide a case*. Venial means "slight, pardonable, excusable," or, of sins, "not mortal": *He forgave his wife's flirtations as merely venial offenses*.

worth while/worthwhile Worth while is used only predicatively, e.g., *Nobody had thought it worth while to call the police,* and means "worth the time or effort spent." Worthwhile also has this meaning but can be used both predicatively and attributively, e.g., *Only in unusual circumstances would investment be worthwhile* (predicative), or *He was a worthwhile subject for the experiment* (attributive). In addition, worthwhile has the sense "of value or importance," e.g., *It's great to be doing such a worthwhile job*.

⊙ Garner, Bryan A. *A Dictionary of Modern American Usage*. New York: Oxford University Press, 1998.

℘	delete	
℘	delete and close up	
℘#	delete and leave space	
∧	insert	
#	space	
⊙	period	
ˆ	comma	
ˆ	semicolon	
ˆ or ⊙	colon	
˅	apostrophe	

⁶⁶ ⁹⁹	quotation marks	
( )	parentheses	
[ ]	square brackets	
=	hyphen	
Ⅰ/M	em-dash	
Ⅰ/N	en-dash	
¶	new paragraph	
dictionary	break line or word	
⌄	set as superscript	
∧	set as subscript	

diction(r/a)y	transpose
(tr)	transpose (note in margin)
(3)	spell out
(SP)	spell out (note in margin)
dictionary	capitalize
(cap)	set as capitals (note in margin)
Dictionary	make lower case
(lc)	set in lower case (note in margin)
dictionary	make boldface
(bf)	set in boldface (note in margin)
dictionary	make italic
(ital)	set in italic (note in margin)
dictionary	small caps
(sc)	set in small caps (note in margin)
(lf)	lightface (note in margin)
(rom)	set in roman (note in margin)

⊙ University of Chicago Press. *The Chicago Manual of Style*. 14th ed. Chicago: University of Chicago Press, 1993.

WORK AND HOME: *Measurement*

Common English Measures

Length

12 inches	= 1 foot	
3 feet	= 36 inches	= 1 yard
5,280 feet	= 1,760 yards	= 1 mile

Area

144 square inches	= 1 square foot	
9 square feet	= 1,296 square inches	= 1 square yard
4,840 square yards	= 43,560 square feet	= 1 acre
640 acres	= 1 square mile	

Volume

3 teaspoons	= 1 tablespoon
16 tablespoons	= 1 cup
2 cups	= 1 pint
2 pints	= 1 quart
4 quarts	= 1 gallon
2 gallons	= 1 peck
4 pecks	= 1 bushel

Weight

437 1/2 grains	= 1 ounce
16 ounces	= 1 pound
2,000 pounds	= 1 ton

⊙ English Weights and Measures. http://home.clara.net/brianp/index.html.

Metric Measures

The metric system, a decimal (based on powers of 10) system of measurement, uses the same prefixes for each kind of measure. The root of the word indicates the measure in question:

-meter is for length
-liter is for volume
-gram is for weight

The chart below uses meter as an example. The root *meter* and symbol *m* can be changed to *liter (l)* or *gram (g)* as needed.

Symbol	Prefix	Value	Symbol	Prefix	Value
Km	kilometer	1,000 meters	dm	decimeter	.1 meter
Hm	hectometer	100 meters	cm	centimeter	.01 meter
Dm	decameter	10 meters	mm	millimeter	.001 meter
m	meter	1 meter			

Multiplying or dividing by factors of 10 reveals equivalent metric measures. Thus, 27 kilometers = (27 × 1,000) = 27,000 meters; 5 meters = (5 /.01) = 500 centimeters, and so on.

⊙ The World of Chemistry. "Metric System and Unit Conversion," http://edie.cprost.sfu.ca/~rhlogan/metric.html

English–Metric Conversions

Common Metric-to-English Conversions

Length

1 centimeter	≈ .3937 inch	≈ .0328 foot	≈ .0109 yard
1 meter	≈ 39.37 inches	≈ 3.28 feet	≈ 1.09 yards
1 kilometer	≈ .62 mile		

Weight

1 gram	≈ .035 ounce	≈ .0022 pound
1 kilogram	≈ 2.2 pounds	

Volume

1 liter	≈ 1.057 quarts	≈ .264 gallon

Common English-to-Metric Conversions

Length

1 inch	≈ 2.54 centimeters	≈ .0254 meter
1 foot	≈ 30.48 centimeters	≈ .3048 meter
1 yard	≈ 91.44 centimeters	≈ .9144 meter
1 mile	≈ 1,609 meters	≈ 1.609 kilometers

Weight

1 ounce	≈ 28.35 grams	≈ .02835 kilogram
1 pound	≈ 453.6 grams	≈ .4536 kilograms

Volume

1 quart	≈ .946 liter
1 gallon	≈ 3.785 liters

⊙ Heddens, James W. and William R. Speer. Today's Mathematics, 7th ed. New York: Macmillan, 1992.

Common Cooking Measures

Volume

3 teaspoons	= 1 tablespoon	16 tablespoons	= 1 cup	
4 tablespoons	= 1/4 cup	2 cups	= 1 pint	
5 1/2 tablespoons	= 1/3 cup	4 cups	= 2 pints	= 1 quart
8 tablespoons	= 1/2 cup	4 quarts	= 1 gallon	

Liquid weight

8 ounces	= 1 cup	64 ounces	= 1/2 gallon
16 ounces	= 1 pint	128 ounces	= 1 gallon
32 ounces	= 1 quart		

Dry Weight

8 ounces	= 1/2 pound	16 ounces	= 1 pound

⊙ English Weights and Measures. http://home.clara.net/brianp/index.html

Temperature Conversions

Celsius to Fahrenheit: [(C × 9) / 5] +32 = F
Fahrenheit to Celsius: [(F − 32) × 5] / 9 = C
Celsius to Kelvin: C + 273.15 = K
Kelvin to Celsius: K − 273.15 = C
Fahrenheit / Kelvin: convert Fahrenheit or Kelvin figure to Celsius, then calculate

Degrees Fahrenheit	Degrees Celsius	Degrees Kelvin
−25	−31.67	241.48
−20	−28.89	244.26
−15	−26.11	247.04
−10	−23.33	249.82
−5	−20.56	252.59
−4	−20.00	253.15
−3	−19.44	253.71
−2	−18.89	254.26
−1	−18.33	254.82
0	−17.78	255.37
1	−17.22	255.93
2	−16.67	256.48
3	−16.11	257.04
4	−15.56	257.59
5	−15.00	258.15
6	−14.44	258.71
7	−13.89	259.26
8	−13.33	259.82
9	−12.78	260.37
10	−12.22	260.93
11	−11.67	261.48
12	−11.11	262.04
13	−10.56	262.59
14	−10.00	263.15
15	−9.44	263.71
16	−8.89	264.26
17	−8.33	264.82
18	−7.78	265.37
19	−7.22	265.93
20	−6.67	266.48
21	−6.11	267.04
22	−5.56	267.59
23	−5.00	268.15
24	−4.44	268.71
25	−3.89	269.26
26	−3.33	269.82
27	−2.78	270.37
28	−2.22	270.93
29	−1.67	271.48
30	−1.11	272.04
31	−0.56	272.59
32	0.00	273.15
33	0.56	273.71
34	1.11	274.26
35	1.67	274.82
36	2.22	275.37
37	2.78	275.93
38	3.33	276.48
39	3.89	277.04
40	4.44	277.59
41	5.00	278.15
42	5.56	278.71
43	6.11	279.26
44	6.67	279.82
45	7.22	280.37
46	7.78	280.93
47	8.33	281.48
48	8.89	282.04
49	9.44	282.59
50	10.00	283.15
51	10.56	283.71
52	11.11	284.26
53	11.67	284.82
54	12.22	285.37
55	12.78	285.93
56	13.33	286.48
57	13.89	287.04
58	14.44	287.59
59	15.00	288.15

WORK AND HOME: *Measurement*

°F	°C	K
60	15.56	288.71
61	16.11	289.26
62	16.67	289.82
63	17.22	290.37
64	17.78	290.93
65	18.33	291.48
66	18.89	292.04
67	19.44	292.59
68	20.00	293.15
69	20.56	293.71
70	21.11	294.26
71	21.67	294.82
72	22.22	295.37
73	22.78	295.93
74	23.33	296.48
75	23.89	297.04
76	24.44	297.59
77	25.00	298.15
78	25.56	298.71
79	26.11	299.26
80	26.67	299.82
81	27.22	300.37
82	27.78	300.93
83	28.33	301.48
84	28.89	302.04
85	29.44	302.59
86	30.00	303.15
87	30.56	303.71
88	31.11	304.26
89	31.67	304.82
90	32.22	305.37
91	32.78	305.93
92	33.33	306.48
93	33.89	307.04
94	34.44	307.59
95	35.00	308.15
96	35.56	308.71
97	36.11	309.26
98	36.67	309.82
99	37.22	310.37
100	37.78	310.93
105	40.56	313.71
110	43.33	316.48
115	46.11	319.26
120	48.89	322.04
125	51.67	324.82
212	100	373.15

⊙ Perfectly Useless Software. "Handy-Dandy Super-Nifty Temperature Conversion Table,"
http://students.washington.edu/kyle/temptable.jpg
Also see: www.nws.mbay.net

WORK AND HOME: *Education and Learning*

College: Information Sources

With a high school diploma or equivalent, a student may pursue undergraduate studies toward an associate's degree (typically requiring two years of full-time coursework) or a bachelor's degree (typically requiring four years of full-time coursework). Most students earn undergraduate degrees while attending school full-time, while others take night or weekend classes while working. Financial assistance is available through loans, grants, and work-study programs.

Online Sources	*Website/Phone*
The Center for All Collegiate Information *a Web-only source*	www.collegiate.net/
Back to College c/o WD Communications P.O. Box 2001 Fullerton, CA 92837	www.back2college.com/ (714) 447-0734
CollegeDegree.com *a Web-only source*	www.collegedegree.com/
U.S. News Online *a Web-only source* *a service of:* U.S. News & World Report, Inc. 1050 Thomas Jefferson Street, NW Washington, D.C. 20007	www.usnews.com/usnews/edu/ college/cohome.htm (202) 955-2000
CollegeView *a Web-only source* *created by:* Hobsons 10200 Alliance Road Cincinnati, OH 45242	www.collegeview.com/ 800-927-8439
Overview *a Web-only source*	www.overview.com/
Universities.com *a Web-only source*	www.universities.com/

⊙ Aviezar, K. Patricia. *Peterson's Game Plan for Getting into College.* Lawrenceville, N.J.: Peterson's, 2000.
    Barron's. *Barron's Compact Guide to Colleges,* 12th ed. Hauppauge, N.Y.: Barron's Educational Series, 2000.
    Fiske, Edward B. *The Fiske Guide to Colleges 2001.* New York: Time Books, 2000.
    Princeton Review. *Pocket Guide to Colleges.* New York: Random House, 2000.
    Yale Daily News. *The Insider's Guide to the Colleges 2001.* New York: Griffin Trade Paperback, 2000.

Graduate School: Information Sources

With a four-year college degree or equivalent, a student may pursue graduate studies toward a masters, doctorate, or other higher degree. Most require at least two years of full-time coursework. Many students earn graduate degrees while attending school full-time, while many others take night or weekend classes while working. Financial assistance is available through loans, grants, and work-study programs.

Online Sources

Website/Phone

Council of Graduate Schools
One Dupont Circle NW, Suite 430
Washington, D.C. 20036-1173

www.cgsnet.org/ResoucesForStudents/index.htm
Phone: (202) 223-3791
Fax: (202) 331-7157

GradView
a Web-only source

www.gradview.com/

Gradschools.com
a Web-only source
a service of:
Educational Directories Unlimited, Inc.
University Technology Park
1450 Edgmont Avenue, Suite 140
Chester, PA 19013

www.gradschools.com/linkus.html

Phone: (610) 499-9200
Fax: (610) 499-9205
E-mail: info@edudirectories.com

Peterson's: The Grad Channel
a Web-only source

iiswinprd01.petersons.com/
GradChannel/

U.S.News Online
a Web-only source
a service of:
U.S. News & World Report, Inc.
1050 Thomas Jefferson Street, NW
Washington, D.C. 20007

www.usnews.com/usnews/edu/ beyond/bchome.htm

Phone: (202) 955-2000

**Graduate Record Examinations
(Educational Testing Service)**
a Web-only source
General inquiries:
GRE-ETS
P.O. Box 6000
Princeton, NJ 08541-6000

www.gre.org/

Phone: (609) 771-7670
Fax: (609) 771-7906
E-mail: gre-info@ets.org

All About Grad School
a Web-only source

www.allaboutgradschool.com/
usgradschools/

⊙ Barron's. *Barron's Profiles of American Colleges*, 23rd ed. Hauppauge, N.Y.: Barron's Educational Series, 1998.

Bloom, Dale F., Jonathan D. Karp, and Nicholas Cohen. *The Ph.D. Process: A Student's Guide to Graduate School in the Sciences.* New York: Oxford University Press, 1999.

Doughty, Harold R. *Guide to American Graduate Schools*, 8th ed. New York: Penguin, 1997.

Gourman, Jack. *The Gourman Report: A Rating of Graduate and Professional Programs in American and International Universities*, 8th ed (revised). New York: Random House, 1997.

International Universities: Information Sources

The opportunity to study abroad for a four-year or post-graduate degree is available in nearly every country, in every language, including English.

Online Sources

Website/Phone

International Association of Universities
IAU/UNESCO Information Centre
on Higher Education
UNESCO House
1, rue Miollis
75732 PARIS Cedex 15 France

www.unesco.org/iau
Phone: 011-33-1-45.68.26.12
Fax: 011-33-1-47.34.76.05
E-mail: centre.iau@unesco.org

EI Education International, Ltd.
205-5325 Cordova Bay Road
Victoria, British Columbia V8Y 283
Canada

www.eiworldwide.com
Phone: (250) 658-6283
Fax: (250) 658-6285
E-mail: info@educationinternational.com

The Internationalist
"International Business Schools"
a Web-only source

www.internationalist.com/
COMPANIES/Schools.html

Studyabroad.com
a Web-only source
a service of:
Educational Directories Unlimited, Inc.
University Technology Park
1450 Edgmont Avenue, Suite 140
Chester, PA 19013

www.studyabroad.com

Phone: (610) 499-9200
Fax: (610) 499-9205
E-mail: info@edudirectories.com

World Universities
a Web-only source
a service of:
Bauhinia World Connection
Kee Wah Industrial Building
666 Castle Peak Road
Kowloon, Hong Kong

www.bauhinia.com/university

Phone: (852) 2785-6081
Fax: (852) 2785-1401
E-mail: info@bauhinia.com

Central and Eastern European Directory On-Line
a Web-only source

www.ceebd.co.uk/ceeed/educatio.htm

⊙ Education International. *The Guide to Universities and Colleges in Canada.* Brussels, Belgium: Education International, 1999.
    Gourman, Jack. *The Gourman Report: A Rating of Undergraduate Programs in American and International Universities,* 10th ed. New York: Random House, 1997.
    International Association of Universities. *World List of Universities,* 21st ed. New York: Grove's Dictionaries, 2000.

Student Financial Aid: Information Sources

Financial assistance for post-secondary education in the United States is available in the form of grants, loans, and work-study programs. The primary criteria for funding are financial need and merit.

Online Sources	Website/Phone
U.S. Department of Education 400 Maryland Avenue, SW Washington, D.C. 20202-0498	www.ed.gov/prog_info/SFA/ StudentGuide/ www.ed.gov/finaid.html www.ed.gov/offices/OSFAP/Students/ www.fafsa.ed.gov/ Phone: 800-433-3243 800-730-8913 (for TTY users) (319) 337-5665 (if no 800 access)
National Association of Student **Financial Aid Administrators** 1129 20th Street NW, Suite 400 Washington, D.C. 20036-3489	www.nasfaa.org/nasfaa/ Phone: (202) 785-0453
Nellie Mae 50 Braintree Hill Office Park, Suite 300 Braintree, MA 02184	www.nelliemae.com/ Phone: 800-367-8848 Fax: 800-931-2200
Sallie Mae 11600 Sallie Mae Drive Reston, VA 20193	www.salliemae.com/ 800-239-4269 (info about financing a college education) 800-891-1410 (info about PLUS*) *Parent Loans for Undergraduate Students*
FinAid! ("The SmartStudent™ **Guide to Financial Aid")** *a Web-only source*	www.finaid.org/
Student Loan Funding Resources, LLC One West Fourth Street, Suite 200 Cincinnati, OH 45202	www.studentloanfunding.com Phone: 877-477-7537 (toll-free) Fax: (513) 763-4340

⊙ Cassidy, Daniel J. *The Scholarship Book 2001: The Complete Guide to Private-Sector Scholarships, Fellowships, Grants, and Loans for the Undergraduate.* Upper Saddle River, N.J.: Prentice Hall, 2000.

College Board. *College Cost & Financial Aid Handbook 2001.* New York: Henry Holt, 2000.

Davis, Herm, and Joyce Lain Kennedy. *College Financial Aid for Dummies.* Foster City, CA: IDG, 1999.

Standard Admission Tests

For students entering undergraduate and graduate schools, standardized entrance examinations are typical requirements. For the schools' admissions officers, the scores on these tests provide a basis on which to judge students from varying educational backgrounds with a common yardstick. Different admissions tests are designed to satisfy different academic criteria, so it is important that prospective students familiarize themselves with the examination requirements of their chosen schools. Twelve of the standard admissions tests administered in the United States are discussed here.

Pronunciation note: These tests are best known by their abbreviated names, which are not pronounced as words, but as initials, letter by letter. For example, the ACT is not pronounced like the word "act"; rather, each letter is spoken: "A-C-T."

ACT (or ACT Assessment) (American College Testing)
- Administered by ACT (a nonprofit organization that, until 1996, went by the name American College Testing Program), for college-bound students (typically high school juniors and seniors).
- Measures proficiency in English, mathematics, reading, and science.
- Many schools that require the taking of SAT II tests will accept the ACT in lieu of the SAT IIs.

AP (Advanced Placement)
- Sponsored by the College Examination Board and administered in high schools, for college-bound students.
- AP exams are available for more than 30 subjects.
- A passing score on an AP exam in any given subject typically earns either college credit or advanced placement in that subject.

DAT (Dental Admissions Test)
- Administered by the American Dental Association (ADA), as required for admittance into dental school.
- Measures academic aptitude, scientific comprehension, and perceptual ability.

GMAT (Graduate Management Admissions Test)
- Administered by the Educational Testing Service (ETS), for prospective business-school graduate students.
- Measures verbal, mathematical, and analytical writing skills.

GRE (Graduate Record Examination)
- Administered by the Educational Testing Service (ETS), for prospective graduate students.
- Measures verbal, quantitative, and analytical reasoning skills.
- Many graduate schools base the student's eligibility for merit-based grants, fellowships, and assistantships partly or largely on GRE scores.

LSAT (Law School Admissions Test)
- Administered by Law School Admission Services (LSAS), as required for admittance into law school.
- Measures critical reading, logical reasoning, analytical reasoning, and strategic thinking skills.

MCAT (Medical College Admissions Test)
- Administered by the Association of American Medical Colleges (AAMC), as required for admittance into medical school.
- Measures proficiency in the basic sciences, general problem-solving, critical thinking, and communication.
- The MCAT is often considered the most intensive of the admissions examinations.

OAT (Optometry Admission Test)
- Administered by the Association of Schools and Colleges of Optometry (ASCO), as required for admittance into optometry school.
- Measures proficiency in physics, chemistry, biology, reading comprehension, and quantitative reasoning.

PCAT (Pharmacy College Admissions Test)
- Administered by the Psychological Corporation, for prospective pharmacy-school graduate students.
- Measures scientific, mathematical, and verbal skills.

PSAT (Preliminiary Scholastic Assessment Test)
- Administered by the Educational Testing Service (ETS), for college-bound students (typically high school sophomores and juniors).
- Shorter than (but very similar in content to) the SAT, the PSAT is often taken as practice, in preparation for the SAT.
- PSAT scores are commonly considered by scholarship committees.

SAT (or SAT I) (Scholastic Assessment Test)
- Administered by the Educational Testing Service (ETS), for college-bound students (typically high school juniors and seniors).
- Measures proficiency in mathematics, vocabulary and reading.
- The SAT is the most widely distributed college admissions test in the United States.

SAT II (Scholastic Assessment Test II)
- Administered by the Educational Testing Service (ETS), for college-bound students (typically high school juniors and seniors).
- SAT II exams are available for more than 20 subjects.
- Unlike the SAT I, which measures general math and verbal skills, each SAT II exam measures the student's knowledge of a specific discipline.

⊙ Kaplan. "Test Prep Info Center," www.kaptest.com/
  Paul, William Henry. *Getting In: Inside the College Admissions Process.* Cambridge, Mass.: Perseus, 1997.
  TurboGrad. "SAT Prep & More," www.turbograd.com/default.asp

Libraries: Dewey Decimal System

The Dewey Decimal System (or "Dewey Decimal Classification") is based on a library classification system formulated in 1873 by American librarian Melvil Dewey (1851–1931). First published in 1876, the Dewey Decimal System uses numerical categorization for organizing, as well as locating, the contents of a library and has been adopted by more than 200,000 libraries in nearly 140 countries. In simplest terms, the system divides all subject matter into ten main classes, which are then divided and subdivided, making the classification progressively more specific. The listing that follows gives the main classes and their primary divisions.

000	Generalities		100	Philosophy
000	Generalities & Computer Science		110	Metaphysics
010	Bibliographies		120	Epistemology
020	Library & Information Sciences		130	Paranormal Phenomena & Occult
030	General Encyclopedias		140	Specific Schools of Philosophy
040	*Unassigned*		150	Psychology
050	General Periodicals		160	Logic
060	General Organizations and Museums		170	Ethics
070	Journalism & Publishing		180	Ancient, Medieval, & Oriental Philosophy
080	General Collections		190	Modern Western Philosophy
090	Manuscripts & Rare Books		200	Religion
100	Philosophy & Psychology		200	General Religion

210	Natural Theology	540	Chemistry & Allied Sciences
220	Bible	550	Earth Sciences
230	Christian Theology	560	Paleontology
240	Christian Moral & Devotional Theology	570	Life Sciences
250	Christian Religious Orders & Local Church	580	Botanical Sciences
		590	Zoological Sciences
260	Christian Social and Ecclesiastical Theology	600	Applied Sciences & Technology
		600	General Technology
270	Christian Church History & Geography	610	Medical Sciences
		620	Engineering
280	Christian Denominations & Sects	630	Agriculture
290	Non-Christian and Comparative Religion	640	Home Economics & Family Living
		650	Management
300	Social Sciences	660	Chemical Technologies
300	Sociology, Anthropology, & Culture	670	Manufacturing
310	General Statistics	680	Application-specific Manufacturing
320	Political Science	690	Building
330	Economics	700	Arts
340	Law	700	Art Theory, History, & Education
350	Public Administration	710	Civic & Landscape Art
360	Social Concerns & Services	720	Architecture
370	Education	730	Sculpture
380	Trade, Commerce, & Communications	740	Drawing & Decorative Arts
390	Customs, Etiquette, & Folklore	750	Painting
400	Languages	760	Graphic and Printed Arts
400	Language	770	Photography
410	Linguistics	780	Music
420	English (& Old English) Language	790	Sports, Recreation, & Performing Arts
430	Germanic & Scandinavian Languages	800	Literature
440	French Language	800	General Literature & Rhetoric
450	Italian, Romanian, & Rhaeto-Romantic Languages	810	American Literature
		820	English (& Old English) Literature
460	Spanish & Portuguese Languages	830	Germanic Literature
470	Latin Language	840	French Literature
480	Classical Greek Language	850	Italian, Romanian, & Rhaeto-Romantic Literature
490	Other Languages		
500	Natural Sciences & Mathematics	860	Spanish & Portuguese Literature
500	General Science & Mathematics	870	Latin Literature
510	Mathematics	880	Classical Greek Literature
520	Astronomy & Allied Sciences	890	Literature of Other Languages
530	Physics		

900	History & Geography	950	Asian History
900	General History	960	African History
910	Geography & Travel	970	North American History
920	Biography, Geneaology, & Insignia	980	South American History
930	Ancient World History	990	History of Other Areas
940	European History		

⊙ Fowler, Allen. *The Dewey Decimal System*. Danbury, Conn.: Grolier, 1997.
Mortimer, Mary. *Learn Dewey Decimal System*, 21st ed. Lanham, Md.: Scarecrow, 1999.
Online Computer Library Center, Inc. "Dewey Decimal Classification," www.oclc.org/oclc.fp/

Library of Congress Classification System

The Library of Congress Classification System (also known as the LCC) is the library classification system that was designed and developed for the U.S. Library of Congress in Washington, D.C. Much of the groundwork for the current system was laid by Librarian of Congress Herbert Putnam (1861–1955) a hundred years ago. Used in many academic libraries, the LCC is an alpha-numeric system, in which each book (or magazine, etc.) is assigned a "call number" comprised of letters and numerals. The first level of classification is identified by one letter (using all letters of the alphabet except I, O, W, X, and Y). The second, more specific level uses two or three letters, and the next level introduces numerals, making the classification progressively more specific. The listing that follows gives the main classes and their primary alphabetic divisions.

A	General Works	BQ	Buddhism
AC	Collections; Series; Collected works	BR	Christianity
AE	Encyclopedias	BS	The Bible
AG	Dictionaries; Other General Reference Works	BT	Doctrinal Theology
		BV	Practical Theology
AI	Indexes	BX	Christian Denominations
AM	Museums; Collectors & Collecting	C	Auxiliary Sciences of History
AN	Newspapers	CB	History of Civilization
AP	Periodicals	CC	Archaeology
AS	Academies & Learned Societies	CD	Diplomatics, Archives, Seals
AY	Yearbooks; Almanacs; Directories	CE	Technical Chronology, Calendar
AZ	History of Scholarship & Learning; The Humanities	CJ	Numismatics
		CN	Inscriptions, Epigraphy
B	Philosophy; Psychology; Religion	CR	Heraldry
B	Philosophy (General)	CS	Genealogy
BC	Logic	CT	Biography
BD	Speculative Philosophy	D	History: General & Old World
BF	Psychology	D	History (General)
BH	Aesthetics	DA	Great Britain
BJ	Ethics; Social Usages; Etiquette	DAW	Central Europe
BL	Religion; Mythology; Rationalism	DB	Austria; Liechtenstein; Hungary; Czechoslovakia
BM	Judaism		
BP	Islam; Bahaism; Theosophy, etc.	DC	France

DD	Germany
DE	Mediterranean Region; Greco-Roman World
DF	Greece
DG	Italy
DH	Belgium; Luxemburg
DJ	Holland
DJK	Eastern Europe
DK	Russia (& former Soviet Union); Poland
DL	Northern Europe; Scandinavia
DP	Spain; Portugal
DQ	Switzerland
DR	Balkan Peninsula
DS	Asia
DT	Africa
DU	Oceania (South Seas)
DX	Gypsies
E	History (General): North America; United States
F	History: United States Local History; Latin America; South America
G	Geography; Maps; Anthropology; Recreation
G	Geography (General); Atlases; Maps
GA	Mathematical Geography; Cartography
GB	Physical Geography
GC	Oceanography
GE	Environmental Sciences
GF	Human Ecology; Anthropogeography
GN	Anthropology
GR	Folklore
GT	Manners & Customs
GV	Recreation & Leisure
H	Social Sciences
HA	Statistics
HB	Economic Theory; Demography
HC	Economic History & Conditions (by region)
HD	Economic History & Conditions
HE	Transportation & Communications
HF	Commerce
HG	Finance
HJ	Public Finance
HM	Sociology
HN	Social History & Conditions; Social Problems
HQ	The Family; Marriage; Women
HS	Societies: Secret, Benevolent, etc.; Clubs
HT	Communities; Classes; Races
HV	Social Pathology; Social & Public Welfare; Criminology
HX	Socialism Communism; Anarchism
J	Political Science
J	General Legislative & Executive Papers
JA	Collections & General Works
JC	Political Theory; Theory of the State
JF	Constitutional History & Administration (General)
JK	Constitutional History & Administration: United States
JL	Constitutional History & Administration: British America; Latin America
JN	Constitutional History & Administration: Europe
JQ	Constitutional History & Administration: Asia; Africa; Australia; Oceania
JS	Local Government; Municipal Government
JV	Colonies and Colonization; Emigration & Immigration; International Migration
JX	International Law
JZ	International Relations
K	Law
K	Law (General)
KD	United Kingdom; Ireland
KDZ	America; North America
KE	Canada
KF	United States
KG	Latin America (General)
KH	South America (General)
KJ-KK	Europe
KL	History of Law: The Ancient Orient

KM	General
KN-KP	South Asia; Southeast Asia; East Asia
KQ-KT	Africa
KU	Australia
KV-KW	Pacific Area Jurisdictions
KZ	Law of Nations
L	Education
L	Education (General)
LA	History of Education
LB	Theory & Practice of Education
LC	Special Aspects of Education
LD	Educational Institutions: United States
LE	Educational Institutions: America (outside of United States)
LF	Educational Institutions: Europe
LG	Educational Institutions: Asia; Africa; Australia; Oceania
LH	School Magazines & Papers
LJ	Student Fraternities & Societies in United States
LT	Textbooks
M	Music (and Books on Music)
M	Music (General); Instrumental Music; Vocal Music
ML	Literature of Music
MT	Musical Instruction and Study
N	Fine Arts
N	Visual Arts (General) [for Photography, see "TR"]
NA	Architecture
NB	Sculpture
NC	Drawing; Design; Illustration
ND	Painting
NE	Print Media
NK	Decorative Arts; Applied Arts; Decoration & Ornament
NX	Arts in General
P	Language & Literature
P	Philology & Linguistics (General)
PA	Classical Languages & Literature
PB	Celtic Languages & Literature
PC	Romance Languages
PD	Germanic Languages
PE	English

PF	West Germanic
PG	Slavic, Baltic, & Albanian Languages & Literature
PH	Finno-Ugrian & Basque Languages & Literature
PJ	Oriental Languages and Literature (General); Semitic Languages & Literature
PK	Indo-Iranian Languages & Literature
PL	Languages & Literature of Eastern Asia, Africa, & Oceania
PM	Hyperborean, Indian, & Artificial Languages
PN	Literature (General)
PQ	Romance Literature
PR	English Literature
PS	American Literature
PT	Germanic Literature
PZ	Juvenile Belles Lettres
Q	Science
Q	Science (General)
QA	Mathematics
QB	Astronomy
QC	Physics
QD	Chemistry
QE	Geology
QH	Natural History (General); Biology (General)
QK	Botany
QL	Zoology
QM	Human Anatomy
QP	Physiology
QR	Microbiology
R	Medicine
R	Medicine (General)
RA	Public Aspects of Medicine
RB	Pathology
RC	Internal Medicine; Practice of Medicine
RD	Surgery
RE	Ophthalmology
RF	Otorhinolaryngology
RG	Gynecology & Obstetrics
RJ	Pediatrics
RK	Dentistry

Library of Congress Classification System *(cont.)*

RL	Dermatology	TR	Photography
RM	Therapeutics; Pharmacology	TS	Manufactures
RS	Pharmacy; Materia Medica	TT	Handicrafts; Arts & Crafts
RT	Nursing	TX	Home Economics
RV	Botanic, Thomsonian, & Eclectic Medicine	U	Military Science
		U	Military Science (General)
RX	Homeopathy	UA	Armies: Organization, Description, Facilities, etc.
RZ	Other Systems of Medicine		
S	Agriculture	UB	Military Administration
S	Agriculture (General)	UC	Maintenance & Transportation
SB	Plant Culture	UD	Infantry
SD	Forestry	UE	Cavalry; Armored & Mechanized Cavalry
SF	Animal Culture		
SH	Aquaculture; Fisheries; Angling	UF	Artillery
SK	Hunting	UG	Military Engineering; Air Forces; Air Warfare
T	Technology		
T	Technology (General)	UH	Other Services
TA	Engineering (General); Civil Engineering (General)	V	Naval Science
		V	Naval Science (General)
TC	Hydraulic Engineering; Ocean Engineering	VA	Navies: Organization, Description, Facilities, etc.
TD	Environmental Technology; Sanitary Engineering	VB	Naval Administration
		VC	Naval Maintenance
TE	Highway Engineering; Roads & Pavements	VD	Naval Seamen
		VE	Marines
TF	Railroad Engineering & Operation	VF	Naval Ordnance
TG	Bridge Engineering	VG	Minor Services of Navies
TH	Building Construction	VK	Navigation, Merchant Marine
TJ	Mechanical Engineering; Machinery	VM	Naval Architecture; Shipbuilding; Marine Engineering
TK	Electrical Engineering; Electronics; Nuclear Engineering		
		Z	Library Science
TL	Motor Vehicles; Aeronautics; Astronautics	Z	Books in General; Book Industries and Trade; Libraries & Library Science; Bibliography
TN	Mining Engineering; Metallurgy		
TP	Chemical Technology	ZA	Information Resources (General)

⊙ The Library Corporation (TLC). "LC Classification Outline, 6th Edition: Contents," www.tlcdelivers.com/tlc/crs/lcs00001.htm

U.S. Library of Congress. "The Library of Congress Cataloging," lcweb.loc.gov/catdir/catdir.html

U.S. Library of Congress (Office for Subject Cataloging Policy, Collection Services). *LC Classification Outline,* 6th ed. Washington, D.C.: Library of Congress, 1990.

Index

A

Abe, Kobo, 443
Abidjan, Côte d'Ivoire, 159
Abu Dhabi, United Arab Emirates, 146
Abuja, Nigeria, 108
Abzug, Bella Savitzky, 224
Academy Awards, 643–49
Accra, Ghana, 67
Achebe, Chinua, 443
Acheson, Edward Goodrich, 435
acids and bases, 393
acne vulgaris, 317
acquired immune deficiency syndrome (AIDS), 318
ACT assessment, 752
actinium (element), 395
actors, 523–26, 532–37
Actors Theatre of Louisville, 521
Acts, Books of, 176
Adak Island, 279
Adams, Abigail Smith, 189
Adams, John, 188, 191, 230, 488
Adams, John Quincy, 188, 230
Adams, Louisa Catherine Johnson, 189
Adams, Maude, 523
Adamstown, Pitcairn Islands, 117
Adès, Thomas, 488
Admiralty Island, 279
Adonis (Greek deity), 186
advanced placement test (AP), 752
Advisory Council on Historic Preservation, 195
Aeolus (Greek deity), 186
Aeschylus, 454
Aesculapius (Roman deity), 187
Afghanistan
    foreign embassy in the U.S., 202
    general information, 24
    population of, 156
    telephone dialing codes, 716
    travel requirements for, 541
    UN membership, 1
AFL-CIO affiliates, 685
Afognak, 279
Africa, 9, 22. *See also* specific countries

African Development Bank (AfDB), 4
Agee, James, 443
Agnew, Spiro Theodore, 192
Agriculture, Nutrition, and Forestry Committee, 226
Agriculture Committee (House), 218
Ahmedabad, India, 159
AIDS (acquired immune deficiency syndrome), 318
Ailey, Alvin, 510
air bags, 710
air conditioning, 706–7
aircraft types, 423–25
Air Force (U.S.), 271
airlines, 551
air pollution, 377
airports, 550
Akron, Ohio, 303
Alabama
    area codes, 714–15
    area of, 286
    capital, 286
    date of admittance, 285, 289
    electoral votes, 233
    features and attractions, 290
    income tax rates, 698
    membership in Congress, 222
    motto and nickname, 288
    poison control center, 337
    population of, 307
    postal abbreviation, 722
    racial makeup of, 308
    sales tax rates, 700
    state flowers, birds, and trees, 287
    time zone, 344
    tourism department, 556
Alabama Shakespeare Festival, 521
Alaska
    area codes, 714–15
    area of, 286
    capital, 286
    date of admittance, 285, 289
    electoral votes, 233
    features and attractions, 290
    income tax rates, 698
    membership in Congress, 222

telephone dialing codes, 716
travel requirements for, 541
UN membership, 1
Anti-Masonic Party, 234
antimony (element), 395
Antoinette Perry Awards (Tony awards), 667–74
Antonines dynasty, 170
AP (advanced placement test), 752
Aphrodite (Greek deity), 186
Apia, Samoa, 124
Apocalypses, Books of, 177
Apocrypha, Books of, 176
Apollo (Greek deity), 186
Apollo (Roman deity), 187
appellate courts, structure of, 268
Appleton, Edward Victor, 435
Appropriations Committees (Congressional), 218, 226
Aquarius (zodiac sign), 357
Arab Bank for Economic Developments in Africa
      (ABEDA), 5
Arab League (AL), 5
Aral Sea, size of, 14
arch bridges, 434
Archimedes, 435
Archipenko, Aleksandr Porfiryevich, 471
architecture, 481–85, 684
Arctic Ocean, 17
area codes (U.S. and Canada), 714–15
areas and volumes, 379, 382, 744
Arena Stage, 521
Ares (Greek deity), 186
Argentina
   foreign embassy in the U.S., 202
   general information, 28–29
   population of, 156
   telephone dialing codes, 716
   travel requirements for, 541
   UN membership, 1
   visitors' and convention bureau, 562
argon (element), 395
Aries (zodiac sign), 356
Aristarchus, 435
Aristophanes, 454
Arizona
   area codes, 714–15
   area of, 286
   capital, 286
   date of admittance, 285, 289
   electoral votes, 233
   features and attractions, 290
   income tax rates, 698
   membership in Congress, 222
   motto and nickname, 288
   poison control center, 337
   population of, 307
   postal abbreviation, 722
   racial makeup of, 308

sales tax rates, 700
state flowers, birds, and trees, 287
time zone, 344
tourism department, 556
Arkansas
   area codes, 714–15
   area of, 286
   capital, 286
   date of admittance, 285, 289
   electoral votes, 233
   features and attractions, 290
   income tax rates, 698
   membership in Congress, 222
   motto and nickname, 288
   poison control center, 337
   population of, 307
   postal abbreviation, 722
   racial makeup of, 308
   sales tax rates, 700
   state flowers, birds, and trees, 287
   time zone, 344
   tourism department, 556
Arkwright, Richard, 435
Arlington, Texas, 303
Armed Services Committees (Congressional), 218, 227
Armenia
   foreign embassy in the U.S., 202
   general information, 29
   population of, 157
   telephone dialing codes, 716
   travel requirements for, 541
   UN membership, 1
arms, right to bear, 246
Arms Control and Disarmament Agency, 195
Armstrong, Edwin Howard, 435
Armstrong, Neil A., 431
Army Corps of Engineers campgrounds, 565
Army (U.S.), 271–78, 278
Arne, Thomas Augustine, 489
arsenic (element), 395
Artemis (Greek deity), 186
Arthur, Chester Alan, 188, 191
arts, 461–74
   architecture, 481–85, 684
   dance, 509–13
   film, 527–37
   literature, 443–60
   painting, 461–71
   photography, 474–76
   sculpture, 471–74
   theater, 513–26
Aruba
   general information, 29–30
   population of, 158
   telephone dialing codes, 716
   travel requirements for, 541
asbestos, 406

Ascension, dialing codes, 716
ASCII, 417–18
Asclepius (Greek deity), 186
ascorbic acid (vitamin C), 332
Ashbrook, Jean Spencer, 224
Ashgabat, Turkmenistan, 144
Ashton, Sir Frederick, 510
Asia, 9, 23. *See also* specific countries
Asia Pacific Economic Corporation (APEC), 5
Asimov, Isaac, 443
Asmara, Eritrea, 58
Aspdin, Joseph, 435
assembly, freedom of, 246
assembly language, 419
Associated Press Poll Champions (football), 601
associate justices (Supreme Court), 262–64
Association of American Universities (AAU), 200
Association of Southeast Asian Nations (ASEAN), 5
Astaire, Adele, 510
Astaire, Fred, 510, 532
Astana (Akmola), Kazakhstan, 83
astatine (element), 395
asteroids, 390–92
asthma, 318
astrological signs, 356–57
astronomy, 383–91
Asuncion, Paraguay, 115
Athabaska (lake), 15
Athena (Greek deity), 186
Athens, Greece, 68, 159
athletics. *See* sports and games
Atka Island, 279
Atlanta, Georgia, 159, 303
Atlantic hurricane names, 368–69
Atlantic Ocean, 17
Atlantic Theatre Company, 521
atmosphere, 411
Attu Island, 279
Atwater, Richard and Florence, 458
Atwood, Margaret, 443
Auber, Daniel-Francois, 489
Augusta, Georgia, 304
Aurora, Colorado, 303
Aurora (Roman deity), 187
Austen, Jane, 443
Austin, Alfred, 453
Austin, Texas, 302
Australia
    foreign embassy in the U.S., 202
    general information, 9, 30
    population of, 156
    telephone dialing codes, 716
    tourism department, 560
    travel requirements for, 541
    UN membership, 1
    visitors' and convention bureau, 564
Australia Group, 5
Australian Open (tennis), 621–23

Austria
    foreign embassy in the U.S., 202
    general information, 30–31
    population of, 156
    telephone dialing codes, 716
    travel requirements for, 541
    UN membership, 1
authors
    children and young adult, 458–60
    novels and short stories, 443–52
    playwrights, 454–57
    poet laureates, 452–53
automobiles, 414–15, 710
Avarua, Cook Islands, 50
aviation, 419–25
awards and prizes, 643–84
Azerbaijan
    foreign embassy in the U.S., 202
    general information, 31
    population of, 156
    telephone dialing codes, 716
    travel requirements for, 541
    UN membership, 1
Azores, 202, 541

B
Babbage, Charles, 435
Babcock, George Herman, 435
Bacall, Lauren, 532
Bacchus (Roman deity), 187
Bach, Johann Sebastian, 489
Bacon, Francis, 461
Bacon, Roger, 435
bacterial diseases, 317
Baekeland, Leo Hendrik, 435
Baffin, 11
Baghdad, Iraq, 78, 159
Bagnold, Enid, 458
Baha'i holidays and festivals, 173
Bahamas
    foreign embassy in the U.S., 202
    general information, 31–32
    population of, 157
    telephone dialing codes, 716
    travel requirements for, 541
    UN membership, 1
Bahrain
    foreign embassy in the U.S., 203
    general information, 32
    population of, 157
    telephone dialing codes, 716
    travel requirements for, 541
    UN membership, 1
Baikal (lake), 14
Baird, John Logie, 435
Baker, Howard H., Jr., 228
Baker, Irene Bailey, 224
Bakersfield, California, 303

Bellona (Roman deity), 187
Bellow, Saul, 443
Belmopan, Belize, 35
Belo Horizonte, Brazil, 159
Bemelmans, Ludwig, 458
Benét, Stephen Vincent, 443
Benin
    foreign embassy in the U.S., 203
    general information, 35–36
    population of, 157
    telephone dialing codes, 716
    travel requirements for, 542
    UN membership, 1
Bennett, Michael, 511
Bennett, Willard Harrison, 435
Bentley, Helen Delich, 224
Benton, Thomas Hart, 462
Benz, Carl Friedrich, 435
Bergman, Ingrid, 532
Beriosova, Svetlana, 511
berkelium (element), 395
Berlin, Germany, 66, 159, 562
Berliner, Emile, 435
Berlioz, Hector, 489
Bermuda
    foreign embassy in the U.S., 203
    general information, 36
    population of, 158
    telephone dialing codes, 716
    travel requirements for, 542
Bern, Switzerland, 137
Bernhardt, Sarah, 523
Bernini, Gianlorenzo, 471
Bernoulli, Daniel, 435
Berstein, Leonard, 489
Berthollet, Claude-Louis, 435
beryl, 406
beryllium (element), 395
Bessemer, Henry, 435
Betjeman, Sir John, 453
Bhutan
    foreign embassy in the U.S., 203
    general information, 36–37
    population of, 157
    telephone dialing codes, 716
    travel requirements for, 542
    UN membership, 1
Bible, 175–76, 175–77
Bierce, Ambrose, 443
Big Seven, 5
Bill of Rights, 246–47
Bingham, George Caleb, 462
Binnig, Gerd Karl, 435
biochemistry, 393
biology, 399–405
biotin, 332
Bird, Forrest M., 435

birds, endangered, 373, 374–75
Birdseye, Clarence, 435
Birmingham, Alabama, 159, 303
birthstones and flowers, 358
Bishkek, Kyrgyzstan, 86
bismuth (element), 395, 406
Bissau, Guinea-Bissau, 72
bits and bytes (computer), 417
Bizet, Georges, 489
Black, Harold Stephen, 435
Black, Hugo Lafayette, 262
Black, Joseph, 435
Blackmun, Harry Andrew, 262
Blackwood, Algernon Henry, 443
Blaine, James G., 221, 231
Blair, John, 262
Blatchford, Samuel Milford, 262
bleeding, first aid for, 322
Blitch, Iris Faircloth, 223
Blitzstein, Marc, 489
blood pressure test, 312
Blumberg, Baruch Samuel, 435
Blume, Judy, 458
boats and boating, 415–17
Boccioni, Umberto, 462, 471
Bogart, Humphrey, 532
Bogata, Columbia, 48, 158
Boggs, Corinne Claiborne, 224
bohrium (element), 395
Boland, Veronica Grace, 223
Bolivia
    foreign embassy in the U.S., 203
    general information, 37
    population of, 156
    telephone dialing codes, 716
    travel requirements for, 542
    UN membership, 1
Böll, Heinrich, 443
Bolton, Frances Payne, 223
Bombay, India, 158
Bonaparte, house of, 168, 172
Bond, Michael, 458
bonds, 690
bone mineral density test, 312
Bonnard, Pierre, 462
Bono, Mary, 226
Booker Prize, 661
books. See literature
Booth, Edwin, 523
Booth, John Wilkes, 523
borax, 406
Bordeaux, France, 562
Borges, Jorge Luis, 443
Borglum, Gutzon, 471
Borgnine, Ernest, 532
Borneo, 11
Borodin, Alexander, 489

Burbank, Luther, 436
Burchfield, Charles Ephraim, 462
Burdick, Jocelyn, 229
Burger, Warren Earl, 261
Burgess, Anthony, 444
Burke, Yvonne Brathwaite, 224
Burkina Faso
    foreign embassy in the U.S., 204
    general information, 40
    population of, 156
    telephone dialing codes, 716
    travel requirements for, 542
    UN membership, 1
Burma. *See* Myanmar (Burma)
Burnett, Francis Hodgson, 458
Burnford, Sheila, 458
Burr, Aaron, 191, 230
Burroughs, William Seward, 436, 444
Burstyn, Ellen, 532
Burton, Harold Hitz, 262
Burton, Richard, 532
Burton, Sala, 224
Burton, Virginia Lee, 458
Burton, William Meriam, 436
Burundi
    foreign embassy in the U.S., 204
    general information, 41–42
    population of, 157
    telephone dialing codes, 716
    travel requirements for, 542
    UN membership, 1
Bush, Barbara Pierce, 190
Bush, George Herbert Walker, 189, 192, 232
Bush, George W., 189, 232
Bush, Laura Welch, 190
Bushfield, Vera Cahlahan, 229
Bushnell, David, 436
business and labor, 685–86
Butler, Pierce, 262
Byrd, Robert C., 228
Byrd, William, 490
Byrne, Leslie, 225
Byrnes, James Francis, 262
Byrns, Joseph W., 221
Byron, Beverly Barton Butcher, 224
Byron, Katherine Edgar, 223

C
cable-stay bridges, 434
Caccialanza, Gisella, 511
cadmium (element), 395
Cage, John, 490
Cage, Nicholas, 532
Cagney, James, 532
Caicos. *See* Turks and Caicos Islands
Cain, James M., 444
Caine, Michael, 532

Cairo, Egypt, 57, 158
calcite, 406
calcium (dietary), 333
calcium (element), 395
Calcutta, India, 158
Caldecott Medal, 680–81
Calder, Alexander, 471
Calderón de la Barca, Pedro, 454
Caldwell, Erskine, 444
calendars, 345–52
Calhoun, John Caldwell, 191
California
    area codes, 714–15
    area of, 286
    capital, 286
    date of admittance, 285, 289
    electoral votes, 233
    features and attractions, 290
    income tax rates, 698
    membership in Congress, 222
    motto and nickname, 288
    poison control center, 337
    population of, 307
    postal abbreviation, 722
    racial makeup of, 308
    sales tax rates, 700
    state flowers, birds, and trees, 287
    time zone, 344
    tourism department, 556
californium (element), 395
Calliope (Greek deity), 186
Cambodia
    foreign embassy in the U.S., 204
    general information, 42
    population of, 156
    telephone dialing codes, 716
    travel requirements for, 542
    UN membership, 1
Cameroon
    foreign embassy in the U.S., 204
    general information, 42–43
    population of, 156
    telephone dialing codes, 716
    travel requirements for, 542
    UN membership, 1
Campbell, John Archibald, 262
Campbell, Mrs. Patrick, 523
Campbell Donald, 436
campground associations, 565–66
Camus, Albert, 444
Canada
    area codes, 714–15
    foreign embassy in the U.S., 204
    general information, 43
    population of, 156
    telephone dialing codes, 716
    tourism department, 560

travel requirements for, 542
UN membership, 1
visitors' and convention bureau, 564, 565
Canberra, Australia, 30
cancer
breast, 312, 315
cervical, 315
colorectal, 313, 314
ovarian, 315
prostate, 316
skin, 316
testicular, 316
Cancer (zodiac sign), 356
Cancun, Mexico, 563
C and C++ (programming languages), 419
Cannon, Joseph G., 221
cantilever bridges, 434
Cantwell, Maria, 225
Capetian, house of, 168
Cape Town, South Africa, 159, 563
Cape Verde
foreign embassy in the U.S., 204
general information, 43–44
population of, 157
telephone dialing codes, 716
travel requirements for, 542
UN membership, 1
Capito, Shelly, 226
Capote, Truman, 444
Capps, Lois, 226
Capricorn (zodiac sign), 357
Caracas, Venezuela, 150, 159
Caravaggio, 462
Caraway, Hattie Wyatt, 229
carbon (element), 395
cardiopulmonary resuscitation, 320–21
Cardozo, Benjamin Nathan, 262
Carle, Eric, 458
Carlisle, John G., 221
Carlson, Chester F., 436
Carolingian, house of, 168, 169
Carothers, Wallace Hume, 436
Carpo (Greek deity), 186
Carrel, Alexis, 436
Carrier, Willis Haviland, 436
Carson, Julia, 226
Carter, Eleanor Rosalynn Smith, 190
Carter, James Earl, Jr. (Jimmy), 189, 232
Cartwright, Edmund, 436
Carver, George Washington, 436
Casablanca, Morocco, 159
Caspian Sea, size of, 14
Cass, Lewis, 231
Cassatt, Mary Stevenson, 463
Castle, Irene, 511
Castle, Vernon, 511
Castries, Saint Lucia, 123

cataracts, 314
cat breeds, 712
Cather, Willa, 444
Catholicism
Holy Roman emperors, 170–71
Patron saints, 181–85
popes (listed), 177–80
Catron, John, 262
Cavendish, Henry, 436
Cayenne, French Guinea, 62
Cayman Islands
foreign embassy in the U.S., 204
general information, 44
population of, 158
telephone dialing codes, 716
travel requirements for, 542
Celebes (Sulawesi) Island, 11
cell biology, 400
Cellini, Benvenuto, 471
Celsius, Anders, 436
cemeteries, national, 574
Central African Republic
foreign embassy in the U.S., 204
general information, 44–45
population of, 157
telephone dialing codes, 716
travel requirements for, 542
UN membership, 1
Central America, map of, 20
Central and Eastern European Directory, 750
Central Intelligence Agency, 195
Ceres (Roman deity), 187
cerium (element), 395
Cernan, Eugene A., 431
Cervantes Saavedra, Miguel de, 444
cervical cancer, 315
cesium (element), 395
Cézanne, Paul, 463
Chad
foreign embassy in the U.S., 204
general information, 45–46
population of, 156
telephone dialing codes, 716
travel requirements for, 542
UN membership, 1
Chad (lake), 15
Chagall, Marc, 463
championship cat breeds, 712
championships
Australian Open (tennis), 621–23
Du Maurier Classic (golf), 630
French Open (tennis), 618–20
LPGA Championship (golf), 629–30
Masters Tournament (golf), 626
Nabisco Championship (golf), 629
NBA (basketball), 588–89
NCAA (basketball), 592–94

Clark, Champ, 221
Clark, Tom Campbell, 262
Clarke, Arthur C., 444
Clarke, John Hessin, 262
Clarke, Marian Williams, 223
classical instrumentalists, 496–98
classical orders, 486
classical singers, 498–99
classification systems, 399–400, 753–58
Clavell, James, 444
Clay, Henry, 220, 230
Clayton, Eva, 225
Cleary, Beverly, 458
Cleveland, Francis Folsom, 190
Cleveland, Grover, 231
Cleveland, Ohio, 302
Cleveland, Rose Elizabeth, 190
Cleveland, Stephen Grover, 188
Cleveland Public Theatre, 521
Clifford, Nathan, 262
Clift, Montgomery, 532
climate, weather, and environment, 358–78
    Beaufort Wind Scale, 364–65
    climate types, 359–61
    cloud types, 362–63
    earthquakes, 371–72
    endangered animal and birds, 373–76
    environmental hazards, 704–5
    heat index, 362
    hurricanes, 366–69
    meteorology symbols, 358–59
    pollution, 377–78
    storms and storm warnings, 363
    tornados, 369–71
    wind chill index, 361–62
Clinton, DeWitt, 230
Clinton, George, 191, 230
Clinton, Hillary Diane Rodham, 190
Clinton, William Jefferson, 189, 232
Clio (Greek deity), 186
Close, Glenn, 532
cloud types, 362–63
cobalt (element), 395, 406
Cobb, Howell, 220
Cobb, Lee J., 523
COBOL (Common Business-Oriented Language), 419
Cocteau, Jean, 444
Coelus (Roman deity), 187
Colbert, Claudette, 532
Coles, Charles, 511
Colette, (Sidone-Gabrielle Colette), 444
Colfax, Schuyler, 191, 220
college information sources, 748–53
college sports. See NCAA (National Collegiate Athletic Association)
Collins, Barbara-Rose, 225
Collins, Cardiss, 224
Collins, Susan, 229

Cologne, Germany, 159
Colombo, Sri Lanka, 133
Colonial Williamsburg, 479
Colorado
    area codes, 714–15
    area of, 286
    capital, 286
    date of admittance, 285, 289
    electoral votes, 233
    features and attractions, 291
    income tax rates, 698
    membership in Congress, 222
    motto and nickname, 288
    poison control center, 337
    population of, 307
    postal abbreviation, 722
    racial makeup of, 308
    sales tax rates, 700
    state flowers, birds, and trees, 287
    time zone, 344
    tourism department, 556
Colorado Springs, Colorado, 303
colorectal cancer, exam for, 313, 314
Colt, Samuel, 436
Colton, Frank B., 436
Columbia
    foreign embassy in the U.S., 204
    general information, 47–48
    population of, 156
    telephone dialing codes, 717
    travel requirements for, 542
    UN membership, 1
Columbus, Ohio, 302
columns, types of, 486
Commerce, Science, and Transportation Committee (Senate), 227
Commodity Futures Trading Commission, 195
Common Cause, 200
common cold, 318
Commonwealth (Commonwealth of Nations), 5
Commonwealth of England and Britain, 167
Commonwealth of Independent States (CIS), 5
communications, 713
Communist Party of the USA, 234
Comoros Islands
    foreign embassy in the U.S., 205
    general information, 48
    population of, 157
    telephone dialing codes, 717
    travel requirements for, 542
    UN membership, 1
composers, 488–94
composite numbers, 379
computer languages, 419
computers, 417–19
Conakry, Guinea, 71
Concorde Coalition, 201
conductors, 495–96

Crompton, Samuel, 436
Cronus (Greek deity), 186
Cronyn, Hume, 523
Crosby, Bing, 532
Crossroads Theatre Company, 521
Cruzan v. *Director, Missouri Department of Health*
    (1990), 265
Cuba
    foreign embassy in the U.S., 205
    general information, 52
    population of, 156
    size of, 11
    telephone dialing codes, 717
    travel requirements for, 543
    UN membership, 1
Cubin, Barbara, 225
cumulonimbus clouds, 362
cumulus clouds, 363
Cunningham, Merce, 511
Cupid (Roman deity), 187
Curaçao, Netherlands Antilles, 563
    foreign embassy in the U.S., 205
    travel requirements for, 543
Curie, Marie, 436
Curie, Pierre, 436
Curitiba, Brazil, 159
curium (element), 395
Curry, John Steuart, 463
Curtis, Benjamin R., 262
Curtis, Charles, 191, 228
Curtis, Tony, 532
Cushing, William, 262
Cyprus
    foreign embassy in the U.S., 205
    general information, 53
    population of, 157
    telephone dialing codes, 717
    travel requirements for, 543
    UN membership, 1
cytology, 400
czars and czarinas of Russia, 171
Czech Republic
    foreign embassy in the U.S., 205
    general information, 53–54
    population of, 156
    telephone dialing codes, 717
    travel requirements for, 543
    UN membership, 1

D
Dahl, Roald, 458
Daimler, Gottlieb, 436
Dakar, Senegal, 126
Dali, Salvador, 463
Dalian, China, 159
Dallas, George Miflin, 191
Dallas, Texas, 159, 302

Dall Island, 279
Damadian, Raymond V., 436
Damascus, Syria, 138, 160
dance, 509–13
Daniel, Peter Vivian, 262
Danish, house of, 167
Danner, Pat, 225
Darby, Abraham, 437
Dar es Salaam, Tanzania, 139
Dartmouth College v. *Woodward* (1819), 265
Daschle, Thomas A., 229
data information, 417
DAT (dental admissions test), 752
Daumier, Honoré, 463
David, Jacques-Louis, 463
Davies, Charles Gates, 191
Davies, Peter Maxwell, 490
Davies, Robertson, 445
da Vinci, Leonardo, 436
Davis, Bette, 532
Davis, David, 262
Davis, Jo Ann, 226
Davis, John W., 220, 231
Davis, Ossie, 524
Davis, Susan, 226
Davy, Humphry, 437
Day, William Rufus, 262
Day-Lewis, Cecil, 453
Day-Lewis, Daniel, 532
Dayton, Jonathan, 220
Dean, James, 533
Dean, Mark, 437
death, causes of (U.S.), 327
De Brunhoff, Jean, 458
Debussy, Claude, 490
De Chirico, Giorgio, 463
Declaration of Independence, 236–38
Dee, Ruby, 524
Deere, John, 437
deficiency diseases, 317
Defoe, Daniel, 445
Deforest, Lee, 437
Degas, Edgar, 463, 471
degenerative disorders, 317
DeGette, Diana, 226
de Haviland, Olivia, 532
de Kooning, Willem, 463
Delacroix, Eugene, 464
DeLauro, Rosa, 225
Delaware
    area codes, 714–15
    area of, 286
    capital, 286
    date of admittance, 285, 289
    electoral votes, 233
    features and attractions, 291
    income tax rates, 698

travel requirements for, 543
UN membership, 1
Donatello, 472
Donelson, Emily, 188
Donizetti, Gaetano, 490
Doric order, 486
Dos Passos, John, 445
Dostoyevsky, Fyodor Mikhaylovich, 445
Douglas, Emily Taft, 223
Douglas, Isle of Man, 96
Douglas, Kirk, 533
Douglas, Michael, 533
Douglas, William Orville, 262
Dove, Rita, 453
Dow, Herbert Henry, 437
Doyle, Sir Arthur Conan, 445
Dr. Seuss (Theodore Seuss Geisel), 459
Draper, Charles Stark, 437
Dred Scott v. *Sandford* (1857), 265
Dreiser, Theodore, 445
Drew, Richard, 437
drugs (pharmaceuticals), 322–25
Drummond Island, 279
Dryden, John, 452, 454
dry weight measurements, 745
Dublin, Ireland, 79
dubnium (element), 395
Dubuffet, Jean, 464, 472
Duchamp, Marcel, 464, 472
due process, 247
Dufy, Raoul, 464
Dukakis, Michael S., 232
Duke, Charles M., Jr., 431
Dumas, Alexandre père, 445
Du Maurier, Daphne, 445
Du Maurier Classic (golf), 630
Dunaway, Faye, 533
Duncan, Isadora, 511
Dunham, Katherine, 511
Dunlop, John Boyd, 437
Dunn, Jennifer, 225
Durand, Asher Brown, 464
Dürer, Albrecht, 464
Duse, Eleonora, 524
Dushanbe, Tajikistan, 139
Dusseldorf, Germany, 159
Duval, Robert, 533
Duvall, Gabriel, 262
Dvořák, Antonin, 490
Dwyer, Florence Price, 223
dynamics, musical, 487
dynasties, 167, 169
dysprosium (element), 395

E
Eakins, Thomas, 464
ear, anatomy of, 405

ear infection (otitis media), 319
Earth (planet), 383
earthquakes, 371–72
earth sciences, 406–11
Eastman, George, 437
Eastman, P. D., 458
Eastwood, Clint, 533
eclipses, solar, 387–88
Eco, Umberto, 445
Economic and Social Council (UN), 3
economics
    global, 8
    Nobel Prize, 642
Ecuador
    foreign embassy in the U.S., 206
    general information, 56
    population of, 156
    telephone dialing codes, 717
    travel requirements for, 543
    UN membership, 1
eczema, 319
Edgar, Edward, 490
Edgerton, Harold E., 437
Edison, Thomas Alva, 437
editing, proofreader's marks, 743
education and learning, 748–53
    college information sources, 748–53
    education IRAs, 691
    financial aid, 751
    standard admission tests, 751–53
Education and the Workforce Committee (House),
    218
Edwards, Elaine S., 229
Edwards v. *Aguillard* (1987), 265
Egypt
    foreign embassy in the U.S., 206
    general information, 56–57
    population of, 156
    telephone dialing codes, 717
    tourism department, 561
    travel requirements for, 543
    UN membership, 1
EI Education International, Ltd., 750
Einstein, Albert, 437
einsteinium (element), 395
Einthoven, Willem, 437
Eirene (Greek deity), 186
Eisenhower, Dwight D., 189, 232
Eisenhower, Mamie Geneva Doud, 190
elections. *See also* presidency (U.S.)
    article 1 of the Constitution, 238–42
    article 2 of the Constitution, 242–44
    electoral college, 233, 242–43
    12th Amendment, 247–48
    24th Amendment, 251
electricity, 413, 702–3
elementary particles, 398
elements, 395–97

Elion, Gertrude Belle, 437
Eliot, George (Mary Ann Evans), 445
Ellesmere, 11
Ellis Island, 479
Ellison, Harlan, 445
Ellison, Ralph, 445
Ellsworth, Oliver, 261
El Paso, Texas, 302
El Salvador
    foreign embassy in the U.S., 206
    general information, 57
    population of, 157
    telephone dialing codes, 717
    travel requirements for, 543
    UN membership, 1
e-mail, 713
emergency information, 337–42
Emerson, JoAnn, 226
Emmy Awards, 662–67
emperors, Roman, 170–71
endangered animal and birds, 373–76
Energy and Natural Resources Committee (Senate), 227
Engelbart, Douglas, 437
Engel v. *Vitale* (1962), 265
England, Great Britain, and the United Kingdom
    British poet laureates, 452–53
    foreign embassy in the U.S., 206, 217
    general information, 147
    monarchs of, 167–68
    population of, 156
    Protectorate of, 168
    size of, 11
    telephone dialing codes, 719
    tourism department, 561
    travel requirements for, 548
    UN membership, 2
    visitors' and convention bureau, 564
English, Karan, 225
Ensemble Studio Theatre, 521
Ensor, James Sydney, 464
environment. *See* climate, weather, and environment
Environmental Protection Agency, 196
Environments in Public Works Committee (Senate), 227
Enyo (Greek deity), 186
Eos (Greek deity), 186
Epistles, Books of, 177
Epstein, Jacob, 472
equal protection in the U.S. Constitution, 248–49
Equal Rights Party, 235
Equatorial Guinea
    foreign embassy in the U.S., 206
    general information, 57–58
    population of, 157
    telephone dialing codes, 717
    travel requirements for, 543
    UN membership, 1

Erato (Greek deity), 186
erbium (element), 395
Ericsson, John, 437
Erie (lake), 14, 282, 286
Eris (Greek deity), 186
Eritrea
    foreign embassy in the U.S., 206
    general information, 58
    population of, 157
    telephone dialing codes, 717
    travel requirements for, 543
    UN membership, 1
Ernst, Max, 464, 472
Eros (Greek deity), 186
Escapees RV Club, The, 566
Esfahan, Iran, 160
Eshoo, Anna G., 225
Eslick, Willa McCord Blake, 223
Essen, Germany, 158
estate and gift taxes, 701
Estonia
    foreign embassy in the U.S., 206
    general information, 58–59
    population of, 157
    telephone dialing codes, 717
    travel requirements for, 543
    UN membership, 1
Ethiopia
    foreign embassy in the U.S., 206
    general information, 59
    population of, 156
    telephone dialing codes, 717
    travel requirements for, 543
    UN membership, 1
ethnic makeup of states, 308–9
Euripides, 454
Europe. *See also* specific countries
    European Monetary Union (EMU), 6
    European Union (EU), 6
    general statistics, 9
    map of, 21
europium (element), 395
Eusden, Laurence, 453
Euterpe (Greek deity), 186
exosphere, 411
Ex Parte Merryman (1861), 266
Ex Parte Milligan (1866), 266
Eyck, Jan van, 464
eyes, physiology of, 314, 405
Eyre Lake, 15

F
factors, 379
Fagan, Garth, 511
Faggin, Federico, 437
Fahrenheit, Daniel Gabriel, 437
Fairbanks, Charles Warren, 191

flowers, 287–88, 358
fluorine (dietary), 333
fluorine (element), 395
fluorite, 407
Fokine, Michel, 511
Foley, Thomas S., 221
folic acid, 332
Fonda, Henry, 533
Fonda, Jane, 533
Fontanne, Lynn, 524
Fonteyn, Margot, 511
food. *See* diet
football, 594–604
Ford, Elizabeth Ann Bloomer Warren, 190
Ford, Ford Madox, 445
Ford, Gerald Rudolph, Jr., 189, 192, 232
Ford, Harrison, 533
Ford, Henry, 437
foreign films, 530–31
Foreign Relations Committee (Senate), 227
forests, national, 569–71
Forest Service campgrounds, 565
Former Yugoslav Republic of Macedonia. *See*
    Macedonia, former Yugoslav Republic of
Forrest, Edwin, 524
Forrester, Jay Wright, 437
Forster, E. M., 445
Fortaleza, Brazil, 159
Fortas, Abe, 262
Fort-de-France, Martinique, 97
FORTRAN (FORmula TRANslation), 419
Fortuna (Roman deity), 187
Fort Wayne, Indiana, 304
Fort Worth, Texas, 302
Fosse, Bob, 511
Foster, Jodie, 533
401k, 403b plans, 692
Fowler, Tillie, 225
Fowles, John, 446
fractions, mathematical procedures on, 380–81
Fragonard, Jean-Honoré, 464
Frahm, Shelia, 229
France
    foreign embassy in the U.S., 207
    general information, 61–62
    kings and emperors of, 168–69
    population of, 156
    telephone dialing codes, 717
    tourism department, 561
    travel requirements for, 543
    UN membership, 1
    visitors' and convention bureau, 562, 564
francium (element), 395
Franck, César, 490
Franco, Francisco, 172
Franconia, house of, 169
Frankfurt, Germany, 159, 563

Frankfurter, Felix, 262
Franklin, Benjamin, 438
Freeman, Morgan, 533
Free-Soil Party, 234
Freetown, Sierra Leone, 129
Fremont, California, 303
Fremont, John C., 231
French Antilles, 717
French Guiana
    foreign embassy in the U.S., 207
    general information, 62–63
    population of, 157
    telephone dialing codes, 717
    travel requirements for, 543
French Open (tennis), 618–20
French Polynesia
    foreign embassy in the U.S., 207
    general information, 63
    population of, 157
    telephone dialing codes, 717
    travel requirements for, 543
Fresno, California, 302
Friedrich, Caspar David, 464
Frontiero v. *Richardson* (1973), 265
Fuentes, Carlos, 446
Fugard, Athol, 454
Fuller, Melville Weston, 261
Fulmer, Willa Lybrand, 223
Fulton, Robert, 438
Funafuti, Tuvalu, 145
fungal diseases, 317
Furman v. *Georgia* (1972), 265
Furse, Elizabeth, 225

G
Gable, Clark, 533
Gabon
    foreign embassy in the U.S., 207
    general information, 63–64
    population of, 157
    telephone dialing codes, 717
    travel requirements for, 543
    UN membership, 1
Gaborone, Botswana, 38
gadolinium (element), 395
Gág, Wanda, 458
Gainsborough, Thomas, 464
Galapagos Islands. *See* Ecuador
galaxies, 388
Galileo, 438
Galle, Johann Gottfried, 438
gallium (element), 395
Galsworthy, John, 446
Galvani, Luigi, 438
Gambia, The
    foreign embassy in the U.S., 207
    general information, 64

population of, 157
telephone dialing codes, 717
travel requirements for, 543
UN membership, 1
games and sports, 578–633
Garbo, Greta, 533
Garcia, Márquez Gabriel, 446
García Lorca, Federico, 454
Gardner, Ava, 534
Garfield, James Abram, 188, 231
Garfield, Lucretia Rudolph, 190
Garis, Howard, 458
Garland, Judy, 534
Garland, Texas, 304
Garner, John Nance, 191, 221
Gasque, Elizabeth Hawley, 223
Gauguin, Paul, 465
Gaza Strip, 64–65, 157
Geiger, Johannes, 438
Gemini (zodiac sign), 356
General Assembly (United Nations), 3
General Services Administration, 196
genetics, 399
geography
    global, 8–23
    United States, 279–85, 283–88
geology, 409–11
geometric shapes, 382
George Street Playhouse, 521
George Town, Cayman Islands, 44
Georgetown, Guyana, 73
Georgia (country)
    foreign embassy in the U.S., 207
    general information, 65
    population of, 157
    telephone dialing codes, 717
    travel requirements for, 543
    UN membership, 1
Georgia (state)
    area codes, 714–15
    area of, 286
    capital, 286
    date of admittance, 285, 289
    electoral votes, 233
    features and attractions, 291
    income tax rates, 698
    membership in Congress, 222
    motto and nickname, 288
    poison control center, 338
    population of, 307
    postal abbreviation, 722
    racial makeup of, 308
    sales tax rates, 700
    state flowers, birds, and trees, 287
    time zone, 344
    tourism department, 556
Gérard, François, 465

Gerbert of Aurillac, 438
Géricault, Théodore, 465
germanium (element), 395
Germany
    foreign embassy in the U.S., 207
    general information, 65–66
    population of, 156
    telephone dialing codes, 717
    travel requirements for, 543
    UN membership, 1
    visitors' and convention bureau, 562, 563
Germer, Edmund, 438
Gerry, Elbridge, 191
Gershwin, George, 490
Gettysburg, 479
Gettysburg Address, 252
Ghana
    foreign embassy in the U.S., 207
    general information, 66–67
    population of, 156
    telephone dialing codes, 717
    travel requirements for, 543
    UN membership, 1
Ghiberti, Lorenzo, 472
Ghirlandaio, Domenico, 465
Giacometti, Alberto, 472
Gibbons v. *Ogden* (1824), 265
Gibbs, Florence Reville, 223
Gibraltar
    general information, 67
    population of, 158
    telephone dialing codes, 717
    travel requirements for, 543
Gide, André, 446
Gideon v. *Wainwright* (1963), 265
Gielgud, John, 524
Gilbert Islands. *See* Kiribati
Gillette, Frederick H., 221
Gillette, William H., 524
Gilpin, Charles, 524
gingivitis, 319
Gingrich, Newt, 221
Ginsburg, Charles P., 438
Ginsburg, Ruth Bader, 262
Giotto, 465
Gipson, Fred, 458
Girardon, François, 472
Giraudoux, Jean, 455
Gish, Lillian, 534
Glass, Philip, 490
glass, recycling, 708
Glauber, Johann Rudolph, 438
glaucoma, 314
Glendale, Arizona, 303
Glendale, California, 304
Glinka, Mikhail, 490
global statistics, 8

Glover, Savion, 511
Gluck, Christoph Willibald, 490
Goddard, Paulette, 534
Goddard, Robert Hutchings, 438
Godunov, Alexander, 511
Godunov, house of, 171
Gogh, Vincent van, 465
Gogol, Nikolai, 446
Goldberg, Arthur Joseph, 262
Goldberg, Whoopi, 534
gold (element), 395, 407
Golding, William, 446
Goldsmith, Oliver, 446
Goldwater, Barry M, 232
golf, 625–31
Goodman Theatre, 521
The Good Sam Club, 566
Goodspeed Opera House, 521
Goodyear, Charles, 438
Gordimer, Nadine, 446
Gore, Albert A., Jr., 192, 232
Gorky, Maxim, 446
Goslar, Lotte, 511
Gospel, Books of, 177
Gounod, Charles, 490
gout diet, 334
Governmental Affairs Committee (Senate), 227
government and history (U.S.), 188–258
Government Reform Committee (House), 219
Goya y Lucientes, Francisco José de, 465
Grable, Betty, 534
Graceland, 479
Graces (Greek deities), 186
Graces (Roman deities), 187
graduate school information sources, 749
Graham, Martha, 511
Graham, Thomas, 438
Grahame, Kenneth, 458
Gramatky, Hardie, 458
Granahan, Kathryn Elizabeth, 223
Grand Princess of Moscow-Vladimir, 171
Grand Rapids, Michigan, 304
Grand Turks, Caicos Islands, 144
Granger, Kay, 226
Grant, Cary, 534
Grant, Julia Dent, 188
Grant, Ulysses Simpson, 188, 231
graphite, 407
Grass, Günther, 446
Grasso, Ella Tambussi, 224
Graves, Dixie Bibb, 229
Graves, Robert, 446
Gray, Horace, 262
Great Basin Desert, 280, 284
Greatbatch, Wilson, 438
Great Bear Lake, 14

Great Britain. *See* England, Great Britain, and the United Kingdom
Great Salt Lake, 282, 286
Great Slave Lake, 14
Greco, El, 465
Greece
    foreign embassy in the U.S., 207
    general information, 67–68
    gods of Greek mythology, 186–87
    population of, 156
    telephone dialing codes, 717
    travel requirements for, 543
    UN membership, 1
Greeley, Horace, 231
Green, Edith Starrett, 223
Greenback Party, 234
Greene, Enid, 226
Greene, Graham, 446
Greenland. *See also* Denmark
    general information, 68
    population of, 158
    size of, 11
    telephone dialing codes, 717
    travel requirements for, 543
Greenough, Horatio, 472
Green Party, 234
Greenpeace, 201
Greensboro, North Carolina, 304
Greenway, Isabella Selmes, 223
Grenada, 68–69
    foreign embassy in the U.S., 207
    Operation Urgent Fury, 276
    population of, 158
    telephone dialing codes, 717
    travel requirements for, 543
    UN membership, 1
Grenadine Islands, 2, 717
Grieg, Edvard, 490
Grier, Robert Cooper, 262
Griffiths, Martha Wright, 223
Grimm, Wilhelm and Jacob, 458
Gris, Juan, 465
Grisham, John, 446
Grisi, Carlotta, 511
Grosz, George, 465
Grow, Galusha A., 220
Guadalajara, Mexico, 159
Guadeloupe
    foreign embassy in the U.S., 207
    general information, 69
    population of, 157
    telephone dialing codes, 717
    travel requirements for, 543
Guam
    general information, 69–70, 299–300
    population of, 157
    telephone dialing codes, 717

Guangzhou, China, 159
Guantanamo Bay, 717
Guatemala
    foreign embassy in the U.S., 208
    general information, 70
    population of, 156
    telephone dialing codes, 717
    travel requirements for, 544
    UN membership, 1
Guatemala City, Guatemala, 159
Guericke, Otto von, 438
Guernsey, 70–71, 158
Guinea
    foreign embassy in the U.S., 208
    general information, 71
    population of, 156
    telephone dialing codes, 717
    travel requirements for, 544
    UN membership, 1
Guinea-Bissau
    foreign embassy in the U.S., 208
    general information, 72
    population of, 157
    telephone dialing codes, 717
    travel requirements for, 544
    UN membership, 1
Guinness, Alec, 524, 534
Guiyang, China, 160
Gulf War, 276
gum disease, 313
Gutenberg, Johannes, 438
Guthrie Theatre, 521
Guyana
    foreign embassy in the U.S., 208
    general information, 72–73
    population of, 157
    telephone dialing codes, 717
    travel requirements for, 544
    UN membership, 1
gypsum, 407

H
Haas, Robert, 453
Habsburg, house of, 169–70, 172
Habsburg-Lorraine, house of, 170–71
Hackman, Gene, 534
Hades (Greek deity), 186
Hadley, John, 438
hadrons, 398
hafnium (element), 395
Hagatna, Guam, 70, 300
Hagen, Uta, 524
Haiti
    foreign embassy in the U.S., 208
    general information, 73
    Operation Uphold Democracy, 276
    population of, 157

telephone dialing codes, 717
travel requirements for, 544
UN membership, 1
Hall, Charles Martin, 438
Hall, Katie Beatrice, 224
Hall, Robert N., 438
Halley, Edmund, 438
Hals, Frans, 465
Hamburg, Germany, 159
Hamilton, Bermuda, 36
Hamilton, Virginia, 458
Hamlin, Hannibal, 191
Hammarskjöld, Dag, 4
Hammer v. *Dagenhart* (1918), 265
Hammett, Dashiell, 446
Hancock, Winfield S., 231
Handan, China, 159
Handel, George Frederic, 491
Hangzhou, China, 159
Hanks, Tom, 534
Hanoi, Vietnam, 151
Hanover, house of, 167
Hansen, Julia Butler, 224
Harare, Zimbabwe, 155
Harbin, China, 159
Harden, Cecil Murray, 223
Harding, Florence, 190
Harding, Warren Gamaliel, 188, 231
Hardy, Thomas, 446
Hargreaves, James, 438
Harlan, John Marshall, 262, 263
Harlow, Jean, 534
Harman, Jane, 225
Harris, Joel Chandler, 459
Harris, Julie, 524
Harris, Rosemary, 524
Harrison, Anna Symmes, 188
Harrison, Benjamin, 188, 231
Harrison, John, 438
Harrison, Rex, 524, 534
Harrison, William Henry, 188, 230
Hart, Melissa, 226
Hartford Stage Company, 521
Harvey, William, 438
hassium (element), 395
Hastert, John Dennis, 221
Havana, Cuba, 52, 159
Hawaii
    area codes, 714–15
    area of, 279, 286
    capital, 286
    date of admittance, 285, 289
    electoral votes, 233
    features and attractions, 291
    income tax rates, 698
    membership in Congress, 222
    motto and nickname, 288

Hawaii (*cont.*)
poison control center, 338
population of, 307
postal abbreviation, 722
racial makeup of, 308
sales tax rates, 700
state flowers, birds, and trees, 287
time zone, 344
tourism department, 556
Hawkins, Erick, 511
Hawkins, Paula, 229
Hawthorne, Nathaniel, 446
Haydn, Franz Joseph, 491
Hayes, Helen, 524
Hayes, Lucy Webb, 190
Hayes, Rutherford Birchard, 188, 231
Hayworth, Rita, 534
Hazen, Elizabeth Lee, 438
Health, Education, Labor, and Pensions Committee
(Senate), 227
health, nutrition, and fitness, 327–42
heart, anatomy of, 401
Heart of Atlanta Motel v. *U.S.* (1964), 265
heat, physical laws regarding, 412
heat index, 362
heating systems, 706
Hebe (Greek deity), 186
Hecate (Greek deity), 186
Heckler, Nargaret M., 224
height and weight standards, 328
Heisman Memorial Trophy, 604–4
Helios (Greek deity), 186
helium (element), 395
Heller, Joseph, 446
Hellman, Lillian, 455
Helsinki, Finland, 61
Hemingway, Ernest, 446
Henderson, David B., 221
Hendricks, Thomas Andrews, 191
Henley, Beth, 455
Henri, Robert, 465
Henry, O. *See* Porter, William Sydney
Henry Ford Museum, 480
Henze, Hans Werner, 491
hepatitis, 319
Hepburn, Audrey, 534
Hepburn, Katharine, 534
Hephaestus (Greek deity), 186
Heracles (Greek deity), 186
Hera (Greek deity), 186
Hercules (Roman deity), 187
herding dogs, 711
hereditary disorders, 317
Hermaphroditus (Greek deity), 186
Hermes (Greek deity), 186
herpes, 319
Herschel, William, 438

Hertz, Heinrich, 438
Herzegovina. *See* Bosnia and Herzegovina
Hesse, Herman, 447
Hestia (Greek deity), 186
Heston, Charlton, 534
Hewlett, William R., 438
Hialeah, Florida, 303
Hicks, Edward, 465
Hicks, Louise Day, 224
high-calcium diet, 334
high-fiber diet, 334
Highsmith, Patricia, 447
Higonnet, René Alphonse, 438
Hillier, James, 438
Hilton, James, 447
Himes, Chester, 447
Hindemith, Paul, 491
Hindu holidays and festivals, 174
Hines, Gregory, 511
Hinton, S. E., 459
Hipparchus, 438
Hispaniola, 11
history (world), 160–73
Hoban, Russell, 459
Hobart, Garret Augustus, 191
Ho Chi Min, Vietnam, 159
hockey, 605–12
Hockey Hall of Fame, 609–12
Hockney, David, 465
Hoe, Richard March, 438
Hoff, Marcian, 439
Hoffman, Malvina, 472
Hoffmann, Dustin, 534
Hogarth, William, 465
Hohenstaufen, house of, 169
Hokkaido, 11
Holbein, Hans (Elder and Younger), 465–66
Holden, William, 534
holidays (U.S. and global), 353–55
Hollerith, Herman, 439
Holliday, Judy, 524
Holm, Hanya, 512
Holmes, Oliver Wendell, Jr., 263
holmium (element), 395
Holocaust/World War II history (museum), 480
Holst, Gustav, 491
Holstein-Gottorp-Romanov, house of, 171
Holt, Marjorie Sewell, 224
Holtzman, Elizabeth, 224
Holy See. *See* Vatican City
home buying, 694–95
Homer, Winslow, 466
home safety, 701–2
Honduras
foreign embassy in the U.S., 208
general information, 74
population of, 157

telephone dialing codes, 717
travel requirements for, 544
UN membership, 1
Honeyman, Nan Wood, 223
Hong Kong
foreign embassy in the U.S., 208
general information, 74–75
population of, 157
telephone dialing codes, 717
travel requirements for, 544
visitors' and convention bureau, 563
Hong Kong, China, 158
Honiara, Solomon Islands, 131
Honolulu, Hawaii, 303
Honshu, 11
Hooley, Darlene, 226
Hoover, Herbert Clark, 188, 231
Hoover, Lou Henry, 190
Hope, Laura Lee, 459
Hopkins, Anthony, 534
Hopper, Edward, 466
Hopper, Grace, 439
Horn, Joan Kelly, 225
Horton, Lester, 512
Hosmer, Harriet Goodhue, 472
Houdry, Eugene, 439
hounds, 711
House Administration Committee, 219
household budgeting, 687–88
House of Representatives. *See* United States House of
    Representatives
Houston, Texas, 159, 302
Howe, Elias, 439
Howells, William Dean, 447
Hubble, Edwin Powell, 439
Huck, Winnifred Sprague Mason, 222
Hughes, Charles Evans, 261, 263
Hughes, Ted, 453
Hugo, Victor Marie, 447
human immunodeficiency syndrome (HIV), 315
humidity (heat index), 362
Humperdinck, Engelbert, 491
Humphrey, Doris, 512
Humphrey, Hubert Horatio, 192, 232
Humphrey, Muriel, 229
Hungary
foreign embassy in the U.S., 208
general information, 75
population of, 156
telephone dialing codes, 717
travel requirements for, 544
UN membership, 1
visitors' and convention bureau, 562
Hunt, Walter, 439
Hunt, Ward, 263
Hunter, Holly, 534
Hunter, Robert M. T., 220

Huntington Beach, California, 304
Huntington Theatre Company, 521
Huron (lake), 14, 282, 286
hurricanes, 363
Hurricane Intensity Scale, 366
names of, 368–69
strongest in U.S. (listed), 367
Hurston, Zora Neale, 447
Huston, Angelica, 534
Hutchison, Kay Bailey, 229
Huxley, Aldous, 447
Huygens, Christiaan, 439
Hyatt, Anna Vaughn, 472
Hyderabad, India, 158
hydrogen (element), 395
Hygeia (Greek deity), 186
Hymen (Greek deity), 186
hypercholesterolemia, 313
hypertension, 312
hyperthyroidism, 316
Hypnos (Greek deity), 186
hypotenuse, 379
hypothyroidism, 316

I
Ibsen, Henrik, 455
Iceland
foreign embassy in the U.S., 208
general information, 75–76
population of, 157
size of, 11
telephone dialing codes, 717
travel requirements for, 544
UN membership, 1
Idaho
area codes, 714–15
area of, 286
capital, 286
date of admittance, 285, 289
electoral votes, 233
features and attractions, 292
income tax rates, 698
membership in Congress, 222
motto and nickname, 288
poison control center, 338
population of, 307
postal abbreviation, 722
racial makeup of, 308
sales tax rates, 700
state flowers, birds, and trees, 287
time zone, 344
tourism department, 557
Iliamna (lake), 282, 287
Illinois
area codes, 714–15
area of, 286
capital, 286

features and attractions, 292
income tax rates, 698
membership in Congress, 222
motto and nickname, 289
poison control center, 339
population of, 307
postal abbreviation, 722
racial makeup of, 308
sales tax rates, 700
state flowers, birds, and trees, 287
time zone, 344
tourism department, 557
Kenya
foreign embassy in the U.S., 209
general information, 83
population of, 156
telephone dialing codes, 718
travel requirements for, 544
UN membership, 1
Kerouac, Jack, 447
Kerr, Michael C., 221
Kesey, Ken, 447
Kettering, Charles Franklin, 439
Keys, Martha Elizabeth, 224
Khachaturian, Aram, 491
Khartoum, Sudan, 134, 159
Kidman, Nicole, 535
Kiev, Ukraine, 146, 159
Kigali, Rwanda, 121
Kilby, Jack S., 439
Kilpatrick, Carolyn Cheeks, 226
King, DeVane, 191
King, Stephen, 447
kings and emperors, 167–73
Kingston, Jamaica, 81
Kingston, Norfolk Island, 110
Kingstown, Saint Vincent and the Grenadines, 124
Kinshasa, Democratic Republic of the Congo, 159
Kirchner, Ernst Ludwig, 466
Kiribati
general information, 84
population of, 158
telephone dialing codes, 718
travel requirements for, 544
UN membership, 2
Kirkland, Gelsey, 512
Kitakyushu, Japan, 159
Klee, Paul, 466
Klimt, Gustav, 466
Kline, Franz Joseph, 466
Knowland, William F., 228
Knowles, John, 447
Knutson, Coya Gjesdal, 223
Koch, Robert, 439
Kodály, Zóltan, 491
Kodiak Island, 279
Kokoschka, Oskar, 466

Kolff, Willem J., 439
Kollwitz, Käthe Schmidt, 466
Konigsburg, E. L., 459
Korea, Democratic People's Republic of (North Korea)
foreign embassy in the U.S., 210
general information, 84–85
Korean Conflict, 275
population of, 156
telephone dialing codes, 718
travel requirements for, 544
UN membership, 2
Korea, Republic of (South Korea)
foreign embassy in the U.S., 210
general information, 85
Korean Conflict, 275
population of, 156
telephone dialing codes, 718
travel requirements for, 544
UN membership, 2
Korean War Veterans Association, 277
Korematsu v. U.S. (1944), 266
Koror, Palau, 113
Krantz, Judith, 447
krypton (element), 396
Kuala Lumpur, Malaysia, 94, 563
Kuiu Island, 279
Kunitz, Stanley, 453
Kupreanof Island, 279
Kushner, Tony, 455
Kuwait
foreign embassy in the U.S., 210
general information, 85–86
Gulf War, 276
population of, 157
telephone dialing codes, 718
travel requirements for, 544
UN membership, 2
Kwolek, Stephanie Louise, 439
Kyrgyz Republic (Kyrgyzstan)
foreign embassy in the U.S., 210
general information, 86
population of, 157
telephone dialing codes, 718
travel requirements for, 544
UN membership, 2

L
labor force, global, 8
labor unions, 685
Lachaise, Gaston, 472
Laclos, Pierre Choderlos de, 447
lactose-restricted diet, 334
Ladies Professional Golf Association (LPGA), 629–30
Ladoga (lake), 15
Laënnec, René T.H., 439
Lagos, Nigeria, 158
Lahore, Pakistan, 158

Lahr, Bert, 525
La Jolla Playhouse, 521
Lake Albert (lake), 15
Lake of the Woods, 282, 287
lakes, largest, 14–15, 282, 286–87
lakeshores, national, 575
Lalo, Édouard, 491
Lamar, Joseph Rucker, 263
Lamar, Lucius Quintus Cincinnatus, 263
L'Amour, Louis, 447
Lampedusa, Tomasi di, 447
Lanai, Hawaii, 279, 283
Lancaster, Burt, 535
Lancaster, house of, 167
Land, Edwin Herbert, 439
Landon, Alfred M., 231
land pollution, 378
Landrieu, Mary, 229
land-use, global, 8
Lane, Harriet Rebecca, 189
Lane, Nathan, 525
Lange, Jessica, 535
Langley, Katherine Gudger, 223
Langmuir, Irving, 439
Langtry, Lillie, 525
language, 724–27. *See also* literature
    American sign language, 726
    confused and misused words, 738–42
    NATO alphabet, 727
    proofreaders marks, 743
    punctuation, 733–38
    style and usage, 728–43
Lansbury, Angela, 525
lanthanum (element), 396
Lao People's Democratic Republic (Laos), 2, 86–87
    foreign embassy in the U.S., 210
    population of, 157
    telephone dialing codes, 718
    travel requirements for, 544
La Paz, Bolivia, 37
Lares (Roman deities), 186
Lasso, Orlando di, 491
Las Vegas, Nevada, 302
Latvia
    foreign embassy in the U.S., 210
    general information, 87
    population of, 157
    telephone dialing codes, 718
    travel requirements for, 545
    UN membership, 2
Laughton, Charles, 535
Lawrence, D. H., 447
Lawrence, Ernest Orlando, 439
Lawrence, Gertrude, 525
lawrencium (element), 396
laws of physics, 412–13
lead (element), 396, 407

League of Conservation Voters, 201
League of Women Voters (LWV), 201
Lear, William Powell, 439
Lebanon
    foreign embassy in the U.S., 210
    general information, 87–88
    peacekeeping mission in, 275
    population of, 157
    telephone dialing codes, 718
    travel requirements for, 545
    UN membership, 2
Le Carré, John, 448
Lee, Barbara, 226
Lee, Harper, 448
Leeuwenhoek, Antonie van, 439
Lefkosa, Cyprus, 53
Le Gallienne, Eva, 525
legal terms, U.S., 259–61
Le Guin, Ursula K., 448
Leibniz, Gottfried Wilhelm, 439
Leigh, Vivien, 535
Lemmon, Jack, 535
Lemon v. *Kurtzman* (1971), 266
Lemures (Roman deities), 186
L'Engle, Madeline, 459
length measurements, 744–45
Leonardo de Vinci, 466
Leoncavallo, Ruggero, 491
Leo (zodiac sign), 356
leptons, 398
Lesotho
    foreign embassy in the U.S., 210
    general information, 88–89
    population of, 157
    telephone dialing codes, 718
    travel requirements for, 545
    UN membership, 2
Lessing, Doris, 448
Leutze, Emanuel Gottlieb, 466
Levin, Ira, 448
Lewis, C. S., 459
Lewis, Edmonia, 472
Lewis, (Harry) Sinclair Lewis, 448
Lexington-Fayette, Kentucky, 303
Liberal-Republican Party, 234
Liberia
    foreign embassy in the U.S., 210
    general information, 89
    population of, 157
    telephone dialing codes, 718
    travel requirements for, 545
    UN membership, 2
Liber (Roman deity), 187
Libitina (Roman deity), 187
Library of Congress classifications, 755–58
library organization, 753–58
Libra (zodiac sign), 357

Lully, Jean Baptiste, 491
Lumière, Auguste, 439
Lumière, Louis, 439
Luna (Roman deity), 187
lunar phases, 387
Lunt, Alfred, 525
LuPone, Patti, 525
Lurton, Horace Harmon, 263
Lusaka, Zambia, 155
Lusk, Georgia Lee, 223
lutetium (element), 396
Luxembourg
    foreign embassy in the U.S., 210
    general information, 91
    population of, 157
    telephone dialing codes, 718
    travel requirements for, 545
    UN membership, 2
Luxemburg, house of, 169–70
Luzon, 11
lyme disease, 319

M
Macau
    foreign embassy in the U.S., 210
    general information, 91–92
    population of, 157
    travel requirements for, 545
Macedonia, former Yugoslav Republic of
    foreign embassy in the U.S., 207
    general information, 92
    population of, 157
    telephone dialing codes, 718
    travel requirements for, 545
    UN membership, 2
Machaut, Guillaume de, 491
machine language, 419
MacLachlan, Patricia, 459
MacLaine, Shirley, 535
Macon, Nathaniel, 220
Macready, William Charles, 525
macular degeneration, 314
Madagascar
    foreign embassy in the U.S., 211
    general information, 92–93
    population of, 156
    size of, 11
    telephone dialing codes, 718
    travel requirements for, 545
    UN membership, 2
Madeira Islands, 211
Madeline Island, 280, 283
Madison, Dolley Payne Todd, 189
Madison, James, 188, 230
Madison, Wisconsin, 303
Madras, India, 158
Madrid, Spain, 133, 159, 564

magnesium (dietary), 333
magnesium (element), 396, 407
Magritte, René, 467
Mahfouz, Naguib, 448
Mahler, Gustav, 491
Mailer, Norman, 448
mailing rates, 721–22
Maillol, Aristide, 472
Maiman, Theodore Harold, 439
Maine
    area codes, 714–15
    area of, 286
    capital, 286
    date of admittance, 285, 289
    electoral votes, 233
    features and attractions, 293
    income tax rates, 698
    membership in Congress, 222
    motto and nickname, 289
    poison control center, 339
    population of, 307
    postal abbreviation, 722
    racial makeup of, 308
    sales tax rates, 700
    state flowers, birds, and trees, 287
    time zone, 344
    tourism department, 557
major league baseball, 578–84
Majuro, Marshall Islands, 97
Makarova, Natalia, 512
Malabo, Equatorial Guinea, 58
Malamud, Bernard, 448
Malawi
    foreign embassy in the U.S., 211
    general information, 93
    population of, 156
    telephone dialing codes, 718
    travel requirements for, 545
    UN membership, 2
Malaysia
    foreign embassy in the U.S., 211
    general information, 94
    population of, 156
    telephone dialing codes, 718
    travel requirements for, 545
    UN membership, 2
    visitors' and convention bureau, 563
Maldives
    foreign embassy in the U.S., 211
    general information, 94–95
    population of, 157
    telephone dialing codes, 718
    travel requirements for, 545
    UN membership, 2
Male (Maale), Maldives, 95
Mali
    foreign embassy in the U.S., 211
    general information, 95

population of, 156
telephone dialing codes, 718
travel requirements for, 545
UN membership, 2
Malkovich, John, 535
Maloney, Carolyn B., 225
Malpighi, Marcello, 439
Malta
foreign embassy in the U.S., 211
general information, 95–96
population of, 157
telephone dialing codes, 718
travel requirements for, 545
UN membership, 2
Mamet, David, 455
mammals, endangered, 373–74
Mamoutzou, Mayotte, 99
Managua, Nicaragua, 108
Manama, Bahrain, 32
Manchester, England, 159
Manet, Édouard, 467
manganese (dietary), 333
manganese (element), 396, 407
Manhattan Island, 280, 283
Manhattan Theatre Club, 522
Manila, Philippines, 116
Manitoba, 714–15
Manitoba (lake), 15
Mankin, Helen Douglas, 223
Mann, Thomas, 448
manned space missions, 426–28
Mansfield, Katherine, 448
Mansfield, Mike, 228
Manship, Paul, 472
Mantegna, Andrea, 467
Mapp v. *Ohio* (1961), 266
Maputo, Mozambique, 103, 159
Maracaibo (lake), 15
Marbury v. *Madison* (1803), 266
Marc, Franz, 467
March, Frederic, 525, 535
Marconi, Guglielmo, 439
Marenzio, Luca, 491
Margolies-Mezvinsky, Marjorie, 225
Mariana Islands
general information, 110–11, 300
population of, 158
telephone dialing codes, 718
Marines (U.S.), 271
Marini, Marino, 472
maritime law, 415–17
Markova, Alicia, 512
Mark Taper Forum, 522
Marlowe, Christopher, 455
Marsh, Reginald, 467
Marshall, John, 261
Marshall, Thomas Riley, 191
Marshall, Thurgood, 263

Marshall Islands
foreign embassy in the U.S., 211
general information, 96–97
population of, 158
telephone dialing codes, 718
travel requirements for, 545
UN membership, 2
Marsh Island, 279, 283
Mars (planet), 383
Mars (Roman deity), 187
Martha's Vineyard, 280, 283
Martin, Ann M., 459
Martin, Homer Z., 440
Martin, Joseph W., 221
Martin, Lynn Morley, 224
Martin, Mary, 525
Martinique
general information, 97
population of, 157
telephone dialing codes, 718
travel requirements for, 545
Martin v. *Hunter's Lesee* (1816), 266
Marx Brothers, The, 535
Maryland
area codes, 714–15
area of, 286
capital, 286
date of admittance, 285, 289
electoral votes, 233
features and attractions, 293
income tax rates, 698
membership in Congress, 222
motto and nickname, 289
poison control center, 339
population of, 307
postal abbreviation, 722
racial makeup of, 308
sales tax rates, 700
state flowers, birds, and trees, 287
time zone, 344
tourism department, 557
Masefield, John, 453
Maseru, Lesotho, 88
Mashhad, Iran, 160
Mason, James, 535
Massachusetts
area codes, 714–15
area of, 286
capital, 286
date of admittance, 285, 289
electoral votes, 233
features and attractions, 293
income tax rates, 698
membership in Congress, 222
motto and nickname, 289
poison control center, 339
population of, 307
postal abbreviation, 722

Massachusetts (*cont.*)
  racial makeup of, 308
  sales tax rates, 700
  state flowers, birds, and trees, 287
  time zone, 344
  tourism department, 557
Massenet, Jules, 491
Massine, Léonide, 512
Masters Tournament (golf), 626
Masyas (Greek deity), 186
Mata-Utu, Wallis and Futuna, 152
mathematics, 379–82
Matisse, Henri, 467
Matthau, Walter, 535
Matthews, Stanley, 263
Maugham, William Somerset, 448
Maui, Hawaii, 279, 283
Maupin, Armistead, 448
Maurer, Robert D., 440
Mauritania
  foreign embassy in the U.S., 211
  general information, 97–98
  population of, 157
  telephone dialing codes, 718
  travel requirements for, 545
  UN membership, 2
Mauritius
  foreign embassy in the U.S., 211
  general information, 98
  population of, 157
  telephone dialing codes, 718
  travel requirements for, 545
  UN membership, 2
Maxim, Hiram Stevens, 440
May, Catherine Dean, 223
Mayotte
  general information, 99
  population of, 157
  telephone dialing codes, 718
Mazor, Stanley, 440
Mbabane, Swaziland, 136
McCarter Theatre Center for the Performing Arts, 522
McCarthy, Carolyn, 226
McCarthy, Karen, 225
McCarthy, Mary, 448
McClellan, George B., 231
McCloskey, Robert, 459
McCollum, Betty, 226
McCormack, Cyrus Hall, 440
McCormack, John W., 221
McCormick, Ruth Hanna, 223
McCullers, Carson, 448
McCulloch v. Maryland (1819), 266
McDaniel, Hattie, 535
McDonald, Audra, 525
McDonald's LPGA Championship (golf), 629
McElroy, Mary Arthur, 190

McFarland, E. W., 228
McGovern, George, 232
McKenna, Joseph, 263
McKinley, Ida Saxton, 190
McKinley, John, 263
McKinley, William, 188, 231
McKinney, Cynthia, 225
McLean, John, 263
McMillan, Clara Gooding, 223
McNally, Terrence, 455
McNary, Charles L., 228
McReynolds, James Clark, 263
Mead (lake), 283, 287
mean (mathematical), 379
Mears, Helen Farnsworth, 472
measurements, 744–47
mechanics, physical laws regarding, 413
Medellin, Columbia, 159
median (mathematical), 379
medicine and drugs, 312–27, 640–42
Meek, Carry P., 225
Meikle, Andrew, 440
meitnerium (element), 396
Melbourne, Australia, 159, 564
Melpomene (Greek deity), 186
Melville, Herman, 448
Memphis, Tennessee, 302
mendelevium (element), 396
Mendelssohn, Felix, 492
menopause, exam for, 315
Menotti, Gian Carlo, 492
Mercator, Gerardus, 440
merchant Marine, global, 8
mercury (element), 396, 407
Mercury (planet), 383
Mercury (Roman deity), 187
Mergenthaler, Ottmar, 440
Merman, Ethel, 525
Mesa, Arizona, 303
mesons, 398
mesosphere, 411
Messiaen, Oliver, 492
Mestral, George de, 440
metals, recycling, 708–9
meteorology symbols, 358–59
Metis (Greek deity), 186
metric measurements, 744
Metro Manila, Philippines, 158
metropolitan areas (U.S.), 304–6
Mexican War, 274
Mexico
  foreign embassy in the U.S., 211
  general information, 99–100
  population of, 156
  telephone dialing codes, 718
  travel requirements for, 545
  UN membership, 2
  visitors' and convention bureau, 563

Mexico City, Mexico, 99, 158
Meyerbeer, Giacomo, 492
Meyers, Jan, 225
Meyner, Helen Stevenson, 224
Miami, Florida, 160, 303
Michelangelo Buonarroti, 467, 473
Michener, James, 448
Michigan
    area codes, 714–15
    area of, 286
    capital, 286
    date of admittance, 285, 289
    electoral votes, 233
    features and attractions, 293
    income tax rates, 698
    membership in Congress, 222
    motto and nickname, 289
    poison control center, 339
    population of, 307
    postal abbreviation, 722
    racial makeup of, 309
    sales tax rates, 700
    state flowers, birds, and trees, 287
    time zone, 344
    tourism department, 557
Michigan (lake), 14, 282, 286
microbiology, 400
Micronesia, Federated states of
    foreign embassy in the U.S., 211
    general information, 100
    population of, 157
    telephone dialing codes, 718
    travel requirements for, 545
    UN membership, 2
Midler, Bette, 535
Midway Islands, 718
Mikulski, Barbara Ann, 224, 229
Milan, Italy, 159
military, 271–78
    "commander in chief" established, 243
    global expenditures, 8
    military sites, national, 574
    personnel and pay grades, 272–73
    retiree organizations, 276–78
    service academies, 278
    veterans organizations, 276–78
    wars and conflicts, 274–76
Military Order of the Purple Heart, 277
Military Order of the World Wars, 277
Milland, Ray, 535
Millender-McDonald, Juanita, 226
Miller, Arthur, 455
Miller, Henry, 448
Miller, Samuel Freeman, 263
Millet, Jean, 467
Millman, Irving, 440
Milne, A. A., 459
Milwaukee, Wisconsin, 302

Mindanao, 11
minerals (dietary), 333–34
Minerva (Roman deity), 187
Mink, Patsy Takemoto, 224
Minneapolis, Minnesota, 159, 303
Minnesota
    area codes, 714–15
    area of, 286
    capital, 286
    date of admittance, 285, 289
    electoral votes, 233
    features and attractions, 293
    income tax rates, 698
    membership in Congress, 222
    motto and nickname, 289
    poison control center, 339
    population of, 307
    postal abbreviation, 722
    racial makeup of, 309
    sales tax rates, 700
    state flowers, birds, and trees, 287
    time zone, 344
    tourism department, 558
Minor v. *Happersett* (1875), 266
Minsk, Belarus, 34
Minton, Sherman, 263
Miquelon, 718
Miranda v. *Arizona* (1966), 266
Miró, Joan, 467
Mishima, Yukio, 449
Mississippi
    area codes, 714–15
    area of, 286
    capital, 286
    date of admittance, 285, 289
    electoral votes, 233
    features and attractions, 293
    income tax rates, 698
    membership in Congress, 222
    motto and nickname, 289
    poison control center, 339
    population of, 307
    postal abbreviation, 722
    racial makeup of, 309
    sales tax rates, 700
    state flowers, birds, and trees, 287
    time zone, 344
    tourism department, 558
Missouri
    area codes, 714–15
    area of, 286
    capital, 286
    date of admittance, 285, 289
    electoral votes, 233
    features and attractions, 294
    income tax rates, 698
    membership in Congress, 222
    motto and nickname, 289

National League (baseball), 579
National Museum of the American Indian, 480
National Organization for Women (NOW), 201
National Partnership for Reinventing Government, 197
National Priorities Project, 201
National Recreation Reservation Service, 565
National Rifle Association (NRA), 201
National Science Foundation, 197
National Security Agency, 197
National Technology Transfer Center, 197
National Theatre of the Deaf, 522
National Veterans Legal Services Program, Inc., 277
National Veterans Organization of America, 277
nations and territories (listed), 24–160, 156–58
Native American tribes, 309–10
NATO alphabet, 727
Natsume, Soseki, 449
Nauru
    foreign embassy in the U.S., 212
    general information, 104–5
    population of, 158
    telephone dialing codes, 719
    travel requirements for, 546
    UN membership, 2
Navy (U.S.), 271
Nazimova, Alla, 525
NCAA (National Collegiate Athletic Association),
    592–94, 600–602
N'Djamena, Chad, 45
Nebraska
    area codes, 714–15
    area of, 286
    capital, 286
    date of admittance, 285, 289
    electoral votes, 233
    features and attractions, 294
    income tax rates, 699
    membership in Congress, 222
    motto and nickname, 289
    poison control center, 340
    population of, 307
    postal abbreviation, 722
    racial makeup of, 309
    sales tax rates, 700
    state flowers, birds, and trees, 287
    time zone, 344
    tourism department, 558
Nellie Mae, 751
Nelson, Samuel, 263
Nelson Island, 279, 283
Nemerov, Howard, 453
Nemesis (Greek deity), 186
neodymium (element), 396
neon (element), 396
Nepal
    foreign embassy in the U.S., 212
    general information, 105
    population of, 156

telephone dialing codes, 719
    travel requirements for, 546
    UN membership, 2
Neptune (planet), 383, 386
Neptune (Roman deity), 187
neptunium (element), 396
Nereids (Greek deity), 186
Nereus (Greek deity), 186
Netherlands
    foreign embassy in the U.S., 212
    general information, 105–6
    population of, 156
    telephone dialing codes, 719
    travel requirements for, 546
    UN membership, 2
    visitors' and convention bureau, 563
Netherlands Antilles
    foreign embassy in the U.S., 212
    general information, 106
    population of, 157
    telephone dialing codes, 719
    travel requirements for, 546
    visitor's bureau, 563
Nettilling (lake), 15
Neuberger, Maurice Brown, 229
Nevada
    area codes, 714–15
    area of, 286
    capital, 286
    date of admittance, 285, 289
    electoral votes, 233
    features and attractions, 294
    income tax rates, 699
    membership in Congress, 222
    motto and nickname, 289
    poison control center, 340
    population of, 307
    postal abbreviation, 722
    racial makeup of, 309
    sales tax rates, 700
    state flowers, birds, and trees, 287
    time zone, 344
    tourism department, 558
Nevelson, Louise, 473
Nevis. See Saint Kitts and Nevis
Newark, New Jersey, 303
Newbery Medal, 678–80
New Brunswick, 714–15
New Caledonia
    general information, 106–7
    population of, 157
    telephone dialing codes, 719
Newcomen, Thomas, 440
New Delhi, India, 76
Newfoundland, 11, 714–15
New Guinea, 11
New Hampshire
    area codes, 714–15

Niihau, Hawaii, 280, 283
Nijinsky, Vaslav, 512
Nike (Greek deity), 186
nimbostratus clouds, 362
Nin, Anaïs, 449
niobium (element), 396
Nipigon (lake), 15
nitrogen (element), 396, 407
Niue, 109–10, 719
Nixon, Richard Milhous, 189, 191, 232
Nixon, Thelma Catherine Ryan, 190
Nobel, Alfred Bernhard, 440
nobelium (element), 396
Nobel Prize, 634–42
Noguchi, Isamu, 473
Nolan, Mae Ella, 222
Nolte, Nick, 536
Noma, Hiroshi, 449
non-governmental organizations, 3
non-sporting dogs, 711
Norfolk, Virginia, 303
Norfolk Island
    general information, 110
    population of, 158
    telephone dialing codes, 719
Normandy, house of, 167
Norrell, Catherine Dorris, 224
North America
    general statistics, 9
    map of, 20
North Atlantic Treaty Organization (NATO), 7, 727
North Carolina
    area codes, 714–15
    area of, 286
    capital, 286
    date of admittance, 285, 289
    electoral votes, 233
    features and attractions, 295
    income tax rates, 699
    membership in Congress, 222
    motto and nickname, 289
    poison control center, 340
    population of, 308
    postal abbreviation, 722
    racial makeup of, 309
    sales tax rates, 700
    state flowers, birds, and trees, 288
    time zone, 344
    tourism department, 558
North Dakota
    area codes, 714–15
    area of, 286
    capital, 286
    date of admittance, 285, 289
    electoral votes, 233
    features and attractions, 295
    income tax rates, 699

    membership in Congress, 222
    motto and nickname, 289
    poison control center, 340
    population of, 308
    postal abbreviation, 722
    racial makeup of, 309
    sales tax rates, 700
    state flowers, birds, and trees, 288
    time zone, 344
    tourism department, 559
Northeast Campground Association, 565
Northern Ireland, 2, 213
North Korea. See Korea, Democratic People's Republic of (North Korea)
Northup, Anne, 226
Northwest Territories, 714–15
Norton, Eleanor Holmes, 225
Norton, Mary, 459
Norton, Mary Teresa, 222
Norway
    foreign embassy in the U.S., 213
    general information, 111
    population of, 157
    telephone dialing codes, 719
    travel requirements for, 546
    UN membership, 2
notes, musical, 487
Nouakchott, Mauritania, 98
Noumea, New Caledonia, 107
Nova Scotia, 714–15
novelists, 443–52. See also literature
Nox (Roman deity), 187
Noyce, Robert N., 440
nuclear physics, 413
Nuclear Regulatory Commission, 197
Nuku'alofa, Tonga, 141
numbers, 380
Nunivak Island, 279, 283
Nureyev, Rudolf, 512
nutrition, health, and fitness, 327–42
Nuuk (Godthab), Greenland, 69
Nyasa (lake), 14
Nymphs (Greek deities), 186
Nyx (Greek deity), 186

O
Oahu, Hawaii, 279, 283
Oakar, Mary Rose, 224
Oakland, California, 303
Oates, Joyce Carol, 449
O'Casey, Sean, 455
Oceania, 9, 18
oceans, general statistics, 17
O'Connor, (Mary) Flannery, 449
O'Connor, Sandra Day, 263
O'Day, Caroline Love Goodwin, 223
Odets, Clifford, 456

over-the-counter pharmaceuticals, 322–23
Owasco (lake), 282, 287
Owen, Ruth Bryan, 223
oxygen (element), 396
ozone layer, 411

P

PABA (paraaminobenzoic acid), 332
Pacific hurricane names, 368–69
Pacific Ocean, 17
Pacino, Al, 536
Padre Island, 280, 283
Paganini, Niccoló, 492
Page, Geraldine, 525, 536
Page, Thomas Nelson, 449
Pago Pago, American Samoa, 26, 299
painters, 461–71
Pakistan
    foreign embassy in the U.S., 213
    general information, 112–13
    population of, 156
    telephone dialing codes, 719
    travel requirements for, 546
    UN membership, 2
Palace of Versailles, 480
Palau
    foreign embassy in the U.S., 213
    general information, 113
    population of, 158
    telephone dialing codes, 719
    travel requirements for, 546
    UN membership, 2
Palestrina, Giovanni Pierluigi da, 492
Palikir, Micronesia, 100
palladium (element), 396
Panama
    foreign embassy in the U.S., 213
    general information, 113–14
    Operation Just Cause, 276
    population of, 157
    telephone dialing codes, 719
    travel requirements for, 546
    UN membership, 2
Pan (Greek deity), 186
pantothenic acid, 332
Papeete, French Polynesia, 63
paper, recycling, 707–8
Papin, Denis, 441
Papua New Guinea
    foreign embassy in the U.S., 213
    general information, 114–15
    population of, 157
    telephone dialing codes, 719
    travel requirements for, 546
    UN membership, 2
paraaminobenzoic acid (PABA), 332

Paraguay
    foreign embassy in the U.S., 213
    general information, 115
    population of, 157
    telephone dialing codes, 719
    travel requirements for, 546
    UN membership, 2
Paramaribo, Suriname, 135
parasitic diseases, 317
Paris, France, 62, 158, 564
Parker, Alton B., 231
Parker, Dorothy, 449
Parker, Louis W., 441
Parkes, Alexander, 441
parks, national, 567–69
Parrish, Maxfield, 468
Parsons, Charles Algernon, 441
Parsons, John T., 441
particles, elementary, 398
Pascal, Blaise, 441
PASCAL (computer language), 419
Passport America, 566
Pasternak, Boris Leonidovich, 449
Pasteur, Louis, 441
patent law, 270
Paterson, William, 263
Patinkin, Mandy, 525
Paton, Alan Stewart, 449
patron saints, 181–85
Patterson, Elizabeth J., 225
Patterson, Katherine, 459
Pavlova, Anna, 512
Peace Corps, 197
peace (Nobel Prize), 634–35
Peale, Charles Willson, 468
Peale, Raphaelle, 468
Peale, Rembrandt, 468
Peck, Gregory, 536
Peckham, Rufus Wheeler, Jr., 263
Pelosi, Nancy, 225
Penderecki, Krzystof, 492
Penn, Sean, 536
Pennington, William, 220
Pennsylvania
    area codes, 714–15
    area of, 286
    capital, 286
    date of admittance, 285, 289
    electoral votes, 233
    features and attractions, 296
    income tax rates, 699
    membership in Congress, 222
    motto and nickname, 289
    poison control center, 341
    population of, 308
    postal abbreviation, 722
    racial makeup of, 309

Rhode Island (*cont.*)
  sales tax rates, 700
  state flowers, birds, and trees, 288
  time zone, 344
  tourism department, 559
rhodium (element), 396
Rice, Anne, 450
Richardson, Ralph, 526
Richmond, Virginia, 304
Riga, Latvia, 87
Riley, Corinne Boyd, 224
Rimsky-Korsakov, Nikolai, 493
Rio de Janeiro, Brazil, 158, 564
Ritter, Johann Wilhelm, 441
Rivera, Chita, 513, 526
Rivera, Diego, 469
rivers, 15–16, 283–85, 287–89
Rivers, Lynn, 225
Riverside, California, 303
Riyadh, Saudi Arabia, 126, 159
Road Town, Virgin Islands (British), 151
Robards, Jason, 526
Robbins, Jerome, 513
Robbins, Tom, 450
Robertian, house of, 168
Roberts, Owen Josephus, 263
Robertson, Alice Mary, 222
Robeson, Paul, 526, 536
Robinson, Bill Bojangles, 513
Robinson, Joseph T., 228
Rochester, New York, 303
Rock and Roll Hall of Fame, 480
Rockefeller, Nelson Adlrich, 192
rocks, types of, 410
Rockwell, Norman, 469
Rodgers, Richard, 493
Rodin, Auguste, 473
Roebuck, John, 441
Roemer (Rømer), Ole, 441
Roentgen, Wilhelm Conrad, 441
Roe v. *Wade* (1973), 267
Rogers, Edith Nourse, 222
Rogers, Ginger, 513, 536
Rohrer, Heinrich, 441
Roman Catholic patron saints, 181–85
Roman Catholic popes, 177–80
Roman emperors, 170–71
Romania
  foreign embassy in the U.S., 214
  general information, 119–20
  population of, 156
  telephone dialing codes, 719
  travel requirements for, 546
  UN membership, 2
Roman mythology, 187
Roman numerals, 380
Romanov, house of, 171
Rome, Italy, 80, 159

Rooney, Mickey, 536
Roosevelt, Anna Eleanor, 190
Roosevelt, Edith Kermit Carow, 190
Roosevelt, Franklin Delano, 188, 231, 232
Roosevelt, Theodore, 188, 191, 231
Roseau, Dominica, 55
Ros-Lehtinen, Ileana, 225
Rossetti, Dante Gabriel, 469
Rossini, Gioacchino, 493
Rosso, Medardo, 473
Rostand, Edmund, 456
Roth, Philip, 450
Rothko, Mark, 469
Roukema, Margaret Scafati, 224
Roundabout Theatre Company, 522
Rousseau, Henri, 469
Rowe, Nicholas, 452
Rowling, J. K., 459
Roybal-Allard, Lucille, 225
Rubens, Peter Paul, 469
rubidium (element), 396
Rubin, Benjamin A., 441
Rudolf (lake), 15
Rufus, William, 191
Rules and Administration Committee, 227
Rules Committee, 219
rules of the sea, 415–17
Rurik, house of, 171
Rushdie, Salman, 450
Russell, Rosalind, 536
Russia (Russian Federation)
  czars and czarinas of, 172
  foreign embassy in the U.S., 214
  general information, 120–21
  population of, 156
  telephone dialing codes, 719
  travel requirements for, 546
  UN membership, 2
ruthenium (element), 396
Rutherford, Daniel, 441
Rutherford, Ernest, 441
rutherfordium (element), 396
Rutledge, John, 261, 263
Rutledge, Wiley Blount, Jr., 263
RV organizations, 566
Rwanda
  foreign embassy in the U.S., 214
  general information, 121
  population of, 156
  telephone dialing codes, 719
  travel requirements for, 546
  UN membership, 2
Ryder, Albert Pinkham, 469

S
Sacramento, California, 302
safety tips, 701–5
Sagan, Francoise, 450

Sagittarius (zodiac sign), 357
Saiki, Patricia Fukuda, 225
St. Clair (lake), 282, 287
Saint-Denis, Reunion, 119
St. Denis, Ruth, 513
Saint-Gaudens, Augustus, 473
St. George, Katharine Price Collier, 223
Saint George's, Grenada, 69
Saint Helena, 121–22, 158
St. Helena, 719
Saint Helier, Jersey, 82
Saint John's, Antigua and Barbuda, 28
Saint Kitts and Nevis, 2, 719
    foreign embassy in the U.S., 214
    general information, 122
    population of, 158
    telephone dialing codes, 719
    travel requirements for, 546
St. Lawrence Island, 279, 283
St. Louis, Missouri, 160, 303
Saint Lucia
    foreign embassy in the U.S., 214
    general information, 122–23
    population of, 157
    telephone dialing codes, 719
    travel requirements for, 546
    UN membership, 2
Saint Martin (Saint Maarten), 214, 546
St. Paul, Minnesota, 303
Saint Peter Port, Guernsey, 71
Saint Petersburg, Russia, 159
St. Petersburg, Florida, 303
Saint Pierre and Miquelon
    foreign embassy in the U.S., 214
    general information, 123
    population, 158
    telephone dialing codes, 719
    travel requirements for, 547
saints, patron, 181–85
Saint-Saëns, Camille, 493
Saint Vincent and the Grenadines, 2
    foreign embassy in the U.S., 214
    general information, 123–24
    population of, 158
    telephone dialing codes, 719
    travel requirements for, 547
Saipan, Mariana Islands, 111, 300, 719
Sakhalin, 11
Saki (Hector Hugh Munro), 450
Salacia (Roman deity), 187
Salian, house of, 169
Salinger, J. D., 450
salt, 408
Salton Sea, 282, 287
Salvador, Brazil, 159
samarium (element), 396
Samoa
    foreign embassy in the U.S., 214

general information, 124
population of, 157
travel requirements for, 547
UN membership, 2
Sanaa, Yemen, 154
San Antonio, Texas, 302
San Bernardino, California, 304
Sanchez, Loretta, 226
Sand, George (Amadine Lucie Aurore Dupin), 450
Sandburg, Carl, 450
San Diego, California, 159, 302, 480
San Diego Zoo, 480
Sanford, Edward Terry, 263
San Francisco, California, 159, 302
San Jose, California, 302
San Jose, Costa Rica, 51
San Juan, Puerto Rico, 118, 301
San Marino
    foreign embassy in the U.S., 214
    general information, 124–25
    population of, 158
    telephone dialing codes, 719
    travel requirements for, 547
    UN membership, 2
San Salvador, El Salvador, 57
Sansovino, Andrea, 473
Sansovino, Jacopo, 473
Santa Ana, California, 303
Santa Cruz Island, 279, 283
Santiago, Chile, 46, 159
Santo Domingo, Dominican Republic, 55, 159
São Paulo, Brazil, 158
São Tomé and Príncipe
    foreign embassy in the U.S., 214
    general information, 125
    population of, 157
    telephone dialing codes, 719
    travel requirements for, 547
    UN membership, 2
Sarajevo, Bosnia and Herzegovina, 38
Sarandon, Susan, 536
Sarett, Lewis Hastings, 441
Sargent, John Singer, 469
Saroyan, William, 450
Sartre, Jean-Paul, 450
Saskatchewan, 714–15
satellites of the planets, 383–86
Satie, Erik, 493
Saturn (planet), 383, 384–85
Saturn (Roman deity), 187
Satyrs (Greek deities), 187
Saudi Arabia
    foreign embassy in the U.S., 214
    general information, 125–26
    Gulf War, 276
    population of, 156
    telephone dialing codes, 719

Tahiti, 216, 547
Tahoe (lake), 283, 287
Taipei, Taiwan, 138, 159
Taiwan
    foreign embassy in the U.S., 216
    general information, 138
    population of, 156
    telephone dialing codes, 720
    travel requirements for, 547
Taiyuan, China, 159
Tajikistan
    foreign embassy in the U.S., 216
    general information, 138–39
    population of, 157
    telephone dialing codes, 720
    travel requirements for, 547
    UN membership, 2
Takemitsu, Toru, 494
talc, 408
Tallinn, Estonia, 59
Tallis, Thomas, 494
Tampa, Florida, 303
Tanaga Island, 279, 283
Tandy, Jessica, 526
Taney, Roger Brooke, 261
Tanganyika (lake), 14
Tanguy, Yves, 470
Tanizaki, Jun'ichiro, 451
tantalum (element), 397
Tanzania (United Republic of)
    foreign embassy in the U.S., 216
    general information, 139–40
    population of, 156
    telephone dialing codes, 720
    travel requirements for, 548
    UN membership, 2
Taoist holidays and festivals, 175
Tarawa, Kiribati, 84
Tartarus (Roman deity), 187
Tashkent (Toshkent), Uzbekistan, 149, 159
Tasmania, 11
Tate, Nahum, 452
Tatlin, Vladimir, 473
Taurus (zodiac sign), 356
Tauscher, Ellen, 226
Taverner, John, 494
taxes and taxation
    establishment of, 239
    poll taxes, 251
    tax rates, 697–701
taxonomic classifications, 399–400
Taylor, Elizabeth, 537
Taylor, Frederick Winslow, 442
Taylor, John W., 220
Taylor, Laurette, 526
Taylor, Margaret Smith, 189
Taylor, Paul, 513

Taylor, Zachary, 188, 230
T'bilisi, Georgia, 65
Tchaikovsky, Peter Ilyich, 494
technetium (element), 397
technology, 414–34
teeth, anatomy of, 405
Tegucigalpa, Honduras, 74
Teheran, Iran, 159
Tehran, Iran, 77
Tel-Aviv-Yafo, Israel, 160
Telemann, Georg Philipp, 494
telephone dialing codes, 714–20
television, 538–39, 662–67
tellurium (element), 397
temperature conversions, 746–47
Temple, Shirley, 537
Templeton Award for Progress in Religion, 661–62
tempo indicators, 487
Tennessee
    area codes, 714–15
    area of, 286
    capital, 286
    date of admittance, 285
    electoral votes, 233
    features and attractions, 297
    income tax rates, 699
    membership in Congress, 222
    motto and nickname, 289
    poison control center, 341
    population of, 308
    postal abbreviation, 722
    racial makeup of, 309
    sales tax rates, 701
    state flowers, birds, and trees, 289
    time zone, 344
    tourism department, 559
tennis championships, 612–25
Tennyson, Alfred Lord, 453
Tentings Plus of the Northwest, 566
terbium (element), 397
Terminus (Roman deity), 187
Terpsichore (Greek deity), 187
terriers, 711
territories, 156–58, 299–301
Tesla, Nikola, 442
testicular cancer, 316
Texas
    area codes, 714–15
    area of, 287
    capital, 287
    date of admittance, 285
    electoral votes, 233
    features and attractions, 297
    income tax rates, 699
    membership in Congress, 222
    motto and nickname, 289
    poison control center, 342

population of, 308
postal abbreviation, 722
racial makeup of, 309
sales tax rates, 701
state flowers, birds, and trees, 289
time zone, 344
tourism department, 559
Texas v. Johnson (1989), 267
text file codes, 417–18
Thackeray, William Makepeace, 451
Thailand
    foreign embassy in the U.S., 216
    general information, 140
    population of, 156
    telephone dialing codes, 720
    tourism department, 561
    travel requirements for, 548
    UN membership, 2
    visitors' and convention bureau, 562
Thalia (Greek deity), 187
thallium (element), 397
Thanatos (Greek deity), 187
Thant, U, 4
Tharp, Twyla, 513
theater
    film actors, 532–37
    plays and musicals, 513–20
    stage actors, 523–26
    theater companies, 521–22
    Tony awards, 667–74
Theatre Museum, 480
Theiler, Max, 442
Themis (Greek deity), 187
thermosphere, 411
Theroux, Paul, 451
Thimphu, Bhutan, 37
Thomas, Clarence, 264
Thomas, Lera Millard, 224
Thompson, Emma, 537
Thompson, John Taliaferro, 442
Thompson, Kay, 460
Thompson, Ruth, 223
Thompson, Smith, 264
Thompson, Virgil, 494
Thomson, Joseph John, 442
thorium (element), 397
thulium (element), 397
thunderstorms (severe), 363
Thurber, James, 451
Thurman, Karen, 225
Tianjin, China, 158
Tiepolo, Giovanni, 470
Tilden, Samuel J., 232
time, 343–52
Timken, Henry, 442
tin (element), 397, 408
Tintoretto, 470

Tirana, Albania, 24
titanium (element), 397, 408
Titans (Greek deity), 187
Titian, 470
Titicaca (lake), 15
Tobago. *See* Trinidad and Tobago
Todd, Thomas, 264
Togo
    foreign embassy in the U.S., 216
    general information, 140–41
    population of, 157
    telephone dialing codes, 720
    travel requirements for, 548
    UN membership, 2
Tokyo, Japan, 81, 158, 565
Toledo, Ohio, 303
Tolkien, J. R. R., 460
Tolstoy, Leo, 451
Tompkins, Daniel D., 191
Tonga
    foreign embassy in the U.S., 216
    general information, 141
    population of, 158
    telephone dialing codes, 720
    travel requirements for, 548
    UN membership, 2
Tony Awards, 667–74
tooth decay, 313
tornados, 363, 369–71
Toronto, Canada, 158, 565
Torrens (lake), 15
Torricelli, Evangelista, 442
Torshavn, Faroe Islands, 60
Toulouse-Lautrec, Henri de, 470
tourism departments, 556–61
Tourmanova, Tamara, 513
Tower of London, 480
Townes, Charles Hard, 442
toy dogs, 712
Tracy, Spencer, 537
Transportation and Infrastructure Committee, 219
travel and transportation
    air travel, 419–25, 550–51
    boats and boating, 415–17
    campground associations, 565–66
    destinations, U.S., 567–77
    distances between cities, 552–55
    railroads, 8, 431–32
    requirements for, 541–48
    RV organizations, 566
    subways, 432–33
    visitors' bureaus, 562–65
Travers, P. L., 460
Tree, Herbert Beerbohm, 526
trees, state, 287–88
Trevithick, Richard, 442
trials and courts, 247, 268

Trimble, Robert, 264
Trinidad and Tobago
    foreign embassy in the U.S., 216
    general information, 142
    population of, 157
    telephone dialing codes, 720
    travel requirements for, 548
    UN membership, 2
Trinity Repertory Company, 522
Tripoli, Libya, 90
Triton (Greek deity), 187
Trivia (Roman deity), 187
Trollope, Anthony, 451
troposphere, 411
Truman, Elizabeth Virginia Wallace, 190
Truman, Harry S., 189, 191, 232
Trumbell, John, 470
Trumbull, Jonathan, 220
Trusteeship Council, 3–4, 4
Ts'ao Hsueh-ch'in, 451
Tucson, Arizona, 302
Tudor, Anthony, 513
Tudor, house of, 167
Tull, Jethro, 442
Tulsa, Oklahoma, 303
Tune, Tommy, 513
tungsten (element), 397, 408
Tunis, Tunisia, 142
Tunisia
    foreign embassy in the U.S., 216
    general information, 142–43
    population of, 156
    telephone dialing codes, 720
    travel requirements for, 548
    UN membership, 2
Turgenev, Ivan, 451
Turkey
    foreign embassy in the U.S., 216
    general information, 143
    population of, 156
    telephone dialing codes, 720
    travel requirements for, 548
    UN membership, 2
    visitors' and convention bureau, 563
Turkmenistan
    foreign embassy in the U.S., 216
    general information, 143–44
    population of, 157
    telephone dialing codes, 720
    travel requirements for, 548
    UN membership, 2
Turks and Caicos Islands
    foreign embassy in the U.S., 216
    general information, 144
    population of, 158
    telephone dialing codes, 720
    travel requirements for, 548
Turner, Joseph Mallord William, 470

Turner, Lana, 537
Tuvalu
    foreign embassy in the U.S., 217
    general information, 144–45
    population of, 158
    telephone dialing codes, 720
    travel requirements for, 548
Twain, Mark (Samuel Clemens), 451
Tyche (Greek deity), 187
Tyler, John, 188, 191
Tyler, Julia Gardiner, 189
Tyler, Letitia Christian, 189
Tyson, Charles W., 442

U
Uganda
    foreign embassy in the U.S., 217
    general information, 145
    population of, 156
    telephone dialing codes, 720
    travel requirements for, 548
    UN membership, 2
Ukraine
    foreign embassy in the U.S., 217
    general information, 145–46
    population of, 156
    telephone dialing codes, 720
    travel requirements for, 548
    UN membership, 2
Ulaanbaatar, Mongolia, 102
ulcer (peptic), 320
Umnak, 279, 283
Unalaska, 279, 283
Underwood, Oscar W., 228
Unimak, 279, 283
unions, 685
United Arab Emirates
    foreign embassy in the U.S., 217
    general information, 146–47
    population of, 157
    telephone dialing codes, 720
    travel requirements for, 548
    UN membership, 2
United Armed Forces Association, 277
United Kingdom. See England, Great Britain, and
        the United Kingdom
United Nations, 1–4
United RV Campers Club, 566
United States, 147–48. See also states and cities
        (U.S.)
    American poet laureates, 453
    area codes, 714–15
    cabinet departments, 192–95
    Congress, 218
    Constitution, 238–52
    Declaration of Independence, 236–38
    elections, 230–33

V

vaccines, childhood, 325–26
Vaduz, Liechtenstein, 90
Valentino, Rudolph, 537
Valletta, Malta, 96
The Valley, Anguilla, 27
Valois, house of, 168
vanadium (element), 397
Van Allsburg, Chris, 460
Van Buren, Angelica Singleton, 189
Van Buren, Martin, 188, 191, 230
van der Weyden, Rogier, 470
Van Devanter, Willis, 264
Van Duyn, Mona, 453
Van Dyck, Sir Anthony, 470
Vänern (lake), 15
Vanuatu
    general information, 149–50
    population of, 157
    telephone dialing codes, 720
    travel requirements for, 548
    UN membership, 3
Varèse, Edgard, 494
Varnum, Joseph B., 220
Vatican City
    foreign embassy in the U.S., 208
    general information, 73
    telephone dialing codes, 718
    travel requirements for, 544
Vaughan Williams, Ralph, 494
Vega, Lope de, 457
vegetarian diet, 334
Velásquez, Diego Rodríguez de Silva y, 470
Velazquez, Nydia M., 225
Venezuela
    foreign embassy in the U.S., 217
    general information, 150
    population of, 156
    telephone dialing codes, 720
    travel requirements for, 548
    UN membership, 3
Venus (planet), 383
Venus (Roman deity), 187
Verdi, Guiseppe, 494
Verdon, Gwen, 526
Vereen, Ben, 526
Vermeer, Jan, 470
Vermont
    area codes, 714–15
    area of, 287
    capital, 287
    date of admittance, 285
    electoral votes, 233
    features and attractions, 297
    income tax rates, 699
    membership in Congress, 222
    motto and nickname, 289

poison control center, 342
population of, 308
postal abbreviation, 722
racial makeup of, 309
sales tax rates, 701
state flowers, birds, and trees, 289
time zone, 344
tourism department, 559
Verne, Jules, 460
Veronese, Paolo, 470
Verrocchio, Andrea del, 473
Vesta (Roman deity), 187
Veterans' Affairs Committee, 219, 227
Veterans News and Information Service, 277
Veterans of Foreign Wars of the United States, 277
Veterans Resource Network Association, 278
vice presidents (U.S.), 191–92
Victoria, Canada, 11
Victoria, Hong Kong, 74
Victoria, Seychelles, 128
Victoria, Tomás Luis de, 494
Victoria (lake), 14
Victoria (Roman deity), 187
Vidal, Gore, 451
Vienna, Austria, 31, 160
Vientiane, Laos, 87
Vietnam
    foreign embassy in the U.S., 217
    general information, 150–51
    population of, 156
    telephone dialing codes, 720
    travel requirements for, 548
    UN membership, 3
    Vietnam Conflict, 275
Vietnam Veterans of America, 278
Villard, Paul, 442
Vilnius, Lithuania, 91
Vinson, Frederick Moore, 261
viral diseases, 317
Virginia
    area codes, 714–15
    area of, 287
    capital, 287
    date of admittance, 285
    electoral votes, 233
    features and attractions, 297
    income tax rates, 699
    membership in Congress, 222
    motto and nickname, 289
    poison control center, 342
    population of, 308
    postal abbreviation, 722
    racial makeup of, 309
    sales tax rates, 701
    state flowers, birds, and trees, 289
    time zone, 344
    tourism department, 560